The University of Georgia
College of Agricultural and Environmental Sciences
Cooperative Extension

Georgia Master Gardener Handbook
Seventh Edition

Compiled and edited by

Robert R. Westerfield
Extension Horticulturist and
Interim State Master Gardener Coordinator

Marco T. Fonseca
Extension Horticulturist and
State Master Gardener Coordinator (2002-2011)

Kristin L. Slagle
State Master Gardener Program Assistant

Horticulture Department
University of Georgia
Athens, GA

Copyright © 2011 University of Georgia College of Agricultural and Environmental Sciences
ISBN 978-0-9746963-4-8

Annual Publication 106   Revised October 2011

Dedicated to
Marco T. Fonseca
State Master Gardener Coordinator 2002-2011

INTRODUCTION TO THE GEORGIA MASTER GARDENER EXTENSION VOLUNTEER PROGRAM

In 2011, the Georgia Master Gardener Extension Volunteer Program celebrated 32 years of commitment to community volunteer service (1979-2011). Under the leadership of the University of Georgia Cooperative Extension, more than 10,000 Master Gardeners have been trained and certified to help provide horticultural information to the public. For over a quarter of a century, these dedicated gardeners have conducted educational workshops, staffed booths at county fairs and flower shows, hosted plant clinics, developed community gardens, written newsletter/newspaper articles, and operated hotlines at county offices. The Master Gardener Extension Volunteers of Georgia are invaluable for their assistance to local Extension agents in helping to meet the public demand for gardening information.

Mission Statement

To assist Cooperative Extension by training Master Gardeners to provide unbiased and up-to-date horticultural information to the community through volunteer service in educational gardening projects and by using applied research and resources of the University of Georgia.

Cooperative Extension

In 1914, Senator Hoke Smith of Georgia and Senator Frank Lever of South Carolina coauthored national legislation that was to impact farming as well as rural America. The Smith-Lever Act created the Cooperative Extension Service to serve as a vital link between the United States Department of Agriculture and land grant colleges, and to fulfill the mandate through outreach programs of sharing useful and practical information on agriculture and home economics. In particular, it was to provide agricultural information on innovative practices such as crop rotation, seed selection, land management, and diversification.

During WWII, the Georgia Cooperative Extension Service assumed a leadership role in the state's agricultural practices and food production. Over the years, university budgets and human resources were unduly strained due to societal changes in economics, politics and demographics. However, the Cooperative Extension vision, purpose, and practice of "putting knowledge to work" have remained strong.

Through innovation and dedication, Cooperative Extension has adapted its programs in order to maintain the informational dialogue between researchers, educators, extension agents, and community citizens.

Today, Cooperative Extension programming targets a wide range of issues such as rural and community development, food and nutrition education, family and youth development (4-H), natural resources, and crop production.

The Master Gardener Program

The Master Gardener Program was created in Tacoma, Washington in 1972 in response to increasing demands for horticultural information by a growing urban population. Innovative Extension agents with Washington State University developed the concept of training volunteers to help them respond to the public's numerous questions on gardening. The program was so successful and popular that it extended to every U.S. state, several provinces of Canada, and internationally.

In Georgia, a Master Gardener Program concept was introduced by Dr. Butch Ferree and was first organized in 1979 in the Metro-Atlanta area. Led by County Extension Agents Newton Hogg, Gary Peiffer, and Robert Brannen, the first class had 140 participants. In later years, the program spread to Savannah, Macon, and Columbus. Master Gardener Extension Volunteers are active in over 70 counties statewide.

Training Volunteers

The training of Master Gardener Volunteers is a serious and thoughtful process in accordance with the higher educational standards of the University of Georgia. The emphasis of training is to prepare volunteers to respond to the demand for horticulture information by a rapidly growing population. As representatives of the University of Georgia, Master Gardener Extension Volunteers provide the public with the latest research-based information using a variety of programs and projects.

Extension staff in participating counties recruit applicants, and select participants through an interview process. Each county Extension program is provided with statewide policies and guidelines, while allowed the flexibility to address local needs. In accordance with University of Georgia policies, the Georgia Master Gardener Extension Volunteer Program provides training and assistance to its citizens without regard to race, color, nationality, age, disability, or gender. Participants are selected on the basis of a variety of factors. The applicant's availability and willingness to volunteer, suitability for volunteer assignments, previous volunteer experience and special skills are all important factors in the selection process.

Most participating counties conduct Master Gardener Extension Volunteer training in the spring and fall on an annual or biannual basis. Classes typically meet once or twice weekly for 12 weeks. Participants are required to attend at least 80% of the classes and pass 2 written exams. The class instructors include UGA faculty and/or specialists, CEA's, Master Gardeners, industry experts, and teachers from local colleges. The training curriculum undergoes periodic redevelopment to meet changes in technology and informational delivery. The core curriculum includes a minimum 50 hours of instruction; 40 hours in core subjects covered in this handbook, and the remaining 10 hours are elective or selected to meet local needs.

After training, the Master Gardener Extension Volunteer Intern must complete 50 hours of volunteer service within the first year. To remain active, he or she must contribute 25 hours of Extension-approved volunteer service each year thereafter. Active Master Gardeners assist with the operational and educational programs of their local County Extension Offices throughout the state.

Due to changing structure in state Cooperative Extension systems, innovative specialty training programs are being utilized in order to extend outreach program information to more people using volunteers. After the initial training, there are plenty of opportunities for Master Gardeners to continue to learn through local group meetings, state, regional and international conferences and the Advanced Master Gardener Extension Volunteer Training Program. Advanced Training is a series of workshops designed to teach Master Gardeners advanced information in specialty subject areas of expertise such as water quality and management, urban forestry, sustainable gardening and landscape, youth gardening, diagnostics and technology. After training, the Master Gardener subject specialists will be called upon to teach/lecture at community centers, garden demonstrations, local schools, Master Gardener training classes, and more.

Handbook

The Georgia Master Gardener Handbook is the official reference text produced by the University of Georgia and is developed specifically for use by the Master Gardeners of Georgia during training and for future reference. The handbook evolved from merely the grouping of allied publications into units to the more specialized and organized individual thematic chapters written by different authors reflecting different writing styles.

Each of the previous State Master Gardener Program Coordinators merit appreciation for their accomplishments in developing the Georgia Master Gardener Handbook editions one through six: Dr. Gary Wade (first and second), Dr. Wayne J. McLaurin (third), Dr. "Butch" Ferree (fourth and fifth), and Mr. Marco Fonseca (sixth and seventh). The Georgia Master Gardener Handbook is a valuable reference tool for all Master Gardener Extension Volunteers who, as representatives of the University of Georgia, must provide clients with reliable, up-to-date, unbiased, and research-tested horticultural information.

Sale of the handbook to the public is available through the State Master Gardener Program Office.

ACKNOWLEDGEMENTS

Volunteerism and community participation have been fundamental to the American culture. "Though government has an important role to play in meeting the many challenges that remain before us, we are coming to understand that no organization, including government, will fully succeed without the active participation of each of us. Volunteers are vital to enabling this country to live up to the true promise of its heritage" --Bill Clinton

The Master Gardener Program represents an effective volunteer partnership between dedicated citizens and the Cooperative Extension of Land Grant Universities nationwide. In 1979, County Extension Agents with the University of Georgia Cooperative Extension Service made a decision to train volunteers to expand outreach of the knowledge generated by the researchers of the University of Georgia. Well over twenty five years later, Master Gardeners are still an integral part of Cooperative Extension, delivering community programs that 'reach out' to the public.

The Georgia Master Gardener Handbook is the result of volunteer effort by dedicated professionals; faculty specialists and county Extension agents wrote or updated the chapters. Other specialists, agents and Master Gardeners spent many hours reviewing the manuscript and suggesting changes to make the chapters even better. Finally, Krissy Slagle, Master Gardener Program Assistant spent many hours formatting and correcting all the chapters.

Thank you to all of you who so unselfishly contributed to make it a reality.

Published by the Horticulture Department
Douglas A. Bailey, Department Head

Technical Assistance - Office of Communications & Technology Services
Jay B. Bauer, Senior Graphics Designer
Dana M. Mays, Senior Graphics Designer
Amanda Swennes, Managing Editor - CAES Publications

Front Cover
LaMont Sudduth—LaMont Sudduth made Griffin, Georgia his home after 12 years of travel as a rock guitarist. Complementing his decision to leave the music business was his contrasting passion in plants, which led him to the Horticulture Department at the UGA-CAES Griffin campus in 1987. During this period his interest in rock gardening and landscape design began to flourish. In the year 2000 his design tendencies develop into a newer realm of expression, that of paint and canvas. Whether his inspiration is fed by the beauty of nature, the spiritual, or the emotion, his artwork has been exhibited regionally in galleries, and has earned a place in the homes of private collectors as far away as South Korea and Poland. Currently LaMont, his wife and two children are living in Williamson, GA

Contributing Authors
David Adams, (Retired) Professor, Entomology
Lisa M. Ames, Homeowner Diagnostician
David C. Berle, Associate Professor, Horticulture
George Boyhan, Professor, Horticulture

Kris Braman, Professor, Entomology
Matthew Chappell, Assistant Professor
Mark A. Czarnota, Extension Horticulturist
L. Paul Guillebeau, Extension IPM/Pesticide Coordinator, Entomology
James Harris, Professor Emeritus, Extension Education
Peter G. Hartel, Associate Professor, Crop and Soil Sciences
Frank P. Henning, EPA Region IV Liaison
Wade Hutcheson, County Extension Coordinator
Anthony Johnson, Horticulturist, Field Research Services
Gerard W. Krewer,(Retired) Professor, Horticulture
Elizabeth L. Little, Distance Education Instructor
Alfredo Martinez-Espinoza, Extension Plant Pathologist, Plant Pathology
Patrick E. McCullough, Assistant Professor, Crop and Soil Sciences
Wayne J. McLaurin,(Retired) Professor Emeritus, Horticulture
Michael Mengak, Associate Professor - Wildlife Specialist, College of Forest Resources
James T. Midcap, (Retired) Professor, Horticulture
Gary R. Peiffer, County Extension Agent
Bodie V. Pennisi, Extension Horticulturist- Floriculture
J. Faith Peppers, Director of Public Affairs CAES
Daniel P. Rahn, (Retired) Public Service Associate, Office of Communications
F. Richard Rohs, (Retired) Professor, Agricultural Leadership, Education & Communication
Beverly Sparks, Associate Dean for Extension
Dan Suiter, Extension Entomologist
Paul A. Thomas, Extension Horticulturist - Floriculture
Gary L. Wade, Extension Horticulturist
Clint Waltz, Extension Specialist - Turfgrass, Crop and Soil Sciences
Sheryl Wells, Public Service Representative -Biological & Agricultural Engineering
Robert Westerfield, Extension Horticulturist
Jean Williams-Woodward, Extension Plant Pathologist - Ornamentals, Plant Pathology

Volunteer Reviewers
Caley Anderson, Carolina Arnold, Ann Beccia, Leslie Bendell, Victoria Blackstone, Deborah Callahan, Gena Courtney, Marty Crouch, Sandra Davis, Gayle Dean, Paul Desaulniers, Ted Emig, Russ England Terry Lee Fonseca, Yvonne Godwin, Sandy Golden, Marian Gordin, Ellen Grandgenett, Angie Hart, Carla Harward, Rachel Hendee, Joel Hitt, Beverly Howerton, Cheryl LaValley, Katy Lazar, Lisa McKinney, Louise Miller, Judy Moll, Leslye Queen, Kathy Scott, Pat VanGorder, Lucy Whelchel, Frances Winslow

Contents

1. The Soil Ecosystem   1

2. Basic Botany   25

3. Plant Physiology: Growth and Development   41

4. Plant Propagation   65

5. Basic Entomology   77

6. Basic Plant Pathology 89

7. Weed Science   103

8. Principles of Integrated Pest Management 117

9. Ornamental Plants in the Landscape: Site Analysis, Planting and Management 137

10. Herbaceous Plants: Annuals and Perennials   165

11. Selecting Woody Plants for Georgia Landscapes 195

12. Trees   229

13. Diagnosing Ornamental Plant Problems 261

14. Turfgrass 319

15. Insects and Diseases of Turfgrasses 345

16. Vegetable Gardening 359

17. Diagnosing Vegetable Garden Problems 397

18. Principles of Organic Gardening 415

19. Fruit Gardening   425

20. Insects and Diseases of Fruit 461

21. Landscape Design Principles 475

22. Developing a Water Smart Landscape   483

23. Rainwater Harvesting and Rain Gardens 503

24. Ponds and Water Gardening 519

25. Indoor Plants 533

26. Composting 555

27. Nuisance Wildlife   573

28. Structural and Household Pests   607

29. Leadership and Communication   635

Glossary 653

Index 663

1

The Soil Ecosystem

Peter G. Hartel

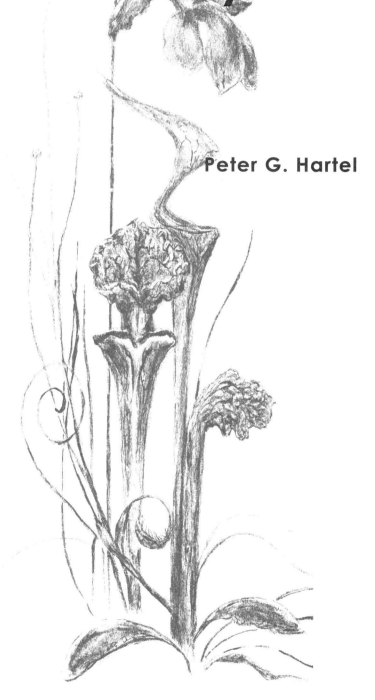

LEARNING OBJECTIVES

Describe soils properly.

Identify the six abiotic factors affecting soil.

Identify the six abiotic and biotic factors affecting soil organisms and plants, and give an example of each.

Integrate soil description and the six abiotic and biotic factors affecting soil, soil organisms, and plants.

Understand how some abiotic soil factors will change in the future.

TERMS TO KNOW

Amensalism biotic factor where one organism is harmed while the other is unaffected.

Anion ion with a negative charge.

Anion exchange capacity (AEC) total amount of exchangeable anions a soil can hold.

Cation ion with a positive charge.

Cation exchange capacity (CEC) total amount of exchangeable cations a soil can hold.

Commensalism biotic factor where one organism benefits while the other is unaffected.

Competition biotic factor where two organisms vie for the same resource (for example, nutrients).

Ecosystem interactions of a biological community with its physical environment.

Field capacity amount of water a soil can hold against the force of gravity (for plants only); in term of water potential: -0.01 MPa in sandy soils and -0.03 MPa in all other soils.

Food web complex interactions of food chains in an ecological community.

Gravitational potential force of gravity pulling water towards the earth's center.

Matric potential force arising from the adsorption of water to the surfaces of soil particles and water being trapped in fine pores (capillary force).

Mutualism biotic factor where both organisms benefit (synonym, symbiosis).

Osmotic potential attraction of solute ions (for example, fertilizer) for water molecules.

Parasitism a biotic factor where one organism feeds on another.

Predation a biotic factor where one organism feeds on another.

pH the negative logarithm of the hydrogen cation (H^+) in soil solution.

Redox potential a measure of a compound's tendency to accept or donate electrons. Measured in millivolts.

Rhizoplane root–soil interface.

Rhizosphere zone of soil under the influence of plant roots.

Soil texture proportion of sand, silt, and clay in soil.

Symbiosis biotic factor where both organisms benefit (synonym, mutualism).

Water potential mainly, the sum of the osmotic, matric, and gravitational potentials.

Wilting point the point at which there is so little water in the soil that plants wilt irreversibly (for plants only); in terms of water potential: -1.5 MPa.

Introduction

In 1938, the Soil Conservation Service, sent its assistant chief, W. C. Lowdermilk, to investigate land practices in western Europe, North Africa, and the Middle East. One of the conclusions he reached in his agricultural classic, *Conquest of the Land through 7,000 Years*, was that civilizations that did not care about their soils inevitably failed, while those civilizations that did care about their soils flourished. Civilizations discovered, one way or the other, the Chinese proverb that soil is the mother of civilization.

Master Gardeners know that soil is their greatest resource. But beyond this idea, every Master Gardener knows that soil is not dead; it is alive; it is dynamic, and describing soil solely on the basis of its physical and chemical characteristics is obvious nonsense. Therefore, this chapter looks at soil as alive and considers soil as part of food web, at least as part of a tripartite relationship with soil organisms and plants (Figure 1). Looking at soil in this way helps us understand, even in the space of a fraction of an inch, how we can have a myriad of possible interactions among the soil, soil organisms, and plants, and why soil is considered the most complex of all habitats.

This complexity is intimidating. One way to make this complexity less intimidating is to look each of the tripartite relationships in terms of their abiotic and biotic factors. When combined with soil description, this approach uncovers a wonderful gardening secret: if we look at the relationships this way, then there is very little that happens in our gardens that we cannot explain.

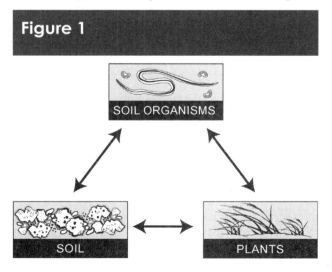

Figure 1. Soil as part of a tripartite relationship among soil organisms and plants. (Original drawing by Wendy Giminski.)

The secret of soil is revealed because, unless we are dealing with extremely rare circumstances like radioactive soils, there aren't any other possibilities because there aren't any other factors. Therefore, we begin with describing soil and then look at factors that influence it.

SOILS, THE FIRST PART OF THE TRIPARTITE RELATIONSHIP

Describing Soil

Soil is a mantle of weathered rock, which, when organic matter is added, contains minerals and nutrients capable of supporting plant growth. Soil forms as the rock minerals and organic matter interact with climate, living organisms, and topography over time.

There are two types of soil: mineral and organic. Generally, an organic soil contains at least 20% organic carbon, and a mineral soil contains less than 20% organic carbon. Less than 1% of all soils are organic soils. Therefore, the vast majority of Georgia soils are mineral soils. In Georgia, a good place to find an organic soil would be the Okefenokee Swamp.

Like a cake, a soil is composed of layers, and each layer is called a horizon. Each soil horizon has its distinct characteristics. Together, all of the soil horizons constitute a soil profile. Each horizon in the profile has a letter; beginning from top to bottom, the horizons are O, A, E, B, or C. Not every soil has every horizon. The O horizon is the "organic" horizon and is formed from plant and animal litter. The A horizon is a mineral horizon, and is unlike the O horizon because it has less organic matter. The E horizon is like the A horizon, but has even less organic matter. Assuming a reasonable amount of rainfall, minerals and nutrients typically leach from the O, A, and E horizons into the B horizon. For this reason, the O, A, and E horizons are considered the zone of eluviation, where nutrients leach, while the B horizon is considered the zone of illuviation, where nutrients accumulate. Below the B horizon is the C horizon, or unconsolidated parent material.

Soils have a phase name, which include its series name and its texture. For example, a soil may be a Tifton loamy sand (Figure 2). The series name is Tifton, and the name is usually taken from near where the soil was first identified. The texture of our Tifton soil is a loamy sand. The texture of a soil based on the proportions of three different particles: sand, silt, and clay. For the U.S. Department of Agriculture (USDA) system of classification:

- sand is soil particles with diameters from 0.05 to 2.0 mm (50 to 2,000 µm; 2.0 mm is a bit more than ⅟₁₆")
- silt is soil particles with diameters from 0.002 to 0.05 mm (2 to 50 µm)
- clay is soil particles with diameters less than 0.002 mm (less than 2 µm)

Particles larger than 2.0 mm, like stones and gravel, are ignored. For a frame of reference, if we were to pluck out a human hair and look at it, its diameter would be about 100 micrometers (µm). Therefore, the diameter of a human hair would be twice the size of the smallest sand particle.

The particle size distribution in a soil allows it to be placed into one of 12 textural classes. The textural class of a soil is determined by means of a soil textural triangle (Figure 3). Our Tifton soil contains 5.4% clay and 82.5% sand, and therefore it is a loamy sand. It is understood that the remaining percentage, 12.1%, is silt because the total percentage of sand, silt, and clay must equal 100%.

The texture of a soil does not change quickly with time and is considered a fixed basic soil property. In old terminology, soils were described as "coarse" or "fine." A coarse-textured soil had more sand, and a fine-textured

Figure 2

Figure 2. Tifton loamy sand. The tape measure is in meters, where 1 meter (or 100 centimeters) equals about 39 inches, or a little more than a yard. The top 30 cm (or 11 inches) is the A horizon, and the rest is the B horizon. The B horizon extends down (off the figure) to about 1.65 meters (65 inches), to where the C horizon finally begins. Tifton soil is the State Soil of Georgia. (Picture courtesy of Bill Miller, University of Georgia.)

soil had more clay. A soil whose properties are equally influenced by sand, silt, and clay was a loam or a loamy soil. It is important to note that these classes of soil texture do not apply to organic soils: an organic soil is classified as a muck or peat depending on the state of decomposition of its organic matter; mucks have well-decomposed organic matter and peats do not.

The Natural Resources Conservation Service (formerly the Soil Conservation Service) classifies all our soils, locates them on a map, and gives the general chemical and physical characteristics of each soil. This valuable information is available online at <http://soils.usda.gov/survey/printed_surveys>. Choose the state (Georgia) and then follow the directions. For Master Gardeners with GPS-enabled smartphones, download the free application, SoilWeb. Assuming you have cell phone coverage, this application supports on-demand access to soil survey information for Georgia (and anywhere else in the contiguous 48 states).

Bulk Density

A typical mineral soil contains 50% solid material (45% minerals and 5% organic matter) and 50% pore space. The pore space will be occupied by air or water, and these two are inversely related: as the volume of soil water increases, the volume of soil air decreases, and vice versa. The total space that the solid materials and pore space occupy defines the bulk density, which is the weight per unit volume. The bulk density for mineral soils typically ranges 1.00 to 1.80 grams per centimeter. As a frame of reference, a penny weighs 2.5 grams, and 1 centimeter is a little bit more than ⅜". Because organic material is highly porous and has a low bulk density, incorporating organic matter into the soil decreases the bulk density of a soil.

Soil Pores

Pores in the soil affect water and air movement. Sandy (coarse-textured) soils have higher bulk densities and less total pore space (35 to 50%) than clayey (fine-textured) soils that have lower bulk densities and more pore space (40 to 60%). The size of the pores, however, is just as important as the total quantity of pore space.

Large pores characteristically allow the rapid movement of soil gases and soil water. Sandy soils have less total pore space, but those spaces are mostly large pores. For this reason, sandy soils usually drain rapidly. In contrast, clayey soils have more total pore space, but these spaces are mostly small pores. Soils high in clay usually drain slowly because the small pores restrict the water flow.

This difference is why sandy soils hold relatively less water than clayey soils, which hold relatively more water.

Soil Structure

When soil particles cohere more strongly to each other than to other adjoining particles, these particles form a soil aggregate. These aggregates can range in size from 0.5 to 5.0 mm (0.02 to 0.2") in diameter and can even form clusters of aggregates. Depending on their shape, these aggregates define soil structure. For example, aggregates shaped like spheres have more pore space and more rapid permeability than aggregates that are shaped more like blocks.

SOIL ABIOTIC FACTORS

At this point, we can describe soil, and we now need to consider how abiotic factors affect soil. The six abiotic factors that affect soil are pH, nutrients, water (moisture), oxygen (redox), temperature, and light.

pH

Water (H_2O) has the ability to dissociate in ions, one positively charged (H^+) and one negatively charged (OH^-). A positively charged ion is called a cation; a negatively charged ion is called an anion. Because water is composed of two elements, hydrogen (H) and oxygen (O), the H^+ is called a hydrogen cation; the remaining OH^- is called a hydroxyl anion.

Figure 3

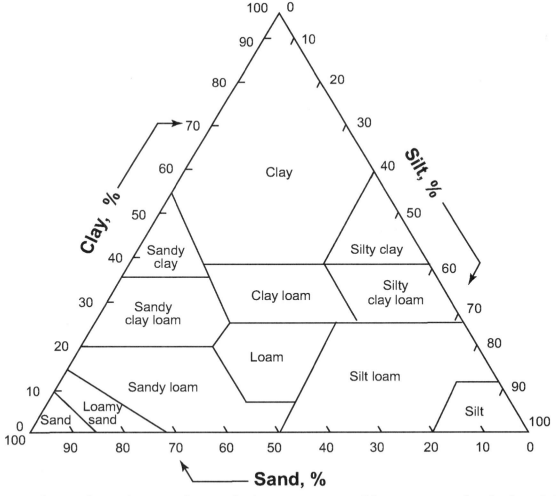

Figure 3. Soil textural triangle. To use the triangle, determine any two of the percentages of sand, silt, and clay in a soil. Follow the arrow in the direction of the tic marks at the appropriate percentage. The texture of the soil is identified at the intersection of the two lines. (Adapted from Soil Survey Staff, 1975. Used with permission.)

pH is defined as the negative logarithm of the hydrogen cation (H+) concentration in solution, where the concentration is in moles per liter. A logarithm is the exponent to which a base number must be raised to equal a given number. Therefore, if the base number is 10 and the given number is 100, then the logarithm is 2, because $10^2 = 10 \times 10 = 100$. We use the negative logarithm because the concentrations are less than 1 mole. A mole (M) is the molecular weight of a substance. Therefore, if the concentration of hydrogen cations in pure water is 0.0000001 M and the base number is 10, then 0.0000001 M = 1×10^{-7} or pH 7.0. This pH is considered neutral.

The hydrogen cation concentration typically ranges from pH 1 (1.0 M H+), which is acid, to pH 14 (0.00000000000001 M H+), which is alkaline or basic. What is important here is that that pH is a base 10 logarithm scale; if two solutions differ by 1 pH unit, then one solution has 10 times more H+ than the other.

Nutrients

In order to understand nutrients in soil, it is important to understand chemical charge. Soils possess both positive and negative charge. The ability of a soil to hold onto positively charged cations (for example, potassium or K+) is the cation exchange capacity (CEC) of the soil, and the corresponding ability of soil to hold onto negatively charged anions (e.g., nitrate or NO_3^-) is the anion exchange capacity (AEC). Because the ability of a soil to hold cations usually exceeds its ability to hold anions, soil testing laboratories typically report only the CEC of a soil. Both the AEC and CEC are important because they can alter soil physical properties.

The type and amount of clay and organic matter affect the CEC and AEC of a soil. We begin with clay. Most clays are composed of crystalline sheets of silica and alumina. One sheet of silica and one sheet of alumina give a 1:1 clay like kaolinite, which is common in Georgia, and one alumina sheet between two silica sheets gives a 2:1 clay like smectite, which is common in the midwestern United States.

Clays have two sources of charges. First, each silica atom in a silica sheet is held within a tetrahedron of negatively charged oxygen atoms (O^{2-}); similarly, each aluminum atom in an alumina sheet is held within an octahedron of negatively charged oxygen atoms. The charge on a silica atom is +4 (Si^{4+}) and the charge on an alumina atom is +3 (Al^{3+}), and because of the way the charges are shared among the oxygen atoms, the net charge in either a silica tetrahedron or alumina octahedron is 0.

However, in some cases, atoms of similar size can fit in the space designed for a silica or alumina atom. In the case of silica, alumina (Al^{3+}) and iron (Fe^{3+}) can fit; in the case of alumina, magnesium (Mg^{2+}), iron (Fe^{2+}), and zinc (Zn^{2+}) can fit. With each substitution, there is a -1 charge because the total negative charges of the oxygen are no longer satisfied. This substitution, called isomorphous substitution, means that clays are negatively charged. This charge is permanent and is not affected by soil pH.

Second, alumina and silica sheets have edges. In an acid soil (pH of less than 6.0), the charge of exposed, negatively charged oxygen atoms (O^{2-}) is satisfied by hydrogen cations (H+). However, when the soil pH is more than pH 6.0, there are not enough hydrogen cations to go around, and other cations like calcium (Ca^{2+}) or magnesium (Mg^{2+}) take the place of hydrogen cations. This difference in charge is the charge attributed to broken edges. This charge is pH-dependent and this pH dependency is what distinguishes it from isomorphous substitution. Most of the charge in 2:1 clays is because of isomorphous substitution, and most of the charge in 1:1 clays is because of broken edges. Because Georgia has a lot of 1:1 clays, most of the CEC in Georgia soils is because of broken edges. What is important is that we have an explanation why clays can hang onto cations.

In addition to hanging onto cations, clays can hang onto anions. This association comprises the AEC, and the AEC is also located at broken edges. Wherever Al^{3+} or Si^{4+} is exposed, some anions (for example, orthophosphate, $H_2PO_4^{2-}$) have the right size and geometry to be adsorbed, whereas other anions (for example, nitrate, NO_3^-) do not fit well and are not adsorbed. What is important is that we now have an explanation why clays can hang onto anions, and why nitrate, a good source of nitrogen for many plants, leaches so quickly in soil..

There is an important relationship between the exchange capacity of a soil and soil texture. Because the adsorption of water, nutrients, and gases are all surface phenomena, the greater the surface area of the soil particles, the greater the adsorption. When we look at the size of the particles that comprise soil texture, we see an interesting relationship: the particle surface area per unit mass increases logarithmically as the particle diameter decreases (Table 1). Therefore, particle size and surface area are inversely related, and clay has many, many times more surface area than the equivalent amount of silt or sand. For this reason, clay dominates the adsorption of water, nutrients, and gases in a soil, and sand and silt are relatively unimportant.

Organic matter is the other source of charge that affects the CEC and AEC of a soil. Organic means that a compound contains carbon (C). In this case, organic matter is composed of a heterogeneous mix of carbon (C), hydrogen (H), and oxygen (O). Because of this heterogeneity, we do not understand the structure of organic matter well. We do know that the source of the charge in organic matter is primarily carboxyl groups (COOH). These groups are typically attached to a larger molecule, and, by convention, the attachment is typically written as (R—COOH). As the pH increases, the carboxyl group dissociates into ions, just like water (R—COOH $\leftrightarrow$ R—COO$^-$ + H$^+$). Under acid conditions, the H$^+$ ions are strongly held and are not easily replaced by other cations, but as the pH increases, the H$^+$ ions are replaced by other cations, just like what happens to clay particles and broken edges.

There are two important points to understand about organic matter. First, like broken edges in clay particles, the charge of organic matter is entirely pH-dependent. Second, the CEC of organic matter far exceeds that of clay. When we integrate the CEC of organic matter with the CEC of isomorphous substitution and the broken edges of clay (Figure 4), we see, at least on a chemical basis, one reason why all gardeners value organic matter: assuming the pH isn't too acid, organic matter increases CEC and the soil's ability to hold on to nutrients.

Now that we have clarity about soil pH and soil charge, we can integrate the two and look at specific nutrients over a range of pH for almost all agricultural soils (pH 5.0 to 9.0; Figure 5). What we see are two striking features. First, most nutrients are most available at neutral or near-neutral pH. Second, there are notable exceptions to this rule: with the exception of molybdenum, heavy metals are more available at low pH (less than pH 5.0) than at neutral or near-neutral pH. Heavy metals are elements that have a specific gravity equal or greater that 5.0 g per cubic centimeter, where the specific gravity of water is 1.0 g per cubic centimeter. Now we have an understanding, at least on a chemical basis, why Master Gardeners should or should not try to alter the soil pH through liming: it depends on which nutrients need to be maximized.

Water

Understanding soil water requires an understanding of energy. Energy is the ability to do work. There are two kinds of energy: kinetic and potential. Kinetic energy is the energy something possesses because of its motion and mass. Potential energy is the energy something possesses because of its position or arrangement with respect to other bodies. Therefore, potential energy is not a constant property, but a relative measure of one object to another. Thus, the potential energy of an apple in a tree and the ground depends on the relative height of the apple to the ground. When the apple falls from a tree, the apple's kinetic energy increases and its potential energy decreases. This idea is important is because water in soil flows from an area of higher energy to an area of lower energy (this idea is an expression of the Second Law of Thermodynamics that processes in na-

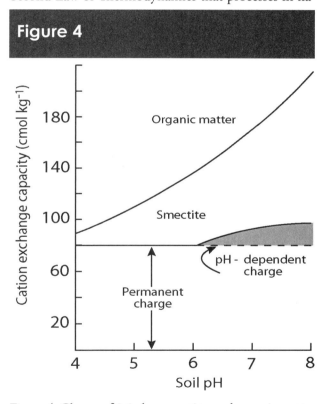

Figure 4

Figure 4. Charge of 2:1 clay, smectite, and organic matter with varying pH. (Adapted from Brady and Weil, 2010. Used with permission.)

Table 1. Number and surface area of particles according to the United States Department of Agriculture (USDA) soil classification scheme.

PARTICLE	USDA SIZE	PARTICLES	SURFACE AREA
	millimeters	number	centimeters per gram
Sand	0.05 to 2.00	5,700	45
Silt	0.05 to 0.002	5,776,000	454
Clay	Less than 0.002	90,260,853,000	8,000,000

ture increase in entropy or disorder). Therefore, a water potential is the measure of the potential energy (per unit mass or volume) of water at a point in a system relative to the potential energy of pure, free water. Water potentials are typically expressed in terms of pressure as kiloPascals (kPa) or MegaPascals (MPa). A Pascal is a Newton per square meter; a Newton is a measure of force required to accelerate 1 kilogram (2.2 lbs.) one meter per second per second. Previously, soil water was measured in bars, where 1 bar equaled 0.987 atmosphere. To convert bars to kPa or MPa, multiply bars by 100 or 0.1, respectively (for example, -1 bar = -100 kPa or -0.1 MPa).

Pure, free water is usually assigned a water potential of 0 Pa. Because the water potential in soil is usually lower in potential energy than pure, free water, the water potential in soil is usually a negative number. The water potential of a soil is the sum of many forces, of which three are important in soil:

- osmotic potential
- matric potential
- gravitational potential

The osmotic potential is primarily the attraction of solute ions (for example, fertilizer) for water molecules and is always a negative number. Remember that, in osmosis, pure water always wants to move in the direc-

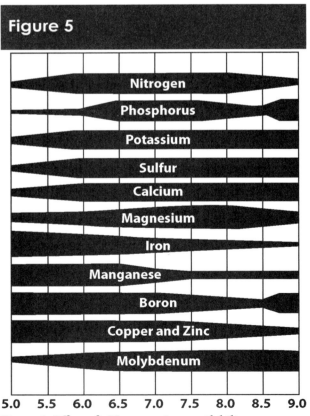

Figure 5

5.0 5.5 6.0 6.5 7.0 7.5 8.0 8.5 9.0

Nitrogen
Phosphorus
Potassium
Sulfur
Calcium
Magnesium
Iron
Manganese
Boron
Copper and Zinc
Molybdenum

Figure 5. Effect of pH on nutrient availability.

tion of salty water in order to dilute it. Therefore, the osmotic potential is significant in saline soils or in soils amended with organic wastes or fertilizer.

The matric potential is the sum of adsorption of water to the surfaces of soil particles and capillary forces arising from water being trapped in fine pores. For example, if a fine glass tube is placed in water, the water rises in the tube because of the surface tension of water and the attraction of water molecules to the sides of the tube. The smaller the tube, the greater the rise of water. Like the osmotic potential, the matric potential is always a negative number. The matric potential is most significant in unsaturated soils. Again, water will move from a more saturated soil (high free energy; high potential) to a less saturated soil (low free energy; low potential).

The gravitational potential is the force of gravity pulling water towards the earth's center and may have a positive or negative potential depending on the reference level of the water. If the reference level is the lower edge of the soil profile (the usual case), then the gravitational potential will be positive.

In addition to the energy potential, soil water can be measured in terms of its volumetric or gravimetric water content, which is the water lost from the soil upon drying to a constant mass at 221°F (105°C). In this case, the soil water is expressed either as the mass of water per unit mass of dry soil or as the volume of water per unit bulk volume of soil.

Soil texture affects soil water. Over the entire range of water pressure, a soil high in clay, with its greater percentage of small pores, retains a larger amount of water than a soil high in silt, which, in turn, retains a larger amount of water than a soil high in sand. These curves are called soil water characteristic curves or water release curves (Figure 6). The water release curves of most garden soils lie between the curves for clay and sandy soils. If we added organic matter, then the curve would shift upward. This shift upward is another reason why Master Gardeners value organic matter: it increases the water-holding capacity of the soil, but does so without increasing the bulk density of the soil because organic matter has a lower bulk density than clay.

Generally, water moves through the soil by either unsaturated or saturated flow. Under unsaturated conditions, the water moves into and through the soil. Under saturated conditions, the soil pores are water-filled, and water move by mass flow, that is, it flows with the water. Compared with saturated soils, water moves more slowly in unsaturated soils and the soil shows a wetting front as the water moves to drier regions in the soil. The wetting front moves more slowly in clayey soils compared with sandy soils because clayey soils have smaller pores than sandy soils.

There is another effect as water moves through soil. Where rainfall is sufficient, it leaches basic cations from the O, A, and E horizons into the B horizon and makes the topmost horizons more acidic; where rainfall is insufficient, this leaching of basic cations doesn't occur and the topmost horizons stay alkaline. Thus, we have an explanation why a majority of Georgia's soils are acid, and why a majority of soils in Texas are alkaline.

Oxygen

Soil aeration measures how well a soil is oxygenated, and this oxygenation depends on soil moisture, soil texture, and soil porosity. The earth's atmosphere is the major source of oxygen; thus, oxygen can get into the soil only by mass flow or diffusion. Because mass flow is based on differences in air pressure, mass flow of oxygen into the soil is relatively unimportant beneath the top inch of soil. Therefore, diffusion is the major way oxygen is replenished in soils. Soil texture affects this diffusion. If the soil has a high percentage of clay, then it will have a high percentage of small pores. The small diameter of these pores will slow diffusion. Soil water affects this diffusion of oxygen because the diffusion coefficient of oxygen in air is 0.189 per square centimeter per second, but in water, it is only 0.000025 per square centimeter per second. In other words, oxygen diffuses 10,000 times more slowly through water than it does through air. This 10,000-fold difference means soil pores filled with water will reduce the diffusion of oxygen into the soil. Because the water release curves are higher for clayey soils than sandy soils, it is no surprise that clayey soils, with their higher percentage of small pores, are often poorly aerated. Soil depth also affects soil aeration. Generally, soil oxygen declines with depth, especially in soils with high clay contents.

Soil aeration is commonly measured in terms of a redox (**red**uction—**ox**idation) potential. The redox potential is the measure of the tendency of a compound to accept or donate electrons. As a substance loses electrons (for example, $Fe^{2+} \rightarrow Fe^{3+}$), it becomes more positive (more oxidized); as it gains electrons (for example, $Fe^{3+} \rightarrow Fe^{2+}$), it becomes more negative (more reduced). Waterlogged soils, especially those with a lot of organic matter, generally have a low redox potential. So, in general, drier soils are "oxidizing" environments and wetter soils are "reducing" environments.

Another way to think about redox is to think of electrons as cash. As cash, electrons can do a lot, like drive a system. In this cash system, any element in its free state is worth zero (0). Therefore, elemental sulfur (S) and free oxygen (O^2) are each worth 0. Each charged element by itself is worth its charge. Therefore, magnesium (Mg^{2+}) is worth +2. If elements are combined, then every hydrogen (H) is +1 and every oxygen (O) is -2 (there are exceptions to this rule, but they needn't concern us here). If hydrogen or oxygen or both are combined with another elements, these other elements must equal the overall charge. Thus, even carbon (C) in a complicated molecule like glucose ($C_6H_{12}O_6$) means that the C = 0, because H_{12} = +12 and O_6 = -12. Something simpler like carbon dioxide (CO_2) means that C = +4, because O^2 = -4. What is important is that if glucose ($C_6H_{12}O_6$) is converted to carbon dioxide (CO_2), then C goes from 0 to +4. The only way for C to go from 0 to +4 is to give up 4 electrons (or cash). Chemically, a reduced compound, glucose, was oxidized to carbon dioxide, and it gave up a lot of energy (cash, in the form of electrons) and this energy is available for use.

We can now also apply the idea of redox to soil color. When soil is well-aerated, elements in the soil like iron and manganese are oxidized and the predominant soil colors are red, yellow, and reddish-brown. However, when soil is poorly aerated, elements in the soil like iron and manganese in the soil are reduced, and the predominant soil colors are blue and gray. If the soils have mixed zones of good and poor aeration, then the soils will have a mottled appearance.

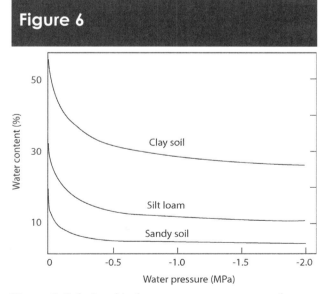

Figure 6

Figure 6. Relationship between water content and water potential for a sandy soil, a silt loam, and a clay soil. (Adapted from Papendick and Campbell, 1981. Used with permission.)

Temperature

Generally, temperatures increase the rates of physical and chemical processes in soil. In addition, soil temperature and soil moisture are inextricably linked. Water has a high specific heat, that is, it requires a considerable amount of energy to raise 1 cubic centimeter of water by 1°C. When water is added to soil, it is easy to understand how the high specific heat of water and the natural high density of soil combine to moderate rapid changes in soil temperature. This effect increases with soil depth. As soil depth increases, the temperature of the soil below the soil surface lags behind the temperature of the soil surface and the temperature fluctuation is reduced. This lag is another important way that soil differs from water: the mass of soil moderates the rapid fluctuation of temperature more commonly found in water bodies.

Light

As a form of energy, light from the sun heats the soil and dries it out. This light also increases mineral decay. Theoretically, the soil emits a portion of this energy (as infrared radiation) back into space, but actually greenhouse gases capture the majority of the energy and only a small portion makes it back into space. Because the concentration of greenhouse gases in our atmosphere is increasing, it traps more heat, and our atmosphere is becoming warmer.

DESCRIBING SOIL ORGANISMS, THE SECOND PART OF THE TRIPARTITE RELATIONSHIP

At this point, we have described soil and considered six abiotic factors, pH, nutrients, water, oxygen, temperature, and light. Because we have already agreed that soil is alive, we must add soil organisms to our description. However, soil organisms can also interact with each other, and, for this reason, we must also consider six biotic factors: symbiosis, commensalism, amensalism, neutralism, competition, and predation/parasitism. Again, although there are potentially other biotic and abiotic factors (for example, ionizing radiation in an uranium-rich soil), these factors are so rare that we really do not need to consider them.

Before considering all these factors, there are three important points to consider. First, we need to identify the major groups of organisms in the soil, their size, and their numbers (Table 2). The table shows that soil organisms are both diverse and numerous. Viruses are obligate intracellular parasites composed of a protein coat and a genome of either DNA or RNA. They are extremely small (only 0.03 to 0.20 micrometers in length). Bacteria are predominantly single cell, prokaryotic organisms. Prokaryotic means that they do not have a membrane-bound nucleus or other organelles, and their DNA is a single molecule. Fungi are nonmotile, filamentous, eukaryotic organisms that do not contain chlorophyll (therefore they cannot carry out photosynthesis) and reproduce by spores. Eukaryotic means that they do have a membrane-bound nucleus and other organelles, and their DNA is more than a single molecule. Single filaments of fungi are called hypha (plural, hyphae) and a mass of hyphae is called a mycelium. Protozoa are aquatic, unicellular, eukaryotic organisms that predominantly eat bacteria. There are three main types found in soil, amoebae, ciliates, and flagellates, and these are mostly identified by their morphology and means of locomotion. Nematodes, also called roundworms, are aquatic, eukaryotic, cylindrical, unsegmented worms with tapered ends. They feed on bacteria, fungi, plant roots, and other nematodes. Earthworms are eukaryotic, segmented worms. Because they cannot regulate their water content and temperature, their activities are highly dependent on soil moisture and temperature.

Using our human hair reference of 100 μm in diameter, it is apparent that most soil organisms cannot be seen with the naked eye. Another good way to compare sizes of soil organisms is available online at http://www.cellsalive.com/howbig.htm. But just to rely on numbers is misleading, because it is important to consider their function as well. As we shall see, soil organisms have some important functions to perform in soil, especially for cycling nutrients.

Second, all soil organisms must live in soil pores. Unless a soil organism can make its own pores (for example, an earthworm), chemical and physical forces limit movement of most soil organisms in these pores. Soil pores usually offer only a tortuous path to movement. Therefore, it is only when soils are saturated or when larger soil organisms actively or passively transport smaller soil organisms that smaller soil organisms overcome these forces to move great distances (inches or more). Therefore, if a soil factor becomes bad for a small soil organism, then it is usually stuck in place and cannot escape to better conditions elsewhere.

Third, biotic and abiotic factors in soil can range from essential to unimportant. If they are important, then soil organisms—like Goldilocks—prefer these factors to be "just right." For an organism to be outside the boundary of an essential biotic or abiotic factor means diminished activity, and, if sufficiently far outside the boundary, death. For example, human beings require temperatures within a certain range to survive: assuming that we have no protection, if the temperature is too cold, then we will freeze to death; if the temperature is too hot, then we will die of heat stroke or heat exhaustion. Some factors may only have a limit in one direction. For example, as human beings we require oxygen to breathe: if there is not enough oxygen, then we suffocate; if there is too much oxygen, then we will breathe just fine.

ABIOTIC FACTORS FOR SOIL ORGANISMS

pH

Although some soil organisms tolerate low pH (these are called acidophiles and are able to grow at pH 3 or lower) or high pH (these are called alkaliphiles, and are able to grow at pH 9 or higher), most soil organisms are neutrophiles and prefer a near-neutral pH range of 6 to 7. The reason that many soil organisms prefer this pH range is because soil nutrients are most available at this pH. Furthermore, a neutral pH avoids heavy metal toxicity because almost all these metals are only active in acid soils (pH less than 5). Thus, bacteria in soil are most abundant at pH 7 and decrease as the soil becomes more acid. The notable exception to this rule for soil organisms is soil fungi. Fungi are acid tolerant (pH 4 to 7) and tend to be abundant in acid soils where there is less competition from other soil organisms.

pH is also related to soil water potential: when soils are saturated, the hydrogen cation concentration is diluted; when soils are dry, the hydrogen cation concentration is concentrated. This concentration affects the ability of soil organisms to control anions and cations in soil solution.

Depending on the buffering capacity of the soil, some soil organisms have the capacity to change soil pH. A good example of this change is in the nitrogen cycle. When a waste containing nitrogen is placed on the soil, for example, urea, microorganisms in the soil convert the urea to ammonium (NH_4^+). This process, called ammonification, yields a highly basic cation NH_4^+, that will raise the soil pH. However, this rise is temporary because the next group of bacteria, the nitrifiers, will convert the ammonium to nitrite (NO_2^-) and then to nitrate (NO_3^-). This process, called nitrification, acidifies the soil as the H^+ is released. Therefore, Master Gardeners must realize that the practice of adding organic or synthetic fertilizer nitrogen to soil will ultimately acidify the soil and, unless the soil is highly alkaline or highly buffered, it will need to be limed at some future date.

The AEC and CEC we observe in soil with respect to anions and cations also apply to soil organisms because the surfaces of soil organisms are composed of organic molecules, which can be positively or negatively charged (for example, R—COOH $\leftrightarrow$ R—COO$^-$ + H$^+$) depending on the soil pH. At typical soil pH values (pH 5 to 8), soil microorganisms are negatively charged. Because clays and organic matter are negatively charged at these pH values as well, it seems reasonable that soil and soil organisms would naturally repel each other. However, this repulsion is not what is observed; instead, soil and soil organisms readily bind chemically with each other. How this binding occurs is not fully understood. Some scientists suggest that divalent cations "bridge" the negative charges of soil organisms and clay particles or organic matter, but evidence for this binding is unconvincing. It is more likely that a variety of mechanisms are responsible for soil organisms chemically binding to clay and organic matter.

Table 2. Size, number, and wet weight of various organisms in soil. To convert kilograms of wet weight per hectare to pounds per acre, multiply by 0.89.

ORGANISMS	LENGTH OR WIDTH	NUMBER	KILOGRAMS OF WET WEIGHT
	micrometer	per gram of soil	per hectare
Viruses	0.02 (width)	10,000,000,000 to 100,000,000,000	Not applicable
Bacteria	1 (width)	10,000,000 to 100,000,000	300 to 3,000
Fungi	10 (width)	100,000 to 1,000,000	500 to 5,000
Protozoa	100 (length)	1,000 to 100,000	5 to 100
Nematodes	1,000 (length)	10 to 100	1 to 100
Earthworms	100,000 (length)	Not applicable	10 to 1,000

In addition to chemically binding, soil organisms can also produce an array of substances that allow them to bind to surfaces physically. For example, some bacteria produce biofilms. These biofilms can serve a variety of functions, but one use is to create a nice home for the bacteria to buffer themselves from adverse abiotic and biotic factors.

Nutrients

Soil organisms must obtain nutrients from their environment to survive and grow. Some of these nutrients provide energy, whereas others provide cell constituents. In terms of energy, all soil organisms are either chemotrophs that derive all their energy from organic and inorganic sources (sometimes also called organotrophs and lithotrophs, respectively), or they are phototrophs that convert light energy into chemical energy. Because carbon is the most common element in all soil organisms, chemotrophs and phototrophs are typically further divided into autotrophs, which convert inorganic carbon (i.e., CO_2 or carbonates) into organic compounds, or heterotrophs, most of which feed on nonliving plants and animals or on organic matter in the soil.

In terms of cell constituents, nutrients are divided into macronutrients, substances required in large quantities by organisms, and micronutrients, substances required in small quantities. Besides carbon, the major macronutrients for soil organisms are nitrogen, phosphorus, and sulfur, and to a lesser extent, calcium, magnesium, potassium, and sodium. The major micronutrients are cobalt, copper, iron, manganese, molybdenum, and zinc. Macronutrients comprise the vast majority of the structural components like carbohydrates, proteins, lipids, and nucleic acids, while micronutrients are typically found in growth factors and enzymes.

The degree to which soil organisms enjoy nutrients will depend not only on chemical characteristics of the nutrients, but also how accessible they are. Not surprisingly, soil organisms have developed an array of different mechanisms to deal with periodic, episodic, or steady flow of nutrients. Some soil organisms opt for rapid growth only when nutrients are plentiful. Some organisms, by virtue of being left with "crumbs from the table," opt for a slower growth rate and tend to metabolize more complex nutrients. The remaining organisms lie on the continuum between these two strategies.

For autotrophs, there is no problem of limited carbon because CO_2 and bicarbonate are plentiful. For heterotrophs, activity depends on the quality and quantity of available carbon. Readily available natural organic compounds like simple sugars are degraded quickly and activity is high. For natural organic compounds that are resistant to degradation (for example, organic matter), activity is low.

Oxygen

There are four groups of soil organisms with respect to soil oxygen. Obligate aerobes require oxygen to grow, facultative anaerobes can grow both in the presence or absence of oxygen, microaerophiles prefer or require low oxygen, and obligate anaerobes grow only in absence of oxygen.

Most soil organisms are obligate aerobes because they use oxygen exclusively as a terminal electron acceptor in respiration. In aerobic respiration:

$$C_6H_{12}O_6 + 6O_2 \rightarrow 6CO_2 + 6\,H_2O + \text{lots of energy}$$

Here glucose, a sugar, is oxidized in the presence of oxygen to carbon dioxide and water with the production of energy (and heat). However, when oxygen is not present, then fermentation results:

$$C_6H_{12}O_6 \rightarrow 2\,C_6H_{12}O_6 + 2CO_2 + \text{little energy}$$

Here glucose, a sugar, is oxidized to ethanol and carbon dioxide with the production of energy (and heat). Because aerobic respiration produces more energy than fermentation (because the product is highly oxidized CO_2, not a reduced intermediate), the population densities of obligate aerobes are relatively higher than those of anaerobes. In addition, obligate anaerobes cannot survive the presence of oxygen because aerobic respiration temporarily yields hydrogen peroxide (H_2O_2) and superoxide (O_2^-), toxic products to which obligate anaerobes cannot break down. As a result, obligate anaerobes live strictly by fermentation. However, some obligate aerobes can respire anaerobically by substituting nitrate (NO_3^-), sulfate (SO_4^{2-}), or carbonate (CO_3^{2-}) for oxygen as the terminal electron acceptor. This anaerobic respiration is restricted to bacteria, and for this reason, these bacteria dominate in anaerobic soils. Many bacteria and a few fungi are facultative anaerobes, which grow in the presence or absence of oxygen. When oxygen is available, the organisms grow aerobically; when oxygen is unavailable, the organisms grow by either fermentation or anaerobic respiration. Finally, aerotolerant anaerobes lack an electron transport system and function solely by fermentation (bacteria only).

Redox potential can also give some insight as to which organisms are likely to be active in a particular soil. Soils with a high redox potential (400 to +700 millivolts) are "oxidizing" habitats and are conducive to aerobic processes, and soils with a low redox potential (+400 to -300 millivolts) are "reducing" habitats and conducive to anaerobic processes like methane production. However, the idea that highly aerobic soils contain a few anaerobes would not be true. The ability of soils to contain water-filled pores restricts oxygen diffusion and guarantees that anaerobic microsites exist. Thus, it is common to find oxygen concentrations in soil ranging from fully aerobic (oxic) to low levels (hypoxic) to completely anaerobic (anoxic), even over distances of 0.1". In fact, oxygen gradients spanning these extremes in soil are probably the normal state of affairs.

Water

All soil organisms—without exception—require water to live. Like soil, soil organisms have their own water potentials, composed primarily of a osmotic or turgor potential. The osmotic or turgor potential is created because soil organisms typically contain more salts than the soil solution, and because these organisms have a semipermeable membrane, water will naturally flow from the soil solution into the organisms, turning them into little balloons. Only a cell wall or, in the absence of a cell wall, a way to excrete excess water, keeps this from happening. The theoretical limits for soil organisms in soil are between 0 and −81 MPa. At 0 MPa, soil is completely saturated; at −81 MPa, DNA is denatured.

Besides the effect of water potential on microbial activity, it is also important to simultaneously consider oxygen and nutrients. As already mentioned, when soil is saturated, diffusion of oxygen into the soil is slowed, and if the oxygen consumption rate exceeds the diffusion rate, the soil, regardless of its texture and porosity, becomes anaerobic. Soil organisms that require oxygen fare poorly. Soil organisms capable of surviving under low oxygen conditions fare better but still show diminished activity because the amount of energy produced under anaerobic conditions is less than under aerobic conditions. Phototrophs on the soil surface (for example, algae) fare well, and in fact prefer saturated conditions. Movement by aquatic soil organisms is maximal because the water film thickness around soil particles is maximal. Texture plays a role because soil organisms move more easily in sandy soils than in clayey soils (again, because sandy soils have larger pores). Concentrations of water-soluble nutrients are low. Water stress for almost all soil organisms is minimal.

Once water drains from the large soil pores, the water potential becomes negative (approximately −0.01 MPa for sandy soils and −0.03 MPa for other soils), and oxy-

gen diffusion increases. Sandy soils, which contain more large pores than clayey soils, are more oxygenated than clayey soils. Except for movement by aerial (i.e., living in air-filled spaces) soil animals like microarthropods (for example, mites), movement by aquatic soil organisms like nematodes, protozoa, and bacteria becomes more difficult as the water film thickness dwindles to only a few micrometers. However, the combination of aerobic conditions, concentrated nutrients, and good water relations means microbial activity is near maximal.

As the total soil water potential decreases from −0.01 to −0.1 MPa, oxygen diffusion improves, but water films become discontinuous, and consequently, nutrient availability and movement by aquatic organisms decrease. Because matric potential is related to capillary forces and these forces are directly related to the soil pore diameter, clayey soils, by virtue of their more numerous micropores, contain more water than sandy soils and dry more slowly. This drying rate is important because the slower the rate of drying, the greater the ability of an organism to survive. Because microbial activity depends on each soil organism maintaining proper turgor pressure for cell functioning, soil matric and osmotic potentials increase in their importance. Except in saline soils, matric potentials are more important than osmotic potentials.

By −1.5 MPa, water is gone from the small pores and only water bound to soil solids is available for soil organisms. The soils are relatively oxygenated. Movement stops. Diffusion of nutrients is so restricted that starvation conditions are created. Furthermore, because all soil organisms contain semipermeable membranes that allow water to enter and exit in near equilibrium with the environment, osmotic potential becomes critical as soil ions become more and more concentrated. To avoid contraction of the cytoplasm from the cell wall (this is called plasmolysis), most soil organisms divert their energy to accumulating solutes to counter this negative potential.

By −4.0 MPa, most biological processes (for example, nitrification) stop. Unless an organism can form a resistant structure (for example, spores in bacteria and fungi, cysts in the protozoa), most organisms desiccate and die.

Temperature

Soil organisms are divided into psychrophiles, mesophiles, and thermophiles. Psychrophiles do not grow above 20°C (68°F), have minima of 0°C (32°F) or lower, and optima around 16°C (60°F). Mesophiles have minima of above 0°C (32°F), maxima below 50°C (122°F), and optima between 15 and 40°C (59 and 104°F). Finally, thermophiles have minima at or above 20°C (68°F), maxima at or above 50°C (122°F), and optima between 40 and 50°C (104 and 122°F). Because most soil temperatures correspond well with the temperature optima of mesophiles, it is not surprising that most soil organisms are mesophiles. However, some specialized habitats (for example, volcanic soils) do favor thermophilic bacteria and fungi.

There is an important relationship between temperature, water potential, and microbial activity. Both water potential and temperature must be within critical range for microbial activity to occur. Assuming water potential is within this range, at one extreme, reduced temperatures slow cellular processes. On the other extreme, excessive temperatures denature proteins and alter cell membrane permeability. Between these extremes is the "Q10 rule for biological systems," where Q10, the temperature quotient, equals 2. This rule states that within a limited range, activity doubles for each 10°C increase in temperature. For example, mesophilic organisms at 30°C will have twice the activity as the same organisms at 20°C.

Light

For phototrophs like soil algae, light is an essential because it is required as a source of energy. The amount of light on soil varies because soil constituents absorb or reflect it (this is the albedo effect), and gardening practices like tilling the soil affect how far light penetrates into the soil. Even so, phototrophs decrease with increasing soil depth and decreasing light intensity. Except for a few phototrophs capable of heterotrophy, phototrophs deep in the soil are unlikely to be metabolically active.

For chemotrophs, light is important for a different reason. Although visible light may be important for certain functions like spore formation, UV B light (290 to 320 nanometers) is a source of non-ionizing radiation. This irradiation splits water molecules into free radicals that damage DNA. Therefore, this irradiation links light to water potential: the higher the water content, the more free radicals produced, and the higher the DNA damage. Although ozone screens out most UV-B light in our atmosphere, ozone depletion offsets this. Therefore, it is likely that this abiotic factor will increase its deleterious effect on microbial activity in the photic zone, and only soil organisms that produce UV-absorbing pigments or develop rapid mechanisms of DNA repair will be relatively unaffected.

BIOTIC FACTORS

Soil organisms can also interact with other organisms, and, with one exception, these interactions affect their activity. These biotic interactions can also include larger soil fauna, and at their most complex, populations of organisms or consortia. These interactions are mutualism, symbiosis, commensalism, competition, amensalism, predation, and parasitism (Table 3). The one exception is neutralism, where both organisms interact with each other, but do not affect each other. Because neutralism has no effect, it is not further considered here.

Symbiosis or Mutualism

In symbiosis or mutualism, both organisms benefit. This association can be so specific that one or both organisms are obligate symbionts and cannot live without the other or the relationship can be more general. A well-known symbiosis is a lichen, which consists of a fungus and an alga. The alga provides the fungus with food, and, in return, the fungus provides the alga a home.

Commensalism and Amensalism

In commensalism, one organism benefits while the other is unaffected. For example, one organism can provide an essential growth factor, like a vitamin, for another organism. This type of cross-feeding is common for soil organisms. The opposite of commensalism is amensalism, where one organism is harmed while the other is unaffected. A good example of this interaction is when one organism produces an antibiotic against another organism. Such an interaction is often the basis of biological control. For example, some isolates of the bacterium, *Pseudomonas fluorescens*, can suppress the fungal pathogen, *Gaeumannomyces graminis*, responsible for "take-all" in wheat (*Triticum aestivum*).

Competition

In competition, both organisms vie for the same re-

Table 3. All possible interactions between two organisms.			
Organism #1↓ Organism #2 →	**Positive interaction**	**No effect**	**Negative interaction**
Positive interaction	mutualism, symbiosis		
No effect	commensalism	neutralism	
Negative interaction	predation, parasitism	amensalism	competition

source. This resource can be for any one of the abiotic factors as well as space. In the case of nutrients, the three factors that govern competitive success are growth rate, substrate affinity, and efficiency. If nutrients are unlimited, then microbial activity is governed by the maximal growth rate. This maximal growth rate is rarely the case in soil; the norm for most organisms in soil is starvation. Under these circumstances, substrate affinity and efficiency govern the ability to compete. In the case of substrate affinity, assuming an organism can metabolize a substrate, an organism that recognizes a substrate at a low concentration outcompetes an organism that only recognizes a substrate at a high concentration. In the case of efficiency, an organism that is more efficient in its carbon and energy use outcompetes a less efficient organism.

Predation and Parasitism

Finally, in predation and parasitism, one organism feeds on another. The most common example of predation in soil is protozoa and nematodes preying on bacteria and fungi. Predator responses follow classic predator–prey curves: increases and decreases in numbers of predators lag behind increases and decreases in numbers of prey, respectively. Numbers may not be a good reflection of microbial activity, however. The C:N ratio of soil fauna is approximately 20:1, whereas the C:N ratio ranges from 4:1 to 5:1 for bacteria and up to 15:1 for fungi. When protozoa prey on bacteria and fungi, nitrogen is in excess and is excreted into the environment. This nitrogen is then available to promote microbial activity.

The most common example of parasitism in soil is viruses. Even though viruses are considered nonliving (because they have no intrinsic metabolism or ability to replicate), they parasitize numerous soil bacteria, fungi, and soil fauna. This parasitism is normally a negative interaction. However, occasionally viruses can interact positively with soil organisms because they are capable of adding of a new gene or modifying an existing gene in the host DNA. If this addition or modification (called transduction) makes the host organism more competitive than before, then a seemingly bad thing becomes beneficial.

PLANTS, THE THIRD PART OF THE TRIPARTITE RELATIONSHIP

Early in the 20th Century, scientists observed that plants did a seemingly stupid thing: they exuded as much as 40% of their photosynthate into the soil. The effect of exuding all of these nutrients into the soil was to turn the soil around the roots into to a fabulous oasis for soil organisms. For example, counts of bacteria were often a hundred-fold higher near the roots than in root-free soil. This release of photosynthate led to a new term, rhizosphere, or zone of soil under the influence of plant roots. Seeds in soil did exactly the same thing, and the parallel term was the spermosphere.

Why would a plant exude its hard-won photosynthate into the rhizosphere? The answer was simple: when experiments were done with plants growing with or without soil organisms, more often than not, plants grew better with soil organisms than without them. The soil organisms were providing the plants with plant growth hormones, suppressing plant pathogens, sequestering essential plant nutrients like iron (Fe^{+3}) with special chemicals called siderophores, or releasing essential plant nutrients like phosphorus (P) with organic acids. Although the rhizosphere was limited to short distances around the root (typically less than $\frac{1}{8}$"), the effects were so great that they inspired whole new fields of study. For example, scientists now study plant growth-promoting rhizobacteria (usually called PGPR).

Besides affecting soil organisms, plants also exerted considerable effects on soil. Plant roots bound soil particles, thus promoting soil aggregation, which, in turn, affected soil porosity and oxygen relations. Decaying plant roots created channels in soil, such that when water flowed in the soil, it flowed preferentially through these channels because water "prefers" the path of least resistance. This water flow, called preferential or bypass flow, is important because it describes a way that soil contaminants can move through soil without soil organisms degrading them.

Just these initial interactions among plants, soil organisms, and soil underscore the limitations of considering plants separately from soil and soil organisms, and why plants need instead to be considered as part of a tripartite relationship with soil and soil organisms.

ABIOTIC FACTORS

pH

Like soil organisms, plants prefer a particular pH range. Most plants prefer a near-neutral soil pH (6.0 to 6.5) because nutrients are most available at this pH. Good examples of plants that require this pH range are corn, onions, and tomatoes. However, some plants require a lower pH to grow well. For example, blueberries, rhododendrons, and azaleas have a high requirement for iron (Fe) and this heavy metal is much more available in acid soil than in neutral soil. For this reason, these plants grow better in acid soils (pH 5.0).

Roots have adsorption sites that allow them to change their rhizosphere pH. However, their ability to make this change depends on the buffering capacity of the soil and plant's preference for ammonium or nitrate as a source of N. If the plant prefers ammonium as its nitrogen source, then the plant releases acid from its roots and the rhizosphere pH decreases; if the plant prefers nitrate as its nitrogen source, then the plants releases OH^- anions and the rhizosphere pH increases. Under these conditions, soil pH can vary as much as one or two pH units (because pH is logarithmic, this is a 10- or 100-fold change in H^+ concentration) in the rhizosphere compared with nonrhizosphere soil.

Nutrients

There are 16 nutrients essential for the growth and reproduction of plants, which grouped into two categories, macronutrients and micronutrients. The distinction between a macronutrient and a micronutrient is based on dry weight: if a nutrient is measured in parts per hundred (%), then it is a macronutrient; if nutrient is measured in parts per million, then it is micronutrient. However, the important distinction is not if a nutrient is a macro- or micro-nutrient, but that it is essential: if any nutrient is missing, then the plant cannot grow or complete its life cycle.

The macronutrients are carbon (C), hydrogen (H), oxygen (O), nitrogen (N), phosphorus (P), potassium (K), calcium (Ca), magnesium (Mg), and sulfur (S), and the micronutrients are boron (B), copper (Cu), manganese (Mn), zinc (Zn), iron (Fe), molybdenum (Mo), and chloride (Cl-). One common mnemonic to remember these nutrients is:

C HOPKiNS CaFe, Mg B Mn CuZn Mo, pass the Cl, please

(See Hopkin's Cafe, managed by my cousin Mo, pass the salt, please)

The first three macronutrients, carbon, hydrogen, and oxygen are considered non-mineral macronutrients because the plants obtain these nutrients from air and water and combine them through the process of photosynthesis:

$$6 \, CO_2 + 6 \, H_2O \rightarrow C_6H_{12}O_6 + 6O_2$$

Here, in the presence of light energy, plant combine carbon dioxide and water to form a sugar, glucose, and

oxygen. In this reaction, the oxygen actually comes from the breakdown of water, not carbon dioxide. For this reason, plant do not "breathe" in CO_2 and "breathe" out O_2. The non-mineral macronutrients are obtained from air and water and comprise about 94% of a plant's dry weight; the remaining 15 macro- and micronutrients come from the soil and comprise the remaining 6% of a plant's dry weight.

Water

Like soil organisms, all plants—without exception—require water to live. With respect to plants, two terms have persisted because they are useful for relating soil water to plant growth. The first is field capacity, sometimes also called water-holding capacity. In terms of water potential, field capacity is approximately -0.03 MPa (-0.33 bar), except for sandy soils where field capacity is approximately -0.01 MPa (-0.10 bar). At this point, water has drained from the large pores, but other soil pores are still full of water, which is available for plant growth.

The second term is "permanent wilting point." In terms of water potential, the permanent wilting point is approximately -1.5 MPa (-15 bar). This point occurs when a plant has used all of the water from the micropores and the only water remaining in the soil is hygroscopic water, water bound too tightly to the soil solids for plants to use. At this point, plants permanently wilt and do not recover, even when water is added. "Field capacity" and "permanent wilting point" remain in use because they are still good terms for gardeners to describe the upper and lower limits of plant available water but they should not be confused with water potential because they do not have the word "potential" (or pressure) associated with them.

Because plants transpire water as they grow, it is also important to consider what is happening to water in the rhizosphere. In soils above or near field capacity, even considerable plant transpiration has little effect on soil water potential. However, when the water potential is -0.2 MPa or an even more negative number, the water potential at the soil–root interface (or rhizoplane) can stress microbial cells because the diffusion of nutrients is reduced. Also, as the pores empty of water, the motility of some soil organisms is reduced (nematodes) while the motility of others (mites) is enhanced. This scenario does not mean that having soils at field capacity is necessarily at good thing: if all the pores are water-filled, then diffusion of oxygen into the soil is reduced, and the normal respiration of plants (next section) is blocked.

Oxygen

Like all aerobic organisms, plants use the energy from the oxidation of sugars (here, glucose) for growth:

$C_6H_{12}O_6 + 6O_2 \rightarrow 6CO_2 + 6 H_2O$ + lots of energy
(This chemical equation, of course, is exactly the same as the reaction of aerobic respiration for soil organisms, except plants are able to use a small portion of the oxygen generated by photosynthesis for the reaction. More importantly, plants show the carbon cycle: the reduction of an inorganic molecule, carbon dioxide (CO_2), to an organic molecule (here, glucose), which is called immobilization, and the oxidation of an organic molecule (here, glucose) to CO_2, which is called mineralization. All nutrient cycles, without exception, have immobilization and mineralization. Furthermore, all major nutrient cycles, with the exception of phosphate (which cycles back and forth through orthophosphate, $H_2PO_4^{2-}$) have reduction and oxidation.

Temperature

Temperature affects plants because it affects photosynthesis. Like soil organisms, the rate of this process is temperature dependent: to a certain point, the higher the temperature, the faster the rate. However, if the temperature is too high, then respiration exceeds photosynthesis, and growth slows. Conversely, if the temperature is too low, photosynthesis is slowed, and growth slows. In addition, many temperate plants exhibit vernalization, which means that they require a cold period, typically between 40 and 50 °F, to break dormancy or to begin germination or flowering.

Light

Plants exhibit three responses to light: photosynthesis, phototropism, and photoperiodism. In photosynthesis, plants harvest light energy with the pigment chlorophyll, which is embedded in membranes of chloroplasts of plant cells. Since light only occurs during the daytime, photosynthesis only occurs during the daytime. In phototropism, plants move towards light. Finally, in photoperiodism, some plants react to the dark. For example, a long-day plant requires a short night to flower, whereas a short-day plant requires a long night to flower. In contrast, other plants are day neutral and flower regardless of night length.

BIOTIC FACTORS

Symbiosis

Because of its importance to gardening and agriculture in general, the most well known symbiosis for plants is biological nitrogen fixation. In this symbiosis, nitrogen-fixing bacteria enter the plant and incite a nodule to form. In return for the bacteria fixing atmospheric nitrogen, the plant supplies the bacteria with nutrients. A good agricultural example of this symbiosis is between the bacterium, *Bradyrhizobium japonicum*, and the legume, soybeans (*Glycine max*) (Figure 7); a good forestry example is the symbiosis between the bacterium *Frankia* and a range of angiosperms like alder (*Alnus* sp.).)

Another well known symbiosis is various mycorrhizal associations where several genera of soil fungi colonize plant roots. In return for giving the fungi a home and supplying them with nutrients, the fungi allow roots to explore a much greater soil volume, thereby enhancing its water and mineral uptake, principally for phosphorus. It is estimated that as many as 95% of all plants are mycorrhizal.

It is important to note that these symbioses are dependent on the availability of soil nutrients. Thus, if a plant has a plentiful supply of available nitrogen, then nitrogen fixation is inhibited; similarly, if the plant has a plentiful supply of phosphorus, then mycorrhizal associations are inhibited.

Figure 7

Figure 7. Nodules on soybeans after inoculation with Bradyrhizobium japonicum.

Commensalism and Amensalism

Like soil organisms, plants have commensalistic and amensalistic relationships. For Georgia, a good example of a commensalistic relationship is the growth of the epiphytes, Spanish moss (*Tillandsia usneoides*) and resurrection ferns (*Polypodium polypodioides*) on southern live oaks (*Quercus virginiana*). The Spanish moss and resurrection ferns gain a home for aerial feeding, while the oak receives nothing in return. A good example of

amensalism in plants is the production of the chemical juglone by eastern black walnuts (*Juglans nigra*). Thus, at little expense to the walnut, it increases its ability to survive by producing a compound that inhibits or kills many other species of plants. This amensalism is also a form of negative allelopathy In allelopathy, one plant produces a chemical that affects the ability of another organism to grow, survive, or reproduce.

Figure 8

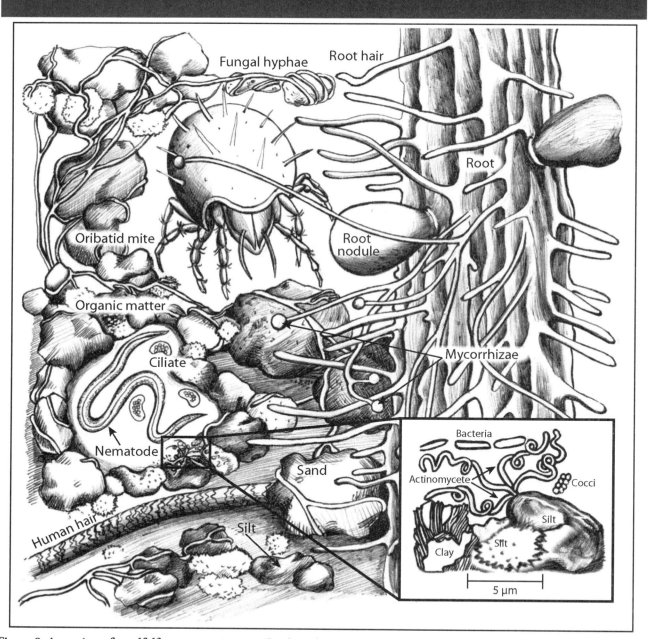

Figure 8. A portion of an alfalfa root growing in a Cecil sandy loam, a common soil in the Piedmont, containing less than 1% organic matter. The soil is well-aggregated and not compacted. A human hair (diameter, 100 micrometers) is included for comparison. (Original drawing by Wendy Giminski.)

Competition

Like soil organisms, plants compete for nutrients, water, and space both with each other (intra-species competition) as well as with other plants (interspecies competition). Unlike most animals, plants cannot move. Therefore, if conditions are sufficiently crowded, then plants may compete for light as well. Plants may also compete for animals to pollinate them or to disperse their seeds.

Predation and Parasitism

As a good source of nutrients, plants are eaten by animals or parasitized by a number of organisms. Plant parasites range from obligatory to facultative; a facultative plant parasite can live on its own. A good example of a plant that parasitizes another plant is mistletoe.

INTEGRATING ABIOTIC AND BIOTIC FACTORS

In order to truly understand what is happening in any garden soil, it is important not only to consider each of the six biotic and abiotic factors separately, but also to integrate them with each other. Furthermore, it is important to remember to include soil properties like soil texture, bulk density, and soil structure in this integration because these features affect soil organisms and plants as well. For example, soil texture affect plants because soils with more clay may restrict root growth, as do compacted soils with their high bulk densities.

With this chapter as a guide, now consider a plant (here, alfalfa) growing in a Cecil sandy loam (Figure 8). Everything in the figure is properly scaled. Given the dimensions of a human hair (added to the figure for comparison), the total area is slightly less than ⅛ by ⅛". Alfalfa grows poorly in acid soil (as does its bacterial nitrogen-fixing symbiont), so the soil must have been limed to a fairly neutral pH. Assuming it is cool spring day aboveground, light is driving photosynthesis and warming both the plant and the soil, although the soil is slightly cooler under the plant because the plant canopy is shading the soil. Belowground, alfalfa has formed two symbiotic relationships, one with a bacterium (*Sinorhizobium meliloti*) and another with a mycorrhizal fungus. Within the nodule, the bacterium is fixing atmospheric nitrogen for the plant and, in return, the plant is supplying the bacterium with nutrients. The plant is also providing a home and furnishing nutrients to the mycorrhizal fungus, which, in return, is exploring a greater volume of soil to provide the plant with water and a variety of mineral nutrients,

especially phosphorus. These associations suggest that the soil lacks nutrients as these associations would not have formed if the soil had had sufficient qualities of nitrogen and other mineral nutrients. The plant is also exuding a portion of its photosynthates from its roots and creating a typical rhizosphere effect, where fungal and bacterial populations are enhanced as these organisms dine on the increased carbon. In return, the fungi and bacteria may be providing the plant with plant growth hormones and other minerals. Because plant roots and soil organisms are respiring, soil oxygen is decreasing and carbon dioxide is increasing. However, the increased carbon dioxide is being offset in the rhizoplane because it is during the day and the plant is transpiring water. Therefore, oxygen diffusion is increasing in this area as the water potential becomes more negative and the water-filled pores drain. In pores that remain water-filled, bacterial-eating nematodes and protozoa are dining on the increased bacterial populations. Another predator, an oribatid mite, is taking advantage of a now-drained soil pore to prepare to eat mycorrhizal hyphae. The mycorrhizal and other fungal hyphae are binding soil particles, thus promoting soil aggregation. This aggregation is affecting soil porosity, which, in turn, is affecting soil water and oxygen relations. Because the C:N ratio for bacteria is much smaller than the predators eating them, the protozoa and nematode are excreting excess ammonia for nitrifiers to convert to nitrate. These acidifying reactions will lower the soil pH in this area.

Unlocking the Gardening Secret

The interactions between and among soil, soil organisms, and plants are the equivalent of an intricate and elegant dance. Knowing these interactions—how some plants and microorganisms will grow and others will die, and how some processes will begin and others will stop—is the key to understanding the soil ecosystem. However, given the number of factors in soil and their possible interactions among soil, organisms, and plants, it may seem intimidating to try to figure out what is happening in a particular soil. We are not Superwoman or Superman with X-ray vision capable of seeing what is happening in the space of a few fractions of an inch. Yet as the swirl of cream in a cup of coffee is the same as the swirl of galaxies, scaling up works well because the interdependencies at the micro level are the same at the macro level. Here are four keys to unlocking biotic and abiotic interactions.

First, follow the adage is that the best fertilizer is the gardener's footstep. Always begin with good observation. There are only a few soil properties and six abiotic and biotic factors; unless there are extremely unusual circumstances, there aren't any others. Therefore, if something is happening in the garden it must because of one of these factors or the interaction of one or more of these factors. Weather provides immediate information on three abiotic factors, light, temperature, and water.

Second, sample the soil and get a routine soil test. It is important that the soil be sampled correctly, and the University of Georgia Extension Service has a publication on this at http://pubsadmin.caes.uga.edu/files/pdf/C%20896_3.PDF. Information from this publication follows this chapter. While digging for a soil sample, the color of the soil will give insight to soil aeration, another abiotic factor. The routine soil test will give soil pH, lime buffering capacity, and six of the 13 of the soil mineral macro- and micro-nutrients (phosphorus, potassium, calcium, magnesium, manganese, and zinc) and insight into the final two soil abiotic factors, pH and nutrients. If the soil has never been sampled before, include a separate test to determine the percentage of organic matter. Both a routine soil test and a test for organic matter are relatively inexpensive.

Third, go through each factor and apply the Goldilocks principle: if something is out of range, then it needs to be adjusted until it is "just right." In the case of plants, there are a number of well-known symptoms for a variety of biotic and abiotic factors. For example, a plant with stunted growth and yellow leaves may not only be exhibiting symptoms of nitrogen deficiency, but also too much water in the soil. However, if it hasn't rained and the soil is dry, then it is more likely that nitrogen deficiency is the problem.

Fourth, adhere to Wendell Berry's maxim: if you do not know where you are, then you do not know who you are. Become a student of place and time. Up to now, the factor of time has been ignored, yet it too has a place in understanding our gardens. For example, years and years of long-ago agricultural production has allowed much of our beautiful Georgia topsoil to slip seaward. As a result, many of our soils are so badly eroded that their official descriptions begin with the awful words, "In much of the acreage, so much material has been lost through erosion that the plow layer now extends into the subsoil." It is hard to believe that when famed botanist William Bartram came through Georgia over 200 years ago, he wrote about our soils as a "deep, rich dark mould on a deep stratum of reddish brown tenacious clay…" Now we realize that it is not the "deep, rich dark mould" that we are looking at, but the "reddish brown" subsoil. Therefore, instead of a Georgia soil

with 4 to 6% organic matter (the historic average), the organic matter in our soils is often less than 1%. The effect is that we start our gardens automatically with a lowered CEC, a higher bulk density, and a reduced water-holding capacity, all traits attributable to a loss in organic matter. Therefore, one of best actions any Master Gardener can do to any Georgia soil is to restore this lost organic matter back to the soil.

Becoming a student of place and time requires that we look to the future as well. Three abiotic factors will become increasingly important in the future: temperature, water, and nutrients. For temperature, the levels of greenhouses gases like carbon dioxide and methane in our atmosphere continue to increase, and because we have incontrovertible proof that these gases trap heat, Georgia's climate will become warmer. Gardeners who are old enough can already see this effect of this warming because spring is now coming approximately one week earlier than it was 25 years ago. For example, Figure 9 shows what is happening in Athens, Georgia: while the date of the first frost in the fall has remained the same, the date of the last frost in the spring is approximately one week earlier than before. Master Gardeners need to consider the effects of this future temperature increase. For example, use of mulches to keep soils cooler in summer will become more important in the future.

For water, Master Gardeners need pay close attention whenever climatologists predict El Niño (Spanish for "the boy") and La Niña (Spanish for "the girl") weather

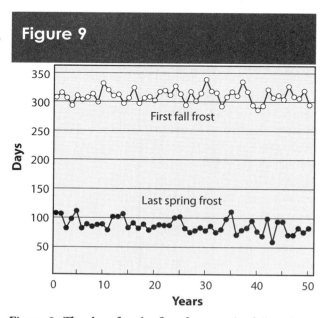

Figure 9. The date for the first frost in the fall and the last frost in the spring in Athens, Georgia, for the last 50 years. (Data courtesy of Dorinda Dallmeyer, University of Georgia).

patterns for the Southeast. El Niño and La Niña refer to the warming and cooling of the surface waters of the tropical central and eastern Pacific Ocean, respectively. In Georgia, El Niño generally means that we will have wetter and cooler weather than normal, and La Niña means that we will have significantly warmer and drier weather than normal. For La Niña weather conditions, Master Gardeners will need to embrace methods like drip irrigation and sensor technology to reduce the amount of water needed for irrigation that will become an inevitable part of water conservation.

For nutrients, if they are petroleum-based (for example, synthetic fertilizers), then they will become more expensive because the supply of petroleum is finite. Sooner or later, the petroleum will run out. Therefore, gardening practices will become more sustainable and practices like rotating crops to reduce disease, using cover crops to take advantage of biological processes like nitrogen fixation, and recycling nutrients with composting will become increasingly commonplace as the petroleum-based alternatives of synthetic herbicides, pesticides, and fertilizers become too expensive.

Soil Is Beautiful and It Does Beautiful Things

In the end, Lowdermilk was right: civilizations that did not care about their soils inevitably failed, while those civilizations that did care about their soils flourished. We will never achieve this caring if we see soil solely as a jumble of physical and chemical characteristics. We need to see soil as interacting with soil organisms and plants as part of a much more complex food web. When we see soil this way, then eventually we will see that we are part of this web as well. When we realize this truth, we will then soil in a different light: that soil is beautiful and it does beautiful things. Therefore, the true task of Master Gardeners to get others to see this picture as well because, literally, our civilization depends on it.

RESOURCES

Bartram, W. 1791. *Travels through North & South Carolina, Georgia, East & West Florida, the Cherokee Country, the Extensive Territories of the Muscogulges, or Creek Confederacy, and the Country of the Chactaws; containing an account of the soil and natural productions of those regions, together with observations on the manners of the Indians.* James and Johnson, Philadelphia.

Brady, N. C., and R. R. Weil. 2010. *Elements of the nature and properties of soils, 3rd ed.* Prentice Hall, New York.

Lowdermilk, W. C. 1953. *The conquest of the land through 7,000 years.* Agriculture Information Bulletin No. 99. Government Printing Office, Washington, DC.

Sylvia, D. M., J. J. Fuhrmann, P. G. Hartel, and D. A. Zuberer. 2005. *Principles and applications of soil microbiology, 2nd ed.* Pearson, Upper Saddle River, NJ.

DISCUSSION QUESTIONS

1. A sample of the Cecil soil from the Georgia Piedmont contains 10.0% clay and 70.0% sand. Using the soil triangle in Figure 3, determine the textural class of this soil.

2. The CEC of the A horizon of a Tifton sandy loam is 2.15 cmol kg^{-1} of soil. What is CEC and if you wanted to change it, what could you add?

3. Name the six abiotic soil factors and give an example for each.

4. Name six *different* kinds of organisms in soil.

5. Name the six biotic soil factors, and give an example of each for soil organisms and plants.

6. What is the rhizosphere and why is it so important?

7. What are the 16 nutrients essential for the growth and reproduction of all plants?

8. Draw the carbon cycle, showing immobilization and mineralization, and oxidation and reduction.

9. Why is a routine soil test essential as one part in determining problems in a garden?

10. What three abiotic factors are likely to be a problem in our future and why?

SOIL TESTING FOR HOME LAWNS & GARDENS

Soil tests such as those conducted by the University of Georgia Soil Testing and Plant Analysis Laboratory will help you develop and maintain a more productive soil by providing information about the fertility status of your soil. Information from a soil test will help you select the proper liming and fertilization program to obtain optimal growth of lawn, garden, and ornamental plants.

One of the most important steps in soil testing is collecting the sample. Soil test results can be no better than the sample submitted to the laboratory for analysis. A soil sample weighing about 1 pound is used to represent thousands of pounds of soil in the landscape or garden. Therefore, it is extremely important that soil samples be properly and carefully taken.

A Good Soil Sample Should Be Representative of the Area

Take soil from a minimum of 10 random locations (x) in the sampled area and mix together in a clean bucket.

For trees and shrubs, take soil from six to eight spots around the dripline of the plants and mix.

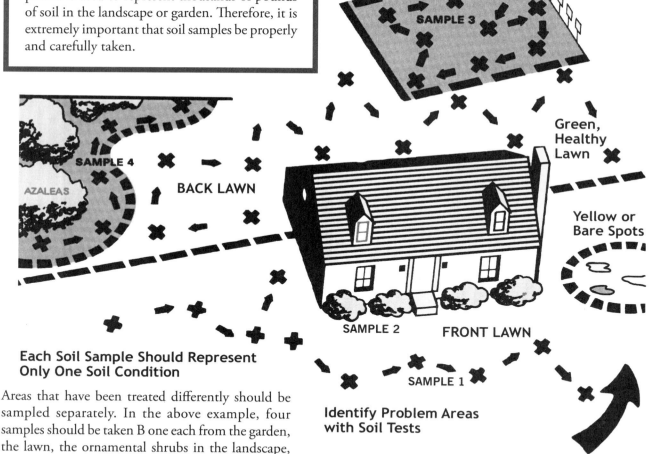

VEGETABLE GARDEN

SAMPLE 3

SAMPLE 4

AZALEAS

BACK LAWN

Green, Healthy Lawn

Yellow or Bare Spots

SAMPLE 2

FRONT LAWN

SAMPLE 1

Each Soil Sample Should Represent Only One Soil Condition

Areas that have been treated differently should be sampled separately. In the above example, four samples should be taken B one each from the garden, the lawn, the ornamental shrubs in the landscape, and the azaleas. If the front and back lawns have been treated differently or if they are seeded to different grasses, then take a separate sample from each.

Identify Problem Areas with Soil Tests

Areas where plants grow differently or the soil appears different should be sampled separately.

Adapted from University of Georgia Cooperative Extension Circular 896

Do Not Contaminate The Sample

Use clean sampling tools and containers.

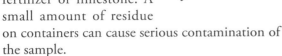

Never use tools or containers that have been used for mixing or applying fertilizer or limestone. A small amount of residue on containers can cause serious contamination of the sample.

Sample to the Proper Depth

Remove any surface litter such as turf thatch or mulch.

For lawns, sample to a depth of 4 inches. For gardens, ornamentals and fruit trees, sample to a depth of 6 inches.

Use a trowel or sampling tube to collect soil samples. To use a trowel or spade, push the tool to the desired depth into the soil.

Then push the handle forward, with the trowel or

spade still in the soil, to make a wide opening. Cut a thin slice from the side of the opening that is of uniform thickness about 3 inch thick and 2 inches wide, extending from the top of the ground to the depth of the cut. Scrape away any grass thatch or mulch, and place the slice of soil into a clean bucket or other container. After the soil is taken, remove the shovel or spade and let the soil fall back in place.

Soil Samples Should Be Carefully Mixed and Packaged

Do not use sample bags other than those provided by the University of Georgia Soil Testing and Plant Analysis Laboratory. All cores taken for a given sample should be collected in a clean bucket and **thoroughly mixed.**

Fill the soil sample bag to the indicated line with the mixed soil.

Supply all the information asked for on the soil sample bag. List your **Name** and **Address, Plant to Be Grown, Sample Number** (please use a simple code and do not exceed 3 digits, *e.g.* 1, 2, 3, ... 20, 21, 22, ... 321, 322 ... 32A, 32B ...) and your **County**. This information is essential for the return of your sample results and fertilizer recommendations to the proper county extension office. On the bag, indicate tests desired by checking the proper box. For lawns, gardens and shrubs, a routine test will suffice. If a special analysis, *e.g.,* nitrate-nitrogen (NO_3-N), organic matter (OM) or boron (B) is needed, first consult your local county extension office. Samples should be dropped off at your county extension office for mailing to the laboratory. Soil sample bags and other pertinent information are available at your county extension office.

When and How Often Should Soils Be Tested?

Soils can be tested any time during the year; however, be sure to sample well in advance of planting or spring green-up. This sampling is particularly important on areas where lime is likely to be needed. Lime reacts fairly slowly and should be mixed with the soil several weeks before planting. Generally, fall is the most desirable time to sample soils, because landscapes and gardens are usually dry and easily accessible. Soils should be dry enough to till when sampling. If wet samples are collected, they should be air dried before being placed in the soil sample bag.

Once medium or high fertility levels are established, lawn and ornamental areas only need to be sampled every two to three years. Vegetable gardens should be sampled every one to two years.

NOTES

2
Basic Botany

James T. Midcap

Matthew Chappell

LEARNING OBJECTIVES

Learn to identify basic plant parts and types/variations of plant parts: stems, leaves, buds, flowers, fruit, and roots.

Understand what vascular tissue is and its function in the plant.

Understand what the cambium is and its function in the plant.

Understand the difference between dicots and monocots.

Develop an appreciation for the necessity and benefits of binomial nomenclature.

TERMS TO KNOW

Binomial nomenclature system in which the scientific name of a plant consists of two parts indicating the genus and species.

Cambium tissue in a plant that produces new cells.

Corm short, thickened, underground, upright stem in which food is stored.

Cotyledon l eaf or leaves of the embryo, also called seed leaves.

Crown part of a plant where the root and the stem meet.

Cultivar cultivated variety; a subdivision of a species, a result of human-manipulated hybridization.

Deciduous plants that drop their leaves at the end of each growing season.

Dicot dicotyledon; flowering plants with embryos that have two cotyledons.

Dioecious plants that have only male or only female flowers on an individual plant.

Genus groups of closely related species clearly defined from other plants.

Hybrid first generation cross between two genetically diverse parents.

Latent bud dormant bud that is capable of growth and development.

Lateral bud buds on the sides of stems, responsible for growth of leaves and side branches.

Meristem region of cell and tissue initiation; cells that do not mature, but remain capable of further growth and division.

Monocot monocotyledon, flowering plants that have embryos with only one cotyledon.

Monoecious plants that have both male and female flowers on the same plant.

Pistil female part of the flower, consisting of one or more carpels and enclosed ovules.

Pollen microspores that carry the male gametophyte of seed plants.

Rhizome underground, horizontal stem.

Root portion of the plant usually found below ground; distinguished from stem by not having nodes.

Root hairs tubular outgrowths of surface cells of the root.

Seed the organ that forms after fertilization occurs.

Sepals structures that usually form the outermost whorl of a flower. Together, they are called the calyx.

Species group of closely related individuals that have the potential to reproduce with each other; a unit of classification.

Stamen the male part of the flower. It consists of the anther and the slender filament that holds it in position.

Stem main trunk of a plant. It develops buds and shoots.

Stigma part of the pistil that receives the pollen grains; usually the top of the pistil.

Style slender part of a pistil between the stigma and the ovary.

Taproot a stout, tapering primary root that has limited side branching or fine roots.

INTRODUCTION

Botany is the science of understanding plants and how they grow. Under the umbrella of botany are many other more specific plant related fields including: plant taxonomy (the study of plant classification and nomenclature), plant morphology (the study of plant forms), genetics (how plants reproduce and how new cultivars are formed), and plant physiology (the study of plant functions). Basic botany is important in understanding horticulture, which deals with the art and science of cultivating plants, such as flowers, vegetables, fruits, and woody ornamentals. Botany helps us understand how and why plants react to cultural practices and their environment.

Plant Names

Plant nomenclature, or the naming of plants uses both common names and botanic names. Both types of names serve useful roles in plant communication. Common names are used in general conversation by gardeners talking about their tomatoes, roses or flowering shrubs. Botanical names are used to convey an exact species identification, and only one botanical name is given to each species of plant on Earth.

Common Names—Most plants have common names, especially popular plants that are attractive or useful. Common names are easy to use because they are derived locally using the local language and/or dialect. However, they do not guarantee the exact identification of the plant. Different common names arise for the same plant in different regions. Common names usually change from one country to another, even if the plant does not. Problems arise when more than one name for the same plant exists or the same name is used for two different plants.

As an example, "Tulip tree" can refer to *Magnolia soulangiana* or *Liriodendron tulipifera*, both widely grown in Georgia. In the case of *Magnolia soulangiana*, with its large pink spring flowers, three common names are used interchangeably: Japanese magnolia, saucer magnolia, and tulip tree. The Liriodendron, a tall native tree, is known by three different common names: yellow poplar, tulip tree and tulip poplar. These common names can cause confusion about the true identity of a particular plant.

Botanical names— Botanical names are precise, using only one name for each plant. The botanical community has developed a set of rules for naming plants, known as The International Code of Botanical Nomenclature.

These rules provide guidelines for everyone as to how plants are named. When landscape architects, nurserymen or gardeners need to be precise and accurate with plant identifications or specifications, they use botanical names. Most reference books use botanical names as well as some common names. There are no rules that specify correct common names.

Nomenclature and Classification: History and Relevancy

Nomenclature deals with the science of naming plants, while classification is the grouping of similar plants based on their phenotypic (physical appearance) and/or genetic (similar hereditary traits) relationship to each other.

Scientists in the late 1600's and early 1700's became increasingly vocal about the problems of long plant names (descriptions) because without a standardized system of nomenclature, classification of plants was nearly impossible. Carl Linnaeus (1707-1778), a physician and professor of botany and medicine at the University of Uppsala in Sweden, revamped the naming and classification of plants by instituting a universally understood system of nomenclature that also afforded scientists the ability to classify similar plants. Linnaeus is remembered today as the "father of taxonomy".

Linnaeus accomplished two things: a standardized method of naming plants, and a classification scheme. He developed the binomial system of nomenclature which uses two words to name a population of closely related plants, genus and species. Originally, the currently recognized 300,000 plant species were grouped into species based on the ability of plants within a species to interbreed. This species definition (concept) survives in part today and forms the basis for the taxonomy of all living organisms, not just plants. However, plants can also fall into the same species based on a myriad of other factors and more than 100 definitions of "species" have been recorded in scientific literature.

Linnaeus proposed that Latin be the language for naming plants and be the standard worldwide. It was a good choice, since Latin was a "dead language" (not spoken), and the names and their meanings would not change or evolve as with a spoken language. Latin was also a good choice on political grounds, since it was a universal language among medical scholars regardless of their native language.

Because of Linnaeus and his binomial system, the genus for the oak was named Quercus. The white oak species became *Quercus alba*. The scarlet oak became *Quercus coccinea* and the red oak *Quercus rubra*. The Latin "alba" refers to the white undersides of the leaves while "rubra" refers to the red fall color. "Coccinea" refers to the brilliant scarlet fall color. In this manner, unique names for each oak species were formulated, as well as the names for other plants.

Linnaeus classified many plants and groups of plants. He created a classification system based on the sexual and phenotypic characteristics of the flowers. His system was later replaced by a natural classification system that was based on overall phenotypic similarities of the species, although floral classification is still a dominant feature used in classification. Similar species are placed into a common genus, similar genera were placed into a family, and so on, up the classification ladder. Taxonomists soon realized that this natural system did not always work, so a phylogenetic system (based on evolution)was developed that gave a truer picture of the relationships of plants to one another. Today's classification system is based on a combination of natural classification and the phylogenetic system, since the evolution of all plants is not completely understood.

The plant classification system illustrated shows the major groups.

MAJOR TAXA

Plant Kingdom

   Division

      Class

         Order

            Family

MINOR TAXA

Genus (Genera)

   Species

      Subspecies

         Variety

The genus is a simple concept. All maples that we see in nature and in horticulture belong to the maple genus, *Acer*. In similar fashion, all oaks are found in the oak genus, *Quercus*. The pine and its relatives comprise the genus *Pinus*. Each species is comprised of a population of plants possessing unique identification characteristics capable of breeding among themselves. The species may

be assumed to represent a succession of plants from one generation to the next.

The species is always written with the genus to which it belongs. For example, the red maple species is *Acer rubrum* and the sugar maple is *Acer saccharum*. The species botanical name is the genus *Acer* and the specific epithet (specific name) is rubrum for red maple.

When a species is made up of distinct, geographically isolated groups that are not phenotypically distinct enough to constitute separate species, the term "subspecies" is employed. In the past, botanists would either not use the term or use it interchangeably with "variety." More recently, a variety is usually considered to be less distinct than a subspecies. Thus, just as a species can have several subspecies, a subspecies can have several varieties. This practice is sometimes used in the USDA PLANTS online database. Be careful not to confuse the abbreviation "ssp." (subspecies) for "spp." (species, plural). You can also find subspecies abbreviated as "subsp." in many recent works, an innovation which makes the ssp./spp. distinction less problematic.

Below the species level are varieties, often of considerable interest to horticulturists. Botanical varieties are recognized as changes in natural (wild) populations that do not modify the essential identifying features of the species. If a group of individuals within the species shows minor but consistent differences, they may be called a variety.

Hybrids may result as cross breeding occurs between two species, thus requiring special distinction. The names of these " interspecific hybrids" are designated by an "×" (multiplication sign) preceding the specific epithet, such as *Clematis × jackmanii*, a hybrid between *C. lanuginosa* and *C. viticella*. Did you notice that the second and third time the genus *Clematis* was mentioned, it was abbreviated with a "C."? It is acceptable to abbreviate a species name to the first letter of the genus name if used two or more times in sequence.

Hybrids between genera, or "intergeneric hybrids" occasionally occur but are very rare. These hybrids are designated by an "×" preceding the genus. For example, the leyland cypress, × *Cupressocyparis leylandii*, is an inter generic hybrid between *Cupressus macrocarpa* and *Chamaecyparis notkatensis*. This cross of *C. macrocarpa* native to California Monterey peninsula, and *C. notkatensis*, native from Alaska to Washington, occurred in Wales, England.

The Cultivar

Many cultivated plants are selected or developed by man. A special horticultural taxonomic category is used to designate these plants. The cultivar, an abbreviation for "cultivated variety", differs from naturally occurring botanical varieties. Cultivars are plants that originate and persist under cultivation. They are clearly distinct from the species. Modern cultivars can be patented or the names copyrighted and/or trademarked. Cultivars are maintained by man since oftentimes they cannot maintain themselves through natural pollination and seed production in environments outside the native range of the species that the cultivar was derived from.

The cultivar name uses the language of the country where it originated. It can consist of up to three words, is set off in single quotes and is not italicized. Examples include *Fothergilla major* cv. 'Mt. Airy' or the coral bark Japanese maple, *Acer palmatum* 'Sango Kaku'. A cultivar can develop from a botanical variety. For example, rose glow barberry developed as a sport from the purple leaf Japanese barberry. The botanical name for rose glow barberry is *Berberis thunbergii var. atropurpurea* 'Rose Glow'.

Most cultivars are clones. Clones are plants that are reproduced by asexual means and are genetically identical to the parent plant. Most clones are reproduced by cuttings, grafting, budding, layering, division or tissue culture. However, not all cultivars are clones. Cultivars that come true from seed, particularly vegetables, annuals and some herbaceous perennials are not clones.

PLANT PARTS AND FUNCTIONS

Horticulture crops include a widely diverse collection of plants. However, these plants carry out the same basic processes and possess great similarity in the construction of their parts.

Most horticulture plants are either gymnosperms, which include the conifers or cone-bearers, or angiosperms, which produce seeds inside a fruit. The angiosperms are further divided into plants classed as dicotyledons (dicots), flowering plants that possess two seed leaves, and monocotyledons (monocots), flowering plants that possess one seed leaf. Dicots include beans, peas, and many ornamentals while monocots include corn and grasses.

The plant body has two basic parts: the below ground part (the root) and the above ground part (the shoot) as shown in Figure 1. Roots anchor a plant in the soil,

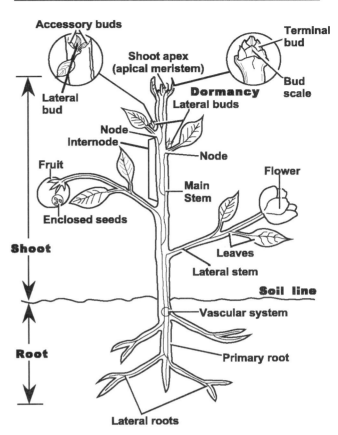

Figure 1. A diagram of the vascular plant with buds, nodes, reproductive structures, roots, shoots and vascular system.

absorb water and nutrients from the soil, and conduct the absorbed materials to the base of the stem. Roots can also serve as food storage structures.

The shoot functions to provide structural support to foliage, flower and fruit/cone; manufacture food; move food, water and nutrients; reproduce; and sometimes store food. The shoot is made up of stems, leaves, buds, and sometimes reproductive structures. The areas of the stem where leaves are attached are called nodes. The space between two nodes is called the internode. A terminal bud is usually present at the apical/terminal meristem (tip of shoot). Lateral buds are located at the nodes between the leaf and the stem. Buds are capable of developing into shoots, reproductive structures, or both. Reproductive structures include flowers, fruits, and seeds on flowering plants (angiosperms), and cones and seeds on conifers (gymnosperms). The vascular system moves water from the roots up to the leaves and floral structures via the xylem, and food from the leaves down to the roots via the phloem.

The whole plant can be broken down into smaller and smaller units. The roots, shoots, buds, leaves, flowers, fruits, cones and seeds can all be broken down into the tissues, cells, and cell parts. We will only discuss the organs and their tissues in this basic botany section.

Roots

Root Structure—The very tip of actively growing young roots is important for plant survival because the tip of a root is the actively growing portion of the root (think the opposite of a human hair). The root apex, an apical meristem, is only one to several cells thick and initiates cell division to produce new cells (Figure 2). The root apex is protected by the root cap that acts as a lubricant as the root pushes through the soil column. Once cells are produced in the root apex, these cells begin a maturation process. First, these cells stretch and elongate in the zone of elongation, pushing the root tip further through the soil. The zone of elongation is therefore directly responsible for root lengthening (growth). Next, in the zone of maturation, the cells attain physiological maturity and stop stretching. The easiest way to tell where the zone of maturation begins is to look for the presence of tiny root hairs (often less than 1 mm long) that are produced to absorb and translocate water and minerals from the soil into the root.

Taproots and Fibrous Roots—The root initially arises from the lower end of the embryo during germination of the seed. This primary root grows downward in the soil, and the root system of the plant begins. When the primary root grows down with minimal branching, it develops a taproot system. When the root system consists of mostly lateral roots near the surface, it is called

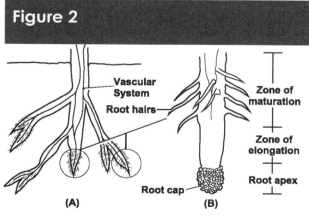

Figure 2

Figure 2. A diagram of plant roots with the developmental stages of young roots. The root hairs absorb much of the water and nutrients used by the plant.

a fibrous root system.

Taproots are found on carrots, dandelion, hickory, and white oak as opposed to fibrous rooted plants like fescue and vinca. Plants with fibrous shallow roots respond more quickly to fluctuations in water and nutrients than plants with taproots. Taprooted plants do well during droughts because their roots penetrate deeply into the soil. Some plants have both a lower taproot and an upper fibrous root system with recent research indicating that many trees initially produce a taproot that rots as the tree ages, leaving only a fibrous root system.

Adventitious Roots—Adventitious roots are produced by many plants that root quickly and easily when asexually propagated. They usually develop on aerial portions of the stem, such as prop roots on corn or on horizontal stems of ivy. Adventitious roots originate within or near the vascular tissues of the stem.

Adventitious rooting allows commercial propagation of many herbaceous and woody plants. Adventitious roots form on cuttings and can be enhanced with hormonal treatment. Gardeners take advantage of the plant's ability to form adventitious roots, to produce annuals, perennials, and woody plants by asexual cutting propagation.

Root Function—Root systems can account for more than half the dry weight of the whole plant. The primary function of the roots is to absorb water and nutrients, and transport the absorbed materials to the base of the stem. Roots anchor the plant in place and support the shoots. Roots may serve as food-accumulating organs in some species.

Some roots become rich in accumulated foods in the form of sugars and starch. Plants with food storage roots can provide a valuable addition to our diet. Food storage roots become enlarged and fleshy and form thick taproots in some plants. Plants with edible taproots include beets, carrots, parsnips, radish, rutabaga, salsify, and turnips. In other plants, the branch roots can become swollen and function as storage organs. Roots of this type are known as tuberous (or storage) roots and occur on dahlia, Jerusalem artichoke, and sweet potato.

Root systems are ideally suited to absorption. Their complex branching and the presence of root hairs in the zone of maturity creates very large surface areas that are in contact with the soil. Much of this surface area depends upon the root hairs associated with areas of new growth. Root hairs slough away as they get older and farther back on the maturing root. Much of the absorption is through the root hairs although some absorption occurs in young roots through their surface epidermis.

Horticultural Implications—The type of root system does affect horticultural practices. A plant with a taproot system is difficult to transplant (moving the plant by digging it up and placing it at a new site). The problem is that much of the deep taproot gets cut off and left behind in the soil. The plant is unable to survive this setback. Plants with taproots are frequently grown in containers to eliminate this problem. The whole taproot is intact in the container when you transplant it to your garden. Plants with fibrous roots are much easier to transplant, because most of the root system is moved during transplanting.

Loss of root hairs explains why transplanting a plant causes a setback. No matter how careful you are when digging the plant, you do some damage to root hairs and lose some absorption capability. Depending on the extent of the root hair loss, the plant may or may not wilt. Time is needed to restore this loss. For this reason, plants grown in individual containers transplant better than field-dug plants. Nursery stock in containers is preferred over balled and burlapped stock, and bedding plant plugs over bare root transplants.

The instant lawn from sod rolls is made possible because grasses have a fibrous root system. Grass is grown on huge sod farms. When orders arrive for sod, a machine with a sharp blade slices through the soil just below the crown of the grass. While slicing the sod from the soil, the machine also rolls the sod. The sod rolls are transported by truck to various nurseries and sold either directly to consumers or to landscape contractors who install instant lawns.

Certain fungi, known as mycorrhizae, grow in contact with plant roots. They increase the absorption of water and nutrients by the roots of many plants. The term myco means "fungus" in Latin, and rhizae means "root," hence myco-rhizae essentially means fungus-root. In exchange for their help in absorption, the fungus utilizes some products from the plant, primarily sugars and carbohydrates. These plant products increase the growth and reproduction of the fungus. These fungal partners can actually live separately from plants in the soil. When they exist apart, the growth and reproduction of these isolated fungi are much slower.

Mycorrhizae can be especially important in mature root areas that no longer have root hairs. It is estimated that some 90% of horticultural plants have mycorrhizal partners. This knowledge helps explain why certain plants propagated in nurseries and grown in home landscapes do not grow as well as their counterparts in natural environments. The nursery plants are missing their mycorrhizal partners. Home landscape soils may have mycorrhizae waiting to inoculate new plant roots, and many mycorrhizae products are available for purchase to 'prime' soil for planting ornamentals.

Stems

Stem Structure and Function—Shoots are composed of stems, leaves, buds, and sometimes flowers, fruits/cones and seeds. The stem supports the leaves and reproductive structures. It also conducts the nutrients and water absorbed by the roots up to the leaves and reproductive structures. Some stems have limited food production abilities when young and green. Modified stems may act as food storage organs. Plant forms are determined by the structure and growth of the stems.

The stem has many specialized tissues (Figure 3) because of complex stem functions such as growth, support, and conduction. Herbaceous stems grow primarily in length, and woody stems in length and diameter. Growth in length is initiated by the apical meristem, and growth in

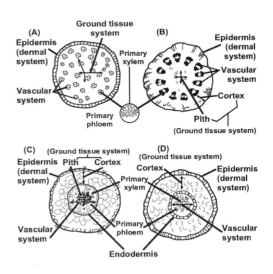

Figure 3. Cross sections of a herbaceous monocot stem (A) and root (C), a herbaceous dicot stem (B) and root (D). There is no vascular cambium developed in monocots and the vascular tissues are scattered. The dicots have aligned vascular tissues with xylem produced to their inside and phloem produced to the outside of the stem and root.

diameter by lateral meristems (as in vascular cambium and cork cambium). Upright growth of plants results from a rigid stem with one actively growing point. Multiple stems and several growing points produce shrubby or bushy growth.

Buds

A bud is an embryonic structure (either stem, flower, or both) that can grow actively or maintain the potential for growth while dormant. Terminal (apical) buds occur at the tips of stems and lateral (axillary) buds are found in the leaf axils (above where the leaf is attached to the stem) as shown in Figure 4. Some species have accessory buds that are located above or to the side of the axillary bud. Many buds develop into leafy stems; these are termed "leaf buds". Flower buds, such as those found on elm or cherry, produce flowers. Mixed buds, such as those found on the apple, can give rise to leafy stems and flowers.

Bud scales often overlap each other and cover the buds of most woody plants. Bud scales reduce water loss from the bud and protect it from mechanical injury. The buds of some woody plants have no bud scales, and are called naked buds. In these buds the outer embryonic leaves are well-developed typically and covered with hairs to protect the younger, enclosed leaves. Herbaceous plants have less conspicuous buds than woody plants.

Adventitious buds arise as new buds from roots or stems. Many cells, even mature ones, can return to a meristematic state (totipotency) and produce adventitious shoot buds (or roots). This makes vegetative propagation possible. Many roots, including food storage roots, can also be useful for propagation if they have the capability of producing adventitious shoot buds.

Stem Modifications—Many modifications of the normal upright stem exist. These include both above ground and below ground modifications. Such changes arose as plants evolved under changing conditions. Stem alterations are of interest to the horticulturist,

Figure 5

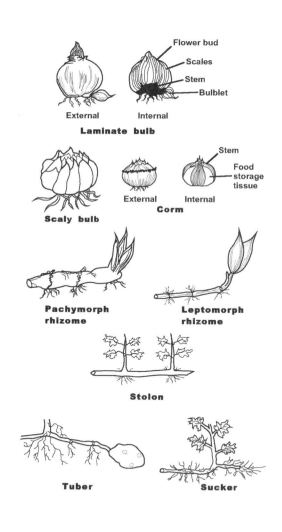

Figure 5. Underground modified stems. Bulbs store food in leafy scales while corms store resources in stem tissue. Rhizomes run underground while stolons spread on the soil surface. Tubers may form from stems or roots. Suckers originate from underground roots.

Figure 4

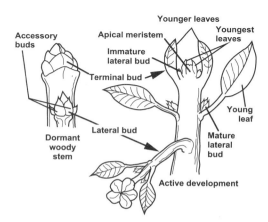

Figure 4. Buds and shoot development. Buds develop into shoots with leaves and flowers. Dormant buds are usually well-developed on woody stems.

since many are useful as food sources or for propagation purposes (Figure 5).

Climbing Stems—Above-ground modifications include climbing and succulent stems. The advantage enjoyed by the first climbing stems was their ability to literally grow over the competition. This led to a successful niche in the plant community. Several types of climbing stems developed. Types include those that lean or clamber over supports (allamanda), those that twine around supports (bougainvillea, clematis, wisteria), and those that grasp supports with tendrils (grape) or holdfasts (Boston ivy).

Succulent Stems—Succulent stems are enlarged, with small or no leaves. This modification permits food manufacture and water storage in the stem, and minimal water loss through leaves. Plants with succulent stems are highly adapted to survive in arid desert areas. Such stems arose as areas suffered prolonged drought. Plants that survived formed stems suitable for water storage (thick stems) and minimal loss of water (tiny or no leaves). Examples are cacti and *Euphorbia*.

Offsets—Another above-ground modification of the stem include offsets. Offsets arise from the crown, the portion of the stem near the ground. The crown gives rise to new shoots, such as with herbaceous perennials. Crowns of many herbaceous perennials (asparagus, chrysanthemum, daylily, and rhubarb) can be divided to produce new plants. Offsets (sometimes called offshoots) are shortened, thickened rosette-like stems produced from the crown of some plants, such as the bromeliads and succulents. These are useful for propagation by simple division.

Runners—Specialized stems that arise from leaf axils at the crown of a plant, such as is seen with ajuga and strawberry, are called runners. A common house plant, the spider plant (*Chlorophytum comosum*), also has runners. When grown in a hanging basket, the runners dangle like spiders on a web. In their natural habitat, runners grow horizontally above the surface of the ground, giving the appearance of "running" along the surface. At the nodes of the runner, new plants arise and develop roots.

Bulbs—Modified stems that develop underground include bulbs, corms, rhizomes, suckers, and tubers. A bulb consists of a short, fleshy stem basal plate containing a flower or growing point at its apex, plus overlapping of fleshy scales. Bulbs are produced by some monocots for food storage and reproduction. Bulbs are valued for propagation and some for food. Their food storage ability and being deep in the soil give bulbs the ability to survive harsh winters or dry periods in a dormant stage. When conditions improve, the bulb begins growth and sends up leaves through the soil.

Scales of bulbs may be present in continuous, concentric layers that are dry and papery outside and fleshy inside, as in tunicate bulbs. Examples are the amaryllis, daffodil, hyacinth, onion, and tulip. Scales are easily seen in the onion when you slice it. The concentric arrangement of scales also enables the preparation of onion rings.

Bulbs without an outer dry covering and a less-structured arrangement of the scales are known as scaly or non-tunicate bulbs. When cut in half lengthwise, the bulb appears as layers of fleshy scales over a small, triangular piece of tissue at the base. This tissue is actually stem tissue. An example is the lily. Miniature bulbs developing below ground from the parent bulb are referred to as bulblets and offsets when mature, or as bulbils when formed above ground on the stem.

Corms—A corm is the enlarged base of a stem enclosed by a few, dry scales. Corms are mostly stem structure with obvious nodes and internodes, in contrast to the bulb, which is mostly scales. The corm appears solid. Examples are the Crocus, Colocasia, Gladiolus, and Tritonia.

Rhizomes—A rhizome is a specialized stem that grows horizontally underground. Instead of being compressed, like bulbs and corms, the rhizome is equivalent to laying the whole stem on the ground and covering it with soil. Leaves and flowers appear directly from underground. The rhizome, while root-like in appearance, differs from roots by having nodes and internodes. Buds and scale-like leaves are sometimes found at the nodes. The production of roots, shoots, and flowering stems from rhizomes makes them useful for propagation.

Stolons—Stolons are modified stems similar to rhizomes, except they occur above ground. Stolons also tend to be numerous, often forming a crawling mat of surface-hugging stems. Because of their ability to root and form new plants, stolon-producing plants tend to be weedy and invasive. Stolons are useful for propagation of Bermuda grass and mints.

Suckers—A sucker is a shoot that arises underground from an adventitious bud on the root. However, in practice, shoots arising from the crown near the soil's surface are also called suckers. Suckers are used for propagation of blackberry and red raspberry.

Tubers—A tuber is a modified underground stem, essentially a terminal swelling of a rhizome. Tubers are useful for propagation. A true tuber is distinguished from a tuberous root. A true tuber has all the parts of a stem, that is, "eyes" which are actually buds at nodes, where a tuberous root has the external and internal structure of a root. The Irish potato has tubers; the sweet potato and dahlia have tuberous roots.

Leaf Form & Structure

The leaf serves to expose a large surface area to absorb the light energy needed for photosynthesis. The three main leaf functions are food manufacture (photosynthesis), transpiration (water loss by evaporation) and air exchange (carbon dioxide vs. oxygen). Sometimes leaves are needle-like or scaly, as seen on conifers such as pines and juniper, respectively. The leaf-like structure of ferns is called a frond.

The typical leaf has two parts: the blade, a thin, flattened expanded portion, and the petiole, a stalk that attaches the blade to the stem. Leaves without petioles are said to be sessile. This condition is found in grasses, including corn. The base of the petiole sometimes has leaf-like or scale-like structures called stipules. This feature is especially prominent in the garden pea, *Pisum sativum,* where the stipules are actually larger than the leaf parts.

On the lower and often the upper surface of the leaf are lines or ridges called veins. These are a continuation of the vascular system of the stem. The vein arrangement (venation) is usually parallel in monocots, and net-like

Figure 6

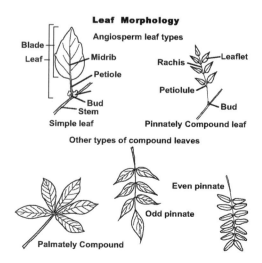

Figure 6. Simple and compound leaves and their parts.

Figure 7

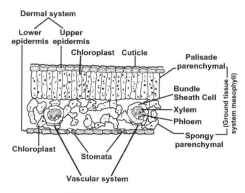

Figure 7. The leaf blade is a series of layers of cells. The waxy cuticle protects the surface. The stomates allow exchange of oxygen and carbon dioxide. The vascular system moves food and water while photosynthesis takes place in the parenchyma cells.

in dicots. This characteristic makes it very easy to tell a monocot from a dicot just by examining the leaf. Net-like veins may assume either the form of a feather with a strong main vein with lateral smaller veins (pinnately veined), or the form of the fingers spreading from the palm of the hand (palmately veined). Veins are usually less conspicuous and parallel on conifers.

Leaves are either simple or compound (Figure 6). A simple leaf has a single individual blade. The compound leaf consists of many blades divided into leaflets. Compound leaves can be either palmately or pinnately compound. In a palmately compound leaf, all leaflets are attached at the end of the petiole. In a pinnately compound leaf, leaflets are attached to the sides of a central segment (called the rachis) like the barbs of a feather.

The leaf blade is usually surrounded by an upper and lower single cell layer called the epidermis that is covered by a waxy coat, called the cuticle. (Figure 7) A few plants have a multiple layer epidermis, such as oleander. The lower epidermis is rich in pores (stomata or stomates) through which gases and water vapor move. The upper layer usually has fewer or no stomates. Sandwiched between the epidermal layers is the mesophyll layer, the site of photosynthesis and water/nutrient transport.

Flowers

The reproductive structures of angiosperms vary greatly in appearance. However, they share fundamental similarities in their basic structural plan (Figure 8). The stalk of a solitary flower or a collective mass of flowers (inflorescence) is called a peduncle. The stalk of one of the flowers in an inflorescence is called a pedicel. The receptacle is an enlarged area at the top of the flower stalk, to which the floral parts are attached. Four kinds of floral organs arise from the receptacle. These structures are the sepals, petals, pistils, and stamens.

Sepals—Sepals are found at the base of the flower and enclose the blossom when it is in bud to protect the floral parts from dessication. Collectively, the sepals are called the calyx. In some flowers the sepals can be mistaken for petals because of their similarity in color and size. In this case the individual parts are not called sepals and petals, but are referred to as tepals (examples include lily, tulip, and magnolia).

Petals—Above the calyx and toward the center are the petals, collectively known as the corolla. Petals are usually brightly colored, sometimes fragrant and sticky with a sugary nectar produced by glands. Together the calyx and corolla are called the perianth. Petals play a key role in those flowers that depend on bees or other creatures for pollination (transfer of pollen) as petal color as utilized as a pollinator attractant.

Color and Pollination—Color serves to attract pollinators such as honeybees, which unlike most insects, have color vision. Bees are the dominant pollinators of plants. Many flowers have "honey guides", a series of lines that lead the bee along the petals to where the pollen and nectar are found. We cannot see these lines, but the bee can, because bees see ultraviolet light. If we shine ultraviolet light on petals and photograph them with ultraviolet-sensitive film, we can see these lines on the photograph.

Fragrance and Pollination—Some insects, such as moths and butterflies, have keenly developed senses of smell. They are attracted by the fragrance of flowers. Some fragrances are pleasant and we also enjoy them, such as roses and hyacinths. Other flowers have unpleasant smells, such as the carrion flower, which smells like rotting meat. The flower also looks like rotting meat, with its mottled brown color. Carrion flowers are pollinated by flies, which are attracted by the stench.

Nectar and Pollination—Nectar and pollen (to a lesser extent) are used as food sources by the visiting insects and other pollinators. Bees convert the nectar into honey and hummingbirds use nectar to fuel their very high metabolism. Nectar is sugar and water and is a high energy food. Nectar is produced at the base of petals in glands called nectaries. Finding the nectar is the reward that reinforces the visits of the pollinators.

Figure 8

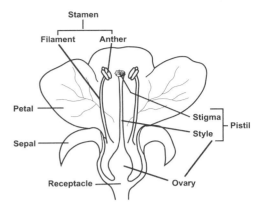

Figure 8. A typical flower with all the possible structures.

Stamens and Pistils—The stamens (male reproductive organs) are located above the petals. Typically, they consist of an elongated stalk, the filament that supports an enlarged pollen-containing structure called the anther. In the center of the flower is the female reproductive organs or the pistil(s). This structure is somewhat flask-shaped. The swollen, basal part (the ovary) is connected by a stalk (the style) to an enlarged terminal end (the stigma). The mature pollen grains are released from the disintegrating anther and carried to the stigma of the same or another flower by insects, wind, or rain, and pollination takes place. If the stigma is receptive, fertilization follows. The ovary when fertilized then gives rise to the fruit and seeds. *Think hand polination*

Pistils may be either simple or compound, depending on the numbers of carpels present in the structure. A simple pistil has one carpel (the structure that bears the ovaries), and a compound pistil bears two or more fused carpels. Pistils having multiple carpels possess several compartments in the ovary. The arrangement of the ovules on the carpels is used for classification.

The floral organs are usually arranged in whorls. In dicots (apple, cabbage, cacti, carnation, columbine, magnolia, maple, and poppy), the number of floral organs (sepals, petals, and so on) in each whorl is four or five or multiples thereof. In monocots (corn, lily, orchid, and palm), the number is three or multiples thereof.

Flower Modifications—Modifications of the floral organs are common. In some flowers the petals are fused to form a lobed tube called a corolla. Examples are the petunia and morning glory. These lobes correspond to the number of petals. Fusion of the other floral organs is possible.

Flowers that contain all four floral organs are called complete flowers (lily and cherry); incomplete flowers (grasses, maple, and willow) lack some of the floral organs.

Monoecious and Dioecious Plants

Flowers that have both functional stamens and pistils, such as the tomato flower, are said to be perfect or hermaphroditic. Flowers lacking either the stamens or pistils are termed imperfect. Complete flowers contain all the flower parts. All complete flowers are perfect in that they contain both stamens and pistils. The converse is not true; some perfect flowers might be missing petals. All imperfect flowers are incomplete, but not all incomplete flowers are imperfect.

Incomplete flowers without pistils are called staminate flowers (tassel of corn). Those without stamens are called pistillate flowers (silk of corn). Plants with both pistillate and staminate flowers on the same plant are termed monoecious (begonia, corn, cucumber, oak, squash, and walnut); dioecious plants (holly and spinach) have pistillate flowers and staminate flowers on separate plants.

Understanding monoecious and dioecious plants is important with regard to ease of pollination, productivity of fruits and vegetables, and production of seeds (especially hybrid seed). For example, holly plants are dioecious. If you have only one holly plant, you will not get the colorful red berries. You need to have a female plant for berry production and second male plant to provide the pollen necessary for fertilization and fruit development.

Flower Symmetry

Flowers may be singular or borne in groups or clusters, termed inflorescences (Figure 9). The arrangement of the flowers in the inflorescence varies, which provides the basis for several recognized forms: catkin, corymb, dichasium, head, panicle, raceme, spike, and umbel. Because these may exhibit a degree of constancy for a genus or even family, the type of inflorescence is often useful in plant identification.

Fruits

A fruit is the ripened ovary or group of ovaries and its contents. Some fruits fuse with adjacent parts of the ovary and are termed accessory fruits. Seeds are usually present in the ovary. Botanically, fruits arise only from flowering plants, since floral organs are needed for fruit production. Botanical fruits are distinguished from the popular horticulture use of terms: fruits and vegetables. Some botanical fruits are called vegetables, such as corn, cucumber, eggplant, squash, and tomato.

Fruits may be classified as simple, aggregate, or multiple fruits. Simple fruits in turn may be fleshy or dry. Dry fruits are either dehiscent (open at maturity) or indehiscent (not open at maturity).

Simple Fruits—A simple fruit develops from the ovary of one simple or compound pistil and can be either fleshy or dry. The grape, peach, and tomato are all fleshy, simple fruits. When simple fruits have other floral parts fused to the ovary, they are termed simple accessory fruits. In simple fruits, the ripened, enlarged ovary wall is termed the pericarp; it may contain up to three distinct layers from the outside and inward: exocarp (skin), mesocarp, and endocarp. The soft or hard pericarp can be either dry or fleshy. Dry tissue consists of dead sclerenchyma cells with suberized or lignified walls. Fleshy tissue is composed of living parenchyma cells.

The three kinds of simple fleshy fruits are the berry, drupe, and pome (Figure 10). The berry (eggplant, grape, and tomato) has a fleshy pericarp with a thin skin. The pepo is a berry fruit with a hard rind (cucumber, pumpkin, and squash), and the hesperidium is a berry

Figure 9

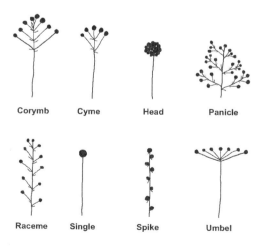

Corymb   Cyme   Head   Panicle

Raceme   Single   Spike   Umbel

Figure 9. Types of inflorescences. The peduncle is the main stalk of an inflorescence. Pedicels are attached to the individual flowers in the inflorescence. The central flower of a cyme opens first while the outer flowers opens first in the corymb.

fruit with a leathery skin and radial partition (citrus fruits). Note that the botanical berry is not the same as the horticulture berry.

Drupes, also called stone fruits, have a thin-skinned exocarp, a fleshy mesocarp, and a stony endocarp. Examples are the almond, apricot, cherry, coconut, olive, peach, and plum. Pomes have an endocarp that forms a dry, paper-like core, such as the apple and pear. Because pomes have other floral parts fused to the ovary, they are simple accessory fruits. In the apple, the white fleshy part comes from the flower petals that became fleshy. The core comes from the pistil. If you turn the apple over and see little, black triangular dry parts in the base indentation, you are looking at the remains of the sepals. Other simple accessory fruits that are completely fleshy are termed false berries (banana and cranberry), since in the true berry the ovary is the only fleshy part.

Simple dry fruits are either dehiscent or indehiscent (Figure 11). Dehiscent fruits open at maturity and release several to many seeds while still attached to the plant. Seeds are released later with indehiscent types after fruits have fallen off the plant. Dehiscent forms include the legume (found in the pea), which has one carpel and two dehiscing sutures (open at maturity); follicle (found in columbine), with one carpel and one dehiscing suture; silique (found in mustard), with two carpels and two dehiscing halves and a membranous portion remaining with attached seeds; and capsule (found in the Brazil nut), with two or more carpels and dehiscing pores, slits, or top.

Indehiscent forms include the achene (found in sunflower), which has one carpel and one loose seed; samara (found in maple), which is a winged achene with sometimes two carpels; nut (found in walnut), which is a large achene with a thick, hard pericarp; -grain (found in corn), which has one carpel and one seed, with the seed and pericarp joined at all points; and schizocarp (found in parsley), which has two or more carpels, each usually containing one seed, that separate at maturity, but each retains its seed.

Aggregate and Multiple Fruits—Aggregate fruit consists of clusters of individual fruits that develop from the several pistils of a single flower. These pistils share a common receptacle. These fruits may consist of individual fruits that are drupes or achenes. Examples are the raspberry, blackberry, and strawberry. Aggregate fruits can also be accessory fruits. For example, the red fleshy part of the strawberry comes from the receptacle of the flower, while the hard, tiny crunchy parts comes from the ovaries.

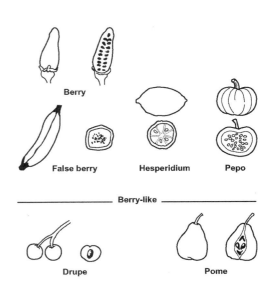

Figure 10. Examples of fleshy fruits.

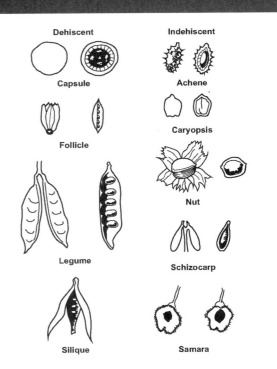

Figure 11. Examples of dry fruits.

Multiple fruits arise from the many flowers found on a compact inflorescence. The fleshy parts of these fruits are often fused floral organs (accessory structures). The pineapple is an example.

Parthenocarpic Fruits—Parthenocarpic fruits are seedless. These result from the phenomenon called parthenocarpy, or the production of fruit even though fertilization does not take place. Some seedless fruits are not naturally parthenocarpic, since they have resulted from the abortion of the young, fertilized ovaries, such as by spraying with growth regulators. Certain varieties of seedless grapes ('Thompson Seedless') are induced. Other varieties of seedless grapes and cultivated varieties of the pineapple, banana, clementines, the Washington navel orange, and some kinds of fig are parthenocarpic fruits. These types of fruits are highly valued in horticulture because many people prefer their fruits and preserves free of seeds.

Cones—The conifers do not have flowers or fruits. Instead these plants have two types of cones. One cone produces pollen (microsporangiate cone) and is smaller and less scaly than the other. The second cone produces ovules (ovulate cone) that, after a single fertilization, bear seeds on the cone scales. Pollen-bearing cones are usually on the lower branches and appear yellowish when the pollen is mature. Ovulate cones are found on the upper branches and are brown and scaly. This arrangement promotes wind-assisted cross-pollination. These cones are typical of pines.

Not all conifers have "pine cones." Some, such as juniper, have cones with fused, fleshy scales. These cones look more like blueberries.

Seeds—A seed is an embryonic structure developed by flowering plants and conifers after fertilization. (Figure 12). Seeds have the potential to develop into a plant. Seeds differ so much in shape, size, seed coats, and other characteristics that it is difficult to form any meaningful classification.

Seeds are bounded by a seed coat that has developed from the integuments of the ovule. Seed coats vary from thin and papery, such as found on peanuts after removal of the shell, to hard and thick, such as the coconut. On some seed coats the micropyle, the opening in the integuments of the ovule through which the sperm enters, is still seen as a small pore. The hilum, or scar left by the stalk that attached the seed to the placenta, is usually visible. Both the micropylar and hilum scars are visible on bean seeds.

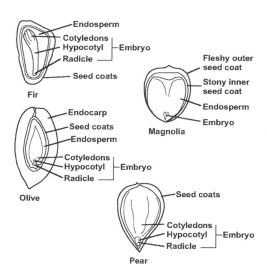

Figure 12

Figure 12. Structures of seeds of horticulture crops.

The seed embryo is usually fully developed when the seed is mature and ready for dispersal. A few plants, such as the orchid, have immature embryos that develop after dispersal. The structural features of the embryo vary somewhat. Conifer seeds have cotyledons, a simple apical meristem, and a hypocotyl. Embryos in the flowering plants have three basic parts: cotyledon(s), epicotyl, and hypocotyl.

Cotyledons are specialized seed leaves: one is found in seeds of monocots, two in seeds of dicots, and several in seeds of conifers. In some plants, cotyledons function as a food source during germination. In others, cotyledons serve as absorbing organs to transfer food from the endosperm to the developing embryo after germination. In some seeds, the cotyledons also become green and leaf-like, and photosynthetic for a short time. Cotyledons, when green, bear no resemblance in shape to the true leaves that follow.

The epicotyl is the region above the cotyledon(s). It varies in complexity from being only a basic apical meristem to a full-formed shoot bud, the plumule. In simpler seeds, the area below the cotyledon(s) is the hypocotyl-root axis. The end of this structure has an apical meristem that becomes the root. In more complex seeds the hypocotyl is a transition zone between the cotyledons) and radicle. The radicle is an embryonic root.

A nutrient tissue, the endosperm, is present in many seeds. Endosperm is rich in oil and/or protein. In some seeds, the embryo and seedling use the endosperm during germination. In other seeds, the endosperm has been utilized during the development of the seed prior to germination. Seeds that have depleted the endosperm utilize the cotyledons as food storage organs. These seeds have thick fleshy cotyledons, as found in bean and pea seeds. Seeds with rich endosperm often have thin, papery cotyledons.

Endosperm-rich seeds form an important part of our diet. Seeds with oil-rich endosperm are the sources of cooking oils, such as olive, peanut, sunflower, and canola seeds. Seeds with protein-rich endosperm are often used as foods, such as rice and wheat. Some seeds are rich in both; corn, cotton, and soybean are used as both oil and protein sources.

RESOURCES

Raven, Peter, et al. *Biology of Plants. 6th Ed.* W.H Freeman & Co. 944 pages.

DISCUSSION QUESTIONS

1. Discuss why plant nomenclature might be important to a gardener.

2. Discuss the differences between monocots and dicots.

3. In which areas of a root and shoot does growth originate?

4. Name three examples of modified root structures and their purposes.

5. Plants with which kind of root system are easier to transplant and why?

6. What purposes does the plant's stem serve?

7. Discuss the purpose of a leaf and the types of leaves a plant might have.

8. What are the 3 types of buds?

9. Discuss the difference between monoecious and dioecious plants?

10. What is a "perfect flower"?

NOTES

3

Plant Physiology:Growth and Development

Gary L. Wade

Matthew Chappell

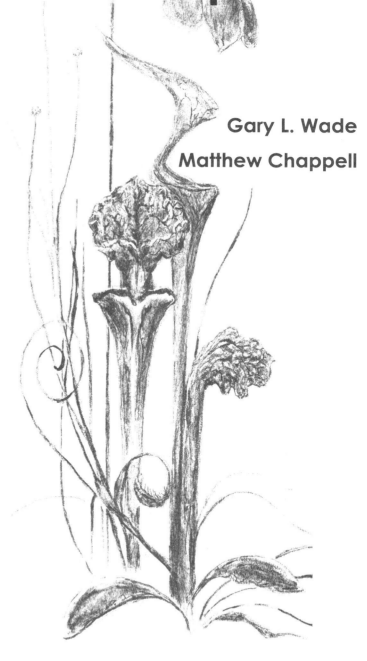

LEARNING OBJECTIVES

Understand the process of photosynthesis and be able to tell functions of xylem and phloem.

Know where the inputs to photosynthesis come from and where the outputs go.

Know where the inputs from respiration come from and where the outputs go to.

Understand the role of stomata in photosynthesis, respiration, and transpiration.

Understand how photosynthesis and respiration are affected by environmental factors.

Understand the wavelengths of light and their effect on growing plants indoors or in greenhouses.

Understand the term Etiolation and the concepts of Phototropism and photoperiod.

Understand the meaning behind the terms day neutral, long day, and short day.

Understand the many functions of water in plants and the process of transpiration.

TERMS TO KNOW

Anion negatively charged ion.

Anthocyanin pigment in plants that gives them their red color.

Auxin plant hormone that promotes cell elongation.

Carbohydrate group of foods composed of carbon, hydrogen and oxygen with the hydrogen and oxygen in the ratio of 2 to 1.

Carotene pigment in plants that imparts yellow and orange coloration.

Cation positively charged ion.

Chlorophyll green pigment which occurs chiefly in chloroplasts and is involved in photosynthesis.

Chloroplast specialized cytoplasmic bodies containing chlorophyll.

Cutin waxy substance of which the cuticle of plants is composed

Etiolation morphological response to low light levels, including long, slender stems, small leaves and a deficiency of chlorophyll.

Grana stack of thin discs within the chloroplasts containing chlorophyll and serving as the site of photosynthesis.

Hardiness ability of a plant to adapt to the extreme temperatures of a region.

Lamella thin plate, sheet or layer-like structure within the chloroplast.

Phloem conducting tissue, consisting principally of sieve cells and sieve tube cells; the chief function is food conduction.

Photoperiodism growth and development response of plants to differing lengths of exposure to light.

Photosynthesis manufacture of carbohydrates from carbon dioxide and water in the presence of chlorophyll, utilizing light energy and releasing oxygen.

Phototropism bending growth resulting from unequal illumination.

Phytochrome plant pigment existing in two interchangeable forms, one absorbing primarily red light and the other primarily far-red light.

Protein complex, organic, nitrogenous substance built up from amino acids, constructing the major portion of the organic materials in living protoplasm.

Respiration chemical oxidation process; living protoplasm breaks down certain organic substances with the release of energy, which is used in various anabolic activities, movements, etc.

Stoma pore controlled by guard cells in the epidermis of a leaf or other plant parts.

Transpiration emission of water vapor from aerial parts of plants, chiefly through leaf stomata.

Vessel conducting tube in the xylem tissue.

Xylem complex plant vascular tissue that conducts water and minerals from the soil to aerial parts of the plant.

INTRODUCTION

It is appropriate to begin your Master Gardener experience by reviewing some of the basic plant sciences you may have learned in a high school biology class but have long forgotten. By gaining a basic understanding of plant physiology, you will understand why and how plants respond and adapt to their environment and how environmental factors influence physiological responses and growth changes in plants. This is particularly useful when you are called upon to diagnose a plant problem. Your knowledge of plant physiology will help determine the environmental cause of the visible effect/response and aid in your ability to find an appropriate solution to the problem.

We will begin this chapter by looking at the early years of plant physiology and some of the pioneers who set the stage for our understanding of how plants respond to their environment and how they grow and develop. Next, we will review the dynamic processes called photosynthesis and respiration and learn how plants manufacture their own food. We will discuss the mechanisms plant use to transport nutrient elements, water, gases and food substances from one location to another. Then we will focus on three environmental factors that have a pronounced effect on plant growth processes: light, water and temperature. Finally, the sixteen essential elements for plant growth will be discussed, including examples of their essential role within the plant and factors that influence their availability in the soil.

The Early Years of Plant Physiology

Our early understanding of plant growth processes was grounded in traditional plant lore, passed from generation to generation. The *Old Farmer's Almanac* still contains many tried and true beliefs that have proven their worth again and again, yet have few scientific explanations. In decades past, many persons planted by the phases of the moon and were successful in following this practice. So why should we question what past generations of gardeners have proven? Until the late 17th century, man believed plants grew by consuming soil and organic matter, just as a cow consumes grain for energy and growth. Then a French chemist, von Helmont, conducted an experiment with a willow tree which marked the beginning of plant physiology as we understand it today.

Von Helmont oven-dried 200 pounds of soil, placed it in a container, and planted in it a small willow tree weighing just 6 ounces. For five years, the tree received only rain water. Then, he carefully removed the willow tree from the container, washed the soil from its roots, oven-dried the soil, and weighed both the plant and soil once again. After five years, the soil had lost only four ounces, while the tree had gained 162 pounds, 6 ounces. Von Helmont concluded from this study that plants did not consume soil. Instead, he believed their sustenance was provided by water. Although we know today that von Helmont's conclusions are not entirely true, he was the first to scientifically prove the essential role water plays in plant growth.

A hundred years after von Helmont's willow tree experiment, a scientist by the name of Joseph Priestly found a definite relationship between plants and animals living together. He placed a potted plant in a sealed glass container and found that it wilted and died within a short time. Similarly, a mouse placed by itself in the sealed glass container died soon after the container was sealed. However, when a plant and a mouse were placed in the container together, they were able to live indefinitely when given food and water. Priestly concluded that plants and animals have a symbiotic relationship, and he theorized that each was purifying the air for the other. Although he knew nothing of the process of photosynthesis, his research led to the discovery of oxygen and the essential role plants play in helping animals breathe and survive.

For the next 150 years, scientists continued to explore animal/plant relationships, adding bits and pieces of new knowledge to the complex puzzle. It was not until the 1940's that scientists really began to unravel the mysteries of plant growth through the dynamic process called Photosynthesis.

Photosynthesis and Respiration

All life on earth depends directly or indirectly on photosynthesis - the process by which plants transform light energy from the sun into chemical energy that drives plant growth processes. The chemistry for this to occur is complex, involving more than 16 chemical reactions, but it can be summarized by the following simplified equation:

$$Chlorophyll + 6\ CO_2 + 6\ H_2O \xrightarrow{Light} C_6H_{12}O_6 + 6\ O_2 + energy$$

Light energy trapped by the chlorophyll molecule causes carbon dioxide and water to combine and form glucose and other sugars, ultimately leading to carbohydrate production. In turn, oxygen is given off and a high-energy molecule (ATP) is produced.

Figure 1

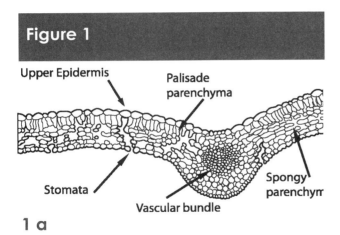

Upper Epidermis
Palisade parenchyma
Stomata
Vascular bundle
Spongy parenchym

1 a

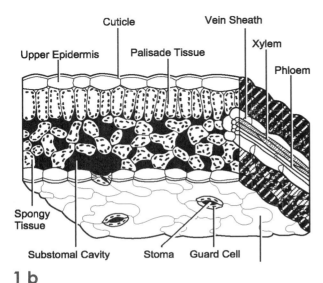

Cuticle
Vein Sheath
Upper Epidermis
Palisade Tissue
Xylem
Phloem
Spongy Tissue
Substomal Cavity
Stoma
Guard Cell

1 b

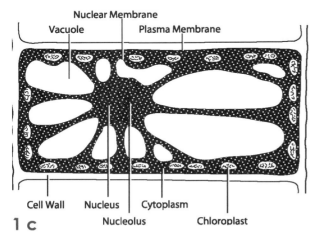

Nuclear Membrane
Vacuole
Plasma Membrane
Cell Wall
Nucleus
Cytoplasm
Nucleolus
Chloroplast

1 c

Figure 1. 1a shows cross section of a leaf. In 1b the cross section is shown in medium detail with the palisade tissue located just below the upper epidermis. The black dots are chloroplasts. Note how the chloroplasts are predominately in the palisade cells near the top of the leaf and how they are aligned along the perimeter of each cell so they can efficiently trap light. 1c shows a single palisade cell in detail.

In vascular plants, photosynthesis occurs in chloroplasts, which are structures found mainly in green leaves. However, chloroplasts can also be found in other green plant parts, including stems and developing buds. Chloroplasts contain the chlorophyll pigment and are the site of photosynthesis. Figure 1 shows a cross-section of a leaf. Note the cells containing chloroplasts and how the chloroplasts are arranged along the perimeter of the cell wall so they can trap light more efficiently.

Figure 2 shows what a single chloroplast might look like under an electronic microscope.

In natural environments, photosynthesis starts as daylight begins to impact the surface of the leaf and ends at dusk. Soon after the photosynthetic process begins generating carbohydrates in the morning, respiration kicks in, and the two processes go on simultaneously. In respiration, the energy generated in photosynthesis is used to break down the carbohydrates and combine them with nutrients (elements coming from the soil) to form plant food substances, such as amino acids, proteins and fats. Water and carbon dioxide are given off and are recycled back into the photosynthetic mechanism. Unlike photosynthesis, respiration can occur when there is no sunlight or artificial light present.

Excess water is excreted through the stomata on leaves and evaporated in a process called transpiration. Have you ever noticed how some plants generate water droplets along their leaf margins at night? This is partly due to excess water from respiration being exuded by the

Figure 2

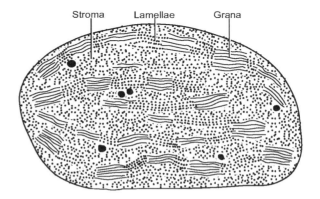

Stroma
Lamellae
Grana

Figure 2. Magnified view of a chloroplast showing the internal structure. The grana house the chlorophyll molecule and are the site for photosynthesis. The lamellae connect the grana, and all are suspended in a substance called stroma. The physiological function of the lamellae and stroma are not clearly understood.

plant. Have you ever left plants in your car overnight and found the windows steamed up the next morning? This is caused by respiratory water loss from the plants and the transpiration of the water into the air, increasing the humidity within the car. Night-time dew results from respiratory (transpiration) water loss from plants.

Respiration is an oxidation process. It requires oxygen to occur. When an energy-containing carbohydrate is enzymatically broken down by the addition of oxygen, there is a release of energy (as heat) and the formation of carbon dioxide and water, as shown by the equation below. Some of the carbohydrate is recombined with other elements (from the soil, soil solution or fertilizers) to form amino acids, proteins and fats. These are plant foods. Fertilizer is not plant food. Plants manufacture their own food.

Note how the equation for respiration shown below is the reverse of the equation for photosynthesis. Therefore, photosynthesis may be called an energy building process, while respiration is a process of releasing energy. But remember that while respiration breaks down energy, it also builds tissues and therefore increases plant size.

PLANT RESPIRATION

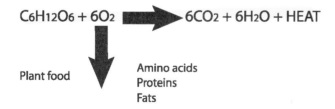

$$C_6H_{12}O_6 + 6O_2 \rightarrow 6CO_2 + 6H_2O + HEAT$$

Plant food   Amino acids
                    Proteins
                    Fats

Proteins are essential for all living cells, both in plants and animals. They contain carbon, hydrogen, oxygen, nitrogen, sulfur, phosphorus and other macro and micro nutrients that we will discuss shortly. The average protein is about 16 percent nitrogen, so right away you should see a connection to the nutrient elements applied via fertilizers. Proteins are composed of amino acids linked together in various numbers and ways. Proteins make up a large portion of the genetic substance in cells. Young green plants may contain 15 to 20 percent protein, while older, more mature plants may have only 3 percent protein or less.

Fats are common to both plants and animals. Their function in the plant is similar to that of carbohydrates -- largely as a source of energy. Fats have less oxygen than the carbohydrates, so they are a more concentrated source of energy. A pound of fat has about 2¼ times as

Table 1. A comparison of photosynthesis and respiration	
PHOTOSYNTHESIS	**RESPIRATION**
Occurs only in cells containing chlorophyll	Occurs in all living cells
Occurs only in the light	Occurs in both light and darkness
Raw materials are water, carbon dioxide and oxygen	Raw materials are carbohydrates
Energy is stored	Energy is released
Increases dry weight	Decreases dry weight

Figure 3

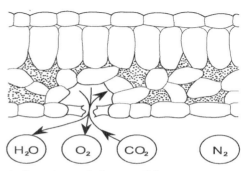

Figure 3. Opening and closing of the stomata is governed by the concentration of solutes in the guard cells and their diffusion outward from an area of high concentration to an area of low concentration.

much stored energy as a pound of carbohydrate. Fats are often found in high concentration in the endosperm tissue of seeds.

Table 1 compares photosynthesis to respiration. While photosynthesis occurs only in light, respiration goes on round-the-clock, during both day and night.

Movement of Nutrient Elements and Food in the Plant

Nutrient elements move into the plant via two primary pathways: through pores called stomata on the leaves, and through the roots. The atmospheric elements, carbon, hydrogen and oxygen move in and out of the stomata as CO_2 (carbon dioxide) or H_2O (water). Figures 1, 3 and 4 show stomata on a leaf surface (just one is called a stoma). Stomata cannot be seen with the naked eye, just as the pores in our skin are microscopic and cannot be seen with the naked eye. However, there may

See slides 1/8/13

Figure 4

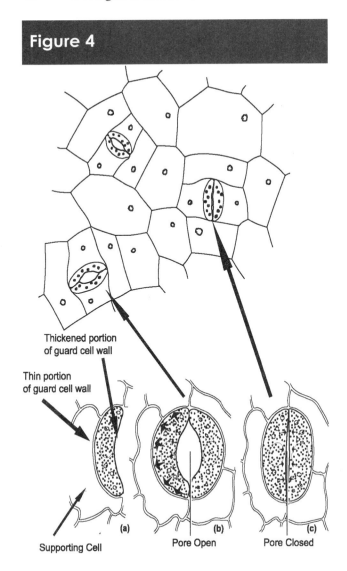

Thickened portion
of guard cell wall

Thin portion
of guard cell wall

Supporting Cell

(a)

(b)
Pore Open

(c)
Pore Closed

Figure 4. Opening and closing of the stomata is governed by the concentration of solutes in the guard cells and their diffusion outward from an area of high concentration to an area of low concentration.

Table 2. Number of stomata per square inch on the leaves of various plants

PLANT	UPPER EPIDERMIS	LOWER EPIDERMIS
Apple	None	250,000
Bean	26,000	160,000
Corn	39,000	64,000
Black oak	None	375,000
Orange	None	290,000
Pumpkin	18,000	175,000
Sunflower	55,000	100,000

be millions of them on a single leaf surface. Usually the stomata are more numerous over the abaxial (lower) side of the leaf than the (adaxial) upper side. An exception is floating leaves where almost all stomata are on the upper surface. Vertical leaves, such as those of many grasses, often have equal numbers of stomata on both sides. Table 2 shows the number of stomata per square inch on the upper epidermis and lower epidermis of several plants. As shown in Figure 3, stomata are surrounded by guard cells containing chloroplasts, which swell and shrink in response to the diffusion of water and carbohydrates in and out during photosynthesis and respiration.

When conditions are conducive to stomatal opening (e.g., high light intensity and high humidity), a proton pump drives protons (hydrogen H+) out of the guard cells, causing the cell's contents to become increasingly negatively charged. This negative potential opens potassium channels and the uptake of potassium ions (K+) occurs to balance the cell's charge. To maintain this internal negative charge so that entry of potassium ions does not stop, negative ions balance the influx of potassium. This in turn increases the osmotic pressure inside the guard cells, drawing in water through osmosis. This increases the cell's volume and turgor pressure and the increased pressure causes the cells to bow apart from one another, creating an open pore through which gas can move.

When roots begin to sense a water shortage in the soil, abscisic acid (ABA) is released. ABA binds to receptor proteins in the guard cells' plasma membrane and causes the inside of the cell to increase. This in turn causes a release of Ca^{2+}(calcium) from internal stores such as the endoplasmic reticulum and vacuoles. This causes chloride (Cl^-) and inorganic ions to exit the cells. Secondly, this stops the uptake of any further K^+ into the cells and subsequently the loss of K^+. The loss of these solutes (elements) causes a reduction in osmotic pressure, thus making the cell flaccid and so closing the stomatal pores. Generally, stomata are open during the day and close at night. Figure 4 shows a close-up view of stomata in the open and closed position.

Other elements (also called nutrient elements or plant nutrients) move into the plant through the root and are transported upward in the plant via a vascular system called the xylem. The xylem consists of a series of vessel elements joined together much like a pipeline for transporting water and nutrients to the above-ground portions of the plant. The elements take part in the food manufacturing process during respiration, or they may be involved in other chemical reactions within the plant.

Plant food manufactured during respiration is transported within the plant via another vascular transport system called the phloem. Food is transported wherever it is needed; from where it is produced, called the source, to where it is used, called the sink. It may go to developing buds and flowers in the spring, elongating stems or expanding leaves in summer, or it may be transported to nearby buds or roots and stored for next season's growth. Interesting research has shown that the majority of carbohydrates produced in a deciduous woody plant actually are not sent to the root system in the fall but rather to buds to be stored for next year's growth. The veins in a leaf are a good visual representation of the xylem/phloem transport system. Just like millions of fiber optic lines carrying phone and video signals to our homes, the xylem/phloem transport systems are two distinctly different transport systems within the vein, directing different growth substances to different places for different purposes. They are separated only by a thin membrane.

Figure 5 shows the location of the xylem and the phloem in a woody plant. Generally, the xylem is inside the cambium while the phloem is just outside the cambium and under the bark.

The heartwood of a tree, showing the growth rings from year to year, is layer upon layer of xylem. When a tree is girdled and the external bark is removed, phloem transport to the roots is disrupted. A tree may often live several months after it is girdled, because it can continue to transport water and nutrients upward via the xylem. However, no new food substances can go to the root. Therefore, food stored in the root will gradually be depleted, and the tree will die.

In monocotyledonous plants with vascular bundles (those having parallel veins in foliage) rather than rings of growth; like corn, iris, daylilies and snake plant, there is not one central transport system for water, nutrients and food, so the cross-section of the stem will show a series of bundles (the veins). The xylem will be toward the inside of each bundle and the phloem will be toward the outside.

PHYSIOLOGY AND PLANT GROWTH: LIGHT, TEMPERATURE AND WATER

Light

Light is an environmental factor that has one of the most pronounced effects on plant growth and life in

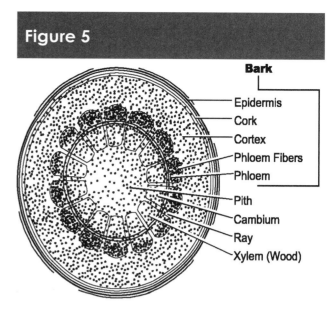

Figure 5. Cross-section of a woody plant.

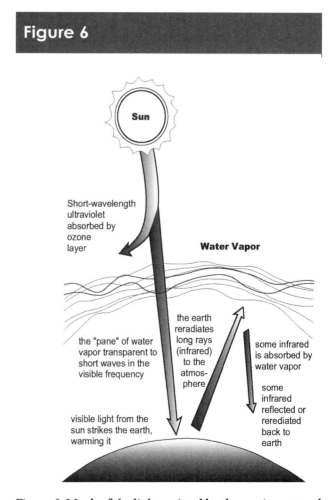

Figure 6. Much of the light emitted by the sun is scattered back into space by the Earth's upper atmosphere. Only 1% to 2% of the light energy reaching earth makes its way to leaf surfaces.

Figure 7

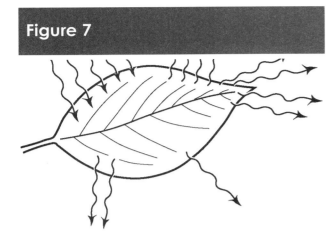

Figure 7. Most of the light energy striking a leaf is absorbed, while some is reflected or transmitted right through the leaf. Only 0.5% to 2.0% of the light energy reaching the leaf is used in photosynthesis.

Figure 8

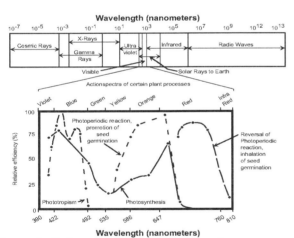

Figure 8. Only a small portion of the electromagnetic spectrum of energy emitted by the sun is visible light. Research has shown that plants absorb light primarily in two regions of the visible spectrum - the red and blue regions.

Table 3. Average light intensity foot candles (fc) for various lighting situations	
Sunny Day	10,000 fc
Cloudy Day	500-2,000 fc
Conference Room	20-30 fc
Reading in the Home	20-30 fc
Retail Stores	30-100
Church Chapels	5-10 fc

general, so we will spend a considerable portion of this chapter discussing light and its many effects on plants. Virtually all life on earth depends directly or indirectly on light and the radiant energy from the sun. Light energy from the sun is emitted in a series of pulses, called photons. When photons of similar energy combine, they form wavelengths. These wavelengths vary from very long radio wavelengths to the more penetrating and rapid wavelengths of light called x-rays, gamma rays and cosmic rays. Fortunately for us, most of the energy emitted from the sun is reflected back into space by the earth's upper atmosphere and does not reach the earth's surface. Otherwise, we all would have been irradiated like a microwave oven long ago. Only about 20% of the sun's energy actually reaches earth, and only 1% to 2% of that energy actually reaches plant surfaces. The remaining 98% of the light energy reaching the earth is scattered, absorbed as heat energy, or reflected. See figure 6.

The light energy that reaches the leaves of plants may be reflected, absorbed or transmitted through the leaf (see Figure 7). Only 0.5% to 2.0% of the light energy reaching the leaf is trapped by chlorophyll molecule and used in photosynthesis. Chlorophyll is very efficient at trapping light, even in the most dense shade.

Most of the light energy striking a leaf is absorbed, while some is reflected back upward or transmitted right through the leaf. Scientists use the electromagnetic spectrum to classify the different wavelengths of energy emitted by the sun (see Figure 8). Only a small portion of the electromagnetic spectrum is visible light. When this visible light is passed through a prism, it can be further separated into wavelengths that are visible as distinctly different colors - the colors of the rainbow - ranging from infrared to red, orange, yellow, green blue and violet. During the middle part of the last century, scientists made an interesting and historical discovery. They found that plants absorb light primarily in two regions of the visible spectrum - the red region and the blue region. This led to the development of gro-lights, also called full-spectrum bulbs, specifically designed to produce photosynthetic-specific wavelengths.

Measuring Light Intensity—Today, three units of measure are used to determine light intensity, or irradiance. Most gardeners use an old English unit for measuring light - the foot candle. A foot candle is defined as the unit of light, or illuminance, emitted by a candle on a one square foot surface that is one foot from a candle. On a bright, sunny day, light intensity may be 10,000 foot candles. The intensity of light a particular plant needs to grow and flower is genetically determined. Some plants can grow in as little as 50 foot candles of light while others may need 1,000 or more foot candles of light energy. A device called a light meter is used to measure light intensity. Table 3 is a comparison of average light intensities in different lighting situations using foot candles as the unit of measure. Scientists however, use two other units of measure to quantify light intensity. Watts per square metre (W/m^2) is a measure of optical brightness hitting any surface (e.g. a plant or a car surface). It translates directly into the rate at which energy is transferred, since one watt is simply one joule per second. In plant science, Photosynthetic Photon Flux Density (uE) is helpful to measure the intensity of light in the wavelength range most important to plants, namely 400 to 700 nm (nanometers). In this measurement, scientists use a unit micromole per square metre per second (umol/m^2/s). This quantity is the number of photons which would fall on (or pass through) one square metre of leaf each second, one mole being 6.02 x 1023 (Avogadro's number). On the Earth's surface, the noontime brightness of the Sun is 1060 W/m^2 or 2000 uE.(This varies with location and season, so we are using this number for purposes of comparison.)

Growers of foliage plants have tables available to them which show the light intensity required by various foliage plants. Each plant may have one light level for maintenance, one for optimum growth, and one to induce flowering. Table 4 shows various light intensities for maintenance and optimum growth of selected foliage plants. Note how light intensities for optimum growth are higher than those required just to maintain the plant. In the commercial foliage plant industry in central Florida, plants are grown outdoors under shade cloth. Shade cloth is manufactured to provide different levels of shade, ranging from 20% shade to 80% shade, so each plant can be provided just the right light intensity.

Similarly, professionals who maintain interior plants in shopping centers, hotel lobbies and atriums can obtain information on the light requirements of interior foliage plants and know whether they need to provide artificial lighting. Lighting manufacturers have reference tables that show how far a particular type of light needs to be placed from a plant's foliage in order to provide the plant its needed light intensity. Spotlights you sometimes see directed to plants in interior environments are not there just to show off the plants. They are there to provide the plants the minimum light intensity required for photosynthesis and growth.

When providing supplemental lighting to plants,

Table 4. Recommended light intensities (fc) for maintenance or optimum growth of selected plants

PLANT NAME	MAINTENANCE (fc)	OPTIMUM GROWTH
Asparagus Fern	100-200	200-400
Shefflera	150-200	200-400
Parlor Palm	50-75	75-100
Ty Plant	75-100	100-150
Red Edge Dracaena	100-150	200+
Weeping Fig	100-150	150-400+
Boston Fern	50-100	150-200+

light duration is another consideration. Since plants photosynthesize during light periods, the longer you light them, the more carbohydrates they will produce. Therefore, increasing light duration from eight to 14 hours will provide more foot candles, watts per meter square, and photosynthetic photon flux density of energy overall and may allow you to grow plants at lower light intensities. Conversely, as the output or intensity of light is increased, the duration of the lighting can be decreased. Table 5 shows minimum light levels required for maintenance of selected foliage plants. Most publications on foliage plants will have more extensive listings for your reference.

Generally, plants for low light areas can be placed six feet or more from windows where they get some light, but little direct light. They would be good choices for conference rooms, lobbies and hallways. Plants for medium light levels would be placed about three to 6 feet from a window, while those requiring high light would be placed within 3 feet of south, east or west facing windows which are brightly lit. If natural light is not available, supplemental lighting can be provided.

Similarly, we know that landscape plants differ in their preference for sun, shade or partial shade. Some woody ornamentals adapted to shade are camellia, gardenia, and aucuba. Azalea, dogwood and camellia prefer filtered shade, while crape myrtle, flowering cherry and rose prefer six to eight hours of full sunlight for best growth and flowering. Most plant lists show light level preferred by each plant.

Symptoms of Too Much or Too Little Light— When growing plants in light levels different from those to which they are adapted, morphological changes sometimes occur in the leaves. For instance, dogwood prefers filtered shade in its native habitat. In a shaded environment, it has larger and thinner leaves arranged in planes perpendicular to the sun angle. This allows maximum capture of available light.. However, when grown in full sun, the leaves of dogwood become thick, coarse-textured, and hang downward (parallel to light angle) on the branches in an effort to escape the intense sunlight. Other symptoms of too much light are chlorotic (yellow) leaves or brown spots on leaves. For example, if a Dracaena (Corn Plant) is taken from an indoor environment and placed outside in full sun for several hours, its leaves will develop brown spots. This phenomenon is actually the result of a process called photoinhibition whereby chlorophyll can not keep up with the high light intensity and the xanthophyll cycle is initiated to reduce the energy reaching the chlorophyll

molecule. Unfortunately, the xanthophyll cycle creates heat in cells and over long periods can lead to cell death. Essentially, prolonged high light level results in high heat levels that eventually break down of chlorophyll and cause death of cells within the plant.

When young seedlings are grown under low light levels, their stems will stretch and the plants will grow spindly. This is called **etiolation** (see Figure 9). Increasing light intensity and duration will correct the problem.

Phototropism—Another light response of plants is called phototropism, the movement of plants toward a light source. Have you ever noticed how chrysanthemums or sunflowers rotate their flowers and follow the sun throughout the day? This is an example of phototropism. The mechanism for phototropism was explained by F.W. Went in a 1928 experiment with oat seedlings (see Figure 10). He discovered that when oat seedlings were lighted from one direction, they bent toward the light source. If he removed the terminal part of the seedling, the shoot tip, it did not bend toward the light.

Therefore, he concluded that there is some sort of stimulus produced in the terminal bud of plants that governs their movement toward light. Next, he inserted a small mica chip into the stem a short distance from the tip on the side opposite the light source and found that the seedling would again not bend toward the light. However, when the mica chip was inserted into the stem on the side of the light source, it bent toward the light. He concluded that there was some stimulus produced in the terminal bud that moved downward in the stem on the side opposite the light source. The stimulus caused the cells along the side of the stem opposite the light source to elongate and push the plant toward the light. It was later discovered that this stimulus was auxin, a natural plant hormone produced in the terminal bud (apical meristem) of plants. The blue light receptor Phototropin 1 (phot1), a photoreceptor kinase, drives this reaction by regulating turgor pressure of cells on specific sides of the stem.

Photoperiodism—One of most significant scientific discoveries of the 20th century was the effect of day length on flowering plants. Called "photoperiodism," this light effect has enabled greenhouse growers to develop production schemes for flowering plants whereby day length can be manipulated to force plants to flower at various times of year.

Photoperiodism was discovered in 1906 by Garner and Allard, researchers at the USDA Agricultural Research Station in Beltsville, MD. They observed that a variety

Figure 9

Figure 9. Etiolation is a symptom of insufficient light. Symptoms include internode stretching, spindly growth, and leaves not fully expanded.

Table 5. Light requirements of selected foliage plants

LOW LIGHT (50-100 fc)	MEDIUM LIGHT (100-200 fc)	HIGH LIGHT (200+ fc)
Chinese Evergreen	Rex Begonia	Zebra Plant
Cast-iron Plant	Wandering Jew	Croton
Parlor Palm	Schefflera	Ti Plant
Jade Plant	Dracaena	African Violet
Snake Plant	Weeping Fig	Cactus
Bamboo Palm	Philodendron	Staghorn Fern
Pewter Plant	Spider Plant	Swedish Ivy
Bird's-nest Sansevieria	Pothos	Tricolor Bromeliad

fc = foot candle

Figure 10

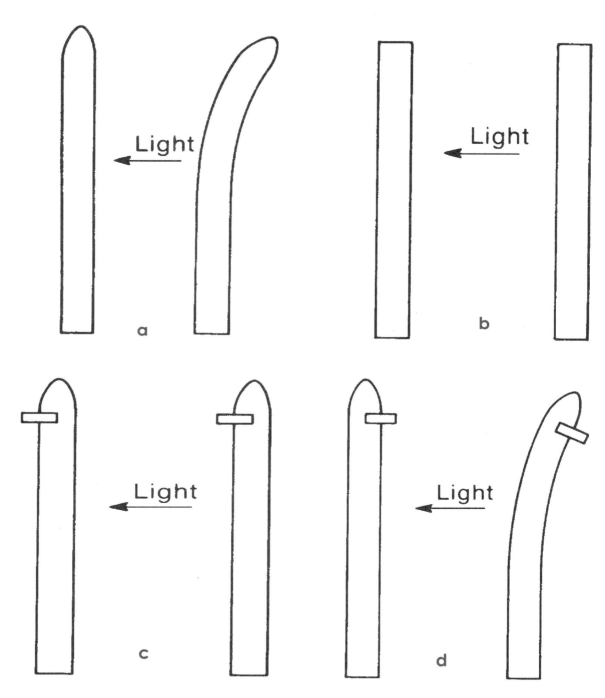

Figure 10. Phototropism—When oat seedlings were lighted from one direction, they moved toward the light (a). When the shoot tip was removed, no movement occurred (b). When a mica chip was placed just below the tip on the side opposite the light source, no movement occurred (c). When the mica chip was placed below the shoot tip on the side toward the light source, the plant moved toward the light (d). Conclusion: Light causes a stimulus (auxin) produced in the shoot tip to move downward on the side of the stem opposite the light source. The stimulus causes cell elongation on the site opposite the light source, so the plant is pushed toward the light. Although the plant appears to be pulled toward the light, it is actually pushed toward the light.

of tobacco, called Maryland Mammoth, flowered only in late fall or winter. They tried forcing plants to flower in a greenhouse by changing the temperature, changing light intensity or giving it supplemental fertilizer, but the plant remained vegetative and would not flower. Then they discovered that if they pulled black cloth over the plant at 4 o'clock in the afternoon, giving the plant a long period of uninterrupted darkness, it would flower. They concluded that the length of the night influenced floral initiation, and they coined this phenomenon 'Photoperiodism.'

Soon it was discovered that a number of flowering ornamental plants were just as dependent on day length as tobacco for floral initiation. It was also found that plants varied greatly in the length of darkness required for floral initiation. Scientists began grouping plants into three categories based on their photoperiodic responses: long day plants, short day plants or day neutral plants. Long day plants are those that initiate flowering when the night length is shorter than some critical minimum, while short day plants flower when the night length is longer than a critical minimum. Day neutral plants flower over a wide range of photoperiods; with day length not affecting flowering. Table 6 shows the photoperiodic response of some flowering plants.

The critical photoperiod required to initiate flowers, and the length of time a plant must be exposed to the uninterrupted darkness to initiate flowers varies by species. Spinach, a long day plant, cannot flower in the tropics because days never get longer than 14 hours.

Table 6. Photoperiodic response of certain flowering plants

LONG DAY PLANTS	SHORT DAY PLANTS	DAY NEUTRAL PLANTS
Spinach	Chrysanthemum	Tomato
Radish	Poinsettia	Corn
Petunia	Christmas Cactus	Snapdragon
Rose Mallow	Soybean	Garden Bean
Garden Phlox	Rice	Peas
Larkspur	Kalanchoe	Cucumber
Clover	Strawberries	Squash
Black-eyed Susan	Coffee	Pepper

Ragweed rarely flowers in Maine because it's a short day plant. If ragweed does have time to flower in early fall, a killing frost usually occurs, which prevents the plant from setting seed.

The number of cycles of uninterrupted darkness (called induction cycles) required to initiate flowering also varies by plant species. Chrysanthemum, a short day plant, requires at least 9 hours of uninterrupted darkness to initiate flowers. Because of this, chrysanthemum growers that provide cut flowers usually provide at least 13 hours of darkness by pulling black cloth over the plants from 5 p.m. to 8 a.m. However, growers of chrysanthemum for homeowner markets do not need to

Table 7. Flower or Vegetative Response of Chrysanthemum at Various Lighting Regimes

Chrysanthemum (a short-day plant)
Initiates flowers when day length is 14 hours or less or night length is 9 ½ hours or more. The length of the night period is the critical factor.

14.5 HOURS LIGHT		9.5 HOURS DARK	FLOWER INITIATION
15 HOURS LIGHT		9 HOURS DARK	VEGETATIVE
9 HOURS LIGHT	15 HOURS DARK		FLOWER INITIATION
9 HOURS LIGHT	7 HOURS DARK	1 HOUR LIGHT — 7 HOURS DARK	VEGETATIVE
9 HOURS LIGHT	4 HOURS DARK — 1 HOUR LIGHT	10 HOURS DARK	FLOWER INITIATION

treat their mums because night length occurs naturally in the southeastern U.S. as day length shortens in the fall. Cultivars of chrysanthemum vary as to the length of the induction cycle. Some cultivars require as little as 6 weeks on the light/dark cycle while others require as much as 15 weeks.

Sometimes growers need to delay flowering for a later market. To keep plants vegetative, they extend the photoperiod with artificial lighting. Light bulbs are placed over the plants in a greenhouse and timed to come on in the middle of the night for 2 to 4 hours. This disrupts the dark cycle and prevents the plants from flowering. Although growers typically provide 100 to 200 foot candles of light intensity during the dark period, some plants can be prevented from flowering with as little as 10 footcandles of light during the dark period. Table 7 illustrates plant responses of chrysanthemum under various lighting regimes. Once flower induction occurs, it can not be turned off and the plants can be given normal day-length and will flower normally.

Light receptors that drive photoperiodism are proteins called phytoreceptors. Phytochrome is the most common photoreceptor, a pigment that plants use to detect light. It is sensitive to light in the red and far-red region of the visible spectrum. Many flowering plants use it to regulate the time of flowering based on the length of day and night (photoperiodism) and to set circadian rhythms. It also regulates other responses including the germination of seeds, elongation of seedlings, the size, shape and number of leaves, the synthesis of chlorophyll, and the straightening of the epicotyl or hypocotyl hook of dicot seedlings. It is found in the leaves of most plants. Other plant photoreceptors include cryptochromes and phototropins, which are sensitive to light in the blue and ultra-violet regions of the spectrum. These proteins change their chemistry within the plant according to light intensity and duration and serve as a signal to developing buds to either remain vegetative or develop into flowers.

Seed Germination—Still another effect of light on plants is in seed germination. Light enhances germination of some seeds and inhibits germination of other seeds. Most seed catalogs have charts listing the light requirement of seed.. It's important to always read the seed packet for special lighting instructions. Lettuce seed is a well-known example of a seed that requires light for germination. For best germination, lettuce seed is broadcast on the soil surface and not covered with soil. Pansy seed, on the other hand, requires darkness for germination. It is a common practice in the greenhouse industry to place seeded flats of pansies in dark, humid

Table 8. Light requirement for germination of various seeds

SEED	LIGHT REQUIREMENT	SEED	LIGHT REQUIREMENT
African Violet	Light	Hollyhock	Dark or Light
Ageratum	Light	Impatiens	Light
Alyssum	Dark or Light	Lobelia	Dark or Light
Calendula	Dark	Marigold	Dark or Light
Candytuft	Dark or Light	Morning Glory	Dark or Light
Celosia	Dark or Light	Nasturtium	Dark
Chinese Lantern	Light	Nicotiana	Light
Coleus	Light	Pansy	Dark
Columbine	Light	Perennial Aster	Light
Coneflower	Dark	Petunia	Light
Coral Bells	Light	Phlox	Dark
Coreopsis	Light	Red-hot Poker	Light
Corn Flower	Dark	Rudbeckia	Dark or Light
Cosmos	Dark or Light	Snapdragon	Light
Cyclamen	Dark	Statice	Dark or Light
Dianthus	Dark or Light	Strawflower	Light
Dusty Miller	Dark	Sweet Pea	Dark
Galliardia	Dark or Light	Tuberous Begonia	Light
Geranium	Dark or Light	Verbena	Dark
Globe Amaranth	Dark	Vinca (annual)	Dark
Gloxinia	Light	Vinca	Dark

growth chambers to enhance seed germination. Home gardeners can obtain the same results by covering seeded flats with moist newspaper to block out light during germination, then removing it once the germination has occurred.

Table 8 shows the light and dark requirement of a wide variety of seeds. Like photoperiodism, this light response is controlled by the plant protein phytochrome. Phytochrome has two forms within the seed - phytochrome far-red and phytochrome red. During light periods, phytochrome red predominates while the far-red form is dominant in the dark. In the case of lettuce, phytochrome red stimulates the plant hormone ethylene to soften the seed coat and to enhance germination. When lettuce seeds are covered and shielded from light, phytochrome far-red in the seed coat predominates and germination is often poor.

Temperature

A second environmental factor influencing plant physiology and plant growth and development is temperature. Most chemical reactions in plants are mediated by enzymes that are influenced by temperature. The classic example is RuBisCO, the most abundant protein on Earth that is responsible for capturing and 'fixing' carbon dioxide from the atmosphere to create carbohydrates within a plant. RuBisCO has an optimum temperature range of 28 to 40°C (82-104°F); too cool or too hot leads to less efficient carbon fixation and hence slower growth. . When looking at the plant as a whole; as temperature increases beyond the optimum (which is different for different species), the rate of respiration begins to exceed the rate of photosynthesis and plant growth stops. At very high temperatures, above 100°F, enzymes and proteins may be inactivated and/or broken down, and toxic substances may be produced which are lethal to plant cells, causing them to die. Under high heat, transpiration also increases to the point where net water loss through the stomata exceeds water gain through the roots and the plant wilts. Many plants have the ability to close their stomata when temperatures rise to undesirable levels, thereby conserving water. However, when plants close their stomata, internal heat increases and can permanently damage important enzymes and proteins.

Hardiness—Hardiness is a term used to describe a plant's ability to adapt to the average minimum and maximum temperatures of a region. The onset of winter hardiness is triggered by shorter days and cooler temperatures in fall. During the fall months, growth begins to subside, photosynthesis declines and chlorophyll begins to degrade as a result of night temperatures below optimum levels. With the onset of frosts, plants become more hardened. Woody plants usually require one or more hard freezes before they are fully hardened to the average winter temperatures of the region. A few mild frosts help move the plant toward its winter state, but it usually requires one or more hard freezes to place plants in full winter hardiness. Plant parts vary in their ability to harden and resist cold. Generally, roots are less hardy than leaves, and leaves are less hardy than stems, and stems are less hardy than buds.

Since roots are the least hardy part of the plant, growers of containerized plants often take precautions to protect plants from winter freezes. Growers will jam the pots together to minimize air flow and will place pots filled with sand around the perimeter of the block to add extra insulation. Some growers will cover entire blocks of plants with white plastic sheeting or white fiber sheeting to shield them from winter cold and excessive wind. This covering can be left in place the entire winter in northern areas or placed on and taken off multiple times in the southern regions of the U.S. Moisture held by the covering will prevent the plants from dehydrating, and the white color lets in sufficient light to allow the plants to photosynthesize. Although the plants winterized under plastic often look ratty when uncovered the following spring, a far greater percentage will survive cold temperatures than if not covered.

Just as nurserymen protect the roots of containerized plants from freezing, home gardeners should be prepared to move patio plants into a heated basement or garage when temperatures drop below freezing. The smaller the container, the more rapidly the soil will freeze. When roots freeze, either the entire root or more often the root hairs can die, and the top of the plant begins to suffer when the roots are unable to supply it with sufficient water and nutrients. (See section on cold protection for additional information).

Freezing injury is a complex phenomenon governed by a number of factors, including genetics, the minimum temperature level, the speed at which the temperature dropped, the duration of below freezing temperatures, and the degree of hardiness of the plant at the time of the freeze and the nature of the freeze (i.e., whether the freeze is accompanied by wind or occurs suddenly following several days or weeks of warm weather). Have you ever wondered how pansy plants can freeze solid in winter, then bounce back without a scratch when weather warms? Unlike other plants that freeze when ice crystals form within their cells, causing them to rupture, pansies have the ability to sense cold and move water out of their cells into the spaces between the cells. As a result, carbohydrates within the cells concentrate, and as they concentrate they act like antifreeze in a car, lowering the freezing point of the cell. The inter-cellular spaces freeze but not the cells themselves. The cells remain intact, and the plant appears unaffected when temperature warms.

Throughout this manual you will be advised to consider the hardiness of plants and their ability to adapt to average minimum and maximum temperatures of a region. Here in Georgia, there are five cold hardiness zones, ranging from zone 6b in the northern part of the state to zone 8b in southern Georgia. It's extremely important to select plants having winter hardiness at least to your zone or above. It would be a mistake to grow a zone 8 plant in zone 6 because the plant is likely to die due to winter cold. Figure 11 shows the plant hardiness zones for Georgia.

In 1998, the American Horticulture Society developed and released a Heat Hardiness Zone Map for the United States. This map was based on national weather data compiled over 21 years by Dr. Marc Cathy, former director of the U.S. National Arboretum. The map divides the U.S. into 12 zones and shows the average number of days above 86°F in each zone. A Georgia adaptation is shown in Figure 12.

Fall Leaf Color —Temperature has the greatest influence on fall leaf colors. As days get shorter and temperatures cool, the production of chlorophyll ceases. The chlorophyll remaining in the leaf breaks down as temperatures dip below 50 degrees Fahrenheit and disappears, allowing other pigments within the leaf to become visible. Carotene and xanthophyll give leaves their yellow and orange color, and anthocyanin makes leaves red and purple. These pigments are in the leaves throughout the growing season, but they are masked by an overabundance of chlorophyll, which gives leaves their green color. Anthocyanin increases as sugar content of the leaves increases, so if we have bright, sunny days and cool nights, a surplus of sugar is produced during photosynthesis and leaves become more brilliant red or orange. Plants that produce excess sugars, such as maple, tupelo, oaks and Winged Euonymus, often appear on fire with reds and purples when nights are cool and days are sunny. Ginkgo produces mostly xanthophyll which accounts for its glowing yellow color in fall.

Chill Hours of Fruit—Winter temperature fluctuations have a pronounced effect on certain fruit crops; like peaches and apples. You will often see peaches and apples listed in catalogs as low-chill varieties or high-chill varieties.

Both of these fruits require a certain number of chill hours below 45°F before they will break dormancy and flower, and each variety in commercial production is rated for its chilling hour requirement. Once the tree's

Figure 11

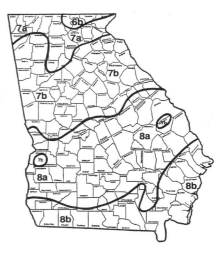

Figure 11. Plant hardiness zones in Georgia. Average minimum temperature (°f) by zone

Zone	Range in Degrees Fahrenheit
6b	- 5 to 0
7a	0 to 5
7b	5 to 10
8a	10 to 15
8b	15 to 20

Figure 12

Figure 12. Heat hardiness zone map for Georgia. Average number of days/year above 86°f.

Zone	Ave. No. of Days
5	30 - 45
6	45 - 60
7	60 - 90
8	90 - 120
9	120 - 150

chill hours are satisfied, it breaks dormancy and flowers. Chill hours vary from about 350 hours (low chill varieties) to more than 1200 chill hours, depending on variety. It would be a mistake to grow a low-chilling peach or apple that requires 400 chill hours in an area that gets 1000 chill hours on average because the plants will get their chill hours satisfied early in their dormancy, break bud and flower long before the cold temperatures are over, making them susceptible to freeze injury and crop loss. Typically, low-chill varieties are grown in southern Georgia, while those with a higher chilling requirement are grown in the central and northern parts of the state.

Cold Protection—In the commercial horticulture industry, growers sometimes provide cold protection to sensitive crops. Previously we discussed some of the measures taken by nurserymen to protect containerized plants from winter freezes. Citrus growers in Florida protect their crops by burning smudge pots throughout the grove to help mix air layers in the grove to moderate air temperature around the tree canopy. Another cold protection measure sometimes used is icing. This involves turning on overhead irrigation when temperature drops below freezing to form a layer of ice on the foliage. As water freezes, it releases heat, so the temperature adjacent to the leaf and fruit remains near the freezing point, even when the surrounding air may be well below freezing. However, the secret to success with this cold protection measure is to provide a sufficient volume of water at all times to keep the water constantly freezing and accumulating. If the ice is allowed to evaporate, it will cool the surrounding area, pulling heat from the plant. This can result in more severe damage than if no protection at all had been applied. In addition, the ice load may break limbs and branches. Homeowners should be wary of this technique because the risks typically outweigh the benefits and more harm than good may be done to plants. Most cold protection measures work as long as the temperature does not drop much below 25°F and as long as there is not a strong wind. When strong wind accompanies freezing temperature, damage is often most severe.

Cold-sensitive plants in the landscape can be protected from severe freezes by covering them with old blankets, quilts or corrugated cardboard boxes. The thicker the covering, the better insulator it will be. Make certain the covering is left open to the ground to allow heat escaping from the ground to radiate upward under the canopy. Plastic is not a good covering for landscape plants because heat will be lost readily through the plastic while moisture will be trapped under the plastic. Foliar damage may result when the trapped water freezes on the foliage and gradually evaporates, pulling heat from the plant.

Another cold protection technique involves placing a hoop of chicken wire around the plant and filling it with fall leaves, wheat straw or pine straw. This helps minimize the flow of cold air around the leaves and stems.

Water

A third environmental factor having a pronounced effect on plant physiology, plant metabolism, plant growth and development is water. Water has been called the lifeblood of plants since it plays a major role in transporting nutrients and food throughout the plant, just as our blood transports nutrients, waste products and oxygen throughout our bodies. Water is a major component of plant cells. By creating turgor pressure within the cells, water helps plants stand upright, much like an inflated tire. When water loss exceeds water gain, cells deflate and the plant wilts. Water movement through plants is based on the concept of water potential, the tendency of water to move from one area to another due to osmosis, gravity, mechanical pressure, or matrix effects such as surface tension.

Fruit and vegetables contain large quantities of water in relation to their weight. A fresh apple, for instance, is 84% water, a banana is 75% water, a peach is 87% water, strawberries are 92% water, and iceberg lettuce is 96% water. This factor, along with their low caloric value and high nutritive value is why fruit and vegetables are great diet foods. Water cools plants during transpiration as it moves outward through the stomata in the form of water vapor. Just as we perspire on a hot summer day, plants transpire. This evaporative loss of water cools the leaf surface and prevents the plant from overheating.

Have you ever wondered how water reaches the top of some of our tallest trees, like the California redwoods, which may reach heights in excess of 300 feet? Do the roots act like a pump, sending water under pressure upward to the top? No, root pressure has been found in only a few plant species and in those plants where it has been found, the pressure has only been great enough to force the water to a height of 64 feet.

In 1937, a scientist by the name of Phillip Kramer determined that shoot tension, not root pressure is responsible for water movement in plants. He called it the transpiration-cohesion-tension mechanism. Although it sounds complex, the process is rather simple. Essentially, water movement within a plant is based on water potential, or the direction that water will flow

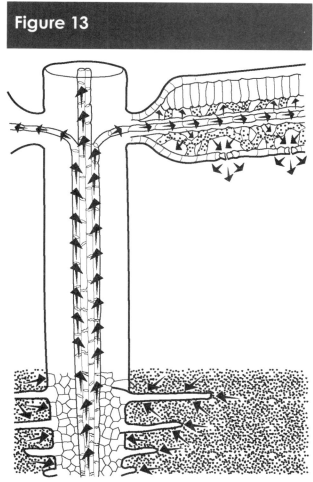

Figure 13

Figure 13. Transpiration - Cohesion - Tension Mechanism. As water vapor moves out through the stomata, a vapor pressure deficit pulls water upward to replace the water lost.

through a plant, with a more negative value indicating "drier" conditions and less negative values indicating more "saturated" conditions. Water flows from high to low water potential. The symbol for the water potential and other energy potential in cells is represented by the Greek letter psi which is usually expressed in kilopascals (kPa) or megapascals (MPa). Water potential ranges from -100 to 1 MPa. The water potential of air at 50% humidity is approximately -100 MPa and this drives water movement from the soil to the stomata and out into the ambient air. As water vapor is transpired through the stomata in the upper plant parts, it creates a water (vapor) pressure deficit within stomatal cavity, where water potential ranges from -6 to -8 MPa. Because water molecules have great cohesive strength and are linked together like chains (see figure 13), the tension created by the loss of water through the stomata pulls more water upward through the xylem, where water potential is also -6 to -8 MPa, to replace the water that is lost. A good way to visualize this is by imagining a never-ending

rope being thrown out a window. As water loss occurs, more water is pulled up to take its place. Kramer's studies proved that water is pulled upward in the plant, not pumped upward by the root. Water's natural tendency to 'stick' to the walls of this straw-like xylem elements is called adhesion, and in tandem with cohesion, can move water up to heights of 406' (the tallest known tree; Sequoia sempervirens - Coast Redwood).

Although some water moves in and out of the plant via the stomata on the leaves, stems and fruit, most absorption of water and nutrients occurs in the root hair region of the root, found just behind the root tip in the zone of elongation. Root hairs are long extensions of the epidermal cells on the root that are in intimate contact with soil particles (see figure 14). Because the water potential of roots (-2 to -4 MPa) is less than that of soil (0.6 tp -0.1), roots are able to out compete soil for the water molecule and the water consequently moves from the soil into the root. The number of root hairs on a single root is often in the billions. A single rye plant, for instance, was found to have over fourteen billion root hairs, having a combined surface area of over 4,000 square feet. Can you imagine how many root hairs some well established trees must have? Since most root hairs are found on the secondary and tertiary roots growing off the main root, the majority of the absorptive root system on a large tree is mainly at the drip line (tips of the canopy) and beyond. The location and sheer volume of root hairs are what allows a plant to take up such high volumes of water from the soil. There are very few absorptive roots near the main trunk of trees. Roots do not have stomata like the upper plant surfaces. Epidermal cells (cells along the outer edge) are generally one-cell thick. They lack the waxy coating (called cutin) found on epidermal cells of the upper plant parts. Therefore, there is little to no impediment of water movement into the root. As water moves in, it carries valuable nutrients extracted from the soil and soil solution. Once inside the plant, water moves in the xylem stream to wherever water potential is lowest in the plant canopy.

Plants native to arid regions of the world have developed morphological features that help them cope with low water availability. Have you ever noticed how Purple Coneflower and Black-eyed Susan (plants native to the arid southwestern regions of U.S.) have hairy leaves that feel somewhat like sandpaper when you run your fingers across them? These leaf hairs (termed pubescence) serve to reduce the air flow near the surface of the leaf, thus reducing the evaporative loss of water from the leaf. The leaf hairs also trap water vapor arising from the stomata and hold it adjacent to the leaf. Succulents, like cacti and sedum, have a thick, waxy cuticle on their leaves that serve as a barrier to water loss. Have you ever noticed the round nodules on liriope roots that are sometimes the size of marbles? A principle function of these nodules are to hold water.

ESSENTIAL ELEMENTS FOR PLANT GROWTH (Nutrients)

It is impossible to talk about plant physiology without discussing the essential role certain chemical elements play in plant metabolism, plant growth and plant structures. There are 21 elements, also referred to as nutrients, known to have an essential role in plant growth and development. Each element is essential because no other element can substitute for it in 100% of its plant functions, and each one has a unique role in plant metabolism and physiology. Furthermore, a plant cannot complete its life cycle without them. *Note: various scientists will list varying numbers of essential elements or nutrients- however, the three essential atmospheric elements and eighteen essential soil elements covered in Tables 9-10 are comprehensive and cited across literature as of 2010.*

Three essential atmospheric elements - carbon, hydrogen and oxygen, make up approximately 95 percent of the dry weight of plants. We have already seen in the previous discussion on photosynthesis and respiration how vital these elements are in plant metabolism [water (H_2O), carbon dioxide (CO_2), and plant sugars ($C_6H_{12}O_6$)]. In fact, they are major part of most chemical compounds in the plant.

The eighteen additional essential elements are obtained primarily from the soil, the soil solution or fertilizers. They are grouped into three classes: major elements -- nitrogen (N), phosphorus (P) and potassium (K); secondary elements -- calcium (Ca), magnesium (Mg) and sulfur (S); and micro elements -- boron (B), copper (Cu), manganese (Mn), zinc (Zn), iron (Fe), molybdenum (Mo) chlorine (Cl), Sodium (Na), Cobalt (Co), Silicon (Si), Selenium (Se), and Nickel (Ni) (see Table 9). This classification is based on the concentration of each element found in the plant, not on its level of importance. Major elements are required in largest quantities by the plant, so when we buy a bag of fertilizer, we generally buy it according to its content of N, P and K. Secondary elements are required in somewhat lower amounts than the major elements, while micro elements are required in very small quantities, often measured in parts per million (ppm) or parts per billion (ppb). **See table 10 on the following pages for specific nutrient uses.**

Figure 14 shows the structure of the chlorophyll molecule and illustrates the role several essential elements play in the structure of this compound. Note the essential roles of magnesium, nitrogen, carbon, oxygen, hydrogen. Without these elements, there would be no chlorophyll and photosynthesis could not occur.

Essential elements are present in the soil solution and on soil particles in ionic forms having positive charge (cation) forms or negative charges (anions). See Table 11.

Soil particles generally have a negative charge and have a strong affinity for positively charged ions. When we lime a soil, we are applying calcium and magnesium which have strong positive charges. These tend to knock other positively charged elements off the soil particles and into the soil solution, making them more available to the plant. The plant root also assists in bringing many of the nutrient ions into the soil solution by releasing carbon dioxide during respiration which combines with water to form carbonic acid. The acid environment increases the solubility of some essential elements, causing them

Table 9. Range in concentration within plant tissue(s) of both atmosperic (italicized) and soil essential plant elements

ELEMENT	PPM	%	TYPE
Hydrogen	*60,000*	*6.0*	*Atmospheric*
Carbon	*420,000*	*42.0*	*Atmospheric*
Oxygen	*480,000*	*48.0*	*Atmospheric*
Nitrogen	14,000	1.4	Major
Potassium	10,000	1.0	Major
Calcium	5,000	0.5	Major
Magnesium	2,000	0.2	Secondary
Phosphorus	2,000	0.2	Secondary
Sulfur	1,000	0.1	Secondary
Chlorine	100	0.01	Minor
Iron	100	0.01	Minor
Manganese	50	0.005	Minor
Boron	20		Minor
Zinc	20		Minor
Copper	6		Minor
Molybdenum	0.1		Minor
Sodium	trace		Minor
Cobalt	trace		Minor
Silicon	trace		Minor
Selenium	trace		Minor
Nickel	trace		Minor

to leave the soil particles and enter the soil solution. It is important to note however that a generally accepted pH range should be between 5.2 - 6.5. Within this pH range, optimal nutrient availability will be achieved. A pH too low or two high can result in some nutrients becoming available at toxic levels while others being completely bound by the soil and unavailable to plants.

Environmental factors, such as soil aeration, temperature and soil moisture influence the rate and extent of nutrient absorption. One of the essential requirements for nutrient uptake is a supply of atmospheric air. Adequate soil aeration for the development of healthy and vigorous roots is emphasized many times throughout this manual. The rate of nutrient absorption by plant roots is correlated to the respiration rate of the absorbing cells. In turn, the respiration rate is influenced by the supply of oxygen. Reduced root growth is common on compact, poorly drained soils. Restricted root systems can hardly be expected to absorb sufficient nutrients for normal plant growth.

Temperature also has a marked effect on respiration and, therefore, nutrient uptake. The effects of low soil temperatures in early spring often reduce nutrient uptake.

An oversupply of one element in the soil may reduce the

Table 11: Ionic forms of some essential elements absorbed by plants

ELEMENT	IONIC FORM
Nitrogen	NH_4^+, NO_2^-, NO_3^-
Phosphorus	HPO_4^-, $H_2PO_4^{2-}$
Potassium	K^+
Calcium	Ca^{2+}
Magnesium	Mg^{2+}
Sulphur	SO_4^{2-}
Iron	Fe^{2+}, Fe^{3+}
Copper	Cu^2, Cu^{2+}
Zinc	Zn^{2+}

uptake of certain other elements. For instance, too much potassium may result in magnesium deficiency. Excess calcium carbonate (from lime) may cause deficiencies of other elements such as magnesium and potassium as the elements become bound up in the soil and unavailable to the plant. Excess phosphorus may also cause iron deficiency by tying up iron in the form of iron phosphate, making iron unavailable in the soil solution. Nutrient interactions and soil pH effect on nutrient availability are two important reasons for having a soil test done through your local county Extension office before applying fertilizer or lime to the soil.

Figure 14

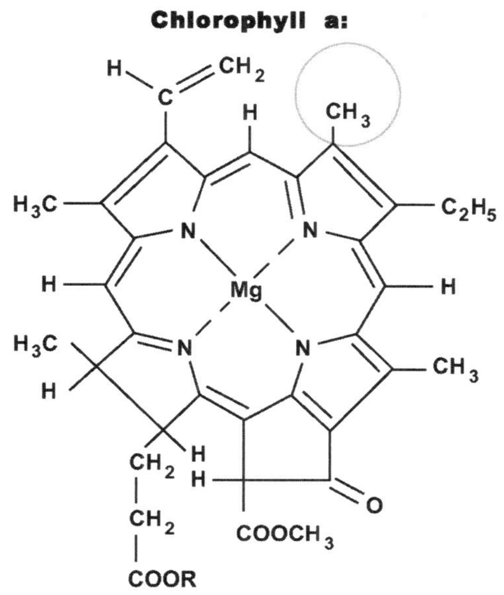

Figure 14. The structure of the chlorophyll molecule.

Table 10. Essential soil nutrients, nutrient functions, deficiency symptoms, and nutrient antagonism & interactions.

NUTRIENT	FUNCTIONS IN THE PLANT	DEFICIENCY SYMPTOMS	NUTRIENT ANTAGONISM AND INTERACTION
Nitrogen (N)	An essential element in all living systems; Occurs in the living substance (protoplasm) of cells; A major component of all proteins; A major component of chlorophyll which converts sunlight into plant energy; Affects both yields and quality of seeds.	Lighter green or yellow colored leaves (first evident in older leaves); Some plants (eg. berries) can develop red or orange colors; Stunted growth; Lower protein levels in pasture and grain; Delayed maturity; Decreased resistance to disease and/or insect attack; Smaller fruit and lower yields; Shorter storage life of fruit/seed.	When high levels of Nitrogen induce accelerated growth rates; Levels of micronutrients that would normally be marginal can become deficient; High soil levels of Nitrogen can assist Phosphorus, Calcium, Boron, Iron and Zinc but an excess can dilute these elements; Low soil levels can reduce Phosphorus, Calcium, Boron, Iron and Zinc uptake; Ammonium Nitrogen can make Molybdenum deficiency appear less obvious.
Phosphorus (P)	Phosphorus is important in plant bioenergetics. As a component of ATP, phosphorus is needed for the conversion of light energy to chemical energy (ATP) during photosynthesis. Phosphorus can also be used to modify the activity of various enzymes by phosphorylation, and can be used for cell signalling. Since ATP can be used for the biosynthesis of many plant biomolecules, phosphorus is important for plant growth and flower/seed formation.	Reduced growth; Sometimes stunted and other times only evident from shortened internodes.	High levels of Phosphorus reduce Zinc and, to a lesser degree, Calcium uptake; It is antagonistic to Boron in low pH soils.
Potassium (K)	Aids photosynthesis and the functioning of chlorophyll; Important for the formation and translocation of starches; Potassium regulates the opening and closing of the stomata by a potassium ion pump. Since stomata are important in water regulation, potassium reduces water loss from the leaves and increases drought tolerance.	Yellow scorching or firing (chlorosis) along the leaf margins. Symptoms usually occur first on the lower leaves of the plant and progress toward the top as the severity of the deficiency increases. Older leaves may wilt, look scorched. Interveinal chlorosis begins at the base, scorching inward from leaf margins.	High levels of Potassium reduce Magnesium and to lesser extent Calcium, Iron, Copper, Manganese and Zinc uptake; Boron levels can either be low or toxic; Low levels can accentuate Iron deficiency.

Table 10. Essential soil nutrients, nutrient functions, deficiency symptoms, and nutrient antagonism & interactions.

NUTRIENT	FUNCTIONS IN THE PLANT	DEFICIENCY SYMPTOMS	NUTRIENT ANTAGONISM AND INTERACTION
Calcium (Ca)	Necessary for the proper functioning of growing points- particularly root tips; Forms compounds which strengthen cell walls; Aids in cell division and elongation; Neutralizes organic acids; Aids in the proper working and permeability of cell membranes; Regulates protein synthesis and slows aging process; Calcium regulates transport of other nutrients into the plant and is also involved in the activation of certain plant enzymes.	Terminal buds and root tips fail to develop normally; Lodging(stem flopping); Stunted root systems; Leaves of grasses do not open properly- the tips of which stick to the next lowest leaf; Soft fruit; Senescent breakdown and poor storage life of fruit; Internal and external disorders of many fruit and vegetables.	High levels of Calcium can accentuate Boron deficiency; Liming can decrease the uptake of Boron, Copper, Iron, Manganese and Zinc by raising soil pH.
Magnesium (M)	The only mineral constituent of the chlorophyll molecule; Aids plants to form sugars and starches; Plays an important part in the translocation of phosphorous; Aids several plant enzymes to function.	Interveinal chlorosis(yellow or pale color) beginning in the tips of older leaves; Veins remain green.	At high levels can interfere with uptake of potassium, calcium, zinc, manganese, and copper.
Sulfur (S)	Similar requirements to phosphorus in plants; A constituent of several amino acids which are essential for protein production; Aids the activities of some enzymes and vitamins; Needed for chlorophyll formation; Deficiency adversely affects the oil content in some oil crops and the baking quality in wheat crops; Aids efficient nitrogen stabilization; Needed for nodule formation in legumes.	Generally very similar to nitrogen deficiency - a uniform pale green to yellow leaf but the difference is sulfur deficiency starts in the new leaves whereas nitrogen deficiency starts in the old leaves; Root nodules produced are smaller, pale rather than pink and reduced in number; Deficiencies in field crops include poor low yielding plants, low protein and pale green and yellow leaves in wheat.	Unknown
Silicon (Si)	Silicon is deposited in cell walls and contributes to its mechanical properties including rigidity and elasticity.	Affects the development of strong leaves, stems, and roots leading to drooping foliage and a reduction in photosynthesis; Increases susceptibility to fungal and bacterial diseases and insect and mite pests.	Unknown

Table 10. Essential soil nutrients, nutrient functions, deficiency symptoms, and nutrient antagonism & interactions.

NUTRIENT	FUNCTIONS IN THE PLANT	DEFICIENCY SYMPTOMS	NUTRIENT ANTAGONISM AND INTERACTION
Boron (B)	Plays a role in cell division; Aids efficient translocation of calcium; Protein synthesis; Carbohydrate metabolism; Pollen viability; Flower and fruit set and formation; Hormone formation.	Thick, curled and brittle tissues – cracking and splitting, sometimes with gummosis; Surfaces of leaf, petioles, stems and midribs develop cracks or a corky appearance; Reduced flowering, seed set and fruit set; Growth points can die, forming multiple side shoots; Small misshapen fruit; Internal flesh disorders and cracking in fruit and vegetables.	Unknown
Chlorine (Cl)	Chlorine is necessary for osmosis and ionic balance; Plays a role in photosynthesis	Abnormally small and oddly shaped leaves, with distinct interveinal chlorosis	Unknown
Copper (Cu)	Required for chlorophyll production; Helps with photosynthesis; Aids in the production of enzymes & proteins; Involved in several enzyme systems; Involved in several oxidation reduction reactions and the formation of lignins; Required for seed coat production.	Marginal chlorosis of young leaves; Sometimes necrotic tips (if severe); Twig dieback. Sometimes necrotic and brown spots over leaf surface. Reduced growth and yields.	High levels of Copper can accentuate Molybdenum and to a lesser degree Iron, Manganese and Zinc deficiency.
Iron (Fe)	Necessary for the formation of chlorophyll; Aids in photosynthesis; Involved in the oxidation process that releases energy from starches and enzymes; Aids in the formation of proteins; Involved in the conversion of nitrate to ammonia in the plant; Aids respiration.	Young leaves have interveinal chlorosis with green veins; Later in season visible yellowing of leaves (margins and tips can scorch); Stunted growth.	Iron deficiency can be accentuated by liming, low Potassium levels or high levels of Copper, Manganese or Zinc.
Manganese (Mn)	Essential for chlorophyll production and photosynthesis; Aids nitrogen and carbohydrate metabolism; Oxidation reduction; Involved in the activity of several enzymes; Combines with copper, iron and zinc to aid plant growth processes.	Chlorosis of recently matured leaves with no reduction in leaf size; Less pronounced mottling in some broad leaf plants; Grasses can show a longitudinal striping; Chlorosis in broadleaf evergreens (more evident on the shady side of the tree).	High levels of Copper, Iron or Zinc can accentuate Manganese deficiency – especially repeated soil applications of Iron; Uptake can be decreased by liming or increased by Sulfur applications (because of the affects on pH).

Table 10. Essential soil nutrients, nutrient functions, deficiency symptoms, and nutrient antagonism & interactions.

NUTRIENT	FUNCTIONS IN THE PLANT	DEFICIENCY SYMPTOMS	NUTRIENT ANTAGONISM AND INTERACTION
Molybdenum (Mo)	Is a cofactor in the enzyme nitrate-reductose; Aids in the conversion of nitrates of ammonium (the initial stage of synthesis of proteins) essential for Rhizobia to enable legume crops to fix aerobic (atmospheric) nitrogen; Helps plants to utilize nitrate nitrogen; Involved in phosphate and iron metabolism.	In general, similar to nitrogen deficiency - yellowing or pale leaves stunting, necrotic leaf margins and tips (this is because without molybdenum plants cannot metabolize nitrogen) – symptoms start in older leaves first; Flowers can wither or be suppressed.	Deficiencies can be accentuated by high levels of Copper and to a lesser degree Manganese; Uptake can be adversely affected by sulfates; Uptake can be increased by applying phosphates and liming.
Zinc (Zn)	Necessary for the formation of chlorophyll; Involved in several enzyme systems, the growth hormone auxins and the synthesis of nucleic acids; Plays a part in the intake and use of water in by plants.	Stunted growth; Leaves reduced in size and misshapen; Chlorosis (leaf mottling) leading to necrosis and premature leaf fall; Rosetting and/or little leaf in fruit trees; "tram lining" or light striping both sides of the midrib in grasses; Bronze spotting on older leaves later giving a mottled appearance in legumes; Reduced development and size of fruit.	Uptake can be decreased by high Phosphorus levels, liming or high levels of Copper, Iron or Manganese; Zinc deficiencies are often associated with Manganese deficiencies, especially in broad leaf evergreens.
Nickel (Ni)	Nickel is essential for activation of urease, an enzyme involved with nitrogen metabolism that is required to process urea. Without Nickel, toxic levels of urea accumulate, leading to the formation of necrotic lesions; In lower plants, Nickel activates several enzymes involved in a variety of processes, and can substitute for Zinc and Iron as a cofactor in some enzymes.		Unknown
Selenium (Se)	Incorporated it into several amino acids replacing sulfur as part of the normal structure	Similar to nitrogen and sulfur deficiency - a uniform pale green to yellow leaf starts in the new leaves; Rarely seen due to abundance of sulfur in GA soils.	None reported although in low sulfur soils can be preferentially taken up by plants.
Sodium (Na)	Sodium can replace potassium's regulation of stomatal opening and closing; Sodium is involved in the regeneration of phosphoenolpyruvate in certain plants.	Reduction in plant size (biomass) and seed weight.	Unknown

DISCUSSION QUESTIONS

1. Describe the Von Helmont experiment and what it proved.

2. Can you write the summary equation for photosynthesis and explain it?

3. What are two differences between photosynthesis and respiration?

4. What is a stoma and what is its function?

5. What are xylem and phloem and how do they differ?

6. What two regions of the visible spectrum do plants absorb most?

7. What is a foot candle and how is it used?

8. What is phototropism?

9. What is a short-day plant? What is a day-neutral plant?

10. Why is light important in seed germination?

11. Define hardiness and hardiness zones.

12. Where is Auxin produced in the plant?

13. How does water move upward in the plant?

RESOURCES

Grelach, Victor A. *Botany Made Simple*. Doubleday & Company Books, New York, ISBN:68-11764.

Salisbury, Frank B. and Cleon Ross. *Plant Physiology*. Wadsworth Publishing Company, ISBN: 68-17381.

Leopold, Carl. *Plant Growth and Development*. McGraw-Hill Publishing Company, ISBN:64-21071.

Copies of the *Hardiness Zone Map* are available from the American Horticultural Society, 7931 East Boulevard Dr., Alexandria, VA 22308-1300, Ph.: 1-800-777-7931, E-mail: gardenahs@aol.com

4
Plant Propagation

Bodie V. Pennisi

LEARNING OBJECTIVES

Understand basic principles of sexual plant propagation.

Be familiar with how plants are asexually propagated.

Be familiar with techniques for stem, leaf and root cutting propagation.

Know basics of seed germination.

Be familiar with layering, grafting and budding as methods for plant propagation.

TERMS TO KNOW

Adventitious root root that develops on any part of the plant other than from other roots.

Aleurone layer outermost layer in cereal seeds and other taxa, which contains enzymes concerned with starch digestion and subsequent seed germination.

Apical bud bud on the top of a shoot

Asexual propagation done by removing and planting part of the vegetative plant body and generating a complete replica of the original plant.

Auxins plant hormones involved in adventitious root formation.

Axillary bud bud in the axil of a leaf.

Callus undifferentiated tissue usually associated with adventitious root formation.

Cotyledons seed leaves.

Cutting any portion of the vegetative plant body used for propagation.

Double dormancy combination of endodormancy and exodormancy.

Enhanced seed commercial seed that have been treated in a certain way, in order to increase germination and/or achieve uniform germination, and/or improve seedling survival.

Endodormancy imposed by the embryo itself.

Epicotyl part of the seed embryo below the cotyledons.

Exodormancy imposed by factors outside the embryo.

Gibberellins plant hormones involved in cell elongation and seed germination.

Hardwood cuttings taken in the dormant season.

Hybrid seed seed produced by crossing parents of two different plant species.

Hormones substances involved in regulation of physiological processes in plants.

Indole-3-acetic acid (iaa) naturally-occuring auxin.

Indolebutyric acid (iba) synthetic auxin used in commercial rooting hormone preparations.

Naphtaleneacetic acid (naa) synthetic auxin used in commercial rooting hormone preparations.

Intermediate seed seed, which can tolerate some combinations of desiccation and low temperatures, but tolerate freezing poorly.

Orthodox seed seed which can be dried to very low moisture levels. Once desiccated, they withstand freezing.

Photodormancy type of dormancy where the ability of the seed to germinate is controlled by the wavelength and duration of light received by the embryo.

Phytochrome pigment involved in perception of red light; also controls seed germination and flowering in many plant species.

Primary dormancy develops when the seed is attached to the plant and exists when first harvested.

Quiescent seeds readily able to germinate upon absorption of water.

Recalcitrant seed seed, which will die if dried below critical moisture level, and cannot tolerate low temperatures.

Rooting hormones synthetic root-promoting chemicals that stimulate adventitious root formation.

Scarification methods aimed at overcoming seed dormancy induced by mechanical factors, such as hard seed coat.

Seed dormancy condition, in which seeds will not germinate even when most of the environmental conditions are favorable for germination.

Secondary dormancy condition that prevents germination after the seed has been detached from the plant and is exposed to specific unfavorable conditions.

INTRODUCTION

Plant propagation is the creation of new plants from existing ones. It can be used to multiply the numbers of a species, perpetuate a species, or maintain plant vigor. Plants can be propagated in two ways: by seed or sexual propagation and vegetatively or asexual propagation.

Seed Propagation

Sexual propagation is the union of pollen from the male anthers with the egg of the female ovary to produce a seed. A seed carries genes from both parent plants, and appearance of resulting plants reflects the gene combination. When both parents come from the same species, the offspring resembles this species. If, however, parents belong to two different species, the offspring looks like a mixture of the species. This unique appearance results only if the cross is achieved every time a seed is produced. Hybrid seeds are a result of such crosses.

Seeds are infinite in variety, size, and shape. Orchid plants contain over one million seeds in one ounce. In contrast, Double coconut, the world's largest known seed, may weigh more than fifteen pounds.

Collecting Seeds—Seeds may be collected or purchased commercially. Provenance is a term used to describe seeds' origin, in terms of climate and geographic location. It can have profound effects on seed germination and plant survival. For example, Hemlocks grown from southern North Carolina seed sources are more heat tolerant than Hemlocks grown from Pennsylvania seed sources.

Seeds should be completely mature when collected. Leave the fruits on the plant until they are dry, crisp, papery, or stiff. Usually the ripe seeds are exposed. The best time to gather seeds is in the afternoon on a sunny, dry day, as wet seeds often mold in storage. Clean the seeds by pouring them from one jar to another in front of a low-speed fan; this removes any dry plant parts. After cleaning, spread the seeds on newspapers to dry for one to two weeks. They can then be stored in small, dry bags or placed in jar or other airtight containers. Store the jars in a cool, dry basement, vegetable crisper of the refrigerator, or an interior closet.

Extracting Seeds—Seeds develop from fruits, and upon ripening, these can remain fleshy, such as in berries, or dry out and become part of the seed coat, such as in grains and grass seed. Thirdly, the fruits may dehisce, or open and release the seeds. Upon ripening, gymnosperm seeds are exposed to the environment.

Cleaning Seed—Cleaning seed reduces disease and weed seed from growing along with the selection. For dry seeds, simply crush dried material and blow gently, transferring the seeds from hand to hand.

Enhanced Seeds—Enhanced seeds from commercial sources may be treated in a certain way, to increase germination and/or achieve uniform germination, and/or improve seedling survival. Seeds can be coated with fungicides or beneficial soil organisms, which serve to protect the young seedling after germination. The seeds may have several coats of different materials, including nutrients. Seeds also may be pre-germinated, that is, they have been exposed to conditions favorable for germination, which would initiate the germination process, then they have been dried to suspend the process. All of this has been aimed at improving germination.

Seed Storage—Seed storage is critical, especially with respect to the amount of moisture in the seeds and temperature. Seeds lose half their storage life for every 1% increase in seed moisture between 5 and 14%.

Seeds lose half their storage life for every 5 degrees C increase in storage temperature between 0° and 50°C (32-122°F).

For storage purposes, seed scientists divide seeds into three standard categories based on their tolerance to drying and low temperature. These categories are called orthodox, recalcitrant, and intermediate.

- **Recalcitrant seeds** will die if dried below critical moisture level, and cannot tolerate low temperatures. They are usually short-lived and therefore not easy to store.

- **Orthodox seeds** can be dried to very low moisture levels. Once desiccated, they withstand freezing. Under proper conditions, they can be stored for a long time. Most temperate crop seeds are orthodox.

- **Intermediate seeds** can tolerate some combinations of desiccation and low temperatures, but tolerate freezing poorly. There is in fact a gradient from orthodox to recalcitrant, with no sharp boundaries between the categories.

Seed Viability—Plants differ in their seed viability for extended periods of time. When purchasing pre-packaged seeds, examine the label carefully as it contains important information, such as planting directions, expiration date, seed source, germination percentage, and lot number.

Preconditioning Seeds—To induce more uniform germination, seeds can be preconditioned. The methods used are: mechanical scarification, acid scarification, soaking in water, moist pre-chilling or freezing.

Mechanical scarification is one way to weaken the seed coat. You can file the seed coat with a metal file, rub the seed with sandpaper, nick it with a knife, or crack it gently with a hammer.

Commercial growers use **acid scarification** by soaking seeds in concentrated sulfuric acid. Sulfuric acid, however, can be very dangerous if not handled with extreme caution. Vinegar is safer to use. Place the seeds in a glass container and cover with vinegar. Stir the seeds gently and soak for 10 minutes to several hours, depending on the species. Various reference books provide information on soaking time. When the seed coat has been thinned, remove the seeds, wash, and sow as soon as possible because scarified seeds do not store well.

A third method is **hot water scarification.** Bring water to a boil, remove the pot from the stove, and place the seeds into the water. Allow the seeds to soak until the water is at room temperature. Remove the seeds from the water and sow. Following scarification, the seeds should be dull in appearance, but not deeply pitted or cracked. Sow as soon as possible because scarified seeds do not store well.

Cold stratification (moist pre-chilling) involves mixing seeds with an equal volume of a moist medium (sand or peat, for example) in a closed container and storing them in a refrigerator (approximately 40° F). Alternatively, seeds can be wrapped in moist paper towels. Periodically, check to see that the medium is moist but not wet.

Warm stratification is similar except temperatures are maintained at 68° F to 86° F, depending on the species.

Germination Process—A seed is composed of a seed coat (also called testa), cotyledons, seed leaves (sources of food for the developing young embryo), the embryo itself (consisting of a shoot, epicotyl, hypocotyls), and radicle (embryo root).

Upon imbibing water, the seed coat swells and ruptures, allowing for water to enter into the seed. The water triggers a chain of reactions, which bring about development of the embryo and eventual emergence from the seed coat. Water stimulates production of the hormones gibberellins, which then diffuse to the aleurone layer, and stimulate the synthesis of various enzymes. Enzymes are released into the endosperm, where starch is stored and break it down to simple sugars, which are then transported to the developing embryo.

Seed Dormancy—Dormancy is the condition in which seeds will not germinate even when most of the environmental conditions are favorable for germination.

Some seeds germinate readily and are said to be nondormant, while others do not germinate and are said to be dormant. Seed dormancy is nature's way of setting a time clock that allows seeds to initiate germination when conditions are normally favorable for germination and survival of the seedlings. Many trees and shrubs have dormant seeds. Dormancy favors seedling survival, creates a seed bank, and helps seed dispersal, mostly through birds.

It is important to know if your seeds are dormant and which treatment will break that dormancy and allow them to germinate. The recalcitrant seed are able to germinate without desiccating. They lose viability after drying and must be planted quickly. Examples are Oak, Maple, and Coffee. The orthodox seeds desiccate after reaching full development to allow the seed to be quiescent or dormant until conditions are right to germinate. Examples are legumes.

Types of Seed Dormancy

Quiescent seeds are readily able to germinate upon absorption of water.

Primary dormancy develops when the seeds are attached to the plant and exists when first harvested. If seeds are not exposed to sufficient moisture, proper temperature, oxygen, and light for some species, they will not germinate. In this case, the seeds' dormancy is due to unfavorable environmental conditions.

Secondary dormancy is a condition that prevents germination after the seed has been detached from the plant and is exposed to specific unfavorable conditions.

When seeds ripen they may be dormant or not dormant. If they are dormant, they are referred to as having primary dormancy. Some seeds are not dormant when mature and they are known as quiescent. They germinate readily when given the proper environmental conditions. Seeds that do not have primary dormancy often acquire dormancy as they dry.

Primary dormancy is caused by various factors. In exogenous dormancy the hard seed coat, which is impervious to water and gases, is the reason for the dormancy. The seeds will not germinate until the seed coat is broken or scratched to make it permeable to water. In endogenous dormancy the embryo itself is not well developed. Lastly, **double dormancy**, a combination of internal and external dormancy, may exist.

External or **exogenous dormancy** may be due to physical factors, such as an impermeable seed coat. Examples are legumes. In this case, a process of scarification will remove the dormancy. In nature, this often occurs by fall seeding. Scarification can be forced, rather than waiting for nature to change the seed coats. Mechanical factors, such as seed coat restricting the radicle from emerging and thereby inhibiting germination, also can cause external dormancy. An example is olive. In nature, seed coats are softened by environmental agents such as acid in guts of birds, microorganisms in warm, moist soil, or forest fires.

The seed coat also may contain substances, chemical factors, which may inhibit germination. This occurs in fleshy fruits, hulls, and capsules of many dry fruits. Examples are apples, citrus, grapes, and desert plants. In nature, this type of dormancy is overcome by heavy rains, which can leach the inhibitors. Chemically-related exogenous dormancy can be overcome by leaching with running water, while changing water every few days; chilling for a few days; excising the embryo; or using hormones.

Internal or **endogenous seed dormancy** may be due to morphological or physiological factors. The embryo may not be well developed at the time of ripening, and it may need additional growth after the seed is separated from the plant. Morphologically-related internal dormancy occurs in several herbaceous plants such as Ranunculus, poppy, and also in woody plants such as holly. In this case warm stratification is needed.

Physiological factors can be **non-deep dormancy**, which is short-termed and disappears with storage. Photodormancy is imposed by the inner membranes of freshly harvested seed and is typical of herbaceous plants such as annuals and veggies. It can be overcome by exposing the seed to red light. Red light plays an important role in seed germination (see Photodormancy).

Intermediate dormancy is caused by the embryo-seed coat separation and can be overcome by cold stratification. It is typical of conifers.

Lastly, **deep physiological dormancy** is caused by the embryo itself. It is characteristic of many temperate trees and it can be overcome by cold stratification.

Double dormancy is due to some combination of underdeveloped embryo and physiological dormancy. Examples are *Viburnum*, *Lilium*, Peony. Seeds with double dormancy require a chilling period for embryo growth, followed by a warm period for root growth, then a second cold period for shoot growth. Trillium and other native perennials are examples.

Exo-endodormancy, as the name implies, is caused by both external and internal factors. This type can be overcome by sequential scarification and stratification treatments.

Secondary Dormancy—Thermodormancy is an imposition of new dormancy mechanism during unfavorable conditions. The critical point is that this dormancy occurs after the seeds have been separated from the plant. Thermodormancy prevents germination during unfavorable conditions in seeds that have overcome primary dormancy. As an example, Maple seeds germinate in spring, but with insufficient water or too high temperatures, a secondary dormancy will set in which will require chilling for the seed to germinate.

Photodormancy is a type of dormancy where the ability of the seed to germinate is controlled by the wavelength and duration of light received by the embryo. Examples are lettuce, butterfly weed and tobacco. Plants differ in their requirements for light during germination. Some species require light some need dark, and others germinate under either light or dark conditions.

In order to understand how red light affects seed germination, we need to examine the role of light in a plant's life cycle. Plants perceive and respond not only to light intensity but also to light quality.

Photodormancy and **photoperiodism** (sensitivity of a plant to the duration and timing of day and night) are under the control of a pigment called **phytochrome**.

VEGETATIVE PROPAGATION

Vegetative propagation is done by removing and planting part of a plant, and generating a complete replica. The offspring is identical to the parent because there is no mixing of the gene pools as in seed propagation. Also, with vegetative propagation a larger plant can be obtained in a shorter period of time.

The vegetative plant part is placed under conditions favorable for rooting. Size of the plant part varies from as large as the mature plant (e.g. division) to as small as a piece of the leaf. The plant part must develop its own roots to allow for water and mineral absorption.

Vegetative propagation may be done for several reasons. It is the only way to reproduce an exact replica of the parent plant. Vegetative propagation produces a clone, which is genetically and physically identical to the parent plant. Commercially, nurserymen can generate higher profits with cuttings compared to grafting. Lastly, it can be used to avoid graft or bud incompatibility with the stock.

"Cutting" is a general term applied in vegetative propagation, it can be any portion of the vegetative plant body. In most plants the areas, which contain meristems (growing points), have to be included in the cutting. The meristems are found at the shoot tip, the tips of side branches, and the root tips.

Herbaceous plants—A typical herbaceous stem has an apical bud from which the plant grows in height. The nodes are places on the stem where leaves are attached. Axillary buds are found at each node. Shoot cuttings may be made from tip cuttings, which consist of the apical bud and the first one or two nodes on the stem, or they may be made from a stem section containing a single node or several nodes.

Woody plants—Woody plants have different types of shoot cuttings, depending on the season.

Softwood cuttings are taken early in the growing season; they are the emerging shoots of shrubs, trees and evergreens. The wood is still green and easily bruised with a fingernail. They root faster compared to other types but need to be kept cool and moist because once cut, they lose water quickly. Examples of woody plants that can be propagated by softwood cuttings are beautyberry, crape myrtle, and butterfly bush.

Semi-hardwood or greenwood cuttings are taken later in the growing season. This category applies to broadleaf evergreens such as rhododendron, photinia, holly, magnolia, and camellia taken in summer. The growth flush is completed, the wood is firm, and leaves are mature.

Hardwood cuttings are taken later in the dormant season. This category applies to deciduous and broadleaf and needle evergreens. Generally, last season's growth is collected in fall through winter.

Taking Cuttings—When taking the cutting, make a slanting smooth cut with a sharp knife or clippers. Remove any flower buds. The angled cut serves to increase the surface area of the cut. Wound the lower half-inch of stem on the opposite side of the last node by gently scraping the epidermal layer. The scraping of the stem exposes the cambial layer (tissue layer composed of thin-walled cells involved in cell division) underneath the bark to the rooting hormones. This layer also generates the roots. Remove bottom leaves and/or cut bottom

leaves in half to reduce transpiration. Some leaves should be left because they are the source of internal hormones that help initiate **adventitious** roots.

Rooting Hormones—Although factors, which trigger adventitious root formation are still unknown, plant hormones play a role. Hormones occur naturally in plants and are known to regulate various physiological processes. Some hormones are present in buds and in leaves and are involved in the formation of adventitious roots. Synthetic rooting hormones are root-promoting chemicals that stimulate adventitious root formation.

Plant-rooting response to rooting hormones falls into one of three classes:

1. Plants that have all essential endogenous root substances plus auxins. Cuttings rapidly form roots.

2. Plants that have all essential endogenous root substances but no auxins. When cuttings are treated with auxins, they rapidly form roots.

3. Plants that lack an endogenous root substance(s) and/or lack the sensitivity to respond to this substance(s), even though natural auxins may or may not be present in abundance. External application of auxins has little or no effect.

Auxins such as indole-3-acetic acid (IAA), indolebutyric acid (IBA), and naphtaleneacetic acid (NAA) have greatest effect on initiating roots in cuttings. The response, however, is not universal across plant species. Some are difficult to root and require special combination of hormones. Two hormones are sometimes more effective than either one alone, which is called a synergistic effect. For example, IBA and NAA together are better at inducing adventitious roots than either hormone used alone.

In general:

• Auxin concentrations of 500 to 1,250 ppm are used to root the majority of softwood and herbaceous cuttings.

• Auxin concentrations of 1,000 to 3,000 ppm with a maximum of 5,000 ppm are used to root semi-hardwood cuttings.

• Auxin concentrations of 1,000 to 3,000 ppm with a maximum of 10,000 ppm are used to root hardwood cuttings.

Rooting hormones are available as powder or liquid formulations. Some of the popular brands are Rootone, Rhizopon, Dip'n Grow, and Hormex. Rooting hormones are available from most garden stores.

Methods of Vegetative Propagation

Plants may be propagated from: **plantlets, divisions, layering, root cuttings,** or **shoot cuttings**. Shoot cuttings may be tip, stem, or leaf cuttings. Vegetative propagation generates a complete replica of the parent plant. Sometimes, however, when the parent plant contains tissues and cells with differing genetic makeup, the new plant generated from that tissue might look different than the parent plant. An example is a chimeral African violet, which is propagated from leaf cuttings may generate two or more distinct flower color forms from a single leaf. A chimeral plant contains cells with differing genetic makeup.

Plantlets—Plantlets are miniature, but complete plants, which grow by the side of, or on the top of the mother plant. Other names for them are "runners" or "suckers."

Division—Division is one of the surest and easiest methods of plant propagation. It is used almost exclusively with herbaceous plants. It is important to divide plants when they are dormant in spring or fall. A good general rule to follow is to divide early-blooming species in the fall, and late-blooming species in the spring. For example, Bearded Iris may be divided from July to September; Oriental poppy and Madonna lily should be separated when the foliage becomes yellow. An exception is Primrose, which can be divided immediately after the flowers fade in the spring before growth starts, or early in the fall. Greenhouse and houseplants can be divided in the spring, when their new growth is about to begin.

Root Cuttings—Root cuttings are portions of underground plant parts, which in a botanical sense are diverse group. Commercial catalogs often put bulbs, corms, tubers, rhizomes, and rootstocks together under the category "bulbs". Botanically speaking, each of these structures is different.

- **Bulbs** are made up of closely packed, fleshy scale leaves attached to a small basal plate of solid tissue. Examples are Amaryllis, Onion, Tulip, Narcissus and Lily.

- **Corms** are similar in appearance to bulbs but they are solid throughout with small buds ultimately forming on the top. Examples are Gladiolus and Crocus.

- **Tubers** are swollen stems, as in Potato.

- **Tuberous roots** are swollen roots, as in Dahlia and Begonia.

- **Rhizomes** are thickened shoots, which grow underground or along the soil surface, producing roots from their undersides and leaves or shoots above-ground. Examples are Iris, Solomon's seal.

Shoot Cuttings—This method of propagation is very popular with herbaceous plants. Tip cuttings should contain the very tip and the subtending two pairs of mature leaves. Remove the lowermost leaves, as they tend to rot once under the soil line. Some people remove the smallest leaves along with the tip, because they tend to lose water very quickly and wilt. This practice may be used with plants with tender young growth. When taking stem cuttings, include at least two nodes as the lower node should be beneath the soil surface. Also remove any flower or seed heads, as they draw energy to themselves instead of to making roots.

Leaf Cuttings—Some plants can be propagated from leaf cuttings, such as Mother-in-law's tongue, Sansevieria, African violets, and many succulents, such as Jade plant, and Christmas cactus. Leaf cuttings from succulent plants and those with a multitude of epidermal hairs, generally do not need misting to form roots. In fact, they tend to rot if placed under excessive moisture.

The ability of plants to propagate via leaf cuttings is related to a quality called **adventitious buds.** Not all plants have these small, dormant meristematic areas in their leaves, most plants do not. Under favorable conditions the adventitious buds within the tissues of the leaf "awaken" and prompt development of an entire miniature plant. If the baby plant is separated from the parent leaf and that leaf is placed back under favorable conditions for root formation, another plant will form. This is because the meristematic areas are numerous.

Adventitious roots are wound-induced or preformed, and formation of these roots is a prerequisite to successful cutting propagation. Wounding induces hormones to form in the cutting at the wound site. These hormones in turn cause cells to proliferate and form a dense mass of tissue, called callus. Callus is required for adventitious roots to develop.

Many woody ornamental plants are propagated from cuttings. However, two things are crucial to success: taking the cuttings at the right time and providing a suitable environment for root initiation and develop-ment.

Ilex and *Loropetalum*, for instance, are propagated from the flexible young growth, or semi-hardwood. The best time to take semi-hardwood cuttings is from June to September. In the spring, the growth is often too tender and succulent and will not propagate well. If working with larger branches, use only the semi-hardwood cuttings.

Some woody plants are propagated by **ground-layering.**

It works best with plants that have arching branches that can be brought down in contact with the ground. Make a diagonal cut halfway into the stem of the selected branch at a point where you desire roots to form.

GRAFTING AND BUDDING

Grafting and budding are methods of asexual plant propagation in which plant parts are joined so that they grow as one plant. These techniques are used to propagate cultivars that do not produce satisfactory results when propagated by cuttings, layering, division, or other asexual methods. Grafting and budding also are used on cultivars whose own root systems are inadequate. Many species of fruit and nut trees and woody plants are propagated by grafting and budding.

The **scion**, the portion of the cultivar that is to be propagated, is a part of shoot with dormant buds that will produce the stem and branches. The **rootstock**, or stock, provides the new plant's root system and with some techniques, the lower part of the stem. All methods of joining plants are types of grafting, but when the scion is simply a piece of bark (and sometimes wood) containing a single bud, the propagation method is called **budding.**

Grafting and budding are preferred to planting seeds of a named variety of fruit tree because of the large variability in the resulting offspring. More than 99 percent of all seedling trees bear fruit inferior to that produced by the parent trees. The fruit of seedlings is the same species, but it is unlike that of the parent tree in flavor, color, date of ripening, and many other characteristics. To obtain a true-to-type fruit tree that is a clone of the parent-tree, it is necessary to graft or bud onto the desired rootstock.

Certain trees selected for their desirable fruits or ornamental qualities may have root systems that are less desirable. Other varieties of the same species may have desirable root systems that resist soilborne pests, fungus, and viral pathogens and may withstand unfavorable soil conditions (drought, high salinity) more effectively than their cousins that have the better fruit and ornamental appearance. When the better scions are grafted onto the better rootstocks, a more vigorous variety of higher commercial value can be developed.

The grafting process involves the **cambium**, a thin layer of meristematic cells located between the wood (xylem) and bark (phloem) of a stem. Cells in the cambial area produce callous tissue, which heals the scion (the new top) to the stock. After successful grafting, cambium will produce new bark cells (to the outside) and new wood cells (to the inside). Certain conditions to ensure successful grafting are:

1. The cambial layers of the scion and rootstock must come into good contact under favorable environmental conditions (both temperature and relative humidity).

2. The scion and rootstock must be compatible for cambial cells to establish the new vascular tissue connection between them.

3. Both the scion and stock must be at the proper physiological stage (usually the scion buds are dormant).

4. The graft union must be kept moist until the wound has healed. New vascular tissue, xylem (water-conducting tissue) and phloem (sugar-conducting tissue), must develop to allow the passage of nutrients and water between the stock and scion.

Whip and Tongue Graft—Whip and tongue graft is often used for small material ¼ to ½ inch (6 to 12 mm) in diameter. The scion and rootstock are usually of the same diameter. The technique results in a strong graft that heals quickly because of the large contact area of the cambia of the stock and the scion. Make one 2 ½-inch-long sloping cut at the top of the rootstock and a matching cut at the base of the scion. On the cut surface, slice downward into the stock and up into the scion so the pieces (tongues) will interlock. Fit the pieces together, then tie and wax the union or wrap with plastic tie tape. It is critical that the scion is dormant. The best season for whip graft is January through March. Collect the scion in January and use it immediately, or store it wrapped in moist paper and a plastic bag in the refrigerator for use in February or March. About a month after grafting, the buds on the scion will start to grow. At that time, use a sharp knife to cut through the material tying the graft union. If necessary, use a stake to support the new top.

Cleft Graft—Cleft graft is often used in topworking trees to change the cultivar or top growth of a shoot or a young tree (usually a seedling). It is common graft method for peach and ornamental trees, such as camellia and crape myrtle. It is especially successful if done in later winter or early spring when the buds of the rootstock are swelling but not actively growing. Collect scion ⅜ to ⅝ inch in diameter. Cut the limb or small tree trunk to be reworked (the rootstock) perpendicular to its length. Make a 2-inch (5-cm) vertical cut through the center of the previous cut, being careful not to tear the bark, and keep this cut wedged apart. Prepare two scion pieces 3 to 4 inches long. Cut the lower end of each scion piece into a wedge. Insert the scions at the outer edges of the cut in the stock. Tilt the top of the scion slightly outward and the bottom slightly inward so that the cambia of the scion and stock touch. Remove the wedge and cover all cut surfaces with grafting wax.

Side or Bark Graft—Unlike most grafting methods, bark graft can be used on large limbs. The technique works well with persimmon, apple, and pear trees and does not require special equipment or training. The technique depends on separating the bark readily from the wood; therefore, it can be done only in the spring after the rootstock has started active growth. Collect scion wood ⅜ to ½ inch in diameter in January when the plant is dormant, and store the wood wrapped in moist paper in a plastic bag in the refrigerator. In the spring when the bark is easy to separate from the wood ("slipping"), make a slanted 1- to 1 ½-9 inch cut at the end of the scion. Cut through the bark of the stock a little wider than the scion and remove the top third of the bark from this cut. Insert the cut surface of the scion against the wood of the stock. Secure the graft with tape and apply grafting compound.

Four-flap or Banana Graft—Four-flap or banana graft can be used on small-diameter wood as well as large limbs. The technique depends on separating the bark readily from the wood of the stock; therefore, it is done when the bark is "slipping". The scion and rootstock are usually of the same diameter. Collect scion wood 3/8 to ½ inch in diameter in January when the plant is dormant, and store the wood wrapped in moist paper in a plastic bag in the refrigerator. Make four 2-inch long cuts at the bottom of the scion to expose the cambial layer. The cuts should strip away the bark and expose the cambial layer. Make similar cuts in the stock to achieve four flaps but preserve the bark. Cut off the stripped wood of the stock to allow for inserting the scion inside. Arrange the four flaps close around the scion and secure the graft with elastic band. Wrap tape and apply grafting compound.

Graft Care—Proper care should be maintained for the year or two after the grafting is done. If a binding material, such as strong cord or nursery tape, is used on the graft, it must be cut shortly after growth starts to prevent girdling and dying of the graft. Rubber budding strips are superior to other materials in that they expand with growth and usually do not need to be cut because they deteriorate and break after a short time. Inspect grafts after a 2- to 3-week period to see if the wax has cracked. Apply new wax to exposed areas, if necessary.

After this period, the graft union will probably be strong enough so that more waxing is not necessary. For the first year, one or two limbs of the old variety that were not selected for grafting should be maintained as nurse limbs. The total leaf surface of the old variety should be reduced gradually as that of the new one increases. Completely removing all the limbs of the old variety at the time of grafting increases the shock to the tree and causes excessive suckering. The scions may grow too fast, making them susceptible to wind damage. By the end of 1 or 2 years, the new variety will have taken over.

Budding

Budding, or bud grafting, is the union of a bud and a small piece of bark from the scion with a rootstock. The nursery industry uses this technique for propagating roses and fruit trees sold to home gardeners and orchardists. Budding involves the same physiological processes as grafting, but it is faster and forms a stronger union than grafting. It is especially useful when scion material is limited. Commonly used budding techniques depend on the bark's slipping. Slipping occurs from spring to fall when the plant is growing, cambial cells are dividing actively, and newly formed tissues can be torn as bark lifts from the wood.

To bud trees from June through August, select bud wood from the current season's growth that is 2 to 10 months old and can easily be cut. Use wood that is ¼ to ⅜ inches in diameter, and cut off the leaves. Good bud wood is firm and has narrow, pointed leaf buds, not flower buds. If budding in April, collect wood from dormant trees in January. Wrap the dormant wood in moist (not wet) paper and place it in a plastic bag in a refrigerator set at 32° to 35°F (0° to 2°C) until needed.

T-Bud—The budding technique most commonly used by nurserymen in propagating roses, fruit trees, and ornamental shrubs is called T-budding, because of the T-like appearance of the cut in the stock. Its use is limited to actively growing stocks that are ¼ to 1 inch in diameter and have fairly thin bark that separates easily from the wood. In Georgia, T-budding is done in June.

Chip Bud—Chip budding can be done when the bark is not slipping, during the dormant season. Slice downward into the stock at a 45° angle through one-fourth of the wood. Make a second cut upward from the first cut, about 1 inch long. Remove a bud and attending chip of bark and wood from the scion shape so that it fits the rootstock wound. Fit the bud chip to the stock and wrap the union.

Graft Care—For trees budded from April through June cut off the top of the stock just above the bud, forcing the bud to grow. To bud trees in August, however, do not cut off the top of the seedling until the following spring because the bud should remain dormant. In March, cut August-budded trees above the inserted bud to force growth of the bud. About a month after budding an actively growing tree, cut the ties around the bud, beginning on the side opposite the bud, so that they do not girdle or choke the growth of the tree. Remove sucker shoots that grow on the rootstock after budding. To force the bud to develop the following spring, cut the stock off 3 to 4 inches above the bud. The new shoot may be tied to the resulting stub to prevent wind damage. After the shoot has made a strong union with the stock, cut the stub off close to the budded area.

SOILS AND GROWING MEDIA FOR PROPAGATION

Any substance which provides air/water relationships of 25 to 40% air space is suitable for plant propagation, including soil, sand, pumice, and bark. Homeowners often use homemade mixes, made of garden soil. Garden soil needs to be sterilized before use. Put moist soil through a ¼-inch sieve, place a layer up to 3-inch deep in a baking tray, and bake for 30 minutes at 400°F. Microwave also may be used — seal the soil in a pierced roasting bag and heat on high power for 10 minutes.

Commercial growers use **soilless** media when producing plants. These media have numerous desirable qualities, i.e., free of pathogens and weed seeds, lightweight, well-aerated, and good water and nutrient retention. Soilless media and individual constituents are also available for sale in garden stores.

They have the following major components.

Inorganic components

• **Sand** should be sterile; use sharp builder's sand with a particle diameter of 0.5 - 2 mm. Sand has no buffering capacity; its pH varies with source and can change with the water being applied to the plant. Sand contains no nutrients and has no water-holding capacity. It is suitable when mixed with peat, perlite, and other components.

• **Perlite** is a crushed aluminum-silica volcanic rock, heated rapidly to 1800 °F. It is sterile, lightweight and chemically inert. Perlite contains no nutrients, has low water-holding capacity, and a pH of 7-7.5. For propagation, use horticultural grade #2.

• **Vermiculite** is a clay mineral, heated to 1400 °F. It is sterile and lightweight. Vermiculite has high nutri-ent- and water-holding capacity, and a pH of 7-7.5. For propagation, use coarser grades.

• **Scoria** is a naturally occurring volcanic rock, crushed and screened for size. **Pumice** is a white, natural glass. Both have similar qualities to perlite

Organic components

• **Peat** may come from several types of plants, sphagnum moss, hypnaceous moss, reed and sedge, and humus or muck, all collectively called peat. Peat moss is excellent when mixed with sand and perlite; peat provides water and nutrient-holding capacity, while perlite provides aeration.

• **Bark**, hardwood, or pine bark is relatively sterile and lightweight when dry has high nutrient- and water-holding capacity, and a pH of 3-4.5. The fine shredded form is popular for propagation, containing 70-80% of the particles in the ¼₀ to ⅜-inch size, and 20-30% of the particles less than 1/40-inch size. Bark can be used alone or mixed with others.

• **Amendments** (used to adjust pH, provide calcium, magnesium, and other nutrients, and improve the wettability of the mix)**Lime, gypsum, starter charge** (fertilizer)**, wetting agents**

A popular recipe is:

> 3 parts bark: 2 parts peat: 2 parts perlite

For most plants a good propagation mix is:

> 2 parts coarse perlite: 1 part peat.

The propagation medium should have a pH of 5.0 to 6.5.

Propagation Systems

In propagation by cuttings, mist is needed to keep leaves wet to maintain a favorable water status and to cool the leaves. The objective is not to water the cuttings, but to minimize transpiration and loss of moisture from the plant tissues. A **mist system** is composed of a cut-off valve, a pressure regulator, a filter (to screen small particles), a solenoid valve and mist nozzles. A timer is also needed, which should be installed away from the mist. It is important is to use a timer designed for mist systems as it can be set for short durations, such as 20 seconds every 10 minutes.

Bottom heat is helpful, especially when propagating during the cold months. Temperature controls plant development and if the roots are cold, they will be slow to develop. This is true for both seed and vegetative propagation. Optimal root zone temperature is 10 to 15 degrees higher than the air temperature, generally 65 to 75°F. The thermostat placement should be positioned close to the roots.

Tips for Success

Do not use cuttings from unhealthy plants, especially if infected with pests and or diseases. Propagating infected plants will likely spread the disease to the new cuttings or divisions. Before you take a cutting, inspect the plant very carefully.

• Be especially careful when cuttings are shared with friends. Discard any plant material that appears unhealthy or shows pest infestation.

• Use only clean, disinfected tools when taking cuttings. Dip tools in rubbing alcohol or a weak (10%) bleach solution after moving from one plant to the next.

• Wash hands with soap and water before taking cuttings, especially when working with herbaceous plants. People who smoke may spread viral particles from their hands to young plants through the cuts.

• Maintain a clean and organized environment. Keeping detailed records of seed and cutting sources, time of the year when propagation was made, rooting hormones and concentrations used, environmental conditions, germination percentage, seedling growth, and percent rooting, are all useful information that may make seed and vegetative propagation efforts successful.

DISCUSSION QUESTIONS

1. What are the methods of plant propagation?

2. What are the different types of seed dormancy?

3. What are the three standard categories of seeds based on their tolerance to drying and low temperature?

4. What are the methods used to overcome seed dormancy imposed by hard seed coat?

5. How does the mechanism of regulation work in photodormant seeds?

6. What are the types of herbaceous cuttings?

7. What are the types of woody cuttings?

8. What are rooting hormones?

9. How should you treat cuttings of woody plants?

10. What are the most common soilless growing media components?

11. Why is bottom heat needed?

RESOURCES

Cathey, H. M. 1991. *Temperature and Lighting Requirements for Germination of Selected Annual Flowering Plants.* Washington, DC. USDA.

Dirr, M A., and C. W. Heuser Jr. 1987. *The Reference Manual of Woody Plant Propagation: From Seed to Tissue Culture.* Varsity Press: Athens, GA.

Frey, D. 1993. Plant Propagation. In D. D. Sharp, ed., *Maryland and Delaware Master Gardener Handbook.* College Park: University of Maryland Cooperative Extension.

Geisel, P.M. 2002. Plant Propagation. In D.R. Pittenger, ed., *California Master Gardener Handbook.* Publication 3382. Oakland: University of California Division of Agriculture and Natural Resources.

Hartman, H. T., D. E. Kester, F. T. Davies, and R. L. Geneve. *Plant Propagation: Principles and Practices.* 1997. 6th ed. Prentice Hall, Englewood Cliffs, NJ.

NOTES

NOTES

5
Basic Entomology

Kris Braman
Beverly Sparks
David Adams

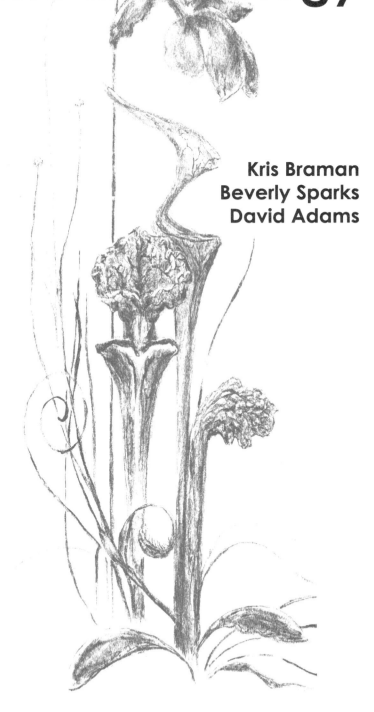

LEARNING OBJECTIVES

Understand the basic classification system of insects.

Have an appreciation for the multitude of insects in existence.

Know the basic form and structure (morphology) of insects.

Understand the concept of metamorphosis and the different types of metamorphosis.

Understand the types of injury insects can cause regarding feeding and secondary damage.

Understand the benefits and value of insects.

Have an appreciation for how proper pest identification fits into a pest management plan.

TERMS TO KNOW

Gall an abnormal swelling or growth of plant tissue that is initiated by a pathogen, insect or mite.

Gallery a tunnel made by a wood-boring insect. The galleries of some insects have characteristic patterns.

Honeydew the sugary liquid excrement of some sucking insects.

Horticultural oil a contact insecticide made from petroleum oils, summer oils, or superior oils and one of the oldest forms of pesticides.

Insecticidal soap a type of contact insecticide made from the potassium salt of oleic acid which is present in high quantities in olive oils and other vegetable oils.

Insecticide a chemical used to kill insects.

Instar the stage of an insect between successive molts (loss of skin). The molting process allows for insect growth.

Larvae the newly hatched, wingless, often wormlike form of many insects before metamorphosis. It is a stage of rapid feeding.

Leaf mine an area of a leaf characterized by insect larval feeding between upper and lower layers of the leaf. May be blotched, linear or serpentine in shape.

Metamorphosis the changes of form insects go through in their life cycle from egg to immature stages to adult.

Morphology study of the major structures and organ systems of an insect.

Nymph immature insect which looks like the adult of the same species in general body shape and habits.

Oviposit to lay eggs.

Pest an injurious plant or animal.

Phylum a major division of the animal or plant kingdom.

Pupa resting stage of an insect between larva and adult.

Resistant plant the capacity of a plant to withstand the effects of a harmful condition or biological agent such as insects or disease.

Sooty mold one of several species of fungi with black fruiting bodies that grow on the sugary liquid excrement of sucking insects.

Spot treatment application of a pesticide to restricted area or areas of a whole unit. For example the treatment of spots or patches in a home lawn.

INTRODUCTION

Insects and mites are among the oldest, most numerous and most successful animals on earth. It is estimated that over 100,000 different species live in North America. In the typical backyard, there are probably 1,000 insects at any given time. While insects which cause problems for man are heard about most often, it is important to note that the vast majority are either beneficial or harmless. Insects pollinate fruits and vegetables, they provide food for birds and fish, and produce such useful products as honey, wax, shellac, and silk. In addition, some insects are beneficial because they feed on insects that are considered pests by man.

Although the number of pest species compared to the total number of insect species is very small (less than 3% of all insects are classified as pests), the troubles for man wrought by this group reach astonishing proportions. Insects annually destroy millions of dollars worth of crops, fruits, shade trees and ornamental plants, stored products, household items, and other materials valued by man. They carry diseases of man and domestic animals. They attack man and his pets causing irritation, blood loss, and in some instances, death.

Insect Damage

Injury by Chewing Insects—Insects obtain their food in a variety of ways. One method is by chewing off the external parts of a plant. Such insects are called chewing insects. It is easy to see examples of this injury. Perhaps the best way to gain an idea of the prevalence of this type of insect damage is to try to find leaves of plants which have no sign of injury from chewing insects. Cabbageworms, armyworms, grasshoppers, the Japanese beetle, the Colorado potato beetle, and the fall webworm are common examples of insects that cause injury by chewing.

Injury by Piercing Sucking Insects—A second important way insects feed on growing plants is by piercing the plant tissue and sucking sap from cells. In this case, only internal and liquid portions of the plant are swallowed and the insect feeds externally on the plant. These insects have a slender and sharp pointed portion of the mouthpart which is thrust into the plant and through which sap is sucked. This results in a very different looking, but nonetheless severe injury. The hole made in this way is so small that it cannot be seen with the unaided eye, but the withdrawal of the sap results in either minute spotting of white, brown, or red on leaves, fruits or twigs; curling of the leaves; deforming of the fruit; or a general wilting, browning and dying of the whole plant. Aphids, scale insects, squash bugs, leafhoppers, and plant bugs are well known examples of piercing sucking insects.

Injury by Internal Feeders—Many insects feed within plant tissues during a part or all of their destructive stages. They gain entrance to plants either in the egg stage when their mothers thrust into the tissues with sharp ovipositors and deposit them there, or by eating their way in after they hatch from the eggs. In either case, the hole by which they enter is almost always minute and often invisible. A large hole in a fruit, seed, nut, twig, or trunk generally indicates where the insect has come out and not the point where it entered.

The chief groups of internal feeders are indicated by their common group names: (a) borers in wood or pith; (b) worms or weevils in fruits, nuts or seeds; (c) leaf miners; and (d) gall insects. Each group contains some of the foremost insect pests of the world. In nearly all of them, the insect lives inside the plant during only a part of its life, sooner or later emerging, usually as an adult. Control measures for internal feeding insects are most effective if aimed at adults or the immature stages prior to their entrance into the plant.

A number of internal feeders are small enough to find comfortable quarters and an abundance of food between the upper and lower epidermis of a leaf. These are known as leaf miners.

Gall insects sting plants and cause them to produce a structure of deformed tissue. The insect then finds shelter and abundant food inside this plant growth. It is not known exactly what makes the plants form these elaborate structures when attacked by the insects. However, it is clear that the growth of the gall is initiated by the oviposition of the adult and its continued development results from secretions of the developing larva. The same species of insect on different plants causes galls that are similar, while several species of insects attacking the same plant cause galls that are greatly different in appearance. Although the gall is entirely plant tissue, the insect controls and directs the form and shape it takes as it grows.

Injury by Subterranean Insects—Almost as secure from man's attack as the internal feeders are those insects that attack plants below the surface of the soil. These include chewing insects, sucking insects, root borers, and gall insects. The method of attack differs from the above ground forms only in their position with reference to the soil surface. Some subterranean insects spend their entire life cycle below ground. For example, the woolly apple aphid, as both nymph and adult, sucks sap from roots of apple trees causing the development of tumors and subsequent decay of the tree's roots. In other subterranean insects there is at least one life stage that has not taken up subterranean habit. Examples include wireworms, root maggots, strawberry root weevils, Japanese beetles, and grape and corn rootworms. The larvae are root feeders, while the adults live above ground.

Injury by Laying Eggs—Probably 95% or more of insect injury to plants is caused by feeding in the various ways just described. In addition, insects may damage plants by laying eggs in critical plant tissues. The periodical cicada deposits eggs in one year old growth of fruit and forest trees and in doing so they split the wood so severely the entire twig beyond the oviposition site often dies. As soon as the young hatch, they leave the twigs and cause no further injury to the plant.

Use of Plants for Nest Materials—Besides laying eggs in plants, insects sometimes remove parts of plants for the construction of nests or for provisioning nests. Leaf cutter bees nip out rather neat circular pieces of rose and other foliage which are carried away and fashioned together to form thimble shaped cells in the stem of a plant.

Insects as Disseminators of Plant Diseases—In 1892 it was discovered that a plant disease (fire blight of fruit trees) was spread by an insect (the honeybee). At present there is evidence that more than 200 plant diseases are disseminated by insects. The majority of these diseases, about 150, belong to the group known as viruses, 25 or more are due to parasitic fungi, 15 or more are bacterial diseases, and a few are caused by protozoa.

Insects may spread plant diseases in the following ways: (a) by feeding, laying eggs or boring into plants they create an entrance point for a disease that is not actually transported by them; (b) they carry and disseminate the causative agents of the disease on or in their bodies from one plant to a susceptible surface of another plant; (c) they carry pathogens on the outside or inside of their bodies and inject plants hypodermically as they feed; or (d) the insect may serve as an essential host for some part of the pathogens life cycle and the disease could not complete its life cycle without the insect host.

Benefits and Value of Insects

Insects must be studied carefully to distinguish the beneficial from the harmful. People have often gone to great trouble and expense to destroy insects, only to learn later that the insect destroyed was not only harmless but was actually engaged in saving their crops by eating destructive insects.

Insects are beneficial to the gardener in several ways:

1. Insects aid in the production of fruits, seeds, vegetables, and flowers by pollinating the blossoms. Most common fruits are pollinated by insects. Melons, squash, and many other vegetables require insects to carry their pollen before fruit set. Many ornamental plants, both in the greenhouse and out of doors, are pollinated by insects (chrysanthemums, iris, orchids, and yucca).

2. Parasitic insects destroy injurious insects by living on or in their bodies. Insects also act as predators, capturing and devouring other insects.

3. Insects destroy various weeds in the same ways that they injure crop plants.

4. Insects improve the physical condition of the soil and promote its fertility by burrowing throughout the surface layer. Also, the dead bodies and droppings of insects serve as fertilizer.

5. Insects perform a valuable service as scavengers by devouring the bodies of dead animals and plants and by burying carcasses and dung.

Many of the benefits from insects enumerated above, although genuine, are insignificant compared with the good that insects do fighting among themselves. There is no doubt that the greatest single factor in keeping plant-feeding insects from overwhelming the rest of the world is that they are fed upon by other insects.

Insects that destroy other insects are considered in two groups known as predators and parasites. Predators are insects (or other animals) that catch and devour other creatures (called the prey), usually killing and consuming them in a single meal. The prey is generally smaller and weaker than the predator.

Parasites are forms of living organisms that live on or in the bodies of living organisms (called the hosts) from which they get their food, during at least one stage of their existence. The hosts are usually larger and stronger than the parasites and are not killed promptly but continue to live during a period of close association with the parasite.

Insect Form and Structure - Morphology

All adult members of the class Insecta possess the following characteristics: a) three body regions; b) three pairs of legs; c) one pair of antennae; and d) none, one or two pairs of wings. Legs and other appendages are often greatly modified to suit the environment in which the insect lives and these appendages are often used as tools for classification.

Head, Thorax, Abdomen—While the adult insect's body is made up of three parts (head, thorax, and abdomen), the division is not always obvious between thorax and abdomen. (Figure 1.) An insect's body is not supported by a bony skeleton but by a tough body wall or exoskeleton. The tough covering of skin is referred to as the cuticle. The cuticle contains a layer of wax which determines its permeability to water and prevents desiccation or drying. The cuticle of each segment is formed into several hardened plates called sclenites which are separated by infolds or sutures which give them flexibility. The cuticle of the immature stage is not usually as hardened as that of the adult.

The thorax is made up of three segments: prothorax, mesothorax, and metathorax. Each of these segments bears a pair of legs. The wings are attached to the mesothorax and metathorax, never to the prothorax or first segment.

The abdomen may have eleven or twelve segments, but in most cases they are difficult to distinguish. Some insects have a pair of appendages at the tip of the abdomen. They may be short, as in grasshoppers, termites, and cockroaches; or extremely long, as in mayflies; or curved, as in earwigs.

Legs—The most important characteristic of insects is the presence of three pairs of jointed legs. These are almost always present on adult or mature insects. In addition to walking and jumping, insects often use their legs for digging, grasping, feeling, swimming, carrying loads, building nests, and cleaning parts of the body. The legs of insects vary greatly in size and form and are used in classification. (Figure 2.)

Wings—Venation (the arrangement of veins in wings) is different for each species of insect; thus, it serves as a means of identification. Systems have been devised to designate the venation for descriptive purposes. Wing surfaces are covered with fine hairs or scales, or they may be bare. Note that the names of many insect orders end in "ptera," which comes from the Greek word meaning "with wings." Thus, each of these names denotes some feature of the wings. Hemiptera means half winged; Hymenoptera means membrane winged; Diptera means two winged; Isoptera means equal wings. Names of insect orders ending in "aptera" means without wings.

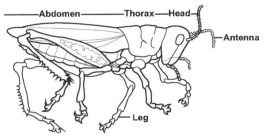

Figure 1. Insect body parts.

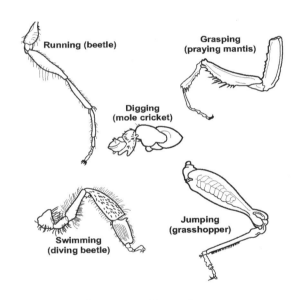

Figure 2. Leg adaptations of some insects.

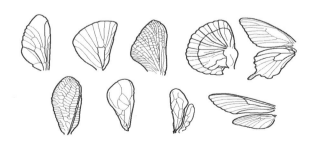

Figure 3. Examples of various insect wings.

Figure 4

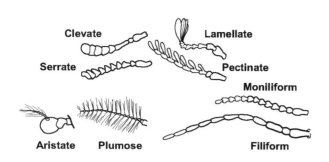

Figure 4. Different types of insect antennae.

Antennae—The main features of the insect's head are the eyes, antennae, and mouthparts. The antennae (Figure 4) are a prominent and distinctive feature of insects. Insects have one pair of antennae located on the adult's head usually between or in front of the eyes. Antennae are segmented, vary greatly in form and complexity, and are often referred to as horns or "feelers." They are primarily organs of smell but serve other functions in some insects.

Mouthparts—The most remarkable structural feature of insects and the most complicated is the mouth. Great variations exist in form and function of insect mouthparts. Although insect mouthparts differ considerably in appearance, the same basic parts are found in all types. Most insects are divided into two broad categories by the type of mouthparts they possess — those with mouthparts adapted for chewing and those with mouthparts adapted for sucking. (Figure 5.)

There are intermediate types of mouthparts: rasping-sucking, as found in thrips; and chewing-lapping, as found in honey bees, wasps, and bumble bees. Sucking types are greatly varied. Piercing-sucking mouthparts are typical of the Hemiptera (bugs), Homoptera (aphids, scales, mealybugs), blood-sucking lice, fleas, mosquitoes, and the so-called biting flies. In the siphoning types, as seen in butterflies and moths, the mandibles are absent and the labial and maxillary palpi greatly reduced. Houseflies have sponging mouthparts.

The mouthparts of immature insects can vary from those found in the adult form. Although nymphs have mouthparts similar to those of the adults, larval forms generally have the chewing type regardless of the kind possessed by the adults. For some adult insects the mouthparts are vestigial (no longer used for feeding).

Figure 5

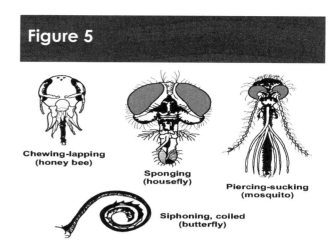

Figure 5. Insect mouthparts.

INSECT CLASSIFICATION SYSTEM

Identification of thousands of species of insects would be impossible to deal with if they were not organized around a standard classification system. By grouping organisms based on the degrees of similarity among them we can arrive at a system of classification.

Kingdom

    Phylum

        Class

            Order

                Family

                    Genus

                        Species

At the highest level of this classification system organisms are divided into two **Kingdoms**- Animal and Plant. There are often additional groups used that are intermediate to the groups listed. These groups often use a prefix of super- (above) or sub- (below) to indicate the position of the new group in the above list. Thus, superfamily groups fall between order and family while subfamily groups fall between family and genus. An insect name is complete if the genus, species and author names are given because of the rules that govern taxonomy.

Phyla—Obviously, insects belong to the Animal Kingdom. The Animal Kingdom has major divisions known as **phyla** (singular- phylum). Several of the phyla which contain agricultural pests are:

- Arthropoda (insects, spiders, crayfish, millipedes)
- Aschelminthes (roundworms, trichina)

- Platyhelminthes (flatworms, flukes, tapeworms)
- Mollusca (snails, slugs, clams)

Insects belong to the phylum Arthropoda. Arthropods are a very important group of animals as they represent more than three fourths of the animal species known to exist. Characteristics that place an animal in the phylum Arthropoda include segmentation of the body and skeletons that are located on the outside of their bodies.

Classes—The Phylum Arthropoda is divided into **classes**. Entomology is concerned primarily with the study of two classes of arthropods:

Class Insecta - (insects)

Class Arachnida - (spiders, ticks, mites, scorpions, and relatives).

However, some other arthropod classes like Diplopoda (millipedes) and Chilopoda (centipedes) are often considered by entomologists. Even a few non-arthropod groups like snails and slugs (Phylum - Mollusca) are sometimes referred to entomologists.

Table 1 describes a few of the more important classes and presents some characteristics that are used to distinguish between the various Arthropod classes. Insects belong to the class Insecta. For an Arthropod to be further classified in the class Insecta, it must have 3 body segments and 3 pair of legs.

Orders—Classes are further divided into orders. The more important orders of the class Insecta are described in Table 2. The Class Insecta is generally studied under a classification system with approximately 30 orders. Many of these are of minor importance and are studied only from the standpoint of scientific interest. Many taxonomists disagree on the number of orders and their names. Thus, this scheme will often vary with different authors.

Families, Genera, and Species—Insect Orders are further broken down into a classification known as Family. The family is a more finite grouping of very closely related insects. Family names end with "idae." Aphidae (aphids), Muscidae (houseflies), and Blattidae (cockroaches) are examples of families of insects.

Families are further divided into **genera** and **species.**

These are the most finite levels of our classification system. The housefly, *Musca domestica,* serves here as an example of classification:

Phylum: Arthropoda

Class: Insecta

Order: Diptera

Family: Muscidae

Genus: *Musca*

Species: *domestica*

Common name: housefly

The most commonly found insects also acquire common names and sometimes one species will have several common names. For example, *Helicoverpa zea* on corn is called the corn earworm, but when it is found on tomatoes it is called the tomato fruitworm. Often common names are used to refer to large groups of insects, such as families or orders. The term beetle refers to the order Coleoptera, which includes thousands of different species. The term moth refers to thousands of species in the order Lepidoptera.

Insect Development-Metamorphosis

In higher animals, the most important development takes place before birth (in the embryonic stage); in insects, it occurs after birth or egg hatch. The immature period of an insect is primarily one of growth, feeding, and storing up food for the pupal and adult stages. Many insects feed very little or not at all during their adult lives.

One of the distinctive features of insects is the phenomenon called metamorphosis. The term is a combination of two Greek words: meta, meaning change and morphe,

Table 1. Classes of the phylum Arthropoda				
CLASS	**EXAMPLE**	**BODY SEGMENTS**	**PAIRS OF LEGS**	**AGRICULTURAL IMPORTANCE**
Crustacea	Crayfish	2	5	Sowbugs can be minor pests
Arachnida	Spiders, Mites, Ticks	2	4	Some mites are major plant pests
Insecta	Bugs, Beetles, Butterflies	3	3	Large numbers are pests

Figure 6

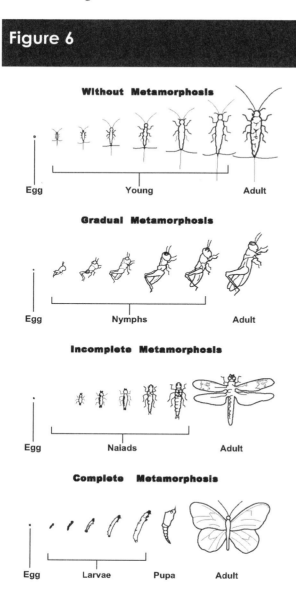

Figure 6. Different types of insect metamorphosis.

meaning form. It is commonly defined as a marked or abrupt change in form or structure and refers to all stages of development. Insects undergo one of four types of metamorphosis.

Some insects do not go through a metamorphosis but rather gradually increase in size while maintaining the same characteristics. Others experience a gradual metamorphosis, going through a nymph stage.

• In the case of gradual metamorphosis the stages are: egg, nymph, and adult.

• Insects that undergo complete metamorphosis go through the following stages: egg, larvae, pupae, and adult.

• The immature insect sheds its outer skeleton (molts)

at various stages of growth, since it outgrows the hard covering or cuticle more than once. Most insects do not grow gradually as many other animals do. They grow by stages. When their skeleton gets too tight, it splits open and the insect crawls out, protected by a new and larger skeleton that has formed underneath the old one. The stage of life between each molt is called an instar. Following each molt, the insect increases its feeding. The number of instars, or frequency of molts, varies considerably with species and to some extent with food supply, temperature, and moisture.

The pupal stage is one of profound change. It is a period of transformation from larva to adult.

Many tissues and structures, such as prolegs, are completely broken down and true legs, antennae, wings, and other structures of the adult are formed.

The adult insect does not grow in the usual sense. The adult period is primarily one of reproduction and is sometimes of short duration. Their food is often entirely different from that of the larval stage.

IDENTIFYING INSECTS

Most home gardeners can classify an insect by the common name of its order, identifying it as a beetle, wasp or butterfly. The ability to classify an insect to the order level gives one access to much valuable information. This information would include the type of mouthparts the insect has (this tells us how it feeds and gives clues towards methods of control), its life cycle (and proper timing for best control), and type of habitation.

Insect Orders Important to the Gardener

Dermaptera—Earwigs.

(1) Adults are moderately sized insects.

(2) Chewing mouthparts.

(3) Gradual metamorphosis.

(4) Elongate, flattened insects with strong, movable forceps on the abdomen.

(5) Short, hardened outer wings; folded, membranous, "ear-shaped" inner wings.

(6) Adults and nymphs similar in appearance.

Diptera—Flies, Mosquitoes, Gnats, Midges

(1) Adults have only one pair of wings, are rather soft-bodied and often hairy.

(2) Adults have sponging (housefly) or piercing (mosquito) mouthparts.

(3) Larvae may have mouth hooks or chewing mouthparts.

(4) Most larvae are legless.

(5) Larvae of advanced forms, housefly and relatives, have no head capsule, possess mouth hooks, and are called maggots; lower forms such as mosquito larvae and relatives have a head capsule.

(6) Complete metamorphosis.

Hemiptera—suborder Heteroptera-Stink Bug, Plant Bug, Squash Bug, Boxelder Bug

(1) Have gradual metamorphosis. Stages are egg, nymph, adult.

(2) Have two pairs of wings; second pair is membranous, the first pair are "half-wings"-membranous with thickening on basal half.

(3) Adults and nymphs usually resemble one another.

(4) Have piercing-sucking mouthparts.

(5) Adults and nymphs are both damaging stages.

Hemiptera—suborders Auchenorrhyncha and Sternorrhyncha-Cicadas, leafhoppers, spittlebugs, aphids, mealybugs, scales, whiteflies

(1) Generally small, soft bodied insects; cicadas may be large and hard bodied.

(2) Winged and unwinged forms.

(3) All stages have sucking mouthparts.

(4) Have gradual metamorphosis.

(5) Many are carriers of plant diseases.

Hymenoptera—Bees, Ants, Wasps, Sawflies, Horntails

(1) Adults with two pairs of membranous wings.

(2) Larvae with no legs (wasps, bees, ants), or with 3 pair of legs on thorax and more than 4 pair of legs on abdomen (some sawflies).

(3) Generally with chewing mouthparts.

(4) Rather soft bodied or slightly hardened bodied adults.

(5) Complete metamorphosis.

Lepidoptera—Butterflies, Moths

(1) Adults soft bodied with four well developed membranous wings covered with small scales.

(2) Larvae with chewing mouthparts.

ORDER	COMMON NAME	METAMORPHOSIS	MOUTHPARTS	WINGS
Orthoptera	crickets, grasshoppers	gradual	chewing	2 pair
Isoptera	termites	gradual	chewing	2 pair
Thysanoptera	thrips	gradual	sucking (punch-suck)	2 pair
Hemiptera	true bugs, aphids, scale	gradual	piercing-sucking	2 pair
Coleoptera	beetles, weevils	complete	chewing	2 pair
Lepidoptera	butterflies, moths	complete	chewing (larva) siphoning (adult)	2 pair
Hymenoptera	ants, wasps, bees	complete	chewing-lapping	2 pair
Diptera	flies	complete	chewing or piercing-sucking	1 pair
Siphonaptera	fleas	complete	chewing or piercing-sucking	none
Dermaptera	earwigs	gradual	chewing	2 pair
Thysanura	silverfish	gradual	chewing	2 pair

Table 2. Orders of the class Insecta

(3) Adult mouthparts are a coiled, sucking tube. Adults feed on nectar.

(4) Larvae are caterpillar, worm-like, variable in color and voracious feeders.

(5) Larvae generally have legs on the abdomen, as well as the thorax.

(6) Complete metamorphosis.

Neuroptera—Lacewings, Antlions, Snakeflies, Mantispids, Dustywing

(1) Insect predators, many are aquatic.

(2) Two pair of membranous wings.

(3) Chewing mouthparts.

(4) Complete metamorphosis.

Orthoptera—Grasshopper, Cricket

(1) Adults are moderate to large, often rather hard bodied.

(2) Have simple metamorphosis.

(3) Adults usually have two pairs of wings. Forewings are elongate, narrow and hardened; hindwings are membranous with extensive folded area.

(4) Chewing mouthparts. Both adults and nymphs are damaging.

(5) Legs often enlarged for jumping or running.

(6) Immature stages are called nymphs and resemble adults but are wingless.

Thysanoptera—Thrips

(1) Adults are small, soft bodied insects.

(2) Mouthparts are sucking (a punch and suck-type mechanism).

(3) Varied metamorphosis (a mixture of complete and gradual).

(4) Found on flowers or leaves of plants.

(5) Wings in two pairs, slender, feather-like with fringed hairs.

Other Insect-Like Creatures

Spiders, Spider Mites, Ticks, and Scorpions: Order Arachnida

a. Spider mites: tiny soft bodied animals with two body regions, thick waists, four pairs of legs, and are without antennae.

Common species:

(1) The twospotted mites and near relatives. These mites have two spots on the back and may be clear, green, orange, or reddish. Usually hard to observe without a hand lens.

(2) The European red mite: This mite is carmine red with white spines.

(3) Clover mites: These mites are brownish or grayish, flat and have very long front legs.

b. Spiders: Resemble mites except that most are larger and the two body regions are more clearly distinct from one another (thin waist). Most spiders are beneficial predators. Two poisonous spiders are found in Georgia.

c. Ticks: Resemble large mites and are important agriculturally and medically in that they are parasites of man and animals.

d. Scorpions: have a large pair of appendages on the body which are modified into pincers and a long tail.

Millipedes: Order Diploda—These are elongate invertebrates with two visible body regions, a head and a body. They are generally rounded in cross section and, with the exception of the first four or five segments, all body segments possess two pairs of legs. Millipedes are generally inoffensive creatures that feed on fungus and decaying plant material. At times, they can be fairly destructive to vegetables or other plants in greenhouses.

Centipedes: Order Chilopoda—Centipedes strongly resemble millipedes. They are different in that they have longer antennae, are flattened in cross section and have but one pair of legs on each body segment. They are beneficial in that they are predators of other arthropods.

Sowbugs and Pillbugs: Order Crustacea—These are oval with a hard convex outer shell made up of a number of plates. Sowbugs are highly dependent on moisture. Generally, they feed on decaying plant material, but they will attack young plants in greenhouses and gardens.

Summary

Insects constitute one order of the phylum, Arthropoda, and yet they are one of the largest groups in the animal kingdom. The insect world is made up of individuals that vary greatly in size, color, and shape. Although most insects are harmless or beneficial to man, the few that cause damage have tremendous impact. Harmful species can usually be recognized with some basic knowledge of their hosts, habits, life cycle, and the type of damage they inflict.

RESOURCES

Cranshaw, Whitney. *Garden insects of North America: the ultimate guide to backyard bugs.* Princeton University Press.

Imes, R. *The Practical Entomologist.* Simon and Schuster.

Milne, Lorus and Margery. *The Audobon Society Field Guide to North Americal Insects and Spiders.*

Http://WWW.Bugwood.org contains educational resources including digital images of insects and damage for forestry, ornamentals and agriculture. The site also includes information on other pests such as weeds, diseases and exotic invasives.

DISCUSSION QUESTIONS

1. What are the ways in which insects damage plants?

2. Discuss the benefits of insects in agriculture/horticulture.

3. Why is insect morphology important in insect damage identification?

4. How does knowing which order an insect belongs to help in planning a control strategy, if necessary?

5. Discuss the different types of insect metamorphosis.

6. Why is it important to know the difference between the life cycles of insects?

7. Which common insect orders are characterized by rasping-sucking mouthparts?

8. Name the insect order of which many members are carriers of plant disease.

9. Name the non-insect order to which spiders, spider mites, ticks and scorpions belong.

NOTES

6

Basic Plant Pathology

Elizabeth Little

Alfredo Martinez-Espinoza

LEARNING OBJECTIVES

Define the term plant pathology.

Understand the impact of plant diseases.

Know the difference between pathogenic (biotic) and non-pathogenic (abiotic) diseases.

Understand the concept of the disease triangle.

Know the basic differences between fungal, bacterial, viral, and nematode plant pathogens.

Understand how each type of pathogen can survive, spread, and cause disease.

Begin to develop a working knowledge of disease management strategies.

TERMS TO KNOW

Blight sudden and rapid death of leaves, flowers, stems, or fruits, often affecting whole portions of a plant.

Blotch large and irregularly shaped spot on leaves, shoots, or stems.

Canker dead, sunken lesion affecting the underlying cambial tissues on a stem, branch, or twig of a plant.

Chlorosis yellowing of normally green tissue due to chlorophyll destruction or failure of chlorophyll formation.

Damping-off death of seedlings due to a soil-borne infection at soil line, resulting in the seedling falling over.

Dieback death of entire stems and branches starting from tip and moving downward.

Galls or **tumors** localized swellings of plant tissue caused by the overstimulation of plant auxins and cytokinins.

Lesions and **spots** localized areas of discolored or dead plant tissue as a result of injury or disease.

Mosaic and **mottle** common symptoms of many virus diseases characterized by intermingling patches of normal and light green or yellowish color.

Mummy dried shriveled fruit composed of both plant and fungal material.

Ringspot circular area of chlorosis with a green center on the foliage; is symptomatic of a virus.

Rot softening, discoloration, and often disintegration of succulent plant tissue as the result of fungal or bacterial infection.

Scab roughened crust-like area on the surface of a plant organ.

Scorch death and browning of interveinal leaf tissue, often starting at the margins and progressing inwards, as a result of certain diseases or environmental conditions.

Stunting retardation of normal growth resulting in a subnormal sized plant or plant parts.

Wilt loss of rigidity and drooping of plant parts generally caused by insufficient water or blockage of the water-conducting elements by a pathogen.

INTRODUCTION

Healthy plant: a plant that can carry out its physiological functions such as growth, differentiation, development, absorption of nutrients and minerals, photosynthesis, reproduction etc. to the best of its genetic potential.

Diseased plant: a plant with normal physiological functions interrupted by an organism (pathogen) or certain environmental conditions.

Plant Pathology is the study of:

• The organisms and the environmental conditions that cause disease in plants.

• The mechanisms and interactions by which these factors produce disease in plants.

• The methods of preventing and managing plant diseases.

History of Plant Pathology-a few examples

370 A. C. Theophrastus first wrote about diseases on trees, cereals, and vegetables.

1743 First report of nematodes associated with a plant disease.

1755 The French scientist Tillet successfully infected wheat plants by dusting wheat seeds with smut spores before planting. Prevost (1807) repeated the experiments and correctly concluded that the smut spores were the cause of the disease. He also developed seed treatments using copper sulfate to kill the spores on the wheat seed.

1844-1845 The Irish Potato Famine, caused by the Late Blight Fungus, *Phytophthora infestans*, struck Ireland resulting in the acceptance of the germ theory and the study of plant diseases. Between 1845 and 1850 the famine resulted in more than 1 million deaths and forced 1.5 million people to emigrate from Ireland.

1885 Bordeaux mixture originates in France. Downy mildew of grape became a tremendous problem in France after the pathogen was accidentally introduced on American rootstocks. Growers would apply a mixture of copper sulfate and lime to the vines to prevent people from stealing the grapes. A French botanist, Millardet, observed that the treated plants had less disease and developed the mixture into a fungicidal compound called Bordeaux mixture that is still commonly used today.

1904-1940 Chestnut blight caused by *Crypthonectria (Endothia) parasitica* killed many thousands of mature chestnuts in Eastern North America. The disease devastated the people and the wildlife that relied on the chestnut tree for their livelihood.

1946 W. M. Stanley received a Nobel Prize for his work with the isolation and elucidation of the nature of viruses using tobacco mosaic virus (TMV).

1970 Southern corn blight devastated the corn crops in the U.S. resulting in around $1 billion in losses.

1985-Present Lethal yellowing of palms was first detected in the Caribbean. The disease subsequently destroyed the tall coconut palms in the Caribbean, Central America, Mexico, and Florida, and continues to spread around the world. Lethal yellowing is caused by a type of small systemic bacterium called a phytoplasma.

2001 Daylily rust was first observed in the continental United States, specifically in the state of Georgia, and was found to be caused by the fungus *Puccinia hemerocallidis*.

2003 Bacterial wilt on geranium caused by the bacterium *Ralstonia solanacearum* race 3 (a quarantine pathogen) was re-introduced to USA, causing millions of dollars in losses.

2004 *Phakopsora pachyrhizi*, the causal agent of soybean rust was first reported in the continental United States after the spores were blown into the gulf coast states on a hurricane.

2005 The disease citrus greening (Huanglongbing) caused by a phloem-limited bacterium was discovered in Florida. The disease is vectored from plant to plant by insects called psyllids. By 2010 the entire state was under quarantine.

Plant diseases are extremely important and are a major limiting factor in the production of many crops in the United States with about 30,000 diseases of economic importance. In Georgia alone, plant diseases account for over 150 million dollars in damage each year.

TYPES OF PLANT DISEASES

To diagnose and manage a plant disease it is necessary to first determine whether the disease is caused by a pathogen (biotic cause) or an environmental factor (abiotic cause).

NON-PATHOGENIC (ABIOTIC) DISEASES

Non-pathogenic diseases are plant disorders caused by poor environmental conditions for plant growth (temperature or moisture), nutritional imbalances (too much or too little), or chemical toxins (herbicides, air pollution). Non-pathogenic causes can result in stress and predispose a plant to pathogenic diseases.

Environmental Stress

Lack or Excess of Soil Moisture—A plant can dehydrate when adequate moisture is not provided during drought periods resulting in the browning of foliage and possible death. Excess water caused by poor drainage can reduce oxygen around the roots and cause suffocation. Excess water from rain, irrigation, or poor drainage can also predispose plants to attack by living pathogens.

Too Low or Too High Temperature—Some plants are adapted to cool climates and others to warm climates. If plants are grown out of their adapted habitat, they can be overcome by extremes in temperature.

Nutrition Deficiencies and Toxicities— Plants need a balance of essential nutrients for optimal growth. A lack or excess of any of these nutrients can cause a disease-like disorder resulting in poor or abnormal growth. For example, iron deficiency results in an interveinal yellowing of the young leaves while a nitrogen deficiency causes the yellowing of the older leaves. Boron toxicity caused by an excess of boron is common in some soils and can distort the shoots on susceptible crops such as corn.

Soil Acidity or Alkalinity— Some plants prefer acid soil and others do better in alkaline soils. A pH out of the optimum range can interfere with the ability of a plant to take up nutrients resulting in plant injury.

Chemical Toxins

Air Pollution— Air pollutants such as ozone, sulfur dioxide, or nitrogen dioxide produced from the combustion of fossil fuels can injure plants and cause poor growth. These detrimental effects occur downwind and often many miles from the sources.

Herbicides— Herbicides are used widely and are designed to kill plants. The inadvertent use on non-target plants is very common in the landscape and in cropping situations. Herbicides applied as liquid sprays can easily drift to non-target plants. Some herbicides can remain active for several years resulting in symptoms on crops planted in the same spot the next year or when contaminated plant material is used as compost.

PATHOGENIC DISEASES

Pathogenic diseases are caused by a live organism that invades the host plant resulting in the interruption of the plant's normal function. Pathogens are parasites that obtain nutrition from another organism (the host) at the expense of the host. In the process of feeding, the plant parasite not only consumes plant tissue, which weakens and damages the host, but also produces toxins, enzymes, and growth-regulating substances that disturb the normal metabolic processes in the plant. Over time, the actions of the parasite result in the production of disease symptoms.

Most plant pathogens infect only one species of host or closely related species of hosts (narrow host range) while others can attack many different unrelated hosts (wide host range). Each plant has a particular set of pathogens that could potentially cause disease, and usually the disease that occurs on a particular plant species will not spread to unrelated host plants. Some pathogens may only cause lesions on leaves or stems while others may only infect flowers or fruit. Some pathogens survive only in the soil and infect plant roots. Some enter the plant's vascular system and infect the entire plant systemically (Figure 1).

Disease Triangle

In order to have a pathogenic disease, three factors must always be present: (1) a susceptible host, (2) a parasitic organism, and (3) environmental conditions favorable to the pathogen and disease development. If a susceptible host and organism are present, a disease will only develop if moisture and temperature conditions are favorable for that organism to infect (Figure 2). Disease management is based on the elimination or modification of any one of these factors. Breeding a resistant host, using chemicals to destroy the organism, or altering the environment are just a few of the tactics used to lessen disease.

Disease Cycle

The first step in understanding how a particular pathogen can be managed is to understand how that pathogen survives, spreads, and infects. The life cycle of a plant pathogen is usually tied to the availability of suitable host tissues to colonize and eventually reproduce. Therefore, the life cycle and the disease cycle are often synonymous.

Figure 1

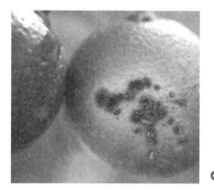

a

b

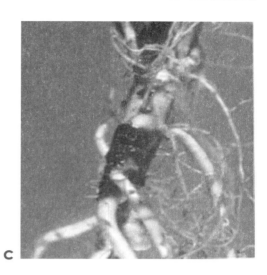

c

Figure 1. Disease symptoms on different plant parts. 1a shows lesions on fruit, 1b leaf spot on leaves, and 1c root rot.

A disease cycle is usually broken down into the survival phase, when suitable plant material is not available, and the active infection phase. The active infection phase can be further broken down into steps: dissemination (movement of the pathogen to an infection site), penetration into the plant, invasion and colonization of plant tissues, production of reproduction structures, secondary spread during the same season, and production of survival structures at the end of the season (Figure 3).

Understanding how, when, and where each of these steps occurs for a particular disease can present opportunities for disrupting the disease cycle. For instance, if the pathogen survives on the dead infected leaves on the ground, then destruction of the leaves before the following season can reduce the amount of pathogen inoculum and disease development.

The major groups of plant pathogens are fungi, bacteria, viruses, and nematodes.

DISEASES CAUSED BY FUNGI

A fungus (plural=fungi) is a non-photosynthesizing, multicellular organism that excretes cell-degrading enzymes and absorbs food. The body of most fungi

Figure 2

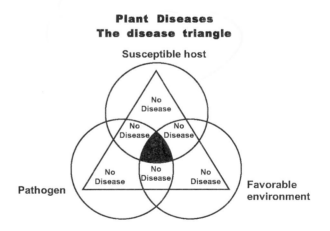

Figure 2. Disease triangle

Figure 3

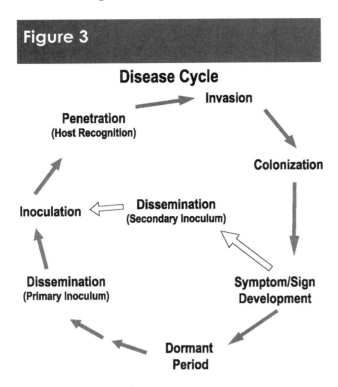

Disease Cycle

Penetration
(Host Recognition)

Invasion

Colonization

Inoculation ⇐ Dissemination
(Secondary Inoculum)

Dissemination
(Primary Inoculum)

Symptom/Sign
Development

Dormant
Period

Figure 3. Disease cycle

Figure 4

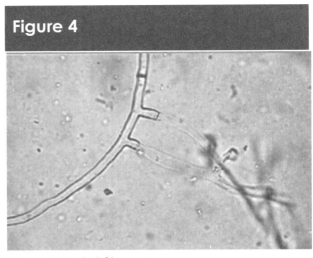

Figure 4. Hyphal filaments

Figure 5

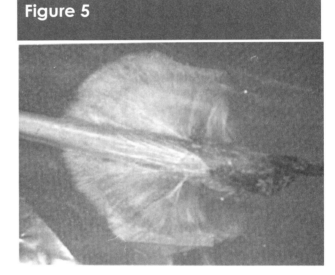

Figure 5. Mycelial (filamentous) growth of fungi

consists of a web-like mass of thin, branching tubes called hyphae. The entire mass of hyphae (Figure 4) of an individual fungus is called a mycelium (pl. mycelia) (Figure 5). Most fungi reproduce and spread by producing spores.

Properties of fungi:

• Cause the majority of all plant diseases.

• Characterized by a mycelial (filamentous) growth habit.

• Consume organic matter from either dead (saprobe) or live organisms (parasites).

• Reproduce primarily by the means of spores.

• Most are identified based on the appearance of their spores and how they are produced.

• Most are saprobes and are an essential part of most ecosystems where they decompose dead plant material.

Plant pathogenic fungi cause a wide variety of disease types including spots on foliage, root and crown rots, cankers, blights, and systemic wilts.

Plant-associated fungi:

Beneficial Fungi— Most fungi are harmless saprobes, but some actually form beneficial symbiotic relationships with plants. The most common group of beneficial fungi is the **mycorrhizal** fungi. Mycorrhizal fungi form a superficial infection of plant roots and help the plant

to better absorb nutrients and water, and protect the plant from stress and disease. Many plants, especially trees, rely on these beneficial fungi to compete and survive. A few types of fungi live inside plants as endophytes and protect the plant from disease, insects, and harsh environmental conditions. Many types of grasses commonly have **endophytes**.

Disease-Causing Fungi (parasites)—Over 8,000 species of parasitic fungi and fungal-like organisms are capable of causing plant diseases in Georgia. Some fungal pathogens attack only one plant species, while other can attack many different species or even families of plants. Some plants are susceptible to more than 50 fungal diseases while other plants have only a few fungal parasites of any concern. Some fungi, called **obligate parasites**, have a very highly specific relationship with a plant species and can only feed on the live plant cells of that species. Once the plant dies, an obligate pathogen dies unless it can produce a survival spore or find another live plant of that species.

Non-obligate parasites require a live host plant to complete their life cycle, but they can survive for a period of time as a saprobe on dead plant tissues waiting for a new plant to infect. A small group of soil-inhabiting fungi can survive almost indefinitely on dead organic material in the soil, but under very favorable conditions they can opportunistically attack a live plant and cause disease.

Methods of survival and spread

Most plant pathogenic fungi need a live host plant to complete their life cycle. Surviving periods when host plants are not available and finding ways to find new host plants are essential for the long term survival of a plant pathogen. Most pathogenic fungi survive from one season to the next as one of several types of durable, weather-resistant fungal structures. Once new hosts are available and the environmental conditions are correct, the fungus breaks dormancy and seeks out a new host.

Many fungal pathogens can survive for a time as mycelium in dead host debris. These fungi do not need a resistant structure but survive only as long as the dead plant material is intact, generally no more than a year or two. Many common foliar diseases, such as black spot of rose and early blight of tomato, survive as mycelium in the infected leaves that fall to the ground. Some fungi infect or infest seed or other propagation materials, which places the pathogen with the host when growth starts.

Once plants are again available to infect, fungi must move long or short distances to find a suitable host. Most fungi produce **spores** as a means of spread and infection. Spores are to fungi what seeds are to plants. Spore appearance (shape, size, color, etc.) is often unique for a particular species and many fungi are identified based on the appearance of the spores (Figure 6). Spores are produced in large numbers and are spread most commonly through air movement, but some are also spread by water or even animals, to another infection site. Most air-borne spores are produced on stalks which hold the spores up off the plant surface so that they can be released into the air to be carried long or short distances to plants.

Some fungi produce spores that are enclosed and protected inside fungal spore structures called pycnidia and acervuli. Under wet conditions, the spores are ejected from an opening in the spore structure and carried by

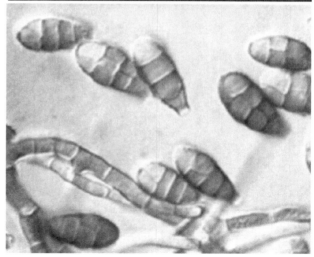

Figure 6

Figure 6. Fungal spores

wind and/or water splash to suitable sites for infection. These structures can often be seen in foliar lesions as minute black dots (Fig. 7).

A special group of fungi are only found in the soil and cause disease in roots, lower stems, or other plant parts that are in contact with the soil. These fungi are called **soil-borne pathogens** and they do not move from plant to plant through the air. Instead they wait for a suitable host to come to them. Some of these fungi can survive for years in the soil as **sclerotia**, which are hardened, compact masses of mycelium, or as other types of resistant survival structures (Figure 8). The resistant structures germinate with hyphae when the roots of susceptible plants grow near them and the hyphae can grow short distances through the soil toward the host.

Sclerotium rolfsii, which causes Southern blight or white mold on many plants such as vegetables and ornamentals, is a good example of a sclerotia-producing soil-borne fungus. *Rhizoctonia*, which is also an important root pathogen of many plant species, can survive in the soil as sclerotia or as mycelium on organic matter. The mycelium can grow directly into plant parts that are in contact with the soil. Oomycetes (a water-loving group of fungus-like pathogens) such as *Phythophthora* or *Pythium* survive as oospores in the soil. Under wet conditions the oospores germinate to produce motile spores called zoospores that swim short distances to attack roots and stems.

Infection

In order for infection to occur, the spore must germinate

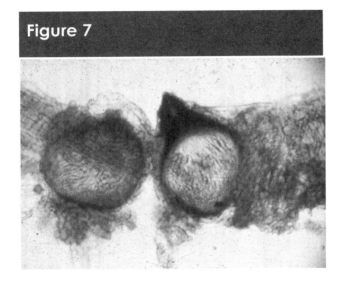

Figure 7. Pycnidia in plant tissue.

Figure 8. Sclerotia.

and penetrate the plant tissue. Some spores form a germ tube that directly penetrates an intact plant surface by producing a cuticle-digesting enzyme. Young, tender leaves and blooms are more likely to be invaded by direct penetration. This is why most foliage infections occur in early spring while new growth is tender and conditions are wet. Once leaves become mature, infection is less likely to occur.

Other fungi penetrate plants indirectly through natural openings such as stomata or through wounds. Fungi that enter plants through stomata can attack older and tougher leaves. Wounds, such as those caused by tools or equipment, make an excellent avenue of penetration. Many fruit rots occur when fungal spores come

in contact with bruised areas. Insect or hail damage can also increase fungal infections.

Once inside the plant, the fungus produces mycelium that starts to feed on plant tissues creating cell death and disease symptoms. Eventually more spores are produced on the surface of the infection site. Most fungi can produce several generations of spores during a growing season and disease can increase quickly when the environmental conditions are suitable. Environmental and host factors determine how extensive the infection becomes and the amount of damage that results.

DISEASES CAUSED BY BACTERIA

Bacteria (singular = bacterium) are single-celled microscopic organisms that can multiply rapidly by simple cell division to form colonies with millions of individuals. Bacterial division can occur in as little as every 20 minutes, and one cell can increase to 17 million cells in 12 hours under warm conditions. About 200 species of bacteria cause a variety of disease types in plants including leaf spots, blights, cankers, root rots, vascular wilts, and diebacks. While there are far fewer diseases caused by bacteria than by fungi, bacterial diseases can cause serious damage since there are fewer effective management options when conditions are conducive for infection.

How Bacteria Survive and Spread

Bacteria do not make survival structures like fungi, but they are able to survive for years as groups of cells in a hibernation-like state in protected places on plant surfaces, in plant debris, on or in seed, or even on equipment. Once the warm, wet conditions that bacteria favor return, the bacteria resume growth and spread to new infection sites by wind-driven rain or water splash.

If a susceptible plant is found and conditions remain favorable, the bacteria increase quickly to high numbers and move into the plant through natural openings or wounds. The bacteria grow in the spaces between cells and their large numbers overwhelm the host's defenses, causing cell death and disease. As more bacteria are produced within the plant, excess bacteria ooze out of the plant and are carried to other infection sites by wind driven rain, water splash, and, in some cases, by insects (Figure 9). Bacteria will continue to spread and cause disease as long as the environmental conditions are suitable and plant host is susceptible.

Just like fungi, some bacterial pathogens are soil-borne and enter the roots to cause serious diseases. Crown gall and southern bacterial wilt of tomato are both soil-borne diseases. These bacteria survive for long periods of time in the soil waiting for a susceptible plant to arrive in their vicinity.

Bacteria often contaminate seed and can be spread long distances with the seed to establish new populations each year. This is especially problematic on annual vegetables. In Georgia, the most serious foliar disease in commercial tomato production is bacterial spot, which is carried on the tomato seed.

Some bacterial pathogens are only spread by insects. These bacteria infect the host systemically, either the xylem or the phloem. There is no cure for systemic infections and little can be done to prevent them except to avoid planting susceptible plants in areas where the disease is common. Pierce's disease of old world grapes (*Vitus vinifera*) and bacterial scorch of many species is caused by a xylem-inhabiting bacterium (*Xylella fastidiosa*) and is spread by leafhoppers. This disease is always fatal to non-native grapes, and the bacterium and leafhoppers are so prevalent in Georgia that wine grapes can only be grown successfully at high altitudes in the mountains where the disease does not occur.

The **phytoplasmas** are an interesting group of phloem-inhabiting bacterial pathogens that are also spread by leaf hoppers. These bacterial pathogens cause symptoms that resemble virus infections and were mistaken for viruses for many years. In Georgia, the most common phytoplasma disease is aster yellows. The symptoms of the disease are stunting, the greening of the flowers (virescence), and the production of leaves from flowers (phyllody). *Echinacea* (cone flower) is a common host for this pathogen (Figure 10).

DISEASES CAUSED BY VIRUSES

Viruses (singular = virus) are very small, simple life forms that consist of genetic material (DNA or RNA) encased in a protein capsule. Just like human viruses, plant viruses take over a cell's machinery to reproduce themselves. Therefore, viruses must have a live host to continue to survive. Viruses eventually infect entire plants systemically in the phloem and there is no cure for a virus infection. Common virus disease symptoms include mosaic, yellowing, ringspots, and stunting (Figure 11). Many vegetables and ornamentals are susceptible to a variety of viral diseases and these diseases are very problematic in warmer regions where the constant availability of hosts and vectors allows for continual spread.

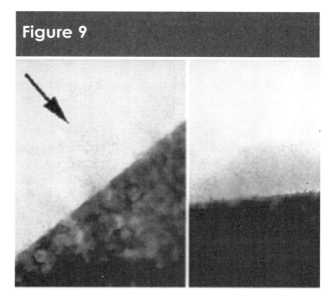

Figure 9. Bacterial cells.

Figure 10. Phyllody on cone flower caused by aster yellows.

How Viruses Survive and Spread

Viruses must have a live plant to survive. Viruses overwinter in perennial crops and weeds, sometimes in infected seed, or in the insect vector that spreads the viruses. Most viruses can only infect a limited number of plant species while a few viruses have a wide host range and can survive in many different plant species. Tomato spotted wilt virus is an example of a virus with a large host range and this virus can be especially problematic in crops such as peanut, tomato, and tobacco in areas where the virus has become well established in a variety of hosts.

Viruses are spread by vectors, most commonly by aphids, but also by whiteflies, thrips, leafhoppers, nematodes, and even beetles. Some plant viruses, such as tobacco mosaic virus, are quite infectious and are spread easily from diseased to healthy plants by human activities. Vegetative propagation from infected plants is a major source of virus infections in clonally produced plants such as potatoes, strawberries, fruit trees, and ornamentals produced from cuttings.

DISEASES CAUSED BY NEMATODES

Nematodes are microscopic, worm-like animals that are found abundantly in all soils. Most are saprobes or predators, and perform important ecological functions. There are over 4000 species of plant parasitic nematodes, but only about twelve genera are economically important in Georgia. Nematodes are found in all soils, but

Figure 11

Figure 11. Viral symptoms on fruit and leaves.

are most problematic in sandy soils, and the amount of crop damage and yield loss caused by nematodes makes them one of the most important groups of pathogens worldwide.

Nematodes Survival and Spread

Plant parasitic nematodes must have a live host plant in order to feed and survive. Plant pathogenic nematodes have a spear-like mouth part called a stylet that works like a hypodermic needle (Figure 12). The nematode inserts this stylet into plant cells and feeds on the contents of the cells causing cell death and disease.

Most plant parasitic nematodes feed on the roots resulting in root dieback and a gradual decline of the host. Some nematode species can enter the foliage, seed, or vascular system of the plant host and feed exclusively on above ground plant parts. When a host is not available, nematodes can survive short periods of time as an egg in the soil. Once the egg hatches, the immature nematode must immediately find a host in order to survive and become an adult nematode.

Nematodes are found in the highest numbers in warm, porous soil that is moist but not saturated. Nematodes can move short distances through soil pores to find new roots. Plant parasitic nematodes are often introduced into new areas on the roots of transplants or by movement of contaminated soil from one area to another. Once nematodes infest new areas they generally cannot be exterminated. Nematodes feed on many ornamentals, vegetables, and fruit trees resulting in unhealthy plants that do not produce well and are more susceptible to other diseases.

Symptoms of Nematode Injury

High numbers of nematodes on the roots results in the generalized above-ground symptoms of any root problem including yellowing of foliage and poor growth. Therefore, nematode infestations are often mistaken for other problems such as nutritional imbalances or root rot. The root system often becomes stunted with the presence of lesions and a lack of feeder roots. Affected plants will wilt and appear drought-stricken because the injured roots cannot take up enough water

The soils of Georgia contain a wide variety of nematodes such as lesion, ring, dagger, sting, and root knot. One of the most common and damaging nematodes in the landscape and vegetable garden is the root knot nematode. These nematodes make deforming galls on the roots that are visible to the naked eye. This nematode is

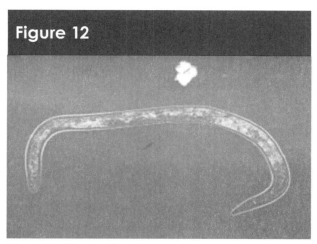

Figure 12. Nematode.

particularly problematic since it can attack most plant species, although some plants, such as Japanese hollies, boxwoods and tomatoes, are particularly susceptible to the damage.

FACTORS NECESSARY FOR INFECTION BY PLANT PATHOGENS

As explained for the disease triangle, each pathogen must have suitable environmental conditions and a susceptible plant host in order to cause disease. For virus diseases, the conditions that influence abundance and feeding ability of the vector must be considered as well. Understanding the requirements for disease can help in making management decisions to lessen disease.

Moisture

Excess moisture from rain or irrigation is most often the environmental factor associated with disease outbreaks. This is especially true for fungal and bacterial foliar diseases, and for root diseases. In order for most fungal spores to germinate and penetrate plant tissue or for bacteria to increase and infect, free water must be available on the surface of the plant. Very few new infections develop during dry periods. A dry spring can lessen disease development for the entire season because even if sufficient moisture becomes available later, the foliage is no longer young and tender, and there will be less of the pathogen available to cause infections.

Powdery mildew fungi are unusual and need only high humidity to infect. Powdery mildew disease is most common during humid, but dry summers. On the other hand, downy mildew disease is favored by cool and very wet periods, and this disease often lessens during the summer.

Temperature

Each pathogen has a minimum and optimum temperature for ideal development. Most disease-causing organisms grow well at temperatures between 70 and 90 F, although this can vary for particular pathogens. At temperatures outside of the optimum, disease may still develop if conditions remain wet for extended periods. Temperature and moisture generally work together in promoting or preventing disease.

Stage of Plant Growth

A pathogen must have susceptible plant tissue in order to establish an infection. Many fungi and bacteria attack young, tender leaves. Others prefer new shoot growth, young feeder roots, or ripe fruit. If the plant passes through the susceptible stage before the pathogen finds the host or during unfavorable weather conditions for infection, then it might escape injury for the entire season.

MANAGING DISEASES

The preceding information on plant pathogens should be useful in understanding how to effectively manage plant disease. Plant pathologists have developed procedures for breaking the life cycle of pathogens, thus lessening the harmful effects of plant disease. These practices can be broken down into the following categories: **Exclusion** includes methods to exclude the pathogen from areas where it does not occur, **Eradication** is the destruction or reduction of the survival sites of the pathogen before infection occurs, **Resistance** is the use of plants or plant cultivars that can resist or tolerate pathogen infections, and **Protection** are methods used during the season to reduce the impact of disease.

There are some basic principles to consider in disease management:

• Complete elimination of disease is usually not possible or practical. The goal for the management of most diseases is to lessen damage to an acceptable level.

• Healthy plants are better able to resist disease than a stressed plant.

• Put the right plant in the right place. Choose plants that are proven to thrive in your area.

• Where feasible, integrate a variety of disease management methods for the best results.

Exclusion

Some pathogens may not be present in a certain area

and steps can be taken to prevent the introduction of the pathogen. Many pathogens can be carried on seed and some are introduced each year into a garden on contaminated seed. This is especially true for vegetables. For this reason, gardeners should not save seeds from diseased plants in their garden and, if possible, buy seeds that claim to be free of pathogens. These pathogen-free seeds should be grown in areas where diseases are not present. If the only means of survival for the pathogen is the seed, using clean seed can entirely prevent the disease.

Other pathogens can be accidentally carried into the garden on infected transplants and potted plants. Vegetable or annual transplants may already be infected with a foliar disease. Soil-borne diseases can be introduced into a new site in the garden by planting potted plants or transplants containing soil-borne disease organisms. Accidental pathogen introductions can be avoided by examining potted plants and transplants for disease, and purchasing plants from reputable nurseries.

Eradication

These methods are designed to target the survival sites of plant pathogens. An understanding is needed of where particular pathogens may be surviving in order to target these sites and break the disease cycle. For many plant diseases, prevention of the first infections can lessen disease impacts for the entire season.

Rotation—Disease pathogens that survive the winter in or on old diseased leaves, branches, mummified fruit, and other infected debris only survive as long as the debris is intact. In the case of annuals such as vegetables, growing the same plant species year after year in the same spot puts the plant next to the source of disease. Two to three year rotations where related plants are not planted in the same spot allows the debris to decompose and can reduce disease, especially if the pathogen cannot move far from the survival site. Planting of a cover crop during part of the time not only reduces pathogen survival but also adds to soil fertility. In a small garden space, rotation may not be as feasible so targeting the most important disease problems for rotation and using other methods of eradiation can help.

Root and crown infected soil-borne fungi often make long-term survival structures and longer rotations may be needed to reduce disease. In addition, some soil-borne pathogens, such as *Rhizoctonia* and *Sclerotium*, have very wide host ranges that can reduce the effectiveness of rotations. Nematode populations can also be reduced by rotation; although some nematodes, such as

the very important root knot nematode, have very wide host ranges and can survive on many rotation crops or weeds. Some grasses such as bahigrass and bermudagrass are effective rotational crops to reduce high populations of root knot nematodes.

While perennial plants cannot be rotated each year, when perennials such as vines, brambles, fruit trees, and ornamental plants do not thrive in a spot and need to be replaced, replacement with another plant species can prevent future problems. For instance, many fruit trees, such as peach, can have what is called transplant disease when replanted in the same spot due to a build-up of pathogens in the soil.

Mulch—Placing mulch (shredded leaves or wood, pine needles, straw, bark chips etc.) beneath shrubs or between the rows in the garden forms a barrier that prevents organisms from moving from soil to plants. This can be very effective for diseases that survive in the debris. Before new mulch is laid down under plants that have had disease problems, all plant debris and old mulch materials should be removed. Mulch has the added benefit of improving plant health by conserving moisture, keeping roots cool, and providing additional organic matter.

Sanitation—Removing and destroying the old leaves and other diseased plant debris from beneath trees and shrubs, and in garden spaces lessens the ability of the pathogen to survive. Mowing the old leaves under trees and shrubs in the fall can help break down the leaves more quickly. Cultivating the soil in vegetable gardens may help to destroy and/or bury fungal survival sites. Some pathogens survive in diseased perennial plants and cutting out diseased canes or branches lessens disease. For instance, powdery mildew and black spot can survive in infected rose canes. Fire blight of apple and pear can survive in blighted branches. Peach brown rot survives in mummified fruit left hanging in the tree.

Suppressive Soils—An effective long term approach to reducing soil-borne pathogens and improve plant disease resistance is to increase the soil organic matter and quality of the soil. Healthy soils that contain plenty of organic mater encourage a high diversity of the soil microbial populations. Many of these microbes have a suppressive effect on disease. This goes back to the old saying, "healthy soils, healthy plants." Plant pathogenic organisms are generally poor competitors in microbial rich soils, and in some cases resistant survival structures can be broken down more quickly. There are also beneficial microbes that form relationships with plant roots and provide a barrier against pathogen invasion and also promote plant health.

Resistance

Resistant plants are able to prevent attack by pathogens, either partially or totally, resulting in less disease. Using resistant plants, if available, is one of the easiest, safest and most effective means of managing plant diseases. Some plant species or cultivars may be naturally more resistant to disease. For example, native rabbiteye blueberries have very few disease problems while highbush blueberries, which are adapted to a cooler climate, have problems with several different diseases in Georgia.

Resistance can also be incorporated into certain plants or cultivars against specific diseases through breeding and selection efforts. Often, the diseases that are targeted in resistance breeding programs are difficult to manage any other way. For example, Fusarium wilt is a soil-borne fungal disease that can survive in the soil for many years. An effective wilt resistant gene was identified and has been bred into most commercial and hybrid tomato cultivars. Many vegetables, in particular tomatoes and cucurbits, are particularly plagued by a number of diseases in Georgia and using available disease resistant vegetable varieties is recommended for the homeowner.

Protection During the Growing Season

Not all survival structures may be destroyed through eradication efforts and eventually disease many develop during conducive environmental conditions such as warm, wet weather. Also, spores may blow in each year from other locations. For many diseases, in particular foliar diseases that can spread quickly during the season and some root diseases, additional protections against disease may be needed during the growing season.

Cultural methods—As discussed above, each pathogen has a certain requirement for temperature and, in particular, moisture. Proper irrigation can prevent many problems. Sprinkler irrigation should be avoided when possible, especially on shrubs, flowers, and in the vegetable garden. Overhead irrigation wets the leaves and creates infection conditions for fungi and bacteria, even during dry periods when disease would not normally be active.

If overhead irrigation is needed, water in the morning when the leaves will dry most quickly. Water deeply and less frequently. Situating plants in open areas with good air movement, pruning to decrease canopy density, and staking plants off the ground are all ways to reduce the amount of moisture on the leaves and decrease disease.

Overwatering and/or poorly drained soil are the leading causes of root rot in plants. Many established plants need little if any supplemental water, especially if adequately mulched. In our heavy clay soils and hot, humid climate, root disease can develop quickly in saturated soils. When plants start to succumb to root disease with symptoms of wilting and dieback, the reaction is often to apply more water resulting in the death of the plant. Improving drainage or not placing susceptible plants in wet areas are other ways to avoid root rot.

Stressed plants are more susceptible to all types of pathogen infections. Fertilizer should be applied in balanced amounts and when indicated by a soil test. Maintaining a proper pH for the plant species will allow for adequate uptake of nutrients and improve plant health. Excessive nitrogen can increase foliar disease by increasing the amount of tender growth. The underlying cause for most lawn diseases in the Southeast can be attributed to poor cultural conditions such as excess moisture and nitrogen, improper pH, and compacted, poor quality soils.

Biological and Chemical Applications—Fungicides and bactericides are used most often on foliar diseases that can build up during the growing season. These products should be used as a last resort when all else fails. Fungicides and bactericides only give temporary relief, are not always effective, may have environmental and health consequences, and need to be applied repeatedly if the underlying host or environmental cause of the problem is not addressed.

There are some plants which have chronic in-season problems in Georgia, such as rose cultivars susceptible to black spot, apple and pear varieties susceptible to fire blight, and powdery mildew on squash. In most cases, there are at least partially disease-resistant cultivars available which reduces the need for chemical applications.

All fungicides, bactericides, and microbial-based biological products work best if applied before disease appears and have little effect on active infections. Predicting when these infections may occur and knowing how to apply these products effectively can be tricky for the homeowner. In addition, some diseases are not harmful to the plant at low levels, such as many leaf spot diseases, and not all diseases should or can be treated with fungicides. Over-application or inappropriate use of pesticides is common around the home, and before using any fungicides or bactericides, an accurate diagnosis and recommendation should be obtained from current your Cooperative Extension agent.

RESOURCES

National Sustainable Agriculture Information Service (ATTRA) has a large number of homeowner appropriate plant growing and pest management publications on their website, mainly for food crops: http://attra.ncat.org/index.php

The American Phytopathological Society has an on-line education center including in depth articles and lessons on important plant diseases: http://www.apsnet.org

Pirone, Pascal P., *Diseases and Pests of Ornamental Plants*, 5th Edition. Discusses diagnosis and treatment of organisms afflicting nearly 500 genera of ornamental plants.

Plant Pathology Extension Websites at State Universities have great on-line resources and PDF's on plant diseases. Look at Georgia, Florida, South Carolina, North Carolina, and Alabama for southeast-specific information.

DISCUSSION QUESTIONS

1. How can Plant Pathology be defined?

2. What are the two types of plant diseases?

3. What three factors are required for a pathogenic disease?

4. What are the properties of fungi?

5. Describe the reproductive process of fungi.

6. What are some ways in which a fungus enters a plant?

7. How do bacteria differ from fungi?

8. How are viruses spread?

9. What are nematodes and how can they cause plant disease?

10. How can plant diseases be controlled?

7
Weed Science

Mark A. Czarnota

Patrick McCullough

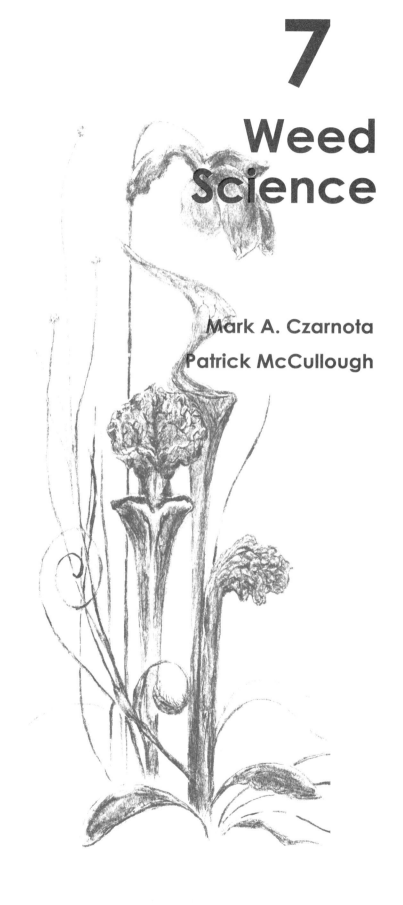

LEARNING OBJECTIVES

Understand the growth characteristics of weeds including growth habit and reproduction.

Know basic techniques for weed identification and basic weed control methods including mechanical and chemical controls.

Understand the difference between pre-emergent and post-emergent herbicides and the difference between selective and non-selective herbicides.

Have an understanding of the most effective use of herbicides and be familiar with herbicide application methods and equipment.

Know the commonly used herbicides and their classification and nomenclature.

Be familiar with herbicide application methods and equipment.

Know methods of weed control for vegetable gardens, orchards, turf and landscapes including acceptable herbicide options and benefits of mechanical weed control.

TERMS TO KNOW

Contact herbicide herbicide that kills primarily by contact with plant tissue.

Cultural weed control supression of weeds by using mulches and other non-chemical methods.

Fallow not planted in a crop.

Herbicide chemical applied to plants that prevents or suppresses their growth and development, or a chemical that when applied to plants kills them.

Landscape fabric loosely intertwined fabric of various material that is placed over the soil as a mulch to reduce weed invasion.

Mechanical weed control removal or supression of weeds by hoeing, pulling, burning, digging, or tilling.

Over-the-top application use of a selective herbicide sprayed directly over an area containing desired and undesired plants.

Phytotoxicity ability of a material to cause injury to plants.

Selective herbicide pesticide that kills only one type of plant. (For example broadleaf herbicides only kill broadleaf weeds, not grasses).

Weed unwanted plant.

INTRODUCTION

There are various definitions for a weed, as the following examples show:

"'Any plant out of place."

"'A plant whose virtues have not yet been discovered." (Emerson)

"'No more than a flower in disguise." (Lowell)

"'But an unloved flower." (Wilcox)

"'In nature there is no such thing as a weed."

"'Weeds - Adam had'em; and the Garden of Eden became a garden of weedin'." (McGlamery)

"'Even crabgrass has not always been considered a weed, as it is reported to be the first grain cultivated by man during the Stone Age in Switzerland. It was introduced to the U.S. in 1849 by the U.S. Patent Office as a forage plant." (Weeds Today)

Why Worry about Weeds? In nature, no such thing as a weed exists! For some people, plants are just plain interesting. Many people often ask, "Why do you want to get rid of those beautiful flowers growing in your lawn and landscape?". As with most things in life, it is a matter of opinion! Many serious gardeners, however, are only interested in growing certain varieties of turfgrass or landscape plants, and cringe when they see unwanted plants interfering with their cherished landscape and garden plants. Weeds in the landscape and garden should be controlled for 4 reasons, and they include:

• Weeds compete with desirable plants for nutrients, water, and light

• Weeds cause economic loss in the landscape and vegetable garden

• Weeds are hosts for insect and disease

• Weeds can deface a well planned landscape

Table 1. Examples of seed production in common weeds

COMMON NAME	APPROXIMATE NUMBER OF SEED PRODUCED PER PLANT
common lambsquarters	72,000
pigweed	117,000
curly dock	40,000
sandbur	1,110

How Do Weeds Reproduce?

Weeds may reproduce vegetatively or by seed. It is important to understand the dynamics of weed reproduction. For example, nutsedge tubers planted on a spacing of one per sq. ft. on one acre have produced over three million plants and four million tubers in one season. Weeds also produce a tremendous number of seed.

Some examples of the number of seed produced per plant are listed in Table 1.

How Do Weeds Survive? Although tubers and rhizomes can remain alive for many years, seeds are highly specialized structures that, under the right conditions, can remain alive in the soil for many years (in some cases thousands of years). An old study found that pigweed and ragweed would still germinate after 40 years, mustard and knotweed after 50 years, and evening primrose, curly dock and common mullein after 70 years. Seeds of lupines have been found from Roman times (about 2000 years ago) that were still viable and germinated. There are several different mechanisms which seeds employ to keep them dormant but alive. These include a thick seed coat that inhibits the movement of water or oxygen, or chemicals within the seed coat that inhibit germination. For germination to occur, many of these mechanisms need to be disrupted. Thick seed coats can be worn down (or scarified) by either weathering or the digestive system of an animal. Once the seed coat is broken, water and oxygen can enter the seed, and remove any inhibitory compounds. Some seeds require freezing and thawing (the process known as stratification) in order to germinate. Others require a flash of light. All of these characteristics enable weed seed to survive in the soil for many years.

How Are Weeds Classified? Weeds are classified in several different ways, so that we may develop effective control strategies. Following are some of those ways:

Weed Types

Grass weeds—Grasses are monocots, and among other characteristics, monocots are plants that emerge as one single leaf at germination. Grasses have round or flattened stems, nodes (joints), and parallel veins in leaves. An example is crabgrass.

Sedge weeds—Sedges are also monocots but have three ranked leaves (leaves that emerge in a triangular pattern, triangular stems without nodes (usually only seen when the plant is flowering), and have parallel veined leaves. An example is purple nutsedge.

Broadleaf weeds—Broadleaf plants are dicots. There are many characteristics that make plants dicots. A few of them are seedlings emerge with two leaves, leaves have netted vein patterns, nodes (joints) with one or more leaves. Some dicots can also produce woody (or secondary) growth. Examples are ivyleaf morningglory, and common privet.

Lifecycle

Annual weeds germinate from seeds, produce seed and die in one season. There are two types of annual weeds. Winter annuals are adapted to cool temperatures of fall, winter, or spring, usually dying in late spring or early summer. An example of a winter annual is annual bluegrass. Summer annuals are adapted to warm temperatures of spring, summer and fall, dying by late summer or fall. Southern crabgrass is classified as a summer annual.

Biennial weeds germinate from seed and produce a cluster of leaves near the soil surface during their first year of growth. In the second year, biennial weeds flower, produce seed and die. Wild carrot (Queen Anne's Lace) is a biennial.

Perennial weeds germinate from seed or vegetative parts, such as tubers or rhizomes, and establish underground plant parts which allow them to live for an indefinite number of years. Wild garlic and yellow nutsedge are examples of perennial weeds.

Weed Control Methods

Weed control, by hand or with mechanical or cultural methods (such as plowing or mulching), can be accomplished without knowing the "name" of a weed. All that is necessary is to recognize that there is a plant you do not want. Where herbicides are used, the specific name of a weed becomes important. The reason is simple: many herbicides may control one kind of plant, but not another. If you decide to use a selective herbicide, two pieces of information are required: (1) Will the herbicide control the targeted weed? (2) Will the herbicide injure desirable plants growing in my garden (turfgrass, ornamentals or vegetables)? Answering these two questions is required if control is to be successful. Names of weeds susceptible to a given chemical are usually listed on the herbicide product label, or in other literature such as Extension publications. Information on plant tolerance is also available on the herbicide label. It is your responsibility to be able to recognize weeds by name and match them to the specific herbicide. Also, you need to determine if the herbicide is safe around desirable plants.

Weed control is the process of limiting a weed infestation so that a landscape planting can grow, develop properly, and be aesthetically appealing. There are several methods to control weeds in landscape plantings, which include preventive practices, cultural practices, mechanical means, and the use of herbicides. To control weeds consistently, one must understand the contribution of each method in controlling weeds. A combination approach that uses the various methods is always more successful than only using one control method. This approach is referred to as "integrated weed management (IWM)".

Preventive Practices

Preventive practices are aimed at preventing the introduction of or spread of weeds over a given land area. Preventive practices include:

Using weed-free seed, sod sprigs, container plants, mulches, and topsoil —There are state and federal laws that prohibit the presence of noxious weed seeds in seed that is sold for agricultural purposes. The homeowner should purchase high-quality seed and vegetative planting materials that do not contain weed seeds. Similarly, only mulches and topsoil that do not contain problem weed species should be purchased.

Prevent weeds from spreading —Common approaches include: preventing weeds from going to seed, cleaning mowers and earth moving equipment before moving to different sites, and if possible, controlling weeds along ditch banks, fence rows, and other adjacent areas.

Cultural Practices

The second line of defense against weeds is to follow cultural practices that promote vigorous growth and development of the landscape planting. For example, weeds do not easily infest turfgrasses that are properly fertilized, watered, and mowed at the correct height and frequency. Most weeds appear primarily in bare or thin areas of the turfgrass. Many weeds are not shade-tolerant. Properly spacing annual and herbaceous perennials will enable these plants to quickly shade the soil surface and limit weed establishment. Adherence to the following guidelines will increase the competitiveness of turfgrasses and/or ornamentals with weeds.

Plant Adapted Species—Many plants will only grow in certain situations. Make sure that you plant the right plant in the right location. Georgia contains 2 major hardiness zones, zones 7 and 8. There are many plants that grow in zone 8, but do not do well in zone 7.

Ground covers (Algerian Ivy) and turf grass adapted to zone 8 (St Augustine) do not do well on the fringes of zone 6 and in zone 7. When plants are not growing in optimal environments, they generally do not do well and do not compete well with weeds. One should always be vigilant about choosing plant material that will thrive in your location. Healthy plants are a defense against weed growth as well as disease and insect infestation.

Fertility Management—Fertilization should be based on the turfgrass or ornamental plant requirements, maintenance practices, and desired appearance. A soil test is the best method to determine the fertility levels of a growing area. The fertility levels will also help determine the fertility needs for growing a particular plant. The University of Georgia Cooperative Extension Service provides soil tests at a nominal fee to Georgia residents. Instructions, soil test bags, and assistance are available at Extension offices. Proper fertilization encourages proper growth of turfgrass, ornamental, and vegetable plants. A healthy plant is competitive with weeds.

Irrigation—Due to seasonal variations in rainfall distribution, supplemental irrigation is required in most crops in Georgia. Infrequent water applications that soak the soil to a depth of 5 to 7 inches promotes deep root development and improves turfgrass and ornamental plant competition with weeds. Shallow, frequent watering results in shallow roots and promotes germination of some weed species.

Insect and Disease Control—Landscape plants and turfgrasses can be severely weakened or killed by insects and diseases. The resulting bare or thin areas are easily invaded by weeds. Approved insect and disease management programs maintain turfgrasses and ornamental plants in a healthy, vigorous condition and aid in the prevention of weeds.

Mechanical Removal and Physical barriers

Frequent mowing at recommended clipping heights helps limit the development of many weed species in turfgrasses. Mow turfgrasses often enough so that only 1/3 of the leaf area is removed at any one time. Mowing above or below the recommended clipping height decreases the competitive ability of the turfgrass.

Cultivation—The act of tilling or preparing land to maintain or grow a crop exists in many forms. Cultivation can be utilized to eliminate unwanted vegetative growth. In ornamentals it is usually employed before planting, and is seldom used after that. In vegetable plantings many people will cultivate before planting, and maintain bare soil there after. Cultivating to a depth of 1 to 2 inches can be used to control emerged weeds in non-mulched plantings. Deeper cultivation brings weed seeds near the soil surface and may injure ornamental roots. Before an ornamental planting is installed, cultivation can be used to eliminate emerged weeds In turfgrass, vertical mowing, aeration, and top dressing are sometimes necessary to reduce surface compaction and thatch accumulation, and to improve soil aeration and water infiltration. Of course, one should never forget hand-removal for those easy to remove annual weed in just about any situation.

Mulches are an extremely valuable method to control weeds in ornamental plantings. Mulches physically interfere with seed germination and weed emergence. They block sunlight from the soil surface and inhibit the reception of light by developing weed seedlings. The combination of physical interference and blocking of sunlight by mulches prevents the germination and emergence of many annual weeds. Mulches also help maintain soil moisture and temperatures. There are many types of organic mulches, including pine straw, pine bark, and shredded hardwood, just to name a few. Most organic mulches should be maintained at a depth of 2 to 4 inches. Inorganic mulches, such as stone and river rock, can be effectively used to prevent weed emergence. Inorganic mulches do not decompose and therefore do not require replacement as much as organic mulches. Inorganic mulches are commonly maintained at a depth of 1 and 4 inch layer. Also, use caution when using rock mulch around tender plants, as rocks re-radiate heat which may damage these plants. Limit use to shady areas.

Landscape fabrics may also be used to control weeds in ornamentals. Fabrics are usually manufactured from polypropylene or polyester and usually allow moisture, nutrients, and oxygen to reach the roots, while preventing most weeds from emerging. Fabrics can be installed before or after planting. With woody ornamentals, fabric is commonly installed after planting. With mass plantings of annuals or herbaceous perennials it is usually easier to install fabric before planting. Once installed, slits or holes are cut into the fabric through which the herbaceous ornamental is planted. After the fabric is installed, mulch is placed on the surface to improve the aesthetic appeal of the planting. Some weed species will be able to penetrate the fabric or will be able to derive enough moisture and nutrients at the interface of the fabric and overlying mulch. Limited weed removal will still be required with landscape fabrics.

Chemical Control—A herbicide is a chemical used to prevent, suppress, or kill the growth and development of a weed. Prior to a herbicide being labeled for use in the landscape, it is investigated thoroughly by the chemical company, land grant universities, and various federal agencies. The herbicide must be proven to cause no adverse risk to humans, the environment, or desirable plants, and to effectively control weeds. Final approval for use as a herbicide is under the direct control of the United States Environmental Protection Agency. Table 2 shows the relative toxicity of some commonly used lawn and garden herbicides.

In 1944, it was discovered that 2,4-D controlled dandelion and plantains in established Kentucky bluegrass. Since the introduction of 2,4-D, chemical weed control has gained widespread acceptance by landscape managers and homeowners. Continued discovery and registration of new herbicides has enabled the landscape manager to control weeds that previously were not controlled by existing herbicides. Herbicides are valuable components of a landscape weed control program. The use of herbicides in the absence of following approved preventive, cultural, and mechanical weed control practices, however, will not result in a high quality, weed-free landscape planting.

All herbicides may be grouped into various categories based on their general mode-of-action or time of application.

Preemergence—Preemergence herbicides are applied to the turfgrass or ornamental site prior to weed seed germination. This group of herbicides controls weeds during the weed seed germination process. Weeds that have emerged at the time of application are usually not controlled by preemergence herbicides. Most herbicides may be classified as preemergence or postemergence. A few have both preemergence and postemergence activity on selected weeds. Currently, preemergence herbicides are our best line of defense for weed control as our arsenal of selective postemergence herbicides is very limited.

Preemergence herbicides form the base of a chemical weed control program in landscape sites, and are used primarily to control annual grasses and broadleaf weeds. Due to their persistence in the soil, preemergence herbicides control susceptible weeds for an extended period of time. Preemergence herbicides used in landscapes generally persist in the soil for two to four months. The soil persistence characteristics of these herbicides is advantageous in terms of length of weed control; however,

Table 2. Relative toxicity of some commonly used herbicides

COMMON NAME	TRADE NAME	ORAL ACUTE VALUES
atrazine	Purge II	1,869
2,4-D (ester)	Various	500-1200
Aspirin Comparison		750
dithiopyr	Dimension	>5,000
oryzalin	Surflan	>10,000
simazine	Princep	> 5,000
trifluralin	Treflan	>10,000
Table Salt Comparison		3,320

it may be a disadvantage if seeding, sprigging, sodding, or other types of replanting operations are planned for a particular site. Newly-seeded and sprigged turfgrasses have a low level of tolerance to most preemergence herbicides. The herbicide label should be consulted to determine the length of time required before establishment operations can be safely conducted.

Postemergence—Postemergence herbicides are applied directly to emerged weeds. In contrast to preemergence herbicides, this group of herbicides has little, if any, soil activity. A complete chemical weed control program can be accomplished with postemergence herbicides provided multiple applications are used throughout the year. Postemergence herbicides are useful at controlling perennial grass and broadleaf weeds that are not controlled by preemergence herbicides.

Both Pre- and Postemergence herbicides can be further subdivided into two other groups: Selective and Nonselective herbicides.

Selective—A selective herbicide controls one plant species without seriously affecting the growth of a different plant species. The majority of postemergence herbicides used in turfgrasses are selective herbicides. Examples include 2,4-D (various trade names) to control most broadleaf weeds without severely injuring most landscape grasses.

Nonselective—A nonselective herbicide controls plants without regard to species. Nonselective herbicides are used as "spot treatments" for difficult-to-control weeds. In ornamentals and turfgrass, nonselective herbicides can cause severe plant injury if the spray solution contacts the foliage or green bark of desirable plants. Avoid using nonselective herbicides around turf and ornamentals during windy conditions. Glyphosate (Roundup and other trade names) is an example of a nonselective herbicide.

Contact—Contact herbicides affect only the portion of green plant tissue that is contacted by the herbicide spray. These herbicides are usually not translocated in the vascular system of plants. Therefore, they will not kill underground plant parts such as bermudagrass rhizomes. Adequate spray volumes and thorough coverage of the weed foliage is necessary for effective control. Contact herbicides kill plants quickly, often within a few hours of application. Contact herbicides can be classified as selective or nonselective. They generally do not work well at controlling perennial type weeds as do the systemic type herbicides. Diquat (i.e. Reward) is an example of a contact herbicide.

Systemic—Systemic herbicides move through the plant vascular system. The vascular system transports inorganic nutrients, sugars, hormones, and water which are required by plants for normal growth and development. In contrast to the "quick kill" observed with contact herbicides, systemic herbicides kill plants over a period of days or a few weeks. Systemic herbicides are also classified as selective or nonselective. Glyphosate is a nonselective systemic herbicide. 2,4-D and dicamba are examples of selective, systemic herbicides.

Herbicide Nomenclature

Each chemical that is used as a herbicide has at least three different names. For example:

1. Brand or Trade Name: Treflan

2. Common Chemical Name or Active Ingredient: trifluralin

3. Full Chemical Name: 2,6-dinitro-N N-dipropyl-4-(trifluoromethyl) benzenamine

The brand or trade name is used by the chemical company to promote the sale of a specific product, and is often the most recognizable name of a herbicide. Trade names can, and often, change with the sale of a product to a different manufacturer or if the herbicide goes off patent and is sold by a different company. The common chemical name is a generic name that is given to a long, more complex chemical name. The full chemical name describes the exact chemistry of the compound. The names of both the common or full chemical name seldom change. Only one common and chemical name exist for each chemical that is used as a herbicide. However, numerous brand or trade names can usually be found for each chemical that is used as a herbicide. Knowledge of the common name will help you to select various brands of the same herbicide, and may save money, or unnecessary trips in searching for a specific brand name product.

Herbicides are labeled by brand name for the site of application. For example, glyphosate is the common name of the chemical in the herbicides Roundup and Rodeo. Roundup may be used for weed control around ornamentals and many other terrestrial uses. Rodeo is labeled for controlling emerged weeds in aquatic situations. Even though the same chemical, glyphosate, is the active ingredient in both products, Roundup may not be used for aquatic weed control, and Rodeo may not be used for weed control around ornamentals.

Herbicide Selection

A large number of herbicides are available to control weeds in landscape plants (see the *Georgia Pest Management Handbook Commercial Edition* and the *Georgia Pest Management Handbook Homeowner Edition*). There is no single herbicide that is appropriate for all landscape weed control situations. The following guidelines should be considered for the selection of a herbicide.

Landscape Plant Tolerance—Turfgrass and ornamental plant species vary in their tolerance to herbicides. For example, centipedegrass and St. Augustinegrass have excellent tolerance to atrazine; however, tall fescue and other cool-season turfgrasses will be severely injured or killed by atrazine. Most broadleaf ornamentals have excellent tolerance to over-the-top applications of postemergence grass control herbicides such as sethoxydim (Vantage), fluazifop (Flusilade, Ornamec, Take-Away) and fenoxaprop (Acclaim). Most turfgrasses and ornamental grasses, however, can be severely injured by these postemergence grass control herbicides. Always refer to the label or various weed control guides to determine if a herbicide may be used on a specific turfgrass or ornamental plant species.

Time of Application—The time of year that a herbicide is applied can influence turfgrass or ornamental plant tolerance. For example, dormant bermudagrass has excellent tolerance to glyphosate. However, severe injury will occur if glyphosate is applied to semi-dormant or to actively-growing bermudagrass. Turfgrass tolerance to postemergence herbicides is generally less at elevated air temperatures (>90° F) than at more moderate air temperatures. Herbicides that contain 2,4-D, MCPP, dicamba, or MSMA should not be applied at air temperatures greater than 90° since there is a strong possibility of increased turfgrass injury. Similarly, certain ornamental plants, such as prostrate forms of juniper with blue-green foliage, can be injured by postemergence grass control herbicides if applications are made in the summer months under high air temperatures and high relative humidities.

Rule of Thumb— Avoid over-the-top applications to ornamental plants if the sum of the air temperature plus relative humidity is greater than 150. For example, an application on a summer day when the air temperature is 95°F and the relative humidity is 80% (95 + 80 = 175) would not be advisable. Additionally, some postemergence herbicides should not be applied during the green-up (transition from winter dormancy to active growth) of warm-season turfgrasses. Certain postemergence herbicides, such as imazaquin (Image) can delay active turfgrass growth if applications are made during or just prior to green-up. Consult the herbicide label to determine if applications during green-up are recommended.

Weed Species—There is no single herbicide that will control all weed species. Correct weed identification is a prerequisite for the selection of an appropriate herbicide. Weed identification manuals and assistance are available at county Extension offices. Weed response ratings for commonly used turfgrass herbicides are shown in various weed control publications available at county Extension offices. Additionally, the herbicide label will list the weeds controlled by a particular herbicide. Careful study of these references or herbicide labels will enable the selection of the appropriate herbicide for a specific weed.

Application Frequency—With some weed species and herbicides, a repeat application is necessary to effectively control the weed. Refer to the herbicide label.

Application Equipment—The availability of application equipment may dictate the selection of either a granular or sprayable herbicide formulation. Many herbicides are available in both forms.

Non-target Plant Tolerance—Turfgrass herbicides are commonly applied to sites that contain ornamental plantings. Foliage or green bark of many ornamentals can be injured through contact with herbicide vapor and spray drift and by root absorption. Vapor drift is the movement of herbicide vapors from the area of application. Herbicides vary in their volatility or their potential for vapor drift. Ester formulations of the phenoxy herbicides (2,4-D, 2,4-DP) easily volatilize and herbicide vapors can injure sensitive ornamentals, vegetables, and fruit trees. Ester formulations should not be used

during the warm months of the year when conditions are favorable for volatilization. Spray drift damage can be prevented by spraying on calm days when the wind velocity is less than five miles per hour, and by selecting a nozzle tip and spray pressure that produces large droplets. Large spray droplets are much less subject to spray drift than small, fog-like spray droplets.

Due to their soil residual characteristics, certain herbicides can injure ornamentals via root uptake. Avoid applications of herbicides that contain dicamba or atrazine over the root zone of desirable ornamentals. Injury to ornamentals by root uptake is most likely to occur on sandy soils when heavy rainfall immediately follows a herbicide application.

Some turfgrass herbicides are also labeled for use around landscape ornamentals. The use of these herbicides is safe for applications to or near ornamentals that are listed on the herbicide label.

Fertilizer-Herbicide Mixtures

Selected preemergence and postemergence herbicides may be applied with either liquid or dry fertilizers. Fertilizer-herbicide mixtures allow a "weed-n-feed" treatment to be applied in the same application. "Weed-n-feed" treatments may be convenient; however, certain factors must be considered prior to application. Depending upon the turfgrass or ornamental, the time of year that a herbicide should be applied may not coincide with the time of year that a fertilizer should be applied. For example, centipedegrass should not receive spring fertilization until the grass has fully greened-up or has recovered from winter dormancy. At the full green-up stage of centipedegrass, it is usually too late to apply a preemergence herbicide since many summer annual weeds have already emerged. An exception is atrazine. This herbicide has preemergence and postemergence activity, and can be applied with fertilizer carriers after centipedegrass green-up to control emerged summer annual broadleaf weeds.

Atrazine, however, will not provide effective control of emerged annual grasses, such as crabgrass and goosegrass. Many herbicides are formulated with a fertilizer as the carrier. When using these products, it is important to determine if the manufacturer's recommended rate of the product supplies the amount of fertilizer needed by the turfgrass or ornamental and the amount of herbicide that is required for weed control. Supplemental applications of fertilizer or herbicide may be required if the fertilizer-herbicide product does not supply enough fertilizer or herbicide to meet the fertility needs of the turfgrass or ornamental or the amount of herbicide needed for weed control.

Certain turfgrass fertilizer-herbicide products should be used with caution near ornamentals. Products that contain dicamba or atrazine can be absorbed by the roots of ornamentals and cause severe injury.

GUIDELINES FOR HERBICIDE USE

Certain herbicides may be used before or after turfgrass or ornamental establishment. For a list of ornamental and turfgrass herbicides please refer to Tables 3 and 4, respectively.

Preplant Herbicides

Emerged weeds may be killed prior to establishment with nonselective herbicides, such as glyphosate (Roundup and others) and glufosinate (Finale).

Newly-Established Turfgrasses—The growth and development of newly seeded or sprigged turfgrasses can be severely inhibited by weeds. Ideally, it would be advantageous to apply a preemergence herbicide immediately after seeding or sprigging. However, newly seeded and sprigged turfgrasses are much less tolerant to preemergence herbicides than established turfgrasses. Most preemergence herbicides cannot be safely used on newly-established turfgrasses. Weed control in newly-established turfgrasses can be accomplished by mowing and timely application of postemergence herbicides. Due to extensive soil preparation, many weed species, such as morningglories and sicklepod, which are not a problem in established turfgrasses, may be present in newly established turfgrasses. Mowing is an effective control for these non-traditional weeds.

Rule of Thumb: Delay the application until after three or four mowings, or until sprigged turfgrasses have rooted and are actively growing. Delaying the application allows the turfgrass seedlings or sprigs to become established, and improves their tolerance to postemergence herbicides.

Newly-Planted Ornamentals—Many preemergence herbicides may be applied to newly-planted ornamentals. Applications to new transplants should be delayed until the soil has settled and no cracks are present. Watering the site after planting is an excellent way to firm the soil around newly-planted ornamentals.

Established Landscape Sites—Numerous preemergence and postemergence herbicides are available for use in established turfgrass and ornamental plantings.

Preemergence herbicides are applied in the fall (ornamental plantings and non-overseeded turfgrasses) and in the spring according to the following schedule:

Fall—When temperatures drop to 55-60° F at night, apply preemergence herbicides to control winter annual weeds such as annual bluegrass, henbit, and common chickweed. Recommended dates are: September 1-15 in North Georgia; October 1-15 in South Georgia.

Spring—When day temperatures reach 65-70° F for four to five days, apply preemergence herbicides to control summer annual weeds, such as crabgrass and goosegrass. Recommended dates are: March 1-20 in North Georgia; February 15 - March 1 in South Georgia.

Postemergence Herbicides

Postemergence herbicides are applied after annual weeds emerge or when new growth of perennial weeds appear. Follow these guidelines to increase weed control and improve desirable plant tolerance:

1. On turfgrasses, apply postemergence herbicides in the fall and late spring months. Air temperatures are cooler at this time of year which results in better turfgrass tolerance to herbicides. Also, perennial weeds and many annual weeds are actively growing and are easier to control with postemergence herbicides at these times of the year.

2. Do not apply postemergence herbicides to turfgrasses, ornamentals, and weeds that are stressed due to high air temperatures or drought. Turfgrass tolerance to postemergence herbicides decreases at air temperatures greater than 90° F and when turfgrasses are drought-stressed. Under high air temperatures and high relative humidities, the tolerance of some ornamentals to postemergence grass control herbicides decreases. Many herbicide labels include warning statements relative to the use of the product at high air temperatures. Always follow the most restrictive warning that is on the label. Control is also poorer when herbicides are applied to environmentally stressed weeds than when applied to actively growing weeds.

3. Certain postemergence herbicides can delay the green-up process of warm-season turfgrasses. The risk of injury from postemergence herbicides is greater during the green-up process than when the turfgrass is fully dormant or actively growing. The herbicide label should be consulted to determine if applications during green-up are recommended. Repeated applications at low rates will generally improve control and turfgrass

Table 3. Examples of ornamental herbicides available for homeowner use

PREEMERGENCE HERBICIDES

Trade Name	Active Ingredients	Remarks
Surflan	oryzalin	Controls many annual grasses and small seeded broadleaf weeds. Excellent tank mixed with Roundup.
Preen	trifluralin	Weed control spectrum similar to that of Surflan. Applied prior to planting, and incorporate into soil.
Casoron	dichlobenil	Spectrum of weed control is limited, but controls many difficult weeds, such as bracken fern, Florida betony, and horsetails in many established woody ornamentals. Volatile, and should only be used in the late fall, winter or early spring.

POSTEMERGENCE HERBICIDES

Trade Name	Active Ingredients	Remarks
Segment	sethoxydim	Controls many actively growing grasses. Does not control broadleaf weeds or sedges. Can be used over the top of broadleaf ornamentals and centipedgrass.
Ornamec, Grass-B-Gon	fluazifop	Control spectrum similar to that of Vantage. Does not control broadleaf weeds or sedges. Can be used over the top of broadleaf ornamentals.
Scythe	potassium salts of fatty acids	Provides contact control of actively growing weeds. Does not control perennial type weeds. Do not allow spray to contact foliage of actively growing, desirable plants.
Roundup	glyphosate	Many formulations available. Provides control of most actively growing weeds. Control may take 10 to 14 days, but provides excellent control of annual perennial weeds. Provides no preemergence weed control Do not allow spray to contact foliage of actively growing, desirable plants.
Finale	glufosinate	Provides control of most emergent weeds. Does not control established perennial type weeds. Do not allow spray to contact foliage of actively growing, desirable plants.
Reward	Diquat	Provides control of most emergent weeds. Does not control established perennial type weeds. Do not allow spray to contact foliage of actively growing, desirable plants.

Table 4. Examples of turf herbicides available for homeowner use

PREEMERGENCE HERBICIDES

Trade Name	Active Ingredients	Remarks
Surflan	oryzalin	Controls many annual grasses and small seeded broadleaf weeds in established turf. Do not apply to newly seeded or new sprigged turf. Reseeding must be delayed after application.
Balan	benefin	See above.
Halts	pendimethalin	See above. Available under various names and formulations.
Bonus S., Purge, and various others	atrazine	Will control many annual weeds in warm-season grasses. many restrictions, make sure to read the label.

POSTEMERGENCE HERBICIDES

Trade Name	Active Ingredients	Remarks
Vantage	sethoxydim	Will control many annual grassy weeds in centipede and fine fescue turfgrass. Other turfgrasses will be severely injured by an application of this herbicide.
Crabgrass Killer and other names	MSMA	Provides good control of emerged annual grasses, bahaiagrass, dallisgrass, and fair control of nutsedge. Usually, temporary turf discoloration occurs after application of this herbicide. Do not apply to St. Augustine, centipede or carpetgrass.
Weed-B-Gon , and various others	2,4-D	Controls a broad spectrum of annual and perennial broadleaf weeds. Available in many formulations and combined with many other herbicides to increase spectrum of weed control. Can be used on most turfgrass, but depends on the formulation and other herbicides it is combined with. Make sure to read and follow the herbicide label.
Weed-B-Gon Chickweed, Clover and Oxalis Killer	triclopyr	Controls a broad spectrum of annual and perennial broadleaf weeds in tall fescue, Kentucky bluegrass and zoysiagrass. Restrictions on newly sodded furfgrass and reseeding turf.
Purge II	atrazine	Mainly used for the control of many winter annuals and annual bluegrass in dormant bermudagrass, centipedegrass and zoysia.
Image	imazaquin	Controls nutsedge(s), wild garlic and selected broadleaf weeds in bermudagrass, centipedegrass and zoysia. Do not apply to turfgrass emerging from dormancy or newly seeded or sprigged turfgrasses.
Manage	halosulfuron	Provides excellent control of sedges in all turfgrass species.
Basagran T/O	bentazon	Provides good control of yellow nutsedge and select broadleaf weed in all turfgrass species.

tolerance. Single applications at high rates generally cause more turfgrass injury than repeat applications at low rates. Refer to the label for information regarding repeat treatments.

4. Mowing schedules will need to be coordinated with postemergence herbicide applications. A general recommendation is to delay mowing 3 to 4 days prior to or after a postemergence herbicide application. The delay prior to treatment will increase the leaf surface area of the weed and result in better spray coverage and control. The delay after treatment is necessary to allow adequate time for herbicide absorption and translocation in the target weed species.

5. Do not apply postemergence herbicides immediately before rainfall or irrigation. Generally, the performance of most postemergence herbicides is better when rainfall or irrigation does not occur for 6 to 24 hours after an application. Rainfall or irrigation immediately after treatment can wash the herbicide from the treated foliage and decrease control.

6. Do not contact the foliage or green bark of ornamental plants with spray solutions that contain glyphosate, glufosinate, or diquat. These non-selective herbicides can easily penetrate green immature bark and cause injury to ornamentals. Additionally, glyphosate should not be sprayed at the base of ornamental plants to control suckers.

Note: This list of ornamental and turf herbicides is brief and incomplete. It is meant to expose new herbicide users to the horticultural field and to common herbicides that they many encounter. More information, and a more complete list may be found in the *Georgia Pest Management Handbook*, published by The University of Georgia.

Table 5. Common vegetable garden weeds and control methods

Weeds Controlled By:	trifluralin (Treflan)	DCPA (Dacthal)	Hand or Cultivation	Other Methods
ANNUAL WEEDS (from seed)				
crabgrass	E*	G*	X	X
goosegrass	E	G	X	X
PERENNIAL WEEDS (established plants)				
fescue	-	-	X	X
nutsedge	-	-	X	X
bermudagrass	-	-	X	X
johnsongrass	-	-	X	X
SMALL-SEEDED BROADLEAF WEEDS (from seed)				
carpetweed	E	E	X	X
chickweed	E	E	X	x
henbit	G	G	X	X
pigweed	E	G	X	X
ragweed	-	-	X	X
cutleaf evening primrose	-	-	X	X
common lambsquarters	E	-	X	X
LARGE-SEEDED BROADLEAF WEEDS (from seed)				
sicklepod	-	-	X	X
common cocklebur	-	-	X	X
morningglories	-	-	X	x
prickly sida	-	-	X	X

*E=Excellent control, G=Good control. If no symbol is shown, control by that method is poor. Where X is shown, control or suppression results.

VEGETABLE GARDEN WEED CONTROL

The choice of herbicides for weed control in vegetable gardens is very limited. Mechanical cultivation and the application of a weed-free mulch will generally control most weeds in home gardens. Herbicides can be used along with other practices as discussed earlier. A complete and current list of herbicides may be found in the *Georgia Pest Management Handbook Homeowner Edition.*

Table 6. Common vegetables and tolerance to Trifluralin and DCPA

Vegetable Crop	(Treflan)	(Dacthal, others)
Beans	X	X
Cabbage	X	X
Eggplant		X
Greens (collards, mustard, turnips)	X	X
Okra	X	
Onions		X
Peas, English	X	
Peas, Southern	X	X
Peppers	X	
Potatoes, Irish	X	X
Potatoes, Sweet		X
Tomatoes	X	

An X in the column indicates that the herbicide is labeled on the corresponding vegetable

Herbicides used in vegetable gardens usually will control grasses and certain small-seeded broadleaf weeds. Hard-to-kill perennial weeds, such as bermudagrass or nutsedge, may be controlled when the garden plot is fallow (not planted in a crop) with glyphosate (Roundup) in combination with cultivation. Moreover, with the limited selection of selective herbicides, certain weeds will have to be controlled by hand removal or cultivation. A list of common garden weeds and control methods are listed in Table 5.

Herbicides may temporarily reduce early vigor and growth of some vegetable plants, particularly under cool, wet conditions which often occur in early spring. Timing of the herbicide application and seed planting sequence may vary and can determine whether or not a temporary reduction of plant vigor will occur. The greatest potential for vigor reduction occurs when cool, wet weather follows an application of either a preemergence or preplant incorporated herbicide. Additionally, severe injury can occur by not following label directions for rate and application timing, using a herbicide on a species of vegetable not shown on the herbicide label, or by not correctly calibrating application equipment. The least potential for vigor reduction occurs when a labeled herbicide is used according to label directions. Herbicides are not universally labeled for use on all vegetable crops, because (among other reasons) different crops have differences in tolerance, just as weeds may vary in tolerance. Trifluralin and DCPA are labeled on many homeowner vegetable crops. Table 6 contains common vegetables and tolerance to trifluralin and DCPA.

Vegetable weed control tables are based on tables prepared by Dr. Stanley Culpepper.

Table 7. Examples of herbicides labeled for use in home fruit gardens

Crop	Herbicide Common Name	Small Package Product	Large Package Product
Apples, grapes, peaches, pecans, pears	glyphosate	Roundup	Roundup
	oryzalin	Surflan	Surflan
	simazine	-	Princep
	diuron	-	Karmex
	DCPA	Garden Weed Preventer	Dacthal
Blackberries	simazine	-	Princep
	oryzalin	Surflan	Surflan
Blueberries	simazine	-	Princep
	diuron	-	Karmex
	oryzalin	Surflan	Dacthal
Strawberries	DCPA	Garden Weed Preventer	Dacthal

- indicates that herbicide is not available in small packaging

HOME ORCHARD WEED CONTROL

The choice of herbicides for use in home orchards is limited primarily by availability of small packages. There is a wide variety of herbicides for use on fruit and nut crops, but the large packages for agricultural use are too costly and wasteful for homeowners (unless several neighbors jointly purchase and use the product).

Research has shown there is a great benefit in increased growth and vigor of woody plants when weed growth is eliminated from the base of the plant. Herbicides such as glyphosate are most often used for this purpose. However, herbicides such as glyphosate should not contact the foliage or green bark of desirable plants or severe injury can occur. Application is repeated only as necessary to suppress regrowth. In this situation, pre-emergence herbicides such as simazine (Princep) and oryzalin (Surflan) are commonly applied as a tank mix to provide control of annual weeds before they emerge. Also, maintaining a 2 to 4 inch layer of mulch to the drip line of fruit or nut trees can be used to suppress weed growth. Cultivation with hand or mechanical tools is generally discouraged, since the root system is very shallow and may be damaged, encouraging disease and insect attack. Reducing vegetative growth under fruit and nut trees also eliminates the need for mowing close to the plant, and reduces mower strikes against the tender bark.

For additional information refer to Circular 569, *Weed Control in Fruits and Nuts*, available from your local county Extension office.

DISCUSSION QUESTIONS

1. What is the defintion of a weed?

2. What are the 3 weed types?

3. Why is it important to know the difference between the life cycles of annual, perennial, and biennial weeds?

4. How can ornamental plants become weeds?

5. Tell how preventative practices can be effective in controlling weeds in the garden or landscape.

6. Discuss the difference between contact and systemic herbicides.

7. In what instances would preemergence herbicides be most effective in controlling weeds?

8. When are postemergence herbicides commonly used?

9. Name the factors that influence how well a herbicide will work.

10. Discuss how proper timing is important when using a herbicide for weed control.

11. What is the difference between selective and nonselective herbicide?

RESOURCES

Several weed identification guides created by the Georgia Cooperative Extension Service may be ordered for a nominal fee through Georgia County Extension Offices.

1. *Weeds of the Southern United States*.

2. *Weeds of Southern Turfgrasses*.

3. *Identification and Control of Weeds in Southern Ponds.*

Other excellent weed control manuals are available from any good bookstore and they include:

1. *Color Atlas of Turfgrass Weeds*, by McCarty, Everest, Hall, Murphy and Yelverton.

2. *Weeds of the West*, by Whitson, Burrill, Dewey, Cudney, Nelson, Lee, and Parker

3. *Weeds of the Northeast*, by Uva, Neal, and DiTomaso

8

Principles of Integrated Pest Management

L. Paul Guillebeau

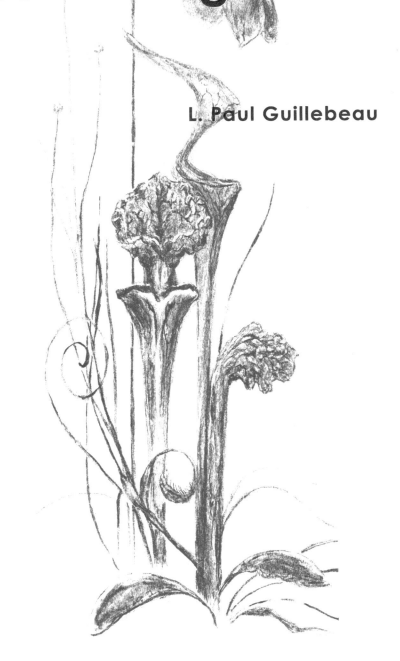

LEARNING OBJECTIVES

Define pest, IPM and understand the concepts of IPM.

Understand the concept of scouting for pest problems.

Understand what natural controls are available and their benefits and limitations.

Be familiar with the *Georgia Pest Management Handbook* and how to use it.

Learn the pesticide formulations and be able to read a pesticide label and know what the signal words are.

Know factors that can cause pesticide applications to fail to control pests.

Know why a sprayer should be calibrated, how to properly clean pesticide equipment, and how to safely store pesticide and the importance of safety equipment.

Be able to recognize pesticide poisoning symptoms and know who to call in a pesticide emergency.

Understand the impact of pesticides on the environment and the role and benefits of beneficial insects in the landscape.

TERMS TO KNOW

Acute effects illnesses or injuries that may appear immediately after exposure to a pesticide (usually within 24 hours).

Delayed effects illnesses or injuries that do not appear immediately (within 24 hours) after exposure to a pesticide.

Exposure coming into contact with a pesticide.

Host living plant or animal a pest depends on for survival.

Labeling pesticide product label and other accompanying materials that contain directions that pesticide users are legally required to follow.

Parasite organism that lives and feeds on or in another species, which it usually injures.

Pathogen any disease-producing organism.

Pesticide chemical used to destroy pests, control their activity, or prevent them from causing damage.

Precautionary statement pesticide labeling statement that alerts user to possible hazards from use of the pesticide product.

Prevention keeping a pest from becoming a problem.

Nonselective pesticide pesticide that is toxic to most plants and animals.

Selective pesticide pesticide that is more toxic to some kinds of plants and animals than others.

Systemic pesticide pesticide that is taken into the blood of an animal or sap of a plant. It kills the pest without harming the host.

Translocated pesticide that kills plants by being absorbed by leaves, stems, or roots and moving throughout the plant.

INTRODUCTION

Integrated pest management (IPM) is a program for managing pests that utilizes a variety of techniques to manage pest populations. Some components of IPM include plant health, host plant resistance, biological controls, cultural controls, and pesticides. Initially, IPM was developed in agricultural production to maximize efficiency. In more recent times, IPM is seen as the best way to balance the needs of pest management with protection of human health and the environment.

IPM Basics

The basic concepts of IPM depend on knowledge of the pest's biology and the ecology of the surrounding system.

There are four components to an IPM system:

Pest Identification

Monitoring

Control Guidelines

Methods of Prevention and Control

As a gardener develops an IPM program, he or she should consider the following questions.

1. What pests are most likely to cause problems in the yard and garden?

2. When are problems with these pests most likely to arise?

3. What factors attract these pests?

4. What can I do to make my plants or area less attractive to pests?

5. What nonchemical methods can be used to avoid or correct a pest problem?

6. What natural factors (e.g., biological control agents) are present that will help to manage pest populations?

7. What can I do to encourage the development of populations of biological control agents?

8. What treatment threshold(s) will determine if and when pesticides will be applied?

9. When is the best time to control the pest(s)?

10. What pesticide choices will minimize the risks to human health and the environment?

11. How can I best combine the components of my IPM program to manage pests most effectively and minimize the risks of pesticides?

We can use a common pest, the corn earworm, to illustrate the development of an IPM program.

1. Corn earworm.

2. Anytime of the gardening season, but more likely later in the season.

3. Corn earworms locate host plants through a variety of visual cues and plant volatiles.

4. Plant diversification in the garden can dampen or confuse the cues that attract corn earworms to the garden.

5. Cultural controls (e.g., tillage), mechanical controls (e.g., tying corn silks), and biological controls can help manage corn earworm populations.

6. Many predators and parasitoids attack corn earworm larvae.

7. Plant diversification and a water supply will help build beneficial populations.

8. Depending on the plant to be protected, the threshold might be based on the number of corn earworm larvae present or the amount of plant injury.

9. Corn earworm larvae are much easier to control when they are small.

10. Corn earworm larvae are susceptible to pesticides containing *Bacillus thuringiensis*. If this pesticide is appropriate for the situation, *B. thuringiensis* has little no impact on nontarget organisms. Otherwise, apply a pesticide that breaks down quickly or apply the pesticide as spot applications to minimize the impact on nontargets.

11. In this hypothetical situation, a gardener could:

a. Plant corn early,

b. Plant a variety of food plants and flowers,

c. Till to kill corn earworm pupae in the soil,

d. Check corn plants several times each week to monitor corn earworm larvae, corn injury, and biological control populations,

e. Apply *B. thuringiensis* when corn earworm larvae are small.

Although simplistic, this example shows how various

components are used to devise an IPM program. Other chapters in this book will help in devising an appropriate IPM program for the situation.

Pesticides play an integral role in many IPM situations. Keep in mind, however, that pesticides are only one of the tools in the IPM toolbox. Pesticides must be chosen and applied in the context of the overall IPM program. The wise use of pesticides can help manage pest populations with minimal threat to human health or the environment.

PESTS

A pest is anything that:

• competes with humans, domestic animals, or desirable plants for food or water,

• injures humans, animals, desirable plants, structures, or possessions

• spreads disease to humans, domestic animals wildlife, or desirable plants

• annoys humans or domestic animals.

Types of Pests

Types of pests include:

• Insects, such as roaches, termites, mosquitoes, aphids, beetles, fleas, and caterpillars,

• Insect-like organisms, such as mites, ticks, and spiders,

• Microbial organisms, such as bacteria, fungi, nematodes, viruses, and mycoplasmas,

• Weeds, which are any plants growing where they are not wanted,

• Mollusks, such as snails, slugs, and shipworms, and

• Vertebrates, such as rats, mice, other rodents, birds, fish, and snakes.

Most organisms are not pests. A species may be a pest in some situations and not in others. An organism should not be considered a pest until it is proven to be one. Categories of pests include:

• Continuous pests that are nearly always present and require regular control.

• Sporadic, migratory, or cyclical pests that require control occasionally or intermittently.

• Potential pests that do not require control under normal conditions, but may require control in certain circumstances.

Pest Identification

Accurate identification is the first step in an effective pest management program. Never attempt a pest control program before the identity of the pest has been established. The more information about the pest and the factors that influence its development and spread, the easier, more cost-effective, and more successful the pest control will be. Correct identification of a pest makes it possible to determine basic information about it, including its life cycle and the time that it is most susceptible to being controlled. To identify and control pests, one needs to know:

• The physical features of the pests likely to be encountered,

• Characteristics of the damage they cause,

• Their development and biology,

• Whether they are continuous, sporadic, or potential pests, and what the control goal is.

Pest Control

In considering whether pest control is necessary, remember:

• Control a pest only when it is causing or is expected to cause more harm than is reasonable to accept.

• Use a control strategy that will reduce the pest numbers to an acceptable level.

• Cause as little harm as possible to everything except the pest.

Even though a pest is present, it may not do much harm. It could cost more to control the pest than would be lost because of the pest's damage.

Pest Control Goals

In trying to control a pest, try to achieve one of these three goals, or some combination of them:

1. **Prevention**— keeping a pest from becoming a problem,

2. **Suppression**— reducing pest numbers or damage to an acceptable level, and

3. **Eradication**— destroying an entire pest population.

Prevention may be a goal when the pest's presence or abundance can be predicted in advance. Continuous pests, by definition, are usually very predictable. Sporadic and potential pests may be predictable if the circumstances or conditions are known that favor their presence as pests. For example, some plant diseases occur only under certain environmental conditions. If such conditions are present, steps can be taken to prevent the plant disease organisms from harming the desirable plants.

Suppression is a common goal in many pest situations. The intent is to reduce the number of pests to a level where the harm they cause is acceptable. Once a pest's presence is detected and control is deemed necessary, suppression and prevention often are joint goals. The right combination of control measures can often suppress the pests already present and prevent them from building up again to a level where they are causing unacceptable harm.

Eradication is a rare goal in outdoor pest situations because it is difficult to achieve. Usually the goal is prevention and/or suppression. Eradication is occasionally attempted when a foreign pest has been accidentally introduced, but is not yet established in an area. Such eradication strategies often are supported by the government. The Mediterranean fruit fly, gypsy moth, and fire ant control programs are examples.

Eradication is a more common goal indoors. Enclosed environments usually are smaller, less complex, and more easily controlled than outdoor areas. In many enclosed areas, such as dwellings, schools, office buildings, and food preparation areas, certain pests cannot or will not be tolerated.

Threshold Levels

Thresholds are the levels of pest populations at which pest control action should be taken to prevent the pests in an area from causing unacceptable injury or harm. Thresholds may be based on aesthetic, health, or economic considerations. These levels, which are known as "action thresholds," have been determined for many pests.

A threshold often is set at the level where the economic losses caused by pest damage, if the pest population continued to grow, would be greater than the cost of controlling the pests. These types of action thresholds are called "economic thresholds." For example, when the number of insects on a particular crop exceeds a given quantity, an insecticide application to prevent economic damage could be justified.

In some pest control situations, the threshold level is zero: even a single pest in such a situation is unreasonably harmful. For example, the presence of any rodents in food processing facilities forces action. In homes, people generally take action to control some pests, such as rodents or roaches, even if only one or a few have been seen.

Pest Monitoring

Regular monitoring or scouting can answer several important questions:

• What kinds of pests are present?

• Are the numbers great enough to warrant control?

• When is the right time to begin control?

• Have the control efforts successfully reduced the number of pests?

Monitoring of insect, insect-like, mollusk, and vertebrate pests usually is done by trapping or by scouting. Monitoring of weed pests usually is done by visual inspection. Monitoring for microbial pests is done by looking for the injury or damage they cause.

Monitoring also can include checking environmental conditions in the area. Temperature and moisture levels, especially humidity, are often important clues in predicting when a pest outbreak will occur or will hit threshold levels.

Useful tools for pest monitoring include: notebook, hand lens of at least 10x magnification, collection bags and bottles to hold specimens for identification, small forceps, sweep net, plastic coated pest flash cards and a beating sheet. Place the sheet under the leaves of the plant and tap or shake the branch or plant to dislodge the pests onto the sheet. This is helpful in determining whether or not a pest is present on the plant). Yellow and blue sticky cards are helpful in determining whether certain pest populations are increasing. Place the cards in areas of suspected infestation and change regularly (yellow for whiteflies and blue for thrips).

Steps in Pest Monitoring

1. Identify the pest.

2. Identify the current stage in the pest's life cycle.

3. Note the location(s) of the pest.

4. Determine the number of insects, weeds or disease infected plants.

5. Inventory the environment surrounding the pest, as well as the entire area that might be affected by control actions. This might include chemically sensitive family members or neighbors. Remember to look for beneficial

and non-target plants, insects and animals.

6. Identify Key Hosts. These are plants or other hosts that have a history of problems or in some other way indicate the presence of the pest.

7. Identify existing damage from the pest.

8. Keep accurate records of findings and controls, if used. The same problems may appear on the same hosts year after year. Good records will help in timing future control measures.

Avoiding Harmful Effects

Pest control involves more than simply identifying a pest and using a control tactic. The treatment site, whether it is outdoors or indoors, usually contains other living organisms: people, animals, and plants and nonliving surroundings: air, water, structures, objects, and surfaces. All of these could be affected by pest control measures. Unless the possible effects are considered on the entire system within which the pest exists, a pest control effort could cause harm or lead to continued or new pest problems. Rely on good judgment and, when pesticides are part of the strategy, on the pesticide labeling.

Most treatment sites are disrupted to some degree by pest control strategies. The actions of every type of organism or component sharing the site usually affect the actions and well-being of many others. When the balance is disrupted, certain organisms may be destroyed or reduced in number and others — sometimes the pests — may dominate.

To solve pest problems:

• identify the pest or pests and determine whether control is warranted for each,

• determine pest control goal(s),

• know what control tactics are available,

• evaluate the benefits and risks of each tactic or combination of tactics,

• choose a strategy that will be most effective and will cause the least harm to people and the environment,

• use each tactic in the strategy correctly,

• observe local, state, and federal regulations that apply to the situation.

The strategy chosen will depend on the pest identified and the kind and amount of control needed.

Natural Controls

Some natural forces act on all organisms, causing the populations to rise and fall. These natural forces act independently of humans and may either help or hinder pest control. It may not be possible to alter the action of natural forces on a pest population, but be aware of their influence and take advantage of them when possible. Natural forces that affect pest populations include climate, natural enemies, natural barriers, availability of shelter, and food and water supplies.

Climate—Weather conditions, especially temperature, day length, and humidity, affect pest activity and rate of reproduction. Pests may be killed or suppressed by rain, freezing temperatures, drought, or other adverse weather. Climate also affects pests indirectly by influencing the growth and development of their hosts. A population of plant-eating pests is related to growth of its host plants. Unusual weather conditions can change normal patterns so that increased or decreased damage results.

Natural enemies—Birds, reptiles, amphibians, fish, and mammals feed on some pests and help control their numbers. Many predatory and parasitic insect and insect-like species feed on other organisms, some of which are pests. Pathogens often suppress pest populations.

Geographic barriers—Features such as mountains and large bodies of water restrict the spread of many pests. Other features of the landscape can have similar effects.

Food and water supply—Pest populations can thrive only as long as their food and water supply lasts. Once the food source — plant or animal — is exhausted, the pests die or become inactive. The life cycle of many pests depends on the availability of water.

Shelter—The availability of shelter can affect some pest populations. Overwintering sites and places to hide from predators are important to the survival of some pests.

Applied Controls

Unfortunately, natural controls often do not control pests quickly or completely enough to prevent unacceptable injury or damage. Then other control measures must be used. Those available include: host resistance, cultural control, mechanical control, sanitation, chemical control, and biological control.

Host resistance—Some plants, animals, and structures resist pests better than others. Some varieties of plants, wood, and animals are resistant to certain pests. Use of resistant types, when available, helps keep pest populations below harmful levels by making conditions less favorable for the pests.

Host resistance works in three ways:

1. Chemicals in the host repel the pest or prevent the pest from completing its life cycle.

2. The host is more vigorous or tolerant than other varieties and thus less likely to be seriously damaged by pest attacks.

3. The host has physical characteristics that make it more difficult to attack.

Cultural control—Cultural practices sometimes are used to reduce the numbers of pests that are attacking cultivated plants. These practices alter the environment, the condition of the host plant, or the behavior of the pest to prevent or suppress an infestation. They disrupt the normal relationship between the pest and the host plant and make the pest less likely to survive, grow, or reproduce. Common cultural practices include rotating crops, cultivating the soil, varying time of planting or harvesting, planting trap crops, adjusting row width, and pruning, thinning, and fertilizing cultivated plants.

Mechanical (physical) control—Devices, machines, and other methods used to control pests or alter their environment are called mechanical or physical controls. Traps, screens, barriers, fences, and nets sometimes can be used to prevent the spread of pests into an area.

Lights, heat, and refrigeration can alter the environment enough to suppress or eradicate some pest populations. Altering the amount of water, including humidity, can control some pests, especially insects and disease agents.

Sanitation—Sanitation practices help to prevent and suppress some pests by removing the pests or their sources of food and shelter. Urban and industrial pests can be reduced by improving cleanliness, eliminating pest harborage, and increasing the frequency of garbage pickup. Carryover of agricultural pests from one planting to the next can be reduced by removing crop residues.

Other forms of sanitation that help prevent pest spread include using mulches, pest-free seeds or transplants and decontaminating equipment, animals, and other possible carriers before allowing them to enter a pest-free area or leave an infested area.

Chemical control—Pesticides are chemicals used to destroy pests, control their activity, or prevent them from causing damage. Some pesticides either attract or repel pests. Chemicals that regulate plant growth or remove foliage also are classified as pesticides. Pesticides are generally the fastest way to control pests. In some instances, they are the only tactic available.

Biological control—Biological control involves the use of natural enemies — parasites, predators, and pathogens. Supplement this natural control by releasing more of a pest's enemies into the target area or by introducing new enemies that were not in the area before. Biological control usually is not eradication. The degree of control fluctuates. There is a time lag between pest population increase and the corresponding increase in natural controls. But, under proper conditions, sufficient control can be achieved to eliminate the threat to the plant or animal to be protected.

Biological control also includes methods by which the pest is biologically altered, as in the production and release of large numbers of sterile males and the use of pheromones or juvenile hormones.

Pheromones can be useful in monitoring pest populations. Placed in a trap, for example, they can attract the insects in a sample area so that pest numbers can be estimated. Pheromones also can be a control tool. Sometimes a manufactured copy of the pheromone that a female insect uses to attract males can be used to confuse males and prevent mating, resulting in lower numbers of pests. Applying juvenile hormones to an area can reduce pest numbers by keeping some immature pests from becoming normal, reproducing adults.

Pest Control Failures

Sometimes even though a pesticide was applied, the pest has not been controlled. Review the situation to try to determine what went wrong. There are several possible reasons for the failure of chemical pest control.

Pest Resistance—Pesticides fail to control some pests because the pests are resistant to the pesticides. Consider this when planning pest control programs that rely on the use of pesticides. Rarely does any pesticide kill all the target pests. Each time a pesticide is used, it selectively kills the most susceptible pests. Some pests avoid the pesticide. Others withstand its effects. Pests that are not destroyed may pass along to their offspring the trait that allowed them to survive.

When one pesticide is used repeatedly in the same place against the same pest, the surviving pest population may be more resistant to the pesticide than the original population. The opportunity for resistance is greater when a pesticide is used over a wide geographic area or when a pesticide is applied repeatedly to a rather small area where pest populations are isolated. A pesticide that leaves a residue which gradually loses its effectiveness over time will increase its resistance. Rotating pesticides may help reduce the development of pest resistance.

Other Reasons for Failure—Not every pesticide failure is caused by pest resistance. Make sure the correct pesticide was used and the correct dose and that it was applied correctly. Sometimes a pesticide application fails to control a pest because the pest was not identified correctly and the wrong pesticide was chosen. Other applications fail because the pesticide was not applied at an appropriate time — the pest may not have been in the area during the application or it may have been in a life cycle stage or location where it was not susceptible to the pesticide. Also remember that the pests that are present may be part of a new infestation that developed after the chemical was applied.

Georgia Pest Management Handbook

Published annually, this manual gives current information on selection, application, and safe use of pest control chemicals. The Handbook has recommendations for pest control on farms, around homes, urban areas, recreational areas, and other environments in which pests may occur. Cultural, biological, physical, and other types of control are recommended where appropriate.

Recommendations are based on information on the manufacturer's label and on performance data from Georgia research and Extension field tests. Because environmental conditions and methods of application by growers vary widely, suggested use does not imply that performance of the pesticide will always conform to the safety and pest control standards indicated by experimental data.

The *Georgia Pest Management Handbook* is intended to be used only as a guide. Specific rates and application methods are on the pesticide label. Refer to the label when applying any pesticide.

INTRODUCTION TO PESTICIDES

The term "pesticide" is a broad term that refers to any substance used to manage pests. Many pesticides can be identified by the "-icide" suffix. Insecticides control insects. Herbicides control plants. Fungicides control fungi. Not all pesticides carry the "-icide" suffix. Other general names include disinfectants, growth regulators (prevent or enhance development), pheromones (attractants, usually used in traps), and repellents.

Note: the use of product names as examples is not an endorsement of those products.

Grouping Pesticides Based on the Source

Inorganic pesticides come from minerals, such as boron, copper, or sulfur. Other inorganic pesticides, such as lead arsenate, were once widely used in the cotton and fruit production; this practice was discontinued as safer products became available. Compounds made with copper, sulfur, or boron (e.g., boric acid) are commonly used as pesticides today.

Naturally derived organic pesticides are natural compounds that come directly from plants or micro-organisms. Pyrethrins, for example, come directly from chrysanthemums. Pyrethrins are active ingredients in wasp and hornet sprays. Neem is another common example of a plant derived organic pesticide. Spinosad is a fermentation product from actinomycete bacteria.

Synthetic organic pesticides are man-made compounds with an organic chemical structure. In some cases, synthetic organic pesticides are based on naturally occurring chemicals. For example, pyrethroids are active ingredients in many common insecticides. Their structure is modeled after pyrethrins.

Microbial pesticides include bacteria, fungi, nematodes, and viruses. Most of these products can be applied with conventional application equipment. In some situations, certain microbials can be established in the lawn or garden. Most of the time, however, repeated applications will be necessary in response to pest problems. *B. thuringiensis* is the most common microbial pesticide. Various strains are effective against caterpillars, mosquitoes, or beetles. In general, microbials are safer than other types of pesticides. Remember that the effectiveness of a microbial depends on a living organism. Buy fresh products and protect them from extreme temperatures.

Grouping Pesticides Based on Activity or Timing

Protectants are applied to plants, animals, structures, or products to prevent pest injury. For example, termiticides are applied to buildings before termite infestation occurs. To be effective, most fungicides must be applied before the plants or infected. In most situations, the application of prophylactic pesticides is contrary to IPM principles, but sometimes it is necessary to apply a pesticide before the pest causes damage.

Contact poisons work by simply touching the pest. Most synthetic organic insecticides work this way. Insects are killed when they walk across a leaf or other surface that has been treated with the insecticide.

Stomach poisons must be eaten by the pest. These pesticides are often more compatible with biological controls. Caterpillars have to eat B. thuringiensis before it will kill them. Baits typically contain stomach poisons.

Systemics are absorbed by the plant or animal that is being protected. The pesticide will be moved through the plant. Some systemics are only transported locally; others move throughout the entire plant or animal. The pest is killed when it feeds on the animal or plant. Systemic pesticides are often combined with fertilizers.

Translocated herbicides are moved throughout the plant after they are applied to leaves, roots, or stems. The entire plant is killed. Glyphosate (e.g., RoundUp) is a common example.

Selective pesticides are less likely to harm nontarget organisms. An herbicide that contains only 2,4 D will kill most broadleaf plants, but it will not kill grasses. Most microbial insecticides are only effective against certain kinds of insect pests.

Nonselective pesticides affect a wide range of similar organisms. Most insecticides are nonselective. For example, carbaryl (e.g., Sevin) can be used to control pest insects, but it will also kill bees and many beneficial species. Glyphosate (e.g., RoundUp) will kill or injure nearly every type of plant.

Fumigants are gases that kill pests when they are inhaled or absorbed. Very few pesticides are available as fumigants. Some "bug bombs" products are fumigants.

Preplant pesticides are applied before the crop is planted. Preplant pesticides may be part of a combination product that also contains fertilizer.

Preemergence herbicides are applied before the weeds emerge. Some preemergent herbicides are applied before the crop emerges; some are applied after the crop emerges.

Postemergence herbicides are used after the target plant emerges.

When and Where to Apply Pesticides

The timing and placement of pesticide applications are critical. Follow the label directions, the advice of the County Extension Agent and the *Georgia Pest Management Handbook*. Many pesticides work well at very low rates. There is often great temptation to use more pesticide that the label indicates. It is illegal to exceed the label rate, and damage to nontarget plants or animals is likely to occur.

Pesticides work best when they are applied at specific times in the pests' life cycle. Most pesticides are more effective when the pests are small. Insect growth regulators have little or no effect on adult insects. It is important to be familiar with the pesticide activity and the biology of the pest.

Be careful to treat only the intended target. Some pesticides (e.g., 2,4 D) can harm nontarget organisms at very low concentrations. If an insect or mite pest occurs on the underside of leaves, pesticide applications to the upper side of leaves may be ineffective. Avoid pesticide applications when the wind speed or direction will carry the pesticide from the target area. Some pesticide labels will prohibit applications above a certain wind speed. Some pesticides are likely to leach from sandy soils. Do not apply pesticides when rain is imminent. The pesticide will be less effective, and the pesticide is more likely to run off into waterways or leach into groundwater. Read the pesticide label and consult the appropriate *Georgia Pest Management Handbook*.

Factors that Affect Pesticide Activity

Human error is a common reason for pesticide failures. If the pesticide does not provide satisfactory control, review these questions.

1. Was the problem correctly identified? It may seem reasonable to attribute yellow leaves to an aphid infestation if these insects are present. However, if low soil fertility is causing the problem, an insecticide will not help. If you are unsure of the source of the problem, consult your Extension agent.

2. Did you use the appropriate pesticide? Check the label and consult Extension recommendations. B. thuringiensis is very effective against some kinds of caterpillars, but it has little or effect on mites. The homeowner edition of the *Georgia Pest Management Handbook* contains the recommendations of Extension specialists. Be sure to refer to the current edition.

3. Was the pesticide applied properly? Check the pesticide label to be sure you applied the proper rate. Never apply more pesticide than the label directs.

4. Was the pesticide delivered to the target site at the appropriate time? Many weeds are difficult to control if they are large. Some insect and mite pests occur in areas that are difficult to treat effectively (e.g., on the underside of leaves).

Soil type can be an important factor in pesticide decisions. You may need to use higher pesticide rates in soils high in organic matter or clay. Pesticides are more likely to leach from sandy soils. Read the pesticide label and consult your Extension agent.

Weather conditions can reduce the effectiveness of pesticides. If it rains before pesticide residues dry, the active ingredient is likely to be carried away. Sunlight breaks down some pesticides (e.g., pyrethrins) quickly. Wind increases the likelihood of drift, and it accelerates the loss of some pesticides.

Pesticide resistance occurs when resistant traits become common in the pest population. Pesticide applications rarely kill every pest. The more sensitive individuals are more likely to die, and the more resistant individuals are more likely to live and reproduce. The resistant traits may be passed to their offspring, and the next generation has fewer individuals that are sensitive to the pesticide. After repeated cycles, many individuals in the population may have the resistant traits, and the pesticide no longer provides satisfactory control. Resistance to one pesticide usually conveys some resistance to other pesticides in the same chemical class. An IPM program makes resistance less likely because the pests are subjected to a variety of control methods.

Pesticide Formulations

A pesticide formulation is a combination of active ingredients and inert ingredients.

Active ingredients are the substances that control the pest. A product may have one or more active ingredients. The active ingredients are always specified on the pesticide label.

Inert ingredients are added to make the pesticide more effective or easier to use. An inert ingredient may be added to make the pesticide mix with water or to retard breakdown by sunlight. Other inert ingredients added to make the pesticide stick or spread on leaves. The inert ingredients are usually not listed on the pesticide label.

A particular active ingredient is usually available in several different formulations. Liquid and solid formulations are both common. Some products are ready to use, and others must be diluted with water or a petroleum

solvent. The label will tell you how to use a pesticide formulation. Each formulation has advantages and disadvantages that make it appropriate for a particular situation. Consider which formulation is best for your circumstances before you buy the pesticide. You may have to purchase additional equipment to apply a particular formulation. The lists below include only the most common pesticide formulations. The pesticide label will provide additional information.

Liquid formulations—Emulsifiable concentrates (E or EC) are the most common liquid formulation. They are mixed with water to form an emulsion. Most ECs appear oily before they are mixed with water; the resulting water emulsion is usually white. If a number appears before the letter abbreviation, the number indicates the number of pounds of active ingredient per gallon of product. For example, "4EC" indicates four pounds of active ingredient per gallon.

• Advantages: mixes well with water, requires little agitation.

• Disadvantages: more likely to injure some plants, more likely to penetrate the skin directly.

Ready to use (RTU) aerosols— are prepackaged liquid pesticides. They may be a premixed EC or some other formulation.

• Advantages: no mixing or measuring required, easy disposal.

• Disadvantages: very expensive relative to most other pesticide products, many aerosols are flammable.

Dry formulations—Dusts (D) are usually ready to use without mixing or dilution. A powdered dry inert (e.g., talc, clay, or ash) is combined with the active ingredient(s). The amount of active ingredient is usually less than ten percent. The abbreviation "10D" indicates that product has ten percent active ingredient. Do not mix dust formulations with water.

• Advantages: no mixing, little or no waste.

• Disadvantages: leave a visible residue, may easily drift into a person's breathing zone (wear a dust mask).

Granular (G) formulations—are made by combining the active ingredient(s) with coarse granules of an inert (e.g., ground corncobs, clay, or nutshells). The concentration of active ingredient may be as high as 40 percent. The abbreviation "20G" means the product is 20 percent active ingredient. Granules are usually applied dry.

• Advantages: no mixing, spills are usually easy to clean up.

• Disadvantages: applications usually limited to horizontal surfaces or plant whorls.

Wettable powders (WP)—are finely ground particles made to mix with water. Most wettable powders are much more concentrated than dust formulations; the active ingredient(s) are commonly more than 50% of the WP formulation. The abbreviation 50WP means the product is 50% active ingredient.

• Advantages: usually safer for plants and man than EC formulations.

• Disadvantages: water mixture requires regular agitation to maintain suspension, leaves visible residue on sprayed surfaces.

Baits (B)— combine a pesticide with some food or other attractive substance. Bait products are commonly used for slugs/snails, rats/mice, and some insects. The concentration of active ingredient is usually less than five percent.

• Advantages: less active ingredient usually needed, less area usually treated with pesticide.

• Disadvantages: nontarget animals may be attracted to the bait. Pets may eat slug/snail bait, and other rodents may eat baits intended for rats or mice.

Pesticide Labeling

The pesticide "label" is the information attached to the pesticide container. Other information may also come with the pesticide product, or the pesticide label may refer the user to other information. This body of information is the "labeling". Federal and state regulations require all pesticide users to follow the directions on the pesticide label. Failure to follow label directions increases the risks of the pesticide and may result in civil and/or criminal penalties.

NEVER recommend that a client ignore or deviate from the pesticide labeling.

Sometimes pesticide labeling is confusing. However, it is important to understand all of the labeling information before using a pesticide or before recommending a pesticide to someone else. If one does not understand the labeling, he or she should consult the Extension agent or the Georgia Department of Agriculture. The Georgia Department of Agriculture regulates the sale and application of pesticides in the state.

All pesticides sold in the United States must be registered with the U.S. Environmental Protection Agency (EPA). The EPA requires that certain information must appear on all pesticide products. Consider this information before deciding which pesticide product is appropriate for the situation.

Signal words indicate the acute toxicity of the pesticide product. Acute toxicity is the likelihood that a single overexposure to the pesticide will injure a person or pet. Acute toxicity is related to the weight of a person or animal. The amount of pesticide needed to injure a child or pet may be much less than the exposure that would injure an adult.

"DANGER-POISON" (along with the skull and crossbones) appears on a pesticide product that can kill a person in very low doses. The amount of a DANGER-POISON pesticide required to kill a 180-pound man may be less than 4000 milligrams (one extra-strength headache capsule is usually 500 mg). The amount to kill a child or pet would be much less.

"DANGER" without the word "POISON" indicates a pesticide that can cause irreversible eye damage and/or severe injury to the skin.

Most DANGER-POISON and DANGER pesticides are not available to the general public. The Extension Service never recommends DANGER-POISON or DANGER pesticides for use around the home.

"WARNING" indicates a pesticide of intermediate toxicity. They may still cause severe injury, but greater exposure would be required.

"CAUTION" indicates a pesticide of low toxicity. Exposure is much less likely to cause injury.

The EPA has offered some pesticide companies the option of deleting the CAUTION signal word if the acute toxicity of the product is shown to be very low. These pesticide products will have no signal word.

Brand names are the company's identifier for that particular product. Usually the brand name will be the most prominent word on the product. "RoundUp" is the brand name for one herbicide that contains the active ingredient glyphosate. Other products may have the same ingredients with a different brand name and price.

Active ingredient(s) must be listed on the pesticide label along with their concentration. The ingredients may be listed by a complicated chemical name or a common name (e.g., carbaryl or glyphosate.) Regulations do not require identification of the inert ingredients, but the percentage of inerts must be indicated.

The formulation will be identified on the pesticide label. It is helpful to know the common abbreviations for various formulations, but the information is also specified on the pesticide label.

Hazards to Humans (and Domestic Animals) will provide information about specific risks associated with the pesticide. Common statements include "Harmful if absorbed through skin" or "Avoid contact with skin or eyes." This section will indicate precautions and protective clothing needed to avoid injury. The protective clothing as directed by the pesticide labeling MUST be worn. If one is unable or unwilling to wear the specified protective gear, do not buy that pesticide.

Environmental hazards will also be specified. This section will caution the user about risks to birds, fish, bees, or other wildlife. The user will also be advised about other environmental concerns, such as potential leaching.

Physical and Chemical Hazards will be indicated for some pesticides. Some pesticides are highly flammable, or they may be corrosive to certain types of metals. Common statements include "Keep away from open flame" or "Do not incinerate".

Statement of Practical Treatment or First Aid instructions will be included on every pesticide label. Be familiar with these directions before using the pesticide. Quick action may be necessary if someone is exposed, and inappropriate action could exacerbate the injury. For example, the label may advise against vomiting is a person swallows the pesticide. This section may also contain important information for medical personnel. Take the label along when taking a victim to seek medical attention.

Directions for Use will tell the applicator how to use the product safely and effectively. This section contains the following information.

1. Where the pesticide may be used. It is illegal to apply a pesticide to a use site that is not indicated on the label. If a pesticide indicates beans but not corn, that pesticide may not be used on corn even if the same pest is on both crops. Some labels will indicate some specific plants and a generic group (e.g., daffodils and other flowering plants). The product may be legally used on any plant in the generic group; the manufacturer has tested the product on the specified plant. Before spraying a large number of unspecified plants, test the product on one or two plants.

2. How much pesticide may be used. The labeling will tell how to mix the pesticide and indicate a maximum rate. The directions may tell how many teaspoons are needed for a gallon or how many pounds are needed for 100 gallons. An Extension agent can help calculate how much pesticide is needed.

3. How often the pesticide may be applied. The labeling will indicate how often the pesticide may be applied and/or the maximum number of applications.

It is illegal and dangerous to apply a pesticide at a rate or frequency higher than the label maximum. The pesticide may legally be applied at a rate or frequency below the labeling directions, but the pesticide may not be effective. Do not advise a client to use less than the label rate before consulting with the Extension agent.

4. Other restrictions. Most pesticides will indicate a reentry interval and/or a preharvest interval. Do not allow anyone to enter the treated area before the reentry interval expires. If the labeling does not specify a reentry interval, stay out of the treated area until the spray dries completely. Do not consume a food treated with pesticide until the preharvest interval expires. If the labeling does not indicate a preharvest interval, the food may be eaten right away, but it should be washed thoroughly.

5. Pests that the product will control. The labeling will indicate which pests can be expected to be controlled with that product if it is applied at the specified label rate. It is legal to apply the pesticide for pests that are not on the label if the use site is indicated on the label. However, the product may not be effective.

6. Storage and disposal. Some pesticide labels will include information about proper storage and disposal. In many cases, however, the directions provide little specific advice.

Application Equipment

The proper application equipment will help in applying a pesticide safely and more effectively. A pesticide may be applied with any equipment that is not prohibited on the label. Be sure to select and maintain the appropriate application equipment.

Hand or backpack sprayers for liquid pesticides are relatively inexpensive and easy to operate. Operation of these sprayers is uncomplicated. Most applicators can repair the equipment with parts available through local retailers. Look for a tank with a large opening. Select a tank size that is appropriate for the situation. Remember that a five-gallon sprayer full of water and pesticide weighs about 40 pounds. If it is necessary to mix and carry several gallons of pesticide solution, a backpack sprayer may be a better choice.

Test the sprayer with water at the beginning of each season. Check for leaks and a regular spray pattern. Flush the tank and lines with water after each use. It may be necessary to wash the sprayer out with water and detergent when switching pesticides. Apply the wastewater to a use site indicated on the pesticide label. NEVER dump the wastes down the drain or into a sewer.

Phenoxy pesticides (e.g., 2,4 D) are active in very low concentrations. It is best not to apply other pesticides with sprayer that has been used with phenoxy herbicides. Many people keep one sprayer for phenoxy herbicides, another sprayer for other herbicides, and a third sprayer for insecticides and fungicides.

Dusters may be as simple as a shaker can. Other types of dust application equipment may include a bellows or fan to distribute the dusts. This type of equipment is usually very simple to operate and maintain. Be careful to keep the pesticide dust off of the skin and nontarget areas.

Granular applicators may be a shaker can or rolling spreader equipment. Drop spreaders distribute pesticide directly below the spreader. Rotary spreaders throw the granules over a wider area.

USING PESTICIDES SAFELY

Pesticide safety begins even before purchasing a pesticide. First, consider nonchemical options that may manage the pest problem. Sometimes nonchemical options are less effective than chemical pesticides, but the risks of pesticides are almost always greater.

Read the pesticide labeling. If one is unwilling or unable to follow the labeling directions, do not buy that product. Look for a CAUTION pesticide that is recommended for the situation. If no CAUTION product is recommended or available, it may be necessary to buy a WARNING pesticide. Cooperative Extension does not recommend the purchase of a DANGER pesticide for household use.

Do not transport pesticide in the passenger compartment of a vehicle. Secure the package so it will not break or leak. Do not transport pesticide near food, feed, clothing, or other household products.

Store pesticides in a secure area out of the reach of children and pets. Keep bottles of liquid pesticide in a plastic tray so that any leaks will be contained. Protect pesticides from extreme temperatures, and protect dry pesticides from excessive humidity.

Pesticide Toxicity

Acute toxicity is the likelihood of injury from a single or short-term exposure. If a person becomes ill shortly after applying a pesticide, consider acute toxicity. Common symptoms include nausea, dizziness, and headache. Refer to the pesticide label and consider how the person may have been exposed. It may be necessary to seek medical attention. Poison Control (1-800-222-1222) can advise about human or animal exposure

Chronic toxicity is the likelihood of injury after repeated or long-term exposure. One cigarette or a single alcoholic drink is unlikely to cause injury, but long-term exposure can cause serious health problems. Repeated exposure to small amounts of pesticide may cause illness. There is little specific information about the long-term effects of pesticide exposure. The signal word (e.g., WARNING) on a pesticide label is based only on acute toxicity; it provides no information about chronic risks.

Pesticides are most dangerous as concentrates. Be especially careful when measuring and mixing pesticides.

The EXTOXNET EXtension TOXicology NETwork web site is an excellent source for additional information about pesticide toxicity and environmental risks.

Routes of Exposure

Skin is the most common route of pesticide exposure. Some pesticide formulations (e.g., emulsifiable concentrates) can penetrate the skin directly, and many pesticides can penetrate through a wound.

Swallowing pesticide can be very serious. NEVER store any pesticide in a food or drink container. Pesticides in soft drink bottles have killed both children and adults. Be sure that implements used to measure or mix pesticides are not confused with kitchen equipment.

Inhaling pesticides can cause serious injury. Keep out of pesticide drift and pay attention to changes in wind direction.

Eye injury can occur very quickly with some pesticides. Always pour pesticides below the waist.

Inattention and poor work habits cause most pesticide exposure. When handling pesticides, always wash hands before eating, drinking, using tobacco, or using the toilet. Keep people and pets out of the spray area. Close house and car windows before applying pesticide. Be careful not to carry pesticide indoors on shoes or clothes.

First Aid for Pesticide Exposure

Act quickly if someone is exposed to pesticide. Be familiar with the first aid directions on the pesticide label.

Skin—Rinse the exposed area with clean water immediately. Wash the area with soap and water as possible.

Swallowed pesticide—Consult the pesticide label and call Poison Control (1-800-222-1222) immediately.

Inhaled pesticide—Move the victim to fresh air. If the symptoms do not abate right away, seek medical attention.

Pesticide in eye—Rinse the eye gently with clean water for at least 15 minutes. Seek medical attention.

Protecting the Body from Pesticides

The pesticide label will provide some precautions; follow these label directions. Also, use common sense to minimize pesticide exposure.

Clothing—At a minimum, wear a long-sleeved shirt, long pants, shoes, socks, and gloves. Wear a wide-brimmed hat if spraying overhead.

Gloves are the most important piece of protective equipment because most pesticide exposure occurs on the hands and forearms. Wear plastic or rubber gloves that are long enough to protect the wrists. Cloth or leather gloves do not prevent pesticide exposure. Keep shirtsleeves outside the gloves unless spraying overhead. When wearing reusable gloves, wash them before removing the gloves.

Wear rubber boots or shoe covers that repel liquids. Leather or cloth shoes will absorb pesticides. Wear pant legs outside of the boots.

Wear any additional protective clothing as directed by the pesticide label.

Wash the entire body with soap and water in the shower after completing a pesticide task. Wash the clothes separately from other laundry and dry them outside. Throw away any clothes that are heavily contaminated with pesticide.

Pesticide Spills

Dry spills are relatively easy to clean up. Scoop up the pesticide with a shovel or paper. In most cases, the pesticide can still be used as planned.

Be prepared for spills of liquid pesticide. DO NOT hose down a pesticide spill. For spills on a hard surface, use rubber/plastic gloves and other protective equipment indicated on the pesticide label. An absorbent material, like cat litter, can be used to soak up the spill. Scoop the absorbent material and pesticide into a heavy-duty garbage bag. Clean the contaminated area with detergent and apply the absorbent material again. Scoop the material into the garbage bag. Place the garbage bag into the outdoor garbage can and throw the materials away with other household trash.

If a liquid pesticide spills on soil, usually it is not necessary to take any action. Remove the contaminated soil and dispose of it with household trash.

If one is unsure of how to clean up a pesticide spill, call CHEMTREK 24 hours a day (800-424-9300) or the local Extension agent.

Pesticide Disposal

Do not buy more pesticide than needed. Measure pesticides carefully to avoid excessive leftover pesticide mix. Apply the leftover pesticide mix to a site indicated in the pesticide labeling. Do not exceed the label rate.

Give excess usable pesticide to someone who will use it properly. The Extension agent may be able to assist with giving away unwanted pesticide.

If the pesticide cannot be used by anyone, carefully add some absorbent material (e.g., cat litter) to the container, or pour the pesticide into a leak-proof, disposable container with some absorbent material. When all of the liquid is absorbed, throw away the materials with other household trash.

Rinse containers of liquid pesticides thoroughly. Rinse them at least three times. Add the water to the pesticide spray tank. Empty containers of dry pesticides thoroughly. Dispose of empty, clean pesticide containers with other household trash.

BENEFICIAL INSECTS AND BIOLOGICAL CONTROL OF MITES AND INSECTS

More and more emphasis is being placed on reducing the use of pesticides to prevent excess from running off landscapes into surface and groundwater in Georgia, particularly in urban areas. In addition, homeowners are becoming increasingly aware of nonchemical means of pest control. Government regulation of pesticides is becoming more and more restrictive, providing further incentive to use biologically-based pest management methods. These tactics may include the use of pest-resistant plants or the use of parasites, predators, and pathogens to reduce numbers of unwanted insect or mite pests.

Reduction of pest insects or mites below a damaging level through biological control may be achieved by conservation of existing natural enemies, augmentation of their numbers, use of products containing pathogens or nematodes, or through importation of natural enemies from the native location of an exotic pest.

Conservation

The protection of existing natural enemies may be accomplished by using management practices that favor their survival and minimize harmful effects. This includes the use of pesticides only when necessary and then, as spot sprays rather than blanket coverage of an area. Pesticide choice can be selective to reduce toxicity to beneficial insects and mites.

Avoid or be very selective in applying broad-spectrum or persistent pesticides. Often natural enemies are even more susceptible to these types of pesticides than are the pests one is trying to control. Natural enemies may be killed immediately and toxic residues will further reduce the beneficial population. Dust interferes with the activity of many natural enemies and can contribute to an outbreak of mites. Planting groundcovers and reducing dust favors the activity of beneficial insects and mites. Similarly, planting a variety of flowering species can provide additional nectar sources and sources of alternative prey for generalist predators and parasites.

Augmentation

Augmentation of natural enemies may be considered when the resident populations are insufficient to reduce pest numbers to an innocuous level. In this case, natural enemy numbers can be increased (augmented) through the purchase and release of commercially available beneficial species.

Although this method has been widely used in the management of greenhouse pests, there has been relatively little research on the use of commercially produced beneficials in landscape settings. Natural enemy releases are most likely to succeed on plant materials in areas where a certain amount of infestation and pest damage can be tolerated.

Situations where high numbers of pests and a high degree of damage are already apparent are not good candidates for natural enemy releases. Two tactics for augmenting beneficials are inoculative releases and inundative releases. An inoculative release occurs when a small number of individuals of a beneficial species is released into a low level pest infestation. The progeny of these beneficials may be sufficient to keep pest levels at or below the desired level. An inundative release is when large numbers of natural enemies are released, often several times in a season.

Importation

Importation, or classical biological control, is used most often against pests that have been accidentally introduced to the area where they are currently a problem. Insects that are not pests in their native habitat may explode in a new area where the regulation of population size by natural enemies has been removed. Natural enemies collected from the pest's native region and studied for potential to suppress the pest can be introduced in the new environment. Introduction of exotic natural enemies must be done by qualified scientists as required by law, but represents another category of natural enemies that should be recognized and conserved.

Formulated products containing entomogenous (insect-eating) nematodes or bacteria are available for the control of many insect pests. These are produced commercially and may be applied in a manner very similar to that used for conventional pesticides. These types of products, however, often require a much more restrictive set of environmental conditions to function optimally. Nematodes, for example, require a high moisture environment in order to move and locate insect hosts. If soils are too dry, the product may not work as well. In other cases, products may be sensitive to high temperatures or ultraviolet (UV) light, or may require refrigeration. Most nematodes and pathogens are relatively slow acting. Patience is required. A quick knock-down of pests should not be expected; a reduction in pest numbers will occur over time. Usually a particular life stage of the pest is the only one vulnerable to a nematode or pathogen, thus requiring repeat applications to allow for the appropriate stage or stages to be targeted.

Types of Biological Control Agents

Three general categories of natural enemies may occur or be used in managed landscapes: predators, parasites (or, more correctly, parasitoids), and pathogens or disease-causing agents.

Predators are generally insects, spiders, or mites that must find and kill several prey individuals in order to complete their life cycle. This might be a ladybird beetle that consumes hundreds of aphids as both a larva and an adult, or an insect like the minute pirate bug that feeds voraciously on thrips and insect eggs. Predators are usually larger than the prey they eat, although there are exceptions. Predators that feed on insects also occur among the birds, reptiles, amphibians, mammals, and fish. Some can cause significant reductions in insect numbers. Most often we are talking about invertebrate predators in insect and mite control.

Parasites are defined as organisms that live in or on the body of the host during some part of the parasite's life cycle. **Parasitoid**s are a type of parasite that may consume part or all of its host's tissues—resulting in the death of the host. The most abundant parasitic insects are flies and wasps. Parasitic insects usually require only one host to complete their development in contrast to predators, which require several. Parasitic insects may be responsible for controlling several pests, however, when they oviposit, or lay eggs, on a number of new hosts.

Pathogens may be bacteria, viruses, or fungi that cause disease in insects. Nematodes that infect insects are often included in this category, too. Many pathogens that attack insects exist in the landscape and several have been formulated and are commercially available for use in agriculture, greenhouses, nurseries, and the landscape.

The first step in being able to more effectively use biological control in landscape management is to be able to correctly identify certain common natural enemies and to know what pests they may be active against. Many natural enemies are generalists, feeding on a wide variety of prey or, in the case of parasites, parasitizing several host species. Some, on the other hand, are very specialized in the type of prey or host they can successfully overcome. Knowledge of the life cycle is important, too. Many natural enemies attack only a particular stage of a pest, perhaps the egg or the larval stage.

Identification of Some Important Predators

Spiders are all predators, but have many different lifestyles. Some make webs and wait for prey to come to them while others are active hunters. Spiders are important predators in the landscape and are very common in trees, shrubs, grass, and herbaceous plant beds. Most spiders are general predators, feeding on a wide variety of prey. There are a number of spider species that may be found in the landscape. All have two body parts, an abdomen and a cephalothorax (combined head and thorax), and eight legs. Spiders tend to avoid people and most are harmless to humans. Spider complexes are believed to be important in reducing several kinds of landscape pests.

Mites are more closely related to spiders than they are to insects. Mites do not have antennae like insects do, or segmented bodies, or wings. They usually are very small and often go unnoticed. Most mites have an egg stage, a six-legged larval stage, and two eight-legged stages before becoming an adult. Phytoseiid mites are the major group of natural enemies that attack certain kinds of pest spider mites. It is especially important to conserve predatory mites in the landscape to prevent pest mite outbreaks. Other insect pests are also eaten by predatory mites, including whiteflies, thrips, and certain insect eggs.

Most predaceous mites are somewhat pear-shaped and shiny, with noticeably long legs. They may be bright red, yellow, or green depending on what they've been eating and appear transparent. Predaceous mite eggs usually are oblong; the eggs of pest mite species generally are spherical. Predaceous mites are also much more active and mobile than pest mite species.

True Bugs (Heteroptera) is a group that contains several generalist predator species. These insects all have piercing-sucking mouthparts which they use to impale their prey and extract fluid. The beak is usually carried beneath the body, but can be pointed forward or downward while feeding. The usual prey for these insects are soft-bodied insects of small to intermediate size. The next six insects are representatives of these predators:

Stink Bugs Although many stink bugs are plant feeders, there are some predaceous species, including the spined soldier bug. This is a known predator of more than 100 pest species. Adults are about ½ inch long, light brown, and somewhat dorsoventrally flattened. The shoulders are drawn out into the appearance of a spine, hence the name. Both the more colorful nymphs and the adults feed on and may attack prey much larger than themselves. Adults overwinter and become active in the spring when new eggs are deposited. Caterpillars and leaf beetle larvae are common prey items for stink bugs.

Predaceous Damsel Bugs are ⅛ - ⅜ inch long and may be cream colored to dark brown to black, depending on the species. The most common species are slender, elongate insects that are most active in mid-summer. They feed on eggs and immature stages of many pest insects.

Minute Pirate Bugs are ⅛ - ¼ inch long. These insects are black and white as adults and have colorful yellow-orange-brown nymphs, depending upon instar. Gardeners notice the painful puncture that this small insect inflicts. It is an effective predator of thrips and of the eggs of many insect and mite species.

Assassin Bugs generally appear oval or elongate and are often black and orange-red or brown. They are larger than most of the other predaceous bugs, especially the giant wheel bug. Assassin bugs have a head that has a particularly long and narrow appearance. They feed on most other insects and will inflict a painful bite if handled.

Predaceous Plant Bugs are less well-known than other predaceous true bugs, but have been shown to be active predators of thrips, lace bugs, aphids, moth eggs, and other insects of importance in the landscape.

Big-Eyed Bugs are stout-bodied insects, about ⅛ inch long with prominent eyes that give the insect its name. These insects are slightly larger than chinch bugs. They may have similar coloration, but are always broader across the head than the area just behind (shoulders). Chinch bugs, on the other hand, have a narrow head, never broader than the area directly behind. Often, big-eyed bugs can be found with populations of chinch bugs and it is important to be able to distinguish predator from pest. Big-eyed bugs also feed on caterpillars and insect eggs.

Lacewings (Neuroptera) Both green lacewings and brown lacewings are predators; green lacewings are more common. They often are found on weeds, shrubs, and other cultivated plants. Adult green lacewings are about ¾ inch long; brown lacewings are smaller. Adult and larval brown lacewings and larval green lacewings feed on soft-bodied insects, especially aphids, and mites. Adult green lacewings may be pollen-feeders or they may be predaceous. Most are greenish with copper-colored eyes and the network of veins in the wings that gives them their name.

Lacewing eggs are attached to leaves by a long hair-like stalk. This raises the eggs off the surface of the leaf and helps prevent cannibalism when the young predators hatch. Larvae are oblong and soft-bodied, with distinctive sickle-shaped mandibles. They are often called aphid lions because of their habit of feeding on aphids. Some brown lacewings adhere the skins of their prey and other matter to their backs as a form of camouflage.

Praying Mantids (Mantodea) are comparatively large insects. Some may be as long as 3 inches. Our native species are much smaller, however. Usually they are green, gray, or brown. Their raptorial (prey-catching) front legs are covered with stout spines that help them grasp their prey. Mantid egg capsules contain 200 or more eggs neatly arranged in rows. The capsules are deposited on twigs and stems in a tan-colored frothy mass which hardens. It is very unlikely that praying mantids can suppress key pests in the landscape to the extent necessary.

Several families of flies (Diptera) contain predaceous members.

Robber Flies are ¾ - 1¼ inch long and vary in appearance. Some are quite stout, while others are long and slender. The face is usually bearded and the head is hollowed out between the eyes. Adults are predaceous on many kinds of insects and usually capture their prey in the air. Larvae are soil-dwelling and predaceous on white grubs and other organisms.

Syrphid Flies are sometimes called flower flies because they commonly are found on flowers, or hover flies because of their behavior in flight. Most of these flies are yellow with brown or black bands on the abdomen. Some resemble wasps; many mimic bees. Syrphid larvae are maggot-like and predaceous on aphids and other soft-bodied insects. They have no legs or visible head capsule and are translucent.

Predaceous Midges Most members of this group are gall makers on plants, but there are some predaceous members of the family that feed on aphids. These larvae look much like syrphid larvae, but smaller.

Long-Legged Flies are small, about ¼ inch with very long legs in relation to the body and usually metallic blue or green in color. Adults and larvae are predaceous and are often found near woodland streams or other wet areas.

Paper Wasps (Hymenoptera) are important predators of caterpillars. The caterpillars are paralyzed when the wasp stings them and then are transported to the nest to serve as food for the developing wasps.

Earwigs (Dermaptera) of many species are predaceous. One common species was found to eat 50 chinch bugs per day in laboratory tests. Earwigs vary in size—some of the larger species are ¾ -1 inch long. They are usually brown and may have stripes. Earwigs have pincers, or forceps, at the end of the abdomen.

Beetles (Coleoptera) contain many families that are comprised partially or entirely of predaceous species. Some common representatives are mentioned here:

Ground Beetles are predaceous as adults and as larvae. There are some seed-feeding species. They are active on the ground primarily at night. Adult beetles vary in size from ¼ to 1 inch or longer. Many species are metallic, while others are plain brown or black. They prey on armyworms, cutworms, small mole crickets, and other insects.

Rove Beetles have shortened elytra (wing covers) that leave the segments of the abdomen visible, giving these beetles their characteristic appearance. Most species are slender and elongate from ¹⁄₁₆-½ inch long. Typically they are reddish-brown to black. Many species are predaceous, some feed on decaying organic matter helping to recycle needed nutrients in the landscape.

Lady Beetles are among our most important beneficials. Adults and larvae feed on aphids, scale insects, mites, mealybugs, other soft-bodied insects and their eggs. Lady beetle adults are oval-shaped. Most are orange or reddish with black markings.

Lady beetle larvae are elongate, covered with spines, and dorsiventrally flattened, i.e., they are wider than they are thick. Often they are brightly colored with spots. Some larvae are covered with white waxy secretion like mealybugs. Adults and larvae are voracious feeders on aphids. A single individual may consume hundreds of aphids during its lifetime.

Tiger Beetles are very active, often metallic beetles ½ - ¾ inch long. They are difficult to collect because of the speed with which they run or fly. Larvae, commonly called doodlebugs, live in burrows in the soil and ambush prey as it goes by. Some species are often well represented in landscape beds.

Identification of Some Parasitic Insects

Parasitic wasps are a large group of beneficial insects and are extremely important in biological control. Although nobody knows for sure, there are likely more than 1 million species of parasites. Every insect has one or many different species of parasites that attack them. Many wasp families contain representatives of the parasitic lifestyle. Most of these wasps are very small, <⅛ inch, and are, therefore, rarely seen. A large number, in fact, attack the egg stage, completing their entire life cycle inside tiny insect eggs. Parasitic wasps lay their eggs in or on the host and the immature stage of the wasp feeds on the host's tissues. The parasitic wasp may emerge from its host to pupate, or it may pupate within the body of its host.

Wasp larvae that develop inside the host are called endoparasitic. They leave evidence of parasitism when they chew a small hole in their host's body to emerge. That small circular hole indicates that parasitism is occurring in the pest population. Insects that may be parasitized this way include scales, aphids, whiteflies, lace bug eggs, leafminers, and caterpillars. Other parasitic larvae live on the outside of the host's body and are called ectoparasites. Both endo- and ectoparasites may spin numerous white cocoons for pupation, another obvious indication of parasitism.

Field evaluation of parasitism usually has to be made on the basis of evidence of parasitism—signs that the parasites leave behind. Adults are usually too small to be seen or easily sampled, and the larvae are generally not visible inside the host insects. Often we look for evidence such as aphid "mummies" (brown, swollen, hollowed-out remains of parasitized aphids), or darkened scales or whiteflies, or exit holes to help us assess the presence and abundance of parasites.

Parasitic wasps are the best natural control for scale insects. When large numbers of armored scales have exit holes in the scale covers, it is recommended that spraying be avoided, especially if the scale population is low to moderate. Scale parasites will be very active at least twice during a scale generation. The mature female scale may be attacked and the emerging crawlers (the mobile immature stage of scale insects) are attacked by parasites. Application of a pesticide during peak crawler emergence, although our traditional recommendation, can have very negative effects on parasitism by these very susceptible wasps. Try a 3% - 4% horticultural oil during late winter. If scale populations are heavy and rate of parasitism does not appear to be high enough, follow with one or more 2% oil applications later in the summer after crawlers have ceased activity, giving parasites a chance to build. If parasites and predators appear to be absent and scale populations are heavy, an oil application targeting the crawler stage and incorporating a half rate of insecticide may be necessary for suppression.

Parasitic flies are abundantly represented by the family Tachinidae, with about 1,300 North American species. They vary tremendously in appearance. Many just resemble a common housefly, while others look like bees or wasps. These flies deposit an egg or in some cases, a live larva, on or near the body of their host. The tachinid larva burrows into its host and consumes the internal tissues. Numerous insect pests are attacked by tachinids.

Types of Pathogens

Insects get diseases just like we do. Microorganisms that cause disease in pest insects include bacteria, fungi, viruses, nematodes, and others. Disease outbreaks can cause spectacular "crashes" in large pest populations with no interference by man. Often, disease is maintained at low levels within an insect population. Representatives of each group mentioned has been developed for use as microbial insecticides.

Viruses in the Baculoviridae family have been developed for use in insect pest control because of their high virulence in insects and demonstrated safety to humans. Commercial use has been limited by high cost of production and a high degree of environmental instability of viruses. None of the few virus products that have been registered is available for use on landscape plants at this time. Infected larvae turn dark and become shiny, revealing evidence of infection. Viruses are usually quite host specific.

Bacteria are available for control of caterpillars, fly larvae, and most recently, new strains have been discovered that are effective on beetles, including leaf beetle larvae and white grub larvae. These are all strains of *Bacillus thuringiensis* Berliner. The original strain, *B.t.* kurstaki, is active against caterpillars, including many which are pests of ornamentals. *B.t.* israeliensis kills fly larvae, while the strains sandiego and bui-bui affect leaf beetle and grub larvae, respectively.

Fungi that attack insects belong to the Deuteromycetes and Entomophthoraceae. Fungal spores usually require water to germinate and invade new hosts. Although sudden, severe outbreaks of fungi are often involved in high insect death, the high moisture requirement has limited commercial development. Symptoms of fungal infection vary. Often the infected caterpillar's body becomes hard, brittle, and covered with first white, then green, powdery spores.

Nematodes are microscopic roundworms that live in the soil. Like fungi, they also require a high moisture environment for movement and survival. They have been most effective in soil or other moist habitats. Some success in controlling wood-boring caterpillars in the landscape has been reported, however.

Managing Naturally-Occurring Parasites & Predators

Natural enemies will be at their most effective if the use of broad-spectrum, high toxicity products that destroy them are avoided. The biological insecticide *Bacillus thuringiensis*, for example, is very effective against caterpillar pests, but leaves most natural enemies unharmed. Selective insecticides may work more slowly than broad-spectrum sprays, but long-term control is better achieved by using methods that conserve natural enemies and promote balance.

Spot treat or remove infested plants. Use resistant plant varieties that are compatible with biological control. Stop treating minor pests and focus management on key pests. Keep a garden diary; record what works well. Develop "threshold levels" for treatment; a few insects generally do not merit a pesticide application.

Monitor for beneficial insects and mites the same as for pest insects. Evidence of natural enemy activity includes diseased insects or those that have holes from which parasites have emerged. Determine whether pest numbers are increasing, decreasing, or staying the same. Make the same assessment for associated natural enemies. Predators and sometimes parasites can be sampled in much the same way as pests in the landscape are sampled. A sweep net is useful and foliage can be shaken or beaten over a white tray where dislodged insects and mites become very visible. Direct visual observation is often the most effective sampling method. Insects can be counted as number per leaf or terminal, for example, or number spotted during a three minute observation period. If the ratio of pests to natural enemies is low, spraying should be delayed. Frequent (weekly or biweekly) monitoring is necessary to take fullest advantage of natural control.

Methods to Increase Natural Enemy Populations

Judicious selection and use of pesticides to favor natural enemy survival and reproduction is critical to enhancing natural enemy activity in the landscape.

Nectar and pollen are required by many predators and parasites. Well-designed landscapes feature a variety of plant material, including a season-long bloom of perennials. Those that have been shown to be particularly attractive to beneficials include daisies, Queen Anne's Lace, yarrow, white alyssum, goldenrod, and clover.

RESOURCES

Georgia Pest Managment Handbook: Homeowner Edition. Special Bulletin 48. Published yearly by The University of Georgia College of Agricultural and Environmental Sciences, Cooperative Extension. Available as a printed publication for a nominal fee or free online

DISCUSSION QUESTIONS

1. What are the four components of an IPM system?

2. Why is pest identification important in an IPM program?

3. Discuss the 3 goals of pest control.

4. What are the steps in pest monitoring?

5. How do natural controls affect pest populations?

6. What are some nonchemical methods of pest control?

7. Explain the action of contact pesticides, systemic pesticides, and translocated pesticides.

8. Name and explain the meaning of signal words and symbols you may see on a pesticide product.

9. Where can you find out how much pesticide to apply?

10. List some information that can be found on a pesticide label.

10. Describe actions that a pesticide user can take to avoid contamination of groundwater.

11. Where should pesticides be stored?

12. How should you dispose of excess pesticides?

13. What is the most common route of pesticide exposure and how can pesticide users protect themselves from exposure?

14. What are the 3 principles of using beneficial insects in reducing pesticide use?

15. List 10 beneficial insects you might find in the landscape

9

Ornamental Plants in the Landscape:

Site Analysis, Planting and Management

Gary L. Wade

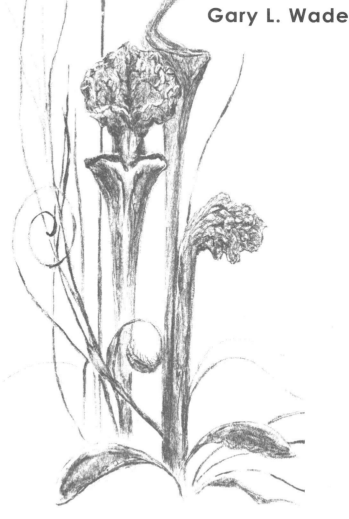

LEARNING OBJECTIVES

Know proper site selection for planting woody ornamentals.

Know proper planting methods for woody ornamental plants.

Be familiar with mulches and their use.

Know the types of fertilizer available and benefits and drawbacks of each.

Know how to calculate fertilizer requirements.

Understand reasons for pruning woody ornamentals.

Be able to demonstrate proper pruning techniques and equipment.

Be familiar with when to prune plants.

TERMS TO KNOW

Balled-and-burlapped (B&B) field grown plants that are dug and roots wrapped in burlap, wire cage or similar material prior to replanting.

Thinning complete removal of branches back to main trunk, a lateral branch or to ground level.

Heading indiscriminately cutting back terminal portion of the branch. Results in thick, dense growth of the outer canopy.

INTRODUCTION

A Master Gardener will be called upon, and often challenged, to provide up-to-date cultural information on ornamental plants in the landscape. It is important that the recommendations provided are accurate, current, and consistent with those of The University of Georgia. Research during recent years has determined that many of the cultural practices we have taken for granted, such as adding peat moss or compost to a planting hole when planting, may not necessarily be the best practices. Furthermore, Master Gardeners may also be asked to troubleshoot a landscape problem. To do this, it is necessary to catalog site characteristics, such as drainage, sunlight exposure, etc. to objectively determine the cause of the problem.

Often plants become stressed and more prone to insect or disease problems when they are forced to grow in soils or climates where they are not accustomed to growing. Spraying a pesticide to control a particular pest when the real problem is soil drainage may not be the best long-term solution to a problem.

This chapter begins with a thorough discussion of site analysis, a critical step in landscape development. Next, the chapter focuses on planting techniques and cultural practices that assure lasting landscape beauty. We will review in detail three of the most common landscape management practices: mulching, fertilization and pruning. Irrigation, turfgrass management and pest control will be discussed elsewhere in this manual.

Site Analysis

Whether planning a new landscape or adding new plants to an existing landscape, site analysis will influence the types of plants selected for the site and changes that need to be made in the site in order to successfully grow the desired plants. Impulse purchasing is easy to do at garden centers. Gardeners often see a plant with outstanding qualities and just have to have it. Then they get it home and wonder where to plant it, walking around the landscape looking for the perfect space to show off the outstanding features of their newfound treasure.

Unfortunately, that perfect spot may not be the best site from the plant's perspective. Forcing plants to grow in harsh environments may cause plant stress and long-term problems. This is proven again and again at the Plant Diagnostic Clinic at The University of Georgia where a large percentage of the plant problems diagnosed result from the inability of the plant to adapt to or tolerate the environment in which it is growing.

Site analysis is the first and most critical step in the landscape process. It involves cataloging the changing environmental factors on the site, differences in soil types, soil drainage characteristics, etc. An individual landscape may have several microclimates, each offering a different growing environment.

Note Changes in Sunlight Patterns—The sun rises in the East and sets in the West, and at midday in summer it is directly over head. Therefore, shade-loving plants would be placed on an eastern exposure where they are shaded from the hot afternoon sun by a building, a structure or a nearby plant. They also can be planted as an understory plant in a shaded woodland where they get filtered shade throughout the day. However, it would be a mistake to plant shade-loving plants on a hot western exposure without offering them some relief from the intense rays of the summer sun in the afternoon. In contrast, flowering sun-loving plants often perform poorly in shade, or even partial shade.

Think about the long-term changes in sunlight patterns in the landscape. As tree canopies mature, sunlight patterns change. Plants initially in full sun may eventually be in full shade. Junipers, for instance, are often planted as a ground cover around the base of trees. They do fine for the first few years, but as the trees grow and cast shade on the junipers, they thin out due to insufficient light and they become stressed and more prone to insect and disease problems. Junipers are full-sun plants; they do poorly in shade.

Peaks, Valleys and Concrete Surfaces Affect Drainage—Most landscapes have a number of topography changes. There will be high spots and low spots, and there may be areas where water stands for periods of time after rain. A walkway from the driveway to the front door often acts like a concrete dam, keeping water impounded after rain. Down spouts often have splash pans, but adjacent plants must be able to cope with flood conditions after heavy rain and wet/dry fluctuations in soil moisture.

Poor drainage is a leading cause of plant problems in the landscape. Look for poorly drained spots or areas that are prone to extreme fluctuations in soil moisture and make changes, when possible, to assure good drainage. Some soils have a hardpan layer or rock under their surface that prevents water from draining.

A good way to assess soil drainage in an area is to do a Perk Test (soil absorption capacity test). This involves digging a hole as if you were planting an ornamental plant, filling the hole with water and observing how the water drains. If most of the water you placed in the hole is still there an hour later, a drainage problem is likely. If water remains in the hole for several hours, action is needed to correct the drainage problem.

There are several ways to correct a drainage problem. First, you can plant on an elevated bed, 12 inches or more above grade, to get the roots of plants out of the poorly drained soil. The bed should be high enough and wide enough to allow good root extension of the ornamental plants. Don't just place the root ball on top of the ground and cover it with a little dirt like a fireant mound. This will result in extreme root stress and will not solve the problem. Another option is deep cultivation to break apart a hardpan layer under the soil. Some landscape firms use large, motorized augers to break up compacted soils before planting. A third option would be to install sub-surface drain pipe to carry water off the site. This would require you to have another area of the landscape where the water can drain, without causing problems in the new area.

If a drainage problem cannot be corrected by mechanical means, there are two additional options you can explore: (1) install mulch on the soil surface and avoid planting it all together, or (2) install plants that are adapted to wet soils. Information on suggested plants for wet sites can be obtained from your local County Extension Agent.

Identify the Direction of Cold Arctic Blasts—Most severe cold snaps we encounter in Georgia originate in Canada and move across the U.S. from the Northwest to the Southeast. When cold temperatures are accompanied by strong wind, damage to ornamental plants can be severe. Therefore, it is best to locate cold-sensitive plants on the south or southeast side of a property, particularly where they are sheltered from the northwestern winds. Planting tall evergreens on the northwest side of the property will also help reduce the effects of the cold arctic blasts.

Identify Undesirable Views or Desired Level of Privacy—A site analysis also will help determine whether screen plants or screening structures are necessary to block undesirable views or to create privacy. In a developed residential community there are always undesirable views, and as property sizes shrink, there is an ever-increasing desire for privacy in one's backyard - a concept called "cocooning" by modern sociologists.

Other Considerations, such as Noise or Deer Browsing—Noise from nearby homes, shopping centers, schools, construction sites, or highways may be a consideration in some landscapes. If noise is an issue,

planning may involve incorporating a wall or planting tall evergreens to help muffle the noise. Another issue in some urban settings is deer browsing. If deer are known to frequent the site, then planning should include the selection of deer tolerant plants or plants known to be unappetizing to deer.

Once site criteria are thoroughly assessed and cataloged, consider two options during the next phase of landscape development: select plants adapted to the site and the local environmental conditions and/or make physical changes to the site to provide a better growing environment for the types of plants to be grown. For instance, if a favorite azalea is a "must have" plant, but the planting site is in hot, baking, afternoon sun, then an option would be to introduce shade, either by erecting a nearby structure to cast shade or by planting a taller shrub or tree to cast shade on the area. On the other hand, a shaded, poorly drained site would spell disaster for junipers because they cannot tolerate shade and wet feet, but it would be great for inkberry or wax myrtle. Appropriate plant selection is an important element in development of a healthy, attractive landscape.

Soil preparation and planting are perhaps the most critical of all landscape practices. Proper planting assures rapid plant establishment and healthy growth, provided other environmental factors are favorable, such as sunlight and moisture. Haphazard planting subjects plants to lifelong stress and makes them more susceptible to other types of environmental injury, including pests, drought and cold.

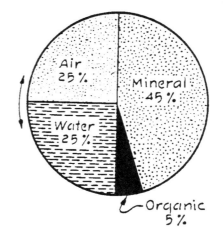

Figure 1. Volume composition of an ideal silt loam surface soil. Source: Buckman, H. O. 1969. The Nature and Properties of Soils. The Macmillan Company.

Proper planting involves more than simply digging a hole and sticking in a plant. The type of soil preparation required and the need for amendments depends on the structure and texture of the existing soil, drainage characteristics, and the type of plants to be grown. No two soils are alike, so there is no cookbook recipe for applying soil amendments. The goal in planting is to provide an ideal soil environment for root growth. An ideal soil has 1) air space for good drainage, yet has good water holding capacity, 2) some mineral matter to provide the soil chemistry necessary for nutrient absorption, and 3) a small amount of organic matter to supply slow-release nutrients and to improve soil structure and texture (Figure 1).

When is the Best Time of Year to Plant? In the professional landscape industry, planting goes on year-round. However, the best time of year to plant, in terms of root growth and plant establishment, is during the fall.

Unlike the tops of ornamental plants that go dormant and cease growth for the winter, roots of ornamental plants continue to grow throughout the winter months. During the fall, the above-ground portion of a plant begins slowing down in its growth and moving toward dormancy, so it makes little demand on the roots. Therefore, the energy produced via photosynthesis during the previous season can be directed to root growth. When spring arrives and a new growing season begins, the plant has a well-established root system ready to provide the necessary water and nutrients for optimum plant growth.

In contrast, spring and summer transplanting results in competition between roots and shoots for water, nutrients and food substances. Roots often cannot satisfy the demand for water and nutrients by the top, so wilting and stress (called transplant shock) often occur. Plant establishment is more difficult and demanding during the spring and summer months.

Container-grown ornamental plants with well-developed root systems can be planted successfully throughout the year, provided water is available during the establishment period. Balled-and-burlapped (B&B) plants, on the other hand, are best planted during the fall and winter months. B&B trees in full leaf have been transplanted successfully during the spring and summer months, but special care must be taken during establishment. A few ornamental plants, i.e., roses and fruit trees, are sold as bare-root plants during the winter months. They should be planted as early as possible during the winter season to allow root growth and establishment prior to spring growth.

Careful Handling Minimizes Transplant Shock— When carrying ornamental plants, always carry them by the root ball or container. Never grab plants by their foliage or trunk without also supporting the root ball. Root damage can occur when the weight of the root ball pulls the roots downward.

Wind exposure during transport from the nursery to the landscape can desiccate (dry out) and damage foliage, so transport plants in the trunk of a car or covered truck when possible. When transporting plants in an open-bed truck, try to minimize exposure to wind by placing them as close to the cab as possible or laying plants on their sides to minimize exposure to wind. Wrap the foliage of trees with a tarp secured with cord to prevent damage. When transporting plants more than five miles, or when transport requires driving at high speeds on an interstate highway, cover the entire load with a well-secured tarp to prevent wind damage.

When arriving home, place the plants in a shaded area away from the afternoon sun. Avoid setting plants on concrete or asphalt in sun because these surfaces radiate large amounts of heat that can dry out the foliage. Large B&B trees held on their side for any length of time in the sun should have their trunks wrapped or covered to prevent sunscald (sun damage to the bark which often results in bark splitting). If planting balled-and-burlapped plants cannot be done right away, "heel them in" by digging a temporary hole in a shaded area and burying the root ball to prevent it from drying out. If planting is to occur within a day or two, leave the root ball on top of the ground in the shaded area, but use the garden hose to wet the burlap two or three times a day.

Always water plants thoroughly before they are planted. It is difficult to re-wet a dry root ball once it is planted.

Take Time to Prepare the Site Thoroughly—When shaping the final grade of the planting beds, remember the importance of good drainage. Few ornamental plants can tolerate long periods of standing water.

Good drainage is critical for most ornamental plants, particularly annuals and herbaceous perennials. The previous section on site analysis discusses options for dealing with poorly drained soils.

When planting after new construction, remove any debris left on the site that may cause plant growth difficulties. Chunks of concrete, roofing shingles, globs of tar, oil spills, and sheetrock are often encountered on new construction sites. These materials may be toxic to roots or can cause long-term growth problems.

Do Not Guess Fertility and Lime Needs: Get a Soil Test—In addition to examining the physical properties of the soil and taking corrective measures to improve poorly-drained soils, a soil test will show which types of fertilizer are best and whether it is necessary to add lime to the soil. A soil test is recommended at least two to three weeks before planting to know how to treat the soil at planting time. However, if new soil is brought onto the site at planting time, or if soil is moved around during the final grading, it is best to wait until all the soil is in place before sampling. Fertilizer and lime can be surface applied at the recommended rate later, even after plants are established.

Should Organic Amendments Be Added to the Soil?
Organic matter is appropriately referred to as "Black Gold" by many gardeners. It improves the water and nutrient-holding capacity of a soil, improves soil structure, and adds valuable microorganisms that enrich a soil. Unfortunately, there is no cookbook recipe for amending all soils. The type of amendment and amount used depends on the structure and texture of the existing soil, soil drainage, and the type of plant to be grown. Amendments generally fall into two categories: organic amendments, such as peat moss or compost, and inorganic amendments, like pea gravel, coarse sand or rock.

When adding organic matter to a soil, research has shown that it is best to incorporate it throughout the rooting zone, to a depth of 8 to 12 inches, if possible, instead of placing it in individual planting holes. By incorporating an amendment uniformly into the soil, the entire rooting area becomes a homogenous growing environment for roots. On the other hand, when a planting hole alone is amended, the structure and texture of the soil in the hole differ from that of the surrounding native soil. This encourages the roots to stay within the confines of the hole and discourages them from exploring the surrounding native soil. It also upsets the water equilibrium between the surrounding native soil and the soil in the hole. In some soils, fine-textured organic matter, like peat moss or compost, added to the planting hole may act like a sponge in a bathtub when they are added to the planting hole, holding excess moisture after rain or irrigation. On the other hand, adding a coarse aggregate to a planting hole in an effort to improve drainage may cause the soil in the hole to dry out more rapidly than the surrounding soil. This may result in plant stress during periods of limited rainfall.

A general rule of thumb for applying organic matter is to add 25% by volume. This equates to 3 inches of an organic material incorporated to a 12-inch depth.

Generally, one cubic yard of organic matter will cover 100 square feet to a 3-inch depth. An area 1,000 square feet in size will require 10 cubic yards. If purchasing compost or other amendments in 3 cubic feet bags, one would need to buy nine 3-cubic feet bags per 100 square feet (27 cubic feet in 1 cubic yard divided by 3). A forty-pound bag is generally equivalent to a volume of 2 cubic feet, so 14 bags per 100 square feet would be necessary to provide the recommended 3-inch depth.

In some heavy soils, inorganic amendments, such as builder's sand or pea gravel are sometimes used to improve drainage. However, avoid incorporating sand into clay soils because it may result in a concrete-like soil structure.

Do not use uncomposted bark products as amendments. Freshly milled bark that has not been composted robs plants of nitrogen when used as an amendment. As microorganisms in the soil feed on bark to decompose it, they utilize nitrogen in the soil. Also, the pH of the soil often drops dramatically below the desirable range when uncomposted materials are used as amendments. Use uncomposted organic material as a mulch, and decomposed organic matter as a soil amendment. Decomposed or "composted" organic products have a rich, earthy smell and a crumbly appearance, and the original organic materials are no longer recognizable.

Planting Procedures

Woody Ornamental Trees and Shrubs—Once the site is prepared, plant beds are shaped and appropriate amendments incorporated, it is time to plant. The following are current recommendations for successful planting of trees and shrubs.

When Planting an Individual Tree or Shrub in Undisturbed Soil, Dig a Wide Planting Hole—Although it would be desirable to cultivate a large area when planting a solitary tree or shrub, it may not be practical. Therefore, when planting an individual tree or shrub in native, undisturbed soil, dig the planting hole at least two times wider than the root ball of the plant. Simply changing the structure of the soil adjacent to the roots of the plant provides a favorable environment for early root growth and plant establishment. In one study at The University of Georgia, a group of red maple trees was planted in soil that had been thoroughly tilled, while another group was planted in holes dug no wider than the root ball in undisturbed soil. After five months, the roots of trees planted in the disturbed soil had grown five feet beyond the planting hole. Those in the undisturbed soil had only extended about two feet beyond the planting hole.

Dig the Hole to the Depth of the Root Ball—Dig the hole to the depth of the root ball and no deeper. This assures that the top of the root ball will be level with the soil surface and that it will not settle over time. When planted too deeply, the root system will struggle to obtain sufficient oxygen, plant establishment will take longer, and long-term plant stress may result.

If the planting hole is dug deeper than the root ball, backfill with some of the soil removed from the hole until the top of the root ball is level with the soil surface. Then, firm the soil with your foot in the bottom of the hole to minimize settling.

Remove Wire or Cord from the Trunk of B&B Plants—Nylon cord or wire securing burlap around the trunk of balled-and-burlapped plants should be cut and removed from the trunk area.. f the nylon cord is not removed, it can girdle and injure the trunk as the trunk expands.

Pull back the burlap or remove it entirely from B&B plants. In poorly-drained areas it would be wise to re-move the burlap entirely, if possible, to prevent it from holding too much moisture near the roots (some of the newer burlaps contain nylon and are slow to decom-pose). When planting large trees in wire baskets, it may not be practical to remove the wire or burlap completely. In this case, use wire snips to cut the wire and pull it and the burlap away from the top ⅓ of the root ball.

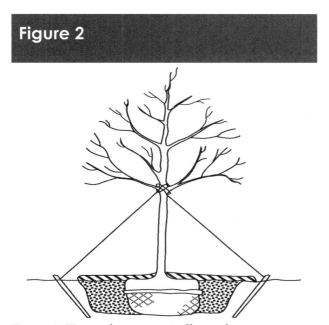

Figure 2

Figure 2. Two stakes are typically used on trees one to three inches in trunk diameter while guy wires are used to support trees larger than 3 inches in trunk diameter.

Some nylon-based burlap is slow to decompose and can be an impediment to root growth.

Disturbing the Root Mass of Container-Grown Plants—To slice or not to slice the root mass of container-grown plants is a very controversial subject fueled by a number of conflicting research studies and recommendations. Some landscapers will consistently slice the root ball of container-grown ornamental plants by cutting a vertical slice approximately 2 inches deep on two to four sides of the root ball. Research has not determined that this practice consistently results in better root growth and more rapid plant establishment. However, one study at The University of Georgia showed that disturbing the roots of pot-bound plants (those having a dense external root mass) allowed better water movement into the internal portions of the root ball. Also, container-grown trees having a thick outer root mass of roots and a strong secondary root system have been observed to have a difficult time breaking free of the circling behavior of the root system when not disturbed.

The majority of research to date suggests that it is best to disturb the roots of container-grown plants when the outer root mass is pot-bound. Otherwise, if the roots do not appear pot-bound, leave them undisturbed.

Backfill With the Same Soil Removed from the Hole—As discussed previously, it is not necessary or advantageous to amend soil added back to the plant-ing hole. Simply backfill with the same soil removed from the hole after breaking apart clods to improve the structure of the soil.

Install Staking or Guy Wires if Necessary—At this point in the planting operation, stakes or guy wires are sometimes used on trees and large evergreen shrubs in exposed windy sites to hold them in place during establishment. Large shrubs, 5 to 15 gallon sizes, are often held in place with a single stake attached in a lean-to fashion.

Trees having a trunk diameter greater than one inch and a height exceeding four feet will probably need some sort of staking or guy wires to hold them in place until they are established. Trees having a trunk diameter between one and three inches usually can be supported by two to four stakes, depending on the size of the top. Stakes may be metal rods or wooden stakes 2 x 2 inches in diameter and 6 feet in length. Place the stakes in the ground at planting time several inches below the depth of the planting hole and along the perimeter of the root ball. To avoid damaging the roots, avoid driving the stakes into the root ball.

Three guy wires are commonly used on trees larger than three inches in trunk diameter (see Figure 2). Use heavy wire, such as 12-gauge, to secure the tree to three wooden stakes pounded into the ground at a 45 degree angle just outside the planting hole. Place the wire inside a piece of old garden hose where it touches the tree to prevent it from damaging the bark. If possible, place all three wires just above the lowest scaffold branches to prevent them from slipping up and down on the trunk. The wires should support the tree firmly but should not be too taut. The goal is to keep the tree from blowing over and uprooting itself during the establishment phase. Research has shown that trees allowed to move slightly with the breezes during establishment develop a larger root system and a stronger trunk than those held firmly during establishment.

Remember, stakes and guy wires are only temporary and should be removed as soon as a tree is established. As a general rule, remove guy wires by mid-spring from trees planted the previous fall or winter, and 8 to 10 weeks after transplanting in spring and summer. Research at The University of Georgia with red maple has shown that the roots of spring-planted trees are well established and growing three to four feet beyond the planting hole within three months of transplanting, provided the soil environment is favorable for root extension.

Water Saucers (basins)—It is often recommended that a ring of soil or berm be shaped around the edge of the planting hole to act like a saucer, holding water after rain or irrigation and funneling it to the roots. However, the International Society of Arborists (ISA) no longer recommends that water rings be formed around the perimeter of the planting hole when planting trees. They feel a soil ring enhances the interface difference between the soil in the hole and the surrounding native soil and can actually be an impediment to outward root growth (sort of like putting excess fill dirt over tree roots). Furthermore, a water ring encourages an imbalance of water between in the hole and the surrounding native soil which, in some cases, may be detrimental to root growth (remember the sponge in a bathtub effect discussed under Soil Amendments?). Also, it is the observation of the author that water rings can erode inward over time, covering the surface roots with excess soil and blocking air flow to the roots, an effect similar to planting too deeply. However, shaping a ring of soil along the planting hole and creating a water saucer remains a common practice in the landscape industry, and many planting specifications still require it. Therefore, if it is used, the soil ring should not exceed 4 inches in height, and it should be removed 8 to 10 weeks after planting

to prevent it from eroding over the planting hole. Use a stiff rake to pull it outward and away from planting hole.

Water Immediately After Planting to Settle the Soil—A thorough watering is one of the most critical steps in the planting operation. Watering immediately after transplanting settles the soil and eliminates air pockets that may dry out the roots. Three to five gallons of water will be required when planting one-gallon and three-gallon size plants. Water slowly to allow the water to penetrate to the base of the planting hole.

Fertilization at Planting Time—Fertilizer is not essential for plant establishment. During establishment, the roots draw on their stored carbohydrates and derive little immediate benefit from applied nutrients. This is particularly true for trees and shrubs transplanted during the fall and winter months when there is little demand for nutrients by the canopy.

If possible, wait until spring to fertilize fall-planted trees and shrubs, and wait 6 to 8 weeks before fertilizing trees and shrubs transplanted during the spring and summer. Then apply fertilizers lightly in a band along the perimeter of the planting hole.

Annual and perennial flowers have a more immediate need for fertilizer than woody ornamentals and are fertilized when planted. Slow-release type fertilizers are incorporated into the soil at planting time, and liquid fertilizer supplements are often applied during the growing season. The type and rate of fertilizer applied is tailored to the individual needs of the flowers being grown (see section on fertilization).

Apply Mulch to the Soil Surface—Mulching is the final step in the planting process and one of the most important. Mulch maintains a uniform moisture level and prevents wet/dry fluctuations in soil moisture. It insulates the roots of plants from extreme summer heat and winter freezes, and it provides a barrier to weed growth and certain soil-borne diseases. Mulch placed around shrubs and trees in turf areas prevents bark injury from weed eaters and lawnmowers.

There are two general types of mulches on the market: organic mulches and inorganic mulches. Examples of organic mulches are pine straw, pine-bark, hardwood bark and cypress mulch. Inorganic mulches include rock, gravel, marble and recycled tire chips. Generally, organic mulches are preferred in the Southeast, not only because they are readily available, but also because they absorb moisture and release it back slowly to the atmosphere, helping cool the landscape. Inorganic rock-type mulches, on the other hand, tend to absorb and re-radiate heat, which can cause plant stress on a hot summer day. Their use should be limited to small, shaded areas.

The best mulches are fine-textured, organic, and non-matting. Examples are pinestraw, pine bark mulch, pine bark mini-nuggets and shredded hardwood mulch. Grass clippings and sawdust should be avoided because they are too fine-textured and can form an impervious mat that inhibits water flow into the soil. Grass clippings may also introduce weed seeds to ornamental plantings, and sawdust has been reported to harbor termites.

Today, a growing number of municipalities are grinding yard trimmings and providing it to citizens to use as mulch. In Athens, a pick-up load of mulch is available for $5 at the local landfill. Consider using these materials if they are available in the local area.

Recycled rubber mulch, sometimes dyed in a variety of colors, is also available in some areas. It is often used on playgrounds and walks. Some people object to its use, calling it an environmental contaminant because it may take thousands of years to decompose. Another concern is the unpleasant odor emitted by the rubber on a hot sunny day.

Table 1. Advantages and disadvantages of commonly used mulches

MULCH	ADVANTAGES	DISADVANTAGES
Pine straw	An excellent mulch for water conservation	Flammable when extremely dry. Fades to a dull gray-brown color with age. Decomposes rather quickly and requires annual top-dressing with additional pine straw to maintain a fresh appearance.
Pine bark	Mini-nuggets conserve moisture better than large nuggets. They also stay seated better on the landscape than large nuggets. Lasts longer than pine straw.	None
Shredded or chipped hardwood bark	Provides a durable, long lasting mulch. Available free or at a low cost in many municipalities.	None
Fall leaves	An overlooked and readily available mulch. Shredded leaves stay seated better and conserve moisture than unshredded leaves. To shred them, place them in long, narrow rows on the lawn and run over them with the lawnmower set at the highest wheel setting.	Not as neat and uniform in appearance as pine straw or pine bark.
Grass clippings	None	Decompose quickly, mat down and mold. Not recommended. Compost them instead.
Pecan hulls	An acceptable and economical mulch where available.	Rough looking. Mold with age and attract wildlife when fresh.
Gravel, marble chips, volcanic rock	Long lasting	Absorb and re-radiate heat. Unnatural in appearance. Not recommended.
Newspaper	Placed two sheets thick under organic mulch, newspaper helps conserve moisture while adding water and nutrients to penetrate. A good way to recycle newspapers	When placed too thick (>2 layers) can serve as a barrier to water and nutrients.
Landscape fabric	Helps conserve moisture when installed under organic mulch. Allows nutrients and water to penetrate to plant roots. Prevents most weeds.	Aggravating to install. Does not prevent nutsedge and other persistent weeds. Over time weed seeds can sprout on top of fabric and become difficult to remove.
Plastic film	None	Prevents oxygen, nutrients and water from reaching plant roots. Not recommended.

Each mulch has advantages and disadvantages, as shown in Table 1.

Whatever mulch is used, apply it 3 to 5 inches deep under newly-planted ornamental plants. As plants get established and their roots explore the native soil, gradually expand the mulched area, if possible. When applying mulch around trees and shrubs, pull it back a few inches from the base of plant because it may encourage bark-rotting fungi if the trunk area is kept too moist.

Research at the University of Florida determined that the roots of newly-planted trees extended up to 7 feet beyond the planting hole one year after transplanting. Therefore, applying a narrow ring of mulch around the base of a tree no larger than the planting hole has little long-term benefit to the tree.

Black or clear plastic placed under mulches to prevent weeds is not recommended. Plastic prevents water, nutrients, and oxygen from penetrating the soil to the roots. Plastic also traps excess moisture in the soil and encourages root rot diseases. Landscape fabrics (geotextiles) placed under mulch are alternatives to black plastic. They allow water, nutrients, and oxygen to penetrate to the root system.

Most landscape fabrics are made of polypropylene, a by-product of the petroleum industry. They are composed of filaments that are woven or spun bonded together. Although they help prevent weeds, they do not prevent all weeds; nutsedge and Bermudagrass can penetrate most fabrics. Furthermore, weed seeds can sprout on top of the fabric as the mulch layer decomposes.

Newspaper placed under mulch can serve as an added barrier to moisture loss, and it is a great way to recycle newspaper. To help the newspaper stay seated on the bed, moisten it in a bucket of water. Then apply it two sheets thick over the bed, overlapping the edges slightly. Avoid using more than two sheets thickness because it may serve as a barrier to moisture movement into the soil.

Seasonal Color Beds—Seasonal color displays with annual and perennial flowers are a big investment in any landscape. In order to achieve the maximum return on the investment, seasonal color plants must be provided their optimum growing requirements at all times.

Herbaceous flowering plants are generally more demanding than woody ornamentals. In the commercial landscape industry, bed preparation for seasonal color displays begins with deep cultivation to break up the native soil and to assure good drainage. Next, the bed is elevated six to twelve inches above the surrounding soil by adding well-drained top soil. This not only improves the visibility of the display but also assures good drainage.

Good drainage is essential.

Seasonal color beds are amended with composted organic matter, such as composted animal manure and/or composted bark. If drainage of the native soil is poor, large-particle granite sand or shale is sometimes included in the mix. The type and amount of various amendments used depend on the type of plants grown, the structure and texture of the native soil, and whether the bed has been previously planted and amended. Organic amendments are generally applied 3 inches deep and incorporated to a 12-inch depth.

Next, a slow-release fertilizer is applied to the bed. Slow-release fertilizers provide plants with a constant supply of nutrients throughout the growing season. Osmocote is a commonly used slow-release fertilizer. Tablet forms of slow-release fertilizers such as Agriform tablets, Osmocote pellets, and fertilizer briquettes are also used. These are placed in the planting hole directly beneath the plant. Release durations of the slow-release products vary from 4 to 12 months. Most seasonal displays require a product with at least a 6-month release duration.

Slow-release fertilizers are best used on annuals planted in spring and summer because their release is governed by warm temperature. On winter beds of pansies, kale, etc. slow-release fertilizers are generally ineffective due to cooler soil temperatures. For these plants, it's best to apply a 10-10-10 fertilizer on the planting bed, then follow-up applications of liquid feed throughout the growing season.

After planting, pine straw or pine bark mini-nuggets are added to the soil surface. These fine-textured mulches stay seated better on the bed than coarse-textured mulches. Some landscapers install a roll of pine straw along the perimeter of the bed to prevent bark mulch from washing from the bed and to give the bed a finished appearance.

The final step in the planting operation is to water immediately after transplanting. A liquid fertilizer is often applied to provide the plants some immediate nutrients until the fertilizer added to the soil begins releasing.

Soil preparation and planting are cultural practices that cannot be short-changed. The time and effort spent planting will determine the future health of a landscape plant and its maintenance requirements. Plants improperly installed on a poorly prepared site will often suffer long-term growth difficulties and will be more prone to environmental stress and pest injury.

Review the Steps for Successful Planting

1. Assure good drainage by deep tilling, sub-soiling, elevating planting beds, or installing subsurface drainage pipe. A thorough tilling of the native soil provides a favorable environment for root growth.

2. When using amendments, incorporate them uniformly throughout the soil as opposed to placing them in the planting hole.

3. When planting individual plants in undisturbed soil, dig a wide planting hole, at least two times wider than the root ball. Dig the hole only as deep as the root ball, making certain the soil in the bottom of the hole is packed firmly to minimize settling.

4. Make certain the top of the root ball is level with the soil surface.

5. Backfill with the same soil removed from the hole, after breaking apart clods and improving its structure.

6. Water immediately and thoroughly to settle the soil and to eliminate air pockets. Water is critical throughout the establishment period.

7. Trees and large evergreen shrubs planted in exposed windy sites may require staking or guy wires to hold them in place during establishment. Remove these supports as soon as the trees are established.

8. Apply 3 to 5 inches of an organic mulch to the soil surface.

Planting is a simple process, but it is so often done haphazardly. Like a skilled surgeon, the reputation of a Master Gardener depends on the planting operation being a success.

FERTILIZATION

Fertilization is an important part of landscape management, particularly in urban areas where much of the native topsoil is removed during land development and replaced with subsoil that is often deficient in essential plant nutrients.

Unfortunately, fertilization is a rather simple cultural practice that has become increasingly complex and confusing due to the wide variety of fertilizers on the market today - from general-purpose garden fertilizers to slow-release granules, pellets or spikes, specialty products, such as azalea/camellia fertilizer, bulb booster, and rose special, or organic fertilizers and liquid fertilizers. Also, there is a wide array of weed-and-feed combination fertilizers. It is no wonder gardeners get confused!

Adding further to the confusion are several environmental factors and circumstances which influence the type and quantity of fertilizer applied. For instance:

• Plants growing in shade generally require less fertilizer than those grown in sun because they have a lower metabolic rate.

• Plants growing in sandy soils generally require more frequent fertilization than those in clay soils, due to nutrient leaching from sandy soils.

• Fertilizing during the dormant winter season provides plants little benefit because they are not actively absorbing nutrients from the soil. Much of the nitrogen and potassium (two very soluble nutrients) applied in winter will simply leach from the soil.

• Fertilization rates for trees growing in turf areas cannot exceed the rate recommended for the turfgrass. Otherwise, injury to the turf may result.

• Fertilization rates for street trees in restricted root environments must be greatly reduced when compared to trees growing in open areas.

Selecting a Fertilizer

Generally, plants do not care whether a fertilizer is granulated, encapsulated, briquetted, pelletized, organic or water-soluble! All they want are nutrients in any form possible.

Like amendments, there is no cookbook formula for determining which fertilizer is best for each landscape. The fertilizer selected generally depends on cost, the type of plants being fertilized, the existing nutrient content of the soil, the length of nutrient release, site conditions, and the growth response desired from the plants. A soil test, available through the county Extension office, is the most scientific way to determine the type of fertilizer to use and rate of application. Fertilizers are available in a number of different formulations, including granular, slow-release, organic, or water soluble.

Granular fertilizers are also called "general purpose" fertilizers. Examples are 16-4-8, 8-8-8 and 10-10-10 that you purchase in 40lb. bags in the garden center. They are generally the most cost-effective ways of applying nutrients on a wholesale basis in the landscape. When selecting general-purpose fertilizers, don't let cost be the only consideration. The cheapest general-purpose fertilizers usually contain only N, P and K. More costly products contain slow-release forms of nitrogen, such as IBDU (Isobutylene Diurea), sulphur-coated urea, and urea formaldehyde. Look for these on the fertilizer label. Generally, granular fertilizers formulated with slow-release nitrogen, particularly the synthetic forms, like IBDU and sulphur-coated urea, cost more than the basic general-purpose fertilizers, but their extended release often justifies the added cost. Some granular fertilizers also contain secondary nutrients (calcium, magnesium or sulphur) and minor nutrients, such as iron, manganese or zinc. The rule of thumb when purchasing general-purpose fertilizers is to get the most nutrients for your fertilizer dollar. Look at the tag before purchasing the product to see how many nutrient elements are in the bag. It is better to pay $8 and get six or more nutrients than $5 and get only N, P and K. The more nutrients you can get per dollar, the better.

Slow-release type fertilizers are a popular technique for applying nutrients. Even though they generally cost more per pound than granular fertilizers, their release duration exceeds that of granular fertilizers by several weeks, or even months, depending on the product. In fact, some of the new slow-release briquettes release nutrients up to three years after application. Therefore, their higher initial cost may be justified by less frequent application and savings in labor.

One type of slow-release fertilizer has its nutrients microencapsulated in porous membrane coating that look somewhat like fish eggs. Osmocote is an example. Fertilizer is released slowly through the pores of the granules, and the release rate is influenced by soil temperature and moisture (release increases as soil temperature and soil moisture levels increase). Since the fertilizer oozes through the pores gradually, they can be placed directly in the planting hole without injuring the roots.

Other types of slow-release fertilizer are tablets, briquettes and spikes. You have probably seen the tree food spikes that can be pounded into the ground under the tree canopy to provide slow-release nutrients. There also are tablets and briquettes that can be placed in the planting hole or applied to the soil surface on established plants. Studies have yet to indicate whether the concentration of fertilizer near the roots is better for the plant than broadcast application. However, studies with annuals showed that applying a slow-release product in the planting hole when planting annuals resulted in significantly fewer weeds than when a fertilizer was broadcast over the bed.

Liquid fertilizers are often used on annuals and perennials immediately after transplanting, so some nutrients can be absorbed and utilized right away. Liquid fertilizers can be absorbed through both foliage and the roots for a quick response. A disadvantage of liquid fertilizers is that their solubility also causes them to leach readily from the soil. This may result in a "feast then famine" condition unless they are reapplied according to a routine schedule. On the other hand, because they are quickly absorbed, they can be used to correct nutrient deficiencies.

In this age of environmental awareness, many people prefer to use natural organic fertilizers instead of synthetic or manufactured fertilizers. Organic fertilizers are made from composted animal products, animal by-products, naturally occurring minerals, or plant products. Generally, organic fertilizers are lower in nutrient value than synthetic fertilizers, but their nutrients are released slowly over a long period of time. Some organic fertilizers, such as composted animal manures, also function as soil-building amendments that improve the structure, texture, and microbial activity of the soil. Table 2 shows the approximate nutrient content of several organic fertilizer sources.

Specialty fertilizers are formulated for plants that have a higher demand for a particular nutrient, like iron or

Table 2. Average nutrient content of various organic fertilizer sources.

	NITROGEN	PHOSPHORUS (P_2O_5)	POTASH (K_2O)
Blood dried	13.0	---	---
Bone meal (raw)	3.5	22.0	---
Bone meal (steamed)	2.0	2.0	28.0
Cottonseed meal	6.6	2.5	1.5
Fish scrap (dried)	---	9.5	6.0
Soybean meal	7.0	1.2	1.5
Horse manure	0.7	0.3	0.6
Cow manure	0.6	0.3	0.6
Pig manure	0.5	0.3	0.5
Sheep manure	0.8	0.3	0.9
Chicken manure	1.1	0.8	0.5
Duck manure	0.6	1.4	0.5

Source: Soil Fertility and Fertilizers. SL Tisdale and W.L. Nelson, Macmillan Publishing Co,. 1975

zinc. Like slow-release fertilizers, price goes up as the content of secondary and minor elements increases. Special fertilizer formulations are available especially for pecans, roses, azaleas and camellias. These fertilizers have been formulated for the specific nutrient needs of these plants.

Adjusting Soil pH—Soil pH is a measure of the chemical reaction of soil on a scale of 0 to 14. Values below 7 are considered acid, and values above 7 are alkaline. The pH level of a soil can be determined from a soil analysis.

Optimum growth occurs when the soil pH is within a specific range for the crop in question. Most ornamental plants prefer a pH in the range of 5.2 to 6.5. When the pH of soil drops below 4.5, aluminum, iron and manganese become soluble and may become toxic to the plant. Also at low pH, levels of certain nutrient elements, like phosphorus and magnesium, may become unavailable. On the other hand, as pH increases above 7.0, a deficiency of iron, manganese, boron and molybdenum is likely to occur. Also at elevated pH, phosphorus combines with calcium to form insoluble calcium phosphates, so phosphate deficiency may develop. Figure 3 shows the availability of various nutrient elements at different pH levels.

The pH of mineral soils can be lowered by the addition of sulfur. Table 3 shows the approximate amount of sulfur to apply per 1,000 square ft. to lower the pH by one unit on a silt loam soil. Other soil types may require different amounts of sulfur. Ammonium sulfate can also be used to lower soil pH, but it does not react as quickly with the soil as wettable sulfur. Exercise caution when using wettable sulfur because it becomes sulfuric acid when it contacts moisture, including perspiration on the skin. Apply it on a calm day and use protective gloves, clothing and goggles.

Soil pH can be increased by the addition of lime, preferably dolomitic lime that contains both calcium and magnesium. Generally, about 30 pounds of dolomitic lime per 1,000 square feet are required to increase the pH of the soil by one unit (from pH 5.0 to pH 6.0, for instance).

Selecting a Fertilizer Analysis—For general fertilization of ornamentals without the benefit of a soil test, a fertilizer having its primary nutrients (nitrogen, phosphorus and potassium) in a 3-1-2 or 4-1-2 ratio is recommended. A 12-4-8 fertilizer, for instance, is a 3-1-2 ratio while a 16-4-8 fertilizer is a 4-1-2 ratio. Research has shown that phosphorus, the middle number in the analysis, is held by soils and does not leach as readily

Table 3. Approximate amounts of sulfur necessary to lower pH of silt loam soil.

	POUNDS PER 1000 SQUARE FEET	POUNDS PER ACRE
8.0 to 6.5	30	1300
8.0 to 6.0	40	1750
8.0 to 5.5	55	2400
8.0 to 5.0	70	3000
7.5 to 6.5	20	870
7.5 to 6.0	35	1525
7.5 to 5.5	50	2175
7.5 to 5.0	65	2830
7.0 to 6.0	20	870
7.0 to 5.5	35	1525
7.0 to 5.0	50	2175
6.5 to 5.5	25	1090
6.5 to 5.0	40	1750

Figure 3

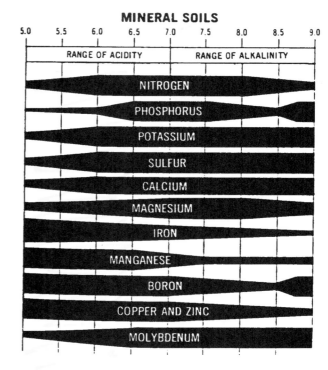

Figure 3. Relative availability of essential elements to plant growth at different pH leves for mineral soils.

with rains or irrigation as nitrogen or potassium does. On new sites where phosphorus has never been applied, a complete, balanced fertilizer, such as 8-8-8 or 10-10-10, is sometimes recommended.

Without the benefit of a soil test, one can only guess the existing nutrient content of a soil and the best fertilizer formulation to use. Never lime a soil unless a soil test indicates a need for lime because nutrient deficiencies may result.

When to Fertilize—Research has shown that plants actively absorb nutrients from the soil during the growing season and that they derive little benefit from nutrients applied during the dormant winter season (see Figure 4). When nitrogen is applied during midwinter, much of it is lost to leaching and vaporization. Fertilization can begin three or four weeks before the plants begin breaking bud in the spring and continue through mid-summer. Fertilizing in late summer (September and October) could promote a late flush of growth which may not acclimate before the first freeze. Some studies have shown that fall fertilization also results in less winter hardiness on some woody plants.

During periods of limited rainfall, reduce the amount of fertilizer applied and the frequency of application in non-irrigated areas. Not only do fertilizers encourage water-demanding new growth, they also can dehydrate

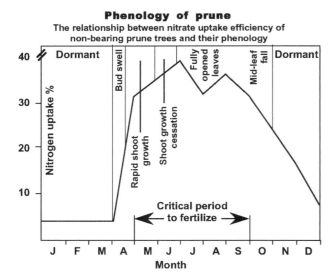

Phenology of prune
The relationship between nitrate uptake efficiency of non-bearing prune trees and their phenology

Fig. 4.   Uptake of nitrogen throughout the year. Source: S.A. Weinbaum et al. 1986. J. Amer. Soc. Hort. Sci. 111(2):224-228.

the roots of plants, making drought stress symptoms more severe. Furthermore, from the environmental standpoint, avoid fertilizing prior to rain, because leaching and run-off of fertilizer may occur. When this happens, fertilizer becomes an environmental pollutant.

How Frequently to Fertilize—The frequency of fertilization depends on the type of plants being fertilized, the desired growth rate, and the type of fertilizer used. If slow-release fertilizers are used, one application should be sufficient for the entire growing season. General-purpose fertilizers, like 10-10-10, may need to be applied two to three times during the growing season or perhaps monthly on plants like annuals and roses. In the professional landscape industry, liquid fertilizers are often applied to annual flowers every two weeks during the growing season. To encourage the spread of newly established ground covers, light applications of a general-purpose fertilizer made monthly would be beneficial. Newly planted ornamental plants usually require more frequent fertilization to promote optimum growth, but once they achieve the desired size, the frequency of fertilization can be reduced to once or twice a year.

How Much Fertilizer to Apply

During Establishment—Woody ornamental trees, shrubs and groundcovers generally do not need fertilizer during the establishment period because they have enough stored energy in their roots to get established. However, if some initial fertilizer is desired, light applications are recommended. For example, on newly planted one-gallon size plants, apply one teaspoon of a 12% to 16% nitrogen fertilizer or one level tablespoon of an 8% to 10% nitrogen fertilizer around the perimeter of the planting hole in March, May, and July. Small trees 12 to 14 inches tall should receive no more than one tablespoon of a 12% to 16% nitrogen fertilizer two to three times during the first growing season. On newly planted large trees, apply two to three tablespoons of a 12% to 16% nitrogen fertilizer uniformly along the perimeter of the planting hole. Remember, newly transplanted ornamentals are under stress while they are getting established and they can be easily injured by over-fertilization.

Never apply weed-and-feed type fertilizers to turfgrasses adjacent to newly planted ornamental plants. Weed-and-feed fertilizers contain herbicides that kill broadleaf weeds, and since most ornamentals are broadleaf plants, they can be damaged by these materials.

Once Established—The quantity of fertilizer to apply to established ornamentals depends on the nitrogen content of the fertilizer used, the area fertilized, and the amount of new growth desired. Nitrogen stimulates vegetative growth, so application rates are based on this primary nutrient.

Generally, application rate is calculated on the basis of area (square feet) to be fertilized and nitrogen content of the fertilizer used. It is given in pounds of nitrogen per 1,000 square feet. Rates vary from 1 lb. to 6 lbs. N per 1,000 sq. ft. per year. If you are following a low-maintenance approach to landscape management and want to keep the plants healthy but minimize the amount of new growth, then fertilize at the lower end of this range (1 to 3 lbs. of nitrogen/1,000 square feet/ yr.). However, when fertilizing to encourage optimum growth of a new planting, higher application rates (4 to 6 lbs. of nitrogen/1000 square feet/yr.) may be used.

Optimum growth fertilization is usually done only on herbaceous ornamentals, such as annual flowers, roses, or on newly planted groundcovers to encourage their spread. Applying more than 1 pound of N per 1,000 square feet at each application is not cost effective since excess nitrogen may leach from the soil, and higher rates may result in root injury. Therefore, to apply 4 lbs. N, four applications at the 1 lb. N rate would be done in four separate applications throughout the growing season, perhaps at 4 to 6 week intervals.

When using a general-purpose granular fertilizer, calculate the quantity to apply by using the following technique. First, determine the area to be fertilized in square feet. This involves measuring the length and width of a bed area and multiplying the two numbers to determine square feet. Not all beds are perfectly rectangular or square, so simply estimate the width and length as accurately as possible. For instance, if a foundation planting is approximately 6 feet wide and 100 feet long, then the total area to be fertilized is 600 square feet (6 X 100). After cataloging the sizes of various beds of the landscape, draw a map or keep a log of them and their size for future reference. Trees, shrubs and ground covers growing within the same bed usually can be fertilized at the same rate with the same fertilizer.

Once you know the area to be fertilized, calculate the amount of fertilizer to apply by dividing the first number in the analysis (nitrogen percent) into the number 100 (a constant). For instance, when applying a 16-4-8 fertilizer, the amount to apply would be 100 divided by 16 = 6 pounds per 1000 square feet or approximately ½ pound per 100 square feet (move the decimal one

Table 4. Recommended application rate of various complete granular fertilizers in the landscape

	Application rate per*				
	1,000 square feet		100 square feet		10 square feet
SOURCE	LBS	CUPS	LBS	CUPS	TBS[†]
10-10-10	10	20	1	2	4
8-8-8	12.5	25	1.2	2.5	5
13-13-13	12.5	25	1.2	2.5	5
12-3-6	8	16	.75	1.5	3
12-4-8	8	16	.75	1.5	3
12-6-6	8	16	.75	1.5	3
16-4-8	8	12	.75	1	2
4-12-12	25	50	2.5	5	10
5-10-10	20	40	2	4	8

[†]TBS=Tablespoons * This rate will supply 1 lb. actual nitrogen per 1000 sq. ft. For optimum growth of young shrubs, ground covers, trees- 3 to 6 applications are recommended at 4 to 6 week intervals from March to August. Established trees and shrubs will benefit from 1 to 2 applications during the growing season. Annual flowers and roses should receive monthly applications from March to August. The volume measurement assumes that 2 cups of a dry granular fertilizer weighs about 1 lb.

place to the left, i.e. 6 lbs./1,000 sq. ft. = 0.6 lbs./100 sq. ft.). This amount of fertilizer would equal 1 pound of actual nitrogen per 1,000 square feet. Applying this amount of fertilizer three times during the growing season would provide 3 pounds of actual nitrogen per 1,000 square feet. Table 4 lists the amount of fertilizer to apply per unit area for various granular fertilizers using this calculation.

Avoid over-fertilization, because fertilizers are chemically salts and, when used in excess, can injure roots. Excess fertilizer also can run off the property during rain or irrigation and become an environmental pollutant when it enters streams and rivers.

When applying water soluble fertilizers, slow-release fertilizers, or organic fertilizers, it is best to follow the label recommendations on application rate.

Trees growing in turf areas will obtain nutrients from the fertilizer that is applied to the turfgrass, so avoid applying excess fertilizer on turfgrasses in an effort to feed trees. Excess fertilizer can damage turfgrass. Research at the University of Florida has shown that tree roots, on average, extend two to three times the canopy spread.

Therefore, if the distance from the main trunk to the drip line (tip of the canopy) is 40 feet, then fertilizer would be broadcast up to 80 feet from the main trunk, if possible. Using the formula for the area of the circle (3.14 x radius squared), the area in square feet to fertilize in this case is $3.14 \times 80^2 = 20,096$ square feet. Of course, there are many instances where the area that can be fertilized is restricted, such as a parking lot island or on street trees. In these cases, simply calculate the area available for fertilization. There are few absorptive roots within 3 feet of the trunk, so there is little benefit from broadcasting fertilizer close to the trunk of established trees.

How to Fertilize—For trees and shrubs, research has shown that it is best to broadcast fertilizers uniformly over an area as opposed to concentrating fertilizers in holes under the canopy. However, root feeding in holes may be advantageous in certain heavy, compact soils.

The most efficient method of fertilizing is with a fertilizer spreader. A push-type cyclone or drop spreader are good choices for turf areas. For broadcasting fertilizer over shrubs and ground covers, a hand-crank spreader with shoulder harness may be used. Broadcasting fertilizers by hand can also be done, but it results in less even application.

When fertilizing over the top of shrubs and groundcovers, make certain the foliage is dry, and use a leaf rake or broom to brush fertilizer off the foliage and onto the ground after application. Some plants, such as liriope and azaleas, can trap fertilizer granules in the whorls of their foliage, and foliar injury may result.

It is not necessary to remove mulch when fertilizing established plants. Removing mulch may expose tender roots near the surface thereby increasing the risk of fertilizer burn.

Whatever fertilizer or method of application is chosen, irrigate soon after applying it to wash residual fertilizer from the foliage and to help nutrients penetrate through the mulch and soil to the roots. Without irrigation, some of the nitrogen applied may volatilize and may be lost to the atmosphere without benefitting plants.

PRUNING

Ornamental plants in landscapes are pruned for many reasons. Some plants are pruned routinely to maintain a desired size or shape. Others are pruned to promote healthy vigorous growth, flowering, or fruiting. Sometimes it is necessary to prune shrubs that overgrow their sites, crowd other plants or limit the view from windows. Plants damaged by insects, diseases, or freezing injury may require corrective pruning.

Each plant in the landscape has its own growth habit and different requirement for pruning. Some shrubs have dwarf growth habits and may never require pruning, while vigorous large-growing shrubs may require frequent pruning.

Anyone can prune, but not everyone prunes properly. Improper pruning, or pruning at the wrong time of year, can result in misshapen plants, reduced flowering or plants that are more likely to be damaged by insects, diseases or winter cold.

Remember the three T's for proper pruning: tools, technique and timing. Use the proper tools, apply the appropriate technique on each pruning task, and prune at the best time of year in relation to flowering.

Pruning Tools

Like other products on the market today, pruning tools are available in a wide range of brand names, styles and prices. When purchasing tools, shop for quality and durability before price. Look for tool manufacturers that provide replacement parts on request and offer warranties against faulty materials and workmanship.

Most pruning tasks in the landscape can be accomplished using hand pruners, lopping shears, pruning saws, pole pruners, or hedge shears. (see Figure 5).

There are two basic types of hand pruners: 1) scissor-action or draw-cut pruners and 2) anvil action or snap-cut pruners. Scissor-action pruners have a sharpened blade that cuts by gliding against a thicker sharp blade. Anvil-action pruners have a sharp blade that cuts against a broad, flattened, grooved blade. Scissor-action pruners usually cost more than anvil-action pruners, but they make closer and smoother cuts.

Hand pruners cut small twigs and branches up to ½ inch in diameter. For larger branches, of ½ to 1½ inches in diameter, lopping shears are best.

Lopping shears, sometimes called loppers, are like scissor-action hand pruners except they have larger blades and long handles that increase leverage. When using loppers, cut in one smooth stroke to avoid injuring the branch.

A pruning saw is used for branches larger than one-and-a-half inches in diameter. A pruning saw has a

Figure 5

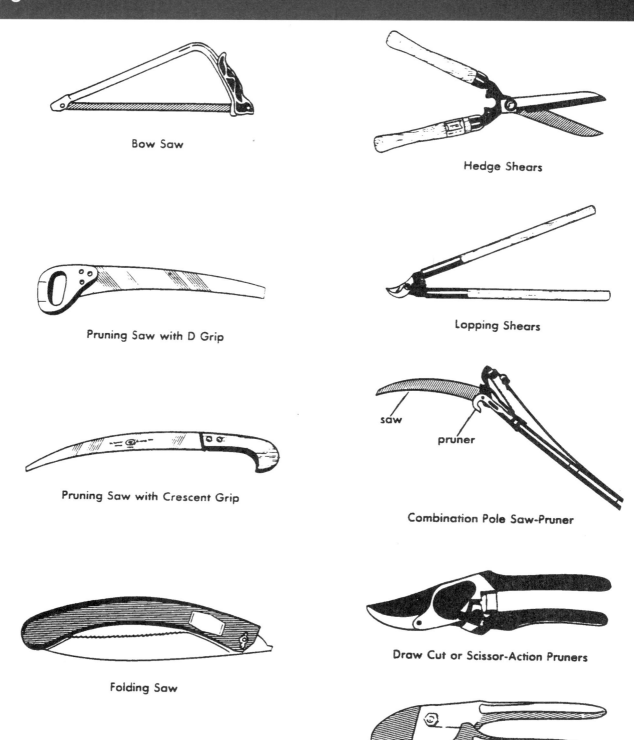

Bow Saw

Hedge Shears

Pruning Saw with D Grip

Lopping Shears

Pruning Saw with Crescent Grip

saw

pruner

Combination Pole Saw-Pruner

Folding Saw

Draw Cut or Scissor-Action Pruners

Anvil or Snap Cut Pruners

Figure 5. Pruning tools.

narrower blade (for easier maneuvering) and coarser points or teeth than a common carpentry saw. Most pruning saws also have curved blades that cut on the draw stroke (pulling the blade toward oneself). Handle shapes vary among pruning saws and are a matter of personal preference. The bow saw, another type of pruning saw, makes large cuts, but may be awkward to maneuver in tight areas.

Pole pruners remove branches from trees that cannot be reached from the ground. Most pole pruners have both a cutting blade and a saw. The cutting blade is operated from the ground by a long rope or lanyard that is pulled downward. The pole can be made from aluminum, fiberglass or plastic. Some poles fit together in three six-foot-long sections, while newer models have a telescoping type of extension. Due to the risk of electrocution, avoid using aluminum handled pole pruners near power lines.

Use hedge shears (manual, gasoline-powered or electric)

Figure 6

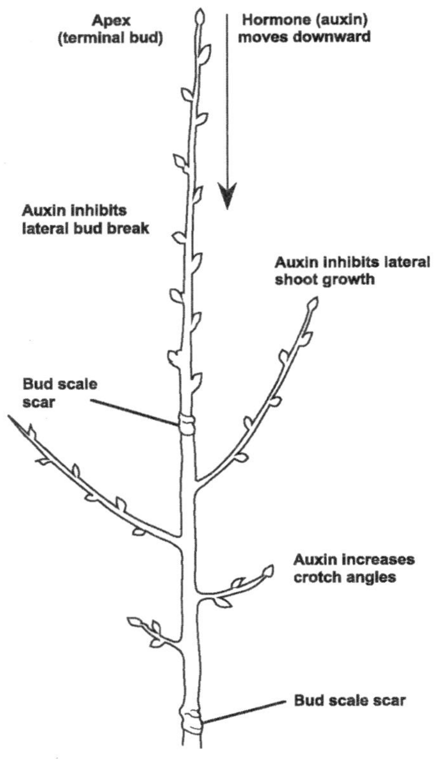

Figure 6. Apical dominance of stems. When a terminal bud is removed, auxin flow downward is disrupted and lateral shoot growth occurs. Most of the new growth occurs within 6 to 8 inches of the pruning cut.

to shear or clip hedges or other plants when a neatly trimmed appearance is desired. Do not attempt to cut large branches with hedge shears.

To keep all pruning tools in good shape, sharpen and oil their blades at the end of each season. When sharpening loppers, hedge shears and scissor-action hand shears, sharpen only the outside surfaces of the blades so the inside surfaces remain flat and slide smoothly against one another. It is best to have pruning saws sharpened by a professional. Oil blades by wiping them with a cloth saturated in household oil, and treat wooden handles with linseed oil.

Pruning Technique

To understand why one pruning technique is preferred over another for a particular plant and why cuts are made the way they are, it helps to review a basic botanical principle of pruning. The terminal bud (the bud at the end of a branch or twig) produces a hormone called auxin that directs the growth of lateral buds (buds along the side of the branch or twig). As long as the terminal bud is intact, auxin suppresses the growth of lateral buds and shoots behind the terminal (Figure 6). However, when the terminal bud is removed by pruning, the inhibiting effect of auxin is eliminated and lateral buds and shoots below the pruning cut grow vigorously. The most vigorous new growth always occurs within 6 to 8 inches of the pruning cut.

Shearing vs. Thinning—When shrubs are sheared routinely, a lot of dense, thick, new growth is produced near the outer portions of the canopy. As a result, less light reaches the interior portions of the plant, and foliage within the canopy becomes sparse. Air circulation within the canopy is reduced, and the likelihood of insect and disease infestation increases.

Thinning (cutting selected branches to a lateral branch, a lateral bud, or main trunk) is usually preferred to shearing. Thinning encourages new growth within the interior portions of a shrub, reduces size and provides a fuller, more attractive plant (figure 7).

Making the Cut—A second botanical principle explains what happens when a pruning cut is made. When a branch is cut back to the main trunk, to a lateral branch, or to a lateral bud, a higher concentration of hormones in these areas causes the wound to heal rapidly. When a stub is left, the distance from the hormonal source increases and the wound heals slower, if it heals at all. Insects and diseases may enter the cut portion of a stub and cause it to die back.

Figure 7

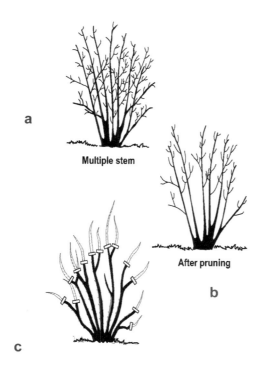

a — Multiple stem

b — After pruning

c

Figure 7. Multiple stem shrub before pruning(a), after pruning-thinning (b), or heading (c).

Therefore, regardless of whether pruning a small twig or a large branch, a gardener can avoid leaving a stub by always cutting back to a bud, a lateral branch or the main trunk.

When pruning back to a bud, make the cut at a slight angle just above the bud. This allows moisture to flow readily off the wound. A hormonal stimulus from the nearby bud accelerates the healing process. However, avoid making the cut at a sharp angle because in will result in a larger wound for healing (Figure 8).

Pruning Large Tree Limbs—When large limbs are removed from trees, the bark along the main trunk may tear due to the weight of the falling limb. Bark damage can be avoided by making a jump cut, which consists of three separate cuts (Figure 9). First, cut about one-fourth to one-half way through the lower side of the limb about a foot from the main trunk. Then make a second cut on top of the limb a few inches beyond the first cut. The weight of the branch will break the limb back to the first cut. Then, remove the remaining stub

by cutting it back to the branch collar, a swollen area where the branch is attached to the trunk. Cut just outside the branch collar. Avoid making a flush cut into the collar and too close to the main trunk because the wound will not heal properly.

Research shows that wound dressing compounds do not promote healing or protect a wound from decay, regardless of the size of the cut. Aesthetically, wound dressings may have some merit, but if pruning is done properly, the wound heals rapidly and a wound dressing is not needed.

Shaping Tree-form Shrubs—Common landscape shrubs like crape myrtle, yaupon holly, wax myrtle, and wax-leaf ligustrum are often pruned as tree forms (shrubs shaped like a tree with one or more main trunks). The best time to begin a tree form is late winter before spring growth begins.

It is easiest to start a tree form from a one-year old plant, but mature plants can also be re-shaped into a tree form with a little extra effort. Select one to three of the most vigorous growing branches (depending on the number of main trunks desired) and prune all other branches to ground level. Remove lateral branches that are less than four feet off the ground along the main trunk and thin the canopy by getting rid of inward growing branches or branches that cross one another. Avoid shearing unless you want a high-maintenance topiary.

A multiple-trunk tree-form also can be developed by pruning all branches back to ground level, selecting three to five of the most vigorous new shoots during the growing season to serve as main trunks and removing all others.

Be prepared for an abundance of new suckers to sprout from the base and waterspouts along the trunk. These

Figure 8

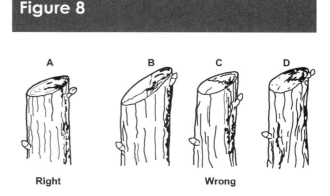

A   B   C   D

Right   Wrong

Figure 8. Proper pruning angle. A is cut correctly, B is too slanting, C is too far from the bud, and d is too close to the bud.

Figure 9

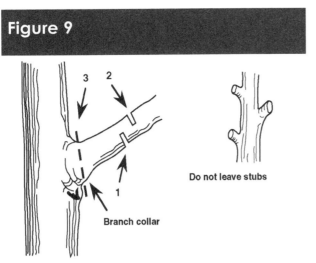

Do not leave stubs

Figure 9. To remove heavy branches without damaging the tree, a three-cut sequence is recommended. Cut to the branch collar (swollen area where the branch joins the trunk).

undesirable shoots are easily removed by hand when they are young and succulent. On some vigorous plants, like crape myrtle, it may be necessary to remove undesired shoots weekly. Diligence will eventually pay off as the energy of the plant will gradually be diverted into the new main trunks.

It may take three to five years to shape a tree-form plant, but the interest and accent it lends to the landscape may be worth the extra effort.

Pruning Overgrown Shrubs—Homeowners and inexperienced landscapers will sometimes make the mistake of planting large-growing shrubs along the foundation of a building or home. As the plants mature they overgrow the site, crowd other plants, hide windows and appear out of scale with the building. When this occurs, it may be necessary to prune severely to bring the plants within bounds (Figure 10). This is called renewal pruning.

Renewal pruning involves cutting the plants back to within 6 to 12 inches of ground level. In this instance, timing is more important than technique. The best time to prune severely is when spring growth begins - mid-March in north Georgia and mid-February in south Georgia. Pruning in late fall or mid-winter may encourage new growth which can be injured by cold. Renewal pruning results in abundant new growth by mid-summer. Once the new shoots are 6 to 12 inches long, prune the tips to encourage lateral branching and a more compact shrub.

Most broadleaf shrubs, such as azaleas, camellias, ligus-

trum, glossy abelia, nandina, cleyera and crape myrtle, respond well to renewal pruning.

Avoid renewal pruning on boxwoods because they are slow to recover from severe pruning. It also should NOT be done on conifers, including junipers, pine, spruce, fir, cedar, arborvitae, leyland cypress and yew, because these plants are not capable of forming new growth from old wood. When these plants are pruned severely, all the plant's energy goes to the shoots adjacent to the cut instead of new shoots. When the terminal branch of a pine tree is removed, a lower lateral branch tries to become dominant. The result is a lop-sided tree as the lateral branches assume a more vertical position. Topping a leyland cypress will cause the plant to look unsightly for a period of time, but the branches close

Figure 10

Figure 10. Renewal pruning is sometimes necessary to bring overgrown broadleaf shrubs back into scale with their surroundings.

to the cut will eventually shift to a more vertical position, fill in the void, and continue the upward growth. When a juniper is pruned back to the ground and no green growth remains, the plant will likely die. When a conifer overgrows its site, it may be best to cut it down and replace it with a more suitable plant.

Skirting, lifting the canopy by removing low-growing branches and shaping a tree form, is an alternative to renewal pruning. A tree form may adapt well to the landscape scheme and will appear less harsh than a severely pruned shrub.

Pruning Time

Because flowering ornamentals form their flower buds at different times of year, pruning times must be adjusted accordingly. Many spring-flowering plants, such as azalea, dogwood, forsythia, redbud and rhododendron, set flower buds in the fall; therefore, pruning during the fall and winter months eliminates or decreases their spring flower display. Plants that typically flower during the summer form flower buds on new growth and can be pruned during the winter with no effect on their flowering. Examples of this type of plant are crape myrtle, hibiscus, and glossy abelia.

As a general rule, plants that flower before May should be pruned after they bloom, while those that flower after May are considered summer-flowering and can be pruned just prior to spring growth. Exceptions to this rule are late-flowering azalea cultivars which bloom during May, June, or even July. Always prune azalea cultivars after they bloom.

Ornamental plants that are not grown for their showy flowers can be pruned during the late winter, spring or summer months. Avoid pruning during the fall or early winter because new growth may emerge before the plant goes dormant, and the new growth may not have time to sufficiently harden to resist winter freezes. Table 5 lists suggested pruning times for selected flower plants.

Some shade and flowering trees tend to bleed or exude large amounts of sap from pruning wounds. Among these trees are maple, birch, dogwood, beech, elm, willow, flowering plum, and flowering cherry. Sap exuded from the tree is not harmful, but it is unsightly. To minimize bleeding, prune these trees after the leaves have matured. Leaves use plant sap when they expand, and the tree exudes less sap from the wound.

Guidelines for Pruning Specific Plant Groups

Deciduous Shade and Flowering Trees—Trees are like children; training at an early age will influence how they develop. Many landscapers are reluctant to prune a young tree, particularly when it is nothing more than a single stem or a few scrawny branches, but this is precisely when pruning should begin.

Ideally, deciduous shade trees (those that lose their leaves during the winter) and flowering trees should have one central trunk (leader) and five to eight strong lateral branches along the main trunk. Major limbs should begin about five feet above the ground and have good spacing around the main trunk.

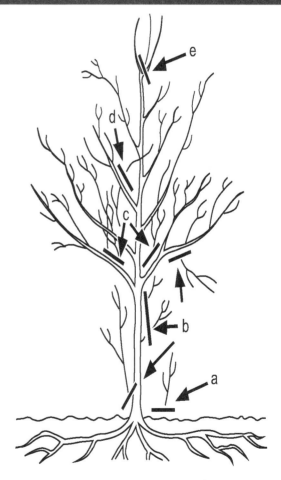

Figure 11

Figure 11. Tree pruning. Remove suckers originating from below-ground roots (a), low-growing branches which interfere with maintenance practices (b), upright growing shoots or watersprouts (c), crossing branches (d), and branches that compete with the central leaders for dominance (e).

Once the framework (trunk and main branches) of the tree is established, some annual maintenance pruning is required (Figure 11). Each tree is different in its growth habit, vigor and pruning requirements, but there are some general considerations that may help direct your pruning decisions:

1. A major limb growing at a narrow angle to the main trunk (less than a 45 degree angle) is likely to develop a weak crotch and may split during heavy winds and ice loads. Remove branches that have narrow crotch angles.

2. Remove branches that grow inward or threaten to rub against nearby branches.

3. Remove branches that grow downward from the main limbs which may interfere with mowing and other maintenance practices.

4. Prune branches damaged by insects, diseases, winter cold or storms below the damaged area. Prune branches of pear, pyracantha, or loquat damaged by fireblight disease several inches below the infection. To prevent spreading the disease, sterilize pruning tools between cuts by dipping the blades in rubbing alcohol or a solution prepared from 1 part household bleach to 10 parts water.

5. Trees such as Bradford pear, ornamental cherry, crabapple and ornamental plum form vigorous shoots (suckers) at the base of the trunk and many upright succulent shoots (watersprouts) along the main branches. These shoots starve the tree of valuable nutrients and detract from the tree's overall appearance. Remove them while they are young.

6. Some trees develop lateral upright shoots which compete with the main trunk for dominance. Remove these shoots to maintain a conical or pyramidal growth habit.

Broadleaf Evergreen Trees—Broadleaf evergreens, like magnolias and hollies, usually require little or no pruning. In fact, most broadleaf evergreens develop a naturally symmetric growth habit when left alone. Low-sweeping branches at ground level lend a natural Southern charm to our landscapes.

A small amount of pruning may be necessary during the early life of the tree to balance the growth or to eliminate multiple trunks and/or multiple leader branches. Otherwise, routine annual pruning is not recommended.

Deciduous and Broadleaf Evergreens—Some shrubs in the landscape have an inherently dwarf growth habit and require little or no pruning. Japanese boxwood, dwarf yaupon holly, and Helleri holly are a few examples. Although selective thinning is the best pruning technique to use on these shrubs, it is also time-consuming. Shearing is often the most cost-effective and efficient pruning method for these plants. However, as noted previously, shearing increases maintenance requirements and results in a formal, unnatural appearance.

Broadleaf evergreens with coarse-textured foliage, such as Indian Hawthorne, Osmanthus, and Burford holly are best pruned with thinning cuts. Shearing cuts the foliage and causes it to appear tattered and brown.

Large, established shrubs differ in their pruning requirements due to their age, growth habit, vigor, flowering time, and location in the landscape. Begin pruning shrubs when they are young to encourage vigorous, compact growth. Occasional thinning cuts control shrub size, and decrease the need for severe pruning as

Table 5. Suggested pruning time for common flowering trees, shrubs and vines

PRUNE AFTER FLOWERING	
Azalea	Japanese pieris
Beautybush	Mockorange
Bigleaf hydrangea	Oakleaf hydrangea
Bradford pear	Pearlbush
Bridalwreath spirea	Pyracantha
Clematis	Redbud
Climbing roses	Saucer magnolia
Crabapple	Star magnolia
Deutzia	Shrub honeysuckle
Dogwood	Thunberg spirea
Doublefile viburnum	Vanhoutte spirea
Flowering almond	Weigela
Flowering cherry	Winter daphne
Flowering quince	Wisteria
Forsythia	Witchhazel
PRUNE BEFORE SPRING GROWTH BEGINS	
Beautyberry	Goldenrain tree
Camellia	Japanese barberry
Chaste tree (Vitex)	Japanese spirea
Crape myrtle	Nandina
Floribunda rose	Rose of Sharon (Althea)
Fragrant tea olive	Sourwood
Grandiflora rose	Anthony Waterer spirea
Glossy abelia	Sweetshrub

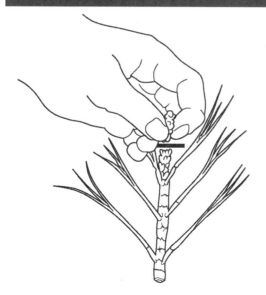

Figure 12. Prune pines and spruce in the candle stage.

the plant matures.

Use hand pruners to cut back shoots that are dying from disease or winter cold or that have become leggy. Always cut dying shoots back to healthy green wood to prevent further dieback. Once new shoots are six to eight inches long, they can be pinched or 'tip pruned' to encourage branching, compact growth and more blooms. A young, vigorous azalea may require light pruning several times to develop a dense, compact growth habit, but avoid pruning after July 1 to avoid interfering with bud set for the following year.

Conifers (Needle Evergreens)—Most upright-growing plants in this group, such as spruce, pine, cedar and fir, have branches spaced evenly around the main trunk. They develop symmetrical growth habits and become quite large at maturity. If planted in open areas and given plenty of room to grow, they require minimal pruning.

By removing about one-half of the new shoots while new growth is in the candle stage (small immature needles packed around the stem resembling a candle), it is possible to thicken the growth of pines and spruce (Figure 12). Avoid cutting back into the hardened older wood because new shoots will not grow from old wood. Pruning conifers in the candle stage will only thicken their growth and control height temporarily. A loblolly pine will eventually reach 60 feet tall despite the best efforts to keep it small.

Upright and broad-spreading junipers, such as Torulosa,

Pfitzer, Hetzi and Parsoni, sometimes overgrow their sites and must be reduced in size. Make thinning cuts within the canopy to reduce plant size without destroying the natural shape by cutting selective branches back to lateral branches. This technique maintains a natural appearance while decreasing the size of the shrub.

Vines/Groundcovers—Certain vines in the landscape, such as honeysuckle, English ivy, clematis, wintercreeper euonymus and trumpetcreeper climb trees or other supports and can grow rampant if they are not controlled. The amount of pruning these plants need every year depends on their vigor, growth habit and spread. Vines trained to an arbor (to shade a patio or deck) may require only minor thinning or tip pruning to encourage branching, while those growing in trees or competing with other plants may need more severe pruning to control their size.

Pruning time is important for flowering vines. Prune summer-blooming vines, such as clematis and trumpetcreeper, before new growth begins. Prune spring-blooming vines, like wisteria, Japanese honeysuckle, winter jasmine and periwinkle, after they flower.

Groundcovers are pruned primarily for three reasons: to thin their canopy when they grow thick and dense, to keep them within bounds, and to rejuvenate their growth after a harsh winter has damaged their foliage.

Horizontal junipers, like Blue Rug, Bar Harbor and

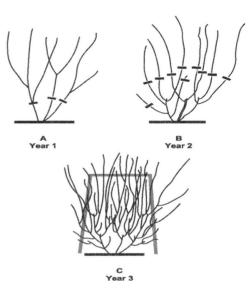

Figure 13. Developing a hedge over a 3-year period

Prince of Wales, tend to form new foliage on top of older foliage and become thick and dense once their canopies meet. Thinning cuts improve air circulation within the canopy and prevent insect and disease problems.

Prune liriope and mondo grass to rejuvenate them after a harsh winter has damaged their foliage. Mow off the foliage of these ground covers with a lawn-mower set at the highest possible cutting height. This would be done in early to mid-February in south Georgia, and late February in north Georgia.

Hedges—Because hedges are used primarily as privacy screens, begin pruning them early to encourage a compact growth habit. Head back newly planted hedge plants to within 12 inches of ground level and prune new shoot tips during the growing season to encourage branching. To develop a dense, compact hedge that provides privacy, prune regularly while the plants mature. Figure 13 illustrates a 3-year pruning sequence to produce a hedge.

Once a hedge reaches the desired height, decide whether an informal or formal pruning style are desired. An informal style is best for a low-maintenance landscape. Informally pruned hedges assume a natural growth habit. Prune only "as needed" to remove dead or diseased wood, to thin branches, or to tip prune selected branches where more dense compact growth is needed.

Formally pruned hedges, on the other hand, require frequent shearing, sometimes three to five times during the growing season, to maintain their shape. If a formally pruned hedge best fits the style of landscaping, prune it in a pyramidal shape with the narrowest part of the hedge at the top tapering to a wider base (Figure 14). A pyramidal shape allows adequate light to reach the lower portion of the canopy. As a result, the foliage will remain dense all the way to the ground.

To Paint or Not to Paint Wounds—Research has shown that it is not necessary to put pruning paint on pruning cuts, regardless of the size or type of wound. In fact, some of the asphalt based pruning paints can crack over time, trap moisture, and encourage wood decay. Pruning paints do not encourage wound healing. They are simply cosmetic. If pruning is done properly and according to the guidelines provided in this chapter, wounds should heal completely.

Figure 14

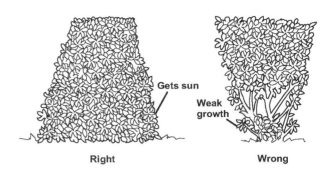

Figure 14. Formal pruning of a hedge.

Suggested Guidelines For Pruning Selected Ornamental Plants In The Landscape

For additional information on pruning, refer to Georgia Cooperative Extension Bulletin 961: *Pruning Ornamental Trees and Shrubs in the Landscape.*

ARBORVITAE—An evergreen, the exterior foliage can be pruned lightly when it needs shaping. Avoid making major cuts.

AZALEA—Prune by thinning after bloom if necessary. Do not prune at all if the plant looks good. Old overgrown plants can be renewed by cutting back close to ground level in February.

BEAUTYBERRY—Thin out growth prior to spring growth. Flowers and fruits on new growth

BIRCH—Make major cuts when dormant. Light pruning in full leaf will minimize sap flow (bleeding) from wound.

BOXWOOD—Prune by thinning or shearing most any time of year. Avoid heavy pruning, because the plant is slow to recover or may decline.

CAMELLIA—Thin out branches after bloom if necessary. Camellias generally require little pruning.

CHERRY (Ornamental)—Make major cuts in late winter. Use light pruning after bloom to remove suckers or to shape.

CLEMATIS—Some bloom on old wood, and some

on new wood, depending on species. It is best to wait until after bloom to prune this plant. Thin out the old wood. Some vigorous varieties can be pruned within 12 inches of ground level.

CLEYERA—Prune by thinning during the growing season to maintain a natural shape.

COTONEASTER—Make thinning cuts to remove old wood and to shape in late winter or early spring.

CRABAPPLE (Flowering)—Prune when fully dormant to remove suckers and to produce a desirable shape. Young suckers can be easily removed by hand during the growing season.

CRAPE MYRTLE—Crape myrtle tolerates severe pruning abuse in the landscape. It can be pruned to a tree form by selective thinning, or to a shrub form by pruning it within a foot of ground level. It is a summer-flowering shrub, so prune it during late winter or early spring. Research has shown that late summer pruning of crape myrtle decreases its winter hardiness.

Encourage a second flush of bloom during late summer by removing the seed clusters after the flowers fade and thinning some of the new growth.

Crape myrtle shaped as a tree form often sends up vigorous shoots or suckers from the base that can easily be removed by hand when they are young and succulent. To prevent regrowth of suckers, apply a sprout-inhibiting compound containing NAA to the base of the plant.

Crape myrtle is best pruned by selective thinning cuts that will maintain the natural form of the plant (figure 15). Too often landscapers make heading cuts on main branches, leaving nubs that result in a poodle-like growth habit and unnatural appearance.

DEUTZIA—Make thinning cuts after flowering if shaping is necessary.

DOGWOOD—This tree sets blossom buds in late summer. Make major cuts when dormant, even though that may sacrifice some blossoms. Otherwise, prune it after flowering.

ELAEAGNUS—A very vigorous summer grower. It may grow a foot or more a week during the growing season. Thin out long shoots as necessary. Do not try to maintain a formal shape.

EUONYMUS—Growth habit of this plant ranges from upright shrubs to ground covers. Prune by thinning as necessary any time during the growing season.

FRINGETREE—Prune by thinning to achieve desired shape in late winter. Birds enjoy the late summer fruit, so avoid pruning after flowering.

GOLDENRAIN TREE—Prune to tree form in late winter.

HEMLOCK—This plant normally needs no pruning. Light shearing of the outer canopy may be necessary to correct form. Avoid major cuts.

HOLLY—There are many different growth habits and forms. Most are evergreen, but some species are deciduous. If plants are prized for berries, prune them in late winter, before spring flowering. If berries are not a concern, thinning (or shearing of small-leaf types) can be done any time during the growing season.

HONEYLOCUST—Maintain desired shape by thinning in late winter.

HYDRANGEA (Bigleaf, French, Oakleaf)—Flower buds form on old wood. Prune after flowering.

HYDRANGEA (Panicle, Smooth)—Blooms on new wood. Prune when dormant, and remove spent blossoms after flowering.

JASMINE (Winter)—Thin out after flowering to maintain a desired shape.

JUNIPER—Maintain shape or eliminate undergrowth of groundcover types by thinning during the growing season. Avoid heavy pruning to old wood because new growth will not occur.

LAUREL (English)—Prune by thinning as needed during the growing season.

LIRIOPE—Remove old foliage 4 to 6 weeks before the spring growing season. On level ground, set the lawnmower to make the highest cut, for an efficient way of pruning this plant.

MAGNOLIA (Japanese)—Prune to desired shape after flowering.

MAGNOLIA (Southern)—Generally requires little pruning. Shape by thinning during the growing season, preferably after bloom.

MAPLE—Prune in late winter if major cuts are necessary. Light pruning in mid-summer can also be done. Avoid early spring pruning because unsightly sap will flow from the pruning wounds.

MOCKORANGE—Prune after flowering by thinning

out old wood. It may be cut back to ground level if desired.

MOUNTAIN-LAUREL—Prune lightly by thinning to desired shape after flowering.

NANDINA—As plants age, thin out old canes by cutting them back to ground level. Then selectively cut back one-third of the remaining canes by half their length to encourage a full dense canopy. Do this pruning in late winter or after fruiting.

OAK—Prune to desired shape when dormant.

OLEANDER—Flowers on new growth, so prune it just prior to spring growth. Thin out old wood and head back top for desired shape and height.

OSMANTHUS—Shape by thinning during the growing season. The plant responds well to heavy pruning.

PEAR (Ornamental)—Make major cuts in late winter (when dormant), even though some blossoms may be sacrificed. Lightly prune after flowering if necessary.

PHOTINIA (Red-tip)—Prune any time during the growing season. Early spring and late summer pruning results in new growth that turns brilliant red.

PINE (Also spruce, fir)—Prune to desired shape by removing all or part of the new growth (called "candles") in spring. Avoid pruning into old wood.

PITTOSPORUM—Prune to desired shape any time during the growing season.

PYRACANTHA—Prune after fruit set to remove non-fruiting wood.

QUINCE (Flowering)—Prune after flowering. Thin out old branches and head back others to desired form and size.

REDBUD—Make major cuts in late winter. Light pruning can be done after flowering.

RHODODENDRON—Prune, if necessary, to desired shape and to increase branching after bloom.

ROSE (Hybrid tea, grandiflora, floribunda)—Prune in early spring when new growth begins.

ROSE (Climbing)—After flowering, thin out old canes and head back remaining shoots by about one-third, depending on their vigor.

ROSE-OF-SHARON—This plant flowers on new growth, so prune it in late winter.

SPIREA—Prune by thinning after bloom. Most species respond well to severe pruning.

TRUMPETCREEPER—Flowers on new growth, so prune it during the dormant season. This plant will tolerate severe pruning.

VIBURNUM—Prune after flowering or fruit set to thin out oldest, non-fruiting wood and to improve shape.

WAXMYRTLE—Prune to desired shape during the growing season.

WISTERIA—Prune after flowering. This is a very vigorous vine. It can be heavily pruned.

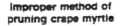

Figure 15

Improper method of pruning crape myrtle

Proper method of pruning crape myrtle

1. Cutting on line shown by dashed line is too often done when pruning shrubs.

1. Shrub before pruning. Remove all weak and dead branches.

2. Same plant after being pruned as indicated above. All sucker growth remains.

2. Same shrub after removal of weak and interfering branches and with base sucker growth removed.

3. Final result: beautiful natural shape of shrub is lost and bloom is sparse and ineffectual.

3. Final result: beautiful natural and distinctive form of plant retained. Vigorous growth and prolific and effective flowering.

Figure 15. Pruning crape myrtle

RESOURCES

Wade, Gary L. *Soil Preparation and Planting Procedures for Ornamental Plants in the Landscape.* Georgia Cooperative Extension Bulletin 932.

Wade, Gary L. and James T. Midcap. *Pruning Ornamental Plants in the Landscape.* Georgia Cooperative Extension Bulletin 961.

Wade, Gary L. and Beverly Sparks. *Care of Ornamental Plants in the Landscape.* Georgia Cooperative Extension Bulletin 1065.

Wade, Gary L. and Robert R.Westerfield. *Basic Principles of Pruning Woody Plants.* Georgia Cooperative Extension Bulletin 949.

Feucht, James R. and Jack D. Butler. *Landscape Management: Planting and Maintenance of Trees, Shrubs and Turfgrasses.* Van Norstrand Reinhold Company.

Harris, Richard W. *Arboriculture: Integrated Management of Landscape Trees, Shrubs and Vines.* Prentice Hall.

DISCUSSION QUESTIONS

1. Why is site analysis important?

2. Describe how sunlight influences plant selection and placement in the landscape.

3. What is a Perk test?

4. Where would it be best to locate tender vegetation in the landscape?

5. When is the best time of year to plant?

6. Describe the step-by-step planting procedure for woody ornamentals.

7. How are guy wires installed on a large tree, and how long should they be left in place?

8. List three common mulches and their advantages and disadvantages.

9. Give some examples of an organic fertilizer, a general-purpose fertilizer, and a specialty fertilizer.

10. How much 12-4-8 fertilizer should be applied per 1,000 square feet?

11. Describe the proper procedure for fertilizing a large, established tree.

12. What are some problems of overfertilization?

13. Describe the difference between heading and thinning.

14. Describe the jump cut technique for removing large limbs from trees.

15. When is the best time to prune spring flowering plants? summer flowering plants?

10

Herbaceous Plants: Annuals and Perennials

Paul A. Thomas

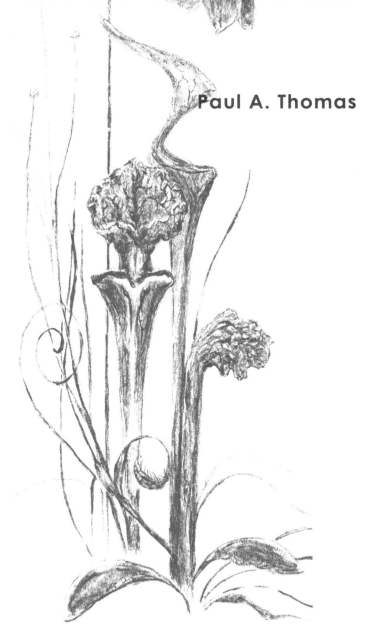

LEARNING OBJECTIVES

Understand the unique lifecycles of annuals, perennials & biennials.

Understand cultural requirements that should be considered.

Understand bed layout and planning considerations and planting techniques for annuals.

Understand basic annual bed fertilization and maintenance including weed control.

Have an appreciation for the common annuals available in Georgia and the benefits of annuals in container gardening.

Understand the qualities of perennials, why and where you would grow them.

Understand cultural requirements of perennials, bed layout and planning considerations.

Know basic planting techniques for perennials including division.

Understand basic perennial bed fertilization, maintenance, and weed control options for perennial beds.

TERMS TO KNOW

Annuals plants that complete their life cycle in a year or less.

Biennials plants that complete their life cycle in two years or growing seasons

Cool Season annuals certain flowering annuals grow and flower more profusely in comparatively cool weather.

Hardy Annuals plants that tolerate frost and some freezing weather.

Foliage Plant plants grown primarily for ornamental foliage such as coleus and hosta.

Herbaceous a nonwoody plant.

Perennials plants that do not die after flowering, but live from year to year.

Vegetative Annual annual flowers that cannot be produced from seed.

Warm Season Annuals annuals that grow

and flower well during the summer.

ANNUALS AND ANNUAL BEDS

What are annual flowers and why are they so important? They are plants that provide color and beauty in the landscape during spring, summer, and fall. In recent years, plant breeders have improved to perfection the numerous types and forms of annual flowers that bloom. Annual plants now grow more compactly, produce more blooms, tolerate more heat or shade, and above all, flower more profusely. These annual flowers and are eagerly sought and planted in the spring to renew and brighten the landscape scene.

Although annuals are primarily used to provide color, they can also add rhythm, harmony, contrast, and accent to the garden landscape. Basic plant selection is the foundation to success. Each selection will have different needs and preferences; hence, it is incorrect to group all annuals together when discussing watering and fertilization. Most annuals are planted in full sun, but there are many selections that will provide color in shade or in wet locations. Tables are provided at the end of each chapter to assist you in plant selection for different conditions.

Some examples of how annuals can be used in the landscape include the following:

• Attract attention and lead the eye to a focal point within the landscape.

• Divert attention from necessary but unattractive objects, such as railroad tracks or parking lots.

• Relieve monotony by using different annual flowers in adequately sized containers. These containers with their colorful plants provide interest on steps, patios and plazas.

• Tie together a shrubbery planting composition and unify the entire landscape design around a commercial building.

• Extend the season of interest into the summer and fall months by planting annuals with perennials and bulbs.

• Add interest to border plantings.

Using Color In Design

Using the range of colors available in modern flowering annuals can be a daunting challenge. A brief review of color principles may help. Primary colors are red, yellow and blue. Colors opposite one another in the color wheel are said to be complementary and when used side by side produce a strong but pleasing contrast.

Following the principle of combining complementary colors, it would be possible to use blue (violet) Agera-tum in the foreground of yellow Marigolds to produce a striking contrast. A similar contrast could be obtained by using red Petunias or Geraniums in front of a green hedge. Combinations of primary colors also provide a striking contrast.

Colors that lie between any two primary colors on the color wheel are said to be in harmony with one another. This is a principle that can be applied to produce an effective display of annual flowers. For example, a combination of the red violet and violet portion of the color wheel produces a harmonious display.

A few design factors to consider when using annuals:

• Red, orange, and yellow are warm colors and produce excitement in the landscape.

• Blue, green and violet are cool colors, imparting a "visual" cooling effect.

• Annual flowers are most effective when seen against a background that shows off their colors. Most flowers need a darker background. Backgrounds such as green shrubs or brown fences are very effective.

• A flower border located in front of a shrub border as a part of a long, sweeping curve is much more restful to the eye than a flower border with sharp, angular lines.

• Like many other areas of horticulture, there is much to learn to become a proficient gardener. This chapter only provides a basic outline for growing annuals. You will need to read about and discover on your own the diversity and intricacies of the more than 3200 annual cultivars on the market.

Terms to Know

There are a few terms involved with annual gardening. Annuals are highly variable and can be divided into several categories. Major categories include:

Hardy Annuals—Hardy annuals are those that tolerate frost and some freezing weather. In warmer areas of the state, they can be sown outdoors in the fall. Seedlings tolerate some cold and overwinter to resume growth in the spring. Examples include Delphinium, Larkspur, and Sweet Pea. Some hardy annuals are planted as small plants in the fall in mid and South Georgia. In mild winters these may even bloom by late fall. If cold weather comes earlier, they produce stocky growth and then branch and flower prolifically in the spring. Examples of hardy annuals include Sweet Alyssum, Calendula, Pansy, Stock, Snapdragon, and certain types of Dianthus.

Cool Season Annuals—Certain flowering annuals grow and flower more profusely in comparatively cool weather. Warm days in the 70's and 80's, followed by cooler nights, conserve carbohydrates produced by the plant. The important issue is cool soil temperatures in the lower 60's to mid 50's. These cool temperatures help reduce respiration at night and preserve carbohydrates that serve as a source of energy for growth and more intense flower coloration. Examples of annuals that grow and flower best during cooler periods of the year include Pansy, Snapdragon, Violas, Petunia and Alyssum.

Warm Season Annuals—Warm season or summer annuals are numerous and grow and flower well during the summer when air temperatures range in the high 80's and 90's during the day and the 60's and 70's during the night. Soil temperatures are usually in the low 70's at night most of the summer. These plants have adapted to produce sufficient carbohydrates and store them in such a way as to keep them available for growth, even when it's really hot. A few examples are Marigold, Vinca, Tithonia, Zinnia, and Salvia. They are best purchased as larger plant materials such as 4 inch or 6 inch pots. Many growers sell the larger warm season annuals late in the spring, as it is easier to grow them, and it is not too late to establish them. Warm season annuals establish well in warm soils and do not suffer transplant shock if watered.

Vegetative Annuals—Vegetative annuals are annual flowers that cannot be produced from seed, and must be produced from rooted cuttings or tissue cultured plantlets. You will hear this term bantered about often given the number of specimens on the market today. They are usually tropical in origin, unusual in form, and often more expensive than seed-produced annuals. Sun-loving Coleus, some cultivars of Petunia, Scaevola and many, many more are becoming quite popular. Many of our most popular hanging basket plants are vegetatively propagated annuals

Invasive Annuals (Reseeders!)—As responsible gardeners, we need to keep in mind that some annuals can become quite a nuisance if left on their own. Many of our popular annuals re-seed, and generate thousands of seedlings. Selections such as Melampodium, Cleome, Cosmos, Celosia and Amaranth can take over a garden in a year. Yet, each garden is different, and plants may reseed heavily in some years and not at all in others. This makes it impossible for us to know which annuals can become a problem in any one location. Therefore it is the responsibility of each gardener to make every effort to prevent them from spreading into undisturbed, wild areas, such as local forests or prairies.

Planting Annuals

Plant Size Makes a Difference—When deciding how to plant annuals, it is essential to know how large your plants will grow during the intended growing season. Pansies and most other cool season annuals will grow slowly and can be planted on 6 to 8 inch centers. By doing this, the plants will grow into each other and form a solid carpet of color by the end of the growing season although many spring, summer, and fall annuals can grow rapidly. Some common annuals such as Tithonia and the Mexican Sunflower may grow to a height of 6 feet and a width of 3 feet. This often surprises the gardener who purchased a small seedling in a 4-inch pot. Know your plants and their habits, and space them accordingly.

Growing from Seed—Gardeners often derive pleasure from starting their own seed. However, many bedding plant seeds are difficult to maintain after germination, and cause frustration. Planting a great many seeds in a common pot may seem efficient; however, separating the seedlings is the cause of much damage to young roots and allows disease to take hold. A much better practice is to use cell trays (sometimes called plug trays) for seedlings, and to put two or three seeds per plug. This allows you to thin without doing much damage, and gives each seedling its own root system. All seedlings require a moist environment with adequate light. However, almost all annuals have slightly different germination requirements, which means there is a lot to learn before beginning a seed germination project. It may also be necessary to use fungicides to control loss from disease.

Plugs, Flats and 4-inch Pots—A more simple and efficient way to establish a garden is to purchase young plants that have already been grown. These seedlings can range in size from starter plants or plugs grown in cell trays to mature bedding plants in 4-inch plastic pots. The overall fact to remember is that the more root system a plant has, the more likely it is to survive and adapt to the new location in which it is planted. Use this fact in the planning stage. With an early start, plugs or flats of bedding plants will do nicely, as they cost less and have plenty of time to grow. However, with a late start, using well-established 4-inch pots is the best decision, although it does incur a greater expense. In fact, some private theme parks plant 12-inch hanging basket material in the ground to establish instant color beds. Remember that planting small plants in mid-summer will not likely yield the expected results. Planning a proper planting schedule with the correct sized plant is essential for success.

Growing in Containers—Many gardeners do not have a great deal of space, but they wish to have color on their patios or balconies. Most annuals adapt well to container gardens, and there are quite a few choices one can employ. Container gardens can be constructed from large ceramic or cement planters, large plastic pots, small and flat colorful bowls or hanging baskets. Hundreds of odd materials including old tires, tennis shoes, and just about anything that will hold soil can be recycled into containers. The "artist" in the gardener comes into play here, as matching the size, color, and habit of the annual to the container is quite a challenge. The reward is a dramatic conversation piece in which the gardener creates something beautiful from discarded or plain items.

The key to growing in containers is drainage. Be sure that the pot has drainage holes for water to drain from. Select a growing medium that is porous, with sufficient different sized particles so that the soil will remain friable and well-drained throughout the season. Bark mixes and even good garden compost will be excellent materials. Also, be sure the container will hold some water when irrigated. Leave at least ½ inch of open space between the soil line and the top of the container, so that water can be added, and allowed to pool and absorb into the soil easily without overflowing.

Bed Preparation—Bed preparation is essential for a successful annual bed. In South Georgia, the general rule is that each bed should be tilled, and amendments added each year before planting. The reason is simple. Soils are sufficiently warm, allowing organic matter to break down quickly. This is good for the growth of annuals, but once the organic matter is gone, it causes a drainage problem. The Georgia clay soils of the Piedmont dry out very quickly and heat up unless sufficient organic matter is present. For optimal performance, beds should be amended with at least 2" to 4" of organic matter (such as compost) each spring season.

Tilling down to a depth of 12" is recommended though tilling to a depth of 6" is essential. This provides a large area for root growth, and for water-holding organic matter to preserve moisture while allowing excess water to drain away from the bulk of the plant roots. Be sure to till thoroughly, and then rake each bed to make sure excess surface water drains away. A slight mound of a few inches is best. If water drains into the bed and forms wet spots or standing water, the excess moisture can ruin the plants.

Mulching after planting is also advised. 2" to 4" of any porous mulch, (a mulch material that allows water to drain easily and allows some air movement) such as pine straw, will reduce wind and sun-driven evaporation, and lower soil temperature. Be careful not to use fine or highly composted materials. When dry, fine particle mulches, can actually repel water or may absorb rainfall from brief summer showers and thus prevent the water from reaching the plant roots. In wet weather, such mulches can also prevent soils from drying out, thus increasing chance for disease.

Planting Technique—If you have properly constructed a bed, planting annuals should be an easy task. It is most important to handle the plant carefully. Try to minimize handling of the root system by holding the plant by the stem. The first task is to establish a hole in the soil for the plant. Since the bed has already been tilled, it is not essential to dig a large hole as you might for shrubs or trees. Dig a hole just large enough for the root ball and deep enough to allow the soil to just cover the root ball. Failure to cover the root ball will cause "wicking" or rapid drying of the root ball. Gardeners place slow-release fertilizer pellets or pearls in the holes before planting. This is fine as long as a small amount of soil covers the fertilizer pearls. Roots that have direct contact with slow- release fertilizer can be damaged.

It is imperative to firm the soil around the root ball to assure good soil contact with the established roots. This can be done by hand, or with the back of a trowel. Once this is done, the plant is ready for irrigation.

Irrigation—Newly planted annuals should always be watered in thoroughly. The next three weeks may require the gardener to water often to allow the plants to establish, depending on the weather. However, the most common mistake made when caring for a bed of annuals is overwatering. Begin to cut back on watering three weeks after installation. It is quite normal for bedding plants to "flag" (or wilt) slightly in afternoon sun. Even Impatiens in a shade garden will wilt in the high heat of a Georgia summer afternoon. By watering only when the plants actually need water, a strong healthy root system will be established

One rule of thumb is to water in the mornings on days when the plants have not "perked up" after wilting the day before. This nightly recovery is quite normal and it is only when insufficient water is present in the soil that the plants will remain floppy or wilted. Water thoroughly early in the morning by applying 1" to 2" of water so that the entire bed will be moistened, and the water will penetrate to the lower soils. This motivates the roots to grow deeper as the upper soils dry out again. Mid- to late- afternoon irrigations or frequent irrigations during the week will only enhance the spread of disease, cause weak root systems, and flush out important nutrients leading to more frequent fertilization.

Fertilization—Fertilization of annuals should be performed when transplanting in the early spring. Fertilization should also be continued throughout the summer. Usually 2 to 3 pounds of a complete granular fertilizer may be applied per 100 square feet for adequate fertilization at the garden construction stage. Supplemental applications can be applied on a monthly basis at the rate of ½ to 1 pounds per 100 square feet of area for June and July. After July, it is usually not essential to fertilize annuals as most have reached maturity and do not need as much fertility. Many gardeners use liquid feed systems to fertilize their bedding plants. A 150 part per million solution of 20-20-20 is preferred every three weeks until August. Directions on how to make up this solution is usually on the product bag. Be sure to rinse the fertilizer off the foliage and flowers with clear water after application. Soil-incorporated slow release fertilizer products are also good. However, if the season is very wet and soil temperatures are very warm, the fertilizer can be depleted more quickly than the manufacturers suggest. Be careful not to place fertilizer products directly against plant stems or roots. This will cause damage and can cause death.

Maintenance Considerations

Insects and Disease—In general, most bedding plants do not have serious problems with disease or pests if the garden is properly established. However, weather and other local conditions such as nearby fields can cause problems to arise. (See Chapter 13 in this book *Diagnosing Ornamental Plant Problems.*) There are several products that gardeners can use to control insects. Refer to the *Georgia Pest Management Handbook* for specific recommendations.

Diseases are more problematic in that they can be stopped from spreading, but the damage rarely can be repaired. This is especially true for root diseases caused by overwatering or poor bed preparation. The best approach is to provide drainage by using proper bed preparation techniques, and by using porous mulches. Avoid watering plants overhead after 1:00 PM in the afternoon. Wet foliage at night is a perfect environment for foliar diseases to establish. Removing spent flowers as well as avoiding application of grass clippings from unbagged lawn mowers will also reduce disease potential. Remove any diseased or individually wilted plants that appear sickly. This will reduce the potential for spread of the disease.

For a suspected, serious plant disease that appears to be spreading, contact your county agent. Specific recommendations for disease control can only be made after suspected disease samples have been identified by a professional. Recommendations can then be made from the *Georgia Pest Management Handbook.*

Weed Control—Weeds can be a nuisance in flower beds and most annuals are sensitive to post emergent herbicides. The best approach is to use pre-emergent herbicides early in the spring prior to planting the annuals. Follow up with appropriate amounts of mulch and/or weed control cloth. Scouting for weeds early is also important. Weeds rob nutrients and water from flower beds. For specific recommendations for weed control, refer to the *Georgia Pest Management Handbook.*

Deadheading—"Deadheading" is a term that refers to the act of removing spent flowers before they start producing seeds. This is important to many species of annuals, as it prevents the plants' food reserves from being put into seed production rather than allowing new growth and flowers. Disease potential can also be reduced by deadheading plants with large flowers. Deadheading only takes a few minutes, and can be a fairly simple task, if done as part of the weekly scouting of an annual bed.

Trimming—Some annuals, especially petunias, benefit from being cut back or trimmed mid-summer. This allows long, leggy growth to be removed and replaced with a more highly-branched set of stems, and hence, more flowers. Many annuals also benefit from the reduction of foliage. This increases the "root-to-shoot ratio", which means that in summer drought and heat there are more roots than shoots, and the plant can deal with the increased water loss more efficiently.

Popular Annuals

Some of the most popular annuals used throughout Georgia include:

Ageratum—There are few annuals with blue flowers. This explains why Ageratum (or floss flower) is so popular. Ageratum will grow in partial shade, but prefers full sun for a large portion of the day. Most varieties are low-growing and bloom constantly because the bushy plants continue to put out new shoots that end in a cluster of fuzzy flowers. Individual blossoms are exceptionally long lasting. While most varieties produce light or deeper blue flowers, there are varieties that produce white or pink blooms. A popular use of the blue variety is in combination with yellow marigolds.

When these two primary colors are used in combination, they produce a strong but pleasing contrast. Because ageratum grows more slowly than marigolds, plant it several weeks earlier.

Alyssum—If there is an ideal annual for edging flower beds, it is alyssum. It is low-growing, ever-blooming, and produces fragrant blossoms. Because of this fragrance, it is called Sweet Alyssum. It is classified as a hardy annual and because of its tolerance of light frost can be set out in early spring. In the more southern areas of the state, plants started from seed in August or early September make a fall showing and may actually overwinter and resume vigorous growth in the spring. Alyssum fades in the southern areas of the state once high temperatures prevail.

Amaranth—Spectacular and colorful are descriptive terms that suit amaranth. The flowers offer little interest, but the upper, cascading leaves contribute their brilliance to the summer landscape. Space these colorful plants at least 12 to 18 inches apart, and provide a contrasting background for exhibiting these eye catchers. A green hedge or contemporary wooden fence is a perfect backdrop. Choose a sunny location and avoid over-fertilization, which can cause foliage to be dull.

Angelonia—Angelonias are interesting annuals that have tall racemes of flowers resembling open flower varieties of snapdragons ranging in color from bright white to purple to pink, with bicolored selection now available. They are excellent container garden plants that unfortunately do not appear showy in mass bedding situations. They are easy to grow and generally stand about 18 inches tall at maturity.

Balsam—Waxy, camellia-like flowers are tucked rather tightly between leaves of balsam. This annual will grow in light shade or full sun, but requires fertile soil and adequate moisture to thrive. The dark green foliage makes a nice contrast with the red, pink, lavender or white flowers.

Begonia—Fibrous rooted begonias have become immensely popular. This is not surprising, for this plant is quite versatile. Newer sun-tolerant varieties such as Whiskey, Vodka, Gin and others are available. The major requirements of these varieties are good drainage, a good mulch, and irrigation when needed. Begonias have always been a good choice for shady locations, where they seem to flower exceedingly well. Nothing seems to produce as many flowers and to last as long as begonias. The old saying, "You get your money's worth with begonias," is true.

Celosia—Celosia in its various forms, such as the cockscomb and plume types, are colorful garden plants. The cockscomb types are a bit more exotic in their appearance, while the plume type seems to blend in with other flowers. Once the terminal flower appears, the plants begin to branch nicely resulting in additional shoots and many more plumes. When they mature, celosia blooms can be dried by hanging them upside down in a dry location. After drying, the foliage is removed and the flowers are ready to use in dried arrangements.

Cleome—Cleome, more commonly known as spider flower, is an old-fashioned annual. Because of its coarse foliage and ability to grow three to four feet tall, it is ideal for hiding unsightly spots and well suited as a background for lower growing annuals. A white and rose bicolored flowering variety is now available that imparts high impact. This well-liked annual thrives in sandy and clay soils in full sun

Coleus—Colorful foliage rather than interesting flowers is the appealing characteristic of coleus. Standard series coleus such as Fuji, Carefree, Saber and Wizard, are ideal for moderately shaded areas, but require moderate light to develop a more intense coloration of the leaves. Moisture stress for these cultivars is decreased in the shade. Newer, interesting forms of coleus have joined the old standbys. The Sunlover and Solar series are Coleus that can be grown in full sun and which sport very dramatic colors and sharp contrasts, increasing the versatility of these plants. Oddly enough, coleus is one of the few annuals from which flowers should be removed as they emerge.

Cosmos—Cosmos are easy to grow and can be used when temperatures are high. Most of the cosmos varieties, such as Diablo (burnt orange), grow from two to three feet tall and require a bit of room. A newer dwarf form called 'Sunny Gold' grows about 18 inches high and is perfect in the foreground of border areas.

Cupheas—There are many annual Cupheas that are worth growing in the garden. *C. Micropetalum* is a tall orange and yellow cigar flowering type that can stand three feet tall, and is very showy. *C. hyssopifolium* is the common purple flowering Mexican Heather. *C. laevia* is a red and black flowering Cuphea that resembles the head of Mickey Mouse. All these Cupheas require full sun and adequate moisture to perform well.

Dusty Miller—Senecios are bedding plants grown for their hairy, silvery foliage. The gray foliage is a great contrast to dark foliage of some amaranths and celosias, coleus, and any other dark foliaged annual or perennial. They require full sun, good drainage and low to moderate fertility. Dusty Miller does not like prolonged periods of rain and may look scraggly until new foliage is produced.

Evolvulus—Evolvulus is a plant primarily used for a hanging baskets or as a container annual. It has deep blue flowers and a relatively compact and slow growing habit that makes it ideal for small containers. Evolvulus requires full sun and can withstand occasional drought. It is a wonderful companion plant for bacopa, neirembergia and vinca.

Geranium—A great number of geraniums are sold each spring. Flower color ranges from red to pink to salmon and white. Geraniums bloom best when night temperatures are cool. This explains why these plants renew their vigor in the fall as night temperatures drop. Botrytis (gray mold) causes leaf disorders and flower discoloration. Porch geraniums usually escape this malady because the foliage stays dry and discourages the spread of this disease.

Hyacinth Bean—This wonderful vine is a relative of our common pole bean and grows in a similar fashion. The flowers are a combination of light and dark purple, and the vine blooms in profusion all summer. The resulting seed pods are deep purple and quite decorative. It is very easy to grow and tolerates most conditions, as long as full sun is available and it is irrigated when the soil is dry. Seeds are easily collected and stored for next year's garden.

Gomphrena—Gomphrena is a very unusual annual which produces round to oblong, lavender, red or white clover-like blooms. It is heat tolerant and does very well in hot sunny spaces. Dwarf varieties such as the Gnome series, grow 10 inches tall, while full-sized varieties can get up to 30 inches tall. This annual makes a good cut flower, and is also a good flower to dry.

Impatiens—What more can one say to describe impatiens other than "spectacular"? Impatiens, sometimes called Sultana, were designed for shaded areas. They come in many bright as well as pastel colors. Soil should be prepared to provide good drainage. This eliminates root rotting problems and leads to healthy, blooming plants. Water impatiens, but not every day. Plants naturally wilt in the heat of the day, but recover by morning. If plants wilt in the early morning, they need watering. Too much fertilization promotes leaves and stems at the expense of blooms.

Marigold—Marigolds have to be included in the five most popular annuals because they are easy to grow and flower profusely. Several types such as African (large flowers), hybrids (medium-sized flowers), and countless other varieties are available. The Ladybird series is a dwarf, heat-tolerant series worth looking into. Marigolds like hot temperatures and well-drained soils. Mites can discolor the foliage but can be controlled by periodic spraying with a miticide.

Mandevilla—Mandevilla is a large pink flowering vine that is commonly used on mailboxes and trellises in the South. It is a tropical vine, so it requires frequent watering and steady fertility to perform well. Total vine length can be as long as 15 feet per season. To keep it compact, most gardeners train the vine to wind around stakes, a trellis or a mailbox post. This annual can be brought indoors and kept in a sunny window all winter.

Melampodium—Melampodium is truly a superior poor-location plant. It thrives in poor soil, full sun, and hot, dry locations. Thousands of dime-sized yellow flowers appear in May through frost. Plants form a large three-foot wide mound. Drought and disease resistant, this is one of the easiest plants to grow. Word of caution: Melampodium reseeds freely and one plant will generate millions of seeds. It will take over if seedlings are not weeded out in spring.

Nasturtium—We seem to have gotten away from this old favorite for many years now. Nasturtiums are very easy to grow, and seem to do well even in poor soils. Early cultivars formed thick masses of vine sporting yellow to red flowers. More modern varieties are compact and well-behaved. 'Whirlybird' blend is one of the most common series for use in small to mid-sized gardens. Nasturtium flowers and leaves are edible, and often used in salads.

Pansies (and Violas)—What would Georgia be like in the winter without pansies? This annual is rapidly becoming an economically important greenhouse crop. Series such as 'Universal', 'Crystal Bowl' and 'Crown' are favorites with landscapers. For something unusual, try pastel or 'Antique Shades'. Violas are close relatives of the pansy and, although the flowers are smaller, they are produced in greater number. Johnny jump-up types include 'Alpine Summer' and 'Cuty'. The Jewel series is a good viola series for mass planting. Remember to continue to feed Violas and Pansies throughout the winter months for maximum flowering.

Petunia—Petunias grow and flower best under conditions of cool nights and warm days. They will tolerate light frost. In the extreme southern part of Georgia they should be planted in early spring; however, they may not tolerate the summer heat. They will perform throughout the summer in the mountains where nights remain cool. The multiflora petunias produce smaller blooms, but in greater profusion than the larger, grandiflora types. The cascade types are used extensively in hanging baskets and planters, where a trailing effect is desired.

Pentas—Pentas are tropical annuals that make wonderful butterfly attractors for the garden. They come in colors of red white, pink and purple. There are tall types, (24-30") such as the Nova series, and many shorter varieties (5-inch) that are used in mass beddings. Pinching early on helps this plant branch and produce profuse blooms. It requires frequent irrigation in hot weather, and requires full sun.

Portulaca—Experts agree that portulaca, or moss rose, is an excellent choice for a less than desirable spot. It thrives in poor soil and hot, dry locations because of its succulent nature. This low-growing annual, suitable for edging beds or in planters, produces brilliant flowers of unusual color. Both single and double flowering varieties are available. The flowers of most varieties open fully in bright sun and close at night or under cloudy conditions. Plants should therefore be exposed to full sun. A breakthrough in plant breeding has resulted in a variety called 'Afternoon Delight' that remains open longer than most.

Salvia—Red Salvia is a favorite of all. While this colorful annual is most often planted in full sun, it flourishes in light shade or half a day of sun. Plant breeders have produced short, medium and tall varieties. Not all salvias are red; varieties producing purple and white blooms are available. The white variety prefers some shade. Deadheading (removing spent flower stalks) and light fertilization every four to six weeks keep salvia in constant flower.

Scaevola—Recently introduced from Australia, Scaevola "Blue Wonder" is a patented plant. It is, without a doubt, one of the best bedding plants to be used in the garden. It is relatively pest free, grows fast and produces a thick carpet of blue trumpet-like flowers. With frequent irrigation and fertilization, one plant can spread over four feet in area. The color blue that the flower imparts is a rare addition to summer gardens in Georgia. More varieties are being bred and distributed each year.

Snapdragon—Snapdragons too, like pansies, are best planted in early fall. Fall bloom is followed by a winter rest. With warming spring temperatures will come a dramatic display of flowers. Snapdragons come in tall

sizes such as the Rocket series, to the dwarf, Tahiti series. Butterfly type snapdragons have flowers that are permanently open resulting in impressive flower displays, but do not snap open when the sides of the flowers are pressed in. Like pansies, snapdragons benefit from midwinter fertilization.

Tithonia—Mexican sunflowers (*Tithonia rotundifolia*) are wonderful butterfly attractors. Plants are very tall, reaching six feet or more in good soil. Numerous, long-lasting orange flowers appear in July and continue until frost. If grown in less than full sun, the plants will be smaller and weak- stemmed, but if staked will bloom nicely.

Torenia—The "wish-bone" flower is perhaps the best alternative to impatiens one could find for southern shade gardens. Attractive to butterflies and available in many colors from deep blue to a pure white, Torenia can bring brightness to a fairly drab, dark green planting. When used in combination with annuals such as Cat-Whiskers, it can make a very enticing flower display all summer. Irrigate regularly and fertilize periodically for best results.

Verbenas—Verbena, an old-time favorite, has a long blooming season. The low spreading types are used to edge beds. They tolerate full sun well. Bushy, upright varieties are also available. Recent introductions have extended the available color range of flowers from red to wine, pink, blue, and amethyst. Brightly colored flowers with contrasting white centers (Bright Eyes) are also available and quite eye-catching.

Vinca—Vinca, which is often called annual periwinkle, is one of the better flowering annuals because of its ability to withstand high summer temperatures and dry conditions. These plants seldom suffer from insect or disease problems. Varieties of vinca are available which produce white, pink, or rose-colored flowers with a contrasting red eye. Some rather fine, low, compact varieties are available.

Zinnia—Zinnias of all descriptions are available for summer and fall flowering. Varieties are available which produce large, medium, or small flowers on tall, medium, or short plants. Most varieties perform well under a variety of conditions. Zinnias make excellent cut flowers for summer and fall arrangements. They can be seeded directly into the garden during any summer month. Mildew may be a problem during rainy periods; however, fungicidal sprays can be applied as a preventative measure to protect and extend the life of plants.

Table 1. Annuals for Georgia gardens

COMMON NAME	BOTANICAL NAME	HEIGHT (INCHES)	SPACING (INCHES)	COLOR	EXPOSURE (SU S-S SH)	SEASON C/W
Abelmoschus	Abelmoschus moschatus	12-15	18	P/W, RU	SU	W
Ageratum	Ageratum houstianum	6-12	6-8	B, L,PW	SU/S-S	W
Alyssum, Sweet	Lobularia maritima	4-8	4-6	L, P, W	SU/S-S	C
Amaranthus	Amaranthus caudatus	24-48	12-24	F	SU	W
Balsam	Impatiens balsamina	12-30	8-18	-B	SH, S-S	W
Basil	Ocimum basilicum	12-24	12-24	F	SU	W
Begonia, Wax	Begonia x semperflorens-cultorum	6-12	8-12	P, R, W	S-S SH	W
Bells-of-Ireland	Moluccella laevis	24-36	12	P, W		
Black-eyed-Susan	Rudbeckia hirta	12-36	12-24	G,O,R,Y	SU	W
Black-eyed-Susan vine	Thunbergia alata	Vine	12-18	O, W, Y	SU	W
Browallia	Browallia speciosa	12-36	6-8	B, W,Pu		
Calendula	Calendula officinalis	12-24	10-12	G, O, W,Y	SU	C
Calliopsis	Coreopsis tinctoria	18-24	10-12	O,Y	SU	W
Candytuft	Iberis umbellata	8-12	6-12	L, P, Pu,R,W		
Castor bean	Ricinus communis	60-144	24-48	F	SU	W
Cleome	Cleome hassleriana	36-60	12-24	L,P,PU,W,Y	SU	W
Cockscomb	Celosia aigentea var. cristata	18-24	12	F	SU	W
Coleus	Solenostemon scutellarioides	12-30	6-18	F	SH S-S	W
Cornflower	Centaurea cyanus	12-36	8-12	-0,-G,-Y	SU	C
Cosmos	Cosmos bipinnatus,	12-48+	10-12	G,L,P, Pu,R,W	SU	W
	C. x sulphureus	12-48+	10-12	G,O,,R,Y	SU	W
Cup-and-saucer vine	Cobaea scandens	Vine	-	L, W		
Cypressvine	Ipomoea quamoclit	Vine	-	R	SU	W
Dahlberg daisy	Dyssodia tenuiloba	4-8	8	Y	SU	
Dusty-miller	Senecio cineraria	6-12	8	F	SU	W/C
Evolvulus	Evolvulus glomeratus ssp. grandiflorus	12	12-24	B	SU, S-S	W
Forget-me-not	Myosotis sylvatica	6-12	12	B, P, W		
Four-o'clock	Mirabilia jalapa	18-36	18-24	P, R, WY	SU	W
Foxglove	Digitalis purpurea	12-60	8-12	-B	SU S-S	C
Gaillardia	Gaillardia pulchella	12-30	8-15	O,R,Y		
Geranium	Pelargonium x hortorum	12-24	12	-B,-Y		
Gomphrena	Gomphrena globosa	8-24	10	L,P,Pu,R,W	SU	W
	G. haageana	24	10	O,PR		

Table 1. Annuals for Georgia gardens

COMMON NAME	BOTANICAL NAME	HEIGHT (INCHES)	SPACING (INCHES)	COLOR	EXPOSURE (SU S-S SH)	SEASON C/W
Heliotrope	*Heliotropium arborescens*	8-24	12-18	B,Pu,W		
Hollyhock	*Alcea rosea*	12-48+	12-24	PR,W,Y	SU	W
Hyacinth bean	*Dolichos lablab*	Vine	-	P, W	SU	W
Impatiens	*Impatiens wallerana*	6-24	10-15	L,O,PR,W	SH	W
Larkspur	*Consolida ambigua*	24-48	8-12	B, L, P, W	SU	C
Lobelia	*Lobelia erinus*	6-12	4-6	B, W	SU S-S	C
Mandevilla	*Mandevilla laxa etc.*	Vine	12-18	P, R, W	SU	W
Marigold	*Tagetes spp.*	6-36	6-18	G, O, R, Y	SU	W
Melampodium	*Melampodium paludosum*	24-30	15	Y	SU	W
Mexican heather	*Cuphea hyssopifolia*	10	18	L, P, W	SU	W
Mexican sun-flower	*Tithonia rotundifolia*	48-72	24	R	SU	W
Moneyplant	*Lunaria annua*	12-36	12	F		
Monkeyflower	*Mimulus x hybridus*	6	6-12	O,R,Y	SH	
Moonflower	*Ipomoea alba*	Vine	-	W	SU	W
Morningglory	*Ipomoea purpurea*	Vine	-	-G, -Y	SU	W
Nasturtium	*Tropaeolum majus*	12-72+	8-12	O, P, R, W, Y	SU	C
Nicotiana	*Nicotiana alata*	12-36	12-24	G, P, Pu, R, W	SU S-S	C
Ornamental cabbage and kale	*Brassica oleracea*	12-18	18	F	SU	C
Ornamental pepper	*Capsicum annuum*	6-12	10-12	F	SU	W
Pansy	*Viola x wittrockiana*	6-10	6	ALL	SU S-S	C
Pentas	*Pentas lanceolata*	24-30	12-18	L, P, R, W	SU	W
Petunia	*Petunia x hybrida*	6-24	10-12	-G, -0	SU	C W
Phlox	*Phlox drummondii*	6-24	6-8	ALL		
Pinks	*Dianthus hybrids of D. barbatus, D. chinensis, and D. deltoides.*	6-18	8-12	--B	SU	C/W
Polkadot plant	*Hypoestes phyllostachya*	18-30	6-12	F	SH	W
Portulaca	*Portulaca grandiflora*	4-6	8-12	O, P, R, W, Y	SU	W
Sanvitalia, Creeping zinnia	*Sanvitalia procumbens*	6-9	8	G,O, W, Y	SU	W
Scarlet runner bean	*Phaseolus coccineus*	Vine	-	R	SU	W
Scarlet sage	*Salvia splendens*	12-18	8-12	B, Pu,R, W	SU	W

Table 1. Annuals for Georgia gardens

COMMON NAME	BOTANICAL NAME	HEIGHT (INCHES)	SPACING (INCHES)	COLOR	EXPOSURE (SU S-S SH)	SEASON C/W
Scaveola	*Scaveola aemula*	12	12-24	B, W	SU	W
Snapdragon	*Antirrhinum majus*	6-36	10-12	-B,--G,-L	SU	C
Snow-on-the-mountain	*Euphorbia marginata*	30-48	12-24	F		
Statice	*Limonium sinuatum*	18-24	12-24	B,L,R,W,Y	SU	
Stock	*Matthiola incana*	12-30	10-15	ALL	SU	C
Strawflower	*Helichrysum bracteatum*	12-36	9-12	O, P, R, W, Y	SU	W
Summer-cypress	*Bassia scoparia f. trichophylla*	24-36	18-24	F		
Sunflower	*Helianthus annuus*	24-120+	12-24	G, O, R, W Y	SU	W
Sweet pea	*Lathyrus odoratus*	12-60+	6-12	ALL	SU	C
Verbena	*Verbena x hybrida*	6-12	12-18	B, P, Pu, R, W	SU	W
Vinca, Annual	*Catharanthus roseus*	6-18	10-12	L, P, W	SU	W
Wallflower	*Erysimum hybrids*	6-12	12	G,O, P, R, Y	SU	C
Torenia, Wish-boneflower	*Torenia fournieri*	6-12	6-12	B, W	SH	W
Zinnia, Garden	*Zinnia elegans*	6-36	10-12	-B, -G, -Pu	SU	W

PERENNIALS & PERENNIAL BEDS

In years past, perennials were the primary source of spring and summer color for the flower border and rock garden. Many of these trusty plants could be counted on to welcome spring with colorful blooms each year. Others provided spectacular flowers of unusual color and form in the summer landscapes

Unfortunately, perennials lost their popularity during the 1960's and 1970's, due perhaps to the introduction of many new annuals and to the perceived difficulty in maintaining large perennial beds properly. Interest in perennials is at an all time high now, as many gardeners are rediscovering the benefits of perennial gardens and installing some of the newer cultivars. At the same time, new gardeners are finding that tending a well-designed perennial border is both fun and rewarding.

Terms to Know

Perennial—A perennial is a plant that will consistently survive more that one year and have sufficient health to reproduce within three years. There are many other definitions, but just surviving is not a clear criterion as we have mild winters that allow even tropical plants to occasionally survive more that one year.

Hardy Perennials—A hardy perennial is one that can survive the coldest Georgia winters and the hottest summers too. Perennials must be able to reproduce successfully in Georgia most years to be considered hardy. You can imagine that given the differences in the environment between Savannah and Rome, Georgia, that exactly what constitutes a perennial is a difficult and localized issue. A hardy perennial in Savannah may be an annual in Rome!

Tender Perennials—Plants that will survive given average winters and summers in Georgia. However, occasionally we have a late spring cold snap that sends temperatures into the teens or lower. Tender perennials do not survive these cold snaps. Thus, a Tibouchina might live 6 years and be killed by the cold snap on the seventh. It is also true that many hardy annuals may survive for several ears if the winters or summer are mild. Therefore you must consult with your local county agent or other Master Gardeners to determine what is or is not truly perennial in your area.

Invasive Plant—An invasive plant is one that is not native, has been introduced by mankind, and has the ability to grow and reproduce sufficiently in undisturbed areas to upset or alter the habitat and the life cycles of native plant and animal life.

Native Plant—A native plant is one that is naturally found growing is a specific environment, and has been growing in that area prior to the arrival of mankind. As it is difficult to determine when mankind started bringing plants to the US, most folks suggest that we arbitrarily set the date at the early 1400's. Many of our perennials are native, however some are not, and some sold in the trade can be invasive and damaging to the environment. It is essential to know the difference and not use or promote invasive plants.

Planting Perennials

Bed Preparation Technique—It is convention to plan to renovate a perennial bed every three years. Thus, perennials require a slightly different approach to bed preparation as the plants will remain in the bed without additional amending for up to three years. Prepare the soil carefully before attempting to establish a perennial bed. Incorporate three to four inches of large particle sized or "rough" composted organic matter into the soil to improve soil aeration and drainage. Fine particles of highly composted material will break down and disappear too quickly, and the heavy, compacted soils will cause decline in growth of your perennials.

Since the bed soil will remain unamended, soil pH can change over time. The addition of both large particle lime and fertilizer at the time the bed is prepared will insure an adequate fertility and pH level. Add a complete fertilizer at the rate of two to three pounds per 100 square feet of area. Dolomitic lime is applied at the rate of 3 to 4 pounds per 100 square feet of area. (A soil analysis is preferred in order to determine the proper amounts of fertilizer and lime to apply.) Fertilizer, lime, and organic matter should be incorporated into the soil together to a 12 inch depth, just as is recommended for annuals. This can be accomplished by spading or roto-tilling.

Planting Schedule & Technique—Planting perennials properly and at the right time can determine whether and how prolifically they bloom the first year. Fall is considered the best time to plant perennials in the south. In the coastal areas, planting can continue from September through November. In the mountains, it would be advisable to plant in September since hard-freezing weather comes early. In general, planting should be accomplished at least six weeks before hard-freezing weather occurs.

Fall established perennials continue to develop after planting. An extensive root system is produced during fall and spring, enabling the plants to become established before hot weather. Plants continue to develop above-ground parts. This development, although slow, accounts for the initiation of flower buds and stocky, vegetative growth. This explains why well-branched plants emerge in the spring and flower profusely at the proper time.

Early spring is also considered a good time to plant perennials. Planting early, just after killing frosts have passed, is preferable. Use perennials that were seeded the previous fall and overwintered in protective structures (such as cold frames). They will bloom the first season.

If plants are somewhat pot bound at planting time, simply loosen the roots around the bottom and sides of the root ball and spread them out in the bottom of the planting hole. Cover and firm the soil lightly around the plant. Be sure the crown of the plant is at or slightly above ground level.

Irrigation—Periodic irrigation, especially during the summer, is necessary for plants to grow well. However, it is very common to find perennial gardeners overwatering their perennials. Most perennials are plants that can withstand brief periods of dry weather. Watering established perennials more that twice a week is not usually necessary or advisable. Watering thoroughly by applying 1 to 2 inches of water per weekly irrigation during dry weather facilitates good root production

Fertilization—Fertilization of established perennials can be done in the early spring. Usually two to three pounds of a complete fertilizer per 100 square feet is adequate. A supplemental application during midsummer can be surface applied at the rate of 1 to 2 pounds per 100 square feet of area. Slow release fertilizers work well with perennials, as most show growth during spring and early summer. It is not advisable to fertilize perennials in fall or late summer, as this may stimulate soft new growth just before first frost.

Maintenance

As with annuals, deadheading and trimming are essential practices in the perennial garden. Many perennials such as purple cone flower will regenerate new flowers if spent flowers are deadheaded. Trimming back Salvia guaranitica in late July will allow a new flush of blue flowers in September. You will have to learn how to approach each specimen in your garden, but the basic principle holds for most mid-summer blooming perennials.

Weed Control Options—Since we cannot till a perennial garden each year, weed control is even more important in the perennial garden. Following the basic principles of applying good porous mulch, using pre-emergent herbicides in fall or very early spring, and scouting for young weed growth in early spring is essential for successful gardens in Georgia. For specific recommendations, consult with your County Extension Agent or see the *Georgia Pest Management Handbook.*

Perennials started from seed in greenhouses during January and February become available as small plants in late spring. These can be planted in April and May. Many of these will not bloom prolifically the first year and in some cases not before the following growing season. Be sure the area selected for perennials drains well. When drainage is poor, plants can be expected to suffer from both root and crown rots.

Perennials should be mulched lightly following planting. Mulches keep down weeds and prevent the rapid loss of moisture. However, heavy mulching in the fall can encourage crown rot. Plants will need to be watered thoroughly following planting, to settle the soil around the roots. Check plants closely every few days following planting to prevent them from drying out. Supplying adequate water during the establishment period is essential.

One secret to growing perennials successfully is watering and controlling weeds. Excessive weeds can crowd out perennials and destroy the attractiveness of these plants. Mulching and occasional weeding are the solutions to this problem.

Recommended Perennials

A few of the better perennials for Georgia gardeners are listed below.

Achillea (*Achillea filipendulina*) (*A. millefolium*) Achillea or Yarrow is recognized for its ability to tolerate both infertile and dry soils once established. The fern-like foliage, especially of the silver-gray leaved type (*A. taygetea*), contrasts nicely with the flat, yellow flowers. Flowering begins in July and often extends into September. Height ranges from 24 to 30 inches. Some staking may be required if heavy rains beat the plants down. The foliage is aromatic and flowers remain attractive for several weeks. Achillea is an aggressive spreader, so plants may need thinning periodically. Yarrow flowers can be dried for use in fall and winter arrangements.

Bee Balm/Oswego Tea/Bergamont (*Monarda didyma*) Bee Balm is often referred to as an aromatic herb, because of the pungent smell of the crushed leaves. Early settlers of Oswego, New York, used its leaves to brew tea, hence Oswego Tea. It grows well in all areas of the state and is another perennial that attracts bees and hummingbirds. Bee Balm is a rather vigorous perennial growing to three feet tall in height. Flowers are borne terminally on the main stem and branches and may be pink, red, purple or white, depending on the cultivar. Blooming may occur during June through August. Being a member of the mint family, Bee Balm spreads rapidly by rhizomes and may become invasive. Plants do best in full sun but will grow in moderate shade. Plants prefer moist sites but will grow on dry ones. Space 12-15 inches apart.

Butterfly Weed (*Asclepias tuberosa*) Butterfly Weed can be found growing wild in most parts of Georgia. It is generally associated with dry, sandy sites. Plants are difficult to transplant due to a taproot. Plantings are best established from seedlings in fall or spring. The brilliant orange clusters of flowers, borne in umbels during early to mid summer, attract butterflies and hummingbirds. While deep orange is the predominant flower color, varieties are available from pale yellow to oxblood. Plant in full sun where drainage is good. Space plants 12 inches apart.

Candytuft (*Iberis sempervirens*) Candytuft is often used as a low-growing evergreen shrub substitute to edge foundation plants or perennial borders. It is a welcome perennial for the rock garden. Candytuft is outstanding when the flat, dense clusters of white flowers cover the plant for 10 to 14 days in early spring. Keep plants compact and neat by shearing lightly after blooming to remove seed heads and encourage branching. Candytuft seems to prefer light shade in Georgia.

Columbine (*Aquilegia sp.*) Columbine produces lacy foliage and showy flowers on wiry stems. As a result of hybridization, the spurred flowers come in a wide color range. The flowering period is early (May-June) and foliage may fade somewhat after blooming. Columbine prefer a cool moist soil that is fairly rich. If plants are to survive they must have excellent drainage. If planted in the hotter areas of the state, locate in light shade. Space plants 12-24 inches apart and locate in the front or middle portion of the border.

Coral Bells (*Heuchera sanguinea*) Coral Bells is quite effective as a ground cover along a path or as a specimen in the front of the border. Evergreen leaves and crowns hug the ground. Flower clusters on rangy stems rise above the plants. Flower colors range from pink to red to white and chartreuse. Plant in shady or partially shady areas in well-drained soils. Coral Bells may be less adaptable to hot, dry soils of South Georgia due to the shallow fibrous root system. Plant 9-15 inches apart and set crowns at ground level when transplanting.

Coreopsis (*Coreopsis grandiflora*) Coreopsis is a highly-praised garden perennial. It produces yellow, daisy-like flowers freely during late spring and early summer (late May through July). Flowers are borne on wiry stems well above the lance-shaped leaves. Light breezes cause stems and flowers to nod gracefully.

Deadheading (removing spent flowers) is recommended to prolong the flowering period. Plants may grow from 1 ½ to 3 feet tall, depending on the species or variety selected. Newer varieties such as Sun Ray and Baby Gold are lower-growing (18 to 20 inches). Coreopsis should be planted in full sun and prefers a well-drained location. Plants should be irrigated during periods of sparse rainfall.

Daylily (*Hemerocallis sp.*) The most popular perennial in Georgia is the Daylily. Individual flowers last for only a day. However, a sizable clump will bloom for several weeks by producing a number of flowering stems and buds. While daylilies will grow with little care, they respond to irrigation and fertilization. Plant in full sun or light shade, and mulch.

Dianthus (*D. deltoides and plumarius*) Meadow pink and grass pink has long been a favorite perennial for use in rock gardens and as an edging plant for the border. The trailing growth habit, grayish green foliage and fragrant carnation-like flowers, make both species welcome additions to the garden. Plant in full sun in well-drained locations. Lime is often recommended as a soil amendment when growing these plants. Plants bloom in late April or early May.

Many of the newer hybrid Dianthus overwinter nicely under Georgia conditions. The foliage may be burned slightly by extremely hard freezes, but it quickly recovers. They bloom profusely in April and May when established during the fall. The blooming period may be somewhat later when established from small plants during the spring. Varieties such as Snowfire and Magic Charms are somewhat heat tolerant. They bloom sporadically during the summer, especially if plants are cut back after their first blooms fade.

False Spirea (*Astilbe x arendsii*) Astilbe is noted for its glossy green foliage and fluffy plumes of white, pink, lavender or red flowers on erect stems. The feathery effect is due to the tiny flowers. This perennial is more adaptable to the Piedmont and mountainous areas where deeper and cooler soils of higher moisture content are available. Plants prefer some shade and should not be allowed to dry out excessively. Foliage may reach a height of 1-2 feet with flowers reaching another foot. Plant 1-2 feet apart.

Foxglove (*Digitalis purpurea*) Foxglove, with its tall flowering spikes and strong vertical lines, provides both emphasis and stateliness. The unique finger-like flowers open progressively from the lower part of the flower spike upward in late spring or early summer. The flowering habit has the effect of lengthening the blooming season. Even the coarse, downy, greenish-gray leaves, which form a rosette at ground level, provide interest to the border. Foxglove can be used in full sun or partial shade in South Georgia. It flourishes in rich, well drained soil with adequate moisture. It is considered a biennial.

Gaillardia (*Gaillardia grandiflora*) Gaillardia or Blanketflower is regarded as an excellent perennial for sandy soils and full sun exposure. It blooms throughout the summer and even during dry periods. Petals may be wine red, red, or red with yellow borders. Varieties grow as low as 12 inches or as tall as 30 inches.

Gaura (*Gaura lindheimerii*) Gaura plants send up tall thin branches that possess hundreds of pure white flowers. This heat and drought tolerant plant blooms all summer long, and gets to be three to four feet in diameter within two years of growth. This is a very good plant for sunny locations where a bright spot is needed. Remove old flowering branches to encourage secondary flowering.

Gayfeather/Blazing Star (*Liatris spicata*) The tall lavender or purple flower spikes provide an appealing, vertical accent in the garden. Blooming may commence as early as June in lower Georgia. Uniquely, flowers unfold from the top of the spike downward. The spike can be cut and used in fresh arrangements or dried for similar use later.

Plants respond to moist, well-drained soils in full sun or light shade. It does, however, survive in drier sites but needs moisture during the flowering period. Remove spent flower spikes to encourage secondary flowering. Plant 12-15 inches apart. Mature plants grow 2-3 feet tall.

Gerbera Daisy (*Gerbera jamesonii*) Gerbera Daisies produce beautifully colored and artistic flowers highly prized by homeowners. Flower arrangers are especially fond of these flowers. The flowers are borne on 15 to 18 inch stems that rise from a low-growing mass of coarse but attractive leaves. Single and double flowering varieties are available with red, pink, yellow, white and orange flowers. Gerbera grow best in full sun; however, they do well in light shade in the more southern areas of the state where summer temperatures are excessive. Irrigation and periodic fertilization during the growing season are essential for continued flower production. Good drainage and light protective winter mulches are recommended. Most Gerberas are planted in the spring. However, plants can be successfully transplanted in the early fall (September). If planted in protected, well-drained locations and mulched, they seem to survive well. With fall planting, plants emerge in early spring and start blooming quite early. Crown rot, which develops as a result of poor drainage, causes the greatest loss of these plants. Planting too deeply can also be detrimental.

Hardy Mums (*Chrysanthemum sp.*) The hardy or outdoor garden Chrysanthemum ("mum") is an ideal perennial for furnishing fall color in the landscape. Among the most decorative mums in this group are the "cushion" or "azalea mums." These low-growing, compact plants produce many blossoms in the fall, literally covering the foliage. The blooming habit is similar to that of azaleas, hence the name "azalea mum."

Outdoor mums are herbaceous perennials. The tops are killed by frost; however, new growth originates from the crown of the plant in early spring. The small plants originating from the crown may be separated and replanted in early spring. Cuttings can be rooted from the same plants in May and early June. Because of the long growing season, plants may be cut back to ground level in mid June. If cut back, they should be re-mulched and fertilized. Pinch the new growth as it reaches four to six inches in length to promote branching. Pinching is discontinued after mid to late July so that flower buds will develop for fall flowering.

Cushion mums are often purchased as budded plants in four to six-inch pots in early fall and transplanted to the flower border or foundation planting.

Hosta/Plantain Lily (*Hosta plantaginea*) As one writer explains, "plants in this genus have a noble appeal; flowers and foliage connote grandeur when used in appropriate plantings." Various cultivars are available with varying leaf patterns and coloration. Leaf texture may be smooth, ribbed, or seer suckered, flat, wavy or twisted. Leaf coloration includes light green, dark green, gray or bluish-green. Variegated forms are also available. As an added bonus, lily-like flowers are borne on stalks above the 1-3 foot foliage during the summer.

Hostas are recommended for shaded areas with moist, rich soils; however, certain varieties need some sun if foliage is to color properly. Plant 24-36 inches apart, depending on variety.

Hardy Lantana In Georgia, one particular cultivar of *Lantana camara* just happens to be very hardy and worthy of mention. Lantana 'Miss Huff' is a very popular cultivar that is hardy as far north as Kentucky. It grows very large (4' diameter) and literally has thousands of blooms per plant. It is drought resistant, insect and disease resistant and deer resistant. Do not trim the stems in winter. Mound leaves in the stems and trim after new growth emerges in early May.

Obedient Plant/False Dragonhead (*Physostegia virginiana*) Obedient plant flowers in mid to late summer, with white flowering cultivars flowering earlier than pink ones. Tubular flowers, arranged in rows on the spike remain in place when pushed aside, hence the name obedient plant. This is another of the spike flowering perennials that is easy to grow and does well in most areas of Georgia. It prefers moist soil or at least soils that do not dry out excessively. Plants grow from 1 ½—2 ½ feet tall. Plant 15-18 inches apart in full sun. In southern Georgia plants may benefit from late afternoon shade.

Purple Cone Flower (*Echinacea purpurea*) Purple cone flower is one of the more striking, but lesser-known perennials. The purplish pink petals surrounding a central bronzy cone are eye-catching as they droop naturally. The tough, deep green foliage contrasts nicely with the flower color. This perennial grows 2 to 2 ½ feet tall and performs well under hot dry conditions. Blooming occurs during June and July. Staking may be required to support the heavy flowers. (Purple cone flower is an herbaceous perennial, which means that the top dies after frost, and new growth is produced from the crown in early spring.)

Ruellia (*Ruellia* spp.) Mexican petunia is a wonderful new addition to the gardener's inventory. It is a heat resistant, tall perennial that produces many purple or pink flowers. Flowers begin to show mid summer and continue until frost. This plant has few diseases or pests, and appears to tolerate most Georgia soils well. It forms a colony that spreads slowly. Propagation is by division of the rather massive root systems.

Rudbeckia (*Rudbeckia sp.*) Rudbeckia, more commonly known as Brown-Eyed-Susan or Coneflower, is native to Georgia. The beautiful yellow flowers punctuated with the brownish central cone are borne during mid to late summer. The new improved cultivars are preferred and include taller varieties (two to three feet) such as Gloriosa Daisy, Double Gloriosa Daisy, and Goldstrum (*R. fulgida* 'Goldstrum'). Lower-growing varieties (1 to 2 feet) suitable for bedding use include: 'Orange Bedder,' 'Rustic Colors,' and 'Marmalade.' Rudbeckia grows well in full sun or light shade, and withstands dry soils comparatively well once established. Plants may be established in the fall; however, they will bloom the first season when sown from seed in early spring or planted as small bedding plants.

Mealy Cup Sage, Salvia (*Salvia farinacea*) Mealy cup salvia offers light blue flowers which contrast with grayish stems. These colors are a relief from the more conventional hot colors such as red and orange. Individual plants branch readily and reach 15 to 20 inches in height. Each of these branches produces a terminal flower spike. A newer variety called Victoria produces spectacular lavender-blue flower spikes during the summer months. The perennial salvias tolerate dry conditions well.

Blue Sage (*Salvia Guaranitica*) This specimen is an outstanding new plant for gardeners looking for adding blue to the garden pallet. It is one of the Georgia Gold Medal Selections and excellently suited for Georgia gardens. It is heat tolerant, drought tolerant, and very long lived. Best flower production comes if the plant is trimmed back in mid July. Full sun or partial shade works well for this plant.

Shasta Daisy (*Chrysanthemum maximum*) (C. X *superbum*) Shasta daisy is a most popular perennial grown in Georgia. The foliage is dark green and low growing. The white daisy-like flowers with yellow centers are borne on relatively tall stems (two feet) in the spring. They make excellent cut flowers and arrange nicely.

Shastas normally bloom in May and June. However, specific varieties can be selected to extend the blooming period into July and August. Example:

Period of Bloom	Variety
May	Chrysanthemum May Queen
June-July	Chrysanthemum Secundum

Speedwell (*Veronica sp.*) Colorful flower spikes are the trademark of Veronica. Diversity of this perennial is another virtue. Various species and cultivars are available that produce blue, purple, pink or white flower spikes at the end of branches, beginning in June and ending in August. Cultivars are available ranging in height from 12-30 inches. Plants like full sun but will grow in partial shade. Removing spent flower spikes prolongs the blooming season. Space plants 12-18 inches apart.

Stokesia (*Stokesia cyanea*) Stokesia or Stoke's Aster is an extremely hardy perennial for Georgia. It withstands dry conditions as well. Plants are low growing initially, stretching to 15-18 inches at blooming time. The most common variety produces light blue blooms. However, other varieties produce white or rose-colored flowers. Plants may begin blooming in May and continue sporadically into October. Plant in well-drained locations.

Summer Phlox (*Phlox paniculata*) Hardy or summer phlox is called the backbone of the perennial garden. This summer flowering perennial has been vastly improved. Many outstanding varieties produce large, exquisitely colored flower heads. Summer phlox grows from two to three and one half feet tall depending on variety. Consequently they are used in the mid to rear sections in the border. They prefer full sun, good moisture, and an occasional spraying for mildew. Benlate is recommended. The flowering period of summer phlox is usually in July and August.

Sweet William (*Dianthus barbatus*) Sweet William is an old-fashioned garden favorite. Taller varieties such as Scarlet Beauty and Newport Pink grow 12 to 18 inches tall and are suitable for massing and background use, while Indian Carpet, the dwarf form, can be used in containers or for edging borders. Plant in full sun in a well-drained soil. Sweet William flowers in late April-early May and is considered a biennial.

Thrift (*Phlox subulata*) Moss Phlox or Thrift, as it is commonly called in the South, is a low-growing, spreading perennial. It is often seen growing on sand or clay banks, where it seems to thrive under these dry and infertile conditions. Moss phlox is selected for rock gardens because of its ability to thrive under adverse conditions and neglect. The needle-like foliage forms a dense, low mat of growth. It covers itself with lavender-pink blooms for a two week period in March to April. Varieties producing white or blue flowers are also available.

Tritoma (*Kniphofia uvaria*) Tritoma, Torch Lily, or Red Hot Poker produces sword-like leaves and poker shaded flower spikes which are creamy-yellow topped with bright orange to red. A border spot exposed to full sun and offering good drainage should be selected for this perennial. As a rule, Red Hot Poker blooms in late summer. However, certain varieties (T. 'Springtime') bloom in the spring. Regardless of time of bloom, the plants are striking accents and show up splendidly against a dark green background. Variously colored tritomas are available, depending on cultivar or variety selected. Even a white-flowering type is available. Once established, tritoma is drought resistant.

Verbena (*Verbena tenuisecta*) A wonderful, low-growing perennial that has few pests. Once established, this species of verbena is extremely tough and long lived. It requires dry, sunny, sandy locations so some bed preparation is required. Blooms from early spring to frost. It is a wonderful butterfly attractor and comes in white, pink and lavender as well as dark purple.

Table 2. Perennials for Georgia gardens

COMMON NAME	BOTANICAL NAME	HEIGHT	COLOR	BLOOM TIME	EXPOSURE
Ajuga	*Ajuga reptans*	4-12 in.	B, P, W	Sp	SH
Artemisia	*Artemisia* spp.	1-3+ ft	I.F.'	Su/	SU
Aster	*Aster* spp.	1-6+ ft	All	Su /+F	SU
Astilbe	*Astilbe japonica*	1-3 ft	P, R, W	Sp	SH
Babysbreath	*Gypsophila paniculata*	2-3 ft	W	-Su/F	SU
Baptisia	*Baptisia australis*	3-4 ft	B	Sp	SU, S-S
Bee-balm	*Monarch didyma*	2-4 ft	P, R, W	+Sp/Su	SU, S-S
Coneflower	*Rudbeckia* spp.	2-7+ ft	G, O, Y	Su/F	SU
Bordergrass and creeping-lilyturf	*Liriope muscari* and *L. spicata*	1-2 ft	L, P, W	+Su	SH, S-S, SU
Butterfly weed	*Asclepias tuberosa*	2-3 ft	O	Su/+Su	SU
Candytuft	*Iberis sempervirens*	9-12 in.	W	Sp	SU, S-S
Cardinal flower	*Lobelia cardinalis*	3-4 ft	R	+Su	SH, S-S
Columbine	*Aquilegia* x *hybrida*	1-3 ft	B, P, W, Y	Sp	SH, S-S
Common thyme	*Thymus vulgaris*	3-12 in.	B, L	Su	SU
Coreopsis	*Coreopsis* spp.	1-3 ft	Y	Su	SU
Daylily	*Hemerocallis* spp.	1-4 ft	-B	Su	SU
Delphinium	*Delphinium* spp.	1-5 ft	B, L, W	Sp	SU
False aster	*Kalimeris pinnatifida*	12 in.	W	Sp/Su/F	S-S
False sunflower	*Heliopsis helianthoides* ssp. *scabra cv.* Summer Sun	2-4 ft	G, Y	+Su	SU
Foxglove	*Digitalis purpurea*	2-6 ft	L, P, W, Y	Sp+	SU, S-S
Fringed-bleeding heart	*Dicentra eximia*	1-3 ft	P, W	Sp+/Su	SH
Garden chrysanthemum	*C.* x *morifolium*	1-3 ft	-B	Su/F	SU
Gaura	*Gaura lindheimeri*	3-4 ft	W	Su-	SU
Goldenrod	*Solidago* spp.	1-3 ft	G	Su+/F	SU
Green-and-gold	*Chrysogonum virginianum*	6-9 in.	Y	Sp/-Su	SH
Hardy ageratum	*Eupatorium coelestinum*	2-3 ft	B, W	F	SU,
Hardy iceplant	*Delosperma cooperi*	3 in.	Pu	-Sp/F	SU

Table 2. Perennials for Georgia gardens

COMMON NAME	BOTANICAL NAME	HEIGHT	COLOR	BLOOM TIME	EXPOSURE
Hardy lantana	*Lantana camara* cv. Miss Huff cv. Mozelle	4-6 ft 4-6 ft	O, Y O, Y	Sp/Su/F Sp/Su/F	SU
Hosta	*Hosta* spp. and hybrids	1-3 ft	B, L, W	-Su/+S	SH, S-S
Iris	*Iris* spp. and hybrids	1-3 ft	All	Sp/-Su	SU
Japanese anemone	*Anemone* x hybrida	2-3 ft	P, W	+Su/F	S-S
Japanese pachysandra	*Pachysandra terminalis*	8-12 in.	W	+Sp	SH, S-S
Leadwort	*Ceratostigma plumbaginoides*	8-12 in.	B	Su+	SU, S-S
Lenten-rose	*Helleborus orientalis*	15-18 in.	L, P, W	W/-Sp	SH, S-S
Mondograss	*Ophiopogon japonicus*	6-15 in.	L, W	Su	SH, S-S,
Obedientplant	*Physostegia virginiana*	3-4 ft	P, R, W	Su	SU
Oriental poppy	*Papaver orientate*	2-3 ft	O, P, R, W	Sp+	SU
Peony	*Paeonia lactiflora*	3-4 ft	P, R, W	Sp/+Sp	SU, S-S
Phlox	*Phlox paniculata, P. subulata, P. divaricata*	6-36 in.	All	-Sp/Su	SU
Pink/white boltonia	*Boltonia asteroides* cv. Pink Beauty and cv. Snowbank	3-6 ft	P, W	+Su	SU
Pinks	*Dianthus* spp.	12 in.	P, R, W, Y	Sp/Su	SU
Purple Coneflower	*Echinacea purpurea*	2-35 in	UP, R, W	Su	SU
Red-hot poker	*Kniphofia uvaria*	3-5 ft	O, R, Y	Su	SU
Rose-mallow	*Hibiscus moscheutos*	3-4 ft	P, R, W	Su	SU
Russian sage	*Perovskia atriplicifolia*	4-5 ft	L	Su/F	SU
Salvia	*Salvia* spp.	6 in.-5 ft	B, L, R, W	Su/F	SU
Sedum	*Sedum* spp.	1-24 in.	P, R, W	Sp/F	SU
Shasta daisy	*Chrysanthemum* x *superbum*	2-3 ft	W	-Su/Su	SU
Smooth white-beard-tongue	*Penstemon digitalis*	2-3 ft	W	Su	SU, S-S
Stoke's aster	*Stokesia laevis*	1-2 ft	B	Su	SU, S-S
Swamp-sunflower	*Helianthus angustifolius*	5-7 ft	Y	F	SU
Tall gayfeather	*Liatris spicata*	2-3 ft.	L, P	Su/+F	SU
Verbena	*Verbena canadensis, V. tenuisecta, & hybrids*	3-24 in.	B, L, P, Pu, R, W	Sp/F	SU
Veronica and hybrids	*Veronica spicata*	1-3 ft	B, P, W	Su	SU
Yarrow	*Achillea filipendulina*	3-5 ft	Y	So	SU

GROWING BULBS

Bed Preparation

The majority of bulbous plants are actually less particular about soil than many other cultivated plants. Most, however, prefer a moist, well-drained medium sandy loam which does not remain wet and sticky after heavy rain or dry out too quickly. Good drainage is essential. If in doubt, test for drainage before planting. Dig a hole about a foot deep and fill it with water. The next day fill the hole with water again and see how long it remains. If the water drains away in eight to 10 hours, the soil is sufficiently well drained to grow most bulbs.

If drainage is a problem or if the soil is too sandy or a heavy clay, you may need to use a soil amendment. Peat moss, bark, rotted sawdust, compost, perlite, vermiculite, coarse sand and many other materials have been used successfully. The type of amendment needed depends on the structure and texture of the existing soil, drainage, and the type of bulbs to be grown. Spread several inches of material on the soil surface and thoroughly incorporate it. In extreme cases, you may need to install drainage lines or construct raised beds to ensure good drainage.

A pH of 6.0 to 6.8 is best for most bulbs. Incorporate lime if a soil test indicates a need for it. In the absence of a soil test, add one to two pounds of 5-10-10, 10-10-10, or 8-8-8 fertilizer per 100 sq. ft. of bed space. Organic fertilizers, such as bone meal, are often recommended for bulbs but are probably no better than inorganic sources used at the proper rates. Incorporate lime, fertilizer, and any soil amendments thoroughly and deeply, at least 12 inches. Do not attempt to work the soil when it is too wet. If you can crumble the soil between your fingers, it is dry enough for digging and planting.

Selecting Bulbs

Bulbs are sold in a variety of retail outlets. Always buy from a reputable dealer. Avoid bulbs that are soft, look molded or discolored. Bulbs should be firm and have unblemished skin. There is a direct correlation between the quality of the bulb and the quality of the flower produced; bargain bulbs are no bargain! Spring-flowering bulbs purchased in the spring are often leftovers from the previous fall and are virtually worthless.

Bulbs are generally graded and sold according to size. Large bulbs produce larger and/or multiple flowers. The largest bulbs are not necessary for good landscape effect. In most cases, medium grades are entirely satisfactory.

Planting

Plant spring-flowering bulbs in the fall. In Georgia, spring-flowering bulbs can be planted from October through late December in most areas. If you cannot plant the bulbs right away, store them at around 60-65 degrees F. in a dry area. Temperatures above 70 degrees F. may damage the flower buds. In areas of the state with extremely mild winter climates, it may be desirable to pre-cool some bulbs. Most spring-flowering bulbs require a 12-16 week cold period in ventilated packages in the bottom of your refrigerator at 40-50 degrees F. before planting. Check with your bulb supplier to determine whether the bulbs you purchase have been precooled or whether you may need to give them a cold treatment. Summer-flowering bulbs are planted in spring after the danger of frost has passed.

Planting depth and spacing are very important to the success of bulbs. A general rule of thumb for planting depth (from top of bulb to soil surface) is two to three times the greatest diameter for bulbs two inches or more in diameter and three to four times the greatest diameter for smaller bulbs.

Spacing will vary from one to two inches to as much as several feet. When spacing bulbs, consider not only how much space each plant needs, but also how frequently it will be dug and divided. Also, consider the landscape effect. Avoid spotty or line-out arrangements. It is sometimes suggested that bulbs be broadcast over the area to be planted in order to achieve a naturalistic look; this is inadvisable, however, because dropping or throwing the bulbs may bruise or injure them.

Plant the bulbs upright (rhizomes and tuberous roots are usually planted on their side), and press the soil firmly around them. Water the beds thoroughly to help settle the soil.

Care and Maintenance

Mulches or ground covers may be necessary to ensure winter survival of some bulbs. They not only minimize winter injury, but also provide a background against which little bulbs show to better advantage.

A well-prepared bed should require little cultivation except periodic weeding. Many spring-flowering bulbs are "over planted" with other plants, frequently annuals. Be sure not to dig so deeply as to damage the bulbs. When the bulbs flower, fertilize them again using the fertilizers and rates previously mentioned. When the flowers fade, cut them off to prevent seed formation.

It is best not to cut or remove the foliage until it dies naturally. Most spring-flowering bulbs produce foliage in fall or early spring which dies by late spring or early summer. Summer-flowering bulbs produce their foliage in spring; it usually remains until cold weather kills it in the fall. Most of the fall-flowering bulbs produce foliage when the spring-flowering bulbs do; they simply flower at a different time.

Normal rainfall usually provides enough moisture for spring-flowering bulbs but not for summer-flowering bulbs. During dry weather, provide supplemental irrigation at weekly intervals. Soak the ground thoroughly. Bulbs have a much higher water requirement when in active growth than when dormant.

Disease and Insect Control

Good cultural conditions eliminate many disease problems. Discard any diseased bulbs at planting. Aphids, thrips, Japanese beetles, slugs, stem and bulb nematodes, narcissus bulb fly larvae, wireworms, bulb mites, mosaic virus, botrytis and various bacterial and fungal rots can sometimes be a problem.(See Chapter 13 in this book *Diagnosing Ornamental Plant Problems*.) Because the recommendation for control of these pests is constantly changing, you should contact your Extension agent for current recommendations or consult the *Georgia Pest Management Handbook*.

COMMONLY USED BULBS AND TUBERS

Achimenes—Achimenes are widely grown indoors, but are suitable for outdoor pots on shaded porches or patios when night temperatures remain above 60 degrees F. Most plants grown today are hybrids; numerous varieties and colors are available. They are propagated from seeds or rhizomes.

Agapanthus—Several species, hybrids and varieties are cultivated. Leafless flower clusters bear 12 to 30 blue or white flowers. Often grown as tub plants, they are hardy outdoors only in Zone 9. Plant shallow outdoors. In containers, leave the nose of bulb protruding above soil surface.

Allium—Lilac-pink flower clusters are five to six inches in diameter. A very showy plant in the landscape, it is usually used in the background of borders. The Allium (onion) genus is best known for its edible members -- onions, garlic, chives, shallots, and leeks -- but many ornamental species are also cultivated.

Anemone—Blue, red, white, and pink cultivars of *A. blanda* are available. Plants form small compact mounds of flowers, and are frequently used with early tulips. *A. coronaria* (Poppy anemone) blooms later and has larger flowers, but is less hardy than *A. blanda*. Soak tubers overnight before planting.

Begonia(Tuberous)—Almost all colors of tuberous begonias are available in upright or trailing types with several distinctly different flower forms. Grown as a pot plant, in window boxes, or as a bedding plant in shaded areas outdoors, it is a handsome plant in bloom. Plants are somewhat brittle. Well-drained soils are essential. Presprout tubers indoors to increase length of the growing season outdoors. Plant shallow so that the top of tuber is slightly above the soil surface.

Caladium—Caladiums are grown for their foliage, the flowers being rather insignificant. Individual leaves are 6 to 24" long and come in an endless combination of red, pink, white, silver, and green. Caladiums should be dug and stored over winter. They may be presprouted indoors to extend the growing season. They should be grown in shade and are well adapted to pot culture.

Canna—Canna is a favorite summer blooming plant because of its long bloom time and because it thrives in hot weather. Numerous varieties and colors are available ranging from dwarf to very tall varieties. The rhizomes are generally hardy in Zones 8 and 9, but should be lifted and stored during winter at 45-50 degrees F. in Zone 7.

Chionodoxa—Blue and white varieties are available. The flowers are small, thus masses are usually necessary for a good display. Chionodoxa is an excellent bulb for naturalizing and will increase by bulblets and self-seeding.

Colchicum—Colchicums are one of the few fall-blooming bulbs. Bright flowers, usually white or lilac, appear suddenly, rising from the soil without foliage. The flowers look much like crocus and are often confused with true autumn crocus. Plant colchicums immediately upon receipt as they will bloom without being planted.

Convallaria—Usually grown for its fragrant bell-shaped flowers, Lily-of-the-valley is also an excellent ground cover for shady locations. It is best propagated in the fall by dividing the pips (shoots that appear on the rhizome) when the foliage has developed fully and begun to yellow. Double-flowered and pink varieties are also available.

Crinum—Crinums thrive in the South with little care.

The plant is grown primarily for its long flowers stalks which bear umbels of as many as 30 lily-like white, pink, or rose-red blooms. Several species and varieties are cultivated; the variegated pink and white is more common. The bulbs are very large, sometimes exceeding six inches in diameter.

Crocus—Numerous crocus species, hybrids and varieties are cultivated. The large-flowered Dutch crocus is largely hybrids derived from *C. vernus*. Many colors are available. The fall, winter, and early spring flowering varieties are particularly valued for their time of bloom. Many species naturalize freely from cormels and by self-seeding.

Cyclamen—Miniature relatives of the florists' cyclamen, hardy cyclamen are excellent for naturalizing in shady areas. Colors range from white to crimson. Tubers may go dormant in mid summer under high temperatures and low moisture. *C. purpurascens*, *C. hederifolium*, *C. cilicium*, and *C. repandum* are readily available.

Dahlia—Dahlias are grown primarily as bedding plants or for cut flowers; some of the dwarf varieties are suitable for tub culture. Most bedding types are seed-grown while most cut types are propagated by division of tuberous roots. Many colors and varieties are available with many flower types. Dahlias are not reliably winter hardy outside Zone 9 and should be dug and stored under dry, cool conditions. Tall varieties require staking.

Endymion—Sometimes confused with Siberian Squill, Spanish Bluebell bears much taller flower spikes and blooms much later. Blue, pink, and white varieties are available. It too is an excellent choice for naturalizing in wooded areas.

Eranthis—Winter Aconite is valued for its very early flowering habit. The bright yellow flowers cover the ground even when ice and snow are still present. A good naturalizing plant, it will self-seed. Soak tubers 24 hours before planting.

Fritillaria—This is one of the showiest spring-flowering bulbs. The flower stalk is topped by a crest of leaves beneath which hang large clusters of two inch reddish orange, bronze, red, or yellow flowers. *F. meleagris* is also cultivated and produces unusual purple and white checkered flowers.

Galanthus—Snowdrops are among the first flowers to bloom in spring. They grow well under deciduous trees and are good for naturalizing and random planting. The drooping white flowers have a green splotch around the inner segments. *G. elwesii* (Giant Snowdrop) is larger and flowers slightly later.

Gladiolus—Gladiolus is best grown as a cut flower. Because the lower florets wither well before the upper ones open, it is generally not an attractive plant in the landscape. You should make successive plantings to ensure flowers for continuous cutting. Numerous varieties and colors are available. The corms are not reliably winter hardy in Zone 7 and should be lifted and stored at 35-40 degrees. Mounding the soil around the base of the plants will help prevent them toppling over.

Hippeastrum—A spectacular plant in bloom, amaryllis has long been cultivated indoors. They can be grown outdoors as summer blooming bulbs. Some hybrids and species are hardy outdoors in Zone 9. When planted outdoors, the nose of the bulbs should be just at the soil surface. In pots, leave about half the bulb above the soil surface.

Hyacinthus—Few flowers can boast the extensive color range and fragrance of hyacinths. *H. orientalis* is hardy but not notably persistent; the bulbs eventually decline becoming too small to flower. *H. orientalis albulus* (French-Roman Hyacinth) has smaller flowers but is said to be more persistent.

Hymenocallis—It produces fragrant three- to four-inch intricately arranged white flowers in midsummer on tall leafless stalks. Several varieties are available, one with yellow flowers. The plant is not reliably winter hardy outside Zone 9 and should be lifted and stored at 65-70 degrees F.

Ipheion—Starflower produces abundant bluish white flowers. It is excellent for naturalizing and multiplies rapidly. It is sometimes used in lawns which can be a problem since the grass usually needs cutting before the plant's foliage matures.

Iris—The Iris genus is extremely diverse and many species and hybrids are cultivated. Several classification schemes exist. They are loosely divided into bulbous iris and rhizomatous iris. The bulbous iris, e.g. *I. danfordiae* (Danford Iris) and *I. reticulata* (netted Iris), are small and generally bloom very early. The rhizomatuous iris, e.g. I. hybrids (Bearded Iris), *I. siberica* (Siberian Iris), and *I. kaempferi* (Japanese Iris), are taller (up to three feet) and bloom from mid spring to early summer. The cultural requirements and differences are too diverse to discuss here.

Leucojum—Small white bell-shaped flowers tipped

with green are borne on each stem. They are good for naturalizing and random planting in shrub borders. *L. aestivum* (Summer Snowflake) is taller and blooms later. *L. autumnale* (Autumn Snowflake) is fall blooming.

Lilium—Numerous lily species and cultivars are available. Bloom times range from May to September. All colors are available except blue. Various flower forms exist. It is an excellent border plant and cut flower. The larger hybrids are effective as single specimens; the species are more often used in mass. Tall varieties should be staked.

Lycoris—In late July or early August, *I. squamigera* suddenly appears. Long leafless flower stalks bear four to 12 lilac-pink, lily-like flowers. The foliage appears in early spring and dies back to the ground by early summer. *L. radiata* (Red Spider Lily) and *L. aurea* (Yellow Spider Lily) are also members of this genus. Both bloom later. *L. aurea* is less hardy.

Muscari—The tiny purple flower clusters resemble clusters of grapes. Common Grape Hyacinth is easy to grow, and naturalizes quickly. It is frequently interplanted with other spring bulbs. A white variety is also available. *M. armeniacum* (Armenian Grape Hyacinth) is larger and more robust; several blue and double-flowered varieties are available.

Narcissus—There are 11 major divisions of the genus Narcissus. Confusion often arises because the generic name Narcissus is also used as a common name. Daffodils, like jonquils, are but one type of narcissus. Hundreds of varieties are available. The cultural requirements for all divisions are essentially identical, but the size,

color, time of bloom, etc. vary and are too complex to discuss here.

Polianthes—The fragrant tuberose became so associated with funerals that its popularity declined. It is a superb cut flower, however, and grows well in Georgia. It is usually treated as tender bulbs. Large size bulbs have a tendency to split into smaller bulbs which may require an additional year or two to reach flowering size.

Scilla—Siberian Squill is valued for its early bright blue flowers. It is excellent for naturalizing, especially in wooded areas. Several varieties are available including one with white flowers.

Sternbergia—An underused bulb, Sternbergia, is valued for its fall-flowering habit. It is frequently mistaken for autumn crocus. The plant grows best in full sun and can remain undisturbed for years. Foliage is produced in the fall and remains green during winter.

Tulipa—Numerous tulip species and cultivars exist. The classification scheme for cultivated tulips list 15 divisions based on time of bloom and parentage. More than 4000 varieties are in existence. Virtually all colors are represented. The tulip is considered by many the premier spring bulb. Most tulips also make excellent cut flowers. Many tulips are not notably persistent in the south and usually decline after the first year. Size, flower type, time of bloom, etc. are too complex to discuss here.

Zephyranthes—*Z. atamasco* (Atamasco Lily, Rain Lily, Fairy Lily) is often seen along the roadsides of Georgia, frequently along drainage ditches and wet meadows. Flowers often appear following a soaking rain. Other species and hybrids are also available.

Table 3. Bulbs for Georgia gardens

COMMON NAME	BOTANICAL NAME	COLD HARDI-NESS	PLANTING TIME	PLANTING DEPTH (INCHES)	SPACING (INCHES)	FLOWERING TIME	HEIGHT AT FLOWERING
Giant onion	*Allium giganteum*	H	F	8	12	late	3-4 ft.
Greek wind-flower	*Anemone blanda*	H	F	5	1-2	early	6 in.
Glory-of-the-snow	*Chionodoxa luciliae*	H	F	5	2	early	5 in.
Crocus	*Crocus species & hybrids*	H	F	5	1-4	very early to mid*	4 in.
Hardy cyclamen	*Cyclamen species*	H	S	see text	4	early-mid	4-5 in.

H=Hardy, F=Fall

Table 3. Bulbs for Georgia gardens

COMMON NAME	BOTANICAL NAME	COLD HARDI-NESS	PLANTING TIME	PLANTING DEPTH (INCHES)	SPACING (INCHES)	FLOWERING TIME	HEIGHT AT FLOWERING
Winter aconite	*Eranthis hyemalis*	H	F	5	2	very early	4 in.
Crown imperial	*Fritillaria imperialis*	H	F	8	12	mild	3 ft.
Common snowdrop	*Galanthus nivalis*	H	F	5	2	early*	6 in.
Amaryllis	*Hippeastrum hybrids*	T	S	8	6-12	late*	1-2 ft.
Spanish bluebell	*Hyacinthoides hispanica*	H	F	5	1-2	late	8 in.
Hyacinth	*Hyacinthus orientalis*	H	F	8	3-4	mid*	10 in.
Spring starflower	*Ipheion uniflorum*	H	F	5	2-4	mid*	6 in.
Iris	*Iris species & hybrids*	H	F	varies	varies	very early to late	see text
Spring snowflake	*Leucojum vernum*	H	F	5	2-4	mid	9 in.
Common grape hyacinth	*Muscari botryoides*	H	F	5	1-3	early	6 in.
Narcissus, daffodil, jonquil	*Narcissus species & hybrids*	H	F	5-8	1-4	early-mid*	6-24 in.
Tulip	*Tulipa species & hybrids (Summer/Fall Flowering)*	H	F	5-8	2-4	early-late*	6-30 in.
African lily	*Agapanthus africanus*	S (see text)	S	see text	24	summer	1-5 ft.
Tuberous begonia	*Begonia x tuberhybrida*	T	S	see text	12-15	until frost*	12-18 in.
Caladium	*Caladium bicolor*	T	S	see text	12	-	6 in.-2 ft.
Canna	*Canna x generalis*	SH	S	5	>12	until frost	1 1/2-5 ft.
Milk-and-wine lily	*Crinum* spp.	H	S or F	8	>12	middle	2-4 ft.
Autumn crocus, Meadow saffron	*Colchicum autumnale*	H	F	5	1-2	early	4-8 in.

H=Hardy, F=Fall

Table 3. Bulbs for Georgia gardens

COMMON NAME	BOTANICAL NAME	COLD HARDI-NESS	PLANTING TIME	PLANTING DEPTH (INCHES)	SPACING (INCHES)	FLOWERING TIME	HEIGHT AT FLOWERING
Autumn crocus	Crocus species	H	F	5	1-4	early	4 in.
Hardy cyclamen	Cyclamen species	H	S	see text	6-	8 early-late	4-5 in.
Dahlia	Dahlia hybrids	SH	S	4-6	12-18	until frost	1-5 ft.
Gladiolus	Gladiolus x hortulanus	SH	S	4-6	6	see text	1-5 ft.
Peruvian daffodil	Hymenocallis narcissiflora	SH	S	4	12-15	early*	18-24 ft.
Lily	Lilium species & hybrids	H	F or S (see text)	8; see text	4-6	varies	2-6 ft.
Red Spider lily	Lycoris radiata	H	F	see text	5-8	early	2 ft.
Magic lily	Lycoris squamigera	H	S	see text	12	middle	2 ft.
Tuberose	Polianthes tuberosa	T	S	see text	6-8	mid-late	1-4 ft.
Winter daffodil	Sternbergia lutea	H	F	5	4-6	early	6 in.
Rain lily	Zephyranthes species & hybrids	H	F	2	3-6	middle	6-8 in.

H=Hardy, F=Fall

PLANT SELECTION GUIDES: ANNUALS FOR SPECIFIC USES

ANNUALS FOR SHADE OR PARTIAL SHADE

Ageratum*
Alyssum, Sweet
Balsam
Begonia
Browallia
Candytuft*
Chinese-forget-me-not
Coleus
Forget-me-not*
Heliotrope
*Impatiens
Larkspur
Lobelia
Monkeyflower

ANNUALS FOR DRY AREAS

Babysbreath, Annual
Black-eyed-susan
California poppy
Cleome
Cornflower
Cosmos
Dahlberg daisy
Dusty-miller
Gaillardia
Gomphrena
Portulaca
Sanvitalia
Snow-on-the-mountain
Strawflower
Summer-cypress
Verbena, Annual
Vinca
Zinnia

HEAT-LOVING ANNUALS

Abelmoschus
Amaranthus
Black-eyed-susan
Black-eyed-susan vine
Begonia
Celosia
Cleome
Cosmos

Creeping zinnia
Dahlia
Dahlberg daisy
Four-o'clock
Gaillardia
Gomphrena
Impatiens
Mandevilla
Wax Marigold
Melampodium
Mexican heather
Mexican sunflower
Morningglory
Nicotiana
Petunia
Phlox, Annual
Polka dot plant
Portulaca
Sage
Sanvitalia
Scaveola
Snow-on-the-mountain
Statice
Summer-cypress
Sunflower
Verbena
Vinca
Zinnia

ANNUALS/BIENNIALS TO SOW IN FALL

Alyssum, Sweet
Candytuft
Calendula
Cornflower
Foxglove
Larkspur
Poppy
Stock
Moneyplant
Phlox, Annual
Sweet pea

ANNUAL GROUNDCOVERS

Alyssum, Sweet
Candytuft
Portulaca
Sanvitalia

Verbena
Vinca
Zinnia, Creeping

ANNUALS THAT MAY RE-SEED YEAR AFTER YEAR
Abelmoschus
Alyssum, Sweet
Baby'sbreath
Black-eyed-susan
Black-eyed-susan vine
Browallia
Calendula
Cleome
Cornflower
Cosmos
Forget-me-not
Gaillardia
Impatiens
Larkspur
Melampodium
Morningglory
Nicotiana
Pansy and Viola
Portulaca
Snow-on-the-mountain
Summer-cypress
Verbena
Vinca (Catharanthus)
Zinnia

ANNUALS USEFUL FOR CUT FLOWERS
Aster, China
Babysbreath
Browallia
Calendula
Celosia
Cornflower
Cosmos
Dahlia
Dianthus
Larkspur
Marigold
Nasturtium
Snapdragon
Statice
Stock

Sweet pea
Verbena
Zinnia

ANNUALS SUITABLE FOR DRYING
Babysbreath
Bells-of-Ireland
Celosia
Cornflower
Gomphrena
Moneyplant
Statice
Strawflower
Sunflower

ANNUALS GROWN FOR FRAGRANCE
Alyssum, Sweet
Dianthus
Four-o'clock
Heliotrope
Nasturtium
Nicotiana
Petunia
Phlox, Annual
Stock
Sweet Pea
Verbena

ANNUAL VINES
Balsam apple
Black-eyed-susan vine
Canarybirdvine
Cup-and-saucer vine
Cypressvine
Hyacinth bean
Mandevilla
Moonflower
Morningglory
Scarlet runner bean
Sweet pea

ANNUALS USED FOR EDGING
Ageratum
Alyssum, Sweet
Aster, China
Begonia, Wax
Browallia

Calendula
Candyuft
Coleus
Dahlila
Dusty-miller
Gomphrena
Lobelia
Marigold (dwarf varieties)
Monkeyflower
Nasturtium
Ornamental cabbage and kale
Pansy and viola
Petunia
Phlox, Annual
Pinks
Portulaca
Snapdragon (dwarf varieties)
Strawflower
Torenia
Verbena
Vinca
Zinnia (dwarf varieties)

ANNUALS GROWN FOR COLORFUL FOLIAGE

Amaranthus
Basil
Castor bean
Coleus
Dusty-miller
Hyacinth bean
New Guinea impatiens
Ornamental cabbage and kale
Polkadotplant
Snow-on-the-mountain
Summer-cypress
Zonal geranium

ANNUALS FOR CONTAINERS

Ageratum
Alyssum, Sweet
Aster, China
Balsam
Begonia, Wax
Black-eyed-Susan vine
Browallia
Calendula

Calliopsis
Candytuft
Celosia
Coleus
Cosmos
Dahlia
Dusty miller
Gaillarda
Geranium
Gomphrena
Impatiens
Lobelia
Marigold
Mexican heather
Monkey flower
Nasturtium
Nicotiana
Ornamental cabbage and kale
Ornamental pepper
Pansy
Pentas
Petunia
Phlox, Annual
Pinks
Poppy
Portulaca
Salvia
Scaveola
Strawflower
Stock
Summer cypress
Sweet pea
Torenia
Verbena, Annual
Vinca
Zinnia

ANNUALS FOR HANGING BASKETS

Alyssum, Sweet
Begonia, Wax
Browallia
Geranium, Ivy
Impatiens
Lobelia
Marigold
Monkey flower
Nasturtium

Pansy and viola
Petunia
Phlox, Annual
Pinks
Portulaca
Salvia
Sanvitalia
Verbena
Zinnia, Creeping

ANNUALS/BIENNIALS THAT ATTRACT BUTTERFLIES
Alyssum, Sweet
Begonia, Wax
Ageratum
Black-eyed-Susan
Coreopsis
Cosmos
French Marigold
Gomphrena
Heliotrope
Hollyhock
Impatiens
Mexican sunflower
Money plant
Nasturtium
Nicotiana
Pentas
Petunia
Phlox, Annual
Scarlet sage and others
Snapdragon
Sunflower
Statice
Verbena
Zinnia

ANNUALS/BIENNIALS THAT ATTRACT HUMMINGBIRDS
Cypress vine
Nasturtium
Pentas
Petunia
Phlox, Annual
Scarlet sage

EASY-TO-GROW ANNUALS FROM SEED SOWN IN THE GARDEN
Ageratum
Alyssum, Sweet
Babysbreath, Annual
Black-eyed-susan vine
Calendula
Candytuft
Celosia
Cleome
Coleus
Cornflower
Cosmos
Four-o'clock
Gaillardia
Nasturtium
Poppy
Portulaca
Sunflower
Sweet pea
Verbena
Zinnia

DISCUSSION QUESTIONS

1. Give three examples of cool season annuals.

2. Why is good soil preparation important when planting a perennial bed?

3. Give three examples of spring-flowering bulbs that can be grown in full sun

4. What is the definition of deadheading plants?

5. What are the consequences of improper spacing?

6. When is the best time to water "established" perennials?

7. Why is Spring too late to plant most species of flowering bulbs?

8. Give three examples of summer flowering bulbs.

9. When is the best time to plant perennials and why?

10. What is the main advantage to mulching annuals, perennials and bulbs?

RESOURCES

UGA Trial Gardens are located on the campus of The University of Georgia in Athens. www.uga.edu/ugatrial

Armitage, Allan M. *Herbaceous Perennial Plants: A Treatise on Their Identification, Culture, and Garden Attributes*. 3rd Edition. 1141 pages. Timber Press Publishing Company.

11

Selecting Woody Plants for Georgia Landscapes

James T. Midcap
Matthew Chappell

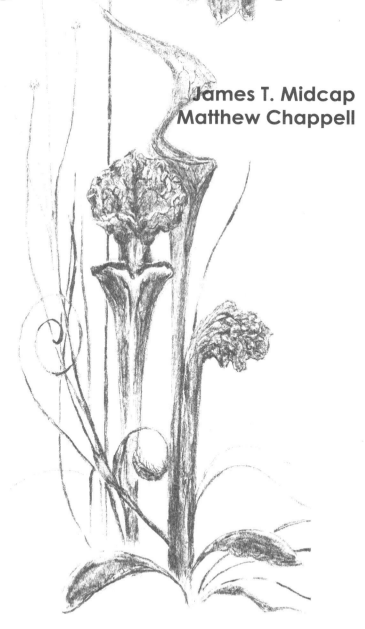

LEARNING OBJECTIVES

Know the difference between evergreen and deciduous plants and landscape considerations of both.

Be familiar with terms such as cold hardiness, heat tolerance, watering requirements, soil preference, light requirements.

Understand the factors of plant selection.

Be able to identify the factors to consider in plant selection.

Identify shrubs, and vines and groundcovers that are suitable for Georgia landscapes.

Know how to select healthy plants from a nursery.

TERMS TO KNOW

Disease resistance the tendency not to be infected by a particular pathogen.

Hardiness the ability to withstand harsh environmental conditions.

Native inherent and original to an area.

Woody plant a plant that uses wood composed of cellulose and lignin as its structural tissue and grows from above ground stems each year.

INTRODUCTION

Georgia's temperate climate affords residents the ability to grow a wide variety of woody ornamentals. Sites in the Georgia mountains are well suited for hardy evergreen and deciduous plants, while coastal areas permit the use of many subtropical species. The typically mild winters across the majority of the state are suitable for a broad selection of herbaceous and woody plants. The 50+ inches of annual rainfall that occurs over a majority of the state are adequate for excellent growth, however, periods of spring and summer drought commonly occur.

Despite relatively mild winters and adequate rainfall across the state, Georgia's climate differs widely among mountain, piedmont and coastal landscapes. This does necessitate some planning before planting a landscape to ensure plants are selected that are adapted to either the north Georgia mountains, the central Piedmont or the Coastal Plain. In addition to the differences in winter temperatures, the northern GA mountain slopes tend to be thin, rocky and well-drained while in the Piedmont, heavy, poorly drained, silty clay loam soils predominate. The coastal plain region often has deep sands and perched water tables that dictate changes in the native plant communities as well as landscape plant selections.

General Plant Selection & Use

A list of plants suitable for the environmental conditions of the site is developed based on cold hardiness, light exposure, rainfall and soil moisture. Plants are then selected which satisfy the basic landscape needs or the planting design. The planting design is based on solving environmental problems, providing structural and architectural features, and aesthetic appeal.

Plants can help overcome a number of environmental problems. Plants modify temperatures by providing shade and windbreaks. All plants provide natural air conditioning by actually cooling the air through transpiration (evaporation through stomata). They also may be used to reduce sound and control traffic noise. Plant foliage filters dust and dirt particles from the air before they infiltrate outdoor living areas. Shrubs and groundcovers selected for slopes can control soil erosion once established.

Landscape architects use plants to articulate space (form floors, walls and overhead canopies) and to build outdoor living areas. Screening hedges and shrubs are used as walls to provide privacy in the outdoor living area. The trees form the ceiling while turfgrasses and groundcovers act as the floor. Scenic views may be framed as focal points with proper placement of trees and shrubs while unsightly views are screened from sight or transferred from focal points to background noise.

Many plants are selected for their aesthetic beauty. Specimens may be chosen for their outstanding leaves, flowers, bark, form or branching habit. Attractive flowers, glossy or colored foliage and brightly colored fruit are powerful visual stimuli. Plants used as living sculptures need strongly defined branching patterns. Green foliage plants provide backgrounds for bold splashes of color or foregrounds (foundation plantings) for many buildings and homes. Today, many plants are selected for their ability to attract wildlife. Fragrant flowers, flowers with particular color/shape combinations, edible fruit and dense branching for nesting sites are likely considerations to attract wildlife.

As the plant selection process nears completion, evaluate your selections based on their maintenance requirements. Consider the pest problems associated with each plant as well as the severity of infestations. Plants with strong pest resistance and few serious pest problems should be given preference over those requiring frequent pest control to maintain their health and beauty.

Select plants that will not overgrow their allotted space. Otherwise, frequent pruning is required to keep them within bounds and to prevent them from crowding other plantings. Many species have multiple cultivars available that offer a variety of mature heights and widths. Start with healthy plants to encourage rapid establishment. To ensure proper establishment plant most trees and shrubs in the fall. This will allow the roots to get a jump start on growing during the winter and spring months before high light and high heat conditions require a large amount of water resources. The exceptions to this rule are 'tender' trees and shrubs that are marginally winter hardy in your area. These should be planted in spring to allow for maximum establishment prior to winter temperatures.

Selecting Plants for the Site

Plants should first be selected based on the conditions of the planting site, next the landscape functions which they are required to fulfill, and lastly the maintenance requirements necessary to keep them healthy and attractive. Plant cold hardiness should be a primary consideration. All perennial plants, herbaceous and woody, must be able to endure the lowest temperatures which occur at the planting site if they are to be permanent. Marginally cold hardy plants may be planted in protected sites; however, they may still be killed during severe winters. There are currently two versions of a minimum temperature hardiness zone map; the 1990 USDA Plant Hardiness zone map and the 2006 Arbor Day Foundation Plant Hardiness map. The USDA revised their plant hardiness zones in 1990 and it is based on average minimum winter temperature over the 1960-1990 time period. Upon its release in 2006, the Arbor Day Foundation map was meant as a replacement to the USDA map with updated climate data over the previous 15 year period; utilizing average minimum winter temperature over the 1990-2005 time period. However, most horticulture professionals and gardeners still prefer the USDA map system because it breaks the U.S. into 20 hardiness zones and uses a 30 year average whereas the Arbor Day Foundation map only includes 10 zones and uses a 15 year average. For the purposes of this publication, the USDA hardiness map will be discussed.

USDA Hardiness Zone Map (Page 56)

The northeast mountains occupy plant hardiness Zone 6b and 7a while most of the Piedmont is in Zone 7b and the Coastal Plain in Zone 8. The average annual minimum temperature for Zone 6b is -5° to 0°F., Zone 7a is 0° to 5°F, zone 7b is 5° to 10°F, Zone 8a is 10° to 15°F and zone 8b is 15° to 20°F. Plants are assigned to a hardiness zone based on the minimum winter temperature they are able to survive.

Trees, shrubs, or herbaceous perennials essential to the landscape should be hardy and able to survive the lowest winter temperatures every year. Non-essential plants or plants under trial may be marginally hardy. Their demise in the landscape due to cold temperatures should not decimate the landscape or remove the focal point(s) of a landscape. Selected trees and major shrubs should always be very cold hardy.

Plants are also selected based upon the moisture levels they require and will receive. With present day emphasis on water efficient and low maintenance landscapes, plants are selected based upon the irrigation to be provided and the normal rainfall of the site. Planting areas are typically designated as one of three water use categories: low, moderate and high. Water efficient plants are placed in low water use zones of the landscape where they receive no additional irrigation once they become established. Plants that require additional water during droughts to look acceptable are planted in moderate water use zones where additional moisture is provided when the plants are stressed. Plants in high water use

zones are provided regular and optimum moisture to keep the plantings in peak condition.

Plant selections are also based upon the moisture holding capacity of the soil. Wet or flood-prone sites and swales require special attention. For these sites select shrubs, vines and ground covers that tolerate standing water as well as the conditions which follow drying of the site. Poorly drained clay soils require plants tolerant of wet saturated conditions. Sandy soils which are not irrigated, on the other hand, require deep rooted and water efficient plants. Native trees and shrubs growing under these conditions may suggest potential plants adapted to the site.

The amount of light at the planting site dictates selecting plants adapted to full sun or deep shade, as well as to all degrees of partial shade. Certain plants are very specific in their light requirements while others tolerate a wide range of light conditions. Aucuba (*Aucuba japonica*), for instance, thrives in partial and deep shade but will sunburn and die when placed in full sun. Flowering dogwood (*Cornus florida*) does best in partial shade but will survive in full sun. However, many dogwoods are stunted and dwarfed when grown in full sun with existing root competition. Full sun requiring plants, when grown in shade, become open and leggy, and more susceptible to insects and disease infestations (E.g. *Juniperis conferta*). Therefore, proper plant selection based on light exposure is necessary for healthy plant establishment and development.

Selecting Plants for Specific Uses

Plants are selected based upon the owners needs or the plants function in the landscape. Shrubs, vines and ground covers are used to achieve different results, both functional and aesthetically. With proper selection for height and spread, texture and color attributes, all can be effective in enhancing the landscape.

Shrub Uses—Shrubs typically fit below the trees and rise above the lawn or ground covers in the landscape. Some develop into small trees while others may only reach one to two feet in height.

However, shrubs are very important in developing a landscape. They provide the garden with structure, such as walls and hedges. Shrubs can be used to develop the outdoor rooms of the garden. Tall shrubs prevent us from seeing from one room to another (screening), while short walls (hedges) allow us to look over into another area but prevent direct entry. A perimeter hedge provides privacy from the outside while allowing us to screen out unwanted views.

Deciduous shrubs provide the garden with vivid reflections of the seasons. They have a sequence of flowers, summer foliage and fruit, and often vibrant fall colors. Their overall appearance changes dramatically from spring to summer to winter. The continual progression insures constant change and continuing interest in the landscape. With appropriate selection, one can have shrubs in bloom all year long, spring, summer, fall and winter. Many gardens are designed to extend the flowering season. In the garden we can enjoy fruit in abundance to feed the songbirds, spectacular fall foliage, fragrance to attract pollinating insects, colors and nectar to attract hummingbirds.

Evergreen shrubs provide full foliage throughout the year and have become indispensable in creating the Southern garden. They are used to define spaces and establish privacy. They also form a permanent background for other features and plants. Well placed groups of evergreens screen unwanted views or create privacy from neighbors. Small and intermediate sized evergreens can be used as ornaments as single specimens or groups of plants. They are frequently used as foundation plantings. An enclosure of intermediate to low shrubs can be used to give a sense of separation without totally interrupting one's view. Small evergreens are used near the house or path where they can be observed up close. They work as accent plants near steps, a garden gate or patio entrance. They are used in formal gardens to create patterns of foliage in living knot gardens. Many small shrubs are planted in handsome pots and combined with other plants for spectacular accents.

The interaction using plants for structural or functional use and combining the ornamental features of plants is key to effective design. Selecting plants adapted to the site and those that fulfill the functional design needs are vital to effective plant selection. Our motto is "select the right plant for the right place" while fulfilling the gardener's needs.

Many of our common ornamental plants such as boxwood, camellia, evergreen azaleas, and evergreen hollies were introduced into our gardens from Europe or Asia. These plants and others have served in historic landscapes for a century or more, and are now commonly called heritage plants. Many heritage plants have been used in our gardens for so long that we think of them as being ours. For example, the American boxwood (*Buxus sempervirens*) is commonly sold, however there is no boxwood native to America. The state flower of Georgia is our Cherokee rose (*Rosa laevigata*), which is native to China, Formosa and Burma. These heritage plants are all from other continents, but have endured and delighted our garden senses for more than a century. Heritage plants are proven introductions that are still landscape favorites.

Not all introduced plants are good, and not all are bad. Introduced plants occasionally have escaped from cultivation and become naturalized as wild populations competing with native plant communities. We term these plants "invasive exotic". Such plants as the Chinese privet (*Ligustrum sinense*), giant reed grass (*Arundo donax*), Chinaberry (*Melia azedarach*) and empress tree (*Paulownia tomentosa*) have all escaped and are no longer recommended for planting. We need to remain alert to the possibility of other plants escaping from cultivation and invading native habitats.

Using native plants provides the opportunity to restore and maintain a Southern plant habitat. Selecting native plants that blend together with natural landscapes create harmony with the existing Southern plant communities. Use of introduced plants in the landscape can introduce a more exotic feeling. Most landscapes effectively combine both native and introduced plants growing side by side. For either native or introduced plants to become established and effective in their landscape roles, the individual plants must be carefully selected for the site and local environment.

Both native plants and introduced species are available to the landscaping public. Many native plants such as inkberry (*Ilex glabra*), summersweet clethra (*Clethra alnifolia*), Carolina jessamine (*Gelsemium sempervirens*) and fothergilla (*Fothergilla gardenii* & *F. major*) are not well known but can be valuable landscape additions. Many introduced plants are well adapted to our landscapes (but not all) and provide color, foliage and fruit. New and improved selections of native and introduced plants are constantly being developed and introduced. The evaluation process is not very extensive, and the home gardener becomes the ultimate evaluator. The reputation of superior plants spreads slowly at first by word of mouth. Soon the gardening magazines are helping to promote these plants. Some of these plants may have the potential to become invasive.

Vine Uses—Vines are among the most versatile plants in the landscape. Most people associate vines with arbors or trellises. They can also be used to screen unsightly views and to provide privacy on patios or decks. They can lend character to stone, brick or stucco walls, break up the monotony of a long chain link fence, or accent or soften the architectural details of buildings.

Vines are sometimes allowed to ramble through shrubs or trees to surprise us with their flowers or foliage. Some vines, like bougainvillea (*Bougainvillea* spp.) or allamanda (*Allamanda cathartica*), are excellent in patio pots or hanging baskets. Honeysuckle (*Lonicera* spp.) adds a wonderful fragrance with there blossoms. Honeysuckle and trumpet creeper (*Campsis radicans*) are prized for their showy flowers, while other vines, like five-leaf akebia (*Akebia quinata*) and climbing fig (*Ficus pumila*) are grown for their foliage. American wisteria (*Wisteria frutescens*) is can be trained as a single-standing specimen or small tree in the landscape [*EDITOR'S NOTE:* Chinese wisteria (*Wisteria sinensis*) has been classified as an invasive exotic by the GA Exotic Pest Plant Council].

Select vines by considering their intended use, light exposure, soil adaptability, type of support needed and color of flowers or foliage. In addition, consider their maintenance requirement. Will the vine require constant pruning to keep it within bounds? Fast-growing vines, such as wisteria and common honeysuckle, require a great deal of routine pruning. If allowed to spread without restraint, their profuse growth can cover trees and shrubs, reducing light and aeration within the canopy. Some vines can even injure or kill small trees by wrapping around them and cutting off nutrient flow. Other vines, like autumn flowering clematis (*Clematis terniflora*), will disperse its seeds and result in many seedlings.

Consider the training required to maintain the selected vine. Some vines cling and climb naturally while others must be trained on support wires, poles or other structures. Therefore, the type of structure will influence the vine you choose.

Vines requiring support can be classified as three basic types: clinging, twining and grabbing.

Clinging vines grasp onto a rough surface by means of rootlets or adhesive disks. Climbing fig, confederate jasmine (*Trachelospermum jasminoides*), Virginia creeper (*Parthenocissus quinquefolia*) and trumpet creeper are examples of clinging vines. These types of vines are often used to cover solid surfaces, such as walls and fences. However, clinging vines may loosen mortar between bricks over time and are difficult to remove once they become anchored. Their methods of climbing also can damage wood by preventing good air circulation and promoting wood decay. Therefore, clinging vines are best suited for trellises or arbors away from solid surfaces.

Twining vines climb by winding their stems around upright supports, such as poles, wires or lattice. These vines require training and may need to be tied in place. Examples are mandevilla (*Mandevilla splendens*), Carolina jessamine and roses (*Rosa* spp.)

Grabbing vines climb by means of tendrils or leaf petioles wrapping around (grab on) anything they contact. One example of this type of vine is the muscadine grape (*Vitis rotundifolia*). Ornamental vines that fall into this category include maypop (*Passiflora* spp.), trumpet honeysuckle (*Lonicera sempervirens*), and clematis (*Clematis* x *hybrida*).

Twining and grabbing vines are supported best on wires, lattice, trellises and arbors. They need support when grown on a flat surface. Vine supports should be constructed from sturdy, durable materials. Always use treated lumber for outdoor structures. Redwood, cedar and cypress are particularly durable lumber materials in the outdoor environment. A wood preservative/water seal applied after construction will also help prolong the life of the structure. Wrought iron also makes an excellent support. Use aluminum or copper wire to attach plants because it is resistant to rusting.

Flowering vines require at least a half day of sun to grow vigorous and bloom abundantly. Shade tolerant vines, like Climbing hydrangea (*Hydrangea anomala* subspecies *petiolaris*), will develop more vivid leaf patterns when provided a few hours of direct morning sun.

Vines have different pruning requirements. Generally pruning is done to remove dead, diseased and damaged wood, to reduce size and to promote branching. Vigorous vines, such as honeysuckle, trumpet vine and American wisteria require regular pruning to keep them confined to the support.

As a general rule, flowering vines should be pruned after they bloom. This is particularly true for wisteria and spring-flowering clematis that bloom on their previous season's wood. Pruning these vines before they bloom will reduce flowering.

Ground Cover Use—Ground covers add texture, color and richness to the landscape. These low-growing plants contribute to the overall effect of the garden. Many ground covers are bright and cheerful and can be deliciously fragrant. A ground cover can be any type of low shrub or vine. These plants are used to carpet the ground as an alternative to lawn or mulch.

Ground covers are usually selected to supply special definition and character to the garden. They provide unity and pattern to a variety of plants. A wide variety of shrubs and trees can be planted within any ground cover planting while retaining the garden's unity and function. A chaotic planting can be pulled together into a functional landscape planting merely by unifying the entire bed with one plant material underneath.

A ground cover planting requires a large mass of plants which will significantly affect the appearance of the landscape. It is important to balance 1) the plants appearance, 2) the purpose of the planting and 3) the horticulture requirements.

The plant's character creates the feel of the landscape. Each ground cover projects its distinctive qualities into the landscape. So, study each selection to ensure that it will harmonize with the desired overall garden effect.

The purpose of the ground cover planting will also affect the plant selection. If the planting is to stabilize the soil on a steep embankment, then a rapidly spreading, easily rooting groundcover is needed. If the planting is to take the place of the lawn and eliminate the mowing, then a spreading grass-like plant such as mondo grass (*Ophiopogon japonica*s) will work since these plants will spread and gradually cover the soil.

Ground covers need to be selected based on the amount of light available. Even in excellent soil, a ground cover will not look its best if planted under unfavorable conditions. Sun-loving junipers (*Juniperis conferta* and *Juniperis horizontalis*) can take the summer's heat and drought while developing a thick carpet of ground cover. However, if planted in shade, these junipers will become leggy and diseased. Conversely, shade loving plants will burn if planted in direct sun. There are a many selections available that fit your functional and aesthetic needs as well as the specific site.

Ground covers must be selected for their cold tolerance and light exposure. Check your local nurseries to see what is available. An investment in a ground cover planting is usually substantial. Be sure that your selections are adapted and will do well before you make a purchase. Watch existing plantings and become familiar with their requirements as well as their seasonal changes. For example, some of the ground cover junipers suddenly change foliage color with the beginning of cold weather, which dramatically changes the look of the landscape.

Selecting Plants From the Nursery

Once the plant list is complete, it is time to select quality plants from the nursery that fit the following criteria. Select plants that are pest free and have no existing insects, diseases and no evidence of past infestations.

Young plants should exhibit healthy vigorous growth, dark green foliage and stout twigs. Plants should be free of mechanical injuries like broken branches, crushed foliage or scarred stems. Select plants that are well-branched and have maintained their lower branches.

A healthy root system is important on young plants since it provides the primary means for rapid establishment and good plant growth at the new site. The root system should be large enough to support the plant top and have active white root tips. The roots of container stock should be examined to make sure they are not diseased or pot bound. Pot bound container plants are more difficult to establish and may develop girdling roots which will shorten the life of the plant. The selection of healthy, quality, young plants for the landscape completes the plant selection process.

The following plant reference lists are not all inclusive; however, they include most of the landscape plants commonly available at many retail nurseries. The categories of plants available in the following reference lists include shrubs, vines and ground covers. Shrubs help provide the frame work of the garden and much of the color. Ground covers unify landscapes with sweeping beds of foliage. Finally, vines act as accents and use the vertical space in the landscape. Trees, lawns, and herbaceous plants (bulbs, annuals, and perennials) are discussed in other chapters of this book.

Table 1. Vines and their characteristics

BOTANICAL NAME AND COMMON NAME	GEORGIA'S HARDY ZONE	TEXTURE	GROWTH RATE	CLASS	REMARKS
Antigonon leptopus Coral Vine	8	medium to coarse	fast	deciduous	Blooms in late summer with coral pink-flowers.
Bignonia capreolata Cross Vine*	entire state	medium	fast	evergreen	Red, orange or yellow spring flowers.
Clematis x armandii Armand Clematis	7,8	coarse	medium to fast	broad-leaved evergreen	Large glossy leaves.
Clematis x jackmanii Jackman Clematis	6b, 7	fine	medium	deciduous	Large purple flowers.
Clematis terniflora Sweet Autumn Clematis	entire state	medium	medium to fast	deciduous	Fragrant white flowers in late summer.
x *Fatshedra lizei* Fatshedra	7b, 8	coarse	medium slow	broad-leaved evergreen	Semi-climbing shrub or vine. Needs support.
Ficus pumila Climbing Fig	8	fine	slow to medium	broad-leaved evergreen	Clings close to wall.
Gelsemium rankinii Swamp Jessamine*	entire state	fine	medium	broad-leaved evergreen	Yellow trumpet flowers in spring and fall.
Gelsemium sempervirens Carolina Yellow Jessamine*	entire state	fine	medium	broad-leaved evergreen	Yellow trumpet-like flowers in spring. Hardy, one of our best vines.
Hedera canariensis Algerian Ivy	8	coarse	medium	broad-leaved evergreen	Very coarse foliage. Sun or semi-shade.
Lonicera x heckrottii Goldflame Honeysuckle	entire state	medium	slow to medium	semi-evergreen	Coral-red flowers in summer.
Lonicera sempervirens Trumpet Honeysuckle	entire state	medium	slow to medium	deciduous	Red, orange to yellow spring flowers.

* Denotes native plant

Table 1. Vines and their characteristics

BOTANICAL NAME AND COMMON NAME	GEORGIA'S HARDY ZONE	TEXTURE	GROWTH RATE	CLASS	REMARKS
Parthenocissus quinque-folia Virginia Creeper*	entire state	coarse	medium	deciduous	Large palmately compound leaves. Good red fall color. Can become invasive.
Parthenocissus tricuspi-data Boston Ivy	entire state	coarse	medium	deciduous	Lustrous three lobed leaves wuith good fall color.
Rosa banksiae 'Lutea' Lady Banks Rose	7b, 8	fine	fast	semi-evergreen	Yellow double flowrs.
Rosa species Climbing Roses	entire state	fine to medium	fast	deciduous	Numerous varieties and colors. Subject to disease and insects.
Smilax lanceolata Lanceleaf Greenbrier*	entire state	medium	fast	broad-leaved evergreen	Bright green foliage for cutting.
Trachelospermum jasminoides Star or Confederate Jasmine	8	medium	medium	broad-leaved evergreen	Good foliage. White fragrant flowers in spring. Variegated form available.
Wisteria frutescens American Wisteria*	entire state	medium	fast	deciduous	Lilac purple last spring flowers. More restrained than others.

* Denotes native plant

Table 2. Groundcovers and their characteristics

BOTANICAL NAME AND COMMON NAME	GEORGIA'S HARDY ZONE	EXPOSURE	TEXTURE	NORMAL GA HEIGHT	GROWTH RATE	CLASS	REMARKS
Ajuga reptans Carpet Bugle	entire state	semi-shade	medium	2-4"	medium to fast	eg	Needs good drainage. Blue or white flowers.
Ardisia japonica Japanese Ardisia	8b	semi-shade	medium	8-12"	slow	eg	Excellent evergreen ground cover.
Aspidistra eliatior Cast Iron Plant	7b, 8	shade	coarse	18-24"	medium	eg	Drought tolerant, bold texture.
Dryopteris ludoviciana Southern Shield Fern	entire state	shade	fine	24-36"	medium	d	Mass plantings, good green filler with fine texture.
Cotoneaster species Groundcover Cotoneaster		see Small Shrubs Table					
Cyrtomium falcatum Holly Fern	8b	semi-shade to shade	coarse	12-24"	medium	eg	Dark green foliage.
Festuca ovina var. *glauca* Blue Fescue	6b, 7a	prefers some shade	fine	6-8"	slow	eg	Small ornamental grass. Best with irrigation.
Gardenia augusta 'Radicans' Creeping Gardenia	7b, 8	sun to semi-shade	fine	18-24"	slow	eg	Small, white, fragrant flowers in summer.
Hedera canariensis Algerian Ivy	8	shade to sun	coarse	6-8"	slow to medium	eg	Good groundcover.
Helleborus orientalis Lenten Rose	6, 7	semi-shade to shade	medium	12-15"	slow to medium	eg	White to rose colored flowers in late winter.
Hemerocallis species Daylily	entire state	sun to semi-shade	medium	24 - 36"	medium to fast	d to eg	very hardy. Numerous flower colors.
Hypericum calcynium Aaron's Beard St. Johnswort	6b, 7	sun to semi-shade	fine	6 - 8"	medium to fast	semi-eg	Yellow flowers in summer.
Iberis sempervirens Evergreen candytuft	6b, 7	sun to semi-shade	fine	6 - 8"	medium	eg	White flowers in spring.

* Denotes native Georgia plant ** Can be grown in full sun in North Georgia with proper care. Should have partial shade or irrigation in South Georgia.

Table 2. Groundcovers and their characteristics

BOTANICAL NAME AND COMMON NAME	GEORGIA'S HARDY ZONE	EXPOSURE	TEXTURE	NORMAL GA HEIGHT	GROWTH RATE	CLASS	REMARKS
Juniperus chinensis var. sargentii Sargent Juniper	entire state	sun	fine	18 - 24"	medium	eg	Conifer. Very hardy. Good winter color. Needs good drainage.
Juniperus conferta Shore Juniper	entire state	sun	fine	18 - 24"	medium	eg	Conifer. Hardy to sandy shore.
Juniperus conferta 'Blue Pacific' Blue Pacific Juniper	entire state	sun	fine	10 - 12"	medium	ef	Conifer. Blue gray foliage. Short vertical stems.
Juniperus conferta 'Emerald sea' Emerald Sea Juniper	entire state	sun	fine	10 - 12"	medium	eg	Conifer. Bright gree foliage. Compact
Juniperus davurica 'Expansa' Parsons Juniper	entire state	sun	fine	18 - 24"	medium to fast	eg	Conifer. Very hardy. Good winter color.
Juniperus horizontalis 'Plumosa Compacta' Andorra Compact Juniper	entire state	sun	fine	12 - 24"	slow	eg	Conifer. Denser, more compact than Andorra.
Juniperus horizontalis 'Wiltoni' Blue Rug Juniper	entire state	sun	fine	4 - 6"	medium	eg	Conifer. Hugs ground.
Juniperus procumbens Japanese Garden Juniper	entire state	sun	fine	12 - 24"	slow	eg	Conifer.Handsome in beds, terraces and slopes.
Juniperius procumbens 'Nana' Dwarf Japanese Garden Juniper	entire state	sun	fine	6 - 8"	very slow	eg	Conifer. Only spreading juniper suitable for restricted spaces.
Ophiopogon japonicus Lilyturf or Mondo Grass	7, 8	semi-shade to shade	medium	8 - 12"	medium	eg	Hardy, makes dense mat.
Ophiopogon japonicus 'Nana' Dwarf Mondo Grass	7, 8	semi-shade to shade	medium	3"	slow	eg	Dwarf form.
Pachysandra terminalis Pachysandra	6b, 7a	shade	medium	6 - 12"	medium	eg	Requires moist shade in warm climate area.

* Denotes native Georgia plant ** Can be grown in full sun in North Georgia with proper care. Should have partial shade or irrigation in South Georgia.

Table 2. Groundcovers and their characteristics

BOTANICAL NAME AND COMMON NAME	GEORGIA'S HARDY ZONE	EXPOSURE	TEXTURE	NORMAL GA HEIGHT	GROWTH RATE	CLASS	REMARKS
Phlox subulata Moss Phlox or Thrift*	entire state	sun	fine	4 - 8"	medium to fast	eg	Rose, white, lilac flowers.
Santolina chamaecyparissus Gray Lavender Cotton	enire state	sun	fine	12 - 24"	medium	eg	Good for hot, dry sites. Gray foliage, yellow-orange flowers.
Santolina virens Green Lavender Cotton	entire state	sun	fine	12 - 24"	medium	eg	Good for hot, dry sites. Green foliage, orange flowers.
Saxifraga stolonifera Strawberry Geranium	7b, 8	shade	fine	4 - 6"	medium	eg	White flowers in summer.
Trachelospermum asiaticum Asiatic Jasmine	7b, 8	sun to semi-shade	fine	4 - 6"	medium	eg	Excellent groundcover.
Yucca filamentosa Adam's Needle or Beargrass*	entire state	sun	coarse	24 - 36"	slow	eg	White flower spikes in summer.
Zamia integrifolia Coontie Palm	8b	sun to shade	coarse	24- 36"	slow	eg	Cycad. Accent plant, native groundcover.

* Denotes native Georgia plant ** Can be grown in full sun in North Georgia with proper care. Should have partial shade or irrigation in South Georgia.

Table 3. Ornamental grasses and their characteristics

BOTANICAL NAME AND COMMON NAME * Denotes native Georgia plant.	GEORGIA'S HARDY ZONE	TEXTURE	HEIGHT	SPREAD	PANICLE LENGTH	EXPOSURE	LANDSCAPE REMARKS	CULTURAL REMARKS
Chasmanthium latifolium Upland Sea Oats	entire state	fine	30 - 36"	18 - 24"	8"	sun to light shade	Very attractive seed heads. Can become invasive.	Will tolerate wet feet. Self sows. Shade for zone 8.
Cortaderia selloana Pampas Grass	7b, 8	fine to medium	7 - 8'	5 - 6'	20"	sun	Male and female plants. Female has fuller plumes.	Most drought tolerant.
Cortaderia selloana 'Nana' Dwarf Pampas Grass	entire state	medium	3'	3.5 - 4'	2"	sun	White female plumes.	Very cold hardy.

++ All Miscanthus have a very prominent white midrib.

Table 3. Ornamental grasses and their characteristics

Botanical Name / Common Name	Georgia's Hardy Zone	Texture				Exposure	Remarks	
Elymus glaucus Wild Blue Rye	entire state	medium	4 - 5'	3 - 4'	10"	sun	Bluish-gray foliage.	Spreads slowly by rhizomes.
Panicum virgatum 'Prairie sky' Prairie Sky Switchgrass	entire state	fine	4 - 5'	3'	12"	sun	Outstanding blue foliage on arching plant.	Golden fall foliage.
Pennisetum alopecuroides Dwarf Fountain Grass	entire state	fine	24 - 30"	2'	3"	sun	Plumes less showy than annual species.	Good companion for perennials.
Pennisetum setaceum Fountain Grass	an annual	fine	4 - 4.5'	4'	12"	sun	Rose-colored foliage and panicles.	Must replant every year.
Pennisetum setaceum 'Rubrum' Crimson Fountain Grass	an annual	fine	4 - 4.5'	4'	12"	sun	Crimson or burgundy foliage and panicles.	Must replant every year.
Pennisetum villosum Feathertop Grass	7b, 8	fine	2 - 3'	2'	3	sun	Showy creamy panicles.	Even with dead heading, blooms once per year.
Saccharum ravennae Ravenna Grass (Hardy Pampas)	entire state	medium to coarse	8 - 9'	3 - 4'	20"	sun	Robust plant.	Clump forming. Divide every 3-4 years.

++ All Miscanthus have a very prominent white midrib.

Table 4. Small shrubs (1-4 ft)

BOTANICAL NAME COMMON NAME * Denotes native Georgia plant	GEORGIA'S HARDY ZONE	TEXTURE	FORM	NORMAL GA HEIGHT	GROWTH RATE	EXPOSURE	CLASS	REMARKS
Abelia x 'Edward Goucher' Edward Goucher abelia	entire state	fine	irregular to oval	4 - 5'	slow	sun, semi-shade	semi-evergreen	Lilac pink flowers.
Abelia x *grandiflora* 'Sherwoodii' Sherwood dwarf abelia	entire state	fine	irregular to spreading	2 - 3'	slow	sun, semi-shade	semi-evergreen	White flowers.
Aucuba japonica 'Nana' Dwarf aucuba	entire state	coarse	oval		slow	shade, semi-shade	broad-leaved evergreen	Attractive foliage and berries.

Table 4. Small shrubs (1-4 ft)

BOTANICAL NAME / COMMON NAME * Denotes native Georgia plant	GEORGIA'S HARDY ZONE	TEXTURE	FORM	NORMAL GA HEIGHT	GROWTH RATE	EXPOSURE	CLASS	REMARKS
Buxus microphylla var. *japonica* Japanese boxwood	7, 8	fine	rounded	3 - 5'	slow	sun, semi-shade	broad-leaved evergreen	Good color and easy to maintain.
Buxus microphylla var. *koreana* Korean Boxwood	6b, 7	fine	rounded	2 - 3'	slow	semi-shade	broad-leaved evergreen	Very hardy, useful for low hedges.
Buxus sempervirens 'Suffruticosa' True dwarf boxwood	6b, 7	fine	rounded	2 - 4'	very slow	semi-shade, shade	broad-leaved evergreen	Will grow large with age.
Camellia hiemalis Dwarf sasanqua	7b, 8	medium	spreading compact	3 - 5'	very slow	sun, semi-shade	broad-leaved evergreen	Foliage very similar to Sasanqua.
Cultivars including Shi Shi Gashira (Beni-Kan-Tsubaki)								Red flower, double-formal to rose form. More compact shape.
More compact. Showa-No-Sakae (Usubeni)								Soft pink flower, Semi-double to double rose form. Suitable for espalier.
Cephalotaxus harringtonia var. *drupacea* Japanese Plum Yew	entire state	medium to fine	spreading	2 - 3'	medium	sun, semi-shade	evergreen conifer	Vase-shaped. Shade in Zone 8.
Cephalotaxus harringtonia 'Fastigiata' Upright plum yew	entire state	medium to fine	upright	3 - 5'	slow	sun, semi-shade	conifer	Accent for restricted spaces. Shade in zone 8.
Cephalotaxus harringtonia 'Prostrata' Spreading plum yew	entire state	medium to fine	spreading	2 - 4'	medium	sun, semi-shade	evergreen conifer	Prostrate in habit. Shade in zone 8.
Chanomeles japonica Japanese flowering quince	entire state	medium	oval	30 - 36"	slow	sun	deciduous	Orange or scarlet red flowers in spring.

Table 4. Small shrubs (1-4 ft)

BOTANICAL NAME COMMON NAME * Denotes native Georgia plant	GEORGIA'S HARDY ZONE	TEXTURE	FORM	NORMAL GA HEIGHT	GROWTH RATE	EXPOSURE	CLASS	REMARKS
Chamaerops humilis European fan palm	8b	coarse	upright-clumping	2 - 4'	slow	sun, semi-shade	evergreen palm	Multi-trunk die to suckers.
Clethra alnifolia 'Hummingbird' Hummingbird summersweet	6b, 7	fine	upright spreading	2 - 3'	medium	sun, semi-shade	deciduous	White fragrant flowers in midsummer.
Cotoneaster dammeri Bearberry cotoneaster	6b, 7	fine	spreading	12 - 18"	medium	sun	broad-leaved evergreen	Some cultivars reach 4' tall. Susceptible to mites.
Cotoneaster horizontalis Rockspray cotoneaster	6b, 7	fine	spreading	2 - 3'	medium	sun	semi-ever-green	Fishbone branching pattern. Susceptible to mites.
Daphne odora Winter daphne	7, 8	fine to medium	rounded	3 - 4'	slow	semi-shade	broad-leaved evergreen	Fragrant flowers in winter. Needs excellent drainage.
Deutzia gracilis Slender deutzia	6b, t	medium to fine	rounded	3 - 4'	slow	sun, semi-shade	deciduous	Very hardy with pale green foliage.
Fothergilla gardenii 'Mt. Airy' Mt. Airy Fothergilla	entire state	medium	rounded	4 - 5'	medium	sun, semi-shade	deciduous	Abundant white spring flowers, great fall color.
Gardenia augusta 'Radicans' Creeping gardenia	7b, 8	fine	spreading	18 - 24"	slow	sun, semi-shade	broad-leaved evergreen	Fragrant white flowers.
Hydrangea arborescens 'Annabelle' Annabelle Hydrangea	6b, 7	coarse	rounded	3 - 5'	medium	semi-shade, shade	deciduous	Large heads of white flowers in early summer.
Hydrangea macrophylla 'Pia'	entire state	coarse	rounded	2 - 3'	slow	semi-shade	deciduous	A true dward with heavy flowering.
Ilex vomitoria 'Nana'' Dwarf yaupon holly	7, 8	fine	rounded	3 - 5'	slow	sun, semi-shade	broad-leaved evergreen	Hardy tough shrub. New-growth green.
Ilex vomitoria 'Schillings' Schillings Dwarf Yaupon	7, 8	fine	rounded to spreading	3 - 4'	slow	sun, semi-shade	broad-leaved evergreen	New growth red.
Ilex vomitoria 'Bordeaux'[tm] Bordeaux dwarf yaupon	7, 8	fine	rounded	3 - 4'	slow	sun, semi-shade	broad-leaved evergreen	New growth on branch tips is red.
Itea virginica 'Henry's Garnet' Henry's Garnet sweetspire	entire state	medium	rounded	3 - 4'	medium	sun	semi-ever-green	Great fall color, tolerates moist sites.
Jasminum floridum Showy jasmine	7, 8	fine	weeping	3 - 5'	slow to medium	sun	semi-ever-green	Yellow flowers in spring.

Table 4. Small shrubs (1-4 ft)

BOTANICAL NAME COMMON NAME * Denotes native Georgia plant	GEORGIA'S HARDY ZONE	TEXTURE	FORM	NORMAL GA HEIGHT	GROWTH RATE	EXPOSURE	CLASS	REMARKS
Jasminum nudiflorum Winter jasmine	entire state	fine	weeping	3 - 4'	medium	sun, semi-shade	deciduous	Yellow flowers late winter. Tenacious shrub.
Juniperus species Spreading junipers	See ground-covers							
Leucothoe axilliaris Coastal leucothoe	entire state	medium to coarse	weeping to irregular	3 - 4'	slow to medium	semi-shade, shade	broad-leaved evergreen	Good drainage on moist locations required.
Leucothoe fontaniesiana Drooping leucothoe	6b, 7	medium to coarse	weeping to irregular	3 - 4'	slow	semi-shade, shade	broad-leaved evergreen	Naturalistic or small gardens with good drainage on moist sites.
Mahonia fortunei Chinese mahonia	8	medium	upright	3 - 5'	medium	semi-shade, shade	broad-leaved evergreen	Graceful evergreen in well drained sites.
Nandina domestica 'Firepower' Firepower dwarf nandina	entire state	fine to medium	rounded	2 - 3'	medium	sun, semi-shade	broad-leaved evergreen	Red fall color. Good for mass plantings.
Nandina domestica 'Harbour Dwarf' Harbour Dwarf nandina	entire state	fine to medium	spreading	2 - 3'	medium	sun, semi-shade	broad-leaved evergreen	Spreads by rhizomes.
Osmanthus heterophyllus 'Rotundifolius' Little leaf tea olive	7, 8	fine	rounded	4 - 5'	very slow	sun, semi-shade	broad-leaved evergreen	Specimen for restricted spaces.
Pinus mugo var. mugo	6b, 7	fine	rounded	3 - 5'	slow	sun	evergreen conifer	Use grafted plants only for dwarf form.
Pittosporum tobira 'Wheeler's Dwarf' Wheeler Dwarf Pittosporum	8	medium	rounded	2 - 3'	medium	sun, semi-shade	broad-leaved evergreen	Mass plantings or low borders.
Prunus laurocerasus 'Otto Luyken' Otto Luyken laurel	6b, 7	medium	rounded	3 - 4'	slow to medium	sun, semi-shade	broad-leaved evergreen	Mass plantings.
Prunus laurocerasus 'Schipkaensis' Schip laurel	6b, 7	medium	rounded	4 - 5'	slow to medium	sun, semi-shade	broad-leaved evergreen	Naturalistic or mass plantings.

Table 4. Small shrubs (1-4 ft)

BOTANICAL NAME COMMON NAME * Denotes native Georgia plant	GEORGIA'S HARDY ZONE	TEXTURE	FORM	NORMAL GA HEIGHT	GROWTH RATE	EXPOSURE	CLASS	REMARKS
Punica granatum var. *nana* Dwarf pomegranate	7b, 8	fine	upright-irregular	3 - 4'	slow	sun	deciduous	Red-orange flowers and fruits.
Rhaphiolepis spp. Indian hawthorne Cultivars including 'Clara' White 3 - 4' 'Eleanor Taber'™ Pink 'Georgia Charm' White 3 - 4' 'Georgia Petite' Light Pink 2 - 3' 'Olivia' White 4 - 5' 'Snow White' White 2 - 3'	7b, 8	medium	spreading to rounded	2 - 5'	slow	sun	broad-leaved evergreen	Glossy foliage, white or pink flowers. Questionable hardiness in zone 7.
Rhododendron Glenn Dale hybrid Azaleas Cultivars include several hundred which offer great range in color and blooming season.	entire state	fine	upright-spreading	3 - 5'	slow to medium	semi-shade	broad-leaved evergreen	Mass flowering effects.
Rhododendron Gumpo azaleas	7, 8	fine	spreading	10 - 12"	slow to medium	semi-shade	broad-leaved evergreen	Late season, large white or pink flowers.
Rhododendron Kurume azaleas Cultivars including: Christmas Cheer' Brilliant Red 'Hino Crimson' Red 'Coral Bells' Shell Pink 'Hinodegiri' Vivid Red 'Flame' Orange Red 'Mothers Day' Red 'Hershey Red' Bright Red 'Pink Pearl' Salmon Rose 'Hexe' Red 'Salmon Beauty' Salmon Pink	entire state	fine	rounded	3 - 5'	slow to medium	semi-shade	broad-leaved evergreen	Mass flowering effects.

Table 4. Small shrubs (1-4 ft)

BOTANICAL NAME COMMON NAME * Denotes native Georgia plant	GEORGIA'S HARDY ZONE	TEXTURE	FORM	NORMAL GA HEIGHT	GROWTH RATE	EXPOSURE	CLASS	REMARKS
Rhododendron Girard hybrid azaleas	entire state	fine	rounded to spreading	3 - 5'	slow to medium	semi-shade	broad-leaved evergreen	Cold hardy and striking flower color.
Rosa (Floribunda) Floribunda rose	entire state	medium	rounded	2 - 4'	slow to medium	sun	deciduous	Mass flowering effects.
Rosmarinus officinalis Rosemary	entire state	fine	irregular	3 - 4'	slow to medium	sun	broad-leaved evergreen	Grayish foliage. Requires well drained soils.
Ruscus aculeatus Butcher's broom	entire state	fine	irregular	2 - 3'	slow	sun	broad-leaved evergreen	Specimen accent in low border.
Santolina species Lavender Cotton	See ground-covers							
Spirea thunbergii Thunberg Spirea	entire state	fine	irregular	3 - 4'	medium	sun	deciduous	Masses, borders.

Table 5 Medium shrubs (5-8 ft)

BOTANICAL NAME COMMON NAME * Denotes native Georgia plant.	GEORGIA'S HARDY ZONE	TEXTURE	FORM	NORMAL GA HEIGHT	GROWTH RATE	EXPOSURE	CLASS	REMARKS
Abelia x grandiflora Glossy Abelia	entire state	fine to medium	rounded	5 - 6'	medium	sun, semi-shade	broad-leaved evergreen	Hedge plant.
Aucuba japonica Japanese Aucuba	entire state	coarse	upright	6 - 8'	medium to fast	semi-shade, shade	broad-leaved evergreen	Green and variegated foliage.
Berberis julianae Wintergreen Barberry	entire state	medium	oval	5 - 6'	slow to medium	sun	broad-leaved evergreen	Rich green foliage, thorns.
Buddleia davidii Butterfly Bush	entire state	fine to medium	rounded	6 - 8'	medium	sun	deciduous	Fragrant summer flowers attract butterflies.
Buxus sempervirens Common Boxwood	6b, 7	fine to medium	rounded	5 - 8'	slow to medium	semi-shade	broad-leaved evergreen	Useful in formal plantings.
Callistemon citrinus Crimson Bottlebrush	8b	fine	irregular	6 - 8'	medium to fast	sun	broad-leaved evergreen	Flowers very showy.
Calycanthus floridus Sweet Shrub*	entire state	coarse	rounded	5 - 6'	slow to medium	semi-shade	deciduous	Fragrant flowers.
Chaenomeles speciosa Flowering Quince	entire state	medium	upright-rounded	5 - 8'	slow	sun, semi-shade	deciduous	White, pink to red flowers.
Clethra alnifolia 'Ruby Spice' Ruby Spice Summersweet	6b, 7	medium	rounded	4 - 8'	slow to medium	sun, semi-shade	deciduous	Pink fragrant flowers, moist soils.
Cycas revoluta Sago palm	8	fine	upright	4 - 6'	very slow	sun, semi-shade	evergreen cycad	Single or multi-trunk specimens.
Fatsia japonica Japanese Fatsia	8	coarse	irregular	4 - 8'	medium to fast	semi-shade, shade	broad-leaved evergreen	Specimen. Zone 7 with protection.
Forsythia x intermedia Border Forsythia	entire state	medium	irregular	5 - 8'	fast	sun	deciduous	Yellow spring flowers.

Table 5 Medium shrubs (5-8 ft)

BOTANICAL NAME COMMON NAME * Denotes native Georgia plant.	GEORGIA'S HARDY ZONE	TEXTURE	FORM	NORMAL GA HEIGHT	GROWTH RATE	EXPOSURE	CLASS	REMARKS
Gardenia jasminoides Cape Jasmine	7b, 8	medium	rounded	4 - 6'	medium	sun, semi-shade	broad-leaved evergreen	Fragrant white flowers.
Hydrangea macrophylla French Hydrangea	entire state	coarse	rounded	4 - 6'	medium	semi-shade	deciduous	Red, pink, blue and white flowering types.
Hydrangea paniculata 'Grandiflora' Pee Gee Hydrangea	6b, 7	coarse	rounded	8 - 15'	medium	sun	deciduous	Flowers open white, turn pink, then bronze.
Ilex cornuta 'Dwarf Burford' Dwarf Burford Holly	7, 8	medium to coarse	rounded	5 - 8'	slow	sun, semi-shade	broad-leaved evergreen	Foundations. Glossy foliage.
Ilex crenata 'Hetzii' Hetz Holly	7	medium	rounded	6 - 8'	medium	sun, semi-shade	broad-leaved evergreen	Dark green foliage.
Ilex crenata 'Sky Pencil' Sky Pencil Holly	entire state	medium	upright	6 - 8'	medium	sun, semi-shade	broad-leaved evergreen	Narrow and strongly upright.
Ilex glabra 'Nigra' Nigra Inkberry*	entire state	medium	rounded	5 - 6'	medium	sun, semi-shade	broad-leaved evergreen	Borders, naturalistic areas and wet sites with good green winter color.
Juniper chinensis "Pfitzeriana" Pfitzer Juniper	entire state	medium	spreading	5 - 6'	medium	sun	evergreen conifer	Mass planting sunny slopes.
Kalmia latifolia Mountain Laurel*	6b, 7	medium	upright	5 - 8'	slow to medium	semi-shade	broad-leaved evergreens	Naturalistic gardens.
Lagerstroemia x 'Tonto' Tonto Crape Myrtle	entire state	medium	upright	6 - 10'	medium	sun	deciduous	Red flowering specimen or border shrub.
Lagerstroemia indica 'Victor' Victor Crape Myrtle	entire state	medium	upright	4 - 6'	mdeium	sun	deciduous	Compact form with dark red flowers in July.

Table 5 Medium shrubs (5-8 ft)

BOTANICAL NAME COMMON NAME * Denotes native Georgia plant.	GEORGIA'S HARDY ZONE	TEXTURE	FORM	NORMAL GA HEIGHT	GROWTH RATE	EXPOSURE	CLASS	REMARKS
Lonicera nitida Box Leaf Honeysuckle	6b, 7	fine to medium	rounded	5 - 6'	medium	sun, semi-shade	broad-leaved evergreen	Attractive foliage.
Loropetalum chinense var. rubrum 'Ruby' Ruby Fringe Flower	7, 8	fine	rounded	6 - 8'	medium	sun, semi-shade	broad-leaved evergreen	Bright pink spring blooms. New leaves ruby red.
Myrica cerifera 'Fairfax' Fairfax Wax Myrtle	7, 8	medium	rounded	6 - 8'	medium	sun, semi-shade	broad-leaved evergreen	Compact form with good foliage.
Osmanthus heterophyllus 'Gulftide' Gulftide Tea Olive	7, 8	fine	rounded	6 - 8'	slow	sun, semi-shade	broad-leaved evergreen	Specimen or hedge.
Osmanthus heterophyllus 'Variegatus' Variegated False Holly	7, 8	fine	rounded	6 - 8'	slow	sun, semi-shade	broad-leaved evergreen	Leaf margins creamy white.
Philadelphus x 'Natchez' Natchez Mockorange	6b, 7	medium	irregular	6 - 8'	medium	sun	deciduous	Large white flowers.
Pieris japonica Japanese Pieris	6b, 7	fine	irregular	5 - 6'	medium	semi-shade	broad-leaved evergreen	Naturalistic. Sun possible in mountains.
Pyracantha koidzumii 'Low-Dense' Low-Dense Pyracantha	8	fine	rounded	6 - 8'	medium to fast	sun	broad-leaved evergreen	Berries hidden by foliage.
Rhaphiolepis umbellata Yeddo Hawthorn	7b, 8	medium to coarse	upright to rounded	6 - 8'	medium	sun	broad-leaved evergreen	Nice texture and dark green foliage with spring flowers.
Rhododendron arborescens Sweet Azalea*	6b, 7	medium	upright to irregular	5 - 8'	slow to medium	semi-shade	deciduous	Fragrant white to pink flowrs.
Rhododendron austrinum Florida Azalea*	7, 8	medium	upright to irregular	6 - 8'	slow to medium	semi-shade	deciduous	Fragrant yellow cream to orange flowers.
Rhododendron calendulaceum Flame Azalea*	6b, 7	medium	upright to rounded	5 - 8'	slow to medium	semi-shade	deciduous	Flowers yellow to orange and scarlet.

Table 5 Medium shrubs (5-8 ft)

* Denotes native Georgia plant.

BOTANICAL NAME COMMON NAME	GEORGIA'S HARDY ZONE	TEXTURE	FORM	NORMAL GA HEIGHT	GROWTH RATE	EXPOSURE	CLASS	REMARKS
Rhododendron Southern Indian	8	medium	rounded to irregular	5 - 8'	medium to fast	semi-shade	broad-leaved evergreen	Mass plantings, borders.
Cultivars including: 'Elegans' Pink 'Iveryana' White to rose 'Fielders White' White 'Judge Solomon' Pink 'Fisher Pink' Light Pink 'Lawsal' Salmon Pink 'Formosa' Purple 'President Clay' Red 'George Lindsey Tabor' Light Pink Effect 'Pride of Mobile' Deep Rose Pink 'G. G. Gerbing' White 'Southern Charm' Pink								
Spirea x vanhouttei	6b, 7	medium	rounded	5 - 8'	medium to fast	sun	deciduous	Arching branches of mass white flowers.
Trachycarpus fortunei Chinese or Fortunes Windmill Palm	7b, 8	coarse	upright	6 - 8'	very slow	sun	evergreen palm	Specimen. Slender trunk with fibrous cover.
Viburnum x burkwoodi Burkwood Viburnum	6b, 7	coarse	rounded	6 - 8'	medium	sun	deciduous	Fragrant white spring flowers.
Viburnum suspensum Sandankwa Viburnum	8	medium to coarse	rounded	5 - 8'	medium	sun, semi-shade	broad-leaved evergreen	Mass plantings, borders.
Weigela florida	entire state	coarse	irregular	5 - 8'	medium to fast	sun	deciduous	Borders for spring flowers.
Yucca gloriosa Mound-lily Yucca*	entire state	coarse	upright	6 - 8'	slow	sun	broad-leaved evergreen	Pale green spine-tipped foliage.

Table 6. Large shrubs 8 feet and up

BOTANICAL NAME COMMON NAME *Denotes native plant	GEORGIA'S HARDY ZONE	TEXTURE	FORM	NORMAL GA HEIGHT	GROWTH RATE	EXPOSURE	CLASS	REMARKS
Acca sellowiana (Feijoa sellowiana) Pineapple Guava	8	medium	rounded	8 - 10'	medium	sun, semi-shade	broad-leaved evergreen	Grayish foliage. Hedges and borders.
Aesculus parviflora Bottlebrush Buckeye*	entire state	coarse	rounded	8 - 12'	medium	sun, semi-shade	deciduous	Specimen, naturalistic settings.
*Agarista populifolia** Florida Leucothoe	entire state	coarse	irregular	8 - 10'	medium	semi-shade, shade	broad-leaved evergreen	Naturalistic settings.
Camellia japonica Japanese Camellia Cultivars that produce cold hardy flower buds: Adolphe Audusson Var.' Variegated 'Are-jishi' Red 'Bernice Boddy' Pink 'Daikagura' Red 'Daikagura Var.' Variegated 'Donckelari' Variegated 'Dr. Tinsley' Pink 'Firebrand' Red 'Flame' Red 'Gov. Mouton' Red 'Gulio Nuccio' Red 'Gulio Nuccio Var.' Variegated 'High Hat' Pink 'Kumasaka' Pink 'Lady Clare' Pink 'Magnoliaeflora' Pink 'Rev. John G. Drayton' Pink 'Tricolor' Variegated 'Ville de Nantes' Variegated 'White Daikagura' White 'White Empress' White	7, 8	medium to coarse	rounded to oval	8 - 15'	slow to medium	semi-shade	broad-leaved evergreen	Specimen.

Table 6. Large shrubs 8 feet and up

BOTANICAL NAME COMMON NAME *Denotes native plant	GEORGIA'S HARDY ZONE	TEXTURE	FORM	NORMAL GA HEIGHT	GROWTH RATE	EXPOSURE	CLASS	REMARKS
Camellia sasanqua	7, 8	medium	irregular to upright	8 - 10'	slow to medium	sun, semi-shade	broad-leaved evergreen	Good foliage and flowers. Hedges, borders.
Sasanqua cultivars Including: Cultivar, Flower color, Flower form, Plant form 'Bettie Patricia', Light pink, Rose form, Double upright to spreading 'Bonanza', Deep red, Semi-peony, Compact form 'Cleopatra', Rose Pink, Semi-double, Compact to spreading 'Cotton Candy', Pink, Semi-double large, Loose upright to spreading 'Jean May', Shell Pink, Semi-double to double large, Upright to spreading 'Mine-No-Yuki', White, Double large, Irregular to spreading 'Pink Snow,' Light Pink, Semi-double large, Irregular young -compact older upright 'Setsugekka', White, Semi-double large ruffled petals, Upright 'Sparkling Burgundy', Ruby, Rose peony form large, Irregular to Spreading 'Yuletide', Red, Single, Upright								
Camellia vernalis Vernal Camellia	7, 8	medium	upright	8 - 10'	medium	sun, semi-shade	broad-leaved evergreen	'Dawn' blooms Sept.-March.
Chimonanthus praecox Wintersweet	entire state	coarse	irregular	10 - 15'	sun, semi-shade	deciduous	deciduous	Fragrant January flowers.
Hamamelis x intermedia Hybrid Witch Hazel	6b, 7	coarse	upright spreading	12 - 15'	medium	sun, semi-shade	deciduous	Red to yellow, winter to spring flowering.
Hamamelis virginiana Common Witch Hazel	entire state	coarse	irregular	12 - 15'	medium	sun, semi-shade	deciduous	Naturalistic sites.
Hydrangea paniculata 'Tardiva' Tardiva Hydrangea	entire state	coarse	upright	8 - 15'	medium	sun, semi-shade	deciduous	Showy white flowers in summer.
Hydrangea quercifolia Oakleaf Hydrangea*	entire state	coarse	rounded	8 - 10'	medium	semi-shade	deciduous	Naturalistic. Large white flowers, wine red fall color.

Table 6. Large shrubs 8 feet and up

BOTANICAL NAME COMMON NAME * Denotes native plant	GEORGIA'S HARDY ZONE	TEXTURE	FORM	NORMAL GA HEIGHT	GROWTH RATE	EXPOSURE	CLASS	REMARKS
Ilex x 'Mary Nell' Mary Nell Holly	7, 8	medium	upright pyramidal	10 - 15'	medium	sun, semi-shade	broad-leaved evergreen	Glossy foliage with bright red fruits.
Ilex x 'Emily Bruner' Emily Bruner Holly	7, 8	medium	pyramidal	12 - 15'	medium	sun, semi-shade	broad-leaved evergreen	Dark foliage with large red berries.
Ilex x 'Nellie R. Stevens' Nellie R. Stevens Holly	entire state	coarse	upright	10 - 20'	medium to fast	sun, semi-shade	broad-leaved evergreen	Dark foliage with red large red berries.
Ilex x attenuata 'Fosteri' Foster's Holly	entire state	medium	upright pyramid	10 - 15'	medium	sun, semi-shade	broad-leaved evergreen	Specimen or hedges with red berries.
Ilex cassine Dahoon Holly*	7, 8	medium	upright	10 - 15'	medium	sun, semi-shade	broad-leaved evergreen	Hedges, borders.
Ilex cornuta 'Burfordii' Burford Holly	7, 8	coarse	oval	8 - 12'	medium to fast	sun, semi-shade	broad-leaved evergreen	Specimen or hedges with heavy red fruit.
Ilex cornuta 'Anicet' Delcambre Needlepoint Holly	7, 8	medium	upright	8 - 15'	medium	sun, semi-shade	broad-leaved evergreen	Excellent for screens and hedges.
Ilex latifolia Lusterleaf Holly	7, 8	coarse	upright pyramidal	10 - 20'	medium to fast	sun, semi-shade	broad-leaved evergreen	Specimen or espalier with bold foliage.
Ilex myrtifolia Myrtle Holly*	7, 8	fine	upright	10 - 12'	medium	sun, semi-shade	broad-leaved evergreen	Naturalistic. Berries red, orange or yellow.
Ilex vomitoria Yaupon Holly*	7, 8	fine	upright	10 - 15'	fast	sun, semi-shade	broad-leaved evergreen	Hedges, borders.Clipped effects.

Table 6. Large shrubs 8 feet and up

BOTANICAL NAME COMMON NAME * Denotes native plant	GEORGIA'S HARDY ZONE	TEXTURE	FORM	NORMAL GA HEIGHT	GROWTH RATE	EXPOSURE	CLASS	REMARKS
Illicium parviflorum Small Anise-Tree*	7, 8	coarse	upright	8 - 12'	medium	sun, semi-shade	broad-leaved evergreen	Light green fragrant foliage.
Illicium floridanum Florida Anise*	7, 8	coarse	upright	8 - 10'	medium	semi-shade	broad-leaved evergreen	Naturalistic.
Juniperus chinensis 'Torulosa' Hollywood Juniper	entire state	fine	upright irregular	10 - 15'	medium	sun	evergreen conifer	Specimen.
Juniperus chinensis 'Robusta Green'	entire state	fine	upright irregular	10 - 15'	slow	sun	evergreen conifer	Specimen.
Loropetalum chinese var. *rubrum* Pink Chinese Fringe Flower	7, 8	medium	irregular rounded	8 - 12'	fast	sun, semi-shade	broad-leaved evergreen	Bright pink spring flowers.
Michelia figo Banana Shrub	8	fine to medium	rounded	10 - 12'	slow	sun, semi-shade	broad-leaved evergreen	Fragrant flowers.
Myrica cerifera Southern Wax Myrtle	7, 8	medium	upright rounded	15 - 20'	medium	sun, semi-shade	broad-leaved evergreen	Borders, hedges and screens.
Nerium oleander Oleander	8	medium	oval	8 - 12'	medium	sun	broad-leaved evergreen	Red, white and pink summer flowers. Poisonous plant.
Osmanthus americanus Devilwood Osmanthus*	entire state	medium	upright	10 - 15'	medium	semi-shade	broad-leaved evergreen	Borders, naturalistic sites.
Osmanthus x *fortunei* Fortune's Osmanthus	7, 8	medium	rounded	10 - 15'	slow to medium	sun, semi-shade	broad-leaved evergreen	Tough border or specimen plant.
Osmanthus fragrans Tea Olive	8	medium	upright	10 - 15'	medium to fast	sun, semi-shade	broad-leaved evergreen	Fragrant, specimen.

Table 6. Large shrubs 8 feet and up

BOTANICAL NAME COMMON NAME * Denotes native plant	GEORGIA'S HARDY ZONE	TEXTURE	FORM	NORMAL GA HEIGHT	GROWTH RATE	EXPOSURE	CLASS	REMARKS
Osmanthus heterophyllus Holly Osmanthus	7, 8	medium	rounded	8 - 10'	slow to medium	sun, semi-shade	broad-leaved evergreen	Foundations, hedges, borders.
Pittosporum tobira Tobira Pittosporum	8b	medium	rounded	8 - 12'	medium to fast	sun, semi-shade	broad-leaved evergreen	Glossy, green foliage.
Podocarpus macrophyllus Southern Yew	8	medium	upright	8 - 15'	medium	sun, semi-shade	evergreen conifer	Foundations, hedges or borders.
Podocarpus macrophyllus 'Maki' Chinese Podocarpus	8b	medium	upright	8 - 15'	medium	sun, semi-shade	evergreen conifer	Smaller leaves.
Punica granatum Pomegranate	8	fine to medium	rounded	10 - 15'	medium	sun	deciduous	Specimen. Orange flowers.
Pyracantha koidzumii Formosa Firethorn	8	medium	irregular	10 - 12'	fast	sun	broad-leaved evergreen	Large red berries.
Pyracantha x 'Mohave' Mohave Firethorn	7, 8	medium	upright	8 - 12'	fast	sun	broad-leaved evergreen	Masses of orange red fruit.
Rhododendron canescens Piedmont Azalea*	entire state	medium	upright to irregular	8 - 12'	slow to medium	semi-shade	deciduous	White, pink to rose flowers.
Rhododendron prunifolium Plumleaf Azalea*	entire state	medium	upright to rounded	8 - 10'	slow to medium	semi-shade	deciduous	Flowers orange red in July and August.
Rhododendron maximum Rosebay*	6b	coarse	irregular	10 - 15'	medium	semi-shade, shade	broad-leaved evergreen	Specimen.
Rhododendron (Hybrids) Hybrid Rhododendrons	6b, 7	coarse	oval to rounded	8 - 10'	medium	semi-shade, shade	broad-leaved evergreen	Require excellent drainage. Use H-1 & H-2 hybrids.
Syringa vulgaris Common Lilac	6b, 7a	coarse	irregular	8 - 10'	slow to medium	sun, semi-shade	deciduous	Fragrant lilac flowers.

Table 6. Large shrubs 8 feet and up

BOTANICAL NAME COMMON NAME * Denotes native plant	GEORGIA'S HARDY ZONE	TEXTURE	FORM	NORMAL GA HEIGHT	GROWTH RATE	EXPOSURE	CLASS	REMARKS
Ternstroemia gymnanthera (Cleyera japonica) Japanese Cleyera	7b, 8	medium	upright	8 - 15'	slow to medium	sun, semi-shade	broad-leaved evergreen	Glossy foliage.
Viburnum awabuki Awabuki Viburnum	8	coarse	upright	8 - 15'	medium	sun, semi-shade	broad-leaved evergreen	Lustrous dark green foliage.
Viburnum odoratissum Sweet Viburnum	8	coarse	rounded	10 - 15'	fast	sun, semi-shade	broad-leaved evergreen	Borders, hedges.
Viburnum opulus 'Roseum' European Snowball Viburnum	6b, 7	coarse	irregular	8 - 10'	medium	semi-shade	deciduous	Borders. "Snowball" flower clusters.
Viburnum plicatum var. tomentosum Doublefile Viburnum	6b, 7	medium	rounded	8 - 15'	medium	sun, semi-shade	deciduous	Abundant snow white spring blooms.
Viburnum x rhytidophyllum Leatherleaf Viburnum	6b, 7	coarse	irregular	8 - 10'	medium	semi-shade	broad-leaved evergreen	Dark green foliage. Borders.
Viburnum tinus Laurustinus	8	medium	upright	8 - 10'	medium	sun, semi-shade	broad-leaved evergreen	Borders, screening.
Viburnum trilobum American Cranberry Bush Viburnum	6b, 7	coarse	irregular	8 - 12'	medium to fast	sun, semi-shade	deciduous	Red fruit in fall.
Yucca aloifolia Spanish Dagger*	entire state	coarse	upright	8 - 12'	medium	sun, semi-shade	broad-leaved evergreen	Hardy. White flowers.

Table 7. Small trees 10 - 40 feet

BOTANICAL NAME COMMON NAME *Denotes native Georgia plant	GEORGIA'S HARDY ZONE	TEXTURE	FORM	HEIGHT	SPREAD	GROWTH RATE	CLASS	REMARKS
Acer buergerianum Trident Maple	entire state	medium	oval	20 - 35'	15 - 35'	slow to medium	deciduous	Specimen or naturalistic sites. Tough tree for urban sites.
Acer palmatum Japanese Maple	entire state	fine to medium	horizontal branching	15 - 20'	10 - 15'	medium	deciduous	Specimens with red or green foliage.
Amelanchier arborea Serviceberry*	6b, 7	medium	oval	30 - 40'	15 - 20'	medium	deciduous	Borders. White flowers in early spring.
Butia capitata Pindo Palm	8	medium	weeping	15 - 20'	10 - 15'	medium	evergreen palm	Specimen.
Carpinus caroliniana American Hornbeam	entire state	medium	irregular	20 - 30'	15 - 20'	slow	deciduous	Tough, urban tolerant tree. Wet site tolerant.
Cedrus deodora Deodar Cedar	7, 8	medium	pyramidal	30 - 50'	20 - 30'	medium	evergreen conifer	Specimen, screening.
Cercis canadensis Eastern Redbud*	entire state	medium	oval	20 - 30'	18 - 20'	medium	deciduous	Spring flowering.
Cercis chinensis Chinese Redbud	entire state	medium	oval	15 - 20'	10 - 12'	medium	deciduous	Small spring flowering tree.
Cercis reniformis 'Oklahoma' Oklahoma Redbud	7, 8	medium	spreading	15 - 20'	15' - 20'	medium	deciduous	Glossy foliage with rosy red spring flowers.
Chionanthus retusus Chinese Fringe Tree	entire state	medium	spreading	15 - 25'	10 - 15'	medium	deciduous	Bright white spring flowers.
Chionanthus virginicus White Fringe Tree Grancy Gray-beard*	entire state	coarse	irregular	12 - 20'	10 - 15'	slow to medium	deciduous	White spring flowers.
Cladrastis kentukea American Yellowwood	6b, 7	coarse	oval	25 - 30'	10 - 12'	slow	deciduous	White flowers and yellow fall color. Specimen.
Cornus florida Flowering Dogwood	entire state	medium	horizontal branching	15 - 25'	15 - 20'	slow	deciduous	Specimen or small grove.
Cornus kousa Kousa dogwood	6b, 7	medium	horizontal branching	15 - 25'	15 - 20'	slow	deciduous	Specimen or small grove.

Table 7. Small trees 10 - 40 feet

BOTANICAL NAME / COMMON NAME (*Denotes native Georgia plant)	GEORGIA'S HARDY ZONE	TEXTURE	FORM	HEIGHT	SPREAD	GROWTH RATE	CLASS	REMARKS
Crataegus phaenopyrum / Washington Hawthorne	6b, 7	medium	upright to rounded	25 - 30'	15 - 20'	medium	deciduous	Red berries in fall.
Eriobotrya japonica / Loquat	8	coarse	rounded	10 - 20'	10 - 15'	medium to fast	broad-leaved evergreen	Dark green foliage with bold features.
Halesia tetraptera / Silverbell*	6b - 8a	medium	spreading	20 - 30'	15 - 20'	medium	deciduous	White flowers.
Ilex x 'Nellie R. Stevens' / Nellie R. Stevens Holly	entire state	medium to coarse	upright	10 - 20'	8 - 10'	medium to fast	broad-leaved evergreen	Specimen, screening.
Ilex x attenuata HYBRID HOLLY / Cultivars include: East Palatka' 'Fosteri' 'Savannah'	entire state	medium to coarse	upright pyramidal	10 - 40'	6 - 15'	medium	broad-leaved evergreen	Specimen, screening. Red berries. (Leaves single spined) (Very pyramidal and dense) (Light green foliage)
Ilex cassine / Cassien Holly*	7, 8	medium	pyramidal	10 - 20'	8 - 10'	medium	broad-leaved evergreen	Screening.
Ilex opaca / American Holly*	entire state	coarse	pyramidal	20 - 50'	15 - 30'	medium	broad-leaved evergreen	Dark green foliage. Specimen, screening.
Ilex opaca 'Greenleaf' / Greenleaf Holly	entire state	coarse	pyramidal upright	20 - 30'	10 - 15'	medium	broad-leaved evergreen	Compact habit of growth.
Ilex vomitoria / Yaupon Holly*	7, 8	fine	irregular	15 - 20'	8 - 10'	fast	broad-leaved evergreen	Screening with bright red fruit.
Ilex vomitoria 'Pendula' / Weeping Yaupon Holly*	7, 8	fine	weeping	15 - 20'	8 - 10'	medium to fast	broad-leaved evergreen	Distinctive weeping habit.
Juniperus virginiana / Red Cedar*	entire state	medium	pyramidal	25 - 40'	15 - 20'	slow	evergreen conifer	Screen.

Table 7. Small trees 10 - 40 feet

BOTANICAL NAME COMMON NAME *Denotes native Georgia plant	GEORGIA'S HARDY ZONE	TEXTURE	FORM	HEIGHT	SPREAD	GROWTH RATE	CLASS	REMARKS
Koelreuteria bipinnata Chinese Flametree	7, 8	medium	upright	20 - 30'	15 - 20'	fast	deciduous	Yellow flowers followed by pink pods.
Koelreuteria paniculata Goldenrain Tree	6b - 8a	medium	rounded	20 - 30'	10 - 15'	medium	deciduous	Yellow flowers in early summer.
Lagerstroemia indica Common Crapemyrtle	entire state	fine	upright	6 - 30'	4 - 15'	medium to fast	deciduous	White, pink, lavender or red flowers. Powdery mildew and aphids may become a problem.
Lagerstroemia indica x L. fauriei Hybrid Crapemyrtle	entire state	fine	upright	15 - 30'	10 - 15'	fast	deciduous	White, pink, lavender or red flowers. Hybrids have mildew resistance and bloom longer.
Magnolia grandiflora 'Little Gem' Little Gem Southern Magnolia	7, 8	medium	upright	15 - 20'	8 - 10'	medium	evergreen	Dark green evergreen foliage on compact plant.
Magnolia soulangiana Japanese Magnolia	entire state	coarse	rounded	20 - 30'	15 - 20'	medium	deciduous	Pink saucer-like blooms.
Magnolia stellata Star Magnolia	entire state	coarse	rounded	12 - 20'	10 - 15'	slow to medium	deciduous	Pink saucer-like blooms.
Magnolia virginiana Sweetbay Magnolia*	7, 8	coarse	upright	15 - 20'	10 - 20'	slow	semi-ever-green	White flowers in summer.
Malus x 'Dolgo' Dolgo Crabapple	6b, 7	medium	rounded	15 - 20'	10- 15'	medium	deciduous	White flowers followed by red to purple fruits. Disease resistant.
Malus floribunda Japanese Crabapple	6b, 7	medium	rounded	15 - 20'	15 - 20'	medium	deciduous	Pinkish-red flowers fading to white. Fruit yellow, red. Mostly disease resistant.
Malus 'Callaway' Callaway Crabapple	6b, 7	medium	rounded	15 - 20'	15 - 20'	medium	deciduous	Pink buds, white flowers. Large 1" reddish fruit. Disease resistant.
Oxydendrum arboreum Sourwood*	entire state	medium to coarse	upright	25-30'	15-20'	medium	deciduous	Red fall color.
Parkinsonia aculeata Jerusalem Thorn	8b	fine	spreading	15-20'	20-25'	rapid	deciduous	Yellow flowers in spring and summer.

Table 7. Small trees 10 - 40 feet

BOTANICAL NAME COMMON NAME *Denotes native Georgia plant	GEORGIA'S HARDY ZONE	TEXTURE	FORM	HEIGHT	SPREAD	GROWTH RATE	CLASS	REMARKS
Phoenix canariensis Canary Date palm	8b	coarse	upright	30-40'	12-18'	medium	evergreen palm	Used as accent specimen.
Pinus virginiana Virginia Pine*	6b, 7	medium	pyramidal	20-40'	15-20'	medium	evergreen conifer	Good for screening.
Pistacia chinensis Chinese Pistache	entire state	fine	rounded	30-40'	30-40'	fast	deciduous	Yellow to bright orange-red fall color. Hardy and heat tolerant.
Prunus x 'Okame' Okame Cherry	entire state	medium	upright	20-30'	15-20'	fast	deciduous	Early spring rosy pink blooms.
Prunus caroliniana Carolina Cherrylaurel*	7, 8	medium	oval	20-30'	15-20'	fast	broad-leaved evergreen	Susceptible to ice damage.
Prunus cerasifera 'Thundercloud' Purpleleaf Plum	entire state	medium	upright	20 - 30'	15 - 20'	medium	deciduous	Purplish foliage.
Prunus mume Japanese Apricot	entire state	medium	irregular	15 - 20'	10 - 15'	slow	deciduous	Blooms very early in spring.
Prunus serrulata 'Kwanzan' Kwanzan Cherry	6, 7	medium	rounded	20 - 30'	15 - 20'	medium	deciduous	Deep pink double blooms.
Prunus subhirtella var. *autumnalis* Fall Blooming Cherry	6b, 7	medium	spreading	20 - 30'	15 - 25'	medium	deciduous	Specimen.
Prunus x *yedoensis* Yoshino Cherry	6b - 8a	medium	weeping	30 - 40'	15 - 20'	medium	deciduous	Specimen.
Quercus myrsinifolia Chinese Evergreen Oak	7, 8	medium	oval	30-40'	20 - 30'	slow	broad-leaved evergreen	Screen, specimen or small street tree.
Salix babylonica Weeping Willow	entire state	fine	weeping	30 - 40'	25 - 35'	fast	deciduous	Specimen.
Salix matsudana 'Tortuosa' Contorted Willow	entire state	fine	weeping	20 - 30'	10 - 15'	medium to fast	deciduous	Short-lived.

Table 7. Small trees 10 - 40 feet

BOTANICAL NAME COMMON NAME *Denotes native Georgia plant	GEORGIA'S HARDY ZONE	TEXTURE	FORM	HEIGHT	SPREAD	GROWTH RATE	CLASS	REMARKS
Sabal palmetto Cabbage Palmetto	8	coarse	upright	30 - 40'	8 - 10'	medium	evergreen palm	Specimen, groups.
Vitex agnus-castus Chastetree	entire state	fine	vase-shaped, spreading	10 - 15'	10 - 15'	fast	deciduous	Blue flowers in mid summer. White and pink flower forms available.

DISCUSSION QUESTIONS

1. What are some factors to consider in selecting woody ornamental plants for the landscape?

2. How important is plant hardiness in selecting woody ornamentals for the landscape?

3. What are things you should look for in selecting healthy plants from the nursery?

RESOURCES

Church, Thomas Dolliver; *Gardens Are for People: How to Plan for Outdoor Living, 3rd ed.*; University of California Press,

Dirr, Michael; *Manual of Woody Landscape Plants, 5th ed.*; Stipes Publishing Co.;

Greenlee, John; *The Encyclopedia of Ornamental Grasses: How to Grow and Use over 250 Beautiful and Versatile Plants*; Rodale Press, Inc.;

Lawrence, Elizabeth; *A Southern Garden, 50th anniversary edition*; University of North Carolina Press; 1991

Motloch, John L.; *Introduction to Landscape Design, 2nd Edition.*Wiley; ISBN: 0471352918

Tripp, Kim E. and Raulston, J. C.; *The Year in Trees: Superb Woody Plants for Four-Seasons Gardens*; Timber Press.

Wilder, Louise Beebe; *Color in My Garden: An American Gardener's Palette, reprint ed.*; Atlantic Monthly Press; 1990 (original 1918)

12
Trees

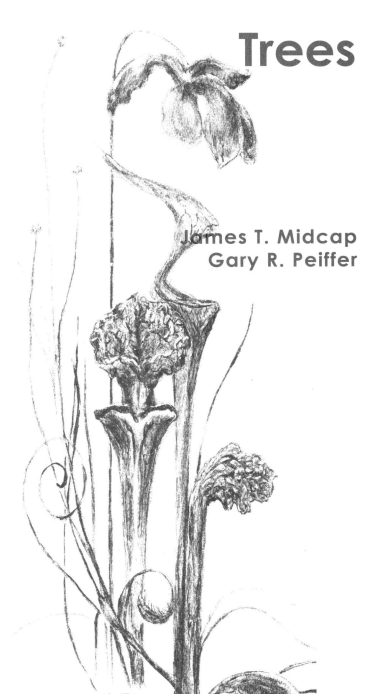

James T. Midcap
Gary R. Peiffer

LEARNING OBJECTIVES

Understand the social, economic, and the environmental value of urban trees.

Be familiar with the concepts of a tree program and tree ordinance for suburban and urban areas.

Understand the importance of protecting trees from damage and hazards and the impact of construction on trees.

Be familiar with the services provided by an arborist.

Know the importance of proper tree selection and characteristics of common trees recommended for Georgia.

Understand why compacted soil slows tree establishment and growth.

Know the advantages of fall planting.

Know the proper way to plant a tree and the impact of soil amendments.

Understand the proper way to care for a tree after planting: staking, watering, fertilization, pruning.

TERMS TO KNOW

Auxin plant hormone that stimulates and regulates growth.

Cambium layer of cells that rapidly divides and produces wood to the inside and inner bark to the outside.

Cytokinins plant hormones produced by the roots and traveling upward through the xylem, promote tissue growth and budding.

Heartwood hard central wood of the trunk of a tree.

Meristem growing points of a plant.

Phloem vascular tissue through which food is conducted from the leaves to plant parts.(down)

Xylem woody tissue that conducts water and serves as a support, as for a stem.(up)

INTRODUCTION

Trees affect the well-being and appearance of our Georgia communities. One of the most effective ways to improve community appearance is to plant trees. Planting trees can have a great visual and economic impact. Many people visualize the ideal community as one with tall, spreading, stately trees lining their streets of well-kept homes and prospering businesses.

Trees provide shade and beauty as well as assume many environmental functions. Trees remove carbon dioxide from the atmosphere and replace it with oxygen. They remove air pollutants and dust particles while softening the microclimate by buffering climate extremes. Trees help save energy by providing shade for people and buildings, and serving as wind breaks.

Trees improve the community's overall quality of life. Quality of life includes "community wellness". Nothing creates a more positive impression than walking or jogging through tree filled landscapes. Trees contribute an atmosphere of peace of mind and relaxation. Even parking lots lined with trees can make a positive impression on shoppers and employees arriving at their destinations.

The pride of planting trees as a community creates a sense of working and pulling together. Trees planted in memory of loved ones or to commemorate special dates become lifelong additions to the community. Youth are motivated into planting when trees are given as a prize or planted in recognition of their community support. Planning these opportunities creates a coordinated treescape as an investment for the future.

Community involvement helps to ensure an organized program for community tree planting and maintenance. Urban trees must be suitable both biologically and environmentally for the site. Tree form, height and color can enhance an appropriate location. Selected trees must be hardy and adaptable to the harsh environments encountered in urban areas - air pollutants, reflected heat, soil compaction and limited rooting space. Professional planning, selection and design are crucial for success.

A critical step in developing an active tree planting program is knowing the resources already in place. Tree inventories provide information on the urban forest and suggest where improvements can be made. They allow us to focus on existing problems and plan for the future. Inventories can provide data to support budgets for tree planting and maintenance.

Opportunities for Trees

Residential Areas—Community residential areas benefit from tree planting. A coordinated addition of trees on residential streets will greatly enhance the neighborhoods. An agreement on standard trees for curbside plantings should be reached. Communities which are considering plantings probably should choose six to twelve shade trees, as well as a similar number of flowering and specimen trees. When choosing specific trees consider the street's appearance as the proposed trees mature. Maturing shade trees will have a unifying effect on the street because of their size and uniformity. Spacing the large trees 60 to 100 feet apart on both sides of the street will still allow plenty of room to plant flowering and specimen trees between them.

Also plan to plant new trees on older residential streets. Once the existing street trees pass maturity they begin to decline and eventually die. Replacement trees should be continually planted so catastrophe or old age does not leave the streets treeless.

Schools—Most school buildings are in desperate need of trees. Trees planted at the schools provide shade for classrooms and outdoor play areas. They can screen objectionable views, serve as buffers for noise and unify the buildings and grounds into an attractive setting. Strategically located shade trees will provide a more comfortable, enjoyable environment. Classes may use the trees to learn about the kinds of trees and their effect upon our environment.

Select deciduous trees that provide shade in the warm months but allow winter sun to heat the buildings in the winter. Plant shade trees close to metal play equipment to prevent excessive heat buildup in mornings and afternoons. Plant screening trees to lessen the visual impact of large parking lots on the school ground. Seasonal accents can be added by planting flowering trees such as crape myrtle and dogwood. Shade trees with attractive fall color also provide accents. Lastly, use large growing trees to provide a background for the building and to frame the sides.

The Business District—The central business district is often almost totally void of vegetation. Establishing trees is an important first step to add vegetation and make the area more attractive. Trees provide interest, variety and an invitation to the shopping area. Importantly, trees begin to create a feeling of unity and harmony in the central business district.

Select deciduous trees rather than evergreens for planting in the business district. They provide shade in the summer and let in the warming winter sun. These trees will form a buffer between the automobile and the pedestrian traffic while offering attractive shade with seasonal color and a decorative accent.

Public Buildings—The appearance of most public buildings can be enhanced by a few well placed shade and flowering trees. The available space will largely determine which trees can be used. Consider the size, shape and location of the trees keeping in mind the buildings' function and surroundings.

Trees soften abrupt changes of contrasting buildings while providing cooling shade from the afternoon sun on the building and sitting areas. They can function as street trees and as foreground plantings for large buildings.

Parking Lots—Trees between the street and parking lot lessen the visual impact of the parking area. Large shade trees planted in the parking area break up the open expanse of paving. To ensure visibility for drivers near entrances and exits, trees should be limbed up. Where no access problems exist and where space permits, plant several species of trees to partially screen the parking lot.

Use large growing trees, evergreens, berms, plant screens or architectural barriers to lessen the visual impact. Trees and shrubs with attractive flowers or fall color add diversionary interest.

Water is necessary to successfully establish and maintain trees in parking lots. Plan to make watering easy by including an irrigation system or at least a hose bib. Parking lot trees need supplemental water to dissipate the heat in addition to normal water requirements.

Family Homes—In the deep South, the foliage of trees provide relief from the hot summer sun, making shade trees a welcome addition to the landscape. Large growing trees should be chosen with care, so they do not overgrow the space available and cause high maintenance costs. Many small trees are important on residential properties to provide flowers and excellent foliage. Small trees provide the proper scale for smaller areas.

Planting Guidelines For The Business District

Trees planted in the business district must not become an obstacle in the sidewalk for shoppers. No tree plantings should be installed unless sidewalks are at least 8 feet wide.

The presence of overhead structures will dictate the height of the tree species to be used. Small growing trees with an upright habit can be planted in sidewalks that are 10 to 12 feet wide. Make the openings or planting pits a minimum of 4 feet by 8 feet and 3 feet deep. Planting holes or pits should be a minimum of 100 cubic feet to provide an extended life for the trees. Follow good planting practices and be sure to provide drainage. Planting under trees is discouraged.

Cover the openings around the tree with brick or other pavers and fill the joints with sand. Metal grates which still allow air and water to reach the plant roots can also be used. The pavers and grates should be flush with the surrounding pavement to allow safe traffic movement. Many sidewalks are too narrow to accommodate trees. Planting space can be gained from the street adjacent to the curb. Parking spaces located at the intersections can be planted without significantly reducing the total amount of parking. Annexing the end parking spaces at the intersection and expanding the curb protects the trees from automobiles and provides additional areas for root development (Figure 1). Extend the curb out into the street to create a larger planting site.

If the sidewalks are wider than 12 feet other alternatives exist. Larger growing trees may be planted as well as groupings of small to medium sized trees. Be sure to increase the size of the planting pit to accommodate these larger trees. Also include benches, trash receptacles and other desirable street furnishings when space is available.

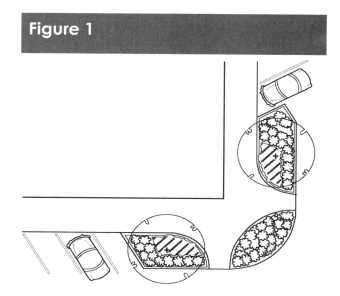

Figure 1

Figure 1. Increase planting space by annexing the end parking spaces and extending the curb into the street.

SELECTING TREES

Trees selected for planting throughout the community should be attractive. The specific tree or trees selected for a street or site must be adapted to that location and its climate extremes. A tree should be selected to fulfill the basic landscape functions for which they are being planted. They should also be relatively maintenance free or selected for the maintenance program to be provided long term. The selection of the right tree for a planting site is one of the most important decisions to ensure long term benefits, beauty and satisfaction with the planting.

The Planting Site—Each planting site has a set of environmental characteristics which define it. Temperature extremes, soil pH, and light levels can limit the plants which will thrive on a site. Every tree has cultural requirements which must be met for the tree to do well. These requirements include light intensity, water availability, soil drainage and soil fertility. Therefore an early step in our tree selection process is to identify tree species or selections whose cultural needs match the planting site so that survival and growth can take place.

Another site consideration is the amount of growing space that is available, both height and width. Large trees planted for shade can fit in well as long as they have room to mature. Tall growing trees should never be planted beneath utility wires. Trees without sufficient space between the sidewalk and the curb cause sidewalk breakage and curb damage as growth increases trunk and root size. Planting a tree too close to a building leads to roof or siding damage by rubbing branches. By knowing the mature height, branch spread and trunk size, problems are avoided.

Because temperature extremes kill trees, it is important to select plants that are hardy to the site. This means they must be able to endure the lowest possible temperatures without injury as well tolerate the stress caused by high temperatures. The USDA Plant Hardiness Zone Map (page 56) allows selection of trees hardy to the site. The plant selection lists provide hardiness zones for each plant.

Soil conditions such as texture, pH, soluble salts and nutrients all affect how trees grow. These characteristics must be evaluated for each site and then trees are selected that will tolerate them. Soil pH and nutrient levels can be modified to improve tree growth prior to planting. Soil compaction must be alleviated to insure proper tree growth.

Light levels affect plant growth and plant survival. Trees planted under an existing foliage canopy must tolerate lower light levels. Trees planted in full sun and high heat must be able to withstand the temperature extremes as well as high light.

In urban sites compacted soils become a major cause of early plant death. Tough trees must be selected which will endure these compacted soils. Alleviate compacted soils when possible and increase the volume of the planting pit before planting trees. These measures will increase tree longevity and increase the selection of tolerant trees.

Functions and Maintenance—Plant selection must consider the design and functions of the planting. These functions may include 1) providing shade for reduced temperatures, 2) developing wind screens to divert winter winds and 3) erosion control to reduce soil movement. Other considerations include providing a feeling of shelter and protection, framing views or buildings, and allowing privacy. Aesthetic features such as colored foliage and showy flowers may be part of the design criteria.

Maintenance considerations generally focus strongly on resistance or susceptibility to insects and diseases. Plants which are susceptible to or have severe pest and major disease issues should be eliminated from a tree selection list. Plants resistant to stress on a given site are important, since stressed trees are more susceptible to insect infestation and disease infection. Maintenance considerations also include early pruning and training to develop a strong branch framework, which will be resistant to future storm damage. Susceptibility to branch breakage and blow down greatly increase maintenance costs.

Selection At The Nursery—The last selection criteria is the selection of the tree from the nursery. First look for a vigorous tree with good twig growth and dark green foliage. The tree should have good branch spacing and trunk taper as well as a strong single trunk or leader. Spreading branches are much stronger than strongly upright branches. Foliage should be evenly distributed over the upper two thirds of the canopy.

Avoid plants that have been mishandled, meaning they have mechanical damage or scarred trunks and limbs. Check the foliage, both top and bottom to detect any insect or disease problems that could be carried to the planting site. Lastly, examine the root ball or root system of the tree. Balled and burlapped trees should have a solid root ball that has been kept moist, and protected from drying or freezing. Container plants should not be heavily pot bound with large circling roots in the

Table 1. Small trees 10 - 40 feet

BOTANICAL NAME COMMON NAME	GEORGIA'S HARDY ZONE	TEXTURE	FORM	HEIGHT	SPREAD	GROWTH RATE	CLASS	REMARKS
Acer buergerianum Trident Maple	entire state	medium	oval	20 - 35'	15 - 35'	slow to medium	deciduous	Specimen or naturalistic sites. Tough tree for urban sites.
Acer palmatum Japanese Maple	entire state	fine to medium	horizontal branching	15 - 20'	10 - 15'	medium	deciduous	Specimens with red or green foliage.
Amelanchier arborea Serviceberry*	6b, 7	medium	oval	30 - 40'	15 - 20'	medium	deciduous	Borders. White flowers in early spring.
Butia capitata Pindo Palm	8	medium	weeping	15 - 20'	10 - 15'	medium	evergreen palm	Specimen.
Carpinus caroliniana American Hornbeam	entire state	medium	irregular	20 - 30'	15 - 20'	slow	deciduous	Tough, urban tolerant tree. Wet site tolerant.
Cedrus deodora Deodar Cedar	7, 8	medium	pyramidal	30 - 50'	20 - 30'	medium	evergreen conifer	Specimen, screening.
Cercis canadensis Eastern Redbud*	entire state	medium	oval	20 - 30'	18 - 20'	medium	deciduous	Spring flowering.
Cercis chinensis Chinese Redbud	entire state	medium	oval	15 - 20'	10 - 12'	medium	deciduous	Small spring flowering tree.
Cercis reniformis 'Oklahoma' Oklahoma Redbud	7, 8	medium	spreading	15 - 20'	15' - 20'	medium	deciduous	Glossy foliage with rosy red spring flowers.
Chionanthus retusus Chinese Fringe Tree	entire state	medium	spreading	15 - 25'	10 - 15'	medium	deciduous	Bright white spring flowers.
Chionanthus virginicus White Fringe Tree Grancy Gray-beard*	entire state	coarse	irregular	12 - 20'	10 - 15'	slow to medium	deciduous	White spring flowers.
Cladrastis kentukea American Yellowwood	6b, 7	coarse	oval	25 - 30'	10 - 12'	slow	deciduous	White flowers and yellow fall color. Specimen.
Cornus florida Flowering Dogwood	entire state	medium	horizontal branching	15 - 25'	15 - 20'	slow	deciduous	Specimen or small grove.
Cornus kousa Kousa dogwood	6b, 7	medium	horizontal branching	15 - 25'	15 - 20'	slow	deciduous	Specimen or small grove.
Crataegus phaenopyrum Washington Hawthorne	6b, 7	medium	upright to rounded	25 - 30'	15 - 20'	medium	deciduous	Red berries in fall.

Table 1. Small trees 10 - 40 feet

BOTANICAL NAME COMMON NAME	GEORGIA'S HARDY ZONE	TEXTURE	FORM	HEIGHT	SPREAD	GROWTH RATE	CLASS	REMARKS
Eriobotrya japonica Loquat	8	coarse	rounded	10 - 20'	10 - 15'	medium to fast	broad-leaved evergreen	Dark green foliage with bold features.
Halesia tetraptera Silverbell*	6b - 8a	medium	spreading	20 - 30'	15 - 20'	medium	deciduous	White flowers.
Ilex x 'Nellie R. Stevens' Nellie R. Stevens Holly	entire state	medium to coarse	upright	10 - 20'	8 - 10'	medium to fast	broad-leaved evergreen	Specimen, screening.
Ilex x attenuata HYBRID HOLLY Cultivars include: East Palatka' Leaves single spined 'Fosteri' Very pyramidal and dense 'Savannah' Light green foliage.	entire state	medium to coarse	upright pyramidal	10 - 40'	6 - 15'	medium	broad-leaved evergreen	Specimen, screening.Red berries.
Ilex cassine Cassine Holly*	7, 8	medium	pyramidal	10 - 20'	8 - 10'	medium	broad-leaved evergreen	Screening.
Ilex opaca American Holly*	entire state	coarse	pyramidal	20 - 50'	15 - 30'	medium	broad-leaved evergreen	Dark green foliage. Specimen, screening.
Ilex opaca 'Greenleaf' Greenleaf Holly	entire state	coarse	pyramidal upright	20 - 30'	10 - 15'	medium	broad-leaved evergreen	Compact habit of growth.
Ilex vomitoria Yaupon Holly*	7, 8	fine	irregular	15 - 20'	8 - 10'	fast	broad-leaved evergreen	Screening with bright red fruit.
Ilex vomitoria 'Pendula' Weeping Yaupon Holly*	7, 8	fine	weeping	15 - 20'	8 - 10'	medium to fast	broad-leaved evergreen	Distinctive weeping habit.
Juniperus virginiana Red Cedar*	entire state	medium	pyramidal	25 - 40'	15 - 20'	slow	evergreen conifer	Screen.
Koelreuteria bipinnata Chinese Flametree	7, 8	medium	upright	20 - 30'	15 - 20'	fast	deciduous	Yellow flowers followed by pink pods.
Koelreuteria paniculata Goldenrain Tree	6b - 8a	medium	rounded	20 - 30'	10 - 15'	medium	deciduous	Yellow flowers in early summer.
Lagerstroemia indica Common Crape myrtle	entire state	fine	upright	6 - 30'	4 - 15'	medium to fast	deciduous	White, pink, lavender or red flowers. Problems-Powdery mildew and aphids.

Table 1. Small trees 10 - 40 feet

BOTANICAL NAME / COMMON NAME	GEORGIA'S HARDY ZONE	TEXTURE	FORM	HEIGHT	SPREAD	GROWTH RATE	CLASS	REMARKS
Lagerstroemia indica x L. fauriei / Hybrid Crape myrtle	entire state	fine	upright	15 - 30'	10 - 15'	fast	deciduous	White, pink, lavender or red flowers. Hybrids have mildew resistance and bloom longer.
Magnolia grandiflora 'Little Gem' / Little Gem Southern Magnolia	7, 8	medium	upright	15 - 20'	8 - 10'	medium	evergreen	Dark green evergreen foliage on compact plant.
Magnolia soulangiana / Japanese Magnolia	entire state	coarse	rounded	20 - 30'	15 - 20'	medium	deciduous	Pink saucer-like blooms.
Magnolia stellata / Star Magnolia	entire state	coarse	rounded	12 - 20'	10 - 15'	slow to medium	deciduous	White star-shaped blooms. Early spring bloomer.
Magnolia virginiana / Sweetbay Magnolia*	7, 8	coarse	upright	15 - 20'	10 - 20'	slow	semi-evergreen	White flowers in summer.
Malus x 'Dolgo' / Dolgo Crabapple	6b, 7	medium	rounded	15 - 20'	10- 15'	medium	deciduous	White flowers followed by red to purple fruits. Disease resistant.
Malus floribunda / Japanese Crabapple	6b, 7	medium	rounded	15 - 20'	15 - 20'	medium	deciduous	Pinkish-red flowers fading to white. Fruit yellow, red. Mostly disease resistant.
Malus 'Callaway' / Callaway Crabapple	6b, 7	medium	rounded	15 - 20'	15 - 20'	medium	deciduous	Pink buds, white flowers. Large 1" reddish fruit. Disease resistant.
Oxydendrum arboreum / Sourwood*	entire state	medium to coarse	upright	25-30'	15-20'	medium	deciduous	Red fall color.
Parkinsonia aculeata / Jerusalem Thorn	8b	fine	spreading	15-20'	20-25'	rapid	deciduous	Yellow flowers in spring and summer.
Phoenix canariensis / Canary Date palm	8b	coarse	upright	30-40'	12-18'	medium	evergreen palm	Used as accent specimen
Pinus virginiana / Virginia Pine*	6b, 7	medium	pyramidal	20-40'	15-20'	medium	evergreen conifer	Good for screening.
Pistacia chinensis / Chinese Pistache	entire state	fine	rounded	30-40'	30-40'	fast	deciduous	Yellow to bright orange-red fall color. Hardy and heat tolerant

Table 1. Small trees 10 - 40 feet

BOTANICAL NAME COMMON NAME	GEORGIA'S HARDY ZONE	TEXTURE	FORM	HEIGHT	SPREAD	GROWTH RATE	CLASS	REMARKS
Prunus x 'Okame' Okame Cherry	entire state	medium	upright	20-30'	15-20'	fast	deciduous	Early spring rosy pink blooms.
Prunus caroliniana Carolina Cherrylaurel*	7, 8	medium	oval	20-30'	15-20'	fast	broad-leaved evergreen	Susceptible to ice damage. Can be invasive
Prunus cerasifera 'Thundercloud' Purpleleaf Plum	entire state	medium	upright	20 - 30'	15 - 20'	medium	deciduous	Purplish foliage.
Prunus mume Japanese Apricot	entire state	medium	irregular	15 - 20'	10 - 15'	slow	deciduous	Blooms very early in spring.
Prunus serrulata 'Kwanzan' Kwanzan Cherry	6, 7	medium	rounded	20 - 30'	15 - 20'	medium	deciduous	Deep pink double blooms.
Prunus subhirtella var. autumnalis Fall Blooming Cherry	6b, 7	medium	spreading	20 - 30'	15 - 25'	medium	deciduous	Specimen.
Prunus x *yedoensis* Yoshino Cherry	6b - 8a	medium	weeping	30 - 40'	15 - 20'	medium	deciduous	Specimen.
Quercus myrsinifolia Chinese Evergreen Oak	7, 8	medium	oval	30-40'	20 - 30'	slow	broad-leaved evergreen	Screen, specimen or small street tree.
Salix babylonica Weeping Willow	entire state	fine	weeping	30 - 40'	25 - 35'	fast	deciduous	Specimen.
Salix matsudana 'Tortuosa' Contorted Willow	entire state	fine	weeping	20 - 30'	10 - 15'	medium to fast	deciduous	Short-lived.Best in wet areas
Sabal palmetto Cabbage Palmetto	8	coarse	upright	30 - 40'	8 - 10'	medium	evergreen palm	Specimen, groups.
Vitex agnus-castus Chastetree	entire state	fine	vase-shaped, spreading	10 - 15'	10 - 15'	fast	deciduous	Blue flowers in mid summer. White and pink flower forms available.

Table 2. Medium And large trees 40 feet and larger

Botanical Name Common Name	GEORGIA'S HARDY ZONE	TEXTURE	FORM	HEIGHT	SPREAD	GROWTH RATE	CLASS	REMARKS
Acer rubrum 'Franks Red' Red Sunset Red Maple	6b, 7	medium	rounded	45-50'	35-40'	medium	deciduous	Shade tree with bright red fall color.
Acer rubrum 'October Glory' October Glory Red Maple	entire state	medium	oval rounded	40-50'	25-35'	medium	deciduous	Shade tree with excellent late red fall color.
Acer saccharum Sugar Maple*	6b, 7	medium	oval	50-60'	25-40'	medium to fast	deciduous	Yellow to reddish fall color. Shade tree.
Acer saccharum ssp. *Floridanum* Southern Sugar Maple*	entire state	medium	oval	40-50'	25-35'	medium to fast	deciduous	Shade tolerant. Usually yellow fall color.
Acer saccharum 'Legacy' Legacy Sugar Maple	6b, 7	medium	oval	40-50'	25-35'	medium	deciduous	Drought resistant with dark green leathery leaves.
Betula nigra 'BNMTF' Dura-Heat River Birch	entire state	medium	oval	40-50'	30-40'	fast	deciduous	Specimen with good heat tolerance.
Betula nigra 'Cully' Heritage River Birch	entire state	medium	oval	40-50'	25-35'	fast	deciduous	Specimen.
Carpinus betulus 'Fastigiata' Upright European Hornbeam	6b, 7	medium	oval-vase	30-40'	20-30'	medium	deciduous	Narrow when young, spreads with age.
Carya illinoinensis Pecan	entire state	medium	rounded	50-60'	30-40'	medium	deciduous	Nuts and shade. Branches subject to breakage.
Cedrus atlantica Atlas Cedar	6b, 7	fine to medium	pyramidal	60-80'	25-30'	slow to medium	evergreen conifer	Specimen tree.
Celtis laevigata Sugar Hackberry*	entire state	medium	upright to rounded	60-80'	25-35'	medium	deciduous	Street and shade tree.
Cercidiphyllum japonicum Katsura Tree	6b, 7	medium	upright	40-60'	30-40'	medium	deciduous	Shade tree, requires ample moisture.
Cinnamomum lanceolata Camphortree	8b	medium	oval	40-50'	20-30'	fast	broad-leaved evergreen	Screening. May self sow.
Cryptomeria japonica 'Yoshino' Japanese Crytomeria	entire state	fine	pyramidal	50-60'	20-30'	fast	evergreen conifer	Specimen and screening.

* Denotes native Georgia plant throughout this table.

Table 2. Medium And large trees 40 feet and larger

Botanical Name / Common Name	GEORGIA'S HARDY ZONE	TEXTURE	FORM	HEIGHT	SPREAD	GROWTH RATE	CLASS	REMARKS
x Cupressocyparis leylandii / Leyland Cypress	entire state	fine	pyramidal	50-60'	20-30'	fast	evergreen conifer	Specimen and screening.
Fagus grandifolia / American Beech*	entire state	coarse	rounded	60-80'	35-45'	medium	deciduous	Shade tree.
Ginkgo biloba / Ginkgo or Maiden Hair Tree	entire state	medium	irregular	50-70'	30-40'	very slow	deciduous	Yellow fall color. Specimen. Select male trees.
Liquidambar styraciflua / Sweetgum*	entire state	coarse	oval	60-80'	40-50'	fast	deciduous	Yellow to orange to purple fall color. Specimen.
Liriodendron tulipifera / Tuliptree Or Yellow Poplar*	entire state	coarse	pyramidal	80-100'	30-40'	fast	deciduous	Shade tree, needs adequate moisture.
Magnolia grandiflora / Southern Magnolia*	entire state	coarse	horizontal branching pyramidal	60-80'	40-50'	slow to medium	broad-leaved evergreen	Specimen with large white flowers.
Magnolia grandiflora 'Bracken's Brown Beauty' / Bracken's Brown Beauty Magnolia	entire state	course	pyramidal	40-60'	15-30'	medium	broad-leaved evergreen	Compact, dense pyramidal specimen.
Metasequoia glyptostroboides / Dawn Redwood	6b, 7	fine	upright	80-100'	25-30'	fast	deciduous conifer	Specimen or screen, tolerant of wet sites.
Nyssa sylvatica / Black Tupelo*	entire state	medium	oval	40-50'	25-30'	medium	deciduous	Naturalistic gardens.
Pinus elliottii / Slash Pine*	8	medium	horizontal branching	80-100'	15-20'	fast	evergreen conifer	Mass plantings.
Pinus palustris / Longleaf Pine*	8	medium	horizontal branching	80-100'	20-25'	fast	evergreen conifer	Mass plantings.
Pinus strobus / White Pine*	6b, 7	medium	pyramidal	50-80'	20-40'	medium	evergreen conifer	Specimen or screening tree.
Pinus taeda / Loblolly Pine*	entire state	medium	horizontal branching	60-80'	20-30'	fast	evergreen conifer	Mass plantings and screening.

* Denotes native Georgia plant throughout this table.

Table 2. Medium And large trees 40 feet and larger

Botanical Name / Common Name	GEORGIA'S HARDY ZONE	TEXTURE	FORM	HEIGHT	SPREAD	GROWTH RATE	CLASS	REMARKS
Platanus occidentalis Sycamore or Planetree*	entire state	coarse	upright	80-100'	40-50'	fast	deciduous	Shade tree.
Platanus x acerifolia London planetree	entire state	coarse	upright	70-100'	50-60'	fast	deciduous	Shade tree with urban tolerance.
Quercus alba White Oak*	entire state	medium to coarse	rounded	60-100'	40-60'	slow	deciduous	Shade tree, difficult to transplant.
Quercus coccinea Scarlet Oak*	entire state	medium	rounded	60-80'	30-40'	medium	deciduous	Scarlet fall color. Shade.
Quercus falcata Southern Red Oak*	entire state	coarse	rounded	70-80'	30-60'	medium	deciduous	Sheds old leaves in early spring. Shade tree.
Quercus hemisphaerica Laurel Oak Or Darlington Oak*	7, 8	medium	rounded	60-80'	40-60'	medium	semi-ever-green	Drought tolerant street tree.
Quercus laurifolia Swamp Laurel Oak*	7, 8	medium	rounded	60-80'	30-40'	medium	semi-ever-green	Shade. Sheds leaves earlier than Laurel Oak.
Quercus lyrata Overcup Oak*	entire state	medium	rounded	40-60'	30-40'	medium	deciduous	Transplants well, adapts to poor sites. Strong oval form when young.
Quercus nigra Water Oak*	entire state	medium	rounded	50-80'	40-50'	medium to fast	deciduous	Shade tree.
Quercus nuttallii Nuttall Oak	entire state	medium	rounded	40-60'	30-40'	fast	deciduous	Shade tree with red fall color. Transplants well.
Quercus palustris Pin Oak	6b, 7	medium	pyramidal	50-60'	25-40'	medium	deciduous	Shade or specimen tree.
Quercus phellos Willow Oak*	entire state	fine	rounded	40-60'	30-60'	medium	deciduous	Yellow fall color, shade tree.
Quercus shumardii Shumard Oak*	entire state	medium	pyramidal to rounded	60-80'	50-60'	medium	deciduous	Russet red fall color. Good street tree.
Quercus virginiana Live Oak*	7, 8	medium	rounded, spreading	40-80'	60-100'	medium	broad-leaved evergreen	Shade or specimen tree.
Taxodium distichum Bald Cypress*	entire state	fine	pyramidal	50-70'	20-30'	medium	deciduous	Specimen with small bright green leaves.

Table 2. Medium And large trees 40 feet and larger

Botanical Name / Common Name	GEORGIA'S HARDY ZONE	TEXTURE	FORM	HEIGHT	SPREAD	GROWTH RATE	CLASS	REMARKS
Tsuga canadensis Canadian Hemlock*	6b, 7	fine to medium	pyramidal	40-70'	25-35'	medium	evergreen conifer	Specimen, screening. Best in filtered shade in piedmont.
Ulmus parvifolia True Chinese Elm or Lacebark Elm	entire state	fine to medium	vase shaped	40-60'	30-40'	fast	deciduous	Quick shade. Often con-fused with Siberian elm.
Ulmus parvifolia 'Elmer I' Athena Lacebark Elm	entire state	fine	rounded	30-40'	40-55'	fast	deciduous	Specimen or shade for urban areas. Drought tolerant and pest free.
Ulmus parvifolia 'Elmer II' Allee Lacebark Elm	entire state	fine	vase shaped	50-75'	40-60'	fast	deciduous	Specimen or shade for urban areas. Drought tolerant and pest free.
Zelkova serrata 'Green Vase' Green Vase Japanese Zelkova	entire state	fine to me-dium	vase shaped	60-80'	40-60'	fast	deciduous	Shade or street tree with fast growth.
Zelkova serrata 'Village Green' Village Green Japanese Zelkova	entire state	fine to me-dium	vase shaped	40-60'	30-40'	fast	deciduous	Excellent street tree with rusty red fall color.

* Denotes native Georgia plant throughout this table.

bottom of the container. Selection of an individual tree can be as important as selection of the tree species. Trees which are healthy, well formed, and are free of pests and injury have a better chance of becoming established in the landscape and performing as expected.

Tree Selection—Tables 1 and 2 list trees which can be planted in Georgia. The plant hardiness zones in Georgia begin at 6b in North Georgia and end at 8b on the Florida border according to the USDA Plant Hardiness Zone Map. The average mature height is listed above the average mature canopy spread. Individual trees may be found which exceed these ranges. Information in the drought tolerance, texture, form, growth rate, group and exposure columns are presented to provide a quick overview and to assist in making preliminary choices. Additional information may be necessary to select the right tree for your site.

How Trees Grow

It is essential to understand how trees relate to their environment in order to understand how trees grow and their proper care. Trees are complex and highly adaptable organisms. Knowing how trees function can help insure tree establishment and continued health.

Tree shoots grow upward into the air and light. The leaves collect carbon dioxide gas from the air and capture light. Roots grow downward and outward into the soil and survive where there is moisture and oxygen. Roots absorb water and essential elements, while providing structural support. Hormones govern the timing of shoot and root growth produced by the tree.

Leaves and Buds—Green leaves contain chlorophyll which captures light. The chlorophyll pigment holds light long enough for other molecules to absorb the light energy. Captured light energy activates carbon dioxide molecules gathered from the air. Carbon atoms in each molecule string together like beads and release oxygen. Strings of carbon form sugar, starch and other compounds used by the tree. Sugar and starch are carbohydrates used by trees as food.

Leaves produce carbohydrates throughout the year. Carbohydrates move from the leaves through the twigs, branches and the trunk to the roots. Carbohydrates move down the tree in the inner bark. Along the way, living cells use carbohydrates as food. Unused food is stored as starch. Food for next spring's growth is stored in the last few annual rings of wood close to the branch tip. A branch or twig must make and store all its own food. Food does not move from the roots to the tree top.

Leaves develop in the growing tip of the shoot, called the bud. Hardened bud scales cover and protect each growing tip (meristem) and the developing leaves inside. Each bud consists of protective covers, new stem pieces, new leaves and the growing meristem. Buds form in the axil (stem connection) of every leaf. Buds produce hormone signals to keep the top of the tree in communication with the root system.

Each bud has developing leaves inside. In the axil of each developing leaf is a developing bud. Within every bud you will find new leaves with new buds at their base (Figure 2). This redundancy (nesting one bud inside another) allows trees to survive stressful environmental conditions and twig dieback.

Buds failing to expand into shoots may be overgrown by bark. Every year bark-overgrown buds grow only enough to keep pace with tree expansion. These buds are called latent buds. Latent buds occur around each branch base since every branch originated from a single bud. Branch pruning can release latent buds near the pruning wound.

Trees maintain thousands of growing points (meristems). Few have the opportunity to expand and grow since they are carefully controlled. The terminal bud on a branch controls and repress the buds below. The most active buds control the tree. Removing a dominant terminal bud releases the lower controlled buds to develop into shoots.

Cambium—The cambium is a layer of cells that rapidly divides and produces wood to the inside and inner bark

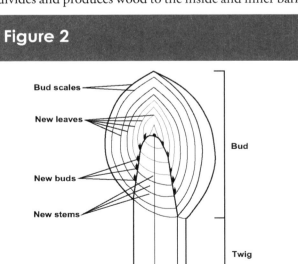

Figure 2

Bud scales

New leaves

New buds

New stems

Bud

Twig

Figure 2. Tree buds contain growing points that produce leaves and shoots. Buds can be grown over with bark and released to grow at a later time.

to the outside. The cambium layer is responsible for expanding twig, branch and trunk diameters every year.

Trunk and Branches—Tree bark insulates the living tree against the environment. Old corky bark consists of wax and oil-impregnated walls of collapsed cells. Bark is the waterproof shell that keeps water in. Specialized air channels called lenticels occur in the bark and allow trees to receive oxygen. The living cells of the inner bark transport carbohydrates.

Trees have massive branches to support and elevate the leaves. The tree stem includes a main trunk, branches and twigs (branches being large twigs and twigs being small branches). All increase annually in diameter.

The stem is the transport system for moving materials from the roots to the leaves and back down again. Water and essential elements move up the trunk and out the branches to the leaves.

These materials move in the outermost annual rings of wood. Carbohydrates move in the inner bark from the leaves down the branch and trunk to the roots.

Tree stems must grow every year. Each spring and summer a new sheath of living wood covers last year's stems. This year's tree is last year's tree refurbished with new tissue. If a tree cannot grow every year, the tree declines and dies.

A cross-section of a tree trunk has many layers (Figure 4). The outside of the tree is dead bark which protects the tree. The inner bark is alive and carries food from the top of the tree, to the base and into the roots. Food and other materials move downward in the inner bark and then toward the tree center through ray cells.

The layer between the bark and wood is the cambium. The cambium produces wood cells to the inside and bark cells to the outside. Active cambium growth increases stem diameter. The cambium is a major reaction site that responds to injury.

Inside the trunk are annual rings of wood. The large pores in each annual ring carry water up to the leaves. These large pore cells are dead. Some fiber cells surrounding the large pores are living. Ray cells distribute food to the living cells. The outer four to 20 annual rings are usually alive and light colored. These young annual rings are called sapwood. The trunk center of large trees is usually darker colored and is dead heartwood. Many chemicals are produced or deposited in the heartwood. Heartwood in some trees is resistant to decay.

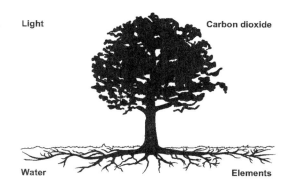

Figure 3

Light   Carbon dioxide

Water   Elements

Figure 3. Tree functions. Absorbing roots collect water and elements, move them up the trunk and branches. The leaves lose water, collect carbon dioxide and light, and manufacture food.

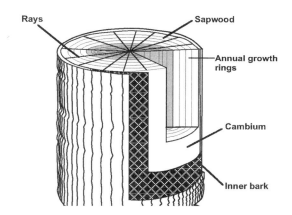

Figure 4

Rays   Sapwood

Annual growth rings

Cambium

Inner bark

Figure 4. Tree stem structure showing the position of major parts.

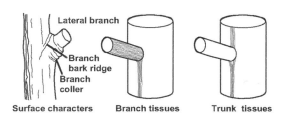

Figure 5

Lateral branch

Branch bark ridge

Branch collar

Surface characters   Branch tissues   Trunk tissues

Figure 5. Branches join trunks in a specific way. Trunk tissues overlay the branch base forming the branch collar. The trunk and branch bark push against each other forming a branch bark ridge.

Branches attach to the tree trunk by interlocking branch and trunk tissues (Figure 5). A woody branch collar produced by the trunk holds the branch base. The branch collar is trunk tissue. Branch tissues move down along the branch and down the trunk.

Branch and trunk tissues expand against each other in the branch crotch. Bark pushes up into a ridge called the branch bark ridge. The bark ridge may become unable to push outward when the bark becomes surrounded by woody trunk and branch tissue. This overgrown bark is referred to as "included bark." Branches with included bark are weak and likely to split apart as they age.

Leaves on every branch or twig must produce enough food to feed its branch or twig. Food does not move from roots or other branches to supply a starving branch. Branches unable to support themselves are sealed-off. Branches which lose their connection to water and elements cannot produce food. Only productive branches survive.

Roots—Roots are active and aggressive. Roots develop and survive where there is plenty of oxygen and moisture. Root tips grow and colonize soil areas. Roots grow most of the year and stop only when soil temperatures are cold.

Most tree roots extend out two to five canopy diameters from the main stem. Most active roots occur in the top 12 inches of soil. The heavier the soil, the closer to the surface the active roots will be. Roots grow near the surface because they need oxygen. Roots cannot grow well below heavy hard pans or in flooded or compacted soils.

Roots occur as perennial woody roots and annual absorbing roots. Woody roots become thicker every year with wood and bark just like branches. Woody support roots grow downward and outward to anchor the tree in place. Massive numbers of annual absorbing roots develop from woody roots.

Annual absorbing roots form shallow, horizontal fans growing in the soil. Absorbing roots take-up water and essential elements. Thousands of annual root fans develop and then die during the growing season. Root fans occur where there is plenty of water and essential elements; as one would find beneath decomposing litter on the soil surface.

Tree roots try to avoid each other when young. As roots grow larger, they may be forced together and form a graft union. Root grafting can cause problems under special circumstances. For example, all elms on a street may be connected by root grafts. These grafts can conduct diseases from one tree to the next.

Roots absorb and transport water and essential elements. Elements move slowly downward with water from one soil particle to another. Tree root fans lie horizontally near the soil surface to capture water and dissolved elements as they move past.

Leaves control water absorption in the root. Water in leaves evaporates (transpires) through leaf pores (stomates). Evaporating water molecules pull up the water molecules behind them. Leaf transpiration pulls long strings of water from the soil into the root, up the stem and into the leaf. During droughts, leaves cannot produce enough force to remove water from dry soils and can be damaged.

Tree Defenses—Trees defend themselves by sealing off problems from the rest of the tree. Trees form barrier walls. These barriers form biologically and physically sealed compartments. Decay, disease, insect and mechanical damage are walled-in to seal damaged portions away from the rest of the tree. These compartments keep pests and decay from spreading. Trees sense and monitor damage, sealing it off quickly. Walls develop anytime damage occurs or when the inside of the tree is exposed to the outside environment.

Communications—Tree branches must communicate with roots and trunks to insure proper growth and defense. Trees do not have a nervous system like animals but trees have a chemical communication system. Buds produce auxin, a communication substance. This substance passes from the shoot tip and leaves to the root tips through living cells. Root tips produce a second

Table 3. Selected tree response to night lighting	
SENSITIVE	**TOLERANT**
Basswood	Ash
Birch	Gingko
Catalpa	Hickory
Dogwood	Holly
Elm	Magnolia
Goldenrain tree	Oak
Hemlock	Pine
Maple	Sweetgum
Redbud	Walnut
Silverbell	
Sycamore	
Yellow poplar	
Zelkova	

communication substance (cytokinin). Cytokinins enter the water stream and move up to the top of the tree.

The ratio of these and other growth hormones changes with both the seasonal activity and the health of the shoots and roots. Each cell in the tree continually reads the combined messages. Responses are dictated by the tree's genetic make-up. Shoots always know what the roots are doing and vice-versa. Synthetic communication substances, such as herbicides, disrupt normal growth.

Growth—Not all parts of the tree grow at the same time. Trees grow in episodes. Roots grow for awhile and then the shoots grow. In a large oak, for example, one branch may grow for a couple of weeks and then another branch will begin to grow.

Growth requires plenty of water. Growing points inside buds create new cells but water must be available to expand these cells. Without water for hydraulic expansion, tissues remain small. Extension growth requires the right chemical signal followed by cell replication and enough water to enlarge the cells.

Tree growth rates change from day to day, day to night and throughout the season. The better the water conditions, the more growth. Water is more available at night and most tree elongation occurs at this time.

Climate and Site Influences

Climate influences tree growth principally through light, temperature, moisture and wind. Seasonal climate changes determine which trees are adapted and thrive. Climate also influences optimum spacing, irrigation, fertilization, pruning and pest control. Shade and street trees must be able to endure and respond to climatic changes over their life spans.

Light—The sunny days of summer may have light intensities four times that needed for maximum photosynthesis. Beneath tree leaves light intensity falls off quickly. Light levels within the canopy may be so low leaves cannot make enough food to survive. Other plants may not be able to grow beneath a tree because of dense shade.

Many trees are sensitive to photo period which is the day length that regulates vegetative and reproductive activity. Photo period can influence leaf shape, leaf drop, fall color and the onset of dormancy. The long days and short nights of spring and summer promote vegetative growth. The short days of late summer and fall slows elongation and initiates overwintering activities. Day

length and the length of the growing season influence the overall rate of plant growth.

The length of the dark period between light periods actually regulates photo period response. Night length shortened by street lights promotes continuous growth. Sensitive trees begin growth early in spring or fail to halt growth in fall. Extended growth results in cold injury to new growth. Table 3 lists light sensitive trees. High-pressure sodium, metal halide and incandescent street lamps are most likely to cause growth problems. Mercury vapor lamps affect trees the least.

Temperature—Temperature is an uncontrollable environmental factor. It is closely related to the amount of sunlight present since visible light energy is absorbed and radiated as heat. Sunlight not reflected or used in the leaf is felt as sensible heat. This heat can be dissipated by water evaporation from leaves or soil.

Low temperatures can kill or injure trees. Critical periods are when spring and fall frosts occur, the coldest portion of mid-winter, and cold periods immediately following winter warming periods. Cold injury causes death of leaf and flower buds, sun scald of tree trunks, dieback of immature stems and frost damage to tender shoots and flowers.

Rapid temperature changes can be especially devastating. Sudden temperature drops in late fall before trees harden-off can result in severe injury. Warmer temperatures in late winter or early spring allow trees to lose hardiness. Extreme temperature drops under these conditions can result in tree death.

Tree species and cultivars exhibit individual hardiness. Growing hardy selections minimizes injury from low temperatures. To enhance fall shoot maturation, reduce water and fertilization of trees sensitive to fall cold injury in late summer and early fall. Once cold weather begins moist soils insure adequate tree water supplies and improve soil heat absorption. Vigorous trees with large food reserves withstand cold temperatures better.

Tree dormancy prevents vegetative and flower bud growth during winter. The dormant resting condition is the key to winter survival because it prevents growth during periods of warm winter weather. During winter, dormancy chemicals are slowly broken down. Serious injury may occur after dormancy inhibitors are gone and warm temperatures initiate growth. Rapidly dropping temperatures can then kill active buds and tissues. Little can be done to prevent this injury. Trees which lose their dormancy inhibitors after only a month or two of cold weather are repeatedly injured by cold.

Cold temperatures are not the only climatic extreme which causes tree injury. High temperatures can cause injury by desiccation (drying out), when transpiration greatly exceeds moisture absorption. As the water content in leaves decreases, stomates close, leaves wilt, transpiration drops and leaf temperatures increase due to reduced evaporative cooling. High night temperatures increase respiration rates and food consumption. Trees under constant high temperatures may exhibit little growth.

Moisture—Natural rainfall usually provides adequate moisture for new and established trees. Periodic droughts can be devastating. Weeks without moisture create problems for trees, especially those with small soil moisture reservoirs (i.e. limited root zone). Many landscaped areas have restricted moisture supplies. Buildings and paving can increase transpiration and reduce moisture in root zones.

Low soil moisture causes leaves to wilt and young shoots to droop. When low moisture persists, leaf margins and tips begin to brown. Browning spreads between the veins and continues until the leaves are completely dead or drop off. Irrigate before permanent injury occurs to the foliage to keep trees healthy.

Soils—The soil supplies trees with water and essential elements. Soils frequently are responsible for the poor performance of many shade and street trees. Site development and building construction compact soils. Adding soil fill around existing trees prevent oxygen and water movement to the roots.

Soil is a complex physical, chemical and biological system. Soils are biologically alive with a wide range of organisms including bacteria and fungi. Beneficial organisms such as mycorrhizae live together with tree roots. This beneficial symbiotic relationship aids the tree in water and nutrient uptake. Nematodes, on the other hand, are parasitic round worms which are detrimental to tree roots.

Soil pore size determines air movement and root growth. Most soil particles are held together as aggregates. Aggregate formation produces large pores which aid in the infiltration and movement of water and the exchange of air. The water and essential element holding capacity of individual soil particles still functions within each aggregate. Soil aggregates are fragile and easily compressed or destroyed. Excessive traffic or construction, especially when wet, readily destroys aggregates reducing water and air movement- compaction.

Soil depth and texture determine the moisture and essential element reservoir while influencing rooting depth. Usually the deeper the soil, the greater the water and essential element supplies. Distinctly different soil layers can interrupt air and water penetration. Subsoil layers with high clay contents cause water to accumulate forming a perched water table. Poor aeration from water collecting above the clay layer restricts root growth. Sand or gravel layers can also interrupt the normal penetration of roots and water.

Soil Elements—Elements in the soil are available to trees in the soil solution. Only a small portion of essential elements in a soil are available for tree uptake at any one time. Essential elements are absorbed by roots, held by the soil, or leached deeper into the soil. As existing elements become depleted, more elements move into the soil solution. Clay particles attract positively charged ions, like potassium, calcium and magnesium, to their negative charged surface. These ions, when released from the clay particles, move into the soil solution and are taken up by trees or move deeper in the soil.

Negatively charged ions, like nitrates, phosphates and sulfates, are held near organic particles with positive charges. These ions are quickly taken up or leached from the soil. Negatively charged ions may combine

Figure 6

Figure 6. A frost pocket can result when cold (heavier) air flows down slopes and forces warmer air to rise.

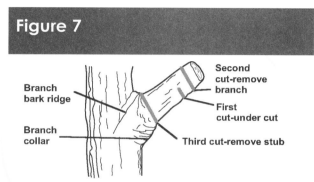

Figure 7

Branch bark ridge

Branch collar

Second cut-remove branch

First cut-under cut

Third cut-remove stub

Figure 7. Remove branches correctly using the three cut technique.

with other elements, precipitate and become insoluble (such as phosphorous). Nitrogen compounds can be quickly changed into inert atmospheric nitrogen by soil microorganisms.

pH—Soil reaction, expressed as pH, refers to the acidity or alkalinity of a soil. Soil pH influences tree growth by affecting solubility of essential elements and the activity of microorganisms. Soils with high pH, above 7.8, are highly alkaline and have little iron or manganese available. Under highly acidic conditions (low pH), manganese and aluminum may reach toxic levels. Microbial activity in soils, especially nitrogen fixing bacteria, decreases as soil pH decreases below 5.5. Most trees grow in the pH range of 5.5 to 6.5. Acid-tolerant trees grow in soils as low as pH 4.0.

Figure 8

Figure 8. Tree topping is not recommended. To lower a tree crown, use the drop-crotch method. Always remove top branches back to larger lateral branches.

Pruning

Pruning determines the future shape, structural design and continued health of a tree. Correct pruning prolongs tree health and reduces future maintenance. Improper pruning may be life- threatening. Flush-cut pruning is severely damaging. These cuts straight down a trunk cause permanent damage.

A proper pruning cut for larger branches has three steps. First, cut on the underside of the branch 8 to 12 inches out from the trunk. Undercut about one-third of the way through the branch. Undercutting prevents bark tearing. Next, move out 2 to 3 inches beyond the first cut and cut down. The second cut completely severs the branch and it falls away without tearing the bark. The last cut removes the remaining stub. Make the cut outside the branch bark ridge and outside the branch collar. Trunk tissue at the bark ridge and in the branch collar remains uninjured. The branch collar tissue forms a natural protective barrier against pests and decay. A proper pruning cut leaves the smallest possible wound to callus over.

Prune twigs, small branches, or large limbs to the outside of the branch collar and bark ridge. Flush cutting a branch even with the stem is unprofessional and abusive to trees. Flush cutting damages the trunk, inhibits natural barrier formation and provides entry to pest or decay organisms. Proper pruning leaves the branch collar intact with no branch stub. Stubs prevent wound closure and can result in decay entering directly into the main stem of the tree. The remaining branch collar may initially bulge out from the trunk but loses its prominence in a few years.

Developing Form—Use proper branch pruning to remove unwanted branches and to develop a good tree form. Never stub back or shear trees. Cutting off the ends of the outside branches leads to dead stubs that become a liability. Dormant buds grow forming new branches around the wounds. These new branches grow rapidly and densely. Repeated and progressively heavier pruning will be required over time. Pests and decay will enter the stubbed branch ends. Large numbers of weak branches will continue to grow.

Developing form removes unwanted branches. Prune branches at the trunk or where attached to a major branch. Pruning wounds are left inside the tree crown, rather than at branch tips, reducing the number of sprouts because of shading. Follow the three-cut pruning technique. Proper branch pruning pays off in good tree health.

Topping—Topping is cutting the main trunk or major branches off below the top of the tree. Improper crown removal results in decay, heavy resprouting, loss of aesthetic form and severely reduced life span. Tree top removal should be done only to save storm damaged trees. Never top a healthy tree, but consider total tree removal before topping. Tree crowns are lowered when growing into overhead wires, buildings or other trees. Drop-crotch crown removal (cutting back to existing large branches) is the best way to lower a tree's crown (Figure 7). Always follow proper pruning techniques by cutting parallel with the branch bark ridge of the branch to remain. Do not leave a flat, horizontal cut.

Wound Paints—Wound paints are not required for treatment of fresh wounds. They do not hasten callus development nor protect from decay; they are cosmetic only. Paints can increase pest problems and prevent wound closure. Tree wound paints are used only to disguise bright pruning cuts.

Girdling—Girdling wounds can kill trees. Girdling prevents trees from transporting food and raw materials. Damage from cuts, lawn mowing, weed removal with a weed eater, or pressure from ties or chains on trunks and branches can damage the inner bark and cambium. Girdling wounds can be caused by tight guy wires, tree wrap fasteners, wire and string. Pressure between the restricting device or wire and the expanding wood will crush the cambium. Immediate removal of restricting items may save your tree.

Fertilization

Proper fertilization encourages rapid development and continued health of trees. Fertilization may improve plant vigor, make trees less susceptible to pests and may help overcome decline. But it can increase susceptibility to diseases such as fire blight. Young trees develop more rapidly when fertilized while mature trees need little fertilization as long as they exhibit good leaf color and reasonable growth.

Tree fertilization needs are difficult to determine based upon growth or off-colored foliage. Essential element deficiency symptoms are also caused by girdling roots, compacted soils, water-logged sites, air pollution, root diseases, nematodes and salt injury. Accurately diag-

Table 4. Essential elements for tree growth			
SOURCE AND ELEMENT	**SYMBOL**	**FORM AVAILABLE TO TREES**	**RATIO NEEDED**
AIR AND WATER			
Carbon	C	CO_2	60,000,000
Hydrogen	H	H_2O	35,000,000
Oxygen	O	O_2	30,000,000
SOIL			
MACRO-ELEMENTS			
Nitrogen	N	Nitrate $\quad$ NO_3^-	1,000,000
		Ammonium $\quad$ NH_4^+	
		Urea $\quad$ $CO(NH_2)_2$	
Potassium	K	Potassium $\quad$ K^+	250,000
Calcium	Ca	Calcium $\quad$ Ca^{++}	125,000
Magnesium	Mg	Magnesium $\quad$ Mg^{++}	80,000
Phosphorus	P	Phosphate $\quad$ $H_2PO_4^-$	60,000
Sulfur	S	Sulfate $\quad$ SO_4^-	30,000
MICRO-ELEMENTS			
Chlorine	Cl	Chloride $\quad$ Cl^-	3,000
Iron	Fe	Iron $\quad$ Fe^{+++}	2,000
Boron	B	Borate $\quad$ $H_4BO_3^-$	2,000
Manganese	Mn	Manganese $\quad$ Mn^{++}	1,000
Zinc	Zn	Zinc $\quad$ Zn^{++}	300
Copper	Cu	Copper $\quad$ Cu^{++}	100
Molybdenum	Mo	Molybdate $\quad$ MoO_4^+	1

nosing the cause of leaf yellowing and poor growth is necessary for proper treatment. It is critical to use soil testing and tissue analysis to determine essential element shortages.

Soils influence the quantity and availability of the essential elements. Trees growing in sandy soils require frequent applications of small quantities of fertilizer. Trees growing in clay soils require less frequent applications but at higher levels. Trees with wide root systems reach more water and elements. Compacted soils restrict root activity and physically impede growth and absorption of essential elements.

Essential Elements—Sixteen elements are essential for tree growth (Table 4). Three essential elements are taken from air and water and the remaining 13 elements are usually derived from the soil. Plants use macro-elements in large amounts and micro-elements in much smaller quantities. Required elements must be available in suitable quantities for proper growth. Any one element will reduce growth when deficient.

Editors note: Some scientists list 18 essential elements or nutrients to include nickel (Ni) and cobalt (Co).

Trees absorb elements as inorganic ions. Organically bound elements are broken down into inorganic forms before tree uptake (except urea). Trees absorb ions selectively. Trees will rapidly absorb and accumulate potassium, nitrate and ammonium ions. Other ions such as sulfate, calcium and magnesium are absorbed less readily. Plants do not distinguish between ions originating from organic or inorganic fertilizers.

Determining Element Levels—Essential element deficiencies and toxicities are diagnosed by soil and/or plant tissue analysis. Soils are tested for pH and the level of the available elements. Interpretation of test results will specify the lime required to adjust the soil pH and the elements required. A good analysis depends upon a representative soil sample. Combine samples from ten locations around each large tree. Samples delivered to your County Extension office will be sent to the UGA soils lab, and the interpretation will be included in the results.

Availability and Function—Nitrogen is commonly deficient in many soils. Nitrogen is available as organic, nitrate and ammoniacal fertilizers. Nitrate fertilizers are readily soluble and available for tree absorption. Ammoniacal nitrogen is held by soil particles. Plant roots readily absorb ammonium ions. Soil microorganisms convert ammonium ions to nitrate in two to three weeks under warm soil temperatures. Other microorganisms can convert nitrate ions to inert atmospheric nitrogen in cool, moist soils.

Organic fertilizers are not immediately available for tree use. To become available to the tree, organic nitrogen must be converted to an ionic form. Urea nitrogen is an exception. Urea is an organic water soluble, tree-available fertilizer. Urea also converts to ammoniacal nitrogen and then to nitrate nitrogen. Trees will absorb urea, ammoniacal nitrogen and nitrate nitrogen.

Slow release fertilizers that break down over 6 to 12 months or longer provide essential elements to shade and street trees. Organic fertilizers release slowly because they must first be converted to ionic forms. Inorganic fertilizers with low solubilities also release slowly. They can be coated with plastic or sulfur, pressed into tablets or enclosed in bags to release slowly. Slow release products provide nitrogen all season long.

Phosphorus occurs in quantities adequate for trees in most non-acidic soils. Trees tend to grow well even when soil phosphorus levels are low. However, newly-planted trees in phosphorus deficient soils may respond to phosphorus applications. As plants increase in size and age, the response usually decreases. Apply phosphorus to trees when soil analysis confirms low levels.

Soils usually contain adequate potassium for tree growth. Potassium deficiencies may occur in acid, sandy and low-organic soils. Top soil removal from construction may leave areas which are deficient in potassium. Where a shortage exists, apply potassium by broadcasting granular fertilizer on the soil surface and incorporating it into the soil.

Complete fertilizers and dolomitic limestone are widely recommended to improve growth, appearance and health of trees. A complete fertilizer contains nitrogen, phosphorus and potassium. Woody plants rarely respond to additions of phosphorus and potassium. Applications of a complete fertilizer when not needed wastes money and essential elements. Depend on a soil test to determine elemental shortages.

Acid soils are usually low in calcium. Highly acidic soils may contain toxic concentrations of manganese, aluminum, copper or other elements. Dolomitic limestone raises soil pH and contains calcium and magnesium. Broadcast applications of dolomitic limestone and incorporate it into the soil.

Iron chlorosis is a common micro element deficiency. The yellowing between leaf veins (interveinal chlorosis) is more pronounced in wet springs or on poorly-drained soils. Iron deficiency occurs when iron in the soil is tied up and unavailable to trees. Iron compounds can be applied to the soil surface, injected into the soil, sprayed on the leaves, or injected in trunks. Iron chelates improve the availability of iron in soils.

Application Methods—Broadcasting fertilizer over the soil surface is the easiest and most cost effective way to fertilize trees. However, specific needs may require other application techniques. Other methods involve soil injection or foliage sprays.

Surface applications are effective for nitrogen and chelated micro-elements. High fertilization rates when used under trees may injure turfgrass and ground covers. Repeat applications of lower rates will lessen the potential for injury to trees and ground covers. Water in surface applications immediately to prevent injury to existing ground covers and lawns.

Trees use essential elements during rapid spring growth and throughout the growing season. Two to three light applications of nitrogen, mid-spring to mid-summer, encourage food production. Large existing trees are usually fertilized once every year or two depending upon soil test results. Slow-release fertilizers cost more but reduce the labor needed for reapplication. Do not over-apply fertilizer or tree decline and death can result. Also, always provide plenty of water with fertilizers.

Irrigation

The amount of water a tree requires is strongly influenced by climate, soils and the tree itself. Trees wilt when water is not available. Their leaves become dull or faded gray-green. Mature leaves turn yellow-brown and fall from the tree while young shoots and leaves die.

Water young trees when they first begin to wilt at mid-

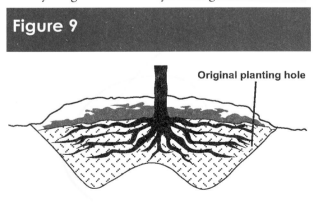

Figure 9

Original planting hole

Figure 9. Basin irrigation is used to water young trees.

day. Water mature trees after two to four weeks without normal rainfall. Apply enough water to recharge the root zone. Water deeply and infrequently. Check the depth of water penetration by pushing a thin steel rod into the soil. The probe pushes easily through wet soil but with difficulty through dry soil. Probe the soil two to three days after watering to determine depth of penetration. Water to 12 or 18 inches deep. Allow the tree to absorb the water before the next irrigation.

Use water basins for newly-established trees. Make the basin larger than the initial hole diameter with a 3 to 5-inch rim. Fill the basin with water. Remove the basin after the first year. Apply water to larger trees with sprinklers or soakers. Do not apply water faster than the soil can absorb it. Mulching will slow water movement on slopes and improve penetration.

Drip irrigation needs to wet only half the soil in the root zone of mature plantings. Water is applied slowly for long periods. Once the root zone is recharged most trees and soils need no further water for several weeks.

Mature landscape trees are frequently not watered. Healthy trees on good sites can withstand short drought conditions without showing undesirable effects. However, trees with inadequate root systems cannot survive without supplemental irrigation. Under saline conditions irrigate frequently to avoid salt injury. Irrigation during droughts in the growing and dormant season will help maintain tree health.

Tree Installation and Establishment

Give your tree a healthy start in a new site with good planting procedures. Proper planting will help reduce plant stress and hasten plant establishment.

Trees are available from nurseries as small bare-root trees, balled and burlapped trees or containerized trees. Each form has its special advantages and disadvantages.

Planting—Bare-root trees are small and easy to transplant. There is no soil on the root system requiring they be protected from drying out. Bare-root trees are best planted during the dormant season. Planting late fall or early winter allows for new root development and establishment well before the buds begin to grow. If bare root trees cannot be planted immediately they should be stored at 34 to 40°F. with moist packing surrounding the roots. If methods of controlling the temperature are not available, they may be healed in or planted temporarily in a trench until the permanent site becomes available.

Bare root trees should be planted at their original depth

in a hole two times the diameter of the root system. Place the tree in the hole on a small compacted mound within the planting hole. The roots should be spread and distributed over the mound. The hole is backfilled with the original soil and watered in to eliminate air pockets and ensure the roots are in good contact with moist soil. Create a basin with a 3 to 5 inch berm, and add 3 inches of organic mulch. Use the basin to water as needed.

Containerized trees have their roots in a potting mix normally of pine bark and sand. Most containerized trees have been growing in the container for a year or more. However, there are some that have been recently planted in the container and have not yet developed a root system throughout the container mix. These trees are best treated as bare-root plants since they do not have an extensive root system.

Container grown trees can be planted throughout the year. When planted in the hot summer months they do require special care to become established. Plants in containers may have circling roots which means roots in the bottom of the container have grown around the sides until they form a circle. These roots are usually cut during the planting procedure. When densely matted roots form on the outside of the rootball they should be sliced vertically on four sides and twice across the bottom to initiate new root development.

Most of our urban trees in large sizes are available as balled and burlapped (B & B) trees. These trees are dug with the rootballs intact and wrapped in burlap and often set in wire baskets. A large portion of the absorbing roots, up to 95%, may have been lost in the digging operation. Surviving transplant shock resulting from this root loss requires proper planting and good care during the next few years. When natural burlap is used it is biodegradable once in the ground and readily rots away. Treated burlap or synthetic burlap must be removed or slits cut in the sides to allow the roots to escape into the landscape soil. All rope or twine tied around the trunk must be removed to avoid girdling the stem. Trees in wire baskets should have the upper 12 to 18 inches of wire removed to avoid injury to enlarged roots ten or fifteen years after planting.

The planting hole is dug once the trees have been selected and are on site. The planting hole should be two times wider than the diameter of the rootball. In compacted soils the hole should be 3 to 5 times the width of the rootball and an area out to ten times the diameter of the rootball can be worked to a depth of 8 to 12 inches for future root growth. To aid the natural extension of the root system, the hole may be wider at the top than the bottom and the walls may be sloped outward since root growth will be shallow and horizontal.

The planting hole should never be deeper than the rootball. A firm base is necessary to set large or small rootballs on to prevent further settling. Plants that settle result in being too deep and are frequently stressed, the roots will drown and suffocate. Holes that have been dug too deeply should be refilled to the proper depth and the bottom firmed to prevent settling when planting takes place. In areas with heavy clay soil the tree may be planted slightly shallower than it existed before. The rootball may be 2 to 3 inches higher than the original grade. The exposed rootball with burlap removed should be covered with 2 to 3 inches of mulch to prevent rapid drying.

The rootballs of trees must be handled carefully. Lift the tree by the rootball and not the stem. Place the tree gently in the planting hole. Be sure the top of the rootball will be no deeper than the soil grade. It is best to use the soil that came out of the hole as backfill. Research has shown that soil amendments (bark and peatmoss) do not aid in the tree establishment and growth. Work the backfill soil around the rootball so there are no air pockets. Firm the soil so the tree is vertical and adequately supported.

For B & B trees, fold back or remove the burlap from the upper 12 to 18 inches of the ball. On large trees with wire baskets now is the proper time to remove the wire with backfill soil supporting the base of the tree and holding it in place. Complete the backfilling operation, water thoroughly to settle the soil around the root system, and add the remaining soil to bring any settlement areas or cracks to grade level.

The remaining soil then is used to create a 3 to 5 inch berm on the outside of the planting hole. The basin will be effective in providing irrigation water during the establishment period. Be prepared to open the basin and let out excess water during periods of high rainfall particularly on heavy soils which become saturated. Lastly, remove all tags and labels so that they will not girdle the trunk or branches of the tree as they increase in diameter.

Staking and Guying—Staking newly planted trees is not always necessary nor beneficial to the tree. Staked trees have been shown to produce less trunk diameter, develop smaller root systems and are more likely to break or become damaged after the stakes are removed. Staked trees are liable to become injured or girdled from the wires or supports.

Staking can be broken down into three main functions. Staking can be used to protect trees from lawn mowers, automobiles or other hazards. Staking can be used to anchor trees until the root system becomes established and is able to hold the entire tree and canopy upright. Lastly, stakes can be used to support trees with a heavy top whose trunks are not yet strong enough to support the top when in foliage.

Protection staking uses 3 to 4 stakes usually 30 to 36 inches long which are placed on the outside of the basin and planting hole. These stakes are to ward off lawn mowers and other equipment which might damage the tree trunk.

On windy sites or sandy soils when trees are tall, staking may be required to hold a plant upright until it can support itself through an expanding root system. Staking should reduce the movement of the rootball and allow roots to become established in the backfill and surrounding soil.

Trees with heavy tops and thin trunks frequently cannot stand upright without staking. Stakes are attached at the point on the trunk where the canopy will remain upright with support. One, two or three stakes may be required depending upon the size of trees being supported.

If a single stake can provide enough support it should be placed on the upwind side of the tree. The stake should be placed several inches back from the trunk and smooth, broad elastic material should be used to tie the tree to the stake in a figure eight loop. Usually the tree is attached to the stake at several points along the trunk.

When two support stakes are used, a single, flexible tie attaches the tops of each stake to the trunk. The stake should be tall enough to keep the tree upright without bending above the tie point. Three stakes provide even greater protection against wind, lawnmowers and vandals.

Trees greater than 3 inches in diameter are often supported with guy wires. The trees are guyed with 3 or 4 wires that are anchored into the ground. Anchoring devices include stakes, land anchors and deadmen. Guy wires should be passed through a section of hose to protect the tree trunk and branches. The wires and hose are passed around the tree at crotches and the wires are twisted to tie them off. Guy wires must not be tied tightly around the tree trunk because this will girdle the trunk.

All stakes and guying systems should be checked frequently to be sure they are not injuring the trees. Support stakes or guy wires are generally removed after one growing season.

Care After Planting—The larger the transplanted tree, the greater the transplant shock. A major portion of the root system is lost in digging and the tree must re-establish roots to support the existing top. The tree's ability to obtain water and essential elements is greatly reduced.

Fertilization is usually not recommended at the time of planting. Excess fertilizer can be damaging by reducing root elongation and increasing top growth. With a limited root system to take up moisture and a larger top requiring more water the tree can suffer severe stress.

Pruning following planting is generally not recommended. There is no advantage to removing one quarter to one third of the canopy to balance the root and shoot systems. Trees will establish most rapidly if pruning is minimized at planting. However, broken or damaged limbs should be removed as well as major faults in the tree structure. The central leader should never be removed.

The area around the tree should be mulched with 3 to 4 inches of organic material. The mulch will help reduce competition from weeds, conserve soil moisture, and moderate soil temperature extremes. The mulch should be pulled back from the stem to allow sufficient drying and prevent trunk or crown rot. Black plastic should not be placed under the mulch since it restricts water movement and oxygen exchange.

Proper watering is necessary for the survival of newly planted trees. When rainfall is less than 1 inch per week, trees should be watered every 5 to 7 days. A slow soaking of their root system is preferred. For clay soils, one must be careful not to overwater and drown the root system.

Young Tree Care

Young trees in the landscape, those that are less than three to five years, require special care to insure establishment and rapid growth. Early care develops an adequate root system and a strong supportive branch structure. The time and expense invested to train a young tree is much less than treating problems as the tree matures.

Young trees may require staking, wrapping and corrective pruning. Proper mulching and control of competition can speed growth. Trees require plenty of available water and essential elements for good growth. Young trees need protection from lawn mowers, weed eaters, vandals and construction activities.

Pruning—Young urban trees require proper pruning. Early pruning improves overall structure and corrects branch defects. Early pruning eliminates problems which become severe in middle and old age. Pruning urban trees develops and maintains a central dominant leader. Double or co-dominant leaders (forks) are removed. Select the main leader early and maintain strong side branches. These side branches become the major branches supporting the weight of the tree later in life. Remove dead, diseased and broken branches. Prune out deformed and crossing branches.

Main side branches should occur singly on street and shade trees. However, trees such as ash and maple frequently have major branches occurring in pairs across the main stem. Select and maintain major side branches spaced 24 to 36 inches apart on alternating sides of the stem. Select branches with wide angles of attachment, 60 to 90 degrees between the trunk and branch. Remove all watersprouts and basal suckers.

Proper pruning for branch removal leaves the smallest possible diameter wound. Small wounds close more rapidly than larger ones. Wound paints are not necessary and are ineffective in reducing wood decay or promoting wound closure. Do not overprune or remove excessive foliage. Always leave ⅔ of the tree height in living crown. Having more leaves, in conjunction with adequate soil moisture and the right amount of nutrients, results in increased tree growth and better health and vigor.

Staking—Most established young trees can stand alone against the wind and need not be staked. Young trees with excessively long new shoots or those exposed to windy sites may require staking to remain upright.

Stake young trees susceptible to blow-over(wind throw). Anchorage staking holds the roots or root ball stationary until roots grow to support the tree. Support staking aids trees whose trunks are not strong enough to stand upright or fail to return to the upright position due to poor form. Support the top about six inches above the lowest level at which the trunk can be held and remain upright. This allows top flexibility while providing support. Support the trunk so it can flex without rubbing against the stakes or ties. Ties must not damage tender bark or girdle the expanding trunk. Support staking holds the tree upright until it can stand alone.

Wrapping—Newly-planted thin bark trees such as red maple or ornamental cherries may benefit from wrap-

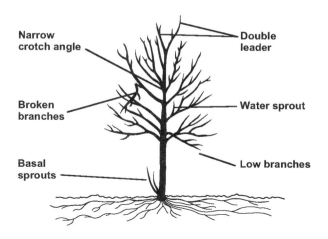

Figure 10

Figure 10. Prune to a central leader. Remove all broken, weak and interfering branches. Prune to maintain the typical form. Remove problem branches as indicated above.

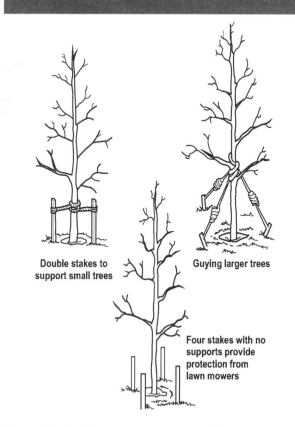

Figure 11

Figure 11. Staking young trees provides support and protection while allowing for top movement to improve stem strength.

ping at planting. Thin barked trees planted on high heat sites are very susceptible to sun scald.

Sun scald occurs when the cambium of thin barked trees heats up during sunny fall or winter days. Cold temperatures following warm periods often kill cambium cells in the trunk. Long vertical scars run down the trunk from the lower most branch to the soil line. Injury usually occurs on the southwest side of the trunk. Thin barked maples and cherries, four to five inches in diameter, may require wrapping in fall to prevent sun scald.

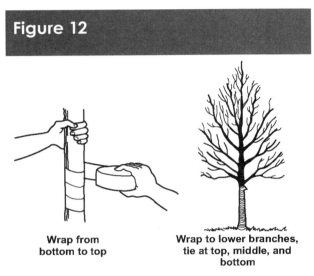

Figure 12

Wrap from bottom to top

Wrap to lower branches, tie at top, middle, and bottom

Figure 12. Trunks of newly planted trees may need to be wrapped. Start wrapping at the tree base working up to the lower most branches. Secure the wrap snugly.

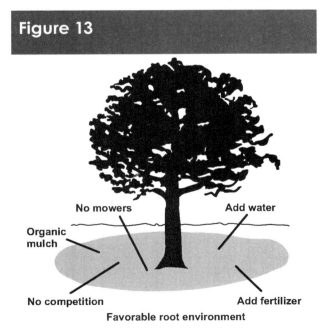

Figure 13

No mowers   Add water

Organic mulch

No competition   Add fertilizer

Favorable root environment

Figure 13. Improve tree growth by mulching beneath the canopy, watering, fertilizing and eliminating competition.

Tree wraps also protect young trees from girdling from rodent chewing such as pine voles. Start at the base of the trunk and wrap up to the lowermost limbs. Overlap each layer one-half inch. Wrap in the fall and leave it on throughout the winter and early spring to prevent sun scald. Tree wrap is temporary and no longer needed once trees develop corky bark.

Fertilization—Young trees growing in maintained lawns that are regularly fertilized do not require additional fertilization. Trees exhibiting poor growth require a soil test to determine if essential elements are in short supply. When nitrogen is required, fertilize trees by applying three pounds of nitrogen per 1000 square feet of root area per year. Make two or three applications, one each in April, June and August at one pound of nitrogen/1000 square feet. Water the site after each fertilizer application. Fertilizing trees with a turfgrass or groundcover understory requires these multiple applications at light rates to avoid injury to the turf.

Mulching—Mulches aid in the establishment and growth of young trees. They conserve moisture by reducing evaporation from the soil surface. Mulches reduce erosion and water run-off. Mulches reduce competition and compaction. Mulches can effectively reduce summer soil temperatures to create a more favorable root environment. However, organic mulches such as sawdust can tie up nitrogen in the soil during their decomposition. These organic mulches eventually break down and add essential elements to the soil. Do not mulch wet sites because mulching keeps soils excessively wet.

To improve growth, mulch young trees to the edge of the canopy. Use three to four inches of an organic mulch. Mulches eliminate the need for groundcovers and turfgrasses beneath young trees thereby reducing competition for essential elements and moisture. Mulching prevents serious injuries to young tree trunks because there is no need to mow or use weed-eaters beneath trees.

Appropriate mulches include pine bark, pine straw and wood chips. Organic mulches more effectively insulate the soil than inorganic or rock mulches. Pull all mulches back from the trunk four to six inches to reduce disease entry into the trunk. Rodents may live and burrow in loose mulches. Be alert for these pests.

Improving Growth—You can improve young tree growth by following a few basic cultural practices. First, eliminate competition from turfgrasses and groundcovers underneath young trees. Second, mulch beneath the canopy out beyond the edge of the foliage to improve the root zone environment. Third, surface apply fertilizers directly to the mulched area. Fourth, water during periods of drought. Fifth, keep lawn mowers and weed-eaters away from tree trunks. These suggestions will improve growth, even on slow growing trees.

Mature Tree Care

Fertilization—Existing urban trees rarely need to be fertilized when growing in maintained turfgrass. These trees absorb and use fertilizer applied to lawns and shrub beds. However, trees not receiving essential elements from existing landscape sources may require fertilization. Test the soil to determine if low element levels exist. Nitrogen can be in short supply. Apply nitrogen at the rate of three pounds per 1000 square feet of area per year. Make three applications during the growing season on trees growing in turf or ground covers. Tree root systems extend well beyond the edge of the canopy. Broadcast the fertilizer ½ the canopy radius distance beyond the canopy edge. Do not fertilize stressed trees before leaves are fully expanded in spring.

Surface Roots—Surface tree roots can be an unsightly problem. Roots do not suddenly grow onto the soil surface. Initially, young tree roots grow one to four inches below the surface. Root expansion causes increased diameter and after 20 or 30 years of growth, roots stick up above the soil level. Erosion speeds root exposure. Exposed roots are easily damaged.

Mulching with pine straw, pine bark, aged wood chips or other organic materials can be beneficial. Mulching exposed roots physically protects them while conserving soil moisture and prevents direct sunlight from heating the roots and soil. Exposed roots need protection from pedestrian and vehicle traffic, including mowers.

Three to four inches of mulch under the tree canopy will keep most weeds and grass out. Eradicate the existing grass and apply the mulch. Ideally, mulch at least half or all the way to the edge of the crown. Mulch to cover all the exposed tree roots. Form mulch islands for groups of trees.

Root Control

Root barriers keep roots from growing beneath driveways or sidewalks. Root barriers are becoming more popular for use around curbs and gutters, parking lots, sidewalks and driveways. Root barriers prevent tree roots from colonizing soil and then breaking paving as they increase in size. Place root barriers in the soil at the edge of concrete, asphalt, or brick paving. Barriers can be thick plastic or metal buried vertically in the soil.

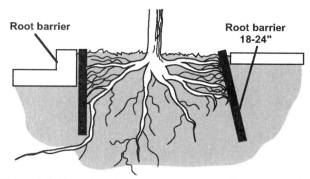

Figure 14

Figure 14. Root barriers prevent unwanted root growth under curbs and sidewalks.

Effective depths depend upon soil texture but usually 18 to 24 inches is required for protection.

Install root barriers by trenching along the area to be protected. Trenching severs the roots growing into the area. The barrier prevents roots from growing back into the protected area. Root barriers can minimize further maintenance expense and liability problems.

Root barriers are used along underground utility corridors and tightly constrained root areas such as around tree islands in parking lots. Seal in-ground tree containers with root barriers to insure the tree stays within the container. Be sure to allow as much space as possible for future root growth. Tree root problems often occur around septic fields and sewer lines.

Tree roots are often blamed for plugging and breaking pipes. Tree roots cannot exert enough pressure to break into a sewer line. Natural settling, age and wear cause lines to crack. Leaking lines encourage roots to grow into the area and penetrate through the crack. As roots increase in size, cracks widen and breaks occur.

A rotary knife can cut roots in sewer lines from inside. Periodic use of specialty root control products will kill new roots moving into the line. Root killing foams can fill the entire line from top to bottom. Foams are effective in keeping tree roots out of the sewer lines. Chronic, long-term problems can be corrected by replacing the line and installing a root barrier. Be aware that severe water pollution can result from the addition of root killing chemicals.

Hollow Trees

Hollow trees are liabilities resulting from earlier tree abuse. Mechanical damage and improper pruning lead to invasion of wood by many organisms. Fungi cause wood decay. Termites, carpenter ants and other insects assist with hollow formation.

A hollow portion of a tree will be the same size as the diameter of the tree when the injury occurred. Decay fungi enter damaged wood but will not move into new wood produced after the injury. The fungi will attack all the wood present at the time of the injury. A tree damaged and invaded when it was six inches in diameter could eventually have a hollow six inches in diameter. If the tree is repeatedly injured, hollows will grow into each newly damaged annual ring.

Do not clean out hollows. Scraping or cutting the inside can break protective barriers. Breaking natural barriers makes the tree susceptible to further decay. Hollows may contain water. Do not drain hollows. If water is present for one or more growing seasons, the tree has already adjusted. Drilling holes or cutting slices for drainage will break protective barriers and allow more decay.

Filling hollows can damage trees. Do not fill hollows with cement, asphalt, gravel or other hard, abrasive material. The strength of a hollow tree comes from the new wood produced around the hollow. Rigid filling leads to tree breakage just above the hollow. Rigid fillings cause internal wounds as trees bend and twist. Remove hollow

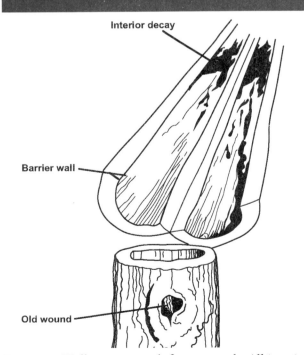

Figure 15

Figure 15. Hollow trees result from wounds. All interior wood present at the time of injury decays leaving only new wood around the outside.

trees which appear weak and likely to fall.

Cover hollow openings to keep out animals and water. A covering of tin or metal window screen filled with plaster can form a waterproof shield. A firm cover allows new tissue (callus) to grow over the opening. The cover prevents the callus from curling or rolling inward which will cause severe structural faults.

Girdling Roots—Tree roots can become tangled, crossed or circled. Major roots crossing or circling the tree base will girdle the trunk and lead to tree decline and death. Cut away girdling roots on older trees. Soil excavation may be necessary to reveal girdling roots at the base of large trees. Flat sided trunks indicate girdling pressure from underground roots. Prune off all roots causing trunk constrictions.

Cabling and Bracing—Cabling and bracing are dangerous and specialized treatments for mature trees. Cables and braces should be prescribed and installed by an expert arborist. Cables and metal rods hold branches together, keep the crown together, and prevent tree splitting. Cabling and bracing is the final attempt to save a tree when it can no longer structurally support itself. Improper installation of cables and braces can lead to branch breakage and tree destruction. Cabling and bracing changes the center of gravity of a tree and the major mechanical stress points. Installing a $2,000 cable job, and then losing the tree to the next storm is not cost effective. Also, attach metal cables in the tree canopy to a surrounding lightning protection system. Seek expert advice for proper cabling, bracing and lightning protection.

Sprouting—Water sprouts on the trunk or in the crown, and suckers around the tree base arise when dormant buds are released. Stress to the tree canopy, trunk or roots by insect, disease, breakage, or water shortage may release latent buds. These buds rapidly grow into long water sprouts or basal suckers.

Prune out water sprouts and suckers or growth control will shift from the crown to these new vigorous branches. Trees under stress will use successful new sprouts to allow shrinkage of their total canopy. The highest branches will be sealed off and die. Excessive sprouting is a sign of serious tree stress. Sprout removal and improving tree vigor are proper treatments.

Wounds—Wounds on trees are serious. The larger the wound, the greater the chance of long-term health problems. Remove loose bark, loose wood and all dead material. Do not aggravate the wound with excessive shaping. Dead tissue will pull away easily. If the tissue is firmly attached, leave it alone. Wounds should not be covered, painted or sealed. Leave wounds open to the atmosphere and allow the tree to seal off the injury. Allow the tree to adjust to the wound without interference. The tree will close the wound.

Tree Wells—Soil fill around existing trees can inhibit gas exchange and soil moisture absorption. Soil aeration is critical. Tree roots must receive adequate oxygen and be able to exchange carbon dioxide. Soil fill also keeps tree trunks moist; this moisture may lead to pest infestations. Trees tolerant of soil fill may be able to survive six inches of well drained soil fill with little harm. Sensitive trees may not survive two inches of fill. The allowable amount of soil fill depends upon soil texture and the reactivity of tree roots to soil fill.

Install a tree well around existing trees where soil filling is planned. A dry well around the trunk will protect the trunk. Aeration spokes of gravel or perforated plastic pipe radiating out from the well to beyond the edge of the dripline allow gas exchange. A properly developed tree well may save existing trees.

Hazardous Trees—Hazardous trees exist on many city streets and home grounds. These trees pose a hazard or a liability risk to property, animals and humans. Hazardous trees may have large dead branches in the crown or along the trunk. Falling wood can damage property and injure people. Hazardous trees with large stress cracks can easily split. Trees with restricted root zones may blow down disrupting above or below ground utilities. Hazardous trees may fall and block streets and highways. Evaluate your trees to detect and correct any hazards that exist. Hazardous trees are usually severely abused trees.

Remove hazardous trees as soon as possible. Removal minimizes liability risks. Do not underestimate the liability problems associated with abused and damaged trees. A limb falling on a car, a child, or house will be damaging. If you have questions about the structural integrity of your trees, seek professional assistance.

Selecting a Tree Care Professional

Trees are a unique and valuable resource. Your tree assets should have the best care available. Select a tree care professional carefully. Tree care professionals include arborists, tree surgeons, ornamental horticulturists, and urban foresters. Check the list below when looking for a good tree care professional.

Professional reputation—Ask for recommendations from neighbors, business associates, professionals caring for trees and the Better Business Bureau.

Customers—Ask for names of customers with similar problems. Call customers and visit sites to determine quality of their work.

Liability insurance—Only hire a firm or individual with liability insurance. The value carried should be great enough to cover all possible damages which might occur.

Workman Compensation Insurance—Hire only firms with this insurance or you maybe liable for workers medical costs if injured.

Review service contracts—Examine contracts for time limits, type of clean-up, and quality guarantees.

Education and experience—Discuss personal experience and areas of specialization. Has the tree professional dealt with problems similar to yours?

Ask for several bids—The lowest bid may not be the best for you and your trees. Research carefully before purchase.

Professionals should not top trees or use metal spikes. Ask for three references and make the follow-up contacts.

Summary—The long term health of your trees, your properties' value, and your liability risks will be affected by your tree care choices. Make financially and biologically sound decisions. Taking proper care of your trees will reward you with healthy attractive shade and street trees.

Acknowledgments—**Material for this chapter was taken from UGA Bulletin 1031, Shade and Street Tree Care by James T. Midcap and Kim D. Coder and from UGA Bulletin 853, Treescape: A Citizen's Guide for Urban Tree Planting by Melvin P. Garber, Kim D. Coder, James T. Midcap and E. Neal Weatherly, Jr.. Appreciation is expressed to the authors for their contributions.**

DISCUSSION QUESTIONS

1. Discuss the values and benefits of trees to communities.

2. List the factors involved in tree selection.

3. Discuss the function of the following tree parts: buds, leaves, roots.

4. What is the purpose of the cambium?

5. What effect does girdling have on tree health and growth?

6. Discuss proper planting procedures for a tree.

7. When is staking a newly planted tree necessary?

8. When are wound paints necessary?

9. Discuss care for a hollow tree.

10. How much fill can be safely piled on the root zone of a tree?

RESOURCES

International Society of Arboriculture provides education, certification and referral of certified arborists. www.isa–arbor.com

Harris, R.W., et. al. *Arboriculture-Integrated Management of Landscape Trees, Shrubs and Vines.* 4th edition. 2003. 592 pages. Prentice Hall.

Environmental Enhancement with Ornamental Plants: Attracting Birds

Mel Garber, Former Extension Horticulturist

Birds can be an important aspect of our backyard environment. In many cases, the quality of our environment is perceived to be directly related to the bird population. The bird population in your yard or neighborhood park can be increased year-round with the proper selection and arrangement of ornamental trees, shrubs and food-producing plants.

To attract and maintain a bird population, a habitat should provide (1) food, (2) cover, (3) nesting areas and (4) water. Ornamental trees and shrubs can supply the necessary cover (shelter) and nesting areas. Many ornamental plants can satisfy more than one habitat requirement. For example, multi-stem plants that form a dense canopy will satisfy the need for a nesting place and also provide cover.

As much as possible, trees and shrubs in your yard should provide birds a year-round food source. The use of native trees and shrubs will help ensure that appro-

priate fruits and berries are available for the local bird population. If the landscape does not supply food during certain periods, you can supplement with commercial bird seed mixes to help keep birds in the vicinity of your yard. Some birds eat a wide variety of seeds while others prefer only one or two types; however, sunflower seeds, proso millet seeds and peanut kernels appeal to the majority of birds.

If they are to become long-term residents, birds require a place of cover or shelter to protect them from inclement weather (sun, heat, wind and rain) and natural predators. This is why birds prefer multi-stem plants that form a dense canopy. The dense canopy also provides an ideal environment for nesting. Since birds require shelter year-round, your yard should have a mix of deciduous and evergreen plants. Evergreen plants include broadleaf evergreens, such as holly, and conifers, such as red cedar. Several references suggest that at least 25 percent of the trees and shrubs should be evergreen.

A source of fresh water is also necessary to maintain your

bird population. The water source should be shallow (no more than 2 to 3 inches deep) and replaced on a regular basis. Running water, such as a shallow fountain, is ideal. The water source should be elevated or in the middle of an open area to minimize predation by cats and other animals. On the next page is a list of recommended trees and shrubs to enhance the bird population. Attributes that must be considered before selecting the trees/shrubs for your yard include: (1) the habitat element provided, (2) fruiting season, (3) deciduous (loses leaves in winter) or evergreen, and (4) size of mature tree (to fit with available space)

To make your landscape more suitable for birds, conduct an inventory of trees and shrubs and develop a table similar to the one above. From this list: a) determine the mix of evergreen and deciduous trees, b) look at the time of fruiting and identify season(s) without a food supply, and c) ensure that adequate cover and nesting habitat is provided. The following two examples describe possible situations in your yard and how to use the table:

• You have very few evergreen trees/shrubs (hence minimal shelter in the winter) but also have only small areas for additional plants. Select plants that are classified as evergreen (E) and are small at maturity. Red cedar, viburnum, pyracantha, Japanese yew, holly and wax myrtle are all relatively small trees.

• You need a food source for the spring but have limited yard area available. An excellent solution is to plant hawthorn, especially mayhaws, which are small multi-stem shrubs that bear fruit in the spring and attract a wide variety of birds.

In most instances, you will find that the addition of a few carefully selected plants can increase the bird population in your yard.

Adapted from University of Georgia Cooperative Extension Circular # 976 revised September 2009.

SOUTHEASTERN TREES & SHRUBS	PROVIDES		FRUITING SEASON	DECIDUOUS OR EVERGREEN	SIZE (SMALL, MEDIUM, LARGE)
	COVER	FOOD			
Beech		X	Fall, winter	D	M
Black cherry	X	X	Summer	D	M
Black gum	X	X	Summer	D	L
Blueberry	X	X	Summer	D	S
Dogwood	X	X	Fall, winter	D	M
Elderberry		X	Summer	D	S
Hawthorn	X	X	Spring	D	M
Holly	X	X	Winter, spring	E	M
Japanese yew	X	X	Summer, fall	E	M
Magnolia	X	X	Summer	E	L
Oaks	X	X	Fall	D	L
Pines		X	Spring, summer, fall	E	L
Pyracantha	X	X	Fall, winter	E	S
Red cedar	X	X	Fall, winter	E	M
Red maple	X		Spring	D	L
River birch	X		Summer, fall	D	M
Sumac		X	Fall, winter	D	M
Sweet gum		X	Summer, fall	D	L
Viburnum	X	X	Winter	E	S
Wax myrtle	X	X	Summer, fall	E	M

NOTES

13
Diagnosing Ornamental Plant Problems

Jean Williams-Woodward

Kris Braman

LEARNING OBJECTIVES

Become familiar with common ornamental plant disorders and their causes.

Be able to recognize insect related injury in common ornamental plants.

Know some common insects and diseases in ornamental plants.

Understand how to prevent or control insect damage on ornamental plants.

TERMS TO KNOW

Blight symptom or disease in which plant parts such as leaves, flowers, and stems are rapidly killed.

Bronze brown discoloration of many small, light, or tan spots caused by spider mite feeding.

Canker localized dead area on woody tissue, often sunken, on a twig, branch, or stem, that can enlarge over time.

Causal agent either a biotic or an abiotic agent that causes a disruption of a plant's normal growth or physical properties.

Chlorotic plant tissues that appear pale green to yellow.

Dieback gradual death of tissues beginning at the tips of branches that can kill part of or entire branches or groups of branches.

Distortion abnormal shape.

Fungicide chemical compound that is toxic to fungi.

Gall an abnormal swelling or growth of plant tissue that is initiated by a pathogen, insect, or mite.

Honeydew the sugary liquid excrement of sucking insects.

Host plant attacked by a pest or pathogen.

Hypha (hyphae) single filament of a fungus.

Leaf scorch leaf browning associated with rapid water loss.

Leaf spot discrete dead area on a leaf.

Lesion wound or delimited diseased area.

Marginal necrosis browning (death) of green tissue around the outer edges of a leaf.

Mildew plant disease in which white mycelium and spores of the causal fungus are visible on the plant surface.

Mosaic pattern of yellow and green tissue intermingled on a leaf; typical of many virus diseases.

Necrosis localized death of tissue, usually characterized by browning and desiccation.

Necrotic showing varying degrees of dead areas or spots. Often used to describe brown spots left by insects or diseases that kill leaf tissue.

Ooze sticky liquid composed of bacterial cells and the polysaccharides they produce.

Phytoplasma microorganism without a cell wall or organized nucleus that causes yellows diseases in plants.

Pustule small swelling similar to a blister or pimple.

Pycnidium (pycnidia) asexual rounded or flask shaped fruiting structure.

Resistance ability to overcome or to slow the development of disease.

Ringspot circular area of chlorosis or necrosis with a green, healthy appearing center.

Rot tissue breakdown.

Sanitation process of removing and destroying old or dead plants or plant parts from a site.

Saprophytic describes any organism that lives on dead or decaying matter.

Sclerotium (pl. Sclerotia) hard, usually darkened and rounded mass of dormant fungal thread like material with hard cell walls that permits survival in adverse environments.

Scorch (leaf) dead (necrotic) tissues on the margins of leaves or between veins that result in browning and shriveling of foliage.

Introduction

Diagnosing plant problems is often a difficult task since there can be many different causes for a given symptom. Soil nutrition and texture, weather conditions, lighting, and many other environmental and cultural conditions influence a plant's overall health. Insect damage can sometimes be confused with plant diseases caused by microorganisms or other factors.

It is difficult to construct a foolproof key for diagnosing plant problems. Even with specialized laboratory equipment, it is often impossible to determine the exact cause of a plant's decline. The following tables provide a key to some common problems of landscape plants. This key was originally constructed for homeowners to help with diagnosing common problems on landscape ornamentals and turf. This key is not comprehensive and other resources will be needed to supplement the diagnostic process.

The key should help homeowners and Master Gardeners ask the right questions to determine the cause of a problem, or at least, narrow down the possibilities. For example, since both dry weather and excess fertilizer can cause marginal leaf burn it would be important to consider recent weather conditions and fertilizer application. Or, since wilt can result from both dry and waterlogged soil, one must consider both rainfall and how well the soil drains.

It is also necessary to examine damaged plant tissues correctly in order to reach a reliable diagnosis. For example, a plant specimen should be examined in the early stages of deterioration to make an accurate disease diagnosis. Once it has decayed, secondary organisms invade the tissue and evidence of the disease organism is obscured.

In many cases you will not be able to determine what caused the problem. Sometimes it is enough to know that you are dealing with a fungal leaf spot, for example, or aphids. Many county Extension offices are equipped with digital diagnostic equipment to assist in problem diagnosis either using office resources or with the aid of a specialist. Frequently the services of a diagnostic laboratory will be necessary. Samples can be submitted to the University of Georgia Homeowner IPM Clinic for diagnosis. If you can narrow down the possibilities and mention these when you send the sample to the laboratory, you will save the diagnostician a lot of time.

IPM Strategies

The control recommendations listed in the diagnostic key are abbreviated to conserve space. A more complete explanation of each control is provided in the following paragraphs. Many of the cultural controls such as plant rotation, removing old plant debris, and planting in well drained soil are repeated many times throughout the key. These are good general integrated pest management practices. Pesticide use is listed only for problems where a pesticide is registered for legal use in Georgia. Pesticide recommendations can be found in the *Georgia Pest Management Handbook* and label directions should always be followed.

Rotate—Plant flowering annuals or biennials in a different area every two to three years. This practice helps reduce the amount of disease organisms that survive in the soil or on plant debris. It is best to grow plants of a different family in the area where plants were removed or rotated due to disease. Some diseases will infect several plant species within the same family. Obviously, rotation of woody plants and perennials is not practical.

Remove Plant Debris—Remove diseased or insect infested plant debris during the season and destroy it by burning or burying. Composting old, diseased plant debris should kill any surviving disease organisms; however, if the compost is not turned properly to keep the pile hot, these organisms will survive and may infect other plants. Burying old plant debris deeply works for some disease organisms that do not survive in the soil, but burning is best for stem and root diseases, and for insect infested woody plant stems and branches.

Remove Affected Plants—It is important to remove plants immediately to prevent the spread of a disease or insect pest to unaffected plants. This often is recommended for viral and soilborne diseases, and some scale pests.

Use Registered Pesticides—Use a pesticide (fungicide, bactericide, insecticide, miticide, or herbicide) according to the label. The name of the plant must be listed on the label for legal use. Remember that most fungicides act as a physical barrier to infection and must be applied on a regular basis to be effective. They should be applied more often during rainy periods both because rain washes the chemical off and because most disease organisms are more active during rainy weather.

Resistant Varieties—Use plants that have been developed for resistance to certain pests. Remember, a resistant variety is not resistant to all pests but only to those for which it has been developed. Also one must understand that a variety sold as "resistant" is not immune, and can, under certain circumstances, become infected with the disease organism, nematode, or insect to which it is resistant.

Pruning—Cut out affected plant parts to control cankers, stem galls on trees, and insect borers in stems and branches. Disinfect pruning tools with diluted liquid bleach (1 part bleach to 9 parts water) or rubbing alcohol between cuts. Make cuts back to live tissue. Cut back to a node or to the branch collar and do not leave stub cuts. Bury or burn pruned branches if burning is permitted in your area.

Soil Test—Submit a soil sample for analysis. Most soil analysis laboratories will test for pH, major nutrients and magnesium. Soluble salt levels and tests for minor elements are usually considered special tests and must be requested. Remember that lack of nutrient availability is caused by improper pH. Apply lime, sulfur or fertilizer as recommended.

Weed Control—Weed control is important for controlling virus diseases as weeds can harbor carriers of certain virus diseases. Insects can spread viruses to garden plants. Control weeds with mechanical cultivation or registered herbicides.

Insect control—Controlling insects is not only important for controlling damaging pests, but can also be important in controlling plant diseases. Viruses, viroids, mycoplasmas, bacteria and even fungi can be spread by insects.

Mulching—Mulching helps control diseases by reducing plant stress due to moisture fluctuations, and it creates a physical barrier against disease organisms surviving on infected fallen plant litter. Mulch keeps moisture in the soil and prevents leaves and flowers from coming into direct contact with soil disease organisms.

The mulch layer should not be more than 3 to 5 inches thick (3 inches for pine bark nuggets and 5 inches for pine straw) and should not be placed right up against the plants.

Submit Sample for Laboratory Diagnosis—The disease may be difficult to diagnose from symptoms or information alone and more sophisticated techniques, such as microscopy or culturing, are necessary to diagnose the problem. Remember that a good specimen and adequate information are of utmost importance to the diagnostician. It is not worth the mailing cost to send a dead twig, a few shriveled leaves, or a diagnostic form without such critical information as when symptoms were first noticed, how much of the plant is affected, etc. The diagnostician does not have the advantage of being able to see the plant in its own environment, so it is very important to submit good specimens. Your local county extension office can provide you with the forms for submitting a damaged plant specimen or an insect sample to The University of Georgia diagnostic facilities.

Experience is the best teacher. The following tables should be helpful as you gain years of experience as a Master Gardener.

Note: Not all controls listed need to be used for a given pest. Give consideration to all possible controls, then decide which one is most appropriate in terms of economics, environmental impact, effectiveness, and the conditions specific to the particular site.

For example, both fungicides and resistant varieties may be listed in the key for one particular disease. If resistant varieties are used, however, fungicides should not be necessary. An appropriate recommendation may be to treat with a fungicide for the current season and use resistant varieties the following season.

Table 1. General problems common to many annual and perennial flowers

SYMPTOMS	POSSIBLE CAUSES	CONTROLS & COMMENTS
Wilting and overall poor vigor		
Plants wilt; flowers may drop and leaves may turn yellow.	**Dry soil.** **Water logged soil.** **Transplant shock**	**If dry, supply water; if too wet, improve drainage and water less frequently. Do not transplant in the heat of the day; water regularly after transplanting.**
Leaves may turn yellow; plant wilts and dies.	**Root, stem or crown rot (fungal or bacterial disease).** **Weather injury (drought).** **Mechanical injury.** **Improper fertilization.** **Natural gas injury.**	**Remove affected plants and surrounding soil. Do not overwater. Use of registered fungicide as soil drench when replanting may be beneficial.**

Table 1. General problems common to many annual and perennial flowers

SYMPTOMS	POSSIBLE CAUSES	CONTROLS & COMMENTS
Seedlings wilt. Stems turn brown and soft and may be constricted at the soil line.	Damping off (fungal disease)	Remove affected plants and surrounding soil. Do not overwater. Use of registered fungicide as soil drench when replanting may be beneficial.

Leaf and flower problems

SYMPTOMS	POSSIBLE CAUSES	CONTROLS & COMMENTS
Plant fails to flower; foliage looks healthy.	Wrong season Cool weather or insufficient light. Too much nitrogen (causes excessive vegetative growth) Immature plants Undersized bulbs	Some plants have specific day-length requirements for flowering. Do not plant sunloving plants in shade. Do not overfertilize (nitrogen stimulates foliage, not flower production). Biennials and perennials often do not flower the first year.
Too many small flowers.	Plants not debudded.	Some flowers, e.g. chrysanthemums need to have some buds removed to produce large flowers.
Tall, "leggy" plant; stem and foliage pale or yellow.	Insufficient light	Pay attention to light requirements of plants.
General yellowing of leaves; yellowing may be interveinal; plant may be stunted; no wilting.	Nutrient deficiency Viral disease	Soil test. Submit sample for laboratory diagnosis.
Grayish white powdery growth on leaves or stems and flowers.	Powdery mildew (fungal disease)	Usually affects new growth. Remove heavily infested leaves and stems. Use resistant varieties if available. Rake up and remove fallen leaves to reduce fungal organisms. Use registered fungicide at the first sign of disease.
Blister containing orange, yellow or brown powdery substance on underside of leaves. Yellow areas opposite pustules seen on upper surface.	Rust (fungal disease)	Remove infected plants. At very lease remove infected leaves. Avoid long durations of leaf wetness; do not water late in the day. Use resistant varieties. Rake and remove fallen leaves. Use registered fungicide to prevent infection.
Random brown, dead spots on leaves.	Fungal, bacterial, or leaf nematode disease (any of several)	Submit sample for laboratory diagnosis. Avoid long durations of leaf wetness; do not water late in the day. Remove affected leaves. Fungicides are ineffective on bacterial or leaf nematode diseases.
Uniform brown, dead areas on margins of leaves.	Scorch due to hot, dry weather Salt injury due to improper fertilization Chemical injury Poor planting site or improper planting depth Mechanical injury	Supply water. Fertilize properly. Do not allow fertilizers or winter salt to accumulate in the soil. Replant in soil with proper aeration and at proper depth. Avoid mechanical damage to plant during maintenance procedures.

Table 1. General problems common to many annual and perennial flowers

SYMPTOMS	POSSIBLE CAUSES	CONTROLS & COMMENTS
Flowers wilt or fail to open; grayish mold appears on flowers in damp weather.	Gray mold (fungal disease)	Pick off and destroy affected flowers. Avoid durations of plant wetness. Remove spent blooms and yellowing leaves.
Yellow and green mottle or mosaic pattern on the leaves.	Viral disease (any of several)	Plants are seldom killed. Affected plants may need to be removed. Do not use tools that have touched diseased plants without cleaning first. Control insects that vector diseases.
Black sooty growth on leaves and stems.	Sooty mold	Control honeydew secreting insects (aphids, soft scales, mealybugs, and some leafhoppers).
Tiny white flecks on white interveinal areas on leaves.	Ozone injury Spider mites	For spider mites use a registered pesticide.
Clusters of insects on stems or underside of leaves; leaf may be curled or distorted.	Aphids or scale insects.	Remove heavily infested leaves and stems. Use registered insecticide.
Leaves chewed or completely eaten.	Various chewing insects. Slugs and sowbugs.	Identify insect and use appropriate insecticide. Use commercial slug bait.
Light colored tunnels or blotches in leaves.	Leafminers	Use registered insecticide.
Tiny white winged insects on undersides of leaves.	Whiteflies	Use yellow sticky cards to monitor infestation. Use registered insecticide as directed on the label.
White cottony masses on leaves or stems.	Mealybugs	Use registered insecticide.
Damage to bark		
Large areas of split bark; no decay evident.	Freeze cracks	Frost can split trunks (especially on thin barked trees; maples, elms); use tree wrap to protect bark from sun to prevent temperature extremes.
Reduced vigor; scraped or split bark.	Sunscald Mechanical injury Lightning injury can cause a tree to explode along the path of the lightning to the ground.	Thin barked trees, especially young ones split when exposed to intense sunlight. Use treewrap or block sun with boards on bright winter days. Avoid heavy fertilization in late summer or fall. Remove grass around trunk and replace with mulch to avoid mowing and trimming close to tree.
Large areas of split bark; decay evident in wood.	Secondary decay of any of the wound described above. Fungal or bacterial canker.	No adequate controls. Water and fertilize tree at appropriate times. Severely affected trees may become a hazard and need to be removed.

Table 1. General problems common to many annual and perennial flowers

SYMPTOMS	POSSIBLE CAUSES	CONTROLS & COMMENTS
Sour smelling sap oozes from cracks in bark.	Bacterial wetwood (slime or alcohol flux); bacterial canker	No control. Prevent damage and stress to a tree's roots and stem; provide adequate water, especially during spring and summer months

DAMAGE TO TWIGS, BRANCHES AND ROOTS

SYMPTOMS	POSSIBLE CAUSES	CONTROLS & COMMENTS
Many small twigs broken off.	Squirrel damage Wind breakage Twig girdler or twig pruner (insect)	Usually not serious. Squirrels prune twigs for nest building and often prune more than they need. If insect pests are suspected, rake up and destroy fallen twigs.
Large corky swellings on roots; plants are weak	Crown gall (bacterial disease)	Fertilize and water properly. Reduce plant stress. Remove affected plants and surrounding soil. Replant with disease free plants.
Large corky galls at base of tree	Crown gall (bacterial disease)	Some galls can be pruned out but it is best consult an arborist. Trees may live for years in spite of galls.
Galls on branches	Fungal disease (any of several). Various insects. Secondary grown gall (bacterial disease).	Submit sample for laboratory diagnosis; prune out galled branches. Most insect induced galls are harmless.
Proliferation of branches at specific points on the plant, forming a witches' broom effect.	Insect injury Fungal, viral or mycoplasma damage	Submit sample for laboratory diagnosis.
Large dead areas in center of trunk or large scaffold limbs.	Heart rot (fungal disease)	Prune out diseased limbs where possible. Fertilize and water properly. Reduce stress. If severely affected, especially on the main trunk, the tree may be a hazard and should be removed.
Sunken cankers (lesions) on trunk or branches. Plant may wilt or have poor growth.	Primary fungal disease Sometimes bacterial disease.	Submit sample for diagnosis. Prune out affected branches at least 6 inches below canker into healthy wood. Disinfect pruning shears between each cut, especially for bacterial cankers
Oozing sap on trunk	Natural causes. Environmental stress Mechanical injury Insect borers Fungal or bacterial diseases	Some trees naturally ooze sap. Drought or waterlogging can cause trees to ooze excessively. Prevent lawnmower or string trimmer injury Use insecticide if insects have been identified as the problem. There are no controls for fungal or bacterial diseases affecting this part of the tree.
Large gathering of caterpillars on tree trunk	Spring cankerworm	Handpick and destroy. Use registered insecticide.

Table 1. General problems common to many annual and perennial flowers

SYMPTOMS	POSSIBLE CAUSES	CONTROLS & COMMENTS
Silk webs containing caterpillars in crotches of tree.	Eastern tent caterpillar	Use registered insecticide; spray surrounding foliage on branch and penetrate web with spray
Tiny wax or pearl covered knobs or bumps tightly attached to leaves, twigs or branches	Various scale insects	Submit sample for diagnosis. Use dormant oil during late winter. Apply registered insecticide when young scales are in the crawler stage.
Brown, gray, green, or yellow crusty leaf like growths on trunks or branches.	Lichens	Lichens are the result of a symbiotic relationship between algae and fungi. They do not harm the plant. Their presence is often due to thinning of the crown and poor vigor of the tree.
Dense, bunchy growth on lower limbs; growth is gray colored; leaves are narrow.	Ball moss	Tufts can increase in size and suppress twig and bud growth. Heavily weighted branches can snap. Remove all the tufts you can reach. Seal them in plastic, and throw them away
Gray growth which hangs down from limbs.	Spanish moss	No control suggested. Seldom becomes dense enough to cause damage

LEAF PROBLEMS

SYMPTOMS	POSSIBLE CAUSES	CONTROLS & COMMENTS
Grayish white powdery growth on leaves; leaves may be distorted	Powdery mildew (fungal disease)	Improve air circulation around plant by selectively pruning branches or increase plant spacing. Use resistant varieties. Use fungicide at first sign of disease.
Black sooty growth on leaves and/or stems	Sooty mold (fungus grows on honey dew substance secreted by aphids and other insects.)	Identify insect pests. Remove heavily infested leaves and stems. Control with insecticide.
Uniform brown dead areas on leaf margins	Leaf scorch caused by insufficient transport of water to the leaves. Cold injury Chemical injury Salt injury	Water deeply during dry periods. Scorch is usually caused by hot dry weather, but root rots and other root damage can also be involved. Chemical injury to trees and shrubs is common on home lawns where herbicides are used too close to root zones. In regions where salty water is used to irrigate, deep watering is recommended to leach salts out of root zone; do not use chemically softened water on plants.
Interveinal yellowing of leaves; no wilting	Yellowing caused by nutrient deficiency or imbalance. Water logged soil, resulting in poor transport of nutrients to leaves.	Treat leaves with spray of chelated iron. Improve drainage.

Table 1. General problems common to many annual and perennial flowers

SYMPTOMS	POSSIBLE CAUSES	CONTROLS & COMMENTS
Blister containing yellow, orange or black powdery substance on leaves; mostly on underside	Rust (fungal disease)	Avoid long durations of leaf wetness; avoid late day overhead irrigation. Remove infected leaves. Rake and remove fallen plant leaves. Use registered fungicide to protect new growth.
Browning on tips of conifers	Ozone injury	No controls
General browning of needles or leaves	Drought Salt injury Gas leak Root feeding nematodes Water logged soil Transplant shock Girdling roots Plant is root bound and root ball center stays dry. Dog urine injury	Water deeply during drought. Do not use de-icing salt near trees and shrubs. Flush soil with water. Check soil around roots for gray, crumbly appearance and foul smell indicative of gas leak. Submit sample for nematode analysis. Improve drainage. Water regularly after transplanting. Be sure main roots are not wrapped around trunk. Cut root ball several places before transplanting. Flush away dog urine with fresh water whenever possible.
Yellow and green mottle or mosaic pattern on leaves; leaves may be distorted	Viral disease	No controls; removal of plant may be necessary if virus is easily spread.
Random brown leaf spots seen on bottom side of leaf	Fungal or bacterial disease (any of several)	See section on specific disease or submit sample for laboratory diagnosis.
Uniform leafspots; spots on one side of the leaf	Chemical injury	Avoid using some products under hot, dry conditions. See pesticide label.
Leaves completely chewed or eaten	Various caterpillars, sawflies, leaf beetles, etc.	Use registered insecticide while insects are small and before damage is extensive.
Silk webs containing caterpillars covering cluster of leaves at tips of branches	Fall webworm	Remove and destroy webs. Use registered insecticide; spray surrounding foliage on branch and penetrate web with spray.
Young leaves puckered, curled or distorted; clear sticky substance on leaves; clusters of small insects on undersides of leaves	Aphids	Spray with strong stream of water or use a registered insecticide.
Leaves off color with tiny white or yellow spots; may appear dirty because of fine webbing and dust that collects on leaves	Spider mites	Use registered pesticide.

Table 1. General problems common to many annual and perennial flowers

SYMPTOMS	POSSIBLE CAUSES	CONTROLS & COMMENTS
Leaf galls (abnormal growth on leaves, stems or other tissues)	Various insects or mites Various fungal diseases	There are no chemical controls for gall insects. Plants are seldom harmed by insect galls. Prune affected leaves or pick off galls for fungal disease control.

DISEASES OF ORNAMENTALS

Introduction

Plant disease is defined as any deviation from normal plant functions. Disease, therefore, can be caused by "**biotic**" or "**abiotic**" agents. However, traditionally plant diseases are caused by biotic agents called **pathogens**, whereas disorders are caused by abiotic agents. Abiotic disorders are those problems not caused by a biological organism and often result from poor site preparation and soil drainage, poor or excessive fertilization or irrigation, or chemical damage such as misapplied pesticides or salt uptake. Diseases on the other hand are biotic, and are the result of biological agents called pathogens, including fungi, bacteria, nematodes, viruses, and phytoplasmas.

This section will describe general ornamental diseases, as well as outline diseases commonly found on woody and herbaceous landscape plants in Georgia. Ornamental plants in the landscape are subject to many diseases. However, in order for a disease to develop, three components are absolutely essential. These include: 1) a susceptible plant (referred to as a "host plant"), 2) a virulent pathogen (one that is capable of causing disease on the host plant), and 3) a favorable environment for disease development. These three components are often referred to as the "disease triangle." Time also is an important component since disease development usually requires a pathogen to be present on its host for a period of time in a conducive environment before infection takes place. For example, for leaf spotting fungi to infect susceptible leaves, water must be present on the leaf surface for several hours. If water is not present for the required time, infection does not take place. See the chapter on **Basic Plant Pathology** for more information on disease development.

When diagnosing plant diseases, act like a detective. Don't limit yourself to looking only at blighted or discolored leaves. Look at the surroundings that the plant is growing in. Ask yourself questions like: Does the soil feel very wet or dry? When did it last rain or when was the last watering? Is the problem affecting the whole plant or just a few leaves? Is the problem affecting both sides of the leaf? Is there a pattern to problem? Does it affect all plants equally or only a few? Answers to questions like these give you clues to the problem and help you formulate disease control recommendations. **In general, abiotic disorders will have very uniform symptoms**. The whole plant will be affected or the entire leaf margin will be discolored. **Diseases typically show random symptoms.** Spots are randomly distributed on the leaf surface or only a few leaves or branches are affected.

This chapter addresses, separately, the effect of host, environment, and pathogen on common disease problems, as well as describes symptoms associated with specific pathogens and gives general control recommendations for commonly seen woody and herbaceous ornamental diseases.

Host Plant

A "happy" plant is a healthy plant. A plant growing under ideal conditions that meet its specific growth requirements is less likely to have a disease (or disorder). Plants that are stressed such as those planted out of its USDA hardiness zone or is planted in the wrong location (too little or too much light or water), as well as injured plants from improper pruning or lawnmowers are more susceptible to diseases because the plant's defenses are weakened and injuries provide a direct entry point for a pathogen into the plant.

A general decline of a plant such as yellowing leaves, thinning foliage, reduced flowering or growth (stunting) may be the result of improper site location or root problems including root rots and nematodes. Often the problem cannot be correctly diagnosed without digging the plant. Sometimes sacrificing one plant may save many, and if the plant is not diseased, it can be replanted.

Some plants also are more susceptible to infection than others. In selecting vegetables, many seed catalogs list whether a particular cultivar is resistant to a disease. Unfortunately with ornamental plants, selection and breeding of cultivars is often based upon flower color, flower size, or other aesthetic qualities rather than disease resistance, but this is changing. For example, there are many crape myrtle and phlox cultivars that are resistant to powdery mildew disease, the primary disease problem on these two hosts. Look for disease resistance information on plant tags and labels when shopping for new plants. Planting a disease resistant plant is the easiest way to avoid or lessen disease problems in the landscape.

Environment

Again, a "happy" plant is a healthy plant. Everything mentioned in the host section can be restated here. In addition, providing plants with proper horticultural needs such as fertilization, water, and pruning will reduce the risk of disease. See specific sections on plant care throughout this book.

Most pathogens require moisture to infect plant tissues. Therefore, anything that reduces the length of time water is present on leaves or roots will reduce pathogen infection. For ornamentals, improving ventilation around plants by selectively pruning or thinning branches of woody ornamentals and increasing plant spacing of herbaceous ornamentals will enable wet plant tissue to dry rapidly. Also, manipulating the environment by watering early in the day so that plants have plenty of time to dry before nightfall reduces the length of time the leaves may be wet and reduces disease.

For root diseases, improving drainage will reduce the risk of developing root rot and nematode damage. Drainage in heavy clay soils can be improved by placing drainage tile under gardens to redirect and remove water or by incorporating pine bark mulch into the soil. The ratio of pine bark to soil should not exceed 25-30% (1 part pine bark to 2-3 parts soil). Other organic amendments such as compost and peat moss also can be used, however, their beneficial effects on improving soil porosity and drainage is short lived and requires incorporation on a yearly basis.

Another observation to be aware of is that plants will often show the same symptom for opposing environmental conditions. For instance, a plant may wilt if it receives too little or too much water. Root rot disease develops when soils are overly wet. The disease collapses the root, so the roots cannot absorb and translocate water through the plant. Therefore, the plant wilts. If you water the wilting plant thinking that it is wilting because it is dry, you would actually be increasing the spread and development of the root rot disease. Be aware of the plant's environment. Don't just treat the symptom, treat the cause for the symptom.

Pathogens

Fungi, bacteria, nematodes, viruses, or phytoplasmas can be pathogens of ornamentals. Many are ubiquitous and are naturally found in soil, vectored by insects or carried on the wind. If environmental conditions favor the pathogen on a susceptible host, disease develops. Other pathogens are introduced via planting of infected plants or re use of contaminated soil.

Fungi

The most common pathogens of ornamentals are fungi. Symptoms caused by fungal infections are leaf spots and blights, petal blights, cankers, vascular wilts, and root and crown rots. Fungal spores (the fungal reproductive unit capable of infecting and causing disease) are disseminated over long and short distances by air movement (wind) and splashing water either from rain or sprinklers.

Fungal leaf spots and blights are favored by leaf wetness and high humidity. A variety of fungi can cause leaf spots including *Alternaria, Septoria*, and *Cercospora*. Some common leaf spot diseases of ornamentals are black spot of rose (caused by *Diplocarpon rosae*) and spot anthracnose on dogwood (caused by *Elsinoe corni*). Typically, fungal leaf spots have a tan to gray center surrounded by a darker reddish, brown or black border. They may be concentrated along the leaf margin and veins. Often the spots will grow together (coalesce), sometimes forming concentric rings of dead, brown tissue. Within the dead tissue, black pimple like fungal fruiting bodies can sometimes be seen. Leaf spots are termed "blights" when the entire leaf or stem is affected. Often infected leaves drop prematurely. Leaf spotting pathogens survive on fallen leaf litter and on dead branches or cankers. Leaf spot diseases rarely kill infected plants, however, they can be aesthetically displeasing.

Powdery mildew is another type of fungal leaf blight. It is probably one of the most troublesome diseases of ornamentals. Plants are rarely killed, but it can cause premature defoliation under high disease pressure. Powdery mildew diseases look the same regardless of host, but the fungi are host specific, meaning that a powdery mildew pathogen on rose is specific to rose and will not infect crape myrtle and vice versa. Leaves develop patches of frosty, white fungal growth primarily on the upper leaf surface and stem. Often the infected tissue is distorted and discolored. Unlike other fungal leaf pathogens, powdery mildew fungi are not favored by wet leaves. Instead symptoms occur under dry conditions in mid to late summer and when humidity is high with warmer daytime and cooler nighttime temperatures.

Rust fungi also cause leaf spots and blights. Pale yellow spots appear on the upper leaf surface while pustules containing rusty, reddish brown powdery spores break through the lower and sometimes the upper leaf surfaces. These spores are easily rubbed off with your fingers or paper. Pustules develop as individual spots or as concentric rings similar to a bulls eye pattern in which an inner pustule is surrounded by an outer ring. This type of ring pattern symptom is especially prominent on geraniums, zinnias, and snapdragons. Rust fungi are host specific. Rust also can be "autoecious" or "heteroecious." Autoecious rusts are those that produce all their spore stages on one host, such as rose, geranium, or snapdragon rusts. Heteroecious rusts are those that produce their spore stages on two different host plants; a primary and an alternate host. For example, cedar apple rust produces leaf spots and pustules on apple and crabapple (the alternate host), but produces hard, gall like structures on cedars (the primary host). In the spring, the cedar galls rupture producing orange, jelly like extensions (similar to tentacles) which release spores that infect apples and crabapples. The spores produced on the apple are then released to re infect cedars during the summer months. These rusts have very complicated life cycles, but are truly very interesting and fascinating pathogens.

Petal blights are primarily caused by the fungus, *Botrytis* spp. The gray, fuzzy fungus often found covering old strawberries is *Botrytis* and is the same fungus that infects leaves, stems, and flowers of numerous ornamentals. This fungus is favored by wet, humid conditions, and under these conditions, the fungus produces an abundant amount of grayish, fuzzy spores that are easily seen and spread by water, wind, and human activity in the garden. Blighted flowers have darkly colored spots that appear water soaked. Eventually, the flowers disintegrate. Other petal blights are common on landscape azaleas and older plantings of camellia. These blights cause the flowers to brown and disintegrate shortly after blooming. Hard, black fungal structures (sclerotia) are produced that can be easily seen embedded in the blighted petals.

Cankers are dead portions of plant stem tissue. When the canker is at the end of a branch or shoot, it is referred to as "dieback." Cankers are brown or blackened areas that become shrunken with time as the healthy adjacent tissue grows around it. Within old cankered tissue, black pimple like fruiting bodies are often seen. Both bacteria and fungi cause cankers. These pathogens enter the stem through wounds made by hail, insects, or mechanical damage from pruning and lawnmowers. As the canker grows, stems are girdled, which causes wilting and death of the tissue above the canker. A common fungal canker is "Bot" canker caused by the fungus, *Botryosphaeria*, that infects numerous hosts, in particular leyland cypress and rhododendron.

Vascular wilts occur when the vascular tissues are infected by fungi and sometimes bacteria. Obvious symptoms of these diseases are wilting because of water stress caused by the pathogen or its by products produced during the disease process which cause blockages in the water conducting vessels of infected plants and death of plant sections. Other foliar symptoms include yellow or scorched leaves and stunting. Sometimes, as with the fungus *Verticillium* spp., wilt pathogens infect the root and move upward to the leaves producing symptoms that appear on only one side of the plant or on one half of a leaf. A lengthwise cut across infected stems shows dark streaks within the vascular tissue. These pathogens are often introduced into gardens from infected plants. Symptom expression is favored by plant stress associated with high temperatures and drought.

Root and crown rots are caused by numerous soil fungi including *Pythium, Phytophthora, Rhizoctonia,* and *Sclerotium*. These fungi have broad host ranges, meaning they are capable of infecting a wide variety of herbaceous and woody ornamentals. Most of these pathogens are favored by cool, wet soil conditions. *Pythium* and *Phytophthora* are classified as "water molds." These pathogens produce a motile spore (zoospore) that can swim in water. The fungi inhabit soil naturally, and under stressful conditions for plant growth such as over watering, over fertilization, and poor soil drainage they infect the feeder roots. Roots are discolored brown or black. Often small feeder roots are sloughed off greatly reducing the plant's ability to uptake water and nutrients. Above ground foliar symptoms are similar to those produced by an unhealthy root system such as yellowing of older leaves, stunting, and general decline of the plant. Often root rot symptoms mimic nutritional deficiencies.

Bacteria

Bacteria are single celled microscopic organisms. Symptoms caused by bacterial pathogens are leaf spots and blights, cankers, and soft rots. Bacteria are disseminated by splashing water, insects, pruning tools, and human activity in gardens. In most cases, bacterial diseases are more serious in hot weather because high temperatures favor bacterial growth. Generally, fungi are most active in cooler weather such as in the spring and fall.

Bacterial leaf spots are not easily distinguished from fungal leaf spots by visual examination. Bacterial infections are characterized as "water soaked" spots. Often brown, dead leaf spots will be surrounded by darker water soaked tissue. Yellow halos sometimes border the spot margin. Spots, tan to black in color, can be irregular in shape along leaf margins or angular and contained within leaf veins. Some of the most common bacterial pathogens are *Xanthomonas campestris* causing leaf spots on zinnia, begonia, oak leaf hydrangea, and geranium, and *Pseudomonas* spp. causing leaf spots on delphinium, poinsettia, and impatiens.

Bacterial cankers can occur on woody landscape plants. The most common bacterial canker is fireblight caused by *Erwinia amylovora*. This disease commonly affects flowering pear, crabapple, quince, cotoneaster, photinia, indian hawthorne, and pyracantha during warmer, wet conditions in the spring. Wetwood or slime flux also is a bacterial disease that is characterized by sweet smelling, sometimes bubbly, ooze from older tree trunks. The disease develops as a result of an internal heart rot. Secondary organisms, including yeasts and bacteria, colonize the internal cavity and their metabolic activity creates gas pressure that is released through a wound or crack in the tree. Sap then flows from the crack, often staining the tree trunk as it runs down the tree over time.

Bacterial soft rot is another common disease on rhizomatous or bulbous herbaceous ornamentals including iris, hosta, and daylily. Soft rot is caused by the bacterium, *Erwinia carotovora*. The bacterium quickly dissolves the rhizome, bulb or corm in warmer, wet conditions. The infected, soft tissues often produce a diagnostic foul, "dead fish" odor.

Nematodes

Nematodes are microscopic, non segmented roundworms. Plant parasitic nematodes usually feed on plant roots, however, some such as the foliar nematode (*Aphelenchoides* spp.) feed on leaf and stem tissue. Symptoms of nematode infestation in the roots are similar to root rots and include stunting, wilting, yellowing of leaves, and nutritional deficiencies. The most easily diagnosed symptom of nematode infestation is galls or knots on the roots caused by the root knot nematode, *Meloidogyne* spp. Another major nematode pathogen of ornamentals, especially boxwoods, is the root lesion nematode, *Pratylenchus*. The feeding of this nematode causes dark brown to black lesions on the secondary roots, often killing the root system. Leaf symptoms of foliar nematode infestations include wedge shaped dead areas bordered by the leaf veins that initially appear reddish or yellowish, but turn brown as the tissue dies. Removal of infected leaves reduces the spread of the nematode within the plant and to adjacent plants.

Nematode control is difficult since infestations often go unnoticed until symptoms are severe. There are no chemical (nematicide or fumigant) control alternatives for landscape garden beds. These products are highly toxic and it is illegal to use the products in residential areas. The best control is to avoid the problem by purchasing healthy, vigorous plants and providing good horticultural conditions that meet the plant's needs. Some plant cultivars are less susceptible to nematodes and should be used if nematodes, particularly root knot nematodes are established in a landscape. Dwarf yaupon and inkberry hollies (*Ilex vomitoria* and *I. glabra*, respectively) can be used as a replacement for the very root knot nematode susceptible boxwood or Japanese holly (*I. crenata*).

Viruses

Viruses are particles of protein and genetic material (RNA and DNA) that are so small that they cannot be seen with ordinary light microscopes. They live and reproduce within living plant cells. Viruses are spread via infected plant material, seed, man, and insect vectors such as aphids, thrips, and leafhoppers. Some viruses have a wide host range, whereas others may only infect one or two hosts. Some of the more common viruses in ornamentals are tobacco mosaic virus (TMV), tomato spotted wilt virus (TSWV), impatiens necrotic spot virus (INSV), and cucumber mosaic virus (CMV). Symptoms of virus infection are easily distinguished from other biotic diseases, but are often confused with abiotic disorders such as herbicide injury or nutrient imbalance. Typical foliar symptoms are mosaic, mottle, or ring spot patterns on the leaf where bright yellow or white areas within the leaf are bordered by darker than normal green areas. Leaf and stem distortions such as cupping and twisting of leaves and thickening of leaf veins also are common symptoms of virus infection that can be confused with 2,4-D or other growth regulating herbicide damage.

Once a plant is infected with a virus, any new plants vegetatively propagated from it will carry the same virus. In addition, a virus infected plant in a garden is the source of inoculum for future spread of the virus by insect vectors. Removal of infected plants and controlling insect pests are the only ways to control the spread of the viral pathogens.

Phytoplasmas

Phytoplasmas are similar to bacteria in shape and structure, but cause virus like symptoms in plants. The most common phytoplasma affecting ornamentals is aster yellows. Aster yellows is vectored by a leafhopper. Symptoms are often dramatic yellowing and proliferation of adventitious leaf and stem buds into a bushy "witches' broom." Flowers also are affected and show the most obvious symptoms, including small flowers and petals that are partially or wholly green. Control of phytoplasmas is the same as for viruses; remove and destroy infected plants as soon as they appear and control insect pests.

Cultural Disease Control

Prevention—The first step in controlling diseases of ornamental plants is to **prevent** the disease from developing. Prevention is the key. Purchase only healthy plants from reputable dealers, practice the good horticultural methods discussed elsewhere in this publication, and avoid environmental conditions that favor disease development. If pathogens are favored by wet leaves and high humidity like bacteria and fungi, reduce the amount of time water is present on leaf surfaces by avoiding overhead sprinkler irrigation and directing water to the base of the plant. Watering in the morning or earlier daylight hours allows plant surfaces to dry quickly and reduces the likelihood of plants having wet leaves in the evening or overnight. Humidity can be reduced by increasing air circulation around plants through increased plant spacing, thinning of overgrown areas, and trellising. Selectively pruning lower branches to allow air circulation within the plant canopy can greatly reduce leaf spot diseases.

Improving soil drainage by installing French drains (tiling) or incorporation of organic material will reduce the risk of developing root and crown rots and nematode problems. Avoid replanting in areas where these diseases have been a problem. Redesigning the garden and replanting these areas with grass may reduce disease and alleviate frustration on the part of the homeowner.

Rotation of plants, such as different flowering annuals, from year to year can reduce the build up of host specific pathogens. Also, use resistant plant varieties where available. Many plants have powdery mildew, rust, and virus resistance bred into them. Fireblight can be reduced by planting resistant crabapple and pear varieties. In addition, control insects and weeds. Insects vector many diseases and weeds can be infected by the same pathogens on ornamentals and serve as a reservoir of inoculum for future infections.

Good care of ornamental plants will prevent many growth difficulties. Remember that perennials (vines, shrubs, and trees) live for many years and their susceptibility to disease is influenced by climatic and environmental conditions, both past and present. Improper management, abuse (from lawnmowers, compaction, or construction injury), and lack of care (water and fertilizer) are the most important factors that contribute to plant decline and disease development. Many problems can be traced back to earlier abuses such as improper site location and preparation, planting too deep, or natural or man made wounds to the stem or roots.

Sanitation

Sanitation is another key component in disease control. Removal and destruction of infected plant material, either infected leaves or whole plants, as soon as it is detected will reduce disease spread. Collection and removal of fallen leaf litter in the fall also reduces disease potential for the following year. Composting of severely infected material is not recommended for the home gardener unless the compost pile is properly cared for and it reaches temperatures in excess of 140°F.

Prune out dead or cankered branches. Make cuts at least 3 to 4 inches below the extent of the canker into healthy tissue for fungal cankers and at least 8 inches below the canker for bacterial cankers like fireblight. Disinfect pruning tools between each cut by dipping the tool in 70% rubbing alcohol or a 1 part household bleach to 9 parts water solution for 10 seconds or spraying liberally with Lysol disinfectant spray. Immediately wash metal tools after use when using bleach as bleach can damage and discolor the tools.

When propagating or dividing plant material, take cuttings from healthy, non infected plants. Cut and remove any diseased or discolored portions. Tubers, corms, rhizomes, and bulbs should be inspected before planting or storage for signs of infection. Rotted and diseased corms and bulbs should be discarded. Rotted sections of rhizomes and tubers can be cut away and wounded areas should be treated with a fungicide dust. Store bulbs, etc. in a cool, dry place.

Always use fresh potting mixes when repotting plants. Never reuse old mixes since they may be contaminated with soil pathogens. Package, soil-less potting mixes cause the least amount of disease problems. Natural soils contain numerous fungi and bacteria that may initiate disease under the right environmental conditions.

Disinfect all old pots, flats, and other supplies with a bleach solution (1 part bleach in 9 parts water) before re use. Change solution every 30 minutes if disinfecting a large number of pots because the chlorine in the bleach volatilizes and the solution loses its effectiveness over time.

Chemical Disease Control

Home gardeners have few alternatives for chemically controlling plant diseases. Prevention and sanitation are the most practical approaches to disease control. Chemicals are not available for control of most bacteria, nematode, virus, and phytoplasma diseases. Fungicides for controlling fungal pathogens are the most widely available chemicals. Copper containing fungicides (copper sulfate or Bordeaux mixture) have some activity against bacterial pathogens. In some cases fungicide application may be worthwhile, but for the home gardener, generally the cost of application exceeds the plant's value. If fungicides or any other pesticide are used, be sure to **read and follow the pesticide label precisely**. Do not apply more chemical than recommended. The "aspirin" approach where "one tablespoon is good, but two is better," does not apply for pesticides. Over application of some chemicals can injure plants or even kill them. Consult your local County Extension Agent for specific chemical disease control recommendations.

Fungicide Classification—Fungicides are classified as either "protectant" or "systemic." Protectant fungicides including Captan, chlorothalonil (Daconil 2787), and mancozeb are applied before infection occurs when conditions are favorable for disease development. These products remain on the leaf surface, they do not penetrate into the leaf tissue, and therefore can be washed off by rain or sprinkler irrigations. These products must be reapplied often, generally every 7 to 10 days. Complete coverage of the plant foliage is essential in protecting the tissue from infection. Systemic fungicides such as triadimefon (FungAway) or myclobutanil (Immunox) are applied before infection occurs when conditions favor disease development or at the first sign of infection. Systemics enter into plant tissue. These products, however, cannot move throughout the entire plant. They are locally systemic, meaning that the fungicide sprayed onto a leaf will move through that leaf, but it is unlikely that it will move into adjacent leaves. Therefore, thorough coverage of the plant material is necessary. Because the fungicides are within leaf tissue, they are not reapplied as often as protectant fungicides, usually every 14 days.

Fungicide Formulations—Fungicide formulations for ornamentals are either sprays or dusts. In general, fungicide sprays are superior to dusts for foliar application and disease control. Sprays provide better coverage, are less likely to drift, and stay on the plant longer. Dusts do give protection, but they are less effective because they don't adhere as well to the plant surface and are more difficult to target accurately. Most fungicides for the home gardener are purchased as prepared mixtures and need no further mixing. Others are concentrated and the user must mix the proper amount of fungicide with water.

Preparing Fungicide Solutions—When preparing a wettable powder for spraying in a compressed air or pump type applicator, first place the required rate of fungicide into a quart jar half filled with water. Make a homogenous slurry. Next pour the slurry into the sprayer tank containing ¾ of the necessary water volume; then top off the tank with the necessary amount of water. Shake tank thoroughly before spraying and agitate it frequently while spraying to keep the fungicide in suspension. Apply to foliage until it drips off; cover all surfaces. Make only enough fungicide solution as you will use because, once mixed, the fungicide cannot be stored. Discard the remainder of the unused fungicide in accordance with the pesticide label recommendations. The entire sprayer should be cleaned after use by triple rinsing. Do not use the same sprayer for fungicides and herbicides. Herbicide residues can remain in the sprayer and can injure plants.

For mixing fungicides for hose end applicators, place the required amount of fungicide and a small amount of water into the reservoir jar of the applicator. Stir until thoroughly mixed. Fill the unit to the desired volume, agitate, and spray according to directions. Keep mixture agitated during spraying. After use, clean and store properly.

For root and crown rot pathogens, fungicides need to be applied to the soil. This can be done using soil drenches or granules or dusts. Dry fungicide formulations (dusts or granules) are incorporated into the soil with a rototiller. Drenches are mixed by adding the required amount of fungicide and water in a bucket. Create a small dike 3 to be 4 inches high around the bed area or just beyond the leaf drop zone (drip line) of the plant and pour the fungicide solution over this area. This dike should help to keep the solution within the desired area. Fungicides to control root rot diseases are often not packaged in small quantities for home use, and therefore are generally not recommended. Root rot diseases can be effectively controlled by changing the environmental conditions that are favoring the root rot disease such as over watering and poorly draining soils.

Fungicide Timing—Timing of fungicide applications is an important component in chemical disease control. Fungicides are applied when conditions favoring disease development are present. They **protect** plants from becoming infected and therefore must be present before infection occurs. Fungicides do not have any curative activity. A diseased leaf will never recover from infection. For example, fungicides applied after powdery mildew is present on a leaf will not return the leaf to its original green color. The leaf and the resulting white fungal growth will remain unchanged. All fungicides can do, if applied after infection takes place, is to be protect new growth from becoming infected. So the plant with the existing powdery mildew infection will show symptoms of powdery mildew on lower, older leaves, but most likely the newer, upper leaves will not be infected.

Rainy, foggy, warm, humid weather conditions generally favor disease development. Whenever possible, spray schedules should be adjusted to provide fungicide protection before rainy periods and fungicides should be reapplied after heavy rains.

REMEMBER WHEN USING ANY PESTICIDE

1. Observe all directions, restrictions, and precautions on pesticide labels.

2. Store all pesticides in original containers with labels intact and behind locked doors. **Keep pesticides out of the reach of children.**

3. Use pesticides at correct label dosage and intervals to avoid illegal residues or injury to plants.

4. Apply pesticides carefully to avoid drift or contamination of nontarget areas.

5. Dispose of surplus pesticides and containers in accordance with label instructions.

Table 2. Diseases of herbaceous ornamental plants

HOST & DISEASE	SYMPTOM DESCRIPTION	SUGGESTED PRACTICES FOR CONTROL
GENERAL DISEASES COMMON TO MANY PLANTS		
A. Leaf spots (fungi; Septoria, Cercospora, Alternaria)	Randomly distributed definitive spots on leaf surfaces. Color ranges from gray to brown or black	Use protective fungicides at first signs of disease. Remove diseased leaves and discard promptly. Severely diseased plants should be discarded. Keep leaf surfaces dry, especially at night; maintain low humidity.
B. Root and stem rot (fungi; Pythium, Thelaviopsis, Rhizoctonia, Phytophthora)	Plants wilt; blackish discoloration of lower stems. Roots are rotting and appear light brown to dark brown.	Improve the structure of soil or non-soil media to improve drainage. Avoid setting transplants too deeply; identify the pathogen to select proper pesticide. Separate infected plants; avoid splashing water.
C. Vascular wilts (bacteria and Fusarium spp., Verticillum spp.)	Sudden wilting or slow stunting of plants. Vascular tissue is usually discolored brown; can be seen by cutting across the stem.	Follow proper sanitation practices. Use either sterile soil or non-soil media. Avoid splashing water. Select resistant varieties if available.
D. Powdery Mildew	White to gray powdery patches on leaves, flowers and new growth.	Lower humidity if possible. Spray with a protectant fungicide. Improve ventilation by increasing plant spacing.
E. Botrytis blight of leaves, stems and flowers (Botrytis cinerea)	Dark, water soaked blight of leaves, petioles and flowers. Gray to buff colored, powdery fungal growth may occur on diseased plant tissue.	Remove and destroy dead plant parts promptly; lower humidity. Keep foliage dry especially at night; spray with an appropriate fungicide when disease occurs.
SPECIFIC HOSTS AND DISEASES		
AFRICAN VIOLET See A, B, D and E under General Diseases		
Ring spot (Physiological)	White, yellow or brown rings on leaves.	Use tepid water for irrigation; keep leaves dry.
AMARYLLIS See B under General Diseases		
Red blotch or Stagnospora leaf spot (fungus)	Red, sunken spots develop on leaves, often in a bull's eye (zonate) pattern, especially in the spring.	Remove affected leaves. Keep foliage as dry as possible, especially at night. Apply fungicides to protect new growth and reduce disease spread.
BEGONIA See A, B, C, D, and E under General Diseases		
Bacterial leaf spot (Xanthomonas)	Small translucent spots enlarge, coalesce to form irregular brownish areas on leaves.	Remove infected leaves.
Foliar Nematodes (Aphelenchoides spp.)	Bronzing, russeting of upper leaf surfaces followed by death of tissue.	Remove infested leaves. Keep foliage dry. Avoid overhead sprinkler irrigation. Discard badly infested plants. Disinfect site.

Table 2. Diseases of herbaceous ornamental plants

HOST & DISEASE	SYMPTOM DESCRIPTION	SUGGESTED PRACTICES FOR CONTROL
CHRYSANTHEMUM See B, D and E under General Diseases.		
Ascochyta stem and ray blight	Flowers have browned, deformed petals which usually occur on one side. Brown lesions on stem.	Must apply fungicides on a regular schedule. Avoid wet leaves at night.
Foliar Nematodes	See Begonia	
CONEFLOWER (ECHINACEA) See A, B and D under General Disease		
Aster yellows (phytoplasma)	Flower parts remain green and may develop additional flowers, leaves or stems from floral parts.	Discard infected plants to reduce disease spread. Disease spread is slow via insect vector (leafhoppers). Do not propagate from infected plants.
COREOPSIS See B and D under General Diseases		
Downy Mildew (fungus)	Lower leaves are purplish or yellow. Whitish, fuzzy fungal growth can be seen on leaf underside during wet, humid, cool weather of spring and fall.	Do not purchase infected plants. Remove affected foliage and discard away from the garden. Keep foliage as dry as possible, especially at night. Avoid overhead sprinkler irrigation.
CYCLAMEN See A, B and E under General Diseases		
Stunt Fungus (*Ramularia cyclaminicola*)	Stunted plants, extreme dwarfing of flower stems, blooms below leaves.	Discard infected plants.
DAHLIA See D and E under General Diseases		
Mosaic (Stunt or Dwarf) (Virus)	Mottled leaf color. Pale green bands of tissues along midribs and larger than ordinary veins on leaves. Common characteristic is stunting/dwarfing, often with many shortened lateral shoots.	Dig up and burn diseased plant. Plant only tubers from healthy plants. Control aphids with approved insecticides.
Ringspot (Virus)	Scattered areas of yellow or light green tissue in the leaves. Ring pattern develops.	Control thrips with approved insecticides.
DAYLILY (HEMEROCALLIS) See A, B and E under General Diseases		
Rust (fungus)	Yellow, raised spots to streaks develop in leaves in the spring and fall. Bright orange spores erupt from pustules on the leaf underside.	Remove infected foliage and discard. Apply fungicides to protect new growth. Plant resistant cultivars.
Leaf streak (fungus; *Aureobasidium*)	Tan to brown sunken lesions develop at leaf tip. Spots coalesce. Eventually a brown streak develops along the leaf mid rib.	Remove affected foliage. Typically affects weakened foliage (drought, nutrition, etc.). Keep foliage as dry as possible; avoid overhead sprinkler irrigation.
DELPHINIUM OR LARKSPUR See A, B, and D under General Diseases		

Table 2. Diseases of herbaceous ornamental plants

HOST & DISEASE	SYMPTOM DESCRIPTION	SUGGESTED PRACTICES FOR CONTROL
Black leaf spot (bacterium; *Pseudomonas*)	Black irregular spots on upper leaf surface, stems, petioles and flowers. Lower leaves infected first; disease progresses upward until the entire stalk is killed.	Remove and destroy infected plants and old residue.
Bud and crown rot (bacterium; *Erwinia carotovora*)	Rapid wilting of the whole plant; plant dies. Softened tissues have a strong offensive odor.	Avoid planting in low, poorly drained areas. Avoid overhead sprinkler irrigation.
FOLIAGE HOUSE PLANTS See A, B, C, D, and E under General Diseases		
Oedema (Physiological problem)	Leaf cells swell, burst and become scab like on the underside of the leaf.	Too much water and high fertility cause problem. Reduce humidity, watering and fertilizer.
Foliar nematode	Tan to black, wedge shaped lesions (bordered by leaf veins) develop in infected leaves.	Promptly remove and discard affected leaves. Keep foliage as dry as possible.
Soft rot (bacteria; Erwinia)	Tissue is soft, water soaked, mushy and may have a foul odor.	Discard plants; avoid splashing water; keep stems, foliage dry; use clean potting mix.
Root knot nematode	Roots are galled. Plants are stunted and often show nutritional deficiencies.	Discard plants.
GERANIUM See A, B, C, D, and E under General Diseases		
Oedema (Physiological)	Same as foliage house plants above.	Remove infected foliage and discard.
Rust	Brown to rust colored powdery pustules in cluster or bull's eye pattern on leaf undersides. May be on stems and petals.	Remove and discard infected leaves. Spray with fungicides at weekly intervals until rust spots are no longer evident.
Bacterial leaf spot (*Pseudomonas* and *Xanthomonas*)	Small brown spots surrounded by large yellow areas. Spots may grow together.	Remove and destroy infected leaves. Keep foliage dry. Avoid overheard sprinkler irrigation.
GLADIOLUS See E under General Diseases		
Corm rots (Fungi)	There are several corm rot diseases; all produce similar brown, sunken lesions on the corms. Leaf spots or rotted stems may later develop.	Avoid injury when digging. Store at 35° to 40° in a dry location. Treat corm with fungicide dust prior to planting.
Cucumber mosaic virus (CMV)	Mottling of leaves, whitish streaks and color break in flowers.	Destroy diseased plants. Control insects, especially aphids.
Rust	Small brown spots on leaf underside. Bright yellow or orange spots with reddish centers on upper surface.	Remove affected foliage and discard. Spray new growth with a protective fungicide.
Bacterial leaf spot (*Xanthomonas*)	Brown to black angular spots with yellow margins on lower section of leaves.	Remove and destroy infected foliage. Keep foliage dry. Avoid overhead sprinkler irrigation.

Table 2. Diseases of herbaceous ornamental plants

HOST & DISEASE	SYMPTOM DESCRIPTION	SUGGESTED PRACTICES FOR CONTROL
GLOXINIA See A, B, C, D and E under General Diseases		
Bud rot	Buds brown to black, fail to open. Gray fungus growth may be present.	Provide good air circulation and low humidity. Remove dead buds and leaves promptly.
Crown rot (Pythium, Rhizoctonia and Phythophthora.	Leaves, petioles, and roots blackened and water soaked.	Avoid use of natural soil in pots. Use non soil potting mixes. Fungicide drenches after proper diagnosis.
Ringspot	See African Violet	
HOSTA See A, B, and E under General Diseases		
Anthracnose (Fungus)	Large, irregularly shaped tan spots with brown borders. Leaves may appear water soaked and yellow to tan in color. Leaf edges are tattered.	Keep foliage dry. Use a protectant fungicide spray under wet and humid conditions.
Sun scorch (Physiological)	Leaf margins brown or yellow associated with dieback of plants.	Avoid direct, full sun exposure. Provide adequate water during dry periods.
Foliar nematode	Yellow to tan lesions bordered by the veins; looks like tan streaks on the leaf.	Remove affected foliage ad discard away from the garden.
Crown and stem rot (Fungus: *Sclerotium rolfsii*)	Petioles wilt a collapse in mid summer. Petioles pull easily from the crown. White fungal threads (hyphae) can be seen on the rotting petiole end. Mustard seed sized, tan round, hard sclerotia (survival structures) can be seen on tissues and on soil surrounding affected plant.	Dig and remove infected plants and discard immediately, away from the garden. Turn soil at least 8 inches deep to bury sclerotia to reduce disease development in the same area. Don't purchase affected plants.
IMPATIENS See A, B, D and E under General Disease		
Impatiens necrotic spot virus (INSV)	Black to tan colored ring spots in bull's eye pattern on leaf surface; can cause color breaks, distortion, and leaf puckering on New Guinea Impatiens.	Discard severely infected plants.
Crown rot (Fungus: *Rhizoctonia solani*)	Causes collapse of entire plant. Lower stem and crown tissue have discolored lesions.	Remove infected plants and soil around plants. Fungus may survive in soil for many years.
Bacterial leaf spot (*Pseudomonas*)	Discrete small, tan, circular spots with purple margins on leaves.	Remove and destroy infected leaves. Keep foliage dry. Avoid overhead sprinkler irrigation.
IRIS See A, B, and E under General Diseases		

Table 2. Diseases of herbaceous ornamental plants

HOST & DISEASE	SYMPTOM DESCRIPTION	SUGGESTED PRACTICES FOR CONTROL
Crown rot (Fungus: *Sclerotium rolfsii*)	Tips of outer leaves die, moving downward until the entire leaf is dead. As rot progresses inward at the base of the plant, the leaves collapse. White fungus growth (later brown) may be seen between leaves near the soil line. Rhizomes are not destroyed but weakened. Light tan to brown bodies, the size of a mustard seed, may be found on rhizome.	Do not overcrowd plants. Thin plants and discard infected plants. Turn soil at least 8 inches deep to bury sclerotia (fungal survival structures) and reduce disease in the same location. Fungus is capable of surviving in location in absence of a host plant for seven years.
Leaf spot or "Fire" (Fungus: *Didymellina* or *Heterobasidium*)	Small brown leaf spots, surrounded by water soaked margin. The spots enlarge, killing the entire leaf. Centers of old spots turn gray and are dotted with small black spore clusters.	Cut off old leaves at the soil line in fall and discard or burn them. Spray with a fungicide in spring to protect new growth. Keep foliage as dry as possible.
Soft rot (Bacterium: *Erwinia carotovora*)	At first, leaves wilt slightly, later become limp and die. Rhizome shows a soft slimy rot and later turns dry and granular, finally decaying entirely. Often associated with wounds or injuries.	Do not overcrowd plants. Dig out infected rhizomes and cut out rotted areas.
Rust	Reddish brown rust pustules appear on lower leaf surface.	Plant rust resistant varieties. Thin plants to improve air circulation. Avoid wetting foliage. Spray with protective fungicides.
LILY See A under General Diseases		
Botrytis blight (Fire) (Fungi: *Botrytis elliptica*)	Orange to red leaf spots. Brown spots on flowers.	See E under General Diseases.
Root and bulb rots	Soft brown decay of roots and bulb scales. Plants stunted.	Discard severely affected bulbs.
IVY, ENGLISH See A under General Diseases		
Bacterial leaf spot and stem canker (*Xanthomas*)	Leaf spots that are brown or black with yellow margins. Spots look greasy when viewed from underneath. Leaf stems are black and shriveled. Canker forms in the woody portion of the vine.	Remove infected plant material. Avoid planting in areas where temperatures may become high or soil too moist. Avoid splashing water and sprinkler irrigation. Keep foliage dry. Apply copper based fungicides in warm, wet weather.
Anthracnose (Fungus)	Spots are round and similar to bacterial leaf spot.	Same as for bacterial leaf spot. Spray with protective fungicide.
MARIGOLD See A, B, C, D, and E under General Diseases		
Aster yellows (Phytoplasma)	Infected plants develop distorted witches' broom growth. Leaf color yellow; abnormal flower color and growth.	Remove and destroy infected plants.
PACHYSANDRA See A and B under General Diseases		

Table 2. Diseases of herbaceous ornamental plants

HOST & DISEASE	SYMPTOM DESCRIPTION	SUGGESTED PRACTICES FOR CONTROL
Leaf and stem blight (Fungus: *Volutella*)	Circular brown blotches on leaves that progresses to a blight. The rest of the leaf turns yellow. A brown stem rot with visible spore pustules.	Remove diseased plants. Improve air circulation by thinning plants. Apply a protective fungicide.
Dieback	Terminal buds and leaves turn brown, roll up and droop. Cankers found on small branches.	Prune out infected twigs.
PANSY See A, B, D, and E under General Diseases		
Downy mildew	Grayish fungal growth on the leaf undersides. Upper leaf surface discolored yellow.	Keep foliage dry. Increase air circulation around plants. Remove infected plants or plant parts.
PEONY See B and E under General Diseases		
Leaf blotch	Glossy dark purple spots on top of leaf, dull brown color below. Problem during moist weather.	Spray with a fungicide. Destroy infected foliage at the end of the season.
Phythophthora blight	Blossoms and succulent growing tips are blighted and become dark brown to black and somewhat leathery. Usually more severe in wet springs or where plants are shaded or crowded. May invade crown, causing a root rot.	Remove and destroy all infected parts as soon as they are detected. Cut off tops at the ground line in fall and burn. Spray foliage with a fungicide. Remove infected plants and soil. Improve drainage of planting site and plant in mounds.
PETUNIA See A and E under General Diseases		
Impatiens necrotic spot virus (INSV)	Circular black spots, may be in ring pattern on lower leaves.	Remove and destroy infected plants. Control insects, especially thrips.
POINSETTIA See A, B, and D under General Diseases		
Bract and leaf spots (Fungus: *Corynespora*)	Brown spots on leaves and bracts.	Keep foliage dry. Remove and destroy infected plant tissue.
Root and stem rots	Plants wilt; blackish brown discoloration of lower stem. Roots rotting.	Improve soil structure and drainage. Avoid setting transplants too deep.
RUDBECKIA See A, B, and D under General Diseases		
Foliar nematode	Purplish, angular leaf spots, often concentrated along the veins.	Promptly remove and discard affected leaves away from the garden.
Downy mildew (Fungus: *Plasmopara*)	Purplish discoloration across the leaf. Grayish to white fuzzy growth on leaf underside in humid, wet, cool weather.	Do not purchase infected plants. Remove infected plant tissue. Keep foliage dry, especially at night. Avoid overhead sprinkler irrigation.
SALVIA See A, B, and D under General Diseases		
Downy mildew (Fungus)	Angular, purple to black spots develop on the leaves during cool humid, wet weather (spring and fall).	Do not purchase infected plants

Table 2. Diseases of herbaceous ornamental plants

HOST & DISEASE	SYMPTOM DESCRIPTION	SUGGESTED PRACTICES FOR CONTROL
SNAPDRAGON See A, B, C under General Diseases		
Downy mildew (Fungus)	Grayish patches appear on lower leaf surface. Upper leaf surface has yellowish discolored patches.	Remove infected plant tissue. Keep foliage dry, especially at night. Avoid overhead sprinkler irrigation.
Rust (Fungus)	Yellow blotches appear on upper leaf surface. Dark brown, dusty pustules on leaf undersides.	Remove infected plant tissue. Keep foliage dry. Improve air circulation. Apply protective fungicide spray.
Impatiens necrotic spot virus (INSV)	Round tan necrotic ring spots on leaves in bull's eye pattern.	Remove and destroy infected plant. Control insects, especially thrips.
TULIP See A under General Diseases		
Botrytis blight or "Fire"	Black, pin head sized sclerotia bodies on brown bulb husks. Sort bulbs carefully and discard diseased ones before planting. Remove infected plants soon after they come up. Remove and destroy all plant debris after blooming. If bulbs are to remain in the soil, cut yellowed tops below ground and burn them. Dust bulbs prior to storage or planting with fungicide. Spray foliage with appropriate fungicide. Practice sanitation.
VERBENA See A, B, and D under General Diseases		
Powdery mildew (Fungus)	The most common disease on verbena. Whitish growth occurs on leaves, stems, and flowers. Leaves may have purplish appearance.	Remove affected foliage from the plants. Increase air circulation around plants by thinning foliage. Apply fungicides to protect new growth at the first sign of disease.
VERONICA (SPEEDWELL) See B and D under General Diseases		
Downy mildew (Fungus)	Angular yellow to purplish lesions develop on the leaves during cool, wet, humid weather (spring and fall). Whole leaves may turn purple.	Do not purchase infected plants. Remove infected plants and/or infected plants if the disease has become systemic. Keep foliage as dry as possible. Avoid overhead sprinkler irrigation.
Foliar nematode	Angular, purplish to black spots develop on leaves, especially along leaf veins. Spot color shades range from very light to very dark on the leaf underside.	Remove infected leaves and discard away from the garden. Keep foliage as dry as possible. Avoid overhead sprinkler irrigation.
VINCA (CATHARANTHUS) See A, B and D under General Diseases		
Phytophthora aerial blight (Fungus)	Stems brown or blacken, wilt and collapse. Typically occurs in mid summer.	Remove infected plants. Avoid overwatering and overhead sprinkler irrigation. Do not plant annual vinca in area for one year.
ZINNIA See A, D, and E under General Diseases		
Bacterial leaf spot (*Xanthomonas*)	Angular to irregularly circular brown spots, surrounded by a prominent yellow halo appear on leaves.	Avoid water splash. Change seed source. Treat seed with a 1 in 5 dilution of household bleach for 10 minutes.
Aster yellows (Phytoplasma)	Flowers are greenish and distorted with excessive petal formation. Witches' broom growth habit.	Remove and destroy infected plants.

Table 3. Common diseases of many woody plants

DISEASE	SEASONAL OCCURRENCE	SYMPTOM DESCRIPTION	SUGGESTED CONTROL PRACTICES
Fungal leaf spots (numerous fungi including *Septoria, Cercospora, Entomosporium, Phyllosticta, Colletotrichum, Macrophoma*)	Year round; peak in April-May and August-September.	Randomly distributed definitive spots on leaves. Spots typically have a tan to gray center with a brown, black or dark purple border; black pimple like fungal fruiting bodies can sometimes be seen in the center of the spot. May be associated with yellowing leaves and premature defoliation.	Rake and remove fallen leaf litter from the base of plants. Avoid long durations of leaf wetness. Do not water late in the day so the plants go through the night wet. Increase plant spacing or selectively prune branches to improve air circulation. Use protective fungicides preventively or at the first sign of disease.
Powdery mildew (*Erysiphe spp., Microsphaera spp., Phyllactinia spp., Podosphaera spp., Sphaerotheca spp., Uncinula spp., Oidium spp.*)	May-October; peak in May-June.	Fungi are mostly host specific. White to grayish powdery patches on leaves, stems, flowers. Mostly seen on new growth.	Remove affected stems or leaves from the plant. Rake and remove fallen plant litter. Increase plant spacing or selectively prune branches to improve ventilation. Apply a fungicide spray at the first sign of infection. Do not wait until the entire leaf is covered with mildew.
Fire blight (*Erwinia amylovora*)	April-June; peak in May-June.	Affects plants in the Rosaceae family (pear, crabapple, Cotoneaster, Rhaphiolepis, Photinia, Pyracantha). Young twigs and branches die from the terminal end and appear burned or deep rust colored. Branch may be dent, resembling a shepherd's crook. Dead leaves and fruit generally remain on the branch. Infection occurs during blooming and is favored by wet conditions.	Prune out branches 6 inches below the signs of damage. Disinfect pruning tool in 70% isopropyl alcohol (rubbing alcohol) or 10% bleach solution between each cut. Avoid heavy nitrogen fertilization, especially in summer. Avoid splashing water. Plant resistant varieties.
Pythium root rot (Pythium spp.)	January-December; peak March-June and August-October	Mostly affects herbaceous plants. Plants may wilt. Roots are light to dark brown and soft. Outer root cortex sloughs off leaving the thread like inner root stele visible. Causes damping off.	Infection is favored by wet soils and high soluble salts. Improve soil structure and drainage. Avoid planting too deeply. Remove infected plants from the area. Avoid plant stress. Fungicide drenches may reduce disease.
Phytophthora root and crown rot (*Phytophthora cinnamomi, P. nicotianae var. parasitica*)	April-September; peak in July-August	Mostly a disease of woody plants. Plants may wilt. Darkly discolored cambial tissue on lower stems. Rotting roots are dark brown or black.	Infection favored by wet soils and stressed roots. Improve soil structure and drainage. Avoid planting too deeply. Remove infected plants from the area. Avoid plant stress. Fungicide drenches may reduce disease.

Table 3. Common diseases of many woody plants

DISEASE	SEASONAL OCCURRENCE	SYMPTOM DESCRIPTION	SUGGESTED CONTROL PRACTICES
Rhizoctonia root rot (*Rhizoctonia solani*)	May-September; peak in July-August	Infects both woody and herbaceous plants. Roots and crown of plant rots. Infected tissues are discolored dark brown. Plants collapse at the soil line. Causes damping off.	Infection is favored by moist soils, root stress and warmer temperatures. Improve soil structure and drainage. Avoid planting too deeply. Remove infected plants from the area. Avoid plant stress. Fungicide drenches may reduce disease.
Crown gall (*Agrobacterium tumefaciens*)	March-October	Roots and base of stems infected with golf ball sized, knobby galls. Secondary galls sometimes seen on branches. Mostly introduced into the landscape through infected nursery stock. May be spread by cutting tools. Infection is favored by wounds and wet conditions. Commonly affects Euonymus, Cleyera, and rose.	Destroy heavily infected plants. Prune out galls, if few present on some branches and lower stems. Disinfect pruning tools between each cut with 70% isopropyl alcohol (rubbing alcohol) or 10% bleach solution. Euonymus elatus not susceptible to infection.
Root knot nematode (*Meloidogyne spp.*)	March-November	Chlorosis and bronzing of foliage, reduced leaf size and eventual defoliation. Root galling and decay. Plants are stunted and slowly decline, often one branch at a time.	Improve drainage; promote good plant growth through horticultural practices. No post plant chemical treatment available.

Table 5. Common diseases of specific woody plants

DISEASE	SEASONAL OCCURRENCE	SYMPTOM DESCRIPTION	SUGGESTED CONTROL PRACTICES
ARBORVITAE (THUJA)			
Bot canker (*Botryosphaeria obtusa, B. dothiodea*)	March-October	Poor growth on some branches. Always associated with a wound on plant from pruning, mechanical damage, freeze cracks, etc. or natural opening (lenticels) following a stress event such as drought. Wounds will sometimes ooze sap and is a possible indicator of canker development. Foliage above canker will die. Black, pimple like fruiting bodies seen on branches.	Prune infected branches at least 4-6 inches below the infected tissue. Avoid plant stress; promote good plant growth. Avoid wounding plants. No fungicides are effective once infection occurs. A protective fungicide application when the injury occurred can reduce possible infection.
ASH			
Anthracnose (*Apiognomonia errabunda; syn. Discula sp.*)	April-June; peak in May	Irregular shaped, light colored spots often with a dark border or chlorotic halo. Spots concentrated along leaf margin and veins. Blotching and distortion of young leaves and shoots. Excess defoliation can occur. Cool, wet weather favors infection.	Fungus survives on infected leaves and in dead twigs and branches. Collect and remove fallen leaf litter before new growth appears in spring. Fungicide application rarely warranted on large, landscape trees. If used, apply to completely cover tree beginning at bud break and continuing through cool, wet weather.
AZALEA AND RHODODENDRON			
Leaf gall (*Exobasidium vaccinii*)	April-June; peak in May	Leaves become distorted with pale green, thickened, fleshy like galls. As galls mature, they turn white, then brown, dry, and fall to the ground. Spores are released when the gall is white. Disease only affects new growth, older leaves are resistant to infection. Infection is favored by cool, moist spring weather. Under dry conditions and in sunny locations, the disease is seldom seen.	Pick off or prune affected leaves from the plant before they turn white. Applications of fungicides after the galls are present will have no effect in controlling the disease. Applying fungicides before and as the leaf buds open and expand in early spring can reduce infection, but timing is critical and sprays are usually not necessary.

Table 5. Common diseases of specific woody plants

DISEASE	SEASONAL OCCURRENCE	SYMPTOM DESCRIPTION	SUGGESTED CONTROL PRACTICES
Petal blight (*Ovulinia e*)	March-May; peak in April	Mostly a problem on . Tiny, round pale spots that rapidly enlarge to irregular blotches are produced on infected flowers. Flowers quickly (1 day after infection) turn brown, limp, and mushy. Under humid conditions, affected flowers are covered in a white mold growth. Affected blooms hang on plants for weeks, even months. Hard, black survival and fruiting bodies (sclerotia) are produced on the affected blooms. Blossoms eventually drop from the plant.	Rake and remove flower debris from underneath bushes. Remove old flowers from plants. Mulch around base of plants. Fungicides can be applied to base of plants to prevent sporulation from sclerotia, but this is marginally effective. On large azalea plantings, make fungicide applications beginning just before blooming and continue at 1 week or less intervals during entire bloom period.
Phomopsis canker and die back (*Phomopsis spp.*)	April-October; peak in July-August	Mostly a problem on Southern Indica type azalea. Death of leaves and stems; reddish brown discoloration of wood on diseased stems. Enters plants through wounds, especially pruning wounds. Stressed plants most susceptible.	Prune wounded, damaged branches. Prevent moisture stress and stem splitting from cold. Mulch plants.
Web blight (*Rhizoctonia solani*)	May-September; peak in July-August	Very rapid symptom development under humid, wet conditions. Small necrotic leaf spots rapidly enlarge, become dark brown to black and advance along leaf margin and midrib. Affected leaves abscise but remain attached to the plant due to the fungus. Leaves are matted or clumped together. In the fall, infected leaves drop as the fungus dies and plants look defoliated.	Crowded, close growing s are most susceptible (e.g. 'Gumpo' s). Avoid prolonged plant wetness; do not water late in the day. Increase plant spacing to prevent plant to plant infection. Apply protective fungicide beginning in mid June when temperatures warm reach about 80°F.

Table 5. Common diseases of specific woody plants

DISEASE	SEASONAL OCCURRENCE	SYMPTOM DESCRIPTION	SUGGESTED CONTROL PRACTICES
Phytophthora dieback (*Phytophthora cactorum, P. nicotianae var. parasitica, P. citricola*)	June-September, peak in July-August	Brown, irregular shaped lesions on leaf margin that progresses along midrib through the petiole into the stem. Brown discoloration extending up and down the stem. Infection only on current season's growth, but slowly moves through plant.	Avoid prolonged plant wetness; do not water late in the day or evening. Prune affected shoots. Excess shade and nitrogen fertilization increases disease susceptibility. Susceptibility varies from cultivar to cultivar. Fungicides can reduce disease incidence.
Botryosphaeria die back (*Botryosphaeria dothidea, B. ribis*)	April-October	Mostly affects rhododendron. Leaves on affected stem droop and roll inward. Reddish black, sunken canker girdles affected stem. Infection develops at pruning wounds, leaf scars, and flower cluster attachment.	Prune stems below the cankered, discolored area. Disinfect pruning tools. Avoid drought stress or freeze injury which predisposes plants to infection. No resistant cultivars or fungicide treatments are known.
BIRCH			
Anthracnose (*Discula betulina; syn. Gloeosporium betulinum*)	May-September; peak June-July	Large tan spots or blotches with brown to dark black margin and yellow halos. Affected leaves fall prematurely, often when much of the leaf is still green.	Collect and remove fallen leaf litter before new growth appears in spring. If small or newly transplanted tree, apply fungicide spray when leaves begin expansion and repeat twice at 10-14 day intervals.
Cylindrosporium leaf spot (*Cylindrosporium betulae*)	June-October; peak in August-September	Small tan to brown to purple spots with no definite margin.	Collect and remove fallen leaf litter before new growth appears in spring. Fungicides not usually necessary. Disease is worse in wet weather.
BOXWOOD			
Volutella blight (*Volutella buxi*)	June-October; peak August-September	Pinkish sporulation seen on leaves and twigs, especially on dead or dying tissues. Discoloration and death of current year's growth.	Prune affected stems below diseased tissue. Heavy pruning of plants promotes infection. Dieback of branches is often due to root rot or other factor that affects good root growth (poor soils, compaction, over watering, poor nutrition, etc.)

Table 5. Common diseases of specific woody plants

DISEASE	SEASONAL OCCURRENCE	SYMPTOM DESCRIPTION	SUGGESTED CONTROL PRACTICES
Root knot nematode (*Meloidogyne spp.*)	March-November	Chlorosis and bronzing of foliage, reduced leaf size and eventual defoliation. Root galling and decay. Plants are stunted and slowly decline, often one branch at a time.	Improve drainage; promote good plant growth through horticultural practices. No post plant chemical treatment available.
CAMELLIA			
Canker and stem die back (*Glomerella cingulata*)	April-September; peak in May-July	Sudden wilting of leaves. Leaves turn brown and remain attached to young twigs. Elliptical and sunken cankers form on infected branches. The bark and wood of infected branches turns brown. Pinkish orange spore masses may be seen around the cankers during extended periods of wet weather.	Prune infected branches four inches below the infected area into healthy tissue and burn or discard disease branches. Disinfect pruning tools in 10% bleach solution or wipe blades with rubbing alcohol between each cut. Fungicides will provide limited effectiveness and can be applied to pruning cuts and wounds.
Leaf gall (*Exobasidium camelliae*)	April-June; peak in May	New expanding leaves are larger, thickened, and pinkish green in color on the upper leaf surface and the lower leaf surface will eventually turn white when the fungus is releasing spores. Infected leaves dry and turn brown to black in late spring. Infection is most severe under cool, moist weather conditions as the leaves expand in the spring.	Remove and destroy (burning or discarding) diseased leaves as they appear in early spring before the lower leaf surface turns white. This will reduce the inoculum source for next year's infection. Do not leave infected leaves or branches on the ground after pruning because spores can still be liberated from the infected clippings. Fungicide applications are seldom necessary and will only provide limited control. Applications must be made as the leaf buds swell in the spring. Spraying after seeing the galls will have no effect on this or next year's infection.

Table 5. Common diseases of specific woody plants

DISEASE	SEASONAL OCCURRENCE	SYMPTOM DESCRIPTION	SUGGESTED CONTROL PRACTICES
Petal blight (*Ciborinia camelliae*; syn. *Sclerotinia camelliae*)	February-April; peak March	Small brown, irregularly shaped spots appear on expanding petals. Spots enlarge rapidly toward the center of flower until the entire flower is dead and brown. Venation is pronounced giving the flower a "netted" appearance in early stages of disease development. This distinguishes petal blight from frost or wind injury. Blighted flowers drop and the fungus produces dark, hard, survival structures (sclerotia) within the tissue which then releases spores and infects flowers the following year.	Remove and destroy infected flowers as they appear. Rake and remove fallen blossoms and other plant debris underneath bushes. Apply a fungicide prior to flower blooming to the soil beneath plants and in an area 10 feet beyond each bush.
Algal leaf spot (*Cephaleuros virescens*)	April-November; peak in July-August	Velvety green, brown or reddish spots develop on the upper leaf surface under wet conditions. Older infections become greenish gray and lichen like in appearance.	Usually does not harm the plant. Fungicides can reduce disease incidence.
Yellow mottle or ring spot viruses	April-September	Irregular yellow or white spots (mottling) or ring spots appear on infected leaves. This is often seen on older winter injured leaves. Affected leaves may drop, but plants are rarely killed.	There is no control for virus diseases, except removing affected plant. Pruning and removing branches showing symptoms does not control viruses.
Oedema Not a disease. It is a physiological disorder.	November-June	Tannish brown, corky or scabby appearance to leaves.	No control is necessary. The problem is favored by high humidity, cloudy weather, poor soil drainage, and excessive watering.
CHERRY (FLOWERING)			
Black knot (*Plowrightia morbusa*; syn. *Dibotryon morbosum*)	January-December	Dark brown to black, hard swellings form on twigs and branches. At first galls are small, but enlarge each year. In spring galls are covered with dark olive green felt like growth. Branches may be girdled and die. Affects numerous Prunus sp.	Prune and destroy galls, cutting several inches below gall during plant dormancy. Usually not necessary to apply fungicides.

Table 5. Common diseases of specific woody plants

DISEASE	SEASONAL OCCURRENCE	SYMPTOM DESCRIPTION	SUGGESTED CONTROL PRACTICES
CRABAPPLE (FLOWERING)			
Fire blight (*Erwinia amylovora*)	April-June; peak in May-June	Young twigs and branches die from the terminal end and appear burned or deep rust colored. Branch may be bent, resembling a shepherd's crook. Dead leaves and fruit generally remain on the branch. Infection occurs during blooming and is favored by wet conditions.	Prune out branches 6 inches below the signs of damage. Disinfect pruning tool in 70% isopropyl alcohol (rubbing alcohol) or 10% bleach solution between each cut. Avoid heavy nitrogen fertilization, especially in summer. Avoid splashing water. Plant resistant varieties.
Apple scab (*Venturia inaequalis*)	April-October; peak in April-June	Dull, olive green, velvety fungal growth develops on upper leaf surface in spring. Leaves yellow and fall prematurely. Trees bare by mid season. Infected fruit have circular rough spots on surface. Infection is favored by cooler temperatures and prolonged leaf wetness.	Plant scab resistant cultivars. Rake and remove fallen leaves and fruit. Beginning at bud break, apply fungicides at 7-10 day intervals. Make 5 to 8 applications through early to mid June.
Cedar Apple rust (*Gymnosporangium juniperi virginiana*)	May-August; peak in July	Bright yellow, yellow orange spots form on leaves. On upper surface of spot, small dark fungal fruiting structures form. Later on underside of infected leaves, clusters of cup shaped structures with fringed edges are observed.	Remove unwanted junipers/cedars from the area. Remove galls from junipers during dormancy. If disease is frequent and severe, apply a fungicide when crabapple flower bud tissue can be seen and again at petal fall.
CRAPE MYRTLE			
Powdery mildew (*Erysiphe lagerstroemiae*)	May-October; peak in June-July	White, powdery spots appear on leaves, stems, flowers. May cause distortion of new growth and suckers	Plant resistant varieties ("Indian" named; Acoma, Tuskeegee, Zuma, etc.). Prune infected sprouts and new growth from plant. Apply fungicides at the first sign of disease (if plants are small). Do not wait until entire leaf is covered.

Table 5. Common diseases of specific woody plants

DISEASE	SEASONAL OCCURRENCE	SYMPTOM DESCRIPTION	SUGGESTED CONTROL PRACTICES
DOGWOOD			
Spot anthracnose (*Elsinoe corni*)	March September; peak in May	Small, reddish spots first appear on flower bracts. Reddish spots on leaves; leaves distorted from infection in bud stage. May cause leaves to drop.	Rake and remove fallen leaves. Disease will not cause significant damage to tree. Fungicides applied at swollen bud stage for flowers and leaves can reduce infection, but are only recommended for young, newly transplanted trees. Kousa variety moderately resistant to disease.
Dogwood anthracnose (*Discula destructiva*)	March September; peak June	Medium to large purple bordered leaf spots develop into large, scorched, tan blotches that enlarge and may kill the entire leaf. Infected leaves cling to stems after normal leaf drop in fall. Symptoms start in the lower crown and progress up the tree. Numerous shoots form along the main stem and on major branches. The shoots frequently become infected and die. Cankers form on main trunk at junction of dead twig or shoot. Trees may die within 2-3 years following infection. Disease is less severe on trees planted in open, sunny sites.	Prune and destroy any dead wood from tree before it reaches the main trunk. Avoid plant stress. Remove severely infected trees and fallen leaf litter and destroy them. Fungicides are often ineffective. In some cases, they may provide some control if applied as buds break in the spring and at least twice thereafter as the leaves expand.
Septoria and Cercospora leaf spots (*Septoria cornicola; Cercospora cornicola*)	June October peak August September	Uniform, medium purplish spots on leaves; spots may be angular. Center of spot turns gray, but spots retain the deep purple border. May cause leaf drop. Mostly seen in late summer/early fall prior to leaf drop.	Chemical control not usually recommended. Disease causes little damage to the tree. Stressed trees more susceptible to the disease. Avoid plant stress.
Algae/Lichens	January December	Greenish gray spots or crusty to feathery growths on stems and branches. Not a disease. Indicates stressed tree.	Improve conditions causing stress.

Table 5. Common diseases of specific woody plants

DISEASE	SEASONAL OCCURRENCE	SYMPTOM DESCRIPTION	SUGGESTED CONTROL PRACTICES
EUONYMOUS			
Powdery mildew (*Microsphaera euonymi japonici*)	May-October; peak in May-June	Small patches of white to gray powdery growth on leaves and stems. Mostly seen on new growth. Infection is favored by high humidity, poor air circulation and cool night temperatures. Most common in early summer and late to early fall.	Remove affected stems or leaves. Improve air circulation around plants by increasing plant spacing or thinning branches. Apply fungicide at the first sign of infection. Do not wait until the entire leaf is covered with mildew. Reapply 10-14 days later.
Crown gall (*Agrobacterium tumefaciens*)	March-October	Roots and base of stems infected with golf ball sized, knobby galls. Secondary galls sometimes seen on branches. Mostly introduced into the landscape through infected nursery stock. May be spread by cutting tools. Infection is favored by wounds and wet conditions.	Destroy heavily infected plants. Prune out galls, if few present on some branches and lower stems. Disinfect pruning tools between each cut with 70% isopropyl alcohol (rubbing alcohol) or 10% bleach solution. *E. alatus* not susceptible to infection.
GARDENIA			
Canker or Galling (*Phomopsis gardeniae*; syn. *Diaporthe gardeniae*)	January-December; peak April-June	Perennial cankers or cankerous rough surfaced galls that enlarge and girdle stems; commonly found near the soil line. Diseased branches lose vigor, may wilt, drop leaves, and die back. Enters plant through wounds.	Prune affected branches from the plant.
Algal leaf spot (*Cephaleuros virescens*)	April-November; peak July-August	Velvety green, brown or reddish spots develop on the upper leaf surface and stems under wet conditions.	Usually does not harm the plant. Fungicides can reduce disease incidence.
HOLLY			
Web or thread blight (*Rhizoctonia solani, R. ramicola*)	May-September; peak in July-August	Very rapid symptom development under humid, wet conditions. Small necrotic leaf spots rapidly enlarge, become dark brown to black and advance along leaf margin and midrib. Affected leaves abscise but remain attached to the plants, matted together, due to the fungus.	Crowded, close growing hollies are most susceptible (Compacta, Helleri, Dwarf Yaupon, etc.). Avoid prolonged plant wetness; do not water late in the day. Increase plant spacing to prevent plant to plant infection. Apply protective fungicide about mid June when temperatures warm to approx.80°F.

Table 5. Common diseases of specific woody plants

DISEASE	SEASONAL OCCURRENCE	SYMPTOM DESCRIPTION	SUGGESTED CONTROL PRACTICES
Sphaeropsis gall or knot (*Sphaeropsis tumefaciens*)	Not certain	Affects American and Dahoon hollies in the South. Young twigs swell, forming galls with witches' brooming of new, leafless shoots from the galled tissue. Infects primarily wounds and can be spread on pruning tools.	Disinfect pruning tools between cuts. Prune affected branches below (4-6 inches) galls.
Black root rot (*Thielaviopsis basicola*; *Chalara elegans*)	January-December; peak in April-July	Chlorotic, stunted foliage. Death of feeder roots. Black lesions seen on washed roots. Dieback of individual branches.	Remove affected plants. Improve soil drainage. Fungicide drenches marginally effective
Anthracnose (*Glomerella cingulata*; syn. *Colletotrichum gloeosporioides*)	March-November; peak in May-June	Irregular leaf spots; scorching along leaf margin. Sunken stem cankers. Die back of branches. Most serious on stressed or weakened plants.	Avoid prolonged plant wetness; do not water late in the day. Avoid plant stress. Prune affected branches from plant if cankers evident. Fungicides are of little benefit and need to be applied as the leaf buds swell and begin expansion. Repeat applications at 7-10 day intervals are necessary until leaf fully expands.
Spine spot (Not a disease)	January-December	Small gray spots with purple halos caused by puncturing of leaves by spines of adjacent leaves or insects.	Prune plants to thin growth and prevent injury. Control insects.
HYDRANGEA			
Cercospora leaf spot (*Cercospora hydrangeae*)	May-October	Randomly distributed leaf spots with a tan center and a dark purplish red border. Spot size may range from small purplish spots to about 1/4 inch across. Infection is favored by cooler temperatures and extended periods of leaf wetness, usually in late spring.	Avoid prolonged periods of leaf wetness. Remove heavily infected leaves. Remove leaf litter under plants. Apply fungicide sprays beginning in early spring as leaves emerge. Repeat application every 10-14 days.
INDIAN HAWTHORNE (RHAPHIOLEPIS)			
Entomosporium leaf spot (*Entomosporium mespili*; syn. *Fabraea maculata*)	January-December; peak in February-April and August-October	Small reddish spots on leaves. Older spots have a tannish center with a purple red border. In some cultivars severe defoliation can occur.	Plant leaf spot resistant varieties (ex. Eleanor Tabor, Olivia, Georgia Petite, Georgia Green). Fungicide application may reduce disease, but it must be reapplied at 10-14 day intervals from spring to late summer.

Table 5. Common diseases of specific woody plants

DISEASE	SEASONAL OCCURRENCE	SYMPTOM DESCRIPTION	SUGGESTED CONTROL PRACTICES
IVY			
Anthracnose (*Colletotrichum trichellum*)	April-October; peak in August-September	Round to large, irregularly shaped, tan to brown spots that have numerous tiny, dark brown, pimple like fungal fruiting structures within spot. Spots often have zonate appearance. Spots may coalesce causing leaf blight.	Remove infected plant material. Avoid splashing water and sprinkler irrigation. Keep foliage dry. Apply protective fungicide in early summer and reapply at 10-14 day intervals.
Bacterial leaf spot (*Xanthomonas campestris pv. hederae*)	April-October; peak in June	Leaf spots are brown to black with yellow halos. Spots look greasy when viewed from underneath. Spots may coalesce causing extensive blighted areas. Leaf stems blacken and shrivel. Cankers may form in woody portion of vine.	Remove infected plant material. Avoid planting in areas that will stress plants (full sun, poor soil conditions, excess water). Avoid splashing water and sprinkler irrigation. Keep foliage dry. Apply copper based fungicides in warm, wet weather.
JUNIPER AND EASTERN RED CEDAR (JUNIPERUS)			
Tip blight (*Phomopsis juniperovora*)	April-September; peak in May	New branch tips turn brown and die. Older, mature growth is resistant to infection. Infections are seen in late spring and early summer following growth flushes. Infected tissue turns gray and black fungal fruiting bodies can be seen on the infected tips.	Prune affected branches when plants are dry. Remove clippings from the area. Avoid wetting plants late in the day or evening hours. Fungicide applications when new growth is present in spring or after pruning can reduce infection. Plant resistant or tolerant juniper varieties.
Cercosporidium needle blight (*Cercosporidium sequoinae var. juniperi*)	April-September; peak June	Progressive browning and loss of foliage beginning on lower branches close to the stem and moving upward and outward until plant dies or only tufts of green shoots remain on upmost branches.	Avoid plant stress. Apply fungicides in early to mid summer can help reduce disease. Remove severely affected plants.
Seiridium canker (*Seiridium unicorne*)	February-December; peak April-May	Yellowing and browning of old foliage precedes fading and death of twigs and branches. Sunken, long cankers develop at wounds or bark openings. Bark is darkened and resin exudes from margins of cankers. Needles on affected branches will fall off easily when rubbed with your hands.	Avoid plant stress and wounding. Irrigate trees during periods of drought. Avoid drought injury. Fungicides ineffective once infection takes place.

Table 5. Common diseases of specific woody plants

DISEASE	SEASONAL OCCURRENCE	SYMPTOM DESCRIPTION	SUGGESTED CONTROL PRACTICES
Cedar apple rust (*Gymnosporangium juniperi virginianae*) Cedar hawthorne rust (*Gymnosporangium globosum*)	March-May; peak in April-May	Hard dark brown galls formed in winter. In spring, galls exude reddish, jelly like "tentacles" of spores (telial horns) that infect apple and crabapple. Infects mostly eastern red cedars and horizontal junipers. Hawthorne rust similar to cedar apple rust, telial horns (fungal structures) are short and blunt.	Usually does not harm junipers. Prune out galls when noticed. See control on crabapple if necessary.
Cedar quince rust (*Gymnosporangium clavipes*)	March-May; peak in April-May	Young shoots infected causing spindle shaped swellings that encircle twigs and small branches. Bright orange pustules expand from diseased bark in early spring. Diseased twigs and branches often die.	Prune affected branches and twigs from cedar trees. Fungicides have limited effectiveness on reducing rust on cedar. Apply fungicides to hawthorne, flowering quince, pear when leaf buds swell and expand.
LEYLAND CYPRESS			
Bot canker (*Botryosphaeria dothidea, B. obtusa, Sphaeropsis, Macrophoma*)	February-November; peak in April-May	Bright rust colored branches most often visible in spring and fall. Infection always associated with wound from pruning, mechanical damage, freeze cracks, etc. or natural opening (lenticels) following a stress event such as drought. A canker develops at the infection site and may ooze sap. Canker darkly discolors cambial tissue. All foliage above canker will die.	Prune affected branches 6 inches below the infected tissue. Avoid plant stress; promote good plant growth. Avoid wounding plants. Avoid planting Leylands too close together (should be planted on at least 8 foot centers or more). No fungicides are effective once infection has occurred. A protective fungicide application when the injury occurred may reduce possible infection.
Cercosporidium needle blight (*Cercosporidium sequoiae*)	June-November; peak in August-September	Foliage in the lower third of tree thins from the inside outward and the bottom upward. Individual needles progressively yellow, then gray, and eventually fall from the tree. Typically infects one year old and older growth; however, current season's growth can also be infected. Branches often look bare with tufts of green growth at the branch tips.	Avoid planting Leylands too close together to allow for air circulation around trees. Fungicides can help reduce infection and disease spread. Begin applications to the lower third of the tree by July 1 and continue at 7 to 10 day intervals through September. Keep foliage as dry as possible to reduce disease spread and development. Avoid using sprinkler irrigation to water trees. The disease may not progress or severely damage landscape trees.

Table 5. Common diseases of specific woody plants

DISEASE	SEASONAL OCCURRENCE	SYMPTOM DESCRIPTION	SUGGESTED CONTROL PRACTICES
Seridium canker (*Seiridium unicorne*)	February-November; peak in April-May	Yellowing and browning of old foliage precedes fading and death of twigs and branches. Sunken, long cankers with a reddish tinge develop at wounds or bark openings. Bark is darkened and resin exudes from margins of cankers. Infection seems to occur from the lower branches and up and from the inside out. Infected trees look thinly branched.	Avoid plant stress and wounding. Keep plants well irrigated during periods of drought. If possible, prune affected branches 6 inches below the canker before infection reaches the main stem. No fungicides are effective in controlling disease once infection takes place.
LIGUSTRUM (PRIVET)			
Cercospora leaf spot (*Cercospora spp.*)	April-October; peak in May and September	Irregularly shaped tan lesions surrounded by a dark brown border. Often lesions develop on leaf margin or tip. Spots may become sunken with age. Most common leaf spot disease. Infection is favored by prolonged leaf wetness. Rarely causes harm to plants.	Avoid prolonged leaf wetness. Selectively prune dense hedges to improve air circulation around plants. Fungicide control not necessary since disease does not significantly harm plants.
MAPLE			
Tar spot (*Rhytisma acerinum*)	April-October; peak in June-July	Raised, black tar like spots develop on the upper side of mature leaves in mid to late summer. Infected leaves may drop prematurely.	Rake and remove fallen leaves. Disease does not cause significant damage to trees. No chemical control recommended.
Phyllosticta leaf spot (*Phyllosticta minima*)	April-October; peak in May-June	Small, round, light colored leaf spots with purple borders. Pycnidia (fungal fruiting bodies) form in a circular pattern within the spot. Infected leaves may drop prematurely.	Control is often not necessary. Disease cause little damage to trees. Rake and remove fallen leaves.
Anthracnose (*Apiognomonia errabunda* or *Kabatiella apocrypta*)	April-October; peak in May-June	Necrotic, irregular, tannish to reddish brown spots concentrated along leaf veins. Fungal fruiting bodies (acervuli) prominent on upper surface of spots. Scorching pattern along leaf margin (Japanese maples).	

Table 5. Common diseases of specific woody plants

DISEASE	SEASONAL OCCURRENCE	SYMPTOM DESCRIPTION	SUGGESTED CONTROL PRACTICES
Verticillium wilt (*Verticillium dahliae, V. albo atrum*) (Not commonly found in Zones 7-10)	April-October; peak in July-August	Small, yellow foliage with marginal scorching or browning. Defoliation and die back of individual shoots and branches. Often, the foliage on one or more branches suddenly wilts. Greenish brown streaking in the vascular tissue or wood.	Fungicides will not cure infected trees. Infected trees should be removed. Plant resistant or immune trees or shrubs in the affected area because the fungus survives in the soil.
OAK			
Oak leaf blister (*Taphrina caerulesence*)	May-June	Bulging, blister like spots on leaves, leaf distortion. Underside of leaf turns brown following spore production. Can be confused with eriophyid mite or midge damage. Affected leaves drop prematurely.	Disease seldom causes significant damage. Apply fungicide spray when leaf buds swell in the spring and reapply at 7-10 day intervals until the leaf fully expands to reduce disease.
Anthracnose (*Apiognomonia quercina;* syn. *Discula quercina*)	April-September; peak in May-June	Young leaves brown and shrivel. Large necrotic areas develop on expanding leaves. Infection of fully mature leaves develop as small necrotic spots. Twigs die back. Infected leaves drop prematurely.	Rake and remove fallen leaf litter. Fungicides may be beneficial to small, newly transplanted trees. Apply as buds swell in spring and reapply at 7-10 day intervals until leaves fully expand.
Hypoxylon canker or oak decline (*Hypoxylon* spp.)	May-October; peak in July-August	Slow growth; chlorotic leaves or leaf scorch; wilting of foliage; "flags" of brown foliage; die back of branches and major limbs. Corky outer bark sloughs exposing smooth, tan to silver gray colored stromata. Old stromata loses its silvery surface and appears black.	Only infects stressed trees. Remove infected trees because it can spread via spores and root grafts with adjacent trees.
Rust (*Cronartium quercum* causes pine oak gall rust; *C. quercum* f. *sp. fusiforme* causes fusiform rust on pines)	May-July; peak in June-July	Small yellow spots with brown centers on the upper leaf surface. Hair like brown telia (fungal fruiting structure) on the leaf under side.	Disease is insignificant on oaks. Damage is primarily on the alternate host (2 and 3 needled pines.)
Oak wilt (*Ceratocystis fagacearum*)	May-October; peak in May-June	Leaves become chlorotic or bronze along leaf veins; leaf tip necrosis. Diseased trees defoliate and show progressive dieback of twigs and branches. Trees may wilt in late spring to late summer. Disease spreads primarily through root grafts and secondly by beetles.	Wilting or recently wilted trees should be removed. Mechanical barriers using a vibratory plow can break up root grafts. Avoid wounding or pruning trees when beetles are active, typically April June. Fungicide injections may reduce disease.

Table 5. Common diseases of specific woody plants

DISEASE	SEASONAL OCCURRENCE	SYMPTOM DESCRIPTION	SUGGESTED CONTROL PRACTICES
PEAR (FLOWERING)			
Fire blight (*Erwinia amylovora*)	April-June; peak in May-June	Young twigs and branches die from the terminal end and appear burned or deep rust colored. Branch may be bent, resembling a shepherd's crook. Dead leaves and fruit remain on the branch. Infection occurs in early spring during flowering and is favored by wet conditions. Pear cultivar Bradford is moderately resistant to fire blight, but it can be infected. Bradford's do not get typical Fire blight symptoms. Infected Bradford leaves are rust colored, scorched, or spotted. Portions of the leaf remain green.	Prune out branches 6 inches below signs of damage. Dip pruning tool in 70% isopropyl alcohol (rubbing alcohol) or 1 part bleach to 9 parts water solution between each cut. Avoid heavy nitrogen fertilization, especially in summer. Avoid splashing water. Plant resistant varieties.
Alternaria leaf spot (*Alternaria alternata*)	May-October; peak July-August	Small, round, tan to brown spots develop on leaves about mid summer. Spots often have zonate appearance. Spots may coalesce and blight leaf. Severely infected leaves drop prematurely. Infection is favored by prolonged leaf wetness, warm temperatures, high humidity and poor air circulation.	Avoid prolonged leaf wetness and wetting leaves during irrigation. Rake and remove fallen leaf litter. Apply protective fungicide applications in early summer and continue through fall.
PHOTINIA (RED TIP)			
Entomosporium leaf spot (*Entomosporium mespili; syn. Fabraea maculata*)	February-November; peak in March-April	Small reddish leaf spots initially. As spots age, center is grayish with a dark purple border. Leaf spots may coalesce causing severe leaf blight. Severely infected leaves drop prematurely. Over time severely infected plants die. Infection is favored by poor air circulation and prolonged periods of leaf wetness.	Selectively prune plants to improve air circulation through plant. Increase plant spacing. Avoid wetting foliage. Apply protective fungicide applications when leaves emerge in spring and continue at 10-14 day intervals throughout growing season.

Table 5. Common diseases of specific woody plants

DISEASE	SEASONAL OCCURRENCE	SYMPTOM DESCRIPTION	SUGGESTED CONTROL PRACTICES
Colletotrichum leaf spot/blight (*Collectotrichum gloeosporioides*)	May-October	Rust colored spots on leaf that coalesce to cover large areas of the leaf. Often concentrated along leaf margin and edge. Leaves may appear scorched along the leaf margins. Infection is favored by prolonged leaf wetness and typically occurs in early spring or late summer.	Rake and remove fallen leaf litter. Avoid wetting foliage. Increase plant spacing or selective prune plants to improve air circulation through plant canopy. Apply protective fungicides in spring and reapply at 10-14 day intervals.
PINE			
Needle rust (*Coleosporium spp.*)	March-May; peak in April	White shelf like projections from the needles. Orange rust spores produced within and rupture through white covering. Affected needles may drop.	Rarely causes significant decline. Eliminate alternate host (Asteraceae family; goldenrod). Fungicides not recommended.
Pitch canker (*Fusarium moniliforme var. subglutinans*)	January-December; peak August-October	Resin soaked lesions on twigs and cankers on larger branches and trunk. Diseased bark turns dark reddish brown. Shoot or limb dieback. Needles yellow then brown and remain on tree glued with crystalline resin.	Avoid wounding plants.
Fusiform rust (*Cronartium quercum f. sp. fusiforme*)	April May; peak April	Stem swellings and spindle shaped galls on branches. Multiple shoots causing witches' brooming grow from galls. Blister-like yellow protrusions from bark in spring. Pine bark dies resulting in cankers.	Remove affected branches or trees. Usually cause minor damage to landscape trees. Fungicides generally not recommended.
Needle cast (*Lophodermium pinastri*)	March-May; peak in April-May	Yellowing and shedding of older needles. Do not confuse with fall needle drop.	Weak pathogen. Rarely causes damage in landscape trees. Fungicides generally not recommended.

Table 5. Common diseases of specific woody plants

DISEASE	SEASONAL OCCURRENCE	SYMPTOM DESCRIPTION	SUGGESTED CONTROL PRACTICES
PYRACANTHA (FIRETHORN)			
Fire blight (*Erwinia amylovora*)	April-June; peak in May-June	Young twigs and branches die from the terminal end and appear burned or deep rust colored. Branch may be bent, resembling a shepherd's crook. Dead leaves and fruit remain on the branch. Infection occurs in early spring during flowering and is favored by wet conditions.	Prune out branches 6 inches below signs of damage. Dip pruning tool in 70% isopropyl alcohol (rubbing alcohol) or 1 part bleach to 9 parts water solution between each cut. Avoid heavy nitrogen fertilization, especially in summer. Avoid splashing water. Plant resistant varieties; P. coccinea cv. 'Sensation', P. koidzumil cv. 'Santa Cruz Prostrata' and hybrids 'San Jose' and 'Shawnee'
Scab (*Spilocaea pyracanthae*)	April-June; peak in May	Fruits covered with scabby lesions and turn black. Velvety, olive green sooty spots form on leaves. Infected leaves turn yellow and fruit and leaves drop prematurely.	Plant scab resistant varieties; 'Shawnee', 'Rutgers', Fiery Cascade'. Avoid wetting foliage when irrigating. Apply fungicide sprays in the spring as leaves emerge.
ROSE			
Black spot (*Diplocarpon rosae*; syn. *Marsonnina rosae*)	January-December; peak in March-June and August-October	Two stages of the disease may be present. 1) Black, round to irregular spots with fringed margins mainly on the upper leaf surface. Tissue around spots turn yellow; causes premature defoliation. Infection is favored by prolonged leaf wetness, poor air circulation and high humidity. It occurs throughout the growing season. 2) Reddish sunken lesions develop on the young canes or on canes overwintering from the fall. These lesions are the primary source of spores to initiate leaf infection in early spring.	Use sanitary measures by destroying infected leaves and canes of the previous year. Mulch under plants. Avoid wetting leaves. Prune canes to allow for better air circulation through the plant. Begin a fungicide spray program before the disease appears in early spring and continue at 7 10 day intervals throughout the growing season.
Powdery mildew (*Sphaerotheca pannosa var. rosae*)	January-December; peak in April-July, November	White to grayish patches appear on the leaves, flowers, and stems. Patches enlarge rapidly and may cover the entire leaf. Affected leaves dry and drop prematurely.	Apply protective fungicides at the first sign of infection and reapply at 10 14 day intervals. Mulch under plants. Remove old fallen leaf litter. Increase air circulation around plants.

Table 5. Common diseases of specific woody plants

DISEASE	SEASONAL OCCURRENCE	SYMPTOM DESCRIPTION	SUGGESTED CONTROL PRACTICES
Downy mildew (*Peronospora sparsa*)	April-July; peak May	Purple irregularly shaped lesions develop on the upper leaf surface. Spots often concentrated along veins and midrib. Grayish, fuzzy growth seen on the leaf underside opposite purple leaf spots in wet weather. Infection is favored by cooler, wet weather. Mostly seen in late spring and sometimes early fall.	Remove affected leaves. Mulch plants and remove fallen leaf litter. Avoid wetting foliage. Apply a protective fungicide application at the first sign of the disease and repeat application 10-14 days later or as label directs.
Rose Mosaic Virus	May-October	Yellow or white mosaic pattern or patches on the green leaf. Does not significantly harm plants. Affected leaves may scorch or drop prematurely.	No control necessary. Pruning will not remove virus from plant. Symptoms may show up more when the plant is stressed (water, cold temperatures).
Common stem canker (*Coniothyrium fuckelii; Leptosphaeria coniothyrium*)	March-October; peak in June-July	Often develops on the canes at the pruning wound. Young cankers are yellowish or reddish. With age, cankers turn brown, sunken, and cracked. Center turns light gray brown with dark border; numerous pycnidia (fruiting structures) develop beneath its upper surface.	Avoid wounding plants. Prune cankers when observed and apply protective fungicide to pruning cut. Avoid wetting foliage and sprinkler irrigation.
Rust (*Phragmidium spp.*)	April-July; peak in June	Bright orange to rust colored pustules develop on the underside of leaves. Yellow spots develop on upper side of leaf. Severely infected leaves drop prematurely. Infection most common in early summer during periods of prolonged leaf wetness, warmer day and cooler night temperatures.	Remove fallen leaf litter. Mulch plants. Apply fungicides at the first sign of disease and reapply at 10-14 day intervals.
Crown gall (*Agrobacterium tumefaciens*)	March-October	Galls form at the soil line, but also can form on branches or roots, are initially white, spherical, and soft. Galls darken with age as the outer cells die.	Purchase and propagate gall free plants. Avoid wounding plants, especially at the soil line. Disinfect grafting tools with 70% isopropyl alcohol (rubbing alcohol) or 10% bleach solution. Remove severely infected plants.

Table 5. Common diseases of specific woody plants

DISEASE	SEASONAL OCCURRENCE	SYMPTOM DESCRIPTION	SUGGESTED CONTROL PRACTICES
SYCAMORE			
Anthracnose (*Apiognomonia veneta*)	April–June; peak in May	Dead twigs and branches have sunken cankers. Bud death followed by new bud formation and death gives witches' broom like proliferation of branch ends. Black fungal fruiting structures visible in spring on bark of newly killed twigs. Leaves, especially in lower and inner branches, are blighted in spring with tan dead areas expanding along leaf veins. Large and irregularly shaped areas are killed along the leaf margins and between the veins.	Prune and destroy dead twigs and branches during dormancy, cutting 3 4 inches below the canker. Plant resistant cultivars that have been propagated from 'Liberty', 'Bloodgood', or 'Columbia' clones of London plane trees. These London plane tree clones are resistant to this disease. Tree injection in the fall before leaf drop has provided some protection.
VIBURNUM			
Downy mildew (*Plasmopara viburni*)	April–June; peak in May and September–November; peak in October	Irregularly shaped purple lesions develop on the upper leaf surface. Under wet conditions, white to grayish patches can be seen on the leaf underside opposite the purple spots. Spots coalesce over time. Severely infected leaves may drop. Infection usually takes place in early summer under cool night temperatures and prolonged leaf wetness.	Remove infected leaves Avoid splashing leaves with water when irrigating. Avoid prolonged leaf wetness. Apply protective fungicides at the first sign of disease.

INSECT PESTS OF ORNAMENTALS

Insects and related pests (mites, slugs, etc.) often reach damaging levels on ornamentals in Georgia. Homeowners who have only one or two shrubs eventually become familiar with major pests and are prepared to take preventive and/or corrective actions. For well landscaped grounds with a large variety of plants, it becomes more difficult to predict problems.

Nature of Damage

Hardly a season passes without pest outbreaks that require control measures to prevent injury to plants. The type and extent of damage to ornamentals by insect pests depends on the pest and ornamental involved. Several insect pests suck plant juices and cause stippling of foliage, stunting, and leaf drop. Pests with chewing mouthparts cause large holes in leaves or chew through stems and petioles. Other pests bore into plant tissue and tunnel through leaves and stems.

Effective management of insect pests of ornamentals requires proper diagnosis of the problem. Often we can make reliable diagnoses based on damage that insects cause. The most reliable diagnosis requires identification of the insect or mite itself. Diagnosis based on symptoms can be divided into damage categories as follows:

- Tattered leaves or flowers
- Stippled, bleached or bronzed foliage
- Die back of plant parts
- Evidence of insects themselves

Pests responsible for each category include:

- Tattered leaves or flowers can be caused by grasshoppers, caterpillars, adult or immature beetles.

- Stippled, bleached or bronzed foliage may be caused by insects with piercing mouth parts such as lace bugs or plant bugs. Mites or thrips may also cause this type of damage.

- Die back of plant parts is often caused by scale insects or by beetles or moth larvae that bore inside the stems.

- Evidence of insects themselves may be webs, tents, cases, flocculence (cottony material), frass (fecal material), sawdust.

Management of Pests

In order to grow attractive pest free plants, homeowners should utilize a pest control program that includes pest prevention, early detection, correct pest identification, proper selection of control materials, and proper application methods. All steps in the control program are interrelated and none can be omitted without jeopardizing control efforts.

Prevention

The most important step in managing insect pests is prevention. Avoid selection of plant materials that are prone to mite or insect problems. Choose plant materials wisely to avoid trouble later. Insects which become established on plants can reproduce rapidly.

Any measures taken to exclude pest establishment will be helpful. Soil sterilization or the purchase of a pest free potting medium is essential to the exclusion of soil insect pests from potted houseplants. For homeowners who enjoy propagating their own ornamentals, the use of clean stock plants is an important step in preventing plant damage. For example, poinsettia stock plants are often infested with whitefly that are capable of causing serious damage to many plants. On hobby greenhouses, screens on doors and vents are helpful in avoiding highly mobile insect pests such as adult leafminers and moths. Weed control around and within landscaped areas and hobby greenhouses reduces the chances of pest population outbreaks. Initial build up of mites, flea beetles, aphids and thrips often occur on weeds and grasses.

Do not overlook the benefits of good cultural plant practices in avoiding pest problems. Healthy, vigorous shrubs and flowers can tolerate light infestations of insect pests without becoming unattractive. For example, flushes of new growth on woody shrubs during spring and early summer may totally mask damage symptoms of a light insect infestation so that chemical controls are not needed. Good cultural management, including optimum fertility and moisture, allows plants to reach maximum tolerance to insect damage. Information on proper cultural management of ornamentals is presented in other sections of this reference manual. Rouging or removal of infested plants or plant parts can quickly reduce an insect infestation and the chances for spread of insects from one plant to another. When plants are inspected for pests, remove and dispose infested leaves and old decaying flowers. Never toss infested plant material on the ground at the base of plants.

Early Detection is Critical—Since the numbers and kinds of insect pests vary considerably, frequent inspection of plants for pest damage is important. During spring and summer some pest species reproduce so rapidly that close visual inspection of plants should be made every other day. Make a general inspection of the plants for loss of color, stunting, or holes in leaves. To detect some of the more unnoticeable pests also exam the undersides of several leaves on each plant.

Correct Identification—Early detection and correct identification of pests are the first two steps to an effective insect management program on ornamentals. Unless an insect is correctly identified, one cannot be certain that the insect found is actually a pest. Consequently, selecting an appropriate control measure becomes difficult. Homeowners should consult county Extension personnel for assistance in identifying unfamiliar insects. It is not unusual to find an unsuspecting homeowner attempting to control beneficial insects! Only after an insect has been correctly identified can one determine if, when, and how it should be controlled.

Proper Selection of Control Materials—Control materials for insect and related pests are listed in separate publications available from county Extension offices. No single pesticide is capable of controlling all major pests without damaging sensitive plants. As new products and research data become available, revisions of control recommendations are made. Consult your county Extension office to be sure you have the latest recommendations.

Correct Application Methods—Regardless of how quickly a pest is detected and how effective the selected pesticide is, pest control will be no better than the method of pesticide application. Pesticides are applied to ornamentals in every conceivable manner. Growers use aerosols, mists, smokes, fogs, dusts, sprays, drenches and granules. For control of foliage feeding pests, most insecticides are applied as sprays. For best performance, an insecticide should be applied at the proper rate and at a time when pests are present and most vulnerable. Sufficient spray volume to permit good and thorough coverage of the upper and lower surfaces of leaves should be used. Spray equipment that produces small diameter droplets provides such coverage.

Due to the difficulty in detecting many of the major ornamental pests, insecticide sprays are occasionally made to prevent damaging infestations of insects. Homeowners should try to detect developing infestations on plantings outside the home as early as possible. Visual inspections should be made twice each week. Examine both sides of the leaves, as well as new growth and stems. During early spring, when scale crawlers are emerging, a hand lens is helpful in detecting the immatures. By examining plants often, homeowners can reduce the use of insecticides. To control pests which are common and abundant in a predictive cycle (for example, a juniper which has mite problems every July), preventive sprays may be the best line of defense.

Aphids

Identification and Biology—Adults may be winged or wingless. The size of most mature aphid species varies from $1/16$ to $1/8$ inch long. The body is oval to pear shaped with two tube like cornicles on the abdomen. Colors are usually green, yellow, orange, red, black, or white. Aphids have several generations a year and overwinter on plants as eggs. Feeding aphids excrete honeydew on which black, sooty mold may grow.

Host Plants—Some aphid species only feed on one plant species, while others may be general feeders. Most deciduous trees and shrubs, as well as conifers, are subject to attack by aphids. Many species alternate host plant species between cold and warm seasons. High nitrogen fertilizer rates can increase aphid reproduction.

Damage Symptoms—Aphids sucking fluids from buds and leaf veins may cause stunting, deformation, discoloration, and leaf death. They do not cause stippling of green tissue. Aphids rarely cause obvious plant injury, but large populations may cause objectionable levels of honeydew (sticky substance) and sooty mold. Leaves damaged early in the season on indeterminately growing plants usually are hidden by healthy leaves produced later in the season after aphid populations decline.

Monitoring Techniques—In spring, look at new growth for curled, discolored leaves. Aphids typically cluster on the top side of curled leaves where white shed skins may be seen more easily than the aphids themselves. In summer, light colored aphids feed on veins on the lower surface of mature leaves. Look for honeydew and sooty mold. If these are present, but aphids are not on leaves, examine the bark for dark colored aphids. Also look for the presence and relative numbers of predators and parasitized aphids (mummies).

Control Strategies—By early summer, aphids are usually controlled in the landscape as a result of the actions of predators and parasites. If excessive honeydew is objectionable, use oil or soap sprays when predators and parasites are present on most terminals and leaves are not curled. Residual or systemics insecticides may be sprayed if leaf curl becomes objectionable, but the use of these insecticides may eliminate beneficials for some time. Dormant oil sprays may be applied when large numbers of overwintering eggs are detected.

Azalea Bark Scale

Identification and Biology—Adult females may be ⅛ inch long. In May, they begin secreting a white, feltlike sac that encloses their bodies and eggs. Overwintering nymphs are about ¹⁄₁₆ inch long, gray, and usually are found in twig forks. Males emerge in early spring, mate, and die. There are two generations a year in Georgia. Immatures overwinter on bark.

Host Plants—This imported scale insect prefers and rhododendron, but also has been found on andromeda (Pieris), maple, arborvitae, fremontia, willow, poplar, and hackberry.

Damage Symptoms—s tolerate low levels of this scale without showing symptoms. Honeydew, sooty mold, leaf yellowing, and dieback have been observed on plants with large populations of this scale insect. Continuous heavy infestations may kill plants in a few years.

Monitoring Techniques—Look for sooty mold on leaves, yellowing leaves, and twig dieback. Stippling of leaves does not occur with this pest. Examine twigs for white egg sacs and the presence of reddish crawlers in May and June. Examine egg sacs closely for holes which indicate the presence of parasites. Look for predators. In light infestations, the scales are found in twig forks. In heavy infestations, they occur anywhere on bark.

Control Strategies—In situations where there are a few egg sacs or scales but no leaf yellowing or sooty mold, do not spray. Beneficial insects usually control this insect. Dormant oil may be used to control overwintering nymphs on twigs. Summer oil or insecticidal soap may be used to control crawlers.

Azalea Caterpillar

Identification and Biology—Adult moths are 1 inch long and brown. Mature larvae may be 2½ inches long. They have reddish brown legs, head, and "neck" area. The body is black with rows of white or pale yellow spots. The larvae feed from late summer through early fall. There is one generation a year. Pupae overwinter in soil.

Host Plants—This native moth prefers but it has been reported on witchhazel, sumac, apple, red oak, and andromeda (Pieris).

Damage Symptoms—The caterpillars feed together when young and then disperse as they mature. Defoliation of entire branches and plants may occur.

Monitoring Techniques—Observe **host plants** for signs of defoliation in late summer and fall. Look for black caterpillars with white spots.

Control Strategies—Hand pick caterpillars from plants when only a few are present. Apply *Bacillus thuringiensis* if caterpillars are numerous and less than ¾ inch in length. Apply residual insecticides on larger caterpillars.

Azalea Lace Bug

Identification and Biology—Adults are ⅛ inch long. The transparent wings are held flat on the back. Their wings are lacy with two grayish brown cross bands connected in the middle. Nymphs are mostly black and spiny. The flask shaped eggs are partially embedded in leaf tissue and often are covered with a black tar like secretion. There are four generations a year. Eggs overwinter in leaf tissue. Lace bug adults and nymphs live and feed on the underside of leaves.

Host Plants—Deciduous and evergreen s.

Damage Symptoms—Nymphs and adults feed on plant juices through leaf tissue, causing white stippling of leaves. Nymphs and adults deposit black excrement spots that stick to the bottom surface of leaves. In heavy infestations, plants are aesthetically damaged and may die back.

Monitoring Techniques—Look for the first signs of damage on plants in full sun or in protected areas beginning in March and continuing throughout the summer. Look for white stippling on older leaves. Turn stippled leaves over to find lace bug stages and black fecal spots. Examine lace bug eggs with a hand lens for signs of parasitism (a round hole in the top of the egg) and look for predators.

Control Strategies—Plant azaleas in partial shade. Time insecticide applications for the presence of the first generation nymphs. Insecticidal soap or horticultural oil sprays will give adequate control if sprayed on the underside of leaves. Beneficials usually are unable to control this pest when **host plants** are located in sunny locations.

Azalea Leafminer

Identification and Biology—Adult moths are about ⅜ inch long with wings folded. They are yellowish brown with purple markings on the wings and stand at a 60° angle when at rest. Mature larvae are about ½ inch long and yellowish brown. There are two generations a year. Pupae overwinter in leaf mines.

Host Plants—Azalea appears to be the only plant attacked by this leafminer. It may be a problem in greenhouses, as well as nursery and landscape settings.

Damage Symptoms—Young larvae form elongate brown blotch mines, usually near the leaf midrib. Older larvae curl the tips of leaves with silk and feed inside the curl. Large populations cause leaves to turn brown and drop prematurely.

Monitoring Techniques—Look for leaf mines in April or May. Curled leaf tips in June indicate completion of the first generation. Second generation leaf mines begin in July. Shake plants in late June and August to make adults fly and to estimate their numbers.

Control Strategies—Since larvae of this pest feed in leaf mines or in curled leaves, systemic insecticides are preferred. Treat in May if numerous developing leaf mines are observed. Evaluate the second generation in July and re treat if needed. Rake and destroy leaves in fall.

Bagworms

Identification and Biology—Adult male moths are about ¾ inch long and black. Adult females do not develop wings. They remain inside their bags Males mate with females in their bags. Larvae and their bags are 1 to 2 inches in length. Larvae begin construction of their bags soon after hatching. Their silken bags are covered with plant parts. One generation occurs each year.

Host Plants—This native bagworm moth seriously damages northern white cedar, red cedar, arborvitae, juniper, and other conifers. Boxelder, sycamore, black locust, willow, elm, poplar, oak, maple, and persimmon may harbor reservoir populations.

Damage Symptoms—Damage is most serious and obvious on foundation conifers, such as arborvitae and juniper, where individual branches and even whole plants are completely defoliated. On large deciduous trees and shrubs, defoliation is less evident.

Monitoring Techniques—In May and June, begin looking for new bags on **host plants**, especially where large, old bags are present. Closely examine outer foliage of plants in full sun. In fall and winter, search for and manually destroy bags, which may contain up to 1,000 overwintering eggs.

Control Strategies—In light infestations, hand pick and destroy bags. In heavy infestations on many plants, spray with *Bacillus thuringiensis* between May and June.

Apply residual insecticides in June and July.

Bark Beetles (Pine)

Identification and Biology—Adult Ips engraver beetles are brown and vary from ⅛ to ¼ inch in length. The head is bent downward, and the wing covers have posterior spines. Larvae are C shaped, legless, and white, with brown heads. There are three to four generations a year. Larvae overwinter in galleries under bark.

Host Plants—Most pines grown under stressed conditions are susceptible to attack.

Damage Symptoms—Adult beetles boring into relatively healthy trees cause sticky white pitch tubes to form. Brown, sawdust like material may be evident from entrance holes in severely stressed trees. Weeks or months later, entire tops of infested trees turn yellowish red and die, usually because of a blue stain fungus introduced by the beetles.

Monitoring Techniques—Look on bark for the first signs of brown dust or white pitch tubes from late March through October. Note the crowns of pines in the area for early warning of a local bark beetle outbreak. Check under bark of dying trees for signs of galleries, larvae, and blue stain.

Control Strategies—Trees should be watered during drought periods to prevent stress. Prevent beetles from building egg galleries by monitoring trees frequently and treating branches and trunks with a residual insecticide when the first pitch tubes appear. Heavily infested or dying trees should be destroyed immediately to prevent adult beetle emergence.

Boxwood Leafminer

Identification and Biology—Adults are orange yellow mosquito-like flies about ⅛ inch long. They swarm around boxwoods for about two weeks in mid March to early April after new growth has flushed on the shrubs. The yellow maggots overwinter in leaf mines. There is one generation a year.

Host Plants—This imported gall fly may damage most boxwood species, but *Buxus sempervirens* 'Argenteo variegata,' 'Pendula,' and 'Suffruticosa' usually are not seriously infested. English boxwoods are less susceptible than American varieties.

Damage Symptons—Larvae feeding inside the leaves cause blisterlike blotch mines to appear on the bottom side of infested leaves. Heavily mined leaves turn yellow and prematurely drop.

Monitoring Techniques—Beginning in mid March, periodically sample boxwood plants to detect flying adults. Examine the underside of the previous year's leaves to detect active mines easily. Look for presence of pupal cases sticking out of mines and the orange colored adults. Mines of the current season do not become obvious until fall. Most damage is done in fall and late winter.

Control Strategies—When adults are detected and are active, apply a contact insecticide. If numerous mines are found in the summer or fall, apply a systemic insecticide. Replace susceptible cultivars with resistant cultivars.

Boxwood Psyllid

Identification and Biology—The light green adults are about ⅛ inch long and resemble miniature cicadas. Nymphs are green and rather flattened, with posterior fluffy white wax. They feed inside cupped terminal leaves. There is one generation a year. Orange eggs overwinter beneath bud scales.

Host Plants—American boxwood cultivars, except 'Suffruticosa', are preferred and most seriously damaged by this imported psyllid. English boxwoods rarely receive serious damage.

Damage Symptoms—The terminal shoots of infested plants develop cupped, stunted leaves.

Monitoring Techniques—Look inside cupped terminal leaves in early spring for nymphs and white wax. Examine plants in early summer for adults. Shrubs usually outgrow damage by mid summer.

Control Strategies—Use horticultural oil or soap sprays to control nymphs when detected in early spring. Use a residual insecticide to control adults that are discovered later in the growing season if the level of damage is intolerable.

Cottony Maple Scale

Identification and Biology—Adult females are about ³⁄₁₆ inch long. They are black, flat, and oval. The ¼ inch white cottony ovisac, or egg sac, is deposited on bark. Crawlers appear in June and immatures in summer on the underside of leaves. There is one generation a year. Immatures overwinter on twigs.

Host Plants—This native soft scale may feed on many different shade trees. Preferred hosts include maple, elm, hawthorn, dogwood, sycamore, poplar, and linden.

Damage Symptoms—Heavy infestations that encrust branches may cause leaf yellowing, stunting, and dieback. Moderate to heavy infestation levels will cause objectionable honeydew (sticky substance secreted on leaves) problems to structures under trees, but usually do not damage trees.

Monitoring Techniques—Look for white eggsacs on bark in early spring. During the summer, look on underside of leaves for flat, yellow immatures sucking sap from leaf veins where honeydew and sooty mold are found on the host plant.

Control Strategies—If infestations are light, honeydew and sooty mold are not objectionable, or if beneficials are abundant, it may not be necessary to treat. Reevaluate the situation within two weeks. If infestations are heavy and stunting, or honeydew and sooty mold are objectionable, apply dormant oils to bark to kill overwintering nymphs. Horticultural oil or insecticidal soap can be applied to leaves during the summer to control crawlers.

Dogwood Borer

Identification and Biology—The adults are clearwing moths about ⅜ inch long. They have two gold bands on a bluish black abdomen. The larva which grows to ½ inch long is white with a brown head and has two reddish brown spots on the back, near the head. There is one generation a year. Larvae overwinter under bark. Adult emergence peaks around early to mid May, but occurs continually from April to October because eggs are laid for several months.

Host Plants—This native clearwing moth primarily attacks stressed or wounded dogwoods. Other landscape trees, such as apple, oak, hickory, cherry, birch, willow, and ash may be attacked.

Damage Symptoms—Larvae bore under bark, causing it to crack. Brown frass around bark cracks usually indicates borers are active. Repeated multiple infestations may cause dieback on large trees, and small trees may be killed.

Monitoring Techniques—Look for brown frass around wounds and bark cracks. Remove loose bark with a knife. Larvae may be found in short tunnels under bark near wounds.

Control Strategies—Plant trees in proper location. Protect tree trunks with mulch bands to prevent wounds from lawn mowers. An early April application of a long residual insecticide to the bark should prevent infestation. An additional application may be necessary in late May. Kousa dogwood appears to be resistant to this borer.

Dogwood Clubgall Midge

Identification and Biology—Adult midges are about ⅛ inch long. They superficially resemble mosquitoes. Mature larvae are yellowish orange maggots. The oval galls are found at branch terminals. There is one generation a year. Pupae overwinter in soil under trees.

Host Plants—This native gall fly infests the flowering dogwood, *Cornus florida*, from New England to Florida.

Damage Symptoms—In spring, newly hatched maggots infest growing tips and cause oval or somewhat tubular green galls to form. Associated terminal leaves slowly wilt and die, and the galls turn brown in summer. Heavily infested young trees are stunted.

Control Strategies—Look for the newly forming green galls in May on terminal twigs of flowering dogwood. Dead terminals with brown galls from the previous year indicate the possibility of an infestation.

Prune out and destroy newly formed green galls in spring. There are no insecticides labeled for control of this minor pest.

Eastern Tent Caterpillar

Identification and Biology—Adult moths are about 1 inch long. They are light brown with two white diagonal stripes across each forewing. Mature larvae may reach a length of 2 inches or more. This is the only common caterpillar with a white stripe down the back. There is one generation a year. Pupae overwinter in cocoons in debris on the ground.

Host Plants—Preferred hosts include wild cherry, crabapple, and apple. In peak years, ash, birch, black gum, willow, maple, oak, poplar, cherry, and plum are attacked.

Damage Symptoms—Silken webs in tree forks at budbreak are indicative of this pest. In peak population years, preferred hosts can be defoliated.

Monitoring Techniques—Look for the black ¾ inch long egg masses on preferred hosts in the dormant season. Look for silken webs in the branch forks of preferred hosts in early March.

Control Strategies—Prune out the egg masses dur-

ing the dormant season. Mechanically destroy the web contents when first discovered. Time insecticide application for the presence of young larvae. Spray *Bacillus thuringiensis* onto foliage where larvae are found feeding.

Euonymus Scale

Identification and Biology—Covers of adult females are about ⅛ inch long, brownish black, and are oyster shell shaped. Male covers are smaller, thinner, and white. Crawlers are yellowish orange and are most often found on new growth. Fertilized adult females overwinter. There are four overlapping generations a year.

Host Plants—This imported armored scale attacks and frequently kills most species of evergreen Euonymus. *E. kiautschovica* is relatively resistant, as are deciduous Euonymus species. Celastrus (Bittersweet) also may be severely attacked.

Damage Symptoms—Light infestations on bark cause no obvious damage. In heavy infestations, the white covers of males are easy to spot on the leaves and the leaves develop yellow spots. After two to three years, even large *Euonymus japonica* usually dieback if intervention does not occur.

Monitoring Techniques—Look for dieback and white male covers on leaves. Look for off color, yellow spotted leaves on unthrifty plants. Always examine *Euonymus japonica* to discover infestations before they cause damage. Carefully examine bark on a few stems to detect light infestations. Examine plants for presence of predators and parasites.

Control Strategies—Replace susceptible Euonymus varieties with resistant or tolerant species where possible. Dormant oil sprays should control light bark infestations. For heavy leaf infestations, remove and destroy heavily infested branches and then follow with an application of a systemic insecticide. Time application of horticultural oil, insecticidal soaps, or other contact insecticides for the presence of crawlers. Do not use contact insecticides if there are numerous predators or parasites present.

Fall Webworm

Identification and Biology—Adult moths are about ¾ inch long with wings folded. Wings are all white or white with black spots. Bases of front legs are orange yellow. Mature larvae are about 1 inch long and may occur in two color forms: those with black heads are yellowish white and those with red heads are brown.

Both forms have paired black tubercles running down the back. They are covered with long, silky gray hairs. There are four generations a year. Pupae overwinter in flimsy cocoons in protected places.

Host Plants—More than 100 species of deciduous forest and shade trees may be attacked by this native tiger moth caterpillar. Preferred hosts include mulberry, walnut, hickory, elm, sweetgum, poplar, willow, oak, linden, ash, and apple and other fruit trees.

Damage Symptoms—The caterpillars produce a "web" of fine silk over terminals. They feed inside the silken web, which they enlarge to take in more foliage as they grow. The webs are aesthetically distracting but rarely is enough terminal foliage consumed to affect tree growth. The dry webs can increase in number over a season and hang on terminals into the winter.

Monitoring Techniques—In early spring, examine the south side of tree crowns for the first signs of webbing over terminals. Continue to monitor host trees throughout the growing season for the presence of webs.

Control Strategies—Prune out webbed terminals as they are detected in the course of regular monitoring visits. When large infestations are present, *Bacillus thuringiensis*, horticultural oil, or insecticidal soap may be used to control young larvae. Use of these products will also protect the numerous species of predators and parasites that normally keep this pest below damaging levels. Insecticides must penetrate the "webs" to provide good control.

Flatheaded Appletree Borer

Identification and Biology—Adults may reach ½ inch in length. They are oval, flattened beetles, metallic greenish bronze above and brassy below. The wing covers have wavy, light colored indentations. The white larvae, commonly called flatheaded borers, are expanded just behind the true head, which is black. There is one generation a year. Larvae overwinter in galleries inside the host plant.

Host Plants—Preferred hosts include sycamore, red maple, silver maple, willow, oak, tuliptree poplar, elm, beech, hickory, apple, pear, dogwood, and black walnut. Newly planted trees are susceptible to these borers until root systems are established.

Damage Symptoms—Larvae bore fairly large, irregular cavities in phloem tissue of the main trunk and larger branches. Young trees and trees under stress are particularly attractive to this pest. Larvae are usually found boring into the base of trees. Small trees often are killed.

Monitoring Techniques—Frequently examine newly transplanted and stressed trees for signs of dieback on branches. Closely examine bark for galleries where cracking and weeping are seen. Adults run over bark and are quick to fly. They are most active on exposed, sunny bark of weakened trees from early March through May and early September through October.

Control Strategies—Plant trees on the proper site. Maintain vigor through use of good cultural practices. If numerous adult beetles are noted on bark, spray the trunk and major branches with an approved residual insecticide. Cut back infested branches below signs of infestation.

Greenstriped Mapleworm

Identification and Biology—Adult moths are about 1 inch long. The front wings are pink with a central yellow band. Mature larvae are about 1½ inches long, pale green with a reddish head, two black thoracic horns, and seven longitudinal greenish black stripes. There are two generations a year. Pupae overwinter in soil.

Host Plants—This native giant silkworm moth prefers maples, especially red maple, sugar maple, and silver maple. It also feeds on boxelder and oaks where they grow mixed in with maples.

Damage Symptoms—The mature caterpillars are capable of devouring leaves down to the midrib. Feeding usually begins on the lower branches. Heavy infestations may strip small trees.

Monitoring Techniques—Look for damage on foliage of lower branches of susceptible maples in early summer. Shake lower branches to knock down camouflaged larvae. Larvae feed singly on leaves. Adults are easily trapped in black light traps.

Control Strategies—Treatment of trees usually is impractical because effective coverage is hard to achieve without special equipment. *Bacillus thuringiensis* may be effective when caterpillars are young.

Native Holly Leafminer

Identification and Biology—Adult flies are about ⅛ inch long and black. The larvae are ⅛ inch long yellow maggots that tunnel through leaves, creating serpentine mines. Eggs are usually deposited in the midrib or leaf margin and early mining occurs there. There is one generation a year. Larvae overwinter in mines.

Host Plants—The native holly leafminer produces mines primarily on American holly. Other Phytomyza species infest Japanese, Chinese, English and yaupon hollies.

Damage Symptoms—Summer to fall mining occurs in the midrib. The obvious, linear, yellowish green mine in the leaf surface occurs the following spring. Several mines per leaf cause premature leaf drop. Adult females of this imported fly puncture tender new holly leaves to feed on plant juices. Parasites often control this pest if insecticide use can be eliminated.

Monitoring Techniques—Look for short mines in late summer. Look at leaves on the south side of holly for expanding yellowish mines in Jan./Feb. Look for adult flies on new terminal leaves beginning in March. Look for numbers of feeding punctures on the underside of new leaves as an indication of fly population size. Adults may be present from March through April.

Control Strategies—In light infestations, pick and destroy mined leaves before March. In heavy infestations, use systemics for larvae in March or late summer. Contact insecticides may be used for adults in early April, but this is the least desirable technique because beneficial parasites may be killed. Typically 70-85%of mines will be parasitized.

Japanese Beetle

Identification and Biology—Adults are nearly ½ inch long, broadly oval, thick bodied, with coppery brown wing covers and a metallic green body. Mature larvae are nearly 1 inch long and white, with brown heads. They resemble several other scarab beetle larvae, but may be identified by the shape of the raster (an area of bare spots, hairs, and spines on the underside of the last abdominal segment). There is one generation a year. Larvae overwinter in soil.

Host Plants—Adults of this imported scarab beetle feed on the flowers and leaves of many plants. Preferred plants include rose, crape myrtle, maples, sycamore, birch, cottonwood, linden, mountain ash, and elms.

Damage Symptoms—Adults prefer tender young leaves, which they may skeletonize completely. Trees may be defoliated in heavily infested areas. Larvae may damage lawns and the roots of small plants seriously. Flowers, such as roses, may be destroyed by large adult populations.

Monitoring Techniques—Look for adults on preferred hosts from early June through August. Examine turfgrass in late summer for presence of grubs. Use a spade to cut three sides of a strip of turf 1 foot square by 2 or 3 inches deep. Force the spade under the sod and lay it back, using the uncut side as a hinge. Use a trowel to dislodge soil from the overturned roots. Count the grubs in the exposed soil, then replace the strip of sod. Treatment of turf is suggested if there are more than six to eight grubs per square foot.

Control Strategies—Milky spore disease is available for control of Japanese beetle grubs. Results with this product have been inconsistent in Georgia. Application of residual insecticides applied to turf in late August or early September has provided more reliable control. Weekly application of residual or contact insecticides to **host plants** in June through July will provide only partial adult control. Traps usually are counterproductive and most often call in more beetles than they trap. Use traps to time insecticide application for adults. Do not use traps for control.

Juniper Scale

Identification and Biology—Mature female covers are circular, white, and about 1/16 inch in diameter. Male covers are smaller, elongate, oval, and white. Shed skins incorporated into the cover are yellow. There is one generation a year. Adult females overwinter on needles.

Host Plants—This imported armored scale insect prefers juniper, but has also been collected from Leyland cypress and cedar. Yellow crawlers are present in late spring.

Damage Symptoms—Light infestations cause no apparent symptoms. Heavy infestations (ten or more scales per ½ inch of twig) cause the foliage to turn yellow and if there is no intervention from beneficial insects or insecticide application, dieback can occur.

Monitoring Techniques—Look for off color foliage. Examine needles closely for minute, white, circular scale covers. Examine infested plants closely for evidence of parasite and predator populations and their activities. Scales usually build up first on the south side of shrubs or on the side against a building.

Control Strategies—Dormant oil spray will reduce the number of adults that successfully overwinter, but usually does not provide adequate control. Use horticultural oil or insecticidal soap to control crawlers in late spring. Systemic insecticides may be used to reduce heavy populations of scales in late summer and fall.

Longtailed Mealybug

Identification and Biology—Adult bodies are about ⅛ inch long. The body margin is ringed with white wax filaments. The last pair is over one-half of the length of the body. The wax filaments are short on crawlers. There are two to three generations a year. Immatures overwinter on bark.

Host Plants—This distinctive, cosmopolitan mealybug is a general feeder. It is usually found in protected locations on pyracantha, holly, yew, and rhododendron.

Damage Symptoms—Moderate to heavy infestations produce much sticky honeydew that fosters a dense growth of sooty mold, and terminal leaves may become yellow and distorted. A heavy layer of sooty mold on leaves of heavily infested plants reduces food production and, therefore, plant vigor.

Monitoring Techniques—Look for honeydew and sooty mold on dense plants growing in sheltered locations. Examine plants closely for active ants and/or presence of honeydew. Examine plants above the areas containing the most honeydew/sooty mold for mealybugs. Mealybugs will be found on the underside of leaves and stems.

Control Strategies—A dormant oil spray will reduce the overwintering population. Summer oil sprays will suppress growing populations. Systemics are preferable if plantings are dense and/or if the pest population is high. Ant control may be indicated if the mealybug problem persists in the presence of ants.

Maple Bladdergall Mite & Maple Spindlegall Mite

Identification and Biology—Adults of these two eriophyid mites are not visible without a hand lens. They live in circular and spindle shaped galls. They are white to clear in color, 0.15 mm long, cigar shaped with only four anterior legs. There are several generations a year. Adult forms overwinter in bark cracks.

Host Plants—The maple bladder gall mite prefers red maple; the maple spindle gall mite prefers silver maple and sugar maple.

Damage Symptoms—Infested leaves develop small circular or spindle shaped galls in spring that turn from green to red to black in one month. The galls are on the top side of the leaf, but the opening is on the bottom side of the leaf. Most infestations cause no other symptoms and are not a serious threat to the health of the host plant.

Monitoring Techniques—Look at new leaves for gall formation in spring as leaves expand. Look at mature leaves in summer to estimate the abundance of galls. Galls can be of cosmetic concern but do not damage plant.

Control Strategies—Control measures usually are not necessary.

Nantucket Pine Tip Moth

Identification and Biology—Adult moths are ¼ inch long with wings folded and silvery gray with rust colored patches. Mature larvae are about ⅜ inch long and tan with dark brown heads. Pupae are brown and overwinter in shoot tips. There are four generations a year. Pupae overwinter on shoots.

Host Plants—This native moth feeds on all pines except eastern white pine and longleaf pine. Mugo, loblolly, pitch, Virginia, scotch, Austrian, and Japanese black pines are preferred.

Damage Symptoms—Newly hatched larvae bore in needles, then buds, and finally into the stem, causing the terminal shoot to die and turn brown. Pines less than 6 feet high that grow in full sun receive the most damage. This pest may prune back, but rarely kills, established pines.

Monitoring Techniques—Look for stunted, brown terminals. Depending on your location, hang a pheromone trap in late February to mid March, depending on temperature, and replace it in mid June. Monitor every one to two days, and record first catch. For a more accurate method, use heat units in combination with trap data to determine egg hatch (i.e., a degree day model).

Control Strategies—In small plantings, destroy brown terminals in the dormant season to kill overwintering pupae. In large plantings, apply a spray to terminals ten days after the first moths are trapped, using pheromone trap catch data.

Oak Lecanium Scale

Identification and Biology—Fully developed adult females are about ¼ inch long. They are oval to almost circular, highly convex and light to dark brown. Crawlers are pale yellow. There is one generation a year. Immatures overwinter on twigs.

Host Plants—This native soft scale is believed to be

restricted to the beech family (Fagaceae), especially oak and chinquapin.

Damage Symptoms—Heavily infested twigs commonly exhibit stunted leaves and dieback due to feeding activities of developing females in the spring. Crawlers spend the summer feeding on leaf veins but usually produce no symptoms of damage.

Monitoring Techniques—Examine host twigs in the dormant season for dead females of the previous season and for immatures that will begin to enlarge and mature in the spring. Look for immatures feeding on leaf veins from mid June through the fall.

Control Strategies—Use horticultural oil as a dormant spray or as a crawler spray in mid June. Using oil will reduce impact on parasite activity that peaks with crawler activity. If **damage symptoms** are evident in July or August and crawlers are present, repeat the oil application to the foliage.

Obscure Scale

Identification and Biology—Fully enlarged adult female covers may reach ⅛ inch in diameter. They are circular, brown to gray, slightly convex, with central skins that are black when rubbed. Male covers are smaller and broadly oval. This species develops in overlapping clusters. There is one generation a year. Immatures overwinter and crawlers appear in July.

Host Plants—This native armored scale feeds on eastern oak species, especially black oaks, and on pecan. In landscapes, pin and willow oaks are frequently damaged by this pest.

Damage Symptoms—Heavy infestations commonly cause branch dieback on oak trees. Pin oak branches may become gnarled where many scale aggregations depress the bark.

Monitoring Techniques—Look on three to four year old branches for overlapping gray scale covers. Scrape off covers to determine viability of a population because covers of dead scales may remain attached. In midsummer, live adult female scales are light purple. Scout in mid July to determine amount of crawler activity. Look under covers in the dormant season for the small, yellow immatures to see if dormant sprays are needed. Look for holes in covers to estimate level of parasitism.

Control Strategies—Concentrate dormant oil sprays on three to four year old growth to reduce overwintering populations. Spray summer oil in late July to kill newly settled crawlers. Over fertilization tends to result in increased scale insect populations. Several parasite species are active when the scale crawlers appear in July. Avoid synthetic insecticide sprays at this time.

Orangestriped Oakworm

Identification and Biology—Adult moths are about 1¼ inches long with wings closed. They are reddish brown, translucent, with a submarginal dark stripe and a white spot on each forewing. Mature larvae are about 1½ inches long. They are black with eight orange to yellow stripes and two black spines behind the head. There are approximately two generations a year in Georgia. Adults first appear in early summer. Pupae overwinter in soil.

Host Plants—This moth caterpillar prefers to feed on oaks, but it also attacks hickory and birch.

Damage Symptoms—The caterpillars are gregarious and the young feed by skeletonizing the leaf surface. Older caterpillars are defoliators and may consume all but the leaf midrib. Defoliation usually occurs one branch at a time when populations are small.

Monitoring Techniques—Look for signs of localized skeletonization turning to defoliation on host tree branches. Where this species is a serious problem, a black light trap can be used to determine the first adult appearance and the relative size of each generation.

Control Strategies—Manually destroy aggregations of young larvae when they are detected on small trees. Application of *Bacillus thuringiensis* or horticultural oil will control young larvae. Contact insecticides often are required to control large caterpillars.

Pine Needle Scale

Identification and Biology—Adult female covers are about ⅛ inch long. They are white, oystershell shaped, and only found on needles. Male covers are similar but smaller. There are two generations a year, with reddish crawlers found in May or June, and July. Red eggs overwinter under scales.

Host Plants—This native armored scale feeds on most needle bearing conifers, including spruce, fir, pine, hemlock, and Douglas fir. White, Mugo, Scots, and Austrian pines are preferred.

Damage Symptoms—Conifers are tolerant of light infestations of this pest. In heavy infestations, several scales per needle may cause yellowing, stunting, and eventual dieback. Trees along roads and against buildings often suffer severe attacks.

Look for obvious white scale covers on green needles. **Monitoring Techniques**—In May and June, turn over scale covers and examine with a hand lens to determine if eggs or crawlers are present. Look for holes in covers that indicate the presence of parasites or predators. Look for active, reddish crawlers and translucent, yellow, settled, and feeding crawlers.

Control Strategies—Many predators and parasites attack this pest. Apply a dormant oil to reduce overwintering populations. Apply a horticultural oil or insecticidal soap when crawlers are present. Application of a long residual insecticide is warranted if no beneficials are found in a scale population that is high enough to cause needle yellowing.

Pine Spittlebug

Identification and Biology—Adults are about ¼ inch long. They are tan with two irregular whitish bands on each wing. Nymphs are mostly black except for whitish abdomens, and they are covered with frothy honeydew called spittle. There is one generation a year. Eggs overwinter on bark.

Host Plants—This native spittlebug prefers Scots pine, but also attacks pine, eastern white, Virginia, jack, slash, loblolly, Japanese, and Mugo pines, as well as Norway, white, and red spruces, balsam fir, larch, eastern hemlock, and Douglas fir.

Damage Symptoms—Both adults and nymphs suck sap from twigs. This feeding activity may cause twig and branch dieback and even tree death. Some flagging injury is due to the fungus *Diplodia pini*, which may enter pines through feeding punctures of spittlebugs in hot spring weather.

Monitoring Techniques—Look for nymphs under spittle on twigs in early spring. Look for adults feeding in the same locations in early summer without a covering of spittle. Nymphs are slow moving and may be collected by hand. Adults are active and may be swept from twigs with an insect net.

Control Strategies—Light spittlebug infestations on small pines may be removed manually. Light infestations have little effect on trees, and chemical control usually is not warranted.

Redhumped Caterpillar

Identification and Biology—Adult moths are about 1 inch long. They are grayish brown with black markings. Fully grown spiny larvae are about 1¼ inches long with many black and yellow longitudinal stripes, a reddish head, and reddish humps on abdominal segments 1 and 8. There is one generation a year. Prepupae overwinter in cocoons in leaf litter.

Host Plants—This native moth is a general feeder attacking plants in the rose family as well as many shade trees, such as poplar, elm, willow, hickory, walnut, sweetgum, persimmon, birch, redbud, and dogwood.

Damage Symptoms—These caterpillars feed together in clusters. When young, they skeletonize the underside of leaves. Older larvae consume leaves to the midrib. On large trees, individual branches may be defoliated. Small trees may suffer complete defoliation.

Monitoring Techniques—Look for the distinctive caterpillars feeding in clusters when branches of **host plants** show skeletonization beginning in June. Later in the summer, defoliation will become obvious as larger larvae consume leaves.

Control Strategies—On small trees and low branches on large trees, prune out clusters of larvae when they first appear. In heavy infestations, spray young caterpillars with *Bacillus thuringiensis* or horticultural oil. Use contact insecticides for older larvae.

Rhododendron Borer

Identification and Biology—Adult moths are about ¼ inch long. The wings are mostly clear and the body is black with three gold abdominal bands. Fully grown larvae are about ½ inch long and white with a brown head and five pairs of short ventral prolegs. There is one generation a year. Larvae overwinter in tunnels in branches.

Host Plants—This native clearwing moth prefers to feed on rhododendron, but occasionally attacks deciduous azalea and mountain laurel.

The boring activities of larvae in branches may cause the bark to crack, revealing tunnels and frass. Heavy infestations girdle branches, causing wilting and eventual branch dieback.

Damage Symptoms—Look for wilting rhododendron leaves and dieback. Prune off suspect branches and dissect them longitudinally to see if larvae are present. Pheromone traps may be used to determine the flight and egg laying period.

Control Strategies—Prune out and destroy wilting branches in late summer or early spring. Hang a pheromone trap in May and treat branches of **host plants** with a systemic insecticide when the first males are trapped, usually in early summer.

Rhododendron Lace Bug

Identification and Biology—Adults are about ⅛ inch long. The body is pale yellow. The lacy, transparent wings have two dark spots and are held flat on the back. Nymphs are black and spiny. Eggs are partially buried in leaf tissue along the midvein. Eggs overwinter in leaves and there are four generations a year in Georgia.

Host Plants—This native pest prefers rhododendron species, but occasionally attacks andromeda and mountain laurel.

Damage Symptoms—Nymphs and adults suck chlorophyll from leaves, causing a coarse, yellowish stippling. Both stages deposit black excrement spots that stick to the underside of leaves. In severe infestations, most leaves turn yellowish brown.

Monitoring Techniques—Look for first signs of stippling damage on plants in full sun. Beginning in early spring and continuing throughout the summer, examine plants closely for signs of stippling on older leaves. Examine the underside of stippled leaves for lace bug stages and black fecal spots.

Control Strategies—Horticultural oil or insecticidal soap will provide control if carefully sprayed on the underside of leaves. Time application for early spring when the first generation of the insect is present. Application of a contact or systemic insecticide may be necessary to control heavy infestations that are present late spring through the fall.

Sawflies

Identification and Biology—Adults resemble bees or small wasps. Larvae resemble caterpillars, except they have more than five pairs of abdominal prolegs. Most species have one to two generations a year, and pupae overwinter in soil. Most sawfly larvae are ½ to 1 inch long. Most are external feeders on foliage. Some eat needles, some eat entire leaves, while others only skeletonize leaves of shrubs and trees. Cocoons may be formed on foliage, twigs, or in the ground.

Host Plants—As a group, sawflies have a wide host range. They feed on conifers, as well as various oaks, roses, black locust, azaleas, ash, black walnut, elm, and other woody ornamentals.

Damage Symptoms—Most sawflies are gregarious feeders. In light infestations, damage may appear as skeletonization or defoliation on leaves or needles of individual branches or shoots. Heavy infestations may cause complete defoliation of conifers and deciduous trees and shrubs.

Monitoring Techniques—Look for symptoms of localized defoliation or skeletonized leaves on exposed branches and shoots of coniferous and deciduous trees and shrubs. Look for clusters of spotted or striped larvae in the vicinity of **damage symptoms**.

Control Strategies—Small infestations may be manually removed and destroyed. Large infestations of young larvae may be sprayed with horticultural oil. Nearly mature larvae may be sprayed with a contact insecticide. Sawfly larvae are not caterpillars; *Bacillus thuringiensis* formulations for caterpillar control will not affect these pests.

Southern Pine Beetle

Identification and Biology—Adults are about ⅛ inch long. They are reddish brown to black, cylindrical, with a median vertical groove in the front of the head. Fully grown larvae are about 3/16 inch long. They are white, legless grubs with reddish brown heads that feed in S shaped galleries under bark. Larvae overwinter in galleries under bark of dying pines, and there are three to nine generations a year, depending on the length of the growing season.

Host Plants—This native bark beetle prefers shortleaf, loblolly, Virginia, and pitch pines. Other yellow pines may be attacked, as well as eastern white, red, and spruce pines, and red and Norway spruce.

Damage Symptoms—When adult beetles bore into pines to lay eggs, vigorous trees repel them with white liquid pitch. Unhealthy trees produce a dryish yellow pitch that forms tubes. Tree crowns turn yellow, then reddish brown as they die from effects of larval girdling and the introduction of a blue stain fungus carried by the adult beetles.

Monitoring Techniques—Examine the trunks of mature pines from May through September for holes in bark exuding white, sticky pitch or dry, yellowish pitch tubes, especially in stressed yellow pines over 15 years of age. Scan the crowns of pines in nearby woods for yellowing and dieback to anticipate a bark beetle attack on landscape pines. Use the oldest, most stressed pines as indicator trees to monitor.

Control Strategies—Maturing pines should be protected from stress factors like drought, flooding, disease, crowding, and site disturbance. Heavily infested and dying pines should be destroyed immediately to reduce beetle reproduction. Spray healthy pine trunks with a residual insecticide at the first sign of pitch tube formation, which usually begins in May.

Southern Red Mite

Identification and Biology—Adults are 0.5 mm long, oval, purplish, or reddish, with eight legs. The red eggs overwinter on the undersides of leaves. There are several generations each year. Most activity occurs in spring and fall.

Host Plants—This imported spider mite has a wide host range, but prefers broad leaved evergreens. It is common on annuals, perennials, azalea, rhododendron, mountain laurel, holly, rose, viburnum, firethorn, and yew.

Damage Symptoms—In light infestations, sap sucked from leaves results in white stippling usually concentrated along the midrib on the lower leaf surface. In heavy infestations, stippling is produced on upper and lower leaf surfaces, and leaves turn gray or brown and die. Lower leaf surfaces often appear dusty because of the numerous egg shells and shed skins.

Monitoring Techniques—Examine plants closely for signs of stippling and the various mite stages on the lower and upper leaf surfaces of broadleaved evergreens in early spring and the fall. When stippling is noticed, tap leaves over white paper to dislodge and count mites, as well as the beneficial insects and predaceous mites. Predaceous mites have longer legs than the southern red mite and move much faster. Look for red overwintering eggs on the lower surface of leaves from November through early spring.

Control Strategies—Application of a dormant oil to the lower surface of leaves when overwintering eggs are numerous will help reduce spring populations. In light infestations, the use of a horticultural oil or insecticidal soap will control these mites with minimal impact on beneficial organisms. When heavy infestations of mites are present, the application of residual miticides often is necessary.

Spruce Spider Mite

Identification and Biology—Adults are about 0.5 mm long. They have eight legs and are yellowish green when young. When mature and fully fed, they are grayish black with a tan area behind the mouthparts. Immature forms are smaller and lighter in color. Eggs are oval to circular and reddish brown. There are several generations a year. Eggs overwinter on bark and needles.

Host Plants—This cosmopolitan pest prefers spruce, pine, hemlock, and arborvitae. Cedar, yew, larch, cryptomeria, dawn redwood, fir, Douglas fir, and false cypress also may be attacked.

Damage Symptoms—These spider mites suck chlorophyll from needles, leaving minute yellowish stipples or flecks at the feeding sites. In heavy infestations, the stipples coalesce and needles turn yellow, then brown. Small trees may be killed, and large trees may suffer dieback. Most damage occurs during the cooler temperatures of the spring and fall.

Monitoring Techniques—At the first sign of stippling on needles, tap branches over white paper and count the dark, slow moving spider mites. Note the presence of white, fast moving predatory mites and the minute, black lady beetle mite predators. Concentrate monitoring activities from March through June and September through November.

Control Strategies—Spraying is not recommended unless stippling damage exceeds ten percent of green foliage; more than ten spider mites, on the average, are tapped from a tree's branches; and beneficial mites and beetles are not found in all branch samples. Use dormant oil sprays when overwintering eggs are abundant. In the growing season, use summer oil or insecticidal soap sprays if predator populations are present.

Thrips

Identification and Biology—Adult thrips are tiny (1/20 inch long), slender insects that have long fringes on the margins of their wings. Adults are commonly yellowish or black and shiny. Nymphs are clear to yellowish and smaller than adults. Females lay eggs within leaf tissue or in curled, distorted foliage caused by feeding nymphs and adults. Thrips have several generations per year.

Host Plants—Thrips attack a wide range of herbaceous and woody landscape plants.

Damage Symptoms—Feeding from adults and nymphs can stunt growth and cause leaves to become stippled and distorted. Infested terminals can become discolored and drop leaves prematurely. Thrips can cause blotches on flowers and in severe infestations buds are distorted and may abort. Thrips can transmit diseases to plants.

Monitoring Techniques—Monitor for thrips by beating branches or shaking foliage or flowers onto a sheet of paper. Adult populations can be monitored using bright yellow or blue sticky traps.

Control Strategies—Healthy woody plants can usually tolerate thrips damage. Provide cultural care to keep plants vigorous. Prune and destroy infested terminals, flowers and buds when possible. When heavy infestations of thrips are present, the application of contact or residual insecticides is often necessary.

Twolined Spittlebug

Identification and Biology—Adults are about ¼ to ½ inch long, smoky brown to black in color, broadly oval, convex, with prominent eyes. They have two bright orange stripes across their wings. Adults sometimes are called froghoppers. Nymphs are smaller, usually pale greenish yellow, and covered by frothy bubbles called spittle. Two generations occur per year.

Host Plants—The immature stages are found in turfgrass and adults may be found on numerous woody ornamentals, especially hollies.

Damage Symptoms—Both nymphs and adults may feed on plant sap. Their feeding destroys plant tissue, causing stunting, distortion, and death of tissues.

Monitoring Techniques—Look for the frothy spittle masses in turf beginning in early spring. The second generation of nymphs usually appears in late summer. Look for active adults beginning in early summer. The second generation of adults usually appears in September.

Control Strategies—Don't allow a heavy thatch layer to accumulate in the lawn. Avoid locating host plants that attract adults, especially Japanese holly, near susceptible turfgrasses. Time insecticide treatment to heavily infested areas of turf for July. Mow and irrigate the grass several hours before applying treatment late in the day.

Twospotted Spider Mite

Identification and Biology—In the growing season, adults are about 0.7 mm long a little larger than a period on a page. They have one oval body segment with eight legs. They are greenish yellow with a black spot on each side of the body. Eggs are white to yellow. Reddish orange adult females overwinter in bark cracks.

Host Plants—Spider mites have a very broad host range. They feed on conifers (see spruce spider mite, above), deciduous trees and shrubs, as well as herbaceous plants.

Damage Symptoms—Spider mites suck leaf juices, causing minute white to yellow stipples to appear. When large spider mite populations feed, the stipples coalesce and leaves may turn white to yellow to grayish brown and then die. Some plants are particularly susceptible to spider mite toxins, and even low populations may cause leaves to die.

Monitoring Techniques—Look for early signs of stippling with the beginning of hot summer weather. Examine the underside of damaged leaves or tap them over white paper and look for spider mites with two spots on the body. Also look for predators, such as phytoseiid mites and lady beetles, and note their relative abundance in relation to the number of mites present.

Control Strategies—In dry, hot, sunny locations, this spider mite may produce one generation a week. Use horticultural oil or insecticidal soap sprays for low mite populations to conserve any beneficials present. When damage becomes objectionable, mite populations are high, and there are no beneficials, consider using a residual miticide spray. Reevaluate in one week.

Wax Scales

Identification and Biology—Adult females are about ¼ inch long and reddish. They are covered with a gummy, white wax that looks like a dunce cap. Immatures resemble cameos with the developing areas of white wax not yet completely covering the reddish body. There is one generation a year. Adult females overwinter on bark.

Host Plants—Wax scales feed on many shrubs and trees, but Japanese holly, Chinese holly, euonymus, boxwood, firethorn, spirea, barberry, and flowering quince are preferred.

Damage Symptoms—Light to moderate infestations may produce nuisance levels of honeydew and sooty mold. Heavy infestations may cause early leaf yellowing and premature leaf drop. Plants become unthrifty with leaves confined to terminals. Eventually dieback occurs.

Monitoring Techniques—Large numbers of foraging bees, wasps, hornets, and ants on dense shrubs may indicate wax scale. Look for honeydew and sooty mold. Look on twigs and small branches for all wax scale stages. Crawlers begin hatching in early summer in Georgia.

Control Strategies—Beginning in May, examine female

wax scales on leaves and branches every one to two weeks and determine when eggs begin to hatch. Remove heavily infested twigs or branches. Infested twigs and branches must be sprayed thoroughly with horticultural oil, insecticidal soap, or a contact or systemic insecticide may be used after egg hatch and when crawlers are present on the plant to achieve effective control.

Whiteflies

Identification and Biology—Adult whiteflies range from $1/16$ to $1/8$ inch in length. Most species resemble tiny white moths. Identification is easiest using the scale insect-like pupal stages.

Host Plants—Whiteflies have numerous hosts, including rhododendron and azalea, ash, dogwood, sycamore, sweetgum, honey and black locust, barberries, redbud, roses, and herbaceous plants like hibiscus and verbena, among others.

Damage Symptoms—Medium infestations may produce objectionable levels of honeydew and sooty mold. Heavy infestations may cause leaves to turn yellow and drop prematurely. All stages feed on the underside of leaves.

Monitoring Techniques—When honeydew, sooty mold, or leaf yellowing is observed, examine the underside of leaves for feeding adult and immature stages of whiteflies. Ants foraging on leaves may indicate the presence of whiteflies.

Control Strategies—Rake up and destroy fallen leaves. If honeydew or damage are objectionable, spray the underside of leaves with soap or oil to conserve beneficials. Remove heavily infested leaves. Predators and parasites usually keep these pests at low levels in the landscape.

White Pine Weevil

Identification and Biology—Adults are about $1/4$ inch long. They are oval and brown with a long snout and two white spots that often run together on the back of the wing covers. Larvae are about $1/8$ inch long. They are C shaped, legless, and white with brown heads. There is one generation a year. Adults overwinter in duff under trees.

Host Plants—This native bark weevil may feed and breed in many native and exotic pine and spruce species.

Damage Symptoms—Adults chew holes to feed on leaders near terminal buds, causing pitch flow. Eggs are laid in holes and the resulting larvae bore in the leader, causing it to stunt, flag, and die. Small trees may be killed. Large trees develop irregular forms.

Look for adults feeding and laying eggs within 12 inches of terminal buds on pines and spruces from March through May.

Monitoring Techniques—Look for infested terminals beginning to flag in June, forming a characteristic "shepherd's crook." Remove and split terminals to be certain weevil larvae, and not diseases, are the problem.

Control Strategies—Prune out and destroy flagging terminals on small trees in June. In heavy infestations, spray terminals in March or April with a residual insecticide when adults are feeding, but before they begin laying eggs.

Discussion Questions

1. What is the cause of most plant diseases?

2. Most crown rots and roos rots are caused by what pathogen?

3. List the most common insect damage symptoms on ornamental plants.

4. List 3 general diseases common to many plants.

14
Turfgrass

Clint Waltz

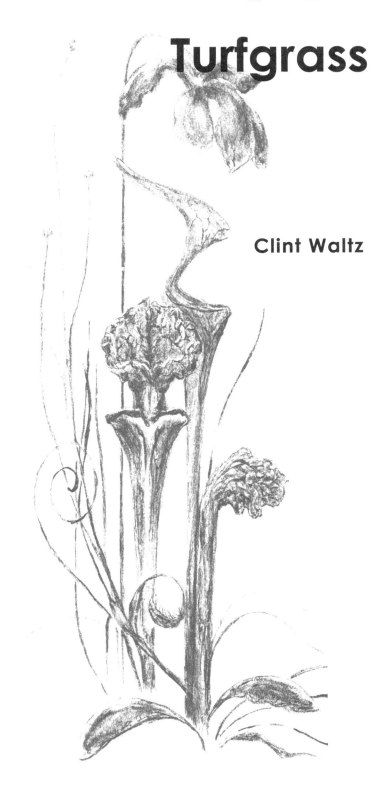

LEARNING OBJECTIVES

Understand the basic function of turfgrass.

Know the names and important characteristics of the recommended cool-season and warm-season turfgrasses.

Know how to select the most appropriate turfgrass for the site.

Know the basic establishment procedures for commonly used turfgrasses.

Understand the basics of turfgrass fertilization.

Be familiar with the recommended turfgrass maintenance practices including: mowing, aerating, dethatching, and irrigation.

Identify the basic steps for renovating an existing lawn

Be able to identify and control common insect and disease related injury in the lawn.

TERMS TO KNOW

Bud leaf arrangement of the leaves in the budshoot.

Cultivation vertical mowing, coring, or topdressing to reduce surface compaction and thatch accumulation and water infiltration, and promote root growth.

Fertilizer analysis numbers representing the percentage of nitrogen, phosphorus and potassium available from the bag of fertilizer.

Ligule structure on a leaf blade which clasps the stem at the junction of the blade and sheath.

Rhizomes below ground stems.

Stolon above ground stems.

Thatch layer of living and dead organic matter that occurs between the green matter and the soil surface.

Vernation arrangement of young leaves within a budshoot.

INTRODUCTION

Turfgrass adds beauty and value to any property and is one of the most versatile and functional plants in the landscape. Turfgrass enhances the environment in ways that can be particularly important in urban areas. Turf is one of the most effective plant covers to reduce soil erosion and surface runoff while recharging ground water, which results in more efficient use of rainfall. A turf area reduces heat by as much as 30°F below that of a concrete or asphalt area and as much as 14°F below that of bare soil. The cooling effect of the average lawn is equal to over eight tons of air conditioning, which is twice that of the average home central air conditioning unit. Turf also absorbs dust and other air pollutants, and produces oxygen. In most landscapes turf also occupies the largest portion and provides the best area for outdoor activities.

TURFGRASS CHARACTERISTICS, IDENTIFICATION, AND SELECTION

Turfgrass identification is one of the first factors needed to objectively evaluate a situation. Although turfgrasses do have many characteristics useful for identification, flowering or seeding parts are generally needed for absolute identification because other plant parts can be affected by environmental factors. Table 1 provides some general characteristics useful for identification of some common turfgrasses and grassy weeds.

Terms used in the table—Stolons are above ground stems and rhizomes are below ground stems. Both are capable of growing a new plant and allow a grass to creep or grow laterally. These can be extremely valuable assets of a plant. However, not all turfgrass species have stolons and rhizomes. Grasses without these characteristics are referred to as "bunch-type" grasses. Texture refers to leaf width. The ligule and bud leaf are important plant identification characteristics. A ligule is the structure which clasps the stem at the junction of the blade and sheath. The vernation, or bud leaf, is the arrangement of the leaves in the budshoot and is characterized as either rolled or folded in the bud. Visit www.Georgia-Turf.com to see line drawings of the morphology of the turfgrass plant.

Selecting the right turfgrass is perhaps the most important factor in developing and maintaining an attractive and problem free turf. Turfgrass selection should be based on environmental conditions, turf quality or appearance desired, and maintenance requirements. The environmental conditions include temperature and moisture, shade adaptation, soil pH, and fertility. It is also important to realize that all turfgrasses have good and bad features. Selection should be based on which turfgrass most nearly meets the criteria considered.

Cool-season Grasses

Cool-season grasses grow well during the cool months of spring and fall when temperatures average 60 – 75° F. They may undergo stress, become dormant, or be injured during the hot months of summer and may require more water than the warm-season grasses. For regional adaptation and general characteristics of cool-season grasses in Georgia refer to Table 2.

Tall Fescue (*Festuca arundinacea*)—Tall fescue is perhaps the most popular grass in the mountain and upper piedmont areas of Georgia, which extend to just south of Atlanta. Its popularity relates to its ease of establishment through seeding and its green color during the spring and fall when warm-season turfgrasses are dormant and brown. Tall fescue is a perennial bunch-type grass which grows rapidly during spring and fall. Because of its bunch-type growth, spring preemergence herbicides are generally necessary to keep a lawn relatively free of weeds. Tall fescue is adapted to a wide range of soil conditions, but grows best on fertile, well drained soils with a soil pH between 5.5 and 6.5. It may need irrigation to remain attractive during the summer; however, excessive irrigation can lead to disease problems. Established tall fescue lawns tend to thin and become "clumpy" and may need periodic reseeding every three or more years.

Kentucky 31 (K 31) is the old, common cultivar or variety of tall fescue. Most of the new and more attractive cultivars referred to as "turf type" tall fescues have a finer leaf blade, lower growth habit, darker green color, and greater density and shade tolerance than K 31. Therefore, if properly managed, new cultivars provide alternatives to K 31.

The introduction of turf type tall fescues, which are frequently promoted as fine leafed, has produced some confusion between tall fescue and fine fescue, which is an entirely different species. It is important to know the difference between tall fescue and fine fescue. The tall fescues have wider leaf blades and better tolerance to Georgia environmental conditions than fine fescues. The fine fescues such as red fescue (*Festuca rubra*) have extremely fine leaves, and are suited to low fertility, low maintenance, and shaded situations. However in Georgia, they generally do not perform as well as tall fescue but are commonly found as part of "shade mixtures" at many retail outlets.

Table 1. Identifying characteristics of certain turfgrasses and grassy weeds.

COMMON NAME	SCIENTIFIC NAME	STOLONS	RHIZOMES	TEXTURE[1]	LIGULE[2]	BUD LEAF[3]	OTHER CHARACTERISTICS
Bahiagrass	Paspalum notatum	yes	yes	C	SH	R	Two to three-spiked seedhead
Bentgrass, Creeping	Agrostis palustris	yes	no	F	M	R	Blue-green colored leaves; grows in patches; stolons usually white
Bermudagrass	Cynodon dactylon	yes	yes	C-F	H	R-F	Tillers grow at 30-60° angle; some hairs on leaf surface; long stolons
Bluegrass, Annual	Poa annua	no	no	F	L	F	Boat-shaped leaf tip; dual veins in midrib; many seedheads in spring
Bluegrass, Kentucky	Poa praetensis	no	yes	M	S	F	Boat-shaped leaf tip; dual veins in midrib; smooth leaf
Carpetgrass	Axonopus affinis	yes	no	C	SH	F	Two to five-spiked seedhead
Centipedegrass	Eremeochloa ophiuroides	yes	no	C	SH	F	Single spike seedhead blades, hairy along edges
Fescue, Red	Festuca rubra	no	few	F	S	F	Leaf is very narrow, needle-like and usually folded
Fescue, Tall	Festuca arundinacea	no	no	C	S	R	Leaf margin rough to touch: red stem base; veins prominent
Orchardgrass	Dactylis glomerata	no	no	C	L	F	Stem very flat; blue-green color; seed contaminant in fescue
Paspalum, Seashore	Paspalum vaginatum	yes	yes	C-F	S	R	Green to dark green in color with a two-spiked seedhead.
Ryegrass, Annual	Lolium multiflorum	no	no	M	S	F	Underleaf shiny; red stem base; veins prominent
Ryegrass, Perennial	Lolium perenne	no	no	C	SH	F	Underleaf shiny; red stem base; veins prominent; claw-like auricles
St. Augustinegrass	Stenotaphrum secundatum	yes	no	C	SH	F	Boat-shaped leaf tip, single spike seed head
Zoysia grass	Zoysia spp.	yes	yes	C-F	H	R	Tillers grow at 90° angle; sheaths compressed; tuft of hairs at collar; hairy on leaf surface; very knotty nodes.

[1] TEXTURE: C=Coarse; F=Fine; M=Medium
[2] LIGULE: S=Short; M=Medium; L=Long; H=Hairy
[3] BUD LEAF: R=Rolled; F=Folded

In older cultivars (e.g. K 31), orchardgrass (*Dactylis glomerata*) was a common weed seed found in tall fescue seed. It is easily seen in lawns because of its blue green color and slightly faster growth rate than tall fescue. Unfortunately, no selective preemergence or postemergence control is available, other than hand weeding. However, the newer turf type tall fescue cultivars are grown and harvested under more rigorous standards, thereby making this weed less of an issue.

Kentucky bluegrass (*Poa pratensis*)—Kentucky bluegrass has a fine to medium leaf texture and bright color. Although it does not perform as well as tall fescue, it can be used in the mountain areas of north Georgia. A major attribute of Kentucky bluegrass is its rhizomatous or creeping growth habit. Kentucky bluegrass can become semi-dormant during hot weather, and grows best in a fertile soil with a pH of 5.5 to 6.5. While it does best in partial shade, it will grow in open sun if adequate moisture is present.

Ryegrasses and Rough Stalk Bluegrass—Perennial ryegrass (*Lolium perenne*), annual ryegrass (*Lolium multiflorum*), and rough stalk bluegrass (*Poa trivialis*) are suited as temporary, cool-season turfgrasses throughout Georgia. They can be used as a winter cover on new lawns where the permanent or base grass has not been established, or for overseeding, to provide a green cover on a warm-season grass during winter. However, overseeding may damage the warm-season grass unless managed correctly in the spring because the ryegrass competes for sunlight, water, space, and nutrients.

Other cool-season grasses include creeping bentgrass (*Agrostis stolonifera*), which is used on golf greens and is becoming a more common lawn weed, and annual bluegrass (*Poa annua*), which is a very common winter annual weed that has a light green color and produces an objectionable seedhead.

Warm-Season Grasses

Warm-season grasses grow best during the warm months when temperatures reach 80 – 95°F in the spring, summer, and early fall. They grow vigorously during this time and become brown and dormant in winter. For regional adaptation and general characteristics of warm-season grasses in Georgia, refer to Table 3.

Bermudagrasses (*Cynodon* spp.)—All bermudagrasses thrive in hot weather but typically perform poorly in shade. They spread by both stolons and rhizomes which can make them difficult to control around flower beds, walks and borders. If fertilized adequately, they require

Table 2. Adaptation and characteristics of cool-season turfgrasses in Georgia

	Fine Fescue[s]	Kentucky Bluegrass[s]	Tall Fescues[s]
ADAPTATION			
Heat hardiness	P - F	P - F	G
Cold hardiness	VG	VG	VG
Drought resistance	G	F - G	G
Sun tolerance	P - G	VG	F- G
Shade tolerance*	P	P	F
Salt tolerance	F - G	G	G
Wear tolerance	F - G	G	G
Establishment rate**	Fast	Medium	Fast
Optimal soil pH range	5.5 - 6.5	5.5 - 6.5	5.5 - 6.5
Region best adapted	Mountains & Piedmont	Mountain	Mountains & Piedmont

Key: E=Excellent; VG= Very good; G-Good; F=Fair; P=Poor; VP=Very poor
[s] = Can be seeded
* Turfgrasses need at least 4 hours of direct sunlight per day.
** Establishment rate is dependent on planting date, seeding rate and environmental conditions

frequent mowing. Bermudagrasses are adapted to the entire state and tolerate a wide soil pH range, but 5.5 to 6.5 is ideal.

Common Bermudagrass (*Cynodon dactylon*)—Also called 'Arizona Common', common bermudagrass is adapted to many soil conditions and makes a good turf if fertilized and mowed correctly. Although common bermudagrass does produce many unsightly seedheads it is often used on home lawns due to the ease of establishment by seeding.

Improved Seeded Types—In the 1980's, research to develop new seeded types from 'Arizona Common' became popular. This research has developed some "improved" seeded bermudagrasses. 'Princess 77', 'Riviera', 'Southern Star', 'Majestic', 'Savannah', and 'Jackpot' have

Table 3. Adaptation and characteristics of warm-season turfgrasses relative to Georgia

	Bahiagrass	Bermuda-grass (common)	Bermuda grass (hybrid)	Carpet-grass	Centipe-degrass	Seashore Paspalum	St. Au-gustine-grass	Zoysiagrass
ADAPTATION								
Heat hardiness	VG	E	E	E	G	E	E	E
Cold hardiness	F	P	F	VP	F	P	P	VG
Drought resistance	E	E	E	P	G	E	VG	G
Sun tolerance	VG	E	E	G	VG	E	VG	VG
Shade tolerance	F	VP	VP	P	F	P	G	G
Salt tolerance	P	G	G	P	P	E	E	G
Wear tolerance	E	E	E	P	P	G	P	G
Establishment rate**	Slow to medium	Fast	Fast	Slow	Slow	Fast	Medium	Very slow
Optimal soil pH range	5.0 - 5.5	5.5 - 6.5	5.5 - 6.5	5.0 - 6.0	5.0 - 6.0	5.5 - 6.5	5.5 - 6.5	6.0 - 7.0
Region best adapted	State-wide, excluding moun-tains	Statewide	Statewide	Piemont	State-wide	Coastal Plain	Piedmont	Statewide

Key: E=Excellent; VG= Very good; G-Good; F=Fair; P=Poor; VP=Very poor
ˢ = Can be seeded
* Turfgrasses need at least 4 hours of direct sunlight per day.
** Establishment rate is dependent on planting date, seeding rate and environmental conditions

performed better than other seeded types in Georgia. Others that have performed similar to or slightly better than 'Arizona Common' included 'Transcontinental', 'Blackjack', 'Sydney', 'Shangri La', 'Pyramid', 'Sundevil II', 'Blue muda', 'Sahara', and 'Mirage'. In general, the better performing cultivars have improved color, density, turf quality, and traffic tolerance; and some have slightly better low temperature survival than 'Arizona Common'. However, these turfgrasses still do not produce the high quality turf of 'Tifway', the industry standard.

Vegetatively Produced Bermudagrasses—Compared with common bermudagrass, these vegetatively produced bermudagrasses have more disease resistance, greater turf density, better weed resistance, fewer seedheads, finer and softer texture, and more favorable color. There are recently released cultivars which have improved cold tolerance and shade persistence compared to older bermudagrasses. The vegetative hybrids typically produce no viable seed and must be planted by vegetative means.

All of the following vegetatively produced bermudagrasses have been developed and released cooperatively by The University of Georgia and the U.S. Department of Agriculture.

'Tifway' (Tifton 419 or Tif-419) Bermudagrass— 'Tifway' bermudagrass grass is the most popular hybrid used because of its outstanding utilitarian features that make it an ideal turfgrass for lawns, golf fairways, and tees, athletic fields, and other recreational areas. It has a darker green color and stiffer leaves than 'Tifgreen', and is more frost resistant than the other bermudagrasses. Therefore, it usually remains green longer in the fall and begins growing earlier in the spring. 'Tifway' can generally be identified by its reddish purple seedheads.

'TifSport' Bermudagrass—'TifSport' bermudagrass is an irradiated mutant from 'Midiron' bermudagrass that looks similar to 'Tifway'. However, when compared to 'Tifway', 'TifSport' has slightly better cold tolerance, greater density, tolerates lower mowing, is more drought tolerant, and is non-preferential to mole crickets.

'Tifgreen' (Tifton 328) Bermudagrass—'Tifgreen' is a low growing, rapidly spreading grass. It is relatively disease resistant and makes a dense, weed resistant turf when properly managed. Its fine texture (leaf width) and soft, green leaves are largely responsible for its excellent putting qualities on golf greens. 'Tifgreen' can easily be identified by its golden seedheads. 'Tifgreen' also tolerates overseeding better than most bermudagrasses.

'Tifton 10' Bermudagrass—'Tifton 10' has a coarse leaf texture similar to common bermudagrass but has a natural dark bluish green color. It establishes rapidly from stolons and performs well in low maintenance conditions. This grass will produce a good quality turf when maintained with 2.5 pounds of N per 1,000 square feet and a mowing height of 1.5 inches. It has a relatively low growing habit which may reduce the need for mowing.

'TifGrand' Bermudagrass—'TifGrand' was released from the UGA Turfgrass Breeding Program in 2009 and became commercially available in 2010. It shares many of the same characteristics as 'Tifway' and 'TifSport' but 'TifGrand' has a genetically darker green color. Other notable characteristics include that 'TifGrand' was bred to have improved persistence in limited light environments (i.e. shade) and has been shown to be non-preferential to the tawny mole cricket.

Other vegetatively produced types that have performed well in Georgia include 'Patriot', 'Celebration', 'Champion', 'MiniVerde', and 'Tifdwarf'. 'Patriot' is a product of the Oklahoma State University breeding program and has cold tolerance and resistance to the disease Spring Dead Spot. 'Celebration' has performed well under limited light environments (i.e. shade) and has a blue-green color. 'Champion' and 'MiniVerde', along with 'TifEagle', are referred to as "ultra-dwarf" bermudagrasses because they can be mowed at ⅛-inch and are used for golf course putting greens. 'Tifdwarf' is an older putting green cultivar which requires less maintenance than the ultra-dwarfs and is well suited for mid- to lower-budget golf courses.

Centipedegrass (*Eremochloa ophiuroides*)—Centipedegrass is a medium textured, low and slow growing but aggressive grass that can produce a dense, attractive weed free turf. It is more shade tolerant than bermudagrass but less shade tolerant than St. Augustinegrass and zoysiagrass. Since centipedegrass produces only stolons, it is easily controlled around borders of flower beds and walks. It is well adapted as far north as Atlanta and Athens.

Centipedegrass is the ideal grass for the homeowner who wants a lawn which needs little care. It can be established by either seed or vegetative parts and does not require much fertilizer. Also, when compared to other lawn grasses, it is generally resistant to most insects and diseases. Since it is slow growing, it takes longer than bermudagrass and St. Augustinegrass to completely establish. Although there are a few different varieties available, common centipedegrass is most commonly used, and 'TifBlair' is the only certified cultivar from cooperative efforts between The University of Georgia and The U.S. Department of Agriculture. 'TifBlair' has improved density and cold tolerance.

Centipedegrass is subject to a condition referred to as "centipedegrass decline." This problem can be prevented by proper management, which includes care not to over fertilize, prevention of thatch accumulation, irrigation during drought stress, (particularly in the fall) and maintaining a mowing height of 1.0 to 1.5 inches. Centipedegrass is adapted to soils of low fertility but grows best at a soil pH of 5.0 to 6.0. When establishing centipedegrass from seed, research has shown improved germination and establishment at a soil pH of 6.0.

Carpetgrass (*Axonopus affinis*)—This is a coarse leaved, creeping grass which grows throughout the state. It will grow well in either sun or shade, but is less shade tolerant than St. Augustinegrass. It strongly resembles and is often confused with centipedegrass. Carpetgrass is recommend only for lawns on wet, low fertility, acid (pH 4.5 – 5.5), sandy soils where ease of establishment and care is more important than quality. Its chief disadvantage is rapid development of seedheads, which are similar in appearance to crabgrass. Carpetgrass readily invades centipedegrass and other turfgrasses because of its ability to spread from seed. Carpetgrass is generally managed like centipedegrass.

Zoysiagrasses (*Zoysia* Spp)—This species is adapted to the entire state and will form an excellent turf when properly established and managed. It is often thought that for the best appearance, zoysiagrasses require cutting with a reel-type mower. In fact, regardless of the turfgrass species, a properly sharpened and adjusted reel-type mower will provide a superior quality cut compared to a rotary-type mower. Zoysiagrass may need periodic thinning or dethatching. The zoysiagrasses form a dense, attractive turf in full sun and partial shade, but often thin in dense shade. Most zoysiagrasses grow slowly compared to other grasses and usually are established by sodding or plugging, although there are seeded types. Plugs, that are 2 inches in diameter planted on 6 inch centers will cover completely in 12 months if watered and fertilized properly. However, it may require several years to cover if not properly maintained.

Zoysia japonica is sometimes called Japanese or Korean lawngrass or common zoysiagrass. It has coarse leaf texture, excellent cold tolerance, and some cultivars (e.g. 'Zenith' and 'Compadre') can be seeded.

'Emerald' Zoysiagrass is a fine textured hybrid. It is well suited for top quality lawns where a good maintenance program is provided. It has a dark green color, very fine leaf texture, good shade tolerance, high shoot density, and a low growth habit. 'Emerald' will develop excess thatch if over fertilized and is prone to winter injury from the Atlanta area and north.

'Meyer' Zoysiagrass, also called 'Z 52' and 'Amazoy', is an improved selection of *Zoysia japonica*. It has medium leaf texture, good cold tolerance, and spreads more rapidly than many other zoysiagrasses. This is the zoysiagrass often advertised as the "super" grass in newspapers and magazines.

'El Toro' Zoysiagrass was developed in California and looks like 'Meyer' zoysiagrass but has a coarser leaf texture. It is a relatively fast growing zoysiagrass, tolerates mowing with a rotary mower, and produces less thatch than 'Meyer'. The winter hardiness of 'El Toro' is better than 'Emerald' but less than 'Meyer'. It is grown throughout the state and has performed well through drought conditions and limited input environments.

'Zeon' Zoysiagrass is a zoysiagrass that was released by a private grower in Texas. It is similar to 'Emerald' in texture and density. Compared to 'Emerald', it has a slightly lighter green color, has softer leaves, and spreads faster. After multi-year evaluations in Georgia it performed better than 'Meyer' and the same as 'Emerald'. It has been used on golf courses, on tees and fairways.

Other vegetatively produced zoysiagrass cultivars that have performed well in Georgia tests include 'Zorro', 'Empire', 'Palisades' and 'JaMur'.

Seeded types generally do not produce as high quality turf as the vegetative types, but are popular because of the ease of establishment, the improved winter hardiness over centipedegrass, and better summer stress tolerance than cool-season grasses. 'Zenith' and 'Compadre' are seeded types. Compared to 'Meyer', 'Zenith' has a slightly coarser leaf blade, is less dense and thus easier to mow. As with all zoysiagrasses, it grows well in full sun or light shade and it also has cold tolerance similar to 'Meyer'.

In general, the zoysiagrasses are: (1) slow to cover completely, thus more costly to establish; (2) less drought tolerant than bermudagrass; and (3) recommended for lawn use only when the homeowner is willing to provide the required maintenance.

Seashore Paspalum (*Paspalum vaginatum*)— Seashore paspalum is used and best adapted for coastal regions due to its salt tolerance and not recommended for Central and North Georgia. Similarly, seashore paspalum is not recommend for homelawns. It is best suited for golf courses and sports fields where it can receive expert maintenance. Also, it does well where poor water quality and sodic soils are a limitation to other grass species. Seashore paspalum has a natural, dark green color that will "stripe up" like many of the cool-season grasses. This is a characteristic that some find attractive, especially those that have moved to the state from northern regions and were accustomed to the appearance of Kentucky bluegrass. Much like bermudagrass, this grass has relatively few pest problems, but broadleaf and grassy weeds, brown patch and dollar spot disease can be problematic. Seashore paspalum is primarily established by vegetative means; sodding and plugging being the most common. Commercially available vegetative cultivars include 'SeaIsle 1', 'SeaIsle 2000', 'SeaIsle Supreme', 'SeaDwarf' and others. 'Sea Spray' is the only commercially available seeded seashore paspalum cultivar.

St. Augustinegrass (*Stenotaphrum secundatum*)—St. Augustinegrass has large flat stems and broad coarse leaves somewhat similar to centipedegrass. It has an attractive blue green color and forms a deep, fairly dense turf. It spreads by long above ground runners or stolons. While aggressive, it is easily controlled around borders. It is planted only by vegetative means. There are no commercially available seed for any St. Augustinegrass cultivar.

St. Augustinegrass is a shade tolerant warm-season grass. It is can be susceptible to winter injury, but cultivars that have performed well in Central and North Georgia include 'Raleigh', 'Palmetto', and 'Mercedes'. Perhaps the greatest disadvantage of this species is its sensitivity to the chinch bug, and gray leaf spot disease. While insecticides can control the insect, frequent applications are required although fewer effective insecticides are available on the homeowner market. Several fungicides are available for the control of gray leaf spot.

The more common St. Augustinegrass varieties are 'Mercedes', 'Palmetto', 'Raleigh', 'Captiva', 'Bitter Blue', and 'Floratam'. 'Raleigh' has good cold hardiness, good shade adaptation, and SADV resistance. 'Mercedes' and 'Palmetto' are varies grown in Georgia. They have performed among the best in Georgia and national trials. They have good shade tolerance,and good cold tolerance, when compared to most other St. Augustinegrasses. 'Bitter Blue' has the best shade tolerance but is sensitive to both chinch bugs and St. Augustinegrass Decline Virus (SADV). 'Floratine' has the finest leaf texture, but is also susceptible to chinch bugs and SADV. 'Floratam' has the coarsest leaf texture, is resistant to chinch bugs and SADV, but is not as shade tolerant or winter hardy as the others.

Bahiagrass (*Paspalum notatum*)—Bahiagrass is more commonly a weed in Georgia but can be used as a turfgrass in South Georgia. It is adapted to drought situations. Its main drawback is its rapid seedhead development and open turf canopy. Common varieties include common, 'Pensacola' (the most widely grown), 'Argentine', and 'Paraguay'.

Georgia Certified Turfgrasses—Specifying turfgrass certified as to varietal purity is the best means of assuring true to type, high quality turf. "Blue Tag" certified turfgrasses are the highest quality grass available because they are grown under rigid specifications verified by field inspections that insure varietal purity, and being free of noxious weeds such as nutsedge and common bermudagrass.

The certifying agency in Georgia is the Georgia Crop Improvement Association (GCIA), an agent of The University of Georgia College of Agricultural and Environmental Sciences. This agency should not be confused with the Georgia Department of Agriculture's live plant certification program. To ensure the consumer they are receiving certified grass, a "Blue Tag" certificate with the GCIA logo and information documenting the harvested field should accompany each load of grass when it arrives from the producer. The issue of varietal identity and purity is becoming more of a concern as landscape values increase and grass contamination becomes more of an issue. Using "Blue Tag" certified turfgrasses is the best means of assuring consistent grass appearance and performance. For more information about benefits of using certified turfgrass visit www.certifiedseed.org.

Establishment

There are three distinct aspects of turfgrass establishment. The first step, soil preparation, is probably the most important. The second step, planting, may involve seeding, sprigging, or sodding. The final step is the care and maintenance during establishment for 2 to 4 weeks after planting.

Soil Preparation—The key to successful establishment is proper soil preparation. The soil should be prepared similarly whether planting by seed, sprigs, stolons, or sod. The following are the steps necessary for proper soil preparation.

1. Take Soil Samples. Fertilizer and lime applications should be based on soil test results. Chapter 1: *The Soil Ecosystem* in this book details procedures for collecting soil samples.

2. Clean Planting Site. Remove all debris from the area to be planted. This includes rocks, bottles and tree stumps. Stumps not removed will eventually decay and leave depressions in the lawn.

3. Rough Grading. If extensive grading is done, remove the topsoil and replace it after the rough grade is set. Rough grading includes sloping the grade away from building foundations, reducing severe slopes, and filling low lying areas. A 1 to 2 percent slope (1 to 2 foot drop

Table 4. Soil amendments and rate of application for soil incorporation

Amendment	Volume (cubic yd) per 1,000 ft^2	Depth (inches) before incorporated 6-8 inches deep	C:N
Composted sludge[1]	3 to 6	1 to 2	
Sawdust[2]	3 to 6	1 to 2	225:1
Composted yard trimmings	3 to 6	1 to 2	27:1
Sphagnum peat moss	3	1	
Rotted farm manure[1]	3	1	13:1

[1]With composted sludge and farm manure, do not apply additional nitrogen at establishment.
[2]Additional nitrogen will be required with the use of sawdust. Apply 2 lbs of actual nitrogen for each cubic yard of sawdust to aid decompostion and to ensure an adequate supply of nitrogen for the grass.

Table 5. Recommended rates of ground scrap wallboard

REGION	RECOMMENDED RATES*
Piedmont, mountains, and ridge and valley	250 lbs / 1000 ft²
Coastal plain	50 lbs/ 1000 ft²

* Rates are for dry ground wallboard

in elevation per 100 linear feet) away from all buildings provides good surface drainage.

This is the best time to install subsurface drainage, if needed, or an irrigation system. Also, the subgrade may become compacted by machinery during rough grading, especially if the ground is wet. This compacted layer should be broken up and loosened before proceeding.

4. Replace Topsoil. Once the subgrade is established, spread the topsoil over the subgrade. On steep slopes or where rock outcrops exist, at least 12 inches of topsoil are needed for proper maintenance.

If organic matter is needed, add 1 to 3 cubic yards per 1,000 square feet of lawn area. Materials such as peat moss, well rotted sawdust (at least 6 to 8 years old; the carbon to nitrogen ratio of the material should be below 40 to 1), or leaf litter serves well as organic materials (Table 4). On heavy soils, add 8 to 10 cubic yards of sand per 1,000 square feet of lawn. All these materials should be mixed thoroughly with the native soil to a depth of 6 to 8 inches. If significant amounts of soil

have been moved, wetting the area with water will help firm the seedbed and identify any low areas that can be fixed before planting.

5. Add Fertilizer and Lime. Once the topsoil is spread and graded, add fertilizer and lime as indicated by the soil test report. Lime and fertilizer should be thoroughly mixed with the top 4 to 6 inches of topsoil. Water in the fertilizer lightly prior to planting. A general recommendation for a starter fertilizer is 20 to 30 pounds of a commercial grade fertilizer, such as 5-10-15, 6-12-12, 5-10-10, or 7-14-21 per 1,000 square feet of lawn. If a soluble source of nitrogen is used, do not apply more than 1 to 1.5 pounds of nitrogen per 1,000 per square feet. If an insoluble source of nitrogen is used, such as urea-formaldehyde, apply 3 to 5 pounds of nitrogen per 1,000 square feet prior to planting.

If the soil test report showed a deficiency of calcium (Ca) or sulphur (S), gypsum (calcium sulfate) can be added to the soil. The calcium in gypsum is also helpful in neutralizing high levels of aluminum (Al). Unlike lime, gypsum does not affect soil pH. However, gypsum applications have been shown to reduce soil crusting, a significant problem in Piedmont soils, increase water infiltration, and improve the overall structure of the soil. Ground scrap wallboard can be beneficial in Piedmont and coastal soils but at varying rates (Table 5), and to maximize its benefits, ground wallboard should be incorporated into the upper 4 to 12 inches of soil. For more information on the use of scrap wallboard refer to UGA Extension Special Bulletin #1223 and UGA

Table 6. Seeding rates for turfgrasses in Georgia

GRASS	SEEDING RATE	PLANTING TIMING	REGION OF ADAPTATION
Tall fescue	5 - 8	September, October, (preferably), or late February to March	Mountain and Piedmont
Kentucky bluegrass	1 - 2	Same as for tall fescue	Mountain
Annual & perennial ryegrass	5 - 10	September to November	All*
Rough stalk bluegrass	5 - 7	September to November	All*
Bahiagrass	3 - 8	May to June	Piedmont to coast
Common bermudagrass	1 - 2 (hulled)	May to June	All
Improved bermudagrass	3 - 5 (unhulled)	May to June	All
Centipedegrass	0.25 - 1.0	May to June	Piedmont to coast
Carpetgrass	1 - 3	May to June	Piedmont to coast
Zoysiagrass	1 - 3	May to June	All

* Annual and perennial ryegrasses and rough stalk bluegrass are used for overseeding, not as a permanent grass.

Extension Circular #857.

6. Final Grading. Final grading and mixing of the fertilizer should be delayed until right before planting. If this is done too far in advance, some fertilizer may be leached and the soil may become crusted. On sandy soils, the seedbed should be firmed. This will help prevent drying of the soil.

Care should be taken not to destroy or damage existing trees. Tilling under a tree may cut tree roots and can damage or kill the tree. Trees can also be suffocated by deeply covering the roots with soil. If additional soil is necessary, the use of a tree well at the base is recommended.

Planting

Cool-season Grasses—In Georgia, most cool-season grasses are established by seeding. In addition to being sold as an individual cultivar, grass seed is sold as either blends or mixtures. A blend contains two or more varieties/cultivars of the same species (e.g. a bag with 'Lexington' and 'Talladega' tall fescues). A mixture contains two or more turfgrass species (e.g. a bag with annual ryegrass and rough stalk bluegrass). For the proper seeding rate and time, see Table 6. Always purchase quality seed, that is certified seed with a high percent germination and purity. Federal and state seed laws assure that the label will provide adequate and correct information about the seed quality. Inexpensive seed often ends up being quite expensive because of low germination and purity. Reputable seed dealers are always willing to help customers select quality seed.

The best way to apply seed is with a mechanical spreader that will distribute the seed uniformly. There are four basic types of mechanical seeders available: (a) drill, (b) gravity, (c) broadcaster, and (d) hydroseeder. For most areas, the broadcaster works best.

When seeding, divide the seed into two equal parts, and then seed in two directions at right angles to each other. Fertilizers and granular pesticides should also be applied in this manner to insure uniform distribution. For some small seed, such as centipedegrass, it may be helpful to mix ¼ pound of seed with a carrier such as one gallon of dry sand to help distribute the seed evenly. If this is done, frequently mix to prevent separation of the seed and sand due to differences in density (density of sand is approximately 1.6 gram per cubic centimeter and density of seed is approximately 0.8 grams per cubic centimeter). Using a carrier material, such as grits (approximately 0.7 grams per cubic centimeter),

with a similar density as seed will reduce separation and improve seed distribution. A mixing ratio of 1 pound of seed to 4 or 5 pounds of grits works well.

Once the seeds are spread, rake lightly to cover with about one fourth inch of soil. On small areas a hand rake works well. This increases the contact of the seed with the soil, thus increasing the chance of the seed surviving. After raking, roll the seedbed lightly to firm the soil. Then place a thin layer of mulch, such as wheat straw, over the soil. Mulch helps prevent soil erosion and retains moisture for seed to germinate. If straw is used, find a source that is free of weed seed. One bale of straw (60 to 80 pounds) will cover approximately 1,000 square feet. The straw can be left on the lawn to decompose if it is not spread too thickly.

Warm-season Grasses—Many of the warm-season grasses in Georgia are established by planting vegetative plant parts. For proper planting rates, see Table 7.

Sprigging is the placing of grass plants, runners, rhizomes, stolons, or small sod pieces (2 to 4 inch plugs) in small holes or furrows on the soil surface. Stolonizing is the broadcasting of vegetative plant parts on the soil surface and covering by topdressing or slicing. To plant sprigs, dig furrows 8 to 12 inches apart and place the sprigs 1 to 2 inches deep every 4 to 6 inches in the furrows. The closer together the sprigs, the quicker the grass will cover. After placing the sprigs in the furrow, cover part of the sprig with soil and firm with a roller or by stepping on the soil around the sprig. To ensure survival, apply water immediately after planting.

Stolonizing or broadcasting requires more planting material but will produce a quicker cover. Stolons are broadcast by hand or by a mechanical spreader over the prepared seedbed. The stolons are then topdressed

Table 7. Sprigging rates for warm-season grasses

GRASS	SPRIGGING RATE* (bu/1000 ft²)	PLANTING TIMING	RATE OF ESTABLISH-MENT
Bermuda-grass	5 - 10	May-June	2 - 3 months
Seashore paspalum	5 - 10	May-June	2 - 3 months

* Based on estimates 1 sq ft of sod = 1 linear foot of sprigs; 1 sq yd of sod (9 sq ft) = 1 bushel of sprigs = 2000 bermudagrass or zoysiagrass sprigs. Broadcast sprigging or stolonizing is used for planting large areas such as gold courses and athletic fields.

lightly with 0.15 to 0.25-inch of soil or sliced into the soil. Machines with vertical blades for slicing the stolons into the soil may be available for this purpose. After topdressing or slicing, roll the lawn to firm the soil around the stolons. Apply water immediately.

Sodding is popular because it produces an instant lawn. Quality sod that is free of weeds, diseases, and insects should be used. Be sure the soil grade is correct before laying the sod. Use freshly harvested sod and store it in the shade until used, since sod that becomes hot will be damaged. Begin installing sod along the longest straight line such as a driveway or sidewalk. Push or butt sod ends against each other tightly without stretching. Avoid gaps or overlaps. Stagger the joints in each row in a brick like fashion, using a large sharp knife to trim corners. On slopes, place sod across, or perpendicular to, the slope. To avoid causing a rough surface or air pockets, avoid walking or kneeling on sod while it is being installed or just after watering. After installing sod, roll the area to improve sod-to-soil contact and remove air pockets. Begin to apply 0.25- to 0.5-inch of water within 30 minutes of installation. Lightly irrigate daily, or more often if necessary, to keep the sod moist until it has firmly rooted (about 2 weeks). Then begin less frequent and deeper watering.

During the first 3 weeks, avoid heavy use of the new lawn. This gives the grass time to become established, and helps the surface remain smooth. Mow the newly laid sod at its recommended height as needed to maintain a proper mowing program.

Plugging is the planting of 2 to 4 inch squares or sod pieces into holes the same size as the plug (Table 8). Plugs are planted every 6 to 12 inches in a row, and rows are spaced 6 to 12 inches apart. Tamp plugs firmly

Table 8. Two-inch plug spacing and sod required for warm-season grasses

TURFGRASS	SPACING (inches)	AMOUNT OF SOD (sq ft) PER 1000 SQ FT*
Bermudagrass	12	30 - 50
Carpetgrass	6	100 - 150
Centipedegrass	6	100 - 150
St. Augustine-grass	6 - 12	30 - 50
Zoysiagrass	6	100 - 150

* Based on estimates of 1 sq yd of sod yields 324 two-inch plugs. The amount of sod refers to the square feet of solid sod from which two-inch plugs can be obtained.

into the soil. Keep the soil moist until the grass is well rooted and spreading vigorously.

Care After Planting

Irrigate newly planted turf lightly and often enough to prevent the surface from drying. This usually means daily irrigations for the first 2 to 3 weeks. As seedlings develop, or as the sprigs or sod begin to take root and grow, decrease the frequency of irrigation and increase the amount applied until well rooted and normal irrigation practices can be followed. Mow grass when it reaches 1.5 times its recommended mowing height (Table 10). Do not mow young grass when it is wet.

Newly planted turfgrasses should be fertilized according to soil test recommendations. In the absence of these recommendations, and in order to obtain rapid cover, monthly applications of a complete fertilizer like 12-4-8 or 16-4-8 at the rate of 1 pound of nitrogen per 1,000 square feet should be used.

Newly planted areas are likely to become weed infested. Many weeds can be controlled by manual extraction or frequent mowing. If chemical weed control is necessary, consult the current *Georgia Pest Management Handbook* or www.GeorgiaTurf.com.

Maintenance

After a lawn is established, its appearance depends on a sound management program. Such a program involves fertilization, irrigation, mowing, and cultivation. No one practice is more important than another because they are interrelated and necessary to obtain an attractive, healthy turf.

Fertilization—Fertilization programs should be based on turfgrass requirements, soil tests, maintenance practices, and desired appearance. Most mixed fertilizers contain more than one source of nitrogen. Applying fertilizer at the right time is as important as knowing what fertilizer to apply. Generally, spring and late summer fertilization with a complete fertilizer (one containing N, P and K) is recommended for the warm-season grasses (Table 9).

The spring fertilizer application for warm-season turfgrasses should be made once the last frost date has past, and soil temperatures at the 4-inch depth are consistently above 65°F. Consult the County Extension Agent for typical frost dates and visit the "Georgia Automated Environmental Monitoring Network" at www.GeorgiaWeather.net. The fall application should be made about 6 weeks before the average first frost date. Normally, the first frost date ranges from the latter part of October in the Piedmont area to the end of November on the coast.

In the absence of soil test recommendations, the complete fertilizer used can range from 16-4-8 to 10-10-10, 5-10-15, etc. Most warm-season grasses require 1 to 5 pounds of nitrogen per 1,000 square feet per year to remain healthy and attractive. A typical example would be 6 pounds of 16-4-8 per 1,000 square feet once soil temperatures at the 4-inch depth are consistently 65°F, then monthly until six to eight weeks before the average first frost date.

Proper fertilization of centipedegrass is important to its survival. Most people tend to over fertilize centipedegrass. One pound of nitrogen per 1,000 square feet per year is ample nitrogen for most established centipedegrass lawns. On sandy soils in high rainfall areas, 2 pounds per 1,000 square feet per year may be needed. Apply 3 pounds of 16-4-8 per 1,000 square feet in the spring once temperatures become conducive and again in midsummer. If the grass shows signs of iron chlorosis, which is observed by the yellowing of leaves, apply ferrous sulfate at the rate of 1 tablespoon per 3 gallons of water to each 1,000 square feet of grass.

The cool-season grasses such as tall fescue and Kentucky bluegrass should receive the majority of their fertilizer requirements in the fall. An example of cool-season grass fertilization would be 6 pounds of 16-4-8 per 1,000 square feet in early September, November, February, and April.

Fertilizer Application—Listed below are some key points to remember when applying fertilizer.

1. Do not apply fertilizer when the grass leaves are wet because foliar burn may result.

2. If possible, water in fertilizer thoroughly with ½ inch of water.

3. Use a mechanical spreader to distribute the fertilizer. Do not fertilize by hand. Split the rate and use the two direction application procedure described for seeding.

4. Never leave unused fertilizer in the hopper. Fertilizer salts are corrosive and could ruin the spreader. Rinse the spreader thoroughly with water, allow to dry, and keep moving parts lubricated with a light machine oil.

Table 9. Suggested fertility program for Georgia lawns

TURFGRASS	Jan	Feb	Mar	Apr	May	Jun	Jul	Aug	Sep	Oct	Nov	Dec	TOTAL LBS N/1000 FT²/YR
Bermudagrass common and hybrid			N†		C	N	N	N	C		N†		2 - 5
Carpetgrass					C		C						1 - 2
Centipedegrass					C	Fe	C	Fe					1 - 2
St. Augustine-grass					C*	C*	C*	C*	C*				2 - 5
Zoysiagrass		N†			C	N	N	C			N†		2 - 3
Tall fescue & Kentucky blue-grass	C	C								C	C		2 - 4

C = Apply complete fertilizer (e.g. 16-4-8) at 1.0 lb N/1000 ft² for high maintenance lawns or .5 lb N/1000 ft² for low maintenance lawns. To improve winter hardiness, an addtional potassium application may be needed at 1.0 lb K/ 1000 ft² in late August through mid-September. Phosphorous is typically not needed on established centipedegrass lawns unless recommended by soil test results.

N = Water soluble inorganic nitrogen source (e.g. ammonium nitrate or ammonium sulfate) is applied at 1.0 lb N/1000 ft² for high maintenance lawns or .5 lb/1000 ft² for low maintenance lawns.

Fe = Apply iron to provide green color without stimulating excessive shoot growth. Ferrous sulfate (2 oz. in 3 to 5 gallons of water /1000 ft²) or a chelated iron source may be used.

† = Fertilizing at this time is only for lawns overseeded with ryegrass.

* = To reduce chinch bugs and gray leaf spot problems on St. Augustinegrass use a slow-release N source.

Table 10. Mowing height for lawn grasses in Georgia

GRASS	MOWER	HEIGHT (inches)	FREQUENCY (days)
Bermuda-grass, common	Rotary or reel	1 - 2	5 - 7
Bermuda-grass, hybrid	Either	1.0 - 1.5	4 - 7
Centipede-grass	Either	1 - 2	5 - 10
St. Augustine grass	Rotary	2 - 3	5 - 7
Zoysiagrass	Reel	1 - 2	4 - 7
Tall fescue	Rotary	2 - 3	5 - 7

5. Collect the unused fertilizer and pour it back into the bag.

6. Sweep or blow fertilizer that has landed onto driveways, walkways, or roads back into lawn. To minimize environmental contamination, fertilizer materials should not be allowed to move into storm sewage or other water systems.

All fertilizers may burn turf if improperly applied. Never exceed the recommended rate or the lawn may be damaged.

Liming—Another important factor in plant growth is the soil acidity level. Most turfgrasses grow best at a pH 5.5 to 6.5. A pH either too low to too high will reduce the availability of plant nutrients. Therefore, it is important to maintain the proper pH. Lime is used to raise soil pH. In most cases a dolomitic source of limestone should be used because it supplies magnesium as well as calcium. Base lime applications on soil test results.

It is important to realize that a plant must have a well developed root system in order to use fertilizer efficiently. No amount of soil testing and fertilization will overcome poor physical conditions of the soil or a poor root system. Soil testing and fertilizer application

Table 11. Mowing calculations for 'One Third' rule

DESIRED HEIGHT	MOW WHEN TURF IS
1	1 $\frac{3}{8}$
1 ½	2
2	2 $\frac{5}{8}$
3	4
INCHES	

cannot overcome poor environmental conditions or management.

Irrigation—Many factors influence the amount and frequency of water needed for a turf. Soil type, type of grass, fertility level, frequency of rain, temperature, wind, and humidity all affect the amount of water needed. A high level fertilization and hot, windy days tend to increase the demand for water, while low level fertilization and cool, cloudy days tend to decrease the demand for water.

To conserve water, wilt is a physiological defense mechanism of the turfgrass plant and allowing some moisture stress actually triggers the plant to initiate rooting, allowing the turfgrass to explore a greater soil volume for water reserves. The key to good moisture management is finding the balance between some wilt and too much that the plant is overly stressed and will not recover from a lack of moisture. Being able to identify wilt within a lawn is the first step toward proper water management. Most grasses appear dark and dull, the leaf blades begin to fold or roll, and footprints remain after walking over the area when the grass is under water stress. Actually observing some wilt, or moisture stress, within the lawn prior to applying irrigation can be a good and improve the sustainability of the turf. Daily irrigation of turfgrass produces short roots incapable of tolerating periodic stresses. Most established turfgrasses in Georgia only need 1.0 inch of water per week. Irrigation should be applied to supplement rainfall.

Apply enough water to wet the soil to a depth of 6 to 8 inches. This is usually equivalent to 1.0 inch of water. Do not apply water until runoff occurs. If water is being applied faster than the soil can absorb it, turn the irrigation off and allow the existing moisture to move into the soil, then apply the remaining irrigation to achieve 1.0 inch.

Prior to sunrise is the best time to water because of less wind and lower temperature. Research indicates water loss at night through evaporation may be 50 percent less than during midday irrigation. Studies also suggest that irrigating after dew develops will not increase disease problems. However, irrigating prior to dew formation or after the dew has dried from the morning sun and/or wind extends the period of free surface moisture and increases disease.

Irrigation is one maintenance practice often done wrong. Light, frequent irrigations produce shallow, weak root systems. A shallow root system prevents efficient use of plant nutrients and soil moisture. The key to success is to condition the grass to require as little extra water as possible. This is best accomplished by developing a lawn with a deep root system. If the soil becomes compacted or crusted, loosen it by coring so that water can penetrate the surface and move into the root zone. Raise the cutting height during water stress periods, and mow less frequently.

Mowing—Proper mowing has a tremendous effect on the appearance of a lawn. Height of cut (Table 10), frequency of cut, and type of mower used are all important factors to consider when mowing.

Reel-type mowers are best suited for the hybrid bermudagrasses and zoysiagrass. Other grasses can be cut satisfactorily with a rotary-type mower. Dull mower blades tear leaves instead of cutting them, thus producing a poor appearance, reducing plant growth, and increasing fuel consumption.

As a general rule, a grass should be mowed often enough so that no more than ¼ to ⅓ of the plant height is removed. For example, if a tall fescue lawn is cut at a height of 2 inches, cut the grass when it reaches 2⅝ inches (Table 11). Removal of too much plant material can damage the grass. The most damaging mowing practice is a sudden reduction in mowing height. This upsets the balance between the grass shoots and roots. If the grass becomes too tall between mowings, raise the cutting height, then gradually lower it with subsequent mowings over time until the recommended height is reached.

During stress periods, such as summer heat, it is a good idea to raise the height of cut slightly. This is especially helpful to the cool-season grasses because it reduces stress. After the stress is gone, lower cutting height gradually. Grasses in shaded areas should be cut higher than normally suggested for better growth. Raising the mowing height of warm-season grasses as fall approaches can help the grass survive the winter months.

If turfgrasses are properly fertilized and mowed, grass clippings will not promote thatch accumulation. In fact, returning the clippings to the soil (grass cycling) will recycle plant nutrients and reduce fertilizer requirements. A "thatch layer" is an accumulation of dead plant material at the soil surface. Thatch is composed of turfgrass stems, rhizomes, stolons, and roots. It prevents penetration of water into the soil, harbors insects and disease organisms, and leads to a shallow rooted grass which is heat, cold, and drought susceptible. Many people like a dense, soft mat of turf, but this is usually a sign of excessive thatch and generally leads to problems.

Following best management practices in mowing, irrigation, and fertilization will minimize the rate of thatch development.

Cultivation—Cultivation of turfgrasses includes vertical mowing, coring, and topdressing. These operations reduce surface compaction and thatch accumulation, improve soil aeration and water infiltration, and promote root growth. All these benefits are essential to producing vigorous, healthy turf.

Vertical mowing or dethatching helps keep turfgrasses healthy by removing the dead vegetation from the thatch layer. This dead material is lifted to the surface by the blades of the vertical mower. This operation should be done in two directions at right angles to each other for bermudagrass and zoysiagrass.

Vertical mowing is best done when the grass is actively growing, and soil temperatures are consistently above 65° F at the 4-inch depth. Vertical mowing during green up can be risky because the grass can be damaged as it begins to grow. Care must be taken not to remove too much from St. Augustinegrass and centipedegrass lawns because they do not have underground runners, or stolons, to rejuvenate new plants. Even though zoysiagrass does have underground runners, it can also be injured by excessive thinning.

Coring relieves soil compaction and increases air and water movement into the soil. It also stimulates decomposition of thatch and organic matter. Proper coring is best accomplished by a power aerator which has hollow tines or spoons that remove a soil core 2 to 3 inches deep and ½ to ¾ inch in diameter.

Coring is best accomplished during periods of active plant growth, and when the soil is moist enough to allow penetration. Coring, also called aeration, is done to correct soil problems and may be the most effective cultivation practice.

Topdressing is a management practice used to aid in the decomposition of thatch, to reduce surface compaction, and to smooth the surface. Topdressing involves spreading a thin layer of topsoil or other soil mix on the soil surface. The topdressing material should have a texture and composition similar to that of the underlying soil. Topdressing rates may range from ½ to 2 cubic yards of material per 1,000 square feet. This produces a layer from ⅛ to ⅝ inch thick. However, it is important that distinct layers are not formed. The topdressing material is worked into the turf by dragging, raking, or brushing.

Fertilization prior to cultivation stimulates rapid turfgrass recovery and promotes a healthy, vigorous turf. However, neither dethatching nor coring should be done during a period of heavy weed germination, or appropriate weed control measures will be necessary. Interestingly, coring has not been shown to reduce the efficacy of previously applied preemergence herbicides.

Renovation—Occasionally a lawn will become thin and spotty and, in some cases, large dead areas may appear. These areas are eventually filled in by weeds. At this point, one must decide if:

1. The lawn can be brought back to the desired appearance through normal maintenance

2. The lawn requires renovation

3. The lawn has to be completely reestablished

First, the cause of the problem must be determined and corrected. Normal causes of decline are:

1. Improper maintenance practices

2. Use of grass not adapted to the area

3. Excessive thatch accumulation

4. Severely compacted soil

5. Disease or insect problems

Cool-season grass lawns should be renovated in early fall (September to October), while warm-season grass lawns should be renovated in early spring (April to May). The renovation steps are as follows:

Step 1. Eliminate all undesirable weeds and/or excessive thatch. Weeds can be removed by either chemical or mechanical means, while thatch will require some mechanical means of removal.

Step 2. Cultivate the soil by coring, slicing, and/or spiking.

Step 3. Correct the soil pH and/or salinity (salt accumulation) problem if one exists. Soil test should be taken to determine the pH and fertility level of the soil.

Step 4. Apply fertilizer as recommended to the area and water. Use a starter fertilizer such as 6-12-12 or 5-10-15 unless soil test recommends otherwise. Apply about 20 pounds per 1,000 square feet.

Step 5. If the lawn is overseeded, drag, rake, or brush the seed into the soil. If the area is planted with vegetative material, place the sprigs in a furrow and lightly topdress.

Step 6. Apply water immediately after planting. Do not allow the newly planted material to become dry. Continue normal mowing practices once the grass reaches 1.5 times its normal mowing height.

Calibration and Application

Failure to apply a material uniformly over an area will produce an irregular response. This can range from a lack of response to a pesticide to leaf burn from over fertilization. Misapplication reduces the effectiveness of the material, may be hazardous to individuals and the environment, and can be costly. Proper application is important whether planting, fertilizing, or applying a pesticide.

First, determine the size of the area by multiplying the length by the width in feet to obtain the square feet involved. Be sure to follow the correct application procedures and recommended rate for the particular material being applied. Finally, proper distribution can be insured by dividing the material into equal parts and applying it in two directions at right angles to each other as previously described.

DISCUSSION QUESTIONS

1. List the names and important characteristics of cool-season turfgrasses commonly grown in Georgia.

2. List the names and important characteristics of warm-season turfgrasses commonly grown in Georgia.

3. Why is it important to select a turfgrass suited to the site?

4. What are the advantages of selecting Georgia Certified Turfgrasses?

5. List the steps in turfgrass establishment.

6. Discuss the differences between seeding, sodding, sprigging and stolonizing in turfgrass establishment.

7. In what instances would sodding be preferable in lawn establishment?

A TURFGRASS MANAGEMENT CALENDAR FOR GEORGIA

Clint Waltz, Extension Turfgrass Specialist

INTRODUCTION

This calendar is a basic guide to turfgrass management in Georgia. The different geographic locations and weather conditions within the state may alter this schedule by as much as four weeks. The schedule can also change within a site because of environmental factors such as moisture, temperature, shade, soil types and conditions, and pest populations. For additional turfgrass management information, contact your county Extension office and visit www. GeorgiaTurf.com.

SELECTION

Turfgrass selection is arguably the most important factor in developing and maintaining a high quality, problem-free turf. Selection should be based on the environment, expected use, and management intensity. Turfgrass "certified" by the Georgia Crop Improvement Association (www.certifiedseed.org) as to varietal purity, freedom from noxious weeds, and documented by the blue certified tag should be used.

ESTABLISHMENT

The three phases of establishment are 1) soil preparation, 2) proper planting, and 3) maintenance for two to four weeks after planting. Cool-season grasses are best established in the fall four to six weeks before the first killing frost date. The best time to plant warm-season grasses is late spring or early summer, once soil temperature at the 4-inch depth is consistently above 65°F. Visit www.GeorgiaWeather.net to find local climatic conditions.

MOWING

Proper mowing involves cutting the grass at the recommended height and often enough to prevent scalping. This means removing no more than ⅓ of the total leaf surface in a mowing. So, if a turf is being cut at 2-inches, mow it when it reaches 2⅝-inches. Not removing clippings and allowing them to naturally filter down into the turf recycles nutrients, is environmentally sound, saves time and energy, and landfill space. Generally raising the mowing height during periods of stress helps maintain turf.

IRRIGATION

Turfgrass water needs depend on grass species, maintenance level, soil type, and weather. Proper irrigation means waiting to irrigate when the turfgrass shows signs of moisture stress, such as a bluish-gray color. Most established turfgrasses require about 1-inch of water per week during the active growth season. Supplemental irrigation should wet the soil to a 6- to 8- inch depth. Multiple start times may be needed to prevent runoff and improve irrigation efficiency on clay based soils. Likewise, two, ½-inch applications are better on sandy soils. The most efficient and effective time to irrigate is after sunset and before sunrise. Irrigating at this time will not increase disease problems.

FERTILIZATION

Depend on soil test analysis to determine the best fertilizer grade, rate, and time of application. Generally, turfgrasses require ½ - to 1-pound of nitrogen per 1,000 square feet per month of active growth. Excess nitrogen increases plant growth which means more frequent mowing, increased plant water needs, thatch formation, and possibly insect and disease problems.

THATCH CONTROL

If the thatch layer is thicker than ½-inch turfgrass vigor can be reduced. Thatch can be effectively controlled by topdressing with a ¼-inch layer of topsoil. Thatch can also be reduced by vertical mowing. Vertical mowing should be done when the turf is actively growing and at least 30 days before the "first killing frost date". Vertical mowing should be avoided during periods of temperature and moisture stress, during periods of weed seed germination, or or when a preemergence herbicide has been used.

Overseeding

Warm-season turfgrasses can be overseeded with cool-season grasses (ryegrass or rough bluegrass) to provide year-long green color. This type overseeding is usually done 2- to 4-weeks prior to the first fall temperature date of 32°F. The bermudagrasses tolerate overseeding best, while it is difficult to get a uniform overseeding in centipedegrass and zoysiagrass turfs. However, overseeding can be problematic for any turfgrass species, especially when already weakened from improper management. Common warm-season grass problems associated with overseeded turfs are weak stands due to competition with the overseeding species and delayed spring green-up.

Renovation

Turfgrass renovation is needed when a turf declines to the point that normal management and cultural practices are not enough to revive the grass but complete re-establishment is not needed. Generally, if 50% or more of the area contains desirable turfgrass, renovation will work. Renovate at the start of the growing season.

Pest Control

Good lawn management can help reduce pest problems. When pest control is needed; (1) identify the pest problem, (2) determine if cultural or other management practices are best suited for control, (3) select the chemical recommended to control the pest, (4) be sure the turfgrass will tolerate the chemical and (5) apply the chemical according to label recommendations. Proper timing of pesticide application is needed for effective and efficient pesticide use.

Weed Control

Preemergence herbicides should be applied before weed emergence. Recommended dates of application for crabgrass and other annual grasses are February 15 to March 5 in South Georgia and March 1 to March 20 in North Georgia. These dates typically correlate to soil temperatures which are below 55°F, the temperature at which crabgrass will germinate.

Recommended dates for annual bluegrass and selected winter annual broadleaf weed control are September 1 to September 15 in North Georgia and October 1 to October 15 in South Georgia. Apply postemergence herbicides to small, actively-growing weeds at air temperatures between 60°F. and 90°F. Applications to turfgrass stressed by high temperature or drought increases the possibility of injury and usually results in poor weed control. Atrazine or simazine can be applied to warm-season turfgrasses for preemergence and/or postemergence control of annual bluegrass and selected winter annual broadleaf weeds from November through February. Avoid all postemergence herbicide applications during spring green-up of warm-season turfgrasses.

Disease Control

The development and maintenance of a healthy, vigorous plant through proper turfgrass management is the best method of disease prevention. Proper fertilization and irrigation are very important disease prevention practices. If a disease is suspected, identification of the disease is needed before treatment can be recommended. (http://plantpath. caes.uga.edu/extension/clinic.html)

Insect Control

Of the many insects and related species living within a turfgrass canopy, very few cause damage. Some insects, such as white grubs and mole crickets, live in the soil and damage turfgrass roots. Others, such as armyworms and chinch bugs, feed on grass leaves and stems by chewing or sucking plant juices. When damage is apparent, an insecticide may be needed.

Bermudagrass Lawn Management Calendar

B BEST MONTH   P POSSIBLE MONTH   M MARGINAL MONTH   X NOT RECOMMENDED

	JAN	FEB	MAR	APR	MAY	JUN	JUL	AUG	SEP	OCT	NOV	DEC
Mowing Height: Common Bermuda 1-2"; Hybrid Bermuda 1.0" to 1.5"; raise .5" higher in hot weather. Remove no more than 1/3 total height at one time.	X	X	X	OK	OK	OK	OK	OK	OK	OK	X	X
Water: 1" per week if no rainfall. Sod laid in fall or winter months must not be allowed to dry out; water as needed.	New sod	New sod	New sod	OK	OK	OK	OK	OK	OK	OK	New sod	New sod
Fertilization: 2 - 4 lb. N/1000 ft²/YR Follow fertilizer recommendations on soil test report. If soil was not tested, use any turf fertilizer and follow label rates. In the spring, do not apply nitrogen-containing fertilizers until soil temperature at the 4" depth is constantly 65°F and rising.	X	X	X	P	B	B	B	B	P	X	X	X
Ideal pH range: 5.5 - 6.5; Use dolomitic lime per soil test recommendation. Can be applied at any time.	B	B	B	P	P	P	P	P	P	P	B	B
Aeration: Use a core aerator during active growth season.	X	X	X	P	B	B	B	B	P	X	X	X
Dethatch: If thatch exceeds .5" deep, use a vertical mower with blades 1" apart; go over the lawn only 2 directions. Top dressing with .25" of soil can be effective.	X	X	X	X	P	B	B	P	X	X	X	X
Seeding- New lawn*: Unhulled seed: 4-8 lb. per 1000 ft². Hulled seed: 1-2 lb. per 1000 ft²	X	X	X	P	B	B	B	P	X	X	X	X
Overseeding-Established Lawns*: 5-10 lb. ryegrass per 1000 ft².	X	X	X	X	X	X	X	X	P	B	P	X
Sodding: 500 ft² per pallet typical.	M	M	M	P	B	B	B	B	P	M	M	M
Weed Control: Read product label carefully to determine which weeds are controlled and on which grasses the product can be used.												
Spring preemergence* prevents crabgrass, goosegrass, and other annual weeds.	X	B	B	P	X	X	X	X	X	X	X	X
Broadleaf postemergence spot spray to kill broadleaf plants like chickweed, wild violet, dandelion, wild onion, etc	OK	OK	OK	OK	OK	OK	OK	OK	OK	OK	OK	OK
Grassy weed postemergence* kills grassy weeds like crabgrass, dallisgrass, etc. Do not apply to drought-stressed bermudagrass	X	X	X	X	B	B	B	B	P	X	X	X
Winter preemergence* prevents chickweed and other winter weeds.	X	X	X	X	X	X	X	X	B	P	X	X

* Read weed control product labels carefully. Some products can not be applied to lawns that will be seeded within a few weeks or when transitioning to active growth.

Centipedegrass Lawn Management Calendar

B BEST MONTH   P POSSIBLE MONTH   M MARGINAL MONTH   X NOT RECOMMENDED

Practice	JAN	FEB	MAR	APR	MAY	JUN	JUL	AUG	SEP	OCT	NOV	DEC
Mowing Height: 1"- 2"; raise .5" higher in hot weather. This is the most important practice for a healthy centipedegrass lawn.	X	X	X	X	OK	OK	OK	OK	OK	X	X	X
Water: 1" per week if no rainfall.	X	X	X	OK	OK	OK	OK	OK	OK	OK	X	X
Fertilization: 1 - 2 lb. N/1000 ft²/YR. Follow fertilizer recommendations on soil test report. If soil was not tested, use any turf fertilizer and follow label rates. In the spring, do not apply nitrogen-containing fertilizers until soil temperature at the 4" depth is constantly 65°F and rising.	X	X	X	X	B	P	B	P	X	X	X	X
Ideal pH range: 5.0 - 6.0; Lime is rarely needed.												
Aeration: Use a core aerator during active growth season.	X	X	X	X	B	B	B	P	X	X	X	X
Dethatch: If thatch exceeds .5" deep, use a vertical mower with blades 1" apart; go over the lawn only 1 direction. Top dressing with .25 inches of soil can be effective.	X	X	X	X	P	P	P	X	X	X	X	X
Seeding: New lawn*: .25 -1.0 LB. per 1000 FT².	X	X	X	P	B	B	P	X	X	X	X	X
Overseeding-Established Lawns*: Overseeding centipedegrass with ryegrass is not recommended.	X	X	X	X	X	X	X	X	X	X	X	X
Sodding: 500 ft² per pallet typical.	X	X	X	P	B	B	B	P	M	M	X	X
Weed Control: Read product label carefully to determine which weeds are controlled and on which grasses the product can be used.												
Spring preemergence*- prevents crabgrass, goosegrass, and other annual weeds.	X	B	B	P	X	X	X	X	X	X	X	X
Broadleaf postemergence- spot spray to kill broadleaf plants like chickweed, wild violet, dandelion, wild onion, etc	OK	OK	OK	OK	OK	OK	OK	OK	OK	OK	OK	OK
Grassy weed postemergence*- kills grassy weeds like crabgrass, dallisgrass, etc. Do not apply to drought-stressed centipedegrass.	X	X	X	X	B	B	B	B	P	X	X	X
Winter preemergence*- prevents chickweed and other winter weeds.	X	X	X	X	X	X	X	X	B	P	X	X

* Read weed control product labels carefully. Some products can not be applied to lawns that will be seeded within a few weeks or when transitioning to active growth.

St. Augustinegrass Lawn Management Calendar

B BEST MONTH   P POSSIBLE MONTH   M MARGINAL MONTH   X NOT RECOMMENDED

	JAN	FEB	MAR	APR	MAY	JUN	JUL	AUG	SEP	OCT	NOV	DEC
Mowing Height: 2" - 3"; raise .5" higher in hot weather. Remove no more than 1/3 total height at one time.	X	X	X	OK	OK	OK	OK	OK	OK	X	X	X
Water: 1" per week if no rainfall.	X	X	X	OK	OK	OK	OK	OK	OK	X	X	X
Fertilization: 2 - 4 lb. N/1000 ft²/YR. Follow fertilizer recommendations on soil test report. If soil was not tested, use any turf fertilizer and follow label rates. In the spring, do not apply nitrogen-containing fertilizers until soil temperature at the 4" depth is constantly 65°F and rising.	X		X	X	B	B	B	B	P	P	X	X
Ideal pH range: 5.5 - 6.5; Use dolomitic lime per soil test. Can be applied at any time.	B	B	B	P	P	P	P	P	P	P	B	B
Aeration: Use a core aerator during active growth season.	X	X	X	P	B	B	B	P	X	X	X	X
Dethatch: If thatch exceeds .5" deep, use a vertical mower with blades 1" apart; go over the lawn only 1 direction. Top dressing with .25" of soil can be effective.	X	X	X	X	P	P	P	P	X	X	X	X
Seeding- New lawn: St. Augustine cannot be established from seed	X	X	X	X	X	X	X	X	X	X	X	X
Overseeding-Established Lawns*: Overseeding St. Augustinegrass with ryegrass is not recommended.	X	X	X	X	X	X	X	X	X	X	X	X
Sodding 500 ft² per pallet typical.	X	X	X	P	B	B	B	P	M	M	X	
Weed Control: Read product label carefully to determine which weeds are controlled and on which grasses the product can be used.												
Spring preemergence* prevents crabgrass, goosegrass, and other annual weeds.	X	B	B	P	X	X	X	X	X	X	X	X
Broadleaf postemergence spot spray to kill broadleaf plants like chickweed, wild violet, dandelion, wild onion, etc	OK	OK	X	X	OK	OK	OK	OK	OK	OK	OK	OK
Grassy weed postemergence* kills grassy weeds like crabgrass, dallisgrass, etc. Do not apply to drought-stressed St. Augustinegrass.	X	X	X	X	X	X	X	X	X	X	X	X
Winter preemergence* prevents chickweed and other winter weeds.	X	X	X	X	X	X	X	X	B	P	X	X

* Read weed control product labels carefully. Some products can not be applied to lawns that will be seeded within a few weeks or when transitioning to active growth.

Zoysiagrass Lawn Management Calendar

B BEST MONTH   P POSSIBLE MONTH   M MARGINAL MONTH   X NOT RECOMMENDED

Activity	JAN	FEB	MAR	APR	MAY	JUN	JUL	AUG	SEP	OCT	NOV	DEC
Mowing Height: .5" to 1.5"; raise .5" higher in hot weather. Remove no more than 1/3 total height at one time.	X	X	X	OK	OK	OK	OK	OK	OK	OK	X	X
Water: 1" per week if no rainfall. Sod laid in fall or winter months must not be allowed to dry out; water as needed.	New sod	New sod	New sod	OK	OK	OK	OK	OK	OK	New Sod	New sod	New sod
Fertilization: 2 - 3 lb. N/1000 ft²/YR Follow fertilizer recommendations on soil test report. If soil was not tested, use any turf fertilizer and follow label rates. In the spring, do not apply nitrogen-containing fertilizers until soil temperature at the 4" depth is constantly 65°F and rising.	X	X	X	P	B	B	B	B	P	P	X	X
Ideal pH range: 6.0 - 7.0; Use dolomitic lime per soil test recommendation. Can be applied at any time.	B	B	B	P	P	P	P	P	P	P	B	B
Aeration: Use a core aerator during active growth season.	X	X	X	P	B	B	B	B	P	X	X	X
Dethatch: If thatch exceeds .5" deep, use a vertical mower with blades 1" apart; go over the lawn only 2 directions. Top dressing with .25" of soil is most effective.	X	X	X	X	P	B	B	P	X	X	X	X
Seeding- New lawn*: 1 - 2 lb per 1,000ft²	X	X	X	X	B	B	P	X	X	X	X	X
Overseeding-Established Lawns*: Overseeding zoysiagrass with ryegrass is not recommended	X	X	X	X	X	X	X	X	X	X	X	X
Sodding 500 ft² per pallet typical.	M	M	M	P	B	B	B	B	P	M	M	M
Weed Control: Read product label carefully to determine which weeds are controlled and on which grasses the product can be used.												
Spring preemergence*- prevents crabgrass, goosegrass, and other annual weeds.	X	B	B	P	X	X	X	X	X	X	X	X
Broadleaf postemergence- spot spray to kill broadleaf plants like chickweed, wild violet, dandelion, wild onion, etc	OK	OK	OK	OK	OK	OK	OK	OK	OK	OK	OK	OK
Grassy weed postemergence*- kills grassy weeds like crabgrass, dallisgrass, etc. Do not apply to drought-stressed zoysiagrass	X	X	X	X	B	B	B	B	P	X	X	X
Winter preemergence*- prevents chickweed and other winter weeds.	X	X	X	X	X	X	X	X	B	P	X	X

* Read weed control product labels carefully. Some products can not be applied to lawns that will be seeded within a few weeks or when transitioning to active growth.

Turf-Type Tall Fescue Lawn Management Calendar

B BEST MONTH P POSSIBLE MONTH M MARGINAL MONTH X NOT RECOMMENDED

	JAN	FEB	MAR	APR	MAY	JUN	JUL	AUG	SEP	OCT	NOV	DEC
Mowing Height: 2"- 3"; raise .5" higher in hot weather. Remove no more than 1/3 total height at one time.	OK	OK	OK	OK	OK	OK	OK	OK	OK	OK	OK	OK
Water: 1" per week if no rainfall. Sod laid in fall or winter months must not be allowed to dry; water as needed.	OK	OK	OK	OK	OK	OK	OK	OK	OK	OK	NEW SOD	NEW SOD
Fertilization: 2 - 4 lb. N/1000 ft²/YR. Follow fertilizer recommendations on soil test report. If soil was not tested, use any turf fertilizer and follow label rates.	X	B	B	P	X	X	X	X	P	B	B	X
Ideal pH range: 5.5 - 6.5; Use dolomitic lime per soil test. Can be applied at any time.	B	B	B	P	P	P	P	P	P	B	B	B
Aeration: Use a core aerator during active growth season.	M	M	B	B	M	X	X	X	P	B	P	M
Dethatch: Generally not necessary.	X	X	X	X	P	B	B	P	X	X	X	X
Seeding- New lawn*: 5 - 6 lb per 1000 ft²	X	P	P	M	M	X	X	X	P	B	P	X
Interseeding-Established Lawns*: 3 - 5 lb seed per 1000 ft².	X	X	X	X	X	X	X	X	P	B	P	X
Sodding-Tall fescue is not available in all months of the year.	X	B	P	P	M	X	X	X	P	B	B	B
Weed Control: Read product label carefully to determine which weeds are controlled and on which grasses the product can be used.	B	B	B	P	M	X	X	X	P	B	B	B
Spring preemergence*- prevents crabgrass, goosegrass, and other annual weeds.	X	B	B	P	X	X	X	X	X	X	X	X
Broadleaf postemergence- spot spray to kill broadleaf plants like chickweed, wild violet, dandelion, wild onion, etc	OK	OK	OK	OK	OK	OK	OK	OK	OK	OK	OK	OK
Grassy weed postemergence*- kills grassy weeds like crabgrass, dallisgrass, etc. Do not apply to drought-stressed tall fescue.	X	X	X	X	P	P	M	M	X	X	X	X
Winter preemergence*- prevents chickweed and other winter weeds.	X	X	X	X	X	X	X	X	B	P	X	X

* Read weed control product labels carefully. Some products can not be applied to lawns that will be seeded within a few weeks or when transitioning to active growth.

Analysis, Rates, And Ratios: Making The Correct Application From A Fertilizer Recommendation

Clint Waltz, Ph.D.Extension Turfgrass Specialist

Plants, like all living things, need nutrients to survive. Many of the elements that are needed to promote and maintain plant growth are already in the soil, but fertilization is often needed to supplement these nutrients. When nutrients are added, care must be taken to apply only what the plants need and will use. Too much fertilizer can cause plant damage, to roots and shoots, and may also impair water quality. Therefore, understanding how fertilizer analyses and ratios are related to recommended application rates is important for maintaining proper plant fertility. Use soil test recommendations to optimize fertility practices and minimize the chances of water pollution.

A fertilizer recommendation from the lab comes as an application rate for a particular nutrient. Seldom do the recommendations, either from a university lab or a private lab, detail the exact amount of a fertilizer product to use. For example, the lab report may recommend applying 1.0 pound of nitrogen per 1,000 ft², but it does not specify the amount of fertilizer product which is needed. The product rate will change based on the fertilizer analysis. When a combination of nutrients is necessary, a comparative ratio is sometimes suggested. Understanding the definitions of these important terms is critical to proper application of fertilizers.

Three numbers on the fertilizer label refer to the percentages by weight of the major nutrients: nitrogen (N), phosphate (P_2O_5), and potash (K_2O). The numbers on the label are listed in that order and are referred to as the fertilizer analysis or grade. Phosphate is the fertilizer form of the element phosphorus (P), and potash is the fertilizer form of the element potassium (K). If the fertilizer contains any one of these, on the label it must include content values for the other elements. If in the fertilizer product the element is nonexistent, then a "0" must appear on the label for that element.

A 50 pound bag of 16-4-8 contains 8 pounds nitrogen, 2 pounds phosphate, and 4 pounds potash. Pound for pound, a 16-4-8 fertilizer contains twice the nutrients of an 8-2-4 fertilizer. Thus, to supply equal amounts of nutrients, half as much 16-4-8 as 8-2-4 is needed to obtain a similar plant response.

For simplicity purposes the analysis is commonly referenced as the amount of N-P-K and disregards the fact that the nutrients exist in their oxide form not in the elemental form. This means that within a fertilizer product there is actually less than the percent by weight of the element. This is because the oxygen must also be taken into account, phosphate is 43% phosphorus and potash is 83% potassium. Any additional nutrients that might be contained in a fertilizer are typically listed in smaller print below these primary three.

Some fertilizer analysis examples are;

10-10-10 – an example of a complete, balanced analysis

16-4-8 – an example of a complete, unbalanced analysis

34-0-0 – an example of an incomplete analysis

15-0-15 – an example of an incomplete analysis, sometimes referred to as a "zero" grade

A fertilizer ratio is the relative amount of nitrogen to phosphate to potassium in a fertilizer product. Evaluating the fertilizer ratio is a method of comparing the amount of one element to another and becomes important when evaluating a fertilizer product for specific plant demands and soil characteristics. The fertilizer ratio is calculated by dividing the lowest analysis number into each of the other analysis numbers. A 16-4-8 analysis fertilizer contains four times more nitrogen as phosphate and twice the amount of potash, the ratio is 4-1-2. Note that fertilizers with the same ratio do not have to have the same analysis. Fertilizer analysis of 8-2-4, 16-4-8, and 32-8-16 all have a 4-1-2 ratio.

A rate is the amount of a nutrient to be applied over a given area. An example of a rate recommendation is to apply 1.0 pound of nitrogen per 1,000 ft². This recommendation describes how much of the nutrient, nitrogen, should be evenly distributed over a given area, 1,000 ft². Using recommended rates specific for individual plant species can produce dense root systems and proper growth while reducing the potential of leaching and runoff. Contact your County Extension Agent for plant specific fertility recommendations.

Using the nutrient rate recommendation from a soil test report, converting to an amount of fertilizer product to supply the nutrients involves some basic math. Inserting the appropriate information into Formula 1 can make the conversion. If the recommendation is to apply 1.0 pound of nitrogen per 1,000 ft² and a 16-4-8 analysis fertilizer is used, first divide the 1.0 pound nitrogen rate by 16% (0.16). The result is the amount of 16-4-8 to apply per 1,000 ft² to obtain 1.0 pound of nitrogen per

Formula 1
Amount of fertilizer to apply / area = [(pounds of recommended nutrient / area) ÷ (% of nutrient in fertilizer product)]

Calculation 1
1.0 pound N / 1,000 ft^2 ÷ 16% nitrogen = <u>6.25 pounds of fertilizer / 1,000 ft^2</u>

Calculation 2
1.0 pound N / 1,000 ft^2 ÷ 8% nitrogen = <u>12.5 pounds of fertilizer / 1,000 ft^2</u>

1,000 ft^2, the total amount of fertilizer product applied for the area is 6.25 pounds (Calculation 1). However, if a fertilizer with the 8-2-4 analysis is used and the same calculations are performed, then 12.5 pounds of fertilizer are needed to achieve the same nitrogen rate and get a similar plant response (Calculation 2). This example demonstrates how the actual amount of fertilizer product applied to an area will vary based on the analysis. Therefore, often it is the nutrient rate that is most important and not the fertilizer analysis; as the same rate can be achieved using several different analysis fertilizers.

NOTES

15

Insects and Diseases of Turfgrasses

Alfredo Martinez

Kris Braman

LEARNING OBJECTIVES

Be able to recognize insect-related injury in turfgrass.

Know some common insects and diseases affecting turfgrass in Georgia.

Understand how to prevent or control insect damage to turfgrass.

TERMS TO KNOW

Blight A symptom or disease in which plant parts such as leaves, flowers, and stems are rapidly killed.

Causal agent Either a biotic or an abiotic agent that causes a disruption of a plant's normal growth or physical properties.

Chlorosis Whitish or yellowish discoloration of normally green plant material due to the lack of chlorophyll.

Chlorotic Plant tissues that appear pale green to yellow.

Coalesce To grow together.

Conidium (conidia) A fungal spore.

Disease Any disturbance of a plant over some period of time that interferes with its normal structure, function, or economic value and that induces symptoms.

Fruiting structure, or fruiting body A fungal structure made of mycelium and containing spores.

Fungicide A chemical compound that is toxic to fungi.

Fungus (fungi) A multicellular lower plant without chlorophyll. The fungus normally consists of strands called mycelium and reproduces through the dispersal of spores.

Grub Immature form of many beetles.

Host Plant attacked by a pest or pathogen.

Infection Process in which a pathogen enters, invades, or penetrates and causes disease with a host plant.

Larva (larvae) Immature form, between egg and pupa, of an insect with complete metamorphosis.

Leaf spot A discrete dead area on a leaf.

Lesion Wound or delimited diseased area.

Mushroom The fruiting structure of many wood-decay fungi, consisting of a rounded cap on a cylindrical stalk.

Nematode A microscopic, wormlike animal that can be parasitic on plants.

Nymph Immature stage of an insect with simple metamorphosis.

Pathogen A microorganism capable of causing disease.

Spore The reproductive or propagative unit of a fungus, which can be formed from a sexual recombination or from cell division.

Susceptible Capable of being injured or killed.

Symptom A plant's reaction to a disorder resulting from a causal agent.

DISEASES OF TURF

Introduction

Turfgrasses are an essential part of home landscapes and recreation areas. Attractive lawns make ideal settings for homes, adding beauty to the neighborhood. Turfgrasses also reduce dust, glare, heat and noise, and prevent erosion and surface runoff. Turfgrasses can also increase the value of properties. Due to Georgia's increasing population, range of climates, and wide variety of turf choices, the popularity of turfgrass has increased tremendously. However, due to the warm and humid weather of Georgia, disease problems can occur in lawns. The key to disease control is a healthy plant. Under proper turfgrass management, disease causing conditions are reduced and a healthy turf is maintained. The following management practices will help produce a vigorous, healthy turf and reduce turfgrass disease problems.

a) **Prepare the soil properly.** The key to successful turf establishment is proper soil preparation.

• Take soil samples to determine proper nutrient requirements.

• Remove all debris such as rocks, tree stumps and other wood debris.

• Provide proper water drainage. The area should be graded to prevent surface water collection.

b) **Plant locally adapted, disease-resistant turfgrass species.** Obtain information for recommended varieties for the area.

c) **Purchase high quality disease free seed, sod or sprigs from a certified producer.** Plant material certified for varietal purity and freedom from noxious pests is recommended when available. Nematodes and disease problems can be brought in on springs and sod.

d) **Follow proper irrigation practices.**

• The most cost effective practice that enhances turf growth is proper irrigation.

• Apply water after observing wilt, the first signs of moisture stress. Typically the turfgrass will become a dull, bluish green color with leaf blade folding or rolling and footprints remaining after walking over the area.

• If the soil becomes compacted, loosen it through cultivation such as core aeration, so the water can penetrate into the soil.

• Irrigate early in the morning. Late afternoon irrigation will encourage disease development. Irrigation after dew development and before sunrise is most efficient and will not increase disease problems. Irrigate deeply and infrequently.

e) **Apply fertilizer according to soil analysis recommendations.**

• Disease incidence is increased by an unbalanced soil fertility.

f) **Mow at the recommended cutting height.**

• Mow turfgrasses no more than ⅓ of the plant. If more plant material is removed, the grass will become stressed and more susceptible to disease causing organisms.

• Keep mower blades sharp. Dull blades shred leaf tips, causing turf to use more water, undergo undue stress, and provide pathogen infection entrances.

• Raise the mowing height during stress periods such as drought.

g) **Remove excess thatch.**

• Excess thatch reduces water infiltration, creates shallow rooted turf, and encourages insect and disease problems. If the lawn is not mowed, irrigated, and fertilized correctly, thatch accumulation could create a problem. Disease causing organisms survive and multiply in thatch. Excess nitrogen is a major cause of thatch accumulation.

• If excess thatch accumulates, the lawn will feel soft and spongy. If the thatch layer is thicker than ½ inch, de-thatching is needed.

h) **Allow for adequate light and air movement in shaded areas.**

• In heavily shaded areas, excessive moisture on grass blades can be a problem.

• Prune trees and shrubs, and design landscape plantings so humidity is reduced by light penetration and air movement.

• Raise the mowing height in shaded areas to help the plant absorb the limited light penetrating the tree canopy.

• Reducing fertilizer amounts by 20 to 50 percent in full areas also helps the grass better cope with the limited light.

i) **Follow recommended disease, insect, and weed control practices.**

Chemicals are not the answer to disease problems. Proper management practices will reduce pest problems and reduce the need for chemicals.

SPECIFIC DISEASES IN GEORGIA TURFGRASSES

Brown Patch and Large Patch

Causal agent—*Rhizoctonia solani, R. zeae, R. oryzae*

Susceptible turfgrasses—Brown patch can infect all species of warm- and cool-season turfgrass in Georgia, including St. Augustinegrass, zoysiagrass, bentgrass, ryegrass, centipedegrass and bermudagrass. It is one of the most common turfgrass diseases in the state.

Symptoms—The symptoms of brown patch can vary depending on grass cultivar, soil, and climatic conditions. This disease typically causes rings and/or patches of blighted turfgrass that measure 5 inches to more than 10 feet in diameter. It also causes leaf spots and "smoke rings", which are thin, brown borders around the diseased patches that appear most frequently in the early morning. After the leaves die in the blighted area, new leaves can emerge from the surviving crowns. On wide bladed species, leaf lesions develop with tan centers and dark brown to black margins.

Conditions Favoring Disease Development—The most favorable conditions for disease development usually occur from late April through October. Brown patch is favored by high relative humidity and temperatures over 80°F during the day and over 60°F at night. This disease can be active on warm-season grasses in the spring and fall. It also occurs in areas that experience more than 10 hours a day of foliar wetness for several consecutive days. Brown patch infestation is more severe when the turf is cut to a height less than the optimum for the turfgrass being grown. Heavy nitrogen applications increase susceptibility to brown patch.

Control—Management plays an important role in brown patch and large patch control.

• Use low amounts of nitrogen, moderate amounts of phosphorous, and moderate to high amounts of potash.

• Avoid nitrogen application when the disease is active.

• Increase the cutting height.

• Increase the air circulation.

• Minimize the amount of shade.

• Irrigate turf early in the day to allow the foliage to dry as quickly as possible.

• Improve turf drainage.

• Reduce thatch.

• Remove dew early in the day by dragging a hose or mat over the turf.

• Fungicides are available to control the disease. Consult the current *Georgia Pest Management Handbook*.

Dollar Spot

Causal Agent—*Sclerotinia homoeocarpa*

Susceptible turfgrasses—All species of warm- and cool-season turfgrass. Tall fescue, bentgrass, zoysiagrass and bermudagrass hybrids are particularly susceptible.

Symptoms—Dollar spot causes sunken, circular patches that measure up to few inches on turfgrass. The patches turn from brown to straw color and may eventually coalesce, forming irregularly shaped areas. Infected leaves may display small lesions that turn from yellow green to straw color with a reddish brown border. The lesions can extend the full width of the leaf. Multiple lesions may occur on a single leaf blade. Abundant white fungus growth may be seen in these areas during periods of severe disease development.

Conditions Favoring Disease Development—Dollar spot is favored by temperatures between 59°F to 86°F, continuous high humidity, and low soil moisture. This disease is particularly favored by warm days, cool nights, and intense dews. It also infects areas with low levels of nitrogen and becomes more severe in dry soils. Dollar spot is more common during the spring and fall months.

Control—Management practices helpful in controlling this disease include the addition of nitrogen and providing sufficient soil moisture.

• Use an adequate level of nitrogen, particularly in the spring and early summer.

• Mow grass at regular intervals.

• Irrigate turf early in the day to allow the foliage to dry as quickly as possible.

• Reduce thatch.

• Increase the air circulation.

• Irrigate turf deeply and as infrequently as possible to avoid drought stress.

• Remove dew from the turf early in the day.

• Fungicides can be used to help bring the disease under control once it is established. Consult the current *Georgia Pest Management Handbook*.

Pythium Root Rot

Causal Agent—*Pythium spp.*

Susceptible Turfgrass—Annual bluegrass, tall fescue,

perennial ryegrass and varieties of bentgrass, bermudagrass, centipedegrass, zoysiagrass and St. Augustinegrass. Pythium root rot is common on highly maintained turf and is throughout Georgia. This may be attributed to over watering.

Symptoms—Pythium root rot is common on highly maintained turf. Although symptoms of Pythium root rot are typically non-distinctive, this disease can appear as yellow, irregularly shaped patches. The affected turfgrass is thin, off color and slow growing, while the root system is stunted with reduced volume and vigor.

Conditions Favoring Disease Development—Wet conditions are required for Pythium blight development. Some Pythium species favor temperatures between 32°F and 50°F while others thrive in temperatures between 70°F and 90°F. In Georgia the disease is most favored by warm temperatures. Cool-season grasses (e.g. ryegrass, tall fescue, and bentgrass) are usually seeded in the fall when temperatures are favorable for disease. For germination, regular irrigation is required following seeding, this watering may promote disease development. Grasses are more susceptible in the young seedling stage, so Pythium occurs most often in the fall and on warm winter days on cool-season grasses. Pythium root rot also infects locations with low mowing height and excessive wear.

Control—Use treated seed. Delay overseeding until the start of cool weather or as late as possible. In Georgia, generally mid-October is the ideal overseeding period.

• Increase the cutting height.

• Apply optimum amounts of nitrogen, phosphorous and potassium.

• Reduce mowing frequency and use lightweight mowers.

• Avoid over watering.

• Apply low amounts of nitrogen in the spring when roots are forming.

• Minimize the amount of shade.

• Improve turf drainage.

• Reduce soil compaction through aerification by using lightweight equipment.

• Fungicides are available to control the disease. Consult the current *Georgia Pest Management Handbook*.

Fairy Ring

Causal Agent—Basidiomycetes of more than 50 species can cause fairy ring; causal agents include: *Agaricus campestris, Chorophyllum molybdites, Collybis spp., Hygrocybe spp., Lepiota sordida, Marasmius oreades, Psalliota spp., Scleroderma spp., Tricholoma spp.,* and *Lycoperdon clitocybe.*

Susceptible Turfgrass—All species of warm- and cool-season turfgrass. The disease is particularly damaging on centipedegrass and St. Augustinegrass in south and coastal Georgia.

Symptoms—The first indication of a fairy ring is a circular or semicircular band of stimulated grass a few inches wide. The band of grass forming the ring is usually greener than the grass in the center. The stimulation of the grass is due to the availability of nutrients resulting from the decomposition by the fungus of organic matter in the soil, and various toxins produced by the fungus itself. Grass inside the ring area may be in a state of decline. In young rings, there may be a dead band of grass a few inches to several feet wide forming a partial or complete ring. The green stimulated ring gradually enlarges, forming an even larger circle. The most characteristic symptom associated with fairy ring is the presence of mushrooms in the stimulated grass ring during rainy, moist periods. However, mushrooms are not always produced and fairy ring may be present yet never produce a mushroom or puffball.

Conditions Favoring Disease—While fairy rings typically occur in the summer, this disease can also occur on cool-season turfgrass in mild winter climates. Once the mushroom fungus becomes established, it can grow and increase the size of the ring in moist, warm weather. The mushroom fungi may produce toxins that inhibit turfgrass growth. The fruiting structures appear during very wet periods, usually in the spring or fall.

Control—Avoid using root zone mixes with high levels of undecomposed organic materials.

• Reduce thatch by vertical cutting.

• Aerate soil.

• Irrigate deeply.

• Use nitrogen fertilizer to mask symptoms on some types of fairy ring.

• Use soil wetting agents to help penetrate hydrophobic areas.

• Fungicides are available to manage the disease. Consult the current *Georgia Pest Management Handbook*.

Fading Out or Melting Out

Causal Agent—*Curvularia spp., Drechslera spp.* and/or *Bipolaris spp.*

Susceptible Turfgrass—Perennial ryegrass, tall fescue

and all varieties of bentgrass, bermudagrass, zoysiagrass and centipedegrass.

Symptoms—Leaf spot (melting out) causes purplish brown to black spots with tan centers on the leaf blade and sheath. The lower leaves of the infected plants become shriveled and blighted. When melting out infection is severe, almost all of the leaves and tillers die, causing severe thinning of the stand—or melting out. On cool-season species, melting out typically follows the appearance of leaf spots.

Conditions Favoring Disease Development—Disease favors temperatures between 40°F and 80°F. It occurs in areas that experience more than 10 hours a day of foliar wetness for several consecutive days. It also favors high amounts of nitrogen and a low mowing height with greater severity on dry soils.

Control—

- Reduce turf stress by using lightweight equipment.
- Increase air circulation to increase canopy drying.
- Avoid the application of high rates of water soluble nitrogen in the spring.
- Minimize the amount of shade.
- Irrigate turf deeply and as infrequently as possible.
- Reduce thatch in the early spring or fall for cool-season turfgrass, and in the summer for warm-season turfgrass.
- Avoid using systemically translocated fungicides, plant growth regulators, and herbicides.
- Fungicides are available to control the disease. Consult the current *Georgia Pest Management Handbook*.

Gray leaf Spot

Causal Agent—*Pyricularia grisea*

Susceptible Turfgrass—St. Augustinegrass, perennial ryegrass, bermudagrass, centipedegrass, bentgrass and various species of fescue.

Symptoms—The symptoms of gray leaf spot vary depending on the grass cultivar. On St. Augustinegrass, gray leaf spot first appears as small, brown spots on the leaves and stems. The spots quickly enlarge to approximately ¼ inch in length, become bluish gray in color, and oval or elongated in shape. The mature lesions are tan to gray in color and have depressed centers with irregular margins that are purple to brown in color. A yellow border on the lesions can also occur. In cool-season turfgrass, the symptoms are similar to those of melting out.

Conditions Favoring Disease Development—Gray leaf spot is favored by temperatures between 80°F to 90°F. It is also found in areas with high nitrogen levels that are also stressed by various factors, including drought and soil compaction. This disease is most severe during extended hot, rainy, and humid periods. The disease is often severe under semi-shade when frequent showers occur or when frequent irrigation produces high relative humidity.

Control—

- Avoid medium to high nitrogen levels during mid summer.
- Irrigate turf deeply and as infrequently as possible to avoid water stress.
- Allow water to remain on leaves for only a short period of time.
- Reduce thatch by vertical cutting.
- When possible, plant turfgrass that is resistant to gray leaf spot.
- Avoid using herbicides or plant growth regulators when the disease is active.
- Fungicides are available to control the disease. Consult the current *Georgia Pest Management Handbook*.

Take All Root Rot

Causal Agent—*Gaeumannomyces graminis* var. *graminis*.

Susceptible Turfgrass—Varieties of bentgrass, St. Augustinegrass, bermudagrass and centipedegrass. Kentucky bluegrass and fescues are rarely affected in Georgia.

Symptoms—Take all root rot causes wilted circular patches that are brown or bronze colored and measure up to several feet in diameter. Infected plants have dark brown roots. Take all patch is common on newly established turf but have also been diagnosed in mature stands.

Conditions Favoring Disease development—Take all root rot typically occurs in wet conditions and in areas with a high soil pH and is severe at pH 6.5 or above. This disease is more severe on less fertile and sandy soils.

Control—

- Use acidifying fertilizers (e.g. ammoniacal based nitrogen sources, urea, sulfur coated urea, etc.).
- Apply moderate to high levels of phosphorous, potash and minor elements, especially manganese (Mn) where these nutrients are depleted from the soil.

- Improve the drainage of the turf.
- Reduce thatch.
- Fungicides are available to control the disease but are minimally effective , especially when applied during the growing season.

Slime Mold

Causal Agent—Mainly *Physarum spp.* and *Fuligo spp.* There are other species causing slime mold.

Susceptible Turfgrass—Warm-season grasses.

Symptoms—Large numbers of pinhead sized fruiting bodies of these fungi may suddenly appear on grass blades and stems in circular to irregular patches 1 to 30 inches in diameter. Affected patches of grass do not normally die or turn yellow, and signs of the fungi usually disappear within 1 to 2 weeks. These fungi normally reproduce in the same location each year. The fungi are not parasitic, but they may shade the individual grass leaves to the extent that leaves may be weakened by inefficient photosynthesis.

Conditions Favoring Disease Development—Slime molds are favored by cool temperatures and continuous high humidity. An abundance of thatch favors slime molds by providing food directly in the form of organic matter.

Management Tips—

- Remove slime mold by mowing.
- Raking and disposing of the slime mold is usually all that is required.
- The slime mold will go away in warm dry weather conditions.

Centipedegrass Decline

Causal Agent—Several Factors

Symptoms—Yellowing or chlorosis is one of the first symptoms which may indicate centipedegrass decline. This is the result of a lack of iron which may be caused by pH or fertility problems. If the grass appears to be spongy, excessively thick, and can be slightly lifted from the soil surface by pulling on the foliage, this is indicative of a poor root system which is generally due to excess thatch, compacted soil, drought, or nematodes. Advanced stages of centipedegrass decline will appear to be randomly placed, irregular dead areas in an otherwise healthy lawn, especially in the spring and early summer.

Conditions Favoring Disease Development—Factors which contribute to centipedegrass decline include improper nutrition, cultural practices, and soil and water conditions. The nutrient requirements for centipedegrass are different from most other turfgrasses. As the pH goes above 5.5, the amount of available iron decreases. Iron deficiency causes the grass to become chlorotic or yellow. Centipedegrass naturally is a lighter green than most other turfgrasses. Centipedegrass is a low growing grass which responds to mowing 1 to 1½ inches. If the grass is mowed often enough so that no more than ¼ to ⅓ of the leaf is mowed, the clippings do not have to be collected. During stress periods such as summer heat or the coming of winter, it is a good idea to raise the mowing height slightly. The brown grass present after winter should be removed in the spring at or just before new growth begins to appear. Removal can be completed by lowering the mowing height ¼ to ½ inch, scalping and collecting the dead plant material.

Care should be taken not to remove too many runners from which growth may occur. If excessive thatch is a problem, two to three years may pass before satisfactory results can be obtained from vertical mowing or dethatching. Use proper water management practices. Proper watering is important to the vigor of centipedegrass because it has a limited root system. This grass should only be watered just before it wilts. Water should be applied to wet the soil to a depth of 5 to 7 inches. If the grass does not receive adequate water during summer dry periods, it may enter the winter weakened and more subject to centipedegrass decline the following spring.

INSECTS OF TURF

Importance of Pests

Home lawns in Georgia are commonly infested with insects and related pests. Several species cause serious damage, while others are simply a nuisance. These pests can be divided into two groups based on where they are found: soil inhabitants and thatch inhabitants. Species within either group can destroy turf. Knowledge of pest biologies, life histories, and habits is needed before effective control programs can be implemented.

Nature of Damage

Damage to turfgrass from insect pests takes many forms. Damage caused by soil inhabitants such as white grubs, ground pearls, and mole crickets usually shows up as patches of wilted, dead, or dying grass. Damage to turf by thatch inhabitants such as sod webworms, armyworms, and cutworms is apparent when grass blades show evidence of chewing or have been cut off close to the ground. Damage by chinch bugs or spittlebugs is similar to damage caused by soil inhabitants. Irregular spots of yellowish turf and dead spots may occur where chinch bug or spittlebug infestations go uncontrolled.

Management of Pests

In Georgia, most insect pests of turf can be controlled when damaging populations are found. However, remember that the first step to management of lawn pests is prevention.

Good cultural practices are essential to prevent insect pests from destroying turf. Use approved methods of fertilization, watering, mowing, etc., to keep grass healthy and growing vigorously. A healthy lawn can tolerate light insect infestation; rapidly growing healthy turf will quickly erase signs of insect damage.

Thatch removal is one means of preventing insect outbreaks. Heavy thatch accumulation, particularly in St. Augustinegrass lawns, provides an ideal environment for chinch bugs, spittlebugs, and caterpillars. Thatch also interferes with insecticidal control.

The next step to management of turfgrass pests is early detection. This is the weakest link in pest management programs for lawns. Pests are difficult to see until damage is observed. There are, however, several techniques which are useful in detection and monitoring insects in turfgrass.

The sweep net is a useful tool for finding caterpillars, aphids, and chinch bugs. The net frame should be sturdy and the net bag should be of solid cloth. Sweep the net back and forth across the turf in areas where you suspect pests. After several sweeps, turn the bag inside out to dump the contents into a container for inspection.

Flotation can be used to detect the presence of chinch bugs. Remove the bottom from an oil can, coffee can, or similar container. Push the can 1 to 3 inches deep into the turf in an area of suspected chinch bug infestation. Fill the can with water and hold the water level above the grass for about five minutes. If chinch bugs are present they will float to the surface.

Irritation is another method of sampling for turf insects. It is particularly useful in mole cricket surveys. Lemon scented dishwashing detergent is a good inexpensive irritant. Mix the detergent with water and pour over a small area of turfgrass. The detergent irritates sensitive soil inhabiting pests causing them to quickly come to the surface. Use one ounce liquid detergent per gallon of water. Use one gallon of water to sample a one square yard area of turfgrass.

Close observations are useful for early detection of potential pest outbreaks. For example, the most critical time for turf damage by chinch bugs is July and August. During this period the turf is frequently under moisture stress and the feeding activity of chinch bugs is greatest. Early stages of chinch bug nymphs are not easily seen and damage symptoms are not severe enough to be noticed. Close observation of susceptible turf during early June is critical in detecting chinch bugs before damage occurs. St. Augustinegrass lawns as well as bermudagrass and zoysiagrass should be closely monitored for the presence of chinch bugs if the pest has been observed during previous years.

Damage symptoms on grasses, sod uprooted by animals feeding on insects, the presence of moths flying over turf areas at night, and birds frequenting a particular area of the lawn are all clues that indicate the presence of lawn pests. By detecting insect pests early, there may be sufficient time to correctly identify the pests, choose an appropriate control, and apply controls before the turf is damaged severely.

Correct Identification—Insect pests must be identified correctly before the appropriate method of control can be chosen. The biology and life cycle of identified pests will provide information on control methods.

Proper Selection of Control Materials—Materials labeled for insect control on home lawns are available in several formulations: baits, emulsifiable concentrates, wettable powders, soluble powders, and granules. The formulation selected, as well as the specific insecticide chosen, determine the level of control. For example, bait formulations are superior in spring and fall for mole cricket control, whereas sprays or granules give better control in the summer.

Correct Application Methods—Application methods are extremely important in turf insect control. The homeowner may use the most effective insecticide available, but if the method of application is poor, the level of insect control will be disappointing.

Distribution—When treating turfgrass, liquid materials should be applied as coarse sprays. Sprays with fine particles may drift and evaporate. The volume of water needed for proper application will vary according to the situation. The greater the thatch accumulation, the higher the spray volume needed. In addition, large volumes of spray are needed for the soil inhabiting pests, such as mole crickets and white grubs. Generally, use of higher spray volumes results in more uniform distribution of insecticide.

Irrigation Requirements—Timely use of irrigation will improve results of application of insecticides for soil inhabiting pests. During dry weather irrigating the turf prior to treatment will help the insecticide penetrate through grass blades and dry thatch. An additional half inch to one inch of irrigation water after treatment will carry the insecticide down through thatch and into the soil to the root zone. Delays in irrigating after insecticide application will greatly reduce the chances of good control.

PEST IDENTIFICATION, LIFE CYCLE AND DIAGNOSIS

Turfgrass pests may be classified by the part of the turfgrass environment that they inhabit.

Soil Inhabiting Insects

Ground Pearls

Identification—These are scale insects that live in the soil. The immature stages are spherical and range in size from a grain of sand to about ¹⁄₁₆ inch in diameter. They are usually yellowish purple in color. The adult female is ¹⁄₁₆ inch long and pink and has well developed forelegs and claws. Adult males are tiny gnat like insects.

Eggs are laid in the soil during spring. The young (nymphs) hatch and feed on fine grass roots. Nymphs cover themselves with hard, globular shells that look like tiny pearls, hence the name "ground pearls." The time required for development from egg to adult is one to two years.

Damage—These insects suck juices from underground parts of warm-season grasses. Centipedegrass is most commonly attacked. Severely infested grass turns yellow, then brown.

Control Strategies—Good cultural practices including proper watering, fertilizer management, and appropriate turfgrass selection. Unnecessary applications of broad spectrum insecticides may suppress natural predators including ants.

Billbugs

Identification—Adult billbugs are weevils ⅕ to ¾ inch long. The reddish-brown to black adults have a pair of jaws at the tip of a long snout or "bill." The young insects are white, legless grubs about ⅜ inch in length with the rear end wider than the head. The "hunting billbug" is the most common type found in Georgia. It occurs throughout the state.

Life Cycle and Biology—Adults feed above ground and deposit eggs in the stems of host grasses. Hatching larvae feed within the stems; larger larvae feed on the crown; mature larvae feed on the roots of the turf. One generation occurs annually, but adults and larvae may be found at any time of year.

Damage—Zoysiagrass and bermudagrass are most often injured, but feeding may occur on many grasses. When infestations are heavy, roots of grass are destroyed and the turf is killed in irregular patches. Early damage resembles dollar spot disease—small spots of dead or dying grass. The most damage occurs in June and July. Damage from billbugs differs from white grub or mole cricket injured turf in that infested soil usually stays firm.

Control Strategies—Varieties of turf resistant to billbug damage are available and should be considered when establishing a new lawn in an area with a history of billbug problems. Maintaining constant soil moisture and moderate fertility levels during the fall months into winter helps mask damage by low-moderate infestations. An insecticide application in mid- to late-May and repeated in June can help reduce adult activity.

Mole Crickets

Identification—Mole crickets are light brown, up to 1½ inches long, have short, stout forelegs, spade-like front legs, and large eyes. The young resemble the adults except that they are much smaller, have no wings, and are sexually immature.

Four species occur in Georgia. Three are pest species in turf: the tawny, southern, and short-wing mole cricket. The fourth is the northern mole cricket, native to the U.S., and is not a pest problem in turfgrass. Mole crickets occur primarily in the sandy soils of the Coastal Plain but have moved into central Georgia.

Life Cycle and Biology—Adults lay eggs in underground cells in the spring. The eggs hatch in two to four weeks, depending on the weather. Nymphs feed and grow through the summer and mature into adults in the late fall or winter. Mole crickets spend the winter deep in the soil, but come to the surface to feed during warm periods. Adult crickets leave the soil on warm spring nights to fly around, sometimes in huge numbers, looking for mates and egg-laying sites. There is one generation per year, and most adults die by early summer.

Tawny mole cricket mating flights occur in March and early April; southern mole cricket flights occur later in April and in early May. Cold or wet spring weather may delay flights.

Damage—The most damaging species of mole crickets feed on grass. Other species don't feed directly on grass, but their tunneling activity damages turf. Both young and adults burrow beneath the soil and make tunnels similar to, but much smaller than, those made by moles. This loosens the soil and causes it to dry out. It also clips the roots of the grass plants. Left unchecked, mole crickets will build up in an area and completely destroy the grass, leaving bare ground.

Control Strategies—Insecticidal control of mole crickets is most effective in summer (late June or early July) when most of the mole cricket eggs have hatched and nymphs are small. Granular or spray insecticides are the formulations of choice for summer

White Grubs

Identification—These grubs are plump, C-shaped insects with three pairs of legs. They are whitish with dark areas near the rear. They have a distinct, brown head. The adults are beetles commonly referred to as chafers, May beetles, June beetles, Japanese beetles or green June beetles. They occur throughout Georgia.

Life Cycle and Biology—Adult female beetles lay their eggs in the soil. The grubs hatch and spend most of their life beneath the soil feeding on underground plant parts. Most have rather long life cycles. The grub stage can last from several months to two or three years. Most species of grubs found in Georgia have a one year life cycle.

Damage—Grub feeding destroys roots, leaving the tops to wither and die. In heavy infestations, roots are pruned off to the extent that turf can be rolled back like a carpet. Symptoms of grub damage include yellowing or browning of the grass and signs of drought stress when moisture levels are good. Grass may feel spongy when infestations are heavy.

Control Strategies—White grub occurrence is sporadic, so applying an insecticide for anticipated grubs is not typically recommended. However, where adult activity has been observed, preventative applications may be warranted. Field trials show preventative insecticides perform best when applied before mid-August, or during egg laying.

Where Japanese beetles are common, do not plant susceptible plants such as roses, grapes, and crape myrtles

near high maintenance turf areas. Most white grub species require moist soil for eggs to hatch. The young larvae are very susceptible to desiccation so if turf can stand some moisture stress, consider withholding water in June, early July and when eggs and larvae are present. Moderate (fewer than 10 per square foot) grub infestation can sometimes be grown out if adequate water and fertilizer is applied from July to August and in April when grubs are feeding. This approach will not work during irrigation bans and where animals dig up grubs.

No registered insecticide is 100% effective; they usually kill 75% to 90% of grubs. Re-applications may be necessary if populations get high. Apply pesticide when grubs are small and actively feeding. Reduce thatch and irrigate after pesticide application.

Leaf, Stem And Thatch Inhabitants

Spittlebugs

Identification—Spittlebug adults, commonly called froghoppers, are about ⅜ inch long, dark brown or black, and have two orange stripes across their wings. The nymph is ivory-colored with a brown head. Nymphs live inside masses of spittle or froth, hence the name "spittlebug." They occur throughout Georgia.

Life Cycle and Biology—Adult females deposit orange eggs in bits of hollow stems and other debris. Nymphs hatch in about two weeks and begin to feed immediately by sucking juices from the grass. They cover themselves with a frothy mass known as spittle. There may be one or several nymphs in each spittle mass. The masses are found from just below the soil surface to a few inches above it. Two generations occur annually in Georgia. Overwintering eggs hatch in March and April. This generation reaches maturity by June. Adult activity is also noticeable in August and September, when the second generation matures.

Damage—Spittlebugs are associated with heavy thatch. A heavily infested area will feel "squishy" when you walk across it due to numerous spittle masses. Centipedegrass is especially prone to spittlebug infestation; zoysiagrass, bermudagrass, and bahiagrass also are susceptible. Populations often begin and increase in shady areas. The second generation appears to cause more injury. Populations, and therefore, damage, can be especially high during years with high spring and summer rainfall.

Control Strategies—Don't allow a heavy thatch layer to accumulate. Adult spittlebugs feed on a number of shrubs and other plants, so avoid locating host plants that attract the adults, especially Japanese holly, near susceptible turfgrasses. Time insecticide treatment in heavily infested areas for July. Mow and irrigate the grass several hours before applying treatment late in the day.

Chinch Bugs

Identification—Adults are about ⅕ inch long and light in color with small black triangular patches on the wings. The wings are carried folded over the back. The nymphs are from ½₀ to ⅕ inch long and vary in color from reddish with a white band across the back to black as they near adult size. Chinch bugs occur throughout the state.

Life Cycle and Biology—The eggs are laid in leaf sheaths or crevices in nodes and other protected places. The young develop into adults in four to six weeks. There are three to four generations a year. The bugs insert their slender beak into the grass and suck the plant juices.

Damage—Typical injury appears as spreading patches of brown, dead grass. St. Augustinegrass is the most seriously injured, but other lawn grasses, including zoysiagrass, bermudagrass, bahiagrass, and centipedegrasses, also are subject to attack. Chinch bug infestations and damage are most often first noticed during hot dry periods in sunny areas of the lawn.

Control Strategies—A common method of determining population levels of chinch bugs is the "flotation technique." A coffee can, or similarly sized can, with its ends cut away, is pushed two to three inches down into turf in a suspected area of chinch bug infestation. The can is filled with water and kept full for about five to seven minutes by adding more water, as necessary. All stages of chinch bugs, if present, will float to the top. A threshold level of 10 to 25 chinch bugs per square foot can cause damage.

This monitoring technique should be repeated in several spots at the edge of the suspected area to increase chances of finding the bugs. Treat if populations are at or above the damage threshold. Insecticides should not be applied to turf in dry soil to avoid potential chemical injury. On the day before treating, thoroughly irrigate the lawn.

Sod Webworms

Identification—Sod webworms are caterpillars of small brown to dull gray moths. Webworms grow to a length of nearly ¾ inch and vary in color from pinkish white to light green to yellowish brown with a light to dark brown or black head. They are covered with fine hairs. The moths (a) have a wingspan of about ¾ inch. They fold their wings closely about their bodies when at rest and have a prominent forward projection on the head. Sod webworms are found throughout Georgia.

Life Cycle and Biology—Moths hide in shrubbery or other sheltered spots during the day. They fly over the grass in early evening. The female scatters eggs over the lawns as she flies. Two to three generations occur each year. Sod webworms feed only at night.

Damage—Damaged grass blades appear notched on sides and are chewed raggedly. Irregular brown spots are the first signs of damage. Large areas of grass may be damaged severely, especially under drought conditions. A heavy infestation can destroy a lawn in only a few days. Damage tends to become visible in mid to late summer and in highly maintained lawns. Sod webworms are partial to newly established lawns.

Control Strategies—Sod webworm populations (and those of other soil-inhabiting insects) can be monitored using the "irritation technique." One ounce of lemon dish detergent is mixed with one gallon of water and the solution is poured over a one square yard area where an infestation is suspected. The detergent irritates the insects, causing them to come to the surface quickly. Damage thresholds vary in different areas. A general guide is 15 or more larvae per square yard.

Insecticide application should be timed for treatment two weeks after peak moth activity and should be made during early evening hours when caterpillars begin feeding.

Armyworms

Identification—Armyworms, which attain a length of ½ inch, are also caterpillars of moths. Their bodies are greenish when small, but become brown when fully grown. Several stripes usually are apparent, extending from the head to the rear. The adult is a mottled brownish-gray moth with a wingspan of nearly 1½ inches. Armyworms occur throughout Georgia.

Life Cycle and Biology—Armyworm caterpillars pupate in the soil. The moths emerge within a couple of weeks. They are active mainly in the early evening and at night, although they have been observed during the day. There are three to six generations a year in Georgia. Female moths lay clusters of eggs on grass blades, lawn furniture, white or light colored walls, and other objects near lawns. Caterpillars hatch and begin to feed on the turf.

Damage—Damaged turf appears ragged with individual blades showing signs of chewing damage. When numerous, armyworms may devour the grass to the ground. Young larvae skeletonize grass blades; older larvae feed on entire blades.

Control Strategies—The irritation technique described above for sod webworm also is effective for sampling armyworm populations. Populations tend to increase after drought conditions; maintain a consistent soil moisture level to help manage this pest. As with sod webworms, time insecticide applications to control armyworms during the early evening when caterpillars are feeding.

Cutworms

Identification—Cutworms, also the caterpillar stages of certain moths, grow to a length of 1½ to 2 inches. The caterpillars are mottled, dull brown, gray, or nearly black and usually appear plump and greasy. If disturbed, the caterpillar usually curls into a C-shaped ball. The front wings of the moth are dark brown to gray, are mottled or streaked, and have a wingspan of 1½ to 2 inches. Cutworms occur throughout the state.

Life Cycle and Biology—Eggs are laid on grass and weed stems or behind the leaf sheath of such plants. Caterpillars usually remain below the ground surface, under clods, or other shelters during the day; they feed at night. Cutworms pupate in the soil. Three to as many as seven generations occur each year. Cutworms can be active all year.

Damage—Foliage or stems may be cut off (hence the name cutworm) by the caterpillars. Circular spots of dead grass or sunken spots are indicative of cutworm infestation.

Control Strategies—The irritation technique described above for sod webworm is also effective for determining cutworm population levels. Insecticide treatment should be made when this technique flushes three to eight larvae per square yard. Due to their nocturnal behavior, it is best to time control measures for early evening when caterpillars are feeding. Do not irrigate turf after treatment is applied for control of caterpillars. For these pests, you want the material to remain at the surface rather than have it move into the soil.

Inhabitants Which Do Not Usually Damage Turf

Cicada Killer Wasp

Identification—This wasp is about 1 ½ inches long. It is marked with yellow and black markings on its body.

Life Cycle and Diagnosis—The wasps dig burrows in the ground and mound the soil at the entrance. The female paralyzes a cicada by stinging it, then places it in the burrow and lays an egg on it. The larval stage of the wasp then feeds on the cicada. Cicada killer wasps usually appear in late July and August when adult cicadas are abundant. Although they generally have a mild disposition they can sting if irritated. They cause no primary damage to lawns. Their presence is sometimes unnerving and their burrows may detract from the appearance of a well manicured turf.

Earwigs

Identification—Earwigs are reddish brown beetle like insects. They are narrow and elongated. Earwigs have a prominent pair of "pinchers" at the rear of their body.

Life Cycle and Diagnosis—Adult females lay their eggs in nests in the soil. The nymphs are cared for by the mother until they are ready to leave the nest. They may become quite numerous in lawns and begin to enter homes, where their presence is objectionable. Some species feed on young roots of plants, however, their value as scavengers and predators of other insects probably outweighs the harm they do.

Millipedes and Centipedes

Millipedes (thousand legged worms) and centipedes (hundred legged worms) are closely related to insects. They are slender, worm like creatures that are dark brown and have many body segments. They differ from insects in the number of legs they have (1 to 2 per body segment). Millipedes and centipedes cause no damage to lawns. Occasionally millipedes migrate from turf areas to inside the home where they become a nuisance pest. Their food is chiefly decaying organic matter.

Sowbugs and Pillbugs

Sowbugs and pillbugs, are similar to millipedes and centipedes and are closely related to insects. Both are brown to light gray in color. They are nearly ½ inch long with segmented bodies and seven pairs of legs. When disturbed, pillbugs roll up into tiny balls. Sowbugs and pillbugs are usually found on damp ground under stones, boards, or dead leaves. They feed on organic matter in the soil, and sometimes on grass and other plants.

DISCUSSION QUESTIONS

1. What is the most common disease of turfgrasses in Georgia usually developing during periods of high humidity, high temperature and contributed to by high nitrogen applications?

2. Which turfgrass disease occurs in areas with high soil pH (alkaline soils), poor fertility and sandy soils?

3. What is the cause of most plant diseases?

4. Most crown and root rots of plants are caused by what pathogen?

5. What are some methods of scouting for turfgrass pests?

6. List the most common damage symptoms on ornamental plants.

7. What are the categories of insect pests of turfgrasses?

8. List 3 general diseases common to many plants.

NOTES

16
Vegetable Gardening

George E. Boyhan

LEARNING OBJECTIVES

Understand the factors to consider in site selection.

Know the benefits of organic matter/soil amendments.

Understand the difference between warm and cool season vegetables.

Understand the concepts of crop rotation, intercropping, and succession planting

Understand considerations of raised bed and container gardening, soil mixes, special cultivars, irrigation requirements.

Know the benefits of using cover crops.

Become familiar with basic vegetable gardening techniques such as transplanting, cultivation, fertilization, harvesting.

Become familiar with the different vegetables and herbs typically grown in Georgia.

TERMS TO KNOW

Banding Placing fertilizer a few inches to the side and below a row at time of planting.

Broadcast A method of fertilizer application whereby the fertilizer is applied uniformly over the entire soil surface.

Compost Organic residue from the aerobic (requiring air) breakdown of formerly living tissue in which air, water, and source material have been brought together to undergo the composting process.

Cool season vegetable Any vegetable that is grown under cool growing conditions of fall, winter, or spring. A vegetable may also be referred to as hardy or half-hardy to indicate their tolerance to frost (half-hardy) or freezing temperatures (hardy

Crop rotation Growing crops of a specific family in different areas of the garden each year to avoid soil-borne diseases and nutrient depletion.

Cultural control The use of good gardening techniques to control pest populations.

Disease resistance The tendency not to be infected by a particular pathogen.

Disease tolerance The ability of a plant to continue growing without severe symptoms despite being infected by a pathogen

Fallow Cultivated land that is allowed to lie idle for a growing season.

Fertilizer A substance that supplies nutrients for plant growth.

Hardening off The process of withholding water and/or reducing the temperature of vegetable plants to prepare them for planting in the field. Seedlings grown under protected conditions are usually too tender to place directly in the field. Hardening off increases cuticle (waxy outer layer) thickness and prepares plants for greater adverse field conditions.

Sidedress A method of fertilizer application in which the fertilizer is placed along the side of plants already established in the field.

Successive planting Planting a series of crops in the same season or planting the same crop every few days or weeks to extend its availability. An example of the former would be to follow an early crop of English peas with summer squash. An example of the latter would be to plant 2 or 3 plants of lettuce every week for a month to extend its availability.

Warm season vegetable Any vegetable that is grown under warmer temperatures of spring and summer. May be referred to as tender (frost damage) or very tender (killed by frost) to indicate frost injury.

INTRODUCTION

Gardening has become a favorite hobby of many families today. One tomato in a flower pot, a garden on the patio, or a planting of several hundred square feet, all require planning, care and attention. The home gardener has many sources of information available including gardening neighbors, seed companies, garden center employees and, most importantly, the Georgia Extension Service, and you, the Master Gardeners of Georgia. The following gardening information should help you, as you assist others in their gardening endeavors.

Vegetable Garden Planning Guidelines

When planning your garden, it is important to ask a few basic questions: Who will be doing the work? Will the garden be a group project with family members or friends? Or will you be handling the hoe alone, in between camping and swimming? Remember, a small weed-free garden will produce more than a large weedy mess.

What do you and your family like to eat? Although the pictures in the garden catalog look delicious, there is no value in taking up gardening space with vegetables that no one eats. Make a list of your family's favorite vegetables, ranked in order of preference. This will be a useful guide in deciding how much of each vegetable to plant. Successive plantings of certain crops, such as beans, can be harvested over a longer period of time and increase your yield. As you plan, list recommended varieties and planting dates.

In addition to considering your favorite vegetables, remember not all vegetables will be suitable for your space and climate. There is no reason to grow tropical cassava that will not survive the winter, nor to grow pumpkins if you only have 100-200 square feet.

How do you plan to use the produce from your garden? If you plan to can, freeze, dry, or store part of the produce, this will be a factor not only in planning the size of the garden, but also in selecting varieties. Some varieties have much better "keeping quality" than others. Care should be used in choosing the seeds, making sure the varieties you select are adapted to your area and intended use.

The amount you grow should also be considered. Lettuce may be one of your favorite vegetables, but having 10-20 heads ready at once will result in a lot of waste. As mentioned above, care should be given to successive planting throughout the season to have smaller quantities of perishable vegetables, such as lettuce, available for a longer period of time.

Some Additional Planning Hints—Plan the garden on paper or your computer first. Draw a map showing arrangement and spacing of crops. If you wish to keep the garden growing all season, you may need a spring, summer, and fall garden plan.

Plan the garden and order seeds well in advance of when you plan on sowing. Some plants may be started indoors as early as January.

• In your plan, place tall and trellised crops on the north side of the garden so they won't shade the shorter vegetables.

• Group plants by length of growing period. Plant spring crops together so that later crops can be planted in these areas after the early crops mature.

• Consider length of harvest as well as time to maturity. Place perennial crops to the side of the garden where they will not be disturbed by annual tillage.

Site Selection

When a choice of locations is available for the garden, there are several things to consider to make certain that the best possible site will be chosen. First of all, most vegetables need full sun to do their best, so the chosen area should have full sun or as nearly full as possible. At least six hours of full sun is required for your garden to be successful. A few of the leafy vegetables will grow under these conditions, but for most vegetables full sun all day is preferable. Early morning sun is important to dry dew from the leaves as soon as possible. Another consideration is proximity to the house. The selected site should be near the house so that the garden can be observed frequently for insect, disease, and weed problems.

In some urban areas, community gardens are grown. If you don't have your own land, you may wish to see if your community has such a garden. These gardens are often looking for volunteers to help with the payoff of free vegetables and/or a great learning experience. Botanical gardens also often offer such opportunities. Such gardens may be raising food for shelters or the poor. They may be involved in educational activities with local schools as well.

Locate near an easily accessible supply of water if possible. Avoid windy locations; if you must plant in a windy spot, build or grow a windbreak. The soil type is also very important. The soil should be fertile, easily worked without leaving a lot of clods, and it should be well-drained. "Well-drained" means that after heavy rains the excess water will drain out of the soil and prevent water-logged soil. The area should also be free of nutsedge, Bermuda grass, and other weeds and grasses that are difficult to control.

The size of the garden may be predetermined by 1) the amount of land available, 2) the amount of time one has to spend in it, and 3) how many vegetables are needed. For those who have a very small area, a few plants can produce fresh vegetables for the family. Two tomato plants properly cared for will provide enough tomatoes for one member of the family. Plants can also be grown in containers. Small patio versions of many vegetables are also available. Trellising can also help with limited space. Many vegetables can be trained to grow on a trellis. These include cucumber, pole beans, and tomatoes.

Soil Preparation and Fertilization

The soil test is a very important tool that can help you determine the kind and amount of fertilizer to use in your garden for different types of vegetables. Since all vegetables do not require the same amount of fertilizer, this can eliminate the guesswork. Also, the soil test evaluates the pH of your soil. Soil pH will tell you whether your soil is very acid, slightly acid, or alkaline. When the soil is very acid, lime will be needed to, as the old-timers say, "sweeten the soil". This is important because when the soil is very acid, the fertilizer in the soil is not as available to the plants and deficiencies often occur. On the other hand, some nutrients may become too available in very acid soil and become toxic to the plant. Get the most out of the nutrients in the soil by maintaining a proper pH of 6.0 -6.5.

Soil sampling bags and instructions on collecting the samples can be obtained at the local county Extension office. Be sure that a uniform sample is taken from each different area or soil type. The results will be mailed to you along with recommendations on how much lime (if any) to apply to adjust the pH, and on the amount and kind of fertilizer to use for the different types of vegetables in your garden. The soil test is inexpensive and should be taken in your garden area at least every two years. When filling out the soil test form, it will ask which crops you are growing. Unless you are growing just one or two vegetables, indicate 'vegetables' on the form. This will insure you get homeowner information on fertility and soil pH on a wide range of vegetables. With one or two vegetables (ex. tomato etc.), indicating the specific vegetable will result in fertility and pH information specific for that vegetable.

Applying Lime

Apply the rate of lime recommended in the soil test report. Since many Georgia soils are deficient in magnesium, dolomitic lime which contains magnesium as well as calcium is recommended. Early lime application (two-three months prior to planting) is best since it allows sufficient time for the lime to adjust soil pH. It takes this long since lime reacts slowly. Incorporation of lime into the top eight inches of soil will speed up the reaction time. Lime as well as all fertilizer materials should be kept dry when stored. This will prevent caking which makes it difficult or impossible to spread.

Add Organic Matter

Organic materials may be added to the garden soil in the form of manure, compost, peat moss, leaves, and green plant material. When organic materials decay, the residue is called humus. This humus improves soil structure and the soil's ability to hold water and nutrients. Application of fresh organic material should be done at least one month prior to planting and worked into the soil. Fresh material applied at time of planting can interfere with seed germination or injure newly planted transplants. Organic matter varies widely from source and type. The nutrient content can vary significantly even from the same material. Rates shown in the table below are minimums; those wishing to significantly increase their organic content should have their soil tested for percent organic matter. Generally increasing and maintaining the organic fraction in Georgia soils to 2-5% in the top 8-12 inches is desirable. This may not always be feasible due to the hot humid weather that occurs over a long period of time in Georgia. Suggested rates of organic materials are listed in Table 1.

Fertilization Placement: Kind and Amount

Placement, kind, and amount of fertilizer are all important if you are to get the most from your fertilizer

Table 1. Suggested rates of organic matter for vegetable gardens

MATERIAL	RATE/100 FT/²
Cattle manure	50-100 pounds
Poultry manure	10 pounds
Sheep manure	10 pounds
Compost	1 bushel
Sewage sludge	not recommended
Bulky material such as leaves and hay should be composted before adding to garden soil.	

dollar. The amount and kind should be based on a soil test. Vegetables are classified into three groups based on fertilizer needs (heavy, medium and light feeders). Heavy feeders require four or five pounds of 10-10-10 or equivalent per 100 square feet. These include tomatoes, Irish potatoes, sweetpotatoes, and cabbage. Medium feeders require 2.25-3.5 pounds of fertilizer per 100 square feet. These include snap beans, carrots, cucumber, and the majority of other vegetables. The only light feeder, which requires about 1.5 pounds of fertilizer per 100 square feet, is southernpea. One pint of fertilizer will weigh about one pound. In most cases, basic fertilizer should contain nitrogen (N), phosphorus (P), potassium (K), and micronutrients. For sidedressing, calcium nitrate, ammonium nitrate, potassium nitrate or sodium nitrate may be used. Potassium-magnesium-sulfate can be used to supply potassium, magnesium or sulfur.

Fertilizer placement is very important. Although fertilizer may be uniformly spread over the entire garden (broadcast), this reduces fertilizer efficiency. Usually, it is better to broadcast part of the fertilizer and sidedress the remainder. This usually involves broadcasting ⅓ to ½ the fertilizer prior to planting and sidedressing the remainder about half way through the crop cycle. Banding is another method of fertilizer placement where the fertilizer is placed three to four inches to the side and below the plant or seed. Usually only part of the fertilizer is banded at time of planting or seeding. Not over 1.25 pounds per 100 square feet should be banded. For example band ⅓ to ½ of the fertilizer and apply the other in one or two sidedressings several weeks after the crop is up. In sidedressing, the material should not be applied too close to the plant since there is danger of burning the plant roots.

Cover Crops

When the garden is not in use as in the winter months, it's a good idea to plant a cover crop. This has several benefits not the least of which is soil conservation. With nothing in the garden to hold the soil in place, there is the possibility of soil washing away. This is particularly true if there is any slope to the garden.

Cover crops can also improve the soil because they can be turned into the soil when its time to plant again. This incorporation of cover crop residue is called, "green manuring". This adds organic matter to the soil which improves the soil's water and nutrient "holding ability".

If the cover crop is a legume, there is the added benefit of additional nitrogen being added to the soil. Legumes are unique among plants in that they form a symbiotic relationship with nitrogen fixing bacteria. These bacteria are able to fix nitrogen from the atmosphere in a form that plants can use. This fixed nitrogen becomes available for subsequent crops when the cover crop residues break down.

Finally, cover crops can help manage soilborne diseases. Nematodes in particular can be greatly reduced in the soil by planting cover crops that are non-hosts. This usually means planting one of the grasses such as wheat or rye.

Because of the relatively mild winters in south Georgia, it is possible to have vegetables growing year round. Winters in south Georgia are suitable for growing overwintering onions and most of the brassicas (collards, mustard, etc.). Most of us however like to give ourselves a rest from the garden as well as resting the garden!

Crop Rotation

Crop rotation is planting different types of plants in a particular space in the garden from one year to the next. This should not be confused with succession planting, which is the planting of different crops in the same place in the garden in a single season. This is often called double-cropping. An example of succession planting is to follow an early crop of English peas with a later crop of cucumbers. The same principles apply however, whether we are talking about succession or rotation. This is done to help minimize the development of soilborne diseases and manage soil fertility. Planting vegetables from the same family on the same spot year after year can result in the build up of soilborne pathogens unique to that family. Cucumbers, squash, cantaloupe, and watermelon should never be followed by these same vegetables in subsequent years. Switching to another family such as the legumes (beans and peas) or the crucifers (broccoli and cabbage) is a good idea.

Preceding the planting of heavy feeder vegetables with a legume is also a good idea. Heavy feeders require a considerable amount of fertilizer, particularly nitrogen, and legumes can boost the amount of nitrogen in the soil.

Fairly detailed and elaborate rotations have been used over the years. Some rotation plans cover only two or three years, while others may be planned out over 5-10 years. Crop rotation should always be part of your garden plan. Planning and keeping records are an integral part of successful gardening, and in successful implementation of crop rotation.

Seed for the Garden

Choosing and purchasing good quality vegetable seeds is important to successful gardening. Seed purchased from a dependable seed company will provide a good start toward a bountiful harvest. Keep notes about the seeds that you purchase: germination, vigor of plants, susceptibility to insect and disease damage, etc. From this information you can determine which seed company is best meeting your needs, and which varieties are most suitable for your area or gardening style. For example, if powdery mildew is a big problem on squash plants in your area, you may want to obtain mildew-resistant varieties for the next season.

Saving Seed

Saving your own vegetable seed is another fun activity. It offers a sense of self-sufficiency and saves money. You can maintain a variety that is not available commercially. This helps to maintain a broad genetic base of plant materials. Participation in a seed-saver's exchange can be a rewarding experience. Extra seeds that you have may be traded for unusual types that are not available through other sources. The Internet can be a good source for finding such organizations.

However, there are certain considerations that should be kept in mind when saving seed. Seed saved from hybrid varieties are not likely to be the same as the parent plants. What does grow may not perform as well as you would like, but can be very interesting to see the diversity that went into developing the hybrid. Some seed dealers have responded to the increasing interest in seed saving by clearly marking open-pollinated varieties in their catalogs. Certain open-pollinated seed may be marked with 'PVP'. This stands for plant variety protection and indicates that there is a patent on this variety. It is illegal to propagate such material without the consent of the developer and there may be a royalty payment required.

Another consideration in saving seed is the possibility of carrying seed-borne diseases into the next year's crop. Many commercially grown seeds are produced in the dry areas of the western U.S. The climate there is less suitable to seed-borne diseases that may be present in Georgia. Take care to control diseases which can be carried in seed. Another weather-related factor is the speed of seed drying, which can be adversely affected by frequent rains and/or humidity.

Finally, if you've ever saved squash seed during a season in which you had more than one type of squash planted, you have probably seen the weird results that may be obtained from cross-pollination! Cross-pollinated crops include squash, pumpkin, sweet corn, watermelon, cantaloupe, and honeydew. Making your own crosses can also be an enjoyable and educational aspect of gardening.

Some common self-pollinated annual plants from which seed may be saved include lettuce, beans, peas, herbs, and tomatoes.

Saving Beans and Pea Seed—Allow seed pods to turn brown on the plant. Harvest pods; after they have dried for 1-2 weeks, shell, and then store in a cool (below 50 °F), dry environment in a paper bag.

Saving Lettuce Seed—Cut off seed stalks when fluffy in appearance, just before all the seeds are completely dried. Seeds will fall off the stalk and are lost if allowed to mature on the plant. Dry the harvested seed stalk further, shake seeds off, and then store in a cool, dry environment in an envelope or small glass jar.

Table 2. Viability of vegetable seeds: average number of years seeds may be saved*

VEGETABLE	YEARS	VEGETABLE	YEARS
Asparagus	3	Leek	2
Bean	3	Lettuce	6
Beet	4	Muskmelon	5
Broccoli	3	Mustard	4
Brussels sprouts	4	Okra	2
Cabbage	4	Onion	1
Carrot	3	Parsley	1
Cauliflower	4	Pumpkin	4
Celery	3	Radish	5
Chinese cabbage	3	Rutabaga	4
Collard	5	Spinach	3
Corn	2	Southernpea	3
Cucumber	5	Squash	4
Eggplant	4	Tomato	4
Endive	5	Turnip	4
English peas	3	Watercress	5
Kale	4	Watermelon	4
Kohlrabi	3		

* Number of years is for optimum germination with storage under optimum conditions. Many seeds will last considerably longer, however germination rates will decline.

Saving Herb Seeds—Herbs vary in the way their seeds are produced. In general, leave herb seeds on the plants until they are almost completely dry. Some seed heads, such as dill, will shatter and drop their seeds as soon as they are dry. Watch the early-ripening seeds; if some begin falling off; harvest the other seed heads, with several inches of stem attached, before they get to that point. Hang several stems upside down, covered with a paper bag to catch falling seed, in a warm, dry place until the drying is complete. Remove seeds from the seed heads and store in envelopes or small glass jars. Some herb seeds, dill, fennel, celery, anise, cumin are used for flavoring, and are ready to use immediately after drying.

Saving Tomato Seeds—Pick fruit when ripe. Cut fruit and squeeze pulp into a container. Add a little water, and ferment two to four days, stirring occasionally, at room temperature. When seeds settle out, pour off pulp and spread seeds thinly to dry thoroughly. Store in an envelope or glass jar in a cool, dry place.

Be sure to mark seed storage containers clearly with permanent (preferably waterproof) ink, indicating the variety and date saved. Seeds will remain viable for some time if properly stored. To test for germination, sprout seeds between moist paper towels; if germination is low, either discard the seed or plant extra, to give the desirable number of plants.

After cleaning and packaging seed, it is a good idea to refrigerate them. This can increase germination rates as well as extend storage life. Every effort should be taken to maintain DRY seed. Even under refrigerated conditions moisture can be detrimental to seed shelf life. Placing paper towels in storage bags or in the crisper (if the seed are kept here) can help maintain dry conditions. Periodically, check on the seeds to ensure there is no mildew, mold, or excessively dried-up seeds.

Table 3. Growth medium for seed starting

MATERIAL	AMOUNT
Shredded peat moss*	1/2 bushel
Horticultural vermiculite	1/2 bushel
5-10-10 fertilizer†	3 tablespoons
20 percent super phosphate	3 tablespoons
Ground limestone	5 tablespoons
Chelated iron	1/2 teaspoon

* If the peat moss is very dry, dampen it by sprinkling with a gallon of water before mixing. Blend the peat and vermiculite thoroughly before adding the dry fertilizer materials.
†At least half of the nitrogen should be in the nitrate form.

Growing Transplants

Vegetables which are available as transplants include tomatoes, pepper, cabbage, eggplant, cauliflower, broccoli, sweetpotato, onions, watermelons, cantaloupes, squash, and cucumbers. Several, such as cabbage, broccoli, sweet potato, and onions are available as bareroot transplants, although this method of production is not as popular as it once was. Most of these vegetables will be available from local stores at the appropriate time of year.

It's not always easy to find the variety and quantity of vegetable plants you want when you need them. To eliminate this problem you can grow your own. Use two to three seeds per pot and thin to one or two plants after germination.

Containers—A variety of containers for seed-starting are available from garden centers, and catalogs.

• Seed Flats –These can be purchased new and re-used each year, but they must be thoroughly cleaned and disinfected before re-use. They are usually 22 inches x 11 inches x 2 inches depth made of rigid plastic. They can be filled with potting soil for germinating seed. In addition, inserts (see plastic cell trays) of various configurations are available for producing individual plants.

• Peat Pellets –Made of compressed sphagnum peat moss that expands when water is applied to make a peat pot ready to receive the plant or seed.

• Peat Cubes –Made of peat moss and already expanded to receive the plant or seed.

• Peat Pots –Made of peat moss and other fiber. Must be filled with soil or growth medium before seed or plants are placed in them.

• Plastic Cell Trays –Must be filled with potting media. Cells come in various sizes.

Select A Growth Medium—Almost all plants for transplanting are grown in artificial mixes. These mixes are usually peat-based, and are available from garden supply stores or the gardening section of many stores. A variety of materials are added to these media to make up their final composition. Materials such as vermiculite, perlite, ground pine bark, wetting agents, and fertilizers may be part of the mix. When purchasing such material, try to buy material that has been formulated specifically for seed germination. This material will have a finer texture and is more suitable for germinating seed particularly small seed. Coarser textured formulations are generally used for potted plants.

You can also make your own growing medium with a number of different formulas giving good results. Table

3 lists ingredients that can be used in either seed flats or pots. When all ingredients have been added, turn the mixture until they are thoroughly blended. Don't contaminate the mixture with outside soil.

Planting—Rows in the seed flat should be ¼ to ½ inch deep, depending on the seed to be sown. Larger seeds are usually sown a little deeper than smaller ones. The edge of a thin board pressed down on the surface of the mix will make a row deep enough for planting.

Sow two to three seeds per inch of row and cover with mixture. Spacing can be adjusted depending on the size of the seed. Then apply a fine stream of water until the entire mixture is moist. Do not soak the mixture because peat moss will hold nine times its weight in water. When these seeds germinate, the small plants are transplanted to individual cells or thinned to 2 to 3 inches apart. Instead of seeding into such a flat and then transplanting or thinning, you can plant one to two seed per cell in plastic cell trays filled with the mix. This saves time and results in no damage to the emerging seedlings as might happen if they are transplanted or thinned.

Place the seeded flats in an area where the temperature is fairly constant. Most vegetable seeds germinate best at temperatures of 75 to 80 degrees F. Bottom heat on flats hastens germination of warm season vegetable seed. You can stack flats (3-5) or individually wrap them with plastic wrap for 48-72 hours. This increases the temperature and hastens the germination process. The wrap should be removed after the 2-3 day period and flats unstacked so as not to interfere with seedling emergence.

It usually helps to cover the containers with plastic wrap to maintain uniform moisture. Seeds and seedlings are extremely sensitive to drying out. They should not be kept soaking wet, however, since this condition is conducive to damping-off disease of seedlings. Damping-off can be prevented or diminished by sprinkling milled sphagnum moss, which contains a natural fungicide, on top of the soil.

Another option is to use peat pellets or cubes, which are pre-formed and require no additional soil mix. The pellets or cubes are soaked until thoroughly wet, then seeds are planted in the holes provided. The whole pellet or cube may then be planted without disturbing the roots. A disadvantage to this method is the expense. In addition, these pellets or cubes have no fertilizer so seedlings will have to be fertilized shortly after emergence with a liquid fertilizer solution.

Transplants should be stocky, healthy, free from disease, and have good roots. They should not be too small or too mature. Tomatoes transplant satisfactorily with small fruits attached, but many other plants will drop flowers or fruit after transplanting. Be sure plants have been hardened-off so they will easily adapt to environmental change. However, they should not be so hardened that they are woody and yellow. Hardening is done by withholding water and exposing the plants to cooler temperatures. This prepares them for transplanting. The process requires three to seven days. Successful transplanting is achieved by interrupting plant growth as little as possible.

Have garden soil well prepared before transplanting. All additives that require time to break down, such as manures, limestone, rock fertilizers, and green manures, should be incorporated at least several weeks before planting. Quick-acting (hydrated) lime, fertilizers, and well-decayed compost may be added just before planting.

Transplant on a shady day, in late afternoon, or in early evening to prevent wilting. It helps to water the plants several hours before transplanting. When using bareroot plants, soak the roots thoroughly an hour or two before setting them out in the garden. You may notice a clear gel on bareroot plants when purchased. This material is a hydrating gel deposited on the roots prior to wrapping and shipping by the grower, and is harmless. The roots should not be allowed to dry out completely at any time. Handle plants carefully. Avoid disturbing the roots or bruising the stems.

Dig holes large enough to accommodate the root system. Set most plants slightly deeper than they grew in the pots or trays. This will insure the plants are well supported. Tomato and pepper transplants may be set several inches deeper. If plants are growing in peat pots be sure the entire pot is covered with soil. After setting plants in the holes, fill in enough soil to hold plant erect,

Table 4. Ease of transplanting vegetables

EASILY SURVIVES TRANSPLANTING	REQUIRES EXTRA CARE	NOT SUCCESSFULLY TRANSPLANTED
Broccoli	Cucumber	Bean
Cabbage	Cantaloupe	Beet
Cauliflower	Pumpkin	Carrot
Eggplant	Squash	Celery
Lettuce	Watermelon	Chard
Pepper		Corn
Sweetpotato		Okra

firming the soil around the plant. About a pint of water should be applied to each transplant. Carefully apply the water so it helps settle the soil and avoids washing the soil from around the plant. Water plants again in one or two days if no rain has fallen. Applying a high phosphorus liquid fertilizer at planting is helpful. This is especially true with plants set out in early spring when temperatures can still be cool.

Care After Transplanting—Once they are established and growing, both direct-seeded and transplanted vegetables can be cared for in the same way. Water only when the surface of the soil feels dry. Experience will tell you when water is needed. If frost or cold weather is expected, tender vegetables can sometimes be protected by covering with a cup or small pot. They should not be left covered during the day if the sun is shining, because high temperatures under such conditions can injure plants. Water the plants once or twice during the next week if there is insufficient rain.

Seeding and Transplanting

These are important factors if you are to use your gardening area to its maximum potential. Planting should be done on a well-prepared, firm seed bed so that the seed will have a good chance to germinate and grow.

Row Planting—A string stretched between stakes will provide a guide for nice straight rows, if desired. Use a hoe handle, a special furrow hoe, or a grub hoe to make a furrow of the appropriate depth for the seed being planted. Sow seed thinly; it may help to mix very small seed with coarse sand to distribute the seeds more evenly. Draw soil over the seed, removing stones and large clods. Firming soil over seeds improves water uptake and hastens germination. Water immediately after planting and as needed to keep the soil moist. Many soils will form a crust at the surface as it dries, which can make it difficult for seed to emerge. Water when this crust appears to soften the soil and allow seedlings to emerge. When plants have grown 4-6 inches tall, thin according to seed packet instructions to provide adequate room for growth.

Row Spacing—Spacing is important. Some plants require more room to grow than others. Large plants, like eggplant and okra, need room and should be placed anywhere from 15-30 inches apart in the row. Running type plants such as cucumbers and cantaloupes should have rows four to six feet wide, and should be spaced two to three feet apart in the row. Small plants such as onions and radishes will need narrower rows, eight or nine inches apart and can be planted from two to four

inches apart in the row. Some crops, such as cabbage, will get too large if too much space is allowed. They should be spaced at the recommended spacing of around 12 inches or less in the row.

Seed Depth—The depth that seeds are planted is also important. Some seeds, such as turnips and tomatoes, are very small, and if they are covered over a quarter of an inch deep, germination will be reduced. Larger seeds such as beans may be planted ¾ to 1½ inches deep. The actual depth will depend on the soil type and moisture conditions. On light soils where moisture could be a factor, seeds might need to be planted deeper, but on heavier soils where adequate moisture is available, they should be planted on the shallow side. Young seedlings can emerge quite easily from a sandy or organic soil. If garden soil is heavy with a high silt and/or clay content, the seeds should be covered only 1-2 times their diameter. In such soils it may be helpful to apply a band of sand, fine compost, or vermiculite 4 inches wide and ¼ inch thick along the row after seeds are planted. This will help retain soil moisture and reduce crusting, making it easier for seedlings to push through the soil surface. Every attempt should be made to place seeds in moist soil and to lightly firm soil, over seeds after planting.

Broadcast Planting—Many crops may be sown in wide rows or beds instead of in long, single rows. Crops such as spinach, beans, peas, beets, lettuce and carrots are especially suited to this type of culture. Seed should be sown evenly over the area, and then raked in with a rake or three-pronged hand cultivator. Firm soil over the seeds and water in. Thin young plants to allow room for growth.

Hill Planting—Larger vegetables, such as melons, squash, and cucumbers, may be planted in hills. Plant 4-6 seeds per hill, firming the soil well. Thin the seedlings to 3-5 plants per hill. Growers and gardeners often refer to hills when talking about widely spaced crops. In many cases no actual mounding of soil occurs even though this term is still used. True hill planting would involve forming hills or mounds. The benefit of doing so is to improve drainage. Beds or ridge planting is also a type of hill planting where a raised bed or ridge is formed for planting for the same reason.

Starter Solutions—Starter solutions are fertilizer solutions intended to feed the plant until new feeder roots are formed. Fertilizers of various analyses are available that are formulated to dissolve in water. Follow directions on the container as to mixing rates and use. These starter solutions will have a relatively large percentage of phosphorus compared to nitrogen and potassium, which helps plants grow during cooler periods of early spring.

Irrigation—Gardens normally need one to two inches of water each week during the growing season. There are two periods during the life of a garden plant when soil moisture is especially critical. The first is during the first two weeks of growth. During this time the plant is becoming established and moisture is vital to the development of a satisfactory root system. The second period is during bloom and "fruit" set. The plant must have enough moisture during this period to set a good crop. Inadequate moisture can result in low yields. Vegetables in which the fruit is not consumed such as cabbage, lettuce, turnips, etc. should be adequately irrigated throughout the growing cycle.

Give the garden a good soaking once or twice a week. Light sprinklings at frequent intervals do little good. A variety of different methods may be employed to irrigate your garden from various types of overhead sprinklers to soaker hoses or drip irrigation. Keep in mind, however, that any method of watering that wets the foliage increases the likelihood of disease, especially if the foliage remains wet for long periods. If you use sprinklers, water the garden in the morning so the foliage will dry before nightfall.

Cultivation Tips

Cultivation and Mulching—Competition with weeds is always a problem for vegetables in the garden. Each time the soil is worked, new weed seeds are brought up to the surface where they soon germinate. The two main reasons for plowing or hoeing the garden are (1) to destroy weeds and (2) to break up soil that has crusted over. Packed crusted soil hampers availability of air and water needed by plant roots. Plowing soils can actually harm vegetables if the equipment is allowed to cut the roots of vegetables. Shallow cultivation, just deep enough to destroy weeds, is recommended.

A good mulch material, applied to weed-free soil, will help control weeds and conserve moisture. Organic mulches include compost, wheat or pine straw, and hay. These should be spread three to four inches deep around plants and between rows. Organic material such as wood chips, wood shavings, and sawdust, may rob the soil of nitrogen. Avoid using these materials unless they have been composted for 2-3 years. Grass clippings may also be used, but care should be taken not to pile the material up around plants. Fresh grass clippings may begin composting, which may be injurious to plants. Some materials such as wheat straw release toxins that inhibit germination. This is advantageous for weed control, but

do not apply these materials adjacent to young seedlings or plant stems.

Manufactured materials that can be used for mulching include black plastic, and heavy Kraft paper. Newspaper can also be used, but should be put down several layers thick. Newspaper must be held in place to prevent it from blowing away. A good method is to wet the paper prior to application. Wet 5-10 sheets at a time and place in the garden. Wetting the whole paper makes it difficult to separate the pages. Plastic mulches usually cause the soil to warm up quickly, and can speed up crop maturity by seven to 10 days. Organic mulches on the other hand usually cool the soil, and can cause a delay in maturity by a few days.

Organic mulches are usually less expensive than manufactured mulches and, as a bonus they can be incorporated into the soil at the end of the growing season. While manufactured mulches cost more and usually must be removed at the end of the gardening period, they are more effective in controlling weeds.

CULTURAL NOTES ON SELECTED VEGETABLE CROPS

Notes on the culture of individual plants have been developed to provide an easy-to-use guide which summarize a wide range of information concerning the culture, nutritional value, harvesting, and storing of specific food crops. Since these notes are not comprehensive, you will need to consult other materials to obtain more detailed information.

Cultural Practices, Issues, and Problems

PLANTING: Indicates if the vegetable is grown from plants or seed and how to propagate. Some vegetables do well started from seed indoors and transplanted to the garden, while others are direct seeded.

SPACING: The in-row and between-row spacing that should give satisfactory results. Closer or wider spacing may be used under some circumstances.

HARDINESS: Very hardy perennial - can withstand winter extremes in most parts of Georgia with only slight protection. Hardy perennial - can withstand winters with protection in colder areas. Hardy annual - can withstand frosts in spring and fall; may need protection from heavy frosts or freezing. Half-hardy annual - can withstand light frosts, but not heavy frosts or freezing. Tender annual - frost will seriously damage plant tissue.

Very tender annual - frost will destroy tissues; needs warm weather for growth.

FERTILIZER NEEDS: Low, medium, or heavy feeder (Refers to relative levels of nutrient uptake from the soil. This information can be used to group similar types of plants, so that fertilizers may be applied to sections of the garden according to plant needs). The low number listed in the fertilizer ranges in the following section would be for heavier soils that are found in north Georgia, while the higher number would be for lighter soils that are found in south Georgia. Soil test results should be the final guide on fertilizer application.

CULTURAL PRACTICES: Gives general growing information. Includes proven methods for increasing production and/or decreasing pest problems. Unique growing suggestions may be included.

COMMON CULTURAL PROBLEMS: This section gives a general list of the most common cultural problems of the crop in the state of Georgia.

DAYS TO MATURITY: This will give an approximate number of days from planting to maturity. Direct seeding or transplanting will result in differences in days to maturity. It should be noted that not all varieties will perform similarly. Many varieties for example are bred to be extra early and will mature in fewer days.

HARVEST: Information on optimum time for harvest. What physical characteristics indicate harvest maturity.

APPROXIMATE YIELDS: These figures are based on the recommended spacing, but can vary considerably because of local conditions. Factors affecting yield include variety, local environmental conditions, soil type, season, planting designs, and cultural practices.

AMOUNT TO RAISE PER PERSON: These figures are average ranges. Specific amounts will vary depending on projected usage, whether fresh or processed, and according to personal preferences.

STORAGE: Optimum storage conditions and expected shelf life.(RH=relative humidity)

PRESERVATION: Suggestions for preserving the crop over an extended period. See Extension publications on food preservation for specific methods.

Asparagus

PLANTING: One-to-two-year old crowns, early spring

SPACING: 12 inches x 5 feet; or in wide beds of three rows with plants 18 inches apart in all directions.

HARDINESS: Hardy perennial, should be mulched in autumn

FERTILIZER NEEDS: Light-medium feeder, high P and K and organic matter at planting; annual nitrogen in late winter or very early spring; may sidedress after harvest; benefits from yearly topdressing of compost. 1.2-1.8 lbs/100 sq. ft. of 5-10-10 applied preplant or late spring and again after harvest.

CULTURAL PRACTICES: Asparagus is a perennial vegetable that will live from 12-15 years or longer. It is one of the most valuable of the early vegetables and freezes well. During the harvest period (traditionally spring, but see below for summer harvest instructions), the spears develop daily from underground crowns. Asparagus does well where winters are cool and the soil occasionally freezes at least a few inches deep.

Start asparagus either from seed or from one to two-year-old disease-free crowns purchased from a well established, reputable nursery. Starting plants from seed requires an extra year before harvest. Seed may be started in peat pots; seeds are slow to germinate, so be patient. Seedlings may be transplanted in May. Crowns are usually shipped and set out in March or April.

Choose a site with good drainage and full sun. The fall ferns of asparagus may shade other plants, so plan accordingly. Prepare the bed as early as possible, and enrich it with additions of manure, compost, bone or blood meal, leaf mold, wood ashes, or a combination of several of these. In heavy soils, double-digging is recommended. To double-dig, remove the top foot of soil from the planting area. Then, with a spading fork or spade, break up the subsoil by pushing the tool into the next 10-12 inches of soil and rocking it back and forth. Do this every 6 inches or so. Double-digging is ideal for the trench method of planting asparagus since a 12" deep trench is usually dug anyway. The extra work of breaking up the subsoil will be well worth the effort, especially in heavy soil. The trench is dug 12-18" wide, with 4-5 feet between trenches. The same method may be used in wide-bed plantings, with plants staggered in three rows. Mix the topsoil that has been removed with organic matter, and spread about two inches of the mixture in the bottom of the trench or bed. Set the plants 15-18 inches apart, mounding the soil slightly under each plant so that the crown is slightly above the roots. Crowns should be of a grayish-brown color, plump and healthy-looking. Remove any rotted roots before planting. Spread the roots out over the mound of soil and cover the crown with 2-3 inches of soil. Firm well. As the plants grow, continue to pull soil over the crowns (about 2 inches every two weeks) until the trench is filled. Water if rainfall is inadequate.

Asparagus shoots or spears should not be harvested the first season after crowns are set. Harvest lightly for 3-4 weeks the second year. The fleshy root system needs to develop and store food reserves to produce growth during subsequent seasons. Plants harvested too heavily too soon often become weak and spindly, and the crowns may never recover. An extra year is added to the above schedule for asparagus started from seed; i.e., do not harvest at all the first TWO seasons, and harvest lightly the third. After the third season, asparagus may be harvested for eight to ten weeks per year.

Weed the bed each spring before the first shoots come up to avoid accidentally breaking off spears. During the production period, it is best to pull rather than hoe weeds, if possible.

Harvest spears daily during the 8-10 week harvest period. Harvest should stop when 40% or more of the spears are the thickness of a pencil or less. The 6 to 8-inch spears are best, and should be snapped off just below the soil surface. If the asparagus is allowed to get much taller, the bases of the spears will be tough and will have to be cut; cutting too deeply can injure the crown buds that produce the next spears. Blanched asparagus is a gourmet item; to blanch (whiten) the spears, mound soil around them or otherwise exclude light from them so that chlorophyll is not formed in the stalks.

When harvest is over (after 8-10 weeks), allow the spears to grow. Asparagus has attractive, fern-like foliage that makes a nice garden border. Some gardeners prefer to support the growing foliage with stakes and strings to keep it tidy. In high-wind areas, it is a good idea to plant the rows parallel to the prevailing winds so that the plants support each other to some extent.

There are several ways to extend the harvest period for asparagus. One method is to plant at different depths (3 inches, 4-6 inches, 6-8 inches, 8-10 inches). The shallow plantings will come up first and can be harvested while the deeper plantings are just forming. This method will result in a slightly longer harvest, but may result in some plants being less vigorous than others.

Another way to extend the harvest for a few weeks is to remove mulch from half of the asparagus bed. Leave the mulch on the other half. The exposed soil will warm up quicker, and induce the crowns to sprout earlier. This

process may be speeded up even further by using black plastic, but be careful not to encourage growth too early, as heavy frost can make spears inedible. Remove mulch from the second bed when spears begin to appear.

A third technique for extending asparagus harvest has been the subject of university research and is highly recommended for home gardeners who have plenty of space. Plant double the amount of asparagus needed for your household. Harvest half of the plants as you normally would in spring and early summer, then allow the foliage to grow for the rest of the season.

During the early harvest period, allow the ferns to grow in the other half of the asparagus planting. Then, cut the ferns in the second half in late July. This causes the crowns to send up new spears, which can be harvested till late in the season. If rainfall is short in summer, it will help to water this bed for good spear production. A light mulch will help keep the soil surface from becoming too hard for the shoots to break through easily. If using this method, harvest the spring bed only in spring and the fall bed only in fall!

Otherwise, you risk weakening the crowns.

In all asparagus plantings, cut the foliage down to 2-inch stubs after frost when the foliage yellows, and before the red berries fall off. The removed tops should be destroyed by composting or removal particularly if foliar diseases were a problem the previous season. In addition, next season's harvest should be shortened by 10 days if diseases were a problem. This helps the plants remain strong. A 4-6 inch mulch of compost, manure, leaves or other material added at this time will help control weeds and add organic matter and nutrients.

COMMON CULTURAL PROBLEMS: Weak, spindly plants and/or too few spears from harvesting too early or too heavy; crown rot or poor production from inadequately prepared, heavy soil.

TIME TO MATURITY: 2 - 3 years

HARVEST: Third year spears; snap off just under soil surface when 6-8 inches tall, before tips begin to separate; use or refrigerate immediately.

APPROXIMATE YIELDS: (per 10 foot row) 3-4 pounds/year.

AMOUNT TO RAISE PER PERSON: 6 lbs.

STORAGE: Process or refrigerate immediately in plastic bag. Asparagus when laid horizontally will curl upward. If not processed immediately, it should be bundled and stored upright to prevent curling.

PRESERVATION: Can or freeze.

Beans

PLANTING: Seed after danger of frost is past.

Rate required to plant 100 ft of row:

Bush Beans	¾ lb
Pole Snap Beans	½ lb (hills at 18 inches)
Lima (small seed)	1 lb
Lima (large seed)	1½ lb
Broad Beans	1¼ lb
Horticultural	½ lb
Soybean	¾ lb
Dry Beans	¾ lb
Mung Beans	1 oz.

SPACING:

Bush snap	2-3 inches x 18-24 inches
Bush limas	4-5 inches x 18-30 inches
Pole beans	4-8 inches x 24-36 inches

HARDINESS: Tender annual, except fava which is a semi-hardy annual; bush snap beans may be planted two weeks earlier than half runner and pole types.

FERTILIZER NEEDS: Beans are medium feeders. Since beans are legumes, they can fix nitrogen after a good root system is established. Roots of legumes are colonized by certain bacteria that fix atmospheric nitrogen which is available to the plant. Nitrogen fixation is reduced when legumes are fertilized, but will generally have better yield when fertilized properly. Bacterial inoculants are available for beans which will improve nitrogen fixation. This can be particularly important for organic growers or those wishing to increase soil nitrogen for subsequent crops. Broadcast 0.7-1.1 pounds 10-10-10 per 100 sq. ft. or use 1.4-2.3 pounds of 10-10-10 per 100 ft. of row. Do not place fertilizer within four inches of seed. Excess nitrogen will delay flowering, but side dress 3-4 weeks after sowing with the same amounts applied at planting. For pole beans increase these recommendations by 50%.

CULTURAL PRACTICES: Snap beans grown for the pod are the most common. (Snap beans are also called "string beans" and "green beans.") Some beans such as limas, soybeans, and dried beans are grown primarily for the seed itself and not the pod. The bush snap bean is the most popular because of its early maturity and because trellising is not required. Types include standard green, yellow wax, and purple-pod types, giving the gardener a larger choice than is generally available in supermarkets. Though wax beans are yellow and waxy in appearance, their flavor is only subtly different from that of regular green snap beans. The purple pod beans are different in flavor and texture and are preferred by many gardeners. These are available in both bush and pole types.

First plantings of bush beans should be made after danger of frost is past in the spring and soil is warmed, since seed planted in cold soils germinate slowly and are susceptible to rotting. Seedling growth may be slow in cool temperatures. Plant several crops of bush beans 2-3 weeks apart, until August 25 for a continuous harvest. Snap beans should be kept picked regularly to keep plants producing heavily.

Half-runner beans (also called field beans) have a growth habit between that of bush and pole beans, producing beans usually used as snap beans. Though they have runners about 3 feet long, half-runners are generally grown like bush beans. Trellising, however, may increase production of these already heavy yielders.

Polebeans come in many varieties, generally bearing over a longer period than bush types. They require trellising, and for that reason generally yield more per square foot of garden. Pole beans are natural climbers but will not interweave themselves through horizontal wires. A tripod support can be made with three wooden poles or large branches that are lashed together at the top. Five to six seeds are planted in a circle 6-8 inches from each support. Trellises should be 6-8 feet tall and sturdy enough to withstand strong winds and rain. Pole beans are often interplanted with corn and squash. Interplanting beans, corn, and squash is an American Indian traditional method of planting and is often referred to as the 'three sisters'. Beans should be planted late enough to allow some growth and development of the corn first.

Popular string-type pole beans are Kentucky Wonder and Blue Lake. Scarlet runner beans are a type of pole bean which is quite ornamental as well as productive and delicious. The vines grow rapidly, producing beautiful red flowers; the beans may be harvested as snap beans when young and as green shell beans later. Beans are ready to pick in 75-85 days, and several pounds are produced per plant. The value of scarlet runner beans is mainly ornamental. The lush 6-15 foot vines can be used to cover arbors, trellises or fences. An added feature is that the flowers are attractive to hummingbirds. According to some sources, the scarlet runner prefers cooler weather than snap beans. In some very hot areas the vines may not keep producing all summer, as they will in cooler regions. Keeping mature beans picked off will prolong the life of the vines.

Lima beans are available in bush or pole types. Bush limas mature about 10-15 days earlier than pole limas. Pole type limas have better yields and produce longer than the bush varieties. Soil temperature must be 65 degrees F for five days in order for the beans to germinate well. Because the large seeds store considerable amounts of carbohydrates, limas are quite susceptible to rot. Pre-germination of seed or starting plants indoors helps if care is taken at planting. Plant carefully, taking care not to damage shoots and roots. Treating seed with fungicides has improved germination rates. Soil should be kept moist (but not soaking wet) until the plants are established. Do not allow a crust to form on the soil, since the seedlings will have trouble pushing through it. Prevent crusting and conserve moisture by spreading ¼ inch of sand, sawdust, or a light mulch over the seeded row. A cold, wet spell or excessively hot and dry periods can cause lima bean flowers to drop.

Southernpeas are widely grown in Georgia. Four bush types, black-eyed peas, cream peas, purple-hull and Crowder peas are commonly grown. Southernpeas may be harvested in the green shell or in the dried stage.

The yard-long or asparagus bean is related to black-eyed peas and has similar flavor, but the entire pod may be eaten. Pods 1½ to 2 feet long are produced on trellised vines. Asparagus beans need warm temperatures and a long growing season to do well. Look for the seeds in novelty, gourmet, oriental, or children's sections of seed catalogs.

Edible soybeans called edamame are increasing in popularity because of their high nutritional value and their versatility. Catalogs often list them as edible soybeans. They require a shorter season, do not grow as tall, and have a better flavor and texture than the field types. Soybeans are less sensitive to frost and may have fewer problems with Mexican bean beetles than standard beans. Soybeans are quite delicious when harvested as green shell beans, but may also be allowed to dry on the vine. The pods of soybeans are quite difficult to open; cook for a few minutes to soften the pod before removing the beans.

Beans used primarily as dried beans are many and varied. Many can be used green, but dry well for easy storage. In the small garden, growing dry beans is somewhat impractical, since the amount of space required to raise a large enough quantity for storage is great. Many types of dry beans may be purchased in supermarkets at a very low cost, so it may be economic to save space for other crops. However, if you have a very large garden area and a desire to sit on the front porch rocking away and shelling beans in the fall, they are worth a try. Some varieties available to gardeners are either rare or completely unavailable in the supermarket.

The horticultural, or October bean, is very widely grown in parts of the state. The colorful pods and beans of the October bean make it an attractive addition to the garden and kitchen. The seeds of pinto beans look similar to those of the horticultural beans, but are smaller. They are widely used as brown beans and as refried beans in Mexican dishes. Black beans or black turtle beans make unusual, delicious black-bean soup. They are easy to grow if given plenty of air movement to prevent disease problems to which they are susceptible. Kidney beans are the popular chili and baking bean, available in deep red or white types. Navy pea and Great Northern beans are used in soups and as baked beans. Cranberry and yellow-eyed beans are heirloom varieties, again gaining favor among gardeners.

Mung beans, native to India, have enjoyed a rise in popularity because of their use as sprouts in oriental dishes and salads. Gardeners now find seeds available for home production. Mung beans require 90 days of warm weather for good yields in the garden. Garbanzos, or chickpeas, produce plants that do not look like other bean plants. Although garbanzos are legumes, they are neither true beans nor peas. The fine-textured foliage is an attractive addition to the garden. Plant many seeds; the meaty seeds, like limas, tend to rot if they don't germinate and grow rapidly. Also, each pod contains only one or two seeds. The nutty-flavored beans of unusual texture are good roasted, in salads, and in soups. They are also the primary ingredient in hummus. Garbanzos also require a warm climate and long (100 day) growing season. If grown as sprouts, be careful to use only untreated seeds. Many seeds are treated with fungicides that will be in the sprouts at harvest.

Fava beans, horsebeans, Windsors or broad beans, are quite hardy. In cool climates they are often substituted for limas. Favas are sown early in spring, since they do not grow well in warm weather. In fact, if sown in March, they may be ready as green shell beans in late

June or early July. It should be noted that some people may have a genetic trait which causes a strong allergic reaction to fava beans. Eating the beans in large quantity has also caused a condition called 'favaism' which is a broadbean induced deficiency in the enzyme glucose-6-phosphate dehydrogenase. For these reasons, they should be eaten in moderate quantities.

COMMON CULTURAL PROBLEMS: Large plants with few beans (excess nitrogen); blossom drop (excessive heat, dry conditions).

DAYS TO MATURITY:

snap beans	50-60 days
pole beans	60-110 days
bush limas	65-75 days
pole limas	85-110 days

HARVEST: Snap beans -full size pods, small beans or larger beans as long as pods are still tender; pods break easily with a snap when ready; seed should not cause pods to bulge. Pods with large seeds should be shelled.

Lima/Dry beans -Seeds will be full sized and pods will be bright green. End of pod will be spongy. For dry beans (of all types) pods should remain on bush until dry and brown.

APPROXIMATE YIELDS: (per 10 foot row) Snap beans 3-5 lbs. Lima beans 4-6 lbs.

AMOUNT TO RAISE PER PERSON: Snap beans 8 lbs.; limas 5-10 lbs.

STORAGE: Can be held for a few days at room temperature and for 1-2 weeks if refrigerated.

PRESERVATION: Drying, freezing, and canning.

Broccoli

PLANTING: Start seeds indoors for early spring transplants. Seed in beds or flats for fall transplants.

SPACING: 12-18 inches x 36 inches

HARDINESS: Hardy annual

FERTILIZER NEEDS: Heavy feeder; fertilize at transplanting at the rate of 4.0-6.7 pounds of 10-10-10 100 foot of row; sidedress with the same amounts after plants become established (two to three weeks). If the crop is direct-seeded, make the second application when plants are about six inches tall. Broccoli will respond to additional nitrogen. Use about 2.2 pounds of calcium nitrate per 10 foot of row. Make the first sidedressing about the time the central head is first seen. Make the second application after the central head is cut and side shoots begin to form.

CULTURAL PRACTICES: There are two types of broccoli: heading and sprouting. Most garden broccoli is of the heading type that is closely related to cauliflower and forms a large central head. When this is removed, side branches will form throughout the summer. Sprouting or Italian broccoli forms many florets, but does not produce a large, central head.

Broccoli raab (turnip broccoli) is not a true broccoli, but is in fact, a type of turnip cultivated for its flower head. It can be sown in spring to raise as an annual, or sown in fall to raise as a biennial. Harvest leaves in fall and flower shoots in spring before they open. Cook and eat like asparagus. Most turnips grown for their greens can also be treated this way. To raise broccoli, buy transplants locally or produce your own.

The home gardener needs to schedule broccoli to mature during cool weather before days become hot. A well-conditioned broccoli plant will tolerate some cold weather and even light frost.

Transplants for a fall setting can be produced along with cabbage and cauliflower transplants, taking about four weeks from seeding to setting into the garden. Set plants 12 inches apart in rows 36 inches apart. Sprouting and perennial broccoli may be sown directly into the garden in spring. Follow packet directions. Broccoli has a relatively shallow, fibrous rooting system. Cultivate carefully or, even better, mulch.

The heads of broccoli are really flower buds. These must be harvested before the flowers open or show yellow. Mature heads measure three to six inches across. Lateral heads that develop later are smaller.

Table 5. Broccoli planting dates		
	SPRING PLANTING DATE	**FALL PLANTING DATE**
South Georgia	Feb 1 - Mar 31	Aug 1 - Sep 30
North Georgia	Mar 15 - Apr 30	Aug 1 - Aug 31
Mountain Area	April 1	July 1

COMMON CULTURAL PROBLEMS: Poor heading (buttoning), and early flowers (interrupted growth due to chilling, extremely early planting, drying out, or high temperatures).

DAYS TO MATURITY: 60-100

HARVEST: Large terminal bud cluster before flowers open, then small side bud clusters as they develop over following weeks. Harvest with three to four inches of stalk. During periods of warm weather and low soil moisture, broccoli will require more frequent harvesting to prevent flower formation in the heads. For the best flavor and texture, harvest each head while the flower buds are still tightly closed. Harvest sprouting broccoli and other types according to packet instructions.

APPROXIMATE YIELDS: (per 10 ft. row) 6-10 bunches or about 4-6 lbs.

AMOUNT TO RAISE PER PERSON: 8 lbs.

STORAGE: Very cold (32 degrees F), moist (95% RH) conditions, 10-14 days.

PRESERVATION: Freeze

Brussels Sprouts

PLANTING: Sow seeds mid to late-summer

SPACING: 12-18 inches x 24-30 inches

HARDINESS: Hardy biennial

FERTILIZER NEEDS: Heavy feeder, follow fertilizer directions for broccoli. Sidedress with about 4.4 pounds of calcium nitrate per 100 ft. of row 2-4 weeks after planting or when plants are 12 inches high.

CULTURAL PRACTICES: Brussels sprouts are grown for harvest in the fall because cool weather during maturity is essential for good flavor and quality. Brussels sprouts are tall erect biennials that are grown as annuals. The sprouts develop in the leaf axils and mature along the stalk. The lowest sprouts mature first and should be harvested when firm and 1 -1½ inches in diameter. Lowest leaves may be removed to permit sprouts to mature. One new variety has a large cabbage-like head on the top which may be harvested anytime. Another has large leaves on the upper part of the plant which fold down over the sprouts to form a protective cover, making this variety even more cold-hardy than the usual varieties. Removing the central leader in early fall will force all the sprouts to develop simultaneously and insure a full harvest.

COMMON CULTURAL PROBLEMS: Sprouts have loose tufts of leaves instead of firm heads (sprouts developed during cooler weather); crop failures can also be due to water stress.

DAYS TO MATURITY: 80-100 days from seed

HARVEST: When sprouts are hard, compact, and deep green about 1-1½ inches diameter, after frosty weather for best flavor. Twist or snap off the stalk. The lowest sprouts mature first.

APPROXIMATE YIELDS: (per 10 ft. row) 4-6 lbs.

AMOUNT TO RAISE PER PERSON: 5 plants

STORAGE: Cold (32 degrees F), moist (95 % RH) conditions, 3-5 weeks

PRESERVATION: Freeze

Cabbage

PLANTING: Start seeds indoors for early spring transplants. Seed in beds or flats for fall transplants.

SPACING: 9-15 inches x 24-36 inches for early plantings, 9-18 inches for late plantings

HARDINESS: Hardy biennial

FERTILIZER NEEDS: Heavy feeder; use starter fertilizer when transplanting; follow recommendation for broccoli. Sidedress three weeks after second sidedress with calcuim nitrate at 4.4 pounds per 100 feet of row.

CULTURAL PRACTICES: Cabbage grows from March to December. It will withstand temperatures as low as 18 to 20°F. Buy locally-grown transplants or produce your own. Start them in growing structures four to six weeks before the first date when plants can be set out, or sow a few seeds in the cold-frame or garden every month in order to have cabbage plants thereafter. It takes about three weeks to get plants ready from seeding to set during the summer months. Plant only the earliest varieties after August 15. It is best not to plant cabbage family crops in the same spot year after year, since diseases and insect pests will build up. Rotate crops within your garden.

Plant spacing affects head size. Close spacing (12 inches apart in the row) produces smaller heads. Average spacing is 12-15 inches apart in rows 30 inches apart. Varieties for sauerkraut are spaced wider. For a smaller family not interested in sauerkraut production, the dwarf varieties may be ideal. The heads are about the right size for a generous bowl of cole slaw, and the fast maturity makes these varieties excellent for succession planting. Cabbage is harvested when it reaches adequate size, depending on variety and growing conditions. Firm heads are preferred, especially for storage. Heads can be left on the plant in the garden for about two weeks in the summer, three to four weeks in the fall.

COMMON CULTURAL PROBLEMS: Head cracking or splitting (excessive water uptake and growth near maturity); root prune with spade or trowel, or twist stalk to break some roots and reduce water uptake.

DAYS TO MATURITY: 70–100

HARVEST: When heads become firm, size will vary with variety, fertility, and spacing. If unable to harvest at maturity, bend over to break part of the roots to reduce head splitting.

APPROXIMATE YIELDS: (per 10 ft. row) 10-18 lbs.

AMOUNT TO RAISE PER PERSON: 15 lbs.

STORAGE: Very cold (32 degrees F), moist (95 % RH) conditions, 4-5 months.

PRESERVATION: Can as sauerkraut

Cauliflower

PLANTING: Plant after danger of frost is past, start seeds indoors for early spring transplanting. Seed in beds or flats for fall transplanting.

SPACING: 18-24 inches x 36-48 inches

HARDINESS: Hardy annual

FERTILIZER NEEDS: Heavy feeder, follow recommendations for broccoli. Use starter fertilizer when transplanting, side dress three weeks later and as needed.

CULTURAL PRACTICES: Spring seedlings should be transplanted after danger of frost is past. Fall cauliflower should be sown in late July to mid-August. Many gardeners experience "buttoning" of cauliflower heads in the spring. Buttoning is a failure of the cauliflower head to gain in size after it reaches about an inch or less in diameter. It is usually due to transplant stress or heat stress during the head formation period. Some cauliflower varieties require too long a growing season for fall production in colder areas of Georgia. Use short-season types or season extenders in these areas.

Cauliflower should be blanched when the flower head is about 2-3 inches. The flower head of cauliflower is often referred to as the curd. Three to four large outer leaves are pulled up over the curd and fastened with a rubber band, or are broken over the top of the cauliflower and tucked in on the other side of the curd. Normal blanching time is 4-8 days and may take longer in the fall. Self-blanching types which have leaves that grow up over the head may eliminate the need for this practice. If weather is warm during the blanching period, tie the leaves loosely to allow air circulation. Harvest while the curd is still firm. If it gets too mature, the curd will become grainy or ricey.

COMMON CULTURAL PROBLEMS: Poor heading (interrupted growth due to chilling from extremely early planting, drying out, or high temperatures).

DAYS TO MATURITY: 55-85 days from transplanting

HARVEST: Cut before flower sections begin to separate. The curd should be compact, firm, white and fairly smooth. Leave a whorl of leaves surrounding the head when harvested to prolong keeping quality.

APPROXIMATE YIELDS: (per 10 ft. of row) 8-12 lbs.

AMOUNT TO RAISE PER PERSON: 8 lbs.

STORAGE: Very cold (32 degrees F), moist (95% RH) conditions, 2-4 weeks.

PRESERVATION: Freeze, pickle

Corn

PLANTING: Seed after danger of frost is past; extra sweet varieties should be planted when soil temperatures reach 65 degrees F.

SPACING: 8-12 inches x 36 inches minimum of three rows side by side (preferably four or five rows) to insure good pollination.

FERTILIZER NEEDS: Heavy feeder; apply 11-18 lbs of 16-4-8 per 1000 sq. ft. preplant; side dress when plants are 12-18 inches high with 3.2-5.3 pounds of 16-4-8 per 100 feet of row.

CULTURAL PRACTICES: Time to maturity and quality differs significantly among sweet corn varieties; Sweet corn is available as yellow, white, or bi-color. Sweet corn is also available in varying degrees of sweetness depending on the underlying genetics. Standard sweet corn varieties are designated 'su' for sugary. There are also sugary enhanced varieties designated as 'se'. These varieties have an additional gene that enhances the sugar content and softens the pericarp or outer layer of the kernel. Finally there are 'sh2' sweet corns, which are often referred to as supersweets. The 'sh2' designation stands for shrunken and reflects the shriveled nature of the kernels when fully mature. The sh2 sweet corns can have double the amount of sugar as the su or se varieties. Standard and extra-sweet varieties are available. Most varieties planted are hybrids that have been bred for greater vigor and higher yields. A continuous harvest can be planned by planting early-, mid-, and late-season varieties, or by making successive plantings of the same variety every two weeks or when the last planting has 3-4 leaves (corn sown in early spring will take longer because of cool temperatures). Use only the earliest varieties for August plantings to assure a good fall crop. Fall-maturing sweet corn will almost always be the highest quality, since cool nights in September increase sugar content. But fall corn will have more insect problems.

Pollination is a very important consideration in planting sweet corn. Because corn is wind-pollinated, block plantings of at least 3 rows are required to insure pollination. Good pollination is essential for full kernel development.

Most of the various types of corn will cross-pollinate readily. To maintain desirable characteristics and high quality, extra-sweet and standard sweet corn should be isolated from each other. Planting varieties 300 feet apart, or planting so that silking dates are 12 days apart, is necessary to insure this isolation. Because they will cross-pollinate, sweet corn plantings must be isolated from field corn.

Early-maturing varieties tend to be relatively small plants and are called "coon corn" by old-timers because the ears are easy for raccoons to reach. These should be planted in rows 30 inches apart with plants 8-9 inches apart. For medium to large plant varieties use a 36 inches row spacing with plants 12 inches apart in the row. Be sure to plant a block of rows for good pollination and full ears.

Some gardeners are interested in growing baby corn such as that found in salad bars and gourmet sections of the grocery store. Baby corn is immature corn, and many varieties are suitable, but 'Candystick', with its ¼ inch diameter cob at maturity, is a good one to try, especially since its dwarf habit means that it takes up less space in the garden. Harvesting at the right time is tricky; silks will have been produced, but ears are not filled out. Experimentation is the best way to determine when to harvest baby corn.

It is not necessary to remove suckers or side shoots that form on sweet corn. With adequate fertility these suckers may increase yield and removing them has been shown in some cases to actually decrease yield.

Mulching is a useful practice in corn because adequate moisture is required from pollination to harvest to guarantee that ears are well filled. Since main crops of corn usually ripen during Georgia's drier periods, it is especially critical to maintain soil water supplies; mulching reduces the need for supplemental watering and keeps the moisture content of the soil fairly constant. Most organic mulches are suitable. Newspaper held down with a heavier material on top is also an excellent moisture conserver in corn.

Normally, sweet corn is ready for harvest about 20 days after the first silks appear. Pick corn that is to be stored for a day or two in the cool temperatures of early morning to prevent the ears from building up an excess of field heat, which causes a more rapid conversion of sugars to starch. Of course the best time to pick is just before eating the corn; country cooks say you should have the pot of water coming to a boil as you are picking the corn and husking it on the way from the garden to the house! This is an exaggeration, of course, but with standard varieties, sugar conversion is rather rapid. Field heat can be removed from ears picked when temperatures are high by plunging the ears in cold water or putting them on ice for a short time. Then store the corn in the refrigerator until ready to use. Extra-sweet varieties will also benefit from this treatment, but they are not as finicky.

COMMON CULTURAL PROBLEMS: Birds eating seed, raccoons eating mature ears of corn, gardener's impatience (picking too soon). Poor kernel development (failure to fill out to the tip); caused by dry weather during silking, planting too close, poor fertility (especially potassium deficiency), too few rows in block resulting in poor pollination; lodging (falling over) from too much nitrogen.

DAYS TO MATURITY: 63-100

HARVEST: When husk is still green, silks dry brown, kernels full size and yellow or white color to the tip of the ear; at milky stage (use thumbnail to puncture a kernel -if liquid is clear the corn is immature, if milky it's ready, and if no sap, you're too late). Cover unharvested ears checked by this method with paper bag to prevent insect or bird damage. Corn matures 17-24 days after first silk strands appear, more quickly in hot weather, more slowly in cool weather.

APPROXIMATE YIELDS: (per 10 feet row) 5-10 lbs. or roughly 10-20 ears

AMOUNT TO RAISE PER PERSON: 20-30 pounds or about 40-60 ears

STORAGE: Refrigerate immediately to prevent sugars from turning to starch; cold (32 degrees F), moist (95 % RH) conditions; will keep 4-8 days, but standard varieties will become starchy after a few days

PRESERVATION: Frozen on or off the cob; canned

Cucumbers

PLANTING: Seed after danger of frost has passed and soil has warmed, or use plants sown indoors 3-4 weeks prior to planting time. Both spring and fall crops may be grown.

SPACING: 9-12 inches x 36-48 inches in rows (slicers), 6-8 inches x 36-48 inches (picklers); closer if trellised (see text)

HARDINESS: Very tender annual

FERTILIZER NEEDS: Medium feeder; apply 9.2-17.2 lbs of 10-10-10 per 1000 sq. ft. preplant. Sidedress at blossom with 4.6-8.6 lbs of 10-10-10 per 1000 sq. ft. and repeat 3 weeks later.

CULTURAL PRACTICES: Varieties include slicers, fresh salad types, pickle types, and dwarf-vined or bush varieties. New varieties of cucumbers are being released which are advertised as all-female, or gynoecious types. On a normal cucumber plant the first 10-20 flowers are male, and for every female flower, which will produce the fruit, 10-20 male flowers are produced. Some of the new varieties produce plants which have only female flowers, while others have a greater proportion of female to male flowers. These plants tend to bear fruit earlier with a more concentrated set and better yields overall. About 10% of the seed in a package of gynoecious cucumbers will produce male flowers. These seed are often left untreated so they won't have the characteristic bright color of treated seed. Make sure some of these are planted in the garden. Failure to include some of these plants will result in no yield.

Parthenocarpic cucumbers are all female and are seedless because the fruit is produced without being pollinated. If this type of cuke is planted near others, pollination will occur and seeds will form. This type is usually grown in greenhouses.

Burpless cucumbers are long and slender with a tender skin. Through plant breeding the bitterness associated with the burp has been removed. Other causes of bitterness in cucumbers include temperature variation of more than twenty degrees, and storage of cucumbers near other ripening vegetables.

Most varieties of cucumber vines spread from row to row. Training on a trellis or fence along the edge of the garden will lift the fruit off the soil and conserve space. If cucumbers are to be trellised, plant four to five seeds per foot in rows spaced 30 inches apart. When plants are four to five inches high, thin so they are nine to twelve inches apart. It may be better to plant a second crop around August 1 than to try to continue harvesting an early planting until frost.

There are many excellent bush varieties of cucumber now available. Most of these produce well for the limited amount of space and may be a desirable alternative in a small garden if trellising is not possible. Bush types have very short vines and do not ramble, therefore conserving space.

In order for the flower to develop into a fruit, pollen must be carried by bees from male flowers, on the same plant or on different plants, to the female flower, the one with the miniature cucumber. Male flowers from other plants pollinate gynoecious cucumber flowers. Poor cucumber set is common during rainy weather when bees are inactive. If insecticides are necessary, use them when bee activity is minimal, this usually occurs at dusk or on overcast days.

Spring planted cucumbers can be harvested earlier if mulched with soil warming black plastic. Organic materials are useful in the summer to return moisture and keep the fruit clean in non- trellised plantings.

Working in the vines when leaves are wet may help spread diseases. Wait until after morning dew or rain evaporates. Trellising gets leaves up off the ground so that they dry off faster. Also, if the vines are trellised, the gardener is less likely to step on the vines, and since there is no need to move the vines for weeding or other purposes, the risk of damage is reduced. If vines are not trellised, avoid destroying blossoms or kinking vines by gently rolling the vines away rather than lifting them when searching for harvestable fruit.

There has been a significant increase in disease resistance in cucumber varieties in recent years. Try to select resistant varieties when possible.

COMMON CULTURAL PROBLEMS: Misshapen cucumbers (low fertility or poor pollination), failure to set fruit (too few bees for adequate pollination, no pollinating plants for gynoecious hybrids, changes in temperature).

DAYS TO MATURITY: 50- 70

HARVEST: From when cucumbers are about two inches long up to any size before they begin to turn yellow, about 15 days. Harvesting cucumbers when too mature results in hard seed in the fruit, which is objectionable. Remove by turning cucumbers parallel to the vine and giving a quick snap. This prevents vine damage and results in a clean break.

APPROXIMATE YIELDS: (per 10 foot row) 8-10 pounds

AMOUNT TO RAISE PER PERSON: 10-15 lbs.

STORAGE: Medium cool (45-50 °F.) and moist (95% RH) conditions.

PRESERVATION: Pickling of pickling types.

Eggplant

PLANTING: Transplant after danger of frost, when soil is thoroughly warm.

SPACING: 18-24 inches X 30-36 inches, 24-36 inches X 48-60 inches if staked

HARDINESS: Very tender annual

FERTILIZER NEEDS: Medium feeder, 0.9-1.3 lbs 16-4-08 per 100 sq. ft. Repeat this application 30-40 days after transplanting.

CULTURAL PRACTICES: The standard eggplant produces egg-shaped, glossy, purple-black fruit 6-9 inches long. The long, slender, Japanese eggplant has a thinner skin and more delicate flavor. Both standard and miniature eggplants can be grown successfully in containers, but standards yield better. White, ornamental varieties are also available, which are also edible. The white colored fruit is where the 'egg' plant got its name.

Warm to hot weather throughout the season is necessary for good production. Seeds germinate quickly at 70-90 degrees F, and plants should be grown for 5-7 weeks before setting them out. Cold temperatures will stop plant and root growth reducing plant vigor and yields. Using hot caps or cloches protects plants from cold conditions.

Eggplants are an excellent vegetable for beginners be-cause they are easy to grow from transplants, are almost indestructible, and are very productive. In fact when they have stopped producing or 'topped out' they can be cut back to 6-8 inches and fertilized with 1.3-1.7 lbs 10-10-10 per 100 sq. ft. This process is called "ratoon-ing" and will result in the plants regrowing to produce a second crop.

Though eggplants do well in hot weather, they must have well drained soil, because they do not thrive in very humid areas. When plants are about 6 inches high, nip back the growing tip to encourage branching. Pick fruits when immature, about ⅔ maximum size. Mature fruit should not be left on the plant as this will reduce overall productivity.

Because of the eggplant's susceptibility to verticillium wilt, rotate plantings with other crops on the same garden soil.

DAYS TO MATURITY: 100-150 days from seed; 70-85 days from transplants

HARVEST: Fruit should be large, shiny, and with uniformly deep purple color. When the side of the fruit is pressed slightly with thumbnail and an indentation remains, the fruit is ripe. Long, slender, Japanese eggplant may be ready to harvest from finger or hotdog size. If fruit is a dull color and has brown seeds, it is too ripe and should be discarded.

APPROXIMATE YIELDS: (per 10 feet of row) 20 pounds

AMOUNT TO RAISE PER PERSON: 12 lbs.

STORAGE: Cool (45-50 degrees F) moist (90% RH) conditions; 1 week

PRESERVATION: Freeze, pickle

English Peas

PLANTING: Direct seed in late winter to early spring (February 1 – April 30) depending on location. For fall production plant from August 1 – September 30.

SPACING: 3-4 inches X 24-30 inches

HARDINESS: Half-hardy annual

FERTILIZER NEEDS: Medium feeder, 1.1-2.3 pounds./100 ft. of row of 10-10-10, incorporated into soil before planting. Sidedress 3-4 weeks later with 1.1-2.3 pounds/100 ft. of row with 10-10-10.

CULTURAL PRACTICES: English or garden peas should not be confused with southernpeas (see beans above), which are warm season legumes. English peas are a cool season legume that should be planted in late winter or late summer for early spring or fall harvest respectively. The sugar content will develop more fully under cool conditions. There are both bush and vining types of English peas so be aware of which type you buy to determine whether trellising will be needed. In addition, there are sugar snap varieties which have an edible pod so they don't have to be shelled.

COMMON CULTURAL PROBLEMS: Unfilled pods-harvesting too early.

DAYS TO MATURITY: 55-75 days

HARVEST: Harvest edible pod types whenever size is convenient for picking. Shelling types should be harvested when shell is filled but before it turns yellow and starchy. This is referred to as the mature green stage.

APPROXIMATE YIELDS: 20 lbs. (per 100 feet of row)

AMOUNT TO RAISE PER PERSON: 15 lbs.

STORAGE: 1-2 weeks under refrigeration

PRESERVATION: Canning or freezing.

Lettuce

PLANTING: Green leaf or butterhead types as soon as soil can be worked in the spring, or in late summer. A small packet of seed will usually supply enough plants for 100 feet of row. Crisphead and Cos types may be transplanted in early spring or fall.

SPACING: Leaf, Cos or Butterhead, 4-10 inches x 12-24 inches; Crisphead, 12-15 inches x 18-30 inches

HARDINESS: Hardy annual

FERTILIZER NEEDS: Medium feeder; use starter solution on transplants. Apply 2.75-5.5 oz of 10-10-10 per 10 ft of row at planting and sidedress 20-40 days later with 2.75-5.5 oz of 10-10-10 per 10 ft of row.

CULTURAL PRACTICES: Lettuce, a cool-season vegetable crop, is one of the easiest vegetables to grow. Lettuce withstands light frost; however, sunlight and high summer temperatures usually cause seedstalk formation (bolting) and bitter flavor. Slow-bolting or heat-resistant varieties are available and are recommended for extending the lettuce-growing season. There are several types of lettuce commonly grown in gardens:

Crisphead, also known as Iceberg, is the lettuce most widely available as a fresh market type. It has a tightly compacted head with crisp, light green leaves. Many Georgia gardeners find this type difficult to grow because it requires a long season. Some of the most advertised varieties are not heat-resistant. It tends to go to seed as soon as temperatures go up. In western states, these types are grown during the winter and may take up to 120 days to mature. Select a slow-bolting variety and start seed indoors in late winter or late summer for best results. Transplant in early spring or fall to take advantage of cool weather, and mulch well to keep soil temperatures from fluctuating and to hold moisture in. After the soil warms up, organic mulch is more suitable than black plastic. Mulching also keeps soil off the leaves, reducing chances of disease from soil-born organisms. Heads of this type of lettuce grown in Georgia may be smaller than western grown lettuce.

Butterhead, or Bibb lettuce, is a loose-heading type with dark green leaves that are somewhat thicker than those of iceberg lettuce. Butterheads develop a light yellow, buttery appearance and are very attractive in salads. A miniature variety of butterhead, Tom Thumb, is very easy to grow, requiring a short growing time. One head of this lettuce is right for one or two servings, so this is one lettuce to plant in succession, about two weeks apart. It may be started indoors for an even longer season. Bibb lettuce will develop bitterness readily if temperatures get too high.

Romaine, or Cos, is less commonly grown by gardeners, but is a very nutritious lettuce that deserves attention. It, too, is relatively easy to grow, forming upright heads with rather wavy, attractive leaves.

Most gardeners who grow lettuce raise the leaf type, either with green or reddish leaves. This type is a fast-growing, long-lasting lettuce used for salads, sandwiches, and in wilted lettuce salads. Leaf lettuce basically needs only to be planted and harvested.

Plants can be grown indoors in a cold frame or in a hotbed. Lettuce is often seeded directly in the soil and thinned. Sow leaf varieties about ¼ inch deep, 10-20 seeds per foot, in rows 12-24 inches apart. Thin individual plants 4-8 inches apart. Plants that are thinned can be transplanted. Do not over water, as this may cause disease of roots or leaves. Overhead watering should always be done in the morning to give plants time to dry off. As mentioned above, mulches are helpful in maintaining soil moisture and keeping leaves off the ground.

Lettuce planted in very early spring should be given full sun so that the soil will warm enough for rapid growth. For long-season lettuces, plant so that crops such as sweet corn, staked tomatoes, pole beans or deciduous trees will shade the lettuce during the hottest part of the day when temperatures are over 70 degrees F. Inter-planting, i.e., planting between rows or within the row of later-maturing crops like tomatoes, broccoli, and Brussels sprouts, is a space-saving practice. Some lettuces, like Tom Thumb and leaf lettuces, are attractive in flower borders. Black-seeded Simpson, a leaf lettuce, is recommended for early plantings.

Try some lettuce in the fall garden as well as in the spring garden. Plant seed in late summer for the fall crop. The fall planting of head lettuce should begin about the last week in July and not much later than the first week in August in the mountain areas. The planting date can be much later in southern counties. The variety 'Summer Bibb' will tolerate warmer weather than the other varieties.

Plant lettuce in succession, or use different varieties that mature at different times. Thirty heads of iceberg lettuce harvested at once can present a major storage problem! Leaf and Bibb lettuces do well in hotbeds or greenhouses during the winter and in cold frames in spring and late fall.

COMMON CULTURAL PROBLEMS: Tip burn (irregular moisture, or lack of calcium); bolting, bitterness due to high temperature or lack of moisture; leaf rots due to soil and/or water on leaves.

DAYS TO MATURITY: 40-80 days, depending on type. Crisphead or iceberg types can take up to 120 days to mature.

HARVEST: Leaf lettuce can be used as soon as plants are five to six inches tall. Use the older, outer leaves which contain high levels of calcium first. You may wish to harvest every other one of the largest plants to accomplish thinning. Bibb lettuce is mature when the leaves begin to cup inward to form a loose head. The heads will never become compact. Cos or Romaine is ready to use when the leaves have elongated and overlapped to form a fairly tight head about four inches wide at the base and 6-8 inches tall. Crisphead is mature when leaves overlap to form a head similar to those available to groceries; heads will be compact and firm. Crisphead lettuce will keep about two weeks in the refrigerator. Leaf and Bibb will store as long as four weeks if the leaves are dry when bagged. If lettuce is to be stored, harvest when dry, remove outer leaves but do not wash, place in a plastic bag and store in the crisper drawer.

APPROXIMATE YIELDS: (per 10 foot row): 5 -10 pounds

AMOUNT TO RAISE PER PERSON: 5 -10 pounds

STORAGE: Cool (32 degrees F), moist (95 % RH) conditions; 2-3 weeks

PRESERVATION: Can not be canned or frozen.

Melons

PLANTING: Seed after all danger of frost is past and when soil warms, or begin transplants three to four weeks before setting out.

SPACING: Cantaloupe (muskmelon) 18-24 inches x 24-48 inches; watermelon 36-48 inches x 72-84 inches apart.

HARDINESS: Very tender annual

FERTILIZER NEEDS: Medium feeder, use a starter solution for transplants. Apply 9.2-17.2 lbs of 10-10-10 per 1000 sq. ft. and till it in prior to planting. Sidedressing with the same amount at fruit set.

CULTURAL PRACTICES: Cantaloupes and watermelons are warm season crops requiring a long growing season of 80 to 100 days from seed to fruit. Although the term cantaloupe is more commonly used, many books and other sources refer to these melons as muskmelons. The term muskmelon refers to the musky odor of these melons. Don't be confused, the terms are interchangeable. Most current varieties are not well suited to small gardens because of the space requirement. Newer bush varieties are available for use in small gardens.

Melons can be produced from transplants or planted directly. Those grown from transplants can be harvested as much as two weeks earlier than melons grown directly from seed, since the gardener must wait until danger of frost is past to plant. Plant or transplant cantaloupe in rows 7-10 feet apart if a path is desired between rows. Seed should be sown ½ to one inch deep after danger of frost has passed and soil is warmed.

Cantaloupes and watermelons are well suited for growing on black plastic mulch. The black plastic absorbs heat readily, allowing the soil to warm quickly. It tends to keep the soil moisture level from fluctuating greatly. In addition, the mulch is very effective in controlling weeds, decreasing the labor necessary to care for melons.

Male and female flowers are produced separately on the same plant. Bees must carry pollen from flower to flower to insure good fruit. Use insecticides late in the evening to prevent killing bees.

Melon plants can be planted in rows for easy harvesting. Growing on a trellis allows closer spacing (rows three feet apart), but each trellised melon must be supported by a sling made of a material which dries quickly to prevent rot. Old nylon stockings, cheesecloth, and other net-like materials make good fruit slings. Very large watermelons probably should not be trellised at all, since the weight of the fruit, even if supported, would likely damage the vine. Fruit produced on trellises will often be smaller than fruit allowed to develop on the ground.

There are a number of fruit types that belong to the same species as cantaloupe. These are often referred to as specialty melons. They include Honeydews, Casabas, Crenshaws, Christmas Melons, Charentais, Galia, Persian, and Canary Melons. Some of these slip (pull from the vine easily when ripe) and some do not (they must be cut from the vine), while some have the characteristic musky odor whiles others don't.

COMMON CULTURAL PROBLEMS: Poor flavor and lack of sweetness due to poor fertility, (low potassium, magnesium or boron); cool temperatures; wet weather; poorly adapted variety; loss of leaves from disease; picking melons unripe; poor pollination caused by wet, cool weather, lack of bee pollinators; planting too close; excessive vegetative growth. A heavy rain when melons are ripening may cause some of the fruit to split open. Fruit in contact with soil may develop rotten spots, or be damaged by insects on the bottom. This is particularly problematic with cantaloupes, which must be picked as soon as they reach maturity or they will begin to rot if they are in contact with the soil. Place a board or a couple inches of light mulching material, such as sawdust or straw, beneath each fruit when it is nearly full-size.

DAYS TO MATURITY: 80-100 days

HARVEST: Cantaloupes are harvested at full-slip; i.e., when the stem separates easily at the point of attachment. Honeydew, Crenshaw, and casaba melons do not slip at the point of attachment and must be cut from the vine. This can make it difficult to assess when the fruit are ready. Honeydew rind will loose its pubescence, Casabas will turn completely yellow, and Crenshaws will have a yellow ground or background color. These melons will rot if left on the ground for too long. For watermelons, become familiar with the variety being grown to determine the best stage for harvesting. Day to harvest on the seed packet can be helpful. Remember to reduce this number by 14-21 days for transplants. The best indicator is a yellowish color on the underside where the melon touches the ground. A dead tendril or curl near the point where the fruit is attached to the vine is used by some as an indicator that the fruit is ready for harvest. You may also thump the fruit, listening for the dull sound of ripe fruit, rather than a more metallic sound; however, this technique takes some practice, and if you have just a few fruit, it is probably wise to include all of the above when making your decision.

APPROXIMATE YIELD: (per 10 foot row) 8 -40 pounds; more if trellised

AMOUNT TO RAISE PER PERSON: 10-15 lbs.

STORAGE: Medium-cool (40-50 degrees F), moist (80-85% RH) conditions

PRESERVATION: Watermelon rind can be pickled

Okra

PLANTING: Seed after danger of frost is past when soil is thoroughly warm.

SPACING: 12-15 inches x 42 inches dwarf types. 18-24 inches x 48 inches medium and tall varieties

HARDINESS: Very tender annual

FERTILIZER NEEDS: Medium feeder, apply 1.1-2.0 lbs of 10-10-10 to 100 sq. ft., preplant and incorporate. Sidedress with 1.0-1.6 lbs of 10-10-10 per 10 foot of row.

CULTURAL PRACTICES: Okra is grown in every county in Georgia. Okra needs a well-drained soil. Since okra is very susceptible to damage by nematodes, follow a crop rotation, using grasses or small grains (i.e. wheat) which prevent a buildup of nematode populations. Okra should not follow vine crops, such as squash and sweetpotatoes. Okra tends to respond to a high phosphate fertilizer. Use 5-10-15 or 6-12-12 initially and as a sidedress. The okra plant has a sensitive balance between vegetation (foliage production) and reproduction (pod production). The use of additional nitrogen should be avoided on vigorous plantings until fruiting begins to check plant growth. Two or more sidedressings with a high analysis nitrogen material may be needed, however, depending on rainfall. It is important to supply additional nitrogen late in the season at the time the "forms" or "blooms" are concentrated in the top of the plant.

COMMON CULTURAL PROBLEMS: They are highly susceptible to root-knot nematodes (causes galling on the roots) which can reduce plant growth and yield. Hard, woody fruit from waiting too long to harvest. Harvest when pods are 2-3 inches long.

DAYS TO MATURITY: 50-60 days to first harvest.

HARVEST: Harvest pods when very small, less than 2-3 inches long. Older pods will rapidly become woody and inedible. Removing old pods and leaves does not result in more production. When plants are past productivity, they can be ratooned (cut back) to 8-10 inches of ground and will grow back.

APPROXIMATE YIELDS: (per 10 feet of row) 6-10 lbs.

AMOUNT TO RAISE PER PERSON: 4-8 lbs.

STORAGE: Room temperature; do not chill or cool; 4-6 days

PRESERVATION: Canning, pickling, or freezing

Onions

PLANTING: Use sets, seeds, or transplants in fall and winter for bulbs and for green or bunching onions. Seeds are sown in September in high density plantings (30-70 plants per ft.), which are pulled and transplanted to their final spacing 8-10 weeks later. Usually 50% of the tops are removed the time of transplanting. Sets and/or transplants should be set in November or December. Overwintering onions are suitable for south Georgia only. Seeding or setting transplants in late winter (February) may be used in north Georgia.

SPACING: Standard 1-6 inches x 12-24 inches. Plant close then thin; use thinnings as green onions.

HARDINESS: Bulb onions – hardy biennial; Green or bunching – hardy biennial; Egyptian or Perennial Tree and multiplier – hardy perennials.

FERTILIZER NEEDS: If growing your own transplants 1.0-1.6 oz. of 10-10-10/10 ft. of row incorporated in the soil prior to sowing. Repeat this at 4 and 6 weeks after seeding. Heavy feeder, apply 0.6-0.9 lbs. 10-10-10/100 sq. ft. before setting transplants, apply again in mid-January and the end of January. Apply 0.4-0.6 lbs/100 sq. ft. of calcium nitrate in February.

CULTURAL PRACTICES: Onions are grouped according to daylength with short-day, intermediate-day, and long-day onions. Each group bulbs according to daylength. Onions suitable for south Georgia are short-day onions that bulb during the relatively short days of late winter and early spring. These onions are famous as sweet Vidalia onions because of their high water content and the low sulfur soils of south Georgia. Sulfur imparts the pungent flavor in onions. Each has three distinct colors; yellow, white, and red. Intermediate onions may be over wintered in north Georgia, however, success is not guaranteed. Long day onions are not suitable for Georgia.

If the seed catalog lists the onion as long day, it sets bulbs when it receives 15-16 hours of daylight and is used to produce onions in Northern summers. Short day varieties set bulbs with about 12 hours of daylight and are used in the deep South for winter production. Long-day onions are typically the hotter common onions, while short-day onions are sweet types.

For green or bunching onions, use sets, seeds, or transplants in the spring and fall. Egyptian (Perennial Tree) and Yellow Multiplier (Potato Onion) onions are specialty items you may wish to try in your garden.. Both sets and plants will require about 12-14 weeks to reach eating size. Sets and plants should be spaced about two inches apart.

For dry bulb production in south Georgia, onions may be direct seeded in October; or transplants may be set out in November or December. The onions will reach maturity in April and/or May. In north Georgia, plants should be set out around the middle of February to the middle of March. Set one to two inches apart and one to two inches deep in the row. Thin to four inches apart and eat the thinned plants as green onions. Avoid sets more than an inch in diameter because they are likely to produce seed stalks. Planting and exposure to cold temperatures also causes seed stalk development. Some people have the best bulb production using seedlings or transplants rather than sets. Egyptian Tree or Multiplier onions should be set in late October or early November. Plant four inches apart in rows one to two feet apart. Distance between rows is determined by available space and cultivating equipment. Bulbs compete poorly with weeds because of upright growth habit.. Shallow cultivation is necessary; do not hill up soil on onions as this can encourage stem rot. Ensure ample moisture, especially after bulbs begin enlarging.

Onions should be harvested when about 20-50% of the tops have fallen over. Use a broom or rake to break over those still standing so that all the onions will mature thoroughly. Tops may be left on or cut off, but leave at least one inch of the top for storage. Careful handling to avoid bruising helps control storage rot. Place the tops over the bulbs to prevent sun scald. Onions may be pulled and left in the garden for a few days to dry, then cured in slatted crates or mesh bags in a well-ventilated attic or porch out of direct sun for one to two weeks. Thorough curing will increase storage life.

COMMON CULTURAL PROBLEMS: Bulb rot from bruising, insufficient drying; split or double bulbs from dry soil during bulb formation; very small bulbs from too late planting or too dry soil.

DAYS TO MATURITY: 150-180 (Mature bulbs) from transplanting for overwintering onions.

HARVEST: Harvest green onions when tops are 6-10 inches tall; bulbs after 20-50% or more of the tops have fallen over. Do not wait more than 1-2 weeks after this occurs. Allow for thorough drying before storage.

APPROXIMATE YIELDS: 10-15 lbs. (per 10 feet of row)

AMOUNT TO RAISE PER PERSON: 10-15 lbs.

STORAGE: Cool (32 degrees F), dry (65-70%RH) conditions; 2-3 months for sweet onions.

PRESERVATION: Onions may be stored dry, or pickled and canned. They freeze well if chopped. For fresh storage, maintain good air circulation. To extend the shelf-life of sweet onions, wrap them individually in paper towels and place them in the crisper drawer of the refrigerator. This will extend their shelf-life 1-2 months. Check them regularly and discard any bulbs that show rot.

Peppers

PLANTING: Set out transplants after soil has thoroughly warmed in the spring, start seed indoors 5-7 weeks prior to this date.

SPACING: 12-18 inches (using double rows) 18-24 inches x 24-36 inches

HARDINESS: Very tender annual.

FERTILIZER NEEDS: Heavy feeder; use starter solution for transplants. Apply 0.5-1.0 lbs/100 sq. ft. of 10-10-10 preplant, sidedress with 0.5-1.0 lbs/100 sq. ft. of 10-10-10 3-4 weeks after transplanting. Sidedress after first fruit reach about the size of a quarter with 1.6-3.2 oz/10 ft of row with calcium nitrate.

CULTURAL PRACTICES: Although types of peppers belong in one of six groups, most are classified according to their degree of hot or mild flavor. The mild peppers include Bell, Banana, Pimento and Sweet Cherry while the hot peppers include the Cayenne, Celestial, Large Cherry, and Tabasco.

Bell peppers, measuring 3 inches wide by 4 inches long, usually have 3-4 lobes and a blocky appearance. They are commonly harvested when green, yet they may turn one of several colors when fully ripe. When fully ripe they may be brown, red, yellow, purple, orange, etc. while still maintaining quality. In grocery stores colored bell peppers have become more popular and are more expensive. Other sweet peppers have conical, 2-3 inches wide by 4 inches long, thick- walled fruit and are used when red and fully ripe. Banana peppers are long and tapering and should be harvested when yellow, orange, or red. Cherry peppers vary in size and flavor. Usually they are harvested when orange to deep red.

Slim, pointed, slightly twisted fruits characterize the hot Cayenne pepper group. These can be harvested either when green or red, and include varieties such as Anaheim, Cayenne, Serrano and Jalapeno. Celestial peppers are cone shaped, ¾ inch to 2 inches long, and very hot. They vary in color from yellow to red to purple making them an attractive plant to grow. Slender, 1 inch to 3 inches long, pointed Tabasco peppers taste extremely hot and include such varieties as Chili Piquin and Small Red Chili.

Peppers generally have a long growing season and suffer slow growth during cool periods. Therefore, after the soil has thoroughly warmed in the spring, set out 5-7 week old transplants to get a head start toward harvest. Practice good cultivation and provide adequate moisture. Mulching can help to conserve water and reduce weeds.

Hot peppers are usually allowed to fully ripen and change colors (except for Jalapenos) and have smaller, longer, thinner and more tapering fruits than sweet peppers. Yields are smaller for hot peppers.

COMMON CULTURAL PROBLEMS: Blossom end rot (moisture irregularities, heavy rains, or calcium deficiency), blossom drop (when night temperatures go above 75 degrees F, or when a full crop of fruit set is excessive).

DAYS TO MATURITY: 100-120 from seed, 70-85 from transplants

HARVEST: Harvest sweet peppers when they reach full size, while still green or they can be left on the plant to change color. When allowed to mature on the plant, bell peppers can be a range of colors depending on the variety. In addition, they usually become sweeter and increase in vitamin A and C content. Cut instead of pulling to avoid breaking branches. Hot peppers are allowed to ripen and change color on the plant. Entire plants may be pulled and hung just before full frosts.

APPROXIMATE YIELDS: (per 10 feet of row) 2-8 lbs.

AMOUNT TO RAISE PER PERSON: 3-10 lbs.

STORAGE: Medium cool conditions (45-50 degrees F), moist (95% RH); 2-3 weeks.

PRESERVATION: Freeze, pickles and relishes, dried spices

Potatoes

PLANTING: 1 - 2 oz. seed pieces with at least one good eye in early spring.

SPACING: 7-12 inches x 24-36 inches

HARDINESS: Half-hardy perennial grown as an annual.

FERTILIZER NEEDS: Medium-heavy feeder, add high phosphorus fertilizer. Apply 1.4-2.3 lbs/100 sq. ft. of 10-10-10 before planting; side dress about 6 weeks after planting when tubers begin forming with 1.4-2.3 lbs/100 sq. ft. of 10-10-10.

CULTURAL PRACTICES: Both white-skinned and red-skinned potatoes can be grown as an early crop for new potatoes and as a late crop for storage. Choose an early maturing variety and a medium to late maturing variety. Plant potatoes early from February 1 to March 15, depending on your location. Hard frosts and freezes may set back growth. Potatoes prefer a cool spring and moisture throughout the growing season.

Avoid a garden site in a turned-under lawn, as grub worms may damage developing tubers unless soil insecticides are used.

A soil pH of 6.0 to 6.5 is most desirable. Scab disease will be less when the pH is between 5.0 and 5.2, but this is impractical for the home gardener practicing crop rotation because most vegetables require a pH of 6.0-6.5.

Purchase certified seed stock. Saving your own seed potatoes is generally not worthwhile because viruses and diseases often show up the next year. Seed potatoes should be firm and unsprouted. Wilted and sprouted potatoes usually have lost vigor from being too warm

in storage. White Irish potato varieties recommended for Georgia include Kennebec and Irish Cobbler. Early red varieties are Red Pontiac and Red LaSoda.

Seed pieces for planting should be cut to about 1½ to 2 ounces or into 1½ inch cubes. Potatoes about six ounces in size can be cut into four pieces nicely. Each seed piece should have at least one good bud or "eye." Plant potatoes in furrows cut-side down, three to five inches deep. Later crops should be planted five to six inches deep. Space the seed pieces eight to ten inches apart.

Pull a ridge of soil over each row when planting. Rake the surface occasionally to kill any weed seeds that germinate before the potato sprouts emerge. Later cultivation should be shallow and far enough from the rows to make certain that no roots are damaged.

Water is critical when blossoms are forming and should be added if the soil at this time is very dry.

Just before the tops have grown too large to allow cultivation, a finishing cultivation, sometimes called "lay by" or "hilling up" is made. "Lay by" is throwing soil over the potatoes to prevent exposure of the potatoes to sun; exposure can cause greening or scalding. Green portions on potatoes taste bitter and contain an alkaloid. Cut off and discard green areas before using.

COMMON CULTURAL PROBLEMS: Green skin (sun exposure), hollow heart (alternate wet and dry conditions), Black Walnut wilt (too close to a Black Walnut tree).

DAYS TO MATURITY: 100-120

HARVEST: Dig early potatoes when tubers are large enough to eat. Potatoes are ready for harvest when plants begin to decline. If conditions are rainy, potatoes should be harvested as quickly as possible at this time to prevent potatoes rotting. Avoid skinning tubers when digging and avoid long exposure to light.

APPROXIMATE YIELDS: (per 10 foot row) 6-15 lbs.

AMOUNT TO RAISE PER PERSON: 75-100 lbs. (plant about 15 lbs. of seed potatoes per person)

STORAGE: Medium-cool (40-50 degrees F), moist (90% RH) conditions; 6-8 months; sprouting is a problem at higher temperatures.

PRESERVATION: Usually stored in medium cool, moist conditions. May also be canned.

Squash

PLANTING: Seed after danger of frost is past and soil has warmed.

SPACING: 16-24 inches X 36-60 inches bush types, 36-48 inches x 120-144 inches vining types.

HARDINESS: Very tender annual

FERTILIZER NEEDS: Medium feeder, 1.0-1.7 lbs/100 sq. ft. of 10-10-10. Sidedress one week after blossoming begins with 4.4-8.3 oz/10 ft of row with 10-10-10.

CULTURAL PRACTICES: Summer squash grows on non-vining bushes. There are many varieties having different fruit shapes and colors. The three main types include the yellow straight neck or crooked neck; the white, saucer shaped, scallop or patty pan; and the oblong, green, grey or gold zucchini.

Winter squash can also be grown throughout the summer. It differs from summer squash in that it is harvested and eaten when the fruit is mature. Also, it has a hard rind and can be stored for use throughout the winter. This type includes Acorn, Butternut, and Hubbard. Some squashes are bush, while others are vining types that need more space per plant. Soil containing plenty of well-rotted compost or manure is ideal, although good crops may be grown in average soils which have been adequately fertilized.

For extra early fruit, plant seeds in peat pots in greenhouses or hotbeds and transplant about three weeks later after danger of frost. Older plants that have hardened off and stopped growth will not transplant well and should be discarded. Squashes are warm season plants and do not do well until soil and air temperatures are above 60 degrees F.

Seed or transplants can be planted through black plastic. Cover seed with one inch of soil. Squash plants have separate male and female flowers on the same plant. Pollen must be transferred from the male flowers to the female by bees. Use insecticides late in the evening to prevent killing bees.

COMMON CULTURAL PROBLEMS: Poor pollination may result in misshapen fruit. Insect pollinators are required.

DAYS TO MATURITY: 50-66 days summer squash, 85-120 days winter squash.

HARVEST: Harvest when immature, only about 6-8 inches long and 1½ -2 inches in diameter for elongated types, 3-4 inches in diameter for patty-pan types, and 4-7 inches long for yellow crooknecks. If the rind is too hard to be marked by the thumbnail, it is too old. Remove old fruit to allow new fruit to develop. Check plants daily once they begin to bear. Winter squash are harvested when the fruit is fully mature. The rind should not give when pressed with the thumbnail. Winter squash are generally harvested all at once when mature.

APPROXIMATE YIELDS: 20-80 lbs. (per 10 feet of row)

AMOUNT TO RAISE PER PERSON: 10-25 lbs.

STORAGE: Summer squash, cool (32-50 degrees F), moist (90% RH) conditions; 5-14 days. Winter squash can be stored for 4 months or longer

PRESERVATION: Usually in cool, moist storage, as pickles or relishes or frozen. Quality may be poor on frozen squash.

Sweetpotato

PLANTING: Set transplants after danger of frost is past and soil has warmed.

SPACING: 10-18 inches X 36-48 inches

HARDINESS: Very tender annual.

FERTILIZER NEEDS: Light-Medium feeder, 0.8-1.4lbs./100 sq. ft. of 5-10-10 preplant incorporated. Sidedress 60 and 90 days after transplanting with 2.3-4.1 lb/100 ft. of row of 5-10-10.

CULTURAL PRACTICES: Sweetpotatoes are a warm season vegetable requiring 120-150 days to mature. They do best on sandy or sandy-loam soils. On heavier clay soils the tubers don't develop as well. Over fertilization with nitrogen fertilizer can result in vegetative growth with reduced tuber development.

Plants are started from slips which are bareroot plants grown from seed tubers. Seed tubers are grown in organic media beds and the emerging plants are 'slipped' from the tuber for sale. When purchasing slips always try to get certified slips which have been checked for disease and insect infestations, as well as being true-to-type.

There are several varieties of sweetpotato; two very popular varieties are Jewel and Beauregard. Varieties can differ as to disease resistance, tuber color, and productivity. Sweetpotatoes are of two basic types the dry-fleshed and moist-fleshed types. Almost all of the varieties grown in Georgia are of the moist-flesh type including Jewel and Beauregard.

COMMON CULTURAL PROBLEMS: Poor tuber development,-too much nitrogen, too much water, soil too heavy.

DAYS TO MATURITY: 90-120 days

HARVEST: Sweetpotatoes will continue to grow right up until frost. After 3 months of growth you can dig a few plants to see the size and quantity of tubers produced and make a judgment whether to harvest or wait. Tubers will continue to enlarge in size and may get too big for convenient harvest and storage.

Within 1-2 hours of harvest the curing process should begin with sweetpotatoes. This involves storing the tubers at 80-85 degrees F for 4-7 days with 90-95% humidity. This will help any cuts or bruises on the tubers to heal and the flavor will improve (sweeten).

APPROXIMATE YIELDS: 100 lbs. (per 100 feet of row)

AMOUNT TO RAISE PER PERSON: 25-50 lbs.

STORAGE: Store at 50-55 degrees F and 80-85% humidity or as close to this as possible. With optimum storage conditions they can be kept for up to 12 months.

PRESERVATION: Canning

Tomatoes

PLANTING: Transplant when all danger of frost is past and when the soil has warmed.

SPACING: 12-24 inches x 36-48 inches.

HARDINESS: Tender annual

FERTILIZER NEEDS: Medium feeder; use starter solution for transplants. Apply 1.1-2.3 lbs/100 sq. ft. of 10-10-10. Repeat this application 3-4 weeks after transplanting.

CULTURAL PRACTICES: Tomatoes are valuable garden plants in that they require relatively little space for large production. Each tomato plant, properly cared for, yields 10 to 15 pounds or more of fruit.

Choose varieties with disease resistance. Fusarium and verticillium wilt are common diseases that can destroy a whole tomato crop. Treating either disease is difficult. Many varieties are resistant to these two diseases - look for VF after the cultivar name, indicating resistance to the wilts. VFN means the plants are resistant to verticillium, Fusarium and nematodes; VFNT adds tobacco mosaic to the list. Recently a viral disease call Tomato Spotted Wilt Virus (TSWV) has attacked tomatoes in Georgia. There is a resistant variety called Southern Star (BHN 444) which growers may wish to try. This is a determinant type (see below) developed for commercial staked tomato production.

The varieties of tomato plants available may seem overwhelming to a new gardener; ask gardening friends for the names of their favorites. This will give you a good idea of what does well in Georgia. Several major types of tomatoes exist that can be chosen according to need:

(a) Midget, patio, or dwarf tomato varieties have very compact vines and grow well in hanging baskets or other containers. The tomatoes produced may be, but are not necessarily, the cherry type (1 inch diameter or less). Some produce larger fruit. These plants are usually short- lived, producing their crop quickly and for a short period.

(b) Cherry tomatoes have small, cherry-sized (or a little larger) fruits often used in salads. Plants of cherry tomatoes range from dwarf (Tiny Tim) to seven-footers (Sweet 100). One standard cherry tomato plant is usually sufficient for a family, since they generally produce abundantly.

(c) Grape tomatoes are a relatively new type that are about the size of cherry tomatoes. The fruit are slightly oblong, low acid, and very sweet. The growth habit is indeterminate and they are a popular commercial type. Seed may be available for homeowners from some seed companies. Several varieties are available, many are named with a Christmas theme such as St. Nick, Jolly Elf, and Santa F_1.

(d) Compact, or determinate tomato plants, may include cultivars of the above two categories. Determinate refers to the plant habit of growing to a certain size, setting fruit, and then declining. Most of the early ripening tomato varieties are determinate and will not produce tomatoes throughout a Georgia summer.

(e) Beefsteak types are large-fruited and produce a tomato slice that easily covers a sandwich. The fruit often weighs as much as two pounds or more. These are usually late to ripen, so plant some standard-sized or early tomatoes for longest harvest.

(f) Paste tomatoes have small pear-shaped fruits with very meaty interiors and few seeds. They are less juicy than standard tomatoes, and are without a central core.

Paste tomatoes are a favorite for canning, since they don't have to be cut up and are so meaty.

(g) Some tomatoes are orange, yellow, pink, or striped, and usually the only way to get these is by growing your own.

(h) Winter storage tomatoes are a relatively new item for gardeners. The plants are set out later in the season than most tomatoes, and fruit are harvested partially ripe. If properly stored, they will stay fresh for twelve weeks or more. While the flavor does not equal that of summer vine-ripened tomatoes, many people prefer them to grocery store tomatoes in winter.

Tomato plants may be started indoors from seed or transplants may be purchased. If starting your own plants, use a light soil mix and give the plants plenty of light. Tall, spindly transplants are usually caused by low light levels in the home. Unless you have a sunny, south-facing window, supplemental light will probably be necessary. The seed are sown 5-7 weeks before the last frost date in your area. A few weeks before transplanting time, harden-off indoor grown plants by exposing them to an increasing number of hours outdoors each day. Bring plants in if there is danger of frost. A few varieties of tomato (the Sub-Arctics) are bred to grow well in low spring temperatures; however, these are rarely available in the usual markets and ordinarily must be grown from seed.

When you are ready to put home-grown or purchased plants into the ground, select stocky transplants about six to ten inches tall. Set tomato transplants in the ground covering the stems so that only two or three sets of true leaves are exposed. Horizontal planting of tomato plants is an effective way to make plants stronger, especially leggy ones. Roots will form along the buried portion of the stem, giving better growth and less chance of plant injury from an excessively weak stem. Do not remove the containers if they are peat or paper pots, but open or tear off one side to allow roots to get a good start. If non-biodegradable containers are used, knock the plants out of the pots before transplanting, and loosen the roots somewhat.

Press the soil firmly around the transplant so that a slight depression is formed for holding water. Pour approximately one pint of starter solution around each plant to wash the soil around the roots. High phosphorus starter fertilizers are particularly useful for tomato production.

If plants are to be staked or trellised, space them 24 inches apart in rows three feet apart. Though it requires more initial work, staking makes caring for tomatoes easier than letting them sprawl. Since they are off the ground, fruit rots are reduced, spraying is easier and less frequently required, and harvesting is much less work. Use wooden stakes six feet long and 1½ or 2 inches wide. Drive them one foot into the soil about four to six inches from the plant soon after transplanting. Attach heavy twine or strips of cloth to the stakes every ten inches. As the plants grow, pull the stems toward the stakes and tie loosely.

Prune staked tomatoes to either one or two main stems. At the junction of each leaf and the first main stem a new shoot will develop. If plants are trained to two stems, choose one of these shoots, normally at the first or second leaf-stem junction, for the second main stem. Remove all other shoots, called suckers, weekly to keep the plant to these two main stems. Pinch shoots off with your fingers. Tomato plants may also be set along a fence or trellis and tied and pruned in a manner similar to that used with stakes.

Growing tomatoes in wire cages is a method which has been gaining in popularity among gardeners because of its simplicity. Cage-growing allows the tomato plant to grow in its natural manner, but keeps the fruit and leaves off the ground, offering the advantages of staking as well. Using wire cages requires a large initial expenditure and a large storage area, but many gardeners feel that the freedom from pruning and staking is worth it. The cages, if heavy duty, will last many years. Be sure to get fencing with at least 6 inches spacing between wires so that you can get your hand inside to harvest the tomatoes. If tomato plants in wire cages are pruned at all, once is enough; prune to three or four main stems. Wire-cage tomatoes develop a heavy foliage cover, reducing sunscald on fruits and giving more leeway when bottom leaves become blighted and have to be removed.

Caged plants are less prone to the spread of disease from plant handling, since they do not have open wounds and must be handled less frequently than staked plants. However, it helps to space the plants somewhat further apart (three feet is good) to allow good air circulation between plants; humidity is higher because of the foliage density, and diseases such as late blight spread rapidly in humid situations. If well-nourished and cared for, caged tomatoes can produce exceptional harvests and make up for the extra space with high production. This type of culture is especially suited to indeterminate varieties.

Blossom-end rot can be a serious problem with tomatoes. To prevent this disorder, maintain a pH of 6.0 to 6.5 and an adequate calcium level by liming. Keep moisture levels fairly uniform (not too wet or too dry), and use calcium chloride (four tablespoons per gallon) once weekly until the condition is corrected.

Tomato blossoms are very sensitive to temperature. At temperatures of 55-60 degrees F., pollination can be severely impaired, and very few fruits will form.

Temperatures of 90-95 degrees F are also very unfavorable for pollination. Night temperatures between 60-70 degrees F are optimum for fruit set. As night temperatures rise above 70 degrees F, flower abortion occurs. In the South these high temperatures are a problem. It is also a good practice to mulch the soil around the plants with several inches of straw, old hay, old sawdust, or black plastic. The mulch will keep the soil temperature uniform and decrease surface evaporation of water, as well as keep down weeds. Use a nitrate top-dressing over the mulch, and water it in.

COMMON CULTURAL PROBLEMS: Blossom-end rot, irregular soil moisture or calcium deficiency; poor color, yellow spots or large whitish-grey spots, sunscald from lack of foliage cover; leaf roll, physiological condition often found in pruned tomatoes; fruit cracking, irregular soil moisture; black walnut wilt, caused by roots of tomato plants coming in contact with roots of black walnut trees.

DAYS TO MATURITY: 55-105

HARVEST: Harvest fully vine-ripened but still firm; most varieties are dark red. Picked tomatoes should be placed in shade. Light is not necessary for ripening immature tomatoes.

Some green tomatoes may be picked before the first killing frost and stored in a cool (55 degrees F), moist (90% RH) place. When desired, ripen fruits at 70 degrees F.

APPROXIMATE YIELDS: (per 10 feet of row) 15-45 lbs.

AMOUNT TO RAISE PER PERSON: 20-25 pounds for fresh used; 25-40 pounds for canning

STORAGE: Green tomatoes -medium cool (50-70 degrees F), moist (90% RH) conditions; 1-3 weeks. Ripe tomatoes - cool (45-50 degrees F), moist (90% RH) conditions; 4-7 days.

PRESERVATION: Can or freeze as sauces or in chunks (whole or quartered), peeled.

When To Harvest Vegetables

As vegetables mature, various physiological processes occur that change the taste, appearance and quality of the product. Texture, fiber and consistency are greatly affected by the stage of maturity.

The stage at which a vegetable is harvested, how it is handled between harvesting and serving, and the elapsed time between harvesting and serving, all will affect the quality of the end product. Some vegetables are more highly perishable than others. Sweet corn and English peas are very difficult to maintain in an acceptable fresh state, even for a short time, while other vegetables may have a much longer shelf life.

Even after harvest, respiration and other life processes continue to take place inside the product, so these processes (in most cases) need to be slowed down in order to increase the shelf life of the vegetable. Lowering the internal temperature of the product is the main way to slow these processes. This is one reason for harvesting vegetables early in the day before the heat from the sun has warmed them.

Some vegetables are harvested at full maturity while others are harvested in the immature state. Watermelon, cantaloupe, and tomato are examples of vegetables harvested at maturity. Summer squash, sweet pepper, and okra are examples of vegetables harvested while immature. The plant part harvested will also play a factor in when a vegetable is harvested and how it is handled. For example, in lettuce the leaves are harvested before sexual maturity. In broccoli and cauliflower the immature flower is harvested. For further information consult Cooperative Extension leaflet 291, *When To Harvest Vegetables*.

HERBS

Herbs are, in general, very easy to grow. They are quite free from damage by diseases and insects. A bountiful harvest can be secured with a minimum of care. A few short rows in the vegetable or flower garden will provide an adequate supply for the average family.

Depending on the species, variety, and growth cycle, herbs are either annual, biennial, or perennial. Keep this in mind while locating them in the garden, along with the following points:

• Group herbs according to light requirements (full sun or partial shade) and locate the planting area accordingly.

• For best results choose a soil that is fertile, well-drained, and loamy.

• Acid soils are unsuitable for herbs. Preferred pH for most herbs is around 6.0-6.5.

• Prepare the soil to a depth of eight inches.

• Give perennial herbs an area which will not be disturbed by tillage. Those that spread by runners, such as mints, should be given a large area, or should be contained in some fashion.

Herbs may be started either indoors or out. For small seeds, the easiest method is to sow them directly into peat pots filled with seed-starting mix or milled sphagnum moss, which has anti-fungal properties. Thin seedlings to four or five per pot. Larger seed may also be started by this method, then thinned to one plant per pot. Keep soil surface moist by misting until plants are established.

Perennials may be started from seed or from cuttings. Root cuttings in a window box or some other suitable container, preferably covered with plastic to maintain high humidity. Four or five inches of clean coarse sand makes a satisfactory rooting medium. Keep the sand moist and keep young plants out of direct sunlight to prevent wilting. In four to six weeks, move the cuttings to pots or cold frames for the winter.

Transplant all herb plants after danger of severe frost. Control weeds during the growing season to prevent competition for water and nutrients. A light, one-inch mulch will conserve soil moisture and help control weeds. Irrigation may be necessary during periods of drought, though once established, many herbs are highly resistant to drought.

Harvesting

Herb leaves which are to be used fresh may be picked whenever the plant has enough foliage to maintain continued growth. Most herbs for drying should be picked just before the flowers open, when the leaves contain the highest content of aromatic, volatile oils. The stems should be selected and cut individually, about 6 inches below the flower buds. Remove dead or damaged leaves, and wipe off any dust or dirt which may be present. If the leaves are very dirty, they may be rinsed gently in cold water and dried with paper towels. You may also spray the leaves with a garden hose the day before harvesting. Discontinue harvesting leaves of perennials by late summer to allow the plants to store enough carbohydrates for overwintering.

Most herbs should be grown on the dry side, which enhances and concentrates the aromatic flavors. Obviously this cannot be done during wet years, but during dry periods harvested herbs will have a more flavorful bouquet.

You may save seed for culinary uses or for starting plants the next year by allowing the plants to completely mature. Harvest seed when they change in color from green to brown or grey, and allow them to dry thoroughly before storing.

Drying and Storage

Herbs may be dried by tying the cut stems in small bunches and hanging them in a well-ventilated, low-dust, darkened room. Each bunch should be labeled, since dried herbs look pretty much the same. The best product will result if leaves are dried rapidly without artificial heat or exposure to sunlight. However, in the case of thick succulent leaves, such as those of basil, rapid drying in an oven, dehydrator, or solar dryer may be the only method of retaining color and maximum aromatic quality.

If leaves are not too small, they may be removed from the stems and dried in a single layer on trays made of window screening or ¼ inches mesh hardware cloth. Label each different herb. Stir the leaves gently once or twice a day to speed the drying operation.

When the drying process seems to be complete, remove the leaves from the stems or trays and place in sealed glass jars in a warm place for a week. At the end of that time, examine the jars to determine if any moisture has condensed on the inside of the glass. If it has, remove the contents and spread out for further drying. If necessary, the final drying may be completed by spreading the leaves on a cookie sheet in an oven set for 110 degrees F or lower.

Herb leaves are dry when they become brittle and will crumble into powder when rubbed between the hands. If you prefer to use herbs in powdered or ground form, crush the leaves with a rolling pin, pass them through a fine sieve, or grind in a blender or with mortar and pestle.

Store herbs in air-tight bottles, preferably brown glass, in as cool a place as possible, out of direct sunlight. By using air-tight containers the herbs will retain their essential oils and flavors.

Herbs as Potted Plants

Most small-sized herb plants may be grown in 4 or 6 inch pots as house plants. When given loving care in a sunny window, they will supply sprigs for culinary use throughout the winter.

If an enclosed porch or sun room is available, larger herbs may be grown. Some of the best to try are basil, sweet marjoram, oregano, rosemary, thyme, and (if you find one) bay laurel (*Laurus nobilis*). Start pot plants from seed, cuttings or divisions in midsummer, or, if available, dig young, vigorous plants from the garden and pot them, being sure to hose off any insects or eggs that might be present.

The Knot Garden

One attractive way to display herbs is the knot garden, in which the various colors and textures of herbs are used to create the appearance of cords looping over and under each other. Herb plants are closely spaced and trimmed to form low hedges. The knot garden is most effective when viewed from above, especially from a second-story window. Plants that work well in knot gardens include spearmint, peppermint, lemon thyme, French thyme, and sage.

Annual Herbs

ANISE (*Pimpinella anisum*) - Spacing: Height 24 inches, Row 18 inches, Plants 10 inches. Cultural Hints: Grows from seed. Plant after frost. Sun. Uses: Leaves for seasoning, garnish; dried seed as spice.

BASIL, SWEET (*Ocimum basilicum*) - Spacing: Height 20-24 inches, Row 18 inches, Plants 12 inches. Cultural Hints: Grow from seed; plant after frost. Sun. Uses: Season soups, stews, salad, omelets.

BORAGE (*Borago officinalis*) - Spacing: Height 24 inches, Row 18 inches, Plants 12 inches. Cultural Hints: Grow from seed, self-sowing. Best in dry, sunny areas. Uses: Young leaves in salads and cool drinks.

CARAWAY (*Carum carvi*) - Spacing: Height 12-24 inches, Row 18 inches, Plants 10 inches. Cultural Hints: Grow from seed. Biennial seed bearer. Sun. Uses: Flavoring, especially bakery items.

CHERVIL (*Anthriscus cerefolium*) - Spacing: Height 10 inches, Row 15 inches, Plants 3-6 inches. Cultural Hints: Sow in early spring. Partial shade. Uses: Aromatic leaves used in soups and salads.

CORIANDER (*Coriandrum sativum*) - Spacing: Height 24 inches, Row 24 inches, Plants 18 inches. Cultural Hints: Grow from seed. Sow in spring in sun or partial shade. Uses: Seed used in confections, leaves in salad.

DILL (*Anethum graveolens*) - Spacing: Height 24-36 inches, Row 24 inches, Plants 12 inches. Cultural Hints: Grow from seed sown in early spring. Sun or partial shade. Uses: Leaves and seeds used flavoring and pickling.

FENNEL (FLORENCE FENNEL) (*Finocchio foeniculum, Foeniculum officianalis*) - Spacing: Height 60 inches, Row 18 inches, Plants 18 inches. Cultural Hints: Grow from seed sown in early spring. Sun, partial shade. Uses: Has anise-like flavor, for salad. Stalk eaten raw or braised.

PARSLEY (*Petroselinum crispum*) - Spacing: Height 6 inches, Row 18 inches, Plants 6 inches. Cultural Hints: Grow from seed started in early spring. Slow to germinate. Sun. Uses: Brings out flavor of other herbs. Fine base and seasoning.

SUMMER SAVORY (*Satureia hortensis*) - Spacing: Height 18 inches, Row 18 inches, Plants 18 inches. Cultural Hints: Grows in well-worked loam. Sow seed in spring. Sun. Uses: Use leaves fresh or dry for salads, dressings, stews.

Perennial Herbs

CATNIP (*Nepeta cataria*) - Spacing: Height 3-4 ft., Row 24 inches, Plants 18 inches. Cultural Hints: Hardy, sun or shade. Grow from seed or by division. Uses: Leaves for tea and seasoning.

CHIVES (*Allium shoenoprasum*) - Spacing: Height 12 inches, Row 12 inches, Plants 12 inches. Cultural Hints: Little care. Divide when overcrowded. Grow from seed or by division. Uses: Favorite of chefs. Snip tops finely. Good indoor pot plant. Can be frozen.

HOREHOUND (*Marribium vulgare*) - Spacing: Height 24 inches, Row 18 inches, Plants 15 inches. Cultural Hints: Grow in light soil, full sun, intense heat. Protect in cold climates in winter. Grow from seed, cuttings, or division. Uses: Leaves used in candy or as seasoning.

HYSSOP (*Hyssopus officinalis*) - Spacing: Height 24 inches, Row 18 inches, Plants 15 inches. Cultural Hints: Grows in poor soil from seed. Hardy. Sun. Uses: A mint with highly aromatic, pungent leaves.

LAVENDER (*Lavandula vera*) - Spacing: Height 24 inches, Row 18 inches, Plants 18 inches. Cultural Hints: Grows in dry, rocky, sunny locations with plenty of lime in soil. Uses: Fresh in salads, or flowers dried for sachets, potpourri.

LOVAGE (*Lavisticum officinale*) - Spacing: Height 3-4 ft., Row 30 inches, Plants 30 inches. Cultural Hints: Rich, moist soil. From seed planted in late summer. Sun or partial shade. Uses: Member of the carrot family cultivated in European gardens as an aquaretic and as a substitute for celery in soups and stews.

OREGANO (*Origanum vulgare*) - Spacing: Height 24 inches, Row 18 inches, Plants 9 inches. Cultural Hints: Grows in poor soil from seed or division. Sun. Uses: Flavoring for tomato dishes, pasta.

PEPPERMINT (*Mentha piperata*) - Spacing: Height 36 inches, Row 24 inches, Plants 18 inches. Cultural Hints: Can start from seed, but cuttings, or division recommended. Sun or shade. Cut before it goes to seed. Sun. Uses: Aromatic-used as flavoring, oil used in products such as chewing gum, liqueurs, toilet water, soap, candy.

ROSEMARY (*Rosmarinus officinalis*) - Spacing: Height 3-6 ft., Row 18 inches, Plants 12 inches. Cultural Hints: Grows in well-drained non-acid soil. From cuttings or seed. Sun. Uses: Leaves flavor sauces, meats, and soups.

SAGE (*Salvia officinalis*) - Spacing: Height 18 inches, Row 24 inches, Plants 12 inches. Cultural Hints: From seed or cuttings. Give full sun. Grows slowly from seed. Renew bed every 3-4 years. Uses: Seasoning for meats, herb teas; used either fresh or dried.

SPEARMINT (*Mentha spicata*) - Spacing: Height 18 inches, Row 24 inches, Plants 18 inches. Cultural Hints: Grows in most soils. Hardy. From cuttings, division. Sun. Uses: Aromatic, for flavoring, condiments, teas.

SWEET MARJORAM (*Marjorana hortensis, Origanum marjorana*) - Spacing: Height 12 inches, Row 18 inches, Plants 12 inches. Cultural Hints: From seed or cuttings, as annual, or overwinter as pot plant. Sun. Uses: Seasoning, fresh or dried.

SWEET WOODRUFF (*Asperula adorata*) - Spacing: Height 8 inches, Row 18 inches, Plants 12 inches. Cultural Hints: Keep indoors or in cold frame over winter. Semi-shade. Uses: Flavoring in drinks.

TARRAGON (*Artemisia dracunculus*) - Spacing: Height 24 inches, Row 24 inches, Plants 24 inches. Cultural Hints: Does best in semi-shade; by division or root cuttings. Protect in cold winters. Uses: European herb of aster family; aromatic seasoning. Note: Russian tarragon is grown from seed and has very little flavor.

THYME (*Thymus vulgaris*) - Spacing: Height 8-12 inches, Row 18 inches, Plants 12 inches. Cultural Hints: Grows in light, well-drained soil. Renew plants every few years. By cuttings, seed, division. Sun. Uses: Aromatic foliage for seasoning meats, soups, sauces, and dressings.

WINTER SAVORY (*Satureia montana*) - Spacing: Height 24 inches, Row 15 inches, Plants 18 inches. Cultural Hints: Grow in light, sandy soil. Trim out dead wood. From cuttings or seed. Sun. Uses: Seasoning for stuffing, eggs, sausage; accents strong flavors.

INTENSIVE GARDENING METHODS

If you don't have space for a vegetable garden, or if your present site is too small, consider raising fresh, nutritious, homegrown vegetables in containers. A window sill, patio, balcony or doorstep can provide sufficient space for a productive container garden. Problems with soilborne diseases, nematodes, or poor soil can also be overcome by switching to container gardening.

Grow vegetables that take up little space, such as carrots, radishes and lettuce, or crops that bear fruits over a period of time, such as tomatoes and peppers. Dwarf or miniature varieties may be utilized as they often mature and bear fruit early, but most do not produce as well overall as standard varieties. With increasing interest in container gardening, plant breeders and seed companies are working on vegetables specifically bred for container culture. These varieties are not necessarily miniature or dwarf, and may produce as well as standard types if properly cared for. Trellising is an excellent way to maximize the use of limited space. Many vegetables such as cucumbers and pole beans can be trained up a trellis.

The amount of sunlight that your container garden spot receives may determine which crops can be grown. Generally, root crops and leaf crops can tolerate partial shade, but vegetables grown for their fruits generally need at least 6 hours of full, direct sunlight each day, and perform better with 8-10 hours. Available light can be increased somewhat by providing reflective materials around the plants, e.g., aluminum foil, white-painted surfaces or marble chips.

Container gardening lends itself to attractive plantscaping. A dull patio area can be brightened by the addition of baskets of cascading tomatoes or a colorful herb mix. Planter boxes with trellises can be used to create a cool, shady place on an apartment balcony. Container gardening presents opportunities for many innovative ideas.

Containers

There are many possible containers for gardening. Clay,

wood, plastic, and metal are some of the suitable materials. Specially made vertical garden containers that snap together are also available. These are often advertised for use with strawberry production, but are suitable for many vegetables. Containers for vegetable plants must (1) be big enough to support plants when they are fully grown, (2) hold soil without spilling, (3) have adequate drainage, and (4) never have held products that would be toxic to plants or people. Consider using barrels, flower pots, cut-off milk and bleach jugs, recycled Styrofoam coolers, window boxes, baskets lined with plastic (with drainage holes punched in it), even pieces of drainage pipe or cinder block. If you are building a planting box out of wood, you will find redwood and cedar to be the most rot-resistant, but bear in mind that cedar trees are much more plentiful than redwoods. Wood for use around plants should never be treated with creosote or other wood preservatives. These may be toxic to plants and harmful to people as well.

Some gardeners have built vertical planters out of wood lattice-work lined with black plastic and then filled with a lightweight medium, or out of welded wire shaped into cylinders lined with sphagnum moss and then filled with soil mix. Depending on the size of your vertical planter, 2 inch diameter perforated plastic pipes may be needed inside to aid watering.

Whatever type of container you use, be sure that there are holes in the bottom for drainage so that plant roots do not stand in water. Most plants need containers at least 6-8 inches deep for adequate rooting.

As long as the container meets the basic requirements described above, it can be used. The imaginative use of discarded items or construction of attractive patio planters is a very enjoyable aspect of container gardening. For ease of care, dollies or platforms with wheels or casters can be used to move the containers from place to place. This is especially useful for apartment or balcony gardening so that plants can be moved to get maximum use of available space and sunlight, and to avoid destruction from particularly nasty weather.

Media

A fairly lightweight potting mix is needed for container vegetable gardening. Soil straight from the garden usually cannot be used in a container because it may be too heavy, unless your garden has sandy loam or sandy soil. Garden soil may also harbor diseases and weed seed which can become problematic. Clay soil consists of extremely small (microscopic) particles. In a container, the undesirable qualities of clay are exaggerated. It holds too much moisture when wet, resulting in too little air for the roots, and it pulls away from the sides of the pot when dry. A container medium needs to be porous, because roots require both air and water. Packaged potting soil available at local garden centers is relatively lightweight and may make a good container medium. Soilless mixes such as peat-lite mix work well, but may be too light to support plants sufficiently. Amending such mixes with ⅓ bagged topsoil will help. If the container is also lightweight, a strong wind can blow plants over, resulting in major damage. Soilless mixes are sterile, which is good since they are generally disease and weed seed free. However they tend to contain few nutrients, other than what the manufacturer adds. This means you will have to supplement with fertilizer. Slow release fertilizers are ideal for this situation. Follow label directions.

For a large container garden the expense of prepackaged or soilless mixes may be quite high. Try mixing your own with one part peat moss, one part garden loam, and one part clean coarse (builder's) sand, and a slow release fertilizer (14-14-14) according to container size. Lime may also be needed to bring the pH to around 6.5. In any case, a soil test is helpful in determining nutrient and pH needs, just as in a large garden.

Planting

Plant container crops at the same time you would if you were planting a regular garden. Fill a clean container to within one-half inch of the top with the slightly damp soil mixture. Peat moss in the mix will absorb water and mix much more readily if soaked with warm water before putting the mix in the container. Sow the seeds or set transplants according to instructions on the seed package. Put a label with the name, variety, and date of planting on or in each container. After planting, gently soak the soil with water, being careful not to wash out or displace seeds. Thin seedlings to obtain proper spacing when the plants have two or three leaves. If cages, stakes, or other supports are needed, provide them when the plants are very small to avoid later root damage.

Watering

Pay particular attention to watering container plants. Early on it is easy to overwater container plants, but as the plants become larger watering must be more frequent. Because the volume of soil is relatively small, containers can dry out very quickly, especially on a concrete patio in full sun. Daily or even twice daily watering may be necessary. Apply water until it runs out the drainage holes. On an upstairs balcony this may mean neighbor problems, so make provisions for drainage of water. Large trays filled with coarse marble chips work nicely. However, the soil should never be soggy or have water standing on top of it. When the weather is cool, container plants may be subject to root rots if maintained too wet. Clay pots and other porous containers allow additional evaporation from the sides of the pots and watering must be done more often. Small pots also tend to dry out more quickly than larger ones. If the soil appears to be getting excessively dry (plants wilting every day is one sign), group the containers together so that the foliage creates a canopy to help shade the soil and keep it cool. On a hot patio, you might consider putting containers on pallets or other structures that will allow air movement beneath the pots and prevent direct contact with the cement. Check containers at least once a day and twice on hot, dry or windy days. Feel the soil to determine whether or not it is damp. Mulching and windbreaks can help reduce water requirements for containers. If you are away often, consider an automatic drip emitter irrigation system.

Fertilizing

If you use a soil mix with fertilizer added, then your plants will have enough nutrients for 3-4 weeks. If plants are grown longer than this, add a water-soluble fertilizer at the recommended rate. Repeat every 2-3 weeks. An occasional dose of fish emulsion or compost will add trace elements to the soil. Do not add more than the recommended rate of any fertilizer, since this may cause fertilizer burn and kill the plants. Slow-release fertilizers, which are manufactured with varying release times, are also available. Check the package for release time and amount to use. Container plants do not have the buffer of large volumes of soil and humus to protect them from over-fertilizing or over-liming. Just because a little is good for the plants does not guarantee that more will be better.

General Care

Vegetables grown in containers can be attacked by the various types of insects and diseases that are common to any vegetable garden. Plants should be periodically inspected for the presence of foliage-feeding and fruit-feeding insects, as well as the occurrence of diseases. Protect plants from very high heat caused by light reflection from pavement. Move them to a cool spot or shade them during the hottest part of the day. Plants should be moved to a sheltered location during severe rain, hail, or wind storms, and for protection from fall frosts.

The purpose of an intensively grown garden is to harvest the most produce possible from a given space. More traditional gardens consist of long, single rows of vegetables spaced widely apart. Much of the garden area is taken by the space between the rows. An intensive garden reduces wasted space to a minimum. The practice of intensive gardening is not just for those with limited garden space. Rather, an intensive garden concentrates work efforts to create an ideal plant environment, giving better yields with less labor.

Though its benefits are many, the intensive garden may not be for everyone. Some people enjoy the sight of long, straight rows in their gardens. Others prefer machine cultivation to hand weeding. There is often less weeding to do in intensive plantings because of fewer pathways and closely spaced plants, and the weeding that must be done is usually done by hand or with hand tools. Still other gardeners like to get their gardens planted in a very short period of time and have harvests come in all at once. The intensive ideal is to have something growing in every part of the garden at all times during the growing season.

A good intensive garden requires early, thorough planning to make the best use of time and space in the garden. Interrelationships of plants must be considered before planting, including nutrient needs, shade tolerance, above- and below-ground growth patterns, and preferred growing season. Using the techniques described below, anyone can develop a high-yielding intensive garden.

The Raised Bed

The raised bed or growing bed is the basic unit of an intensive garden. A system of beds allows the gardener to concentrate soil preparation in small areas, resulting in effective use of soil amendments and creating an ideal environment for vegetable growth.

Beds are generally 3-4 feet wide and as long as desired. The gardener works from either side of the bed, reducing the incidence of compaction caused by walking on the soil. Soil preparation is the key to successful intensive gardening. To grow so close together, plants must have adequate nutrients and water. Providing extra synthetic fertilizers and irrigation will help, but there is no substitute for deep, fertile soil high in organic matter. Humus-rich soil will hold extra nutrients, and existing elements that are "locked up" in the soil are released by the actions of earthworms, microorganisms and acids present in a life-filled soil, making them available for plant use. Large amounts of compost are usually added to such beds. Enough, in fact, to alter the soil texture and structure and creating an ideal soil environment for greatest productivity.

If your soil is not deep, double-dig the beds for best results. Remove the top twelve inches of soil from the bed. Insert a spade or spading fork into the next 10-12 inches of soil and wiggle the handle back and forth to break up compacted layers. Do this every 6-8 inches in the bed. Mix the top soil with a generous amount of compost or manure, and return the mixture to the bed. It should be somewhat fluffy and may be raised slightly. To create a true raised bed, take topsoil from the neighboring pathways and mix it in as well.

This is a lot of work! Try it in one or two beds for some of your most valuable plants. If you like the results you can proceed to other beds as you have time. One nice thing about raised bed gardening is that it breaks work into units. Instead of gazing desperately at a garden full of weeds, thinking you'll never have time to clean it up you can look at each bed and say, "I can do that in half an hour today!" Other chores are accomplished with the same ease.

By their nature, raised beds are a form of wide-bed gardening, a technique by which seeds and transplants are planted in wide bands of several rows or broadcast in a wide strip. In general, the goal is to space plants at equal distances from each other on all sides, such that leaves will touch at maturity. This saves space, and the close plantings reduce moisture loss from surrounding soil.

Raised beds can be built even higher than the usual 6-8 inches and can be constructed to be several feet high with wood, brick, or stone. Such a bed is much easier to work and can allow an older person to continue gardening without having to stoop. A walkway can be constructed around such a bed so that a wheelchair may be accessible.

Vertical Gardening

The use of trellises, nets, strings, cages or poles to support growing plants constitutes vertical gardening. This technique is especially suited, but not limited, to gardeners with a small garden space. Vining and sprawling plants, such as cucumbers, tomatoes, melons and pole beans are obvious candidates for this type of gardening. Some plants entwine themselves onto the support, while others may need to be tied. Remember that a vertical planting will cast a shadow, so beware of shading sun-loving crops, or take advantage of the shade by planting shade-tolerant crops near the vertical ones. Plants grown vertically take up much less space

Table 6. Plants grouped according to nutrient needs			
HEAVY FEEDERS	**MEDIUM FEEDERS**	**LIGHT FEEDERS**	**SOIL BUILDERS**
Broccoli	Cucumber	Asparagus	Beans
Cabbage	Eggplant	Sweet-potato	Southern-peas
Cauliflower	Lettuce	Southern-peas	English peas
Corn	Melons		
Onions	Okra		
Peppers	Potatoes		
	Squash		
	Tomatoes		

Although these plants are grouped by their fertilizer requirements, it is a good idea to follow specific crop requirements as well as soil test results.

on the ground, and though the yield per plant may be (but is not always) less, the yield per square foot of garden space is much greater. Because vertically growing plants are more exposed, they dry out faster and may need to be watered more frequently than if they were allowed to spread over the ground. This fast drying is also an advantage to those plants susceptible to fungal diseases. A higher rate of fertilization may be needed, and soil should be deep and well-drained to allow roots to extend vertically, rather than compete with others at a shallow level.

Interplanting

Growing two or more types of vegetables in the same place at the same time is known as interplanting or intercropping. Proper planning is essential to obtain high production and increased quality of the crops planted. This technique has been practiced for thousands of years, but is just now gaining widespread support in this country. To successfully plan an interplanted garden, the following factors must be taken into account for each plant: length of the plant's growth period, its growth pattern (tall, short, below or above ground), possible negative effects on other plants (such as the allelopathic effects of sunflowers and Jerusalem artichokes on nearby plants), preferred season, and light, nutrient and moisture requirements. Interplanting can be accomplished by alternating rows within a bed (plant a row of peppers next to a row of onions), by mixing plants within a row, or by distributing various species throughout the bed. For the beginner, alternating rows may be the easiest to manage at first. Long season (slow maturing) and short season (quick maturing) plants like carrots and

Table 7. Intensive spacing guide*

PLANT	INCHES	PLANT	INCHES
Asparagus	15-18	Lettuce, head	8-12
Beans, lima	4-6	Lettuce, leaf	4-6
Beans, pole	6-12	Melons	18-24
Beans, bush	4-6	Mustard	6-9
Beets	2-4	Okra	12-18
Broccoli	12-18	Onion	2-4
Brussels sprouts	15-18	Peas	2-4
Cabbage	15-18	Peppers	12-15
Cabbage, Chinese	10-12	Potatoes	10-12
Carrots	2-3	Pumpkins	24-36
Cauliflower	15-18	Radishes	2-3
Cucumber	12-18	Rutabaga	4-6
Chard, Swiss	6-9	Southernpea	3-4
Collards	12-15	Spinach	4-6
Endive	15-18	Squash, summer	18-24
Eggplant	18-24	Squash, winter	24-36
Kale	15-18	Sweet corn	15-18
Kohlrabi	6-9	Tomato	18-12
Leeks	3-6	Turnip	4-6

* Note: to determine spacing for interplanting, add the inches for the two crops to be planted together and divide the sum by 2. For example: if radishes are planted next to beans, add 2" + 4"=6", then divide 6" by 2"= 3". The radishes should be planted 3" from the beans.

radishes, respectively, can be planted at the same time. The radishes are harvested before they begin to crowd the carrots. An example of combining growth patterns is planting smaller plants close to larger plants (radishes at the base of beans or broccoli). Shade-tolerant species, like lettuce, spinach, and celery, may be planted in the shadow of taller crops.

Interplanting can help keep insect and disease problems under control. Pests are usually fairly crop-specific; that is, they prefer vegetables of one type or family. Mixing families of plants helps to break up large expanses of the pest-preferred crop, helping to contain early pest damage within a small area. This gives the gardener a little more time to deal with the problem. One disadvantage is that when it does come time to spray for pests. The gardener cannot be sure that all plants are protected.

Interplanting corn with beans and squash was a common planting scheme among Native Americans. Corn would be planted first and runner beans were allowed to climb up the corn. Squash was then interplanted among the corn and beans. These three crops were often referred to as the three sisters.

Spacing

Individual plants are closely spaced in a raised bed or interplanted garden. An equidistant spacing pattern calls for plants to be the same distance from each other within the bed. That is, plant so that the center of one plant is the same distance from plants on all sides of it. In beds of more than two rows, this means that the rows should be staggered so that plants in every other row are between the plants in adjacent rows. The distance recommended for plants within the row on a seed packet is the distance from the center of one plant to the center of the next. This results in an efficient use of space and leaves less area to weed and mulch. The close spacing tends to create a nearly solid leaf canopy, acting as a living mulch, decreasing water loss, and keeping weed problems down. However, plants should not be crowded to the point at which disease problems arise or competition causes stunting.

Succession and Relay Planting

Succession planting is an excellent way to make the most of an intensive garden. To obtain a succession of crops, plant something new in spots vacated by spent plants. Corn after peas is a type of succession.

Planting a spring, summer, and fall garden is another form of succession planting. Cool season crops (broccoli, lettuce, peas) are followed by warm season crops (beans, tomatoes, peppers), and where possible, these may be followed by more cool-season plants or winter crops.

Relaying is another common practice, consisting of overlapping plantings of one type of crop. The new planting is made before the old one is removed. For instance, sweet corn may be planted at two-week intervals for a continuous harvest. This requires some care, though, because crops planted very early are likely to get a slower start because of low temperatures. In the case of corn, it can be disastrous to have two varieties pollinating at the same time, as the quality of the kernels may be affected. For best results, give early planted corn extra time to get started. Another way to achieve the same result is to plant various varieties of the same vegetable at one time. For example, you can plant an early, a mid-, and a late-season corn at the same time to have a lengthy harvest.

Starting seeds indoors for transplanting is an important aspect of intensive gardening. To get the most from the garden plot, a new crop should be ready to take the place of the crop being removed. Several weeks may be gained by having 6-inch transplants ready to go into vacated areas. Remember to recondition the soil for the new plants.

Planning an Intensive Garden

Begin planning your garden early. In January or February when the cold days of winter seem never-ending, pull out last year's garden records and dig into the new seed catalogs. As with any garden, you must decide what crops you want to grow based on your own likes and dislikes, as well as how much of each you will need. An account of which cultivars were most successful or tasted best is helpful in making crop choices. Use the charts below, and your own experience, to determine which crops are likely combinations. Maintaining your own journal can be helpful in determining good vegetable combinations.

Good gardening practices such as watering, fertilizing, crop rotation, composting, and sanitation are especially important in an intensive garden. An intensive garden does require more detailed planning, but the time saved in working the garden and the increased yields make it well worthwhile. Use your imagination and have fun!

RESOURCES

Bartholomew, Mel. *Square Foot Gardening*. Rodale Books.

Maynard, Donald and George Hochmuth. *Knott's Handbook for Vegetable Growers*, 4th Ed. Wiley.

University of Georgia College of Agricultural and Environmental Sciences. *Herbs in Southern Gardens.*Copies are available for sale from CAES Publications http://www.caes.uga.edu/publications/:

University of Georgia College of Family and Consumer Sciences. *So Easy to Preserve*. Comprehensive guide to preserving fruits and vegetables. Copies are available for sale from CAES Publications http://www.caes.uga.edu/publications/:

University of Georgia College of Agricultural and Environmental Sciences. *Georgia Pest Management Handbook*. Copies are available for sale from CAES Publications http://www.caes.uga.edu/publications/:

DISCUSSION QUESTIONS

1. Why is planning and record keeping so important to successful gardening?

2. What is the difference between succession planting and rotation?

3. Name 3 warm season and 3 cool season vegetables.

4. Why are legumes so important to soil fertility?

5. Name a perennial vegetable crop.

6. What is the final step in producing a quality transplant?

7. Name 2 important criteria in site selection for a vegetable garden.

8. What is the benefit of using a starter solution?

9. What is relay planting and what is intercropping?

10. Name 2 items that would be part of a soilless mix.

17

Diagnosing Vegetable Garden Problems

George E. Boyhan

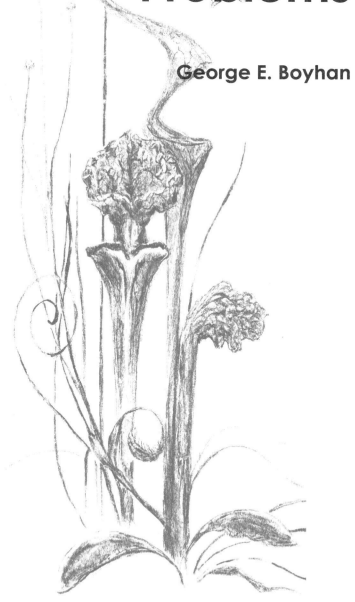

LEARNING OBJECTIVES

Identify common insect pests of small fruit and tree fruit.

Be familiar with common diseases of small fruit and tree fruit.

Identify some common ways to prevent the spread of diseases in tree fruit.

Know some common cultural problems in vegetable gardening.

Know some common insect pests of vegetables and control methods.

Be familiar with common diseases of vegetables.

Know common disease control methods in the vegetable garden.

TERMS TO KNOW

Cover crop crop that improves the soil in which it is grown.

Crop rotation rowing crops of a specific family in different areas of the garden each year to avoid soilborne diseases and nutrient depletion.

Cultural control use of good gardening techniques to control pest populations.

Disease resistance tendency not to be infected by a particular pathogen.

Disease tolerance ability of a plant to continue growing without severe symptoms despite being infected by a pathogen.

Fallow cultivated land that is allowed to lie idle for a growing season.

Inorganic being or composed of matter other than plant and animal; often of mineral origin.

Renovation removing an old planting and putting in a new one or removing and replacing only part of a planting.

Symptom evidence of disease or damage

Vector organism that transmits a disease-causing pathogen.

VEGETABLE PROBLEMS

Diagnosing growth, plant, and fruiting problems will be easier if the person making the diagnosis has experience and knowledge in gardening. Extension publication #577, Home Gardening, can be a valuable reference in gaining this knowledge about vegetable crops. Growth disorders of vegetable crops can be caused by various factors not related to insect or disease damage. Growth disorders can sometimes be the result of a combination of interrelated factors, and a correct diagnosis of the problem can only be determined if all factors are known.

Soil Test

Soil fertility, soil pH, rainfall, temperature, variety, date of planting, and herbicide applications can individually or collectively affect quality. Nutrient deficiencies in vegetable crops caused by a shortage of specific nutrients or low soil pH reduces the plant's ability to function normally. After these factors reach certain critical levels, deficiency symptoms become evident.

Soil testing enables you to supply nutrients in adequate amounts and helps prevent deficiencies. Most all nutrients required for normal plant growth are more readily available at a pH of 6.0 - 6.5. Correcting soil acidity by applying dolomitic limestone to the soil in time to correct an acid condition before the crop is planted can prevent many nutrient deficiency problems.

Deficiency Problems

Magnesium—Low soil pH and a low level of soil magnesium usually result in various foliage and fruit disorders. Soil magnesium levels testing below 60 pounds per acre on the Coastal Plain (south Georgia) soils and below 120 pounds per acre on the Piedmont (north Georgia) soils usually result in magnesium deficiencies in vegetables. For instance, magnesium deficient sweet corn will show a streaked leaf blade. The streaks are characterized by pale streaks between the darker veins and the streaks run the full length of the blade.

Bell pepper plants with a magnesium deficiency will show a pale discoloration beginning at the leaf tip and spreading to areas between the veins. Deficiencies that develop soon after transplanting result in stunted growth; plants do not recover unless magnesium is applied soon after the deficiency develops.

Tomato leaves showing magnesium deficiencies have a blotchy condition between the veins. Severe magnesium deficiency can cause marginal dieback on leaf tips. A calcium deficiency will produce almost the same discoloration, but is usually seen nearer the leaf tip.

Manganese—In very acid soils some microelements such as manganese are made more readily available for plant absorption. When this condition exists, some plants such as snap beans, can absorb this nutrient in excessive amounts to the point that the element becomes toxic to the plant. Bronze-colored, puckered foliage in the bean plant indicates manganese toxicity. Manganese deficiency can occur on very sandy soils with pH of 6.3 or above. The amount of manganese recommended is determined by soil pH, with no manganese recommendation on soils with below a pH of 5.7 regardless if manganese tests low. Nitrogen and phosphorus applications can increase the uptake of manganese.

Phosphorus—Most vegetable foliage showing a phosphorus deficiency will have a bluish purple discoloration. On sweet corn the discoloration will normally be seen on the outer edge of the leaf blade. Phosphorus deficiency symptoms are fairly common on very early planted sweet corn growing in cold soil. If soil phosphorus levels are adequate, this condition usually corrects itself when the soil warms up. Phosphorus deficient tomato leaves will usually show a purple veining effect on the underside of the leaf. This condition is often seen on recently transplanted, young, actively growing tomato plants and usually corrects itself after new feeder roots are established. High phosphorus liquid fertilizers are often applied at transplanting to improve early plant growth. Such high phosphorus fertilizers are referred to as 'pop-up' fertilizers because of the dramatic effect they have on plant growth during the cooler weather in early spring when phosphorus deficiency is most apt to occur.

Boron—Boron deficiency in vegetable crops usually shows up as an internal defect of stems or fruits as they approach maturity. Turnip roots will have a purple ring discoloration that is usually close to the outer surface. 20 Mule Team Borax may be used. White rings that develop just under the tomato skin can be caused by high temperatures. The only control is to keep the tomato plants healthy with a lot of foliage to shade the fruit. Boron deficiency can be affected by a number of factors including high pH, high soil calcium levels, and liberal applications of nitrogen. Dry weather also reduces boron availability.

Molybdenum—If small, individual white spots are seen near the center of the fruit, then a molybdenum deficiency should be suspected. The leaf blade on severely molybdenum-deficient tomato plants will be more narrow than usual.

A condition called 'white core' occurs near the center of the tomato fruit and causes a larger area than that caused by molybdenum deficiencies. White core is a physiological disorder and can be variety-associated. Most tomato varieties recommended for Georgia do not have this condition.

Calcium—A disorder on the blossom-end of tomatoes where the tissues take on a sunken, leathery appearance is called blossom-end rot. This condition is also found on bell pepper and watermelons. Low soil calcium and fluctuating soil moisture aggravates this situation as can heavy rains during periods of rapid growth. Liming to correct soil acidity can help correct this problem. Spraying young plants with calcium chloride (4 tbsp/gal water) may also help. Mulching and irrigating will aid in preventing this condition. (Also seen more on pruned tomato plants.) Blossom-end rot is prone to occur on oblong watermelon fruit, compared to round fruit, especially when plants are grown on soil low in calcium, and also when soils are acid. Calcium chloride sprays may help prevent this problem. Use the same rates as those recommended for tomatoes.

Physiological Disorders

Physiological conditions can result in disorders of vegetables, especially as they approach maturity. Inadequate soil moisture for prolonged periods, followed by excessive water, can cause fruit cracking in tomatoes and watermelons. Mulching plants and timing irrigations to prevent moisture stress in plants can prevent these problems.

Physiological cracking of tomatoes is usually one of two types. Radial cracking and cracks running around the shoulder of the tomato are called 'concentric cracking'. Both types of cracking can be influenced by variety and both can be aggravated by unfavorable growing conditions. Severe pruning of the tomato plant also increases this condition on susceptible varieties. Excessive moisture at or near harvest can increase both radial and concentric cracking. Radial cracking is more prone to occur as fruit near harvest particularly under very hot conditions and wet soil conditions. Fruit expand rapidly resulting in this type of cracking. Concentric cracking is more prone to occur with alternating periods of rapid and slow growth. 'Cat facing' is the distorted growth of the tomato, and is related to fruit set during very cool weather. Adhesion of the flower to the outside of the emerging fruit and inadequate pollination during cool weather are believed to be the cause of this problem.

Irish potatoes that experience drought conditions as they approach maturity can be forced into the semi-dormant state. As temperature and moisture conditions become favorable for growth, the dormant eyes on the tuber can begin to develop on the parent tuber. Results are small tuber development on older tubers. 'Hollow heart' of Irish potatoes is a physiological condition that occurs when slowed growth is followed by rapid expansion of the tubers brought about by excessive moisture and over fertilization. Some varieties are more susceptible than others to this condition.

Tight heads of snow-white color in cauliflower result from excluding all sunlight. Tying wrapper leaves over the heads when they are the size of a quarter as they develop will insure a white cauliflower head, even on the so-called 'self-blanching' varieties. Covering heads with older leaves is extra insurance, since failure to exclude sunlight results in a loose, ricey curd that is brown in color and off-flavor in taste.

Many crops require complete pollination of the female part of the bloom in order to have fruit develop normally. This is especially true with members of the cucumber, watermelon, and squash family. Cross-pollination in the cucumber family is dependent on insects. Members of this family that develop into bottle shapes are the result of incomplete pollination of the female bloom. Tomato blooms are self-pollinating and do not require insects to transfer the pollen.

Both low temperatures (below 55 degrees F) and high temperatures (above 90 degrees F) can damage or kill pollen. Pollen killed by low or high temperatures will result in cracked fruit on the blossom-end of immature fruit. Inadequate pollination in tomatoes can result in the seed cavity not being filled normally; this will result in puffy fruit.

Sweet corn is pollinated by wind-blown pollen. Lack of adequate pollen will result in poorly filled ears. High humidity, foggy mornings and excessive rain during pollination can result in poorly filled ears. A physiological condition that sometimes occurs in sweet corn is one where juvenile corn ears are formed in the tassels. The reason for this condition is not understood, but when this condition occurs, there seems to be little problem with proper pollination of the corn ears. During some seasons, sweet corn plants produce an excessive amount of suckers. These can be removed early in the season or left on the plant. There is no advantage in removal, except to allow equipment to move up and down the row.

'Tomato leaf roll' is fairly common, and may or may not be associated with moisture stress, disease, or nematode problems. If soil moisture is adequate and no disease or nematode problems are present, the leaf roll is usually an indication that the tomato plant is setting a heavy fruit load. Leaf roll is usually more severe on heavily pruned plants.

Hail stones can cause severe crop damage at times. Shredded collard leaves is one example. Immature tomato fruit, when struck by hail stones, will develop a white bruised spot that remains white even after the fruit turns red.

Irish potatoes, exposed to bright light, will turn green on the surface. This green color is due to a chemical called, "solanine" which becomes more concentrated in the presence of bright light. This chemical will be found concentrated just under the potato skin. If these potatoes are to be eaten, it is recommended that they be peeled deeply, cooked in boiling water and the cooking water discarded. Solanine is a poison that is highly water soluble and most will be discarded in the water.

Physical Damage

Rabbits and deer cause considerable damage to gardens each year. Some plants like soybeans and Southernpeas may recover if the tops are eaten after germination. Others may not recover. Human hair has been suggested as a deterrent to both rabbits and deer. Unwashed, non-sprayed hair apparently works best. Wrap small amounts of hair in mesh bags, tie, and hang around outside of the garden. Space bags three to five feet apart and 12 inches from the ground for rabbit problems. For deer, space bags 8 to 10 feet apart and three feet from ground.

Other commercially available animal deterrents are available, which may or may not be effective. The most effective method of control is a fence. Electric fences require less material and can be quite effective. In populated areas, such fences should be clearly marked as electric and may in fact be prohibited.

INSECT PESTS OF VEGETABLES

Importance of Pests—Insect pests are capable of destroying every kind of vegetable grown in the home garden. There are few years when a southern garden can escape damage in appearance. Stand reductions, foliage loss, yield reductions, reduced pod set, pod drop, and fruit rots are but a few examples of insect damage to garden vegetables.

Steps in Managing Pests—Approaches to the management of insect pests by home gardeners in Georgia range from "spray-weekly" to "totally-organic." The main objective should be best control of pests by using all practical approaches (cultural, mechanical, chemical, etc.). A compromise between "spray-weekly" and "totally-organic" approaches is best.

Five basic steps essential to proper management of garden pests are:

1) Prevention

2) Early Detection

3) Correct Identification of Pests

4) Proper Selection of Control Method(s)

5) Correct Application of Control(s)

Prevention

Site Selection—Selection of a good gardening site is essential to successful gardening. Although major considerations should include soil fertility, drainage, accessibility, etc., gardeners may also reduce insect problems with proper site selection and preparation. Several species of soil insects feed on the roots and seeds of garden vegetables. Many of these pests are harbored on weeds or grasses in the garden before vegetables are planted.

Good Cultural Practices—Healthy plants are able to tolerate more pest damage than weak sickly ones. For best results vegetable varieties best suited for the area should be used and the correct amounts of fertilizers, lime, and water should be used. A soil test can be obtained through the county extension office.

Crop Rotation—Under gardening conditions major changes take place in the character of plants grown on the land. These changes affect the insect population of the area in two general ways. Many of those which depend on the plants of one family, or even one species of plant, find their food supply cut off and may nearly disappear from the area, as certain species of billbugs from drained bottom lands. Others take to the cultivated vegetables, closely related to their wild hosts, and find them, perhaps, more palatable. Such insects may become very destructive.

Crop rotations are most effective for insects that are restricted feeders, for those that have limited powers of migration or sluggish habits, and on those which are slow developing in the feeding stage. Many home garden sites become permanent and are never rotated to new areas. Although space restrictions may prevent movement of the garden site, vegetable types within the same garden spot can be grown in a different location each year. Additionally, gardeners may choose to practice diversified planting. Since many insect pests attack plants belonging to a certain species or family, and reject unrelated ones, related vegetable groups should be separated. Groups of related vegetables are as follows:

- Cole crops - cabbage, cauliflower, collards, Brussels sprouts, broccoli
- Solanaceous crops - tomato, pepper, eggplant, potato
- Greens - lettuce, endive, mustard, turnips (tops)
- Root crops - radishes, turnips, beets, carrots, sweet potato
- Bean, pea
- Sweet corn
- Cucurbit crops - cucumbers, gourds, melons, pumpkin, squash
- Alliums - onion, garlic, elephant garlic, leek, chives

Resistant Varieties—Some vegetables are resistant to certain insects. Differences in degree of susceptibility to insect damage may vary considerably with variety or cultivar of vegetable grown. In the southern U.S., where diseases may destroy an entire crop, emphasis has been placed on breeding vegetables which resist disease. Some varieties planted in the southern states are resistant to insects. One word of caution — insect resistance in plants is often interpreted as an absolute protection. In reality, it is a term for distinguishing varieties which show less damage when compared to other varieties under similar growing conditions. Some varieties may be less tasty to insect pests, may possess certain physical or chemical properties which discourage insects from feeding or laying eggs, or may be able to support large populations of insects without suffering much damage.

Before buying seeds or plants, seed catalogs should be checked for information on resistant varieties which will grow well in the area. Some varieties may be resistant to insect attack but subject to certain other restrictions, such as soil pH, drainage, or temperatures. Experience with different varieties will indicate the ones best suited for the area in question.

Sanitation: Destruction of Vegetable Residue—Plant destruction after the last harvest will eliminate or reduce insect buildup. Many insects will mature or overwinter in the stems, leaves, and roots of the plants they feed on. Removing debris will reduce pest populations. Proper composting is an excellent method of disposing of these residues.

Correct Application Methods—The pattern of insecticide treatments (preventive and curative) depends largely on the insect pest involved, its biology, and life cycle. Generally, insecticides are used after an insect infestation is found. Repeat treatments of insecticides may be necessary at specific intervals if the infestation continues. Follow label directions carefully when using insecticides.

GENERAL PESTS OF GARDEN VEGETABLES

Corn Earworm

Description—A fully-grown corn earworm (tomato fruitworm) larvae is up to 1¾ inches long; variable in color from light green to pink to brown to nearly black, marked with alternating light and dark stripes running lengthwise on the body. The head is yellow and unspotted, and the legs are dark or black. The skin of the larva is coarse with short black hairs (like those of a two-day-old beard), but a 10x lens is needed to see them.

Vegetable Hosts—Corn earworms will feed on a wide range of vegetables, including beans, peas, sweet corn, okra, tomatoes, cabbage, eggplant, and pepper.

Damage—Corn earworms chew holes in the pods of beans, peas, okra eggplant and pepper. On sweet corn, earworms chew buds and leaves in the whorl resulting in large ragged holes as the leaves unfold, and possibly, stunted growth. They later feed on the silks and kernels from the tip of the ear downward. There is seldom more than one corn earworm found in each ear since they are cannibalistic. Removal of silks by larval feeding may interfere with pollination, and various mold fungi may be introduced into the ear. Corn earworms rarely feed on cabbage, but when they chew into buds the plant will not cup (head) normally. Instead, a series of "Brussels sprouts" grow around the base. On tomatoes, corn earworms chew holes in leaves, blossoms and fruit. The larva is rather restless and may feed on several fruits, causing them to rot.

Control—Plant as early as the weather permits. Early maturing vegetables will escape damage from earworm infestations occurring late in the season. As soon as larvae are found, a recommended insecticide should be used. In corn, simply cutting off the damaged tip of the ear may be the simplest solution.

Aphids (Plant Lice)

Description—Adult - Aphids are small, soft-bodied, yellow or pale green to black insects about ⅛ inch long with two tail pipes (cornicles). These pests begin damaging vegetables early in the spring when colonies or clusters can be found near growing points and under leaves. They may be found throughout the entire growing season.

Vegetable Hosts—Aphids feed on a wide range of vegetable hosts including cole crops, cucurbits, beans, peas, potatoes, tomatoes, lettuce, turnips, spinach, and other garden crops.

Damage—Adults and young suck plant juices; leaves thicken, wrinkle, and turn yellow or brown. Small plants may be severely weakened or killed. Aphids also vector (carry) plant viruses from diseased to healthy plants.

Control—Observe small plants closely after rapid growth begins in the spring. In some cases, gardeners may be able to wash aphids from plants with a forceful stream of water until the population is no longer a problem. After July 1st, aphids are more likely to be viruliferous (carrying plant viruses) and should be treated with a recommended insecticide as soon as colonies are found. Early detection is very important after July 1st, since a single feeding can introduce a virus to healthy plants. They are particularly problematic for transmitting a number of viruses between squash and related vegetables.

Spider Mites (Red Spiders)

Description—Adults -Spider mites are tiny (barely visible) red, orange, yellow, or green pests that suck juices from the undersides of leaves. As large populations develop during hot, dry weather, leaves of infested plants become covered with fine webs resembling spider webs.

Vegetable Hosts—Vegetables most seriously injured are beans (particularly snap beans), corn, tomato, and eggplant.

Damage—In periods of dry, hot weather the leaves of beans and other vegetables become blotched with white or pale yellow to brown spots ranging from small specks to large areas. This damage results when mites withdraw plant juices. The leaves progressively become pale, sickly yellow and brown before dropping from plants.

Control—Overwintering mites may be reduced in number by destruction of weeds such as pokeweed, Jimson weed, wild blackberry, and wild geranium around and within the garden. Maintaining adequate soil moisture will also prevent the development of mite "explosion". Frequent high pressure syringing of plants with water will reduce mite populations also, but, in most cases, recommended miticides will be needed with applications made on a short (3-4 day) spray interval.

Southern Green Stink Bug

Description—Adult - Adult stink bugs are shield-shaped, flat, bright green insects about ⅝ inch long, with wings and a narrow head. When crushed, stink bugs give off a foul odor. Young - The young or nymphs resemble the adults in shape but are somewhat more rounded than shield-shaped. Nymphs are wingless and green-orange and black in color.

Vegetable Hosts—Lima beans, okra, tomatoes, and cucurbits are favorite hosts. Damage to sweet corn may also occur.

Damage—Stink bugs withdraw plant juices from leaves and fruit of vegetables while injecting a toxic saliva. Feeding on leaves results in yellow spots with a halo. Characteristic damage to fruit varies with the type of vegetable. On lima beans, there is little evidence of feeding on the outside of the pods, but when the damaged beans are removed, they are shriveled and spotted with slick brown stains. Okra pods damaged by stink bugs become distorted with wart-like growths or pimples where feeding occurs. Tomatoes express signs of stink bug feeding as white spots on immature fruit and whitish yellow spots on mature (red) fruit. The leaves of sweet corn become twisted in a spiral fashion when stink bugs withdraw plant juices.

Control—Removal of weeds from within and around the garden may aid in reducing stink bug numbers. But due to the numerous weed hosts, a recommended insecticide should be applied as soon as stink bugs are observed.

Flea Beetles

Description—Adult Flea beetles are very small, black, or striped shiny insects ⅟16 to ⅟18 inch long. These pests jump readily when disturbed. Two species are often seen in large numbers in early spring (May) feeding on weeds.

Vegetable Hosts—Some flea beetles are rather general feeders, but the majority attack only one plant or the closely related crops of a single plant family. Among the most destructive garden species in Georgia are the potato flea beetle, spinach flea beetle, striped flea beetle and sweet potato flea beetle. Tomatoes, peppers, eggplant, and cucumbers are also subject to severe injury.

Damage—Injury to vegetables by flea beetles consists of very small, rounded, or irregular holes eaten in leaves.

Feeding usually results in a shot-hole appearance in leaves. When flea beetles become abundant, the foliage of garden vegetables may be so badly eaten that it can no longer function. These small holes may provide entry of plant pathogens (bacteria, fungi, etc.), and the beetles may carry disease organisms from one plant to another. The potato flea beetle can spread early potato blight in this way, and the corn flea beetle carries bacterial wilt. In addition to damage by adults, the immature flea beetles commonly feed on the roots of the same plants. On sweet potatoes, flea beetle larvae cause long winding trails in the roots. Light damage can often be ignored in a healthy fast growing plant that is rapidly putting out new leaves.

Control—Removal of weed hosts will often reduce flea beetle populations. When heavy beetle populations are observed on weeds surrounding the garden, insecticide treatment of garden margins may prevent entry of this pest. When beetles and damage are seen, recommended insecticides should be applied before serious damage occurs.

INSECTS OF SPECIFIC VEGETABLE CROPS: Beans and Peas

Bean Leaf Beetle

Description—Adult - reddish orange, a black band around outer wing margin and usually three to four black spots where wings meet; about ¼ inch long; adults pass the winter in or near the garden in rubbish and weeds. Larvae - slender white larvae.

Damage—Adults chew rounded holes on the undersides of leaves and on stems of seedlings. Larvae bore into roots and nodules and sometimes chew tissue completely around the stems.

Control—Cleaning up in and around the garden helps to reduce overwintering places for adults. The garden should be plowed or tilled soon after harvest. A recommended insecticide should be applied as soon as beetles are first noticed.

Cowpea Curculio

Description—Adult - black, hump-backed, hardshelled beetles, nearly ¼ inch long, with a slender snout and prominent round punctures (dimples) on the back. Larvae - whitish, legless grubs inside the pods.

Damage—adults cause black, wart-like strings on surface of pods by feeding and egg-laying. Larvae develop

from eggs deposited inside pods. Larvae feed on one or more peas during their course of development.

Control—Where possible, remove broomsedge and bluestem from garden edge to reduce overwintering sites, but this is one pest for which preventive insecticide applications are needed. A recommended insecticide should be applied beginning when the first blooms are found on Southernpeas, and repeat applications are needed on a three-day schedule until four or five treatments have been given.

Mexican Bean Beetle

Description—Adults are coppery-brown rounded beetles about ¼ inch long, with sixteen black spots on the back. Adults spend the winter in rubbish and weeds. Young are yellowish, soft-bodied, and fuzzy. Clusters of yellow eggs are laid under the leaves.

Damage—Leaves appear lacy from adults and young chewing on the undersides.

Control—Handpick adults and young if the numbers are not great and crush the eggs. Clean up plant debris after harvest to reduce overwintering adults. Plant early; pick mature pods promptly. For a heavy infestation apply a recommended insecticide.

European Corn Borer

Description—Larvae - Flesh-colored larvae with rows of small, round, dark-brown spots; dark brown head; up to one inch long.

Damage—Larvae bore into stems and pods of plants and may cause stem breakage. Heaviest damage occurs late in the season.

Control—Apply a recommended insecticide.

Lesser Cornstalk Borer

Description—Slender, bluish-green, brown-striped caterpillars about ¾ inch long when fully grown. These larvae are often found associated with silken tubes beginning at the soil line.

Damage—Stand reduction may occur as larvae bore into stems and kill plants. Damage is most severe on dry, sandy soil.

Control—Winter plowing and early planting of peas will help avoid heavy infestations. Apply a recommended insecticide when characteristic damage is found, or for late plantings use a preventive treatment at planting.

Thrips

Description—Adults - Extremely small (1/25 inch long); yellow or brown active insects with wings. Nymphs are similar to adult but smaller and wingless. Thrips often feed on weeds in and around the garden.

Damage—Adults and larvae suck plant juices and cause whitish blotches; they may distort seedlings and pods and interfere with pollination. Important insect for the transmission of Tomato Spotted Wilt Virus.

Control—Weeds in and around the garden should be removed to reduce the build-up of thrips. Apply a recommended insecticide.

Whiteflies

Description—Adults - Very small sucking insects with two pairs of broadly rounded wings covered with a snow-white, waxy powder. They look like tiny moths and fly out in a cloud when disturbed. Larvae (nymphs and crawlers) - Very small, flat, scale-like insects; difficult to see. All stages feed on the undersides of leaves and excrete honeydew.

Damage—Leaf discoloration and leaf drop; stunting of plants caused by the whitefly sucking plant juices. A sooty mold grows on the honeydew causing a black, unsightly appearance on the leaves.

Control—Use a recommended insecticide. Make sure when you purchase transplants that they are not already infested with whiteflies. Infected transplants can introduce them to your garden early in the season.

Lima Bean Vine Borer

Description—Robust, cylindrical, bluish-green caterpillar that bores into vines of lima beans; about one inch long.

Damage—Bores into vines of lima beans (butter beans) causing enlarged gall-like areas on stems and death of growing points.

Control—Destroy crop residue and cultivate soil during the winter. Use recommended insecticides.

CUCUMBERS, MELONS, SQUASH AND PUMPKINS

Spotted Cucumber Beetle

Description—Adult - Greenish yellow, black heads; slender, about 1/4 inch long. Adults overwinter at the base of plants which are not entirely killed down by the frost.

Damage—The beetles eat holes in the leaves and flowers and carry bacterial wilt. They may attack young seedlings even before they emerge.

Control—Protect young plants by cone-shaped netting or screen protectors until runners develop; clean up weeds to reduce overwintering adults, or apply a recommended insecticide.

Striped Cucumber Beetle

Description—Adult - Pale yellow to orange, three black stripes on wings, black-heads; about 1/4 inch long. Larvae - White, brownish at the ends; slender.

Damage—Adults feed on the leaves, stems, and fruit and carry bacterial wilt. Larvae sometimes feed on underground stems and roots of cucumbers and related plants.

Control—Cover seedlings with netting or cone-shaped screens until runners form or apply a recommended insecticide.

Leafminers

Description—Winding, white trails or broad white spots appear on leaves made by small white or yellow legless maggots feeding between the two surfaces of the leaf. Several generations in a summer.

Damage—The leaves may be greatly weakened. The mines or tunnels which the leafminer makes may serve as points where disease and decay may start; however, a small amount of damage per leaf does not usually justify treatment.

Control—Hand pick infested leaves, if practical, before the larvae pupate and begin another generation, or use a recommended pesticide.

Pickleworm

Description—Yellowish white caterpillar with dark spots when young; old larvae are greenish or coppery; up to 3/4 inch long; overwinters in south Florida and moves northward each year.

Damage—Cucumbers, cantaloupes and squash may be seriously injured; watermelons rarely; pumpkins not at all. The pickleworm burrows into buds, blossoms, vines, and fruits and pushes out small masses of green, sawdust-like excrement from holes in the fruit causing rotting and loss of fruit.

Control—Plant as early as the weather will allow. Apply a recommended insecticide during the fruiting period.

Squash Bug

Description—Adult - The winged adult is dingy gray-black and nearly an inch long, with a narrow head. Adults and nymphs have a very disagreeable odor when crushed. Nymph - Resembles adult in general shape. Newly hatched nymphs have reddish heads and legs and green bodies. Later they become darker, the head and legs turning black and the body light to dark gray.

Damage—Adults and young suck plant juices. Young plants can be severely weakened or killed. Older plants often have one or more runners damaged. Leaves on damaged runners wilt and become crisp and dark brown.

Control—If only a few vines are involved, the easiest control method is hand collection of eggs and bugs. Garden sanitation reduces overwintering populations. For a large infestation, apply a recommended insecticide.

Squash Vine Borer

Description—Thick, white, wrinkled, brown-headed caterpillars, up to one inch long. Produces yellowish, sawdust-like excrement from holes in the vines.

Damage—The larvae bore into the stems of squashes, pumpkins, gourds, cucumbers and muskmelons. Winter squash (in particular Hubbard), pumpkins, and zucchini are quite susceptible to borer damage. Infested vines at first exhibit wilting, and later may be completely girdled, causing the the leaves and stem beyond the point of attack to rot. Late in the season, some tunneling in and damage to fruit may occur.

Control—Plant as early as the weather will allow. With few infested plants, stems can be split and larvae removed. A spade-full of moist soil should be placed over damaged stems to encourage new root growth. Apply a recommended insecticide weekly during the fruiting period.

CABBAGE, COLLARDS, BROCCOLI, AND TURNIPS

Cabbage Maggot

Description—Yellowish white; legless larva; blunt at the rear end and pointed at the front; about ¼ to ⅓ inch long. The adult fly lays eggs in the soil around the base of the plant, and the eggs hatch into the maggots that burrow down to nearby roots.

Damage—The maggots are destructive in seed beds and in young transplants. They feed on the roots and stems just below the surface; seedlings wilt, turn yellow, and die. Infested cabbage rarely produces a head. Maggots are also believed to introduce a fungus causing blackleg and to spread bacterial soft rot.

Control—Treat the soil or the transplants with a recommended insecticide, or protect seedlings from egg-laying adults with a square of tar paper laid flat on the ground around the stem, or cover with mesh or screening to exclude the fly. Seeds planted in cold, damp soil are frequently attacked by cabbage maggots. In the spring, wait until the soil warms up and is sufficiently dry before you plant.

Cabbageworm — Cabbage Looper

Description—Pale green, smooth-skinned worms up to 1¼ inches long, which make a loop in the middle of the body as they move along the plant. Brown pupae are attached to one side of a plant leaf during the growing season.

Damage—Large holes are eaten in leaves. Enough leaf tissue may be consumed to interfere with plant growth. Larvae may be present in the heads and go unnoticed until cooking.

Control—It is very important to control these larvae while they are small, because larger ones are quite difficult to control. Conventional chemical insecticides often fail. Applications of Bacillus thuringiensis (Dipel or Thuricide) are usually needed to keep populations under control.

Cabbageworm — Diamondback Moth Caterpillar

Description—Greenish-yellow with black hairs; slightly pointed at both ends; wiggles rapidly when disturbed and hangs from a silk thread; about ⅓ inch long; overwinters as a pupa in the leaves of the host plant.

Damage—Larvae chew holes in all parts of the plants, but prefer bud area. Larvae may be present in heads but go unnoticed until cooking.

Control—Clean up old plants after harvest to destroy pupae. Apply a recommended insecticide.

Cabbageworm — Imported Cabbageworm

Description—Velvety green with a narrow orange

stripe down the middle of the back and a broken yellowish stripe along each side; about 1¼ inches long; overwinters as pupae in the leaves of the host plant or other objects nearby.

Damage—The larvae chew holes in the leaves and are more likely to feed near the center of the plant. Larvae may be present in the head and go unnoticed until cooking.

Control—Clean up old plants after harvest to remove pupae. Apply a recommended insecticide.

Harlequin Bug

Description—Adult - Shiny red and black flat, shield shaped; about ⅜ inch long. Nymph - red and black, oval, no wings. Eggs - white with black rings; barrel shaped; laid in double rows under the leaves. Adults overwinter around trash and old plants in and around the garden. Bug has a disagreeable odor.

Damage—Sucking adults and nymphs cause yellow splotches; leaves wilt, turn brown, and die.

Control—Handpick bugs and crush their eggs as they appear; if necessary, apply a recommended insecticide.

SWEET CORN

European Corn Borer

Description— Flesh-colored; rows of small, round, dark-brown spots; dark brown head; up to one inch long; overwinters as a caterpillar in the stalk.

Damage—The borer feeds in tassels and young leaves in the whorl, soon moving to tunnel in the stalks and the ear; it may enter the ear at the base, side or tip. Broken tassels and stalks, shredded leaves, sawdust castings outside small holes in the stalk and ear are signs of the borer.

Control—Remove old plants after harvest to reduce borers. Apply a recommended insecticide when the corn borers are first seen in the whorl, and before they enter the stalk and ear.

Fall Armyworm

Description—Adult - light green to black, striped; black head with inverted white Y on the front of the head; about 1½ inches long; feeds at night.

Damage—The armyworm attacks the young emerging leaves in the whorl and the ear in a manner similar to the corn earworm. Fall armyworms will chew through the husks to attack the kernels, whereas corn earworms enter the tip. Often several fall armyworms are found in an ear.

Control—Plant early. Apply a recommended insecticide.

ONION

Onion Maggot

Description—Small white maggots without legs or distinct head, about ⅓ inch long that bore through the underground stems and bulbs.

Damage—Thinning of stands often when maggots tunneling in small bulbs cause the plant to die. Damaged bulbs that are harvested will rot in storage.

Control—Avoid planting onions in an area that is high in partially decomposed organic matter. Cull onions should be removed from the garden after harvest. In areas with a history of onion maggot problems, treat the soil with an appropriate soil insecticide before planting.

Thrips

Description—Adult - Extremely small (1/25 inch long), yellow or brown active insects with wings. Nymph - Similar to adult but smaller and wingless; thrips often feed on weeds in and around the garden.

Damage—Adults and larvae suck plant juices and cause whitish blotches. Tips of leaves may become distorted and die back. With severe infestations entire plants may wither and fall over.

Control—Set onions should not be grown near seed onions. Weeds in and around the garden should be removed to reduce build-up of thrips. Certain varieties of sweet Spanish onions possess considerable resistance to injury. Beginning when thrips are numerous enough to cause scarring of leaves, two or three applications of recommended insecticide should be made at weekly intervals.

POTATO (IRISH AND SWEETPOTATO)

Colorado Potato Beetle

Description—Adult - Yellow and black striped, hard shelled beetle about ⅜ inch long. Larva - Brick-red, humpbacked, soft-bodied larva with rows of black spots along each side of the body. Eggs - Orange, barrel-shaped eggs laid on the leaves.

Damage—Adults and larvae eat holes in leaves, an effect that is especially damaging to small Irish potato plants.

Control—Adults, larvae, and the eggs may be hand-picked from plants and destroyed. Apply a recommended insecticide as soon as adult beetles are seen. If the first application is made before egg-laying, repeat treatments are unnecessary.

Leafhopper

Description—Small, very active, greenish, slender, wedge-shaped jumping insect up to ⅛ inch long.

Damage—The leafhopper sucks sap from undersides of leaves causing leaf tips to turn brown, followed by the browning and curling of entire leaf margin.

Control—Apply a recommended insecticide.

Potato Tuberworm

Description—Adult - White caterpillars up to ¾ inch long with a pinkish or greenish tinge and brown at both ends.

Damage—Larvae burrow into stems and petioles, and mine the leaves of plants. The tubers of Irish potatoes in the field and in storage are riddled with slender, dirty-looking, silk-lined burrows.

Control—Keep potatoes well cultivated and deeply buried in hills during growth. Infested vines should be removed before digging to avoid larval movement to tubers. A recommended insecticide should be used on growing potatoes and on potatoes in storage when infestations are observed.

White Grub

Description—Several species; white or light yellow; hard brown heads; curved; ½ to 1½ inches long when full grown; white grubs live in soil and are larvae of May beetles; they require three years to mature; adult lays eggs in grassy areas.

Damage—Larvae feed on roots and underground parts of potato and many other plants. Adults feed on foliage of trees and ornamentals.

Control—Avoid planting potatoes in an area that has been in sod for the past two to three years. Dig up the soil in the fall and again about two weeks before planting in the spring to reduce white grubs. Keep weeds out of the garden. Use a recommended insecticide prior to planting.

Wireworm

Description—Shiny, slick, reddish-brown, tough, six-legged worm up to 1½ inches long.

Damage—The wireworm tunnels through tubers, making deep, more or less cylindrical burrows.

Control—Avoid planting sweetpotatoes in an area that has been in sod for the past two to three years. If such an area must be used, or if damage from wireworms has occurred in the past, preventive treatments of a recommended soil insecticide should be made before planting.

TOMATOES, EGGPLANTS AND PEPPERS

European Corn Borer (Pepper Only)

Description—Flesh-colored; rows of small, round, dark-brown spots; dark-brown head; up to one inch long.

Damage—Larvae bore into the stems of plants and cause breakage. The heaviest damage occurs late in the season. In addition, larvae may enter the fruit by boring under the calyx (small green leaves under the flower). Tunneling in fruit often causes premature fruit drop.

Control—Plant as early as the weather permits; apply a recommended insecticide when larvae are first found.

Blister Beetle

Description—Adult - Soft, slender beetles with long legs; 1½ - 1¾ inches long; either black, grayish, or black with narrow gray or yellow stripes on margins of the wing covers.

Damage—Loss of leaves from large numbers of beetles feeding on the foliage may result in injury to fruit from sun scald.

Control—Apply a recommended insecticide.

Cutworm

Description—Plump, smooth-skinned, greasy-looking caterpillars up to one inch long, often found curled up at base of plants.

Damage—Young transplants may be cut down at ground level, or branches may be removed from larger plants. Some damage to small fruit may occur on older plants.

Control—Physical barriers consisting of aluminum foil wrapped around a four inch length of stem between leaves and root may be used to protect newly set transplants. Avoid placing transplants in soil recently planted in grass or sod. Baits or spray of recommended insecticides may be needed.

Hornworm

Description—Large, green caterpillars with white bars; up to three or four inches long with a slender horn projecting from near the rear end.

Damage—Hornworms feed on leaves, consuming large amounts of foliage. Loss of leaves may result in stunting and fruit scald.

Control—Handpicking and destruction are often easy because of the size of the caterpillar. If large numbers of hornworms or plants are involved, use a recommended insecticide.

Leafminers

Description—Winding white trails or broad white spots appear on leaves, made by small white or yellow legless maggots feeding between the two surfaces of the leaf.

Damage—The leaves may be weakened, and the mines or tunnels may serve as points where disease and decay may start.

Control—Handpick infested leaves, if practical, before the larvae pupate and begin another generation, or use a recommended insecticide when large numbers of mines are found.

Whiteflies

Description—Adults - Very small sucking insects with two pairs of broadly rounded wings covered with a snow white, waxy powder; they look like tiny moths and fly out in a cloud when disturbed. Larvae - (nymphs or crawlers) - very small, flat, scale-like insects, difficult to see; all stages feed on the undersides of leaves and excrete honeydew.

Damage—Whiteflies suck plant juices, causing leaf discoloration, leaf drop, and stunting of plants. A sooty black mold grows on the honeydew on the leaves.
Control—Use a recommended insecticide. Avoid purchasing transplants already infested with whiteflies.

DISEASES OF VEGETABLES

Introduction

Lack of adequate disease control may be the limiting factor in gardening efforts. The key to controlling vegetable garden diseases is prevention. There are many different diseases which affect the wide variety of plants in home gardens. There are certain diseases which occur each year. Under certain weather conditions and with susceptible plants, some uncommon diseases may cause serious problems. Given the right environment, a susceptible host, and a disease organism, a disease will develop. By altering this disease triangle one can prevent disease. The ultimate goal in accomplishing disease control is through resistant varieties. Certain highly desirable horticultural types may not carry needed disease resistance. When resistance is lacking, we depend on cultural practices and chemicals for disease control.

Nematodes

Among nematodes, root-knot is the most common in home gardens. Nematodes are small, eel-like worms which live in the soil and feed on plant roots. Root-knot causes most problems in home gardens; however, there are two other species which cause yield reduction in garden plants. Reniform and sting nematodes cause serious problems on certain vegetable crops.

Diagnosis—One can find out whether nematodes are causing a problem by observing the root system of susceptible plants and by soil assay. Nematodes damage root systems so that they are not able to pick up nutrients and water as needed, causing yellow and stunted top growth. If you suspect nematode damage, reach down and pull the plant from the soil making sure that the galls will not be stripped from the plant roots. Misdiagnosis is often made by stripping the galls from the roots during the process of pulling the plant. The best method to check plant roots is to use a shovel to loosen the soil around the plant. Remove the plant from the soil keeping all roots intact and looking for swollen galls on the root system. Care should be taken not to confuse nitrogen fixing nodules on legumes with the swollen roots caused by root-knot nematodes. Root-knot galls are made up of large number of cells or cell enlargement.

With experience you will be able to distinguish nematode injury from the physiological nitrogen-fixing nodules associated with leguminous plants. Soil nematode assay is the best way to determine numbers and kinds of nematodes present in the garden. Soil samples for nematode assay should be taken during the months of

July, August and September because root-knot populations are highest during this period. Nematode assay soil samples taken during January and February are of little value since nematodes are practically inactive during these periods of cold weather.

Control—Control recommendations can be made after establishing numbers and kinds through soil assay. There are currently no chemical controls readily available to homeowners. Organic products on the market have not been proven effective in reducing nematode populations. There are however, some biological or cultural ways to reduce nematodes in the home garden. The use of plants resistant to nematode attack offers the best way of avoiding nematode problems. Few resistant varieties are completely immune to nematode attack, but some will still provide acceptable yields. Tomatoes with VFN after their name are resistant to 3 diseases including Verticillium, Fusarium, and nematodes.

Solarization is the use of heat from the sun for killing nematodes in bare soil. This technique involves placing clear 1 mil. plastic sheeting on moist tilled soil and sealing the edges with soil, bricks, sand or other materials. The plastic should be applied in early spring and allowed to remain in place for an entire season. The plastic can then be removed in time to plant a fall garden. The plastic should be removed before cold weather.

Marigolds will kill nematodes, but only if used throughout the garden area and in the absence of other susceptible roots. Planting marigolds in a border around home gardens, down the row, or even in the hole with an individual plant will not control nematodes. Nematodes will feed on the vegetable plant roots and not the marigold roots. Marigolds will only help to control root-knot nematodes if they are broadcast early in spring and left in the area all summer. The best variety is the French dwarf marigold. If other plant roots are allowed to develop in the broadcast marigold area, the nematodes will feed and develop on these roots. Efforts should be made to get rid of all other root systems in the broadcast planted area.

Other cultural practices can help to reduce nematode populations. Crop rotation should be practiced whenever possible in nematode prone areas. Adding organic matter can be particularly beneficial in sandy soil areas. Repeat discing in hot summer months since nematodes require a film of water around their bodies at all times. By eliminating the film of water, we can destroy the nematodes. Discing will bring nematodes to the surface where they will be killed by the hot, drying sun. This method will reduce the population but does not lower

the population enough to avoid reduced yield due to damage to susceptible plants. Good gardening practices such as removing dead plant material, especially the roots and weed control are also beneficial in controlling nematodes.

Soil-borne Diseases

Root-rot and stem rots cause serious damage to garden plants. These diseases occur where rotation is poor, that is, areas that are planted from one year to the next with the same vegetable in the same area. Root-rotting fungi include *Rhizoctonia*, *Pythium*, *Fusarium*, and *Sclerotium rolfsii*. These common soil inhabiting fungi are present in most areas and can cause serious problems when weather conditions are right. Rhizoctonia causes sunken red lesions on the root and stem area of young seedlings. Fusarium causes serious root rot and may cause clogging of water-conducting tissues — thus reducing the growth rate of the plant. Pythium causes long, water-soaked lesions up the stem and occurs primarily in warmer temperatures. Southern blight is also considered a hot weather fungus.

Control—Root-rotting fungi can be reduced by deep-plowing previous crop litter, rotation, and seed and soil treatment. If good cultural practices are followed, seed treatment will usually allow young seedlings to become established before these root-rotting fungi can cause serious problems. It is recommended that all garden seeds be purchased new each year from a western grown source. All seeds should be treated with a chemical to protect against soil-rotting fungi. If root-rot and stem rot are a serious problem and one must replant in the same location, it is advisable to use an in-furrow fungicide to give added protection.

Leaf, Stem and Fruit Diseases

Leaf, stem and fruit diseases affect many different vegetable garden plants. Some are vectored by insects and reducing weed cover in and near the garden can help reduce populations. Others can be controlled by selecting resistant varieties and cultural methods.

Snap Beans

Snap bean rust is about the only disease that can be eliminated once it is established. Other diseases are not usually evident in time to prevent economic loss due to the damage. Bean rust begins with tiny, yellow pimples on the leaves and progresses into ruptured pustules of tiny, brown, seed-like bodies called spores. These spores are able to re-infect unprotected bean leaves within a few days, thus repeating the life cycle and killing the bean leaf as it moves through the planting. Some varieties are more susceptible to rust than others. Most of the improved green bean varieties carry a degree of rust resistance. If rust is diagnosed, measures must be taken to control it. Application of a fungicide will protect clean foliage and prevent future damage by rust.

Lima Beans

Often, **stem anthracnose** of lima beans is confused with rust. Lima beans are not susceptible to rust. The stem anthracnose disease of lima beans is much more serious than the rust of snap beans. Once the symptoms of stem Anthracnose appear, it is often too late to do anything about the disease. Stem anthracnose affects the stems, leaves, petioles, and young developing fruit. The brick-red lesions on the stem, leaves and fruit are characteristic of this disease.

Most gardeners recognize the problem when they find numerous under-developed pods on the soil surface. The time between initial infection and the appearance of symptoms is about fourteen days, which means the fungus is too advanced to stop by using fungicides. The best method of controlling stem anthracnose of lima beans is to purchase western-grown, disease-free seeds, plant them in a new location in the garden and spray with a recommended fungicide. If the disease has not been noticed by the time the first flowers occur, begin the spray program at that point, spraying every seven days until the bean crop is made.

Tomatoes

The tomato is sometimes referred to as King of the Garden. One of the most common diseases affecting tomato is called **early blight**. Early blight usually begins on the lower leaves and moves upward on the plant, depending on the amount of moisture and the overall condition of the plant. A healthy, green, vigorously growing plant is more resistant to disease than one that has become nutritionally deficient or under severe stress. The fungus involved is Alternaria. Target spot is very characteristic and used as a way of identifying early blight of tomato. Early blight can be prevented by mulching, which prevents the fungus from being introduced to the plant by splashing soil and chemical sprays.

Another common disease of the tomato is **southern blight**, caused by the fungus *Sclerotium rolfsii*. Southern blight affects the plant at the soil level causing a mass of white, thread-like mycelium which is visible at the soil surface. Later, tiny, brown, B-B-like structures develop on the white mass of mycelium. These structures are called sclerotia and allow the fungus to over-winter. These tiny bodies are able to live through severe weather conditions, germinate the next year, and cause serious damage to tomatoes, peppers and eggplants, as well as to some other gardening crops. The fungus responsible for causing southern blight in tomato is an oxygen-loving fungus, which means that it can be controlled by deep-plowing. This practice removes the fungus from its oxygen supply, and so stops it from developing. When all other cultural methods have been used, it is sometimes also necessary to use chemicals in the transplant water to aid in the control of southern blight.

There is another way to prevent southern blight in tomatoes, eggplants, and peppers. This involves the use of aluminum foil. Aluminum foil should be wrapped loosely around the stem of the plant. The plant should be planted in the soil so that two inches of the foil is above the soil level and two inches below the soil level. Be careful not to move soil onto the stem above the aluminum foil, since infection can occur at that site. Descriptions of this procedure are available in the county Extension office. This aluminum foil technique will also prevent cut worm damage. We're often asked if materials other than aluminum foil can be used to prevent southern blight infection. The initial research was done with newspaper, waxed paper, and aluminum foil. The results of this study showed almost one hundred percent control with aluminum foil and about sixty percent control with waxed paper. The newspaper was worse than the control plots. If this technique is used to prevent southern blight, aluminum foil will give the best results.

A soil-borne disease which attacks tomatoes is known as **Fusarium wilt**. This fungus is in most garden areas and can be prevented largely through the use of resistant varieties. Be careful to plant those varieties which have the letters VFN at the end of the name in the seed catalogue. This means that they are resistant to Verticillium, Fusarium, and nematodes. In Georgia one need not worry about the Verticillium resistance because our climate is too hot for Verticillium to develop. Fusarium wilt enters plant roots and moves up the vascular system, causing physical clogging of the water-conducting tissues of the plant. This makes the plant slowly turn yellow and eventually die. Other disease organisms enter the sick plant, hastening its death. Fusarium wilt is much worse where nematodes have injured the root system or other physical damage is done to the root system by plows, hoes, etc. Nothing can be done for Fusarium wilt once it enters the plant.

Another disease causing wilt of tomato is known as **Bacterial wilt**. Bacterial wilt usually enters the garden site through contaminated transplants. It is important to grow your own transplants or to buy certified disease-free transplants. Once bacterial wilt enters a garden site, it remains in the soil for a number of years, causing all tomatoes to wilt and eventually die.

The characteristic symptom of bacterial wilt is immediate wilting of green foliage. The plant looks as if someone has poured hot water on it. Gardeners often ask why, if the plant is going to die, it doesn't die while it is still small. The answer is that the bacterium responsible for bacterial wilt develops only after the soil temperature warms in the spring, and this is usually after the plant has become well established. There is no control for bacterial wilt, either in the plant or in the soil. The only method of preventing bacterial wilt is to avoid initial contamination. Bacterial wilt can be positively diagnosed by submerging about an inch of the lower stem in clear water. Usually in two to five minutes, a milky bacterium will stream from contaminated plants. This is the method used in most laboratories for quick identification.

Fruit rots cause numerous problems in tomato plantings. These fruit rots are caused by soil inhabiting fungi such as Rhizoctonia, Pythium, Fusarium and southern blight. The best method of preventing fruit rot in tomatoes is to prevent the fruit from coming into contact with the soil. This can best be done by staking the plant and using a soil mulch. The soil mulch provides uniform soil temperature. This aids in weed control, conserves moisture, and creates a barrier between the fruit and the soil, thus eliminating fruit rots.

Another serious disease of tomato is mosaic. The most common virus affecting tomato is **tobacco mosaic virus.** This disease produces a mottled green and yellow color in the foliage, concentrated in the most recent growth. The crinkling and mottling gets progressively worse as the plant grows. Tobacco mosaic virus enters the plant by physical contact or by insects. If you touch any form of tobacco and then touch transplants, you might transmit tobacco mosaic virus to clean transplants, but this is highly unlikely. In any event, tobacco products should be avoided before handling the transplants. Insects which vector (carry) viruses must be controlled to prevent spread.

Tomatoes are affected by the virus disease **cucumber mosaic virus**. This is another example of a mosaic virus disease that affects tomatoes.

Finally there is a virus disease of tomatoes called Tomato Spotted Wilt Virus (TSWV), which can cause plant stunting, leaf death, and spots or rings on fruit. It is transmitted by thrips and there are now some resistant varieties available.

Herbicides such as 2,4-D can cause symptoms on plants that mimic virus diseases. If such herbicides have been used nearby such as on lawns for weed control, herbicide drift may have caused damage. Usually this damage will be most severe on plants nearest the site of herbicide application.

Turnips, Collards and Cabbage

Major diseases of turnip greens are leaf spotting diseases which render the leaves non-usable. There are four major leaf spotting diseases of turnips. These are **Cercospora leafspot**, **pale spot**, **Anthracnose**, and **downy mildew**. Downy mildew occurs on the underside of the leaf, which means that a spray program should begin early and a preventive program is needed to prevent initial infection of any of these four problems. As soon as a good stand of turnips has been established, it is important to apply a recommended fungicide on a regular basis until harvest. This will prevent any leafspotting causing undesirable leaves. One fungicide controls all four of the turnip leafspotting diseases.

There are several very important diseases affecting cabbage. The one which causes the most serious damage is black rot. **Black rot** is caused by a bacterium which is seed-borne and is transmitted with transplants. Black rot shows up as V-shaped lesions down the leaves. It then moves into the vascular system and causes the heads to deteriorate. Warm, moist weather favors the disease. Cool, dry weather helps to control it, and some crops can be grown under favorable weather conditions even though infection has occurred. Black rot is spread by insect movement, water splashing, and rain. There is no control for black rot once it is established in a cabbage planting. The only way for a home gardener to prevent black rot is to buy certified transplants. These will be marked with a tag indicating that they are certified transplants from the state of origin. Certified transplants will have the certification label either in or on every single container. Without the tag, the plants are not certified.

A common disease of cabbage is **wirestem**. Most serious wirestem occurs in the fall when cabbage is transplanted to hot soils. If one waits until the soils cool in the fall, or uses a fungicide in the transplant water, wirestem can be avoided. Wirestem causes shrinkage of the stem, and the plant dies from a lack of nutrition, often breaking due to the brittle, small stem area just above the root.

Foliage diseases include **downy mildew** and **Alternaria leafspot**. Both of these diseases can be easily controlled with a good fungicide program.

Squash

The major disease affecting squash is mosaic. The symptom of **Squash Mosaic virus** is a mild mottle on older leaves becoming more mottled toward the terminal area of the plant. All fruit produced by this plant will be green and yellow in color and physically distorted. Squash mosaic is caused by a specific virus known as Watermelon Mosaic Virus #1 or Watermelon Mosaic Virus #2. True squash mosaic virus is seed-transmitted. However, 99 percent of the squash virus we see in this area is, in fact, Watermelon Mosaic Virus, which is not seed-transmitted in squash. Western grown, disease-free seeds are recommended. If clean seeds are planted, then mosaic can only be introduced by viruliferous (virus-carrying) insects. The aphid is a primary carrier of Watermelon Mosaic Virus affecting squash. Once a plant is infected with a virus, it is infected for life. There is no recovery. All fruits produced will get progressively worse as the season progresses. There is no control for virus after it enters the plant. Protection must be provided to prevent entry by the virus.

Powdery and downy mildews are two leaf-destroying fungi which affect squash. **Powdery mildew** looks like talcum powder dusted on the leaf's surface. **Downy mildew** usually occurs on the underside of the leaf, causing a gray mold to develop. Both of these diseases can be identified under the microscope or hand lens. A good fungicidal spray program will control downy and powdery mildew. Fruit fungal diseases affecting squash include **Pythium** and **Choanephora**. Both of these diseases occur when the temperature and humidity are high. Pythium causes a white, fuzzy growth on the fruit of deteriorated squash. Choanephora can be easily identified by the black, beard-like fungus growth on the squash. Both of these conditions can be controlled by allowing sunlight to penetrate the center of the plant to dry the area out. Once the area is dry, these problems subside.

Okra

The major problem affecting okra is **root-knot nematodes**. The second most important is **Fusarium wilt**. These two problems must be controlled before the okra is seeded. A pod rot called **Choanephora** sometimes develops on okra because the old, faded bloom has not dropped off the young pod. About the only way to control this is by allowing sunlight to dry the innermost portions of the plant quickly. In some cases, Choanephora has been blamed for the diseased pod when, in fact, a lack of pollination or fertilization caused the abortion. As a result of the young pod's aborting, the fungus grew on the deteriorating tissue. It is always better to diagnose a problem before recommending a control.

Southernpeas

The major problem affecting southernpeas is **Pea Mosaic**. The leading variety of peas in home gardens at one time was knuckle purple hull. Now, 99 percent of all knuckle purple hull seeds are infected with a virus known as a blackeye cowpea mosaic virus. This is a seed-borne virus which has contaminated most seed left of the knuckle purple hull variety. There are other varieties which are susceptible to one or more viruses. There are five major viruses affecting peas in Georgia. The most damaging is **blackeye cowpea mosaic virus**, followed by **southern pea mosaic**, **cucumber mosaic**, and several others. Seed transmission is a major cause of virus spread. Insects play a major role in vectoring viruses. The most important carriers are aphids and leaf hoppers. Some insects can transmit the virus mechanically by introducing the mouth parts into healthy cells. Other insects must acquire the virus and have it incubate in their bodies several days before they are able to transmit it to a new plant. The best method of preventing mosaic in southernpeas is to buy western-grown, disease-free seeds and control insects. One virus may cause a very mild mottling and crinkling, whereas two or more viruses in the same plant will cause severe distortion. Other southern pea diseases include **Fusarium wilt**, which causes vascular clogging and the slow death of the plant. **Southern blight** causes a disease which resembles Fusarium. However, the mycelium of Southern blight is extremely white and coarse, and B-B-like sclerotia are found at the soil surface around the base of the plant.

Disease Management

Irrigation—Irrigation is necessary to supplement natural rainfall in growing a garden, but free moisture on foliage increases the chances of disease. Without free moisture, disease-causing organisms do not germinate and penetrate the host. The best time to irrigate a garden is either at night or after the garden has dried in the morning. Make sure the water is turned off before the plants are wet in the evening by dew. It usually takes 12 to 14 hours of constant wetness for a spore (seed body of fungi) to germinate and get into a leaf. Breaking the cycle of wetness can help to prevent disease.

Control—It is suggested that all cultural practices be followed in gardening. However, we sometimes have to use chemicals. Chemicals should be applied according to label directions and with a sprayer. A sprayer is suggested because one uses less material, gets better coverage, and the fungicides tend to stick to the leaf better and resist wash-off. Most chemicals recommended for the home garden are safe when used according to label directions. Before any chemicals are used, read the labels thoroughly and follow them precisely.

DISCUSSION QUESTIONS

1. What will help to correct the problem of blossom-end rot on tomatoes?

2. Which methods of irrigation will help minimize diseases in the vegetable garden?

3. What is the method used to check a plant for nematode damage?

4. What does the term 'rotation' mean?

5. What is the disease common to beans that begins as tiny yellow pimples on the leaves that progresses to a brown stippled appearance called?

6. What causes 'catfacing' of tomato?

RESOURCES

Bradley, Fern. Ed. *Rodale's All-New Encyclopedia of Organic Gardening: The Indispensable Resource for Every Gardener.*

Greenwood, Pippa, et. al. *American Horticultural Society Pests and Diseases: The Complete Guide to Preventing, Identifying and Treating Plant Problems.*

18
Principles of Organic Gardening

Paul Guillebeau

Elizabeth Little

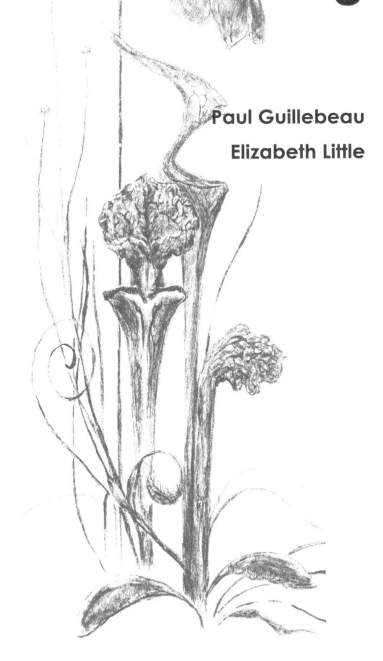

LEARNING OBJECTIVES

Explain what "organic" means to a food producer and how to identify organic foods in the marketplace.

Explain why farmers use conventional pesticides and why home gardeners have more practical options to conventional pesticides.

Design an organic plan for your garden and landscape.

TERMS TO KNOW

National Organic Program (NOP) Develops, implements, and administers national production, handling, and labeling standards.

OMRI Organic Materials Review Institute is a national nonprofit organization that determines which input products are allowed for use in organic production and processing. Publishes two lists of materials approved for organic production.

OMRI Products List The most complete directory of products for organic production or processing and includes over 2,100 products, which are known as "OMRI Listed®." The OMRI Generic Materials List is an authoritative catalog of over 900 materials and their statuses in organic production, processing, and handling.

U.S.D.A. Organic Organic production is a system that is managed in accordance with the Organic Foods Production Act (OFPA) of 1990 (PDF) and regulations in Title 7, Part 205 of the Code of Federal Regulations to respond to site-specific conditions by integrating cultural, biological, and mechanical practices that foster cycling of resources, promote ecological balance, and conserve biodiversity.

INTRODUCTION

This chapter provides the reader a basic understanding of organic production. As you will see, organic gardening requires a great deal of specific knowledge. You will learn the details of weed, insect, and disease management in the other chapters of the Master Gardener Handbook. This chapter will help you plan for a reduced-pesticide garden; the other chapters will help you fill in the details of your plan.

The word "organic" can be confusing because it has multiple meaning and connotations. To a chemist, "organic" refers to carbon compounds. An organic farmer is a producer that does not use synthetic fertilizers or pesticides.

In the world of consumer products, "organic" is a term referred to as "warm and fuzzy". It may difficult for a person to define organic precisely, but buying products labeled as "organic" makes many consumers feel good inside. They often feel like buying organic products helps save the environment or protect human health.

Soon, marketing and advertisers recognized that an organic label could help them command a premium price for their goods. Many different products were identified as "organic", but there were not standards to define what the term meant. Consumers were confused and frustrated, particularly in the grocery store. They wanted to know that organic foods were somehow different from conventionally produced foods.

The United States Department of Agriculture (USDA) agreed to work with the organic community to establish standards for foods that would be labeled as organic. The USDA has never contended that organic foods are better, safer, more nutritious, etc. than foods produced with conventional pesticides and fertilizers. The USDA National Organic Program established rules for commercial organic production that dictate what chemicals and farming practices are acceptable. Fresh foods and food products can carry the USDA seal if they are at least 95% organic ingredients. Products with less than 95% organic ingredients can advertise that the products contain organic ingredients or identify particular ingredients that are organic. For more information about the national organic program, visit www.ams.usda.gov/nop. The USDA organic rules do not apply to home gardeners, but they are a useful guide to choosing organic pest management alternatives.

To better understand and plan an organic garden, it is helpful to consider why farmers use synthetic pesticides. After all, pesticide application is expensive, and many pesticides pose risks to human health and the environment. As you consider this list of reasons for using pesticides, think of strategies that you could use to replace pesticides in each situation.

1. Growers make more money using synthetic chemicals. For commercial growers, farming is the way they pay the mortgage, buy a car, send the children to college, etc. Like anyone else, farmers want to maximize their income.

Generally, a home gardener's income is not tied to their production. Therefore, home gardeners have many options that are not practical for a commercial grower.

2. Growers use pesticides as a substitute for labor. Even if a farmer could find an army of people to hoe weeds from a 100 acre field of cotton, the farmer could not afford to pay them.

You have a home garden because you enjoy the work. If you feel your garden and/or landscape is an unwelcome burden, you need to reduce the size of your garden.

3. Using pesticides usually requires less knowledge and planning. It is less important to identify the pest precisely if you can apply a broad-spectrum pesticide that will kill many different pests. Also, it is less critical to avoid pest problems if you have an effective pesticide.

Without few pesticide options it is critical for organic gardeners to avoid pest problems. Avoiding pest problems usually requires in-depth knowledge of the pest's life cycle and ecology.

4. Farmers use pesticides as rescue treatments when pest populations get out of hand. Often a farmer can eliminate or greatly reduce pest populations very quickly with the application of a pesticide.

Rescue treatments are not typically available in organic production. It is critical, therefore, to plan ahead to prevent pest populations from overwhelming the garden.

5. Growers use synthetic pesticides because the results are often more predictable and consistent.

If your salary varied from paycheck to paycheck, it would make it very difficult to budget effectively or make economic plans. Farmers feel the same way; it is critical for them to be able to accurately predict their income.

For most people, the backyard garden is not a critical source of income or food. Therefore, many more options are available for the home gardener. Because crop failures are not catastrophic, the home gardener can experiment or try chemical-free options.

6. Consumers typically demand perfect produce. Every home gardener is familiar with corn earworm, particularly in sweet corn. There is little or no commercial fresh market for damaged produce.

It is extremely rare to discover corn earworm damage on an ear of sweet corn from the supermarket. When that corn is growing, it is frequently sprayed with insecticide to ensure the perfect ear.

Home gardeners are usually willing to accept less than perfect produce from their own garden in exchange for better quality and fewer chemicals. The difference in the action thresholds for commercial fields and home gardens offers the home gardener more options for reducing chemical inputs.

Organic pest management is not simply replacing a conventional pesticide with another chemical that is labeled 'organic'. Knowledge and planning are the keys to successful organic gardening.

Principles for Organic Gardening

Choose plants/varieties with fewer pest problems.

• When you plan your garden and landscape, ask your Extension agent about plants or varieties that do not require large inputs of pesticides.

• If you discover that you have chosen a plant that requires regular pesticide sprays, replace with a lower maintenance plant.

• Plant selection is particularly important for perennials like trees and shrubs.

• For common problems, pest resistance is often available. Find out what pests you can expect, and look for plants/varieties that are resistant to those pests.

Healthy plants are less susceptible to pests. Stressed plants may attract pests.

• Choose plants that are adapted for your local climate.

• When you buy plants, inspect them carefully for signs of pest infestation.

• Test the soil to make sure the plants are receiving the nutrients they need to stay healthy.

• Plant at the right date and under the proper light/water conditions.

Consult your local Cooperative Extension agent for advice about choosing plants and creating healthy growing conditions.

Anticipate problems

• Find out what pests are common in your area.

• Look for plant varieties resistant to regular pests.

• Learn the life cycles of the pests you expect.

-When/how do they arrive?

-Are any stages of the life cycle vulnerable (or protected)?

Cooperative Extension is your best information source.

Scout for pest problems regularly.

• It is much easier to manage young insects and small populations.

• Scout at least three times per week in warm weather.

• Look at the whole plant, under leaves, and along stems.

Practice good sanitation.

• Dispose of diseased or spent plant materials promptly.

• Many pests will persist over the winter in crop debris.

Use crop rotation.

• Do not plant the same type of plants in the same place each year.

Encourage natural controls.

• An assortment of flowers and herbs will attract beneficial insects.

Use mechanical controls.

• Row covers and hand-picking are practical on a small scale.

• Water spray is effective against many insects if the plants are hardy enough to withstand a vigorous spray.

• Tillage can kill many insects that live in the soil. It will be important for you to know when the insects are in the soil.

Utilize cultural controls.

• An appropriate planting date may avoid peak pest populations.

• Mulch helps keep plants healthy and controls some pests.

• Avoid plants or particular varieties that have a lot of pest problems.

Use chemical controls sparingly. An "organic" listing

Table 1. Organic insecticide/miticide options

Caterpillars	pyrethrins, *Bacillus thuringiensis kerstaki*, spinosad, neem
Thrips	spinosad (fire ant bait formulation)
Aphids, whiteflies, other soft bodied pests	spinosad
Stink bugs	pyrethrins, oils, insecticidal soap, neem
Beetles	neem, pyrethrins, spinosad
Scale insects	spinosad, pyrethrins, neem
Mites	oils
Mosquito larvae	oils, sulfur, insecticidal soap
Yellow jackets	*Bacillus thuringiensis israelensis*
Slugs/snails	traps, pyrethrins
	iron phosphate

USE ALL PESTICIDES ACCORDING TO THE LABEL INSTRUCTIONS!
If used improperly, even natural products may injure your family or pets.

To use this guide, locate your pest problem and identify the chemical options. Review the chemical options for additional information and potential risks. If you need help choosing among several options, consult your local Extension agent.

does not eliminate all risks.

- Spot treat instead of spraying a large area.
- Use pesticides only when other options are not practical.

ORGANIC INSECTICIDE/MITICIDE OPTIONS

Except for spinosad products, nearly all organic insecticides have little or no residual activity. Repeated applications may be necessary before you see results.

Nearly all organic pesticides have a very broad range of use sites, which means you can use them nearly anywhere in the garden or landscape. Check the label to be sure it is labeled for the site you need to treat.

Pyrethrins (pyrethrum)— are produced by some varieties of chrysanthemum. Pyrethrins are often combined with piperonyl butoxide (PBO), which significantly increases the effectiveness of pyrethrins. The PBO is a synthetic chemical; some people do not consider PBO combinations an organic alternative.

Pyrethrins are also available in product combinations with oil or sulfur to give the products greater activity against mites and diseases.

Risks: May kill bees and other beneficials. Extremely toxic to aquatic species. Pyrethrins can be toxic to cats.

NOTE: Very short (hours) residual activity. Insects may recover from pyrethrin exposure unless PBO is added to the product.

Pyrethrin products: Garden Safe, Ortho Ecosense, Bonide, others.

Horticultural oils and dormant oils—are highly refined petroleum products. Oils must be applied to the insects/mites to kill them. No residual activity.

Risks: May kill nontarget arthropods if they are covered with oil. May cause plant injury, particularly if the weather is hot or the plant is water stressed.

NOTE: Be sure you are using the right oil and the right concentrations to minimize the risk of plant injury.

Petroleum oil products – Bonide All Seasons and many others. Note: not all petroleum oil products are considered organic. Check the OMRI list if you want to be sure.

Other oils include sesame oil, soybean oil, and canola oil. We have limited information about their efficacy, but their activity will be similar to the petroleum oils. They can also cause phytotoxicity.

Neem (azadirachtin)— is derived from the Neem tree. Leaf extracts and oils pressed from nuts are available. Neem is an insecticide, an insect growth regulator, and a repellent. An insect growth regulator prevents juvenile insects from maturing properly.

Risks: High concentrations can harm fish. Low risk to bees and other beneficial insects.

Neem products: Green Light, others

Spinosad— comes in two forms. The organic form is derived from a soil bacterium, *Saccharopolyspora spinosa*. The other form is not considered organic even though it is derived in a similar way.

Risks: May harm bees. Low risks for other nontarget species.

Spinosad products: Fertilome, Bulls Eye

Iron phosphate— is the only organic slug bait in U.S. Used for many years in Europe.

Risks: Low risks to nontarget species.

Iron Phosphate products: Ortho Ecosense, Worryfree

Insecticidal soap—may also be called Potassium Salts of Fatty Acids. They must be applied directly to the insects. They have no residual activity.

Risks: May cause plant injury, particularly when weather is hot or plant is water stressed.

Insecticidal Soap products: Ortho Ecosense, Safer, others.

Sulfur—is commonly found in combination with other organic products to provide control of fungal diseases.

Risks: Low risks to nontargets. May cause irritation of skin, eyes, and throat tissue.

Sulfur products: many.

Bt products—*Bacillus thuringiensis kerstaki* is a strain of Bacillus bacteria that only infects caterpillars. The caterpillars must consume the bacteria. Birds, fish, pets, people, etc. cannot catch this strain of bacteria.

Risks: Very low risks to nontarget species (except other caterpillars).

Bacillus thuringiensis kerstaki products: Dipel, Thuricide, others.

Bacillus thuringiensis israelensis is a similar strain of bacteria that controls mosquito larvae. Use it in water containers or ponds where mosquitoes are a problem.

Bacillus popillae is a bacterial strain that infects Japanese

beetle larvae. It will not affect adult insects. There is no clear evidence that using Bacillus popillae will reduce Japanese beetle damage in your yard.

Japanese beetle traps— catch large numbers of Japanese beetle adults attracted from a large area. There is no clear evidence that using Japanese beetle traps will reduce Japanese beetle damage in your yard. On a large property, it may be possible to attract Japanese beetles away from desirable plants; however this strategy is unproven.

Yellow jacket traps—can help to reduce the number of yellow jackets in a local area. May seem ineffective if other foods are nearby that are also attractive to yellow jackets.

Diatomaceous earth—is not recommended. It loses most of its effectiveness in damp/humid conditions, and it is difficult to avoid inhaling the dust.

Home brews— are commonly used and widely touted on the internet. Common brews include garlic, hot pepper, ground insects, etc. Because there is no consistency among brews, there are no reliable data to gauge their effectiveness.

ORGANIC FUNGICIDE/BACTERIACIDE OPTIONS

The products listed in this section are registered by the EPA and are "approved" for use in organic production. However, most of these products are non-specific and are toxic to humans, plants, and many non-target invertebrates and aquatic life. In addition, the effectiveness of most of these products is generally limited when compared to "conventional" pesticides. With this in mind, organic pesticides should not be considered as substitutes for or used as conventional fungicides in a pest control program, and should only be used judiciously and as a last resort in an IPM program.

Table 2. Organic fungicide/bacteriacide options

Type of Pest Controlled	Compound	Notes
COPPERS:		
Many fungal and bacterial diseases, including powdery and downy mildew, fungal leaf spots, anthracnose, bacterial leaf spot and/or blight, fire blight and rust on a wide variety of fruits, vegetables and ornamentals. Effectiveness against most pathogens is often limited. Labeled for many plants	Copper sulfate and fixed coppers (copper hydroxide, copper oxide, copper oxychloride)	Copper is toxic to fish, aquatic invertebrates, and humans. Label directions and harvest intervals should be followed carefully. Copper is a heavy metal and must be used in a manner that minimizes accumulation in the soil. Coppers have the potential to burn the foliage and flowers of many plants. To avoid this problem, do not spray prior to or during the flowering period, or during prolonged cold, wet weather. Refer to individual product label for plants which may be treated.
Various diseases of fruits, vegetables and ornamentals including leaf curl on peaches and bitter rot, black rot and scab on apples. Labeled for many plants.	Bordeaux Mixture (hydrated lime/copper sulfate)	Lime added to copper sulfate increases the effectiveness of the copper. Phytotoxicity (burning of foliage and flowers) can occur on many plants including the young, tender leaves of peach, plum, rose and apple. Some sensitive plants require diluting the product to one half strength (depending on the product used - see label) to avoid phytotoxicity. Should not be used during cool, wet weather since this can increase damage to plant foliage.
SULFURS:		
Used in the dormant season to kill overwintering fungal spores of black spot, powdery mildew and rust of rose, leaf curl and shot-hole of peach, cane blight and leaf spot of brambles. Some brands labeled for delayed dormant and/or growing season applications for scab and powdery mildew of apple, anthracnose, rust and powdery mildew of blackberry and powdery mildew and scab on pear. Some brands labeled for delayed dormant and/or growing season applications for scab and powdery mildew of apple, anthracnose, rust and powdery mildew of blackberry and powdery mildew and scab on pear.	Liquid lime-sulfur (calcium polysulfides)	Labeled for roses, peaches, pears, brambles, fruit trees, deciduous hedge plants, delphinium, lilacs, euonymous, columbine, crape myrtle, sweet peas, zinnias, fruits, ornamentals, and tuberous begonias. Do not spray when temperature is expected to exceed 80°F within 24 hours. Spray early in the morning or late in the evening to avoid burning of foliage Also controls mites and scale.

Table 2. Organic fungicide/bacteriacide options

Type of Pest Controlled	Compound	Notes
	SULFURS:	
Controls fungal diseases including powdery mildew, scab, and cedar apple rust of apples, brown rot and scab of peach, plum and nectarine, powdery mildew on brambles and strawberry. Also labeled for powdery mildew, leaf spots, rust and botrytis on many vegetables and ornamentals (includes black spot of rose).	Elemental sulfur (Dry wettable sulfurs of flowable sulfurs)	Should not be used when the temperature is above 90 degrees or within four weeks of an oil spray as injury to the foliage may occur. Refer to individual product label for plants which may be treated. Do not use on apricots, cucumbers, d'Anjou pears, melons, spinach, squash or viburnum as sulfur causes injury and defoliation to these plants. Sulfur is lethal to beneficial insects, spiders and mites leading to increased problems with certain pests including mites. Residue may be a problem.
	OTHER COMPOUNDS:	
	Oils, horticultural, narrow range oils as dormant, suffocating, and summer oils	Do not apply when sulfur compounds have or will be used. This combination is toxic to the plant.
Controls various foliar fungal diseases, in particular powdery mildew on various hosts.	Potassium bicarbonate	Diluted in water and often mixed with insecticidal soap (surfactant) and horticultural oil to increase effectiveness.
Fire blight control in apples and pears only	Streptomycin	Bactericide/antibiotic compound. Has no fungicidal activity. Fire blight bacteria can develop resistance with prolonged use. When used for fire blight control of apples and pears it must be applied during bloom prior to the appearance of symptoms to be effective. Sprays should begin at 20-30% bloom and continue every 3-4 days until petal fall. Do not apply when fruit is visible. Do not apply within 30 days of harvest for pears. Do not apply within 50 days of harvest for apples.

DISCUSSION QUESTIONS

1. How can you recognize foods in the supermarket that have been produced through accepted practices?

2. Name three reasons why farmers use conventional pesticides?

3. For each of the three reasons in question 2, name an organic alternative that a home gardener could use.

4. Discuss an organic plan for caterpillars, aphids, and mosquitoes. Would organic alternatives be practical in your situation? Why or why not?

5. Name four organic sprays that might be used against fungal or bacterial plant diseases. Discuss the strengths and shortcomings of each option.

RESOURCES

Organic Materials Review Institute and the National Organic Standard. Includes a list of all of the pest management chemicals accepted as organic. http://www.omri.org/

National Sustainable Ag Information Service. This site has a great deal of information about organic production, including pest management. http://attra.ncat.org/organic.html

National Organic Program. http://www.ams.usda.gov/AMSv1.0/NOP - USDA

NOTES

19
Fruit Gardening

Robert R. Westerfield

Gerard Krewer

Marco T. Fonseca

LEARNING OBJECTIVES

Become familiar with cultivars of blackberries, raspberries, blueberries and strawberries suited to local soil and climate.

Understand basic cultural practices for small fruits.

Understand basic cultural practices for muscadine and bunch grapes.

Become familiar with fig culture and varieties suited to local soil and climate.

Become familiar with minor fruit crops suitable for use in Georgia.

Know varieties of pecans available and culture for the home garden.

Become familiar with cultivars of peaches, plums, nectarines, apples, pears suited to local soil and climate.

Understand basic cultural practices for tree fruits.

TERMS TO KNOW

Advective freeze type of freeze that is characterized by cold, dry air masses that move south and east from Canada. Usually these freezes arrive with high winds and generally more common in the winter.

Bud union site where the scion was grafted to the rootstock seedling and is generally obvious at the time of planting.

Cane biennial stem typical of Rubus or Vinis. The green summer shoot matures (hardens off) into a woody, brown one-year-old cane after leaf fall.

Crown compressed modified stem.

Cordons "arms", of the grapevine that extend from grapevine's trunk; they are horizontally positioned along the trellis (arbor) wire.

Curtain trellis vine cordons are trained high up and shoots are encouraged to droop downward.

Floricane second year growth of the cane stem; flowers, bears fruit and dies in this second year.

Fruiting spur short, thickened slow growth; contains the buds that produce fruit on many trees including, apples, pears and cherries.

Fruiting wood one-year-old wood on the grape vine that produces the current season's shoots and fruit.

Node thickened portion of a shoot or cane where the leaf petiole is attached and a compound bud is located.

Primocane first year growth of the cane stem; it is not capable of flowering.

Radiation freeze frost event characterized by a cold air layer that can develop during still nights or early mornings when radiation heat loss occurs from the fruiting zone.

Renewal spur cane pruned to one node with the primary purpose of producing a vegetative shoot (cane) for next year's fruiting wood.

Rootstock seedling base of most cultivated fruit trees, is the bottom portion of the tree and is an integral choice to the longevity of the tree.

Scion fruit bearing portion of the tree, equivalent to the variety; clonally propagated through bud grafting.

Shoot part of the stem extending from the cordon.; is most often pruned in the process of "shoot thinning" to control grape yields.

Spur strain apple type that has fruit spurs and leaf buds that are more closely spaced than on non-spur or standard types. Spur-types have a stiff, upright growth habit that minimizes limb breakage and enables the trees to hold heavy crop loads without having their limbs propped up or tied.

Stolons or runners horizontally oriented stems that grow along the soil surface.

Strain mutation of a certain cultivar selected for an improved characteristic and vegetatively propagated by grafting.

INTRODUCTION

Fruit crops can be a valuable addition to a home landscape if well-adapted types and cultivars are chosen and the plants are well-tended. They may add beauty and interest at several times of the year, especially during bloom, harvest and leaf fall.

Before deciding to grow fruits, a gardener must consider whether he or she is willing to commit to the work that is necessary to produce the quality of fruits generally found in the supermarket. Home-grown fruits can be even tastier and juicier, but only if one is willing to make the commitment to selecting adapted varieties and then caring for the plants.

This work includes fertilizing, pruning, thinning, spraying for insects and diseases, controlling weeds, and supplying adequate water during dry spells. Some species of fruits such as apples, peaches, nectarines, plums, and bunch grapes require much more spraying for pests than species such as pears, muscadines, blueberries, blackberries, and figs. The latter can normally be grown in Georgia even using organic methods if desired.

Site Selection—Choose a site where plants will thrive. Adequate sunlight is the number one condition that must be satisfied; all fruits do best in full sun. An area receiving less than one half day sunlight will produce very small crops of inferior quality fruits. Leaves need bright light to produce a surplus of carbohydrates to feed the developing fruits. Sites that contain too much shade may need to be modified by removing some of the surrounding tree canopy to allow for more sunlight.

Soils—The type of soil and the soil quality are also very important. In small areas, soils can be improved by the addition of organic matter and/or compost. Generally, at least four inches of organic matter tilled into the top six inches of soil is needed to produce a significant change in soil structure. Organic materials are mostly air space, so a large amount is desirable. If compost is used, it also contains a significant amount of nutrients which benefit plant growth. When amending a soil for blueberries, use an acidic organic matter such as peat moss, pine bark, or rotten pine needles.

A soil test is recommended to check available nutrients and pH. Fruit trees need a soil pH of 6.0 to 6.5 and it is very important to maintain pH in this range. Blueberries, however, are an exception and need a pH of 4.0 to 5.2. The pH can be adjusted by adding dolomitic lime to raise the pH or elemental sulfur to lower it. While collecting samples, be sure to take one for nematodes.

If nematodes are present, plant somewhere else that is free of nematodes, or select fruits that are resistant to the nematodes present in the soil. The most common nematode problems with Georgia home garden fruits are root-knot nematodes on figs, peaches, nectarines, and plums. A special rootstock called Nemaguard can be used for peaches, nectarines, and plums when this is a problem.

Problems with poorly drained soils are common in Georgia. Peaches, nectarines, plums, raspberries, and highbush blueberries are very sensitive to inadequate drainage. Apples, rabbiteye blueberries, muscadine grapes, and blackberries are more tolerant of poor drainage, and Asian pears are one of the most tolerant fruits to poor drainage. Drainage problems should be corrected before planting fruit trees.

Planting on raised beds is another possibility for solving poor drainage problems with small fruits. Beds should be wide and high to provide at least 18 inches of well drained soil. For small fruits a bed four feet wide can be used, while for tree fruits a raised bed is not practical. A small ditch between the beds called a "water furrow" will further enhance drainage.

Plant Spacing—Plants need adequate space to develop, so when planning, space them properly to allow development space. Allow easy access for maintenance chores, as well as for harvesting fruit. Planting too far apart will waste valuable space, and planting too closely will cause crowding and shading of neighboring plants. More about spacing is covered in the discussion of each individual fruit.

Variety Selection—Variety selection is extremely important. There is little one can do to make up for a poorly adapted variety. The importance of selecting well-adapted varieties cannot be over emphasized. The fruits discussed in this section are adapted to almost all areas of the state. Exceptions are figs and muscadines, which are poorly adapted to the high mountains. However, variety selection (the search for the best varieties for the area) is very important. The fact that a local nursery or a mail order catalog promotes a specific variety does not mean that it is adapted to every area, regardless of its claims. New and improved varieties may be available for certain areas of the state. It is best to check with your local Cooperative Extension office for variety updates.

Chilling requirements, disease and insect resistance, and weather conditions must be considered before making a choice as to type and variety. This is especially true with peaches, nectarines, plums, apples, blueberries, and bunch grapes. In many cases, different varieties are grown in each section of the state depending on the winter chilling hours (hours at or below 45°F from October 1-February 15) usually accumulated in that area of the state.

In the case of bunch grapes, a bacterial disease (Pierce's disease) kills susceptible varieties in the Coastal Plain and lower Piedmont. Varieties listed in this book are not always the newest ones available; see Extension publications for the latest information.

BRAMBLE FRUITS

Blackberries and raspberries are often referred to as bramble fruits and technically their fruits are not berries, but drupes. Table 1 lists some recommended bramble or cane fruit varieties for Georgia gardens.

Blackberries and raspberries are popular and generally easy to grow. Blackberries and raspberries come as two types: erect types (no trellis required) and trailing types (trellis required), depending on the varieties selected. Certain varieties of erect and trailing blackberries do well in Georgia, while only the trailing raspberry 'Dorman Red' has proven itself for all of Georgia. The erect raspberry variety 'Heritage' is grown commercially in the Georgia mountains and has performed well in North Georgia. For this reason, it is recommended for planting in the mountain and upper Piedmont areas. Blackberries and raspberries are popular and easy to grow.

The general culture of erect and trailing blackberries and the 'Dorman Red' raspberry are very similar.

Site Selection—All brambles should be planted in a sunny spot. They usually grow quite satisfactorily in soils ranging from sand to clay, but do best on sandy loam or clay loam soils. Avoid planting in low areas where water may stand after heavy rains. Before planting time arrives, take a soil sample from the proposed planting site to the local Cooperative Extension office for analysis to determine liming requirements. A pH of 6.0 to 6.5 is best for brambles.

Watering and Mulching—Water brambles during dry parts of the season. Apply enough water to wet the soil at least 8 to 10 inches below the ground surface. This is particularly important for raspberries. All brambles will benefit from mulching, which prevents extremes in soil temperature and helps to conserve moisture.

Trailing Blackberries and The 'Dorman Red' Raspberry

Plant trailing blackberries and raspberries between December and March. Should the plants arrive before time to set them, store them in a cool place (34°F to 40°F), and do not allow them to dry out. When planting time arrives, apply dolomitic lime if necessary to adjust the soil pH to the desired range and thoroughly work the soil to seedbed consistency. After the soil has been firmed by a drenching rain and excess water has drained out of the soil, it is time to build the trellis and do the planting.

Because blackberry and raspberry plants live for many years, the trellis posts should be treated with preservatives and No. 9 gauge wire should be used. Set posts 1½ or 2 feet in the ground spaced 10 to 20 feet apart. (Figure 1) Posts should be 6½ to 7 feet tall. Use three strands of trellis wire, with the first strand being 24 inches off the ground. The other two strands are spaced 18 inches apart. If more than one row is to be planted, the rows should be spaced 12 feet apart. Plant the brambles with 10 feet between plants. The diameter of the hole must be large enough to accommodate all the plant roots in their natural position. If container-grown plants are used, cut the roots off or untwine them so that none remain in a circular position. When planting is complete, the crown (the origin of the mass of roots) of the plant should be ½ inch below the soil line. Some plants will have a "handle" (piece of old stem attached to the plant), and this handle should be above the soil surface. Mulch the planting to conserve moisture and reduce weeds.

Pruning and Training—An understanding of the fruiting habit of brambles is necessary before they can be properly pruned and trained. Blackberry and raspberry plants produce biennial canes, which grow one season (primocanes), and flower, fruit and die the

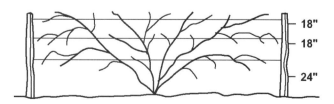

Figure 1. A proper trellis for training blackberries or raspberries.

18"
18"
24"

second season (floricanes). Primocanes are produced each season, so fruiting canes are present annually after the year of planting.

First Year: Little pruning is necessary for trailing brambles the year they are planted. Place a mulch of pine straw, hay, newspaper or plastic on the ground around the plants.

Second Year: After the fruiting season, remove the old (floricane) canes that are in the process of dying. Carefully tie the new canes of trailing blackberries to the trellis and pinch the growing tip, known as 'tipping', six inches above the top wire to encourage branching. During the following winter, train canes in a fan pattern away from the crown and place ties where canes cross each trellis wire. Lateral shoots may be shortened to lengths of 10 to 20 inches, if necessary. In the second year, plants should have a total cane length of 20 to 50 feet with larger vigorous plants retaining more wood. As the plants age, more canes can be left. Exceptionally vigorous plants may be able to support up to 100 feet of canes. Plants with low vigor should be pruned to retain fewer canes.

For 'Dorman Red' raspberries, let the canes lie on top of the mulch until late February, and then tie them to the trellis. This will reduce winter damage to the canes. After the first fruiting season (second year of establishment), the canes that have fruited will die. Prune out these canes. Confine new canes (those that will produce fruit the next season) to the ground under the trellis, to avoid running over them with the mower. In late winter, train the new canes to the wires. Because some of these new canes may be 15 or more feet long, estimate the length of individual canes needed to fit on the trellis. While the canes are still on the ground, cut them to this estimated length, lift them off the ground, and tie them to the trellis.

Harvesting—The berries are ripe and are at the peak of flavor when they lose their high glossy shine and turn slightly dull. Harvesting is best when the berries are juiciest, which is during the late morning hours after the dew has dried. Harvest time for both raspberries and blackberries can vary depending on the cultivar and where they are located in the state. Harvest can range from mid-June to the end of July. In general, the harvest of bramble varieties begins about two weeks earlier in South Georgia, and one to two weeks later in the Georgia Mountains.

Fertilization—Fertilize trailing blackberries, 'Dorman Red' raspberries and erect blackberries twice a year in most situations. Trailing blackberries and 'Dorman Red' raspberry plants should receive about 2 ounces of premium grade (containing micronutrients) 10-10-10 in April and July of the first year. Scatter the fertilizer evenly over a circle 2 feet in diameter centered on the plant. Erect blackberries are usually planted closer together,

Table 1. Recommended bramble fruit varieties

VARIETY	CANE TYPE	COMMENTS
Blackberries		
Choctaw	Thorny, erect	Early blooming, early ripening with good flavor; smaller seeds than other varieties. Rosette resistance unknown.
Rosborough	Thorny, erect	Productive release from Texas; very slightly acidic fruit. Moderately susceptible to rosette disease.
Kiowa	Thorny, erect	One of the best varieties; largefruit; high yielding. Some resistance to rosette.
Arapaho	Thornless, erect	Early ripening; good flavor; medium fruit size; long harvest, moderate yields. Shows resistance to rosettte.
Navaho	Thornless, erect	Late ripening; medium size fruit. Good rosette resistance.
Gem	Thorny, trailing	Excellent quality; good producer; has resistance to rosette.
Hull	Thornless, trailing	Semi-erect; later ripening; high yielding; better flavor if allowed to ripen fully.
Raspberries		
Dorman Red	Trailing	Fruit must be very ripe to be sweet; good producer statewide.
Redwing	Erect	Heritage cross; 10 to 14 days earlier than Heritage with similar quality; recommended for trial in mountains and Piedmont area.
Heritage	Erect	For Georgia mountains and upper Piedmont.

so a banded fertilizer application can be made from the start. The first year, apply one pound of 10-10-10 per 18 feet of row in April and one pound per 36 feet of row in June. For all three types in future years apply one pound of 10-10-10 per 9 feet of row in February or early March and one pound of 10-10-10 per 18 feet of row in June. Spread the fertilizer evenly over the row in a band 2 feet wide. A soil sample will help to determine the correct amount of fertilizer needed.

Erect Blackberries

Planting—Erect blackberries should be planted in late February and early March. If root cuttings or plants arrive before this time, store them in a cool place (34°F to 40°F) until ready to plant. These root cuttings or plants should not be allowed to dry out; keep them damp but not wet during storage. Plants or root cuttings (which are 4 to 6 inches long and about pencil-size in diameter) can be used to establish erect blackberry plantings. Root cuttings cost about a third as much as plants and are preferred for this reason.

Fifteen plants, if properly cared for, will supply berries for an average family of four. If a hedge-row of black-berries is desired, plant the root cuttings or plants 2 to 4 feet apart in the row. For individual planting, keep plants separated, set root cuttings or plants 8 feet apart in the row. Set the root cuttings horizontally 2 inches below the soil surface. If plants are to be used instead of root cuttings, plant them with the root system approximately 2 inches below the soil line. Do not fertilize at planting time; wait until after a drenching rain settles the soil. If more than one row is to be planted, plant rows 12 feet apart.

Pruning—The year of planting, canes produced by the plants will be semi-erect. Contain these semi-erect canes to the row area and do not prune them. They will provide some fruit the following year.

New canes produced the second and succeeding seasons will be erect. They should be cut to a height of 30 to 36 inches in early summer to encourage lateral shoot development. (Figure 2) This practice reduces excessive height of the canes and increases the stability of the hedge. Several prunings may be necessary.

During the dormant season, the dead canes that provided fruit the previous summer should be pruned out. While winter pruning, it is a good idea to shorten any long, lateral branches. Reduce these by one-third to one-half of the length of the branch.

Harvesting—The berries are ripe and at their peak of flavor when they lose their glossy shine and turn slightly dull. Harvesting is best during the late morning hours after the dew has dried. The harvest season for Cherokee and Cheyenne is June 10 to July 5 at Athens. Harvest begins about two weeks earlier in South Georgia and one to two weeks later in the Georgia mountains.

Primocane Raspberries

'Heritage' and 'Redwing' are erect "fall" raspberry varieties that produce fruit in late summer and fall. Planting should be confined to the Piedmont and mountain areas for these red raspberry varieties. These varieties differ from erect blackberries, trailing blackberries and the 'Dorman Red' raspberry because they produce fruit on primocanes (first year canes). Canes emerge from the ground in early spring, grow to a height of 3 to 4 feet and form flower clusters in the terminals of the canes. Once the terminals flower, flower clusters are produced one at a time progressively back down the canes. First fruits of 'Redwing' to ripen are generally ready for harvest in Athens about July 15. Harvest continues until a killing freeze.

Soil Preparation and Planting—Prepare the soil as outlined for erect blackberries. Set the plants 2 feet apart in rows 12 feet apart. Raspberries perform poorly in heavy clay soils. It is critical they be planted in good soil with irrigation and mulching.

Fertilization—Fertilize erect raspberries with 1.5 ounces of premium grade (containing micronutrients) 10-10-10 per foot of row in March and 3 ounces of

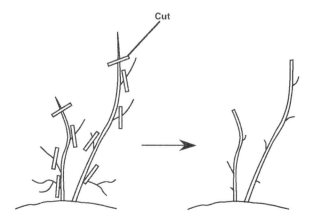

Figure 2

Figure 2. When the new shoots of erect blackberries reach 30-36" in height, cut off the tips. In winter dead or weak wood should be removed and laterals can be pruned to 12-14" for convenient harvesting.

calcium nitrate (or 3 ounces of 10-10-10) per foot of row in June of the first year. From the second year on, increase the March application to 3 ounces of 10-10-10 and continue to use the June application of 3 ounces of calcium nitrate.

Pruning—The best part of growing primocane raspberries is the ease of pruning. In the winter, cut all canes off at the ground line. Primocane varieties can be treated exclusively as a fall fruiting variety when all of the canes are removed each winter. Commercial producers mow the canes at the ground line with a sickle bar mower and rake the old canes out for burning.

BLUEBERRIES

The beautiful rabbiteye blueberry is native to Georgia. Fishermen collected the best wild blueberries growing along our rivers, and later Dr. Tom Brightwell and other horticulturists created improved varieties of rabbiteye blueberries.

Rabbiteyes are generally the best type of blueberries for home gardeners in Georgia. Southern highbush blueberries are grown commercially in Georgia, but require high organic matter soil (at least 3 percent) and are very prone to attack by deer and birds because they ripen early in the season. For this reason, they are usually poor choices from home gardeners. On sites in the mountains of North Georgia, northern highbush blueberries can be grown. Northern highbush blueberries often bloom later than rabbiteyes, so they may be useful on freeze-prone sites in the mountains. Northern highbush blueberries often require deer and bird protection.

Home blueberry plants seldom require spraying for insects or diseases in most areas of the state. A number of nurseries in Georgia propagate and sell blueberry plants. Local garden centers may have them.

Under good management, blueberry bushes will produce some fruit the second or third year after transplanting. By the sixth year they will yield as much as 2 gallons each.

Rabbiteye Varieties—The most important thing to remember about starting rabbiteye blueberries is to plant more than one variety for cross-pollination. Cross-pollination is necessary for fruit set.

'Climax', 'Chaucer', 'Choice', and 'Woodard' are not suggested for mountain areas because they bloom early. 'Austin', 'Climax', and 'Premier' are the earliest ripening rabbiteye varieties. To lengthen the harvest season, select one or more of these varieties, and one or more of the other varieties. 'Baldwin', 'Centurion', and 'Delite' are the latest maturing rabbiteye varieties. By planting early, mid-season and late varieties, fresh blueberries can be enjoyed for six weeks.

'Woodard' is a good berry for fresh eating but develops a tough skin when frozen for future consumption. 'Brightwell', 'Centurion', 'Tifblue', and 'Powderblue' are generally the most spring freeze resistant. Table 2 lists some varieties recommended for Georgia gardens. As with any variety recommendations in this book, consult Extension publications for recommendations on new varieties.

Northern Highbush Varieties—Northern highbush blueberries are, as a rule, self-fertile. However, larger and earlier ripening berries result if several cultivars are interplanted for cross-pollination. They can be grown in the mountains of North Georgia if soil conditions are met and if birds and deer are controlled. Early and mid-season northern highbush varieties ripen ahead of the earliest rabbiteyes.

Obtain plants in time for winter transplanting. Select a site with sun for at least one-half the day. Blueberries will grow in shady spots, but fruit production will be poor.

Soil Preparation and Planting—Blueberries require a soil pH of 4.0 to 5.3 for best growth. If soil pH is in

Table 2. Blueberry varieties for home gardens

Early	Mid-season	Late
Alapaha	Bluebelle	Baldwin
Austin	Briteblue	Centurion
Brightwell	Chaucer	Choice
Climax	Powderblue	Delite
Premier	Tifblue	
Woodard		
Blue Suede[1]		

[1] New southern highbush variety introduced specifically for the home garden market.

the range of 5.4 to 6.0, sulfur can be applied six months before planting to lower the pH. Sulfur may also be applied after planting to the soil surface but not mixed with the soil. Rates of up to 11 ounces per 100 square feet can be used yearly, if needed. If the initial soil pH is above 6.0, growing blueberries will be difficult unless massive amounts of peat moss or milled pine bark are mixed with the soil.

The standard spacing for rabbiteye blueberries is 6 feet in the row with 12 feet between rows. The standard spacing for highbush is 4 feet in the row with 10 feet between rows. For a quicker hedgerow effect, plant rabbiteyes 4 feet apart in the row. If developing individual specimen plants of rabbiteyes, use a spacing of 8 to 10 feet between plants.

Till the soil at least 8 inches deep in a band at least 4 feet wide. If the site is excessively wet, plant on a raised bed 6 to 12 inches high and 4 feet wide.

Mix 2 to 5 gallons of wet peat moss or milled pine bark with the soil in each planting hole. Do not use any agricultural lime; blueberries require an acid soil. Pot-bound plants have roots loosened prior to transplanting. Hold the plant by the base of the stem and beat the root ball on the ground until most of the potting media falls out and the roots are exposed. Spread out the roots. Plants that are not pot-bound can be planted without beating the root ball. Transplant to the same depth that they grew in the nursery. Look for the soil line markings on plants. Firm the soil after planting.

Fertilization—Do not apply any fertilizer at transplanting. After new growth begins (March) and rain or irrigation settles the soil, apply 2 ounces of azalea special fertilizer (4-8-8) or 1 ounce of 12-4-8 or 10-10-10 per plant. Fertilize again at the same rate in May and July if rainfall or overhead irrigation has been good. Spread the fertilizer evenly over a circle 18 inches in diameter with the plant in the center.

In March and July of the second year apply 2 ounces of 10-10-10 or 12-4-8, or use 3 to 4 ounces of azalea special fertilizer (4-8-8). Never over-fertilize; fertilizer damages blueberries easily until they are established. Spread the fertilizer evenly over a circle 24 inches in diameter with the plant in the center.

After the third season, base the amount of fertilizer applied on the size of the bushes. If the soil test results are very high in phosphorus, use 12-4-8. If your soil tests low or medium in phosphorus, use 10-10-10. Use "premium grade" fertilizer if possible; this type contains

secondary and micronutrients that may be needed. Apply 1 ounce of 12-4-8 or 10-10-10 per foot of bush height at the time of bud break in the spring and after harvest in the summer. Continue to increase the amount of fertilizer applied yearly until the bushes are 8 feet tall. Bushes 8 feet tall or taller should receive the maximum rate of 8 ounces of fertilizer per bush. Spread the fertilizer evenly under and around the bushes.

Pruning—After establishment, rabbiteye blueberries require little pruning until they reach about 6 to 8 feet in height. At this point, a cane renewal pruning program should be started. Remove one to three of the largest canes each winter at 0 to 24 inches from ground level or a total of about 20 percent of the canopy. In areas where stem borers are a problem, make the pruning cuts at 24 inches. Over a period of five years the bush will be totally renewed. New, more productive canes will sprout from the old canes and will sprout below ground level. In addition, excessively tall canes can be pruned back to 6 to 8 feet each winter.

Water the plants throughout the growing season when rainfall is not adequate. Irrigation of young plants is especially important. Adequate water is essential for plant growth and important for fruit bud formation that occurs in the fall. Blueberries seldom require spraying for pests.

Cultivated blueberries are an almost perfect fruit. They are easy to pick, and the berries are large. To freeze them, pack the berries dry in plastic containers and place in the freezer. A small amount of frozen berries can be removed from the container and washed as needed.

Additional Recommendations for Highbush Blueberries—Highbush blueberries generally perform more satisfactorily on lighter (sandy to sandy loam) soils because of the need for good internal drainage to avoid infection by Phytophthora root rot. Generally, success with highbush on upland sites also depends on meeting the following conditions:

- Till 6 inches of peat moss, milled pine bark, or well-rotted pine sawdust into the soil in a band 3 to 4 feet wide down the row prior to planting.

- Keep the plants mulched 4 inches deep with pine bark nuggets, pine straw or pine sawdust.

- Install permanent sprinkler or micro-sprinkler irrigation and water regularly if rainfall is insufficient.

- Prune newly set bushes. The next winter, remove all or nearly all flower buds (large plump buds) by tipping the shoots. This will encourage the bush to grow faster by not bearing a crop in the second year. Highbush blueberries often over bear and annual pruning is usually necessary to keep the bushes healthy. On 3- and 4-year-old bearing plants, remove low spreading branches and excessively twiggy growth with too many flower buds.

• When the bushes are about 4 or 5 feet tall, begin a cane-renewal pruning program. First remove the oldest, weakest canes or diseased canes entirely. Then, among the remaining canes, start with the older ones and prune back approximately two per year either to strong laterals or to within 1 foot of the ground. New strong canes will usually develop below the cut. Over a period of four or five years, a new rejuvenated bush framework will be developed.

FIGS

Many people are fond of figs and rightfully so. They are very tasty and can be eaten fresh, preserved, or used for baking and making desserts like ice cream. Figs will do well in most parts of Georgia except the mountainous areas .

Site and Soil Requirements—Figs will grow in many types of soils, but they need a site free of root-knot nematodes. In the colder areas of the state, the ideal site is the south side of a building. Cold injury will be further reduced if the fig does not receive direct sunlight early in the morning or late in the evening during the winter months. However, the site should receive a minimum of eight hours of sunlight daily during the growing season.

Purchasing or Propagating Plants—Fig trees from nurseries may be grown in the field and sold bare-rooted or grown in containers and sold in the container.

Because considerable confusion exists about fig variety names, order fig plants only from reputable nurseries in the Southeast. Never purchase or attempt to grow the kinds of figs grown in California. They require pollination by a tiny wasp that cannot survive under Georgia's climatic conditions. The only types recommended in Georgia are the common ones that produce only female flowers and set fruit without cross-pollination.

Fig trees are easy to propagate, and a home planting can be started at very little expense. The simplest and easiest method of propagating figs is by stem cuttings from an older bush. Make cuttings in late February. The cutting should be 8 to 10 inches long from 1-year-old wood. The upper end should be cut just above a node. Tips and soft growth do not root satisfactorily. Set the cuttings directly in the nursery row in well-drained and well-prepared soil. The cutting length governs the planting depth.

Cuttings should be planted so only one bud is exposed and spaced 10 inches apart in the row. In case of dry weather, watering will aid the growth of the cuttings. These cuttings root early, grow rapidly and make good trees for permanent planting in the fall.

Figs may also be propagated by rooted side shoots. Shoots below the ground's surface frequently root; they may be separated from the parent bush and transplanted.

Figs can also be propagated during the growing season by rooting leafy cuttings under mist, or by air layering. The use of these procedures, however, is seldom warranted.

To propagate by an air layering, a ring of bark ¾ inch wide should be removed from a large twig or small branch. Moist sphagnum moss should be placed over the wounded area and covered with polyethylene film, and the film should be tied at both ends.

Varieties—There are many varieties of figs available, but only a few are well adapted to Georgia. (Table 3) To try growing figs in the mountains, one should select a protected site and try 'Celeste' or 'Hardy Chicago'. In addition, some varieties such as 'Brown Turkey' will produce some figs on the current season's growth after being killed to the ground by a freeze. In the Piedmont, 'Celeste', 'Hardy Chicago', and 'Conadria' are fairly well adapted. South of the Fall Line, any of the varieties listed can be grown, but 'Celeste' and 'Conadria' are two of the best. To extend the season with a late ripening variety, plant 'Alma'.

Soil Preparation and Planting—Soil preparation should always include a preplant soil test. If your soil pH is low, adjust the pH to 5.5 to 6.5 with dolomitic limestone. Spread the limestone evenly over the entire area where the figs will be planted, then till the soil. If possible, till a 6 x 6 foot area 8 inches deep for each bush.

Figs grown in bush form may be set as close as 10 feet apart in the row and 15 feet apart between rows. Figs grown in tree form should be set 15 to 20 feet apart in the row and 20 feet apart between rows. Plant fig trees while they are dormant. In warm areas, bare-rooted trees can be set out in fall or early winter. In middle and northern Georgia, it is best to set them out in spring after danger of hard winter freezes have passed. Container-grown plants can be transplanted later than bare-root plants.

Before planting a bare-root tree, prune about one-third of its top, unless it was topped at the nursery. Container-grown plants can be transplanted without being pruned.

Remove them from the container, spread their roots, and set them in the planting hole. Set trees in the planting hole 4 inches deeper than they were in the nursery to encourage low branching for bush form. Fill the hole with soil; water heavily enough to settle the soil around the roots. Do not apply fertilizer in the hole at planting.

Training and Pruning—Although fig plants can be trained to either tree or bush form, the tree form is not practical for the Piedmont area of Georgia. In this region, fig plants are frequently frozen back to the ground, making the tree form difficult to maintain.

Bush form is generally recommended for other areas of the state as well. In the bush form, more of the fruit will be closer to ground level and easier to pick. Begin training to bush form at the time of planting by cutting off one-third of the young plant. This forces shoots to grow from the base of the plant. Let these shoots grow through the first season. Then, late during the winter after the first growing season, select three to eight vigorous, widely spaced shoots to serve as leaders. Remove all other shoots.

Select leaders that are far enough apart to grow to 3 to 4 inches in diameter without crowding each other. If they are too close together, the leaders cannot grow thick enough to support themselves and their crop, and they tend to fall over or split off under stress of high winds. If this happens, remove the damaged leader and select a new one late the next winter by choosing one of the many suckers that arise annually.

If more branching is desired, head back the bush each spring beginning the second year after planting, after danger of frost is past but before growth has started. Do this by removing about one-third to one-half the length of the last year's growth.

Also, prune all dead wood and remove branches that interfere with the leaders' growth. Cut off low-growing lateral branches and all sucker growth that is not needed to replace broken leaders. Do not leave bare, unproductive stubs when pruning. These stubs are entry points for wood decay organisms. Make all pruning cuts back to a bud or branch.

Recommendations for Figs in South Georgia

Fertilizing—Fig trees grow satisfactorily in moderately fertile soils with limited fertilizer, but fertilizer is needed in soils of low fertility or where competition from other plants is heavy.

Although nitrogen is usually the only needed plant nutrient, other nutrients may be lacking in some areas. If the soil is not very fertile, follow these general guidelines:

* Use a fertilizer with an analysis of 8-8-8 or 10-10-10.

* Apply fertilizer three times a year to bushes to bring them into full production: early spring, mid-May, and mid-July. Mature bushes can be fertilized just once a year in the early spring.

* Fertilize newly set bushes with about 1 ounce of fertilizer at each application. Spread the fertilizer evenly over a circle 18 inches in diameter with the bush in the center. On second-year bushes, increase the amount of fertilizer to 3 ounces at each application and the diameter of the circle to 24 inches.

* To bring 3 to 5 year old bushes into full production, apply ⅓ pound per foot of bush height per application.

Table 3. Fig varieties for Georgia

VARIETY	COLOR OF FRUIT	COLD TOLERANCE	SIZE	Quality of Fruit	
				FRESH USE	PRESERVING
Alma	Greenish brown	Good	Small	Very good	Good
Brown Turkey	Bronze	Good	Medium	Good	Excellent
Celeste	Lt. brown to violet	Good	Small	Very good	Excellent
Green Ischia	Bright green	Fair	Medium	Good	Good (seeds objectionable)
Hunt	Dull bronze with white specks	Fair	Small to medium	Good	Excellent
Kadota	Bright greenish yellow	Poor	Small to medium	Fair	Excellent
LSU Purple	Reddish to dark purple	Poor-Moderate	Medium	Good	Fair
Magnolia	Bronze with white flecks	Poor	Medium	Fair	Excellent

If the fruit are not reaching maturity and ripening properly, excess fertilizer or drought may be the problem; fertilization should be reduced.

- Mature bushes 6 years and older should be fertilized once a year in early spring. On bushes spaced 10 feet apart, apply ½ pound of fertilizer per foot of height, up to 5 pounds per year. On bushes spaced 20 feet apart, apply 1 pound of fertilizer per foot height, up to 10 pounds per year. Scatter the fertilizer evenly under and around the bush. A satisfactory amount of shoot growth for mature plants is about 1 foot per year.

Watering—For highest yields, figs need watering throughout the summer. The frequency and the amount of water depends to a large extent on the soil. As a rule of thumb, 1 to 1½ inches of water per week from rain or irrigation is adequate. Yellowing and dropping of leaves may indicate drought.

In lawns, the grass beneath fig plants may wilt in the heat while the rest of the lawn does not. This indicates that the figs need water. Figs grown with lawn grasses may require watering one or more times a week during hot, dry periods.

Mulching—Figs respond well to mulching with organic materials. Mulch may reduce the effects of nematode problems.

Recommendations for Figs in North Georgia

Winter injury in figs is directly related to the amount of vigor of the plant. A vigorous, fast-growing plant is easily killed by low winter temperatures in the Piedmont. If figs are frequently winter injured in your area, halve the fertilization recommendations.

In attempting to grow figs near the mountains, limited fertilizer should be applied to make the plants as cold hardy as possible.

Fruiting or Lack of Fruiting—If you look for blossoms on a fig tree, you probably will not find them - they are inside the fruit. A number of conditions may cause the fruit not to ripen or to drop prematurely. The following are the most common in Georgia in order of importance:

1. Young, vigorous plants and over-fertilized plants will often produce fruit that drops off before maturing. If the plants are excessively vigorous, stop fertilizing them. Often, three or four years may pass before the plant produces a mature crop because most figs have a long juvenile period before producing fruit. If the distance between the nodes (leaves) on the current season's shoots is more than 3 inches, the plant is probably excessively vigorous.

2. Dry, hot periods that occur before ripening can cause poor fruit quality. If this is the case, mulching and supplemental watering during drought will reduce the problem.

3. The variety Celeste will often drop fruit prematurely in hot weather, regardless of the quality of plant care. However, it is still one of the best varieties.

4. An infestation of root-knot nematodes can intensify the problem when conditions are as described in items 2 and 3 above.

5. The fig plant may be one that requires cross-pollination by a special wasp. If this is the case, then it will never set a good crop. The best way to resolve this is to replace the plant with one from a rooted shoot of a plant you know produces a good crop each year. A fig plant that requires cross-pollination by the special wasp is a rare problem.

BUNCH GRAPES

Three primary species of bunch grapes are grown in the United States: the European bunch grape (*Vitis vinifera*), the American bunch grape (*Vitis labrusca*) and the Summer grape (*Vitis aestivalis*). Bunch grapes are often called "pod" grapes in rural Georgia since they produce large clusters of fruit. Georgia's climate is not well suited to home garden production of European bunch grapes, but American bunch grapes and hybrids between the two species grow well in Georgia. The Summer grape is also an American species and represented by a few varieties that are good for wine production. If grapes are well cared for and sprayed when diseases and insects threaten, yields of 20 to 30 pounds of fruit per vine can be expected.

Site Selection—In the Mountain and Piedmont areas of Georgia, late spring frosts can reduce yields significantly, so plant bunch grapes on elevated sites, if possible. In all areas, avoid low spots where cold air settles. The site should be in full sun. Well-drained, loamy sand, sandy loam, loam or clay loam soils are best for grape production. Avoid areas where water stands after heavy rains.

Rootstocks—American type bunch grapes and summer grapes are usually grown on their own roots in North Georgia. European grapes and French hybrids are usually grafted on rootstocks such as SO4 or 3309 to provide increased Phylloxera resistance. On sandy sites,

Table 4. Grape varieties for the Upper Piedmont & Mountains in order of ripening

VARIETY	RED WINE	WHITE WINE	JUICE/ JELLY	FRESH EATING	COMMENTS
Interlaken				X	Seedless; suffers cold damage often.
Foch (Kuhlman)	X				Blue-black fruit.
Aurora		X		X	Good for wine and fresh eating.
Fredonia*			X	X	Blue fruit.
Baco noir (Baco #1)	X				Blue-black fruit.
Delaware*	X		X	X	Small, sweet reddish fruit; should be grafted on Dog Ridge or similar rootstock for best results
Mars				X	Seedless, blue fruit
Reliance*				X	Seedless red fruit.
Chancellor	X				Dark red fruit.
Niagara*			X	X	Golden fruit; should be grafted on Dog Ridge or similar rootstock for best results.
Catawba	X		X	X	Purplish red fruit; may ripen unevenly; should be grafted on Dog Ridge or similar rootstock for best results.
Vidal	X				Yellow fruit.
Saturn				X	Seedless; red fruit.

* Most outstanding varieties.

test for the presence of root knot nematodes. If they are present, grapes should be grafted on nematode resistant rootstocks such as 'Tampa', 'Florilush' or 'Dog Ridge'.

Varieties—Many varieties of American type bunch grapes will perform well in zones 6 and 7 in Georgia (Table 4). Also, certain selections of French Hybrid grapes (wine grapes) are suggested for trial in these areas. Several hybrid bunch grapes are worthy of trial in zone 8 of Georgia.

Several hybrid bunch grape varieties have been developed which are worthy of trial plantings in Middle and South Georgia. All of these have good resistance to Pierce's Disease, the primary limiting factor to bunch grape culture in the middle and southern portion of Georgia. Table 4 lists suggested varieties for home plantings.

Purchasing Plants—Bunch grapes do not require cross-pollination. Therefore, it is not necessary to buy two or more varieties for pollination. Several varieties can be planted to extend the fruiting season.

Most bunch grapes are sold as one-year-old or two-year-

old plants. Generally, the two-year-old plants get started better and are worth the extra investment. Be sure to purchase them from a reliable source.

Planting the Vine and Plant Spacing—Grapes require a sturdy support structure for their vigorous vines. It is easiest to construct the trellis before planting, but it can be done after planting. Since most bunch grapes are somewhat less vigorous than the native muscadine, only eight to ten feet of row will be required for each vine. Lay out the rows at least 10 feet apart (12 feet on hilly land). Use straight rows for level or slightly rolling land and contour rows for hilly terrain. Prior to setting the vines, soil test and adjust the soil pH to 6.0 to 6.5 with dolomitic limestone. Most Georgia soils are low in magnesium, thus the need for dolomitic limestone.

To plant, prepare a hole large enough to accommodate the entire root system in its natural spread. Set the plant at or slightly below the level it grew in the nursery. Fill the hole with the natural topsoil and firm it. Do not place fertilizer in the hole. (See section on fertilization.) After firming the soil, water liberally.

Following the first growing season, cut the vine back to

a single stem with two to three good buds remaining. After growth begins, select the main trunk of the vine from the stronger of these shoots.

Training and Trellis Systems

American Type Bunch Grapes—American type bunch grapes are vigorous and have a trailing, downward growth habit. Three high trellis systems are commonly used to train home garden American type bunch grapes in the South: the double curtain, the two wire vertical, and the single wire. The top wire is five to six feet above ground level in all three systems.

Double Curtain Trellis—This trellis system is usually the most desirable of the three systems because of increased yields. The canopy is divided between two wires allowing more sunlight to reach the fruit renewal zone. This trellis system has two wires four feet apart and 5½ feet above the ground (Figure 3). A simple "T" bar trellis constructed from treated 4" x 4" posts can also be used.

Two Wire Vertical Trellis—The two wire vertical trellis used for the four-arm kniffin training system is considerably less expensive to construct than the double curtain trellis. However, shading of the foliage on the lower fruiting canes by the upper canes reduces the quality and productivity of the grapes on the lower wire. The primary use for this trellis is in situations where space is limited, but where there is good direct sun exposure. If direct sun exposure is limited because of row orientation, use the double curtain or single wire trellis.

Single Wire High Trellis—This trellis is good where

diseases are a problem. The vines on the single wire dry off more rapidly after a rain. Space the vines ten feet apart when using this trellis. Yields are lower than the other two systems, but construction is easy.

French Hybrid and European Bunch Grapes—Single Wire Low Trellis with Catch Wires (AKA Low Trellis Cordon System): French hybrid and European bunch grapes have new shoots that naturally grow upward. Two or three catch wires above the cordons (arms) further encourage this growth habit and allow good exposure of the fruit to sunlight and fungicide sprays. The low-trellis cordon system establishes the cordons 3 to 3.5 feet above the ground and includes 2 to 3 catch wires positioned at 10 inch intervals above the cordon wire. This system promotes vertical growth, resulting in a narrow, upright vertical canopy.

Training Young Vines

First year—Regardless of the training system, the first year goal is the establishment of a well-developed root system. The strongest cane should be cut back to two or three strong buds. Any other canes present should be removed. However, because it is sometimes difficult to determine the condition of a dormant vine, some growers prefer to leave five to six buds, and then, when growth starts, only allow the most vigorous or desirable buds to develop into shoots. If the trellis cannot be constructed during the first growing season, then a stake four to five feet high should be driven in the soil near each vine and the new growth trained to it. Tie the shoots loosely, or with plastic tape, to avoid the possibil-

Figure 3

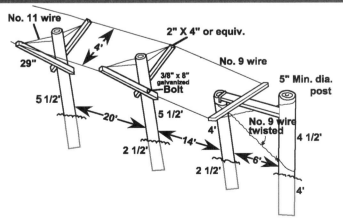

Figure 3. Details for constructing the Double Curtain trellis showing an "h" end post brace. The line posts are 3 to 4 inches in diameter, 8 feet long and placed 2½ feet in the ground and 20 feet apart . The end brace post is 8 feet long with a minimum diameter of 5 inches. It is placed 4 feet in the ground. A 6½ foot post is used as an inside brace post. Place it 2½ feet in the ground, 6 feet from the outside brace post and position a 4" x 4" timber between the top of the two posts as a brace.

ity of girdling. In cool areas of the country, growth rates are slow and vines are often pruned back to near ground level the first winter to help develop a vigorous trunk the second year. In Georgia the growing season is long and vines often make impressive growth the first year.

Double Curtain—Develop a double trunk ("Y"shape) for each vine approximately 30 inches above the ground. This is done by pinching out the growing point and forcing two shoots to develop. One trunk should be allowed to grow to one of the trellis wires and the other trunk to the other wire. Just below the wire pinch out the tip of the growing shoots to encourage side branches. Under good conditions, the trunk system for the grape vine should be developed by the end of the first growing season.

Two Wire Vertical Trellis—Develop a single strong shoot arising from the young plant by removing competing shoots. Train this shoot to a string or stake running from the upper wire of the trellis to the ground. Just below each wire pinch out the tip to encourage two side arms to develop.

Single Wire High Trellis—One shoot should be allowed to develop into the trunk. Train the trunk to a string or a training stake. When the tip reaches the wire, pinch it out and select two shoots growing about eight inches below the wire. Shoots positioned to grow on the trellis wire should be allowed to grow 12 to 18 inches long before they are tied down to the wires. Never tie the growing shoot tips to the wire because they will lose vigor. Always leave at least six inches of shoot tip free

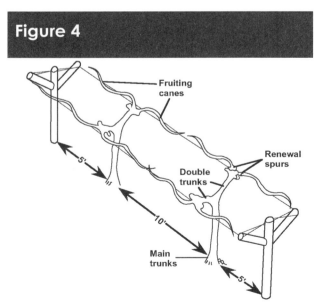

Figure 4

Fruiting canes

Renewal spurs

Double trunks

Main trunks

5'

10'

90°

5'

Figure 4. The Double Curtain trellis showing double trunks, fruiting canes and renewal spurs after pruning.

beyond the last tie so it can grow in an upward direction to maintain vigor.

Second year—The second year should be devoted to training and developing a strong plant structure that can support some fruiting during the third season. Figure 4 illustrates vines properly trained to the double curtain trellis.

Assuming normal growth has been obtained during the first growing season, all buds on the trunk that remain after pruning are capable of developing into shoots and producing fruit. However, fruit production at this stage of vine development will reduce vegetative growth and, therefore, is not desirable. Removal of flower clusters when they occur is recommended. All shoots below the bottom trellis wire should be removed, including suckers from the base of the vine. Continue to develop the permanent cordons (arms). Pinch off developing flowers unless the vines have made tremendous growth the first year. Even then, leave no more than a cluster or two of fruit. Remember that the goal at this point is training and not fruit production.

Pruning the Bearing Vine—Grapes require heavy annual pruning to maintain quality and productivity. Pruning should be done during the dormant season. Because of Georgia's mild climate, pruning should be carried out during February. Late winter or spring pruning will cause "bleeding" (flow of sap through the pruning wounds), but this should not cause alarm since it does not damage the plant.

Pruning

There are two very different types of pruning used on bunch grapes - cane and spur. American-type bunch grapes can be pruned by either cane or spur pruning. French hybrid type bunch grapes are typically spur pruned.

Cane Pruning—(American type bunch grapes) With cane pruning, only the trunk is permanent. The cordons (arms) are formed by leaving several of last year's canes. Do not over crop third-year vines. Thin the fruit clusters to one per shoot.

Most mature vines (typically four years and older) should be pruned to have between 30 and 60 buds. The more vigorous the vine, the more buds should be left. Balanced pruning, a method of pruning to balance production and vine vigor, is recommended. To balance prune, select four canes of last summer's growth, one for each direction on the two wires. These should be selected from canes arising from the head of the vine. Canes about the diameter of a pencil are most desirable. Cut each of these back to leave 15 to 20 buds per cane.

Gather up all of last season's canes pruned from the vine and weigh them. (Note: Do not weigh older wood.) As a rule of thumb, 30 buds should be left on the vine for the first pound of prunings removed, and 10 buds for each additional pound. Vines producing less than ¾ pound of prunings should not be cropped. As an example, suppose a vine after pruning where 60 buds were left yielded 3½ pounds of prunings. Then the number of buds to be left would be about 55 (30 for the first pound and 25 for the other 2½ pounds). Each of the four canes left should be pruned back to about 14 buds each. If balanced pruning is not to be done, then 30 to 60 buds should be left; the greater number being left on the most vigorous vines.

Leave renewal spurs to form canes for next year. These spurs are also canes of last season's growth pruned back to leave only two buds each. From these spurs will grow the fruiting canes for next year. Renewal spurs should be located as near the trunk as possible (Figure 5).

Spur Pruning—(French hybrid bunch grapes and American type bunch grapes) With spur pruning, the trunk and the cordons are permanent and the current season's growth is cut back to short shoots (spurs).

Single Wire Low Trellis with Catch Arms—In late winter cut back side shoots that grew the previous summer. This forms the "spurs". Leave two or three buds per spur for French hybrid grapes and four to six buds on American type bunch grapes. Select shoots that grew upward in a well-lighted environment to have the

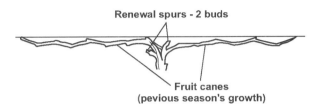

Renewal spurs - 2 buds

Fruit canes
(pevious season's growth)

Figure 5. **Mature grape vine properly pruned showing fruiting canes and renewal spurs. Each cane on the double curtain or 2 wire vertical trellis should be similarly pruned.**

most fruitful spurs. Thin the side shoots to about six inches apart.

The second step is to remove water sprouts, suckers, and any tendrils attached to the trunk or cordons. Finally, prune back cordon growth beyond the four foot point or halfway to the next vine. In the spring allow four to six shoots per foot of cordon to develop, removing shoots where necessary. Also, selectively remove leaves from around the fruit clusters to improve fruit quality and help reduce disease pressure. These leaves can be removed shortly after bloom but before the fruits begin to change color and soften. Do not remove leaves after the fruits begin to soften because sunburn may result.

Fertilization

Establishment of the proper fertility level before planting helps get the young vines off to a good start. Have soil tested prior to planting. After the plants have been settled by a drenching rain and before growth starts, apply ¼ cup of 10-10-10 fertilizer around each plant. Keep the fertilizer at least six inches from the vine. Repeat at six week intervals until mid-July.

On two-year-old vines, double the first-year rate and use the same interval. Bearing vines will need 2½ pounds of 10-10-10 per plant applied in March. If growth is poor on producing vines, apply one additional pound of 10-10-10 per plant in May, as well.

Georgia soils are inherently low in magnesium, and foliar magnesium deficiency frequently becomes noticeable in mid-summer. This deficiency is characterized by a yellowing between the leaf veins on the older grape leaves. If the soil &pH is sufficiently low to warrant liming, use dolomitic lime to help prevent magnesium deficiency in future years. Otherwise, magnesium sulfate (Epsom salts) should be applied and watered in. For young plants, apply two ounces around each vine, keeping the salts away from the trunk six or more inches. Apply 4 to 8 ounces per mature, fruit-bearing vine. It may require 2 to 3 years of magnesium application to bring the level up for the best plant performance.

Cultivation and Weed Control—Every effort should be made to establish a permanent sod between rows before planting the vineyards to reduce soil erosion. After the sod is established and the vines are planted, hand weeding and hoeing, or careful herbicide application will be necessary around the individual vines during the first two growing seasons. The sod should be kept mowed during the summer months.

Once the vineyard is established and producing fruit (generally, by the third season), herbicides can be used to keep the strip along the rows free of weeds and grasses. Several herbicides cleared for use on grapes do an excellent job if properly used. They can be applied with tractor-mounted or hand-operated equipment. Mulching is also useful for improving soil temperature, regulating soil moisture, and reducing weed growth.

MUSCADINE GRAPES

Muscadines are truly a fruit for the South. They were discovered here by the early colonists and have been a favorite fruit of Southerners since. Muscadines are best adapted to the Piedmont and Coastal Plain areas. The severe winters of the Mountain area hamper production.

Muscadines are ideal for backyard gardens because they can be successfully grown with a minimum spray program.

Requirements for Growing Muscadines

A sunny spot—Muscadines do best when they are in full sun for most of all the day. Muscadines do fairly well on most soil types. Do not plant in a spot where water stands after heavy rains.

A good trellis—Muscadine vines may live for decades, so, a strong supporting structure is needed made of materials that will last for many years. Wooden posts should be pressure treated with wood preservatives.

Hand-size pruning shears—If pruning is done properly and on a yearly basis, large pruning tools should not be necessary.

Good plants—Muscadine varieties can be divided into four categories: two based on fruit color (black or bronze), and two based on flower type: perfect flowered or self-pollinating and female. If you plan to grow only one vine, it can be black or bronze, but must be perfect flowered to produce fruit. Female varieties produce no pollen. Therefore, they should be inter-planted with perfect-flowered varieties for proper pollination and fruit set. Recommended Muscadine varieties are listed in Table 5.

Planting the Vines

Muscadines require a minimum 20 feet of trellis per plant. Therefore, measure the area where the vines will be planted to know how many plants to purchase. For more than one row, space the rows 12 feet apart. Once

it is determined how many plants are needed, lay out the area by putting stakes where the trellis posts will go. The posts should be 20 feet apart. Plant the muscadine about one foot from the post since the crop load is usually heaviest in the center of the vine.

To plant, dig a hole large enough to accommodate a bushel basket. The soil pH should be 6.0 to 6.5. For best accuracy of pH, take a soil sample. If no soil sample is taken, thoroughly mix ½ cup of agricultural limestone (dolomitic type) with the soil taken from the hole. Then, plant the vine the same depth it grew in the nursery and water it. After watering, trim the plant, leaving about six inches of the vine above the soil line. Caution: Do not put fertilizer in the planting hole. Do not apply fertilizer immediately after planting.

Trellising

The One Wire Trellis and the Double Curtain Trellis are the two most common trellises used by backyard gardeners. The one wire trellis is easier to construct, but yields are greater from the double curtain. If space is limited, the double curtain should be used to maximize production.

One Wire Trellis—Use the single wire trellis (Figure 6) system in South Georgia because of fruit disease problems. Use five or six inch pressure-treated, eight-foot posts as end posts. Set them three feet deep and angle them slightly away from each other. Line post(s) should be four to five inches in diameter and seven to eight feet long. Set them two to three feet deep in a vertical position. Use no. 9 wire to support the vines.

Figure 6

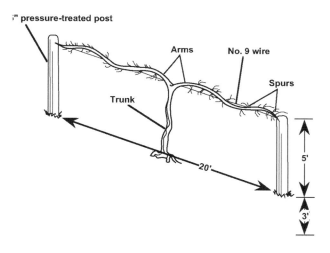

Figure 6. A one wire trellis with established vine.

Table 5. Muscadine varieties

VARIETY	FLOWER TYPE	SIZE	COLOR	MAIN USES	COMMENTS
*Carlos	P.F.	Medium	Bronze	Juice, wine	Productive.
Cowart	P.F.	Large	Black	Fresh eating	Good flavor.
Dixie	P.F.	Medium	Bronze	Juice, wine	Good cold tolerance.
Dixieland (Pat.)	P.F.	V. Large	Bronze	Fresh eating	Vines lack.
Doreen	P.F.y	Medium	Bronze	Juice wine	Very productive. Good winter hardiness.
Dulcet	F.	Medium	Black	Fresh eating	Good flavor.
*Fry	F.	V. Large	Bronze	Fresh eating	Fruit rot & winter injury a problem; excellent flavor.
Golden Isles	P.F.	Medium	Bronze	Juice, wine	Non-musky aroma.
*Granny Val (Pat.)	P.F.	Large	Bronze	Fresh eating	Late season. Vines may lack vigor; cold tender.
Higgins	F.	Large	Bronze-pink	Fresh eating	Mild flavor; late season.
Jumbo	F.	V. Large	Black	Fresh eating	Low sugar content.
*Loomis	F.	Med-large	Black	Fresh eating	Excellent flavor.
Magnolia	P.F.	Medium	Bronze	Juice, wine	Good flavor; good winter hardiness.
*Nesbitt	P.F.	V. Large	Black	Fresh eating	Good cold tolerance.
*Noble	P.F.	Small	Black	Juice, wine	Productive.
Scuppernong	F.	Medium	Bronze	Wine, fresh eating	Very old variety; low yields.
*Summit	F.	Large	Bronze-pink	Fresh eating	Good winter hardiness; more disease-resistant than Fry.
*Tara	P.F.	Large	Bronze	Fresh eating	Fairly good flavor.
*Triumph	P.F.	Med-large	Bronze-pink	Fresh eating	Early season.

* = Probably the best.; y = P.F. = Perfect flowered (pollen and fruit).; F. = Female flowered (fruit only).

Wrap the trellis wire around one end post near the top. Staple it securely several times. Then, run it across the top of the end post and staple it loosely. Next, run the wire over the tops of the line posts. Staple the wire loosely to the tops of these posts. Staple the wire loosely to the top of the other end post. Then, pull the wire tight. Wrap it around the end post and staple it tightly several times. The wire should be five feet above and parallel to the ground.

Double Curtain Trellis—The double curtain trellis provides two wires four feet apart and five feet above

ground (Figure 7). This permits each vine to produce 40 feet of fruiting arm rather than the conventional 20 feet with the one wire system.

Four-inch galvanized pipe welded to form the T-shaped end posts can also be used. The wires should be parallel to the ground.

Training The Vine

Diligent care during the two growing seasons following planting is essential if the vines are to develop into productive additions to the home garden. Vines generally die the year of planting if particular attention is not given to them. Watering as needed, fertilizing as recommended, keeping the area around the young plants weed free, and proper training must be done if success is to be realized.

A properly trained vine has a trunk, two (or four) arms and fruiting spurs. The first two years of training are devoted to developing the permanent trunk and fruiting arms. (see Figure 8)

In the spring following planting, each plant will produce three or four shoots. When these shoots are about 1 foot long, select the strongest and remove all the others. Tie a string to a small stake. Drive the stake into the ground. Place it about 3 inches from the plant.

One Wire Trellis—Tie the free end of the string to the trellis wire. Train the shoot to the string. Pinch off side shoots as they develop. When the shoot reaches the top wire, pinch it off just below the wire. Let the top two buds form the two arms along the trellis wire.

Double Curtain Trellis—Immediately above the young vine, tie a piece of string between the two wires. Then tie the free end of the string attached to the stake to the middle of the string connecting the two wires. The two strings should form a "Y." Train the shoot to the string. When the shoot reaches the string connected to the two wires, pinch out the tip. Let the top two buds develop. Train these shoots to the strings leading to the trellis wire. Once they reach the wire, pinch out the tips and let the top two buds form the two arms along the trellis wire.

For either trellis system, continuously pinch back shoots other than the arms growing from the trunk. Once the trunk and arms have developed, the vine is ready to begin fruiting. Shoots (also called canes) will grow each year from the young arms. Since muscadine fruit are borne on new shoots arising from last year's growth, prune back the canes that grew the previous year, leaving about 3 inches of growth to form spurs. Prune in February or early March. Do not be alarmed if the vines "bleed" at pruning cuts. Bleeding does not harm the vines.

When too many buds are left on the vine, the plant overproduces and fruit are poor. After three or four years of production, remove every other spur cluster to prevent overcrowding. Try to leave spurs that are on the top of the arms. It is a good idea to remove old fruit stems since they are a source of disease.

Remove tendrils that wrap around the arms or spurs.

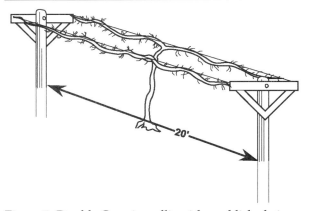

Figure 7. Double Curtain trellis with established vine.

Tendrils are finger-like plant parts muscadines use to attach themselves to their supporting structure. If tendrils are not removed, they will girdle the arms or spurs and cause reduced production. Remove old fruit stems if fruit rots are a problem, as the disease may overwinter in the old stems.

Fertilizing

First year—Apply fertilizer three times: (a) ½ pound of 10-10-10 or equivalent after the plants have been settled by rain, (b) 2 ounces of ammonium nitrate in late May, and (c) 2 ounces of ammonium nitrate in early July. Broadcast each application over a 2-foot circle centered on the plant.

Second year—Timing and method are the same as the first year. Double the rate for each application. Increase the diameter of the broadcast circle to 4 feet.

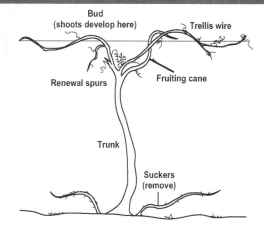

Figure 8. Grape vine.

Third year—If the vine has grown well the first two years and is producing a crop, apply 2 pounds of 10-10-10 or equivalent per vine in March. Apply 1 pound of 10-10-10 per vine in May. Broadcast in a 6-foot circle. If plants have not done well, fertilize as instructed for the second year.

Established vines—Apply 3 to 5 pounds of 10-10-10 or equivalent per plant in March of each year. Then apply ½ pound of ammonium nitrate about June 1. Check the soil pH about every three years. If liming is necessary, use dolomitic lime.

Special Fertilization—Grapes have a relatively high requirement for magnesium. Each year, hundreds of Georgians have grape vines that suffer from a shortage of magnesium. This shows up as yellowing between the veins of older leaves. This yellowing progresses up the shoots as the leaves grow older. Premature fruit fall may also result. To prevent or correct magnesium deficiency, apply Epsom salts (magnesium sulfate) at the rate of 2 to 4 ounces for one- and two-year-old vines; 4 to 6 ounces for older vines. Be sure to evenly broadcast Epsom salts over a 3- to 6-foot area.

STRAWBERRIES

To get a strawberry bed started, all that is needed is a small area that receives full sun most or all of the day. Strawberries will grow well in many types of soil. However, the most desirable soil is fertile, medium-light in texture, well drained and with good moisture-holding capacity. Avoid heavy clays, deep sands and wet soils.

After selecting the site, have the soil tested to determine lime and fertilizer needs. Also, have the soil assayed for nematodes. If lime and/or other nutrients are needed, or nematode treatment is recommended, do not neglect to do as suggested because these treatments are essential to produce good berries. Because of diseases, two very different production systems are used in Georgia. In the matted-row system, plants are set out one spring and fruit the next. This system works best in north Georgia and production may continue for several years. The annual hill system is preferred for middle and South Georgia because anthracnose disease often destroys the matted-row plantings. Plants are set out in the fall and fruit the next spring. The planting is usually destroyed after the crop is harvested.

Varieties

The performance of strawberry varieties can be affected by climate and soil type. Therefore, it is important to use the varieties best suited to a particular area. Buy only certified virus-free plants from a reputable nursery. If the plants arrive and you are unable to plant immediately, store them in the refrigerator. See Table 5 for recommended varieties.

Matted-Row System

The matted-row system works well in north Georgia. The matted-row system involves planting the mother plants 2 feet apart the first spring, then letting runners fill the bed the first summer. The flowers are removed the first year, so no fruit is produced until the second year. An area approximately eight feet wide and 30 feet long will be needed to produce plenty of berries for a family of four for year-round use. Thirty plants will be needed to start the bed. A sunny spot with good soil is necessary to successfully grow strawberries. Avoid planting the berries where pepper, tomatoes, and potatoes have been grown in the last five years, since they and the strawberries are susceptible to verticillium wilt.

Weeds are often a problem in growing strawberries. Thus, you should begin preparing the bed a year in advance of planting. Periodically till or spade the area so that weeds present will not produce seed and cause a future problem. This is also a good time to add lime if soil test results indicate a need.

About a week before planting, broadcast 5 pounds of 10-10-10 or 4 pounds of 13-13-13 slow release fertilizer over the 8 x 30 foot area where the strawberries are to be planted. Till the soil and smooth the bed. Allow the soil to be settled by a rain before planting. When soil moisture conditions are ideal for planting (the soil is not wet), lay off two rows that are 4 feet apart. Each of the rows should be 2 feet from the edge of the bed. Set the plants 2 feet apart in the rows and set the plants at the correct depth.

The top of the crown should be above the soil line. A couple of weeks after the new plants begin to grow, flowers will appear. Remove these flowers the spring of the first year to allow plant development to occur.

During the summer of establishment, allow the strawberry runners to develop to form the matted-row. Strawberries require 1 to 1½ inches of water per week, so water the planting if rainfall is not sufficient. Remember to keep weeds under control. Mulching, hand pulling, hoeing and tilling are the best means of controlling weeds in a small planting although there are a few herbicides available for use on strawberries. Consult the *Georgia Pest Management Handbook* for

Table 6. Strawberry varieties by season and areas of adaptability

VARIETY	EARLY	MIDSEASON
Earliglow	M, N	
Delmarva	M, N	
Allstar		M, N
Chandler	S, M, N (annual hill system only)	
Camarosa	S, M (annual hill system only)	
Sweet Charlie	S, M, N (South Georgia- annual hill system only. All other areas may be grown on either.)	

1 S-South Georgia, M-Middle Georgia, N-Piedmont and North Georgia. A number of varieties traditionally grown in Georgia, such as Apollo, Cardinal, Tioga, Albritton and Delite, have become difficult to obtain.
Apollo should be planted with another variety to ensure fruit set. Other varieties can be planted alone. Sweet Charlie can be grown in both the matted row or the annual hill system.

current recommendations.

The bed should be fertilized twice during the first summer. Broadcast 3 pounds of 13-13-13 or 4 pounds of 10-10-10 over the bed in mid-June and again in late September. Always apply fertilizer to the plants when the foliage is dry, and sweep the plants with a broom or leaf rake immediately following the application. If the soil is extremely sandy, it may be beneficial to fertilize the bed using the above rates in late-May, mid-July and early October. The desired results of the first growing season is to develop matted-rows 2 feet wide with a 2-foot walk space between the rows.

If the planting is vigorous, runners that grow into the aisle will need to be trimmed back. During the winter and spring months, periodically check the planting for the development of winter weeds that should be removed. In the late winter of second and subsequent years (mid-February in middle Georgia and mid-March in the Georgia mountains), broadcast 3 pounds of 13-13-13 or 4 pounds of 10-10-10 fertilizer over the bed. Following fertilization, mulch the bed with a layer (1 to 2 inches) of pine straw before growth begins. Rake most of the straw off the tops of the plants. The strawberry plants will grow up through the straw, and the straw will help keep the berries from getting soiled.

The application of fungicides will be necessary to prevent berry rots if rains are frequent during the harvest period. Insects that feed on the fruit and foliage may also be present.

Renovate after Harvest—The last day of harvesting the crop for the year is the day to get the bed into good shape for the next season. This is in late May to mid-June, depending on the area in the state. If it happens to be too wet to till, wait a few days.

To renovate the matted-rows, mow the leaves from the strawberry plants. Be sure to mow them high enough so that the lawn mower blade does not damage the crowns. Next, narrow the 2-foot wide mats with a tiller or turn the soil with a shovel so that the remaining strip of plants is about 8 inches wide. Save some of the young plants instead of the original mother plants. Remove two-thirds of the plants or there will be too many plants for next year. After tilling is completed, rake out as many of the plants in the tilled area as possible and smooth the soil surface. Broadcast over the bed 3 pounds of 13-13-13 or 4 pounds of 10-10-10 fertilizer, and turn the sprinkler on. One-half to 1 inch of water should be applied immediately following renovation in the form of rainfall or irrigation.

If the bed is still in good condition after two picking seasons, renovate again after harvest and follow the second season recommendations to harvest berries from the same bed a third year.

If a new planting is desired, move it to another area since there may be disease and/or nematode buildup. Always buy new, certified plants to use in the new bed. Old plants may have been infested with nematodes and/or viruses, which will reduce yields and fruit size.

Care after Renovation—Be sure to keep the bed free of weeds and irrigate if the rain is insufficient. Strawberries need 1 to 1½ inches of water per week. Fertilizer should be applied two more times during the second and subsequent growing season. In mid-July, broadcast 2 pounds of 13-13-13 or 3 pounds of 10-10-10 fertilizer over the bed. The last application should be applied in mid to late September by broadcasting 3 pounds of 13-13-13 or 4 pounds of 10-10-10 fertilizer over the bed. Don't forget to apply when the foliage is dry, and sweep the leaves free of fertilizer. By late September, the matted-rows should again be 2 feet wide. Remove any plants that grow into the aisle in late summer.

Winter and Spring Culture—(Third and subsequent years) Check for weeds and remove any that are present. Fertilize using the same rate and timing as the previous winter. Remember to mulch and keep your eyes open for fruit rots, particularly during wet weather, and also insects that may eat the fruit or foliage. A fungicide to prevent rots, or an insecticide to control the harmful insects may be necessary.

Annual Hill System

In middle and South Georgia, and during normal winters in north Georgia, strawberry plants can be set in the fall and harvested the next spring. This reduces the danger of diseases destroying the crop. The 'Chandler' and 'Camarosa' varieties are by far the best for the hill system, but other varieties will produce mediocre to fair results. In north Georgia the 'Chandler' variety is normally more productive than the 'Camarosa'.

Plants are set 12 inches apart in the row and 12 inches apart between rows on beds that contain two rows. The beds should be 6 inches high at the shoulder, 8 inches high in the center, and 26 inches wide. An aisle 22 inches wide between beds should be provided as a place to walk.

Before making the beds, broadcast fertilizer over the plots. Spade or till in 3 pounds of 10-10-10 premium grade fertilizer (contains micronutrients) per 100 square feet of bed. In the spring, if the plants appear to need fertilizer, a pinch of ammonium nitrate can be dropped next to each plant. Best results are usually obtained by mulching the bed with black plastic although pine straw and straw can also be used. A drip irrigation tube should be placed under the plastic. Apply the plastic before planting. Be sure the bed is well formed, firm, fertilized, and very moist. Set plants from September 15 to November 1 in South and Middle Georgia (usually, early October is the best time).

Freshly dug plants are planted and watered intensively for the first week after planting. Potted plants can also be used and require less watering to establish. If the planting is anthracnose disease free, it may live for several years and be managed as a matted-row system. Cut holes in the plastic to allow some of the runners to peg down. The original mother plants will develop many side branches, called "branched crowns." If these are left for a second year, there will be many very small fruit. To carry over these mother plants for the following spring, clip off most or all of the side branches (branch crowns) during the late fall.

Bird Control—Because there is not much food available for birds when strawberries ripen, birds can be a serious problem. The most effective method is to cover the planting with bird netting. The net will have to be anchored all the way around the planting; otherwise the birds will walk under it. To anchor the net, place 6- to 8-inch stakes around the planting every 2 feet. Angle the stakes out away from the rows so that the net can be hooked over the stakes. This will keep the edge of the net close to the ground, and keep the birds from getting under the net. It takes only a few minutes to remove the net for picking, and to replace it after you are through.

TREE FRUITS AND NUTS

A home orchard can provide hours of gardening challenge and enjoyment with plenty of luscious fruit for family and friends. In addition to their edible bounty, fruit trees add beauty to the landscape beginning with bloom and continuing through harvest. For success, it is necessary to understand the requirements for site selection and preparation, variety and rootstock selection, tree planting and training, fertilization and irrigation, fruit thinning, and pest management.

Site Selection—Essential to successful tree fruit culture is selection of a location that provides adequate sunlight, cold air drainage, and water drainage. Fruit trees should receive full-sun light at least 80 percent of the day in order to produce a high quality crop. Full sunlight allows plenty of opportunity not only for fruit formation and development and also supports good fruit health by allowing fruit and leaves adequate drying time. The trees are best located in sites that allow colder, heavier air to drain away from the tree's fruiting zone to lower ground below the orchard. This is due to the incidence of late season cold nights during the spring when flowers or developing fruit would be vulnerable. A radiation freeze occurs when a clear sky and calm winds (less than 5 mph) allow an inversion to develop, and temperatures near the surface drop below freezing.

It has been demonstrated that the average last freeze date is delayed more than five weeks by elevation and solar orientation (Table 7). Hilltops and southern slopes are significantly warmer than northern slopes and low areas.

Proper location in the home garden or landscape can reduce the vulnerability of fruit and flowers to frost. Placement next to a wall can protect against cold winds, mitigate temperature inversions, and allow heat storage. Alternatively, placing fruit trees on a grade that allows

Table 7. Impact of elevation and solar orientation on last freeze date [1]

LOCATION (Orientation)	ELEVATION (ft)	AVERAGE LAST FREEZE (24 degrees F)
Hilltop	803	March 4
S - SE Slope	711	March 28
N- NW slope	724	April 11
River bottom	584	April 12

[1](Johnstone et al., 1968)

the drainage of cold air to lower areas of the yard or garden will provide protection on frosty nights. Another trick that some gardeners use is to keep outdoor Christmas lights on fruit trees to protect on cold nights (Table 8).

Another type of freeze, an advective freeze, can destroy shoots and branches as well as developing flowers and fruit. Advective freezes are characterized by cold, dry air masses that move south and east from Canada. Usually these freezes arrive with high winds and generally are more common in the winter. If this freeze occurs during spring, it can desiccate non-dormant buds or flowers reducing fruit set. If wind speeds are not too high, tarping trees with outdoor-safe mini tree lights, also known as Italian lights, strung on the trees may provide enough heat around buds to save some fruit.

Although fruit trees can be grown on a range of soil types from sand to clay, they thrive best in sandy loam topsoil that is 18 to 24 inches deep underlaid with brightly colored, well-drained clay subsoil. Shallow or poorly drained soils will produce smaller, weaker trees with lower yields. It is essential that the soil profile have adequate nutrient content and water holding capacities throughout. Permeability of the soil profile to water and air is required for proper root growth. A dull-colored soil profile (blue to gray) suggests poor soil drainage. It is particularly important that fruit trees be placed in well-drained soils or on beds raised one to two feet above the typical soil elevation. Since soil moisture can be limiting in some seasons, it is necessary to irrigate bedded trees or rocky sites that tend to be excessively dry.

While fruit trees can be protected against a number of pathogens, there are several that should be avoided through proper site selection. Knowing the history of the site may immediately rule it out as an appropriate orchard locale. If the site is known to have had oak root rot, it should be avoided entirely, or if it is known to be infested with crown gall, special steps are necessary to make a viable location. Root knot and ring nematodes destroy fruit trees within five years of planting them. If nematodes are present, fruit trees can be planted, providing an appropriate rootstock is selected (discussed in Rootstock section).

Site Preparation—Preparation of an orchard should begin one year prior to its planting. After the soil has been analyzed for nutrients, pH and nematodes, amendments of phosphorus, potassium and lime must be made according to test results. Necessary amendments should be applied prior to planting to adjust nutrient levels

Table 8. Timely tips for the home orchardist

SITUATION	CONVENTIONAL CULTURAL PRACTICE	A "MAKE-DO" TIP
Trees need protection from frost events during late winter and early spring.	Select site that allows air drainage away from the fruiting zone of the tree. Use irrigation during the freeze.	String outdoor-safe Italian lights in threes. Turn on the lights when a freeze is expected. A tarp can safely be added to help hold in heat, particularly with advective freezes.
High bloom or fruit count.	Hand remove flowers or very small fruit to allow the fruit to size adequately.	Thin out all short or thin shoots. Shorten length of other shoots toincrease yield by up to 30% and size by up to 16%.
Need to train limb angles of apple trees to 45-degree angle from vertical.	Expensive tree spreaders or tie-downs that can damage shoots.	Clothespins can be used to control the angle of growth by placing them so that the end shoots opposite the pincer end
Need to control weeds, reducing nutrient and water competition.	For young trees or tool weed removal. For older trees careful use of herbicides.	Mulch the 3' x 3' base of tree with wheat straw, being careful not to place mulch next to the trunk.
Brown rot on fruit.	Fungal spray program.	Remove rotting fruit, fruit mummies, and diseased wood. Take out of orchard and burn.

and to achieve a pH of approximately 6-6.5. Proper weed and weed seed removal by herbicide application and fumigation will reduce the level of herbicide usage required once the orchard is established.

The soil should be turned to disturb or remove any compacted layers and ensure adequate drainage in a 4-foot x 4-foot. area for each tree. The hole should be backfilled with the native soil mixed with recommended lime and phosphorus amendments. Do not amend the backfill with organic materials, sand or additives such as perlite, vermiculite, peat, or lava rock. Do not add other nutrients at this time. If several fruit trees are planned, space them appropriately based on their anticipated growth. Pear, peach, plum and nectarine trees are generally spaced 20 feet apart, while seedling apple trees should be spaced 25 feet apart and semi-dwarfing apple trees 16 - 18 feet apart.

Planting—Temperate fruit trees are usually purchased and planted as bareroot trees during the late winter or early spring, while they are still dormant. If one is interested in choosing a particular scion/rootstock combination, it is advisable to purchase from a reputable nursery that specializes in fruit trees. Reserve 2-foot to 3-foot tall, one-year old trees of the desired variety on the appropriate rootstock during early summer. Trees are usually received from the nursery during late December or January. If the trees arrive prior to the completion of orchard preparation or soil conditions are not ideal for planting, they should be opened and examined for signs of diseases or pests. Return any trees that are substandard. They should be kept moist, shaded and cool (but not freezing) up to two weeks prior to planting.

Clip off broken, twisted, or girdling roots, but do not over-prune the roots. Never place bareroot trees in waterlogged soil. Place the bud union about two inches above the settled soil surface at its original nursery depth. Correct depth of planting is important in all soil types, but critical in heavier soils. Studies show that the best growth is achieved when the tree roots are initially planted at a depth of two inches.

Remove any latent buds on the rootstock that could sprout after planting and develop into root suckers. This will reduce the hand labor that will be required later. Do not plant the tree in a basin. If the planting area is too dry, it should be well watered, but not overwatered a few days prior to planting. In addition, the trees should be watered-in just after planting.

For weed and moisture control as well as nutrient enhancement, the soil surface can be covered with 3 to 4 inches of mulch or compost. Take care not to place the organic material close to the trunk, as this encourages pests that invade the crown, such as peach tree borer. A mulch of non-pine materials, such as wheat straw, is preferable to avoid the pH reducing impact of pine. Maintain a 3-foot by 3-foot area weed free around the base of the young tree. To protect the bark from sunscald and damage from herbicides, paint the lower half of the unpruned tree trunk with a 1:1 mixture of water and interior white latex paint. Leaving the upper 6 to 8 inches of the trunk unpainted increases budbreak and avoids damage to those buds that can occur during painting.

Tree Training—Head the tree to 20 to 24 inches from the top of the soil surface to encourage low branching, and to balance the scion and root growth. Cut to two buds any lateral branches below 24 inches from the ground (Figure 9). Alternatively, remove any lateral growth below 24 inches. During the spring and summer the remaining buds will break and push out new shoot growth. In mid-summer the shoots that will form the tree's scaffolds will be selected and trained.

Apples and pears are trained to the modified central leader tree form(Figure 10). After the initial heading cut is made, a bud that produces a strong upright shoot will be the central leader shoot. Four or five lateral scaffolds will be trained to a 45° angle around the leader scaffold. The laterals that are selected should be spaced about 4 to 8 inches apart vertically and well distributed around the trunk. The remaining laterals can be trained to a 45° angle by hanging small weights on the branches or forcing the branches downward with wooden, plastic or metal spreaders. Use clothespins or anchors Very young shoots can be bent to the 45° angle. The leader shoot of second leaf trees (trees in the second season of

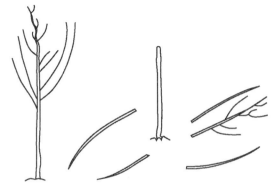

Figure 9

Remove all side shoots at planting

Figure 9. Head the tree at planting

Figure 10

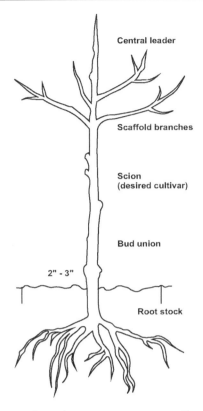

Figure 10. Apple and pear trees are generally trained to the modified central leader.

Figure 11

Figure 11. Mature peach tree trained to the open center form.

growth after planting) is headed, or cut, about 30 to 36 inches above the first tier of laterals that formed during the tree's first summer. This heading cut is made during late winter or early spring the year following planting.

Peaches, plums and nectarines are usually trained to an opened-center form in the Southeast (Figure 11). After the heading cut at planting, laterals are forced out during the spring. These continue to grow during the summer. In mid-summer the 4 or 5 shoots that will become the scaffolds of this tree form can be selected. All other shoots should be removed. The selected shoots should fill the space around the trunk. Upright growing shoots should not be selected, but rather shoots that grow outward or laterally from the trunk

It may be necessary during the first several growing seasons to spend a bit of time removing root suckers. These are vigorous shoots that initiate from the rootstock trunk, at the crown or along the root. Root suckers compete with the rest of the tree, especially the scion, for the sugar and water resources of the tree and can eventually overtake the scion to the extent that the variety of choice is lost. Thus, proper root sucker removal will prevent the competition of that growth with the rest of the tree and reduce your annual work load. It is best to remove suckers when they are less than pencil width in diameter to prevent damage to the tree.

Fertilization—To avoid burning the bare-rooted fruit tree, never mix nitrogen fertilizer in the planting hole or put on top of the loose soil immediately after planting. In March after planting, distribute one cup of 10-10-10 fertilizer around the drip line of the growing tree. Follow this application in May and again in July with one-half cup of ammonium nitrate or one cup of calcium nitrate. Second year trees should be similarly fertilized: 2 cups 10-10-10 in March, ¾ cup ammonium nitrate or 1.5 cup calcium nitrate in May and again in July. Calcium nitrate is the preferred form since it provides necessary calcium and also does not decrease soil pH like ammonium nitrate.

Bearing Tree Care

Pruning—Once trees are bearing fruit, the concern shifts from building tree structure and growing trees to maintaining tree structure and growing fruit. To maintain tree structure, annual pruning is necessary. There are two periods when pruning should be done. During the growing season, upright, vigorous shoots, or water sprouts, should be removed (Figure 12). Water sprouts compete with developing fruit for sugar and water resources from the tree and they shade the fruit reducing peel color. Just at the end of the dormant period, during early bloom, prune the tree to maintain its form. Remove any remaining upright growth and diseased wood. In addition, thin out the canopy so that the tree will not produce so much fruit as to be unable to size the fruit. First remove shoots that are growing into toward the interior of the tree and those shoots that will interfere with the growth of others. Generally, fruiting shoots should be spaced about every 6 to 8 inches along the scaffolds or their branches.

Fertilization—Bearing trees, (trees entering their third leaf) should be capable of producing sufficient fruit to justify a production management program. Fruit trees are fertilized to ensure continued growth and fruit production. Generally, nitrogen, phosphorus, potassium, calcium and magnesium are required annually.

More importantly than any other element, nitrogen controls growth and fruiting in plants. Nitrogen management confronts the fruit grower with a dilemma. When the nitrogen level is optimum for fruiting, vegetative growth may be inadequate and vice versa. Nitrogen interacts strongly with pruning and irrigation. For maximum fruit production, trees should be managed to produce maximum leaf area early in the season. This involves moderate pruning, establishing high nitrogen levels in the tree early in the season, early thinning, maintaining adequate soil moisture, and slowing vegetative growth just prior to harvest by depletion of nitrogen. In the Southeast, this can usually be accomplished with 6 to 12 ounces of ammonium nitrate or 12 to 24 ounces of calcium nitrate per tree annually, with at least half as the calcium nitrate form.

Peach tree survival is greatly improved when the annual nitrogen fertilization is split with some nitrogen being applied in mid to late August (post harvest) and the remainder in late winter. Because the post-harvest nitrogen application is used to help maintain healthy foliage in the fall and improve winter hardiness of the tree, the amount applied at this time should be considered food for next season's crop. Thus, the annual quantity of nitrogen applied to a tree should be figured as that applied before harvest of next season's crop - not the total applied during a calendar year. For example, if 4 ounces of ammonium nitrate are applied in late August to a tree that has performed well over the years with an annual nitrogen application rate of 11 ounces of ammonium nitrate, then 7 ounces (11 - 4 = 7) should be applied in late winter. A rule of thumb on the amount of nitrogen to apply in August is 2 ounces of ammonium nitrate on trees exhibiting healthy foliage and little or no terminal growth, and 4 ounces of ammonium nitrate on trees exhibiting an obvious need for nitrogen. Trees vigorously growing in August should not receive the post harvest application of nitrogen. The post-harvest application should be applied under the drip-line on bare ground, or injected through a drip irrigation system so that the trees (versus trees and sod) get most of the nitrogen.

Weak trees should be supplemented with additional nitrogen: one pound of calcium nitrate or one-half-pound ammonium nitrate. The "spring" application of nitrogen should be applied in mid to late winter, and is twice the suggested amount of ammonium nitrate if calcium nitrate is substituted. This application should be made at least six weeks before bloom for early maturing varieties.

Fruit trees remove small amounts of phosphorus (P) from the soil each year. Only about 12 pounds of phosphorous oxide, or P_2O_5, per acre are removed by a heavy fruit crop. The developing trees have been estimated to retain about 3 pounds of P_2O_5 per acre (not returned to the soil by leaves and pruning). Therefore, no more than 15 to 20 lbs. of P_2O_5 per year should be required to maintain phosphorus once adequate levels (moderate to high) are established in the soil. Many Southeastern soils test "high- plus" for phosphorus. Continued addition of phosphorus to these soils may cause deficiencies in zinc, iron, or copper. Foliar copper levels are marginal or low in many orchards where high levels of phosphorus are present.

Figure 12

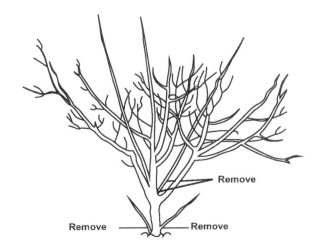

Figure 12. Water sprouts should be removed from fruit trees during the growing season.

The balance between nitrogen and potassium has a strong influence on red color development in fruit. Desirable skin and flesh color has been associated with relatively low nitrogen and high potassium levels in peach leaves. Both trees and fruit buds are more resistant to cold injury when adequate potassium levels are maintained. Foliar potassium levels below 1.0 percent may reduce fruit size. Potassium competes with magnesium and calcium for uptake in peach trees. Excessive levels of one may cause deficiencies of the others. Potassium leaches readily but can accumulate in the subsoil, generally unavailable for tree uptake. Once adequate levels are established, addition of 8-12 ounces of K_2O per tree per year should maintain potassium in most orchards. The source of potassium in commercial fertilizer usually should be based on economics. However, potassium chloride (muriate) should be avoided where large, corrective quantities are added.

Liming annually to maintain the soil pH will maintain the magnesium level if dolomitic lime is used. When magnesium is adequate, hydrated lime may be used. It has a faster reaction time relative to pH adjustment and can provide some of the calcium requirement for the tree. Another source of calcium is calcium nitrate. This form of nitrogen is preferable, because it does not have the pH-lowering impact of ammonium nitrate and it provides some calcium important for fruit set, fruit integrity, and overall tree health.

Thinning—Fruit trees will bear many more fruit than can grow to adequate size if they all make it through the late frosts of February through March. Therefore, proper hand-thinning or judicious pruning can lead to an optimal backyard peach crop. Generally, removal of fruit is advised to a spacing of 6 inches along shoots on the outer portion of the canopy and 8 inches along shoots in the shaded portion. "Timing is everything," they say. And, in the case of thinning fruit, that is absolutely true. As fruits develop, every week after bloom that the tree carries too many fruits can cost the tree 3 to 6 percent in fruit size. Earlier thinning also improves the crop yield and fruit size that can be expected the following year. This is because the following year's fruit buds are being produced while fruit is still on the tree.

If done properly, thinning can increase the tree's yield by 12 percent or more. Ironically, removing shoot tissue that could bear fruit will improve the yield for two reasons. 1) The crop load to which the tree will be distributing water and nutrients will be lowered to a level that the tree's systems can handle. 2) The amount of unnecessary vegetative (shading) growth will be reduced. This pruning can bring a tree into a balance that favors optimum fruit growth. Research has revealed that removing all shoots less than 12 inches long results in greater numbers, size of fruits, and in many more pounds of fruit per tree. In addition to removing these smaller shoots, if the length of remaining shoots is reduced by 50 percent, the yield on some varieties increases by 30 percent and the size by up to 16 percent.

Rootstock Selection—Generally, fruit trees are composed of two parts: the scion and the rootstock (see Figure 10). The scion, equivalent to the variety, is vegetatively propagated through bud grafting. The rootstock, the seedling base of most cultivated fruit trees, is the bottom portion of the tree. The bud union is the site where the scion was grafted to the rootstock seedling and is generally obvious at the time of planting. In general, rootstock affects the tree's resistance to freeze injury, diseases, and pests as well as tree size, vigor and precocity (early production of fruit). For ornamental trees, rootstocks may even impact tree aesthetics.

In peaches and nectarines, rootstocks with nematode resistance are important in the Southeast. The Nemaguard rootstock is valued in sandy sites where root-knot nematodes are particularly troublesome, and the Guardian rootstock is resistant to the ring nematode. The most common rootstock planted in the Southeast at this time for peaches and nectarines is Halford. The trueness of this rootstock relative to seed source is not highly protected and therefore does not carry any reliable resistance and may carry viruses. An old rootstock standard, Lovell is rarely available for trees adapted for the Southeast. Nemaguard and Lovell rootstocks are also recommended for plum trees.

Table 9. Plant sufficiency levels for essential elements.

ELEMENT	SUFFICIENCY RANGES	
	Apple	Peach
N (%)	1.80 - 2.80	2.75 - 3.50
P (%)	0.15 - 0.30	0.12 - 0.50
K (%)	1.20 - 2.00	1.50 - 2.50
Ca (%)	1.30 - 3.00	1.25 - 2.50
Mg (%)	0.20 - 0.40	0.20 - 0.50
Mn (ppm)	22 - 140	20 -150
Fe (ppm)	40 - 100	60 - 400
Al (ppm)	< 300	< 400
B (ppm)	6 - 25	20 - 100
Cu (ppm)	35 - 80	5 - 20
Zn (ppm)	2 - 200	15 - 50

Apple rootstocks are probably most valued for their impact on tree size. The list of common apple rootstocks (Table 10), demonstrates the impact of rootstocks on tree size as well as disease susceptibility. The M7 is semi-dwarfing and provides fire blight resistance. It is commonly used in the apple industry of Northeast Georgia.

Variety Selection—At the core of successful fruit culture is variety selection. To ensure a desired scion-rootstock combination, reserve trees by midsummer at reputable nurseries. Few varieties are adapted to all the fruit growing areas and many are adapted only to a single locality. Difficulty comes in deciding what variety to plant. Several factors are important in variety selection.

The chill requirement for a tree is a physiological need for cool weather in order to break dormancy. Temperatures in the range of 32° to 50°F are the most effective. After a tree has accrued enough chilling hours (generally counted as hours below 45°F) and a period of warm weather has occurred, the tree will bloom and leaf out. If insufficient chilling is received, the tree will respond by blooming out irregularly over a longer than normal period and display delayed leaf development. Generally, a few fruit will set but vary tremendously in size.

As a general rule, the chilling requirements of a desired variety should not be higher than the average chill hours accumulated in the planned locale. For instance, in an area receiving an average of 850 chill hours, a grower could plant varieties ranging from 550 to 850 chill hours.

In South Georgia (lower part of Zone 8a and Zone 8b), varieties with chilling requirements between 350 and 600 hours are recommended.

Growers in the Piedmont area of Georgia (Zone 7a and upper part of Zone 7b) and further north (Zone 6b) seldom have problems with insufficient chilling since they normally receive at least 1200 hours and the

Table 10. Dwarfing effects of apple rootstocks on tree size and fire blight resistance

ROOT-STOCK	ZONE	% OF STANDARD	COMMENTS
Seedling (standard)	6b - 8b	--	18 - 20' tall
MM106ʳ*	6b, 7a, 7b, 8a	70	15 - 18' tall
MM111	6b, 7a, 7b	70	15' tall
M7*	6b, 7a, 7b	60	12' tall
M26ʳ*	6b, 7a, 7b	50	10' tall (require support)
M9ᶠ	6b, 7a, 7b	30 - 40	6 - 8' tall (require support)

ᶠ **Fire blight susceptible, *Collar rot susceptible**

Figure 13

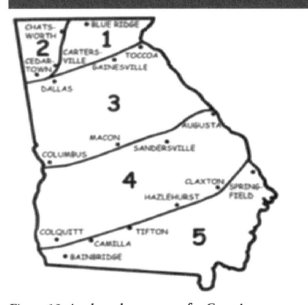

Figure 13. Apple and pear zones for Georgia.

Table 11. Suggested Tree Spacing Based on Rootstock and Tree Form (Non-spur versus spur).

ROOTSTOCK	BETWEEN TREES IN ROW (FEET)		BETWEEN ROWS (FEET)	
Non-spur	Spur	Non-spur	Spur	Non-spur
Seedling	18	12	22	18
MM 106	16	10	20	16
MM 111	16	8	20	14
M 7	12	8	18	14
M 26	10	not recommended	16	not recommended
M 9	8	not recommended	14	not recommended

Table 12. Apple varieties recommended for home use for the different zones in Georgia

VARIETY[1]	ZONE[2]	CHARACTERISTICS[3]	POLLINATION CODE[4]
Anna	5	Excellent shape fruit with blush of red. Ripens mid-June to early July. Spur-type.	A
Dorsett Golden	5	Yellow apple of good quality. Ripens mid-June to early July. Spur-type.	A
Ginger Gold	1-2-3	Very early crisp yellow apple of excellent quality. Good for fresh eating, sauce and pies. Ripens late July-early August. Non-spur.	B
Gala	1-2-3	Excellent quality apple. Good for fresh eating or salads. Ripens early August. Non-spur.	B
Mollie's Delicious	1-2-3-4	A versatile apple. Good for fresh eating, pies and sauce. Ripens late July-early August. Non-spur.	B
Ozark Gold	1-2-3	Matures in early August. Yellow, russet-free apple of excellent quality. Non-spur.	B
Red Delicious	1-2-3-4	Early fall variety ripening in late August-early September. Large, firm, crisp, sweet. Good for fresh eating or salads. Non-spur and spur strains available.	B
Jonagold	1-2-3	Ripens early September. Very large, yellow apple with red blush. Very high quality sweet, juicy apple.	C
Golden Delicious	1-2-3-4	Ripens one to two weeks after Red Delicious. Good producer. Fruit good for sauce, fresh eating and pies. Non-spur and spur strains available.	C
Fuji	1-2-3	Fall variety ripening in early October. Does not color well, but quality is superb. Good for cooking, eating and baking. Non-spur strains available.	B
Mutzu	1-2-3	Ripens early October. Yellow apple of exceptional quality. Crisp and juicy. Slightly tart. All purpose.	B
Rome Beauty	1-2	Ripens early October. Red apple that is primarily grown for baking. Spur and non-spur.	C
Stayman	1-2	Ripens early October. Rusty red finish. Superb quality all purpose apple that is tart. Fruit cracking a problem when dry period followed by rainy period.	C
Yates	1-2-3-4	Late fall variety ripening in late October. Small; dark red. Juicy; mellow, sub-acid. Best keeper. Non-spur.	B
Granny Smith	1-2-3-4	Matures in late October to early November. Yellow-green apple of excellent quality. Good all purpose variety. Non-spur and spur strains available.	B

[1] Listed in order of ripening.
[2] See Figure 13 Apple and pear zones in Georgia
[3] Ripening dates for all varieties except Anna and Dorsett Golden are based on averages from Athens, Georgia. Ripening dates for Anna and Dorsett Golden are based on averages from Monticello, Florida. Non-spur and spur refer to growth habit, as previously described under "Variety Selection."
[4] Varieties followed by a common letter bloom at approximately the same time. Since most apple varieties are self-unfruitful (require pollen from another variety to set fruit), plant two or more varieties that have the same letter so fruit set will result. Stayman, Mutzu and Jonagold have sterile pollen and should not be used as a pollen source for other varieties; therefore, plant at least two other varieties with any or all of these varieties.

higher chilling peach varieties require 1050 hours. But early bloom followed by late frost can destroy a crop. For this reason varieties which require at least 850 chill hours should be planted in the Piedmont of Georgia and further north.

In central Georgia (Zones 7b and 8a), at least 1000 hours are usually accumulated. Varieties ranging in chilling requirement of 500-1000 hours should be chosen. Historical information from central Georgia reveals an average delay in bloom of about three days for each 100- hour increase in chilling requirement of a variety. The capacity for a variety to produce a crop after inclement spring weather is based mainly on bloom date and numbers of flower buds on the tree.

Peach and nectarine varieties are usually listed on the basis of the approximate number of days a variety should ripen before or after 'Elberta'. In central Georgia 'Elberta' ripens in mid-July in most years. Weather conditions, location within the region, crop load, and cultural practices may result in some varieties being earlier or later than expected, thus the listed harvest dates should only be used as guidelines.

A final consideration in variety selection is disease resistance. Avoid varieties that are highly susceptible to bacterial spot. If possible select varieties that are highly resistant. In addition, some relief from brown rot susceptibility can be obtained by selecting varieties that are less susceptible to the disease.

APPLES

The most important difference among apple varieties that should be of concern to the home gardener is spur-strains and non-spur strains. Spur-types are ideally suited for home orchards. Growth on spur-types is more compact as fruit spurs and leaf buds are spaced more closely than non-spur types. On spur-type trees, 2-year-old wood will usually form fruit buds rather than develop side shoots. Several varieties are available in spur and non-spur strains. Refer to Table 11 for suggested apple tree spacing based on rootstock and tree form. Generally, spur strains of the same variety on the same kind of rootstock will result in trees 70% the size of similar non-spur type trees. As with plums, the pollinizer partner must be considered when selecting apple and pear varieties. Varieties with the same pollinizing code should be planted together, with one acting as the pollen parent for the other. If a variety is pollen sterile, it must be planted with another variety of the same code that is pollen fertile. For example, 'Jonagold' can be planted with 'Granny Smith' but not with 'Stayman'. Table 12 lists recommended apple varieties and pollinizing codes.

NECTARINES AND PEACHES

There are peach varieties adapted to most areas of Georgia. Peach cultivars can be divided into 3 groups. Nectarines are "fuzzless peaches". Freestone peaches, usually grown for the fresh market, have a softer flesh that easily separates from the stone. Clingstone peaches have a firm flesh that remains attached to the stone and are good for canning. Table 13 lists some nectarine and peach varieties for Georgia.

Peach trees are short lived, with a 15-20-year average lifespan, and require considerable maintenance in order to produce acceptable fruit. Success with peaches depends on choosing the correct variety, proper pruning, and a regular spray program. The *Georgia Pest Management Handbook*, updated yearly, contains an IPM management guide for fruits and nuts.

PEARS

European or common pears like the Bartlett or Bosc pear are extremely susceptible to fire blight and should not be planted in the Southeast. On the other hand, hybrid pears are resistant and are a good choice for the Southeast.

Certain varieties are self-fruitful; (i.e. they can pollinate themselves). Thus, if you want only one pear tree, a self-pollinating variety should be selected. 'Orient', 'Baldwin', 'Kieffer' and 'Spalding' are at least partially self-fruitful. Other pear varieties require cross-pollination. If you plant varieties that require cross-pollination, be sure to plant varieties that bloom at the same time. Those with a similar pollination code letter generally bloom together. Two varieties, 'Waite' and 'Magness', produce sterile pollen. Plant 'Orient' with them, or two other varieties with a similar pollination code letter to insure pollination of all varieties. (See Table 14).

Asian pears will probably cross pollinate with more common Georgia varieties, but information on this is limited. As such, planting several Asian pear varieties together is recommended.

Hybrids between European and Oriental/Asian pears are most commonly grown in Georgia. These have better resistance to fire blight than most European pears, and some have a low enough winter chilling requirement to be grown in South Georgia.

Table 13. Peach and nectarine varieties with characteristic harvest period, flesh color (Y or W), flesh texture (M or N), pit attachment (C,S or F), and bacterial spot susceptibility (-/+).

Harvest Period	Low Chill <600 Hours	Moderate Chill 600-750 Hours	High Chill 750-900 Hours	Very High Chill >900 Hours
Late April	Flordadawn YMC+ z			
Early May	Sunsplashy YMS+	Mayfire YMC+		
	Gulfcrest YNS+			
	Flordacrest YMS+			
Mid May	Flordaking YMC+	Regal YMS--		
	Gulfking YNS+			
	Regal	YMS--		
Late May	Gulfprince YNC++	Springprince YNC+	Camden YMC-	
	Sunfre YMS-	Empress YMC+	Sunbrite YMC-	
		Gold Prince YMC+	Rubyprince YMC+	
Early June	White Robin WMS+	Junegold YMC+	Summerprince YMS+	Harrow Diamond YMS+
		Juneprince YMS+	Garnet Beauty YMS+	
		Southern Pearl YMS+	Juneprincess YMF+	
Mid June		Coronet YMS+	GaLa YMF-	Surecrop YMS+
		Karla Rose WMS+	Durbin YMS+	
			Summerbeaut YMF+	
Late June		Topaz YMF+	Redtop YMF-	Sureprince YMS+
		Suwanee YMF-	Sunglo YMF+	
			Cary Mac YMF+	
			Harvester YMF+	
			Roseprincess WMF+	
			Fireprince YMF+	
			Winblo YMF+	
Early July		La Feliciana YMF+	Blazeprince YMF+	Redhaven YMS+
		Fantasia YMF-	Redglobe YMF+	

z Y = yellow flesh, W = white flesh / M = melting flesh, N = non-melting flesh / C = clingstone, S = Semi-clingstone, F = freestone / Bacterial Spot Susceptibility: -- = Highly Susceptible, - = Moderately Susceptible, + = Moderately Resistant, ++ = Resistant

y Varieties listed in bold are nectarines; all others are peaches.

Table 13. Peach and nectarine varieties with characteristic harvest period, flesh color (Y or W), flesh texture (M or N), pit attachment (C, S or F), and bacterial spot susceptibility (-/+).

Harvest Period	Low Chill <600 Hours	Moderate Chill 600-750 Hours	High Chill 750-900 Hours	Very High Chill >900 Hours
Late April	Flordadawn YMC+ z			
Early May	Sunsplashy YMS+	Mayfire YMC+		
	Gulfcrest YNS+			
	Flordacrest YMS+			
Mid May	Flordaking YMC+	Regal YMS--		
	Gulfking YNS+			
	Regal YMS--			
Late May	Gulfprince YNC++	Springprince YNC+	Camden YMC-	
	Sunfre YMS-	Empress YMC+	Sunbrite YMC-	
		Gold Prince YMC+	Rubyprince YMC+	
Early June	White Robin WMS+	Junegold YMC+	Summerprince YMS+	Harrow Diamond YMS+
		Juneprince YMS+	Garnet Beauty YMS+	
		Souther Pearl YMS+	Juneprincess YMF+	
Mid June		Coronet YMS+	GaLa YMF-	Surecrop YMS+
		Karla Rose WMS+	Durbin YMS+	
			Summerbeaut YMF+	
Late June		Topaz YMF+	Redtop YMF-	Sureprince YMS+
		Suwanee YMF-	Sunglo YMF+	
			Cary Mac YMF+	
			Harvester YMF+	
			Roseprincess WMF+	
			Fireprince YMF+	
			Winblo YMF+	
Early July		La Feliciana YMF+	Blazeprince YMF+	Redhaven YMS+
		Fantasia YMF-	Redglobe YMF+	

z Y = yellow flesh, W = white flesh / M = melting flesh, N = non-melting flesh / C = clingstone, S = Semi-clingstone, F = freestone / Bacterial Spot Susceptibility: -- = Highly Susceptible, - = Susceptible, + = Moderately Susceptible, ++ = Moderately Resistant, ++ = Resistant

y Varieties listed in bold are nectarines; all others are peaches.

Table 13. Peach and nectarine varieties with characteristic harvest period, flesh color (Y or W), flesh texture (M or N), pit attachment (C,S or F), and bacterial spot susceptibility (-/+).

Harvest period	Variety	Code
	Julyprince	YMF+
	Loring	YMF+
	Majestic	YMF++
	Bounty	YMF+
	Scarletprince	YMF+
	Flamecrest	YMF-
	Redgold	YMF-
Mid July	Dixiland	YMF-
	White Lady	WMF+
	Georgia Belle	WMF+
	Redskin	YMF+
	Honey Dew	WMF+
	Sunprince	YMF+
	Elberta	YMF+
	Ruston Red	YMF++
	Jefferson	YMF++
	Cresthaven	WMF+
	Challenger	YMF++
	Contender	YMF+
	Intrepid	YMF++
Late July	Early Augustprince	YMF+
	Fay Elberta	YMF-
	China Pearl	WMF+
Early August	Augustprince	YMF+
	Flameprince	YMF+
Mid-Late August	Big Red	YMF-
	Parade	YMF-
	Autumnprince	YMF+
	Fairtime	YMF--

z Y = yellow flesh, W = white flesh / M = melting flesh, N = non-melting flesh / C = clingstone, S = Semi-clingstone, F = freestone / Bacterial Spot Susceptibility: -- = Highly Susceptible, - = Susceptible, + = Moderately Susceptible, ++ = Moderately Resistant, +++ = Resistant

y Varieties listed in bold are nectarines; all others are peaches.

Table 14. Pear varieties recommended for home use for the dfferent zones of Georgia

VARIETY	ZONE[1]	CHARACTERISTICS	POLLINATION CODE[2]
EUROPEAN PEARS			
Orient	1-2-3-4-5	An excellent pear for most of thes tate. Resistant to blight. Flesh white; a good keeper. Very large fruit.	B, C
Carrick	1-2-3	Excellent for preserving. Trees resistant to blight.	B
Waite	1-2-3	An excellent pear for the northern half of the state. Resistant to blight, Pollen sterile. Plant with Orient.	C
Kieffer	1-2-3	Large; skin yellow. Poor quality. Subject to blight in wet years. Good for preserves.	A, B
Hood	4-5	Good quality but subject to internal breakdown if allowed to become fully ripe. Blooms early.	A
Flordahome	4-5	New release from Florida. Good quality. Blooms early.	A
Baldwin	4-5	An excellent pear for the southern half of the state. Resistant to blight.	A
Magness	1-2-3-4	Pollen sterile. Plant with Orient. Fruit excellent quality but not very productive.	C
Moonglow	1-2-3-4	Vigorous tree that produces fair to good quality fruit. Nearly free of grit cells.	C
Starking Delicious[3]	1-2-3-4	An excellent pear for the northern half of the state. Fruit excellent quality. Moderately vigorous.	C
Dawn	1-2-3-4	Good quality fruit. Almost entirely free of grit cells. Moderately vigorous tree.	C
Spalding	3-4	High quality fruit that ripens early. Subject to blight.	A, B
Warren	3-4-5	Very high quality fruit. Resistant to blight.	B, C
ASIAN PEARS (trial only)[4]			
Shinko	1-2-3-4-5	Golden russetted fruit.	Hosui
Chojuro	1-2-3-4-5	Brown orange fruit.	Hosui, Shinko
Hosui	1-2-3-4-5	Golden brown fruit.	Shinko, Chojuro
Kosui	1-2-3-4-5	Green yellow fruit.	Hosui, Chojuro

[1] See Figure 13 apple and pear zones in Georgia

[2] Plant two or more varieties followed by a common letter. Multiple letters by some varieties indicate that they will pollinate other varieties followed by either letter.

[3] Starking Delicious is considered by many experts to be the same as Maxine.

[4] Asian pears have juicy, round "apple-like" fruit. Trees may be subject to fire blight in some areas. Trial planting only.

Table 15. Japanese plums for home use in Georgia

CULTIVAR	FERTILITY	SKIN/FLESH COLOR	RIPENING DATE	CROPPING
Dessert/Preserve Quality				
Methley	Self*	Red-purple/Blood	6/03	Reliable
Morris	Not	Dark red/Red	6/16	Productive
AU Rubrum	Not	Dark red/Red	6/15	Reliable
AU Producer	Not	Dark red/Red	6/20	Very Productive
Spring Satin	Not	Red-black/Yellow	6/02	Productive
Byrongold	Not	Yellow/Yellow	6/30	
Rubysweet	Not	Red-bronze/Blood	6/15	Productive
Preferred as Green Plums				
Bruce	Not	Orange-red/Yellow	5/31	Reliable
Six Weeks	Not	Red/Yellow-red	5/25	
Robusto	Not	Bright red/Red	6/05	Productive
Segundo	Not	Yellow-red/Yellow-red	6/11	Productive

* Though self-fertile, the provision of a different variety in the garden will improve pollination and production. Conditions that are not harmful to bees improve production.

PLUMS

Plums are popular for cooking and preserving, and are enjoyed fresh as well. The sweeter varieties are among the more delicious dessert fruits.

The home gardener can choose among several varieties (Table 15), such as 'Methley' (an early season variety that is somewhat self-fertile and crops reliably); 'Morris' is a commercial plum that is very productive and very sweet; two Auburn releases: 'AU Rubrum' and 'AU Producer' produce reliably; and some Georgia releases like 'Spring Satin' (Plum-apricot hybrid), 'Byrongold' or 'Rubysweet', are good for fresh eating and the 'Rubysweet' is particularly sweet. Many gardeners seek plums that are best when eaten green, like 'Bruce', 'Six Weeks', 'Robusto' or 'Segundo'. Whatever you choose, at least two plum varieties are needed for pollination and fruitfulness since plums are generally not self-fertile, i.e. one variety must act as the pollen parent for the other variety.

When considering other varieties, choose trees recommended for your specific zones. Several nurseries sell plum trees appropriate to the Southeast.

PECANS

There are thousands of pecan trees surrounding urban and rural dwellings. These trees can enhance the environment by providing shade and additional income from the sale of nuts. Some of these trees are not profitable because of their susceptibility to disease, particularly scab. Many produce inferior nuts.

For many years, Georgia has been a top producer of improved pecans in the United States. Pecans are recommended for home planting in the Coastal Plain and Piedmont, but are not recommended for the North Georgia Mountains. Here are some tips that should promote successful production.

Varieties—There are numerous pecan varieties from which to choose, but only a few are suitable for yard-tree planting. The primary reason is that many home gardeners will not be able to spray to control destructive diseases. Fortunately, there are scab-resistant varieties which produce high quality kernels.

The varieties recommended for yard-tree plantings are 'Stuart', 'Gloria Grande', 'Curtis', 'Elliott', and 'Sumner'. To ensure good pollination, plant at least two varieties. This is especially important for areas with few surrounding pecan trees. In areas where pecans are common, pollination is not usually a problem. (Table 16)

Site Selection—Tree site is very important because of the ultimate size the tree will reach. Plant the trees well away from the residence and other buildings. Perhaps the biggest obstacle to be avoided is overhead power lines.

Space the trees at least 60 to 80 feet apart so they will

not crowd as they reach maturity. Crowding can cause misshapen trees and decreased production in shaded areas. Unlike commercial situations, yard-trees should be spaced far enough apart so they will never need removing.

Planting Trees—To ensure tree survival, plant freshly dug trees whose roots have been kept moist from digging to planting. If possible, plant trees the day they are received from the nursery. Many trees bought from mail order dealers or garden centers will have been out of the ground for several days. If these trees have been stored and handled properly, they should survive and grow. If the trees appear to have dried, soak them in water for several hours to freshen them prior to planting. Drying before planting and failing to supply adequate moisture for the first two years following transplanting are the major causes for death or very slow growth in young pecan trees.

Pecans by nature have long taproots and require a deep planting hole. The hole should be only as deep as the root system to prevent settling. The hole should be from 12 to 24 inches wide so that all side roots can be properly positioned as the hole is refilled. Never run roots around the hole; instead, prune them at the edge of the hole.

Use the subsoil removed from the hole to build a water-holding basin around the tree. This basin should be 24 to 36 inches across and 6 to 12 inches deep. A reservoir that will hold 10 to 15 gallons of water at each watering is ideal. Remove one-half of the top of the new tree to balance the top with the root system. This is essential for good survival. After the tree becomes established, rake the water basin smooth with the grade of the soil.

Mulch trees with a six-inch layer of pine straw, leaves or old sawdust. This helps hold moisture and limits competition from grass and weeds.

Care Of Young Trees

Watering—The primary after-care chore for successfully growing pecan trees is to supply the trees' moisture

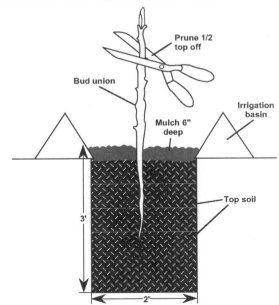

Figure 14. A properly planted pecan tree.

needs for the first two or three years since young trees have lost a large percentage of their roots during digging and transplanting. This limited root system must be supplied regularly to meet the needs of the top. Apply 10 to 15 gallons of water at regular weekly intervals, either by rainfall or irrigation. This is one chore that must not be neglected.

Fertility and pH—Do not place fertilizer in the planting hole as it may injure roots. Young pecan trees do need a ready source of nutrients to promote rapid growth. For accurate determination of fertilizer and lime needs, take a soil sample prior to planting. If no soil test was made, use a general rate of about one pound 10-10-10 fertilizer distributed in a 25 sq. ft. area around the tree. Make this application immediately after planting and again in June or July. The following February, apply four pounds of 10-10-10 fertilizer for each inch of trunk diameter (measured one foot above soil surface).

Table 16. Quality pecan varieties for home gardens				
VARIETY*	**SIZE**	**KERNEL QUALITY**	**SCAB RESISTANCE**	**PRODUCTIVITY**
Elliot	Small	Good	Very resistant	Very good
Excel	Large	Good	Very resistant	Good
Gloria Grande	Large	Excellent	Resistant	Very good
Sumner	Large	Excellent	Resistant	Very good
***To ensure good pollination, plant at least two varieties. This is especially important for areas with few surrounding pecan trees.**				

Do not place fertilizer within 12 inches of the trunk.

Young trees should make from 2 to 4 feet of terminal growth each year. Where growth is less, apply one pound of ammonium nitrate fertilizer per inch of trunk diameter in June or July. As a general recommendation, apply one pound of zinc sulfate per tree for the first three years following planting. Spread the fertilizer and zinc sulfate in a circle around the tree outside of the planting hole.

Care Of Bearing Trees

Fertilizing—Fertilization is one of the most important practices for bearing trees. If the trees are to produce a good crop, terminal growth should be 6 inches each year. In the absence of a leaf analysis or soil test, broadcast four pounds of a complete fertilizer such as 10-10-10 for each inch of trunk diameter (measure 4 ½ feet above soil level). This fertilizer should be applied in mid- to late February. Zinc nutrition is especially important in pecan production. Zinc needs are best determined by analysis of leaf samples taken in late July or early August. Mailing kits and instructions for taking samples are available from your county Extension office. The leaf analysis report will tell you how much zinc to apply. In the absence of a leaf analysis, apply one pound of zinc sulfate to young trees and three to five pounds for large

trees each year. A soil pH of 6.0 to 6.5 assures the availability of essential nutrients. If the pH is too low or too high, uptake and use of nutrients is impaired. Apply lime as suggested in the soil test report to correct low pH.

Other Fruits and Nuts

Although there are other fruits and nuts widely sold in garden catalogs, many are not suitable for home fruit production in Georgia. Climate, soils, and pest pressure make growing fruits such as cherries, apricots, citrus fruits, and tropical fruits and nuts unsuccessful and frustrating for the home gardener. Gardeners in some areas of the state report success with kiwifruit, loquat, mayhaw, and Juneberries.

DISCUSSION QUESTIONS

1. Why is variety selection important in growing fruit?

2. What is the difference between a primocane and a floricane and why are they important in growing bramble fruits?

3. What is the most important factor in choosing rabbiteye blueberry varieties for planting?

4. Is liming necessary in growing blueberries in Georgia?

5. Why are figs grown locally recommended for planting in Georgia?

6. Why is proper trellising particularly important in growing grapes in Georgia?

7. When should grapes be pruned?

8. What is the preferred method for growing strawberries in North Georgia? In South Georgia?

9. Why are muscadines recommended for growing in the South?

10. Why is site selection important for growing tree fruit?

11. What are some tips that can help protect fruit loss during late freezes?

12. What is chill requirement and how does it relate to tree fruit culture?

20

Insects and Diseases of Fruit

Elizabeth Little

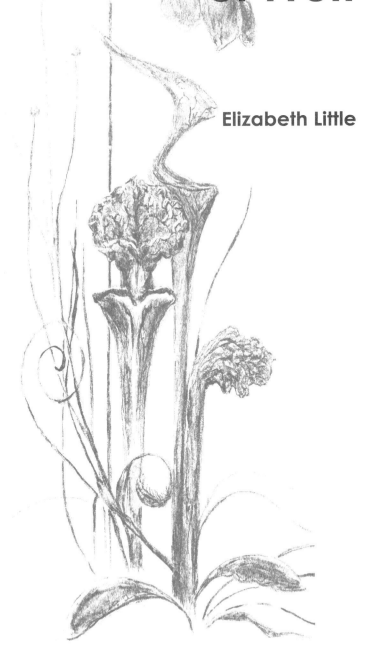

LEARNING OBJECTIVES

Identify common insect pests of small fruits and tree fruits.

Become familiar with symptoms of common diseases of tree fruits and small fruits.

Identify some common ways to prevent the spread of diseases in tree fruits.

TERMS TO KNOW

Calyx end the end of the fruit opposite the stem.

Canker localized area of diseased tissue on a stem.

Cover spray preventative treatment sprayed over surfaces of the leaves as well as leaves in the center of the canopy repeated at prescribed intervals.

Dormant spray preventative treatment applied at various intervals before blossom, ranging from fully dormant up to and during certain states of bud development.

Inoculum pathogen or its parts which can cause infection when transferred to a favorable location.

Pedicel small stalk or stalklike part bearing a single flower.

Pustule small blister-like elevation of the leaf epidermis created as spores emerge from underneath and push outward.

INTRODUCTION

Insects and diseases can affect fruit quality and significantly diminish production in backyard fruit plantings. The keys to keeping backyard fruit crops healthy and reducing pest problems are essentially the same as the IPM methods discussed in other chapters of this book. However, pest pressure is high in the Southeast, particularly on fruit trees, due to warm temperatures and high humidity. Some tree fruits, such as peaches and cherries, will rarely be able to produce an acceptable fruit crop without preventative treatments and homeowners should consider whether the time, effort, and expense are worth investing in high maintenance fruit varieties.

Key principles

- Site selection and preparation
- Proper plant selection, including resistant varieties and rooststocks, if applicable
- Good maintenance practices such as proper pruning, fertilization and weed control
- Sanitation to remove possible sources of pathogens and insects
- Monitoring for problems
- Good record keeping, including notes on weather conditions, fertilizers and pesticides applied and problems encountered
- Choosing pest control methods with the least impacts on natural enemies

SMALL FRUIT PROBLEMS

Blueberry Insects

Blueberries in Georgia are affected by relatively few disease and insect problems. Rarely will a home grower need to spray blueberries for pests. However, a few problems that you may occasionally encounter may require spraying in addition to cultural strategies. Consult the *Georgia Pest Management Handbook* for recommendations.

Blueberry gall midge is a tiny fly. Blueberry gall midge maggots typically feed on vegetative buds. On most varieties vegetative feeding does little harm. On Rabbiteye cultivars, flower-feeding strains of blueberry gall midge occur sporadically. If present, gall midges that feed on flower buds can be serious pests. Feeding injury destroys flower buds before bud scales open in the spring. Orchard sanitation in the form of an herbicide program to chemically mow the entire orchard floor or light cultivation as for mummy berry suppression may offer helpful suppression.

Flower thrips can be damaging to flower buds and blooms. Thrip numbers typically increase dramatically as corollas open and bloom progresses. Determining when or if blueberries should be treated for thrips is difficult. Treatment thresholds to indicate the need for insecticide use do not presently exist. Blueberries are a pollination-sensitive crop. Careless use of insecticide can easily impair pollination and ruin fruit set. Insecticide should not be applied during bloom.

Blueberry bud mite, is an eriophyid mite so tiny that it cannot be seen without magnification. Blueberry bud mite is an occasional pest in Georgia blueberries. Injury may be more visible in late spring. Infested plants are recognized by a clustering or rosetting of buds, which may be abundant. Infested buds become succulent, fleshy, closely packed on stems in clusters or rosettes, and they may redden. Bloom on infested plants is reduced. Affected berries are small, roughened and may have small reddish pimples or blisters on the fruit surface.

Blueberry Diseases

Botrytis flower blight and fruit rot is caused by the fungus *Botrytis cinerea* which overwinters on infected plants. The fungus can affect blossoms twigs and fruit. Tips of infected shoots die back and turn brown to black. Infected blossoms appear water-soaked and turn brown. Brown discoloration can spread down the twig. Immature fruits shrivel and turn bluish-purple or mature fruits turn tan. During damp weather, all infected plant parts become covered with the characteristic gray mold of the fungus. Fungal spores are often disseminated by the wind. Cultural practices are an important key in disease prevention and control. Practice good sanitation, prune to increase air movement, and avoid the use of excessive nitrogen fertilizers in spring as rapidly growing tips are more susceptible to infection.

Mummyberry is a fungal disease that causes infected berries to turn a cream color and drop to the ground; nearly mature berries become dry, shriveled and drop early. In spring, tips of newly infected leaves, buds, stems and flower clusters will suddenly wilt, turn brown, and eventually be covered with spores. The infected fruit form sclerotia, which overwinter and provide a source of infection the following year. Mummyberry is often first introduced into a planting area on the leaves of the blueberry plant. Planting dormant plants can help reduce the potential for introducing spores into an area. Also rake off plant debris from the surface of the potting soil at planting. Sanitation is an important key in helping control infections; rake and destroy mummied fruit each season.

Ripe rot (Anthracnose Fruit Rot) can be a post-harvest problem on blueberries. The fungus overwinters on blighted twigs and spores are released throughout the growing season. The spores infect the green berries, and the berries at or shortly after harvest decay rapidly and exude masses of orange spores.

Septoria leaf spot causes defoliation and poor growth. Spots on the leaves are usually small, up to ½ inch across with a white to tan center and reddish brown margin. The fungus overwinters in infected leaves on the ground, so sanitation is an important control measure.

Rust occurs occasionally and can cause premature defoliation on rabbiteye blueberries. Increasing airflow can help in controlling rust diseases.

Alternaria can sometimes cause both a leaf spot and a harvest or post-harvest problem on blueberries. Leaf spots are circular to irregular-shaped brown to gray lesions surrounded by a red border. Fruit develops sunken lesions and the infected area may be covered with a greenish-black spore mass. Prolonged periods of high humidity promote disease development.

Phytophthora root rot often occurs in areas where blueberries are planted in poorly draining soils. Early aboveground symptoms include yellowing of leaves and lack of new growth. The terminal leaves become small as the disease progresses and excessive defoliation occurs. Older bushes that have been chronically affected appear to be stunted and wilt prone. Improve drainage and incorporate peat or composted bark mulch in heavy clay areas.

Bramble Diseases

Disease Control—Sanitation is the most important means of bramble disease control. The following suggestions will improve your chance of producing healthy berries.

• If cane diseases become a problem, cut off all plants at the soil line just after harvest. For varieties with double blossom, cut canes back to 12 inches above the ground immediately after harvest.

• Fertilize and irrigate the vines to get new growth in the current year for next year's crop. In the absence of diseases, maintain conventional pruning practices.

• Set out only disease-free plants.

• Remove as many wild blackberries growing nearby

as possible.

• Practice good weed control around the plants. Weed removal allows good air circulation.

Anthracnose—Anthracnose first appears as small purplish spots on new canes. As the disease progresses, spots enlarge and become grayish in the center with purplish, slightly raised edges. Cracking bark on diseased canes is common. Badly infected canes may wilt and die. Infections in berry clusters cause withered, dry berries.

Rosette (Double Blossom)—This fungal disease is becoming very serious in Georgia. Buds on vegetative canes become infected during the spring and summer. During the following season, numerous short leafy shoots develop from the infected leaf buds. These shoots become broom-like in appearance. Infected flower buds tend to be larger than normal. Blossoms from infected buds are obviously abnormal, often with numerous extra petals. These flowers do not produce fruit. Of the recommended blackberries, Gem and Navaho are the only varieties resistant to double blossom.

Orange Rust—Leaves on infected canes turn yellow soon after they unfold in the spring. The undersides of the leaves will quickly be covered with orange pustules. In late summer, plants may appear to grow out of the disease, but infected canes will tend to be spindly and bear poorly. Remove infected plants, including the roots, as soon as the disease is detected because the disease spreads readily from one plant to another.

Crown Gall—Crown gall causes tumorous growths in plant crowns and root systems. Once infected, plants cannot be cured. Crown gall will reduce plant vigor, which in turn can increase mortality and decrease productivity. Do not transplant any plants with galls on them or healthy plants out of fields where crown gall is present.

Bramble Insects

Brambles are attacked by two primary insect pests in Georgia - the strawberry weevil and the red-necked cane borer. Cultural control and minimal "as needed" sprays normally control these pests. There are a number of sporadic, but occasionally harmful, pests. Plant bugs, leaf-footed bugs, stink bugs, blackberry psylla, aphids, Japanese beetles, mites, thrips and raspberry crown borers are all potential problem insects.

Strawberry weevils are small, 1/10-inch long weevils or snout beetles. They vary from dull red to nearly black, with a dark spot just behind the center on each wing cover. Strawberry weevil females injure brambles by laying eggs in flower buds and girdling bud stems, which kills the buds. They are normally present just before and during bloom. Treat when weevils are present and an excessive number of cut buds are found.

Red-necked cane borers are ¼-inch long, black beetles that have a red "neck" or thorax. Adults are generally present from May to early June. Larval feeding causes one- to three-inch-long swellings of the canes. The bark often splits in the swollen area. Cane borer is controlled by pruning. Infested canes are unproductive and, if not destroyed, may reinfest other canes for years. Always remove infested canes and burn them as they appear.

Blackberry psyllids are ⅛-inch-long, aphid-like insects that have three reddish stripes running lengthwise on the wings. Adult psyllids jump when disturbed. Blackberry psyllids overwinter in conifers and move to brambles in the spring. Feeding stunts plants and causes leaves to be tightly curled. Treat if leaf distortion is severe and psyllids are present.

Japanese beetles are ½-inch-long, metallic green to greenish-bronze beetles. They feed on and may defoliate a variety of plants. Defoliation may cause stunted, unthrifty plants. Treat as needed.

Raspberry crown borer is a black, clear-winged moth. Females have yellow legs and rings around their abdomens. Larvae are yellowish-white with brown heads and brown on the tip of the thoracic legs. Larval feeding causes weak, spindly canes that break easily. Pull up and burn infested canes and roots.

Spider mites are ¹⁄₅₀-inch-long, spider-like creatures that feed on leaves causing white speckles followed by discolored blotches. Close examination reveals silken threads on the leaf surface. Mites do well in hot, dry weather. Treat if a sharp population increase is noted or if leaf damage appears.

Bunch Grape Diseases

Disease control is a must for Georgia bunch grape producers. Controlling diseases on grapes is not difficult, provided you follow strict disease control practices. These practices are pruning, cultivating and spraying. If you are not prepared to carry out all three of these practices, you will not be a successful grape grower.

Diseases affect European grapes (*Vitus vinifera*) much more severely than they do American bunch grapes (*Vitus labrusca*). Black rot, anthracnose and powdery mildew are of major importance on both types of grapes.

Downy mildew, Phomopsis leaf and cane blight and Botrytis blight cause devastating diseases on European grapes but only minor problems on American bunch grapes, which usually require no special sprays.

Pruning—Severe annual pruning is a very important practice for controlling anthracnose and black rot. Since these two diseases overwinter in old canes, it is necessary to prune out and burn all excess growth. The only part of the vine kept year after year is the trunk.

Select only strong, healthy canes of the previous year's growth to produce the following season's crop. The selected canes should be as free of disease spots as possible. After fruiting canes have been selected, remove excess growth, dried berries and leaves. The remaining vine should contain only the permanent trunk, one-year-old fruiting canes and short spurs to produce new canes. The amount of diseased material left on and around vines after pruning influences the effectiveness of the spray program.

Cultivating—The fungus that causes black rot can also come from old berries and leaves on the ground. Cultivation of the soil just before new growth begins in the spring covers old berries and greatly reduces black rot infection. Timely cultivation or the use of herbicides throughout the spring and summer controls weeds which might prevent good air circulation and hinder spraying operation.

Spraying—You must apply several properly timed fungicide sprays to control grape diseases. Your success as a grape grower will depend on your understanding of spray equipment and the application of spray material. Refer to the *Georgia Pest Management Handbook* for specific fungicide recommendations.

Black rot is the most destructive grape disease in Georgia. Other diseases will be less troublesome when recommended practices for black rot control are carried out. Black rot fungus overwinters in infected canes and grapes, spreading to new growth early in the spring as green tissue appears and suitable weather conditions develop.

After the disease becomes established in new shoots, leaves, tendrils and blooms, the fungus reproduces in great quantity and spreads rapidly in recurring waves during each rain. Grapes become infected by the time they are fully grown, dry and shatter to the ground. There they remain as a source of disease the following year.

The black rot fungus attacks all parts of the grape vine.

Leaf infection appears as tiny, reddish-brown spots on the upper surface in early June. The lesions enlarge to one-fourth inch or more in diameter and become brown with black borders. A ring of black fungus bodies develops near the outer edge of the brown area. Lesions on stems and tendrils are longer and blacker than those on leaves. Stem lesions are narrow, sunken and often split lengthwise on the vine. Infections begin to appear on the fruit when the grapes are about half-grown. Initially, a small, white spot forms. It enlarges rapidly until the entire grape is rotten. Affected grapes soon turn black, shrivel and dry up. Minute, black fungus fruiting bodies develop on the surface of the dried fruit.

Grape Anthracnose may cause extensive losses in poorly kept Georgia vineyards, but it can be controlled. Anthracnose overwinters on infected canes. It spreads to all new growth during wet periods in early spring. The appearance of anthracnose on fruit, stems and leaves is not readily confused with black rot and other diseases. Fruit infections appear as a "bird's-eye" effect, having light-gray centers and reddish-brown borders. Stem lesions are similar in color, sunken, and with slightly raised borders. Severely infected leaves become distorted and curl down from the margins. Individual spots are gray with a dark border. Later, the center of the lesion drops out, giving a ragged effect.

Downy Mildew attacks all green parts of the vine. Initially, lesions are yellowish and oily, and become angular, yellow to reddish-brown spots. Infected shoots thicken and curl, then turn brown and die. Young berries become gray when infected. Rachis infection can spread into older berries causing a brown rot. All infected parts, except older fruit, are covered with white fungal growth during moist weather. The fungus overwinters primarily in infected leaves on the ground. It may survive as mycelium in buds during mild winters. Pre-bloom sprays are necessary for control.

The disease that causes **Phomopsis Leaf Spot** and **Cane Blight** is especially destructive in climates like we have in Georgia. Leaves have small, chlorotic, irregular to circular spots with dark centers. Spots may also occur on veins and petioles, and leaf margins may be turned under. Dead areas may drop out leaving a "shot-hole" appearance. Infected rachis, stems and petioles have dark brown to black streaks or blotches. Cluster stems may become brittle and break. Infected fruit become dark brown and brittle. Proper pruning is essential for the control of this disease. Early sprays are particularly important.

Powdery mildew can infect all green parts of vines.

Symptoms are a white powdery growth on infected parts. Berries infected before they are fully grown split and either dry up or rot. Infection of fully grown fruit results in a blotchy appearance or a netlike pattern of scar tissue. Infected fruit may cause off flavors in wine. The fungus overwinters as black fruiting bodies on the vines and in dormant buds. Sprays starting at petal fall are needed for control of this disease.

Botrytis Blight infects primarily at bloom, killing the flowers. From the blooms it infects the rachis, girdling it and killing the cluster of fruit from that point outward. Fruit may also be infected during ripening. The disease progresses through the whole cluster. White berries turn brown, and dark berries become reddish. The fungus overwinters on hard black bodies, called sclerotia, on the canes or soil surface. Bloom sprays are essential for control of this disease.

Muscadine Diseases

Muscadine grapes are fairly well adapted to production without fungicides. Control weeds with chemicals or mowing, and trim vines so canes terminate 18-24" from the ground. This will promote air movement and drying under vines. It is not known how much this will help in disease control for muscadines, but increased airflow does encourage dryer vines, which should result in less disease. In bunch grapes, similar practices to promote air movement have resulted in a significant reduction of bunch rot.

Design irrigation systems, if needed, to operate under the vines. Overhead irrigation will help spread pathogens and wet vines, thus increasing the level of disease.

As with any crop, balance the need for fungicide treatment with the crop's value relative to the time and money cost associated with a spray program. Muscadine varieties vary greatly in susceptibility to disease. Angular leaf spot may be the only disease that warrants a full spray program.

Even with frequent fungicidal applications, losses may occur in wet years. In dry years, disease losses may be low — even without spraying.

Angular leafspot (*Mycosphaerella angulata*) is the main disease pest of muscadines; it causes a leaf spotting that leads to rapid defoliation. When a muscadine vine defoliates prior to harvest, the development of fruit ceases. To reduce disease problems on muscadines: select varieties for disease resistance, clean up ALL fallen leaves and fruit at season's end and remove diseased leaves that drop early .

Other disease problems that occur on muscadines are bitter rot, black rot, and ripe rot. Proper pruning and removal of infected berries, leaves and rachi may reduce disease. **Bitter rot**, and **black rot** can be a problems on susceptible cultivars such as 'Higgins', 'Magnolia', 'Summit', 'Watergate', 'Carlos', 'Fry', 'Dixieland ', and 'Scuppernong'. **Ripe rot** overwinters in stems that carried rotten fruit. The fruit stems can be clipped and removed as they are discovered. During the dormant season, fruit stems that carried rotted fruit cannot be distinguished from those that carried healthy fruit. Macrophoma rot can also be a problem, particularly on susceptible cultivars such as 'Chowan', 'Higgins', and 'Fry'.

Insect Pests of Bunch Grapes and Muscadines

Mites can become a serious problem and they are capable of explosive population growth. Treat if more than 10 mites per leaf are found, or if mites are present and leaves are webbed or bronzed. Drought and heavy crop load aggravate mite injury, especially early in the growing season.

Green June beetles, Japanese beetles, bees and **wasps** may be pests shortly before and during harvest. They are attracted to and feed on ripening fruit. Green June beetle and Japanese beetle populations can get out of hand rapidly. Moderate defoliation is seldom damaging. Fruit feeding is serious; do not allow these pests to feed heavily on and become abundant in blocks with ripe fruit. Beware of heavy emergence and migration to vines with ripe fruit after rains.

Grape root borers can kill grapevines. Borers tunnel inside vines at or below ground level, weakening or killing them. All grapes- bunch, muscadine and vinifera- are susceptible. Mounding is a technique using layers of soil to make it more difficult for young larvae to reach the roots or adults to emerge. Mound soil 1 foot high and 1½ feet out from the base of each vine by early to mid-June. It is equally important to knock these mounds back down between early November and late December.

Strawberry Diseases

Diseases can be a serious problem on strawberries. Anthracnose, root-knot nematode, Rhizoctonia root and crown rot, Mycosphaerella and Diplocarpon leaf spots, and Botrytis fruit rot are threatening problems for homeowners.

The root-rot phase of **Rhizoctonia Root and Crown Rot** is favored by cool weather while the crown rot is worse during hot weather. Plants typically collapse just as fruiting starts. Bottoms of leaves are purple, and the leaves curl up. The original crown is killed, and numerous side crowns may develop. This disease organism is controlled by soil fumigation. Unless clean plants are purchased, however, the disease may be introduced with the plants and, because of the lack of competition in fumigated soil, it may spread quickly. It is important to buy disease-free plants.

Phomopsis leaf spot has become increasingly important in Georgia in recent years. The disease starts to develop in the fall or spring shortly after planting. It spreads rapidly and can kill much of the foliage. It remains active as long as there is green foliage on the plants. If plants become dormant in winter, the disease will start again in the spring.

Early symptoms are one to six circular, red to purple spots on leaflets. Spots enlarge and develop gray centers. Older spots along veins develop into large V-shaped lesions. Fruit and calyx infection also occurs. The fungus survives in dead leaves attached to the plants. Apply fungicides when new growth starts and continue application in the spring where the disease is a problem. Fruit infection is prevented by controlling foliar infection.

Botrytis fruit rot is the most common and important fruit disease in Georgia. While rot can start on any part of the fruit, it usually starts on the calyx end or the side of fruits touching other infected fruits. Affected fruits become light brown. The fungus can also invade all other plant parts. Survival of the fungus occurs in infected tissue and in large black sclerotia on the ground or plants. It germinates in the spring when bloom starts and infects bloom parts. From these, it moves into the fruit and may rot it immediately, or it may be dormant until the fruit ripens. The disease is most severe in wet weather. Apply protective fungicide sprays starting before bloom and continuing through harvest. This fungus rapidly develops resistance to fungicides, so rotate fungicides.

Angular leafspot bacterium survives in dead plant tissue. The disease starts as small, angular, water-soaked spots on the bottom of the leaves. Spots enlarge but are limited by the veins. Spots are translucent when viewed by transmitted light and dark green in transmitted light. Spots coalesce to cover large portions of the leaf and appear as irregular reddish-brown spots on the top of the leaf. Heavily infected leaves usually die. The disease is favored by wet weather with day temperatures of 70 degrees F and night temperatures near or below freezing. The disease usually stops as temperatures increase in the spring.

Leaf spot and leaf scorch, caused by the fungi *Mycosphaerella fragariae* and *Diplocarpon earliana*, respectively, cause about the same type of damage and are spread in a similar manner. The spores of each fungus are usually brought into a field on new plants or spread to new areas by insects, birds or farm implements. Both fungi overwinter on infected plants.

Leaf spot shows up first on the upper leaf surface as a tiny, round, purple spot about ⅛ inch in diameter. At first, the whole spot is purple. Later, the center of the spot becomes gray and then almost white. The border remains purple.

Leaf scorch forms small, dark purple spots on upper leaf surfaces. These spots remain dark purple. A white center is never formed as with leaf spot. The spots have an irregular outline. When numerous, the spots run together and leaves appear to be scorched.

The loss of foliage due to these two diseases can stunt the entire plant. Severely infected plants may die. During early spring rains, spores from just a few diseased plants can multiply and spread through an entire planting.

The fungus causing **anthracnose** infects stolons, petioles, crowns, fruit and leaves. Small dark lesions appear on stolons and petioles in the summer and girdle them, killing the leaves and unrooted daughter plants. The fungus grows from the infected petioles and stolons into the crown of the plant, causing a reddish-brown firm rot, and the plants wilt and die. The fungus causes round, brown, firm sunken spots on fruit. Normally, death of plants occurs the year after infection occurs. Buying disease-free plants is the best control measure.

Root-knot nematode causes tiny galls (about ⅛ inch in diameter) to form on feeder roots of the strawberry plant. Several short branch roots stick out from each tiny swelling or gall. Injured plants appear stunted, take on an "off" color and produce little fruit. Weakened plants are more subject to drought damage and make fewer runners.

The root-knot nematode is most common in areas where it has been brought in on strawberry plants and in fields where peanuts have previously grown.

Fig Diseases

Root-knot nematodes are the leading killer of fig trees in South Georgia. Root-knot shares this honor with cold damage in North Georgia. An on-the-spot diagnosis of root-knot infection is possible. Dig up a few roots and look for the characteristic galling caused by the nematode Root-knot nematode infected fig trees cannot be cured with chemical treatment. Pruning the tops to balance with the weakened root system and attentive watering and fertilization may prolong the life of root-knot infected fig trees. Usually, however, they will die sooner or later regardless of the care they receive.

In planting a new fig tree, select a site as far as possible from any old garden sites. Take a nematode sample in this site. If root-knot nematodes are present, do not plant figs.

Fig rust attacks the leaves, usually in late summer. Severely infected leaves turn yellow-brown and drop. The underside of the fallen leaves will have numerous small, somewhat raised, reddish-brown spots. These spots are often covered with a dusty golden-yellow mass of rust spores.

Fig rust is usually not fatal, but repeated epidemics will weaken the plant. In any given year, heavy leaf drop from rust will reduce size and quality of the fruit.

Gather all infected leaves from the ground under the bushes in the fall and remove them from the area.

Fig fruit souring is caused by yeasts spread by insects. Souring becomes noticeable as the figs begin to ripen. A souring fig will often show gas bubbles, scummy masses oozing from the eye, or both. These figs will give off an offensive fermented odor. Souring cannot be controlled with chemical sprays. The only control is to grow fig varieties that have a tight or closed eye that prevents insects form entering the fig fruit.

Pink blight appears as a dirty-white to pale-pink velvety growth on dying and dead twigs. It usually occurs in the interior of the tree. Remove infected branches and prune the tree to allow good air movement within the tree.

Leaf blight is another fungus disease that attacks leaves and fruit. Infection may start as a semicircular brown spot at the base of the leaf. Some leaves shrivel and die; others may be covered with brown spots that break out to leave irregular holes. During hot, wet weather, leaves can die and drop very quickly. Dead leaves are often matted together and held to the tree by threadlike strands similar to spider webs.

FRUIT TREE PROBLEMS

A rigid pest management program is essential to the production of top-quality fruit. It is necessary to combine spray management and cultural methods for many tree fruit. Such an integrated management program should begin with the dormant season and be carried beyond the growing season. When chemical management is employed, very good spray coverage will ensure the best results. For this reason, careful management of the size of the fruit tree through rootstock selection and appropriate pruning is important. The focus of the program should not only include the fruit but also the overall health of the tree. Not only will fruit be impacted by diseases like bitter rot in apple or brown rot in peach, but each type of fruit tree is subject to disease that can impact tree longevity; e.g., fire blight of apples and pears, oak root rot of peaches and nectarines, or leaf scald of plum.

Specific products are not recommended in this handbook. The Home Orchard Pest Management Guide in the *Georgia Pest Management Handbook Homeowner Edition* suggests cultural and chemical control practices that offer a reasonable degree of protection from important fruit diseases and insect pests. This guide, which is updated each year by Cooperative Extension specialists, is specific to home fruit production and suggests cultural methods, as well as chemical products used in the control of insects and diseases in the home orchard.

Pre-mixed home fruit or orchard spray products containing pesticides for both disease and insect control are commonly available. In general, home orchard pesticides are often less effective than their commercial counterparts. Using the highest label rate, and spraying more often when the weather is wet, will generally improve disease and insect control. For many fruit trees, the intervals at which the sprays are recommended will depend on certain stages of development in the buds, flowers, or fruit (Table 1). This schedule must be followed in order for the control products to be effective and worth the time and money spent to apply them.

Always consult the label when purchasing or using pesticides. Be sure the label states the material(s) are labeled for use on your crop, whether it be apple, peach, pear, etc. Carefully follow all precautionary statements. They serve to protect you, the environment and those who consume your crop. Label restrictions are legally binding.

Fruit Tree Diseases

Powdery mildew is a problem in all of the fruit crops covered in this chapter and the buds, flowers, leaves, young shoots, and fruits of all these tree fruit are susceptible to the causal agents, *Sphaerotheca pannosa* and *Podosphaeria oxyacanthae*. A fine netlike growth, progressing to large numbers of conidia produced on the leaf or fruit surface results in a white, mealy appearance. Leaves may be chlorotic, eventually necrotic and they may be curled or stunted. Generally, fruit infections are of the greatest economic importance. In apples, buds can become infected as they begin to form until they are matured for overwintering. 'Jonathan', 'Rome Beauty', 'Cortland', Monroe', and 'Idared' apple varieties are particularly susceptible. Peaches and nectarines are particularly susceptible until pit hardening, with necrotic scabby areas developing on peach fruit while nectarines remain green. 'Elegant Lady', and 'O'Henry' are particularly susceptible western peach varieties grown in the east. All nectarines are susceptible to powdery mildew.

Crown gall affects peaches, nectarines, plums, apples, and pears. The disease is present in most tree fruit nurseries and can be transferred to the home garden if infected trees are planted. It is very important to inspect the roots or trunks of purchased trees prior to planting. Return affected trees to the nursery, and do not plant in your orchard to avoid the disease. Crown gall caused by *Agrobacterium tumefaciens* is easily apparent as wart-like swellings or galls on roots or branches. The galls may be ½ to 4 inches in diameter. Affected trees show reduced growth, look generally unhealthy and may appear nutrient deficient. To protect trees in an area already infested with crown gall, dip the roots in No-Gall prior to planting.

Glomerella cingulata is the causal organism of **bitter rot** of apple and pear and **anthracnose** of peach and nectarine. It is first noticed midsummer as a tan circular spot(s) that enlarge to dark brown. As they reach ⅛ to ¼ inch in diameter they appear sunken. Unlike black rot, this lesion will ooze a gelatinous, salmon-pink mass of spores and is light brown underneath. Fungicide sprays may be necessary to control this disease.

Armillaria root and crown rot (Oak root rot), caused by the soil-borne fungus, *Armillaria tabescens*, first kills roots, then the crown and eventually the entire tree. As the root system of uninfected trees grows into the old root cores infected with this fungus, the new roots become infected. Infected trees will survive longer if maintained in an otherwise healthy condition. Oak trees and pecan trees can be carriers of this disease. There is no treatment for oak root rot. Under investigation at this time is the treatment of bareroot trees with *Trichoderma hamatum* to prevent infection by *A. tabescens*.

Table 1. Key growth stages in fruit development

STAGE	FRUIT	DESCRIPTION
Dormant	All	Overwintering stage of fruit buds in which they are not actively growing.
Silver Tip	Apple	Fruit bud scales separated at tip, exposing silver to light gray tissue.
Swollen bud	Pear, plum, peach	Fruit buds swollen, scales separated to expose areas of lighter colored tissue.
Green Tip	Apple	Fruit buds broken at tip, showing about 1/16 inch green
Bud Burst	Pear, plum	Fruit buds broken at tip, showing tips of blossom buds.
Half-inch Green	Apple, peach	1/2 inch of leaf tissue is projecting from the apple fruit buds. Peach, when the leaf bud occurring between a pair of fruit buds has produced about 1/2 inch of new growth.
Tight Cluster	Apple	Blossom buds mostly exposed, tightly grouped, stems short.
Green Cluster	Pear, plum	Blossom buds green, mostly separated in the cluster, stems lengthened.
Pink	Apple, peach	Apple, all blossom buds in cluster pink, stems fully extended. Peach, blossom bud shows a pink tip.
White Bud	Pear, plum	Blossom buds white, separated in the cluster and stems lengthened.
Bloom	All	Blossom buds are all open.
Petal fall	All	After about 75% of the petals have fallen.
Fruit set	All	4-10 days after bloom.
Shuck fall	Peach, plum	Shuck that partially covers the set fruit has begun to split and fall off.

Diseases of Apples and Pears

The **Black rot** fungus, *Botryosphaeria obtusa*, affects fruit, leaves, and bark of apples. In the Southeast, the greatest economic impact is from fruit rot that usually occurs first at the calyx end of the fruit. It may originate from a wound or insect injuries. It usually appears as one lesion per fruit unlike bitter rot, which usually has several. The disease is primarily controlled by sanitation, removal and burning/burial of diseased wood and fruit.

Blossom end rot occurs infrequently. It is caused by *Botrytis cinerea*, a fungus that attacks the blossom end of the fruit. Infection occurs during bloom, but is visible weeks later as a small ¼ to ½ inch diameter lesion next to or including part of the calyx. Usually brown, the spot is slightly sunken and can have a red border. A shallow, dry corky area develops in the flesh beneath the spot. The spot/lesion is initially brown, turning black as it increases in size to form concentric rings that remain firm and leathery. Blossom end rot is more common in 'Red Delicious', 'Rome Beauty', and 'McIntosh' varieties.

Cedar apple rust can cause severe defoliation that can make trees susceptible to winter injury and reduce fruit size and quality. Fruit lesions occur on the blossom/calyx end of the fruit. The lesions first appear as light yellow spots that enlarge and become covered with dark fruiting bodies. The fruit becomes disfigured, developing unevenly. Cultivars with good resistance are available. Fungicide application made at the pink bud stage will control the disease on susceptible varieties.

Collar rot of apple, also known as crown rot, is not typically a major problem in the Southeast. It is a major cause of tree loss in some regions. It can cause tree loss in trees 3 to 8 years of age. MM.104, MM.106, M.7 and MM.111 rootstocks are more susceptible to collar rot than other rootstocks. It is caused by *Phytophthora cactorum*, one of a group of fungi that cause root and crown rot diseases of many tree species. The fungus is most active during moist cool periods. In areas where this disease is known to be a problem, choose more resistant rootstocks such as M.4 and M.9, and avoid sites that are characterized by heavy, poorly drained soils. Where root or crown rot has occurred, remove soil and infected tissue and leave wood exposed to dry. Bridge grafting may also be used to save the tree.

Fire blight is a very serious disease of apple and pear, caused by the bacterium, *Erwinia amylovora* and is a disease of 75 members of the rose family; e.g. pyracantha, spirea, hawthorn, and mountain ash. In apple and pear, the flowers, leaves, shoots, fruit and limbs can all be affected. 'Jonathan', 'Rome', 'Yellow Transparent' and 'Idared' apple varieties, as well as M.26 and M.9 rootstocks are particularly susceptible. All European pears are very susceptible and Asian types are somewhat susceptible. Fireblight is best managed by pruning out all cankers in limbs 1-inch or more in diameter, cutting at least 8 and 12 inches below any external evidence of the canker in apple and pear, respectively. Clean pruning tools between cuts by dipping in rubbing alcohol. At silver tip, apply a dilute Bordeaux spray plus miscible superior oil if the disease was severe the previous season. Miscible oils are 95 to 99% oils that form an emulsion immediately when mixed with water. Antibiotic applications can be made during bloom according to label directions.

Sooty blotch and **Flyspeck** are characterized by sooty or cloudy olive green to black blotches with indefinite borders in addition to small black shiny dots in groups of a few to a hundred. Both are superficial. The causal fungi overwinter in shoots of many woody plants as well as apple and pear. The diseases are spread to apple and pear from alternate hosts by wind. Fruit infection can occur anytime after petal fall. Summer fungicide applications can offer control, but dormant and summer pruning to open up the tree canopy to facilitate air movement, with adequate thinning to separate the fruit in clusters, will reduce the incidence of these diseases.

Root-knot nematodes, *Melodogyne* spp., shorten tree longevity. The roots of nematode-infested trees show numerous small swellings or knots. Diseased trees may grow poorly and appear always nutrient deficient. Nematode diseases can be avoided by testing for the disease prior to planting and choosing resistant rootstocks. The safest planting sites are portions of the yard where Bermuda or other grasses have been established for years. Trees are more tolerant to root-knot nematode if they are grafted on Nemaguard or Guardian rootstocks. Generally, figs, peaches, nectarines, and plums are most susceptible to root-knot nematodes, although they can cause damage or decline in apples and pears, especially in very sandy soils.

Peach, Plum and Nectarine Diseases

Brown Rot is a fungal disease of peach fruit caused by *Monilinia fructicola*. This most common fruit rot of peach causes a tan to brown spot on the fruit surface. Brown rot attacks developing flowers, shoots and fruit. The diseased flowers wilt and turn brown very quickly. Shoot infections result in gummy cankers. Spores form in the cankers and are spread to developing fruit by wind and rain. In the humid conditions of the Southeast, the brownish spores appear on the rotting surface. The airborne spores are carried to other fruit as the disease spreads. If fruit are allowed to rot on the tree, the disease will overwinter on the fruit mummies and spread to buds and shoots to repeat the cycle the next season.

If the mummies and diseased shoots are removed from the orchard and burned, the level of inoculum in the orchard will be reduced substantially. A strict spray program should be followed from floral development through harvest if the site has a history of the disease.

The **Apple Scab** organism, *Venturia inaequalis*, attacks wild and cultivated apple and crabapple. In Georgia, infections may be serious in some years mainly in the mountain areas. Early infections occur on leaves and fruit pedicels during bud break. Secondary infections may occur all season during wet periods on leaves and fruit resulting in cracked or blemished fruit, fruit drop, and leaf defoliation. Fruit lesions are nearly circular, olive green up to ¾ inch in diameter. Apple scab is best managed in the home orchard by selecting resistant cultivars. The fungus overwinters on the fallen infected leaves and mowing or removing leaves under trees will reduce infections the following year.

Peach Scab appears as small dark somewhat velvety spots on the surface of fruit, usually surrounded by a halo. As the closely spaced spots increase, large black areas can result. These symptoms are superficial and do not affect eating quality. For control, apply fungicide at shuck split, the point at which the calyx splits just before falling away from the developing fruit, and every 14 days thereafter for 4-6 weeks.

Bacterial Spot (*Xanthomonas*) occurs on both fruit and leaves of susceptible varieties of peach, nectarine, and plum. This disease can be avoided by choosing moderately resistant varieties. Avoid varieties that are not developed in the humid east, as they will tend to be susceptible. Leaves develop small reddish spots with whitish centers that drop out. The leaves turn yellow and are shed. Trees weakened by stress or in areas where wind blows sand into the trees are more prone to the problem. Overwatering young trees of somewhat resistant varieties can make them susceptible. Fruit symptoms are open spots that have dark middles. These may advance to fruit cracks in severe cases. Use of resistant varieties and managing good fruit health are the most practical methods for reducing the incidence of this disease.

Plum Pox (Sharka) of peach is now an issue in North America. In 1999, plum pox was first detected in Pennsylvania and in Canada in 2000, but by 2003, plum pox was nearly eradicated from other U.S. regions. Plum pox is caused by the plum pox potyvirus. It is vectored by aphids or through budwood. Symptomatic fruit display chlorotic to bluish rings on the fruit surface that can necrose into the fruit flesh, ruining its edibility. Any sighting of this very serious disease should be reported to your county agent and the Georgia Department of Agriculture.

Peach tree short life has been responsible for changing the face of the peach industry in the Southeast. It is a re-plant disease that is associated with sites infested with the ring nematode, Mesocriconema xenoplax. Trees planted in ring nematode infested soil are more likely to come down with the disorder if the pH is 5.5 or lower, the trees are pruned during the months of October - January, or if the trees develop bacterial canker. This disease can be avoided by planting the trees on Guardian rootstock.

Phony peach disease is caused by the xylem-limited bacterium, *Xylella fastidiosa*. It is spread from tree to tree by the glassy winged sharpshooter, *Homalodisca coagulata* (Say) and by other sharpshooter leafhoppers. In zones 8a and 8b, it is unwise to plant plums, carriers of the bacterium as plum leaf scald, with peaches. It is important to remove wild plums and johnson grass (attractive to sharpshooters) in and around the orchard. There is no chemical control for this disease.

Plum leaf scald disease is caused by the xylem-limited bacterium, *Xylella fastidiosa*. It is spread from tree to tree by the glassy winged sharpshooter, *Homalodisca coagulata* (Say) and by other sharpshooter leafhoppers. It is important to remove wild plums and johnson grass (attractive to sharpshooters) in and around the orchard. There is not a chemical control for this disease.

Black knot caused by *Dibotryon morbosum* is present only in the woody parts of trees. Black knot occurs most often on twigs and branches and occasionally on the trunk and scaffolds. Warty swellings become apparent in late summer or the following spring on new shoots, first greenish and corky, hardening to black. They can cover a length of one foot and can completely encircle a branch. Do not plant adjacent to black knot infected trees and remove wild plum to avoid the disease. Prune out diseased branches about 4 inches below the knot. On larger branches and trunks the knots can be cut out. This is done most successfully during September when the fungus is not actively growing and does not extend far beyond the visible swelling. Remove the diseased wood and about 1 inch of clean wood around the knot. Destroy the diseased wood after removal and spray the remaining tissue to control the disease.

Plum Pocket is caused by the fungus, *Taprina communis*. About six to eight weeks following bud break, symptomatic fruit become distorted, enlarging up to 10 times their normal size. Plum pocketed fruit have spongy or hollow centers and may have pits. Early symptoms are small light colored spots that may become blisters. These enlarge rapidly, becoming reddish with a velvety gray appearance. Affected fruit then dry out, leaving only the outer fruit wall that eventually turn brown to black and fall off the tree. Removal of wild plums in and around the orchard reduces potential inoculum. A fungicidal application in the fall or before budbreak in the spring will reduce the incidence of plum pocket in affected orchards.

Insect Pests of Fruit Trees

Many of the insects that impact pome fruits also impact stone fruits. Therefore in the section that follows these insects are being discussed without grouping by crop.

Codling moth occurs in all apple-growing areas across North America. Its damage, evident as stings, lowers fruit value while larval tunneling causes fruit rejection in commercial plantings. Generally, codling moth populations are maintained at a low level due to other insecticidal sprays used in insect management.

Gypsy moth infestations in fruit trees, particularly apple, cause defoliation that can stunt or even kill young trees. Insecticides can be used for gypsy moth control.

Japanese beetle is very familiar to most gardeners. It is a significant problem in tree-ripened peaches, with adults feeding on leaves and fruit, especially in late June and July. Fruit and foliage may be protected from damage by spraying at regular intervals when beetles first cause unacceptable injury.

Lesser peach tree borer is becoming a greater problem in southeastern orchards. These moths lay eggs beneath the bark of peach and nectarine branches. The larvae feed on the underlying wood damaging the tree. These larvae are evidenced by the presence of frass at the wound site. Wounded or weak trees are more likely to be affected by the problem. Limiting heading cuts may somewhat reduce wounds that attract adult females. Thoroughly drenching trunk and scaffold limbs with at least 1 gallon of insecticide mixture applied per tree is necessary for control. For preharvest applications, use insecticides that are appropriate for bearing trees; after harvest, post harvest materials can be used. If applied in late August, the application may protect against peach tree borer as well.

Oriental fruit moth is a pest of most stone and pome fruits. In apples and pears its damage is similar to codling moth. In the Southeast, oriental fruit moth primarily affects succulent shoot terminals. When the females lay eggs in young shoots, these shoots die back and are flagged. Incidental control through control of other insects generally maintains populations at a level that causes acceptable damage.

Peach tree borer females lay eggs beneath trunk bark at the crown of peach and nectarine trees. The larvae feed on the wood damaging the tree. In young trees, if the feeding is extensive enough, the tree can be girdled and killed. Certainly the damage caused by larval feeding weakens the tree. This damage is apparent as a wood-gum mixture called frass. Weakened trees or those suffering from drought or other stresses are most likely to be infested. A drenching application of non-bearing appropriate insecticide applied in late August or early September will protect against this moth.

Pear psylla limits pear production by producing a honeydew on which fungi such as sooty mold thrive. Several cultural practices will reduce psylla populations and dependence on insecticidal control. First, minimize heavy pruning to reduce terminal shoot growth and feeding surface for the psylla. Limit nitrogen fertilization to a minimum required for proper tree growth. Remove water sprouts that provide the succulent leaf feeding surface preferred by psylla.

Plum Curculio injures fruit of apple, peaches, plums and nectarines throughout the Eastern US. The adult beetle is about ¼ inch long, dark brown with whitish patches, with four humps on the wing covers and a protruding snout one-third its body length. They lay their eggs in developing fruit and subsequent larval feeding deforms the fruit. They are best controlled with a petal fall spray-in for apples and a shuck split application in peaches, plums and nectarines.

Scale affects fruit trees as well as other trees and shrubs. **White peach scale** and **San Jose scale** are the two scale insects that are problematic in our area. These very small insects can have devastating effects on tree longevity and fruit quality. Feeding scale reduce tree vitality and cause purplish-red circles on the surface of the fruit. Female scale are capable of producing about 400 young scale each generation with several generations being produced each season in the Southeast. The young scale crawl about on tree branches and then settle in one location where each one secretes a waxy covering that protects the developing organism. This covering blocks the access of aqueous insecticides to the scale. Therefore control sprays must be targeted. The easiest way to control this insect is to make 2 dormant oil applications 2 weeks apart, every winter. If this is done without fail, further control is generally unnecessary.

However, if these sprays are missed, the only control is insecticidal sprays when the scale are crawling uncovered on the branch.

Tarnished Plant Bugs and **Stink Bugs** are shield-shaped greenish to grayish brown, piercing-sucking type insects. They feed by sucking sap and other juices from plants and their fruit. Their feeding is very destructive, causing fruit drop of flowers and very young fruit or entry for fungal disease in mature fruit. Because they seem to inject digestive compounds into the plant, they can cause overall fruit deformation. Reducing broadleaf winter annual leaves and legumes on the orchard floor and around the orchard can reduce the population of these bugs. Insecticides applied at the pink bud stage and petal fall in apples, and at petal fall, shuck off and 10 days after shuck off in peaches can provide good control.

Pecan Insects and Diseases

Diseases of Pecans—The major disease of pecans in Georgia is pecan scab. **Pecan scab** generally shows up as small black spots on the new leaf parts. Later, similar spots may be present on the young nuts. Early lesions may grow together resulting in large irregular black areas on leaflets or nuts. Early infections may become large, ¼ inch or more across, and sunken in the center by late season. Old lesions, particularly in late season, are often overgrown by other fungi, giving them a white moldy look. The best way to control scab is to plant resistant varieties. On susceptible varieties, pecan scab can rarely be controlled without spraying. Spraying of mature pecan trees cannot be accomplished with home spray equipment and hiring of a professional spray company is expensive and may not be advisable in residential neighborhoods. Sanitation can help reduce losses from scab and other minor diseases. Nearly all fruit and foliage diseases of pecans, including scab, overwinter on plant parts infected the year before. Complete removal and destruction of leaves and shucks during the winter can reduce carry-over of scab and other diseases. Removal of limbs touching the ground promotes air movement under the tree, which in turn helps reduce leaf wetness necessary for disease infection.

Insect Pests of Pecans —Although backyard or home orchard pecan trees seldom develop serious insect problems, treating the trees if pests do begin to build can be difficult. Whole-tree spraying is not an option. However, some of the most likely pests can be controlled effectively with insecticides that are available without a pesticide license, using application techniques that are safe to use around children and pets and are compatible with the typical home environment. Follow all label directions to minimize risks.

Weevils—Pecan weevils can be controlled by spraying tree trunks with an insecticide containing the active ingredient carbaryl. Mix the pesticide in a hand sprayer and spray a two-foot-wide band around the tree trunk about waist high, taking care to get thorough coverage. Treatment should usually begin in mid-August and repeated about three weeks later.

Aphids—Pecan aphids can be controlled with root-zone applications of a systemic insecticide containing the active ingredient imidacloprid. Mix the labeled amount in a bucket of water and pour the solution around the base of the tree. For large trees, the insecticide should be mixed in 2-3 gallons of water per tree. Young trees can be treated effectively with 1-2 gallons of solution. Follow the label indications to determine the correct amount of insecticide for the size of tree being treated. Pecan trees can tolerate surprisingly large numbers of aphids, particularly yellow aphids, without loss of yield.

Treat when honeydew accumulation under the tree is heavy, and when sooty mold begins to blacken the lower leaves. Rainstorms will wash off the honeydew and reduce aphid populations directly, so treatment may not be necessary in most years if the weather cooperates.

RESOURCES

Diagnostic Guide to Common Home Orchard Diseases. University of Georgia Cooperative Extension Bulletin 1336

Garden Insects of North America: the ultimate guide to backyard bugs. Whitney Cranshaw. Princeton University Press.

Georgia Pest Management Handbook Homeowner Edition. University of Georgia Cooperative Extension Publications 117 - Hoke Smith Annex, The University of Georgia, Athens, GA 3060

Fruit-specific Cooperative Extension publications are available online or at your local Cooperative Extension office. http://extension.uga.edu/

Bradley, Fern. Ed. *Rodale's All-New Encyclopedia of Organic Gardening: The Indispensable Resource for Every Gardener.*

Greenwood, Pippa, et. al. *American Horticultural Society Pests and Diseases: The Complete Guide to Preventing, Identifying and Treating Plant Problems.*

Jones, Alan. L. *Diseases of Tree Fruits in the East.* Michigan State University Bulletin Office

DISCUSSION QUESTIONS

1. Why is an IPM program vital in producing quality pears, peaches, nectarines, plums and apples?

2. What is a common disease of blueberries grown in poorly drained areas?

3. What is a primary method of controlling cane diseases in bramble fruits?

4. What is an essential part of producing quality peaches, pears and apples in Georgia?

5. What is the main disease of bunch grapes grown in Georgia?

6. What is a disease common to pear that can be spread by pruning called?

7. What is one control that should be practiced in all fruit gardens to prevent insects and diseases?

21

Landscape Design Principles

David C. Berle

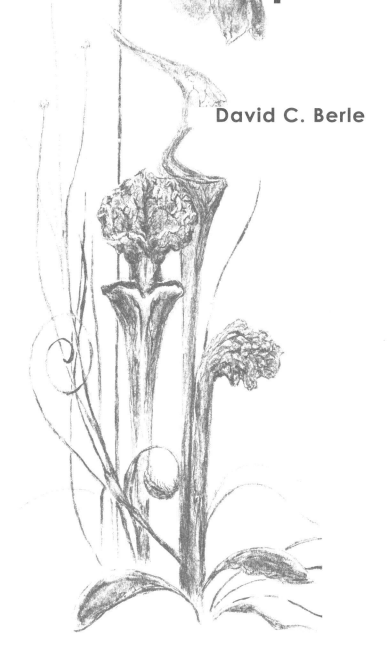

LEARNING OBJECTIVES

Understand the process of site analysis for landscape design.

Know the basic principles of landscape design.

Be familiar with landscape design guidelines.

Understand the factors of plant selection.

TERMS TO KNOW

Base map drawing that incorporates all of the information collected about the landscape and provides the basics to be used in the landscape design process.

Screening plantings or construction used to screen an area to provide privacy, block a poor view, or as a natural boundary or barrier.

Site evaluation collecting and compiling the site information to be used in the development of the landscape plan.

Introduction

Achieving the goal of an attractive, well-arranged landscape is not as easy as it looks. Small landscapes require careful planning for maximum benefit and use; large landscapes can leave homeowners feeling overwhelmed and unsure of how to 'fill' the space. Each individual landscape situation offers both inspiration and challenges for the homeowner willing to develop their own landscape plan. The process of designing an attractive and functional landscape is a matter of gathering information about the landscape, applying some basic design guidelines, and determining the plants and materials to use. The next few sections of this book provide guidance for the landscape design process.

COLLECTING SITE INFORMATION

The first step in developing a landscape plan is understanding the environment. Site information will help inform your overall design as well as help determine plant selection. The most important site considerations are sunlight and soil drainage. Other considerations include things like existing trees, rock outcroppings, streams, and utilities.

Light—Available sunlight is important when it comes to selecting plants for the design. There are some 'swing' plants that will grow well in both sun and shade such as Osmanthus, Nandina, Loropetalum, Liriope, and Ligustrum, but most plants have specific light requirements and their success in the landscape will, in large part, depend on whether those requirements are met.

Determine changes in light by watching the site over a period of time. Ideally, the site should be observed through all four seasons of the year, but this is often not practical. Full-sun (6+ hours) and full-shade (<4 hours) areas are easy to identify. It is the in-between areas that cause problems. The angle of the sun changes with the seasons, so an area that's partially shady in the winter might be in full sun in the summer. Make notes on a map or draw lines on the ground to track the movement of the sun. Remember, early morning sun is not as stressful to plants as late afternoon sun.

Drainage and Runoff—Drainage is more difficult to determine because much of what is happening is underground and conditions vary with the seasons. It is best to observe the site during a downpour and look for water pathways and erosion. Two common problems are poor drainage and stormwater runoff. A standard percolation test might help determine the rate of drainage. If water drains quickly, even during a normal season, it is probably suitable for most plants. If water stands, it could be an indication of drainage. There are many misconceptions about remedies for poor drainage and in extreme cases it is best to consult a professional.

Many homeowners are creating rain gardens to resolve standing water or to collect water where a drainpipe empties. A well-designed raingarden can fit into many different design styles. Runoff issues are becoming more of a concern, and in many municipalities, there are ordinances that require specific action and therefore, it is best to consult your local planning office for more information in cases of extreme water problems.

Existing Trees—If there are existing trees on the site, careful consideration should be given to which trees to keep and which to remove. Trees are valuable and it takes years to replace those destroyed during construction or carelessly cut down. On the other hand, trees damaged during construction or those considered dangerous should be removed. Remember the wide expanse of tree root zones and avoid disturbing tree roots as much as possible.

Natural Landscape Features—Natural features such as streams and rock outcroppings should be considered part of the landscape design and taken advantage of, if possible. Constructing artificial versions of these natural elements can be very costly and should be tastefully designed to avoid a fake or unnatural look.

Slope and Grade—Changes in elevation can add interest and variety to the home landscape. However, excessive grading, terraces, or retaining walls can be expensive and can adversely affect the character of the site. Sometimes, retaining walls, terraces, or banks are needed to facilitate construction or to control water drainage. These features should be designed in concert with the natural landscape.

Utility Lines—It is important to determine the location of underground water, electric, phone, gas and cable lines, as well as sewer or septic tank lines. This information is useful and serves as an aid when determining the location of walkways, patios and larger trees. Most of these can be located at no charge by a locator service listed in the beginning section of the phone book. Water and sewer lines often have to be located by the building contractor or plumber who installed these lines. In today's landscape, there may also be underground fiber optic lines, buried dog fence, and security systems.

Access—Access is a very important consideration when

planning a landscape project. The ability to walk around the perimeter of the house is a requirement, as is access to utility meters, trash and recycling bins, spigots and electrical outlets. Consideration should also be given to areas that may need to be accessed with a pick-up truck or a riding lawn mower. Gates, steps, or narrow paths can become access problems. These issues can easily be avoided with proper planning.

Uses—Consideration of how the landscape will be used is crucial to successful landscape design and, yet, something people often forget. Whether it is done formally or informally, it is always good to think about where everything will go and how a space will be used before starting a landscape project. Sometimes, it is better to put off landscaping an entire yard until the homeowner has lived in the house for a period of time. In this case, starting with a simple foundation planting and waiting long enough to determine the homeowner's needs outside is a wise decision. This is especially true for locating gazebos, walkways and specialty gardens. A common mistake is to locate these elements in areas infrequently used so that the effort is wasted.

Here are a few common questions to consider when determining access and use:

• How will the front yard be used? Formal or informal?

• How will homeowner get from car to house? Is it different for visitors?

• Where will cars be parked, and how will they turn around?

• Will there be outdoor entertaining? If so, how many people and what types of activities?

• Is space needed for a vegetable garden or flower bed or other specialty area?

• What about kids and items such as a swing set, sandbox, trampoline, or soccer net?

• How much time is actually spent in the back yard? Front yard? Doing what?

• Is this a starter house or a house for a lifetime? What about future needs? Resale value?

• Are there hobbies that require space such as boats, a workshop, or equipment?

Additional Information—To dig deeper into the analysis of a site, there are a number of other resources. Soil survey maps and aerial photographs can help locate and identify trees, water sources, and topography. Neighborhood covenants, easements, and roadside setbacks can effect where fences or irrigation pipes can be installed. Most of this information is available from the local government through planning and zoning agencies as well as many public libraries and websites.

Maintenance Considerations

A landscape design determines which plants are used, how they are spaced, the size of the lawn, the types of materials used for walks, patios or walls, and the overall formality of the landscape. All of these landscape features will have an impact on future maintenance requirements.

For example, ignoring the genetic growth habit of plants will most certainly increase the need for pruning. Placing plants with high water needs in dry areas will necessitate more frequent watering. Overcrowding plants may result in the need to thin or transplant in the future and may increase insect and disease problems. Lawn coverage will determine not only mowing time, but also the amount of irrigation, fertilizers and pesticides required to maintain a healthy lawn. Even the type of lawn edging treatment, if any, will have an effect on maintenance time and effort in the future.

Many landscapes include "natural" areas that are less formal than areas with clipped hedges and flower beds. The balance of these two elements is not only a personal preference; it too, can determine the amount and frequency of maintenance. It is important to remember that wooded areas left to grow "naturally" require a certain amount of mulching, weed control, and even pruning, depending on the desired appearance of these areas.

The list below provides some 'food for thought' for landscape maintenance:

Lawns and Mowing

• Lawn size should be manageable for the homeowner and their equipment.

• It is easier to mow around a single, large bed than several small beds.

• Raised edging may require additional work, especially with spreading grasses such as Bermuda grass.

• Edging and walks flush with lawn make mowing easier.

Shrubs and Trees

• Most people use the 80% rule (space plants based on 80% of mature dimensions) when spacing plants.

• Choose cultivars of desired plants that are more compact, have different colors or are better adapted to the site.

• Shade-loving plants growing in full sun require more

watering and often appear wilted. Sun-loving plants grown in shade will flower less and be spindly.

- Locally adapted plants will tolerate the weather and typically require less water.

Watering and Irrigation

- Reduce the NEED for water by selecting plants adapted to the different areas of the landscape.

- Proper mulching reduces watering needs.

- A well-designed irrigation system, with a timer and rain sensor, promotes water conservation.

- Turn run-off and drainage problems into an asset when possible.

Design

- Formal designs usually require more maintenance, especially pruning.

- Massing of plants is good design and allows plants to grow together, reducing pruning needs of individual plants.

- A well-placed, well-designed flower bed does not have to be large to attract attention.

Sometimes the best solution, maintenance-wise, may not be a plant, but rather some other element such as a fence for screening, or a gravel walk instead of turf.

PRINCIPLES OF DESIGN

The number of landscape books that discuss the principles of design are bountiful. These books describe the finer points of landscape design such as scale, proportion, balance, repetition, harmony, and how these elements are brought together to create a pleasing landscape that is unified and orderly. To create a beautiful landscape, these concepts are important and require deeper understanding than this chapter allows. The most important point to remember is that there is a reason some landscapes look better than others. It is partly a matter of personal taste and partly a matter of following these principles. Arrangement, or the way plants are grouped, and how materials go together can make a huge difference in the success of a landscape design. Blending plants together in the landscape requires both knowledge of plants and knowledge of how they will perform. So where does the beginner begin?

There are two basic ways to get landscape design ideas without hiring a consultant – one is to read books, magazines, or the internet, and the other is to examine other landscapes. There are many approaches used to select plant and hardscape materials, but looking for a landscape that is successful, in both appearance and plant health, is a good place to start. Look for plants that combine well with others. Make lists of preferred colors, favorite plants, and desired features. Good landscape design doesn't just happen. It comes from thorough evaluation of site conditions, determining personal needs, and making use of available materials. If homework is done at this stage, applying the principles of landscape design will be easier and make more sense. The following are some design guidelines to consider when designing a home landscape.

Overall Design Guidelines

Ideas—Collect ideas by visiting local nurseries, botanical gardens, and garden tours. Ride around neighborhoods with similar home styles. A good starting point for plant selection is to use combinations of plants you have seen previously or worked for others.

Start small—Begin with a small project, such as a foundation planting or shrub bed. Start with a project that has definite boundaries such as a retaining wall or sidewalk.

Bed lines—The shape of lines around flower and shrub beds, as well as individual trees, can either unify a design or make a design look scattered and 'spotty'. Bed lines should be flowing, not wavy, and they should be able to be maintained with available equipment. Leaving the edging to a novice with a chemical weed killer is a common error that ruins an otherwise good design. Bed lines should also blend with the house and existing driveways and sidewalks as well as the slope of the site. Experiment with various lines using marking paint or a rope before committing to a design. Bed lines are frequently designed first, and then the enclosed area is filled with suitable plants that accentuate the bed lines, making it all work together

Repeat, repeat, repeat—Repetition of shapes, patterns, plants, and even colors can help unify the landscape. For example, the repeated use of curves in the landscape is one subtle way to give a flow or continuity to the design. Alternatively, the repeated use of right angles on a grid design can successfully be used to achieve unity in the landscape. The right angles may begin in the front yard, perhaps the sidewalk, then be used in the bed lines which go around the property, and be picked up again in the backyard. Too much repetition however, can get monotonous.

Keep it simple—Avoid the temptation to get too fancy or use too many different plants. Some people follow the rule of using no more than 5-7 different plants in a foundation planting and no more than 10-12 different plants in a front yard. Avoid cluttering the yard with unnecessary objects. There is a place for bird baths, sculpture, signs, and windmills, but place these items carefully to avoid increasing confusion.

Blending—Continually ask yourself, "How will everything I am planning look together?" Will it blend to create harmony, or will it create a jumble of ideas and elements?

Plant Selection And Use

Familiar plants—Chances are the plants that are familiar are adapted to the area. Save a little room for something exotic or different to experiment with. The Cooperative Extension Office can provide lists of plants, both native and non-native, that will do well in that area in a variety of specific situations. If the plant selected is not on such a list and is hard to purchase in that area, it may not be suited to the local climate.

Group plants—Massing several of the same plants together helps create a certain amount of order in the design. The common rule is to plant the same plant in groups of three, five or seven. This creates the effect of one large group of plants instead of many individual plants.

Plant arrangement—Plants in a straight line create a formal look and make a strong design statement. Straight lines are hard to plant and maintain. Reserve straight lines for the most important areas and consider arranging plants in more relaxed groupings that suggest an informal pattern. When planting in straight lines, be precise, as the human eye can detect even minor variations, and this can make a design look "funny" or "off" even though the viewer may not know exactly why.

Accent—Use an unusual plant or feature to serve as a focus for the eye. Accent curves in walks or beds with curved masses of plants that play off the curve. Reinforce a straight line or curve with a planting of something complementary. Be careful not to overuse this type of design element as the effectiveness would be lost. For example, consider accenting a sidewalk with a wavy bed of Liriope instead of a straight line that simply mirrors the walk.

Room to grow—It is not necessary to plan every square inch of a landscape. Especially in natural areas, but in other areas too, it is important to leave space. Nobody likes to be attacked by plants when they come to a house. Plants have a tendency to fill in available space, so a little extra space may get filled anyway. Why rush things by overcrowding?

Lawn—The homeowner is bombarded with all sorts of conflicting information about lawns. One thing is true — It is better to do a thorough job of caring for a properly sited, smaller lawn, than to try to establish one that's unmanageable or that covers areas not conducive to turf.

Mix it up—Nothing is more boring than a foundation planting using holly, evergreen azalea, and boxwood, all next to each other. When selecting plants to be grouped in the same planting, create more variety by alternating colors, forms, and textures. Combine a burgundy plant with a glossy green plant. Alternate spreading plants with upright plants. Use plants with big smooth leaves next to plants with small spiny-leaf plants. The plant world offers such great diversity there is no reason not to take advantage of it when selecting plants.

Materials

Matching—Matching of materials helps create unity just as it does with plants. Whenever there is an opportunity to select a material for a walk, wall, or patio, consider the existing materials. If the same material such as concrete or limestone can't be used, try to select materials that have similar colors, textures, or patterns as those that already exist in the landscape. For example, if the house has multi-colored brick, select a matching color for patio pavers.

Hardscape Conventions—There are widely accepted standards for things such as the width of walks, height of steps, retaining wall construction and driveway parking space. Look in "how-to" books for ideas or consult a landscape architect to insure that the design falls within accepted standards. Common design mistakes include: no room to back cars, sidewalks too narrow, retaining wall failure, drainage problems, awkward steps, and undersized/oversized patios.

Connections—The location of walks, patios, and driveways should be determined by both need and relationship to the house and landscape. Doors and windows of the house can guide the location of a walk, just as the existing slope can help determine the location of steps. Walks should take people to a clear destination along the simplest path.

ADDITIONAL HELPFUL GUIDELINES

Sunlight—Six hours of direct sunlight each day is considered to be "full sun." Less than 4 hours of direct sunlight is considered "shady." Any amount in between is considered "partly sunny" or "partly shady."

Drainage—Conduct a percolation test to determine soil drainage. Dig a hole about eight inches deep. Fill the hole with water and observe the rate at which the hole drains. If the water drains almost immediately, the soil has excellent drainage. If it takes overnight to drain, then the soil has adequate drainage. If the hole does not drain after twenty four hours, then the soil has poor drainage. This test works best when the soil is already moist.

With the exception of surface grading, it is typically cheaper to select adapted plants rather than attempt to alter existing drainage conditions, unless of course, the drainage problem affects the house. Connect downspouts to a drainage system to direct water away from the house and recycle if possible.

Existing Trees—Proper tree protection during construction requires more attention than most people assume. It is far cheaper to preserve and protect existing trees than to plant new trees. Remove damaged and poor quality trees during the house construction phase to avoid costly removal in the future.

Steps—Steps are easier to walk up than a steep incline, however, a slight incline in a walk is preferred to constructing a single step. The minimum step rise should be no less than six inches and no more than eight inches. Steps should be close together and evenly spaced.

Walks—The minimum width for an entry walk is three feet; four to six feet is preferable. Entry walks should be constructed of solid material to provide sure footing. If stepping stones are used for an entry, they should be secure and evenly spaced. The main entry walk should be a direct route as people grow tired of winding paths. Guidelines for garden walks and paths are more relaxed than entry walks.

Driveways—Make sure the drive is wide enough to park cars side by side. Ten feet is a minimum and twelve feet better. Leave enough driveway room to back up and turn around. Install a four-inch PVC "sleeve" pipe under driveways and sidewalks for later use for irrigation and lighting. Slope driveways and sidewalks so water drains away from the house.

Patios and Decks—Narrow patios and decks feel cramped and confining. Be aware of weather conditions, insects, and views when locating patios and decks. Seating walls should be 16-18 inches in height. Leave about 18-24 inches in length per person.

Retaining Walls—Consider installing drainage systems behind retaining walls. The water pressure and weight of soil are very strong forces against a wall. Retaining walls over four feet should be designed by a professional.

Plants

• Space all plants far enough from the house to maintain a minimum of a two foot space between the house and plant, after the plant matures.

• Large shade trees provide the greatest benefit on the southern and western sides of the landscape, and should be planted at least twenty feet from the house to prevent rubbing against the roof in the future.

• All foundation plants do not have to be evergreen. Consider hardy perennials such as day lily, iris, and black-eyed Susan for use as ground covers.

• Select flower colors that coordinate with existing house colors. Red flowers next to brick can be a problem.

• Smaller plants tend to get established more easily and quickly than very large plants.

• A full-sun plant growing in the shade will not bloom as well as it would growing in better light, and a shade plant grown in full sun will require more water than it would if growing in the shade.

Sustainable Landscape Design

The word sustainable is used frequently and has many meanings that cannot be fully explained in this chapter. However, there are some environmental concerns that should not be ignored when planning new landscape.

First and foremost is concern for water use. All Georgia municipal water providers have water use regulations in effect that influence landscape design. While it may seem like a simple idea, no landscape plant or feature should be used that would require excessive amounts of water. Rain barrels, drip irrigation systems and water recycling systems can help reduce the need for potable water. Several new water collection devices and practices are now available, but costs and returns should be weighed before making any expensive decisions.

A sustainable design considers the suitability of a plant in terms of climate, as well as in terms of susceptibility to pests and need for supplemental fertilizer. Sustainable landscape designs should consider the 'environmental cost' of items. This might include carbon dioxide emissions, fuel for manufacture or shipping supplies, and a new concern- waste disposal. Homeowners are asking questions about the origin of materials and their impact on the environment. There are currently no uniform standards for advertising these costs, but more and more landscape suppliers are sharing this information on their products.

It is worth noting that sustainable landscape design does not mean planting only native plants or never using fertilizer or a pesticide. Some of the hardest landscape plants are not native and almost all of the vegetables and fruits we grow are not native.

Design Implementation

Putting all the information together can be daunting. As mentioned previously, it is often easier to begin with a smaller area and not attempt to design for the entire landscape. There are however, certain stages or steps in developing a design that everyone follows. Some choose to combine all the steps involved in designing and installing a landscape design. Others proceed slowly, taking one step at a time. Below is an outline of the structural elements that should be taken care of first.

1) Conduct a site evaluation, as described earlier in the chapter. Gather information and ideas. Make a notebook or file to keep print-outs, photos, and booklets.

2) Stabilize the site by seeding, mulching, or installing the entire design. Don't let the site become eroded or excessively muddy while developing a plan. Spread mulch or seed bare areas to hold the world together while planning.

3) Determine how the landscape will be used and where each individual component will go. Some people make a sketch of their landscape or use an existing survey map to make a "bubble" drawing of each activity or use.

4) Layout or draw a plan that includes the general plan for bed lines, lawn areas, patios, and walks.

5) 'Play' with bed lines and walks to see how it will all fit together. Some people prefer to do this stage on the ground, using survey marking paint or flags.

6) Locating new shade trees should be the first planting project if possible. Depending on the initial size of the tree planted, it may be years before a tree provides real shade. Red maples and most oaks are the best for fast shade as they will grow several feet per year. Three to five larger shade trees can make a tremendous difference in the overall appearance of a landscape in just a few years.

7) Planting or constructing screens is often a top priority with the smaller landscapes of today. The overall landscape plan should include any screening considered necessary. Often this cost can be shared by agreeable neighbors. Consider views from all the possible angles when determining the desired height. Consider the possibility of feeling too closed in by creating a screen or hedge that is too tall or wide for the site. This is where proportion and scale are important. Also, be sure to check local ordinances and covenants regarding planting or building along property lines.

8) Lawn coverage- The lawn is often the first element installed as part of a new landscape plan. This can be a huge mistake for many reasons. Having turf grass sod damaged by landscape equipment or portions removed when new areas are planted is no fun. It is better to wait for all other landscape work to be completed. If the project will extend over time, then seed all bare areas with turf seed and hold off on the sod.

9) Finally, once the plan is complete and the 'structural' elements installed, it's time to proceed with its implementation. Prioritizing can be difficult. Cost is an important consideration, and it is also important to consider which projects will have the greatest effect. Some components of the landscape design must be done first, such as irrigation or retaining walls.

Conclusion

Landscaping the home grounds is an investment of time and money. To achieve the best results, the site should be looked at in its entirety. The home landscape cannot be developed overnight nor do all of the plants have to be planted at one time. It may take years to reach the full potential of the site, but there is no substitute for good planning. Throughout the design process it is helpful to keep in mind the users of the landscape and how the design will reflect their needs and tastes. Just like the clothes we wear or interior décor we prefer, the home landscape should please the owner first and foremost.

DISCUSSION QUESTIONS

1. What are the factors to be noted in site analysis?

2. How do maintenance considerations affect site design?

3. What are the most important principles in plant selection and use?

22
Developing a Water Smart Landscape

Gary L. Wade

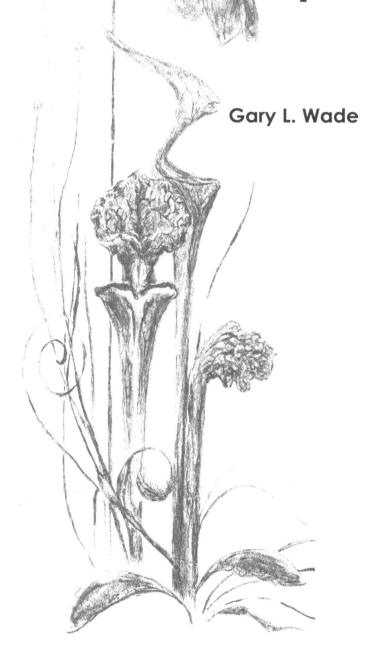

LEARNING OBJECTIVES

Understand the Water Smart concept.

Be familiar with how to develop a Water Smart plan.

Know the importance of establishing water use zones.

Understand the need for soil analysis.

Know how to correct soil problems and improve the soil's ability to hold moisture and nutrients.

Understand the need for appropriate plant selection.

Gain an appreciation for the importance of reducing the need for supplemental irrigation through practical turf areas.

Identify methods and advantages of efficient irrigation.

Know the benefits of use of mulches in a Water Smart landscape.

Be familiar with recommended practices of mowing, pruning, fertilization, etc. as applicable to water-saving.

TERMS TO KNOW

Appropriate plant selection selecting plants that not only are compatible with the design but are also well-suited to the planting site and local environment

Base map a plan of the property drawn to scale on graph paper

Drip irrigation (trickle or micro-irrigation) applies water slowly and directly to the roots of plants

Hydrogels water-absorbing polymers

Public area highly-visible area of a landscape that most visitors see

Service area working or utility area of the landscape

Water Smart/Xeriscape landscape quality landscape that conserves water and protects the environment.

INTRODUCTION

Today, Georgia is facing a serious water supply problem in several urban areas as population growth causes an ever-increasing strain on available water supplies. People are migrating to urban areas for the schools, health care, and goods and services they offer. As a result, over half of the state's 10.1 million residents (2010 Data) reside in just 12 urban counties, while two-thirds of the population lives in just 24 of 159 counties.

Increasing demand for water corresponds to increasing population growth. Table 1 shows population and water demand projections for five counties in northeast Georgia. Similar statistics can be shown statewide for counties in and around urban areas.

Increasing demand for water results in periodic water shortages and restrictions on outdoor water use. Periods of limited rainfall or drought make the problem worse. From 1998 to 2002 and from 2006 to 2008, Georgia experienced two of the worst droughts on record, and restrictions and bans on outdoor water use were common throughout the state. In May 2004, state officials implemented permanent, yet voluntary, odd/even restrictions on outdoor water use to encourage conservation year round. Then, on June 2, 2010 the Georgia Water Stewardship Act went into effect statewide. It allows daily outdoor watering for purposes of planting, growing, managing, or maintaining ground cover, trees, shrubs, or other plants only between the hours of 4 p.m. and 10 a.m. if the water source is from a municipal supply. Persons irrigating from private wells are except from these requirements. For more information, see http://www.gaepd.org/Documents/outdoorwater.html

Household water use increases dramatically during the summer months when irrigation water is applied to the lawn, garden and landscape. In some households, water

"During the 2007 record drought, Georgia still received over 30 inches of rain. Although this was well below normal, it was more rain than two-thirds of the U.S. gets annually. We need to learn how to better manage the water resources we have"

Dr. Carol Couch, former Director, GA Dept. of Nat. Resources

use may be as much as 60 percent higher in summer than in winter.

Tremendous amounts of water may be used outdoors. A typical portable lawn sprinkler applies about 300 gallons of water per hour of operation. Some residential landscapes receive several times this amount of water two to three times a week during the summer. As a result, much water is lost to evaporation or run-off, or it is simply wasted when plants are given more water than they need.

In 1981, a national movement began in Colorado. It was called Xeriscape (pronounced Zera-scape), which means quality landscapes that conserve water and protect the environment. It was derived by merging the Greek word **"Xeros,"** meaning dry, with the word "landscape."

The Xeriscape concept, is a collection of seven common-sense landscape practices that can be applied in every phase of the landscape scheme, from design to installation and maintenance. Each step builds on the one before it, and when applied collectively, water-use efficiency and water conservation can be achieved.

Table 1. Population and water demand projections for five northeast Georgia counties[z]

County	2000 Population	2030 Population	% Change	2000 Water Demand[y]	2030 Water Demand[y]	% Change
Barrow	46,144	173,750	277%+	5.03	23.68	371%+
Clarke	101,489	181,340	79%+	13.67	25.26	85%+
Jackson	41,589	138,480	233%+	3.67	15.88	333%+
Oconee	28,225	51,870	84%+	2.46	9.56	289%+
Walton	60,687	213,880	252%+	6.17	27.91	352%+
Total	276,134	757,320		31.0	102.2	

[z] Source: Northeast Georgia Regional Development Council
[y] Millions of gallons per day

Today, in Georgia and many other states, the Xeriscape concept has been re-named "Water Smart" to make it a more identifiable and environmentally familiar name. The following are the seven steps for developing a Water Smart landscape:

Step 1   Planning and Design

Step 2   Soil Analysis and Improvement

Step 3   Appropriate Plant Selection

Step 4   Practical Turfgrass Areas

Step 5   Efficient Irrigation

Step 6   Use of Mulches

Step 7   Appropriate Maintenance

A Water Smart landscape can reduce outdoor water consumption by as much as 50 percent without sacrific-

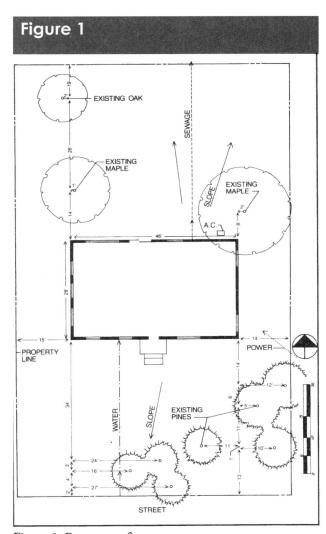

Figure 1

Figure 1. Base map of property

ing the quality and beauty of the home environment. It is an environmentally-sound landscape, requiring less fertilizer and fewer chemicals. A Water Smart landscape also is low maintenance - saving time, effort, and money.

Any landscape, whether newly installed or well established, can be made more water efficient by implementing one or more of the seven practices. It is not necessary to totally redesign the landscape to save water. Significant water savings can be realized simply by modifying the watering schedule, learning how and when to water, using the most efficient watering methods, and learning about the different water needs of plants in the landscape.

The following is a detailed look at each of the seven Water Smart practices.

Step 1: Planning and Design:

Whether developing a new landscape or renovating an existing landscape, proper planning and design are important. It is particularly important when developing a Water Smart Landscape. Before selecting plants, first solve any environmental and physical problems in an attractive and practical manner. Think about the various areas of the landscape in terms of how they should be developed for different uses, and how much space should be allotted to each area.

As you plan each area, consider several different arrangements. For example, is a fence, wall or hedge more appropriate for screening and/or security? How much space is needed for active recreation, a vegetable garden, or patio entertaining? After these decisions are made, begin thinking about what plants to use.

Begin with a Base Map—A base map is a plan of the property drawn to scale on graph paper showing the location of the house, its orientation to the sun, other structures on the site, and unusual features, such as stone outcroppings and existing vegetation (see Figure 1). Accuracy in the base map will help determine if the site will accommodate all current and future plans. Later it will help to determine the quantity of any construction materials and plants needed.

Catalog Site Characteristics—The next step is to lay a sheet of tracing paper over the base map and label it "Site Analysis" (see Figure 2). Use arrows to indicate the direction of desirable views to be emphasized and undesirable views to be screened. Use other arrows to indicate the drainage patterns of the property, including any low spots or eroded areas. Make plans to correct potential drainage problems before planting. This may require re-grading, bringing in additional soil, building retaining walls, or shaping terraces. Any changes in the existing landscape should be subtle so that the natural character of the landscape is retained.

Incorporate as many of the natural elements of the site into the design as possible, such as existing trees and shrubs. Incorporate as many undisturbed native areas into the design as possible. Undisturbed areas of native vegetation will not require supplemental irrigation.

Note the orientation of the home (north-south-east-west). This will help determine where to locate plants best suited for sun or shade. Areas exposed to direct afternoon sun are likely to dry out more rapidly than those in the shade. In these locations, the plan should include drought-tolerant plants, some method of providing supplemental water, or cultural practices that will help conserve moisture. See Chapter 9: *Ornamental Plants in the Landscape: Site Analysis, Planting and Management* for a thorough discussion of site criteria.

Incorporate Shade Into the Design—Shade from trees or structures in the landscape keeps the landscape cooler in summer and reduces water loss while creating a comfortable living environment. A shaded landscape can be as much as 20°F cooler than one in the full sun. Figure 3 compares the heat exchange in an unshaded parking lot, where the soil surface is covered by pavement, to a tree in dry soil and a tree in moist soil.

A person standing in an open parking lot is bombarded with 1,000 heat units from the sun and another 1,000 heat units reflected from the paved surface. (Figure 3) Walking beneath a shade tree provides immediate relief from the sun as the tree acts like an umbrella, blocking light and heat (passive shade). If the tree is growing in moist soil, it will not only block heat but will also dissipate heat by evaporative loss from the leaves (active shade). A moist soil surface also evaporates heat and reduces heat load further. Therefore, a moist landscape with trees can contain one-fourth as much heat as a parking lot in full sun and one-half as much heat as a bone-dry landscape.

In addition to paved areas, shade prevents heat build-up from other hardscape surfaces, such as brick or stucco walls and gravel walks. Whenever possible, shade these surfaces.

Just as we perspire and lose moisture through our pores, plants transpire and lose moisture through their leaves. A mature oak tree, for example, can dissipate as much

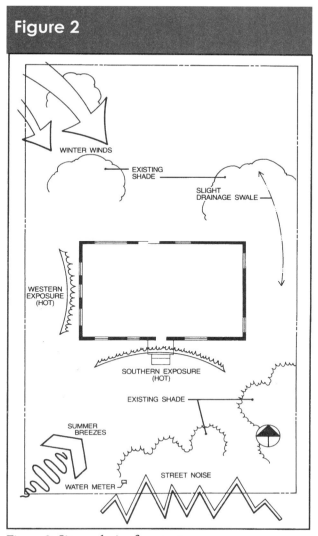

Figure 2. Site analysis of property

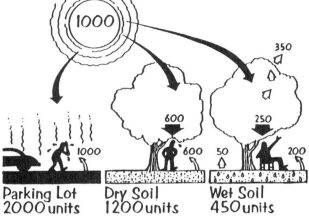

Figure 3. Effects of shade on water loss

heat as four home central air conditioners running 24 hours per day. This evaporative water loss from leaves has a cooling effect on the environment, and cooler temperatures, along with increased humidity, result in less water loss from surrounding plants. Therefore, effective shading makes the landscape more water-efficient, the main objective of a Water Smart plan.

Effective shade management in a Water Smart landscape involves using shade to block sunlight from striking the soil surface and to intercept, scatter, and reflect radiant energy to protect paved surfaces or masonry structures from direct sunlight. Effective shade management also involves managing wind currents that influence heat flow and water loss in the landscape. In addition to trees, structures like trellises, arbors, walls, or fences can provide shade. A vine or espalier on these structures improves their shading and cooling effect.

Plan for Different Use Areas—To begin the plan, overlay the base map and site analysis sheet with another piece of tracing paper. On this sheet indicate the public, private, and service areas of the landscape. (See Figure 4.) Consider how these areas will be developed, based on space requirements for each activity. The public area is the highly-visible area that most visitors see, such as the entry to the home. In a traditional landscape, this area typically receives the most care and the most water. Therefore, the careful design of this area is important for water conservation. It is possible to design this area to require minimal water and maintenance without sacrificing quality or appearance.

The private area of the landscape, usually the backyard, is where most outdoor activity occurs. It is generally the family gathering area. It may also include a vegetable garden or fruit orchard. The landscape in this area needs to be functional, attractive, and durable, but it also should be designed to require less water than the public area of the landscape. The service area is the working or utility area of the landscape, an area usually screened from view and containing such items as garbage cans, outdoor equipment, and air-conditioning units. In terms of routine maintenance, this area would be designed to require the least care and water of the three areas.

Establish Water-use Zones—In addition to dividing the landscape into use areas, a Water Smart plan further divides the landscape into three water-use zones: **high** (regular watering), **moderate** (occasional watering), and **low** (natural rainfall) (see Figure 5). There may be several of these zones within an individual landscape. High water-use zones are small, highly-visible, and

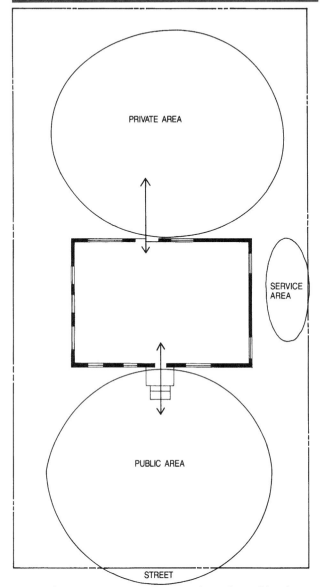

Figure 4. Basic use areas of a typical residential landscape

highly-maintained areas of the landscape, such as the public area and the area around the patio where plants are watered regularly in the absence of rainfall. In the moderate water-use zones, established plants are watered only when they turn a grey-green color, wilt, or show other symptoms of moisture stress. Possible plants for this zone include azalea, dogwood, redbud, Japanese maple, and many herbaceous perennials. Plants in the low water-use zones are not irrigated, except during extreme droughts when plant survival is in jeopardy.

Newly-planted ornamental plants and turfgrasses require regular irrigation during the establishment period, regardless of their intended water-use zone.

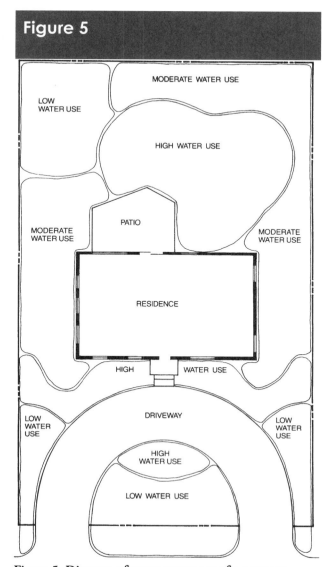

Figure 5

Figure 5. Diagram of water-use zones of a property

beginning to take shape. The form of the various beds can be visualized, even though construction materials and plants have not yet been identified.

Develop a Master Plan—After deciding on a design scheme and a water management arrangement, it is time to give form and definition to the various spaces on the plan. With the identification of planting spaces, edging materials, groundcovers, and paving, the Master Plan begins to take form. This is a plan showing the final product. Straight lines or smooth flowing curves are best —tight curves or unnecessary bends can be maintenance problems. Use right angles and avoid acute angles that are difficult to maintain and irrigate. Remember that simplicity in the design will ensure easy maintenance and water-use efficiency. A prototype Master Plan is shown in Figure 6.

Fit Plants to the Design—After achieving the desired style and overall effect, it is time to select plants to fill the assigned spaces. It is very important to select plants that complement and accent the good features of the architecture and construction materials rather than overpower them.

Group plantings to conform to the shape of plant beds. Avoid rigid, formal, geometric plantings as much as possible. A good approach for most residences is to place the larger plants at the corners with some height at the entrance and low plantings in between. Such arrangements focus attention on the entrance.

For a pleasing visual effect, use odd number groupings (1, 3, 5) when possible. Use bands of low-growing plants or ground covers to tie together and unify groups of taller shrubs.

Place plants at the proper spacing in the landscape to ensure easy maintenance and more efficient use of water. See Chapter 11: Selecting Woody Plants for Georgia Landscapes for information on mature height and spread of commonly-used plants or ask a local nurseryman or County Extension Agent about the plant. It is extremely important to space plants far enough apart so that they can achieve their mature size without being crowded. Over-planting by placing plants too close together increases costs. It also causes long-term maintenance problems and increases the potential for water stress.

Select plants that have a size and form that conform to their location without having to be sheared or frequently pruned to keep them in bounds. Plants, like people, grow in all shapes and sizes. If left unpruned, some plants will be tall and thin, while others will stay

For greatest water conservation, design as much of the landscape as possible into low water-use zones. Most people are surprised to learn that many woody ornamental trees and shrubs, turfgrasses, some herbaceous perennials, and even some annuals, grow well in low water-use zones where they are not irrigated after they are established.

To maximize water savings, concentrate seasonal color beds in areas of the landscape where they can be watered and maintained. Avoid scattering a number of small color beds throughout the landscape. Consider placing seasonal color in containers instead of beds. Containers can be more efficiently watered than beds, and they can be moved to areas where high impact color is needed.

Add a new overlay of tracing paper and sketch the desired water-use zones. At this stage, the landscape is

Figure 6

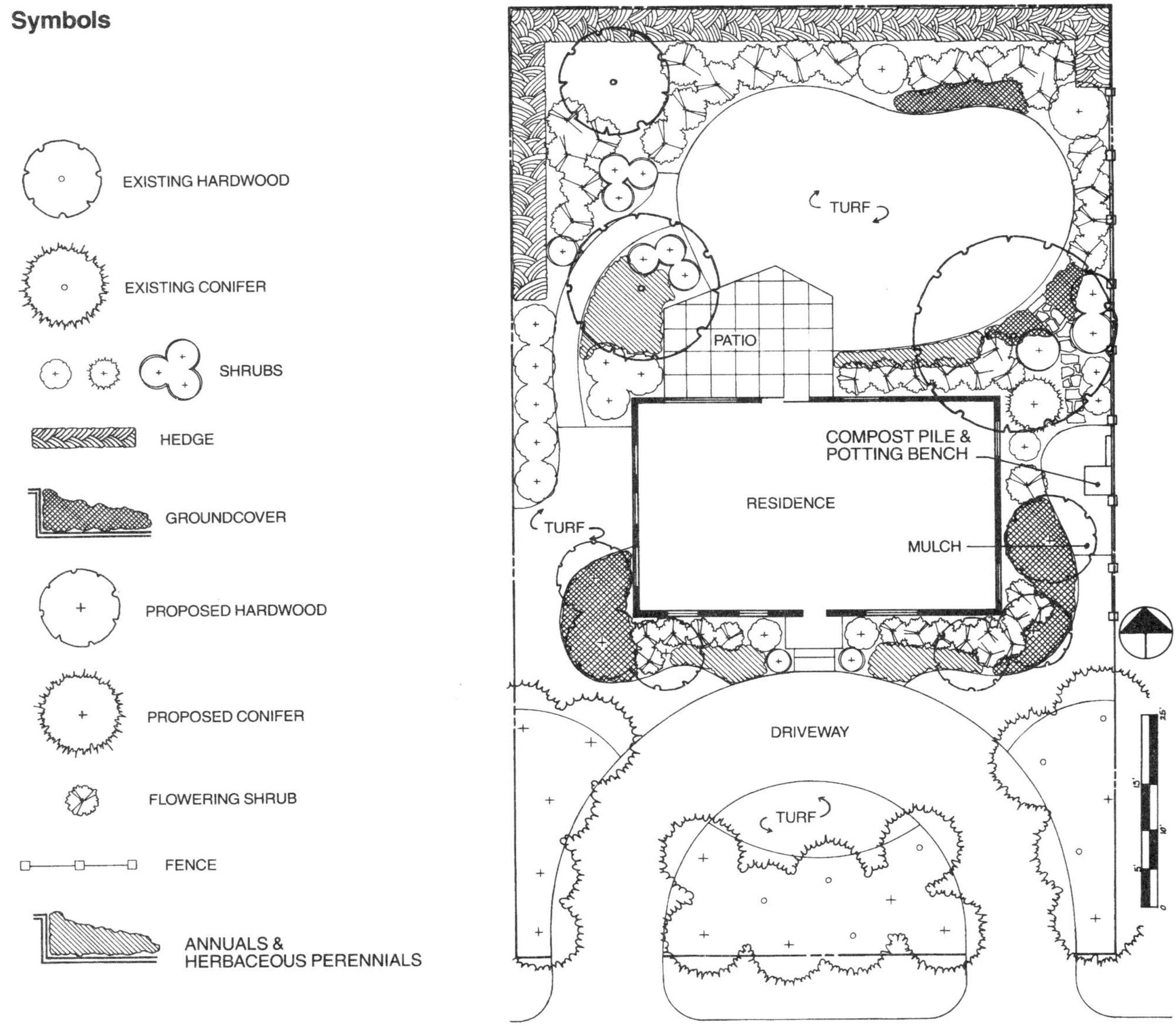

Symbols

EXISTING HARDWOOD

EXISTING CONIFER

SHRUBS

HEDGE

GROUNDCOVER

PROPOSED HARDWOOD

PROPOSED CONIFER

FLOWERING SHRUB

FENCE

ANNUALS &
HERBACEOUS PERENNIALS

TURF

PATIO

COMPOST PILE &
POTTING BENCH

RESIDENCE

MULCH

TURF

DRIVEWAY

TURF

Figure 6. Master Plan for a Watersmart Landscape (note how the character of the landscape is very similar to that of a traditional landscape)

short and spreading. Some will be irregular with open branching while others will be compact with dense foliage. Choose plants with the same shape and ultimate size as the space to be filled. For example, to plant an area in front of low windows, 2 feet above the ground, select spreading, low-growing shrubs with an anticipated height of not over 2 feet.

Avoid using too many different kinds of plants because the landscape may look like an arboretum of plants and will lack unity. For the typical home, three to five different shrubs, in addition to ground covers and trees, are recommended for the basic plantings around the house.

Renovation of an Existing Landscape for Improved Water Conservation—Figure 7 depicts before and after views of a typical residence that has been renovated for water conservation. The before view illustrates a rather dull landscape with foundation shrubs ringing the house, a hedge along three sides, and some native trees along the rear of the property.

The redesign of the residence (after view) shows expansion of the shrub beds in the public and private areas of the landscape to provide seasonal interest, variety, and reduced maintenance. Shade-tolerant ground covers are used under the existing trees on the left side of the front and right rear of the property. A large area in the

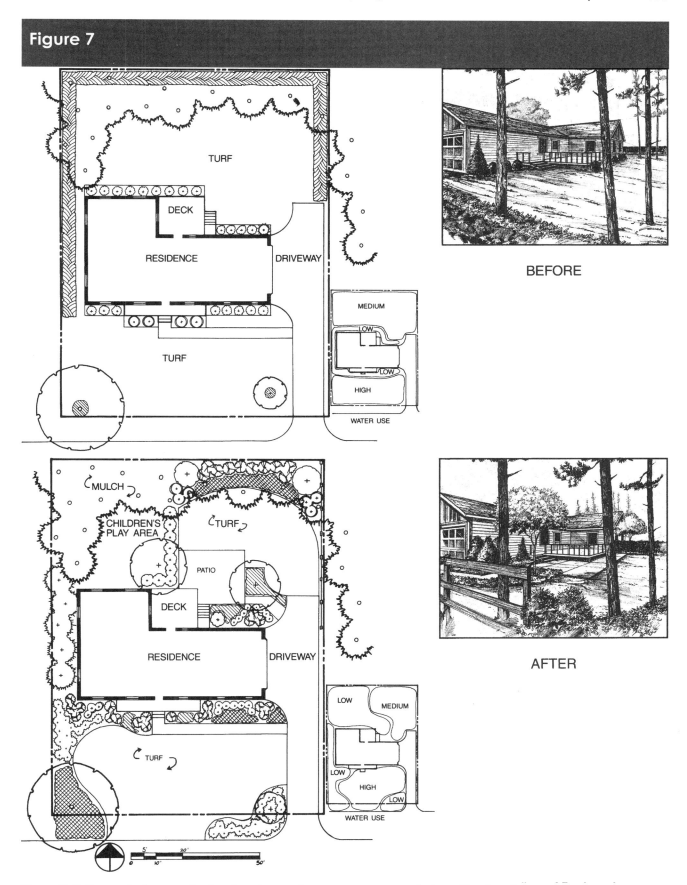

Figure 7

TURF

DECK

RESIDENCE

DRIVEWAY

TURF

MEDIUM

LOW

LOW

HIGH

WATER USE

BEFORE

MULCH

CHILDREN'S PLAY AREA

TURF

PATIO

DECK

RESIDENCE

DRIVEWAY

TURF

LOW

MEDIUM

LOW

HIGH

LOW

WATER USE

AFTER

5'   20'

10'   50'

Figure 7. Before and after retrofit showing changes in water-use zones and view of backyard

left rear of the property was made into a play area for children using mulch. Note how the water-use zones changed during the redesign of the property. The goal was to minimize the irrigated area and irrigation requirements of the landscape.

Tables 2 and 3 show an economic comparison of the landscape before and after renovation. Changes in water-use zones were projected to save over 27,000 gallons of water a year. This equated to an annual savings of $134.90 on water, $151.42 on sewage and $279.66 on landscape maintenance. Although the landscape renovation cost $1,245.00 in plants and supplies, the annual savings brought a total return on investment within 2.2 years. Therefore, a water-wise landscape not only saves water...it saves money!

Table 2. Surface area by water use zone before and after renovation

ZONE	SQUARE FEET BEFORE	SQUARE FEET AFTER
Low	0	3403
Moderate	5788	3403
High	3662	2509
Total irrigated area	9450	6047

*Low = not irrigated; Moderate = irrigated occasionally; High = irrigated regularly

Table 3. Estimated annual water use and annual cost of water, sewage and landscape maintenance before and after renovation

	BEFORE	AFTER	SAVINGS
Water Use (gallons)	81,437	51,733	27,437
Est. annual water[1] cost	$369.84	$234.94	$134.90
Est annual sewage[1] cost	$415.26	$263.84	$151.42
Est. annual maintenance[2] cost	$778.80	$490.14	$279.66
Overall cost	$1563.90	$697.92	$565.98

[1] Water and Wastewater Rate Survey, Metropolitan North Georgia Water Planning District, 2008. Cost based on average charge/7,000 gallons across 16 counties.
[2] HORT Management Cost Estimator, 2009. The University of Georgia Cooperative Extension Special Publication 1, Departments of Horticulture and Agricultural and Applied Economics

The alteration of an existing landscape to conserve water does not have to be as elaborate as that shown. In many instances, it may be as simple as relocating a few shrubs or flowering trees to more environmentally-suitable locations on the property, or improving the shape of plant beds to simplify irrigation. Considerable savings can result by converting irrigated areas to ground covers or natural mulch areas. Often, large amounts of water can be saved simply by changing management practices and watering habits without making any physical changes in the landscape. For each 1,000 square feet of landscaped area converted from an irrigated to a non-irrigated area, it is estimated that more than $90 per year can be saved on annual water and sewage costs.

Step 2: Soil Analysis and Improvement

Inspect The Soil—A thorough analysis of both the physical and chemical characteristics of the soil is important when developing a water-wise landscape. Georgia has a wide variety of soil types, ranging from well-drained coastal sands to poorly-drained clays. Each soil has its own unique structure and texture, drainage pattern, pH, nutrient content, and need for amendments and fertilizer. To complicate matters, there may be several different soil types within an individual landscape, or the soil may consist of fill dirt brought onto the site. Soils are seldom perfect and most of them can be improved in some way to ensure best plant growth.

The goal in a Water Smart Landscape is to create an ideal soil environment for the expanding root system. An ideal soil has good aeration and drainage, yet holds adequate moisture and nutrients for optimum root growth. Research at the University of Florida showed that the roots of trees and shrubs grow outward, approximately seven times the diameter of the root ball, during the first growing season when provided with a good soil environment.

Unfortunately, there is no "cookbook recipe" for soil improvement. Each soil is different, and plants have different requirements for moisture. How to treat the soil depends on the characteristics of the native soil, the type of plants to be grown, and the time of year when planting.

Before planting, check the structure and texture of the native soil by digging a hole 12 to 15 inches deep and examining the soil horizon. Is it loose and granular, or hard and compact? Fill the hole with water and watch how fast it drains. If water remains in the hole after 12 hours, the soil is poorly-drained.

Plants prone to drought stress, such as azalea, dogwood, annuals, and herbaceous perennials, prefer a moist, well-drained soil. On the other hand, plants known to be drought tolerant, such as crape myrtle, ligustrum, and juniper, grow well on dry sites, once established. Soil preparation for summer transplanting, when dry periods are likely to occur, should have a greater water-holding capacity than soil prepared for fall transplanting, when rainfall is generally more regular and irrigation demand is low.

Soil Analysis Saves Guesswork—Before landscaping, get your soil tested. You can either take a soil sample to the County Extension Office for sending to the State Soil testing lab (there will be a small fee for this), or you can order a soil test kit on-line at http://aesl.ces.uga.edu/soiltest123/Georgia.htm The results of the test will go back to your local Extension agent who will provide a recommendation for lime and fertilizer based on the analysis.

Improve the Structure of Poor Soils—Certain native soils, like dense, poorly-drained clays, have such poor structure that plant growth suffers unless they are improved. Poorly-drained soils can be improved in several ways. Sometimes deep cultivation will break apart a hard layer of soil (hardpan) several inches below the soil surface and improve drainage. Another option is to bring in additional soil to raise the planting area 12 to 15 inches above the existing grade. Some professional landscapers also incorporate 3 to 6 inches of a coarse aggregate, such as coarse granite sand or pea gravel, into poorly-drained soils. A final option is to install subsurface drainage pipe to carry excess water off the site after rain.

On the other hand, soils that tend to dry out rapidly and hold little moisture will benefit from organic matter, like compost, incorporated uniformly throughout the planting bed. This is particularly helpful when water-requiring plants, like annuals, are to be grown. For organic matter to be beneficial, apply 3 to 6 inches on the soil surface and incorporate it into the soil to a 12-inch depth.

Water-absorbing polymers, commonly called hydrogels, are popular products on the market today. They are sold under several trade names, including Terra Sorb and Hydrosource. These man-made crystals, absorb several hundred times their weight in water and gradually release it to plant roots. One pound of crystals applied to 100 square feet of bed area will absorb 20 to 25 gallons of water, or about 50 times as much moisture as peat moss. They last from six months to several years in the soil, depending on the product.

Research to date with hydrogels is limited and has provided conflicting results. However, preliminary studies with hydrogels at the University of Georgia show them to enhance the growth of summer annuals in non-irrigated soils. Some professional landscapers use hydrogels in container plantings to extend the time between waterings. Master Gardeners may want to experiment with these products and judge their merits.

STEP 3: Appropriate Plant Selection

Appropriate plant selection means selecting plants that not only are compatible with the design but also are well-suited to the planting site and local environment. It involves selecting plants according to the soil type and light level of the site. Ideally, the plants selected also should be adaptable to local fluctuations in temperature and soil moisture.

Drought tolerance is important in a Water Smart landscape. However, it should not be the only criteria used to select plants. Junipers, for instance, are extremely drought tolerant, but they cannot tolerate wet soils or heavy shade. Red-tip Photinia is drought tolerant, but it is susceptible to a leafspot disease that defoliates it in summer.

Native plants are not necessarily more drought tolerant than introduced exotic species. Even though a plant may be native to the area, it may not adapt to an adverse new environment (micro-climate). To be successful with native plants, the plant's native environment must be simulated. Also, there are some native plants, such as Summersweet Clethra, Inkberry and Swamp Magnolia, that are native to moist sites and are not drought tolerant.

In addition to the adaptability of a plant to the site, several other important criteria should be considered:

Mature size and form— Will the plant remain in scale with the rest of the landscape as it matures, or will it likely overgrow the site and compete with other plants for space, nutrients and water?

Growth rate—Slow-growing dwarf shrubs and ground covers used around the base of the home require little routine pruning.

Texture—Is the leaf texture fine, medium, or coarse; does it combine well with the adjacent plants?

Color—Is the flower or foliage color compatible with other plants or the background color of the building?

Functional Use—Is the plant suitable for the location and intended purpose; i.e. under low windows, along the perimeter of the property as screening hedge, or as a ground cover?

Select healthy, vigorous plants. Examine their root systems for well-developed roots and an abundance of small white roots (absorptive roots) along the exterior of the root ball. Examine the leaves and stems for insects or diseases, and avoid plants that are weak or appear unhealthy.

When selecting plants for a Water Smart landscape, keep in mind this important fact..PLANTS DON'T SAVE WATER....PEOPLE DO! It is not the plants that save water; rather our ability to locate them in the landscape appropriately and to manage them properly that determines their water needs.

Match the water-use zones with the condition of the planting site. For instance, place high water-requiring plants in areas of the landscape that stay moist, and low water-requiring plants in areas that stay drier naturally.

Any ornamental plant or turfgrass presently on the market can be used in a Water Smart landscape. In fact, it may be surprising to learn just how many plants can thrive without any supplemental water once they are established. The key is to identify the water needs of the plant selected, then group it in the landscape with other plants having a similar need for water. By doing this, supplemental irrigation can be applied most efficiently and only to those plants that require it. The result is maximum water conservation in the landscape.

STEP 4: Practical Turfgrass Areas

Turfgrass is one of the most versatile and functional plants in the landscape. It provides one of the best recreational surfaces for outdoor activities. From a water management standpoint, turfgrass is recognized as one of the most effective plant covers to reduce run-off and erosion, while recharging the ground water, which results in more efficient use of rainfall.

Turfgrass has a tremendous mitigating effect on the environment. For example, research documents that a turfgrass area can be as much as 30°F cooler than a concrete or asphalt surface, and 10°F to 14°F cooler than bare soil. This cooling effect from the average lawn is equal to over eight tons of air conditioning while the average home central air unit produces three to four tons. Turfgrass also absorbs dust and other air pollutants, while producing oxygen.

However, in the typical landscape, turfgrass occupies the largest area and, when managed incorrectly, receives the largest amount of irrigation. Considerable water savings can be realized by irrigating only the turfgrass in high impact, highly visible areas of the landscape.

Maximum water conservation with turf is obtained through proper selection, establishment, and maintenance. In addition to differing in appearance, turfgrasses differ in their tolerance to environmental factors such as shade, temperature, soil fertility, water use, and drought resistance. Table 4 shows water use and drought resistance of some turfgrass species and varieties tested in Georgia. The water use is based on the user following recommended irrigation practices. Drought resistance is important when growing turfgrass in non-irrigated areas, although the turfgrasses listed would survive most droughts in Georgia.

Practical turfgrass areas means using turfgrass for a specific function in the landscape. A small "oasis" of turf near the entrance to the home, a playing surface of durable turfgrass in recreational areas, or a blanket of turf on a highly erodible slope are all examples of "practical" turfgrass areas. Also, design turfgrass in practical shapes that can be efficiently irrigated and maintained. Avoid sharp angles and long narrow strips that are difficult to mow and water.

Remember, the goal in developing a Water Smart landscape is to reduce the need for supplemental irrigation, regardless of whether it is in turfgrass or ornamental areas of the landscape.

For additional information on turfgrass selection and maintenance see Chapter 14: Turfgrass in this manual.

Table 4. Average water use and drought resistance of selected turfgrasses in Georgia		
COMMON NAME	**WATER USE**	**DROUGHT RESISTANCE**
Tifway Bermudagrass	very low	very high
Common Bermudagrass	very low	very high
Raleigh St. Augustinegrass	very low	very high
Rebel II tall fescue	very low	medium
Centipedegrass	low	med-high
Meyer zoysiagrass	low	low
K-31 tall fescue	low	low-med

STEP 5: Efficient Irrigation

A Water Smart landscape requires a minimal amount of supplemental water from irrigation. When irrigation is used, water is applied efficiently and effectively to make every drop count.

Just as plants are zoned in the landscape according to their different water needs, zone the irrigation system so that plants with different water needs are irrigated separately. For instance, water turfgrass separately from shrubs and flowers.

The efficient use of irrigation water also requires the selection of the appropriate type of irrigation for the plants in each irrigated area of the landscape. Trees and shrubs in the low water-use zone would need supplemental water only during establishment (first 8 to 10 weeks after transplanting), while plants in moderate water-use zones require water only during periods of limited rainfall when they show signs of stress. For these plants, a temporary system such as a soaker hose or hand watering may be all that is required. Conversely, high water-use zones require frequent watering and may warrant a permanent system with automatic controls. Whenever possible, use highly efficient watering techniques, such as drip irrigation.

Sprinkler Irrigation—Sprinkler irrigation may be as simple as a single sprinkler attached to a garden hose, or it may be a complex system of underground pipes and pop-up spray heads with automatic controls. A Water Smart landscape uses sprinkler irrigation for watering turf where water must be applied uniformly over the entire area. For most other applications in the landscape, drip irrigation is a better choice.

There are many types of sprinklers available for use in the landscape. Permanent systems with pop-up type spray heads are most common. They are installed underground and rise above the ground surface to operate. Some are designed for use in turf (2- to 3-inch pop-up height), while others are designed for use in beds of taller plants (6- to 12-inch pop-up height). Some sprinkler heads are designed for watering small, irregular-shaped areas. These typically have a radius of 15 feet or less. Others, like rotary sprinkler heads, wet a radius of 20 to 50 feet and are used to irrigate large areas. Most sprinklers are available in either full-circle or part-circle models and most have an adjustable radius for watering irregular areas.

Proper Design is Important—The installation of an efficient sprinkler system begins with good design. The system must be capable of applying water uniformly over the desired area with a minimum of overspray into adjacent areas.

Choosing the appropriate sprinkler for a given area is important, but equally important is the location and spacing of sprinklers. It is usually desirable to place part-circle sprinklers along the boundaries of the irrigated area. This allows uniform watering along the edges while avoiding wasteful overspray onto buildings, paved areas, and other adjacent areas.

Proper spacing of sprinklers is crucial in achieving uniform water application. Sprinklers which do not overlap adequately will waste water by applying too much water in some areas and not enough water in others. On the other hand, spacing sprinklers closer than required increases the cost of the system and wastes water. In general, spacing between sprinklers should be about 50 percent of the wetted diameter. For example, sprinklers with a wetted diameter of 80 feet should be spaced 40 feet apart.

Where part-circle sprinklers are used on the same zone with full-circle sprinklers, the sprinklers should be carefully selected to achieve a "matched precipitation rate." A half-circle sprinkler will only water half as much area as a full-circle sprinkler, therefore it should only discharge half as much water. If a full-circle sprinkler discharges 6 gallons per minute, then a half-circle sprinkler should deliver 3 gallons per minute and a quarter-circle sprinkler 1½ gallons per minute. Most manufacturers offer sprinklers with matched precipitation rate (MPR) nozzles.

One other important aspect of proper design is pipe sizing. Selection of pipe sizes should be based on the flow rate through the pipe. If pipes are too small, excessive pressure losses occur. This causes some sprinklers to apply more water than others and results in non-uniform application and waste of water. Additional information on pipe sizing and irrigation system design is available in Georgia Cooperative Extension Bulletin 894, *Irrigating Lawns and Gardens*, http://www.caes.uga.edu/publications/_as well as design manuals available from the sprinkler manufacturers.

Check the Application Rate of Sprinkler Systems—Application rate is the rate at which a sprinkler system applies water to the soil surface, measured in inches per hour (in./hr.). If application rates exceed the intake capacity of the soil, run-off occurs. Problems with run-off are more likely to occur in clay soils which have a low intake capacity.

Rotary sprinklers usually have application rates of 0.25 to 0.50 in./hr. and rarely cause run-off. Spray heads, on the other hand, typically have application rates between 1 and 2 in./hr. and may cause run-off on heavy soils, especially where slopes are greater than 10 percent. If run-off occurs, turn off the system for an hour or two to let the water soak in. Then apply the remainder of the water.

Determine application rate of a sprinkler system by placing three or four rain gauges at random on an irrigated area for a predetermined length of time (usually one hour). By knowing the application rates of the sprinkler system, it can be determined how long to operate the system to apply a given amount of water. This will avoid wasting water. Average water level within the gauges is a measure of the output of the system (inches per hour). Repeat this procedure in each sprinkler zone, particularly if different types of sprinklers are used on different zones.

Adjust Sprinkler Heads As Needed—Improper adjustment of sprinkler heads not only wastes water but also may cause accidents if the water is allowed to spray onto buildings, public streets, or sidewalks. Carefully adjust the radius and arc of part-circle sprinklers to prevent undesirable overspray. Check the system several times during the year to ensure proper adjustment.

Drip Irrigation

Drip irrigation, also called trickle or micro-irrigation, applies water slowly and directly to the roots of plants through small flexible pipes and flow control devices called emitters. Drip irrigation uses 30 to 50 percent less water than sprinkler irrigation and usually costs less to install. Apply water directly to the root zone to minimize evaporative water loss and run-off.

For maximum water-use efficiency, use drip irrigation on trees, shrubs, and flowers in the high and moderate water-use zones of the landscape. There are several types of drip irrigation systems which can be adapted to suit a variety of applications, from watering individual trees and shrubs to beds of annuals, herbaceous perennials, or ground covers.

Components of a Drip System—In a drip system, water is distributed to the plants through small, flexible plastic pipes (⅜ to ¾ inch in diameter) and emitters, or through perforated or porous pipe.

Emitters may be purchased separately from the tubing and placed in the line wherever watering is desired.

Another option is to purchase drip tubing with emitters already installed at the factory, usually spaced 12 to 24 inches apart. Most emitters will discharge water at a rate of ½, 1, or 2 gallons per hour at a pressure of about 20 pounds per square inch.

Perforated or porous pipe discharges water along its entire length to wet a continuous strip. By spacing the pipe 12 to 18 inches apart, it is possible to wet a solid area. It is a good system for closely spaced plantings of annuals, herbaceous perennials, or groundcovers.

Most drip systems will use PVC pipe for main lines and polyethylene tubing for distribution lines. Polyethylene tubing is flexible, easy to cut, and can be connected without glue or clamps. Install emitters by punching a hole in the polyethylene tubing and snapping the emitters into place.

The drip system must have a main valve to turn it on and off. It may be an automatic electric valve connected to a controller, or it can be a manual gate valve. Also, the drip lines may be connected directly to an outside faucet. However, when connecting the system directly to the faucet, use an automated timer to turn the system off after a preset time. Otherwise, it is possible to forget and leave the system on for several days.

Two other necessary components for a drip system are a filter and a pressure regulator. See Figure 8. A drip system uses small passageways to control the rate of water application so that even tiny particles suspended in the water could cause clogging problems. To prevent clogging, use a screen filter with a 150 to 200 mesh screen.

Most drip systems are designed to operate at a pressure of about 20 psi, (pounds per square inch). Household water pressure typically ranges from 40 to 100 psi. A pressure regulator installed immediately after the filter

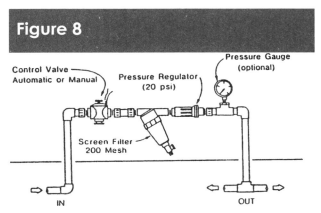

Figure 8. Typical controls required for drip irrigation. These components are usually installed below ground in a valve box.

in the main line will reduce the pressure in the line and ensure efficient operation of the system.

Which Drip System is Best?—Since there are so many different types of drip irrigation components, trying to choose the best system for a particular application is often confusing. The best advice is to keep it as simple as possible, and try to wet only those areas where the water can be taken up by the roots of the desired plants.

For trees and shrubs it is generally best to use a system in which emitters can be inserted wherever water is needed. The number of emitters per plant and flow rate (gallons per hour) per emitter depend on the size and type of plant. Generally, the larger the plant, the more water it requires. Table 4 gives an example of how emitters might be installed based on plant size.

During very dry weather, a drip system would need to run about three times per week for four hours to supply the optimum water needs of the plants. Keep in mind that some species require more water than others. Consider this when installing emitters.

For watering annuals, perennials, and ground covers, it is usually necessary to irrigate a solid area. This can be done using emitter lines with emitters spaced every 12 to 18 inches. By placing emitter lines 12 to 18 inches apart, a uniform wetting pattern can be achieved. Perforated or porous pipe spaced every 12 to 18 inches apart can also be used. In sandy soils, the lines will need to be closer together than in tighter soils. In annual flower beds, the drip lines can be laid aside during bed preparation and replaced afterwards.

Another method of watering that is similar to drip irrigation uses small sprinkler heads, called micro-sprinklers, instead of emitters. All other components are identical to drip irrigation, including the polyethylene distribution lines. Micro-sprinklers spray an area 3 to 12 feet wide and are used for trees and shrubs or beds requiring complete coverage. Micro-sprinklers may be prone to vandalism and are not quite as efficient as emitters, but

they do provide an economical method of achieving uniform watering.

In landscape applications, drip irrigation tubing is usually installed on top of the ground and concealed beneath mulch. This makes the system easy to install and service. However, if vandalism is likely, the tubing can also be installed 4 to 6 inches beneath the soil surface with small microtubing ($1/8$ to $1/4$ inch) protruding to the surface. Running the microtubes above-ground will allow for easy inspection and will prevent dirt from back-siphoning into the emitters and clogging the system.

Guidelines for Irrigating the Landscape

Establish Irrigation Objectives—In a Water Smart landscape, the goal is to minimize the amount of supplemental water applied to the landscape. Therefore, routine irrigation is necessary only in the high water-use zones. Occasional hand watering or a portable irrigation system, such as porous pipe, would be used "as needed" in the moderate water-use zones. Established plants in low water-use zones would receive only natural rainfall and no supplemental irrigation water.

Operate Sprinklers between 9 P.M. and 9 A.M.—Time of application affects water-use efficiency. The best time to irrigate with sprinklers is between 9 P.M. and 9 A.M. During this time there is generally less wind and lower temperatures and therefore less water lost to evaporation. Irrigating during the evening after dew develops (9 P.M.) and before it dries in the morning (9 A.M.) does not increase disease problems.

Drip irrigation systems can be operated any time of day because evaporative water loss is not a problem, and the foliage stays dry.

An Automatic Controller Helps Save Water—An automatic controller attached to the irrigation system turns the system on and off and controls the water flow through the various zones according to a pre-set time clock. It allows for setting the length of time each zone operates, days of the week the system operates, and time of day it operates.

However, an automatic controller does not eliminate the need to closely monitor its operation. Controllers should be re-programmed frequently during the growing season because water needs change from week to week.

A rainfall sensor attached to the controller detects rainfall and prevents the irrigation system from operating if significant rainfall has occurred. Another type of sensor

Table 5. Drip irrigation emitter selection based on plant size

PLANT HEIGHT (ft.)	# EMITTERS PER PLANT
< 2	one - ½ gallon per hour
2 - 4	one - 1 gallon per hour
4 - 6	two - 1 gallon per hour
6 - 7	three - 1 gallon per hour
7 - 8	four - 1 gallon per hour or two - 2 gallon per hour

measures soil moisture and overrides the system when soil moisture is adequate. Sensors are especially useful if the system cannot be monitored and adjusted regularly.

There are many different types of controllers on the market. Make sure to get one with the features needed. When managed properly, an automatic controller can pay for itself in reduced water usage, cost, and labor.

Hand Watering

Hand watering is not just for newly-planted ornamental plants. It is also an effective and efficient way of applying water to selected plants that show signs of stress during dry periods. The direct application of water to the base of the plant, provided it is applied slowly enough to be absorbed by the soil, uses less water and is more efficient than sprinkler irrigation.

To avoid run-off when using the hand-held hose, use a nozzle that divides the spray into rain-size droplets. Some nozzles have built-in spray pattern adjustments.

When watering by hand, apply about 5 gallons of water per 10 square feet, which is approximately the amount of water delivered by a ⅝ inch garden hose operating one minute at medium pressure. Watering small shrubs (less than 4 feet in height) for one minute with the hand-held hose should suffice. Larger shrubs (4 feet and up) will require slightly more water. Increase the watering time by 15 seconds for each foot in height exceeding 4 feet. For large trees, apply about 6 or 7 gallons for each 10 square feet of canopy area. For best results, check the output of the faucet by determining the number of seconds to fill a one-gallon jug and then estimating output per 60 seconds.

Figure 9

Figure 9. The healthy, deep-rooted grass on the left is the result of proper irrigation. The weak, shallow-rooted grass on the right results from light, frequent irrigation.

Irrigating Turfgrass

Turfgrasses used in Georgia can survive seasonal dry periods without irrigation and therefore can be used in any water-use zone. In moderate water-use zones, a turfgrass would be irrigated only when it shows signs of moisture stress. Turf under water stress will appear a dull bluish green color, the leaf blades will roll inward and footprints will remain on the grass after walking over an area. Irrigating turf in the moderate water-use zones with a portable lawn sprinkler, within 24 to 48 hours of these signs, will generally prevent serious loss of turf vigor while maximizing water-use efficiency.

Under optimum growing conditions (high water-use zone), turfgrasses use 1 to 1 ½ inches of water per week during hot dry weather. It is usually best to divide this amount into two applications per week applying ½ to ¾ inch each time. Never apply more than one inch at a time as this will likely result in runoff or deep percolation below the root zone. Early or late in the season, when temperatures are cooler, it is usually adequate to irrigate only once per week.

Never water grass daily except during establishment. Daily irrigation with small amounts of water encourages a shallow root system and reduced drought tolerance as shown in Figure 9. Since roots generally grow where the soil is moist, a shallow root system also prevents efficient uptake of plant nutrients. Shallow, frequent irrigation increases evaporative water loss from the soil.

Irrigating Trees and Shrubs

Woody ornamental trees and shrubs have a deeper, more extensive root system than turfgrasses or herbaceous ornamental plants. The root system of a mature tree, for instance, extends two to three times the canopy spread and may go down several feet into the soil. Woody plants, therefore, can extract moisture from the soil, even when the soil surface appears bone dry, and can survive long dry periods without supplemental irrigation.

Use drip irrigation on trees and shrubs in the high water-use zones of the landscape. Locate the emitters near the drip line of plants where the concentration of absorbing roots is the highest. During extended dry periods, operate the system two to three times per week. Run the system long enough to thoroughly wet the soil 18 to 24 inches deep.

Regular and thorough watering of newly-planted trees and shrubs will encourage good root establishment and greater drought resistance.

Irrigating Herbaceous Ornamentals (Annuals and Perennials)

Herbaceous ornamentals vary widely in their tolerance to drought. Some will perform adequately with a minimum of supplemental water while others require close attention to soil moisture. Irrigation can be provided most efficiently if the plants within a bed have similar water needs.

Herbaceous ornamentals generally have a more shallow root system than woody ornamentals and are among the first plants in the landscape to show water stress during dry periods. Water these plants once or twice a week and use drip irrigation whenever possible. If unable to irrigate because of restrictions, remember that these plants are less costly to replace than trees and shrubs.

STEP 6: Use of Mulches

Mulching is one of the most beneficial landscape practices. Mulches conserve moisture by preventing evaporative water loss from the soil surface and reducing the need for supplemental irrigation during periods of limited rainfall. By maintaining an even moisture supply in the soil, mulches prevent fluctuations in soil moisture that can damage roots (see Figure 10).

Mulches also prevent crusting of the soil surface and allow water to penetrate readily to plant roots. They insulate the roots of plants from summer heat and winter cold and help control weeds that compete with plants for moisture. By serving as a barrier between the plant and soil, mulches help discourage soil-borne diseases that stress plants and cause them to have a higher demand for water.

Islands of unplanted organic mulch, designed to blend with the landscape, are an economical way to retrofit an existing landscape to make it more water efficient while reducing maintenance requirements. Aside from occasional weed control and topdressing with additional mulch, unplanted mulched areas require no water and little routine maintenance.

Pine straw, pine-bark mini-nuggets, and shredded hardwood mulch or chips are some of the best mulches for a Water Smart landscape. These fine-textured mulches hold moisture in the soil better than coarse-textured mulches, such as large-nugget pine bark. They also are non-matting and allow water, nutrients and oxygen to freely move into the soil.

Inorganic mulches, on the other hand, such as rock, gravel, and marble, absorb and re-radiate heat from the

Figure 10

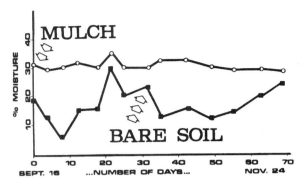

Figure 10. Moisture level of mulched vs. bare soil

sun and increase water loss from plants and soil.

Apply approximately 3 inches of mulch under ornamental plants in the landscape. Avoid applying too much mulch because it encourages shallow roots which are easily damaged by excessive cold, heat, or drought.

Where possible, extend the mulched area two to three times the canopy spread of ornamental trees and shrubs. Research shows that the roots of ornamental plants grow far beyond the canopy spread so it is important to mulch as large an area as practical.

Once mulch is in place, pull it back, 2 to 3 inches, from the trunk of trees and shrubs. This will help prevent-wood rotting diseases.

During periods of limited rainfall, make certain sufficient mulch is maintained beneath plants. If watering restrictions prevent irrigating, mulches will help conserve the moisture remaining in the soil.

Newspapers, 2 sheets thick, placed under organic mulches at planting time, is another water conservation practice. They also may be used on established ornamentals by carefully removing the organic mulch from around the plants, placing the newspapers two sheets thick on the soil surface and reapplying the mulch. Be certain to wet the newspapers thoroughly, immediately after application; otherwise, they may pull moisture from the soil. Also, avoid placing more than 2 layers of newspaper on the surface because it may impede water and nutrient movement into the soil.

STEP 7: Appropriate Maintenance

By following the six previous steps toward water conservation in the landscape, a beautiful landscape can be developed that not only saves water and money, but also requires minimal maintenance.

The objective of Water Smart maintenance is to discourage water-demanding new growth on plants. In other words, keep plants healthy but do not encourage optimum growth at all times. Depending on the current level of maintenance, it may be possible to fertilize less often with less fertilizer, to prune less frequently, and to irrigate less often. Remember, a Water Smart landscape is a low-maintenance landscape. By working smarter, not harder in the landscape, it is possible to save time, energy, and water without sacrificing the beauty of the environment.

Fertilize Less and Use Slow-release Fertilizers—When purchasing a fertilizer, look closely at its contents. Nitrogen, the first number in the analysis, is the element that promotes new growth Purchase a fertilizer having nitrogen in a slow-release form, such as sulfur-coated urea, urea formaldehyde, IBDU (isobutylenediurea), or methylene urea. Some new products on the market feed plants for an entire growing season with one application. Slow-release type fertilizers generally cost more than all-purpose garden fertilizers, such as 8-8-8 or 10-10-10, but they last longer by releasing nutrients gradually. Also, they do not leach from the soil or wash away in run-off as readily as all-purpose fertilizers.

Always check the application rate on the label. The label usually suggests an application rate for optimum growth. This application rate is ideal for newly-planted ornamental plants and turfgrasses to encourage healthy new growth and plant establishment. However, once plants are established, the recommended application rate of fertilizer can be reduced without sacrificing quality or appearance. This reduction in application rate is particularly important prior to, or during, dry periods.

Leaving grass clippings on turfgrass at each mowing, a process called "grasscycling," supplies the grass with recycled nutrients and reduces the need for supplemental fertilizer. Grasscycling does not promote thatch (a spongy condition of the turf). Thatch results from a build-up of grass stems, shoots, and roots, not clippings. As much as one-third of the nutrients applied to the lawn can be recycled back to the grass through grasscycling.

Avoid Shearing Plants—Just like nitrogen fertilizer, shearing promotes water-demanding new growth on plants. When pruning is required, use hand shears or loppers to thin branches and twigs to a side branch or bud. Thinning results in a more open, natural canopy

and is less stressful to the plant than shearing.

Proper Mowing Saves Water—Proper mowing practices are of particular importance in Water Smart landscapes. Mow at the recommended height (Table 6), and mow often enough so that no more than one-third of the leaf tissue is removed at each mowing. For example, if tall fescue is to be maintained at a height of 2 inches, then it should be cut when it reaches 3 inches. Research shows that raising the mower blade during dry weather and cutting the grass higher encourages deeper rooting, increases turf survival during drought, and reduces water demand. Mow turf in shaded areas higher than turf in full sun. Avoid scalping and stressing the grass and make certain the mower blade is sharp at all time.

Aerating Turfgrass Improves Water Movement—Aeration, or coring of turf areas, is sometimes required to relieve soil compaction and to increase air and water movement into the soil. It is particularly helpful on slopes where water run-off is possible and in areas of heavy foot traffic where compaction has occurred. Aeration is best accomplished with a power aerator which has hollow tines that remove small cores of soil. Many rental stores have this type of equipment available. Aeration is best during periods of active plant growth, and when the soil is moist enough to allow deep penetration of the tines. Generally, aeration is used to correct soil problems and is not done on a routine basis.

Other Water-Saving Maintenance Practices

Do Not Let Weeds Compete with Plants for Water—Scout the landscape regularly and do not let weeds take over. Hand-weeding, chemical herbicides, and mulches will help keep weeds in check.

Scout for Pests Before Spraying—While scouting for weeds, also scout for insect and disease pests. Control pests when they begin affecting the appearance and overall health of a plant. Target control measures to the affected plants and avoid spraying the entire landscape if the pest problem is confined only to a small area.

Table 6. Mowing heights for turfgrasses in Georgia	
TURFGRASS	**INCHES**
Centipedegrass	1 to 2
Common bermudagrass	1 to 2
Hybrid bermudagrass	0.5 to 1.5
St. Augustinegrass	2 to 3
Zoysiagrass	0.5 to 2

Make Every Drop Count—Where irrigation systems are used, check nozzles and emitters regularly to see if they are operating efficiently and if they are delivering the right amount of water in the right locations.

Let Plants Show When They Need Water—Learn to identify the symptoms shown by plants under water stress. Shrubs under moisture stress will turn a grey-green color and wilt. Trees will show premature fall color and shed leaves early. Turfgrasses will turn a dull grey-green color and the blades will wilt and roll inward.

Survival Watering During Drought or Watering Restrictions—During drought or watering restrictions, consider the replacement cost of the plants in the landscape and do what is possible to save the most valuable plants. Annual flowers can be replaced more readily than trees and shrubs. If unable to water, cut back annual flowers and mulch them heavily to help them survive a drought.

If you are allowed to water, selectively hand-water shrubs and trees that show drought stress first. Although trees have an extensive "bank account" of roots to absorb water during dry periods, prolonged drought can severely stress and damage a large portion of their surface roots. A thorough watering of three small areas (60 gallons/100 square feet near the dripline), each two weeks in clay soils and once a week in sandy soils, using the hand-held hose, will minimize tree damage during an extended dry period.

If there is a total ban on watering and some plants being to wilt badly or defoliate, consider pruning their canopies by one-third to one-half. This will reduce water demand on the roots and will increase their chances of survival during drought.

Gray Water, defined as waste water discharged from residential lavatories, bathtubs, showers, clothes washers, and laundry trays, can be used in Georgia to water outdoor plants. Bill 463 passed by the Georgia Senate in 2008, provides the following guidelines and requirements:

Private residential direct reuse of gray water shall be lawful if the following conditions are met:

(1) Gray water originating from the residence shall be used and contained within the property boundary for household gardening, composting, lawn watering, or landscape irrigation;

(2) Gray water shall not be used for irrigation of food plants;

(3) The gray water shall not contain hazardous chemicals derived from activities such as cleaning car parts, washing greasy or oily rags, or disposing of waste solutions from home photo labs or similar hobbyist or home occupational activities;

(4) The application of gray water shall be managed to minimize standing water on the surface;

(5) The application of gray water shall be outside of a floodway;

(6) The gray water shall not contain water used to wash diapers or similarly soiled or infectious garments unless the gray water is disinfected before irrigation; and

(7) The gray water shall be applied only by hand watering using garden watering cans or similar hand-held containers.

Summary

Water used on the outdoor landscape is considered non-essential water use, compared to water used for cooking, bathing, cleaning and other life essentials. Therefore, when restrictions are placed on domestic water use (water supplied to citizens by local governments or private utilities), non-essential uses of water are the first to be curtailed. As urban areas continue to grow and develop and increasing demand is placed on municipal water systems, restrictions on water use are likely to become common, even during periods of normal rainfall.

By implementing the seven steps to a Water Smart landscape described in this publication, it is possible to reduce outdoor irrigation by as much as 50 percent without sacrificing the quality or beauty of the home environment.

Remember... the landscape alone does not save water... it is up to us to save water. Considerable water savings can be realized simply by breaking bad watering habits and learning how to water, when to water, the most efficient ways to water, and the water needs of southern ornamental plants.

By putting the Water Smart practices to work in your landscape, you are not only being a good steward of the environment but by preserving and protecting the resources on our planet, you also will help assure our children and future generations the same quality of life that we have grown to appreciate.

ACKNOWLEDGEMENT

Acknowledgement is made to following individuals for their contribution to the original manuscript of this publication:

James T. Midcap, Dept. of Horticulture (retired)

Kim D. Coder, Warnell School of Forest Resources

Gil Landry, Georgia Center for Urban Agriculture

Anthony W. Tyson, Director of County Operations, CAES

Neal Weatherly Jr., UGA College of Environment and Design

DISCUSSION QUESTIONS

1. Why is water conservation important?

2. What is Xeriscape?

3. Name at least three of the seven steps to a water-wise landscape?

4. Why is shade important in a water-wise landscape?

5. Describe the differences between high, moderate, and low water-use zones.

6. Describe some ways to help a soil hold moisture.

7. Are native plants the most drought tolerant?

8. What are some advantages of drip irrigation?

9. When is the best time to irrigate in order to reduce evaporative loss of water?

10. What are the best mulches for water conservation?

11. Should the mower blade be raised or lowered during periods of limited rainfall?

12. What are some symptoms of drought stress?

RESOURCES

The following publications are available from University of Georgia Cooperative Extension at http://extension.uga.edu/

Best Management Practices for Landscape Water Conservations, Bulletin 1329

BMP in the Landscape, Circular 871

Making Every Drop Count Series:

Efficient Landscape Irrigation Systems, Circular 895-5

Managing a Water-Wise Landscape, Circular 895-4

Proper Planting Results in Healthy, Water-Efficient Plants, Circular 895-3

Water Saving Tips When Planting a New Landscape, Circular 895-2

Xeriscape: Seven Steps to a Water-Wise Landscape, Circular 895-1

23
Rainwater Harvesting and Rain Gardens

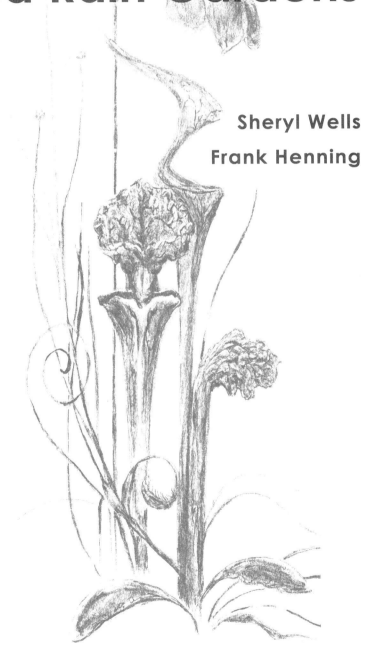

Sheryl Wells

Frank Henning

LEARNING OBJECTIVES

Understand the importance of rainwater harvesting and rain gardens.

Be able to list some of the benefits of rainwater harvesting and rain gardens.

Be able to list the components of a rainwater harvesting system.

Know the area in a landscape in which a rain garden should be located.

Be able to size a rainwater harvesting system and a rain garden.

Know how to design a rain garden.

Know how to maintain a rainwater harvesting system and a rain garden.

TERMS TO KNOW

Basket filter filter in the top of the tank with the purpose of catching debris

Calming inlet device located at the bottom of a storage tank with minimal disturbance to particles that may have settled to the bottom of the tank.

Cistern interchangeable term for a tank and is the central water storage component of the rainwater harvesting system.

First-flush diverter device which removes debris from the collection surface by diverting initial rainfall from entry into the cistern.

Floating intake device used inside cistern to allow removal of water near the surface.

Ponding depth depth from the landscape surface to the depression in the rain garden.

INTRODUCTION

Rainwater harvesting and rain gardens are landscape best management practices designed to slow or reduce stormwater runoff from impervious surfaces. Stormwater runoff can be harvested and stored for later use or can be directed to rain gardens. Rain gardens can improve water quality by acting as a pollution filter bed or vegetated buffer by capturing runoff before it enters lakes, ponds, rivers, or groundwater.

RAINWATER HARVESTING

With recent droughts and increased emphasis on water conservation, rainwater harvesting (RWH) is an alternative source for outdoor irrigation. RWH is the collection of runoff from roofs during a rainfall event. The water is conveyed through a gutter system, filtered and stored in a tank for later use. In Georgia, non-potable harvested water can be an alternative water supply for uses such as washing vehicles, landscape irrigation, livestock and wildlife watering, cooling towers, toilet flushing and other uses.

**Please Note: Georgia plumbing codes do not permit harvested rainwater to be used for potable uses.

History

Rainwater harvesting is not a new concept. It is an ancient technique that has supplied human water needs for thousands of years. According to archeological evidence, RWH took place 4,000-6,000 years ago (Gould and Nissen-Peterson 1999). It is believed that systems were used to collect runoff from hillsides for agricultural and domestic purposes.

Reasons for RWH

Approximately 1% of the water covering the Earth's surface is freshwater that could be collected for human consumption. This water is found in lakes, rivers and underground aquifers. Since the turn of the twentieth century, the population in the United States has tripled, and worldwide water consumption has doubled every 20 years (Van Giesen and Carpenter 2009). Despite individual efforts to conserve water, growth in Georgia and neighboring southern states consistently exceeds the national average, and this growth continues to pressure public-water supplies. Georgia's ever-increasing demand for water is creating a need for alternative sources of irrigation water.

Outdoor water use increases during the summer months

by as much as 50-70% and much of this is attributed to irrigation of residential landscapes. Water used for irrigation purposes does not require the same level of treatment needed for potable water supplies. Harvested water can lower consumer's water bills, reduce demand placed on municipalities when rainfall is below-average and increase the water available when other sources are limited.

Benefits

Some of the most important environmental benefits of having a RWH system are:

* Potable water is conserved and a supplemental water supply is created.

* Stormwater is retained.

* Runoff is slowed and reduced.

* Several green building goals are achieved.

Rainwater harvesting creates an alternative watering source which can be used any time, even when irrigation is restricted. RWH reduces the volume of stormwater that runs off landscapes into streams, and thereby decreases soil erosion, flooding and water pollution. If captured, rainwater can be used for landscape irrigation, and then the soil infiltration that recharges groundwater and supports stream flow is increased.

The National Green Building Standard offers points if rainwater is collected and used as permitted by local building codes (6 points), and an additional 2 points if harvested rainwater is distributed using a renewable energy source or gravity (Van Giesen and Carpenter, 2009). The initial installation cost for RWH systems

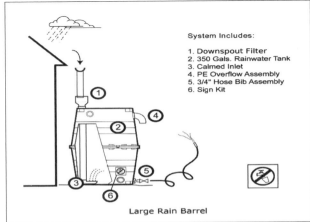

Figure 1. Rain barrel (Van Giensen and Carpenter 2009)

Figure 2

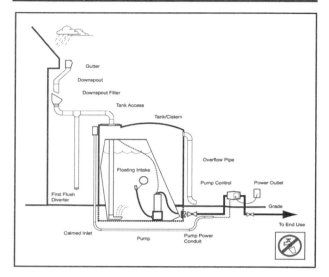

Figure 2. Above ground cistern (Van Giensen and Carpenter 2009)

Figure 3

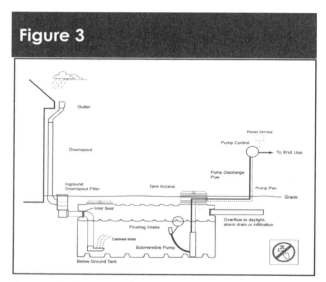

Figure 3. Below ground cistern (Van Giensen and Carpenter 2009)

can vary considerably. However, rainwater is free and the cost of harvesting rainwater is minimal. Electricity for running a pump, if one is needed and regularly scheduled maintenance are all that is required. As a result, RWH installation cost can be recovered over time as municipal water usage is reduced.

Water Characteristics

Rainwater normally has a nearly neutral pH and is low in minerals, salts and does not contain chlorine that treated water does. However, local conditions and the catchment surface can sometimes affect water quality, so

rainwater should be tested through your local Cooperative Extension office to minimize problems with metals or corrosion. Harvested rainwater may also contain pathogens, such as fecal bacteria from birds and other wildlife that may require treatment for certain uses.

System Components

Rainwater harvesting systems can be as simple as a rain barrel or as complex as multimillion-gallon industrial systems. Systems can be placed above (Figure 2) or below ground (Figure 3). Despite the diversity that exists among different RWH systems, the basic components do not change.

Typical Components:

• The catchment surface (normally a roof) which serves as the rainwater collection component.

• Gutters and downspouts which direct the water from the roof to the tank.

• A basket filter or leaf screen, (some of which also include a mosquito screen) which reduce large debris and captured rainwater before it goes to the tank

• Barrels(s) or cistern(s) to store harvested rainwater.

• A pump (if the pressure from gravity is not adequate).

• A delivery system such as outlet pipes, hoses and vents may be needed.

Optional Components:

• First-flush diverters and roof washers which reduce the amount of debris, dust and other pollutants entering the tank.

• Calming inlet that reduces sediment disturbances as water enters the tank.

• Floating intake that reduces the amount of sediment entering the pump intake.

The catchment surface is typically a roof. The roof material, climatic conditions, wildlife and the surrounding environment affect water quality. For example, if a roof is surrounded by trees, debris from the trees as well as fecal matter from birds nesting in the trees may affect water quality. The collection efficiency of the catchment surface is affected by the smoothness of the roof. The smoother the roof surfaces the more water that can be captured. The size of the roof determines the amount of water that can be harvested and will be discussed in the 'System Sizing' section. Roof material found in Georgia may include; composite or asphalt shingle, wood shingle, metal, tile, tar/gravel, slate and vinyl/rubberized. The roof material can have an impact on contaminants in roof runoff. Primary substances of concern in roof runoff include heavy metals, polycyclic aromatic hydrocarbons, microbes, pathogens and pesticides (DeBusk et al 2009) (www.bae.ncsu.edu/stormwater/PublicationFiles/RooftopRunoff2009.pdf).

Gutter size, the number of gutters, location and spacing should be determined by the RWH system supplier or an industry professional. Gutters should be installed so that they are sloping toward the downspout. Water should be encouraged to drain away from the building wall so the outside face of the gutter is lower than the inside face. Gutters, downspouts, and leaf screens should be firmly secured.

Inlet filtration (Figure 4) is used to screen or filter water before it enters the tank. Filtration is necessary to assure high quality water by eliminating debris that washes from the roof. Filters may consist of a coarser-mesh leaf screen, a finer-mesh mosquito screen, first-flush diverters/ roof washers (Figure 5) and downspout filters. Leaf screens (Figure 6) on gutters and downspouts prevent large debris from entering the system. If trees are nearby, leaf screens are recommended. To facilitate regular maintenance and cleaning of the inlet filter and mosquito screen, be sure to mount the screen assembly at a convenient height so it is easily assessable. A first flush diverter (Figure 7) or roof washer is a device that routes the first flow of water which can contain smaller contaminants from the catchment surface down through a pipe away from the storage tank. This device normally has a clean-out valve or pin hole which when opened can be routed to landscape plants via a drain pipe. There are many types of filters on the market and some are self-cleaning and some need to be cleaned. If an irrigation system is used, outlet filtration may be needed to prevent clogging of sprinklers, or drip emitters. Filtration to ensure successful operation of equipment is normally all that is required for outdoor non-potable sources.

The most important component of the system is the tank, which is commonly referred to as a cistern. Before choosing a tank, it is recommended to research local ordinances, covenants, and restrictions concerning tank construction and location. Tanks can be constructed of plastic or recycled material. Other materials include fiberglass, wood, metal, and concrete. It is recommended that tanks not be opaque or clear because this may encourage algal growth. Materials that will resist exposure to thermal and ultra violet sunlight are available. Less expensive tanks can also be wrapped with wood, metal or other facing material in order to present a more pleasing appearance. Aesthetically pleasing tanks can be purchased that will enhance the landscape. Storage tanks

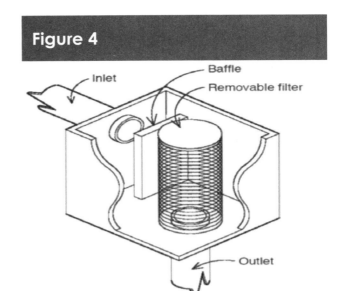

Figure 4. Box filter (Texas Water development Board 2005)

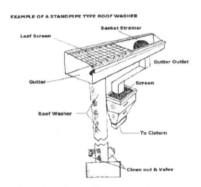

Figure 5. Roof washer (Van Giesen and Carpenter 2009)

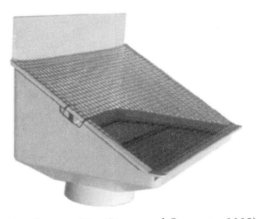

Figure 6. Leaf screen (Van Giesen and Carpenter 2009)

should be labeled with graphics and text that indicate the stored rainwater is a non-potable source.

Tank components include the inlet pipe or access in which the water from the downspout enters. This inlet should have a screen (Figure 8) to keep mosquitoes out or be sealed around the inlet pipe. An overflow is placed near the top of the tank to release water in the event that more is captured than can be stored. All tank overflow outlets should be at least the same diameter as the as the inlets. The overflow can be routed to a rain garden or other landscaped areas via a drain pipe. The overflow should not be routed toward the house foundation or septic field lines. An outlet which can include a hose bibb assembly or shut-off valve is placed toward the

bottom of the tank. This valve should be located at an elevation that is convenient for filling containers or attaching a garden hose. If the outlet is located too close to the bottom of the tank, it will clog with sediments which settle to the bottom.

Other tank components may include a floating intake (Figure 9) and calming inlets. Regardless of filters and screens, some debris can still enter the tank. The small particulates/sediments will sink to the bottom and other debris may float. The cleanest water is in the middle. The floating intake floats in the water in the tank and its sole purpose is to intake water from the calm, clean water that is in the middle of the tank. It connects to the pipe outlet, typically near the very bottom of the cistern, where water is drawn for use. Calming inlets minimize the disturbance of the sediment that settles at the bottom of a cistern. These inlets are designed to mix the anerobic (without oxygen) water at the bottom of the tank with the water closer to the top of the tank which contains more oxygen. The inlet is installed at the end of the inlet pipe and rests on the bottom of the tank. On most systems, this inlet pipe is normally left uncovered.

Delivery pressure may be supplied by gravity or supple-

Figure 7

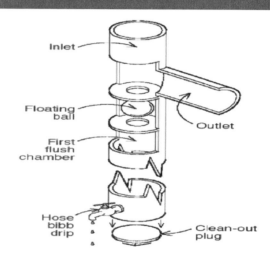

Figure 7. First flush diverter (Texas Water Development Board 2005)

Figure 8

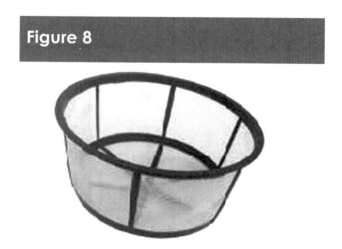

Figure 8. Tank inlet screen (Van Giesen and Carpenter 2009)

Figure 9

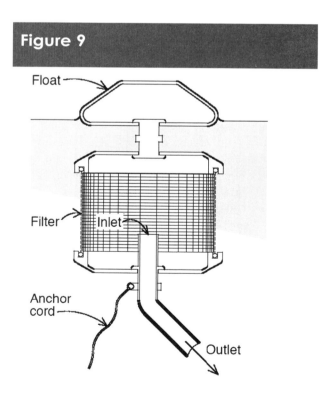

Figure 9. Floating intake filter (Texas Water Development Board 2005)

mented with a pump depending on the location of the tank and intended water usage. Excluding the tank, pumps are typically the most expensive component of the system so choosing the proper pump is important. Pumps have different features that should be considered. Submersible pumps are commonly placed inside RWH tanks. If they are located on the outside of the tank, it is important that they are secure to avoid vibration when operating. Ground fault circuit interrupters are recommended to reduce electrical hazards. Devices such as low pressure switches and temperature switches may also be installed to protect the pump from running dry or being exposed to temperature overloads. Pump sizing will be discussed in the 'Estimating Irrigation Water Demand' section.

Pump Accessories

A pump manufacturer or vendor should be consulted to determine which accessories are needed for specific pumps.

Pressure tank—stores pressurized water to prevent the pump from cycling on and off to meet demands and supplies a constant pressure.

Pressure switch—device which engages the pump when a pressure drop is observed and disengages it when there is no demand.

Check valve—an internal valve which prevents water from flowing back through the pump when it is not running.

Float level switch—switch which disengages the pump when the tank runs dry or water falls below a predetermined level.

Throttling valve—device which controls the flow and pressure of water exiting the pump and is typically in the form of a gate valve.

Delivery systems commonly include pipes connected to an irrigation system and pipes that can be used to drain the cistern for cleaning or for protection from freezing temperatures. Drain pipes should be directed to a rain garden or to another location in the landscape. Hose bibbs may be installed on the tank so that a hose can be connected for outdoor water use.

System Sizing

The first step in designing the best system for your needs is to determine the amount of water you currently use in the landscape for irrigating plants, washing sidewalks,

decks, vehicles, and any other use that does not require potable water. Storage volume or water captured should equal or slightly exceed the amount of water that is used.

Example:

You calculate that you use approximately 400 gallons of water during the summer months to irrigate flower beds and wash vehicles. (see methods of estimating later in text). Furthermore, the roof area you will be harvesting water from is 20' x 20' which equals a total area of 400 ft^2. A 400 gallon storage tank is appropriated for this example. A larger tank could be considered to capture additional volume in case of drought. **Note NCSU has a RWH calculating tool that can be used to simplify storage calculations, (www.bae.ncsu.edu/topic/waterharvesting /model.html).

The catchment area and rainfall amount determine the supply needed and demand dictates the required storage capacity. If the harvested water is the sole irrigation source, monthly rainfall data for the specific area must be known as well as estimated intervals between rain fall events. This data can be obtained from local or state weather sources such as www.georgiaweather.net. The area (length x width) of the catchment surface must be measured. A practical rule of thumb for most homeowners who do not depend totally on RWH for irrigation purposes is the storage tank can be determined by the roof area. Simply measure the length and width of a roof that is draining to specific downspouts. If only one side of the structure is guttered, only the area drained by the gutters should be used in the calculation.

The volume of harvested rainwater can also be calculated. It is impossible to collect 100% of rainfall from a surface due to splashing, evaporation, overshooting gutters, leaking gutters and first flush diverters. Therefore, approximately 0.62 gallons of rain can be collected for each gallon that falls on the roof surface.

Example:

Volume of harvested rainwater (gallons) =

Area of catchment or roof (ft^2) x depth of rainfall (inches) x 0.62(conversion factor)

Example: Roof area is 20 x 20 = 400 ft^2

One inch rainfall event occurs

Volume of harvested rainwater = 400 ft^2 x 1 inch x 0.62 gallons = 248 gallons

An indepth analysis of how to calculate potential

harvested rainwater is available through the American Rainwater Catchment Society Association (ARCSA) website (www.arcsa.org/resources/html) and Georgia Rainwater Harvesting Guidelines (2009) (www.dca. ga.gov/development/ConstructionCodes/programs/ documents/GARainWaterGdlns.040209.pdf).

Estimating Irrigation Water Demand

Water use will be unevenly distributed when water is used for garden and landscape irrigation. Therefore, for the typical homeowner, outdoor water demand can be estimated by using water bills to calculate the difference in summer versus winter water use

Depending on the system design, a pump used for RWH may need to both pull water out of a buried tank and create the pressure necessary for its intended use. Properly sizing the pump for an automatic irrigation system requires detailed knowledge of where the water is stored, pump location and intended use of the water. It is important to choose the correct size and type of pump for the system since irrigation distribution and irrigation efficiency is critical. It may be necessary to consult an irrigation professional, experienced plumber or RWH installer to make sure all applicable codes are met and to determine the proper pump size for the system. In many cases, a ½, ¾, or 1 HP centrifugal pump will be sufficient for homeowners. See other extension publications on irrigation pumps (Harrison 2009); (Thomas et al 2009) www.caes.uga.edu/publications/ and (Jones and Hunt 2006) (www.bae.ncsu.edu/stormwater/pubs. htm). The Texas Manual on Rainwater Harvesting (2005) is another source of information.

Location/Site Preparation

Large systems can be cumbersome and heavy so placement should be planned before installation begins. Utilities should be located and avoided. The tank should be located as close to the supply and demand area as possible. The tank should be below the gutters and downspouts. The soil texture is also important in determining stability. Areas which are highly erodible or in which flooding occur should be avoided. The base or foundation that support the tank should be flat and constructed of a stable material because water is very heavy. A gravel pad is sufficient for tanks that hold up to 3,000 gallons. Excavating about 1 foot of soil and replacing with size 57 stone makes a suitable base for most small tanks. A concrete pad should be constructed for a

tank larger than 3,000 gallons.

To reduce tank temperature and algal growth, tanks should be located in a shaded location when possible. It is also important to be considerate of neighbors and how they will view the system. It may be necessary to camouflage above ground tanks with plant material or fencing.

Tanks can be buried to save space, for aesthetic purposes, or for freeze protection. Underground tanks should be located at least 50 feet from animal stables and areas where wastewater is treated. Underground tanks should be made of a heavily reinforced material and may need interior bracing structures to withstand the weight of backfilled soil. The tank should be compatible with surrounding soils and should be installed in accordance with manufacturer's recommendations and local building codes. If plans include burial or partial burial, it is best to consider the elevation of the seasonally high water table. Tanks that are buried or partially buried can float out of the ground when empty if flotation is not considered in the design.

Maintenance

System inspections and maintenance must be done regularly to ensure proper operation. At a minimum, a monthly inspection is recommended. Also, clogged inlet filters, basket-filters, leaf filters, and mosquito screens are very common in these systems. If possible, debris should be cleaned from all inlet filters and screens before and after every significant rainfall event. It is impossible for filtration to totally eliminate debris and contaminants such as sediment. Hence, RWH systems will require periodic cleaning. A simple method for the homeowner is to mix laundry bleach, which usually has 6 percent available sodium hypochlorite, at the rate of 2 fluid ounces (¼ cup) in 1,000 gallons of rainwater (Texas Water Development Board 2005). If a tank has a submersible pump, the pump can be turned on to stir up the sediments on the bottom. The drain valve can be opened and the tank can be drained. If a pump is used, it should be maintained per the manufacturer's recommendation.

Pollen can also be a problem in spring time. Once inside the tank, pollen will begin to decompose and may produce foul odors if the water is not used. One solution to the pollen problem is to rinse/flush the tank out with potable or chlorinated water. The walls of the tank will need to be rinsed with fresh water. A second solution is to divert rainwater away from the collection tank during the pollen season. Many RWH system installers recommend a complete tank flush twice a year, in spring and fall to eliminate a 'dead zone' in the tank bottom.

Filtration is commonly adequate for systems that are used as non-potable water sources. However, other types of treatment include ultra violet light, chlorination, ionization and iodination. For more information on treatment consult Georgia Rainwater Harvesting Guidelines or The Texas Rainwater Harvesting Manual.

Freeze protection may be necessary in some locations in Georgia. Tanks may be partially buried (see Figure 2) so that the drain outlets are located below the frost line to avoid freeze damage. Systems that are located above ground can be winterized if no irrigation is necessary during the winter months. The system can be drained and the downspout taken out of the inlet so that no water will be harvested. The following spring when irrigation is needed the downspout can be returned to the tank inlet.

Mosquitoes may also be a problem if the inlet screens are not fitted properly and the tank is not totally sealed. For some installations, mosquito briquettes or other forms of larvicide may be labeled for use in RWH systems. Be sure to follow all label instructions when applying any pesticide.

RAIN GARDENS

Introduction

A rain garden is a natural or man-made depression in the landscape with the purpose of capturing rainfall and providing on-site treatment of stormwater runoff. A rain garden is a best management practice which is designed to be aesthetically pleasing and naturally integrated into the landscape (Figure 10). Surface runoff from a roof or other collection surfaces is channeled via rain gutters, pipes swales or curb openings to the garden. The rain garden slows runoff and treats pollutants on site by allowing stormwater to percolate into the soil where

Figure 10. Rain garden (Dietz and Filchak 2004)

it is filtered and treated through natural processes as it infiltrates and recharges groundwater. Rain gardens are designed to allow water to soak into the ground within 24-48 hours to prevent mosquito breeding. A rain garden may be referred to as a bioinfiltration or bioretention cell. However, bioretention cells are normally larger versions of rain gardens that are typically constructed on commercial sites and usually require an engineered design.

History

In 1990, in Prince George's County, Maryland, a developer by the name of Dick Brinker was building a new housing subdivision and had the idea to replace the traditional best management practice ponds with rain gardens. This idea developed into a successful project for Somerset, a residential subdivision, which has a 300-400 square foot rain garden on each house's property (www.wnrmag.com/supps/2003/feb03/run.htm#one). This rain garden system was highly cost effective and resulted in 75-80% reduction in stormwater runoff during regular rainfall events. This community was instrumental in implementing low impact development (LID) which is an ecologically sensitive design approach to stormwater management. Many successful LID case studies were done in this community (cfpub.epa.gov/npdes/stormwater.casestudies_specific.cfm?case_id=14).

Benefits

There are many benefits associated with rain gardens, some of them include:

- Stormwater runoff is reduced.
- Infiltration is slowed and pollutants are reduced.
- Water and energy are conserved.

- Wildlife habitats are created and aquatic ecosystems are improved.
- Property values are increased.

As development increases, impervious surfaces such as streets, buildings, parking lots, driveways, roofs and patios reduce the amount of permeable land surfaces. A one inch rainfall event will produce around 600 gallons of stormwater runoff for every 1,000 square feet of impervious surface. Stormwater runoff can cause flooding, increase erosion and sedimentation and pollute surface and groundwater. Rain gardens are becoming more popular since they are attractive areas in which the property owner can decrease the impact of their impervious surfaces.

Rain gardens allow for and are designed to slow infiltration of water that may carry pollutants such as nutrients, chemicals, bacteria, sediments, litter, oil metals and other contaminants. Rain gardens remove pollutants through physical, chemical and biological processes. Some of these mechanisms include; absorption, microbial processes, plant uptake, sedimentation and filtration. By slowing stormwater so that is can infiltrate into the soil, rain gardens enhance sedimentation and filtration. Vegetation in rain gardens has the potential to reduce or remove dissolved nutrients and pollutants through plant uptake and adsorption. Dissolved metals and nutrients bind or adsorb to soil particles such as clay and organic matter which reduces their impact on surface and groundwater sources. Soil microbes breakdown pollutants and use them as food sources.

Well designed rain gardens will produce more than water quality benefits. Because stormwater and the nutrients it contains are diverted to rain gardens, additional irrigation and fertilization may not be necessary after initial

Figure 11

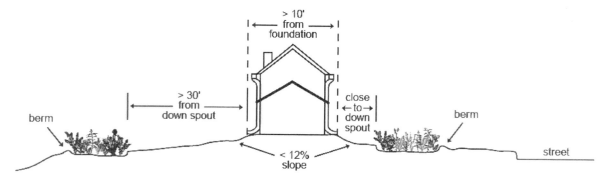

Figure 11. Rain garden location (Dietz and Filchak 2004).

plant establishment. Many forms of desirable wildlife such as birds, butterflies and bees are attracted to diverse habitats. Like the name implies, rain gardens are gardens that can be an attractive addition to any property.

Location/Site

Before selecting a site in the landscape for a rain garden, it is best to observe the direction of surface runoff during a rainfall event. An ideal location is an area downslope of the runoff catchment area where a natural depression exists. Always locate utilities by dialing 811 and check the local building codes before installing a rain garden.

Placement

- At least 10 feet from buildings to prevent seepage into foundations (Figure 11).

- At least 25 feet from septic tank, septic drain field or well head.

- Avoid locations with slopes that are greater than 12%.

- Avoid areas in the landscape that retain water or where ponding occurs.

- Avoid soils that have low or extremely slow infiltration.

- Avoid placing garden on top of underground utilities.

- Avoid placing garden over shallow water tables. In the event the water table is hit when constructing the garden, consider turning it into a wetland garden.

- Choose a location with full or partial sun.

- Do not place directly under trees since the root system may create competition for other plant material and the canopy may create a shading problem.

Sizing

Most contaminants are found in the first inch or first-flush of runoff. Rain gardens are designed to catch the first flush. In the event a storm produces more than a 1 rain fall in a 24 hour period, an overflow should be installed to safely divert the water out of the garden in a manner that minimizes erosion or other damage. The over flow from rain gardens are often delivered directly to nearby streams. Residential rain gardens are typically 100-300 square feet. According to the Center for Watershed Protection, the rain garden area should be between 20 and 30 percent of the drainage area directed to the depression (www.cwp.org/). The size of the garden is determined by the area from which the stormwater runs off of and into the garden, the volume of water it will need to temporarily store, and the type of soil located under the garden. Determine the size of the impervious surface that drains to the garden (refer to the previous RWH system sizing) and simply estimate 20 – 30 percent of that area. The garden should fall within that range. For an in depth sizing discussion refer to (www.legacy.ncsu.edu/classes-a/bae/cont_ed/bioretention/lecture/design_rain.pdf).

To determine soil type under the garden a soil test should be done. An ideal soil type for a rain garden is a sandy loam or loamy sand which results in a permeability rate of 1-6 inches per hour. The soil should be amended if it is not permeable enough to allow water to drain and filter properly. A typical soil mixture should contain 60% sand, 20% topsoil and 20% compost. Mortar sand is not recommended. Table 1 is used to calculate the size of a rain garden based on soil type and impervious drainage area (www.wisconsin raingardenGWQ37.pdf).

Example: A 1,000ft² roof drains into a clay soil rain garden with a 4" ponding depth

Solution: 1,000 ft² x 0.19 = 190 ft² rain garden

A soil percolation test should be conducted to determine infiltration rate. A simple percolation test for the homeowner is to dig a hole with post-hole diggers. The hole should be dug to approximately the same depth as the deepest area that will be excavated during rain garden construction. Saturate the hole by filling with water and allowing this water to drain. Place a yard stick in the hole and refill the hole and determine how many inches of water infiltrates in an hour (www.dnr.sc.gov/marine/NERR/pdf/Clemson_raingardenmanual.pdf). Rain garden soils should drain 1 to 6 inches in an hour. In the event that there is still water in the hole after 48 hours, the site will probably not be suited for a basic rain garden.

Signs of impermeable soils are:

- The site remains saturated or ponds water for several days after a storm event.

- After digging for percolation test water remains in the hole for more than 48 hours, provided it hasn't rained.

- Signs of a wetland soil are evident within 1 foot of

Table 1. Calculating rain garden size based on soil type			
	Rain garden ponding depth		
SOIL TYPE	**4-5 INCHES**	**6-7 INCHES**	**8-9 INCHES**
Clay	0.19	0.15	0.08
Silt	0.34	0.25	0.16
Sand	0.43	0.32	0.20

Figure 12

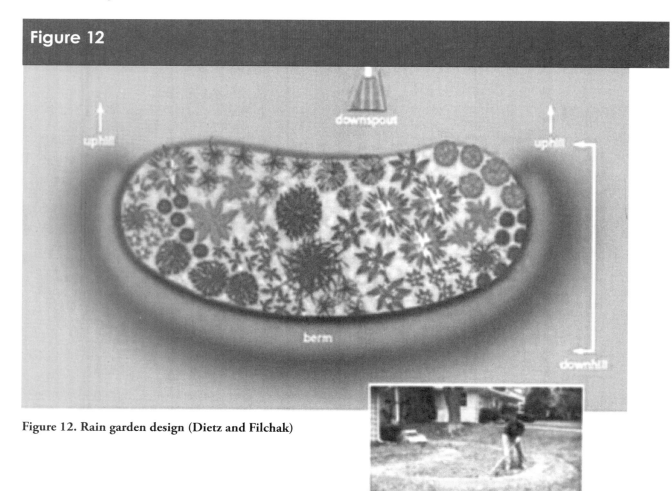

Figure 12. Rain garden design (Dietz and Filchak)

the surface. Wetland soils are often gray with ribbons or areas of brown color.

Sites with poor drainage properties may require either a rain garden with an under-drain system or they may be better suited for wetland gardens. Under-drain installation will not be discussed in this document. Information can be found (www.legacy.ncsu.edu/classes-a/bae/cont_ed/bioretention/lecture/design_rain.pdf).

If the water table is shallow, which is common in coastal areas or soil is not permeable and is unsuitable for a rain garden, a wetland garden may be an option. This document will not discuss wetland gardens but information can be found at (http://legacy.ncsu.edu/classes-a/bae/cont_ed/stormwater/index.htm).

Design

Rain garden design can vary considerably depending on the site constraints and the owner/designer preferences. However, it should naturally compliment the layout of the landscape. Shapes can include oval, round, oblong, kidney- bean or other shapes that flow with the landscape (Figure 12). The longest side of the rain garden should be perpendicular to the slope of the property.

Slope and Ponding Depth

Ponding depth is a term used to describe the depression area between the top of mulch layer and bottom of the overflow outlet. Rainwater is captured in the depression and held there until it infiltrates into the soil. The slope of the garden and the underlying soils determines the ponding depth. The depth of a typical rain garden is normally 4-9 inches (Figure 13). A rain garden less than 4 inches deep will need an excessive amount of surface area to provide enough storage area for large storm events to infiltrate properly. A garden with a depth of more than 9 inches deep might pond water too long. Regardless of the ponding depth, the goal is to keep the garden level. The depth of the rain garden is determined by the slope of the lawn. **To determine the slope of**

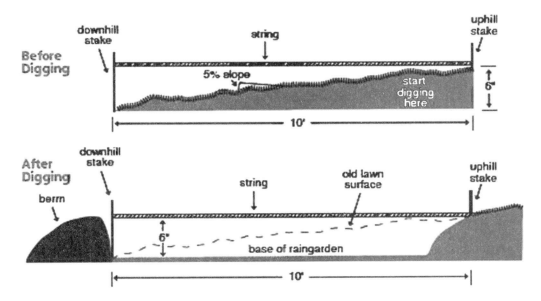

Figure 13. Rain garden depth (Wisconsin Department of Natural Resources 2008)

the lawn, follow these steps (Figure 14):

• Pound a stake in the ground at the uphill and downhill end of the rain garden.

• Tie a string to the bottom of the uphill stake and run the string to the downhill stake.

• Place a string level on the string and tie the string to the downhill stake at the position in which the string is level.

• Measure the width between the stakes.

• Measure the height on the downhill stake between the ground and the string.

• Divide the height by the width and multiply by 100 to find the percent slope of the lawn. Areas with a slope of 12 percent or more are not recommended for rain gardens.

Use the slope of the lawn to select the ponding depth from the following options:

• Slope less than 4%, ponding depth 4-5 inches deep.

• Slope between 5-7%, ponding depths 6-7 inches deep.

• Slope between 8-12%, ponding depths 8-9 inches deep.

Example:

The length of the string between the stakes is 150 inches

and the height is 8 inches;

Height/width x 100 = % slope, therefore 8/150 x 100 = 5% slope

With a 5% slope, the rain garden should be ~ 6 inches deep.

Connecting/ Conveyance of RWH Systems to Rain Gardens

Partnering rain gardens with rainwater harvesting

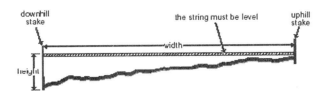

Figure 14. Rain garden slope (Wisconsin Department of Natural resources 2008)

Figure 15

Figure 15. Rock swale (Dietz and Filkan 2004)

systems is a good way to reduce the amount of sediment from entering the garden. The cistern will act as a settling basin as sediment enters the tank and sinks to the bottom. The cistern can drain into the garden via a gutter downspout extension pipe that can be left on top of the ground or buried. Water can also be channeled through downspouts that flow through grass or stone swales (Figure 15). The stone will stabilize the swale and prevent soil erosion. The swales or flow channels should have a minimum 2% slope. The width/depth of the flow channel should be a 2:1 ratio. For example, if the depth of the channel is 1 foot, the width of the channel should be 2 feet. The channel will act as a pretreatment filter for pollutants before they enter the garden.

Garden Construction/Installation

If there is existing vegetation where the garden will be located it will need to be removed. A chemical can be used, but a more environmental approach is to use black plastic to cover the lawn/grass until it dies. After choosing a location, the shape and size of the garden can be outlined with paint or a rope. This can be a boundary outline while digging the garden. Rain gardens are typically dug by hand. Some of the soil that is removed from the depression can be used to create a berm along the downhill slope and on the sides if necessary to help to retain water (Figure 16). The berm on the downhill side should be the same level as the uphill side. The soil that is not needed for the berm can be stockpiled if drains and an overflow are to be put in. The soil can also be left in the depression and amended there. The bottom of the garden can be tilled to improve infiltration, but this is not typically done on small gardens. After the garden has been dug to the proper depth, which is typically 2-3 feet, and soils amended, planting can begin (Figure 17).

Figure 16

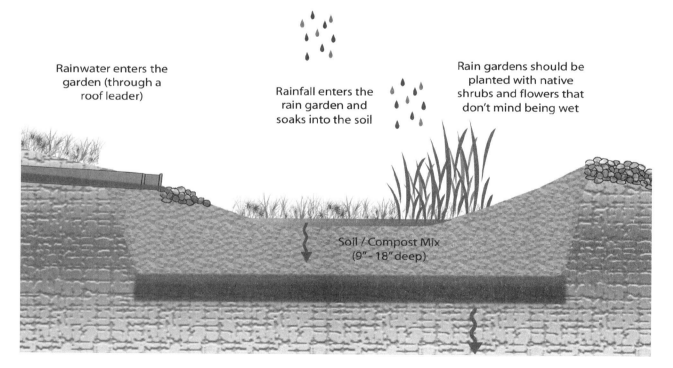

Rainwater enters the garden (through a roof leader)

Rainfall enters the rain garden and soaks into the soil

Rain gardens should be planted with native shrubs and flowers that don't mind being wet

Soil / Compost Mix (9" - 18" deep)

Figure 16 Soil amendment (Dietz and Filchak 2004)

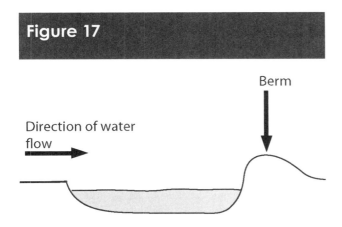

Figure 17

Berm

Direction of water
flow

Figure 17. Berm (Wisconsin Department of Natural Resources 2008

The berm should be mulched or covered with grass.

Plants

The overflow from rain gardens is often delivered directly to nearby streams. Native non-invasive plant species are good choices for rain gardens to reduce the introduction of non-native plants to the natural riparian areas that are found along streams. For a list of Georgia native plants see UGA Cooperative Extension publication *Native Plants for Georgia Part I: Trees, Shrubs and Woody Vines* B 987 or www.gnps.org. Plants that provide a habitat for wildlife are recommended. A variety of plants that are resistant to stress from periods of water pooling and periods between rainfall events should be used. Plants that tolerate both wet and dry conditions are preferable for the bottom of the garden. Plants that tolerate dry conditions should be used toward the edges of the garden. Small trees can be used on the edges or berms. Large trees are not recommended for small rain gardens since the root system will create competition for other plants and could interfere with under drains. Leaf debris and shade can also be a problem with large trees.

Maintenance

Regular visual inspections of the garden should be conducted and include looking for erosion, excessive sediment deposits and dead or diseased vegetation. The plants in the rain garden will need to be watered during establishment to encourage a healthy root system. Once established, plants may need to be water during drought conditions. Annual mulching is recommended with hardwood chips that are less likely to float than shredded hardwood or pine straw. Pruning is typically needed and will be determined depending on the owner's preference. Manually hand pulling weeds may

be necessary. Herbicides are not recommended; however, if they are used choose those with low water solubility characteristics. Fertilizers are not recommended since the plants in the rain garden will receive nutrients in surface runoff. If for some reason water ponds in the garden for more than 72 hours, mosquito briquettes may need to be incorporated until the ponding problem can be corrected.

Resources

American Rainwater Catchment Society of America (ARCSA). (www.arcsa.org/resources/html).

Clemson Public Service. Carolina Clear. 2008. Rain Gardens. *A rain garden manual for South Carolina. Green solutions to stormwater pollution.* Information Leaflet 87. (www. media.clemson.edu/public/restoration/carolina%20clear/toolbox/publication_raingardenmanual_022709b.pdf).

DeBusk, K., W.F. Hunt, D.L. Osmond and G.W. Cope. 2009. *Urban waterways series: Water quality of rooftop runoff and implications for residential water harvesting systems.* North Carolina Cooperative Extension. AG-588-18W. (www.bae.ncsu.edu/stormwater/PublicationFiles/RooftopRunoff2009.pdf).

Dietz, M. and K.. Filchak. 2004. *Rain gardens in Connecticut: A Design for homeowners.* University of Connecticut Cooperative Extension Service. 51130-03108. (www.sustainability .uconn.edu).

EPA "Stormwater Case Studies" (cfpub.epa.gov/npdes/stormwater.casestudies_specific.cfm?case_id=14).

Georgia Automated Environmental Monitoring Network. (www.georgiaweather.net).

Georgia Native Plant Society. (www.gnps.org).

Gould, J, Nissen-Petersen, E. (1999). *Rainwater catchment systems for domestic rain: design construction and implementation.* London: Intermediate Technology Publications.

Harrison, Kerry. 2009. *Irrigation pumping plants and energy use.* University of Georgia Cooperative Extension. B837. (www.caes.uga.edu/publications/).

Hunt, W. F. and N. White. 2006. *Designing rain gardens.* (Bio-retention areas). North Carolina Cooperative Extension Service. AG-588-3. (legacy.ncsu.edu/classes-a/bae/cont_ed/bioretention/lecture/design_rain.pdf).

Jones, M.P. and W.F. Hunt. 2006. Urban waterway series. *Choosing a pump for rainwater harvesting.* North Carolina Cooperative Extension. AG-588-08. (www.bae.ncsu.edu/stormwater/pubs.htm).

Rainwater harvesting at ncsu. (www.bae.ncsu.edu/topic/waterharvesting/model.html).

Texas Water Development Board. 2005. *The Texas Manual on Rainwater Harvesting.* 3rd ed. www.twdb.state.tx.us/publications/reports/rainwaterharvestingmanual_3rdedition.pdf.

Thomas, P.A., R. Seymour, F. Stegelin and B. Pennisi. 2009. *Irrigation and technology assessment.* The University of Georgia The Greenhouse *A* Syst Publication Series. B1275. (www.caes.uga.edu/publications/).

Van Giesen, E. and F. Carpenter. 2009. *Georgia rainwater harvesting guidelines.* (www.dca.ga.gov/development/ConstructionCodes/programs/documents/GARainWaterGdlns.040209.pdf).

Wisconsin Department of Natural Resources. 2003. *Rain Gardens. A how-to manual for homeowners.* University of Wisconsin-Extension. UWEX Publication GW0037.

Wisconsin Natural Resources. February 2003. "Rain gardens made one Maryland community famous". (www.wnrmag.com/supps/2003/feb03/run.htm#one).

Wade, G. E. Nash, E. McDowell, B. Beckham and S. Crisafulli. 2008. *Native Plants of Georgia. Part I. Trees, Shrubs, Woody Vines.* Universtiy of Georgia Cooperative Extension B-987. (www.caes.uga.edu/Publications/displayHTML.cfm?pk_id=7763

DISCUSSION QUESTIONS

1. What are some of the uses of harvested rainwater?

2. How much does outdoor water use increase during the summer months?

3. What are some of the benefits of harvesting rainwater.

4. Why is filtration necessary for rainwater harvesting systems?

5. What is the most important component of the rainwater harvesting system?

6. When choosing a location for a tank, what are some of the things to be concerned with?

7. When choosing a location for a rain garden what are some things to be concerned with?

8. What is the recommended soil type for good drainage in a rain garden?

9. What plant characteristics should be considered when planting in a rain garden?

10. What maintenance practices need to be performed in a rain garden?

24
Ponds and Water Gardening

Tony Johnson

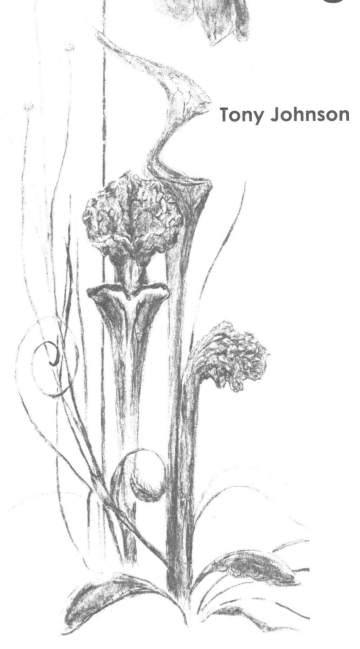

LEARNING OBJECTIVES

Understand the importance of site evaluation in planning a water garden.

Understand the effect of pool design on overall landscape design- a formal vs. informal look.

Understand the considerations of volume of water and surface area.

Understand the basics of water garden installation.

Become familiar with basic pond maintenance.

Become familiar with plant materials for water gardening.

Become familiar with basic water garden problem troubleshooting.

TERMS TO KNOW

Algae simple celled plants and containing chlorophyll.

Algal Bloom rapid growth by algae producing large quantities of plant material.

Ammonia intermediate product of the nitrogen cycle that converts to the more toxic nitrite.

Anaerobic term used to describe a biological process which occurs without the need for oxygen.

Aquatic plant a species of plant that lives in water either floating, submerged, or rooted into the ponds bed.

Biological Filtration loose term that describes the process of removing harmful compounds with bacteria.

Chloramines substance sometimes used as a bactericide in municipal water supplies.

Chlorine chemical added to water in one of a number of forms to destroy or deactivate disease-causing microorganisms

Floating Plant water plant that floats on the surface of a pond with its roots trailing in the water, such as water lettuce and water hyacinth.

Gallons Per Hour (gph) unit of measurement usually used to rate pumps.

Koi fancy-looking, colorful carp.

Marginal plant water plant that grows at the edge of the pond or on the bank where its roots can reach shallow water.

Nitrate relatively safe end product of organic waste degradation.

Nitrite intermediate product in the nitrogen cycle, which is highly toxic to fish, even at low levels.

Nitrifier bacteria that oxidized ammonia to nitrate or oxidizes nitrite to nitrate.

Preformed (pond) tough molded unit, usually made from fiberglass, and available in a variety of formal or irregular shapes.

Submerged plant a plant that remains submerged below the water line.

String Algae, Blanket weed fibrous algae that looks like long strands or filaments.

Water garden usually a small body of water generally used for containing plants, much like a garden, except there is no visible soil.

INTRODUCTION

Ponds, pools and fountains have become popular in recent years as more people look for ways to bring the element of water into the garden. This chapter provides a basic outline for the process of building and maintaining a water garden. For more comprehensive information on construction, there are a number of commercially printed books available.

It is important to put safety first in considering the construction of a water garden. Be sure to contact local code enforcement for permits and codes. Check with your insurance agent about liability issues and if there are small children in your home or nearby, be sure that unsupervised access to the water garden is restricted. Electrical work should be done by licensed contractors familiar with local codes.

Planning and Site Selection

Many important decisions will need to be made before the first item is purchased or the hole is excavated. These decisions will determine the site requirements and materials needed to install the new water garden. What size? Will the design be formal or informal? Will the water garden have Koi or goldfish? Will there be fish at all? Will it have colorful blooming plants or a woodland stream and waterfall? The style of a water garden is a matter of personal taste, although it will be more attractive if it compliments the style of the house, garden and other existing landscape features like decks and patios.

Water gardens are generally classified as either informal (those that imitate nature) or formal (those that reflect a particular architectural style). Whether or not a water garden is considered formal or informal depends largely on its shape and the edging materials used to define and cover the water garden perimeter. Formal water gardens and fountains generally conform to strict geometric shapes such as circles, ovals, squares, rectangles and so on. They may be raised above the ground and contained by a low wall of concrete, brick, cut stone, or stucco. They often include a statuary fountain. They are intended to look man-made and compliment the symmetry of the surrounding garden style and features of the house, patio or deck.

Informal water gardens take a cue from the ponds and streams found in nature. They usually have a curvilinear shape and often they incorporate short streams or small waterfalls. They can also wrap around existing landscape features, such as large boulders or a mass of tall plantings. Overhanging rocks and perimeter plantings are used to

hide the water garden edges above the waterline. These types of water gardens usually look best in landscapes with informal or natural looking gardens. Informal water gardens must be designed carefully to blend into the surrounding landscape. Once decisions are final on the type of water garden, the proper site can be selected. It is best to select a site near the areas where most of the outdoor time is spent gardening, entertaining, and relaxing. Locating it nearby will make the required tasks to properly maintain it easier.

Also consider the views from other areas of the property and from inside of the home. Accessibility to electricity and a water source must be considered. An electrical outlet with a ground fault interrupter will need to be installed if there will be a pump, outdoor or underwater light kits. There should also be a convenient water source to fill the pond and keep it topped off. Another important step is to check on local ordinances relating to the construction of water gardens.

The lay of the land will be an important factor in installing the water garden. A low area on the property may on first thought be an ideal spot for a water garden, but it will make it very difficult to maintain a clear and healthy water garden. Water runoff will contaminate the water garden with the fertilizers and chemicals used to maintain the garden and those of surrounding neighbors. The extra fertilizer will increase the growth of unwanted algae and the chemicals can harm or kill plants and fish. Soil and organic material that wash in will cloud the water. Dig a test hole to determine if there is a high water table and if so install a drain to relive the hydrolytic pressures that will push the liner up form the ground.

Avoid locating the water garden under trees so as not to disturb their root system. Also the leaves, stems, blooms and other debris they shed will end up in the water garden and cause many maintenance headaches. Most aquatic plants require at least 5 to 8 hours of sunlight or more and heavy shade will minimize their bloom production and plant health although some afternoon shade can be beneficial in hot locations.

Selecting Materials and Supplies

Once the style of water garden, formal or informal, has been chosen, the right kind of liner can be selected. Pre-formed liners come in variety of shapes and sizes and have advantage of ready made planting shelves and areas for sitting submersible pumps. They are available in both formal and informal styles. A flexible liner allows for more creativity and a more individual design, especially for an informal or natural water garden. The liner is the most important component of a water garden. It is important to select a high quality liner that is guaranteed fish-safe if fish are to be a part of the water garden. Flexible liners are available in the following materials:

1) PVC (poly vinyl chloride). This is a relatively cheap liner however; it must be protected from UV exposure from the sun.

2) EPDM (Ethylene Propylene Diene Monomer). It comes in various amounts of thickness. It is a superb general-purpose liner material. It is very flexible but large pieces can be very heavy. It must be protected from UV exposure from the sun.

3) Permalon. This liner extremely popular, especially for very large ponds. It is lightweight and pricing is very comparable to other liners, often cheaper. It must be protected from UV exposure from the sun.

Geotextile underlayment is recommended for all water garden liners. It makes liners more puncture resistant and stabilizes ground under the liner to keep pond liners from "over-stretching". A 2 to 3-inch layer of builder's sand may be used. The textile underlayment is preferred by many people and is quick and easy to install.

To calculate the width and length of the liner and underlayment needed:

Water Garden Length + 2 times Depth + 2 foot overlap = Liner Length

Water Garden Width + 2 times Depth + 2 foot overlap = Liner Width

EXAMPLE

Water Garden - 14 feet(L) X 9 feet (W) X 2 feet (Depth)

14 feet + (2x2 feet) + 2 = 20 feet (length)

9 feet + (2x2 feet) +2 = 15 feet (width)

Pump—Choosing a pump for a water garden should be based on a few job requirements. Desired flow, pumping height and electrical costs are all factors that need to be considered. High efficiency pumps are higher quality, will last longer, and use less electricity. Although they reduce operating costs by about one half, they do have a higher initial cost. Low efficiency pumps have a lower initial cost but use more electricity and have a shorter life.

Piping—Spiral tubing is excellent for use in water gar-

dens. It is flexible but will not crimp or collapse around curves. It is reinforced, and can be buried without the fear of tubing walls collapsing. It also dramatically improves water flow. Rigid flexible PVC pipe may also be used.

Filter—A good pond filter system is generally required to keep a water garden healthy and clear. A Koi water garden requires more filtration than a goldfish water garden due to the large mature size of these beautiful fish. Effective water garden filters combine mechanical and biological filtration. Biological filtration involves beneficial bacteria to break down fish waste and other organic matter. Mechanical filtration traps particles in some type of media for later removal during cleaning. Good filters accomplish both.

Skimmer—A skimmer provides several types of filtration. First, it mechanically skims water from the surface of the water garden so that any floating debris such as leaves don't fall to the bottom and decay. Next, the skimmer houses a net or plastic basket that catches the large debris and is easily removed for cleaning. Finally, a filter mat traps small particles. The skimmer also provides a convenient place to house and protect the pump.

Waterfall filtration box—This system is useful for a waterfall and or stream. The waterfall filtration box provides three layers of filtration. First, the water flows through the filter media. Second, the filter mats also provide surface area for bacteria, which break down harmful elements in the water garden and keep the ecosystem balanced. Third, it is easily hidden with stones and plant material.

Installation

Next, determine the size and layout of the water garden. The best way to do this is to use spray paint or a water hose and lay out the shape on the ground. A water garden for goldfish or water lilies need be only about 2 feet deep for zones 5 or greater. Water gardens built in colder areas may need more depth to keep them from freezing solid. Water gardens built for Koi should be close to three feet or deeper to allow these larger fish enough space. The biggest mistake is making the water garden too small. A larger water garden is more stable and easier to maintain. Dig the water garden to the desired shape and dig a shelf around the perimeter about one foot deep and one or more feet wide. **Make sure that the edges of the water garden are level!**

Dig the remainder with a slight slope to the end opposite the waterfall if one is included in the design.

Position any filters and or skimmers and level these in their proper location. Skimmers should be buried to the proper level beside the water garden. A ditch should be dug for the plumbing from the skimmer to the waterfall or external Bio-filter. Line the water garden excavation with the underlayment. This can be cut with scissors or a utility knife. Tape any small pieces together to keep them from moving when the liner is installed. Place the liner into the excavation and unfold. Position the liner evenly in the pond. Try to minimize folds and wrinkles but some will be necessary. After the water is added the folds should flatten out.

Waterfalls and streams can be excavated now. An external filter or waterfall tank can be positioned to create the first waterfall. This can be placed to spill directly into the water garden in which case the liner is held against the filter until the stone can be stacked from the shelf up against the filter to create a waterfall. If a small pool or stream is desired, then excavate this several inches deep and to the desired size and shape.

Position the underlayment and liner allowing extra material to overlap several inches into the water garden. Plumbing from the pump can be connected to an external filter and this can be the start of the waterfall.

Streams should be dug wider than the finished size to make room for stone that will be placed into the stream for the edging. Stone can be secured to the liner with mortar or expandable foam. This will hold back the water allowing it to spill over the stone creating the waterfall. Connect the liner to the skimmer, if one is being used, following the manufacturer's directions. Place the pipe or tubing in place leaving a few inches extra to make connections later. Place the stone or other coping around the edge of water garden. Arrange the copingstone around the edge and fold the liner up behind the stone to slightly above the water level. It is usually not necessary to mortar the stone into place if it is of sufficient size to be stable. If using small stone or if people will be walking around the edge, then mortaring the stone for stability may be required. Back fill with soil to hold the liner again the stone.

Fill the water garden with water to within a few inches from the top and then make corrections if necessary to ensure that the water garden is level. As the water garden is filling, remove wrinkles and make folds as necessary. Having a necklace of stone around the water garden does not create a natural appearance. If the goal is to make the water garden blend into the landscape in a natural setting, consider other methods of edging the water garden. Besides the traditional method of edging with a thin stone on the edge overlapping the water garden, one or more layers of stone can be built up from the shelf. This provides a more natural appearance and will allow the water to fluctuate without seeing the liner. Or, create a cobblestone beach edging by placing a large stone at the inside of a large shallow shelf and filling the area with gravel and cobbles. Naturalize this area by planting shallow water plants. This will create a more natural edge with plants partly in and partly out of the water. Bare root plants plant with some soil still attached can be placed directly into the gravel. This will help the plant to become established more quickly.

AQUATIC PLANTS AND FISH

Aquatic plants are an important part of a water garden's ecosystem. They help shade the water garden, thereby reducing algal blooms, provide oxygen for fish and beneficial bacteria, attract aquatic wildlife, and enhance the water garden's visual appeal.

Water lilies (*Nymphaea spp.*)

Water lilies help the water garden by shading the water from the sun. Algae love sunlight and have a harder time growing if the water garden's surface is partially covered by lily pads. When water lilies begin sending up their first floating leaves the first ones may be smaller or darker in color than later ones. Each leaf lives three to four weeks, then turns yellow and dies. Remove these yellowing leaves to encourage new growth. Later the first flowers reach the surface, opening and closing daily for four days apiece. As a flower fades it sinks into the water garden and should be removed to encourage more flowers to form. Hardy water lilies will flower until late fall. Position the lily so that it receives at least five or more hours of direct sunlight. Some varieties will flower at a reduced rate in less sunlight. More sun will lead to more flowers.

Tropical water lilies add pleasant fragrance and intense colors not found in any hardy lily. These special plants also have attractive mottled foliage to add extra interest to a water garden. Since tropical lilies are separated into day and night blooming varieties, one of each type will extend the beauty around the clock. Once the water temperature consistently reaches 70 degrees, they can be planted and will bloom the entire summer.

Make sure to locate the lily in the water garden where it won't be disturbed by the splashing of a waterfall or fountain. Water splashing on top of the leaves will discolor and eventually kill them.

Hardy Water Lilies—Good quality topsoil is used as the growing medium. Clay-loam soil without organic material is often used. Do not use bagged soil unless it is specifically labeled for aquatic plants. Lightweight soil amendments should also be avoided because they will float to the surface and make a mess.

Use a planting container that is as large as the water garden can accommodate and one that when planted can be easily lifted in and out of the water garden. A larger area for root development will lead to larger flowers and leaves.

Use a three gallon container or larger and pots that are wider than deep are better. Because hardy water lilies grow horizontally, a wider pot is preferred to a tall and narrow one. Fill the container up to two inches from the top with soil. Insert fertilizer tablets according to directions on the bottle. Plant the lily with the end furthest from the point leaves are growing from against one side of the container so the lily will grow across the planting container. Firm the soil around the rhizome leaving the crown exposed and add one inch of large gravel to help keep soil in place and to keep any fish out. (Koi and other fish will 'root around' in the soil and cause the plant to float out of the pot.)

Carefully lower the finished planting into the pool to approximately six inches of water over the top of the pot. This depth can be increased to twelve to eighteen inches after plants are established. For winter care lower pots to the bottom until spring. Fertilize on a regular basis after flush of new growth and plants have broken dormancy.

Tropical Water Lilies—Plant tropical water lilies when the mean water temperature is 70 degrees or warmer. Planting too early will cause dormancy. Use a three gallon container or larger as larger containers produce larger and more abundant flowers. Fill the container to within two inches of the top with the same type of soil as described above. Insert fertilizer tablets according to directions on the bottle. Plant the lily upright in the center of the pot and firm the soil around the roots leaving the crown (where the stems and roots connect)

level with the soil line. Add one inch of large gravel to help hold the soil in place and to keep fish out. CARE-FULLY lower the completed planting into the pool to a depth of six to eight inches over the top of the pot. This depth may be increased to twelve to eighteen inches after plants are established. Fertilize on a regular basis. In cold climates tropical lilies will not over winter in the water garden.

Lotus (*Nelumbo nucifera*)—There are few plants more exotic than Lotus for their captivating flowers, culinary delicacies, and unusual accents in dried flower arrangements. The huge rounded leaves stand proudly above the water's surface providing a coarse texture to compliment any landscape. The flowers are dramatic with unsurpassable beauty and bloom July through the fall! Fertilize regularly for maximum growth and flowering. To increase their blooms, remember to remove the spent leaves and flowers.

They will go dormant after they have finished blooming. Since hardy Lotus can be invasive in soil bottom ponds, be sure to keep them restrained in pots. Lotuses are also excellent candidates for container water gardens. Use the same garden soil and aquatic plant tabs as recommended for the water lilies. Fill the container to within two inches of the top. Plant the tuber horizontally like the hardy water lilies, being very careful not to break the growing tip. If the growing tip is damaged the lotus will die. Add gravel carefully to firm soil and lower the finished planting slowly to a depth of four to five inches over the pot. Lotus need full sun, at least six hours per day. Lotuses are also heavy feeders.

Miniature lotuses are similar to their big brothers in most requirements except that they are, of course, miniatures. Unlike regular sized plants, the miniature bowl lotus, prefer shallow water or simply wet ground. Since the smaller plants are hardy only to zone 6, they will need to be sunk to the deepest part of the water garden to help them from freezing in the winter.

Surface, Bog, and Submerged Plants

Surface Plants—Covering a water garden's surface will cool water and provide shade thereby limiting the ability of algae to grow. These plants will carpet the surface of the water and provide much needed shade. Some have leaves that float on the surface and others have foliage that emerges from the water. These plants add texture to the water garden's surface and provide a break from lily pads. They may also become invasive if they come in contact with soil.

Table 1. Surface plants for water gardens

BOTANICAL NAME	COMMON NAME
Ludwigia peploides	Improved Primrose Creeper
Aponogeton distachyus	Water Hawthorne
Nymphoides cristata	Water Snowflake
Nymphoides geminate	Yellow Snowflake
Nasturtium officinale	Water Cress

Table 2. Perennial bog plants

BOTANICAL NAME	COMMON NAME
Sagittaria latifolia	Arrowhead
Sagittaria japonica flore-plena	Double Flowering Japanese Arrowhead
Sagittaria australis	Arrowhead 'Silk Stockings'
Dulichium arundinaceum	Dwarf Bamboo
Scirpus tabernaemontani	Zebra Bulrush
Ranunculus repens	Buttercup 'Buttered Popcorn'
Phragmites "Candy Stripe"	Candy Stripe Reed
Lobelia cardinalis	Cardinal Flower
Typha minima	Miniature Cattail
Typha angustifolia	Narrowleaf Cattail
Typha japonica variegate	Variegated Cattail
Butomus umbellatus	Flowering Rush
Myosotis scorpoides	Forget-Me-Not
*Orontium aquaticum	Golden Club
Thalia dealbata	Hardy Thalia
Equisetum hyemale	Horsetail
Equisetum scirpoides	Miniature Horsetail
Saururus cernuus	Lizard's Tail
Caltha palustris	Marsh Marigold
Mazus repens	Creeping Mazus
Ludwigia arcuata	Needle-leaf Ludwigia
Hydrocotyle verticillata	Penny Wort
Pontederia cordata	Purple Pickerel Rush
Sagittaria spp.	Sagittaria
Eleocharis montevidensis	Spike Rush
Acorus calmus variegata	Variegated Sweetflag
Peltandra virginica	Water Arum
Eleocharis dulcis	Water Chestnut
Marsilea schelpiana	Ruffled Water Clover
Marsilea drummondi	Water Clover
Iris versicolor	Blue Flag Water Iris
Iris laevigata	Water Iris
Iris laevigata variegata	Variegated Water Iris
Iris pseudacorus	Yellow Flag Water Iris
Iris pseudacorus flore-plena	Double Yellow Flag Water Iris
Iris pseudacorus variegata	Variegated Yellow Flag Water Iris

(*) indicates that the species has marginal cold hardiness. These plants need to be sunk at the bottom of the water garden each winter to increase their chances of over-wintering.

Bog Plants—(Tables 2 and 3) Bog plants are sometimes referred to as marginals or shallow water plants. They provide vertical accent and texture contrast to the water garden. On the edge of the water garden they can hide liner, tubing or a power cord. Some are grown only for their foliage while others have beautiful flowers at different times of the season. When planted in a container their size and spread can be contained. They can be invasive when planted in the soil, however.

Bog plants require fertilizer 2-3 times per year. Plant in as large a container as possible to allow the plants plenty of room to spread and bloom freely. Some plants have spreading root systems that need adequate surface area but not much soil depth. Others have a dense clumping habit that may require less surface area. They should be planted shallow in topsoil. Gently compress the soil into place to anchor the plant. Leave about a half-inch of space at the top to add a layer of gravel. Different species prefer different depths but in general they should be placed between 4 and 15 inches deep on a shelf of the pond or in their own boggy offshoot of the pond.

Submerged Plants—(Table 4) These plants are essential to good water quality and provide shelter and shade for fish. Their natural filtration capabilities help keep the water garden clear. They should be planted in pots in gravel to encourage them to absorb nutrients from the water. Plant several bunches per pot and completely submerge them to the bottom of the water garden.

Floating Plants—(Table 5) Planting is simple with floating plants, just toss them in and let them go their own direction. Buoyant leaves keep these plants afloat, making them great natural spawning areas and hiding places for fish. They also enhance the water quality while their roots dangle in the water readily absorbing organic pollutants, and they provide shade to help limit the growth of algae.

FISH

Though fish are not a necessity in a water garden, many people (especially those who are initially skeptical) find they get tremendous pleasure from watching the relaxed movements of their goldfish or Koi. Fish become family

Table 3. Annual bog plants

BOTANICAL NAME	COMMON NAME
Nymphoides peltata	Floating Heart
Myriophyllum aquatica	Parrot's Feather
Myriophyllum properpinacoides	Miniature Parrot's Feather
Marsilea mutica	Variegated Water Clover
Sagittaria montevidensis	Aztec Arrowhead
Crinum americanum	Bog Lily
Canna spp.	Canna
Ludwigia setoides	Mosaic Plant
Cyperus haspens	Dwarf Papyrus
Cyperus papyrus	Egyptian Papyrus
Thalia geniculata	Red Stemmed Thalia
Hymencallis liriosome	Spider Lily
Colocasia spp.	Black Magic Taro
Colocasia esculenta	Green Taro
Colocasia antiquorum	Imperial Taro
Cyperus alternifolius	Umbrella Palm
Cyperus alternifolius gracilis	Dwarf Umbrella Palm
Hydrocleys nymphoides	Water Poppy

pets, coming when called, following owners around the water garden, taking food from outstretched fingers, even allowing themselves to be petted.

Common types of fish—Because goldfish are inexpensive, hardy, and often colorful, they are the most commonly used fish in water gardens. There are a variety of types, including: Common goldfish; Comets, a stretch version of common goldfish, with longer fins and longer, more deeply forked tails; Shubunkins, which often have matt (non-reflective) scales and are beautifully colored; Fantails, which have fins and tails that are much longer than those of the Commons; Lionheads, which have short, chunky bodies and a "raspberry like" head growth that increases with age. They have no dorsal fin, so they are poor swimmers

Japanese Koi are also wonderful fish for water gardens. They are very colorful and swim in a deliberate, leisurely fashion. It is common for them to grow to 24 inches and

Table 4. Submerged plants for water gardens

BOTANICAL NAME	COMMON NAME
Myriophyllum	----
Anacharis	----
Cabomba	----

Table 5. Floating plants for water gardens

BOTANICAL NAME	COMMON NAME
Pistia stratoides	Water Lettuce
Eichornia crassipes	Water Hyacinth

to live to 60 years of age or more. If they are stocked at a small size, Koi can be used in any water garden. Ponds that are built specifically for Koi, however, are usually at least 3 feet deep, hold at least 500 gallons of water, and have sophisticated filtration systems. Minnows or other small fry can be suitable for tub gardens, though in larger water gardens, when mixed with larger fish, they may get eaten.

Stocking fish—A common rule of thumb for the number of fish to stock is 1 to 2 inches of fish for every square foot of surface area of the water garden. However, a much better method is to start with 3 to 5 fish, see how things go, and add more if desired. The fewer fish a water garden has, the easier it is to keep clean. Fish should be at least 2 to 3 inches when they are stocked. Inexpensive "feeder" goldfish are very young and weak, and have often been roughly handled. Their survival rate is typically very low, and they are not suitable for stocking in a water garden.

Most fish are sold in a plastic bag containing a small amount of water. When transferring fish to the water garden, float the bag on the surface until the water temperature in the bag is the same as that of the pool - at least 20 minutes. Next, open the bag and let the water enter, and then allow the fish to swim out. They'll probably swim off and hide; gradually, over a period of days, they should begin to feed.

Feeding fish—The most important rule of feeding fish is to feed them less. If the fish are overfed, they produce more waste than the water garden can handle, and a significant amount of food falls to the bottoms where it decomposes and fouls the water. If the water garden isn't overstocked, fish can live entirely off the natural production of the pond. Fish may hide out of sight under plants in the pond. To accustom the fish to human presence, feed a small amount at the same time every day, and at the same place in the pond. As a general rule, feed no more than what can be consumed in 2 to 5 minutes.

Goldfish are cold-blooded, so their rate of metabolism depends on water temperature. Do not feed when the water temperature is below 50°F. In spring, when water gets above 55°F (sustained and measured in the morning), resume feeding. Goldfish and Koi are omnivorous: they'll eat almost anything. Packaged fish foods, containing a balance of protein, carbohydrates, and vitamins, are recommended; some Koi foods include spirulina (high-protein algae) or carotene as "color enhancers."

CARING FOR A WATER GARDEN

Water Quality

The water's ability to support aquatic life and its clarity are commonly thought of as water quality. Lack of clarity is usually not a problem for aquatic life, but it limits the ability to see and enjoy Koi and goldfish. The water garden owner should be concerned with both of these aspects.

There are a number of natural processes at work in pond water at any given time. Many of these processes and the elements they create affect water quality.

Nitrogen Cycle—The nitrogen cycle describes how organic wastes are broken down to less toxic compounds in the water garden. Fish wastes (i.e., urea) and other organic matter naturally decompose into ammonia, which is highly toxic. Nitrosomonas bacteria process the ammonia into nitrite, which is also toxic. Nitrobacter bacteria then break down the nitrite into nitrate, which is only mildly toxic.

Ammonia—An intermediate product of the nitrogen cycle that converts to the more toxic nitrite. The toxicity of ammonia depends on the temperature and pH of the water; the higher the pH and/or temperature, the more toxic the ammonia. Ammonia burns the gills and fins of fish and lowers their resistance to disease.

Nitrites—An intermediate product in the nitrogen cycle, nitrites are highly toxic to fish, even at low levels. Decreasing the amount of organic wastes will decrease the amount of nitrites formed.

Nitrate—A relatively safe end product of organic waste degradation, nitrate may be toxic to goldfish at very high levels. Nitrate is a nutrient source for algal and other plant life.

pH—As a measurement of acidity or basicity of water, with 7.0 being neutral, pH is important in water garden management. The pH tolerance of fish varies from species to species. Fish such as goldfish and Koi generally adapt to the pH of local waters but it is important to not make rapid changes in pH. The shock of rapidly fluctuating pH can stress or even kill fish.

Pond pH generally follows a daily cycle of being lowest just before dawn and highest in the afternoon due to photosynthesis and aquatic life respiration. pH increases with plant population and decreases with excessive organic matter and animal population. Low pH water can harm fish gills. High pH water can harm fins and gills and contribute to unwanted algal growth.

For fish to be healthy and also to help with the control of algae, the pH of the water should be monitored using a pH test kit. The pH should be between 6.6 and 7.8, with the ideal being 7 to 7.2. Unless the pH is below 6.5 or above 8, it is usually best not to try and adjust it.

Hydrogen sulfide—This compound can be toxic to fish and occurs as a result of anaerobic bacterial activity or decomposition. Anaerobic bacterial activity occurs in the bottom of water gardens where organic matter is broken down without the availability of oxygen.

Phosphorous—When introduced into the water garden through organic or inorganic means, phosphorous promotes excessive algae growth. Phosphorous can be removed through water changes.

Other elements contained in municipal water supplies can also affect water quality in a pond or water garden.

Chloramines—This substance is sometimes used as a bactericide in municipal water supplies. It is poisonous to fish, but can be removed with many commercially available dechlorinating additives. Unlike chlorine, it will not evaporate from water by itself.

Chlorine—Chlorine in one of a number of forms is added to water to destroy or deactivate disease-causing microorganisms and is the mostly widely used disinfectant in the United States. Chlorine will evaporate from water by letting it stray through the air. It is toxic to fish but can be removed with many commercially available dechlorinating additives.

While it is true that goldfish and Koi can be kept in water gardens with no filtration, it severely limits the number of fish that can be sustained. In the wild, fish have large amounts of water so that toxins from their waste do not build up to dangerous levels. Most hobbyists will want to keep more fish than their water garden will naturally support. Goldfish and Koi excrete waste into the water in the form of ammonia and feces. Also adding to the problem are organic compounds from plant matter, and soil that may flow into the water garden.

In order to provide good water quality, some form of waste removal must be provided. Two methods used in average water gardens are mechanical filtration, and biological filtration. Mechanical filters physically remove solids from the water by trapping the debris in some form of mat, brush, or sponge. Mechanical filters are effective but generally require frequent cleaning to re-move the accumulated matter. Most biological filters are also mechanical filters depending on how they are used.

Filtration

Biological filtration is the most effective method of removing toxins from water gardens by breaking down ammonia into nitrite and then into nitrate. This is accomplished using naturally occurring bacteria called nitrosomonas and nitrobacter. Ammonia is broken down in natural bodies of water, but because of limited space in and around the water garden, this natural process needs some help. An efficient place for the bacteria to live and thrive must be provided. In a biological filter this place is a material on which the bacteria are exposed to large quantities of food and oxygen.

Actually, it is not filtration at all. Instead, it is the mixing of aquarium water with beneficial bacteria that transform wastes in the water into substances which are less toxic to the inhabitants, in a process known as the nitrogen cycle. This process is accomplished by trickle filters (ammonia towers), UGF (undergravel filters) sponge filters, and various other specialty filters.

One of the best materials for accomplishing this is a fiber matting media, which offers a large surface area for the bacteria to colonize and also a large void area to allow large amounts of water to flow through carrying food for the bacteria. Filter materials that are too dense will clog and not allow the water to flow through. Efficiency can also be increased by adding concentrated solutions of bacteria and enzymes.

Biological filters in water gardens must run continuously during the season. If they are shut down for more than a few hours the beneficial bacteria will begin to die. A biological filter should be cleaned using dechlorinated water if possible to avoid removing or killing the beneficial bacteria. Also, the filter should not be over cleaned; rinse the media only enough to allow good water flow though the filter. The brown stain on the filter media is the living bacteria.

Algae and How to Deal with It

Algae are simple celled plants containing chlorophyll. The main form of algae that is of interest to aquaculture is collectively known as unicellular. These consist of free floating cells of algae which make the water look green or brown, depending on the color of the algae. Other forms include filamentous, which are strand like colonies of algae, which usually form dense mats or clumps.

Algal Bloom is caused by rapid growth of algae producing large quantities of plant material, can result in low dissolved oxygen conditions as the algae dies and decays. Low dissolved oxygen can result in the death of fish and other aquatic organisms.

Algae grow quickly in the presence of warm temperatures, sunlight and the accumulation of organic load due the increased metabolism of the fish. Algae thrive in these conditions and will soon turn water pea green making it difficult to see the fish. One of the best things to help clear up green water is to make sure the water garden is properly planted and the biological filter is the proper size and working properly.

Plants will help in controlling algae by taking nitrates from the water, which deprives the algae of the nutrient it depends on for sustenance. Anacharis is one of the best underwater oxygenating plants used for algae control. Floating plants such as water lettuce and water hyacinths are also very good for absorbing nutrients in the water garden to starve algae.

Provide some shade to the water garden with water lilies or other surface plants. Provide 50-60% surface coverage if the pond is in full sun. Shade from trees or other objects will reduce the need for as much surface coverage.

Rain run-off flowing into the water garden will make it difficult, if not impossible, to keep all of the algae in control. This is one of the most common problems that keep a water garden from clearing. If water flows over the lawn or planting beds and into the water garden, it is carrying with it fertilizer in the form of organics or commercial fertilizer which may have been spread to feed the lawn or other plants. Take measures to divert the runoff around the water garden by either constructing a berm or a trench. If the run-off flows over a concrete patio and then into the water garden it can carry nutrients to feed the algae as well as raise the pH of the water, which contributes to algae growth. A pH closer to neutral will decrease algae growth. Cement, limestone, and marble will raise the pH of the water, therefore contributing to algae growth.

Another thing that makes the control of algae difficult is a lot of sludge (dirt and decaying organic debris) in the bottom of the water garden. An inch or so of sludge on the bottom of a water garden should be removed as much possible by siphoning, scooping, vacuuming, or whatever means are available. If the bottom of the water garden is higher than other parts of the yard then, use a section of 1.25 or 1.5" flexible pipe as a siphon. This is much easier with two people. Fill the hose with water and each person will hold their hand over the ends to keep the water in the pipe. One person holds one end in the water and the other will hold the opposite end at the low point in the yard.

Release the hold over the ends of the pipe and the water should start flowing. The end in the pond can be moved about pulling the sludge out of the water garden at the same time. There are also a few types of pond vacs that can be used to remove debris from the water garden bottom. Ultraviolet Sterilizer may help with a constant green water problem. An Ultraviolet Sterilizer will kill all of the algae that pass around the ultraviolet light. These units are sized according to the pump's flow rate and the number of gallons in the water garden. The dead algae are then picked up by the filter to be washed away when the biomechanical filter is cleaned or broken down by the biological filter. The use of a UV sterilizer does not stop the algae problem; it just masks the symptoms.

Filamentous algae are many cells attached together in many forms. It can be long and stringy. It can be short and furry or in the shape of webs or mats. The short velvet type of algae that covers the liner and everything else in the water garden is beneficial. It helps provide a natural appearance to the water garden. It uses nutrients from the water, provides oxygen during the day, and the fish nibble on it. This type of algae cannot be totally eliminated with fish and plants in the water garden.

String algae, which may coat the waterfall, is a little harder to control. Physically remove it from the water garden where possible. Filamentous type algae will flourish on waterfalls and in shallow streams because the sunlight is more intense providing more heat and light than other parts of the water garden and there is a constant supply of nutrients flowing through it.

The fish think that they are getting a real treat when the string algae is dislodged from the waterfall for them to eat. Biological clarifiers help by breaking down the organic material in the water garden, which feed algae. There are other types of products containing bacteria and enzymes that will help in the control of this type of algae. Greenex has proven to be very effective in keeping string algae under control as well as Crystal Clear's Clarity Max and Ecological Laboratorie's Microbe-Lift. Microbe-Lift contains nitrifying bacteria as an added bonus. These products help in the control of algae but are not an algaecide.

The use of these products is a process and will not produce results overnight. The bacteria products should still be used to help with the overall water quality and reduce sludge. For a water garden without fish, use fountain chemicals to control the algae. One product that works very well and economically is Fountec. It is safe for plants, birds and other animals but it MUST NOT be used with fish. In a water garden with fish but no plants, use Pond Blocks. This is a slow release algaecide that will kill the algae (both single cell and multi cell algae). One block will last about a month and treat 250 gallons of water. (Remember this is NOT safe for most plants.)

To summarize, keep the organic load down by keeping runoff out of the water garden and the sludge to a minimum. Don't over feed or keep more fish than a water garden will support. 1 to 2 inches of goldfish per sq. ft. and one Koi per 10 sq. ft. are a good rule for most water gardens. Install an adequate size biological filter and give it time to work. This could take several months. Use enough and the right type of aquatic plants. One bunch of Anacharis per 1sq. ft. of surface area in full sun and 2 bunches per two sq. ft. in shade. Use biological treatments and give them time to work. Greenex, Microbe-Lift and Clarity Max will help but this is an ongoing process and takes time along with the methods outlined above for balancing a water garden.

Typical Pond Calculations

Calculate the width and length of the liner and underlayment needed

Water Garden Length + 2 times Depth + 2' overlap = Liner Length

Water Garden Width + 2 times Depth + 2' overlay = Liner Width

Calculate the number of gallons in a water garden

Rectangle: length x width x depth = cubic feet. One cubic foot of water is 7.5 gallons.

Circle: radius squared x 3.14 x 7.5 gallons

Calculate the square foot surface area of a water garden

Rectangle: multiply average length x average width = square feet of surface.

Round: multiply (half the diameter) x (half the diameter) x 3.14 = square feet of surface.

Cost of Electricity to Operate Pump—Ask the electric supplier for the cost per kilowatt-hour. Multiply amps x volts divided by 1000 x cost per kilowatt-hour x 24 hours x 30 days = cost per month.

Table 6. Tubing flow rates

MAX FLOW (GPH)	REQUIRED TUBING SIZE (INSIDE DIAMETER)
300	1/2"
720	3/4"
1200	1"
3000	1-1/2"
4800	2"

Tubing Flow Rates—(Table 6) The tubing size running from the pump is determined by the maximum flow rate of the pump. Pick the tubing diameter that is most appropriate for the volume of water coming from the pump. A hose adapter or a combination of adapters is required to attach the hose to most pumps.

Helpful Information

Water Garden Depth—Minimum of 18" - deeper (24" to 36") is better for fish

Pump Size—Minimum requirements - ½ the volume of the pond circulated through the pump per hour.

Flow Rate for Water Falls—For every 100 gallons per hour pumped over a falls a ¼" deep, 1" wide spill will be created.

Water Garden Surface—Water plants should cover 50- 60 percent of the water garden surface.

Oxygenating Plants—1-2 bunches per square foot of water garden surface.

Bog Plants—Most can only tolerate 1-2 inches of water above the pot surface.

Water Lilies—Must have 10-24 inches of water above the pot, depending on the variety.

Algae—The best way to keep water clear is to have 50-60 percent of the water garden surface covered with plant material.

Water Garden Tips

• Free-floating algae make the water appear "pea soup green".

• String or Hair Algae floats, usually from the side of the Water Garden, and when removed and dry, resembles fine string or green "hair.

• NEVER empty and refill a water garden to "get rid of green water" ... This just means starting out with new nutrients for MORE algae. Be patient!

• Stock 1 inch of fish for each 1 square foot of water

surface - (a rule that is most often broken)

• Common goldfish breed easily in a water garden. There are many types of goldfish/carp available in many beautiful color combinations — but avoid short bodied ones (difficult for them to compete with other fish or escape predators).

• Koi are the superstars…with a reputation to match when it comes to water gardens. They need heavy filtration, crystal clear and balanced water and like to uproot plants. Koi grow to be extremely large — 20 inches or more.

• Goldfish can easily live off nutrients, insects, and algae in the water garden. However, most people like to feed them. They can be trained to eat from your hand. Do not feed more than fish can eat in about 5 minutes. Treats are brine shrimp, and shredded zucchini.

• Fish will eat mosquito larvae. If there are no fish in the water garden, use mosquito dunks, a Bt product that kills the larvae before they hatch. Dunks look like small 2-inch donut shapes; they can be broken into small bits or chunks and used in the water garden, pot saucers or areas where water stands or collects. They are safe for use around fish, plants, pets, and people.

Exotic Pest Plants

Table 7 contains a selection of plants that are listed as exotic plant pest species in Georgia. Before making a plant purchase, look over this list to see if the plants that you have selected are on it. This list will likely continue to grow if other plants become a problem, and it will vary with different states. Some of the plants listed here, have become "nuisance" or "noxious" plants, from being attached to waterfowl or other wildlife entering a particular body of water. They deposit the plants and then the plants grow where they shouldn't, or where they are not native in that particular body of water (or part of the country). Some plants became nuisance or noxious plants from people unknowingly (or knowingly) releasing them into natural bodies of water.

Today we know that we should protect our environment!

Table 7. Wetland and waterways exotic pest plant species in Georgia

BOTANICAL NAME	COMMON NAME
Alternantheria philoxeroides	Alligatorweed
Hydrilla verticillata	Hydrilla
Salvinia molesta	Giant Salvinia
Eichhornia crassipes	Water Hyacinth
Lythrum salicaria L.	Purple loostrife
Source: Georgia Invasive Species Task Force	

Some state regulators (as well as USDA regulators) are doing something about this issue by banning the sale and/or ownership of these nuisance plants and labeling them as "Prohibited" or "Noxious" plants. Do the environment and the future of water gardening a favor and be responsible ….do not release purchased aquatic plants into natural bodies of water, streams or storm drains, as they are intended for use in a decorative and/or enclosed pond, only. To get rid of excess aquatic plants, put them in the compost pile, give them away to a water gardening friend or kill the plants by drying them on your driveway in the hot sun and compost them.

RESOURCES

Allison, James. *Water in the Garden*. Bullfinch Press.

Nash, Helen. *The Complete Pond Builder*. Tetra Press.

Nash, Helen and Eamonn Hughes. *Waterfalls, Fountains, Pools and Streams*. Sterling Publishing Company.

Nash, Helen and Steve Stroupe. *Aquatic Plants and Their Cultivation*. Sterling Publishing Company.

DISCUSSION QUESTIONS

1. Why is site evaluation important when planning a water garden?

2. Why are volume and surface area important considerations when planning a pond?

3. Why is a complete water change not recommended as a method to get rid of an algae problem?

4. How does overstocking a water garden with fish lead to water quality problems?

6. What are the proper methods of disposing of unwanted aquatic plants?

7. What are the differences between mechanical and biological filtration?

NOTES

25
Indoor Plants

Bodie V. Pennisi
Paul A. Thomas

LEARNING OBJECTIVES

Know how light, temperature, and relative humidity affect plant growth on indoor plants.

Know how to measure light intensity inside your home.

Know how plants are classified according to their light requirements.

Know how to properly water and fertilize indoor plants.

Recognize symptoms of inadequate or excess light, relative humidity, nutrition, and water in indoor plants.

Understand the process of acclimatization and know the symptoms of an acclimatized plant.

Know the techniques of proper pruning, grooming, cleaning and repotting indoor plants.

Know how to select containers for indoor plants.

Know the major pests and diseases on indoor plants and how to keep plants pest- and disease-free.

TERMS TO KNOW

Acclimatization adaptation of a plant to a new environment.

Defoliation loss of leaves.

Fluoride and Chloride chemical elements, which in excess, can cause damage to sensitive plants.

Footcandle light is measured in units called footcandles. One footcandle (ft-c) is the amount of light cast by a candle on a white surface one foot away in a completely dark room.

Gutation water exudates from pores on the leaf surface.

Houseplant a plant grown indoors.

Leaf Marginal and Tip Burn dark brown to black areas found on plant leaves, usually associated with overfertilization.

Relative humidity the amount of moisture contained in the air.

Soluble salts fertilizer salts dissolved in the soil solution.

INTRODUCTION

Much of the scenic beauty of nature has been replaced by densely populated areas that sprawl for miles from urban centers. This visual pollution affects us all and leaves us with a longing for closer contact with nature. We spend about 90% of our time indoors. Interior plants are an ideal way to create attractive and restful settings, and enhance our sense of well being. In addition, houseplants can be a satisfying hobby, and they can help purify the air in our homes. Indoor plants not only convert carbon dioxide to oxygen, but also trap and absorb many pollutants. Many of these chemical compounds are released into our air through a process called "off-gassing" and come from everyday items present in our homes and office.

To be a successful indoor gardener, you need to understand how the interior environment affects plant growth and how that differs from growing plants outside in the garden.

Factors Affecting Plant Growth

Plant growth is affected by **light**, **temperature**, **water**, **humidity**, **nutrition**, and **soil**.

Light—Of all the factors affecting plant growth in interiors, adequate light is by far the most important. Light is needed for the plant to produce food and survive; generally the more light the more food is produced for growth. Light is measured in units called footcandles. One footcandle (ft-c) is the amount of light cast by a candle on a white surface one foot away in a completely dark room. Outdoors, the light levels on a bright day range from 10,000 ft-c in an open sunny area to 250 ft-c or less in the shade of a large tree.

It would be very helpful if you could have some general idea of how much light was present in a given location in your house. You could get a fairly good estimate with a hand-held light meter, or you could use a 35mm camera, and do the following:

• Set film speed indicator to ASA 25 and the shutter speed to 1/60th second

• Place a piece of white paper where you want to measure the light levels, aim the camera toward it close to fill the view, and adjust the f/stop so that meter indicates a correct exposure

• Read the approximate light level from the table

• This table allows you to obtain the light intensity reading practically everywhere in your home. For example, if the f/stop setting is f/16, the approximate light levels are 2,400 footcandles. (see Table 1)

Using the light readings, your home can be divided into four areas, which have the following light levels for 8 hours a day:

1) LOW LIGHT AREAS: 25 to 75 ft-c

2) MEDIUM LIGHT AREAS: 75 to 200 ft-c

3) HIGH LIGHT AREAS: over 200 ft-c but not direct sun

4) SUNNY LIGHT AREAS: at least 4 hours of direct sun

In your home the amount of light in a given location is variable and is affected by the presence of trees outdoors (may shade at certain times), roof overhangs (may shade at certain times), wall color (reflectance), window curtains, day length, time of day, and time of year.

When shopping for indoor plants, select plants for a given location based on the approximate light levels in the spot. The plant label usually contains information on the light requirements of the plant. If the plant label lists 'high light', but the selected area in the home does not provide adequate light for it, artificial light source such as fluorescent and/or special incandescent lights could be used to supplement the natural light. Increasing the number of hours of light also can help, for example, 16 hours of light and 8 hours of dark. This extends the number of hours during which plants receive light.

While adequate light is crucial for plant growth, too much light can be damaging. Indoor plants are classified according to the amount of light needed for growth (list of plants and their light requirements are provided in Table 3). Growers supply this information in general terms on the label with which the plant is sold. Use this information when shopping for indoor plants.

• Low (min. 25-75 ft-c, 75-200 for good growth)

• Medium (min. 75-150 ft-c, 200-500 preferred)

• High (min. 150-1000 ft-c, 500-1000 preferred)

• Very high (min. 1000 ft-c, 1000+ preferred).

Table 1. Aperture settings and light intensity readings

f/2	40 ft-c	f/8	600 ft-c
f/2	75 ft-c	f/11	1200 ft-c
f/4	150 ft-c	f/16	2400 ft-c
f/5.6	300 ft-c		

Generally, windows with eastern exposure provide the best light and temperature conditions for most indoor plants' growth because they receive direct morning light from sunrise until nearly midday. Footcandle readings at these windows can reach 5,000-8,000. As the morning progresses, the direct sun recedes from the room. An eastern room is cooler compared to south or west rooms because the house absorbs less radiant heat. Light from the east is cooler than that from the south or west, and causes less water loss from the plants. Windows with southern exposure give the largest variation in light and temperature conditions. The low winter sun shines across the room for most of the daylight hours. In the summer, when the sun is farther north than in the winter, the sun rises at a sharp angle in the morning and is high in the sky by noon. Direct light comes into a south window only at midday. If there is a wide overhang outside, the sun may not enter the room at all. The sun at noon on a summer day may measure 10,000 ft-c.

Indoors, however, a southern window with wide eaves outside will receive about the same amount of light as a window with northern exposure. Southern and western exposures are interchangeable for most plants. In the winter, most plants but those with definite preference for northern exposure can be placed in a room with southern exposure.

Windows with northern exposure provide the least light and the lowest temperature. Since the USA is in the northern hemisphere, it receives most of its sunlight from the south. Out of the four exposures, the northern exposure receives the least light and least heat the year round. Because of the low light, maintaining healthy plants can be a challenge. A northern windowsill can measure light levels as low as 200 ft-c on a clear winter day. Some indoor plants can tolerate it; others prefer this exposure, e.g. African violets. This exposure is best for plants with green foliage because the coloration on variegated foliage tends to disappear under low light conditions. Although most plants grown indoors will not grow in a northern room, they may tolerate it for short periods of time.

How can you tell if your plant is not receiving adequate light?

- The plant does not grow.
- The internodes (spaces between leaves) are much longer than the internodes on the older part of the plant.
- The new leaves are much smaller than older leaves.
- The leaf color is a lighter green on the newer foliage than on the older foliage.
- The older leaves may die.

Temperature—Temperature is the second most important factor influencing plant growth in interior environments. People feel comfortable in the range 72 to 82 degrees Fahrenheit and interior plants can tolerate and grow well in 58 to 86 degrees Fahrenheit range. This is the case because most indoor plants originate from tropical and subtropical areas of the world.

Temperature and light are linked through the processes of photosynthesis and respiration (see Chapter on Plant Physiology). These processes can be thought of as the "Yin and Yang" of plant life — two parts of a circle. Photosynthesis builds sugars and starch, which are then broken down by respiration to provide energy for developing new tissues (growth) and for maintenance of existing ones. High temperature speeds up respiration. If the plant is not producing sufficient sugars (as under low light), then high temperatures may break down what little sugars are made, leaving little to none for growth. Maintenance takes precedence over growth,

Table 2. Comparison of symptoms of acclimatized plants and non-acclimatized plants	
ACCLIMATIZED PLANTS	**NON-ACCLIMATIZED PLANTS**
Medium to dark green leaves	Yellowish to light green leaves
Large leaves	Small leaves
Flat leaves	Partially folded leaves
Thin leaves	Thick leaves
Widely spaced leaves	Closely spaced leaves
Internodes long	Internodes short
Thin to medium stems	Thick stems
Leaf position horizontal or lightly flexed	Leaf position upright
Few new leaves	Many new leaves
Wide branch angles	Acute angles

therefore under insufficient light plants do not grow. If light is so low that not enough sugars are produced for maintenance, the plant eventually dies.

When sugar levels are low the plant takes nutrients and sugars from older leaves to maintain new leaves. To help plants in a home environment, two options are available: raise light levels to increase photosynthesis and sugar production, or reduce night temperature to lower respiration rates and allow more sugars for growth.

What temperatures are likely to occur in homes? During summer, air conditioning in a house which might be turned off at night or weekend thermostat settings raised result in higher than desirable night temperatures. During winter, heating may be turned off at night or weekend thermostats settings lowered and that might result in lower night temperatures. Chill damage is manifested with yellowing of lower leaves and/or defoliation.

Be especially careful not to allow temperatures to drop below 50°F, or chill damage will result on some sensitive foliage plants (e.g. Chinese Evergreen, Aglaonema). Plants vary in their minimum and maximum requirements. Examples of cool loving plants suitable for locations where temperatures drop to the low 50's at night and 60's during the day are Cyclamen, Wonder Plant, Fatshedera, Japanese Aralia, Fatsia. A list of plants and their temperature requirements are provided in Table 1.

Not all interior plants have the same temperature requirements for optimal growth. For example Cast Iron, Aspidistra and ferns actually grow better with cooler temperatures (72° F), while other tropical plants grow best if the temperatures are 90 to 95° F. Such temperatures are rarely allowed indoors.

The best temperature range for indoor plants is 70° – 80° F day and 65° – 70° F night. You should try to maintain these temperatures even when not in the house.

Relative humidity—Relative humidity (RH) is the amount of moisture contained in the air. For interior plants relative humidity below 20% is considered low, up to 40-50% is medium, and above 50% is high. Relative humidity is a very important factor, but easily overlooked. In the greenhouse relative humidity is 50% or higher. Rapid transpiration and water loss could result when newly purchased plants are placed in 10-20% relative humidity typical of most homes. Most indoor plants come from the tropics where high relative humidity is common. Therefore, you should take steps to help your plants adjust to the low relative humidity in the home by doing one or several of the following:

- Place plants close together to create a microenvironment with a higher RH.
- Place a shallow container filled with water and lava rocks or gravel, which will provide evaporation from a large surface area and increase RH.
- Use a humidifier.
- Use mist bottles to spray water around the plant. In reality, you need to mist every few minutes to make a difference in RH around the plant.
- The foliage and flowers of plants with hairy leaves should not be sprayed with water.

Water

Water Quantity—Learning to water is one of the most important skills in plant care. Applying too much water can suffocate plant roots; too little water causes growth to become erratic and stunted. Watering frequency will depend on the conditions under which the plants are growing. When dealing with how much water to apply, consider the following:

- **Plant type**—(list of plants and their moisture requirements are provided in Table 3). Not all plants are similar in their water requirements. Usually this information, just like the light preference, is included on the plant label. For example a croton, which likes high light, will likely need more frequent watering compared to a succulent plant such as Opuntia cactus. Both have similar light needs, but dissimilar water requirements.

- **Plant size**—Larger plants need more water compared to smaller size plants.

- **Container volume**—If the growing container is too small, more frequent waterings may be needed.

- **Soil moisture**—How much water is already present in the growing medium will also affect your watering frequency.

- **Light intensity**—Plants under high light transpire more water, compared to plants under low light.

Many problems can be traced to improper watering. Containers with saucers may cause an excessive build-up of soluble salts (chemicals coming from the applied fertilizer). High levels of soluble salts can cause damage to the roots and growth decline. To correct this, discard any water in the saucer after each irrigation and apply large quantities of water to the soil to leach the accumulated soluble salts.

In deciding when you should water, feel the soil; push a finger an inch or so below the surface, if it is still moist do not water. Water-devices, or water-meters, also are available to simplify watering.

Water Quality—The quality of the irrigation water is an issue with plants, that are susceptible to fluorine and chlorine, such as Corn Plant, Dracaena, Ti Plant Cordyline, Peacock Plant, Maranta, and Rattlesnake Plant, Calathea. A good solution for these plants is to let the water stand for several days to allow some chlorine and fluorine to be lost from the water before applying it to the plants. If you have susceptible plants close to an open pool, move them away so water splashes do not reach the foliage. If you have an enclosed pool, do not use susceptible plants around it. In general, plants with long linear leaves (e.g., Spider Plant) are more susceptible to fluorine.

Nutrition

Many indoor gardeners have the same problem with fertilizer that they have with water. They want to give their plants too much. The danger from overfertilization occurs because any fertilizer used (whether liquid, powder, or tablet) will dissolve in soil water and will form "salts" in the water. If you continue to add more fertilizer when plants haven't yet used the fertilizer already present, the water in the soil becomes so "salty" that it "burns" the plant's roots by removing water from them. Excess soluble salts accumulate as whitish crust on the surface of the growing medium and/or near the rim of the container.

Before feeding plants, consider the following:

• **Plant type**—Some plants are heavy feeders (e.g., Ficus species), while others need little or no additional fertilizer for months, (e.g., succulents).

• **Volume of soil**—How much growing medium is present—smaller size pots require less fertilizer compared to larger size pots because the first contain less soil.

• **Light intensity**—The higher the light levels, the more nutrients are needed for plant growth.

A newly purchased, healthy plant rarely needs an immediate application of fertilizer. In most cases the amount of fertilizer applied by the commercial producer while growing the plant will supply enough nutrients for two to three months in the home. This rule is flexible and if deficiency symptoms are evident fertilizer application is desirable.

The secret to fertilizing plants indoors is to apply small amounts of fertilizer as the plant grows. Without new growth, the plant has only a limited need for more fertilizer. During winter when light levels are reduced, a plant's need for fertilizer is reduced. During summer when light levels increase and the plant is growing, its need for fertilizer is increased. As a starting point, use about ¼ the label rate for monthly applications.

If the overall plant color becomes lighter green, fertilize every two weeks. If the new growth is dark green but leaves are small and internodes seem longer than on older growth, decrease the fertilizer rate.

Different forms of fertilizer are available to the indoor gardener. Many fertilizers come in a specially designed formula for indoor plants. Generally, they contain less of a percentage of the required mineral elements to help avoid the overfertilization problems.

Growing Medium

The growing medium serves the purpose of providing anchorage, water and minerals. When repotting plants, make sure that the new mix is well drained and aerated, holds water and nutrients well, and is at the right pH (5 - 6.5). Good potting mix provides ample amounts of oxygen to the root system. Most professional mixes are good to use. Some plants require special type mixes, e.g. bromeliads, orchids, and African violets. Either purchase these mixes or prepare your own. Below are some formulas that can be used to prepare a homemade potting mix.

Growing Mix for Flowering Houseplants—The following soil mix will grow acceptable flowering plants in most homes for most gardeners:

Mix   1 part garden loam or potting soil

1 part sand or perlite or vermiculite

1 part peat moss

Add 2 to 3 ounces (by weight) of dolomitic limestone to 4 gallons of soil mix and ¾ ounce (by weight) of either bonemeal or 20% superphosphate. After pasteurizing the soil, add about 3 tablespoons of a 6-6-6 or similar ratio fertilizer to each 4 gallons or ½ bushel of soil and add a minor element mix. Follow the manufacturer's recommendations for minor (trace) elements.

Growing Mixes for Foliage Plants—Although most foliage plants will grow satisfactorily in the soil mix recommended for flowering house plants, they will grow better if the soil mix contains a higher percentage of organic matter.

Mix   1 part garden loam or potting soil

1 part sand or vermiculite

2 parts peat moss

or

1 part pine bark

2 parts peat moss

or

1 part pine bark

1 part sand or vemiculite

1 part peat moss

Add 2 to 3 ounces (dry weight) of dolomitic limestone to 4 gallons (½ bushel) of soil mix. For fluoride sensitive plants, the pH of the soil should be adjusted so it is no lower than 6.5. Superphosphate contains enough fluoride to cause foliar burn on sensitive plants. After pasteurizing the soil, add 3 tablespoons of a 6-6-6 or other fertilizer ratio as 5-10-5 to each half bushel. Plastic coated fertilizers can also be used; most of them require about 2 ounces per half bushel. Add a minor element mix to the soil mix.

Growing Mixes for Bromeliads—Bromeliads are plants from Central and South America, which are either epiphytic (grow on tree branches or in crotches of trees) or terrestrial (grow in the ground). Although most of the bromeliads can be grown successfully in foliage plant mixes, most grow better in specially designed soil mixes. Any mix for bromeliads must be well aerated and drained.

Mix   2 parts peat moss

1 part perlite

1 part fir bark

or

1 part peat

1 part pine bark

or

1 part peat

1 part pine bark

1 part cypress shavings

Add 2 ounces of dolomitic limestone to half bushel (4 gallons) of soil mix and a minor element mix. Dissolve 1 ounce of 10-10-10 water-soluble fertilizer in 3 gallons of water. Use this solution after repotting and once a month to water the soil, and add a little to the water in the vase formed by the overlapping leaf bases.

Growing Mixes for Orchids—Orchids have a great deal in common with bromeliads. They also grow on trees as epiphytes and on the ground as terrestrials. A mix for orchids should have excellent drainage and aeration. Some soil mixes that can be used are:

Mix   3 parts osmunda tree fern fiber (moisten before using by soaking in water for 12 hours)

1 part redwood bark

or

Tree fern slabs may also be used to grow epiphytic orchids.

or

5 parts fir bark

1 part perlite

Add 1 ounce (dry weight) of dolomitic limestone per half bushel (4 gallons). Do not add fertilizer to the mix, but fertilize after the plants are potted. Use ¼ ounce of liquid 10-10-10 with minor elements per gallon of water and fertilize once every 6 weeks if the plants are growing in osmunda fern. If plants are growing in fir bark, use a liquid 30-10-10 with minor elements every 6 weeks instead of a 10-10-10.

Growing Mix for Succulents and Cacti—Cacti and other succulents grow best in a well-drained and aerated soil. A good mix is:

Mix   2 parts garden loam or potting soil

2 parts sand

2 parts peat

1 part perlite (or substitute crushed charcoal)

Add 2 ounces (dry weight) of dolomitic limestone to per half bushel (4 gallons) of soil mix, 2 ounces (by weight) of bonemeal, and ½ ounce of superphosphate. After pasteurizing the soil, add a minor element supplement.

Growing Mix for Ferns—Ferns grow well in most recommended mixes with a high proportion of organic matter with good soil aeration and drainage characteristics. Use any of the suggested foliage plant mixes. However, most ferns kept indoors grow better in the following mix:

Mix   1 part garden loam or potting soil

   1 part peat moss

   1 part pine bark

   1 part coarse sand

Add 2 ounces (dry weight) of dolomitic limestone to per half bushel (4 gallons) of soil mix and ½ ounce of either bonemeal or 20% superphosphate. After pasteurizing the soil mix, add minor elements to the mix. Add 1 tablespoon of a 6-6-6 fertilizer or similar ratio to each half bushel of mix.

Growing Mix for African Violets—Any number of soil mixes for African violets exist and most of them will grow well-formed plants. A good mix should be well drained and aerated. The following soil mix should produce excellent plants:

Mix   2 parts peat moss

   1 part vermiculite

   1 part perlite

Before pasteurizing the soil, add 2½ tablespoons of dolomite and 1½ tablespoons of 20% superphosphate to each half bushel. After pasteurization, add 3 tablespoons of a high phosphorous fertilizer as a 5-10-5 or similar ratio.

Acclimatization

The acclimatization process is very important for the health and growth of indoor plants. Acclimatization is the adaptation of a plant to a new environment. In the greenhouse, plants are accustomed to high light and nutrition, high water supply, high temperatures and high relative humidity, conditions which are ideal for fast growth. The home, with its low light and low relative humidity, is most likely going to be a stressful experience for them. The greater the difference between the previous environment and the environment of the house, the greater the stress the plant endures.

Acclimatization is generally done in the greenhouse or the nursery. Plants are grown for a period of time under low light levels and less nutrients. Since this slows down plant growth, acclimatized plants are not ready for the market as early as non-acclimatized plants. Acclimatized plants cost more compared to non-acclimatized plants but this is money well spent.

You can do your own acclimatization as well. Place newly purchased plants in bright areas in the home, at least for a three to four weeks, then move to a final location. The porch or patio can be the first place for your plants in the warm months, as long as the plants are not in direct sunlight. The most common change occurs to plants once placed indoors is defoliation. As long as it is not extensive, and slows down after a few weeks, the plants are going to be doing well in that particular location. Keep in mind, however, that each time the plant is moved around, it will undergo an acclimatization period, and some changes might become evident.

Learn as much as possible about the extent of acclimatization of the chosen plants. The retailer should be able to provide this information. When shopping for plants at a garden center, ask if the plants have been acclimatized.

Remember that the most important factors about plant growth indoors are adequate light, and fertilizer, and water at reduced rates.

What should you look for when shopping for indoor plants? Buy only healthy-looking plants with medium to dark green foliage (unless foliage is supposed to be of different color). Avoid plants with spotted, yellow or brown leaves. If the plant is unhealthy from the nursery, chances are that it will die before long once placed indoors. Look for pests on the undersides of leaves. Remove the plant from the pot and examine the root system. Healthy roots are generally white; roots should be visible along the outside of the soil ball. Roots should have a healthy, earthy odor.

Any discolorations, generally brown or blackened roots, are signs of problems. Some plants have roots with colors other than white, such as some Dracaenas, which have orange roots. Unhealthy roots also may smell bad. If shopping for ferns do not be alarmed if you see brown-colored spots or long rows of structures on the lower leaf surface. These are reproductive structures.

Selecting Containers

Planters can enhance the decorative value of the plants. In selecting a planter, consider:

• Suitability for the plant's needs
• Suitability for the needs of the individual and the environment
• Cost and availability
• Strength and durability
• Drainage
• Weight

The style and shape of the container should complement the plants grown. The size of the container should match the size of the plants being grown. Small containers are best for small slow-growing plants, while fast-growing plants are better suited for large containers.

Containers can be made from a wide range of materials: terra-cotta, clay, plastics, or ceramic. Terra-cotta pots are made of fired clay and are some of the most popular choices, ranging from plain to ornate in design. Plants perform very well in terra-cotta pots because of the porous surface allowing good air exchange to the plant roots. Other clay containers not considered terra-cotta range in color from gray to brown, depending on the clay used. Clay pots can be glazed or unglazed. The unglazed ones restrict air exchange but they offer more design choices. The disadvantages of clay containers is that they are heavy, especially the large ones, and prone to chipping and breaking.

Plastic pots have evolved from very simple to quite elaborate. They are made of materials such as polyethylene, polyurethane, recycled plastic, fiberglass and other materials. They have the advantage of lightweight and chip- and break-resistant. Air exchange and water evaporation are generally lower in plastic containers compared to clay containers. Plants in plastic pots will not dry out as fast as plants in clay pots and therefore the danger of over-watering is greater.

In general, there are two types of containers: ones with drainage holes and ones without. Do not allow plants in containers with drainage holes to sit in saucers filled with water, unless the plant is suspended above the water level by a layer of rocks. To avoid salt buildup, leach the soil once a month by applying a gallon of water to every cubic foot of potting medium. After a few hours follow with half a gallon of water. If the potting medium contains soil, apply 5 gallons of water per every cubic foot of growing medium.

Containers without drainage holes work well for plants such as Peace Lily, Spathiphyllum, which needs plenty of water. They should not be used for cacti and succulents.

Pruning, Grooming, Cleaning, and Repotting

When is the best time to prune? "When the knife is sharp" goes the old saying, and it means using the natural life cycles as a guide. For example, when the plant is growing rapidly and you want to maintain a certain size, this is a good time to prune. It is advisable to do light, frequent pruning, which is the removal of shoots or shoot tips when they are small, also known as pinching. Pinching also will increase branching on the stem and the result will be a stockier, fuller plant.

When the plant has outgrown its container and needs more space to grow, root pruning should be applied. Do this by pulling away roots from the soil mass and cutting back to within one inch of the soil mass. The alternative method is to make 3 or 4 vertical cuts one inch deep in the soil ball on the opposite sides of the root ball. If re-using containers make sure that they are clean, wash out any old compost, chemical or paint residues.

A clean plant is a healthy plant. Water guttation may accumulate salts along the leaf margins and/or tips creating necrotic areas. Dust dulls normal leaf coloration thus lessening plant value. Dust creates shade on plant surfaces reflecting light that can be used in photosynthesis. Dust on lower leaf surfaces may clog stomata (specialized cells involved in water transpiration), inhibiting gas exchange within the leaf. Leaves with thick, shiny cuticles (Croton, Ficus, Peace Lily, Bromeliads) can be cleaned with a damp sponge.

If the plant is small, dip the foliage in tepid water, and swirl it around. Water should not be used when cleaning cacti, African violet leaves, and other plants with hairy leaves. On these, use a clean, small brush to remove dust. When cleaning a flowering plant, remove dead flowers regularly. Leaves with tip and/or marginal necrosis, such as fluoride damage, should be trimmed to the healthy part. Dead leaves should be either pulled out or cut off.

If the plant has been growing well, it will likely need repotting. The decision to repot should be based on plant appearance; repot if it is top-heavy, if it fills the container with new shoots, or it has extensive root growth out of the pot's drainage holes.

Ideally, plants should be repotted in one-inch increments. Planting into too large container will give the roots more soil than they need initially. The excess soil will hold extra moisture, creating too wet conditions. It is better to increase pot size through smaller increments than to double the pot size in one step.

Pests and Diseases

Very few plants stay pest- and/or disease-free forever. Pests are more likely to be encountered on indoor plants compared to diseases. This is because the interior environment rarely offers favorable conditions for foliar diseases to develop. However, when plants are grown under stressful conditions such as low light and excess water, soil-borne pathogens can be found.

Scales are ⅛-inch to ⅓-inch long, with different color depending on the species.

The three main families of scales are armored (the body covering can be separated from the body), soft (the body covering cannot be separated from the body), and mealybugs. Scales attack leaves and stems, sucking plant juices, causing stunting, leaf discoloration, and death of the tissue. With exception of armored scales, honeydew is also excreted. Scales are usually inconspicuous, and by the time an infestation is noted the population is usually very large.

Mealybugs are soft-bodied, ⅕-inch to ⅓-inch long, covered by white, waxy filaments, giving them a white, cottony appearance. Insects are frequently found on the new growth at the stem apex where they suck plant juices, causing leaf wilting and abscission. Some species of mealybugs appear first on the undersides of leaves. Mealybugs excrete sticky honeydew, which attracts sooty mold.

Aphids are soft-bodied, pear-shaped, ¹⁄₂₅″ to ⅛″ long, usually green in color, may be pink, blue, brown, yellow or black. Insects are found on new growth or on the underside of young leaves, where they suck plant juices, causing deformed, curled growth of new leaves, buds, and flowers. Aphids excrete sticky "honeydew", on which grows a black fungus called sooty mold. Aphids can be wingless or winged. Winged forms develop when colonies become too large.

Spider mites are the most common and destructive mites on foliage plants, referred to as two-spotted spider mites, red spider mite or red spiders. The adult females are about ¹⁄₅₀-inch long, hardly visible with unaided eye. They feed on undersides of young leaves. Infected areas are grayish or yellowed speckled. Webs form as a means of spreading. Hot and dry conditions are favorable for spider mites. Mites are the second most common pest problem on houseplants.

Thrips are not as common pests on houseplants but are common on plants in patios, and other outdoor areas. Thrips are small, slender, ¹⁄₂₅″ to ¹⁄₁₂″ long, tan, black, or brown in color, with lighter markings. Adults and larvae feed on young bud tissue, shoot apex, or flowers and leaves by sucking sap and cell contents. Injured tissue has a whitish or silver-flecked appearance due to the light, which is reflected from the cell walls of the empty cells.

What to Do for Plant Problems

Pests—

• The best method is prevention - purchase pest-free plants.

• Take the affected plant outside in a protected, shaded area, where natural predators will most likely come and rid plant of the pest.

• Treat with insecticidal soap. Best is to treat plants, which have been hardened off in the interior environment. New plants, if they have not been acclimatized (used to lower light, less fertilizer and water), are going to be tender, and should be treated after the first couple of weeks.

• Wipe foliage and stems with soapy water and soft cloth. Use 2 teaspoons of insecticidal soap per gallon of water.

• Remove light infestation of mealybugs or aphids with a cotton swab dipped in rubbing alcohol.

• Heavy infestations may be too extensive to treat. Discard these plants but do not put them in your compost pile.

• Do not use beneficial insects! They may work great in the greenhouse with thousands of plants and pests but there is just not enough food in your home to sustain their population. Most pests can be controlled culturally on indoor plants without the use of chemicals.

Diseases—

Another potential problem in the indoor garden is the occurrence of various diseases. For a disease to happen, three factors must be present: a susceptible plant, a viable pathogen, and a favorable environment. Since the home has very low relative humidity and you are most likely to apply water directly to the growing medium thus keeping the foliage dry, chances of a foliar disease occurring are minimal.

Most commonly, leaf spots will be seen. However, they are usually not caused by a disease. For example leaf scalds occur when leaf water droplets on the leaves act as lenses and focus excessive light in one spot, thus causing bleaching of chlorophyll and death of the underlying tissue. Signs of a disease are spots with patterns: tan center, dark border and a light halo. Often dark structures on the underside of the spot are present. These contain disease spores, means of spreading. Bacterial diseases cause spots, soft spots, and wilts. The signs of a fungal disease are sooty molds, rusts, mildews, rots, cankers, spots, and wilts. Viral diseases cause mottling, distortion, and dwarfing

Most importantly, avoid causing stress to plants; a healthy plant is much more likely to fight off a disease than a stressed one. Use a simplified key for identifying the causal agent for a disease.

When plants are stressed, most commonly you will find soil-borne pathogens. They invade plants at or below the soil line, and disease development is usually well underway before symptoms are noted on plant parts aboveground. This disease type is most common when the growing medium is kept excessively moist. Low light and over-watering are the most frequent causes for creating a favorable environment for soil-borne diseases indoors. **The most common causes of stress in interior plants are low light and over-watering.**

Table 3 on the following pages provides a listing of over 300 plants and their cultural requirements. Guidelines, abbreviations and coding numbers (listed below) are used to simplify cultural care. The cultural care guidelines apply to indoor plants while actively growing.

Summary Of Cultural Care Key

L = Light
(1) Sunny light areas: At least 4 hours of direct sun.
(2) High light areas: Over 200 foot candles, but not direct sun.
(3) Medium light areas: 75 to 200 foot candles.
(4) Low light areas: 25 to 75 foot candles.
T = Temperature
(1) Cool: 50°F night, 65°F day temperatures.
(2) Average: 65°F night, 75°F day temperatures.
(3) Warm: 70°F night, 85°F day temperatures.
H = Relative Humidity
(1) High: 50% or higher.
(2) Average: 25% to 49%.
(3) Low: 5% to 24%.
W = Watering
(1) Keep soil mix moist.
(2) Surface of soil mix should dry before rewatering.
(3) Soil mix can become moderately dry before rewatering.
S = Suggested Soil Mix (Specific ingredients are listed in this chapter. The soil mixes are keyed as follows:)
(1) Flowering house plants
(2) Foliage plants
(3) Bromeliads
(4) Orchids
(5) Succulents and cacti
(6) Ferns
(7) African violets and other Gesneriads

Table 3. Summary of cultural care of indoor plants

BOTANICAL NAME	COMMON NAME	LIGHT	TEMPERATURE	HUMDITY	WATERING	SOIL
				Cultural Care*		
Abutilon hybridum	**Flowering Maple**	1	1	2	2	1
Acalypha hispida	Chenile Plant	1	2	2	2	1
Achimenes hybrids	**Magic Flower**	2	2	2	1	7
Acorus calamus	Sweet Flag	2-3	2	2	1	2
Acorus gramineus	**Minature Sweet Flag**	2-3	2	2	1	2
Adiantum raddianum	Maidenhair Fern	2-3	2	1	1	6
Adromischus cristatus	**Crinkle-Leaf Plant**	2-3	2	2	2	5
Adromischus festivus	Plover Eggs	2-3	2	2	2	5
Aechmea fasciata	**Silver Vase**	2-3	2	2	2	3
Aechmea miniata 'Dis-color'	Purplish Coral Berry	2-3	2	2	2	3
Aechmea 'Royal Wine'	**Royal Wine Bromeliad**	2-3	2	2	1	3
Aeschynanthus marmo-ratus	Zebra Basket Vine	2	2	2	1	7
Aeschynanthus pulcher	**Lipstick Vine**	2	2	2	1	7
Agave Americana 'Mar-ginata'	Variegated Century Plant	1	2	3	3	5
Agave victoriae-reginae	**Queen Agave**	1	2	2	2	5
Aglaonema commutatum elegans	Commutatum	3-4	2	2	2	2
Aglaonema costatum	**Spotted Evergreen**	3-4	2	1	2	2
Aglaonema crispum	Pewter Plant	3-4	2	2	2	2
Aglaonema 'Fransher'	**Fransher**	3-4	2	2	2	2
Aglaonema modestum	Chinese Eergreen	3-4	2	2	2	2
Aglaonema 'Silver King'	**Silver King**	3-4	2	2	2	2
Aglaonema 'Silver Queen'	Silver Queen	3-4	2	2	2	2
Aglaonema simplex	**Simplex**	3-4	2	2	2	2
Allamanda cathartica	Allamanda	1	2	1-2	2	1
Alloplectus nummularia	**Miniature Pouch Flower**	2-3	2	1-2	1	7
Alocasia x chantrieri	Chantrieri	2-3	2	1-2	1	2
Aloe aborescens	**Candelabra Plant**	1	3	3	3	5
Aloe barbadensis	Medicine Plant	1	3	3	3	5
Aloe brevifolia	**Brevifolia Aloe**	1	3	3	3	5
Aloe ciliaris	Climbing Aloe	1	3	3	3	5
Aloe humilis echinata	**Hedgehog Aloe**	1	3	3	3	5
Ananas comosus	Pineapple	1-2	2	2	1	3
Anthurium andraeanum	**Oilcloth Flower**	2-3	2	1-2	1	2

See key in preceding text

Table 3. Summary of cultural care of indoor plants

BOTANICAL NAME	COMMON NAME	LIGHT	TEMPERATURE	HUMDITY	WATERING	SOIL
Anthurium clarinervium	Dwarf Crystal Anthurium	2-3	2	1-2	1	2
Anthurium hookeri	Birdsnest Anthurium	2-3	2	1-2	1	2
Anthurium magnificum	False Crystal Anthurium	2-3	2	1-2	1	2
Anthurium scherzeranum	Flamingo Flower	2-3	2	1-2	1	6
Aphelandra squarrosa	Zebra Plant	2	2	2	1	2
Araucaria heterophylla	Norfolk Island Pine	2-3	2	2	1	2
Ardissa crenata	Ardisia	2-3	2	2	1	2
Ascocentrum miniatum	Miniatum	2-3	2	2	2	4
Asparagus densiflorus 'Myers'	Plume Asparagus	2-3	2	2	2	2
Asparagus densiflorus 'Sprengeri'	Sperengeri Fern	2-3	2	2	2	2
Asparagus falcatus	Sickle Thorn	2-3	2	2	2	2
Aspidistra elatior	Cast Iron Plant	3-4	2	3	2	2
Asplenium daucifolium	Mother Fern	3	2	2	1	6
Asplenium nidus	Bird's Nest Fern	3	2	2	1	6
Astrophytum myriostigma	Bishop's Cap	2	2	3	3	5
Beaucarnea recurvata	Ponytail	1	2	3	3	5
Begonia cubensis	Cuban Holly	2-3	2	2	2	2
Begonia metallica	Metallic Leaf Begonia	2-3	2	2	2	2
Begonia x rex-cultorum	Rex Begonia	2-3	2	2	2	2
Begonia semperflorens	Wax Begonia	1-2	1	2	2	1
Billbergia nutans	Queen's Tears	2-3	2	2	2	3
Billbergia pyramidalis	Urn Plant	2-3	2	2	2	3
Billbergia zebrina	Zebra Plant	2-3	2	2	2	3
Bougainvillea spp.	Bougainvillea	1	2	3	3	1
Brassaia actinophylla	Schefflera	2-3	2	2	2	2
Brassaia arboricola	Dwarf Schefflera	2-3	2	2	2	2
Caladium spp.	Caladium	2	2	1	1	2
Calathea insignis	Rattlesnake Plant	2-3	2	2	1	2
Calathea makoyana	Peacock Plant	2-3	2	2	1	2
Calathea micans	Miniature Maranta	2-3	2	2	1	2
Calathea roseopicta	Rose Calathea	2-3	2	2	1	2
Calceolaria crenatiflora	Slipperwort	2	1	1	1	1
Callisia elegans	Striped Inch Plant	2-3	2	2	2	2
Carissa grandiflora 'Bonsai'	Bonsai Natal Plum	1-2	2-3	2	2	1

See key in preceding text

Table 3. Summary of cultural care of indoor plants

BOTANICAL NAME	COMMON NAME	LIGHT	TEMPERATURE	HUMDITY	WATERING	SOIL
Carissa grandiflora 'Boxwood Beauty'	Boxwood Beauty	1-2	2-3	2	2	1
Caryota mitis	Fishtail Palm	2-3	2	2	2	2
Catharanthus roseus	Madagascar Periwinkle	1-2	2	1-2	2	1
Cereus peruvianus	Peruvian Apple Cactus	1	2-3	3	3	5
Ceropegia woodii	Rosary Vine	2-3	2	2	2	5
Chamaedorea elegans	Parlor Palm	3-4	2	2	2	2
Chamaedorea erumpens	Bamboo Palm	3-4	2	2	2	2
Chamaerops humilis	European Fan Palm	2-3	2	2	2	2
Chirita lavandulacea	Hindustan Gentian	2-3	2	1-2	1	7
Chlorophytum comosum 'Variegatum'	Variegated Spider Plant	2-3	2	2	1	2
Chlorophytum comosum 'Vittatum'	Spider Plant	2-3	2	2	1	2
Chrysalidocarpus lutescens	Areca Palm	2-3	2	2	1	2
Chrysanthemum morifolium	Chrysanthemum	1	2	2	1	1
Cissus antarctica	Kangaroo Vine	2-3	2	2	2	2
Cissus rhombifolia	Grape Leaf Ivy	2-3	2	2	2	2
Cissus rotundifolia	Wax Cissus	2	2	3	3	2
Cissus striata	Miniature Grape Ivy	2-3	2	2	2	2
Citrofortunella mitis	Calamondin Orange	1-2	1	2	2	1
Clivia miniata 'Grandiflora'	Kafir Lily	2	2	2	2	1
Codiaeum variegatum	Croton	1	2	1	1	2
Coffea Arabica	Coffee	2	2	2	2	1
Colummea hybrids	Goldfish Plant	2-3	2	1-2	1	7
Cordyline terminalis	Ti Plant	2	1-2	2	2	2
Crassula argentea	Jade Plant	2-3	2	2	2	2
Crassula falcata	Propeller Plant	1-2	2	2	3	5
Crassula hemisphaerica	Arab's Turban	1-2	2	2	3	5
Crassula lycopodioides	Toy Cypress	1-2	2	2	2	5
Crassula schmidtii	Red Flowering Crassula	2-3	2	2	2	5
Crassula teres	Rattlesnake Tail	2-3	2	3	3	5
Crossandra infundibuliformis	Crossandra	2	2	2	1	1

See key in preceding text

Table 3. Summary of cultural care of indoor plants

BOTANICAL NAME	COMMON NAME	LIGHT	TEMPERATURE	HUMDITY	WATERING	SOIL
Cryptanthus bivittatus 'Minor'	Dwarf Rose Stripe Star	2	2	2	2	3
Cryptanthus fosteranus	Stiff Pheasant Leaf	2	2	2	2	3
Cryptanthus zonatus	Zebra Plant	2	2	2	2	3
Cyrtomium falcatum 'Rochfordianum'	House Holly Fern	2-3	2	2	2	6
Davallia fejeensis	Rabbit's Foot Fern	2-3	2	1	1	3
Dieffenbachia amoena	Giant Dumb Cane	2-3	2	2	2	2
Dieffenbachia x bausei	Bausei Dumb Cane	3	2	2	2	2
Dieffenbachia 'Exotica Perfection'	Exotica Perfection	2-3	2	2	2	2
Dieffenbachia leopoldii	Leopold's Dumb Cane	3	2	2	2	2
Dieffenbachia maculata	Spotted Dumb Cane	3	2	2	2	2
Dizygotheca elegantissima	False Aralia	2-3	2	2	2	2
Dracaena angustifolia honoriae	Narrow-Leaved Pleomele	2-3	2	2	2	2
Dracaena arborea	Tree Dracaena	2-3	2	2	2	2
Dracaena deremensis 'Janet Craig'	Janet Craig	2-4	2	2	2	2
Dracaena deremensis 'Warneckii'	Warneckii	2-4	2	2	2	2
Dracaena fragrans 'Massangeana'	Corn Plant	2-3	2	2	2	2
Dracaena goldieana	Queen of Dracaenas	2-3	2	1-2	2	2
Dracaena hookerana	Leather Dracaena	3-4	2	2	2	2
Dracaena marginata	Marginata	2-4	2	2	2	2
Dracaena surculosa	Gold Dust Dracaena	2-4	2	2	2	2
Dracaena surculosa 'Florida Beauty'	Florida Beauty	2-4	2	2	2	2
Dyckia brevifolia	Sawblade Plant	1-2	2	3	2-3	2
Dyckia fosterana	Silver and Gold Dyckia	1-2	2	3	2-3	3
Echeveria agavoides	Molded Wax	1-2	2	3	3	5
Echeveria elegans	Mexican Snowball	1-2	2	3	3	5
Echinocereus reichenbachii	Lace Cactus	1-2	2	3	3	5
Epidendrum atropurpureum	Spice Orchid	2	2	1-2	1	4
Epiphyllum hybrids	Orchid Cacti	2	2	2	2	1
Epipremnum aureum	Golden Pothos	2-4	2	2	2	2
Epipremnum aureum 'Marble Queen'	Marble Queen Pothos	2-4	2	2	2	2

See key in preceding text

Table 3. Summary of cultural care of indoor plants

BOTANICAL NAME	COMMON NAME	LIGHT	TEMPERATURE	HUMDITY	WATERING	SOIL
Episcia cupreata	Flame Violet	2	2-3	1	1	7
Episcia dianthiflora	Lace-Flower Vine	2	2-3	1	1	7
Episcia reptans	Scarlet Violet	2	2-3	1	1	7
Euphorbia coeralescens	Blue Euphorbia	2-3	2	2-3	2-3	5
Euphorbia mammillaris	Corncob Cactus	1	2	2-3	3	5
Euphorbia milii splendens	Crown-of-Thorns	1	2	2-3	3	5
Euphorbia obesa	Gingham Golf Ball	1	2	3	3	5
Euphorbia pulcherrima	Poinsettia	1-2	2	2	2	1
Euphorbia tirucalli	Milkbush	1-2	2	2	2	1
Fatshedera lizei	Botanical Wonder Plant	2-3	1-2	2	2	2
Fatsia japonica	Japanese Aralia	3-4	1-2	2	2	2
Ficus benjamina	Benjamina	1-3	2	2	2	2
Ficus deltoidea	Mistletoe Ficus	2-3	2	2	2	2
Ficus elastica 'Decora'	Rubber Plant	1-3	2-3	2	2	2
Ficus lyrata	Fiddle-Leaf Fig	1-3	2	2	2	2
Ficus pumila 'Mimima'	Dwarf Creeping Fig	2-3	2	2	2	2
Ficus retusa	Cuban Laurel	2-3	2	2	2	2
Ficus sagittata	Rooting Fig	2-3	2	2	2	2
Ficus willdemaniana	Dwarf Fiddle-Leaf Fig	2-3	2	2	2	2
Fittonia verschaffeltii	Red-Nerved Fittonia	2-3	2	1	1	2
Fittonia verschaffeltii argyroneura	Silver-Nerved Fittonia	2-3	2	1	1	2
Fuchsia hybrida	Fuchsias	2	1-2	1	1	1
Gasteria hybrida	Ox Tongue	2	2	2	3	5
Gastrolea beguinii	Lizard Tail	2	2	2	3	5
Graptopetalum amethystinum	Jewel Leaf Plant	2-3	2	2-3	3	5
Guzmania lingulata 'Major'	Scarlet Star	2	2	1	2	3
Guzmania monostachia	Striped Torch	2	2	1	2	3
Gymnocalycium mihanovichii	Plain Cactus	1-2	2	3	3	5
Gynura aurantiaca 'Purple Passion'	Purple Passion	2-3	2	2	2	2
Haworthia cuspidata	Star Window Plant	1-2	2	3	2-3	5
Haworthia fasciata	Zebra Haworthia	1-2	2	3	2-3	5
Haworthia subfasciata	Little Zebra Plant	2	2	3	2-3	5
Haworthia truncata	Clipped Window Plant	1-2	2	3	3	5
Hedera canariensis	Algerian Ivy	2-3	1-2	2	2	1

See key in preceding text

Table 3. Summary of cultural care of indoor plants

BOTANICAL NAME	COMMON NAME	LIGHT	TEMPERATURE	HUMDITY	WATERING	SOIL
Hedera helix	English Ivy	2-3	1-2	2	2	1
Hemigraphis alternate 'Exotica'	Waffle Plant	2-3	2	2	2	2
Hibiscus rosa-sinensis	Chinese Hibiscus	1	2	2	2	1
Hippeastrum hybrids	Amaryllis	2	2	2	2	1
Howea belmoreana	Belmore Sentry Palm	3-2	2	2	2	2
Howea forsterana	Kentia Palm	2-4	2	2	2	2
Hoya carnosa 'Variegata'	Wax Plant	2-3	2	2-3	2	2
Hoya kerrii	Sweetheart Hoya	2	2	2	2	2
Hyacinthus orientalis	Hyacinth	2	1-2	2	1	1
Hylocereus undatus	Honolulu Queen	2-3	2	2	2	5
Impatiens walleriana 'Variegata'	Impatiens, Busy Lizzie	2-3	2	2	2	1
Ixora coccinea	Ixora	1	2	2	2	1
Jatropha integerrima	Peregrina	1	2	2	2	1
Justicia brandegeana	Shrimp Plant	1-2	2	2	2	1
Kalanchoe blossfeldiana	Christmas Kalanchoe	1-2	2	2	2	1
Kalanchoe fedtschenkoi	Purple Scallops	1-2	2	2-3	3	5
Kalanchoe pumila	Flower Dust Plant	1-2	2	2-3	3	5
Kalanchoe tomentosa	Panda Plant	1-2	2	2-3	3	5
Macropiper excelsum	Lofty Pepper	2-3	2	2	2	2
Malvaviscus arboreus	Turk's Cap	1	2	2	1	1
Mammillaria bocasana	Powder Puff	1-2	2	3	3	5
Mammillaria compressa	Mother of Hundreds	1-2	2	3	3	5
Mammillaria geminispina	Whitey	1-2	2	3	3	5
Manettia inflata	Firecracker Plant	2	2	1-2	2	1
Maranta leuconeura 'Erythroneura'	Red Nerve Plant	2-3	2	2	2	2
Maranta leuconeura 'Kerchoviana'	Prayer Plant	2-3	2	2	2	2
Maranta leuconeura 'Leuconeura'	Silver Feather Maranta	2-3	2	2	2	2
Mikania ternata	Plush Vine	2-3	2	2	2	2
Monstera deliciosa	Philodendron Pertusum	2-4	2	2	2	2
Monstera obliqua	Window Leaf	3	2	2	2	2
Nautilocalyx lynchii	Black Alloplectus	2-3	2	2	1	7
Neoregelia carolinae 'Tricolor'	Tricolor Bromeliad	2-3	2	2	2	3
Neoregelia spectabilis	Fingernail Plant	2-3	2	2	2	3
Neoregelia zonata	Zonata	2-3	2	2	2	3

See key in preceding text

Table 3. Summary of cultural care of indoor plants

BOTANICAL NAME	COMMON NAME	LIGHT	TEMPERATURE	HUMDITY	WATERING	SOIL
Nephrolepis exaltata 'Bostoniensis'	Boston Fern	2-3	2	1-2	2	6
Nephrolepis exaltata 'Fluffy Ruffles'	Fluffy Ruffles	2-3	2	1	2	6
Nephrolepis exaltata 'Whitmanii'	Feather Fern	2-3	2	1	2	6
Nidularium fulgens	Blushing Cup	2-3	2	2	2	3
Nidularium innocentii nana	Miniature Birdsnest	2-3	2	2	1	3
Notocactus rutilans	Pink Ball	1-2	2	3	3	5
Oncidium sphacelatum	Golden Shower	2	2	2	2	4
Opuntia vilis	Little Tree Cactus	1-2	2	3	3	5
Opuntia vulgaris	Irish Mittens	1-2	2	3	3	5
Oxalis braziliensis	Shamrocks	2	2	2	2	2
Oxalis deppei	Good Luck Plant	1-2	2	2	2	1
Oxalis flava	Finger Oxalis	1-2	2	2	2	1
Oxalis hirta	Hirta Oxalis	1-2	2	2	2	1
Oxalis megalorrhiza	Carnosa Oxalis	1-2	2	2	2	1
Oxalis rubra	Red Oxalis	1-2	2	2	2	1
Pachyphytum compactum	Thick Plant	1-2	2	2-3	2-3	5
Pachyphytum oviferum	Pearly Moonstones	1-2	2	2-3	2-3	5
Pachystachys lutea	Yellow Shrimp Plant	2-3	2	2	2	1
Paphiopedilum hybrids	Ladyslipper Orchids	2-3	2	2	1-2	4
Pedilanthus tithymaloides 'Variegatus'	Ribbon Cactus, Devil's Backbone	2-3	2	2	2	5
Pelargonium x domesticum Geranium	Pansy Flowered Geranium	1-2	1-2	2	2	1
Pelargonium graveolens	Rose Geranium	1-2	1-2	2	2	1
Pelargonium hortorum	House Geranium	1-2	1-2	2-3	2	1
Pelargonium peltatum	Ivy Geranium	1-2	1-2	2	2	1
Pellaea rotundifolia	Button Fern	2-3	2	2	1-2	6
Pellionia daveauana	Trailing Watermelon	2-3	2	2	1-2	2
Pellionia pulchra	Satin Pellionia	2-3	2	2	1-2	2
Pentas lanceolata	Egyptian Star Cluster	1	2	2	2	1
Peperomia caperata	Emerald Ripple	2-3	2	2	2	2
Peperomia clusiifolia	Red-Edged Peperomia	2-3	2	2	2	2
Peperomia crassifolia	Leather Peperomia	2-3	2	2	2	2
Peperomia obtusifolia	Baby Rubber Plant	2-3	2	2	2	2
Peperomia obtusifolia 'Variegata'	Variegated Peperomia	2-3	2	2	2	2

See key in preceding text

Table 3. Summary of cultural care of indoor plants

BOTANICAL NAME	COMMON NAME	LIGHT	TEMPERATURE	HUMDITY	WATERING	SOIL
Peperomia orba	Princess Astrid Peperomia	2-3	2	2	2	2
Philodendron bipennifolium	Fiddle-Leaf Philodendron	3-4	2	2	2	2
Philodendron 'Burgundy'	Burgundy	2-4	2	2	2	2
Philodendron 'Emerald Queen'	Emerald Queen	2-4	2	2	2	2
Philodendron 'Florida'	Florida	2-4	2	2	2	2
Philodendron martianum	Flask Philodendron	3	2	2	2	2
Philodendron 'Prince Dubonnet'	Prince Dubonnet	2-4	2	2	2	2
Philodendron 'Red Emerald'	Red Emerald	2-4	2	2	2	2
Philodendron scandens oxycardium	Heart-Leaf Philodendron	2-4	2	2	2	2
Philodendron selloum	Selloum	2-4	2	2	2	2
Phoenix roebelenii	Pigmy Date Palm	2-3	2	2	2	2
Pilea cadierei	Aluminum Plant	2-3	2	1-2	1	2
Pilea microphylla	Artillery Plant	2-3	2	1	1	2
Pittosporum tobira	Japanese Pittosporum	1-3	2	2	2	1
Pittosporum tobira 'Variegata'	Variegated Pittosporum	2	2	2	2	1
Platycerium bifurcatum	Staghorn Fern	2-3	2	2	2	6
Plectranthus australis	Swedish Ivy	2-3	2	2	2	2
Plectranthus australis 'Marginatus'	Candle Plant	2-3	2	2	2	2
Podocarpus macrophyllus 'Maki'	Podocarpus	2-3	2	2	2	2
Polyscias balfouriana 'Marginata'	Variegated Balfour Aralia	2-3	2	2	2	2
Polyscias fruticosa	Ming Aralia	2-3	2	2	2	2
Pteris ensiformis 'Victoriae'	Victorian Table Fern	2-3	2	1	2	2
Punica granatum nana	Dwarf Pomegranate	1	2	2	2	1
Rhapis excelsa	Lady Palm	2-3	2	2	2	2
Rhododendron hybrids	Azaleas	2	1-2	1	1	2
Ruellia graecizans	Red-Spray Ruellia	1-2	2	2	2	1
Saintpaulia hybrids	African Violets	2-3	2	2	1	7
Sansevieria parva	Parva Sansevieria	2-3	2	3	2-3	5
Sansevieria suffruticosa	Spiral Snake Plant	2-3	2	3	2-3	5
Sansevieria trifasciata 'Hahnii'	Birdsnest Sansevieria	2-4	2	3	2-3	5

See key in preceding text

Table 3. Summary of cultural care of indoor plants

BOTANICAL NAME	COMMON NAME	LIGHT	TEMPERATURE	HUMDITY	WATERING	SOIL
Sansevieria trifasciata 'Laurentii'	Gold-Banded Sansevieria	2-4	2	3	2-3	5
Sansevieria trifasciata 'Zeylanica'	Zeylanica	2-4	2	3	2-3	5
Saxifraga stolonifera	Strawberry Geranium	2-3	1-2	2	2	2
Schlumbergera bridgesii	Christmas Cactus	2-3	2	2	2	2
Schlumbergera truncata	Christmas Cactus	2-3	2	2	2	2
Scindapsus pictus	Silver Pothos	3	2	2	2	2
Sedum lucidum	Tortuosum	1-2	2	2-3	2-3	5
Sedum multriceps	Pigmy Joshua Tree	1-2	2	2-3	2-3	5
Sedum spectabile	Showy Sedum	1-2	1-2	2-3	2-3	5
Sempervivum arachniodeum	Cow Web Houseleek	1-2	1-2	2-3	2-3	5
Setcreasea pallida 'Purple Heart'	Purple Heart	1-2	2	2	2	2
Sinningia pusilla	Miniature Slipper Plant	2-3	2	1	1	7
Sinningia speciosa	Gloxinia	2-3	2	1-2	2	7
Soleirolia soleirolii	Baby Tears	2-3	2	1-2	1	2
Spathiphyllum 'Clevelandii'	Peace Lily	2-3	2	2	1	2
Spathiphyllum floribundum	Spathe Flower	2-3	2	2	1	2
Spathiphyllum 'Mauna Loa'	Mauna Loa	2-3	2	2	1	2
Stapelia nobilis	Carrion Flower	1-2	2	2-3	2-3	5
Streptocarpus x hybridus	Cape Primrose	2-3	2	2	2	7
Strobilanthes dyeranum	Persian Shield	2-3	2	2	2	2
Syngonium hoffmanii	Goose Foot	3	2	2	2	2
Syngonium podophyllum	Nephthytis	2-4	2	2	2	2
Syngonium wendlandii	Wendlandii	3	2	2	2	2
Tetranema roseum	Mexican Violet	2-3	2	2	2	1
Trillandsia bulbosa	Dancing Bulb	2	2	2	2	3
Tillandsia lindenii	Blue-Flowered Torch	2	2	2	2	3
Tolmiea menziesii	Piggyback Plant	2	1-2	2	2	2
Tradescantia blossfeldiana	Flowering Inch Plant	2-3	2	2	2	2
Tradescantia sillamontana	White Velvet	2-3	2	2	2	2
Vanilla planifolia	Vanilla	2	2	2	2	3
Vriesea x mariae	Painted Feather	2	2	2	2	3

See key in preceding text

Table 3. Summary of cultural care of indoor plants

BOTANICAL NAME	COMMON NAME	LIGHT	TEMPERATURE	HUMDITY	WATERING	SOIL
Vriesea splendens	Flaming Sword	2	2	2	2	3
Yucca elephantipes	Spineless Yucca	2	2	3	2	2
Zebrina pendula	Wandering Jew	2-3	2	2	2	2
* Adopted from McConnell, D. B. 1978.						
See key in preceding text						

DISCUSSION QUESTIONS

1. How do light, temperature, and relative humidity affect plant growth on indoor plants?

2. What are the guidelines you would use when watering and fertilizing indoor plants?

3. What is acclimatization and how would you recognize an acclimatized plant?

4. How would you select an indoor plant?

5. How often should you prune and what techniques would you use for different indoor plants?

6. How would you repot an overgrown plant?

7. What are the major pests and diseases on indoor plants?

RESOURCES

Manaker, G. H. 1997. *Interior Plantscapes: Installation, Maintenance, and Management.* 3rd ed. Prentice Hall, Upper Saddle River, NJ.

McConnell, D. B. 1978. *The Indoor Gardener's Companion: A Definitive, Color-Illustrated Guide to the Selection and Care of Houseplants.* Van Nostrand Reinhold Company. New York, NY.

D.R. Pittenger, ed., *California Master Gardener Handbook.* Publication 3382. Oakland: University of California Division of Agriculture and Natural Resources.

NOTES

26
Composting

Wayne J. McLaurin

Gary L. Wade

Wade Hutcheson

LEARNING OBJECTIVES

Understand why composting is important in reducing organic waste materials.

Be familiar with how the decomposition processes work.

Know how to build and maintain a compost pile.

Be familiar with benefits and drawbacks of various composting structures.

Know benefits and potential drawbacks of using composted materials in the landscape and garden.

Know how organic materials can be used to amend the soil.

Know how organic materials can be used as mulch in the landscape and garden.

TERMS TO KNOW

Actinomycetes a form of fungi-like bacteria that form long, thread-like branched filaments.

Aerobic composting a decomposition process in the presence of oxygen; the work is done by the combined activities of a wide succession of mixed bacteria, actinomycetes, fungi, and other biological populations.

Anaerobic composting a static method of composting without the presence of oxygen; very little heat is generated, and organic matter is converted into organic acids and ammonia which often results in odors.

Bacteria the smallest living organisms, bacteria are the most numerous decomposers in the composting process.

Compost useable material that is the end product of the decomposition process.

Composting the process by which gardeners convert organic matter into compost.

Fungi a family of simple organisms that lack a photosynthetic pigment.

Heterotrophic capable of deriving energy for life processes only from the decomposition of organic compounds.

Mulching the practice of applying materials such as compost, leaves, or grass clippings to the soil surface to moderate soil temperature and moisture and to control weeds and soil erosion.

Organic matter any material in the soil that was originally produced by living organisms.

INTRODUCTION

Composting is Mother Nature at work. There is nothing secret about it; it happens all the time, all around us, and if it didn't we'd be up to our eyeballs in leaves, limbs, and such.

Landscape refuse, such as leaves, grass clippings, and trimmings, can account for up to 20 percent of the waste being placed in landfills. Bans on outdoor burning and laws that eliminated organic yard debris from being placed into landfills, make compost and mulching attractive alternatives for managing yard refuse and recycling natural materials. Some cities provide composting areas as a means to dispose of grass clippings and leaves; however, many homeowners find it more convenient, economical, and advantageous to compost these materials in their own backyards as finished compost can be used as mulch or as a soil amendment.

Most gardeners know soils can be improved and made more productive by simply mixing organic matter with them. For many years, the most popular source of organic matter for soil improvement has been well-rotted livestock manure, which is now less available, especially for the urban gardener.

Cheaper and more readily available sources of organic residues include plant materials from gardeners' own homes and yards such as grass clippings, uncooked vegetable materials, spoiled fruit and fruit peelings, small twigs, and especially fall leaves. To become usable soil amendments, these materials should undergo a degree of decomposition brought about by certain bacteria, fungi (microbes), and other organisms. Composting is simply a controlled, accelerated version of the natural process of decomposition of organic matter, and the finished product is called compost.

WHY COMPOST?

Composting is the most practical and convenient way to handle yard refuse because it is easier and cheaper than bagging or taking it to a dump site. Compost also benefits soil and the plants growing in it, by improving physical properties such as tilth, infiltration, and drainage and enhancing nutrient and water-holding capacity.

Requirements for Efficient Decomposition

Decomposition of organic material in the compost pile depends on maintaining optimal microbial activity. Any factor that slows or stops microbial growth also impedes the composting process. Composting is probably best described as the farming of microorganisms. Efficient decomposition occurs if aeration, moisture, a food source ("browns" or carbohydrate), and an energy source ("greens" or nitrogen) are available for microbes and other organisms to act upon the small particles of organic material.

Aeration—Oxygen is required for microbes to decompose organic wastes efficiently. Some decomposition can occur in the absence of oxygen (**anaerobic** conditions); however, the process is slow, and foul odors may develop. Because of the odor problem, anaerobic composting is not recommended in a residential setting unless the process is conducted in a fully closed system (see plastic bag method under Composting Structures).

Mixing or turning the pile once or twice a month provides the necessary oxygen and significantly hastens the composting process. A pile that is not mixed or turned may take three to four times longer to decompose. Raising the pile off the ground allows air to be drawn through the mass as the material decomposes. To aid in drawing air into the pile coarse materials should be placed on the bottom as the pile is built, or placed in the pile and raked out after the decomposition starts. Another way to introduce air is to place perforated pipe within the pile.

Moisture—Dry compost will not decompose efficiently. Adequate moisture is essential for microbial activity. The decomposing organisms live on a thin film of water. Proper moisture encourages the growth of microorganisms that break down organic matter into humus. If rainfall is limited, water the pile periodically to maintain a steady decomposition rate. Add enough water so the pile is damp but not soggy; avoid over watering. When placed in the hand, the materials in the compost pile should have the moisture of a wrung-out sponge. Excess water can lead to anaerobic conditions which slow the degradation process and cause foul odors. If the pile should become too wet, turn it to dry it out and restart the process.

Particle Size—Grinding the organic material before composting greatly reduces decomposition time. The smaller the size of the organic refuse particle, the more quickly it can be consumed by the microbes. A shredder is useful for chipping or shredding most yard refuse, and is essential if brush or sticks are to be composted. A low-cost method of reducing the volume of fallen tree leaves is to mow the lawn before raking using the mower's highest mowing setting. Windrow the leaves into long narrow piles one foot high to make the shredding process more efficient. If the mower has an appropriate bag attachment, the shredded leaves can be collected directly. A few twigs and sticks can be left in the pile for aeration.

Organisms Involved in Composting

There are many organisms that break down organic material. Most are not seen by the human eye, but they are present throughout the process. Organisms that are large enough to see are usually associated with the later decomposition stages.

The most important organisms in the breakdown process are the bacteria. The bacteria present in any given compost pile are dependent upon the raw materials present, amount of air in the pile, moisture conditions, pile temperature, and numerous other factors. Bacteria are microscopic: 20,000+ laid end to end may span no more that an inch. Compostable organic materials normally contain a large number and many different types of bacteria, fungi, molds, and other living organisms.

Many types of organisms are required for decomposing different materials, but the necessary variety is usually present in the materials to be composted, and the organisms thrive when environmental conditions are satisfactory. During decomposition, marked changes take place in the nature and abundance of the biological population. Some of the many species will multiply rapidly at first but will dwindle as the environment changes, and other organisms are able to thrive under more varied conditions. Temperature and changes in the available food supply probably exert the greatest influence in determining the species of organisms comprising the population at any one time.

Aerobic composting is a dynamic process in which the work is done by the combined activities of a wide succession of mixed bacteria, actinomycetes, fungi, and other biological populations. Since each organism is suited to a particular environment of relatively limited duration, and each is most active in decomposition of some particular type of organic matter, the activities of one group complement those of another. The mixed populations parallel the complex environments afforded by the heterogeneous nature of the compostable material. Except for short periods during turning, the temperature in a compost pile increases steadily in proportion to the amount of biological activity until equilibrium (state of balance) with subsequent heat loss is reached, or the material becomes well stabilized (humus-like).

In aerobic composting, bacteria, actinomycetes, and fungi are the most active. Mesophilic bacteria (found at lower temperatures, 50 to 115°F) are characteristically predominant at the start and in the early part of the process, soon giving way to thermophilic bacteria (found at higher temperatures, 110 to 150+°F), which inhabit all parts of the stack where the temperature is satisfactory, eventually throughout most of the pile. Thermophilic fungi usually appear after 5 to 10 days, and actinomycetes become prominent in the final stages when short duration, rapid composting is accomplished. Except in the final stages of the composting period when the temperature drops, actinomycetes and fungi are confined to a sharply defined outer zone of the stack, 2 to 6 inches in thickness, beginning just under the outer surface. Some molds also grow in this outer zone. The population of fungi and actinomycetes is often great enough to impart a distinctly grayish-white appearance to this outer zone.

In spite of being confined primarily to the outer layers and becoming active only during the latter part of the composting period, fungi and actinomycetes play an important role in the decomposition of cellulose, lignins, and other more resistant materials, which are attacked after the more readily decomposed materials have been utilized. There are many bacteria that attack cellulose. However, in the parts of compost piles populated chiefly by bacteria, cellulose (paper) breaks down very little, whereas in the layers or areas inhabited by actinomycetes and fungi it becomes almost unrecognizable. Considerable cellulose and lignin decomposition by actinomycetes and fungi can occur near the end of the composting period when the temperatures have begun to drop and the environment in a larger part of the pile is satisfactory for their growth.

It should be noted that since the necessary organisms for composting are usually present and will carry on the process when the environment is suitable, an extensive knowledge of the characteristics of the various organisms is not necessary for understanding a compost pile. Normal maintenance as described in this manual will help to ensure proper balance and numbers of beneficial microorganisms.

Since decomposition is the crux of the composting process, let's take a look at the various organisms that play an essential role in the working compost pile. Most are microscopic, some are large enough to be observed with the unaided eye, but all are beneficial, each having a role in breaking down raw organic matter into finished compost. By far the most important microscopic decomposers are bacteria, which do the lion's share of decomposition in the compost heap. But there are other microscopic creatures such as actinomycetes, fungi, and protozoa, that also play an important role. Together, these are chemical decomposers that change the chemistry of the organic wastes.

The larger fauna in the heap includes mites, millipedes, flatworms, centipedes, sowbugs, snails, slugs, spiders, springtails, beetles, ants, flies, nematodes, and most importantly, earthworms. Collectively, these are called the physical decomposers since they bite, grind, suck, tear, and chew the materials into smaller pieces, making them more suitable for the chemical work of the microscopic decomposers.

All of the organisms, from the microscopic bacteria to the largest of the physical decomposers, are part of a complex food chain in the compost pile. They can be categorized as first-, second-, and third-level consumers, depending upon what they eat and by which group they are eaten. First-level consumers attract and become the food of second-level consumers, which in turn are consumed by third-level consumers. The organisms comprising each level of the food chain serve to keep the populations of the next lower level in check, so that a balance can be maintained throughout the compost. For example, according to Daniel L. Dindal in *Ecology of Compost*, ". . . mites and springtails eat fungi. Tiny feather-winged beetles feed on fungal spores. Nematodes ingest bacteria. Protozoa and rotifers present in water films feed on bacteria and plant particles. Predaceous mites and pseudoscorpions prey upon nematodes, fly larvae, other mites and collembolans. Free-living flatworms ingest gastropods, earthworms, nematodes and rotifers. Third level consumers such as centipedes, rove beetles, ground beetles, and ants prey on second level consumers."

Chemical Decomposers

These organisms are the initial inhabitants of the pile. Many of them are unseen and come in with the materials that make up the pile. These organisms are around all of the time and only need to find conditions "to their liking" in order to start their normal functions of breaking down organic materials.

Bacteria—Bacteria likely to be found in a compost heap are aerobic bacteria that specialize in breaking down organic compounds and thrive in temperatures ranging up to 170°F (77°C). Bacterial populations differ from pile to pile, depending upon the raw materials of the compost, degree of heat, amount of air present, moisture level, geographical location of the pile, and

other considerations. They are so small that it would take 25,000 bacteria laid end to end to equal one inch on a ruler, and an amount of garden soil the size of a pea may contain up to a billion bacteria. Most bacteria are colorless and cannot make carbohydrates from sunshine, water, and carbon dioxide the way more complex green plants can. Some bacteria produce colonies; others are free-living. Under the best conditions, a colony of bacteria can multiply into billions in a very short time. The life span of one generation of bacteria is about 20 to 30 minutes, so that one cell may yield a progeny of billions of individuals in half a day.

Bacteria are the most nutritionally diverse of all organisms as a group and can eat nearly anything. Most compost bacteria are heterotrophic, meaning that they can use living or dead organic materials. Some are so adaptable that they can use more than a hundred different organic compounds as their source of carbon because of their ability to produce a variety of enzymes. Usually, they can produce the appropriate enzyme to digest whatever material they find themselves on. Because bacteria are smaller, less mobile, and less complex than most other organisms, they are less able to escape an environment that becomes unfavorable. A decrease in the temperature of the pile or a sharp change in its acidity can render bacteria inactive or kill them. When the environment of a heap begins to change, bacteria that formerly dominated may be decimated by another species.

Actinomycetes—The characteristically earthy smell of newly plowed soil in the spring is caused by actinomycetes, a higher form of bacteria similar to fungi and molds. Actinomycetes are especially important in the formation of humus. While most bacteria are found in the top foot or so of topsoil, actinomycetes may work many feet below the surface. Deep under the roots they convert dead plant matter to a peat-like substance. While they are decomposing animal and vegetable matter, actinomycetes liberate carbon, nitrogen, and ammonia, making nutrients available for higher plants. They are found on every natural substrate, and the majority are aerobic and mesophilic. Five percent or more of the soil's bacterial population consists of actinomycetes.

Protozoa—Protozoa are the simplest form of animal organism. Even though they are single-celled and microscopic in size, they are larger and more complex in their activities than most bacteria. A gram of soil can contain as many as a million protozoa, but a gram of compost has many thousands fewer, especially during the thermophilic stage. Protozoa obtain their food from organic matter in the same way bacteria do, but because they are present in far fewer numbers than are bacteria, they play a much smaller part in the composting process.

Fungi—Fungi are many-celled, filamentous or single-celled primitive plants. Unlike more complex green plants, they lack chlorophyll, and therefore lack the ability to make their own carbohydrates. Most of them are classified as saprophytes because they obtain energy by breaking down organic matter in dying or dead plants and animals. Like the actinomycetes, fungi take over during the final stages of the process when the compost has been changed to a more easily digested form. The best temperature for active fungi in the compost heap is around 70 to 75°F (21–24°C) though some thermophilic forms prefer much greater heat and survive to 120°F (49°C).

Physical Decomposers

The larger organisms that chew and grind their way through the compost heap are higher up in the food chain and are known as physical decomposers. The following is a list of some of the larger physical decomposers that can be found in nearly any compost heap. Most of these creatures function best at medium or mesophilic temperatures, so they will not be in the pile at all times.

Mites—Mites are related to ticks, spiders, and horseshoe crabs because they have in common six leg-like, jointed appendages. They can be free-living or parasitic, sometimes both at once. Some mites are small enough to be invisible to the naked eye, while some tropical species are up to a half-inch in length. Mites reproduce very rapidly, moving through larval, nymph, adult, and dormant stages. They attack plant matter, but some are also second-level consumers, ingesting nematodes, fly larvae, other mites, and springtails.

Millipedes—The wormlike body of the millipede has many leg-bearing segments, each except the front few bearing two pairs of walking legs. Their life cycles are not well understood, except that eggs are laid in the soil in springtime, hatching into small worms. Young millipedes molt several times before gaining their full complement of legs. When they reach maturity, adult millipedes can grow to a length of 1 to 2 inches. They help break down material by feeding directly on it.

Centipedes—Centipedes are flattened, segmented worms with 15 or more pairs of legs, 1 pair per segment. They hatch from eggs laid during the warm months and gradually grow to their adult size. Centipedes are third-level consumers, feeding only on living animals, especially insects and spiders.

Sowbugs—Sowbugs are fat-bodied, flat creatures with distinct segments. In structure, it resembles the crayfish to which it is related. Sowbugs reproduce by means of eggs that hatch into smaller versions of the adults. Since females are able to deposit a number of eggs at one time, sowbugs may become abundant in a compost heap. They are first-level consumers, eating decaying vegetation.

Snails and Slugs—Both snails and slugs are mollusks and have muscular disks on their undersides that are adapted for a creeping movement. Snails have a spirally curved shell, a broad retractable foot, and a distinct head. Slugs, on the other hand, are so undifferentiated in appearance that one species is frequently mistaken for half of a potato. Both snails and slugs lay eggs in capsules or gelatinous masses, and progress through larval stages to adulthood. Their food is generally living plant material, but they will attack fresh garbage and plant debris and will appear in the compost pile. Look for them when you spread your compost and remove them, for if they are introduced into the garden, they can do damage to crops.

Spiders—Spiders, which are related to mites, are one of the least appreciated animals in the garden. These eight-legged creatures are third-level consumers that feed on insects and small invertebrates, and can help control garden pests.

Springtails—Springtails are very small insects, rarely exceeding one-quarter inch in length. They vary in color from white to blue-grey or metallic, and are mostly distinguished by their ability to jump when disturbed. They feed by chewing decomposing plants, pollen, grains, and fungi.

Beetles—The rove beetle, ground beetle, and feather-winged beetle are the most common beetles in compost. Feather-winged beetles feed on fungal spores, while the larger rove and ground beetles prey on other insects as third-level consumers. Beetles are easily visible insects with two pairs of wings, the more forward-placed of these serving as a cover or shield for the folded and thinner back wings that are used for flying. A beetle's immature stage is a soft-skinned grub that feeds and grows during the warm months.

Once grubs are full grown, they pass through a resting or pupal stage and change into hard-bodied, winged adults. Most adult beetles, like the larval grubs of their species, feed on decaying vegetables, while some, like the rove and ground beetles, prey on snails, insects, and other small animals. The black rove beetle is an acknowledged predator of snails and slugs. Some people import them to their gardens when slugs become a problem.

Ants—Ants feed on a variety of material, including aphid honeydew, fungi, seeds, sweets, scraps, other insects, and sometimes other ants. Compost provides some of these foods, and it also provides shelter for nests and hills. They will remain present only when the pile is relatively cool. Ants prey on first-level consumers, and may benefit the composting process by bringing fungi and other organisms in. The work of ants can make compost richer in phosphorus and potassium by moving minerals from one place to another.

Flies—Many flies, (black fungus gnats, soldier flies, minute flies, and houseflies) spend their larval phase in compost as maggots. Adults can feed upon almost any kind of organic material. All flies undergo egg, larval, pupal, and adult stages. The eggs are laid in various forms of organic matter. Houseflies are such effective distributors of bacteria that when an individual fly crawls across a sterile plate of lab gelatin, colonies of bacteria later appear in its tracks. During the early phases of the composting process, flies provide ideal airborne transportation for bacteria on their way to the pile. Keep a layer of dry leaves or grass clippings on top of the pile and cover your garbage promptly while building compost, so that the pile will not provide a breeding place for horseflies, mosquitoes, or houseflies which may become a nuisance to humans. Fly larvae will not survive the thermophilic temperatures in the well-managed compost pile. Mites and other organisms in the pile also keep fly larvae reduced in number. Though many flies die with the coming of frost, the rate of reproduction is so rapid that a few survivors can repopulate an area before the warm season has progressed very far.

Worms—Nematodes or eelworms, free-living flatworms, and rotifers all can be found in compost. Nematodes are microscopic creatures that can be classified into three categories: those that live on decaying organic matter; those that are predators on other nematodes, bacteria, algae, protozoa, etc.; and those that can be serious pests in gardens where they attack the roots of plants. Flatworms, as their name implies, are flattened organisms that are usually quite small in their free-living form. Most flatworms are carnivorous and live in films of water within the compost structure. Rotifers are small, multi-cellular animals that live freely or in tubes attached to a substrate in the pile. Their bodies are round and divisible into three parts: a head, trunk, and tail. They are generally found in films of water, and many forms are aquatic. The rotifers in compost are found in water that adheres to plant substances where they feed on microorganisms.

Earthworms—If bacteria are the champion microscopic decomposers, then the heavyweight champion is doubtlessly the earthworm. Pages of praise have been written to the earthworm ever since it became known that this creature spends most of its time tilling and enriching the soil. The great English naturalist Charles Darwin was the first to suggest that all the fertile areas of this planet have at least once passed through the bodies of earthworms. A compost pile is incomplete and inefficient without them.

The earthworm is an eating machine consisting mainly of an alimentary canal that ingests, decomposes, and deposits casts continually during the earthworm's active periods. As soil or organic matter is passed through an earthworm's digestive system, it is broken up and neutralized by secretions of calcium carbonate from calciferous glands near the worm's gizzard. Once in the gizzard, material is finely ground prior to digestion. Digestive intestinal juices rich in hormones, enzymes, and other fermenting substances, continue the breakdown process. The matter passes out of the worm's body in the form of casts, which are the richest and finest quality of all humus material. Fresh casts are markedly higher in bacteria, organic material, available nitrogen, calcium, magnesium, and available phosphorus and potassium than soil itself.

Earthworms thrive on compost and contribute to its quality through both physical and chemical processes, and they reproduce readily in the well-managed pile. Since earthworms are willing and able to take on such a large part in compost making, it is the wise gardener who adjusts composting methods to take full advantage of the earthworm's special talents and stops worrying when earthworms appear.

Use of Inocula

Composting developments have been accompanied by considerable discussion of the importance of special inocula (bacterial activators), supposedly containing several pure strains of laboratory organisms or other biological factors essential in the decomposition of organic matter and nitrogen fixation, e.g., "enzymes," "hormones," "preserved living organisms," "activated factors," "biocatalyst," etc. In fact, several commercial composting processes are built around the use of some special inoculum often known only to its discoverer and proponent, who claims it to be fundamental to the successful operation of the process. The need of such inocula has always been debatable, and most composting studies have strongly indicated that they are unnecessary.

In composting organic waste containing refuse, manure, vegetable wastes, etc. inocula are not necessary or advantageous. Bacteria are always present in very large numbers in such material and can be eliminated only by drastic sterilization methods. In any case, the number of bacteria is rarely a limiting factor in composting. Provided that the environmental factors are appropriate, the indigenous bacteria, which are much better adapted than forms produced under laboratory conditions, multiply rapidly. Thus, the rate of composting is governed simply by the environmental conditions.

Special enzyme preparations are also advertised as necessary compost "starters." However, the vast number of enzymes involved in decomposition, as well as the difficulty and expense involved in isolating and synthesizing them, would make initiating the composting process with enzymes alone highly impractical even if satisfactory preparations were available. The addition of enzymes to raw compostable materials is unnecessary because bacteria synthesize efficiently and rapidly to all the enzymes required.

Another popular starter is "hormones," a term popularly used to designate the growth factors and vitamins needed by bacteria or other organisms. The organic constituents of mixed, compostable materials usually contain all the growth factors needed for normal growth. Also, growth factors and vitamins are produced by micro-organisms and will undoubtedly be produced in sufficient quantities in a mixed microbial population to meet normal requirements.

A third group of additives, "bio-catalyst" or "activated factors," contains various biological materials that are supposed to activate and accelerate decomposition and stabilization of organic material. In some cases the "activator" supplies some material that is lacking in the compost. For example, straw or paper, which does not contain the necessary biological nutrients, is not readily composted alone, but if nitrogen and phosphorus are added, the straw and paper will serve as the source of carbon for decomposition.

Agricultural experimentation has found starters or additives usually unnecessary. In one experiment, horse manure, compost material, normal soil, and special commercially prepared bacterial cultures were mixed with garbage and refuse to form one set of compost piles. In another set of piles, materials were composted

without these special commercially prepared bacterial cultures. It was found that, although rich in bacteria, none of the inocula accelerated the composting process or improved the final product. There was no significant difference in the temperature curves or in the chemical analyses of the material at different intervals during the composting period. Therefore, it was concluded that when the environment is appropriate, the varied indigenous biological population will multiply rapidly and composting is not delayed.

Temperature

The temperature of the compost pile is very important to the biological activity taking place. Low outside temperatures slow the activity down, while warmer temperatures speed up decomposition. The microbes that are so essential to the decomposition process fall into two categories: mesophilic, those that live and function in temperatures of 50 to 113°F (10–45°C), and thermophilic, those that thrive at temperatures between 113 and 158°F (45–70°C). A well-mixed, adequately working compost pile will heat to temperatures between 110°F and 160°F (43–71°C) as the microbes actively feed on the organic materials. These high temperatures will help destroy weed seeds and disease organisms within the pile.

MATERIALS FOR COMPOSTING

Many organic materials are suitable for composting. However, organic materials containing both carbon and nitrogen in varying amounts (used by the microorganisms for energy and growth) are preferred.

Carbon-Nitrogen Ratio

Microbial activity is greatest when the carbon-to-nitrogen ratio is 30:1. For proper decomposition the nutrients in the compost heap should be in the right proportions. The carbon:nitrogen (C:N) ratio will determine how long decomposition will take. When the decomposing organisms do not have the proper diet of carbon, the organisms may lose nitrogen to the atmosphere as ammonia. If the initial carbon portion is too high in the compost heap, the process will be considerably slower and very inefficient. Materials can be blended and mixed to achieve a suitable C:N ratio. Over time, the C:N ratio in the pile will generally decrease.

When adding compost to the soil, make sure that it has decomposed "properly." If it is not decomposed or finished it will be high in carbon and will have to use nitrogen from the soil in order to continue decomposition. Table 1 gives estimates of the C:N ratios of some compost ingredients. The higher the number is, the higher the carbon content will be and the longer the breakdown time.

Organic Refuse Materials

Yard refuse, such as leaves, grass clippings, straw, and non-woody plant trimmings, can be composted. The dominant organic waste in most backyard compost piles is leaves. Grass clippings can be composted; however, with proper lawn management clippings do not need to be removed from the lawn. If clippings are used, mix them with other yard debris. Otherwise, the grass clippings may compact and restrict air flow. Branches and twigs greater than one-fourth inch in diameter should be put through a shredder/chipper first. Add small amounts of soil to the compost pile occasionally. Uncooked kitchen wastes such as vegetable scraps, coffee grounds, tea leaves and bags, banana peels, and eggshells are very suitable additions to the compost pile.

Sawdust may be added in moderate amounts if additional nitrogen is applied. Approximately one pound of actual nitrogen (six cups of ammonium nitrate, aka 34-0-0) is required for the breakdown of 100 pounds of dry sawdust.

Wood ashes act as a lime source and, if used, should be added only in small amounts (no more than one-half cup per bushel of leaves). Excessive amounts of wood ashes result in loss of nitrogen from the pile. Also, the microorganisms that break down materials like to work in a slightly acidic condition, and lime or wood ashes would reduce their number.

Ordinary black and white newspaper can be composted; however, the nitrogen content is low and will slow down the rate of decomposition. If paper is composted, it should not be more than 10 percent of the total weight of the material in the compost pile. It is recommended that newspaper be recycled through appropriate community paper-recycling centers rather than through backyard composting.

Other organic materials often used to add nutrients to the pile are blood and bone meal, livestock manure, and excess aquatic plants from ponds or lakes. Spent plants and trimmings from the vegetable garden and flower beds are excellent sources of nitrogen for the compost pile and may be added. Plants or grass clippings previously treated with herbicide or pesticide can be composted in small amounts, but be certain to allow them to decompose thoroughly before adding them back to the soil as compost. Recent research has shown that pesticides are broken down during the composting process and no residuals are left. Ideally, clippings recently treated with herbicides should be left on the lawn to decompose (see section on Alternatives to Composting Grass Clippings).

Because they may pose a health hazard or create a nuisance, certain organic materials should not be used to make compost. Do not use human or pet feces because they may transmit diseases. Do not add meat, bones, grease, whole eggs, and dairy products because they can attract rodents to the site. Also, adding weedy, seedy, or diseased plants may cause later difficulties in the garden. Many plant disease organisms and weed seeds are destroyed during the composting process when temperatures in the center of the pile reach 150 to 160°F (66–71°C). However, in most compost piles, it is impossible to mix the pile sufficiently enough to bring all wastes to the center. Consequently, some weed seeds or disease organisms may survive composting.

Fertilizer and Lime

Microbial activity is affected by the carbon-to-nitrogen ratio of the organic waste. Because microbes require a certain amount of nitrogen for their own metabolism and growth, a shortage of nitrogen slows down the composting process considerably. Material high in carbon and low in nitrogen, such as straw or sawdust, decomposes very slowly unless nitrogen fertilizer is added. Even composting tree leaves, which are higher in nitrogen than straw or sawdust, can still benefit from nitrogen fertilizer. Grass clippings high in nitrogen can aid the composting process, though the homeowner may wish to leave them on the lawn. When mixed properly with leaves, grass will enhance decomposition. Manure or blood meal can also be used as organic sources of nitrogen. Otherwise, use a high nitrogen–containing fertilizer. Phosphorus and potassium are usually present in compostable materials in adequate amounts for decomposition.

During the initial stages of decomposition, organic acids are produced and the pH of the material drops.

Table 1. Carbon: Nitrogen ratio of common composting materials			
Food waste	15:1	Sawdust	500:1
Leaves	60:1	Rotted manure	20:1
Wood	700:1	Straw	80:1
Fruit waste	35:1	Cornstalks	60:1
Grass clippings	19:1	Alfalfa hay	12:1

Lime converts ammonium-nitrogen to ammonia gas and hastens the loss of nitrogen from the pile. Research shows that although lime may speed decomposition, the loss of nitrogen from the pile often offsets the benefits of lime. The pH of finished compost is usually slightly alkaline without the addition of lime. In many areas, the water used to moisten the compost pile is alkaline and may also help increase the pH of the compost. In general, lime is not necessary for degradation of most yard wastes.

COMPOSTING STRUCTURES

To save space, hasten decomposition, and keep the yard looking neat, contain the compost pile in some sort of structure. Structures can consist of a variety of materials and can be made as simple or complex as desired.

Aerobic Structures—A barrel or drum composter generates compost in a relatively short period of time and can provide easy turning (Figure 1). Barrel composting requires at least a 55-gallon barrel with a secure lid. Be sure that the barrel was not used to store toxic chemicals. Drill 6 to 9 rows of one-half inch (.50) holes over the

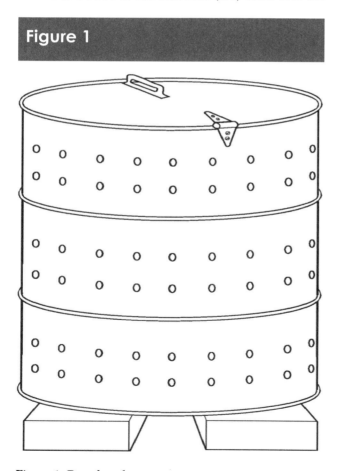

Figure 1

Figure 1. Barrel or drum composter

length of the barrel to allow air circulation and drainage of excess moisture. If the barrel does not come with a rotating foundation, place it upright on blocks to allow bottom air circulation and drainage of excess moisture. Fill it two-thirds full with organic waste material and about one-fourth cup of a high-nitrogen fertilizer. If needed, apply water until the mixture is moist but not soggy. Every few days, rotate the drum (or turn the barrel on its side and roll it around the yard) to mix and aerate the compost. The lid can be removed after turning to allow for air penetration. Ideally, the compost should be ready in 2 to 4 months. The barrel composter is an excellent choice for the city dweller with a relatively small yard.

For larger quantities of organic waste, bin-type structures are the most practical. A circular bin can be made by using a length (11–12 feet) of small-spaced woven wire fencing held together with chain snaps or pieces of fabric (Figure 2). The bin should be about 3 to 5 feet in diameter and at least 3 feet high. To maintain the shape of the pile and facilitate adding water, a stake may be driven in the middle of the bin before adding material. With this design, it is easy to turn the composting material by simply unsnapping the wire, moving the wire cylinder a few feet, and turning the compost back into it.

A very efficient and durable structure for fast composting is a 3-chambered bin (Figure 3). It holds a considerable amount of compost and allows good air circulation. The 3-chambered bin works like an assembly line, having three batches of compost in varying stages of decomposition. A balanced mixture of compost material (see Preparing the Compost Pile section) is started in the first bin and allowed to heat up for 3 to 5 days. Next, that material is turned into the middle bin for another 4 to 7 days, while a new batch of material is started in the first bin. Finally, the material in the middle bin is turned into the last bin as finished or nearly finished compost.

To make this structure, it is best to use rot-resistant wood such as redwood, pressure-treated wood, or a combination of wood and metal posts. Unless the wood is treated or is rot resistant, it will decompose within a few years. Each bin should be about 5 feet by 3 feet and about 3 to 4 feet high. Removable slats in the front offer complete access for turning.

Another structure that has proven successful is the use of wooden shipping pallets. One pallet is used on the bottom with four others making up the sides. Pallets are not rot resistant, but this is an excellent use of a normally expendable item that is crowding the landfills.

There are many other structures for composting and no one structure is best. Invent your own, or consult one of the several books on composting. If you don't want to build a structure, there are several commercial composting units available through local garden stores or mail-order catalogs. Most of these are similar to the barrel composter described previously and are useful for making small amounts quickly.

Pile or windrow composting is another alternative for those with enough room and space. Piles or windrows should measure no less than 5 feet wide by 5 feet high and at least 5 feet long. The length of the windrow can be as long as room allows. The materials can be turned onto adjacent ground (and back again) periodically with a pitchfork. For every large areas, the use of a front-end loader or Bobcat greatly aids in turning.

Anaerobic Structures

Using plastic garbage bags is one way to make compost. The bags are easy to handle and require minimal maintenance. To make compost using this method, fill plastic bags (30- to 40-gallon size and at least 3 ml. thick) alternately with plant wastes, fertilizer, and lime. To each bag of composting material add about one tablespoon of a garden fertilizer with a high nitrogen content. Hydrated lime (one cup per bag) helps counteract the extra acidity caused by anaerobic composting. After filling the bag, add about a quart of water. Close the bag tightly. Set aside for 6 to 12 months. Set the bags in a basement or heated garage for better decomposition during winter months. You will not have to turn the mixture or add water after closing the bag. The main advantage of composting in garbage bags is that it requires little maintenance; however, because oxygen is limited, the process is slow.

Location

Locate the compost pile close to where it will be used and where it will not interfere with activities in the yard or offend neighbors. Examples of good locations for the pile include areas near the garden or kitchen or between the garage and house. The pile will do best where it is protected from drying winds and where partial sunlight will help heat the pile. The more wind and sun to which the pile is exposed, the more water it will need. Avoid placing the compost pile in low spot or area known to have drainage issues as this may contribute to the pile becoming waterlogged.

Figure 2

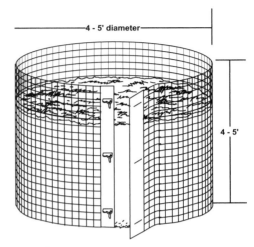

Figure 2. Bin-type Structure.

Figure 3

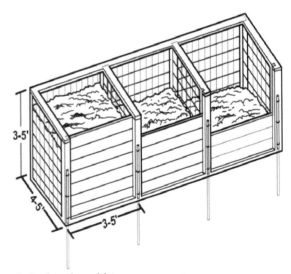

Figure 3. 3-chambered bin.

Preparing the Compost Pile

Prepare the compost pile in layers to facilitate proper mixing. Each pile ideally should be from 4 to 5 feet high. Figure 4 illustrates the layering process. Steps to follow include:

1. Coarser materials decompose faster in the bottom layer. The coarse material also allows air circulation around the base of the pile, creating a chimney effect that will take air up through the pile and heat it up. Moisten all layers as they are put in the pile.

2. Organic wastes, such as leaves, grass, and plant trimmings are put down in a layer 8 to 10 inches deep. This layer should be watered until moist, but not soggy.

3. Apply about a one-fourth-inch layer of soil or completed compost on top of the organic material layer. Adding soil ensures that the pile is inoculated with decomposing microbes. In most cases, organic yard wastes such as grass clippings or leaves contain enough microorganisms on the surface to bring about decomposition. Studies show that there is no advantage to purchasing a compost starter or inoculum. Microbes multiply as rapidly from the soil and/or added organic wastes as from the inoculum. Those microbes already in the soil and on organic materials are just as efficient in decomposing the waste as those provided by a commercial inoculum. Adding soil also helps reduce leaching of mineral nutrients, such as potassium, released during decomposition.

4. Place the nitrogen source on top of the soil layer. Use 2 to 3 inches of livestock manure or a nitrogen fertilizer, such as ammonium nitrate or ammonium sulfate, at a rate of one-third cup for every 25 square feet of surface area. If these nitrogen sources are not available, 1 cup of 10-10-10 fertilizer per 25 square feet of surface area will also suffice. Do not use fertilizer that contains a herbicide or pesticide. Other organic sources of nitrogen are green grass clippings, lake plants, or blood meal.

5. Repeat the sequence of adding coarse material, organic waste, soil, and fertilizer until the pile is completed. Remember to water each section as you make the pile. The pile should be about 5 feet high, topped off with 5 to 8 inches of straw, leaves, or hay, with a scooped out basin on top to catch rain water.

Maintaining the Compost Pile

To hasten decomposition, turn the pile every 7–10 days up to once a month. Turning also exposes seeds, insect larvae, and pathogens to higher temperatures inside

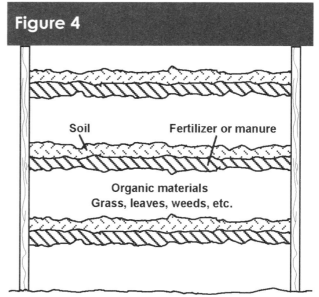

Figure 4. Layering process.

the pile. Turning and mixing can be done by inverting segments of the compost or by shifting the pile into another bin. Shovels, pitch forks, and potato forks are useful turning tools.

A properly mixed compost pile should not have an objectionable odor because elevated temperatures within the pile will destroy odor-causing bacteria. Keep the compost pile moist, but not waterlogged. Odors may arise either from the addition of excessive amounts of wet plant materials, such as fruits or grass clippings, or from over-watering. An actively decomposing pile will reach temperatures of 130°+F in the middle in just a few days. At this time, the pile will begin "settling," a good sign that the heap is working.

If the pile does not heat up, the cause may be one or more of the following: pile is too small; not enough nitrogen; lack of oxygen; too much moisture or not enough moisture. Turn the pile with a spading fork or shovel when the temperature in the center begins to cool. Turning will introduce oxygen and undecomposed material into the center and subsequently regenerate the heating process. The composting process is essentially complete when mixing no longer produces heat in the pile.

When the compost is finished, the pile will be about one-third of its original size and will have an earthy smell. The bin or pile can be screened and used if needed, or stored, or the pile simply can be added to and the process started over. Table 2 lists composting problems and their solutions.

As the decomposition process continues, the pile will

Table 2. Troubleshooting guide to composting problems

SYMPTOMS	PROBLEMS	SOLUTION
Compost has a bad odor	Not enough air	Turn it and add dry material if the pile is too wet
Center of the pile is dry	Not enough water	Moisten and turn the pile
Heap is damp and sweet-smelling but still will not heat up	Lack of nitrogen	Mix in a nitrogen source like fresh grass clippings, fresh manure, or blood meal

begin shrinking and settling. Leaves will shrink to approximately 30 percent of their original volume. As usable compost is harvested from the pile, add small amounts of fresh materials to keep the process going or start a pile and carry to harvest then start over as materials are available.

Bury vegetable wastes 6 inches inside the pile to avoid attracting rodents. If there is enough material, make a new pile instead of combining fresh materials with old compost. Generally, a well-managed compost pile with shredded materials under warm conditions will be ready in about 3 to 6 months but can be ready in 6 weeks for active composters. A pile left unattended with unshredded material may take over a year to decompose. Piles prepared in the late fall will not usually be ready for use the following spring.

SUGGESTED USES FOR COMPOST

Properly decomposed compost has a number of uses in the garden and around the yard. Compost provides economical and efficient ways to recycle organic matter.

Soil Amendment—Compost is used as an organic amendment to improve physical, chemical, and biological properties of soil. Adding compost will increase the moisture-holding capacity of sandy soils, thereby reducing drought damage to plants. When added to heavy clay soils, compost improves drainage and aeration and reduces waterlogging damage to plants. Compost increases the ability of the soil to hold and release essential nutrients. The activity of earthworms and soil microorganisms beneficial to plant growth is promoted with compost additions. Other benefits of

adding compost include improved seedling emergence and water infiltration due to a reduction of soil crusting.

Over time, yearly additions of compost create a desirable soil structure, making the soil much easier to work. For improving soil physical properties, add and incorporate 1 to 2 inches of well-decomposed compost in the top 6 to 8 inches of soil. Use the lower rate for sandy soils and the higher rate for clay soils.

To a limited extent, compost is a source of nutrients. However, nutrient release from compost is slow, and the nutrient content is too low to supply all the nutrients necessary for plant growth. Differences in nutrient content are probably due to several factors including age of the compost, amount of water added, plant species, and the amount of soil that becomes mixed into the pile during turning.

It is usually necessary to supplement compost-amended soils with some fertilizer, particularly nitrogen. If the C:N ratio of the compost is less than 20:1, nitrogen tends to be released rather than tied up. For most yard-trimmings compost, the C:N ratio is less than 20:1. Thus, while compost may not supply significant amounts of nitrogen, especially in the short run, nitrogen tie-up should not be a major concern with most yard-waste compost. Approximately 1 cup of ammonium nitrate (0.15 lb actual nitrogen) per 3 bushels (100 lbs compost) is required to provide the additional nitrogen needed by most garden plants.

Have your soil tested every few years to determine whether supplemental phosphorus and potassium is required. The pH of most finished yard-waste compost is usually around neutral, 7.0. This pH of compost should not pose any problems when diluted by mixing into the soil and, in fact, is beneficial to plants growing on acid soils. However, because of its pH, yard-waste compost does not appear well suited for use around acid-loving plants such as azaleas and blueberries.

Potting Soils—Leaf compost can be used as a component of potting mixes. Generally, no more than one quarter to one third by volume of the potting mix should be compost. Too much compost may result in waterlogging and poor aeration for roots.

Although proper composting destroys most weed seeds and disease organisms, some may still survive due to incomplete mixing. To obtain a completely pasteurized compost for use in the potting mixture, heat the material in an oven at 160°F (71°C) for 30 minutes.

Most compost will be used as soon as it is harvested. If

the finished compost isn't needed immediately cover it or place in an area protected from rainfall to minimize the leaching out of nutrients.

MULCHING

Mulch is organic material, such as wood chips, leaves, pine straw, pine bark, or compost, that is spread over the soil surface. Using mulch is a simple way to recycle yard debris and improve your garden.

The cultural practice of mulching has several advantages. Though mulching requires some labor, mulches save on later cultivation efforts because emerging weeds perish under their dark barrier, reducing tillage and the use of herbicides. Water is conserved because mulches reduce the evaporation of soil moisture. As mulch prevents the formation of impervious soil crusts, water is more easily absorbed by a mulched soil than by an un-mulched soil. Mulch also protects sloping ground from soil erosion, and it stops soil compaction caused by driving rain on any soil surface. Consequently, soil losses from heavy washing and blowing are decreased. Overall, mulches are excellent conservation agents. In addition, mulch provides ideal conditions for earthworms and other soil organisms that are necessary for a healthy soil.

The insulating property of mulch modifies drastic fluctuations of soil temperature, keeping the soil cooler in summer and warmer in winter. During the summer, mulching improves both root growth and nutrient availability. Winter mulches reduce the risk of root damage from low temperatures. Soils are improved with organic mulches as lower layers decompose and become incorporated into the soil. At the end of the growing season, organic mulches can be tilled into the soil to further increase the organic matter content. Also, mulches impart a neat, trim look to lawns and gardens, reduce the incidence of mud-splashed flowers and vegetables after heavy rains, and decrease the frequency of vegetable rot caused by soil contact.

However, mulches do have some disadvantages. Mulch and moisture around newly emerging seedlings or perennials can provide an ideal environment for diseases, such as damping-off or crown rot. The potential of disease is increased by long periods of rain. Diseases may also overwinter in the mulch. Insects and rodents that find mulch an attractive habitat can cause plant damage. These problems can be minimized by avoiding direct contact between the stems of plants and the mulch. Dry mulches that are combustible may be a fire hazard near buildings or in public places. Woody mulches adjacent to buildings can be a vector for termites.

The type of mulch used affects the growth of plants. Premature applications of organic mulches may retard soil warming in the spring and thus slow the growth of plants preferring warmer soils, such as tomatoes, peppers, and eggplants. Mulch applied too thickly or one prone to caking can impede the uptake of water and air by the soil, leading to possible plant damage. Mulches with a carbon-to-nitrogen ratio greater than 30:1 can steal nitrogen from the soil during decomposition, causing nitrogen deficiency in the mulched plant. Prior applications of nitrogen fertilizers can prevent this problem.

A practical mulch should be easily obtained, inexpensive, and simple to apply. Availability and cost vary from region to region. Mulching materials may be found in yards, garden centers, lumberyards, sawmills, dairy farms, tree-service firms, breweries, and food-processing plants. A suggested depth is 2 to 4 inches; too little mulch will give limited weed control, and too much will prevent air from reaching roots. Mulches should be applied prior to active weed growth and summer droughts or before the ground freezes if it is a winter mulch. For warm-season crops, such as tomatoes, mulching should be delayed until blossoms appear. A list of organic mulching materials follows with specific emphasis on advantages and disadvantages.

Some General Rules for Mulching

Annuals and perennials: Both flowers and vegetables should be mulched with a material that breaks down in a relatively short time, such as grass clippings and leaves. Preferably, it would be mulch that decomposes, allows tender plants to break through the mulch surface, and can be turned under when the soil is dug.

Woody plant material should be mulched with a thick layer of shredded or chipped wood that will look good and require little maintenance.

Paths and trails can also be covered with shredded or chipped wood, making it as thick as is practical to wear longer and to keep down weeds. To keep paths weed-free even longer, put down layers of cardboard before spreading mulch.

Mulch Materials and Uses

Availability of many of these products will be limited and perhaps seasonal.

Bark—Small pieces of bark are preferred over large chunks. Bark mulches vary, but all are attractive, durable, and suitable for foundation shrub plantings. Contact with wood framing is to be avoided, since bark can be a termite vector. The high carbon-to-nitrogen ratio of bark requires prior application of nitrogen fertilizer.

Buckwheat hulls—These are light, fluffy, and black. Since buckwheat hulls are prone to caking, they should be applied in a layer no deeper than 2 inches. Forceful watering will cause scattering of buckwheat hulls.

Cardboard—Can be placed on a path area or between garden rows with mulch covering. It will act as a weed barrier and help the mulch last longer.

Coffee grounds—Because coffee grounds cake badly, a depth of no more than 1 inch is recommended. Coffee grounds contain some nitrogen.

Compost—A good mulch, it has some fertilizer value and a soil-like appearance. It is a good organic amendment for tilling into the soil after the growing season ends.

Corn cobs—Ground corn cobs are a good mulch though some find their light color objectionable. Ground corn cobs are in short supply as they are more generally used in feeds and mash.

Grass clippings—Grass clippings, a source of nitrogen, can be spread regularly over vegetables and flower beds or mixed with leaves and spread in a thicker layer. Grass clippings by themselves should be applied no more than 1 inch thick so that they do not mat and stop water from penetrating into the soil or produce a foul odor as they decompose. They should be allowed to brown between each application. If herbicides have been applied to the lawn, it is better to first compost the grass in a hot compost pile.

Leaves—Leaves are free, readily available in many areas, release some nutrients upon decomposition, and spread easily. However, they have a tendency to form a soggy, impenetrable mat. This problem can be overcome by mixing leaves with fluffy materials, such as hay or straw, or by shredding the leaves. Oak leaves are especially good for acid-loving plants, such as azaleas and rhododendrons. Ground and shredded leaves from the lawnmower will not blow around as much as whole leaves.

Newspaper—Readily available and economical, newspaper is somewhat difficult to apply. The high carbon-to-nitrogen ratio necessitates the prior application of nitrogen fertilizer. A good use for newspaper is as an undermulch; that is, place four or five sheets under a thin layer of an attractive, more expensive mulch.

Peanut shells—Attractive and easy to apply, peanut shells also contain nitrogen and are long lasting. However, peanut shells can be a serious source of diseases as well as of weed seed and nutgrass tubers. Peanuts shells composted with other materials are available.

Peat moss—Peat moss is attractive, easy to handle, but somewhat expensive. Dry peat moss requires considerable time and water to become moist, so it should be applied only to a 3 inch or less depth and avoided in areas subject to drought. Its acidic pH makes it especially desirable for acid-loving plants.

Pine needles—One of the most popular mulches, pine needles are readily available in the south. They have an aesthetic appeal and are not prone to forming a soggy mat as are leaves. They are especially good for acid-loving plants.

Polyethylene film—This is one of the few mulches that is readily available and economical enough to be used for larger scale commercial applications. Polyethylene allows passage of gases such as nitrogen, oxygen, and carbon dioxide. Holes or slits facilitate the planting of seeds or plants and water entry. It can last several years if undamaged by machinery. Usually, it is used as black film. Clear film is sometimes used, but permits the growth of weeds unless herbicide is applied before mulching since light passes through it. Earlier crops can be produced with black plastic mulch because it promotes warming of the soil. Drip or seep irrigation may be used under the plastic mulch.

Straw, hay, salt-marsh hay—These materials are lightweight and easy to apply, but their appearance restricts their application mostly to vegetable gardens. They are used more frequently as a winter mulch for protection. They are not long lasting and frequently can contain weed seeds. Do not use Bahaia grass or Common Bermuda due to weed seed problems.

Sawdust—Organic by-products such as sawdust can be obtained from local businesses free of charge. Aged or partially rotted sawdust makes a satisfactory mulch that lasts a long time. Sawdust and other finely ground woody materials can be used on the surface, but should not be mixed into the soil. Materials such as these that have not yet been composted can tie up nitrogen in the soil, causing plants to become yellow and stunted. Since sawdust is prone to caking and has a high carbon-to-nitrogen ratio, apply it only 2 inches deep after adding nitrogen fertilizer to the soil.

Spent hops—These are resistant to blowing and have some nutrient value. However, when fresh they have some odor and may heat up as they decompose, thus causing some plant damage.

Stone—A very durable mulch with an attractive appearance. It should be used with caution in hot sunny areas due to heat absorption. Do not use crushed limestone around acid-loving plants.

Sugarcane—This is a good mulch when available in the crushed form. It has a moderately acidic pH, making it useful around acid-loving plants.

Chipped or shredded woody debris—Since these materials are moderately priced or free, attractive, readily available, and easy to apply, they make an excellent mulch. However, their high carbon-to-nitrogen ratio requires an application of nitrogen fertilizer. Wood chips can last about 2 years. As with a bark mulch, wood chips can be a vector for termites.

Applying Mulch

Always weed the area to be mulched prior to mulching. Mulch can be spread around any plant as far as the drip line (the outside of its outermost branching), or it can cover an entire garden bed. Mulch can be spread thickly if water is able to penetrate and if it does not smother the roots of the plant being mulched. Three inches of mulch is safe for most woody plants, and up to 8 inches can be used for large trees. However, thick mulches are harmful to shallow-rooted plants such as rhododendrons, azaleas, and dogwoods. For woody plants, mulch must be applied very thinly near the trunk to prevent mice from eating the bark of the tree. Avoid allowing mulch to accumulate to a thickness greater than 1 inch close around the trunks of trees and woody ornamentals. Do not make mulch "volcanoes," which are piles of mulch, often pine straw, heaped 12 inches or more directly on the trunk.

ALTERNATIVES TO COMPOSTING GRASS CLIPPINGS

There has been much debate over whether or not to collect grass clippings. However, it is now agreed that as long as the grass is not excessively high and clippings do not thickly cover the lawn surface after mowing, there is no need to collect the clippings. Aside from reducing the work involved in lawn maintenance, leaving the grass clippings on the lawn benefits the turf by returning nutrients and organic matter to the soil. If evenly distributed, clippings left on the lawn can be equivalent to one fertilizer application per year.

In order to keep your lawn looking healthy and to control the amount of clippings generated, several proper maintenance practices should be followed.

It is important that mowing height be correct. The height of the cut depends on the turfgrass variety and whether the lawn is in sun, full shade, or a combination of both. Lawns in full sun have the greatest potential for quick recovery after mowing, and they can be cut shorter. Those in the shade need all available leaf surface possible for photosynthesis. Thus, cut grass in the shade slightly higher than grass in the sun. Where both conditions are present, an intermediate height is recommended.

Mowing frequency also has a direct impact on the amount of clippings generated and depends on the cutting height selected and the turf growth rate rather than on specific time intervals. Ideally, no more than one-third of the leaf surface area should be cut at any one time, and the clippings should be no longer than one inch. A lawn with grass three inches tall should be cut to about two inches. Excessive defoliation in a single mowing can make the lawn more prone to stress and disease problems.

Be careful not to over fertilize the lawn. Over fertilization (primarily nitrogen) will cause excessive growth, and unless the lawn is cut more frequently, the clippings will be slow to reach the soil and decompose. Reducing excessive thatch levels through lawn renovation will improve infiltration of the grass clippings down to the soil surface. It is best to mow your lawn when it is dry so clippings can filter down to the soil without clumping. For more information on lawn fertilization and lawn care, contact your local county Extension office if the Master Gardener experience doesn't fulfill the learning needs.

Two types of mowers are reel and rotary. Either will do an acceptable job when blades are sharpened and adjusted properly. Dull blades "tear" at the grass and can cause the lawn area to deteriorate. Rotary mowers are now available with a mulcher attachment. This attachment reduces the volume of the clippings left behind for faster decomposition. However, mowing on a regular basis and not removing more than the top one third of the grass at a time, makes additional size reduction unnecessary.

If grass growth is excessive, it may be necessary to remove the clippings. In this situation, lawn clippings can be used in the compost pile as previously described or they can be used as mulch in the garden. If used as mulch, take care not to over apply fresh clippings as they tend to inhibit moisture and oxygen penetration into the soil and may produce offensive odors. Fresh clippings mixed with compost makes an excellent mulching material. Do not use grass clippings as a mulch if the lawn has recently been treated with herbicides.

RESOURCES

Ecology of Compost. Daniel L. Dindal, Office of News and Publications, SUNY-ESF, 1 Forestry Drive, Syracuse, NY 13210-2778

Easy Composting - Environmentally Friendly Gardening. 1992. Ortho Books. 96 pages, many color photographs.

Composting to Reduce the Waste Stream - A Guide to Small Scale Food and Yard Waste Composting. 1991. Northeast Regional Agricultural Engineering Service. 44 pages, black & white print, simple explanations, bin plans and diagrams. Available through NRAES, 152 Riley Robb Hall, Cooperative Extension, Ithaca, NY 14853-5701 (607) 255-7654.

The Complete Book of Composting. 1975. by the staff of Organic Gardening and Farming Magazine, Ed. J.I. Rodale. Rodale Books, Inc. Out of print, but still available in libraries and from out-of-print databases on Internet booksellers sites.

The Rodale Guide to Composting. 1979. J. Minnich, M. Hunt. Rodale Press. Out of print, but still available in libraries and from out-of-print databases on Internet booksellers sites.

Worms Eat My Garbage Mary Appelhof. Flowerfield Enterprises/Flower Press. Information on how to set up and maintain a worm composting system.

DISCUSSION QUESTIONS

1. What is compost?

2. Does compost have any value as a fertilizer?

3. Can compost be used as a substitute for fertilizer in the garden?

4. Is it necessary to add lime (calcium) to the compost pile?

5. Is it necessary to add inoculum to the compost pile to activate the composting process?

6. What are the best materials for composting?

7. Is it necessary to shred materials for the compost pile?

8. How often do compost piles need turning?

9. What causes compost piles to have offensive odors?

10. When is compost ready to use?

11. How can compost be used in the landscape and garden?

NOTES

27
Nuisance Wildlife

Michael T. Mengak

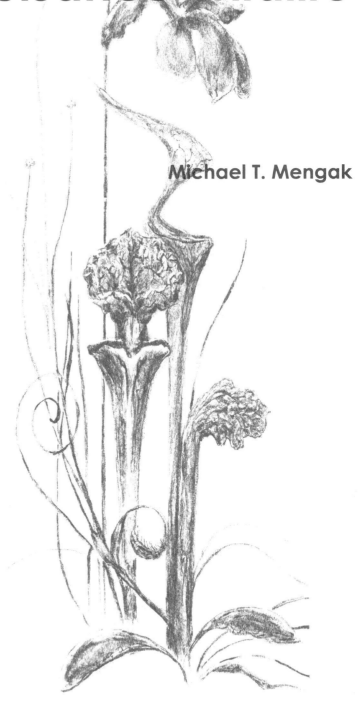

LEARNING OBJECTIVES

Understand common perceptions and myths related to wildlife control.

Be familiar with state laws relating to wildlife control.

Be familiar with some common nuisance wildlife.

Develop knowledge of why some animals become nuisance pests.

Learn ways to discourage wildlife damage to home, landscape and gardens.

Learn some basic guidelines for dealing with nuisance wildlife in and around the home and garden.

TERMS TO KNOW

Fumigant chemical compound used in its gaseous state as a pesticide.

Habitat area or environment where an organism normally lives or occurs.

Repellent substance used to make a surface offensive to animals or insects.

Take to kill, capture, destroy, catch or seize wildlife.

Toxicant poison or poisonous agent.

Wildlife any vertebrate or invertebrate animal life indigenous to this state or any species introduced or specified by the state. Includes fish (except domestic fish produced by aquaculturists), mammals, birds, amphibians, reptiles, crustaceans, and mollusks.

INTRODUCTION

As you read through this chapter, keep in mind some general pieces of information. Gardening is an adventure but, at times, a frustrating activity. There is little we can do about drought, frost, heavy rains or other events of nature. However, we can manage the various animals that will often be attracted to our landscapes and home gardens. This chapter will provide some basic information about a few of our wild neighbors and help you cope with them in your landscape.

All birds except house sparrows, European starlings, and pigeons or rock doves are protected in the United States and cannot be trapped, shot, poisoned, or killed except during legally authorized hunting seasons or under special permit. Since there are no hunting seasons for most birds (songbirds, woodpeckers and the like) we will have to console ourselves with observing and enjoying them in our gardens. Many people spend quite a few hours studying birds; numerous gardens and landscapes are designed with birds (and butterflies) in mind.

Norway rats, black rats, house mice, coyotes, armadillos, groundhogs, beaver, freshwater turtles, venomous snakes, frogs, spring lizards (salamanders), fiddler crabs, fresh water crayfish, freshwater mussels and nutria can be taken by any method unless specifically prohibited (Ga. Code 27-1-28).

Strictly speaking, a permit is necessary to take, harm, harass, trap, or kill any wildlife except those listed in the preceding paragraph. Permits can be obtained from any state wildlife law enforcement officer. Their offices are usually listed in the phone book under state government.

Cooperative Extension provides advice and technical assistance, including training, to homeowners regarding nuisance wildlife control. Cooperative Extension does not conduct wildlife control operations.

Landowners and homeowners needing the services of wildlife control professionals should contact either an independently licensed nuisance wildlife control operator (NWCO) listed in many phone books – often under a heading "Animal Removal Services". A list of NWCO's is also available from the state wildlife specialist, county agents and the state Department of Natural Resources – Wildlife Resources Division.

The US Department of Agriculture – Wildlife Services (USDA-WS) can provide technical assistance for free or operational control for a fee with nuisance wildlife issues on a large scale. Their office is located in Athens, GA.

THE HERL MODEL

The Warnell School of Forestry and Natural Resources (WSFNR) at the University of Georgia and Cooperative Extension can provide brochures or booklets to assist landowners with nuisance wildlife issues. The webpage for WSFNR is http://www.forestry.uga.edu/outreach/index.php. Search under the "Outreach – Publications" library on this webpage. The goal is to effectively reduce human-wildlife conflict in the most efficient way possible. Both WSFNR and Cooperative Extension recommend a 4-step procedure to Master Gardeners and landowners for dealing with nuisance wildlife. The program is known by its acronym – HERL. The letters represent the steps for dealing with human-wildlife conflicts in a landscape setting.

Step 1- H–HABITAT MODIFICATION

Alter the environment around the property to make it less attractive to nuisance wildlife. Clean up debris piles, cut grass and brush, remove hiding places attractive to the wildlife species causing the damage. Specific recommendations are given throughout this chapter under each species review.

Step 2 – E-EXCLUSION

Use fencing and conduct home repairs as necessary to prevent nuisance wildlife from gaining entry to the property and home. This includes locating and sealing all points of entry into a home, shed, barn, siding, shutters, or other structure.

Step 3 – R-REPELLANT

Use registered repellants in a manner consistent with product labeling to discourage unwanted wildlife. The choice of repellants is based on experience and personal preference, but remember that many products on the market have not been rigorously tested in a scientifically controlled manner. Often, if it sounds too good to be true it probably is. Many repellants have limited efficacy. The product washes off in rain, breaks down in sunlight, or the animals simply become accustomed to the product. The landscape should be regularly monitored and repellant applied a needed and in accordance with all labeling precautions. Many outlandish claims are made regarding the efficacy of repellants-most are not effective.

Step 4 – L-LETHAL CONTROL

As a last resort and with proper training and permits, remove offending animals by lethal means. This may include placement of commercially available toxicants (for example, rat poison) or traps (usually easily purchased at garden supply stores and home centers).

DEALING WITH COMMON WILDLIFE SPECIES

Armadillo

Description—The nine-banded armadillo (*Dasypus novemcinctus*) is so named because of the nine moveable rings of armor between the shoulder and the hip shields. It has a long tail that is also protected by rings of armor. Armadillos are about the size of opossums. The ears, tail base, neck, legs, and belly are covered in a sparse yellowish white hair. Three toe prints and sharp claw marks are typical of armadillo tracks.

Habitat—Armadilloes inhabit forests, scrub, and brush lands, but are most abundant in moist, bottomland hardwood forests. The armadillo digs burrows for nesting and for protection during the day. Burrows can be from 4 - 24 feet in length and 20 inches deep, and have several entrances, with a nesting chamber at the very end stuffed full of dried leaves and grasses.

Food Habits—When foraging, an armadillo moves under the cover of shrubs and dense vegetation in an erratic and random pattern. It uses a keen sense of smell to locate prey 5 to 6 inches beneath the soil. The majority of its diet consists of insects, grubs, and worms, but some fruits, bird eggs, and small vertebrates have been recorded.

Behavior—Understanding the life history and habits of armadillos is helpful in developing an effective control program. Armadillos are mainly nocturnal, which means they are active at night. However, they occasionally move about during the day. They burrow in the ground and have strong legs adapted for digging. They root about in ground litter searching for insects, grubs, and other invertebrates. While searching for food, they seem oblivious to anything else and may come very close to human beings before becoming alarmed.

Damage—As armadillos search for food, they dig small holes in the ground. These holes are about 3 inches wide and 5 inches deep. Armadillos will also uproot flowers and other vegetation in loose soils. This characteristic makes them particularly troublesome around gardens.

Prevention and Control—Since they feed on invertebrates in the ground, eliminating the food source will often cause armadillos to look elsewhere for food. However, ridding the soil and vegetation of all insects, worms, and grubs may not be practical and may be detrimental to the plants and other life forms in the area.

Live-traps baited with overripe fruit, such as apples or bananas, may be effective. These traps are more effective when "wings" are added to direct the animal into the trap. Set the traps in the area where the damage is occurring, for example, around the house, in the flower garden, or in the vegetable garden. Captured animals can then be released to another area.

If the damage is isolated to a garden area, an electric fence may be an effective form of control. A single strand 3 to 4 inches off the ground should be sufficient. Polytape electric fence wire with a New Zealand-type charger makes an effective and safe exclusion device. However, be very careful when placing a fence in areas where children may play.

Shooting armadillos at night is an effective and selective method. However, this method requires constant vigilance to find the animal. In addition, local regulations on discharging firearms may prohibit this activity.

No toxicant, fumigants, or repellents are currently registered for armadillo control. However, damage is usually localized, and the control measures suggested here should be useful.

Bats

Description—Bats are small-bodied mammals that fly. They are generally nocturnal and come out at dusk to feed. The world has about 900 kinds of bats, mostly in the tropics. Many of these species are fish and fruit eaters. Bats do not need any light to find their prey. They use sonar. The echoes of their faint squeaks bounce back to their sensitive ears. Blind a bat and he can still maneuver on the wing. Cover his ears and he will crash.

Habitat—There are about 16 species of bats found in Georgia. Our bats are either tree bats or cave bats which readily roost in attics, hollow walls or other dark out of the way places in buildings.

The **Seminole bat**, **hoary bat** and **red bat** are all tree bats. They roost by day in trees and shrubs. These tree bats migrate north for the summer and winter in the South. Tree bats generally live alone or in small groups, well away from people.

The **big brown bat**, **little brown bat**, and **free tail bat** are cave bats. They will also roost in attics and hollow walls. The big brown bat is Georgia's common "attic bat". It is four inches long with a one-foot wingspread. Commonly, big brown bats roost in groups of 100 to 200. Big browns will roost, in the summer, behind shutters and under siding on houses.

Food Habits—Bats are extremely beneficial. Bats of the Southeastern United States consume huge quantities of flying insects including mosquitoes and moths.

Most bats eat insects, like many backyard birds. They catch them in flight with a quick scoop of their winged hands. Some bats in Central and South America eat fruit, and some eat only certain kinds of frogs. Vampire bats of Central and South America live on blood of cattle and other large animals. Fruit eating and vampire bats DO NOT occur in Georgia

Damage—County agents with University of Georgia Cooperative Extension receive about 2,000 calls a year from people wanting to rid their buildings of bats. The smell of bat droppings in an attic can be nauseating. Bats can carry bedbugs and other ectoparasites, rabies and other diseases.

Prevention and Control—The only permanent way to be free from the bat roost nuisance is to shut the bats out.

To shut bats out of a building, find the openings where bats enter. Look for cracks, louvers, knotholes or torn screens. Any crack big enough to admit a pencil can let in small bats. Most bats enter a hole the size of a quarter. Look for openings with "dirty edges" where bats have been squeezing through. Check walls and the ground for bat droppings. They are like a mouse dropping, but shiny and with pointed ends. Unlike mouse droppings, they often stick to surfaces.

All of the holes must be closed to prevent bats from entering.

First, encourage the bats to leave. Try placing lights in the attic. Bats do not like to sleep with the lights on. Turning on a fan in the attic may discourage bats, because they dislike roosting in windy areas. After bats leave, go to work to seal all openings. Stuff stainless steel scouring pads in cracks, and then caulk over them.

If fans and lights do not drive out the bats, close the openings soon after it becomes dark when the bats are out for their evening meal. Don't wait too long, because bats often return to their roost after a good feed.

The best season for closing bats out is late summer or early fall (late August through October). In early summer many young bats will remain in the attic. Their mothers return several times each night to feed them. If the bats are blocked in, they will die and stink. If you wait for cold weather, the bats may not leave. They can hibernate in an attic all winter.

There are no poisons registered for use in Georgia for killing bats.

Bats can bite, but bats do not go out of their way to attack people or entangle in people's hair. Bats may scare people when they dive and swoop for insects or drink from the surface of swimming pools.

There are some good reasons for avoiding bats. Like other mammals, they may carry rabies. It is important to note however, that more people are killed every year by dog attacks or power mowers than by rabies infections caused by bats. Overall, bats are beneficial creatures, consuming many times their body weight in insect pests such as mosquitoes.

Beaver

Description—Beaver (*Castor canadensis*) is the largest North American rodent. Adults can weigh between 60 and 80 pounds although they are generally smaller in the South where typical weights range from 35-45 pounds. Distinguishing features include a flattened head with large, continuously growing incisors, dark brown fur, webbed hind feet, and a large, flattened tail.

Beavers are found throughout North America, except for the arctic tundra, most of peninsular Florida and the southwestern desert areas. The species is locally abundant throughout Georgia wherever aquatic habitats are found, e.g. streams, lakes, farm ponds, wetlands and low lying lands or swamps and along flood prone creek and river bottoms.

Beavers are active for approximately 12 hours each night except for the coldest of winter nights. The phrase "busy as a beaver" is appropriate. However, it is not uncommon to see beavers during daylight hours, particularly in larger reservoirs. Because of the valvular ears and nose and other physical adaptations, they can remain underwater for over 15 minutes when necessary.

Habitat—Beaver habitat is almost anywhere there is a year-round source of water, e.g., streams, lakes, farm ponds, swamps and wetland areas. Beaver have been observed in highway roadside ditches, drainage ditches, canals, mine pits, oxbows, railroad dumps, drains from sewage disposal ponds, and below natural springs or artesian wells. Beavers move into areas because they seem to be stimulated by running water. They will quickly begin building dams to modify the environment more to their liking. Some of the surrounding timber is cut down or girdled by beavers to form dams.

Food Habits—Beavers prefer certain trees and woody species depending on availability, such as cottonwood, willow, sweetgum, tulip poplar, dogwood, blackgum and pine. For some reason beavers seem to like to girdle large pine and sweetgums. They like the gum or sap that seeps out of the girdled area of sweetgum and other species. However, they can and will eat the leaves, twigs and bark of most species of woody plants, which grow near the water, as well as a wide variety of herbaceous and aquatic plants. Beavers often will travel 100 yards or more from the pond or stream to get to cornfields, soybean fields and other growing crops where they generally cut the plant off at the ground and drag the entire plant back to the water. Adding insult to injury, they not only eat part of these plants, they often use the remainder as construction material in the dam.

Damage—Most of the damage caused by beavers is a result of dam building; bank burrowing, tree cutting or flooding. Some individual southeastern states where beaver damage is extensive have determined from surveys that beaver damage estimates range from $3 million to $5 million dollars annually to timber loss, crop losses, roads, dwellings, and property flooded, and other damage.

Subsequent flooding of growing timber causes it to die, and aquatic vegetation soon begins growing. Other pioneer species, e.g., willow, sweetgum and buttonbush, soon are growing around the edge of the flooded area adding to the available food supply. The beaver thus helps create its own habitat.

The habitat modification by beavers, caused primarily by dam building, is often beneficial to fish, furbearers, reptiles, amphibians, waterfowl and shorebirds. However, when this modification comes in conflict with man's objectives, the impacts of damage may far outweigh the benefits.

The damage caused by beavers is not only economically important; it is also very frustrating to landowners and others. They are beavers are hosts for several ectoparasites and internal parasites, which have caused human health problems in water supply systems.

Identifying beaver damage generally is not difficult and includes: dams, dammed-up culverts, bridges, or drain pipes resulting in flooded lands, timber, roads, crops, and cut-down or girdled trees and crops; or burrows

in pond and reservoir levees. If reservoirs are stopped up, it may be very difficult to get the sticks, logs, mud and debris removed so that the water will move out and beaver can be trapped. In large watersheds, it may be difficult to locate bank dens. However, the limbs, cuttings and debris around such areas as well as dams along tributaries usually pinpoint the area.

Prevention And Control Methods

Exclusion—Beavers can be excluded from ponds, lakes or impoundments. However, if the primary reason for fencing is to exclude beaver, fencing is not practical. Fencing of culverts, drain pipes or other structures can sometimes prevent damage, but often results in a dam with the beavers using the fence as construction material. Metal barriers or fencing around valuable trees may prevent damage where feasible.

Cultural Methods—Because beavers usually alter or modify their aquatic habitat so extensively over a period of time, most practices generally thought of as cultural have little impact on beavers. With the exception of the elimination of food sources and in cases where the aquatic habitat can be eliminated, most other cultural practices have no significant impact on beavers. Daily tearing out dams and removing dam construction materials will (depending on availability of construction materials) sometimes cause a colony or individual beaver to move to another site. However, they might be even more troublesome at the new location.

Beavers are adaptable and will use whatever materials are available to construct dams—fencing materials, bridge planking, crossties, rocks, wire, and other metal, wood and fiber materials. Therefore, about the only available aquatic habitat beavers avoid are those systems lacking acceptable foods, lodge or denning sites and where no suitable site exists to construct dams.

Repellents—There are no chemical repellents registered for beavers. The deer repellents Hinder and Ropel may have some potential benefit. Many mechanical devices have been tried in attempts to repel beavers. The only effective and environmentally safe methods known do not actually repel beavers but, in some cases, do prevent damage. These would include fencing of structures in some areas, e.g. drain pipes or structures, fencing or other barriers around valuable trees, shrubs, or other crops, and construction of concrete or other permanent materials in spillways or other drainage systems.

There are no registered toxicants or fumigants for beaver control.

Traps—In Georgia, a good trapper can remove every beaver from a pond if dams are kept broken and the water is kept moving out on a nightly basis. In most cases, a week of trapping is sufficient to remove all the beavers from a single pond. Periodic checks will make sure there are no survivors or that beavers from adjacent areas have not moved in.

The use of traps in most situations where beavers are causing damage is the most effective, practical and environmentally safe method of control. The effectiveness of any type of trap for beaver control is dependent on the trapper's knowledge of beaver habits, including food preferences, ability to read beaver signs, use of proper trap to fit the situation, and trap placement.

Of the variety of traps commonly allowed for use in beaver control, the Conibear type, size 330, is one of the most effective for most situations. Not all trappers will agree that this type trap is most effective; however, it is the type most commonly used by professional trappers and fur trappers who are trapping principally for beavers. This trap kills a trapped beaver almost instantly. When properly set, this type trap prevents any escape by a beaver, regardless of its size. Designed primarily for water use, it is equally effective in deep and shallow water. Because of its size, effectiveness, and mobility – no need for additional apparatus to drown the beaver, and its capability to kill the beaver quickly, traps can be set quickly. Setting several traps in runways and trails along the banks will increase the probability of success. It exerts tremendous pressure and impact when tripped. Therefore, as with most traps, appropriate care must be exercised when setting and placing the trap.

Several other types of traps can be used, including basket/suitcase type (live) traps. However, these are rarely used in beaver damage situations, except by professionals in urban areas where anti-trap sentiment or other reasons prevent killing the beaver. These traps are difficult and cumbersome to use, and will not be further discussed here for use in beaver damage control. Any type of traps used for beavers or other animals should be checked daily.

Shooting—In some states, because of the extent of damage caused by beavers, regulations have been relaxed to allow shooting. Some states even allow the use of a light at night to spot and shoot beavers. Before attempting to shoot beavers, check regulations, and if applicable, secure permits and let the local enforcement officer or game warden know what is being attempted. All shooting should be done with a shotgun. Never shoot a rifle on or across flat water.

Beavers are most active from late afternoon to shortly after daybreak, depending on the time of the year. They begin about 6 to 8 p.m. and are active until about 7 am, when they generally retire to the lodge or bank den for the day. Therefore, if night shooting is not permitted, the early evening and early morning hours are most productive. Generally speaking, the time spent trying to shoot damaging beavers would be much more productive if devoted to trapping. Shooting can be effective and cost efficient.

Other Methods—Beaver damage can be severe and cause extensive economic losses and frustration in many situations. However, the efforts necessary to effect control of beavers causing the damage are most often overestimated. Beaver colonies have a tendency, like other wildlife species, to build up the population to a certain level, then part of the population moves into suitable habitat of nearby water sources. The beavers then develop or modify the habitat to their liking. The Georgia Department of Natural Resources, Wildlife Resources Division publishes a helpful booklet, "Beaver Management and Control in Georgia" which is available from any DNR office.

Legal Status—The legal status of beavers varies from state to state. In some states, the beaver is protected except during furbearer seasons; in Georgia it is classified as a pest and may be taken year-round. Before attempting to trap or otherwise take beavers in any state, always check the existing regulations.

Canada Goose

Description—The Canada Goose is a large bird, usually 25-45 inches in length, with a black head and neck, dark upper parts, white belly, and a black tail, legs, and bill. Commonly heard before it is seen with a loud honk, the Canada Goose is also visible from distances when migrating because of the large "V" formation that the birds make while flying.

Habitat—The Canada Goose occurs throughout most of the United States during the breeding season, and most individuals spend winters in the central and southern latitudes of the country. Within Georgia this species can be found throughout the state all year long in appropriate habitat.

Many of these birds are semi-domesticated or non-migratory individuals and will remain all year in certain areas with open water. The nesting habitat is highly variable, but is usually near water. Nests are on the ground near the water's edge or on muskrat or other mounds within the water. The nest is constructed of plant material, moss, and sticks, and lined with finer material and down.

Food Habits—The main foods eaten by the Canada Goose are plant materials - roots, seed, shoots, bulbs, grain, and berries. A large amount of grain is eaten during the winter. This species gathers food by taking items off the surface or near the surface of the water, "up-ending" (raising its tail end up while moving its head below the surface of the water to eat vegetation), or taking food items off of the ground.

Damage—Because they are generally tolerant of human activity, Canada geese will establish territories and nest around any suitable pond or stream. Their presence on lawns, golf courses, cemeteries, school yards, backyards, and farms can cause problems, including damage to landscaping, gardens, crops, and water quality. Many people find goose droppings to be a nuisance in recreational areas.

Prevention and Control—Habitat modification is the most successful approach to dealing with goose problems. Allowing tall, thick vegetation to grow around ponds or in open areas will deter geese from using an area. If lawn or turf is a must, then geese can be discouraged by (1) reducing fertilizer applications to make grass less palatable and/or nutritious, (2) planting less palatable species (e.g., tall fescue), and (3) eliminating nesting cover. Do not let anyone feed the geese.

Scare Tactics—It is important to begin scare tactics as soon as the geese arrive on your property. Visual repellents include large flags, trash bags, scarecrows, helium balloons, and reflective Mylar tape. Devices should be moved every 2–3 days to prevent habituation and used as soon as a problem is detected. Loud noises from a variety of sources (e.g., propane exploders, leaf blowers, shell crackers, electronic alarms, air horns, or sirens) also can be effective at frightening geese. Dogs, especially border collies, can harass geese until they leave the area. In order to be successful, you need to be persistent with your scare tactics.

Trapping and Shooting—Canada geese are protected by federal and state laws. Check with state wildlife officials for current regulations and special permits.

Goose Attacks—If you encounter an aggressive goose, be sure to maintain direct eye contact with the animal and face your body directly towards the attacking goose. Do not turn your back or shoulders away from the goose, and do not squint, close, or cover your eyes. If the goose makes an aggressive move towards you, you should slowly back away while maintaining a neutral demeanor (i.e., do not shout or kick).

Chipmunks

Description—Chipmunks are small rodents, or gnawing mammals that weigh about 3-5 ounces and are about 5 to 7 inches long with a 3 to 4 inch tail. Chipmunks are reddish brown in color with characteristic black and white facial stripes and several body stripes that end in a reddish rump. They almost always run with their tails erect.

Habitat—The Eastern Chipmunk is found in the Piedmont and mountains of northern Georgia but not on the southeastern Coastal plains. Chipmunks live in suburban yards, wooded parks and forests, near clear cuts and rocky outcrops. Densities can reach 3 to 10 per acre in favorable natural habitat and 20-30 per yard in suburban areas, where they are often caught by house cats and deposited on the cat owner's porch.

Food Habits—Chipmunks spend much time in late summer gathering food. Hard foods are stuffed into their cheek pouches and stored in food caches. Chipmunks are omnivorous; they eat a variety of seeds and nuts in addition to bulbs, fruits, insects, meat, snails, and eggs. They can also be a predator on mice and young songbirds.

Behavior—Normally, just one chipmunk lives in a burrow. Mothers and young are an exception. Outsiders are not welcome. Chipmunks do not share their food very readily. Consequently, once a poison bait has been stored below ground, other chipmunks cannot get it.

Prevention and Control—Often chipmunks create havoc in a landscape or garden. They may dig seeds from the garden, feed on flower bulbs, and burrow into lawns and flower beds. Many calls from homeowners are to request advice about a poison. While it is possible to poison any creature, it is not the best way to eliminate a chipmunk. Chipmunks are hoarders and may hide poisoned food for later consumption. Unlike many other squirrels, chipmunks have cheek pouches. They can carry a lot of food in them. Their burrows, which may be 30 feet long, have side branches leading to little "rooms" which they use for pantries.

Using rodent poisons in backyards can be hazardous to children and pets.

Using standard mousetraps baited with peanut butter is an excellent strategy for control. Place a plastic flower pot with a "door-hole" over the trap to keep other animals from springing the trap.

Even after trapping, the potential for chipmunk pests remains. A good habitat may support 10 to 15 chipmunks per acre, and chipmunks have three to five young per litter. They mature in about three months. With such over production, a chipmunk-less yard in will soon be recolonized. Continue control efforts all year. In the south, chipmunks may hibernate for only a short time period.

In some years chipmunks aren't a problem. Chipmunk populations are always rising and falling. Although a chipmunk has been known to live eight years, the average chipmunk is likely to die within the year. Predators like foxes, bobcats, snakes and hawks are likely to catch them. In the backyard, housecats, disease or food shortage may eliminate them.

Deer

Description—The white-tailed deer is the smallest member of the deer family in North America. White-tailed deer range in size from 4 to 6 ft. in total length and weigh between 85 and 250 pounds. The body color is reddish brown in summer and grayish brown in winter. The belly, chest, throat, chin, and the inside of the back legs are white. The tail is brown above and white below, hence the name.

The breeding season, called rut, occurs from October to January, with a peak in November. Gestation takes approximately 200 days, and one or four young (typically two) are born in May or June. Fawns weigh 5 to 8 lbs. at birth. During the first week the fawn remains hidden in tall grass or under cover of other vegetation while the female forages. Within a month, the fawn accompanies the female at all times. Fawns are weaned at about eight months of age and may remain with the female (doe) for over a year. Fawns are reddish brown and covered in white spots until the fall of their first year. Sexual maturity is reached at about 1.5 years of age, but full size is not attained until 4 to 5 years of age.

Habitat—The white-tailed deer is found in all habitats, from high mountain forests to coastal marshes. Prime areas are those which have a mix of forest, old fields and active crop lands. White-tails range throughout Georgia, and are common in the eastern two-thirds of the United States and southern Canada. It has been recorded in all 48 contiguous states, but is rare in California, Nevada, and Utah.

Food Habits—The white-tailed deer is a browser, feeding on leaves, buds, and twigs of wide variety of plants. It also eats acorns, fruits, mushrooms, and many herbaceous plants. Agricultural crops like alfalfa, corn, milo and soybeans are also eaten. Feeding activity peaks are at dawn and dusk. They generally bed down during the day, but are occasionally seen during daylight hours.

Damage—In many areas of the U.S., deer have become a nuisance, feeding on ornamental plants and fruit and vegetable plants in gardens and landscapes. Deer prefer crops that have been watered and fertilized; they are tastier and more nutritious than untended plants. Deer have certain favored plants, but will eat just about any plant during harsh weather. See pages 599-606 for a list of plants favored by deer.

Male deer, or bucks, damage young trees by scraping against them during the mating season. This shreds and tears the bark and may break branches or the trunk itself.

PREVENTION AND CONTROL

Repellents—There are two types of repellents. Those that are put on the plant to give it a bad taste are called taste repellents. Thiram, capsaicin, and Bitrex® are some examples.

Products that have a bad odor and are designed to keep deer away are called area repellents. Milorganite®, putrefied egg, and tankage (putrefied slaughterhouse wastes) are such materials. Do not put repellents on plants to be consumed by humans unless the label indicates that it is safe to do so.

Many people swear by homemade odor repellents such as soap, human hair, human and animal urine, etc., but research indicates that rotten egg smell is the most effective in repelling deer temporarily.

All repellents are strictly temporary materials. If deer are very hungry, the repellents may not work at all. Repellents are less successful in areas with a high deer density. Rain will wash away most repellants. But, if harvest time is near, a temporary repellent may be a good investment.

To make repellents work better, it is best not to wait for damage to start. If experience shows that deer are going to be a problem in your area, apply the repellent before they arrive. It is difficult to discourage them once they have begun browsing in an area. If deer do catch you off guard and start eating crops, apply repellents right away. Visit the area frequently to scare the deer. Make them associate the repellent with your presence. Reapply repellents frequently; most are not expensive. Repellents cost less than new landscape plants or gardens, especially if you include the cost of your time.

Fences—Electric fences are expensive. However, electric fences are the most effective solution. Sometimes deer will get in anyway, especially if the fence is not built correctly. An electric fence to keep deer out has to be a compromise between price and effectiveness. No single fence design is "best". There are many designs, each with strengths and weaknesses. Visit the University of Georgia - Warnell School webpage for recent publications on deer fence (http://www.forestry.uga.edu/outreach/pubs/wildlife-management.php).

Other fences include a single strand of hot-tape. Hot tape is webbing with thin wires embedded in the nylon or plastic. The wires are charged – sometimes with only 4 "D" cell batteries. When the deer come into contact with the tape they get a mild jolt. Some people spread peanut butter on the tape to encourage deer to touch the tape and this speeds up the learning process.

Other Scare Devices—Dogs can be trained to chase deer, but pie pans and scarecrows lose effectiveness very quickly once the deer become used to the items.

There are new devices such as movement-activated water blasters available in catalogs and garden centers but they are expensive and may or may not work.

In areas with large deer populations, discourage male deer from rubbing bark on young trees by driving tall vertical barrier stakes into the soil around each, about a foot from the trunk. Wrapping a tree trunk with a section of corrugated drain pipe – split vertically – is an effective barrier and will last until the tree is large enough to withstand rubbing.

Shooting—White-tailed deer is managed in Georgia with strictly controlled hunting seasons for both archery and firearms. Many areas in Georgia also prohibit shooting firearms in populated areas.

Gophers

Description—The southeastern pocket gopher (*Geomys pinetis*) is restricted to South Georgia. This mammal is 7-9 inches long with a short tail (usually 2-4 inches in length) and weighs about 10-14 ounces. It is sandy brown in color and has external, fur-lined cheek pouches. That's different from chipmunks and some other rodents that take food into their mouth to stuff their cheek pouches full. Huge front teeth protrude from the front of the pocket gopher's face. Powerful front legs are armed with large clawed forepaws for digging.

"Salamander" is the common word for the Southeastern Pocket Gopher in South Georgia. (In Georgia, the word "gopher" means a certain burrowing tortoise-the gopher tortoise.) Local names can be confusing. To simplify things, keep in mind that in Georgia, spring lizard can mean salamander, and salamander can mean gopher and gopher can mean turtle.

"Gopher" is a confusing word all over the country because the word gopher is used to name various creatures that are not called gophers by biologists. The Richardson's ground squirrel of the West is called gopher. So is the 13-lined ground squirrel of the Great Plains and Midwest. Moles are called gophers in many areas. And voles (certain short-tailed mice) are called gophers in some states.

There are, however, six species of pocket gophers in the United States. One is the **Southern Pocket Gopher** of s. Georgia, s. Alabama and n. Florida. How did the Southern Pocket Gopher get the name salamander? The pocket gopher spends all his time underground making tunnels and nests, eating roots and bearing and raising young. The average person never sees one. All you see are the sandy mounds of excavated earth that the gopher pushes out of the burrows. These sandy mounds gave the name sandy mounder to this unseen animal. In time, the sandy mounder became salamander.

Habitat—Pocket gophers prefer sandy soil which is easier to dig in than clay. Air and gases move through sandy soil more easily than a dense soil. Burrows in clay soil also get very damp and stuffy. They block their tunnels with earth, and then run to escape snakes, weasel and other predators that get into their burrows. They will bite viciously if given a chance. During flash floods they often drown in their burrows.

Damage—While pocket gophers are interesting creatures to most landowners, they sometimes damage trees and other crops.

Prevention and Control—If pocket gophers cause serious problems, control them with special traps called "harpoon traps," or certain poison baits and fumigant tablets. To place these materials, dig down about a foot in front of the mound to intersect the main burrow. Poke the traps, tablets or bait deeply into the burrow in both directions. Then seal the burrow with a plug of earth. If you leave the burrow open, the gopher will see daylight and plug the burrow well back from the opening – and wall himself off form the control materials. Around gardens, use hardware cloth or chicken wire fence buried about one foot deep. This will deter gophers, as well as moles and rabbits.

Lizards

Description—There are approximately 15 species of lizards in Georgia including skinks, anoles, glass lizards.

Scorpion is a local misnomer for the broad headed skink. These lizards may approach 12 inches in length, but are usually 8-10 inches long. Males have a big, bright orange head. They are often on tree trunks.

Perhaps best known is the green anole, often called chameleon, because it can change color from green to brown and all mixtures in between. The true chameleons live in Africa. Then there are the fence lizards – rough and scaly, colored like tree bark. The flanks of the males are brilliant blue. They like to live on log piles.

The six-lined racerunner likes dry, open sandy areas. It is very speedy, and almost impossible to catch. Georgia has six kinds of skinks. They are smooth shiny lizards. The five-lined skinks have brilliant blue tails when they are young. The brown ground skink lives in leaf litter on the forest floor. The mole skink burrows.

Glass lizards may exceed three feet. They look like snakes, because they have no legs. When held, they feel stiff and brittle. They really are. Like other lizards, their tails will break off if they are roughly handled. The story that they can join together after being broken into pieces is false.

How can you tell a glass lizard from a snake if it has no legs? Look at the eyes. Lizards can close their eyes, because they have eyelids, and they have an ear opening. Snakes have neither eyelids nor ears. Snakes can never shut their eyes nor can they hear. Snakes feel vibrations in the ground but they are deaf.

The world has more than 3,000 kinds of lizards. Only two are venomous: the Gila monster of New Mexico and the Mexican beaded lizard. All of Georgia's lizards are beneficial. They eat insects and the law protects them.

Mice

Description—Georgia has 19 kinds of wild mice and rats. Only a few kinds commonly enter buildings and cause trouble. They are the house mouse, the Norway rat and roof rat. House mice (*Mus musculus*) produce about 40 young per female per year. Young mice are ready to bear their own young in a few months.

Habitat—Mice can inhabit a variety of buildings including warehouses, homes, offices, sheds, barns, and garages in any area of the country. Mice can enter buildings through openings as small as ¼ inch.

Food Habits—House mice prefer cereal grains but will feed on about anything. They are sporadic feeders, nibbling bits of food here and there. Mice can live in areas without water because they can get most of the water they need from the foods they eat.

Damage—Mice ruin food, chew insulation off wires, and make nests out papers and other materials. They deposit droppings and can spread disease. Droppings, fresh gnaw marks, and nests made from fine shredded materials are indications of active mouse populations.

Prevention and Control—Sanitation is an important tool in controlling mice. Blocking entrance holes with secured sheet metal can help control rodent access to a building. When you see signs of mice, act immediately to kill the first immigrants. Do not give them time to reproduce.

Traps are not as hazardous to children as poisons. Poisons create dead mice in out-of-the-way places, which lead to odor problems. A mouse in a trap ensures that he has been eliminated. With poisons one never knows for sure.

Most people who have a mouse problem want a super poison for mice that is also safe for children and pets; one that will make the mouse dry up without stinking. There is no poison like that.

Many people think strychnine is good rodent poison. It is not. True, strychnine will kill a mouse, but professionals rate it as only a fair mouse poison. Mice learn quickly not to eat it. Rat populations are almost impossible to kill with it. They do not care for the taste. There are many poisons better than strychnine that are both legal and labeled for rodent control. They have their place but it is not in the home. Traps can work much better.

First, use plenty of traps in a room. Put them along the wall, in cupboards and drawers and other places where mice might run. Make it so a mouse will not have to travel more than 5 or 10 feet to find a trap. Do this because a well-fed mouse has a small home range. It may live for weeks in a very small area. Do not expect the mouse to cross the room to find a trap. The trap must lie in its normal travel path.

A mouse likes to run along a wall. When the mouse comes to a trap, the bait treadle should be across his path. Do not set the trap parallel to the wall and make the mice go around or over the trap to get to the bait.

Make it easy for them.

Multiple catch traps work well but one must remember to use plenty of them. Snap traps are cheaper. Cheeses, peanut butter, bacon, and anything tasty with a strong odor are good baits to use.

Leave the traps in place for a few weeks to be sure that all of the mice have been caught. Find out how they got in and close the openings. Once the house is rid of mice, save the traps. Be prepared for more mice infestations, as they will likely be back.

Moles

Description—There are 2 species of mole found in Georgia. Moles are mammals related to shrews, and have a stout body with short legs. Moles have tiny eyes covered by skin and can only distinguish between light and dark; therefore, moles are confined to their underground burrows. They are well adapted for underground life. Moles literally swim through soft earth with powerful hand-like front feet that are equipped with long, flattened toenails. Moles breed once a year and have three to four young

Habitat—Moles are most common in areas of well drained loam or sand throughout the state.

Food Habits—Moles are insectivores eating mainly insects, grubs, spiders, beetles, worms and other animals. As the mole tunnels along just below the surface, its pointed nose is sniffing among the grass roots. Moles do not eat plants, plant roots, bulbs, tubers, grass or gnaw on plant trunks.

Habitat—Moles spend much time in a deep burrow system a foot or more underground. They have one or more little rooms where they build nests. When a mole is hungry, it moves through tunnels to the upper few inches of soil. There it travels the shallow burrow system to a productive feeding area and begins to plow new ground.

Damage—Raised areas in lawns and gardens may be indicative of runways. Tunnels in lawns and landscapes are unsightly and may cause roots of grass and plants to dry out.

Prevention and Control—Overwatering lawns may force worm and grubs to near the surface where the mole hunts for them. Reduce watering and kill grubs in order to have some success at mole control.

If the thought of killing the mole is unbearable, try

starving it out. Use insecticides, like a grub killer, sparingly in feeding areas to diminish the food supply. This method may have slow and uncertain results.

For a direct approach, there is another method. Check the yard for active mole runways. Use your foot to press down all the runways at intervals of several feet. Place a bottle cap or other marker at those exact spots. The next day check these locations. If the mole has not passed through and the molehill is still flat, pick up the marker. If the mole has raised the hill up again, put a second marker.

After four or five days, it will be apparent which runways the mole uses every day. This is the key to where to put the trap. Then take a harpoon type mole trap and set it in place over the flattened runway. These traps can be purchased at nearly any garden store, home center, or large discount store that has a garden center.

Raise and lower the prongs of the trap until they easily penetrate the soil. Make sure the trap legs straddle the runway, but do not block it. Now the trap is ready for the first intruder.

When the trap is sprung, remove the trap and part the sod to see if it was successful. If the trap does not produce in three to four days and new mole activity is apparent, try another spot. Repeat the process till the molehills do not recur.

Remedies such as chewing gum and ultrasonic repellers have not been proven effective in getting rid of moles and are generally a waste of time and money. Castor oil spray may work in small, localized areas.

Opossums

Description—An opossum is a whitish or grayish mammal about the size of a house cat. Its under fur is dense with sparse guard hairs. Its face is long and pointed with rounded hairless ears. Length is to a maximum of 40 inches; the rat like tail is slightly less than half the total length. Opossums may weigh as much as 14 pounds; males average 6 to 7 pounds and females average 4 pounds.

Tracks of both their front and hind feet look as if little "hands" with widely spread fingers made them. They may be distinguished from raccoon tracks in which hind prints appear to be made by little "feet". The hind foot of an opossum looks like a distorted "hand".

Habitat—Opossums are found in eastern, central, and west coast states. Since 1900 they have expanded their range northward in the eastern United States. They occur throughout Georgia.

Habitats are diverse, ranging from arid to moist, wooded to open fields. Opossums prefer environments near streams or swamps. They take shelter in burrows of other animals-such as woodchucks or armadillos-tree cavities, brush piles, and similar cover. They sometimes den in attics, garages, or storage sheds, where they may make a messy nest.

General Biology and Habits—Opossums usually live alone, having a home range of 10 to 50 acres. Young appear to roam randomly until they find a suitable home range. Usually they are active only at night. The mating season is January to July in warmer parts of the range, but may start a month later and end a month earlier in northern areas. Opossums may raise two, rarely three, litters per year. The opossum is the only marsupial in North America. Like other marsupials, the blind, helpless young develop in a pouch.

Most young die during their first year. Those surviving until spring will breed in their first year. Maximum age in the wild is about 7 years.

Although opossums have a top running speed of only seven miles per hour, they are well equipped to escape enemies. They readily enter burrows or climb trees. When threatened, an opossum may bare its teeth, growl, hiss, bite, screech, and exude a smelly greenish fluid from its anal glands. If these defenses are not successful, an opossum may play dead.

Food Habits—Foods preferred by opossums are animal matter, mainly insects or carrion. Opossums do eat considerable amounts of vegetable matter, especially fruits and grains. Opossums living near people may visit compost piles, garbage cans, or food dishes intended for pets, such as dogs and cats.

Damage—Although opossums may be considered desirable as game animals, certain individuals may be a nuisance near homes where they may get into garbage, bird feeders, or pet food. They may also destroy poultry, game birds, and their nests.

Prevention and Control—Prevent nuisance animals from entering structures by closing openings to cages and pens housing poultry. Opossums can be prevented from climbing over wire mesh fences by installing tightly stretched electric fence wire near the top of the fence three inches out from the mesh. Fasten garbage can lids with a rubber strap or bungee cord.

Traps—Opossums are not wary of traps and may be easily caught with suitable sized wooden box or wire cage traps. Size No. 1 or 1½ leghold traps also are effective. Set traps along fences or trail ways. "Dirt hole" sets or "cubby sets" are effective. A "dirt hole" is about 3" in diameter and 8" deep. It extends into the earth at a 45° angle. The trap should be set at the entrance to the hole. A cubby is a small enclosure made of rocks, logs, or a box. The trap is set at the entrance to the cubby. The purpose of the dirt hole or cubby is to position the animal properly so that it will place its foot on the trap. Place bait such as cheese, or slightly spoiled meat, fish, or fruit in the dirt hole or cubby to attract the animal. Using fruit instead of meat will reduce the chance of catching cats, dogs, or skunks.

A medium-size body grip (conibear-220 or kill type) trap will catch and kill opossums. Place bait behind the trap in such a way that the animal must pass through the trap to get it. Body grip traps kill the captured animal quickly. To reduce chances of catching pets, set the trap above ground.

Laws protecting opossums vary from state to state. Usually there are open seasons for hunting or trapping. It is advisable to contact local wildlife authorities before removing nuisance animals.

Rabbits

Description—There are four species of rabbit found in Georgia. The New England cottontail's range extends down into the southern Appalachians. The marsh rabbit lives in the coastal plain from Alabama to Virginia. The biggest of all the Southern rabbits is the swamp rabbit. A swamp rabbit weighs up to five pounds, twice the size of the others. It inhabits a range bounded by central Texas, southern Illinois, and central Georgia. The Eastern cottontail, the most abundant, occurs throughout the South. If you see that white cottontail as the rabbit bounds away, it's a cottontail. If the tail is not bright white, the rabbit is some other kind.

Surprisingly, rabbits are not rodents. They are lagomorphs. Lagomorphs have an extra set of smaller incisor teeth right behind their two big front teeth whereas rodents do not have them. Lagomorphs recycle their food. They produce soft pellets of partly digested food at night. They take these pellets from their anus and eat them again. The dry rabbit pellets found on the ground have been through the rabbit twice.

Biology—Eastern cottontails reproduce fast and die young. Their gestation period is 30 days. Young weigh about two ounces and are ready to leave the nest in two weeks. In one year females may have three or more litters of three to six young. Most are eaten by predators; others are killed by disease. Lucky rabbits may live a year.

Habitat—Most rabbits live their whole lives in a home range of one to five acres. Swamp rabbits are an exception. They may use a 20-acre home range in the river bottom swamps they inhabit. Rabbits need thick cover and lots of low-growing greens to become numerous. Blackberry thickets in old fields are good habitat. Do not expect to find many rabbits in dense, shady forests with little green growth on the ground. Rabbits do not generally dig tunnels or burrows. They will seek shelter or refuge in old woodchuck, armadillo or tortoise holes. They will usually have their young in a shallow depression or nest lined with the mother's fur. This nest could be in mulch or pine needles or in tall grass.

Damage—Sometimes gardens appeal to rabbits. One rabbit can do a lot of damage; it may eat young sprouts, fell mature plants, and girdle bark from young fruit trees.

Prevention and Control—To get rid of rabbits, eliminate cover wherever possible. Then try trapping. Make a box trap and set it at the edge of the garden. Dry cob corn or an old apple is good bait. Perhaps the best bait is a handful of fresh rabbit droppings. Rabbits will go in to sniff them to see what other rabbit has been in there.

Repellents—Thiram-based repellents will work. Paint them on tree trunks or woody stems. Thiram isn't labeled for edible plant parts. There are many gimmick rabbit repellents, but they generally do not work.

If rabbits are a serious hindrance, a gardener's best bet is to fence the garden with a 30-inch wide strip of one-inch mesh chicken wire. It must be tight to the ground or rabbits will get under. It is best to bury the fence 6-12 inches. A cylinder of the mesh will protect stems of trees and shrubs. This type of fence is inexpensive and very easy to install. Fencing will solve most problems around gardens and chicken houses.

Raccoons

Description—Adult raccoons weigh 8 to 25 pounds and measure 26 to 38 inches long. The black mask and ringed tail are prominent distinguishing characteristics.

Habitat—Raccoons prefer wooded areas near streams, rivers or other water sources. Male raccoons home range extends about 2 square miles, while female ranges do not usually exceed 1.4 miles.

Food Habits—They are omnivorous and eat a variety of foods including fish, clams, crayfish, small mammals, birds, eggs, insects, fruits, vegetables, and grains. Raccoons will also eat pet food and garbage in urban areas.

Damage—Raccoons are garden raiders, devouring sweet corn and watermelons at the peak of ripeness. Raccoons also raid garbage cans at night and may tear off shingles to gain access to a home's attic. Once inside the attic, they tear up insulation and chew holes in walls. Their waste accumulates and creates an odor problem. Raccoons contract a number of diseases including rabies, and carry a roundworm which can cause human encephalitis. Raccoons often build nests in chimneys.

Prevention and Control—Scare devices such as lights and noises are only temporary as raccoons soon get used to them. Place garbage and pet foods in sealed containers. Trim trees to prevent access to the roof if raccoons in the attic are a problem. Electric fences discourage nuisance raccoons from vegetable gardens. Screen chimneys to deny access. Trapping may be necessary to get rid of a nuisance raccoon. Because raccoons are a serious rabies vector in Georgia, relocation is strictly illegal. Trapped raccoons MUST be destroyed. For this reason, raccoon problems are best handled by professional nuisance wildlife trappers.

Rats

Description— There are three species of rat native to Georgia; however, the two species that represent rats to most people are not native. The Norway rat and roof rat have made themselves at home with humans, carrying filth and disease. Rats are larger than mice, sometimes up to one foot long not including the tail. Norway rats are larger and heavier than roof rats. Rats are usually nocturnal. One pair of rats can produce 6 to 12 young in 21 days. A single pair could multiply into more than 640 rats in one year under ideal conditions. Eastern woodrats are really just large mice; they are native and rarely cause damage.

Habitat—Rats and mice are both accustomed to living with humans; rats have been reported living on ships and airplanes, as well as homes, offices and warehouses. Norway rats will nest under buildings and concrete slabs, along stream banks, and in garbage dumps. They tend to inhabit the lower floors of buildings. Roof rats are more aerial and may be found in trees and attics. They often enter buildings from utility lines.

Food Habits—Rats will eat any type of food, but they prefer high-quality foods such as meat and fresh grain.

Rats require more water than mice, usually ½ to 1 ounce daily when feeding on dry food.

Damage—Rats eat and contaminate large amounts of animal feed, damage structures by their gnawing, and may spread diseases. Droppings and fresh gnawing are evidence of rodent infestation.

Prevention and Control—Step One- Consider whether the location is safe for poison baits. Avoid using poison in houses or restaurants. Dead rats can die in the walls and emit a dreadful odor. Use traps for such locations.

Some kinds of poisons are better than others. For example, strychnine will kill mice, but most rats avoid it. They hate the taste. There are poison waters and poison powders, in addition to many kinds of baits. Poisons may be suitable for a location like an outdoor shed. First, lock the door and keep dogs, cats, and children away from the bait. Rats are a lot smarter than mice; they do not rush in and gobble new food. They will let the stupidest rats try a little first. Then, if the food is good, more of the rats try the new food as time goes by.

Because rats are cautious, prebaiting is necessary. That means putting out good, clean food (like corn or grain) to teach the rats where the food is. Many kinds of animal food make good prebait, as do table scraps. Plain garbage will not work well; rats are connoisseurs. They eat the best food they can get.

Put the feed in a good bait box. A large cardboard carton with three-inch holes at ground level works well. Place it near a wall where rats run. Put a little box or old flowerpot inside and fill it with prebait. Put any dog food in the area into a tightly closed garbage pail. This eliminates all competition for the bait stations and control efforts.

Check the bait box each day to see how much food is being consumed. That will indicate how much poison bait will be needed each day. Also, if pets or children discover the bait box, you have time to find a way to keep them out before starting step two.

Step Two- After a week or so, all the rats in the shed will know where the free lunch is. Now, remove the prebait and replace it with poison bait. Make things look just the way they did before. Check the box each day. Keep adding new bait. Never let it go empty so as not to turn any hungry rats away.

A multiple dose rodenticide will work within 4 to 5 days. Keep adding new bait and do not stop until no more rats are coming to the bait.

When bait no longer disappears and there is no new evidence of rat activity, clean up all bait and quit. If rat bait is left out all the time, a whole new generation of bait-wise rats may develop. Do not keep rat bait out if it is not being used and managed well.

This plan may not end a rat problem. New rats will find the area. Make repairs to keep them out. Store all food products so rats cannot get into them. Keep watch for new rats and be ready to start the bait-and-switch strategy again.

Clean out all piles of debris – boards, bricks, rocks, and firewood – anything that makes good rodent habitat. Mow grass low near buildings, clear weeds and vines. A rodent problem can be solved in a few weeks with persistent effort in keeping things neat and tidy.

Skunk

Description—Two species of skunk may be found in Georgia; the **Striped Skunk** and the **Eastern Spotted Skunk**. The Striped Skunks are the most common, and many skunks are more often smelled than seen. The Striped Skunk is about the size of a house cat and covered in long dark fur, except for a white stripe from the tip of its nose to the forehead, a white patch on the head, and two stripes down the back.

Habitat—Striped skunks prefer forest borders, brushy areas, and open grassy fields. Skunks can dig their own dens but prefer to use those excavated by other animals. They may also use stumps, caves, rock piles, junk piles, wood piles and old buildings as den sites. Skunks will generally remain in an area about 1 ½ miles around the den site.

Food habits—Skunks are omnivorous, eating berries, fruits, rodents, frogs, crayfish, birds, eggs, insects and larvae. They also eat carrion, and on occasion, dig in people's garbage for food. Skunks are generally nocturnal.

Damage—Skunks become a nuisance when their burrowing and feeding habits conflict with humans. They may burrow under porches and buildings, and sometimes damage beehives. Skunk problems can be divided into two kinds: before spray and after spray. If you have the first kind, make sure you do not allow it to turn into the second kind.

Prevention and Control—A typical "before spray" skunk problem involves a visiting skunk who is unwelcome but tolerated by a fearful owner. In this case, rule No. 1 is to be nice to the skunk and put out water and food. A small bowl of hamburger, rotten fruit or raw eggs will be hospitable. If the skunk is actually inside the house, this hospitality is essential to maintain a friendly, odorless relationship. Place the food bowl near a door and leave the door open. The skunk will leave on its own.

The purpose of the food offering is to keep the skunk happy. If the skunk is outside, get it in the habit of coming to a certain spot. Once the skunk is dining regularly, step number two is to trap it. By all means use a box or cage trap. A leghold trap will make it mad. Set it at the location where the skunk has been going for dinner. Put the bowl of food inside the trap. With any luck at all, the offending individual will be in the trap the next morning.

Once the skunk is in the trap, move ever so quietly toward the cage trap with an old blanket or gunnysack. Slowly drape the cloth over the trap. Then carefully remove the trap from the house. Do not make sudden moves. The chances of getting sprayed are not great, but it does not pay to take chances. Skunks will generally give warning before spraying by stamping their feet and arching the tail.

Once the skunk is removed to a safe place, far from the house or buildings, you can call your local Game and Fish officer for advice. He may advise you to take the skunk a long way down the road and let her go.

If the skunk is in a burrow, wait until after dark to visit the burrow. Then put a piece of meat at the entrance. Cover the burrow with a board and a big rock. The next day, carefully raise the board and check for the meat. If it's gone, that means the skunk is still at home. Remove the board and try again the next night. When the meat remains uneaten after two days, it's safe to assume the skunk was blocked out. Fill the burrow with earth and cover with a big flat rock.

Skunks that pass through the neighborhood will seek out a vacant skunk palace. After the old skunk is gone, make the premises uninviting to new skunks by covering all openings to crawl spaces.

Should you encounter a skunk out for a stroll, just stop and let it go by. It will not bother you. Never shoot a skunk. A shot skunk always sprays in its death throes; a dead skunk is a much bigger problem than a live one in some places.

If a skunk should spray in a crawl space or if your dog comes home scented, there are deodorants that work. Industrial deodorants used by pest control operators to cover dead rat odor will usually do the job. They consist of the chemical Neutroleum alpha or Neutroleum gamma. These products can be sprayed on surfaces that have been sprayed by the skunk. A professional rat control company may have such a deodorant.

An expert who studies skunk odor recommends the following recipe for cleaning pets that have been sprayed. The recipe is: Mix 1 quart of 3% hydrogen peroxide, ¼ cup of baking soda and 1 teaspoon of any liquid dish detergent in an open container and use immediately. Bathe the animal and wait 5 minutes, then rinse. Do not store this mixture in a closed container-a harmful gas is released.

Snakes

People who fear snakes are sometimes exploited when various devices to guard against snakes are advertised and put on the market. There is only one real defense against snakes: the ability to see one. Should you place your foot beside a rattler, chances are you can withdraw it safely-once you see the snake.

Learn the patterns of venomous kinds and let the others go. The Southeast has 45 species of snakes, 40 of which are in Georgia. Once you know them all, your knowledge will not become obsolete. So get a good book and learn how to identify snakes. Gardeners need not go through life being afraid of them.

Description—Snakes, like other reptiles, are cold-blooded. Snakes have long, cylindrical bodies, and do not have legs. They move about through a combination of five unique modes of terrestrial locomotion. Snakes cannot hear, but they do sense vibrations.

Snakes are either live-bearers or egg layers, but baby snakes are on their own after hatching or birth. Although some species may hibernate in the same den, snakes do not have social bonds.

In Georgia, all non-venomous snakes are protected. The six venomous snakes are **timber rattlesnake**, **pygmy rattlesnake**, **canebrake rattlesnake**, **copperhead**, **cottonmouth** and **coral snake**. Though not legally protected they should be left unharmed. They serve an important role as top predator in their ecosystem. Identification is beyond the scope of this book but many excellent guides are available from Cooperative Extension. Snakes are on the move in the fall when snakes are on the move looking for a place to rest for the winter (Snakes are not true hibernators). A second time of increased snake mobility (and observation by humans) is spring when snakes are searching for mates.

Habitat—Snakes show up in some locations more than

others in the fall. This is because some homes are located in areas where certain kinds of snakes in large numbers pass through on their way to hibernation. They may turn up on the road near a house in the fall or they may appear at the back door if the house is near the woods. Snakes inhabit a variety of habitats besides the woods or forest. In fact, old fields, hedgerows, and the edge of pastures may be more attractive habitat for snakes.

Prevention and Control—Cleaning up the yard by removing all boards and trash and even removing rock gardens and shrubbery will make backyards less inviting to snakes. Still, the odd snake may wander into the yard or house.

Habitat Modification—The primary food of most snakes (especially the larger ones) is rodents, birds, frogs, insects and eggs. No control program is ever complete without removing rodent habitat; this removes part of the habitat of rodent-eating snakes. Put all possible sources of rodent food in garbage containers, plastic containers, or in other ways make it unavailable to rats and mice. Outside the house or other buildings, keep all vegetation closely mowed. Bushes, shrubs, rocks, boards and debris of any kind lying close to the house should be removed, as this provides cover for the rodents and snakes. Be sure to keep all dog or cat food cleaned up after each feeding and keep the stored food unavailable to rodents. In short, remove rodents, rodent food and all objects that lie close to the ground that create cool, damp dark habitat for snakes and keep vegetation mowed close to the ground.

Glue boards: Glue boards have been shown to be useful for trapping snakes in or under buildings. To trap snakes, use a plywood board approximately 24 x 16 inches. Securely tack several rodent glue traps to the plywood, to make a glue patch at least seven by 12 inches. Place the board against a wall where snakes are likely to travel, and the snake will become stuck while trying to cross the board. Do not place the board near any object (pipes, beams, etc.) that the snake can use for leverage in attempting to free itself. A hole drilled through the plywood board will allow removal of the board and the entrapped snake by using a long stick or pole with a hook. Animals trapped in glue can be removed with the aid of vegetable oil, which counteracts the adhesive.

Do not use the glue boards outdoors or in any location where they are likely to catch pets or desirable non-target wildlife. The glue can be quite messy and is hard to remove from other animals.

Napthalene crystals (or Moth Balls): are probably not

effective against snakes. They are not able to smell the way humans do, but they have a sophisticated odor detection organ that allows them to "taste" the air for the presence of chemical compounds.

It sounds trivial, but snakes cannot eat people. They may bite in self-defense, but so do pets, birds and all animals. Do not just arbitrarily kill a snake.

Tree Squirrels

Description—There are three species of squirrels in Georgia: **fox squirrel**, **gray squirrels**, and **flying squirrels**. Fox and gray squirrels are active during the day. Flying squirrels are active at night.

Fox squirrels are about twice as large as gray squirrels and exhibit several color phases. Fox and gray squirrels breed when one year old. They breed in mid-December or early January and again in June.

About three young are born hairless, blind and with their ears closed. Newborn young weigh about ½ ounce at birth. Young begin to explore outside the nest about the time they are weaned at 10 to 12 weeks. At weaning they have reached about half of their adult weight.

Habitat—Squirrels nest in tree cavities, man-made squirrel boxes, or in leaf nests. Leaf nests are constructed with a frame of sticks filled with dry leaves, strips of bark, cornhusks, or other materials. Survival of young is higher in cavities (which are the preferred nest sites) than in leaf nests.

Home range size varies with the season and availability of food. Home ranges have been commonly described from 1 to 100 acres. Squirrels move within their range according to availability of food. They often seek mast-bearing forests in fall, but in spring they may favor tender buds in hardwood forests. Fox squirrels are more common in pine forests.

During the fall of poor mast years, squirrels may travel 5 miles or more in search of better habitat. Over several years squirrel populations may rise and fall dramatically. During periods of high populations, squirrels—especially gray squirrels—may go on mass migrations. At such times many animals die from exposure to bad weather, predators, and automobiles.

Squirrels are a food source for mammalian predators such as bobcats and foxes in additions to hawks, owls, and snakes. Predation seems to have little effect on squirrel populations. Typically about half the squirrels in a population die each year. In the wild, squirrels over four years old are rare, although in captivity individuals may live 10 years or more.

Food Habits—Tree squirrels are active during daylight hours gathering food and building nests. Squirrels flourish where there is an abundant supply of nuts and acorns. They also eat flowers, vegetables, seeds, fruit, mushrooms, insects and bird eggs. Squirrels will chew through bird feeders and seed containers to eat birdseed; store birdseed in tightly covered, sturdy metal containers, preferably indoors.

Damage—In nut orchards, squirrels can severely curtail production by eating nuts prematurely and by carrying off mature nuts. Both fox and gray squirrels can cause losses in pecan orchards and fox squirrels may chew bark of various orchard trees.

In residential areas, squirrels sometimes travel power lines and short out transformers. They may gnaw wires and enter buildings. They will gnaw the aluminum tie wire on chain link fences.

In yards they will chew bark on ornamental trees or shrubbery. Often squirrels take food at bird feeders. Sometimes they chew to enlarge openings of birdhouses and then enter to eat nestling songbirds. Flying squirrels are small enough to enter most birdhouses and are especially likely to eat nestling birds and eggs. In gardens squirrels may eat planted seeds, mature fruits, or grains, such as corn.

PREVENTION AND CONTROL

Exclusion—Prevent squirrels from climbing isolated trees and power poles by encircling them with an 18-24 inch wide collar of metal 3-4 feet off the ground. Attach metal using encircling wires held together with springs to allow for tree growth. Trim trees appropriately to prevent squirrels from jumping onto roofs. Close openings to buildings with heavy ½-inch wire mesh or make other suitable repairs.

Repellents—Thiram painted on plant stems or bark may reduce or prevent chewing.

Toxicants—Use of toxicants in residences may result in undesirable odors from animals that die in out-of-the-way places.

Fumigants—There are no fumigants registered for controlling tree squirrels.

Traps—A variety of traps will catch squirrels; including No. 0 or 1 leg hold trap, box traps, and cage traps. Regular rat size snap traps will catch flying squirrels. Glue traps for rats will catch small squirrels. Good baits are slices of orange and apple, walnuts or pecans removed from the shell, and peanut butter. Other foods familiar to the squirrel may also work well; for example, corn or sunflower seeds.

It is important to "pre-bait" live traps so squirrels will become accustomed to the trap before actual trapping begins. Wire the door open and place bait inside until squirrels freely feed inside. They may then be trapped one at a time and removed.

Shooting—Where firearms are permitted, shooting is effective. A shotgun with #6 shot or .22 rifle with rat shot is suitable. Check with your state wildlife agency for regulations pertaining to the species in your area. A BB-gun or air rifle can be effective.

Other Methods—Often several control methods used simultaneously are more successful than a single control. For example, to remove a squirrel from an attic, watch squirrels to determine where they enter. After squirrels appear to have left, use appropriate exclusion methods to keep them out. One or more baited traps will catch any squirrel accidentally closed in. This last step is very important because locked-in squirrels may cause damage when they try to chew their way out.

Squirrel damage in yards, gardens, forests, and orchards, often is very difficult to control. This is because during population highs, new squirrels arrive quickly to replace those shot or trapped. In high-value crop situations, it may pay to remove woods or other trees near orchards to block the "squirrel highway." Custom designed wire mesh fences topped with electrified wires may effectively keep squirrels out but are expensive.

How to Get Squirrels Out of Attics—Animals often take up residence in the attics of homes. Rat traps baited with cheese or bacon may capture the intruder or the creature may simply spring the traps and take the bait. In this situation, the best suggestion is to use a cage trap. One is likely to find out that the unwanted visitor was a squirrel and perhaps hole where it came and went is found. In this case, it is critical to make repairs to close the hole.

Closing up all entryways is essential to keeping squirrels out of houses. It is especially important to check the repairs carefully for the next week or two as the displaced animals may try to chew their way back in. Even more important is to put dishes of water, nuts, apples, or crusts spread with peanut butter at two or three places in the attic where the squirrel is likely to find them. Do this because it is very easy to lock in a squirrel when closing up holes. Without food the confined animal will get hungry and thirsty and it will run about chewing on window frames and other items, including wiring, in its efforts to escape.

After it dies, usually in some inaccessible place, it will stink. Placing food in the attic will prevent this because the squirrel will advertise his presence by eating it. Check the food dishes to see if any is missing. If there is no sign after a week that the food is being consumed, assume the intruder has successfully been removed and block all the entryways.

If the food is gone or shows telltale tooth marks, you will know a good spot to set a trap. Choose a cage trap for best results. Put a food dish inside and wait. If the squirrel is caught simply take it outside and let it go. Reset the trap; remember, there may be two, three or more animals using the attic.

How can one keep new squirrels from trying to get in? If the house is overhung with large trees, there may be no answer. Isolated trees can be encircled with bands of slippery metal about 18 inches wide nailed about four feet above the ground. If the treetops are near other trees that are part of the branchy squirrel travel ways, this method will not work.

If the squirrels are walking in on wires connected to the house, the plastic tube trick will work. Get 30-inch sections of thin walled plastic pipe 2 to 3 inches in diameter. Slit the tube lengthwise and slip it over the wire. Have a person experienced with working around electricity do this. When the inbound squirrel tries to cross the tube, the tube will rotate and tip the squirrel off the wire.

Trapping squirrels out of the backyard will not work. Squirrels are always overproducing, and the surplus animals continually hunt for vacant back yards. Even in cities, Mother Nature produces a surplus. These extra animals are always looking for a vacant back yard with an accessible attic.

Pine Voles

Description—Voles are small rodents that look like mice. They have blunt noses and short tails. In the Eastern United States the common species are the **Meadow vole** (*Microtus pennsylvanicus*) and the **Pine vole** (*Microtus pinetorum*). The pine vole has very short, fine fur and small indistinct eyes as compared to the meadow

vole, which has coarse fur, and larger eyes. In Georgia, the meadow vole is rare. The Pine vole, also known as the orchard mouse, is locally common in many parts of Georgia. The name is a misnomer—they are not particularly attracted to pines.

Meadow vole's tail – 1 ½ - 2 ½ inches
Weight = 3 ounces.

Pine vole's tail – ½ - 1 inch
Weight = 2 ounces.

Habitat—Voles have a deep burrow system usually one to two feet below the ground under the tree usually within 3 to 4 feet of the trunk. Voles make their nest in a cavity within a deep burrow system. Breather holes extend up from the deep burrow system and connect to the surface. Shallow burrows lead away from the deep burrow system to the grassy strip between the rows. In the grassy strip the tunnels may run an inch or two under the surface. If the thatch is thick, the vole may travel on runways on the surface. The shallow tunnels and runways are where the voles feed on roots, stems, and leaves. Often the floor of runways is littered with cut grass stems. If populations get too high, if drought causes withering of favorite foods, or if for any reason voles run short of food or water they will begin feeding on bark and roots.

Usually up to 10 voles will occupy a home range within 50 feet of a nest. Voles travel less during very cold or very dry weather. When the population expands or when food becomes scarce, they may travel further to new areas. Usually voles travel down a row but they may cross the vegetated strip to adjoining rows. Voles bear an average of 5 young after a gestation period of 23 days. The period of fastest reproduction is usually spring and early summer.

Food Habits—Pine voles feed primarily on herbaceous vegetation—especially roots, stems and leaves of weeds and grasses. In winter when food is scarce, or during summer droughts, they may chew tree roots for food or moisture.

Damage Identification—If chewed roots or stems or runways on the soil surface appear, voles are present. Probe the soil firmly with your fingers in the turf near the trunk. If your fingers break through the turf and you locate a burrow, you have voles. Part the thatch to look for runways. Look for bits and pieces of grass stems (⅛ – ⅜ inch long) littering the trail. Make mats of boards, rubber, opaque plastic, or ⅓ of a roof shingle. The mat makes a shelter at the surface and the voles will burrow up under the mat within a few weeks. When the mat is turned over, the burrows can be easily seen. Cut a one-inch diameter face in a whole apple and place it under the mat or place in a runway. After a day or two, the apple will show vole tooth marks or chewing if voles are present. If more than half of a medium sized apple is consumed within 24 hours, vole populations are high. An apple slice will also work for this purpose. An apple with one or two cut faces about an inch in diameter is best. You can also place apples in runways with the cut faces blocking the runway. The voles may ignore apples not in a runway. Do not confuse feeding by slugs or beetles with vole chewing—look for the tooth marks.

Place a whole apple under each shingle. Check apples 1-5 days later. If there are signs of feeding under any mats the entire area should be treated. Set mouse traps under boards or shingles to confirm that voles are present. Bait traps with a small piece of apple.

Pine voles chew bark from roots below the soil and may girdle the trunk at the ground line. Inspect roots for vole damage if trees wobble in the hole when shaken, if fruit crop is small and drops early, or if leaves wither for no apparent reason. Voles also eat young garden plants, tubers, and bulbs. This damage appears every year on roots of many kinds of plants, shrubs or trees.

Prevention and Control—Remove mulch and till the soil. Kill weeds with herbicides. Water plants to give them extra strength. Trapping may help get rid of some voles. Dig down and expose the burrows and set traps at the entrances. Bait them with a sticky paste of oatmeal and water. It dries hard, holds well, and pine voles like it. They will come out of their burrow at dusk or after dark to take the bait. Cover the trap with a little "tent" made of a shingle or cardboard. Otherwise, you may catch birds instead of voles.

Small Populations in Backyards—Pine voles will sometimes damage ornamental shrubbery or garden vegetables. You can use traps to control such populations. Place shingle or boards in likely places. Dig out a space underneath mats and set snap traps baited with apple fragments. Traps can also be set in runways. Keep trapping until voles no longer appear.

Voles like hostas and tulips, but are less attracted to daffodils. Mowing the grass closely and removing thatch will reduce the attractiveness of the habitat. Burying a fence of ¼ inch mesh hardware cloth around a large garden will prevent access by voles (and moles). Vigilance is the best control.

Predators—Foxes, weasels, hawks, owls, and many kinds of snakes, will eat pine voles. Encourage hawks and owls by installing nest boxes and perches in infested areas. They will decrease chances of a future outbreak. Predators rarely eliminate their prey completely, but they sometimes prevent unusually high populations from developing. They may also slow the rate of population increase.

Woodchuck (Groundhog)

Description—The woodchuck, or groundhog (also known as the whistle pig), is a member of the squirrel family. It has a compact, hefty body, short, strong legs with long, curved claws on the forefeet for digging and a short tail. It is heavily furred and dark brown in color, weighs from five to ten pounds and is 16 to 20 inches long. Although they are slow runners, woodchucks are alert and can quickly move into their dens when alarmed.

Woodchucks hibernate during the winter, becoming active in late February and March. Mating occurs in March and a single litter of two to four young is produced annually. The young are weaned by late June or early July, and soon thereafter strike out on their own—usually occupying old, abandoned dens. The numerous new burrows which appear during the late summer are dug by older chucks. Woodchucks are active during the daylight hours, and their range is 50 to 100 feet from their dens.

Habitat—The den and burrows are extensive and may be used for several years. Burrows may be as deep as five feet and up to 60 feet in length. Woodchucks seem to prefer to construct burrows on or near farm land where crops grow. They frequently may be found in woodlands or in abandoned farm lands and occasionally in urban areas where the combination of food and cover provides a satisfactory habitat. Usually woodchucks are found in north and middle Georgia only.

Food Habits—Woodchucks are voracious feeders. In the early morning and evening periods of the summer, woodchucks actively feed on succulent, green vegetation. They are storing body fat in preparation for hibernation during late fall, usually near the end of October or early November.

Woodchucks feed primarily on vegetables, trees, grasses and legumes. Their favorite foods include various beans, Cole crops, carrot tops, clover, squash and peas.

Damage—Their gnawing and clawing can kill young fruit trees. Gnawing occurs on the main stems of trees and lower branches close to the burrows and is easily distinguished from vole gnawing by the large size of the incisor teeth marks (¼ to ⅜ inch wide). Also, their burrowing habits produce mounds of earth and burrow holes that present hazards.

Prevention and Control—Wire fencing will help keep woodchucks out of nursery areas and small plantings. Bury the lower edge 10 to 12 inches deep in the soil to prevent burrowing under the fence. Because woodchucks are good climbers, the fence should be three to four feet high.

Trapping—Live trapping is an effective method of reducing woodchuck numbers in a small area. Live traps may be of the homemade type or wire mesh commercial variety. The opening for these traps should be eight inches square or larger. Live traps can be effectively baited with apples, carrots, lettuce or other green vegetables, preferably of the type the woodchucks are already eating. Traps should be placed at the burrow opening at dusk when the animal is in the den, in rows where damage is occurring or other areas the woodchucks frequently travel.

Place guide logs on either side of the path between the burrow opening and the trap to funnel the woodchucks toward the trap. Check the trap twice daily, and release during the daytime in a nonagricultural area.

Shooting—In recent years, there have been no closed season and no limit on the number of groundhogs to be taken by individual hunters. If safety requirements are satisfied, landowners can help reduce the number of woodchucks. Even concentrated hunting may not eliminate woodchucks and some of the problems they create. Use of rifles is restricted in some towns. Check with local authorities before hunting.

No toxicants or poisonous baits are registered for woodchuck control in Georgia.

Woodpeckers

Description—About eight species of woodpecker occur in Georgia. Common species are: the **Pileated woodpecker**; adults have a red crest, dark bills, and white chins with a small, white "eye stripe" that extends from behind the eye to the red crest. The **Red-bellied woodpecker** is sandy brown on the belly, throat, chin, and sides of face; light reddish wash on the belly; black-and-white barring on the back and wings. Both males and females have red napes (lower portion of the neck or back of head). The **Red-cockaded woodpecker** has

a white breast and belly, with black spots on the outer breast. The **Northern Flicker** looks more brownish overall, does not have the red nape or crown, has a large white rump patch, and has a black bib. The **Red-headed woodpecker** has a completely red head and a very striking black and white body pattern, with black on the tail, outer flight feathers, and main portion of the wing. The **Downy woodpecker** and the **Hairy woodpecker** both have white backs rather than the black and white ladder found on the Red-cockaded Woodpecker. The **Yellow-bellied sapsucker** has a red forehead and white patches on its wings and rump.

Woodpeckers are not song birds and belong to the order Piciformes. They are uniquely adapted for drilling holes into wood, with stout, chisel-like beaks for pecking into wood and a specially designed tongue for extracting insects or sap from wood. Other distinctive characteristics include short legs with 2 toes directed backward to help the bird grasp branches and trunks. They also have stiff tail feathers useful in supporting the bird as it grasps a trunk.

Habitat—Woodpeckers are very adaptable and can live in wooded areas, utility poles, wooden fence posts and buildings. Woodpeckers may be found in areas where trees are scarce.

Food Habits—Woodpeckers feed primarily on tree-living or wood-boring insects, although they eat other types of insects as well. For example, Northern flickers feed on ground insects including ants. Yellow-bellied sapsuckers eat tree sap and the insects attracted to it. Woodpeckers may also feed on berries, fruit, nuts and seeds.

Damage—Woodpeckers perform a great service to man by eating wood borers, bark lice and other insects harmful to trees. However, when habitat is scarce they can cause severe damage to wooden buildings and commercial or ornamental trees.

Woodpeckers drill holes for a variety of reasons. One of the most obvious is to excavate a cavity for nesting or roosting and another is to search for food. In the spring, woodpeckers also use a rhythmic pecking called "drumming" to establish a territory and attract a mate. Complaints of woodpeckers on houses during this period indicate that the birds are using the house as a "singing" post. Try to convince the bird to move his territory to reduce damage. Whether or not a control measure is used, this noisy irritation usually stops by summer.

Woodpeckers may display drumming behavior on a variety of structures including TV antennas, gutters, or ornamental and orchard trees. Drumming on antennas or gutters is mainly annoying and may not require control; however, drumming that may damage valuable trees and wood siding may require control.

Typical woodpecker damage consists of holes drilled into wood siding or trees. Sapsucker damage, however, is characterized by many rows of closely spaced holes in a tree's trunk or branches.

A woodpecker often selects a tree or house "for no rhyme or reason." The birds usually choose a few favorite areas and attack them repeatedly, leaving nearby areas untouched. Softer woods like cedar or redwood siding seem more susceptible than other types of siding.

Prevention and Control—Woodpeckers are like humans, once a habit begins it is very hard to break. Thus, begin control as soon as the problem begins. Do not wait until a pattern develops. Once you begin using a control, continue for at least 3 days before changing to another control. There is no "cookbook" approach to dealing with woodpecker damage. Evaluate each individual situation separately to determine the most effective, inexpensive control measures. Often more than one technique (for example, using both visual and sound repellents) may provide the best control.

Exclusion—If there is a history of woodpecker damage to wooden siding or ornamental trees, the best long-term solution is to exclude the birds from using the area or tree. You can put hardware cloth, plastic netting, aluminum flashing or metal sheeting around trees, under eaves and on siding. Paint the materials to match the siding or tree color for best results. Once the birds have been discouraged, repair the damaged area immediately so that other woodpeckers are not attracted to the same site.

Repellents—Visual Repellents may discourage them from pecking. Plastic twirlers (windmills), pie pans or strips of brightly colored plastic or aluminum can effectively chase away these pests. You can also buy commercial visual bird repellents.

You can make your own visual repellents with common aluminum foil, which may be the most cost effective.

1) Cut strips of aluminum 2 to 3 inches wide and 2 to 3 ft. long.

2) Attach one end of several strips to a 6 to 8 inch string.

3) Nail small brads or nails 2 to 3 ft. from the damage area. If you put them on a building, place them 6 to 10 ft. apart.

4) Attach each string to the small brad so that the foil strips hang freely and move with the breeze.

Noise Repellents—Loud noises like rock music, or bird distress calls may discourage the birds. You can buy other noise producing devices like propane cannons, fuse ropes, bird banger rockets, screamers and electronic scare devices. Remember to use these techniques as soon as damage begins and continue them for at least 3 days. Understand that when the birds leave one site they simply move to another one.

Tactile Repellents—Sticky repellents like Roost-No-More®, Tanglefoot® and Bird Stop® can also be effective when smeared on the trunk and branches of high value trees and wood siding. These materials may discolor painted or stained wood and may run in warm weather, producing unsightly streaks. Thus, test them on a small area before applying them to house siding.

In most cases you can get control quickly and effectively if you use an integrated approach: put up visual repellents, use a chemical repellent and harass the birds with noise.

Provide Nesting Areas—If it appears that the birds are seeking nesting places, providing them with snags (standing dead trees) or appropriate nesting boxes may be an acceptable alternative.

Legal Status—It is against the law to kill any woodpecker without the proper permit. Woodpeckers are migratory birds and are protected by the Federal Migratory Bird Treat Act. Penalties may range as high as a $500 fine and 6 months in jail for killing a woodpecker. The Red-cockaded woodpecker is a federally endangered species. Killing one of them carries an even stiffer fine and jail sentence. Before you can get a permit to destroy offending animals, you must show that you have used the preceding measures and that they have not been effective.

IDENTIFYING ANIMALS REPONSIBLE FOR DAMAGE

Chewing Damage

Legions of furry and feathered creatures feed on trees. They browse seedlings, girdle saplings, nip twigs, chew bark or roots, and peck holes in bark. Many people bring damaged woody plant materials to Georgia Cooperative

Exension for diagnosis. It is important to identify the mystery nibbler if you want to control damage. Here are some tips on playing detective with only a damaged twig, branch or root for evidence.

First, is the damage above or below ground? If roots are chewed, that simplifies things as Georgia has few subterranean chewers. If the tooth marks are 1/16 inch wide and large roots are chopped through, a pocket gopher is the culprit. If, however, the tooth marks are very fine, a millimeter wide or less, then it's the pine vole. Pine voles may also chew bark above ground up to a height of two or three inches. If your tree loses vigor, leaves wilt, and it wobbles in the hole, check the roots. Something may be eating them. The culprit is not a mole. They don't chew wood; they eat only insects and worms.

Suppose some creature is chewing on the trunk of small trees. If only the bark is chewed within 12 inches of the ground and tooth marks are 1/16 of an inch wide, suspect a cotton rat. If tooth marks are 1/16 to 1/8 inches wide, suspect a rabbit, especially if the chewing extends 12 to 20 inches above the ground.

Rabbits will also clip off pencil-sized stems sharply, at an angle, as with a knife. If stems are broken off bluntly, blame deer or livestock. Deer and cows leave broken ends because they do not have upper front teeth. They must pinch and pull to break sprouts or twigs.

Suppose there are nipped twigs or plates of bark chewed off several feet above ground. Suspect squirrels. If something with big teeth has bitten chunks of bark from tree trunks six or seven feet above ground and left claw marks, it was a bear. If trees are balled and debarked by some coarse toothed chewer, it was a beaver. Birds may also leave their mark on trees. Horizontal rows of small holes indicate sapsuckers. Pileated woodpeckers make rectangular holes approximately large enough to admit the end of a two-by-four stud.

There are other chewers that leave their mark on trees or shrubs. Nearly all can be identified if you know what to look for.

Holes

The hole-in-the-ground question comes to wildlife biologists or county agents in various versions. One goes like this: "Something is digging little holes all over my lawn. What is it and how can I get rid of it?" Or maybe the caller asks, "We found this little hole near the woodpile. Do you think it could be a snake hole?" The second question is easy – snakes don't dig holes, though some may use holes they find.

Identification—But how can you tell what animal made a hole? It's often easy, if you know the animals that live in your area and if you know what to look for. How big is the hole? In north Georgia, big animal like a woodchuck makes a big hole, 6 to 8 inches in diameter. Later, a fox or even a dog might enlarge such a hole. Some burrows are distinctive, like the flat-bottomed, rounded roof style of the gopher tortoise of South Georgia.

Clues—How the hole was dug can also be a clue. Is earth thrown out near the entrance? Norway rats, woodchucks, and red foxes dig in the earth at an angle and leave a mound of fresh earth in front of the burrow. A chipmunk carries his earth elsewhere and leaves little sign. Both pocket gophers and eastern moles push a large mound of earth straight up and out the hole – so much so that it hides the entrance. A crayfish carefully piles mud balls around its entrance to form a chimney.

Habitat—Also consider the animal's habitat. A burrow beside your garbage can might belong to a Norway rat. A cotton rat might make a similar burrow in an old field. If the burrow is at the waters edge, think muskrat.

A pocket gopher likes sandy soil (hence the name salamander which evolved from sandy mounder). A mole likes rich earth with lots of insects. The crayfish likes clay soil near water. Not all animals dig to make homes.

If the hole goes in just a little way and stops, it usually means an animal digging for food made the hole. A skunk in search of grubs in a lawn or pasture leaves a hole a few inches deep with earth scratched out to one side. Snakes do not dig, but readily use existing hole and root channels.

Digging

Go out early in the morning to find out who did it, and you may see crows digging for grubs. If the problem persists, stop this problem by using a soil insecticide to kill the grubs.

Sometimes one might find little conical holes in the garden, perhaps with acorn shells in the bottom of each one. In this case, an observer watched the area and saw a bluejay fly from an oak tree to the ground, set an acorn down, and begin to hammer on it. As the blue jay worked to break the acorn, he drove it into the soft earth with his beak, making a conical hole in the process. Quiet observation yields many clues.

An armadillo will dig a burrow where it can escape the heat during the day. While foraging for insects, bees, beetles and grubs, armadillos will dig a conical shaped hole 3-4 inches deep. These holes may appear overnight in the yard.

Knowing who made a burrow may not tell who is inside. That is because some animals will take over another animal's hole. Remains of prey, bird wings or bones of mammals at the entrance to a den suggest a predator of some kind lives there. You can also scrape the roof of the burrow to find hair and then compare it with hair in a museum collection.

A favorite technique is to scratch up the earth at the burrow entrance with a sharp stick. Then smooth it carefully. Go back later and check the tracks to see what has gone in or out. That may work only once for wary animals like a fox with young. After you disturb the burrow she may move her family.

In very cold winter weather, if animals are not moving, they can still leave evidence. Look for frost clinging to vegetation overhanging the entrance. Such frost often indicates that warm air from an animal's breath is coming out of a burrow.

The latest in technology for burrow studies is a tiny TV camera mounted on a flexible cable. Biologists poke the contraption down a burrow and watch the screen to see what is inside. Wildlife cameras are readily available where hunting equipment is sold.

Identifying Livestock Predators

Seeing a predator does not mean it's guilty. A sign left by a predator is the most important information when determining the cause of predation. Good detective work makes it easier to catch a predator or to prevent another accident. Here are some things to look for when diagnosing a kill.

• Is the animal simply missing?

• Are there animals remaining?

• Do you see bite marks on the carcass?

Skin the carcass if you want an accurate picture. Bites show clearly as punctures, red marks or bruises on the inside of the skin. Bites to a living animal will have blood clots under the skin. Bites to a dead animal will not – indicating that the animal was not killed by the predator but merely scavenged after it died. Where are the bites – on the neck, skull or all over? How far apart are the punctures? This gives a clue to the size of the animal that inflicted the bite marks. Examine the throat

carefully for bites. Skin the neck and cut the windpipe open. Blood and foam in the windpipe indicate injury and death by suffocation.

Did the predator eat any of the prey? Where did it feed on the carcass? Did the animal pick the skeleton clean or did it chew up the bones? Look for more clues- Does the condition of the carcass indicate the animal was healthy – or might it have been sick or dead when the predator came along? Perhaps the animal was dead of bloat, for example, when the predator found it. A healthy animal shows lightweight, pink, spongy lungs with sharp, well-defined edges on the lobes. Look for white or yellow fat around the kidneys in healthy animals. Look for bleeding or large hemorrhages around the fang or bite marks. This indicates the animal was alive when attacked by a predator instead of found and eaten by scavenger.

With the above in mind, here is a list of guesses based on evidence:

Dead Fowl—Suspect a raccoon if penned birds were caught through the wire and parts pulled through the mesh. Likewise, if birds have crops eaten out, but the rest of the bird is left. Raccoons like to eat the grain in a bird's crop.

If remains of birds are under a tree with only intestines, gizzard and feathers left, suspect a predatory bird. Suspect a great horned owl if one bird is taken each night and only the head is eaten. Owls may eat more of the bird, but they eat just the head if surrounded by plenty of food. A fox is a possibility if a single bird disappears every so often with no sign left.

If there is an obvious hole in the pen, many birds are killed, scattered and mutilated, and the place is a mess, with no sign of feeding, somebody's pet dog is more surely the problem. Mink or weasel might be the cause if lots of young chickens are killed with a bite to the throat, and then neatly piled.

Dead Livestock—Pet dogs are suspect if calves or sheep are bitten in many places and not eaten. If livestock are killed with only a bite to the neck, a coyote or an experienced dog may be the killer. Coyotes usually eat a considerable amount from the animal, starting with the internal organs.

Feral hogs (often called wild hogs) sometimes kill livestock, especially when other foods are scarce. This sounds preposterous, but it's true. They often eat the whole carcass including the rumen and its contents. Their tracks usually show well at the site.

Table 1. Identification of animal damage on woody vegetation in the southeast

LOCATION AND DESCRIPTION OF DAMAGE	MOST LIKELY MAMMAL
Below Ground	
Taproot chewed through. Chew marks about 1/16 in. wide.	**Pocket gopher**
Taproots or other roots chewed through, or bark chewed off. Bark or stem chewed up to 2 in. above ground. Toothmarks very fine 1 mm or less.	Pine vole (orchard mouse)
Stem girdling or debarking near the ground within 4 feet.	
Bark chewing up to 1 ft. above ground. Toothmarks less than 1/16 in. wide.	Cotton rat
Bark chewed within 2 ft. from ground. Toothmarks 1/16-1/18 wide.	**Rabbit**
Bark chewed within 2 in. of ground. Toothmarks very fine 1 mm or less.	Pine vole (orchard mouse)
Bark removed up to 3 ft. from ground. Lengthwise rub marks (antler rubbing).	**Buck deer (fall and winter only)**
Bark removed up to 3 ft. above ground. Mostly crosswise parallel toothmarks 1/8 -1/4 in. wide.	Beaver
Irregular strips removed at base of saplings. No toothmarks. Bark removal results from trampling.	**Cattle**
Branch girdling or debarking 4 inches or more above ground	
Irregular plates of bark removed, often measuring several inches on a side. Large toothmarks, few and scattered. Bark may be stripped from base due to inner bark feeding. Claw marks result from climbing.	**Bear**
Bark removed from trunks or branches, often at considerable heights.	Squirrel
Bark removed 2-8 feet above ground. Large irregular toothmarks combined with stripping.	**Horse**
Bark removed from twigs in patches or stems may be girdled. Chewing so fine that no toothmarks show.	European hornet (insect). Ofen mistaken for vertebrate animal damage.

Claw Marks—Claw marks left on the neck, shoulders and ribs, along with a single bite on the throat is typical of a bobcat. Bobcats rarely prey on large, domestic animals. They may occasionally take kids or lambs. Bobcats often feed neatly on one part of the carcass. The carcass may be covered with leaves, sticks and earth. It may be drug several dozen yards from the site of the kill.

If predators are taking livestock, keep chickens and other birds properly penned – there is just no way to guard improperly confined birds. Range turkeys are a problem to protect. A mesh wire fence topped with electrical wire may keep raccoons and dogs out. Trapping predators is your best way to protect livestock in pastures.

USING TRAPS

Many local animal control agencies will provide traps and assistance in dealing with nuisance wildlife. If use of a trap is necessary, it is important to set up and use it correctly to be successful in trapping the intended animal.

Overlooking details can allow a garden thief to escape. For example, animals such as a raccoon will often circle the trap and reach through the mesh from the side after the bait. A raccoon has slender forearms. It can reach three or four inches through a one-inch hole. In the process he could touch the treadle and spring the trap. This closes the door and locks him out. On some trap models (i.e. Hav-a-hart) part of the trigger release mechanism is on the outside of the trap. A raccoon could touch this and spring the trap as he circled.

Try leaning some plywood scraps against the sides and back of the trap to keep the raccoon from reaching through the mesh; be careful to place the wood scraps so they will not interfere with the movement of trap parts. Traps with all the moving parts on the inside are better. Two traps of this type are the Mosby box trap and the Tomahawk.

Make the bait in the trap the raccoon's easiest choice for a meal. Put a chunk of the best melon and some crumbled hamburger in the trap. Place a paper towel used to wipe meat juice from the skillet to lure him to the door—to tempt him-but leave him hungry. Place a trail of hamburger tidbits to the main bait at the back of the trap.

Lure the animal inside; detail is very important when you're making a "set" with a trap. A set with any trap must lure the animal to the spot and then get him in, without anything going wrong.

Cage traps are ideal for catching small animal pests in the garden because they will not harm the family pets. Box traps can also be used for raccoons. Box traps are like cage traps, but they're made of boards instead of wire mesh. Cage or box traps will also catch opossum, skunk, weasels, rabbits, and other small mammals.

After the animal is caught—There are a variety of opinions but the options are very limited. Live wild animals can and do bite when threatened or frightened. Exercise care in transporting or releasing wild animals. Some animal welfare groups would probably recommend that you release the animal in appropriate habitat. There are many problems with this option. In general, it is often illegal to translocate animals.

Other landowners do not want your problem animal. They probably have plenty of their own nuisance ani-mals. The animal being released is unfamiliar with its new habitat and often quickly becomes a meal for a resident predator. It may introduce a disease to the new population, or it may die trying to cross a road as it wanders seeking an unoccupied territory. Occasionally the animal will survive.

A veterinarian could be contacted to euthanize the animal. Bats, raccoons, skunks, and often other species will be tested for rabies. Many people simply drown the animal, although some consider this cruel. Quite probably, many animals are shot. Mice, rats, and snakes are routinely killed and buried or discarded. Larger animals present other challenges. Nature sometimes produces a surplus. When these surplus animals come into conflict with humans, the animal should be eliminated, but this should be the last option.

A successful program of nuisance wildlife management or human-wildlife conflict resolution will require patience, persistence, and, sometimes, imagination. But by using accepted methods at the correct time, one should be able to enjoy many hours of peaceful relaxation in the garden or landscape.

DISCUSSION QUESTIONS

1. What are the basic principles of the HERL model in dealing with human-wildlife conflicts?

2. Where can a land- or homeowner find a listing of licensed Nuisance Wildlife Control Operators?

3. What is the only permanent way to be free of nuisance bat roosting?

4. Beavers may create what kinds of damage for landowners?

5. Why is poisoning not an effective way to get rid of nuisance chipmunks in the landscape?

6. When is the best time to begin using deer repellents?

7. Name the signs that indicate mice or rats may be present in the home, garage, or shed?

8. Why are snake repellents not effective?

9. What are the indications that a tree squirrel may be living in an attic?

10. How would one begin to identify an animal responsible for damage in the landscape?

RESOURCES

City and County Animal Control Offices are listed in the local government pages of the telephone book.

Georgia Wildlife Web http://museum.nhm.uga.edu Provides information concerning the common species of mammals, birds, reptiles, and amphibians found in the state o

Georgia Department of Natural Resources, Wildlife Resources Division http://www.gadnr.org Provides information and on hunting and trapping regulations.

U.S. Department of Agriculture – Wildlife Services (USDA-WS) phone: 706-546-2020 Can provide technical assistance for free or operational control for a fee with nuisance wildlife issues on a large scale.

DEER-TOLERANT ORNAMENTAL PLANTS

**Gary L. Wade, Extension Horticulturist,
Department of Horticulture
Michael T. Mengak, Wildlife Specialist,
Warnell School of Forestry and Natural Resources**
(Adapted from Cooperative Extension Circular C 985)

Deer like nutrition-rich plants, especially in spring and summer when does are pregnant or nursing, when young deer are growing and when bucks are growing antlers. Fertilized plants, such as those in home landscapes, provide protein, energy-rich carbohydrates, minerals and salts. Deer also get about one-third of their water from the moisture in irrigated plants and young, succulent vegetation on expanding leaves, buds and green stems.

Nuisance deer that feast on home gardens and bucks that damage young trees by rubbing them with their antlers during the rutting season are difficult and expensive to control in residential communities. Although there are a number of commer cially available deer repellents on the market, none of them are 100 percent effective. Most "home remedy" repellents, such as soap, human hair and animal dung, are unreliable. Shooting deer or using noise guns is prohibited in most residential neighborhoods, and many citizens are opposed to this method of control. Fencing whole communities or individual properties is often not practical, and may be against local ordinances or community covenants. Trapping and relocating deer is costly and often harmful or fatal to deer.

If deer are overabundant in your neighborhood, and deer herd reduction or management is not feasible, a good way to prevent deer browsing in landscapes is to plant ornamental plants that deer do not like to eat.

There is no such thing as a deer-resistant plant, and when deer populations are high and food becomes scarce, deer may feed on plants that are thought to be deer-tolerant. However, deer generally do not like plants with pungent aromas. Some gardeners have reported success with planting strong-scented plants like lantana, catmint, chives, mint, sage or thyme adjacent to plants that deer frequently browse. Deer also shy away from plants with prickly or rough leaves and plants with a bitter taste. Sometimes, deer browse new plantings or established plants with tender new growth, then avoid those same plants when their leaves are mature.

Over the years, wildlife organizations, universities, botanical gardens and garden writers have constructed many lists of deer-tolerant and deer-susceptible ornamental plants. Because most of these lists are constructed from observational trial-and-error data instead of controlled scientific studies, they are open for criticism. Furthermore, many variables influence deer feeding preferences.

The list below is a compilation of ornamental plants for Georgia hardiness zones that appear in published literature (see Resources) as well as observations by the authors. It is intended to be a guide for selecting ornamental plants for landscapes where deer browsing is a problem. Plants known to be invasive and a serious problem in natural areas, regardless of their level of deer tolerance, were excluded from the list.

Table 1. Plants deer occasionally or frequently browse (protection is recommended)

COMMON NAME	BOTANICAL NAME
American Arborvitae	*Thuja occidentalis*
American Beautyberry	*Callicarpa acmericana*
American Elder	*Sambucus canadensis*
American Sycamore	*Platanus occidentalis*
Arrow-wood	*Viburnum dentatum*
Asiatic Lilies	*Lilium spp.*
Beech (low branches)	*Fagus spp.*
Bittersweet	*Celastrus scandens*
Black-Eyed Susan	*Rudbeckia spp.*
Blackgum	*Nyssa sylvatica*
Blanket Flower	*Gaillardia spp.*
Buttonbush	*Cephalanthus occidentalis*
Carolina Ash	*Fraxinus caroliniana*
Carolina Buckthorn	*Frangula caroliniana*
Carolina Yellow Jessamine	*Gelsemium sempervirens*
Chrysanthemum (fall mums)	*Chrysanthemum spp.*
Coleus	*Coleus spp.*
Cosmos	*Cosmos spp.*

Table 1. Plants deer occasionally or frequently browse (protection is recommended)

COMMON NAME	BOTANICAL NAME
Crossvine	*Bignonia capreolata*
Daylily (prefer flowers and flower buds)	*Hemerocallis spp.*
Eastern Redbud	*Cercis canadensis*
Flowering Crabapple (small trees and low branches)	*Malus spp.*
Flowering Dogwood	*Cornus florida*
Fothergilla (flowers and new growth)	*Fothergilla spp.*
Fringetree	*Chionanthus virginicus*
Gerbera Daisy	*Gerbera jamesonii*
Grape Hyacinth	*Muscari spp.*
Green Ash (tender new growth)	*Fraxinus pennsylvanica*
Greenbriar	*Smilax spp.*
Hawthorn	*Crataegus spp.*
Hibiscus	*Hibiscus spp.*
Some Hollies (some, such as Lusterleaf, Mary Nell, Nellie R. Stevens, Blue)	*Ilex spp.*
Hollyhock	*Alcea spp.*
Honey Locust	*Gleditsia triacanthos*
Hop Hornbeam	*Ostrya virginiana*
Hosta	*Hosta spp.*
Hydrangea (bigleaf, oakleaf, climbing)	*Hydrangea spp.*
Impatiens	*Impatiens walleriana*
Indian Hawthorn	*Rhaphiolepis indica*
Japanese Maple (tender new growth)	*Acer palmatum*
Morning Glory	*Ipomea spp.*
Trumpet Honeysuckle	*Lonicera sempervirens*
Pansy	*Viola spp.*
Petunia	*Petunia spp.*
Redbay	*Persea borbonia*
Red Maple	*Acer ruburm*
Rhododendron	*Rhododendron spp.*
Rose Balsam	*Impatiens balsamina*
Roses	*Rosa spp.*
Sedum 'Autumn Joy'	*Sedum 'Autumn Joy'*
Serviceberry	*Amelanchier arborea*
Solomon's Seal	*Polygonatum spp.*
Sourwood (tender new growth)	*Oxydendrum arboreum*
Strawberry Bush	*Euonymus americanus*
Summersweet Clethra	*Cletra alnifolia*
Swamp Cyrilla	*Cyrilla racemiflora*
Sweetbay Magnolia	*Magnolia virginiana*
Sweetshrub	*Calycanthus floridus*

Table 1. Plants deer occasionally or frequently browse (protection is recommended)

COMMON NAME	BOTANICAL NAME
Titi	*Cliftonia monophylla*
Trumpet Creeper	*Campsis radicans*
Tulips	*Tulip spp.*
Violas	*Viola spp.*
Virginia Sweetspire	*Itea virginica*
Yew (English and Japanese)	*Taxus spp.*

Table 2. Trees deer rarely browse

COMMON NAME	BOTANICAL NAME
Bald Cypress	*Taxodium distichum*
Carolina Silverbell	*Halesia carolina*
Cherry Laurel	*Prunus laurocerasus*
Crape Myrtle	*Lagerstroemia indica*
Dawn Redwood	*Metasequoia glyptostroboides*
Deodar Cedar	*Cedrus deodara*
Eastern Redcedar	*Juniperus virginiana L.*
Falsecypress	*Chamaecyparis spp.*
Fir	*Abies spp.*
Ginkgo	*Ginko biloba*
Goldenraintree	*Koelreuteria paniculata*
Gordonia	*Gordonia lasianthus*
Japanese Cedar	*Cryptomeria japonica*
Katsura Tree	*Cercidiphyllum japonicum*
Kousa Dogwood	*Cornus kousa*
Pawpaw	*Asimina triloba*
Palm	*Many genera and species*
Pine	*Pinus spp.*
Saucer Magnolia, Japanese Magnolia	*Magnolia x soulangiana*
Southern Magnolia	*Magnolia grandiflora*
Smoketree	*Cotinus obovatus*
Spruce	*Picea spp.*
Sugar Maple	*Acer saccharum*
Sweetgum	*Liquidambar styraciflua*
Tuliptree, Tulip Poplar	*Liriodendron tulipifera*

Table 3. Shrubs deer rarely browse

COMMON NAME	BOTANICAL NAME
Banana Shrub	*Michelia figo*
Barberry	*Berberis spp.*
Beautybush	*Kolkwitzia amabilis*
Bottlebrush Buckeye	*Aesculus parviflora*

Table 3. Shrubs deer rarely browse

COMMON NAME	BOTANICAL NAME
Boxwood	*Buxus spp.*
Butterfly Bush	*Buddleia spp.*
Common Witchhazel	*Hamamelis virginiana*
Cotoneaster	*Cotoneaster spp.*
Deutzia	*Deutzia spp.*
Drooping Leucothoe	*Leucothoe fontanesiana*
European Fan Palm	*Chamaerops humilis*
Firethorn (Pyracantha)	*Pyracantha coccinea*
Flowering Quince	*Chaenomeles speciosa*
Gardenia	*Gardenia spp.*
Glossy Abelia	*Abelia spp.*
Some Hollies (yaupon, inkberry, Chinese and Japanese) See occasionally browsed list.	*Ilex spp.*
Japanese Andromeda	*Pieris japonica*
Japanese Plum Yew	*Cephalotaxus harringtonia*
Japanese Rose	*Kerria japonica*
Junipers	*Juniperus spp.*
Needle Palm	*Rhapidophyllum hystrix*
Oleander	*Nerium oleander*
Osmanthus	*Osmanthus spp.*
Pineapple Guava	*Feijoa sellowiana*
Pomegranate	*Punica granatum*
Primrose Jasmine	*Jasminum mesnyi*
Sotol	*Dasylirion wheeleri*
Spirea	*Spiraea spp.*
Sweet Box	*Sarcoccoca hookeriana*
Viburnum	*Viburnum spp.*
Wax Myrtle	*Myrica cerifera*
Weigela	*Weigela florida*
Winter Daphne	*Daphne odora*
Yucca	*Yucca filimentosa*

Table 4. Ornamental grasses deer rarely browse

COMMON NAME	BOTANICAL NAME
Fountaingrass	*Pennisetum alopecuroides*
Feather Reed Grass	*Calamagrostis spp.*
Hakone Grass	*Hakonechloa macra*
Lemongrass	*Cymbopogon citratus*
Little Bluestem	*Schizachyrium scoparium*
Northern Sea Oats	*Chasmanthium latifolium*
Pampas Grass	*Cortaderia selloana*

Table 4. Ornamental grasses deer rarely browse

COMMON NAME	BOTANICAL NAME
Pink Muhly Grass	*Muhlenbergia capillaris*
Purple Moor Grass	*Molinia caerulea*
Ravenna Grass	*Erianthus ravennae*
Sedge	*Carex spp.*
Sweet Flag	*Acorus spp.*
Switch Grass	*Panicum virgatum*

Table 5. Vines and groundcovers deer rarely browse

COMMON NAME	BOTANICAL NAME
Bugleweed (Ajuga)	*Ajuga reptans*
Columbine	*Aquilegia spp.*
Confederate Jasmine	*Trachelospermum jasminoides*
Creeping Raspberry	*Rubus calycinoides*
Creeping Lantana	*Lantana montevidensis*
Dwarf Mondograss	*Ophiopogon japonicus*
Japanese Pachysandra	*Pachysandra terminalis*
Junipers	*Juniperus spp.*
Liriope	*Liriope spicata*
Plumbago	*Ceratostigma plumbaginoides*
Prostrate Rosemary	*Rosemarinus officinalis 'Prostratus'*
Sweet Woodruff	*Galium odoratum (Asperula odorata)*
Thyme	*Thymus spp.*

Table 6. Herbaceous perennials and bulbs deer rarely browse

COMMON NAME	BOTANICAL NAME
Allium	*Allium spp.*
African Lily	*Agapanthus spp.*
Amaryllis	*Hippeastrum spp.*
Anise Hyssop	*Agastache spp.*
Aster	*Aster spp.*
Astilbe	*Astilbe spp.*
Balloon Flower	*Platycodon grandiflorus*
Beebalm	*Monarda didyma*
Boltonia	*Boltonia spp.*
Bush Cinquefoil	*Potentilla fruticosa*
Butterfly Weed	*Asclepias tuberosa*
Candytuft	*Iberis spp.*
Cardinal Flower	*Lobelia spp.*
Catmint	*Nepeta spp.*
Christmas Fern	*Polystichum arcostichoides*

Table 6. Herbaceous perennials and bulbs deer rarely browse

COMMON NAME	BOTANICAL NAME
Cinnamon Fern	*Osmunda cinnamomea*
Columbine	*Aquilegia spp.*
Crinum Lily	*Crinum spp.*
Crocosmia	*Croscosmia spp.*
Crocus	*Crocus spp.*
Daffodils	*Narcissus spp.*
Dahlia	*Dahlia spp.*
Delphinium	*Delphinium spp.*
Elephant Ears	*Alocasia spp. / Colocasia spp.*
False Indigo	*Baptisia australis*
Foamflower	*Tiarella cordifolia*
Forget-Me-Not	*Myosotis spp.*
Four O'Clock	*Mirabilis jalapa*
Foxglove	*Digitalis spp.*
Gay-feather (Liatris)	*Liatris spp.*
Globe Thistle	*Echinops spp.*
Goldenrod	*Solidago spp.*
Green Jerusalem Sage	*Phlomis spp.*
Hens and Chickens	*Sempervivum spp.*
Iris	*Iris spp.*
Jack-in-the-pulpit	*Arisaema triphylum*
Lamb's Ear	*Stachys byzantine*
Lantana	*Lantana spp.*
Larkspur	*Consolida ambigua*
Lavender	*Lavandula spp.*
Lavender-cotton	*Santolina chamaecyparissus*
Lenten Rose	*Helleborus spp.*
Lily-of-the-Nile	*Agapanthus africanus*
Lupine	*Lupinus spp.*
Marjoram	*Origanum marjorana*
May Apple	*Podophyllum peltatum*
Meadow Rue	*Thalictrum aquilegifolium*
Mint	*Mentha spp.*
Money Plant	*Lunaria annua*
Oregano	*Oreganum vulgare*
Peony	*Paeonia spp.*
Perennial Sunflower	*Helianthus spp.*
Pinks	*Dianthus spp.*
Poppy	*Papaver spp.*
Primrose	*Primula spp.*

Table 6. Herbaceous perennials and bulbs deer rarely browse

COMMON NAME	BOTANICAL NAME
Purple Coneflower	*Echinacea purpurea*
Rose Campion	*Lychnis coronaria*
Rosemary	*Rosmarinus officinalis*
Royal Fern	*Osmunda regalis*
Russian Sage	*Perovskia atriplicifolia*
Snowdrop	*Galanthus nivalis*
Society Garlic	*Tulbaghia violacea*
Speedwell	*Veronica spp.*
Sweet Woodruff	*Galium odoratum (Asperula odorata)*
Statice	*Limonium latifolium*
Tansy	*Tanacetum vulgare*
Tarragon	*Artemisia dracunculus*
Threadleaf Coreopsis	*Coreopsis verticillata*
Toad Lily	*Tricyrtis hirta*
Texas Sage	*Salvia greggii*
Wallflower	*Cheiranthus spp.*
Wild Indigo	*Baptisia spp.*
Wormwood	*Artemesia spp.*
Yarrow	*Achillea filipendulina*

Table 7. Annuals deer rarely browse

COMMON NAME	BOTANICAL NAME
Ageratum	*Ageratum houstonianum*
Alyssum	*Lobularia spp.*
Annual Periwinkle	*Catharanthus spp.*
Annual Salvia	*Salvia spp.*
Baby's Breath	*Gypsophila spp.*
Bachelor's Buttons	*Centaurea cyanus*
Basil	*Ocimum basilicum*
Calendula, Pot Marigold	*Calendula officinalis*
California Poppy	*Eschscholzia californica*
Cock's Comb	*Celosia spp.*
Dusty Miller	*Centaurea cineraria*
Flowering Tobacco	*Nicotiana spp.*
Lantana	*Lantana spp.*
Marigold	*Tagetes spp.*
Parsley	*Petroselinum crispum*
Scarlet Sage	*Salvia coccinea*
Swedish Ivy	*Plectranthus spp.*
Snapdragon	*Antirrhinum majus*
Spiderflower	*Cleome spp.*

Table 7. Annuals deer rarely browse

COMMON NAME	BOTANICAL NAME
Strawflower	*Bracteantha bracteata*
Stock	*Matthiola incana*
Sweet Pea	*Lathyrus odoratus*
Verbena	*Verbena x hybrida*

RESOURCES

Adler, Bill Jr. 1999. *Outwitting Deer*. The Globe Pequot Press., ISBN: 1-55821-629-4

Appleton, Forrest. 2008. *Deer in the Urban Landscapes: Coping with the Deer by the Use of Deer-Resistant Plants.*

Halls, Lowell K. and Thomas H. Ripley. 1961. *Deer Browse Plants of Southern Forests*. Published by the Forest Game Research Committee of the Southeastern Section of the Wildlife Society.

Hart, Rhonda Massingham. 1997. *Deer Proofing Your Yard and Garden*. Stipes Publishing Co., ISBN:088266-988-5

Landscape Plants Rated by Deer Resistance. Rutgers University Cooperative Extension.

Larson, Richard. 2001. *Deer-Resistant Plants — Shrubs and Trees for the Deer-Plagued Gardener*. Brooklyn Botanic Garden.

Moreland, David. *A Checklist of the Woody and Herbaceous Deer Food Plants of Louisiana*. Louisiana Department of Wildlife and Fisheries.

Nuss, Robert J. 2001. *Deer Resistant Plants*. Penn State Cooperative Extension Fact Sheet No. GH001.

Perry, Leonard. *Choosing Deer-resistant Landscape Plants*. University of Vermont Department of Plant and Soil Sciences.

28

Structural and Household Pests

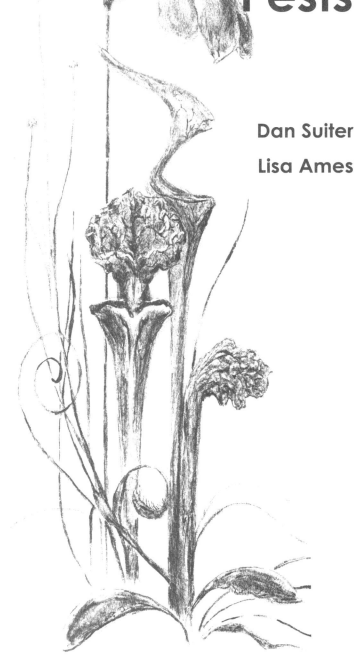

Dan Suiter

Lisa Ames

LEARNING OBJECTIVES

After you complete your study of this chapter you should be able to:

Be familiar with common nuisance pests and serious structural pests.

Be able to distinguish a termite alate from an ant.

Know techniques for preventing and controlling ants and roaches.

Be familiar with stored product and pantry pests and their control.

Be able to identify occasional household invaders and

Understand how some abiotic factors will change in the future.

TERMS TO KNOW

Alate having wings or wing-like attachments.

Concentrates pesticides that must be diluted with water before use.

Emulsifiable concentrates pesticides dissolved in a petroleum-based solvent.

Desiccate to dry up.

Fogger device that spreads a chemical in the form of a fog.

Monomorphic having only one form.

Ootheca case or capsule containing eggs.

INTRODUCTION

Insect pests found in and around the home can be numerous in both number and diversity. The presence of pests is often the result of conditions that promote the pest's survival and/or reproduction. Therefore, it is imperative that homeowners do their best to keep the home environment an inhospitable environment to pests. Homeowners should seal (doors and windows) their homes well, and make their homes difficult for pests to penetrate. Sometimes, however, pest numbers become so great that gaining relief requires chemically-based intervention(s). Although some pest problems can be remedied by the homeowner, in other cases a professional should be consulted.

If a pest problem arises, it is very important that the pest be accurately identified. An Extension Specialist's recommendations for chemical and non-chemical pest control are largely dependent on the pest's identification and a full description of the circumstances surrounding its collection and appearance—i.e., its habits, food, description, where it was found, the number found, and what it was found infesting (if anything). In some cases, chemical control of pests is not needed, and indeed of no use. In other cases, only the use of chemical pesticides will solve the problem. Many cases, however, require a combination of both chemical and non-chemical control techniques.

Homeowners should be encouraged to contact a local county Cooperative Extension agent for help in identifying pests. An Extension agent can identify samples by visual observation or by looking at a photograph. If the homeowner has access to a digital camera, a photograph(s) can be taken and emailed to Cooperative Extension for immediate identification. Specimens can also be collected, placed in a leak-proof vial filled with rubbing alcohol, and mailed to the nearest county Cooperative Extension office.

Hiring a Professional Pest Control Company

It is often best to hire a professional pest control company to tackle pest problems. If a company is hired, it is important to select a company committed to customer service, especially if the homeowner is considering entering into a long-term service contract. Some tips on hiring a pest control company include:

• Ask friends, neighbors, and co-workers about their experiences and interactions with pest control companies. Selecting a professional pest control company is not unlike selecting other service providers, such as electricians and plumbers. Consistently good recommendations are still the most reliable means of selecting a quality pest control professional.

• Avoid going to the yellow pages and selecting a company based solely on an advertisement. Furthermore, do not hire a pest control company based on treatment price alone. A variety of factors should be considered when making a decision on which company to hire.

• Ask prospective companies to describe their commitment to the continuing education of their pest control technicians. Although all technicians in Georgia are required to attend State-approved continuing education seminars, some companies provide in-house training or send their employees to University- or State-sponsored training programs and workshops that are above and beyond that required by the State.

• Ask prospective companies whether they are a member of their state and/or national pest control organization(s) or association. Membership in these organizations suggests that the firm is well-established, and that the owners are active in their profession. Membership also suggests that owners and managers attend national and state conferences where insight into key issues facing the pest control industry are highlighted and discussed, and the most recent findings on pest control research and application technology are presented.

Product Types

There are a number of approaches that can be utilized for the treatment of existing pest infestations, but no single chemically-based approach is completely effective. An integrated approach, therefore, that incorporates both chemical and non-chemical techniques is best suited for the long-term management of urban pests.

Before selecting chemically-based pest control measures, a thorough inspection of the outdoor and/or indoor premises should be conducted to determine the extent of the infestation and to highlight those areas where control approaches should be focused if they are needed. Many indoor infestations of urban pests can be tracked to areas of pest activity (harborage) on the outside of the structure, while still other pests are found only indoors.

Bait products—Over-the-counter bait products are generally limited to ant, cockroach, rat, and mouse control. Most can be used both inside and outside the home. Baits are available in the form of gels/pastes, granules, liquids, stations, or blocks, and are ready-to-use when purchased. Baits are products that kill pests only after being consumed. As such, they are comprised of a toxicant (i.e., active ingredient) incorporated into a food source (i.e., the bait material) that is both palatable and preferred by the target species.

Since baits contain food materials, they are susceptible to spoilage. Read the product's label to determine if the bait has an expiration date. Baits are target-specific, and considered more environmentally-sensitive, than the other chemically-based control tactics discussed hereafter.

Granular products—Granular products are formed by impregnating or coating insecticide onto a small granule of non-active carrier (e.g., clay, corncob, sand, silica, sawdust, etc.). Granular products are applied only on the outside, and are used to control a wide variety of crawling pests by application to places pests live—i.e., mulch, leaf litter, lawn, etc. Granular products are purchased in large bags (10 or 20 pounds) as ready-to-use products.

After application, the insecticide must be released from the granule by allowing water to wash over it and dissolve it. Thus, granular 'activation' requires lawn-watering or natural rain. Unlike liquid sprays (discussed below), granular products may remain active for as long as six to eight weeks. Like liquid sprays, granular products act by contact (killing) and probably by keeping foraging pests out of treated areas (repellency).

Granular products exhibit one distinct advantage over spray formulations—their weight. The weight of the granule allows the chemical to reach deeper into treated areas than would be expected from a liquid spray treatment (discussed below) applied directly to the same area. It is critically important to realize that pests do not eat granular products, as they do some baits that are delivered as small granules. In fact, a granular product is never a bait, but bait can be delivered in the form of a granule.

Dust products—Dust products have the consistency, look and feel of powder and when purchased are ready-to-use. They are not mixed with water, and are applied dry. Dusts are comprised of small particles of active ingredient mixed with equivalently small particles of an inactive carrier material such as talc or clay. Most dusts work because insects pick up the minute particles and ingest them, while others desiccate the insect, causing it to dehydrate and die.

Generally, dusts should be used only in dry voids such as behind brick veneer, drywall, electrical switch-plates, and synthetic stucco to remedy existing pest problems indoors and to prevent the reinvasion of pests into voids from the outside.

Many homeowners make the mistake of over-applying dust. Too much can be repellent, causing insects to avoid dusted areas. Apply dusts so that a very thin film settles in treated voids and on treated surfaces. Ideally, the quantity of dust applied should be only slightly visible in comparison to undusted areas. Some dusts never degrade, while others remain effective for up to a year.

Some dusts contain a high concentration of active ingredient, and should never be applied where they can be accessed by non-target organisms—including the applicator. Misapplication of dusts can result in accidental inhalation and thus unnecessary exposure. Since dusts become airborne very easily, it is advisable to always wear a protective mask and preferably eye protection when applying them.

Aerosol and fogger products—The contents of aerosol cans and total release aerosol foggers are pressurized, usually contain a propellant and the pesticide(s), and emerge as a fine mist or smoke (i.e., microscopic droplets). Aerosol cans are very popular among homeowners because they result in 'revenge' killing—i.e., direct spraying and immediate knockdown and kill of the target pest. Although aerosol cans may be effective in the short-term, they should not be relied upon as the sole means of chemical pest control in and around the home.

Some aerosol cans shoot their contents in a jet stream, and are a good choice when there is a need to treat pests from a distance. Although aerosol cans may be used both indoors and outdoors, the use of foggers is restricted to indoor use especially when treatment requires that a room be filled with pesticide for an extended period of time.

If aerosols are used indoors, never use them in voids or near fires. Wet formulations not only damage drywall, insulation, and wood molding but there is a danger of electrical shock and/or fire when using liquids around electricity. Furthermore, many aerosols and foggers are flammable.

Liquid spray products—Liquid spray products most commonly available to homeowners are emulsifiable concentrates (ECs) and, to a much lesser extent, wettable powders (WPs). ECs are available as concentrates (these products must be diluted with water before use) and ready-to-use products (these products are usable without further dilution). Ready-to-use EC products are commonly sold in 1-gallon jugs. Wettable powders are available only as concentrates.

Emulsifiable concentrates are composed of an insecticide dissolved in a petroleum-based solvent which, when mixed with water, forms a milky-white emulsion that can be sprayed. Wettable powders are created by impregnating or coating an inactive material (clay or silica) with an insecticide. The resultant dust-like powder can then be mixed with water and sprayed. Emulsifiable concentrates do not require agitation (shaking) while wettable powders do because the powder will settle to the bottom of the spray tank if given sufficient time (hours).

The main hazard with undiluted emulsifiable concentrates is that they are readily absorbed should the material come in contact with unprotected skin. They do, however, protect against inhalation hazard. Since wettable powders are dry and the particles small, accidental inhalation may result if precautions are not taken when mixing. To avoid inhalation, always wear a mask when working with wettable powders and dusts.

Emulsifiable concentrates are readily absorbed by porous substrates, making them fairly unsuitable for treating concrete, brick, unpainted wood, mulch, and other porous surfaces because the chemical is unavailable to the target pest(s). **Wettable powders**, on the other hand, are readily available to target pests on these substrates because the powder remains on top of the treated surface after the water evaporates. As such, they are excellent for use on porous materials, and are generally better than emulsifiable concentrates when treatment of porous, outdoor substrates is needed.

Liquid spray treatments are commonly applied to the outside of infested homes in either of two ways. To conduct a **perimeter treatment**, spray the outside walls two to three feet high and spray the ground for three to five feet away from each wall around the entire perimeter of the home. Spray as many areas where pests live or are traveled or potentially traveled as possible. Concentrate spray treatments to areas where pests might enter the structure, such as around doors and windows, inside weep holes, and inside wall penetrations such as gas, plumbing, and exhaust pipes. Perimeter treatments should be re-applied every four to six weeks during the summer and within a week following a heavy rain. Perimeter treatments may require up to 10 gallons of spray, depending on the size of the structure treated.

Spot treatments are limited to those areas where pests are found living and breeding. Typically, no one spot requires more than a quart or so of spray—sometimes less, depending ultimately on the severity of the pest infestation. When spot treating, only those areas considered nests and/or breeding sites or areas where pests are found entering the structure are treated. Breeding sites should be exposed prior to treatment. For example,

exposure of breeding sites in mulch can be accomplished by pulling back the mulch with a stiff rake or similar instrument held in one hand while treating exposed nest sites with the other.

Unfortunately, research has shown that liquid-based spray treatments applied outdoors provide only temporary relief (up to 30 days) against invading pests. Many sprays break down quickly when exposed to intense sunlight, heat, and moisture—dominant outdoor conditions when pest infestations are greatest.

Moisture management—Homeowners should make every attempt to limit the occurrence of excessive moisture in and around their home. It is the most important condition conducive to pest infestation. Since all life forms are dependent upon moisture, its excess not only attracts pests but allows them to thrive. Some common reasons for excessive moisture in and around homes include improper grade/drainage; misdirected sprinklers; clogged gutters and downspouts; and downspout discharge within five feet of the structure. The property owner should ensure that water flows away from the structure, that grade is appropriate, and that gutters and downspouts operate properly.

Property owners should especially keep groundcovers, shrubs, vines, and mulch several feet away from outside foundation walls, as these horticultural practices often retain moisture. Mulch retains moisture in the soil thereby creating zones that provide conditions (high moisture) pests need to explore and thrive in an area. Although no scientific data specifically address the affect that mulch has on pest infestation rates, it is intuitive that mulch placed against a structure's outside walls allow some pests easy access into the house. Excessive moisture also leads to abundant new plant growth, which in turn leads to high populations of honeydew-producing insects, which in turn support large populations of ants.

WOOD DESTROYING INSECTS

Subterranean Termites

Subterranean termites cost the American public over one billion dollars each year to repair the damage they cause and to hire termite control companies to treat infested structures. In the United States subterranean termites are most abundant, and thus cause more structural damage, in the south and southeast. In the southeast, any yard in a suburban neighborhood will likely have a resident population of subterranean termites that can be found feeding on wood fence posts, garden stakes, railroad crossties, tree stumps, fallen limbs, firewood, etc. While subterranean termites are obviously common around homes, structural infestations are not necessarily inevitable. A home's susceptibility to termite attack is dependent upon a number of things, including construction type and perhaps conditions in and around the structure that favor the growth and survival of local termite populations.

Subterranean termites are soft-bodied insects that dehydrate easily, so they must have access to a moisture source. This is usually accomplished by maintaining contact with the soil, but moisture can be obtained from a variety of aboveground sources such as leaky roofs, rain gutters, and condensation from air conditioners. Subterranean termites will eat nearly anything that contains cellulose (e.g., wood and wood products, books, boxes, wicker, paneling, drywall, some carpets, wood cabinets, furniture, mulch, wood flooring, etc.), but prefer to eat softwoods such as pine or fir. Unfortunately for property owners, softwoods are commonly used in structural components such as wall studs, sill plates, joists, headers, window frames, and sub-floors.

The caste system of organization in a termite colony—Termites exhibit a caste system of organization, wherein physically distinct individuals perform different tasks. Generally, three castes are recognized. Worker termites are physically and sexually immature males and females and are the most numerous caste. These wingless, white insects are typically the first termites seen when an active shelter tube, infested log, or piece of infested structural wood is breached. Workers destroy wood because they consume it. They are called workers because they perform most of the labor associated with colony maintenance. Soldier termites are physically and sexually immature males and females whose primary function is colony defense. Soldiers are easily identified by their enlarged, yellowish to yellowish-brown head and long, hard black mouthparts that they use to ward off enemies, primarily ants and termites from other colonies. Reproductive termites, called swarmers, have two pairs of long, narrow wings of equal size. Swarmers are male and female adults produced by mature termite colonies in an attempt to establish a new breeding population.

Shelter tubes—Shelter tubes are composed of soil particles and other debris bound together by termite saliva and fecal secretions. Shelter tubes protect termites from predators and help prevent moisture loss from these soft-bodied insects. They are often constructed on the surface of concrete and other non-food substrates. For a more complete discussion of the biology of structure-infesting subterranean termites, see University of Georgia Cooperative Extension bulletin #1209, *Biology of Subterranean Termites of the Eastern United States.*

First sign of infestation: the swarm—Most often, the first sign of termite infestation that a property owner experiences is the sudden presence of winged termites (reproductives) inside the home, a phenomenon commonly referred to as swarming. During a swarming event hundreds, if not thousands, of winged termites emerge within a very short period of time—usually just minutes. Fortunately, winged termites that emerge indoors are not usually a threat to the structure because they are not likely to find a suitable location to establish a new nest site due to the inhospitable indoor environment. Furthermore, winged termites do not bite or sting, and can be easily removed with a vacuum.

A termite swarm inside the home, or from a structural component outside, is generally accepted as evidence of a structural infestation, and should be considered as such. A swarm observed outside the home from, for example, firewood, stumps, mulch, or railroad crossties is not indicative of a structural infestation. Swarms that occur outdoors simply indicate that a mature termite colony is in close proximity to the site of the flight, but not necessarily one that has or will infest the structure. In this case, however, property owners should consider having their building inspected for termites.

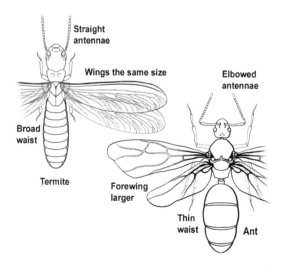

Figure 1

Figure 1. Termite and ant alate comparison. (Illustration by Erin Daniels.)

When swarming, winged termites disperse by flying—usually a short distance because termites are poor flyers—land on the ground, and lose their wings almost immediately. Soon thereafter, females emit a pheromone that attracts male termites for the purpose of mating. After pairing, the termites search for a location to begin a new colony. The most suitable location is one that contains adequate cellulose (a food source) and moisture (for survival), and is protected from natural enemies such as ants, birds, lizards, frogs, etc. The vast majority of winged termites die within a day or so of swarming. Many settle in areas void of moisture and die of dehydration or are consumed by predators. However, if a suitable site is identified, the pair will excavate a small depression and create a closed cell, where they mate. The newly mated pair are now the king and queen of a new termite colony.

A single colony may swarm more than once a year, but second and later swarms often do not match the intensity of the first swarm. It is common for termite colonies in the same area to swarm on the same day, making it difficult to pinpoint the source of the winged exodus.

Depending on the species, winged termites can be black, brown or caramel in color and can be distinguished from winged ants by:

- The presence of straight, bead-like antennae (winged ants have elbowed antennae),
- The lack of a "waist" (winged ants have a distinct constriction between body regions), and
- The presence of two pairs of wings, where all wings are the same size (winged ants have two pairs of wings but the front pair is larger than the hind pair).

It is important that insects suspected of being termites be properly identified. Consider the consequences of an incorrect identification. Any insect misidentified as a termite might result in an unnecessary treatment and needless financial costs and property owner worry. A termite misidentified as any other insect might result in a prolonged infestation, resulting in otherwise avoidable structural damage.

Homeowners and termite control—Although tempting, it is not recommended that property owners treat their own structure for an existing termite infestation. The treatment techniques, products, and equipment needed to rid a building of termites are available only by hiring a professional. One of the most important challenges confronting anyone attempting to control termites lies in locating and properly treating the area(s) where termites are entering the structure. This goal can best be accomplished by a professional.

Termite control service contracts—There are two basic types of contracts offered to consumers by professional termite control companies. Contracts generally state that companies will either (a) treat a recurring termite infestation (the re-treat only contract) or (b) treat a recurring termite infestation and repair new structural damage caused by termites (the re-treat and repair contract). Because the specific terms and conditions of termite control contracts vary considerably from company to company, it is advisable to study and understand each contract type before one is selected.

Contracts offered by termite control companies are typically renewable annually for a set number of years—i.e., the contract's term. Many companies offer a 5-year annually renewable contract term, but shorter and longer terms are also available from some companies. The term for many termite bait contracts has no maturity date, and may remain open-ended for as long as the customer continues to pay the annual renewal fee.

The cost of the initial treatment typically covers the contract for the first year. At the beginning of the second year, and each year thereafter until the contract term expires, an annual renewal fee is usually required. Each year, the contract is considered renewed and thus its active status continued only upon receipt of the annual renewal fee. Most companies may cancel the contract if the annual renewal fee is not paid by its due date.

The annual inspection—Inspections are the cornerstone of prevention and control of termite infestations, and thus the property owner's first line of defense against damage. However, determining a structure's infestation status is often difficult because most wood components are hidden from view and thus not accessible during inspection. Generally though, a cessation or lack of termite activity following treatment may be regarded as evidence of termite control.

Most termite control contracts provide for periodic inspections, whether automatic or when requested by the property owner. If an automatic inspection is not included in the contract's terms and conditions the property owner should request one, in writing, each year at the time the annual renewal fee is paid. Annual inspections usually occur on or around the date of the initial treatment, and are performed only after the annual renewal fee is paid. Termite inspections are not mandatory in Georgia.

Some factors that may affect contracts: type of construction—A structure's susceptibility to termite attack is in large part a function of its construction type. Some construction types (and practices) lend themselves to attack by allowing termites easy and undetectable access into the structure. Any type of siding that extends into the soil, especially synthetic stucco construction, rigid foam board insulation, or pre-formed Styrofoam foundation systems, as examples, are construction types that make buildings more susceptible to termite infestation because they often allow termites easy and undetectable access to wood in the structure. Property owners should keep a six inch gap (minimum) between the soil and the bottom of any type of outdoor siding, and under no circumstance should siding be allowed to extend below grade.

Some termite control companies refuse to treat structures containing one or more of the above-mentioned elements because of their propensity for termite control failure. Even if a company treats, it may not offer the consumer any form of guarantee or warrantee because the risk is too high that termites will return despite a company's best treatment efforts.

Some factors that may affect contracts: wood-to-ground contact—Perhaps the most common, yet avoidable, condition that can be linked to termite infestation is wood-to-ground contact. Wood-to-ground contact allows termites their easiest access into untreated wood and from there to the remainder of the structure. Other forms of wood-to-ground contact that may enhance termite survival and growth include wood debris close to the structure and in contact with the soil—e.g., wood and wood products on the ground in a crawlspace, firewood piled on the ground and next to the structure, stumps, wood fences, etc.

Carpenter Bees

Carpenter bees get their common name because they burrow into wood to create nest sites, referred to as galleries. Carpenter bees are approximately one-inch long and similar in appearance to bumblebees. Both are hairy, however the abdomen of carpenter bees is naked where the abdomen of bumblebees contains fine hairs. The abdomen of carpenter bees is also shiny blue to black or green. If carpenter bee problems are not addressed, damage to wood can become significant since bees return to the same nesting area year after year.

Carpenter bees damage wood because they chew it to create nest sites. They do not eat wood, as do termites. Bees are most noticeable in the spring, and in Georgia the most active month is April. During the spring, property owners often encounter large, aggressive bees hovering around the outside of their homes, especially wood fascia boards, decks, etc. Male bees, although harmless because they lack a stinger, often hover and seemingly attack passersby in defense of nest sites. Female bees are not aggressive are sting only if provoked (e.g., handled).

The entire life cycle of carpenter bees, with the exception of mating, occurs inside infested wood. In the springtime, adult female bees create nest sites by chewing an almost perfectly round, dime-sized hole in the wood. Bees may also commonly utilize old nest sites that they or other bees have created and used in the past. Wood most susceptible to carpenter bees is protected (such as under an eave), horizontally positioned, untreated, and weathered softwoods such as pine, fir, and especially cedar. Wood members attacked include fascia boards, eaves, window sills and trim, doors, headers, siding, shingles, porch ceilings, outdoor wood furniture, decks, etc. Because bees do not eat the wood they chew, they leave behind small piles of sawdust directly underneath the hole created. After entering the wood, typically an inch or so deep, bees then make a 90 degree left or right turn (with the grain of the wood) and chew an additional four to six inches of wood to create a nest gallery. At the end of the gallery, the female bee lays a single egg on a small ball of pollen she has provided. The pollen serves as a food source for the developing larva.

Following egg laying in the first "cell", the female then backs up and seals closed the provisioned cell with a mixture of saliva and wood bits. She then repeats the process until the entire length of the excavated gallery is filled with cells—about six. When the process is finished the eggs hatch, the resultant larvae continue development while feeding on the pollen, and pupation occurs. The next generation of adult bees then emerge in mid- to late-summer. Depending on environmental conditions, development from egg to adult requires one to two months in Georgia. In mid- to late-summer adult bees emerge through the entrance hole originally created by their mother. During the next several months, carpenter bees, like most other bees, spend their time feeding on nectar from flowers. It is at this point that carpenter bees, like bumblebees, can be seen on flowers in vegetable and other gardens in one's yard. At some point in the fall (probably triggered by declining temperatures and/or shorter day lengths), adult carpenter bees return to the same, or similar, gallery where they were born. There they survive the winter season by hibernating (sleeping) inside the protected galleries. The following spring (March and April in Georgia) adult bees (now almost one year old) emerge from their galleries, feed on nectar and mate. Male bees die soon after mating, while newly-mated female bees return to previously-worked nest sites and the cycle re-news. Female carpenter bees die soon after egg-laying is complete.

Control of carpenter bees should consist of a two-pronged approach. First, active bees and their nest sites should be treated with an insecticide to eliminate existing bee activity and stop them from causing further damage. If needed, wood that is severely damaged should be replaced. Second, the environment where bees nest should be altered so that it is no longer conducive to nesting activity.

In the springtime, when bees are actively nesting, galleries should be treated directly with a liquid-based insecticide applied liberally into each hole. Alternatively, dust can be applied into each hole. One or the other, but not both, chemical approaches should be used. Both will work, but may interfere with one another if used simultaneously. Chemical insecticides will kill active bees that return and come in contact with the treated gallery. Some aerosolized products are pressurized so that they will shoot a stream of insecticide 15 to 20 feet. The pressurized spray can be directed towards each hole, and the hole then treated until fully saturated. Aerosol sprays will not only kill actively nesting bees but may also work deep into galleries, killing existing larvae if present. Treating from a distance is important when treating nest sites of insects that may sting. Thorough treatment, with either a dust or aerosol, will contaminate bee galleries, thereby helping to prevent their further use (for at least that season) while killing active bees.

To prevent bees from using the same galleries during the existing season or from chewing new galleries the next season, several days after chemical treatment (above) existing carpenter bee holes should be sealed with a wooden dowel and the wood sanded and painted. Stained, lightly painted, and even some treated woods (such as those used to build decks) remain susceptible to attack, and thus damage. Some stains discourage carpenter bee nesting activity.

Affected surfaces can also be treated with a wettable powder-based pyrethroid insecticide. Wettable powders will not only kill bees that land on the treated surface, but will repel them as well—some pyrethroid insecticides have repellent properties. Pyrethroids break down quickly under common springtime environmental conditions, so they should be reapplied to at-risk wood every 3 weeks or so during the bees' active period. In addition to their repellency, pyrethroid insecticides (including pyrethrins used in jet sprays) are highly toxic to bees.

Plugging holes made by carpenter bees without painting or staining the wood thoroughly may lead to additional damage from returning bees the following spring. Treat with insecticides first, wait a few days (to allow live bees to contact the deposits and die), fill the holes, and then paint or apply a quality stain.

Wood Boring Beetles

Lyctid powderpost beetles infest only hardwoods and mainly those less than 10 years old. This beetle is not a pest of structural wood, but is common in decorative hardwoods found in, but not limited to, staircase banisters, wood floors, doors, gun stocks, picture frames, and hardwood bowls and plates. Adult beetles are 3 to 7 millimeters long, cigar-shaped, have two-segmented, clubbed antennae, are brown to reddish-brown, and their head is visible from above.

Generally the first sign of a lyctid powderpost beetle infestation is the occurrence of very fine powder that shows up on the hardwood item, perhaps a floor; the powder is always accompanied by a small, perfectly round shothole in the wood approximately 1-3 mm in diameter. The hole is created by an adult beetle chewing its way out of the wood. Adult beetles are rarely seen. In Georgia, winter (December to February) is the most common period for beetles to emerge from infested hardwoods.

Lyctid powderpost beetles are problematic, because they desecrate newly-purchased, often expensive, decorative hardwoods. Typically, beetle infestations are first noticed only after the wood is purchased/installed, put in place, and is being enjoyed—usually within a year or two of its purchase.

Well before the wood is made into a purchasable product the female beetle must lay her eggs on an unfinished (no paint, varnish, wax or similar finish) wood surface. She typically deposits up to 50 eggs into the pores that result from the cutting of the hardwood. In fact, the female beetle will not deposit eggs on a finished surface because no pores exist. Therefore, finished pieces of hardwood in the home are not generally susceptible to infestation. After egg laying, the larvae hatch, burrow into the wood, and spend the next year (sometimes longer, depending on sapwood content, beetle species, wood species, temperature, moisture, etc.) inside the wood before it pupates and the adult then emerges. The hardwood is nearly always infested well before it makes it into the home. While inside the wood, the larvae molt several times. It is during this time that they consume the sapwood as their sole food source. After some time, the last instar larva migrates to the edge of the wood where it pupates. The adult beetle then emerges from its pupal case. To free itself, the adult chews a small, almost perfectly round hole (1-3 mm in diameter) in the wood and emerges to the outside air. It is the chewing of the hole in the wood that results in the piles of fine, powder-like frass—thus the name, powderpost beetle. This is typically the first sign of a powderpost beetle infestation, and when the homeowner first takes note.

Often times the best way to remedy a Lyctid powderpost beetle infestation is to replace the wood that the beetles are infesting. Another, much more expensive, alternative is to fumigate. This is the least attractive of all remedies as the cost and hassle associated with fumigation may exceed the cost of infested wood replacement. Lastly, the beetles can be left alone and the problem allowed to run its course. Unfortunately, this may take another year or more and there is no way to determine the eventual, final aesthetic damage to the wood since it is not possible to know the extent of the infestation.

Anobiid powderpost beetles are pests of structural wood, but are not as destructive as subterranean termites. Homeowners diagnosed with an infestation of anobiid powderpost beetles should seek advice and help from a County Extension Agent and/or a pest management professional. Anobiid powderpost beetles infest structural wood and are commonly found in sills, headers, and joists in crawlspaces. Wood suffering from excessive moisture (e.g., result of no vapor barrier in the crawlspace) is most susceptible to attack. Evidence of Anobiid beetles are perfectly round shotholes in wood approximately 1.5 to 3 mm in diameter, with small piles of dust (powder) directly underneath or streaming from each hole. Anobiid beetles are one-eighth to one-quarter of an inch long, elongate and cylindrical, brown to black, and their head is not visible from above.

Perhaps the most important task during inspection for Anobiid powderpost beetles is to determine the status of the infestation—i.e., whether it is active or not. Treatment for both species involves wood replacement, and/or wood treatment, and/or fumigation, and/or installation of a vapor barrier and an appropriate number of crawlspace vents.

ANTS AND COCKROACHES

Ants

Argentine ants—Argentine ants are one of the most common nuisance insect pests encountered by property owners and pest management professionals in the southeastern United States. They are native to South America, and were accidentally introduced into the U.S. in one or more New Orleans, LA coffee shipments in the late 1800s. Argentine ants are three-sixteenths of an inch long (4 mm), monomorphic (i.e., all ants are the same size), and dull or flat brownish-gray in color. Argentine ant colonies are large, and may consist of tens, if not hundreds, of thousands of individuals.

Argentine ants are opportunistic nesters, and outdoors are most commonly found in mulch, in leaf litter on the ground, in the litter of unmaintained rain gutters, in compost piles, in rotted logs, and under rocks, patio stones, potted plants, etc. In buildings, Argentine ants commonly seek nest sites in the voids between block and brick veneer (via weep holes), behind synthetic stucco, in wall voids under window sills, and other warm, protected environments.

In Georgia, pine straw is commonly used as a mulch in flower beds and landscaped areas around the outside perimeter of homes. Mulches are beneficial to plants , because they prevent the loss of soil moisture and thus reduce plant stress during periods of drought and extreme heat. Unfortunately, pests such as ants, termites, cockroaches, millipedes, pillbugs, and springtails are attracted to mulched areas because of their high moisture content and abundance of hiding places. Pine straw not only provides adequate moisture for survival, but the spaces between the pine needles provide an unlimited, protected habitat for ants and other household pests to nest and harbor. Collections of leaf litter and various other organic yard debris behave like mulch by hindering loss of soil moisture, and are likewise excellent nest sites for Argentine ants and other household pests.

When baiting for Argentine ants, place baits where ants are seen foraging (inside and/or outside structures) and if possible always in the shade when baiting outdoors. Most ants do not forage in the direct sun or during the heat of the day, but may be found foraging in shaded locations. During drought or extended periods of moisture stress liquid baits can be used to take advantage of the ants' natural propensity for sweet liquids (i.e., honeydew). Second, it is often advantageous to use several different baits simultaneously to discover one that ants will readily consume since no single bait is consistently eaten by Argentine ants. Try switching baits periodically to provide ants a variety of food materials and the constant presence of "new" food items in their foraging territory. This activity may help sustain bait intake by the Argentine ant colonies. Third, it is advantageous to place a large number of baits or bait placements (at least several dozen) throughout the entire area where Argentine ants have been found. Larger numbers of workers spread throughout large ant colonies will mean that bait material will be diluted among potentially tens of thousands of workers. Finally, when applying granular baits (use them only outdoors), they should be delivered from a number of small piles (about the size of a quarter) placed on the ground in areas where ants have been found. Ants collect more food when they recruit to a single site than if they have to forage for every granule—i.e., when bait granules are scattered.

Granular products should be applied only on the outside of structures for Argentine ants by direct application to ant nest sites such as mulch beds, leaf litter, etc. noted earlier. Most dusts work because the Argentine ants pick up the minute particles and ingest them. Generally, dusts should be used only in voids such as behind brick veneer, drywall, electrical switch-plates, and synthetic stucco to remedy existing Argentine ant problems indoors and to prevent the reinvasion of ants into voids from the outside. From the outside, mortar joints between bricks or blocks may be drilled and dust injected into the void, or the weep holes in brick veneer can be used to introduce dust into voids. Remember that dusts become airborne very easily. It is advisable to always wear a protective mask and preferably eye protection when applying them.

Liquid spray treatments are commonly applied to the outside of infested homes in areas where Argentine ants might enter the structure, such as around doors and windows, inside and around weep holes, and inside and around plumbing and exhaust pipe penetrations.

Spot treatments are less intrusive than perimeter treatments because they are limited only to those areas where Argentine ants are found nesting during inspection. When spot treating, only ant nest sites or areas where ants are found entering the structure require treatment. Nest sites should be exposed prior to treatment. For example, exposure of nest sites in mulch can be accomplished by pulling back the mulch with a rake or similar instrument held in one hand while treating exposed nest sites with the other.

Carpenter ants—Carpenter ants are the largest of the pest ants found in Georgia. They do not eat wood, like termites, but excavate it with their strong, serrated jaws to create galleries where they nest. Because they do not eat the wood they chew, it is common to find sawdust-like wood shavings below an area, such as a tree, where carpenter ants nest. To learn more about carpenter ants and their control, see Georgia Cooperative Extension bulletin #1225, *Biology and Management of Carpenter Ants.*

In Georgia, there are two carpenter ant species of primary pest importance, the **black carpenter ant** (statewide) and the **Florida carpenter ant** (mainly coastal and southern Georgia). Black carpenter ants are dull black and their abdomen is covered by yellowish hairs, while the Florida carpenter ant has a deep reddish-colored head and thorax and a shiny black abdomen. Since ants from a single carpenter ant nest vary greatly in size (i.e., they're polymorphic), ant size alone is usually not a good characteristic for identification. Carpenter ants vary in size from about one-quarter to one-half inch. Carpenter ant colonies are small (up to 10,000 ants) in comparison to the other pest ant species discussed in this chapter.

Carpenter ants are most active at night, when it is not uncommon to see 10 to 20-fold or more ants than would be seen during daylight hours. Ants emerge about 15 minutes after sundown and leave the nest in large numbers in search of food, traveling up to hundreds of feet from the nest on semi-permanent trails. Unlike other pest ant species, carpenter ants create semi-permanent trails from their nest to areas where they feed. Movement between nest sites and between nest sites and feeding sites is often facilitated by the use of these well-maintained, semi-permanent trails. In the evening, ants can be seen using these trails as they emerge from and return to their nest. Colonies may even use the same trail in different years.

Carpenter ants may establish nest sites inside and/or outside the home. Some examples of where carpenter ants have been found nesting inside are in moisture-damaged wood around chimneys and skylights, under bathtubs, inside dishwashers, in wall voids beneath window sills, inside hollow doors and door frames, under fiberglass insulation in crawlspaces and in wall voids, in wood porch supports and columns, under siding and wood shingles, and in moisture-damaged eaves. In general, wood suffering from moisture damage will attract and be used by carpenter ants as nest sites because damp wood is easier for the ants to chew than sound, dry wood. Damp wood, combined with warm temperatures, also promotes the survival, growth, and reproduction of carpenter ant colonies.

Outdoors, nests are most commonly found in hardwood trees containing treeholes. Most large hardwood trees contain a treehole or other imperfection where ants might nest. In treeholes, ants find an environment that is ecologically stable (consistent humidity and temperature) and protected from adverse environmental conditions and natural enemies. There they chew dead wood to create galleries for nest sites. Colonies are less commonly found in stumps, logs, railroad ties, or similar large pieces of wood.

Finding nests is the key to eliminating carpenter ants—The key to eliminating carpenter ant infestations is to find the nest and remove it, either physically or by treating it with an insecticide. To find nest sites indoors, follow a few foraging ants to learn where they might be nesting. Tap the void suspected of harboring the nest. Look for sawdust at the base of trees. Since carpenter ants must excavate wood to expand their galleries, it is common to find piles of sawdust on the ground at the base of a tree where carpenter ants nest. As mentioned previously, carpenter ants do not consume wood but must chew it to build and expand nest galleries. Galleries are created by biting off small pieces of wood and disposing of it to the outside. The small bits of wood often pile up at the base of a tree and take on the appearance of sawdust.

Carpenter ants found in the home often times can be found nesting outdoors in trees. To find outdoor nest sites inspect each large tree (greater than 6 inches in diameter), beginning 15 to 20 minutes after sundown, by walking around it while shining a flashlight up and down the trunk. If a nest is present, ants will be seen moving up and down the trunk as they leave from and return to the nest with food.

Treating carpenter ant nest sites indoors—Either physically remove indoor nests or treat them with an insecticide labeled for ant control indoors. Use insecticidal dusts and/or aerosols to eliminate carpenter ant infestations indoors. Apply small amounts of dust into voids where the ants are known to be nesting, are suspected of nesting, and/or in voids that they use when foraging. Dusts must be placed into voids so that they will not be contacted by non-target organisms. Aerosol formulations may also be used when indoor ant nests are visible and accessible.

Treating outdoor carpenter ant nests—Outdoors, especially in trees, pour a water-based, liquid insecticide directly into carpenter ant nests. Use enough insecticide to thoroughly saturate the entire nest and all ants inside. This may require pouring one gallon or more of liquid insecticide into the nest. It is important to saturate all nest galleries with insecticide.

Control attempts when the carpenter ant nest cannot be found—Often times the nest cannot be found or, if found, cannot be easily treated. Under these circumstances, use baits and/or spot treat outside with a liquid perimeter spray those areas where ants are entering the structure. As part of the perimeter spray program, apply a liquid insecticide to the trunk of each tree on which carpenter ants have been seen. This treatment strategy will kill ants moving up and down the tree trunk.

Selecting a pest control professional to treat for carpenter ants—It is often best to employ a licensed pest control firm, especially when carpenter ant nests are difficult to find. The company chosen should conduct a thorough and complete inspection that results in location of the nest, or at least a probable nest site, before treatment. Avoid having a pest management professional return to spray each month or whenever carpenter ants are seen. The infestation will continue unless nests are found and eliminated. If nests are found and treatment is successful, it is unlikely that additional services for carpenter ant control will be needed since carpenter ant nests are fairly small and grow very slowly.

Red-imported fire ant—The red-imported fire ant is not native to the U.S. It was accidentally introduced into Mobile, AL in the 1930s from South America, and can now be found throughout Georgia as well as most of the rest of the southeastern U.S. Fire ants are not typically considered a structural pest as much as they are a pest of the yard. They are pests, of course, because of the painful sting all worker ants can deliver when their nest is disturbed and they are forced to protect it. This section will concentrate on the existence, and what can be done about it, of fire ants in home lawns.

Ecologically, fire ants are fierce predators and competitors with other ant species. In areas where fire ants are common, there is a marked reduction in the number of ant and other invertebrate species present. In Georgia, a typical fire ant colony consists of 100- to 400-thousand worker ants, brood (eggs, larvae and pupae), and a single queen. The queen's sole function in the colony is egg production. Fire ant colonies are considerably larger than carpenter ant colonies but not quite as big as Argentine ant colonies.

Presence of a visible, dome-shaped mound is a clear indication of the presence of fire ants. The dome is an extension of a series of interlocking, spaghetti-like tunnels underground. These subterranean tunnels radiate from the central dome down and out several feet in all directions. The dome serves to regulate temperature inside the ant nest. The surface area of the dome helps collect and transfer solar radiation into the nest, keeping the inside warm on cool days. Fire ants may move up and down within the subterranean nest to elevations where temperatures and humidities are optimal. On cool days, fire ants can be found at or near the top of the warm dome. On warm days fire ants may move deep into their mound, where temperatures are moderate and cool. Fire ants prefer to locate their nests in open, sunny areas that have recently been disturbed. For example, often times mounds can be found in newer subdivisions but are usually not found in older, well-established neighborhoods.

Soon after a rain it may appear as though new fire ant mounds have "popped up". In fact, the fire ants were present the entire time. The physical action of excessive rain often causes fire ant galleries to collapse. The "new" mounds seen soon after a rain are simply existing fire ant colonies re-building and re-excavating their nest site. There are not new mounds after a rain, only newly built mounds.

Fire ants in and around the home cannot be tolerated due to their painful sting. When stinging, fire ants pinch the skin with their mandibles (jaws) while inserting their stinger and injecting venom into the wound. A single ant may sting multiple times. Fire ant venom results in the intense burning and itching sensation typically associated with a fire ant sting. Most individuals develop a pustule after several days. In severe cases, individuals may succumb to fire ant venom by exhibiting a severe allergic reaction. A single sting to a susceptible individual can be cause for concern. If signs of allergic reaction become evident, seek medical attention immediately. An overwhelming number of fire ant stings, even in individuals not allergic to fire ant venom, can result in hospitalization or death. This phenomenon occurs at least a handful of times each year throughout the southeast, especially in those age groups incapable of escape—i.e., the very young and the very old.

Control of fire ants in the home lawn can be best achieved via a two-step method. When using this method, fire ant baits are first broadcast over the entire lawn. This is followed by treating individual mounds a period of time later.

When applying a granular bait for fire ants, a few recommendations should be followed. First, use a bait labeled specifically for fire ant control, and apply it over the entire yard with the aid of a newly-purchased spreader—i.e., one that has not been previously used. DO NOT use an old fertilizer spreader to spread fire ant bait. Ants are notoriously finicky in deciding what they will and will not collect and return to the nest for consumption. Bait contaminated by any foreign smell,

including fertilizer, may be avoided by foraging ants. Secondly, apply fresh bait, preferably from a newly-opened bag. Bait from a bag that has been opened and that may be rancid (see product directions regarding bait handling and storage) will likely not be collected by foraging fire ants. Third, baits should be applied in the late afternoon when it is dry and ants are active. When the weather is hot, fire ants do not forage in the heat of the day but will forage in the late afternoon and at night. Bait should be applied when fire ants are actively looking for food—i.e., late in the afternoon when it is cool. To determine whether ants are active and foraging, a nugget of hard dog food or similar food can be placed on the ground. If fire ants are actively foraging, the food should be collected within 30 minutes. Baits should also be applied when it is dry outdoors (i.e., later in the afternoon) so that the attractive nature of the granules will not be compromised by excessive wetting. Lastly, bait should be applied when rain is not expected for at 6 to 8 hours following treatment. Following bait application, most of the bait will be picked up by foraging fire ants within an hour. Fire ants do not collect bait over a lengthy period.

The second step involves treatment of individual, active fire ant mounds starting about two weeks after broadcast bait application. Treatment of individual mounds is best conducted with a liquid insecticide drench, a dust, or a granular insecticide. When using a liquid drench at least one gallon of diluted insecticide should be poured directly onto each active mound. It is important that enough liquid be used so that it drains down into the nest and contacts all ants, including the queen. As a non-chemical alternative, extremely hot water may also be used to drench fire ant mounds. Dusts, especially those containing the active ingredient acephate, can be applied directly to the top of each active mound. Granular insecticides, especially those containing fipronil, can be applied directly to the top of each active mound, but must be 'activated' by watering-in the granules. Rain or some type of artificial irrigation (1 gallon from a watering can) must be performed following the application of the granules.

Non-chemical ant control—Some non-chemical practices may make properties not only more inhospitable for ants to nest but may make it more difficult for them to enter the home and allow chemical controls to be more effective. It is advisable to commit to these practices early, and to use these measures in combination with chemical inputs since these measures alone will not rid the home of ants or prevent their infusion from nearby areas. In addition to those general recommendations for managing moisture around the home (see previous section), some specific non-chemical actions can be taken for ant control, including:

• Since ants are attracted to sweets, thoroughly rinse all empty containers (e.g., soda cans) before placing them either in the garbage or in the recycle bin.

• Do not let garbage sit for long periods of time, keep garbage cans away from the structure, and do not let them touch the structure. Ants will establish foraging trails to garbage retention areas. If those areas are near the house, the chance of infestation increases.

• Since ants commonly forage into shrubs and trees to look for food (especially honeydew), keep all vegetation (limbs, branches) from touching the outside wall of the home. Branches in contact with outside walls allow ants easy, direct access into the home.

• Since ants readily consume honeydew, seek the advice of extension horticulturists in selecting species and strains of plants that are less susceptible to aphids, scales, whiteflies and other honeydew-producing insects. Honeydew is nearly pure sugar, and is excreted by aphids and scale insects in large quantities during the spring and summer months. Many ant species, including Argentine, odorous house, and carpenter ants, depend on honeydew as a stable, predictable source of food throughout the warm season.

Cockroaches

Cockroaches are one of the most despised pests in and around homes. The German cockroach, for instance, is generally associated with unsanitary conditions, and is a leading cause of allergies indoors. Only 10 or so of the 4,500+ known cockroach species are considered pests, and most of those were accidentally introduced into the U.S. from tropical regions of the world.

Sixty-nine species of cockroaches are known from the U.S. Since cockroaches are mainly tropical in their natural distribution, it is no surprise that more species are found in the southeastern U.S. than in any other region of the country. Georgia's moderate, year-round climate provides a cockroach fauna richer than many other states. Two cockroach species likely to be encountered by Georgia homeowners include the German cockroach and the smokybrown cockroach. The German cockroach is found indoors only, and mainly in kitchens, while the smokybrown cockroach may be found in any part of the home but prefers to live in areas (excluding kitchens) where moisture is abundant.

German Cockroach—Adults are about five-eighths of an inch long, winged, and easily recognized by the two dark stripes on the shield covering the top of the head.

Immature German cockroaches are black with white bands and are up to three-eighths of an inch long, but are not winged. Originally thought to have evolved in southeast Asia (Vietnam, etc.), aided by human commerce the German cockroach has spread throughout the world.

It is not unusual to see an occasional German cockroach even in homes considered clean and sanitary, since German cockroaches are "hitchhikers"—that is, they hide inside grocery bags, drink cartons, boxes, used appliances and furniture, TVs, radios, etc. that are brought into the home from infested sources (restaurants, neighbors, grocery stores, used furniture stores, etc.). The senior author of this chapter once witnessed a gravid (i.e., pregnant) female German cockroach in a restaurant crawling on and then into a patron's winter clothing. Once infested articles are stored, stowaways begin exploring their new home for food and water. Most die while looking, but some survive if food and water are available. Water is much more critical to cockroach survival than is food. German cockroaches, for example, can live for just 12 days when provided food but no water; 42 days when provided water but no food; and 13 days when provided no food or water.

German cockroaches are normally found in kitchens, and in cases of extreme infestation in bathrooms, bedrooms and living rooms. Conditions favoring the growth of cockroach populations are abundant food, water, and harborage combined with an optimum temperature. When all conditions are present, German cockroach populations quickly expand to fill all available harborage.

German cockroaches prefer to harbor in warm, dark, cracks and crevices close to areas where food and water are readily accessible. When abundant in homes, German roaches are commonly found under the stove and refrigerator; next to the garbage can; behind pots and pans; under stove burners; in cracks and crevices under counter tops, sinks and around plumbing; in voids under cabinets and behind and inside drawers; inside the hollow legs and pipes of kitchen tables and appliances; around hinges on cabinets and closet doors; in and under small electrical appliances such as toasters and kitchen clocks; in stored paper, cans, or grocery bags; on the back of hanging objects such as paintings, clocks, and calendars; and behind molding.

German cockroach females produce 35 to 40 young at a time, once per month for six to eight months. Young cockroaches are contained together in a pouch-like egg case (called the ootheca) that remains attached to the female's abdomen throughout its month-long incubation.

Control—When treating for German cockroaches, use a combination of sticky traps (no toxicant) and gel/paste baits and/or bait stations placed liberally throughout each room where German cockroaches are found. In cases of extreme infestation, a total release aerosol may be needed initially to "clean out" the infestation.

Sticky traps (10-12) can be placed in locations similar to that of baits, checked weekly for the presence of cockroaches, and replaced as needed. Since German cockroaches do not move far, traps that consistently catch the largest number of cockroaches often highlight 'focal points' of cockroach infestation. Concentrate bait placements in these areas. Finally, if German cockroach problems persist, seek the advice and help of a pest management professional.

Smokybrown cockroaches—Throughout the southeastern U.S., smokybrown cockroaches are considered the primary peridomestic cockroach pest in suburban neighborhoods. Smokybrown cockroaches live and breed primarily outdoors, but may invade and form breeding populations indoors in attics, wall voids and basements. Breeding sites of smokybrown cockroaches are those locations characterized by a protected, moist environment—typically crawlspaces or attics with a moisture problem, or outdoors in clogged rain gutters, treeholes, wood & trash piles, underneath wood shingles and wood decks, within weathered decorative crossties, hollow retaining walls, and similarly protected habitats. Smokybrown cockroaches are very susceptible to desiccation. As such, harborage sites are typically those areas where relative humidity is high (moist areas) and the desiccating effects of wind are minimized—attics and crawlspaces with moisture problems fit this description.

Smokybrown cockroach populations in suburban areas can be high. Researchers have removed nearly 2,500 cockroaches from individual homes in the southeast. Smokybrown cockroaches generally do not forage more than a few feet from their harborage, but have been known to move up to 100 feet in search of food, water, and mates. As expected, smokybrown cockroaches are most active at night when it is not uncommon to see large nymphal and/or adult cockroaches crawling on trees, on hollow retaining walls, and on the outside walls of structures. Since small nymphal cockroaches are not as mobile as adults and large nymphs, continued sightings of small nymphs in the same area of the home may indicate a nearby breeding population.

To control smokybrown cockroaches, specific harbor-

ing sites should be identified and treated—preferably with bait. Treatment should be made in early and late summer to prevent the large population buildup that normally occurs from mid-summer to early-fall. Baits provide long-term control while at the same time reducing the amount of insecticide applied to the environment. For smokybrown cockroaches, use mainly gel/paste baits. Place bait wherever cockroaches are seen foraging (see above), particularly at night. Concentrate bait application to these areas, and be liberal with the quantity of bait applied. Again, it is most advantageous to introduce a large number of small bait placements since smokybrown cockroaches generally do not move very far from the area(s) where they live.

Baits conserve smokybrown cockroach natural enemies—The application of liquid sprays to smokybrown cockroach harborage sites kills cockroach natural enemies such as spiders, centipedes, ants, earwigs, parasitic wasps, etc. Baits not only eliminate cockroach populations for a long period, but conserve cockroach natural enemies that would be killed with a spray. Research has shown that smokybrown cockroach populations can be reduced by 90 percent for six months with the targeted placement of bait in locations identified as smokybrown cockroach harborage. Long-term control is directly related to the lengthy generation time of smokybrown cockroaches—one year or more, depending on environmental conditions. Once initial populations are reduced they will not rebound for a long period.

STORED PRODUCT PESTS

Stored product pests usually start out their lives inside a bag of cereal, flour, birdseed or some other similar item tucked away in a pantry or cabinet. There they grow and often multiply until the resource starts to be depleted. Then they either move out to wander and find a place to pupate, or they emerge as adults to find another item to infest. Due to this general behavior, homeowners often aren't aware of a stored product pest's presence until there are many of them flying or crawling around the kitchen or pantry. There are several different kinds of stored product pests, but in general, procedures for controlling them are similar.

The first and most important step is locating the source or sources of the problem. Depending on the species in question, stored product pests can infest a large range of items including anything from cake mixes to dog food to dried fruits and nuts. Even something like potpourri, a dried flower arrangement, or an abandoned rat bait can serve as a food source. Due to the diverse range of items that might be infested, any inspection for stored product pests must be thorough, especially for species that can fly. If all sources of the pest aren't found, there is a possibility that the population might return at a later time. Infested products should either be discarded outside of the home or frozen if the infestation is light and the homeowner wishes to save the item. Uninfested, but vulnerable items should be stored in a refrigerator, freezer, or sealed container at least until the situation is under control.

The next important step in the control process is cleaning up spilled material from cracks and crevices in pantries, cabinets, or other storage areas containing susceptible products. Even a small amount of spilled flour, corn meal, etc. is enough to sustain a few pests until they find a larger source of food and start the infestation over again. Some pantry pests are resourceful and will find their way into packages of crackers, bags of cereal, boxes of dried fruit, etc. so continued vigilance is important. Insecticide applications will kill the adults that the homeowner can see, but will not be effective on the larvae or adults that are hiding in bags of food resources or crevices of pantries, because these will not be reached by the insecticide. Inspection and prevention of future infestation is the most effective approach.

The following is a short description and some specific information for the more common stored product pests found by homeowners. In general, unless indicated, the control process for these pests is like that described in the general description above with inspection, elimination, and prevention being the key elements.

Cigarette and Drugstore Beetles—These common stored product pests belong to the family Anobiidae and share the same hunched over appearance as the anobiids that are pests of wood. Anobiids that infest stored products, however, will not infest wood, and vice versa. Both beetles are small (1/16- 1/8 inch) and brown in color. The main difference is that the **cigarette beetle** (*Lasioderma serricorne*) has serrated antennae and elytra (wing covers) with pits in an irregular pattern if present at all, whereas the **drugstore beetle** (*Stegobium paniceum*) has elytra with pits in longitudinal rows and antennae with a distinctive three segmented club shape. Both fly and both attack a wide variety of stored items including such unusual things as spices, dried fruits, and dried peppers. In addition, cigarette beetles will attack tobacco products, furniture stuffing, and book paste, and drugstore beetles will attack various drugs, hair, horn, and leather. Control procedures above should be followed with the added precaution that since both beetles fly and often

are attracted to light, infestations might be in other parts of the home than only those where they have been seen. Bags of dried dog and cat food are a favored food item and a common item within which these beetles get into a home. Dried pet foods should be stored in large, plastic containers with a good seal.

Flour Beetles—There are two main types of flour beetles that homeowners may see, both in the family Tenebrionidae: the **red flour beetle** (*Tribolium castaneum*) and the **confused flour beetle** (*T. confusum*). Both beetles are small (1/8 inch) and reddish in color. The main difference in appearance is in the antennae: the confused flour beetle has a gradual 4 segmented club whereas the red flour beetle has an abrupt 3 segmented club. More important is that the confused flour beetle does not fly even though it does have wings, but the red flour beetle will fly. They both attack a wide range of stored products and are especially fond of processed items such as flour, cake mixes, and cereals. Neither can attack whole grains, beans, or nuts.

Grain Beetles—There are several species of grain beetles that are pests of stored products in homes, most belonging to the family Cucujidae. The two most common are the **merchant grain beetle** (*Oryzaephilus mercantor*) and the **saw-toothed grain beetle** (*O. surinamensis*). The sawtoothed grain beetle is more common in the southern areas of the country. Both are small (1/8 of an inch) and dark brown with six sawlike teeth along the sides of their upper thorax. The main difference between the two species is that the merchant grain beetle has only a small "cheek" behind its eye, and it is known to fly. The sawtoothed grain beetle has a larger "cheek" behind its eye, and it is not known to fly. The sawtoothed grain beetle is also more cosmopolitan in its food preferences while the merchant grain beetle seems to prefer nuts, cookies, coconut, macaroni, cake mixes, rice flour, and cereals, especially those containing rolled oats.

The standard control procedures above apply to both of these beetles, with the added concern that merchant grain beetles fly and are attracted to light. In addition, the saw-toothed grain beetle has a long-lived adult stage which generally lasts between 6- 10 months, but may be as long as 3 years, so exclusionary practices are especially important for this species. Bird seed is a favored food and is often the original source of grain beetles in homes.

Moths—There are four main stored product moths that can be found in homes. Three of the four belong to the family Pyralidae. These are the **Almond moth** (*Cadra cautella*), the **Mediterranean flour moth** (*Anagasta kuehniella*), and the **Indianmeal moth** (*Plodia inter-*

punctella). The last moth, the **angoumois grain moth** (*Sitotroga cerealella*), belongs to the family Gelechiidae. The indianmeal moth is the most commonly encountered of the four species. It measures about ⅝- ¾ of an inch and has a distinctive wing pattern where the top half is a cream color and the bottom half is a reddish brown with a coppery sheen. The Mediterranean flour moth is larger (about 1 inch) and is a mottled gray color. The almond moth is similar in color to the Mediterranean flour moth, but is just a bit smaller (to ⅞ inch). The angoumois grain moths are the smallest (½- ⅝ inch) and have brownish wings with long fringed scales on the edges. All of these moths leave telltale debris and/or webbing in the infested products which is a good indicator that the moths have infested a product. This is usually helpful when inspecting items for moths.

Standard control procedures are in effect for all of these moths with the following habits to note. The angoumois grain moth requires a whole kernel or caked material to develop, so prefers barley, rye, oats, corn, rice, and various seeds. It is also the most likely of the moths to be active in the wintertime. The almond moth much prefers dried fruits and vegetables. Mediterranean flour moths and especially Indianmeal moths are more cosmopolitan in their food preferences; so many items including unusual things such as potpourri may need to be inspected. As with grain beetles, birdseed is a common item that starts a moth infestation.

Weevils—There are a few types of weevils that attack stored products in homes, but the two most common are the **cowpea weevil** and relatives (family Bruchidae) and the **rice weevil** and relatives (family Curculionidae, genus Sitophilus). The cowpea weevils (*Callosobruchus maculatus*) are short nosed weevils that measure between ¹⁄₁₆ and ⅛ of an inch. They are brownish with cream and black markings and a small yellow, upside down "V" on their pronotum. These weevils and their relatives attack only whole, leguminous products such as black-eyed peas, soybeans, peas, etc., so inspection for these weevils is easier as they will be found only in these types of products. The adults do not feed, but are very good fliers.

The rice weevil (*S. oryzae*) is a long-nosed weevil of only ⅛ inch. It is black with four red markings and has a heavily punctuated upper thorax and elytra. The larvae usually develop in whole or semi whole kernels of grain such as corn, split peas, or rice, but the adults will also feed on items such as wheat products, cereals, nuts, stored cotton and grapes. Rice weevils fly and are attracted to lights. Some of the rice weevil's closely related species have similar habits, but a few do not fly. Standard control procedures should be followed for these weevils, keeping in mind the preferences of each during inspection.

BITING AND STINGING PESTS

Pests that bite or sting come from many different groups, including insects, spiders, centipedes, and scorpions. Some of these groups are discussed in other sections (spiders and occasional invaders). This section will focus mainly on insects that bite or sting. These include the various species of wasps and bees. Insects that bite humans, with the exception of the predatory bugs, generally bite to acquire nutrition in the form of blood. Control is dependent on the type of biting or stinging insect and its association with the home.

Wasps

There are several types of wasps that homeowners may encounter. Many are solitary, including the mason and potter wasps (family Vespidae), the mud daubers (family Sphecidae), the digger wasps (family Scoliidae), the spider wasps (family Pompillidae), and the cicada killers (family Sphecidae, genus Sphecius). Most wasps are beneficial predators of insects and/or spiders and are generally not aggressive. Mason, mud dauber, and potter wasps sometimes build their nests on structures and become a nuisance. An aerosol sprayed into their mud nests can be effective. Digger and spider wasps are solitary wasps that excavate nests underground, usually in sandy areas. If problematic, a light dusting with an appropriate dust is effective.

Cicada killers are predators of cicadas, but often worry homeowners because of their large size (1- 1⅝ inch). They will sting if molested, stepped on, or handled. Cicada killers also excavate holes underground. They can be treated with a granular insecticide or dust if needed. Be cautious when spraying directly with an aerosol. Always follow product label directions.

One of the stinging pests of greatest concern is the group containing the semi-social wasps, such as the **paper wasps** (family Vespidae, genus Polistes). Vespids are medium size (⅝- ¾ inch) and are generally brownish with yellow markings. They build distinctive, open comb nests which several wasps share and use to raise young. When paper wasps build nests on structures, they often build them under the eaves of buildings where the nest is protected from the elements. Many species will defend their nest if it is threatened, some more aggressively than others.

Paper wasps are predators, and are especially beneficial in removing pest caterpillars from vegetable gardens and lawns. However, homeowners may wish to remove nests near and on structures or in frequently traveled locations if there is a threat of injury. Nests should be treated in the early morning or in the evening when a majority of the adult wasps are present. A 20 foot jet spray aerosol pyrethrin or pyrethroid works best, and homeowners should stand back from the nest when treating. It may be necessary to spray "straggler" wasps that return to the nest following its treatment. Following treatment, the nest should be removed to discourage other wasps from returning and to prevent existing pupae from further development.

Hornets

There are two main species known as hornets that homeowners may encounter: the **baldfaced hornet** (*Dolichovespula maculata*) and the **European hornet** (*Vespa crabro*). The baldfaced hornet gets its name from its mostly black color and a contrasting white face. It is the smaller of the two species (⅝- ¾ inch+) and the most likely to be associated with homes. Although called a hornet, the baldfaced hornet is actually a species of above ground yellow jacket. The **European hornet** which is a true hornet, is somewhat larger (¾- 1⅜inch) and will more often be associated with wooded areas. These brown and yellowish striped insects get their name from their native continent of Europe. Like many Hymenoptera, hornets are beneficial predators, feeding on many pest insect species, including caterpillars, grasshoppers, and flies.

In cases when control is necessary, an appropriate fast-acting pesticide should be used, such as a pyrethroid spray labeled for wasp control. Care should be taken when treating hornet nests, especially nests of the bald-faced hornet. Their nests should be treated at night when the hornets are less active. European hornets, however, are more likely to be active at night, so should be treated during the day. European hornets are less aggressive, even around their nests, but caution should still be used. A few days after treatment, nests should be removed (when possible) to prevent remaining pupae from further development.

Bees

There are a few different species of bees that homeowners may encounter including the bumblebee (*Bombus* spp.), the carpenter bee (*Xylocopa* spp.), the ground nesting bees (Andrenidae, Collectidae, Anthophoridae, and Halictidae), and the honey bee (*Apis mellifera*). Most bees are beneficial, either as predators or as pollinators. Bumblebees are rarely a problem, but if a nest is located in a high traffic area, it can be treated much like that of a yellow jacket. Carpenter bees are rarely aggressive and are more of a problem in wood structures. Please see the wood destroying organism section for information on carpenter bee biology and control.

Ground nesting bees are different from the above-mentioned bees in that they are solitary, rather than social. Though many ground-nesting bees might build their underground nests in one area, each is an individual nest without the cooperation found in social bees. Ground-nesting bees are usually small to medium in size (⅛- ¾ inch) and vary in color from brownish to metallic green. They are similar in that they excavate tunnels underground to store pollen and nectar for their developing larvae. Many ground-nesting bees are useful pollinators, and are thus seldom aggressive. Often they can be discouraged from building nests by reducing areas of bare ground. Planting grass or ground cover, or covering bare areas with mulch will often discourage bees from nesting. Seldom is treatment needed, but if it is, lightly dusting nest entrances or broadcast application of a granular insecticide are effective.

Honey bees are beneficial insect pollinators. They can be a problem, however, when they nest in a structure's walls. This situation usually requires professional advice and help to properly extract the bees, especially if they have stored honey. If the problem is a group of swarmers in the yard, a local Extension Agent may be able to provide advice on bee removal.

Yellow Jackets—These yellow and black striped social insects belong to the genera Vespula and Dolichovespula. Adult workers are medium in size (⅜- ⅝ inch). Like many Hymenoptera, yellow jackets are beneficial predators of many types of insects. They do, however, defend their underground nests aggressively, and when nests are located in areas where people often pass, control is usually warranted. They are especially disturbed by vibrations near their nest such as those made by lawn mowers and chain saws. Yellow jackets may also build nests within the exterior walls of structures, and again, should be removed. Worker yellow jackets may also become a nuisance in the autumn when resources become reduced and wasps begin to actively search for food. Treating a yellow jacket nest can be a dangerous undertaking. If control is attempted by a homeowner, ground nests should be treated at night and with an appropriate fast-acting insecticide, such as a pyrethrin or a pyrethroid. Homeowners may wish to seek professional advice and/or help before treating a yellow jacket nest, especially one that is located within the walls of a structure.

Other Biting and Stinging Pests

Bed Bugs—Bed bugs are Hemipterans that belong to the family Cimicidae. The typical species that a homeowner might encounter is *Cimex lectularius*, an oval, flat insect about 3/16 of an inch at maturity. They have vestigial wings that are reduced to wing pads and are not used for flying. They are most often rusty brown at maturity and often have a somewhat sticky appearance. Bed bugs are secretive, nocturnal insects that can sometimes travel long distances to find a blood meal and then scurry back to hiding before being seen. These habits sometimes make it difficult to diagnose bed bugs as the cause of bites. Homeowners can pick up bed bugs as hitchhikers in their suitcases when they travel without being aware of them. The bugs then crawl out and inhabit a new location, often the homeowner's dwelling.

Bed bug control depends on a proper diagnosis and a subsequent inspection of all potential hiding places. Cracks and crevices where bedbugs hide should be treated with an appropriately labeled insecticide. If all potential harborage places are covered, one application should be sufficient for control. Bed bug harborages include: crevices between the mattress and bed frame, the space behind the headboard, cracks beneath baseboards near the bed, spaces behind picture frames, and spaces inside switchplates and electrical outlets near the bed. Care should be taken if treating switch plates and electrical outlets. Vacuuming these harborage areas carefully is preferred to insecticide treatment. All bedding should be thoroughly washed and mattresses and box springs treated when needed. After treatment, mattresses, box springs, and bed frames should be allowed to air before use. Vacuuming and/or steam-cleaning are also effective. When at all possible, a professional should be contacted for bed bug treatment, because an incomplete treatment can lead to bed bugs spreading to other areas and reinfesting at a later time.

Fleas—Fleas belong to the family Pulicidae, and the most common species that homeowners encounter is the cat flea (*Ctenocephalides felis*), even when found on dogs. Fleas may bite humans when they walk on or near flea cocoons, causing the fleas resting inside to emerge and jump onto the nearby warm body. Fleas are attracted to carbon dioxide released as a result of breathing. They may also be attracted to blinking lights.

Flea control involves first finding the most common places a pet sleeps, because this will also be the most likely place that flea eggs, larvae, and flea food are most concentrated. Flea larvae eat debris, but their main food source is dried blood provided by adult fleas. In order for this to be available, a host is needed, and a sleeping or resting pet is ideal for providing dried blood droppings. Frequent vacuuming of pet resting areas is helpful in reducing the larval food source, but treating the areas after vacuuming is also an option. Another important aspect of flea treatment is treating your pet. This is best done with advice from your veterinarian. Cats especially are sensitive to some flea control chemicals that dogs are not, and a cat's health can be severely compromised if the wrong product is used on them. Flea control is often an ongoing process, and vigilance is important to keep the pests from coming back. Outdoor treatments may also be necessary if pets spend a significant amount of time outdoors.

In some cases, pets might not be involved, but fleas might still be in a home. In these unusual cases, wildlife may be the culprit, either nesting in the attic or in a chimney. An apartment renter might also encounter fleas left behind by a previous resident if carpets were not sufficiently cleaned. In such cases, generally a good vacuuming and a spot treatment should take care of the problem. In the first case, however, the wildlife must also be excluded so that there is no further influx of fleas.

Ticks—Ticks that homeowners are likely to encounter belong to the family Ixodidae, including the American dog tick (*Dermacenter variabilis*), the deer tick (*Ixodes scapularis*), the brown dog tick (*Rhipicephalus sanguineus*), and the lone star tick (*Amblyomma americanum*). Prevention is the most important means of preventing bites. Habitat modification, such as mowing grass to 3" or less and reducing brush, can help, but for areas where ticks are plentiful, repellents and vigilance are most important. Homeowners who walk in areas where ticks are plentiful should wear appropriate clothing (long pants tucked into socks, for example) and use repellents. Checking for ticks is also important. Most diseases that ticks transmit, including Lyme disease, require the tick to feed on a person for several hours to a day or two before the disease can be transmitted, so the quicker a tick is found, the better. Checking frequently for ticks after being in an area that might have ticks is important.

If a tick is found biting, it should be removed carefully so that the head is not left behind. Tweezers work best, and removed ticks should be flushed or burned to make sure they can't escape from a drain or waste basket. Most tick bites leave a mark that is visible for up to a few days, but if unusual marks, such as a large "bullseye" develop around the area, or if there are strange symptoms or a rash, consult a doctor.

Predatory Bugs—Unlike the more familiar stink bug, these Hemipterans are beneficial insect predators. Like many insect predators, however, the same things that make them good predators, like their large "beak", can also mean that they can bite if mishandled. The main types of predatory Hemipterans that homeowners are likely to encounter are the **ambush bugs** (family Phymatidae), the **predatory stink bugs** (family Pentatomidae), and the **assassin bugs** and **wheel bugs** (family Reduviidae). Most of these species are small and will in most cases cause very little problem if they bite. The wheel bug, however, can be rather intimidating, mostly due to its size. Adults are over an inch long, sometimes reaching 1 ½ inches in length. They are also stout bodied with a large "beak". They are beneficial predators of caterpillars and other large pest insects in gardens, but if mishandled, these bugs may sometimes bite painfully. Wheel bugs have an enzyme that they use to subdue prey, that will cause a stinging sensation that may last up to 10 days if not treated. Swabbing ammonia on the bite can reduce this significantly, generally reducing the pain to a few hours or less.

Control is rarely necessary. The bugs are not aggressive, and most are solitary predators, so wide-scale pesticide application to control them is not practical. Checking plants placed outdoors before bringing them inside should keep wheel bugs out of the house, and wearing garden gloves should prevent bites from occurring while working among the plants.

Spiders

Spiders found in homes generally fall into two categories: 1) occasional invader spiders such as wolf spiders, jumping spiders, and the less common trap-door spiders and orb weaver spiders, and 2) peridomestic spiders such as comb-footed spiders, cellar spiders, filistatids, sac spiders, and rarely brown recluse spiders.

Most occasional invader spiders, with the exception of orb weavers, don't use webs to trap prey. They hunt mostly on the ground or on foliage, sometimes using ambush techniques. These usually enter homes accidentally through spaces beneath doors and can be managed by installing doorsweeps and by reducing insect and prey populations near doors. (see section on Occasional Invaders). Following is a brief description of the more commonly encountered occasionally invading spiders.

Wolf Spiders—Wolf spiders belong to the family Lycosidae. Some species are large, measuring an inch or more. Wolf spiders hunt by crawling over the ground as they search for prey - typically crickets or cockroaches. The females often carry their egg sac attached to their abdomen by a silken snare. When the spiderlings hatch, they piggy-back on their mother's body until they get a little larger and can venture off on their own.

Jumping Spiders—Jumping spiders belong to the family Salticidae. Most are small (⅛- ¾ inch body size). They have 8 eyes, two of which are larger that they use to visually locate prey. Most species are active during the day and prefer sunny areas when found indoors. They eat a variety of insects including flies and moths which they pounce on to capture. Most jumping spiders have a silken "retreat" which they retire to at night. The more domestic species may spin these in curtain folds or over door frames, but most outdoor species hide them under loose bark, logs, rocks, or any convenient crevice. Females lay eggs inside these retreats and often guard the young spiders after they hatch.

Trap-Door Spiders—These large spiders are in the family Ctenizidae. Their body size can reach 1½ inches in length. Trap-door spiders excavate subterranean tunnels which serve as both a hiding place and a place from which to ambush insects, spiders, and other small animals. When prey approaches, the spider will pop out of its burrow, grab it, and take it into the tunnel. There is usually a "door" that the spider makes out of silk and debris that will fall back into place as the spider returns to its burrow. A few species use the back of their abdomen in place of a door when threatened. Because of their subterranean life-style, trap-door spiders usually go unobserved by most homeowners. Male spiders sometimes leave their burrow and wander, especially after a rainstorm. Wandering spiders may be found indoors and in carports, garages, etc.

Orb Weavers—The members of this family of webspinners belong to the Araenidae. They come in many shapes and sizes (1/16- 1⅛ inch in body size), including the familiar garden spider, and are usually found in garages indoors. They spin large, elaborate webs shaped like a wheel. They can be vacuumed up or removed to outdoors when found. Generally no pesticides are needed for control. If orb weavers are causing problems outdoors in carports, porches, etc., spot treatments are effective. Changing exterior lighting to yellow bug lights will also help by reducing insect prey.

Unlike the spiders above, peridomestic spiders often find themselves at home indoors. The most common of these spiders build the familiar "cobwebs" often seen in corners indoors. Webs are used to catch and store insect prey. These can be vacuumed or spot treated when necessary. Doorsweeps may help to exclude these spiders, but other means of entrance such as vents leading outdoors may also be an avenue for their entrance. Following are some of the more common domestic spiders.

Comb-Footed Spiders—Several members of this family, the Theridiidae, are species often associated with dwellings. Two of the more common genera found in homes are the Arachaearanea (house spiders), and the Steatoda (the false black widow is *S. grossa*). With the house spider, even though it is small (³⁄₁₆- ⁵⁄₁₆ inch body length), its presence can be conspicuous because it uses a trial and error approach when hunting. The spider will abandon a web and build a new one if the first web doesn't catch prey. When these abandoned webs pick up dust and debris, they can become an annoyance. When a house spider finds a successful hunting location, it will stay. Generally this will be an area of high humidity, suitable air currents, or near a consistently open door, all of which have a higher probability of bringing in prey. When pray falls into the web, the spider will often rush down to throw more silk onto the prey, wrapping it up and pulling it upwards into the web. In modern homes, house spiders are generally found in basements, crawl spaces, etc. where humidity may be high and chances of finding prey are better. One genus of this family, the widow spiders, will be discussed separately below.

Cellar Spiders—Cellar spiders belong to the family Pholcidae, and are another domestic spider that prefers damp, more humid areas of homes such as basements and crawl spaces. The body of these spiders is small (¹⁄₁₆- ⁵⁄₁₆ inch), but they have very long legs. Because of their long-legged appearance, they are often confused with harvestmen which are actually not spiders, but a member of the order Opilones. Harvestmen, unlike cellar spiders, have their two body parts fused to resemble a circle in shape. Both creatures share the nickname "daddy-long legs."

Like house spiders, cellar spiders can be a nuisance due to excessive webbing. They continually build on to a web without removing the old webbing, a behavior which can quickly result in a large network of strands. When prey falls into the web of a cellar spider, it often shakes in a rotary motion, which helps to further snare the prey. It will also do this when disturbed, vibrating so quickly that it will blur. If overly disturbed, the spider will drop and may run away.

Funnelweb Spiders—Funnel web spiders are small to medium sized (¹⁄₁₆- ¾ inch). The webs of these spiders often originate out of a crevice such as beneath a window frame. Unlike cobweb spiders, the spider is usually hidden and only part of the web is visible. The web may be vacuumed up, but a spot treatment into the crevice in which the spider is hiding may be necessary.

Filistatids—Like the funnelweb spiders, the Filistatidae build webs wherein the spider is usually hidden from view in a crevice. They are medium sized (½ – ¾ inch). In the southern region, filistatids are one of the more common domestic spiders. The species *Filistada hibernalis* may live several years. They are mostly nocturnal, remaining hidden in their refuge at the center of their web during the daytime. In appearance, they somewhat resemble the brown recluse spider and are often confused with this less common species. Unlike the brown recluse (discussed below), filistatids have eight eyes which are all grouped together in the center of their head. This contrasts with the distinctive three sets of two eyes that are found on the brown recluse. Also unlike the brown recluse, filistatids are not poisonous.

Sac Spiders—These spiders belong to the family Clubionidae. They are small (³⁄₁₆- ³⁄₈ inch in body length). Unlike many of the other domestic spiders, sac spiders do not build traditional webs. Also, unlike most of the other domestic spiders a few species of this family are likely responsible for a great many biting incidents. One species in particular, the **yellow sac spider** (*Chiracanthium mildei*) has been known to be somewhat aggressive. These spiders build retreats in which they hide, and are generally located in upper corners and ceiling/wall junctions. At night, they leave the retreat to hunt along walls and ceilings. Bites occur most often when the spiders take refuge in clothing and then become trapped against a person's skin. Generally, the effects of the bite are temporary, lasting only a couple of days, but some people have a more severe reaction.

Brown Recluse Spiders—Brown recluse spiders may bite if provoked, and their venom is necrotic. They belong to the family Sicariidae and are a special case. They are medium sized spiders (¼- ½ inch in body length). The brown recluse is not widespread in Georgia. Populations in homes where they are found can be high, and professional assistance is often needed for their control. If brown recluse spiders are confirmed in a home, homeowners can reduce the chances of interacting with the spiders by removing items from the floor that spiders can use for harborage, removing dust ruffles from the bed, and moving the bed a couple of inches from the wall so that spiders are not able to bridge from the wall to the bed. Homeowners can also place sticky traps under beds, dressers, sofas, etc, to help reduce the population and to locate those areas where spiders are most abundant. Professional help in controlling brown recluse spiders is recommended.

Widow Spiders—Though part of the comb-footed spider family, the genus Lactrodectus deserves special mention because the members in it are venomous. The females and males greatly differ in size with the female body length reaching ½ inch while the male is about half the size. With legs outstretched, the female spider will be about 1 ½ inches. There are a few species that can be found in the southern states: the black widow (*L. mactans*), the northern widow (*L. various*), and the brown widow (*L. geometricus*). The black widow is the most recognizable with its shiny black body and distinctive red hourglass on the underside of the abdomen. The northern widow is similar but has a divided hourglass and red circles and white markings on the upper side of the abdomen. The brown widow has an hourglass that is yellow or orange, and its body is a matte, mottled, brownish color rather than shiny black. Its egg case is also distinctive in that it bears spiny projections rather than the usual smooth shape of most spider egg sacs.

Unlike the other comb-footed spiders mentioned previously, the widows are less domestic. They are more likely to be found by homeowners in rock piles, wood piles, weedy brush, barns, and building exteriors than inside homes. They may occasionally show up in garages. In most cases, widow spiders are not aggressive, but if they are protecting an egg case, they are more likely to bite. This is truer of the northern and black widows. The brown widow is a more docile species and is more likely to drop when threatened. In most cases, widow bites are not fatal if treated promptly. Whenever possible, if a bite is suspected, the spider should be carefully collected to confirm the species involved.

OCCASIONAL INVADERS

Occasional invaders are pests that enter a home by accident or in an attempt to get away from a negative environmental condition (too much water, too little water, decreasing temperatures). They often enter homes, garages, and basements through spaces beneath exterior doors. General management measures include: 1) implementing good moisture management around the structure (see above section), 2) decreasing leaf litter, mulch, and hiding places such as rocks, potted plants, and landscape elements around the foundation and especially around exterior doors, and 3) installing

doorsweeps beneath exterior doors, especially those that have no accompanying storm door. Alternatively, temporary control can be implemented by treating door thresholds with a residual insecticide. The insecticide won't necessarily prevent the pests from entering, but should kill some pests that do enter for as long as the pesticide remains active. Dead pests can be vacuumed up with a vacuum cleaner.

For cases of extreme outbreaks of most occasional invaders, granulars, spot treatments, or perimeter sprays can be applied to areas where the pests are proliferating for a temporary control measure. Formulations that do not break down under moist conditions are likely to be the most effective.

More invasive occasional invaders such as clover mites, boxelder bugs, and overwintering lady bugs, may require special control measures. These measures may include reducing outdoor populations before they become too numerous, sealing or screening entrance points in the structure, and/or reducing or treating vegetation on which the insects feed. These measures will be discussed in more detail in the corresponding sections below.

One of the first steps in controlling an occasional invader pest problem is identifying the type of pest that has invaded. Some of the more common occasional invaders homeowners may find fall into several different categories of creatures. Insects are the most common. However occasional invaders cover a wide range of other creatures such as mites, crustaceans, centipedes, millipedes, and land planaria. Some of the more common of these animals that might enter homes or structures are discussed below.

Omnivores

Many of the occasional invaders that enter homes are omnivores. They usually feed on decaying organic matter such as dead plant material, dead insects, and fungus. Most of these omnivores are attracted to areas where there is available moisture and harborage. In many cases, these same conditions will also promote the availability of the decaying organic matter on which they feed. Leaf litter and mulch, for example, not only provide moisture and cover, they often promote the growth of fungus, bacteria, and other decaying matter that the omnivores eat. In general, the key to managing omnivorous occasional invaders is to reduce areas around the foundation that attract them. This is especially true of areas near exterior doorways, which are generally the most common means of entrance for occasional invaders. The general management procedures outlined above will in most cases be sufficient to control most of the omnivorous occasional invaders. Some of the more common types of omnivores that might enter homes are described below.

Springtails—These minute organisms (1/32- 1/8 inch) belong to the insect order Collembola. They are primitive insects that often use their furcula or "spring" to leap when disturbed. Springtails are naturally abundant, being found in great numbers in leaf litter and the soil/thatch layer of lawns and vegetation. One of the main factors in their survival is moisture. Most species of Collembola do not possess a tubular respiratory system and instead breathe directly through their skin. Because of this primitive integument (skin), they are unable to manage water like some of the more advanced insects and are therefore vulnerable to desiccation.

When previously moist conditions around a home begin to dry out, springtails may retreat inside to escape the now unfavorable environment. They may enter homes under exterior door thresholds, through screens (especially on ground level patios), or through spaces around utility pipes. They may also piggyback inside in the soil of potted plants. Once indoors, springtails generally do not survive long. Areas of high humidity such as humid bathrooms or kitchens, areas where there are leaks, or damp crawl spaces or basements are the usual places where they might be able to survive.

Most springtails cause no other damage than their occasional appearance in large numbers. In rare instances, they may slightly damage young plants.

Scuds—These creatures, which are also known as amphipods, are crustaceans of the order Amphipoda. Adults measure between 3/16 and 3/4 of an inch and resemble small shrimp. Like the Collembola above, they are very susceptible to detrimental water loss. They are also susceptible to detrimental water gains. Scuds often enter structures to escape conditions that are either too dry, or more often, too wet. Overly wet conditions for scuds may occur after a heavy rain or prolonged irrigation. Most often, they end up inside structures by entering beneath an exterior door. Once inside, the dry conditions usually kill them within 24 hours. They can then be vacuumed up and discarded.

In cases where moisture can not be controlled, organophosphate pesticides labeled for yard or shrubbery use should be effective against scuds.

Pill Bugs and Sow Bugs —These members of the Crustacea are related to crabs and aquatic arthropods. They belong to the order Isopoda. Pill bugs and sow bugs are relatively similar except that pill bugs are capable of rolling into a tight ball for protection whereas sow bugs are not. Sow bugs also have two protuberances called uropoda that can be seen projecting from the tail end of their bodies when they are viewed from above. Adults of both can reach 5/8 of an inch in length. The habits of these two creatures are similar. Their preference for decaying materials often makes them beneficial, because they will "clean up" fallen leaves and debris in gardens. They may even climb onto a plant to feed on dead flower heads while leaving the living plant parts untouched. In times of water stress, however, they might curl up in damage holes left by other pests and therefore get blamed for the damage. Rarely, if populations are large enough, they might do a little grazing themselves in times of water stress, but generally only to plant parts which lie on the ground.

When isopods invade homes, it is often due to moisture stress. In most cases, unless there are places inside the home with leaks or high humidity, the wandering isopods die fairly quickly. They can then be vacuumed up. In severe cases of invasion, a perimeter treatment concentrating on areas around exterior doors should help temporarily until the proper management steps can be taken.

Millipedes—These many-legged creatures belong to the order Diplopoda. They can range in size from very small (1/16 of an inch) to rather large (4½ inches) and can build up impressive populations with the right environmental conditions. Sometimes large numbers of millipedes will migrate. Though the reason this occurs is not always known for sure, there are a few potential explanations: natural hibernation movement has caused their migration, a rising water table from heavy rains has forced them from an area, increasing temperatures have made them search for cooler environments, or high populations suddenly have been faced with increasingly dry conditions and overcrowding of available resources, causing a subsequent search for new resources. Whatever the cause, potentially hundreds or thousands of millipedes may seem to suddenly appear and invade a structure. They generally enter through spaces beneath exterior doors. Like pillbugs and sowbugs, millipedes generally don't survive long indoors unless they find a moist habitat.

Perimeter treatments that especially target the areas around exterior doors may provide temporary relief. During migrations, however, such treatments may not prevent the millipedes from entering structures because they will only be exposed to the pesticide for a short period of time (during their movement). It might be necessary to do a little night time surveillance to find out where the millipedes are coming from and treat that area directly. Millipedes that do enter and die can be vacuumed up with a vacuum cleaner.

Crickets—The three most common types of crickets that enter homes are the camel cricket (family Gryllacridadae), the field cricket (family Gryllidae, species *Gryllus* spp.) and the house cricket (family Gryllidae, species *Acheta domesticus*). Most crickets enter homes seeking moisture. Of the three types, the field cricket is the least likely to survive for long periods indoors, and the camel cricket does best in areas of higher humidity such as basements and crawl spaces. The house cricket, on the other hand, is fairly adaptable and can live for long periods of time inside dwellings. Once they have come indoors, house crickets may feed on a variety of fabrics including cotton, wool, silk, and various synthetic fibers such as acetate.

In addition to the usual harborages that attract occasional invaders, camel crickets especially may sometimes use drainage culverts or the area beneath outside air conditioners as harborage. Both field crickets and house crickets are attracted to lights, so changing outdoor lighting to less attractive, yellow bug lights will make the home less attractive to them.

Land Planaria—There are two species of land planaria that are the most likely to be found around homes, *Dolichoplana striata* and *Bipalium kewenese*. *B. kewenese* is the most common and colorful of the two. Both species can grow to several inches in size. Land planarians feed on earthworms and are found most often beneath rocks and landscape objects. They occasionally invade structures, carports, or garages after a heavy rain. Despite their appearance, they are harmless to humans and pets.

Predators

Unlike the occasional invaders mentioned previously, this group of occasional invaders generally find their way into homes accidentally due to their close proximity with other pests. Centipedes, scorpions, ground beetles, and earwigs are all predators of insects and spiders. They are generally attracted to structures due to availability of harborage and the presence of prey. All of the conditions conducive to the perpetuation of pest insect populations may secondarily invite predators to also take up residence. Most of the predatory occasional invaders are fast moving and, like most predators, may bite and/or sting if mishandled. This is especially true of the scorpions and larger centipedes. Below are some

distinguishing characteristics of these predators.

Centipedes—These multi-legged and fast creatures belong to the order Chilopoda. The most common species invading homes is the house centipede (*Scutigera coleoptrata*). It has unusually long legs and is very fast. They may be found anywhere in a house, but prefer the more humid areas such as basements and crawl spaces where they can find insects and spiders to eat. Another common genus of centipedes, the Scolopendra, has members which can get quite large. Unlike the house centipede, these have shorter legs which are positioned more laterally to the body. They are also more likely to inflict a painful bite if mishandled, so as with all centipedes, removal should be conducted cautiously.

Outdoors, most centipedes will be found in areas such as wood or stone piles, beneath bricks, rocks, or boards in the landscaping, in debris or mulch piles, under fallen logs, or in leaf litter. When working in the garden where many of these conditions may exist, it is a good idea to wear garden gloves to protect against centipede bites.

Scorpions—Like the centipedes, scorpions (order Scorpiones), may be found anywhere in a home, but are partial to areas that provide prey. They may also seek water, and sometimes end up in bathtubs or sinks, because they entered but could not crawl out again. Scorpions have a habit of crawling into the first available harborage area they can find when the sun rises. This sometimes puts them into contact with humans if that first available location is a shoe, folded clothing, or a convenient blanket. Outdoors, scorpions may be found in many of the same situations as centipedes. In the southeast, most scorpion stings result in only a temporary discomfort, much like a bee sting, but in some cases people may have an allergic reaction to the venom. As with the centipedes, scorpions should be removed cautiously.

In cases of severe scorpion problems, pesticide applications may be needed. Void areas of walls may even have to be treated with residual materials or dusts if the population is especially severe.

Ground Beetles—These insects are members of the family Carabidae. They, too, are predacious, especially on insects. They are less likely to inflict damage than many other predators, but they do have powerful jaws and may potentially bite if molested. These beetles do not, however, have venom like scorpions and centipedes.

In most cases, ground beetles worry homeowners, because some species can be rather large bodied and look intimidating. Some species measure over an inch long. They can usually be escorted out of a home with little incidence if they are caught, though many species are very fast and able to avoid capture. Chemical control is not needed for ground beetles, as they pose little threat and are generally not abundant in number.

Earwigs—Like ground beetles, earwigs (order Dermaptera) look more intimidating than they are. Most are medium sized, but some species can reach an inch in length. The large "pinchers" on the rear of their body can pinch, but they do not have any venom. In addition to the usual conditions which attract occasional invaders, earwigs are attracted to lights or to the insects attracted by lights.

In general, predatory occasional invaders will be reduced when prey populations are reduced or eliminated. It is therefore important to observe the conditions necessary for perimeter pest control such as moisture management and exclusion. These same procedures will help to reduce populations of insect predators and are generally sufficient for control.

Seasonal Invaders

This last group of occasional invaders is a bit different from the previous pests mentioned. These pests often require some special precautions when they occur in order to reduce the chances of subsequent invasions. Exclusion is important for all of them, but is sometimes difficult to achieve depending on how they enter a structure. Pesticide applications for control can also be difficult, depending on the situation. The three most common seasonal invaders will be discussed in more detail below.

Clover Mites—These members of the Acari (mites) belong to the family Tetranychidae. They are red in color and larger-sized than many mites, although they still measure only 1/64 inch long. The mites feed only on plants, but that includes more than 200 different plant species. The most preferred plants are white clover and black medic. Slightly less favored are Kentucky bluegrass, bentgrass, chickweed, and red fescue. Other types of flowering plants and ornamentals are less desirable hosts.

Clover mites usually enter structures when vegetation dies off in the autumn, but may also enter structures during the spring, especially if new mulch is added to plant beds around the foundation. The mites generally enter through cracks in the foundation or around windows and doors. They may also crawl up behind siding until they find a way inside. Once the mites are inside, indoor

pesticide applications will only provide temporary relief if conditions conducive to mite invasion remain and outdoor control measures are not conducted. Squashing the mites may result in red stains, so removal via vacuum is a better option.

Outdoors, one of the most effective control measures for clover mites is to leave a 12 - 18 inch grass free band around the perimeter of the home. In most cases, this will reduce the number of invading mites by 90%. A perimeter treatment coupled with this physical barrier is even more effective. The perimeter treatment should reach up the foundation about two feet and encompass the soil/grass junction at the structure's foundation. Timing of the pesticide application is crucial, however, because the mites are only active in cooler weather. They become dormant once the weather gets hot, and perimeter treatments made during their dormancy will not be effective.

Ladybugs—Ladybugs are actually not bugs, but beetles of the family Coccinellidae. A large majority of the species are beneficial, though some have the nuisance habit of overwintering in structures, including homes. Because they are beneficial and pose no health or structural threat, direct control is generally not recommended. It is also a bad idea to trap and/or treat the ladybugs once they have entered wall voids. Dead ladybugs will attract even more undesirable pests such as dermestid beetles which prefer to feed on dead insects and have the habit of wandering around (often into the home) when they are ready to pupate.

Physical exclusion is generally the recommended management option, but timing is critical. Exclusion must be done before the beetles start to enter to structures to overwinter, so June or July is the best time. Unfortunately, exclusionary measures for ladybugs are quite detailed, including using 16 mesh screen on roof vents, caulking around utility entrances, and installing chimney caps. Homeowners should consult their local Extension agent and/or a pest control company for help with the necessary exclusionary measures.

Kudzu Bugs—In October 2009, large aggregations of an insect (*Megacopta cribraria* (F.); Heteroptera: Plataspidae), commonly referred to as the kudzu bug, bean plataspid, lablab bug, or globular stink bug, were discovered in nine northeast Georgia counties. Before discovery in Georgia, *M. cribraria* was not known to occur in the Western Hemisphere. When discovered in Georgia, the insect was flying from nearby patches of kudzu (*Pueraria* spp.) onto the outside walls of houses and other structures. By November 2010 the insect was confirmed from more than 80 north and central Georgia counties as well as limited distributions in North and South Carolina and Alabama. *Megacopta cribraria* adults are 4 to 6 mm long, oblong, olive-green colored with brown speckles, and produce a mildly offensive odor when disturbed. It is related to various species of stink bugs.

In its native Asia, one of *M. cribraria*'s preferred hosts is kudzu, an invasive vine introduced into the U.S. more than 100 years ago as a ground cover to slow soil erosion but that now grows unimpeded throughout the southeastern U.S. Kudzu appears to be a primary host in North America, and we believe *M. cribraria* will continue to spread into most areas where kudzu is established.

Boxelder Bugs—These insects are Hemipterans of the family Rhopalide and the genus Boisea. The primary host for these bugs is the fruit bearing-boxelder tree. They will also feed on fruit-bearing silver maples. The main problem these bugs cause however, is their habit of overwintering in structures in large numbers.

As with ladybugs, boxelder bugs should not be killed once they have entered a structure, because they too, will provide a preferred meal for dermestid beetles which may then later infest the home. Since these insects are not beneficial, however, well-timed chemical measures may be used to reduce populations before they can come indoors. This includes targeting both the bugs on the trees themselves, preferably when they are in younger nymphal life stages, and the outside surfaces of the home where the bugs might congregate before entering. Unfortunately, treating the host trees for boxelder bugs often requires specialized equipment and chemicals, so often a professional must be employed. Effective treatment of the outside surfaces of the home depends on critical timing to coincide with the emergence of the last adults of the season. A local Extension agent should be consulted for advice on when this emergence usually occurs in the homeowner's particular area of the country. Exclusionary practices similar to those used for ladybugs are also suggested.

Conclusions—When managing occasional invaders, perhaps the most important things to ask are why the pests entered the home and why they were able to do so. Conditions that allow pests to proliferate and harbor near a structure are more likely to invite them to take that next step and come inside. Leaving spaces beneath doors and having inadequately sealed vents, windows etc, then provides them with a way to enter. Once inside a home, conditions such as areas of high humidity can allow the pests to survive. By eliminating these conditions, homeowners make their dwellings less hospitable to insects and other invaders.

Since moisture management and harborage reduction are critical, these are important steps in pest management. Please see the section on moisture management for detailed information on this important aspect of occasional invader management. Exclusionary practices such as installing doorsweeps and adequately screening roof and crawlspace vents is also an important step in excluding pests. Unlike chemical means, these are also more permanent solutions in pest management that are effective against a wide range of potential pests.

FABRIC AND PAPER PESTS

Most household pests of fabrics and paper are encouraged by one or both of the following conditions: undisturbed areas or high relative humidity. There are four main groups of fabric and paper pests: the clothes moths, the silverfish and firebrats, the carpet beetles, and the booklice. In general, clothes moths and carpet beetles do not need high humidity, but are more likely to be found infesting clothing, rugs, insect/plant collections, etc. that been in storage for a while. Most booklice, silverfish, and firebrats on the other hand, prefer areas of high relative humidity, and some can not survive without it.

Clothes Moths

There are three main species of clothes moths that are of concern to homeowners, all in the family Tineidae. They are similar in size (⅜- ½ inch) and are streamlined shape and a dull in color. The main difference is that the larvae of the casemaking clothes moth (*Tinea pellionella*) and the household casebearer moth (*Phereoeca uterella*) will be partially covered by a silken case that has bits of material incorporated into it. For the household casebearer moth, the material is usually granular debris from its surroundings. In areas of sandy soil, the debris is often particles of sand. The cases are generally seed-shaped with a small, open tube at either end. The larvae of the casemaking clothes moth generally incorporate fibers from the items they are feeding on. The case is usually rectangular and open at both ends. Both caterpillars will feed from either of the open ends of their case. The larvae of the webbing clothes moth (*Tineloa bisselliella*) also build silken tubes, but they are usually incorporated within the fibers that the moths are feeding on, and the caterpillars travel within the tubes rather than carrying them around with them. Though the diet of the casemaking clothes moth is a bit more diverse and includes some plant materials (tobacco, various spices, hemp) all the species prefer materials such as wool, feathers, and fur. The webbing clothes moth may also feed on meat and fish powders and milk related products.

To manage clothes moths, finding the infestation is important. Clothing or stored items that haven't been disturbed for a while are often the most likely places to find the secretive clothes moth. All three species prefer to feed from hidden areas such as under collars or underneath rugs. Susceptible items should be inspected carefully, especially tight hidden spaces. Infested items can be washed when possible. Nearby susceptible items could be stored in containers with an appropriate repellent/insecticide such as moth balls until the infestation is under control. In cases where pesticide applications are needed, the application should be made to cracks and crevices in the closet or area surrounding the infestation.

Silverfish and Firebrats

Silverfish and firebrats belong to the order Thysanura, family Lepismatidae. They are similar in size (½ to ¾ inch long), though silverfish tend to be a little larger. Both have a long slender body, that is shaped somewhat like a carrot that tapers towards the tail end. They have long antennae up front and three bristled appendages that protrude from their posterior. The main difference in their appearance is that silverfish have a distinctive silvery sheen whereas firebrats are covered with mottled markings and lack the silvery sheen.

Both silverfish and firebrats generally prefer areas of high humidity, but **firebrats** prefer areas of high temperatures (90- 106°F), whereas silverfish prefer room temperatures (70- 85°F). A few species of silverfish, however, can survive even without high humidity. Two of these that can be found inside dwellings are the **fourlined silverfish** (*Ctenolepisma lineata*) and the **gray silverfish** (*C. longicaudata*). They also vary slightly in their preferred diets, but most will feed on wool, various kinds of paper, wheat flour, and beef extract.

There are some interesting facts of note for silverfish and firebrats that impact control endeavors. Both are fairly long-lived species (1 to 8 years in some species) that can often go for long periods of time without food or water. They also continually molt throughout their lifetimes, even after reaching the adult stage. This is of interest, because when an insect molts, it is generally able to repair damaged and missing limbs. Most adult insects are not able to regrow missing legs or antennae if they lose them, but because silverfish continue to

molt, they are able to replace any damaged or missing appendages throughout their lifetime.

As with most fabric pests, finding the material the insects are feeding on is important. Many silverfish and firebrat infestations are localized, and with the case of the firebrats they are usually restricted to areas of high temperature. Microencapsulated pesticides and inorganic dusts generally work best, especially for firebrats, where the pesticide may have to hold up to high temperature conditions. For many silverfish species, reducing humidity will also help in control.

Carpet Beetles

There are several species of carpet beetles, but the two most common are the black carpet beetle (*Attagenus unicolor*) and the varied carpet beetle (*Anthrenus verbasci*). All are in the family Dermestidae.

The **black carpet beetle** adult is a uniform black and measures about ⅛ to ¼ inch long. The larva somewhat resembles a silverfish. It has a similar carrot-shaped appearance with the tail region narrower, but is instead gold in color and has one uniform tuft of hairs protruding from its posterior end. It also lacks the long antennae of the silverfish.

The **varied carpet beetle** adult is smaller (¹⁄₁₆ to ⅛ of an inch) with a multicolored pattern of black, white, and brown. This pattern may vary from beetle to beetle which is where the varied carpet beetle got its common name. The larvae are stouter in appearance than those of the black carpet beetle with a widened posterior region and longish hairs all over their body rather than only predominant at the end. They do, however, have distinctive tufts on their posterior, but these do not stick out far from their body as they do with the black carpet beetle.

Both species have a wide variety of materials that they will eat, but in general, dead insects and fabrics such as wool, silk, fur, and leather are preferred. Both will also feed readily on abandoned rat baits and various types of stored products. Controlling carpet beetles often depends on finding the primary feeding source. Until the source or sources are found, the larvae will continue to feed and more adults will emerge.

Clothing and fabrics should be inspected first, followed by stored products. If carpet beetles larvae or damage is not located in these areas, a more unusual source such as abandoned rat bait or dead insects in the wall voids may be involved.

When carpet beetles have infested fabrics, they should

be cleaned – either through washing or dry cleaning. Some smaller items could be frozen if possible. The homeowner may wish to store other susceptible items, such as wool sweaters, wool blankets, fur coats, etc. in sealed containers with an appropriate repellent (such as moth balls) until the beetles have been found and cleaned out. Outdoors, carpet beetle adults often feed on the pollen of flowers. Both species are especially attracted to the flowers of Spirea, so homeowners that have these shrubs nearby a home may want to be extra vigilant about periodically inspecting for carpet beetles indoors.

Booklice

Booklice belong to the order Pscoptera. Most are relatively small (1/32 – 1/16 of an inch). The species found indoors are usually wingless and somewhat resemble very small termite workers. Most species are susceptible to water loss and require a high relative humidity (> 50%) to survive and proliferate. They feed on fungus that grows due to high humidity.

Most booklice populations can be significantly reduced or eliminated by decreasing relative humidity to below fifty percent. Some methods to help achieve this are: correcting water leaks, increasing ventilation, and using dehumidifiers in trouble areas. Special attention should be paid to areas where books are stored, because booklice are especially fond of grazing on the sizing and glue found in old books. In newer homes booklice may sometimes be associated with plaster or sheetrock walls that are still drying. This generally will be a temporary situation, and decreasing humidity will again help to dry out the area and discourage pscopteran growth.

DISCUSSION QUESTIONS

1. Why is it important to correctly identify a pest before treating it?

2. Why are baits a good pest-control tool?

3. Liquid spray products are most commonly available to homeowners in what formulations?

4. What should a homeowner do if a termite swarm appears in the home?

5. Tell how preventative practices can be effective in controlling wood boring insects in the home.

6. Why is moisture management important in keeping a home pest-free?

7. What are the key features in identifying whether an insect is a termite or an ant?

8. What is the best method for controlling a smoky brown cockroach infestation in the home?

9. What are the steps for controlling a stored product pest infestation such as indian meal moth?

10. What should be the first step in controlling fleas?

RESOURCES

University of Georgia Cooperative Extension. *Biology of Subterranean Termites of the Eastern United States.* Bulletin #1209.

University of Georgia Cooperative Extension. *Termite Control Services: Information for the Georgia Property Owner.* Bulletin # 1241.

University of Georgia Cooperative Extension. *Biology and Management of Carpenter Ants.* Bulletin #1225.

Bugwood Network, online at WWW.bugwood.org

29
Leadership and Communication

RICHARD ROHS

DAN RAHN

JAMES HARRIS

J. FAITH PEPPERS

LEARNING OBJECTIVES

Identify the major factors which determine leadership.

Identify the qualities of a good leader.

Know the five stages of group development.

Identify five tips to communicate effectively.

Know at least one technique to deal with each of the five types of disruptive behaviors.

Be able to identify keys to good writing.

Know some techniques that make a good presentation.

TERMS TO KNOW

Clique   a small exclusive group of friends or associates.

Fog Index   an easy to use readability index.

Interdependent   mutually dependent.

Leadership   interpersonal influence process in a situation within which the leader attempts to gain group support to achieve a specified goal or goals.

Norms   unwritten rules for behavior

PART ONE: INTRODUCTION TO LEADERSHIP

The success of any program depends on how effectively leaders mobilize human and non-human resources. Effective leadership is a key ingredient to effective education and change. An effective leader must understand 1) what leadership is, 2) the qualities a person needs to be an effective leader, 3) how groups grow and operate 4) how to communicate effectively and 5) how to handle disruptive behavior.

A great deal of literature exists on leadership, leadership styles, training of leaders, etc. An individual who does not "study" leadership in the academic setting will soon find a shortage of good leadership books, leaving him or her with the questions, "What is leadership?" and "What does it take to be an effective leader?" It is the intent of this chapter to provide answers to these questions.

Leadership

The final definition of leadership has not been written and perhaps may never be written. A major reason for this is that there are no gauges by which we can accurately measure the effectiveness of a leader. Leadership is an intangible factor that makes one group or individual more effective than another.

Let's take a look at what practical experience and social scientists tell us about leadership.

Leaders are made not born—Many individuals have mistakenly believed that some individuals were born to be leaders and others followers. This belief prevailed in the 1800's because leaders during this period came primarily from the aristocracy. As democracy advanced, individuals not from the aristocracy began to assume leadership positions. Thus, the idea of leadership, as an inborn characteristic began to decline.

Today, social scientists generally agree that while personality characteristics influence a leader's acceptability and influence in situations, no single leadership type of personality exists.

Leadership can be learned—For the past 40 years the idea that leadership is learned has prevailed. That is, one can teach individuals the skills and techniques necessary to be an effective leader. Certainly, acquiring new skills for effective leadership is easier than acquiring a new personality. Today, however, there is growing recognition by social scientists that leadership cannot be treated as either inborn or learned. A combination

of these two basic ideas, plus a third dimension - the situation in which a leader functions - is perhaps the most appropriate orientation.

Leadership varies with specific situations—In addition to the inherited potential and learned skills, another dimension of leadership - the situation - must be considered. There is a growing feeling among social scientists that the specific situation determines who assumes the role of leader. In each situation the leadership role demands certain specific kinds of knowledge and skills from the person fulfilling that role. The relationship between learning and the situation should be obvious.

What is Leadership: a Definition

Though we have identified some of the major factors, which determine leadership, we have not defined it. Although there are many different definitions of leadership, the following one seems to incorporate most of the key elements from the social science viewpoint.

Leadership is an interpersonal influence process in a situation within which the leader attempts to gain group support to achieve a specified goal or goals.

Qualities of a Leader

In any organization of leaders, each leader has a distinctive quality, which supplements the qualities of the others, facilitating teamwork. Their responsibility is to focus their own abilities, as well as the potentialities of the members, on the accomplishment of agreed upon goals. As different persons assume leadership over time, programs vary because personalities, ideas and skills vary, because variety is essential to lively interest and because the needs of the community or organization change. Often individuals ask themselves what caused them to make crucial choices: social pressure? circumstances? home? friends? education? religion? Actually, a person's total background converges to influence what he or she is and does, but particular persons and occasions precipitate decision.

"I was simmering, simmering, simmering,"- said Walt Whitman, "Emerson brought me to a boil."

Whether an Emerson, an Indira Ghandi, or a 'John Doe', every effective leader seems to possess the following attributes:

• **Intelligence** (inquiry, discernment, initiative, viability, adaptability, tenacity) leading to competence, which the group perceives as enhancing achievement of its goals.

• **Faith** in himself and that the belief that persons can be trusted to do what is needed, that through guidance they realize their potentials, and that through consultation, responsibility and cooperation they grow in confidence and ability to serve.

• **Cooperativeness**—readiness to give and take, to share ideas and opportunities, to work harmoniously in a team. It is getting things done regardless of who gets the credit, preferably the group as a whole. It is readiness to see that the spotlight shifts from person to person, rather than being fixed on one or a few.

• **Considerateness**—a generous respect for personality, giving due weight to the opinions and judgment of others.

• **Empathy**—putting oneself in the place of another and looking at life through their eyes. It is responsiveness to the feelings of one's associates, sharing emotionally with them, reacting to their needs or utilizing their readiness of action. Empathy involves listening earnestly to what someone has to say, so that they know that you consider their contributions to be of value. From empathy comes rapport, which is characterized by the kindred feeling that encourages thinking and working together.

• **Goodwill**—concern for the welfare of others, expressing itself through congenial attitudes, a kindly sense of humor and acts of service. When a leader is motivated by goodwill, they learn to enjoy more and more people like them and each other.

• **Fellowship**—a sense of identity with people and enjoyment in being with them. To be in fellowship is to be conscious of mutuality of interests, needs and purposes. Fellowship is the social cement that holds people together. When leaders are men and women of developed fellowship, they will promote human harmony.

How Groups Grow and Operate

As a leader of a group, how can you motivate group members to learn or do anything? How does leadership emerge as a group forms? How do the members bond to form a group? How is trust established? What will cause the group to fall apart or to become truly effective? How can a leader have impact on the formation of the group? These are some of the questions to be addressed in this section.

There are two basic components of groups: the human component and the task component. The classic leadership dilemma is getting the job done (task) while maintaining a humanistic group existence. As groups form, interpersonal relationships must be established (human) and the job to be done must be defined, organized, and accomplished (task).

In order for both of these components to be successful, it is important to monitor the development of small groups. In doing so, a leader can influence a group in such a way as to assure completion of tasks and maintenance of positive human regard.

In monitoring a group, there are two areas upon which to focus: the stage of group development and the factors affecting the group.

All groups develop in a predictable and sequential way. By identifying the stage a group is presently in or is about to enter, a leader can time interventions so that the group will be ready at the appropriate time to move forward. The leader is also better able to diagnose problems, to bring out the human resources of the group, and to increase the group's options by using a developmental model of group development.

Stages of Group Development

During their sequential development, human dimensions, such as individual motivation and abilities, affect all groups. To diagnose difficulties and select interventions, a leader should understand and assess an individual's motivation and abilities.

There are many models of group development available. These models have similarities in that all groups go through various stages of group development in a progressive sequence. The names given to these stages by different theorists vary, but the tasks and human interactions in each stage are similar. Group growth and development consists of five stages: forming, storming, norming, performing, and adjourning.

Stage 1: Forming

During this first phase of group development, group members tend to depend on the group leader to provide all the structure: to set the ground rules, to establish the agenda and to do all the 'leading.' Thus, the major issue in the human component is dependency.

The major issue in the task component is orientation of group members to the work they are being asked to do. The nature of the group's work is explored so there is a common understanding of what the group has been organized to do.

Common behavior at this point is questioning:

1) Why are we here?

2) What are we supposed to do?

3) How are we going to get it done?

4) What are our goals?

5) What are our objectives?

Under the human component, conversations tend to be polite as individuals share information as a way of getting acquainted. This helps group members anticipate each other's future responses to group activities. Stereotyping as a means of helping us to categorize other members is common in this stage. We begin to think, who can I align myself with in this group? Cliques begin to form and the need for group approval is strong.

Stage 2: Storming

Stage 2 is called Storming because in this stage the issues of power and control come to the forefront, and groups are characterized by conflict.

Think of groups that you have been involved with in the past. Can you describe storming as a stage? What happens in the human component? The task component?

Interpersonal conflict is inevitable as a part of small group interaction. It may be hidden, but it is there. Why? Because each of us brings to a group our own unresolved conflicts with regard to authority, dependency, rules, and agenda. These issues cause conflict as we organize to get work done. So the major human component issue is conflict, while the major task component issue is organization.

In the human component we can expect group members to become competitive. Each member would like the group to take the action he/she feels is appropriate. But he/she usually finds other group members close-minded. Why? Because each person wants the group to take a different action!

Cliques at this point become well-formed and begin to wield influence. Hidden agendas can no longer stay hidden, so they begin to come forth. Group identity is still low; but because the need for group approval has declined, members gain the courage to risk displaying their individual commitments. This causes the most active participation and also the most widely different amounts of participation than in any other stage. This is an uncomfortable stage for many people.

Through this process the structure of the group begins to evolve. Questions typically asked within the structure component are:

—Who is going to be responsible for what?

—Who is the leader of this group?

—What are going to be the work rules?

—What are going to be the limits?

—What is going to be the reward system?

—What are going to be the criteria?

—What will be the structure of our group?

In order to move from storming to the next stage of group development, members must utilize their abilities to listen and to stop defending one's own view. They must be willing to risk the possibility of being wrong. Therefore, humility is necessary. Other disruptive behaviors may occur. Techniques to deal with these are discussed at the end of the chapter.

Some groups never move from Stage 2 (Storming) to Stage 3 (Norming). A particularly competitive group member and his/her clique can block the transition.

In other cases, you will observe other members who are ready to move to Stage 3 reject members who stay rooted in Stage 2. This is a time when you will see some group dropouts.

Stage 3: Norming

Stage 3 is called Norming because the group establishes certain norms-the unwritten rules for behavior in both the human component and the task component.

During this stage, because the group has established rules of behavior, the members begin to experience a sense of unity, of having 'gotten together', after the storming stage. The major issue of this human component is cohesion.

The members begin to share and solicit ideas, feelings, and feedback with each other. Members actively question and listen to each other, creating and building group spirit. During this phase people typically feel good about what is going on and are happy about being a part of the group.

There is more openness in the group. Cliques begin to dissolve, and the range of participation among and between members narrows. Once a group enters Stage 3, it is difficult to introduce new members because the group is highly cohesive.

During this stage there might be a brief period of time when the task is abandoned and the group members play and enjoy themselves in the group experience. Some very task oriented leaders become anxious and begin to push during this time. Actually, this period is normally very brief and should not overly concern the leader.

The major issue in the task component is data-flow. The group members will share information concerning the task as freely as they do about themselves. There is a great deal of idea generation and alternative exploration. This is a very constructive period and progress toward goals becomes evident. Leadership no longer resides with any one person, but is shared by many (and sometimes most) of the group members.

Conflict is still a possibility, but when it does arise, it is dealt with as a mutual group problem. Practical creativity and utilization of each person's talents are high in this stage.

Group leaders can be most effective in this stage by

1) asking constructive questions,

2) summarizing and clarifying the group's thinking,

3) trusting the group to achieve its maximum potential, and

4) trying to blend in with the group as much as possible.

Stage 4: Performing

During this stage, the group performs in such a way that its overall goal is met. Experience has shown that this does not always occur. In order to move into this stage, it is necessary for group members to accept one another as distinct individuals -faults and all!

During this phase group members will work singly, in any sub-grouping, or as a total unit, according to what is necessary to accomplish the task. The main issue in the human dimension is Interdependence. The members are, at this point, highly task-oriented and highly people-oriented.

Activities are marked by both collaboration and functional competition. There is a high commitment to common activity; morale is high and loyalty to the group is intense. There is an overall feeling that, "We don't always agree on everything, but we do respect each other's views and agree to disagree." Cliques are absent. Group identity is high and a symbol, formal or informal, of the group may appear. Member participation is as even as it will ever be in the group. The group is strongly unified. A new member will have great difficulty in entering the group. In order for this to occur, the entire group will regress to Stage I and start the process again.

A group leader should weigh the advantages of adding a new member, keeping in mind that the group might regress as a result. The trust level of the group is high. In fact, this is what is necessary to move fully from Stage 3 (Norming) into Stage 4 (Performing) Each member must trust himself and each of the other group members.

In the task component, the main issue is Problem-solving. There is support for experimentation with solving problems. Individuality and creativity levels are high. Groups that make it to Stage 4 usually accomplish more than is expected. The apparent talents of the group members often help, too. This is called synergy. (Sum of the parts is greater than the whole.)

Stage 5: Adjourning

The final stage, Stage 5, is called Adjourning. Once the goals and objectives of a group are accomplished, the group has two options:

1) establish new goals and objectives to work toward.

2) dissolve the group

Either of these is appropriate according to the particular group. If new objectives are to be established, the group will regress to Stage 1, and again move forward. This should occur more quickly. If there is no need to establish new objectives, then the group needs to adjourn.

During this stage, the major issue in the human component is: Separation–Group members begin to move apart, and this process may cause some regression to earlier stages. Conflict may arise again, either spoken or acted out. This serves as a way for group members to release their anxiety over the loss of what has been a meaningful experience for them. A good adjournment includes a review of where the group has been and what it has accomplished. This makes the major issue in the task component-Evaluation–Through this process the members of the group are able to leave with a sense of dignity. Groups which do not have a formalized adjournment stage may informally initiate one, for example, by suggesting that the group go out for coffee and dessert after the final meeting. Other groups do not have an adjournment stage. Members of these groups often feel a 'let-down' following the last meeting as though there were something left 'undone.' A leader can structure some type of closure activity to be sure that there is a sense of completion when a group is dissolving.

PART TWO: COMMUNICATING EFFECTIVELY

Communication impacts our day-to-day lives. The average person may spend up to 40 percent of their typical day communicating one-on-one with others. Despite the emphasis on communication and the delivery of information through various methods, "communication breakdowns" continue to be one of the greatest sources of problems in today's environment. Theses breakdowns can happen unknowingly and often. Consider this example:

Operation: Haley's Comet

A COLONEL ISSUED THE FOLLOWING DIRECTIVE TO HIS EXECUTIVE OFFICER:

"Tomorrow evening at approximately 2000 hours, Haley's Comet will be visible in this area, an event which occurs only once every 75 years. Have the men fall out in the battalion area in fatigues, and I will explain this rare phenomenon to them. In case of rain, we will not be able to see anything, so assemble the men in the theatre, and I will show them films of it."

EXECUTIVE OFFICER TO COMPANY COMMANDER:

"By order of the Colonel, tomorrow at 2000 hours, Haley's Comet will appear above the battalion area. If it rains, fall the men out in fatigues. Then march to the theater where the rare phenomenon will take place, something which occurs only once every 75 years."

COMPANY COMMANDER TO LIEUTENANT:

"By order of the Colonel in Fatigues at 2000 hours, tomorrow evening, the phenomenal Haley's Comet will appear in the theater. In case of rain in the battalion area, the Colonel will give another order, something which occurs once every 75 years."

LIEUTENANT TO SERGEANT:

"Tomorrow at 2000 hours, the colonel will appear in the theater with Haley's Comet, something which happens every 75 years. If it rains, the colonel will order the comet into the battalion area."

SERGEANT TO SQUAD:

"When it rains tomorrow at 2000 hours, the phenomenal 75-year-old General Haley, accompanied by the Colonel, will drive his Comet through the battalion area theater in fatigues."

As a Master Gardener you will be dealing with a variety of people. You may need to communicate with phone clients, class participants, committee members, community leaders and others. Some may be pleasant exchanges, others may not.

The keys to making the most of your interactions are:

1. Think through what you want to say before you say it.

2. Once you have made your point, ask the listener for feedback.

3. Speak clearly and concisely.

Dealing with Disruptive Behavior

A major challenge of meeting management for Master Gardeners may be dealing with disruptive or problem-causing participants. The inappropriate and disruptive behavior of some participants slows the progress of the meeting. The group must be protected from the disruptive actions of individual members, while protecting the individual members from being attacked by others. This can be a delicate matter. Troublesome group members cannot be "turned off" or "tuned out" when they are disruptive. In dealing with the disruptive person the leader can:

• Acknowledge the actions of the person rather than ignoring them. Initially, call attention to the actions by describing them, but make no critical or evaluative comment.

• Let the person know that while you do not agree with him/her, it is acceptable for them to feel a certain way.

• Begin to deal with the problem with the least threatening approach. Use a subtle, low-key intervention technique. Reserve direct confrontation as a final approach.

Types of Problem Participants

Some basic types of problem participants and suggestions for dealing with them include:

The LATE-COMER who always arrives late and makes a big production upon arrival.

• Don't stop the meeting to catch them up or stall the start time.

• Don't confront the person in front of the group.

• Following the meeting, ask the person why they are always late.

• Ask the person to arrive early to help set up the room for the next meeting, to be a recorder, or to assist in facilitation or some other way (if appropriate).

The CRITIC who is always negative.

- Ask the person to defend his/her criticism with facts or offer suggestions.

- Interrupt and cut off the unwarranted criticism.

- Have the group agree to process of "evaluating ideas" during a set period of time.

The LONG-WINDED LOUDMOUTH who dominates the meeting, talks too much and too loudly, and refuses to stop talking.

- Subtly move closer to them while they are talking, maintaining eye contact. When you are standing in front of them, focus on someone else and call on him or her.

- When (if) they quit talking, don't yield the floor to them again.

- Direct your conversation to another person.

- Talk with them outside of the meeting, explaining that their actions are preventing others from participating.

The HARPOONER or ATTACKER who personally attacks other group members or the meeting leader.

- Move between the attacker and the person being attacked. Have them talk to you rather than each other.

- Remind the participants that the meeting is not a forum in which to resolve personal differences.

- When you (the leader) are being attacked, resist becoming defensive. Thank the attacker for the comments and then turn the issue back to the attacker, asking for positive suggestions.

The RABBIT CHASER or WAR STORY TELLER who wanders off the subject.

- Ask the person, "How do you feel that relates to our situation?"

- Clarify the topic under discussion: "We seem to have gotten of the subject."

- Present a summary of progress and suggest moving to the next subject area.

The WHISPERER or SIDE CONVERSATIONALIST who constantly whispers with neighbors and makes side comments.

- Maintain eye contact with the whisperers and allow group to be silent until the side conversations cease.

- Ask the person to share his/her comments with the entire group.

- Make a general announcement: "We have a lot to cover today. Let's hold it down."

- As a final resort, rearrange the seating in the meeting.

WRITTEN COMMUNICATIONS

Part of being a Master Gardener is being a Master Communicator. It is not enough to just know all this great information about the garden. It is important to share it. As a Master Gardener, you have a wealth of garden knowledge to share. Know the best ways to communicate that garden information to the people who need it.

There is no formula, pattern or rule that will guarantee you write well. Keep in mind whenever you're writing that writing is choosing the right words to carry something to somebody.

Consider that guideline. But to do it right, one must start from the end and work backwards.

Knowing Your Reader

Before choosing the right words, first ask yourself, "Who am I writing to? Where is this information going?"

Most life-changing truth is communicated one-on-one, face-to-face, heart-to-heart. And that's one of the beauties of the Master Gardener program. It brings you one-on-one, face-to-face, heart-to-heart with people. Even when writing.

You do not usually pick up the phone and just start talking into the handset. You should not just start writing, either, without first knowing whom you intend to be your reader.

Don't try to write to the world — just pick one real, live, flesh-and-blood human being — a gardener. Then just talk with him. Think of it as dialing the phone and connecting with your reader. What interests that gardener? How could your information affect her? What would get his attention?

Remember your reader. Focus on him. Always ask yourself, why is he going to read this? If you're not always thinking about what your reader wants to read, he is not going to stay tuned to what you are writing.

Conveying Something

Any good writing — all good writing — conveys something to a reader. Information, principles, ideas, thoughts — the words carry something to someone.

What do you want to send your reader?

Before you can interest him in what you have to say, you have to be sincere and interested yourself.

Tell him things that interest him in a way that interests him. He might not care for what you want to tell him, but he's interested in something. If you know what that something is, you can start writing about that and lead him into what you want him to know.

You have something important to tell him. If you don't, don't write. He'll know if you're just wasting his time.

If you lose interest while you're writing — your mind wanders, or you just get tired — don't try to fake it, just to get it finished. If you do, you'll just use any old word, any old tired sentence, any old dull paragraph. And your reader will know. He'll get tired, too. He'll know you aren't interested anymore in what you're writing. And he won't be interested anymore in reading it.

Choosing the Right Words

This section is about writing, but in a larger sense it's really about words. Words are a communicator's wheelbarrow, garden hose and sprayer: they are the things you use to carry information to wherever you want it to go.

You wouldn't choose the wheelbarrow to carry water to your garden or the pump-up sprayer to carry compost. And you wouldn't haul either out to the garden in the Cadillac, just to impress the plants.

Whether you talk with someone on the phone, to a group of people in person, on the radio or TV, or write a letter, newsletter or newspaper article, you will use the same tools: words. So how do you choose the actual words to put on paper?

This is the point where many people get uptight about writing. But there is no reason to. You enjoy gardening. You probably enjoy talking about it, too. What you enjoy is sharing your ideas with others, and that's what writing is all about.

What most gardeners want is good information in a down-to-earth, human sort of way. So just relax, have fun, be yourself and share your knowledge.

Here's a nine-word writing short course to help you get started: Simple words. Active verbs. Short sentences and paragraphs. Stop.

Using Simple Words

Not necessarily short words, mind you. Sometimes long words are simple words. "Simple" is the key. If a short word means the same thing as a long word, though, always use the short one.

That sounds like simple, common-sense advice. But it's the most common mistake we make in writing is using bigger, harder-to-understand words than we need. We say purchase when we mean buy, sufficient when we mean enough, initial when we mean first.

We just naturally want to impress people. But in trying to impress your reader, you often lose him.

It does not matter that you understand the words you use. Look at a story from your reader's point of view. You may like minuscule and know perfectly well it means very small. But don't bother your reader with it. It isn't very small to him. It's very big. So say tiny. Or little.

Don't write "terminated," "deficient," "approximately," "satisfactory," and "agitate the container." They don't impress your reader. They don't get through to him, either. Instead, write "ended," "low," "about," "OK," and "shake the can."

Question every long word you're tempted to use. (Make each word go through a sieve. Many will go through. There is room for the necessary long word if you get rid of those you don't need.)

Using Active Verbs

Another bunch of words we writers overuse, for some reason, is passive verbs.

We write, "There was an increase in the number of carrots being consumed by teenagers." But if we relax and write it the simple, clear way our reader wants it, we'll write, "Teenagers ate more carrots."

The first of those sentences is lifeless and muddled. Don't ask me why we often write like that instead of using sentences like the second one — a simpler, clearer, livelier way to tell something.

Active words pump life into your sentences, but they do more than that — they keep your sentences in their simplest, clearest form. This may be perfectly clear to you: "Only dormant trees should be purchased and should be planted while dormant during late fall to early spring."

But it's much easier and quicker for your reader to understand: "Buy and plant trees only while they're dormant, during late fall to early spring."

Using Short Sentences and Paragraphs

One more mistake we writers make: we use too many words. We get too fascinated with the words themselves and not with the message they carry, and we just use too many of them.

Remember, no one pays your reader to read this stuff. She's a busy person, and if it takes her too long to wade through what you've written she just won't do it.

So keep your sentences and paragraphs short. Don't leave out information. Just remember that each word is supposed to help carry that load of information. If it doesn't carry its share, don't use it.

Here's a sentence to help you see what I mean. See how many unnecessary words you can cut from it: "In the year of 1981, near the city of Athens, a woman by the name of Mary Jones was engaged in building a small-sized pantry for the purpose of storing all her different jars of canned vegetables from her bountiful garden that year."

Maybe you came up with something like this: "In 1981, near Athens, Mary Jones was building a small pantry for her freshly canned garden vegetables." If you did, you gave your reader a break. That's the important thing.

Use short sentences. Notice the number of lines you write. By the time you've written two lines you've written 15-20 words. If you haven't completed a sentence by then, worry about it.

Some sentences need to be long, of course, but keep your average sentence short. If you've written a long sentence, let that be a signal to drop in a short one or two to vary the pattern and lower the average length.

Vary the paragraph lengths, too, but keep the average short. Short paragraphs simplify your writing by grouping the thoughts into compact pieces that the reader can grasp one after another. If you're already full, which would you rather eat, a grape or a watermelon? Well, if your reader's already tired, he's more likely to read the next paragraph if it's just three lines than if it's half a page.

And if the next paragraph is just a little one, too, and the next, and the next ....

Stop

That's simple enough. But it's hard for many writers to do. We want a clever ending, an impressive way to sum everything up. But you don't need to do that.

When you've written all the simple words, short sentences and short paragraphs you need to carry the necessary information to your reader, just stop.

That's all there is to writing: Simple words. Active verbs. Short sentences and short paragraphs. Stop.

OK, it's not all that simple. That nine-word short course in writing is just a set of guidelines. It's not a formula. You just can't reduce good writing to a set of rules. That's why writing is so hard to teach. It's an art governed by many principles.

But if you follow the bottom-line guideline and the nine-word short course above, you'll be well on your way to creating clear and readable (good) writing.

The Good-Writing Formula

Then, after you've written, you can use a formula to see how clear or how foggy your writing is. The formula will tell you if you've geared your words to your intended reader. It will tell you if you need to simplify.

You already know some of the things that make reading hard:

1. The long sentence. (But how long is long?)

2. Unfamiliar words. (Unfamiliar to the reader, not the writer.)

3. Looks dull. (Long paragraphs. Blocks of unbroken writing. Children's books have lots of white space, pictures and dialogue. It just looks more interesting.)

4. Passive verbs.

5. Not enough personal, friendly words. (The most important words in the English language are words like you, me, I, we and us.)

6. Too many slow-down words. (Adverbs and adjectives don't do a lot for you. They mostly get in the way and slow down your reader. Verbs do the work.)

But how can you measure all that? How can you take something as complex as writing and come up with a simple way to figure how readable it is?

The easiest way to check the readability of your writing is simply to use the readability formula in the word-processing software on your computer. Nearly all software now includes some kind of readability check, usually as a part of the spelling or grammar check.

If you don't use a computer, you can still check your readability. You need only check two factors: the average sentence length plus a hard-word factor can be counted as fast as you can skim a page.

The formula is the Fog Index, by Robert Gunning. Applying it to your writing can tell you if you're shooting too high, too low or right on target.

Figuring the Fog Index

1. Count the words in something you've written and divide by the number of sentences.

On a longer piece, you may want a shortcut. Start at the beginning and count 100 straight words — but go on to the end of a sentence. Count the sentences in the passage. Then divide that number into the number of words. This gives the average sentence length of the passage.

2. Count the words in the passage that have three syllables or more. Don't count (1) proper names, (2) combinations of short words that keep their original meaning (like bookkeeper and manpower), or (3) verbs made into three syllables by adding -ed or -es (like created or trespasses).

This gives you the percentage of hard words in the passage. (I know — not all three-syllable words are hard words and not all two-syllable words are simple; but this formula works.)

3. To get the Fog Index, add the average sentence length to the percentage of hard words and multiply by 0.4.

Let's figure the Fog Index of a passage from "The Summing Up," by W. Somerset Maugham:

"I have never had much patience with the writers who claim from the reader an effort to understand their meaning. You have only to go to the great philosophers to see it is possible to express with lucidity the most subtle reflections. You may find it difficult to understand the thought of Hume. If you have no philosophical training, its implications will doubtless escape you. But no one with any education at all can fail to understand exactly what the meaning of each sentence is. Few people have written English with more grace than Berkeley. There are two sorts of obscurity in writers. One is due to negligence and the other to willfulness."

The word numbers in the sentences are as follows: 20, 22, 11, 12, 20, 10, 8 and 10. The total number of

words in the passage is 113. This figure divided by 8 (the number of sentences) gives the average sentence length: 14.1 words.

The words of three syllables or more are underlined in the passage — 15 of them, or 13.3 percent. The average sentence length (14.1) and percentage of hard words (13.3) adds up to 27.4. And this multiplied by .4 results in a Fog Index of 10.96, or 11 (always round it off).

The figure represents the school grade level of reading skill required to read the passage. To read the Maugham passage with reasonable speed and comprehension, you'd need an 11th-grade reading skill.

What Does the Fog Index Mean?

Magazines give us a good idea — they keep a constant level of reading ease week after week, month after month, year after year.

Don't think a constant level of reading ease means a sameness of writing style. Thousands of writers have written for these magazines. Articles and stories reflect the personal styles of each. Each magazine is carefully edited, and each depends mainly on its writing to attract subscribers.

Here's rough comparison of magazines in various groups, along with their circulations, averages for sentence length, percentage of hard words and average Fog Index.

Now go back to your own Fog Index. If your writing has a Fog Index of 13 or more, you're beyond the danger line of reading difficulty. You're writing on a college level, and your reader is likely to find it heavy going. Your friends and neighbors are likely to get the idea you're trying to impress them instead of simply writing what you want to say.

Table 1. Average Fog Index of publications				
TOTAL	SENTENCE LENGTH	HARD WORDS	TOTAL	FOG INDEX
Class (New Yorker)	20	10	30	12
News (Time)	18	10	28	11
Reader's Digest	16	9	25	10
Slicks (Life)	16	7	23	7
Pulps (True Confessions)	15	4	19	7

A Master Communicator

Remember, use the Fog Index as a guide after you've written, not as a pattern before you write. Good writing must be alive. Don't kill it with the system.

When you write, most of your attention must be on what you're saying and who you're saying it to, rather than on how you're saying it. No one should write arithmetic.

You're a Master Gardener! And now you're a Master Communicator!

You've learned:

1. Many things that will make you a better gardener in your own backyard.

2. How to share all that new knowledge with your friends and neighbors, so they can become better gardeners, too.

ANATOMY OF A PRESENTATION

Preparation: Building Confidence and Success

A. **Analyze the audience** in terms of:

• Knowledge of topic.

• Interest in topic or attitude toward it.

• Language: How much expert terminology does the group understand?

• Influential members: Who makes the decisions?

• Situational elements: Size, location, time of day, special nature of the occasion, etc.

B. **Determine your purpose**—Specify your objectives. What do you want to accomplish?

• What points do you want to make to your audience?

• What ideas do you want to persuade them to accept?

C. **Select the right topic**—(if it hasn't been assigned).

• What is the subject?

• What needs to be presented?

• How much to present at one time? The law of limitation.

D. **Research the topic**—How much do you know about it? How much does your audience need to know? If they need to know more than you know, you have a research gap to fill. Which of your ideas will need support, and where can you find that support efficiently?

E. **Select the right material**—Select the most effective pattern of ideas, given your topic, for your audience and your objectives.

Capture and Hold an Audience

A. **Organize your talk**

• The skeleton outline.

• Writing and revising.

• Key ideas only.

B. **Establish rapport**—effective openings. Try to:

1. Arouse interest.

• Project your enthusiasm and interest with vitality and intensity.

• Challenge the audience

2. Orient the audience.

• Tell the group what you're going to tell them. Lay the groundwork for your presentation.

• Review events leading up to the current situation.

• Explain key terms.

• Establish a "common ground" with your audience.

3. Direct attention.

• What main questions must be answered?

• Why are they urgent?

• What is the first question?

4. Reveal yourself.

• In general, let the audience know at the outset who you are. Sense your attitude and conviction toward the subject, and feel your confidence in handling it.

Do You "Get Through" to Others?

The word communicate has the same elements as the word communion, an act or instance of sharing. Both are derived from cum, meaning with, and union, signifying oneness or union. Communicate in its general sense means to get closer to others; to share something with them, thus possessing it in common with them.

The dictionary defines communicate in several ways, such as these: "To transmit, impart, make known, as to communicate news or an idea . . .to interchange thought or intelligence by speech or writing."

Remember, however, that communication is a two-way street. We should be as ready to receive as we are to give.

Techniques for Development and Delivery.

A. **Development**—Think through not only the opening but the main body and conclusions of your presentation. What support do you have for each of the main points, and how do you plan to get from one point to the next?

1. Build support for points you feel the audience may not understand or agree with. Types of support include:

- Facts
- Statistics.
- Illustrations.
- Examples.
- Comparisons (or analogies).
- Testimony of experts.
- Visuals.

2. Use logical transitions to move from one idea to a new one. Types of transitions include:

- Point-by-point buildup.
- Mini-summary.
- Refocus on main theme.
- Question and answer.

Tips on Expressing an Idea—In preparing any talk, first limit your topic to one dominant purpose, one limited idea. Second, select specific material suited to the limited purpose. Third, arrange your material, your illustrations, examples, facts, or statistics in some definite order.

Instead of a skeleton outline using such abstract words as introduction, body, and conclusion (which do not help you much), use phrases like take hold, transmit, drive home. Start with a picture, an image or a story so you will already have gotten into the minds of the audience. Not any picture or any story, but one that suits the particular dominant purpose and takes hold of your listeners' attention. After transmitting your idea and the specific incidents, illustrations, or other evidence to back it up, you're ready to emphasize your point with a brief summary of your idea, a poem, or a call for action. It should be a highlight of your talk as you nail your point with intensity.

Opening Your Talk—Draw your listeners into your talk with your first few words. Don't amble into what you have to say. Get into it quickly, enthusiastically.

There are many ways of opening a talk. Here are a few:

1. Begin with a "slice of life" . . . something from your own experience.

2. Arouse curiosity. For example: "Yesterday afternoon at 4 o'clock something happened at home I'll never forget...."

3. Present arresting facts or startling statistics. For example: "Two-thirds of the world goes to bed hungry every night."

4. Ask a question.

5. Use a prop or a visual aid. Show something.

Do not begin with an apology. If you are not a good speaker or you are poorly prepared, your audience will soon find it out, so do not bother to apologize. Chances are, though, you are a much better speaker than you think and adequately prepared as well. Begin with confidence.

B. Delivery

1. Rehearse the presentation. Make clear, concise, brief notes and go over them "live."

2. Check out the environment.

- Visual equipment ready? Working?
- Lights? Controls? Assistance, if necessary?
- Acoustics? Try your voice on someone sitting in the back of the room. Will you need a microphone?

3. Give the presentation, conveying interest and concern for the ideas you are discussing.

4. Maintain audience contact. Never lose it! Ways of maintaining contact with your audience include:

- Looking for signs of comprehension and eye contact.
- Listening.
- Asking questions.
- Transmitting enthusiasm.

5. Obtain feedback, if possible. Either a question-and-answer period at the end of the presentation or questions following key points will help you find out where you stand; whether the audience understands you and believes you.

6. Follow through.

- Review the presentation in terms of the audience's reaction. How could your presentation have been improved? Where did it fail to meet your objectives?
- Decide what follow-through action is necessary.

What should members of the audience do, and by when? What should you do, and by when?

Special Development Tasks

Specifics make your talk more believable. Generously flavoring the talk with references to everyday experiences often helps people listen to, believe and remember your talk.

A. Don't use broad, obscure statements. They show:

- You're not sure of your facts.
- You didn't take the trouble to check your material.
- You didn't care enough about either your audience or your talk to prepare yourself thoroughly.

B. Don't be guilty of bypassing facts to make a point quickly. Too often that point, unsupported by specific evidence, misses its goal completely. Do not, then, use:

- "They say . . ." Who are "they"? Most of the time we really don't know. It's a convenience to fall back on the mysterious "they," and perhaps we hope our listeners will not ask us to identify our vague authority.
- "A recent survey . . ." How recent? Who made the survey?
- "It is well known . . ." Is it really? By whom? How can you be sure?

C. Do be factual and accurate—To present your good ideas so they'll be remembered, avoid vague generalities and foggy references. "Statistics show ..." But do they? Whose statistics?

D. Use specifics—In all your formal presentations and all your everyday speaking, train yourself to think and speak in terms of specific facts and figures. For instance, use the names of people whenever you can.

Select, Design, and Use Visuals

A. Selection and planning

1. Remember: to use visual aids to support presentations. This means designing each visual for a specific function. A visual aid is just that — not a crutch — not a substitute. Use them where they are needed and relate to the subject.

2. Use visual aids to show what something looks like. Get a picture of it. Use a pie to break down bigness and add interest and clarity.

3. In seeking visuals list your key ideas and then ask: "How could a visual help?" "What visual aid will work best?" Then test the visual to make sure it will be an effective aid.

B. Design and construction

1. Avoid too much detail, illegible writing or printing, wrong emphasis, too small or too crowded a visual.

2. Use capital letters — large ones — and print them.

3. Use numerals when you can.

4. Make any drawings large. Lines should be heavy.

C. Display

1. Blackboard and flip chart materials. If you can, prepare them in advance. Set them up ahead of your talk, but keep them covered until they're needed.

2. Handouts. Ordinarily, do not distribute these until the end of your talk. If you have to give them out during the talk, never give more than one at a time and have your audience read them along with you.

D. Cautions

1. Keep all visuals out of sight until you are ready to use them.

2. Do not talk toward your visual; always talk toward the audience.

3. Do not stand in front of what you are showing.

4. Hold visuals up so that everyone can see them.

5. Keep them from blocking your face.

6. Put all aids aside when you have finished using them.

7. Remember: practice makes perfect.

Close Effectively

A. Summarize key ideas.

B. Develop a "call to action."

C. End on a note of intensity.

End on a High Note—Summarize briefly; or, if your talk was a short one, re-emphasize your major point. End on a high note. Don't run downhill in either the tone of your voice or interest in your subject. A dreary ending leaves your listeners with a dreary impression of you and your topic. When you have said what you had to say, sit down.

SPECIAL ELEMENTS OF A PRESENTATION

Personality: Behavior Manifests Belief

A. Attitude—It must be positive —

• Toward your subject.

• Toward yourself.

• Toward your audience.

B. Fear and how to control it.

1. Fear is normal.

• A little nervous excitement beforehand assures the speaker that he is enthusiastic about the job ahead. The person who no longer finds the experience of speaking before a group stimulating is probably as much of a bore to his listeners as he is to himself.

2. What you can do to minimize fear.

• Harness your nervousness and make it work for you. Do not dissipate its value by wasting it in needless moving about, clearing your throat, or rambling in your presentation while trying to calm your fears.

• Concentrate on your message and the task of getting it over to your audience.

• Remember, your nervousness isn't nearly so evident to your listeners as it is to you.

• Remember, practice makes perfect. Each speaking experience you have will help overcome nervousness.

• As your time and energy permit, accept speaking engagements — all kinds.

C. Appearance

• Facial expression. Are you dead or alive?

• Posture. Does it command attention without being stiff?

D. Voice

• Enunciation. Do you speak clearly, or do you tend to slur certain sounds?

• Speed, pace. Fluent or halting? Rapid? Slow? How about the timing of pauses?

• Tone. Does your voice convey excitement, enthusiasm, seriousness, etc.?

• Precision. Are you using correct, precise words to convey your thoughts?

E. Eye Contact and Communication

• Do you look straight at your listeners when you speak?

• If you find it hard to look at your audience — and even experienced speakers do — try looking at the person sitting in the last row at the extreme left, then slowly turn your gaze toward the person in the same position on the extreme right. Gradually sweep the entire audience with your eyes, resting for a second or two here and there. Try to see facial expressions. Are they with you? Or are they nodding with boredom?

• Communicate with your eyes. Be conscious of your facial expression. Do not be afraid to smile. Facial mobility is a sign of a relaxed speaker. The frozen face begets a frozen response from the audience.

Audience Contact— Are you truly in touch with your audience? Have you established enough rapport to help carry the thrust of your thinking?

To see how important your voice can be in building this rapport, try watching a televised presentation with the sound turned off. How effectively does the speaker communicate without his voice? Now listen to him without the picture. Does his voice dramatize his message?

F. Mannerisms

• Speech habits. Are you slovenly in your speech? Do you use re-worked fad words just to seem with it?

• Body movements. Do your movements distract or irritate the audience? Do they have a communication purpose?

• Gestures. Be conscious of what you do with your hands and head. Do these gestures give point and meaning to what you say?

The Need for Practice

A. Lessons from successful speakers.

B. Modern aids to self-development.

• Cassette player or tape recorder.

• Video equipment.

C. Toastmasters Clubs.

D. Preparation without memorizing-some general rules:

• DO practice your talk once or twice, preferably aloud, before you give it before the group. You can do this privately or before family or friends.

• DO NOT overdo the practicing. Just try to fix the sequence of points in your mind. Too much rehearsing leads to slavish repetition.

• DO NOT memorize what you want to say word-for-word. It will make your talk sound mechanical. Memorized talks are not spontaneous and natural because you concentrate on recalling words instead of ideas.

• AVOID the added strain that memorizing places on you. It keeps you from introducing any new material, such as something said by a previous speaker, or referring to something said by the person who introduced you. If you're distracted by what goes on around you (such as a loud sneeze in the audience, a door slamming, a waiter dropping a tray, etc.), there's a good chance you'll forget what to say next.

Make and Use Notes

These are comparable to the markers along our express-ways. We pick up information at a glance as we whiz by. A few tips on making notes will help you use them more easily:

A. Make your notes on cards (3 x 5 or 5 x 7, or whatever size appeals to you) or on regular letter-size sheets of paper.

B. Keep all notes brief — a few words, a phrase, statistics, etc., but with plenty of space around each point. Don't try to cram all your material on two or three cards; rather use eight, ten, or more so the eye can pick up information quickly.

C. Underline words; use colored pencils and the like —devices that will help direct the eye.

D. Number each card or sheet in the upper right-hand corner. Not numbering them is a needless risk.

E. Type or print in large block letters. Handwriting, even your own, can tax the eyes.

F. Do not fold your notes before your talk; creased papers sometimes present problems when you place them on the speaker's stand.

G. DO NOT STAPLE your notes. Turning pages can be distracting to you and your audience.

Memory Tips

A. What it takes:

• Desire.

• Concentration.

• Repetition.

• Association.

B. Application to speaking– the PREP formula. (Point, Reason, Example, Point)

The Place of Humor

A. Use it sparingly.

B. Make it relevant.

C. Keep it brief.

Techniques for Answering Questions

A. Listen for both content (what is asked) and intent (what is meant).

B. Acknowledge the question; i.e., show that you understand it, if necessary...

C. Ask the questioner to clarify. Paraphrasing the question is one way of seeking clarification.

D. Answer the question briefly, accurately, completely.

E. Verify the questioner's satisfaction. Has your answer been responsive?

F. Be ready to offer proof, clarification, or support of your ideas.

G. *Avoid*:

• Showing you feel the question is stupid or ill-conceived.

• Being unresponsive or flippant. If you cannot answer the question, explain why not, simply and politely.

• Diverting the question needlessly. If you must divert it, be sure to try to give the answer later on.

• Going off on an unrelated tangent.

• Treating two questions as one. This can be confusing.

Involve the Audience

People don't care unless they share. Put yourself out there. What would make you leave feeling fortunate to have been there? When you involve your audience at all stages of preparing and delivering your presentation, you greatly enhance your chance of being successful in the end.

RESOURCES

J.W. Fanning Institute for Leadership at the University of Georgia provides leadership consulting and leadership instruction and training services. http://www.fanning.uga.edu

Elements of Style. Strunk, W.S. and E.B. White.

Developing Instructional Design. Mc Ardle, Geri.

Using Visual Aids. Raines, Claire and Linda Williamson.

DISCUSSION QUESTIONS

1. What are the major factors which determine leadership?

2. Name the qualities possessed by a good leader.

3. The five stages of group development are:

4. What is the first step in writing an article or preparing a presentation?

5. Name three tips for writing.

6. How does using the Fog Index make written communication more readable?

7. What are some good ways to establish rapport with an audience?

8. How and why should you use visuals in a presentation?

9. Name two techniques for handling questions.

NOTES

Glossary

Abdomen - the posterior section of the arthropod body.

Abiotic - nonliving.

Acclimate - to adapt to new environmental conditions.

Achene - a type of simple dry fruit produced by many species of flowering plants.

Acidity - quality of being sour; degree of sourness; having a pH of less than 7.

Actinomycetes - a form of fungi-like bacteria that form long, thread-like branched filaments.

Aerobic - occurring only in the presence of oxygen or requiring oxygen.

Adventitious - plant parts, such as shoots and roots, produced in an unusual position on a plant or at an unusual time of development.

Aeration - to be exposed to air; to cause air to circulate through a medium.

Air layering - a propagation technique in which plant parts are rooted while they remain attached to the parent plant.

Aggregates - (soil); clumps or cemented units of mineral and organic matter.

Aleurone layer - Outermost layer in cereal seeds and other taxa, which contains enzymes concerned with starch digestion and subsequent seed germination.

Algae - aquatic plants that lack a vascular system. Some are microscopic and others are large. Examples are pond scum, kelp and red tides.

Algal bloom - rapid growth by algae producing large quantities of plant material.

Alkalinity - having a pH greater than 7.

Alternate host - a secondary host that becomes infected and is necessary for alternating generations of a disease-causing organism.

Amendment - an alteration or addition to soil to correct a problem.

Ammonia - An intermediate product of the nitrogen cycle that converts to the more toxic nitrite.

Anaerobic - able to live and grow where there is no air.

Anion - an ion having a negative charge

Annuals - plants that complete their life cycle in a year or less.

Anther - the upper part of the stamen where the pollen is produced.

Apical - meaning to be at the apex or tip.

Apical bud - a bud at the apex or terminal position on a plant or branch.

Aquatic plant - species of plant that lives in water either floating, submerged, or rooted into the ponds bed.

Arboretum (pl. arboreta) - a place where trees, shrubs, vines and herbaceous plants are cultivated for scientific and educational purposes.

Arthropod - invertebrate animals (insects, arachnids and crustaceans) that have a jointed body and limbs and usually a hard shell or exoskeleton that is molted periodically.

Asexual propagation - the duplication of a plant from a cell, tissue or organ of the plant.

Auxin - a generic term for a group of plant hormones that regulate plant growth and development.

Available moisture - the amount of water in a soil that roots can absorb.

Axillary bud - Bud in the axil of a leaf.

Bacteria - microscopic organisms having round, rod-like, spiral or filamentous single-celled or noncellular bodies often gathered into colonies.

Balance - in landscape design, the equality or equilibrium of visual attraction.

Balled-and-burlapped (B&B) - field grown plants plants that are dug and roots wrapped in burlap, wire cage or similar material prior to replanting.

Band fertilize - to apply fertilizer in a narrow line along a row of plants or in a circle around individual plants.

Bare root - a plant that is sold or shipped dormant with no soil surrounding its roots.

Bark - dead outer protective tissue of woody plants, derived from the cortex.

Beneficial insects - insects that prey on or parasitize pests.

Bentgrass - a high-maintenance grass used on golf putting greens.

Biennials - plants that complete their life cycle in two years or growing seasons.

Binomial nomenclature - a system in which the scientific name of a plant consists of two parts indicating the genus and species.

Biological control - the use of living organisms or their products to control pest populations.

Biological diversity - presence of many different types of living organisms.

Biological filtration - A loose term that describes the process of removing harmful compounds with bacteria.

Blade - the usually broad, flattened part of a leaf.

Bolt - the tendency of cool-season plants to grow rapidly and produce seeds when exposed to warm temperatures.

Bonsai - a potted plant dwarfed by special cultural practices.

Bract - a modified leaf, usually reduced in size or scale-like. Sometimes large and brightly colored.

Bramble - any shrub with thorns in the rose family; usually refers to blackberries and raspberries.

Branch - one of the coarser divisions of a trunk or main branch.

Branch crown - plant tissue that is the junction of the roots and stem that forms on the side of a strawberry plant. These only form foliage.

Broad spectrum - pesticides that affect a wide variety of pests.

Bud - a structure of embryonic tissues which will become a leaf, a flower, or both or a new shoot.

Bud leaf - the arrangement of the leaves in the budshoot.

Bud scales - specialized tissue that covers the terminal bud and embryonic leaves of a plant during winter.

Bud union - the location of a graft.

Bulb - an underground storage organ made up of enlarged and fleshy leaf bases and a bud.

Bulbil - a small bulb that forms along the stems of certain plants, such as tiger lilies and bladder ferns.

Bulblet - a small bulb that develops around a parent bulb and can be removed to propagate additional plants.

Button - the small heads of broccoli or cabbage that form as a result of seedlings being exposed to freezing temperatures.

Cage - an enclosure used to support a plant.

Callus - wound tissue.

Cambium - the tissue in a plant that produces new cells.

Candle - the new shoot growth on needled evergreens before the needles expand.

Cane - a one-year-old shoot on a grapevine or bramble.

Canker - a localized area of diseased tissue on a stem.

Canopy - the top layer of a tree including branches and foliage.

Capillary action - a force that causes liquids to rise or fall when inside very small tubular spaces.

Carbon dioxide, CO2 - a colorless, odorless gas found in the air. It is absorbed by plants and exhaled by animals.

Carnivore - a flesh-eating animal.

Caterpillar - worm-like larva of various insects, especially butterflies and moths.

Cation - an ion having a positive charge.

Cation exchange - the interchange between a cation in solution and another cation on the surface of a colloidal or other surface-active material such as a particle of clay or organic matter in the soil.

Cation exchange capacity (CEC)- the total amount of exchangeable cations a soil can hold.

Cell - the unit of plants that makes up tissues. Cells have a cell wall that encloses the protoplasm.

Chlorophyll - green pigments in plants that facilitate photosynthesis.

Cloche - a transparent plant cover used to protect plants from cold temperatures.

Cold composting - composting under conditions where the temperatures do not rise to 140° F.

Cold frame - a glass-covered frame without artificial heat used to protect plants and seedlings.

Collar - a band of material used as a mechanical barrier to protect a plant from damage by insects.

Colloids- the very smallest soil particles which are visible only with an electron microscope

Compaction - a state where soil particles are forced closely together, reducing pore space.

Complete metamorphosis - changes in body form of insects that include egg, larva, pupa and adult; also known as complex metamorphosis.

Compost tea - a low-nutrient liquid that results from placing plant debris in water and allowing it to decompose.

Composted manure - animal feces that have been aged in a pile, allowing much of the nitrogen to leach from the feces. A nonburning organic fertilizer.

Compound Leaf - a leaf of two or more leaflets.

Contact insecticide - a poison that must contact the body of the insect to be controlled.

Contractile - drawing together resulting in decreased size or bulk.

Cool-season crop - a crop that grows best during the cool temperatures of spring and fall.

Cool-season grass - turfgrasses that actively grow during the cooler spring and fall weather. These include Kentucky bluegrass, the fescues, ryegrasses and bentgrass.

Compost - the useable material which is the end product of the decomposition process.

Composting - the process by which gardeners convert organic matter for use.

Concentrates - pesticides that must be diluted with water before use.

Cordon - horizontal branches of a grapevine trained along the trellis; also called the arms. The canes left after pruning which will produce fruiting shoots and new canes.

Core aeration - increasing air penetration of the soil by removing plugs of soil. A heavy machine with hollow prongs is moved across a lawn pushing the prongs into the soil and pulling out plugs of soil.

Corm - a short, thickened, underground, upright stem in which food is stored.

Cormel - a small corm that forms around the parent corm. It can be removed and planted to propagate a new plant.

Cotyledon - the leaf or leaves of the embryo, also called seed leaves.

Cover crop - a crop that improves the soil in which it is grown.

Crop rotation - growing crops of a specific family in different areas of the garden each year to avoid soil-borne diseases and nutrient depletion.

Cross-pollination - the transfer of pollen from one plant to the stigma of another plant.

Crotch - the angle measured from the trunk of a tree to the upper surface of a branch.

Crown - the part of a plant where the root and the stem meet.

Culinary - used in cooking.

Cultivar - also cultivated variety; a subdivision of a species, a result of human-manipulated hybridization.

Cultivation - preparation of the soil for growing plants.

Cultural control - the use of good gardening techniques to control pest populations.

Cuticle - a waxy or varnish-like layer covering the outer surface of leaves.

Cutin - the waxy or varnish-like material that makes up the cuticle.

Cutting - any portion of the vegetative plant body used for propagation.

Day-neutral plant - a plant that will flower under any day length.

Days to maturity - the number of days between planting the seed and first harvest.

Deadhead - to remove spent blossoms of herbaceous plants.

Deciduous - plants that drop their leaves at the end of each growing season.

Defoliation - casting off or falling off of leaves.

Dehydration - an abnormal loss of fluids.

Desiccation - drying.

Determinate - growth that is limited.

Diameter breast high - the diameter of a tree trunk at a height of 4-½ feet above the ground.

Dicot - also dicotyledon; flowering plants with embryos that have two cotyledons (seed leaves).

Dioecious - plants that have only male or only female flowers on an individual plant.

Disease resistance - the tendency not to be infected by a particular pathogen.

Disease tolerance - the ability of a plant to continue growing without severe symptoms despite being infected by a pathogen.

Division - a method of propagation by separating and planting segments capable of growing roots and shoots.

Dormancy - a state of suspended growth or lack of visible activity caused by environmental or internal factors.

Double dig - a method of digging a garden bed which involves removing the soil to the depth of one spade blade and then digging down an equal distance, breaking up and mixing the soil.

Drift - when a pesticide is blown by wind onto non-target organisms.

Drip irrigation - a system of tubes with small holes that allow water to drip out onto the root zone of plants. A water-conserving irrigation system.

Drip line - a line encircling a tree corresponding to the furthest extension of the branches of a tree.

Drought - a prolonged period of dryness that can cause damage to plants.

Dwarf - an atypically small plant.

Ecosystem - a system consisting of a community of animals, plants and microorganisms and the physical and chemical environment in which they interrelate.

Element - a substance that cannot be separated into different substances. All matter is made of elements.

Emulsifiable concentrates - pesticides dissolved in a petroleum-based solvent.

Endodormancy - Dormancy imposed by the embryo itself.

Endophyte - a plant living within another plant. In turfgrasses, it is a fungus within the grass plant secreting substances that repel insect pests.

Enhanced seed - Commercial seed that have been treated in a certain way, in order to increase germination and/or achieve uniform germination, and/or improve seedling survival.

Epicotyl - Part of the seed embryo below the cotyledons.

Epidermis - the outer superficial layer of cells.

Epiphyte - a plant that usually grows on another plant and gets its nutrients from the air and water.

Espalier - a plant trained to grow flat against a wall or trellis.

Established - the state of a plant when it is adjusted to the site and thriving.

Eukaryote - organism consisting of one or more cells that contain nuclei.

Evergreen plants - plants that do not drop the current season's leaves at the end of the growing season.

Exodormancy - dormancy imposed by factors outside the embryo.

Fallow - cultivated land that is allowed to lie idle for a growing season.

Fertilization - the application of nutrients for plant growth. The union of the egg and sperm.

Fertilizer analysis - numbers representing the percentage of nitrogen, phosphorus and potassium that is available from the bag of fertilizer.

Fertilizer burn - the browning, and in extreme cases, killing of plants from exposure to excessive nitrogen.

Fibrous root - a root system where the roots are finely divided.

Field capacity - the amount of water soil can hold against the force of gravity.

Filament - the part of the stamen that holds the anther in position for pollen dispersal.

Fine fescue - a fine-leaved turfgrass that grows well in shade, low soil moisture, low fertility and low pH.

Floricanes - on raspberries and blackberries, two-year-old canes which bear fruit and then die.

Flower - an axis bearing one or more pistils or one or more stamens or both.

Fogger - a device that spreads a chemical in the form of a fog.

Foliage - leaves.

Food chain - a sequence of organisms in a community in which each member of the chain feeds on the member below it, as in fox, rabbit and grass.

Footcandle - a unit of light measurement. One footcandle (ft-c) is the amount of light cast by a candle on a white surface one foot away in a completely dark room.

Force - manipulation of environmental factors to make a plant blossom out of season.

Frond - the leaf of a fern; also leaf of a palm.

Frost pocket - a depression in the terrain into which cold air drains, but cannot escape.

Fruiting wood - on grapevine, the one-year-old canes that will produce the current year's fruit.

Fungi - saprophytic and parasitic organisms that lack chlorophyll and include molds, rusts, mildews, smuts, mushrooms and yeast; singular, fungus.

Gall - An abnormal swelling or growth of plant tissue that is initiated by a pathogen, insect or mite.

Gallery - a tunnel made by a wood-boring insect. The galleries of some insects have characteristic patterns.

Gametophyte - the phase of a life cycle which has half the normal number of chromosomes.

Genus - groups of closely related species clearly defined from other plants.

Gibberellins - Plant hormones involved in cell elongation and seed germination.

Girdling - removing the bark from a woody stem to kill the plant. Encircling a stem with a material so that the cambium layer is destroyed, killing the plant.

Grafting - the joining of two separate structures, such as a root and a stem or two stems, so that by tissue regeneration they form a union and grow as one plant.

Green manure - an annual cover crop that is turned into the soil before it flowers.

Greensand - an organic source of potassium. About 7% potash plus 32 trace elements.

Ground cover - a spreading plant that grows near the ground densely.

Grub - short, fat, worm-like larva, especially of beetles.

Guard cells - specialized crescent-shaped cells that control the opening and closing of a stomata.

Gutattion - Water exudates from pores on the leaf surface.

Harden off - to acclimate a plant to harsher conditions.

Hardiness - the ability to withstand harsh environmental conditions.

Hardpan - a hard, compacted, often clayey layer of soil through which roots cannot grow.

Hardwood cutting - a mature, woody piece of a woody plant that is removed to asexually propagate a new individual plant.

Heading - Indiscriminately cutting back terminal portion of the branch. Results in thick, dense growth of the outer canopy.

Heave - the partial lifting of a plant out of the soil as a result of alternating freezing and thawing of the soil.

Heavy metals - the heavy metals of concern to gardeners are lead, zinc, nickel, arsenic, copper and cadmium. These metals can be toxic to plants when they accumulate to high levels in the soil.

Heeling in - covering the roots of dormant plants with soil or mulch for short periods.

Heirloom vegetables - cultivars that were popular a generation or more ago.

Herbaceous - a nonwoody plant.

Herbicide - an agent that stops plant growth or kills a plant.

Herbivore - a plant-eating animal.

Heterotrophic - capable of deriving energy for life processes only from the decomposition of organic compounds.

Hill planting - grouping plants in a cluster, not necessarily on an elevated mound.

Holdfast - a part of a plant that clings to a flat surface.

Honeydew - a sugary substance secreted by aphids and other juice-sucking, plant-feeding insects.

Hormones - Substances involved in regulation of physiological processes in plants.

Hotbed - a bed of soil enclosed by a structure with a top of glass, heated, often by manure, for forcing or raising seedlings.

Houseplant - Plant grown indoors.

Humidity - the amount of moisture in the air.

Humus - brown or black, partially decomposed plant or animal material that forms the organic portion of soil.

Hybrid - a first generation cross between two genetically diverse parents.

Hyphae - pl. of hypha; the threads making up the mycelium of a fungus.

Hypocotyl - Part of the seed embryo between the epicotyl and the radicle.

Incomplete fertilizer - a fertilizer formulation lacking one of the primary nutrients N, P or K.

Incomplete metamorphosis - gradual growth of an arthropod that involves change in size, but not form.

Incubation - the growth of a pathogen so that it can enter a host.

Indeterminate - growth that is potentially limitless.

Indole-3-acetic acid (IAA) - Naturally-occuring auxin.

Indolebutyric acid (IBA) - Synthetic auxin used in commercial rooting hormone preparations.

Infection - the stage when a pathogen is growing in a host and causing damage.

Inoculant - a microorganism which is introduced into the soil to improve growth of legume crops.

Inoculation - the introduction of a pathogen to a host.

Inorganic - being or composed of matter other than plant and animal; often of mineral origin.

Instar - the stage in the life of an arthropod between molts.

Internode - the area on a stem between nodes.

Interplant - growing two different intermixed crops in an area to maximize space usage.

Interstem - an intermediate stem piece that is grafted between the scion and the stock.

Irrigation - to supply water by artificial means, such as with sprinklers.

Landscape fabric - a loosely intertwined fabric that is placed over the soil as a mulch to reduce weed invasion.

Larva s. **Larvae** pl. - a stage of insect complete metamorphosis between the egg and pupal stages. The feeding, growing, nonreproductive stage of insect development.

Latent bud - a dormant bud that is capable of growth and development.

Lateral bud - smaller buds on the sides of stems, responsible for growth of leaves and side branches.

Lath house - a structure consisting of a frame supporting strips of wood which are spaced to provide about 50% shade.

Layering - a method of propagation in which adventitious roots form before the new plant is severed from the parent plant.

Leach - to dissolve in water and wash away.

Leaf mine - an area of a leaf characterized by insect larval feeding between upper and lower layers of the leaf. May be blotched, linear or serpentine in shape.

Leaf scorch - injury to leaves due to lack of sufficient water, excessive transpiration or injury to the water-conducting system of the plant.

Ligule - the structure which clasps the stem at the junction of the blade and sheath.

Long-day plant - a plant that requires a night shorter than its critical dark period, usually 12 hours or less, to develop flowers.

Macronutrients - the nutrients needed in large amounts by plants: nitrogen, phosphorous, potassium, magnesium, calcium and sulfur.

Marginally hardy - close to the limit of hardiness that a plant can withstand.

Matted-row - a system of planting where plants are placed off center or are centered on a diagonal.

Meristem - a region of cell and tissue initiation; cells that do not mature, but remain capable of further growth and division.

Metamorphosis - the changes of form insects go through in their life cycle from egg to immature stages to adult.

Microbe - also microorganism; an organism of microscopic size.

Microclimate - the local climate of a small site or habitat.

Micronutrients - the nutrients needed in small amounts by plants: iron, manganese, zinc, copper, molybdenum, boron and chlorine.

Miticide - a pesticide that kills mites.

Mollusk - invertebrate animals with soft, unsegmented bodies, such as clams and snails, usually enclosed in a calcium shell.

Molt - to shed the exoskeleton to accommodate growth.

Monocot - or monocotyledon, flowering plants that have embryos with only one cotyledon.

Monoecious - plants that have both male and female flowers on the same plant.

Monomorphic - having only one form.

Morphology - the form and structure of an organism or one of its parts.

Moss - small, leafy plants that do not produce flowers or seeds. They grow in moist, shaded areas where fertility is low.

Mulching - the practice of applying materials such as compost, leaves, or grass clippings to the soil surface to modify soil temperature and moisture and control weeds and soil erosion.

Mummy - a dried shriveled fruit.

Mycelium (pl. mycelia) - the vegetative part of a fungus, consisting of a mass of branching thread-like hyphae.

Mycoplasma - disease-causing agents similar to viruses.

Naphtaleneacetic acid (NAA) - Synthetic auxin used in commercial rooting hormone preparations

Native - inherent and original to an area.

Natural - occurring in nature.

Nematodes - microscopic, elongated, cylindrical, parasitic worms that live in water and soil.

Node - the location on a stem where buds form.

Nodules - swellings on the roots of legumes where nitrogen-fixing bacteria live.

Nonselective pesticide - a poison that kills a wide variety of pest species.

Nutrients - substances a plant takes in and uses as food for growth and development.

Nymph - a stage or series of size changes between egg and adult in the life cycle of insects that go through incomplete or simple metamorphosis.

Ootheca - a case or capsule containing eggs.

Organic - of plant or animal origin.

Ovary - the swollen bottom part of the pistil that contains the ovules or immature seeds.

Oviposit - to lay eggs.

Oxygen, O$_2$ - a colorless, tasteless, odorless gas that is ⅕ of the volume of the atmosphere.

Parasitic - an organism that lives on or in another living organism (the host) and obtains nutrition from the host.

Pathogen - a disease-causing organism.

Pelletized - the coating and forming into pellets of very small seed so they are easier to handle.

Penetration - the point at which a pathogen enters a host.

Permanent wilting percentage - the amount of water a soil contains after plants are permanently wilted.

Perennials - plants that do not die after flowering, but live from year to year.

Perithecium - in certain fungi, a flask-like case covering the spore sacs.

Pest - an injurious plant or animal.

Petals - a whorl of structures that surround the inner reproductive organs of a flower. Together they are called the corolla.

pH - a measure of the hydrogen ion activity (H$^+$) in solution.

Pheromone - a chemical substance that convey information to and produce specific responses in certain animals.

Phloem - the part of the vascular system that moves food through the plant.

Photodormancy - type of dormancy where the ability of the seed to germinate is controlled by the wavelength and duration of light received by the embryo.

Photoperiodism - responses of plants to the relative lengths of light and dark cycles.

Photosynthesis - the production of sugar from carbon dioxide and water in the presence of chlorophyll, activated by light energy and releasing oxygen.

Phototropism - the bending of a plant toward the direction of more intense light.

Phylum - a major division of the animal or plant kingdom.

Phytochrome - pigment involved in perception of red light; also controls seed germination and flowering in many plant species.

Pinch - breaking off the terminal growing point of a plant to encourage axillary buds to grow.

Pistil - the female part of the flower, consisting of one or more carpels and enclosed ovules.

Pollard - a tree cut back to the trunk to make a dense cluster of branches and foliage.

Pollen - the microspores that carry the male gametophyte of seed plants.

Pollination - the transfer of pollen from the anther to the stigma.

Pollinator - an insect or other vehicle by which pollen is carried from one flower to another. A plant that provides pollen for a self-infertile plant.

Post-emergent herbicide - a pesticide that kills plants after they have grown to seedling stage or beyond.

Potpourri - a mixture of dried flower petals with herbs and spices used for its fragrance.

Potting medium - material used for growing plants in containers. Mixes may include vermiculite, perlite, sand, peat, charcoal, loam and fertilizer.

Pre-emergent herbicide - a pesticide that kills plants as they germinate.

Primocanes - on raspberries and blackberries, new, first-year canes.

Procumbent - having stems that trail along the surface.

Prokaryote - a single-celled organism without a nucleus; i.e. Bacterium.

Propagation - to increase the number of plants by sexual or asexual means

Protozoans - organisms made up of a single cell or a group of basically identical cells.

Proportion - the size of parts of the landscape design in relation to each other and the design as a whole.

Prune - to cut back parts of plants for better shape, disease control or improved fruiting.

Pupa - a stage in complete metamorphosis when an insect transforms from the larval to adult stage of development.

Radicle - embryonic root.

Raised bed - a gardening area where the soil has been elevated above ground level. Beds may be raised in a structure of wood, brick, cement blocks, etc.

Rasping - mouthparts that are rough and used to scrape a surface to feed.

Recalcitrant seed - seed, which will die if dried below critical moisture level, and cannot tolerate low temperatures.

Reel mower - a mower with multiple blades mounted on a cylinder. The blades cut against a bar.

Relative humidity - the amount of moisture contained in the air.

Renewal spur - on grapevines, the cane pruned to one or two nodes on the cordon; becomes the fruiting cane the following year.

Renovation - removing an old planting and putting in a new one or removing and replacing only part of a planting.

Repetition - repeated use of design features with like or similar qualities.

Resistant plant - the capacity of a plant to withstand the effects of a harmful condition or biological agent such as insects or disease.

Respiration - the process where food is oxidized (burned) to release energy.

Rhizome - an underground, horizontal stem.

Rhythm - a principle of landscape design, that elements of design create a feeling of motion.

Root - the portion of the plant usually found below ground. They are distinguished from stems by not having nodes.

Root girdling - encircling roots at or below the surface of the ground that tend to strangle the plant.

Root hairs - tubular outgrowths of surface cells of the root.

Root prune - to cut back the roots of a plant to encourage them to develop more fibrous roots or to reduce the mass of roots.

Rooting hormone - a chemical that stimulates the growth of roots.

Rootstock - the root onto which a scion or bud is grafted or budded.

Rotary mower - a mower with a blade that spins in a horizontal plane from a central rod.

Row cover fabric - a loosely woven translucent fabric used to keep insect pests off crops. It also functions as a cloche.

Saprophyte - an organism that obtains nutrition from dead organic matter.

Scale - 1. a shelled, sucking insect pest of plants. 2. In design, the size of an object in relation to the surroundings.

Scarification - the physical or chemical treatment given to some seeds in order to weaken the seed coat sufficiently for germination to occur.

Scion - the upper part of the union of a graft.

Sclerotium (pl sclerotia) - a dense mass of branched hyphae that contain stored food and are capable of remaining dormant for long periods.

Scorch - injury to leaves due to lack of sufficient water, excessive transpiration or injury to the water-conducting system of the plant.

Secondary dormancy - Condition that prevents germination after the seed has been detached from the plant and is exposed to specific unfavorable conditions.

Seed - the organ that forms after fertilization occurs.

Seed dormancy - Condition, in which seeds will not germinate even when most of the environmental conditions are favorable for germination.

Seed provenance - Describes seed's origin, in terms of climate and geographic location.

Selective herbicide - a pesticide that kills only one type of plant, for example broadleaf herbicides only kill broadleaf weeds, not turfgrasses.

Self-cleaning - herbaceous plants that drop spent blossoms, thus not requiring deadheading.

Semi-hardwood cuttings - cuttings taken later in the growing season.

Sepals - structures that usually form the outermost whorl of a flower. Together, they are called the calyx.

Sewage sludge - the solid matter that settles out during the treatment of sewage.

Sexual reproduction - production of new generations involving the exchange of chromosomes from both a male and female parent.

Sharp sand - a coarse sand used in building.

Short-day plant - a plant that requires a night longer than its critical dark period, usually 12 hours or more, to develop flowers.

Side-dress - to apply fertilizer to the side of a row of growing plants or around single plants.

Slice seed - a technique used to sow seed. A machine cuts or slices grooves into the lawn or soil and drops seeds directly into the grooves.

Slope - a land elevation change; determines surface water drainage patterns.

Soaker hose - a porous tube that allows water to seep from it; used to irrigate plants. It is used to conserve water and to avoid wetting plant foliage.

Softwood cutting - a nonwoody piece of a woody plant that is cut from the stock plant to asexually propagate a new individual plant.

Soil conditioner - any material added to soil to improve its structure, texture, tilth or drainage.

Soil structure - the manner in which sand, silt, and clay particles are arranged together

Soilless mix - potting medium that contain a mixture of ingredients from the materials listed for potting medium, but no mineral soil.

Soluble salt - salts from fertilizers and tap water that are dissolved in water.

Solvent - a liquid that can dissolve a substance.

Sooty mold - one of several species of fungi with black fruiting bodies that grow on the sugary liquid excrement of sucking insects.

Species - a group of closely related individuals that have the potential to reproduce with each other; a unit of classification.

Specific epithet - the second name of the binomial given to a species; for instance, "rubrum" is the species epithet of Acer rubrum.

Spines - a sharp-pointed woody structure, usually a modified leaf or leaf part.

Spore - a minute reproductive body produced by primitive organisms, such as ferns and fungi.

Sporophyte - the part of a life cycle when the full complement of chromosomes are present.

Spot treatment - application of a pesticide to restricted area or areas of a whole unit. For example the treatment of spots or patches in a home lawn.

Spreader-sticker - substances added to pesticides to make them spread over and stick to a surface more readily.

Spur - on grapevines, canes pruned to 1 to 4 nodes.

Square-foot gardening - a system of gardening developed by Mel Bartholomew that uses 4 foot by 4 foot plots subdivided into 1-foot squares for growing a specific number of a particular type of vegetable to maximize space and facilitate ease of maintenance.

Stake - a piece of pointed wood or metal that is driven into the ground to support a plant.

Stamen - the male part of the flower. It consists of the anther and the slender filament that holds it in position.

State specialists - professors at landgrant universities who provide expertise for Extension workers.

Stem - the main trunk of a plant. It develops buds and shoots.

Sterile - not able to produce seed.

Stigma - the part of the pistil that receives the pollen grains; usually the top of the pistil.

Stock plant - a plant used as a source for cuttings.

Stolon - a horizontal stem that roots at its tip.

Stoma (pl.Stomata) - an opening or pore in leaves that is surrounded by guard cells.

Strain - a subgroup of a species; the descendants of a common ancestor.

Stratification - storing of seeds at low temperatures under moist conditions in order to break dormancy.

Style - the slender part of a pistil between the stigma and the ovary.

Stylet - long mouth part of an organism, normally used to extract fluids.

Succession planting - planting portions of a crop over a period of time to get a continuous harvest over a long period of time.

Succulent - having tender, new growth or thick, fleshy tissues which store water, such as cactus.

Sucker - a shoot arising from the root or lower part of the stem of a plant.

Sunscald - plant injury caused by exposure to bright sunlight, excessive heat and/or wind.

Susceptible host - an organism that can be infected by a pathogen.

Symbiotic - a relationship in which two or more dissimilar organisms live together in close association.

Symptom - evidence of disease or damage.

Synthetic - substances produced by chemical or biochemical means.

Systemic - a group of pesticides that are absorbed into the tissues of plants, thereby poisoning the organisms that feed on the plant.

Taproot - a stout, tapering primary root that has limited side branching or fine roots.

Temperate - moderate; the zones between the tropics and the polar regions of the earth.

Tendril - a slender, coiling modified leaf or leaf part. These help plants climb.

Tepee - a tripod of stakes used to support climbing plants.

Testa - seed coat.

Terminal bud - large, vigorous buds at the tips of stems.

Terrace - a series of flat platforms of soil on the side of a hill, rising one above the other.

Texture - the surface quality of an object that can be seen or felt.

Thatch - an intertwined layer of dead and living roots, stems and blades of grass plants.

Thinning - complete removal of branches back to main trunk, a lateral branch or to ground level.

Thorax - the middle of the three major divisions of the arthropod body.

Topiary - training, cutting and trimming of plants into ornamental shapes.

Topsoil - uppermost layer of soil, usually darker and richer than the subsoil.

Toxicity - intensity of a poison.

Transpiration - the loss of water from plant tissues in the form of vapor.

Transplanting - digging up a growing plant from one location to plant it in another location.

Tree - a woody plant with one main stem and having a distinct head in most cases.

Trellis - a frame of latticework used as a support for climbing plants.

Tropical - regions of the earth lying between the Tropic of Cancer and the Tropic of Capricorn extending around the equator where the temperature and humidity are high.

Trunk - the main stem of a tree, shrub or vine.

Tuber - an enlarged, underground stem that stores food.

Turgid - the condition of a cell, tissue or plant when it is filled with water so that it is firm; not wilted.

Twig - the shoot of a woody plant representing the growth of the current season.

Understock - the part of a plant to which a graft is attached.

Unity - effective use of components in a design to express a main idea through consistent style.

Variegated - plant parts having different pigments resulting in more than one distinct color or shade on the foliage.

Variety - a subdivision of a species; occurs through natural hybridization.

Vascular system - the tissue in a plant that moves fluids through the plant.

Vector - an organism that transmits a disease-causing pathogen.

Vegetative - plant parts and processes concerning growth and nutrition and not reproduction.

Vegetative propagation - See Asexual propagation

Venation - the pattern of veins.

Vernation - arrangement of young leaves within a budshoot.

Viable - capable of growing or developing.

Virus - a group of submicroscopic infective agents that are considered nonliving complex molecules.

Warm-season crops - crops that are harmed by frost and do not grow well until the temperatures are in the 70s.

Whip - a very young tree that still has a flexible trunk.

Wide-row planting - growing the smaller vegetable crops in a space up to 3 feet across to better utilize space while reducing weeding.

Wilting point - the amount of water in a soil when a plant cannot obtain enough water to remain turgid.

Witches'-broom - a dense, bushy growth of branches and foliage caused by a parasitic organism, fungus, mites, or poor pruning techniques.

Wood - a dead hard xylem tissue.

Xylem - the part of the vascular system that moves water and minerals through the plant.

INDEX

Symbols

2,4-D 108, 109, 110, 113, 273, 412

A

Abiotic - *See also* Non Pathogenic
   disease 92
   soil factors 5
Achene 37
Actinomycetes 556, 559
Acute toxicity 127
Adjusting soil pH 149, 362 - *See also* Liming
   ammonium sulfate 149
   using sulfur 149, 427, 432
Advective freeze 446
Adventitious roots 30, 71
Agrobacterium tumefaciens 469
Algae 528
   Algal bloom 528
Almond moth 622
Alternaria 271, 277, 299, 411, 413, 464
Amensalism 2, 14, 18
Ammonification 11
Ammonium sulfate
   to lower pH 149
Angiosperms 29, 34
Angular leafspot 466, 467
Animal damage 594
   Chewing damage 594
   digging 595
   holes 595
   livestock predators 596
Animal traps 597
Anion 2
   exchange capacity 2
Annual bluegrass (Poa annua) 323 -
      See also Bluegrass, Annual (weed)
   Annual ryegrass (Lolium multiflorum) 323 - *See
   also* Ryegrass, Annual
Annuals 167
   bed preparation 169
   cool season 167
   diseases of - *See* Diseases of herbaceous
   ornamentals
   for butterflies 193

   for Georgia gardens 174
   for hummingbirds 193
   for specific uses 190
   growing from seed 168
   growing in containers 169
   irrigation 169
   planting 168, 169
   warm season 168
**Annuals and Perennials, Herbaceous Plants
(Chapter 10) 165–194**
Anthracnose 280, 281, 286, 288, 294, 295, 297, 298,
303, 411, 412, 464, 466, 467, 468
Ants 616
   Argentine 616
      baiting for 616
   carpenter ants 617
   non-chemical control 619
   red imported fire ant 618 - *See also* Fire ants
Aphids 79, 185, 266, 269, 305, 402, 403, 419, 474,
542
   on vegetables 402
Apical bud - *See* terminal bud
Apical meristem 38
Apples 453 - *See also* Fruit trees
   diseases of 470
   dwarfing rootstocks 451
   pollinizing codes 452, 453
   spur types 453
   training 447
   varieties 452
   zones for Georgia 451
Arachnida 86
Armadillo 576
Armillaria root and crown rot 469
Armyworms 355
Arthropoda 82
Aschelminthes 82
Asparagus
   growing 369
   problems 370
   propagating 33
Asparagus bean 372
Assassin bugs 133
Atrazine 110, 336
Auxins 63, 70, 90

Azalea 211, 212
    fertilizer 149
    florist 551
    native 215, 221
    pH 15
    pruning 157, 158, 159, 160
    water use zone for 488
Azalea bark scale 306
Azalea caterpillar 306
Azalea diseases 286
    botryosphaeria die back 288
    leaf gall 286
    petal blight 287
    phomopsis 287
    phytophthora dieback 288
    web blight 287
Azalea lace bug 306
Azalea leafminer 306
Azalea pests
    petal blight 272
    rhodendron borer 314
    sawflies 315
    southern red mite 316
    whitefiles 318

B

Bacillus thuringiensis (Bt.) 119, 135, 306, 307, 309, 310, 313, 314, 315, 406, 419, 420
    israelensis 419, 420
    kerstaki 420
    popillae (milky spore) 420
Bacteria 529
    actinomycetes 559
    anaerobic 12, 528
    as beneficial to control pests 120, 124, 131, 132, 420
    as decomposer 558, 559
    as plant pathogen 93, 96, 135, 270, 271, 272
    biological filtration and 522, 523, 528, 529
    cells 97
    chemical control 275
    C:N ratio and 15, 19
    in composting 556, 558, 562
        aerobic 558, 559
    infection of plant tissue 96, 97, 99
        moisture and 101, 274
    mesophilic 558
    nitrifier 520

nitrogen-fixing 17, 247, 363, 371
    soil 10, 11, 12, 13, 14, 15, 17, 19, 246, 363
        anaerobic 12
        thermophilic 13, 14, 558
Bacterial canker 266, 272
Bacterial diseases
    fire blight 100, 284, 291, 299, 301, 422, 451, 470
    prevention 274
    soft rot 279
Bacterial ooze 273
Bacterial soft rot 273
Bagworms 307
Bahiagrass (*Paspalum notatum*) 327
    identifying 322
    seeding rate 328
    varieties 327
Bark beetles 307
Bats 576
Bean leaf beetle 404
Beans and peas
    diseases of 410, 411
    growing 371
    insect pests of 402, 403, 404
    planting depth 367
    problems 373, 399
    saving seed 364
    when to plant 371
Beavers 577
Bed bugs 625
Bees 624
    carpenter 614
Beetles
    predaceous 133
Beneficial insects
    augmentation 131
    conservation 131
    importation 131
    parasitic 134
    predators 132
Bentgrass, creeping (*Agrostis palustris*) 322
    identifying characterisitics 322
Bermudagrass, common diseases of
    brown patch 348
    dollar spot 348
    fading out, melting out 349
    gray leaf spot 350
    pythium root rot 349
    slime mold 351

take all root rot 350

Bermudagrasses (*Cynodon* Spp -) 323

  common 323

  fertilizing 331

  identifying characteristics 322

  maintenance calendar 337

  pH preferred 323, 337

  sprigging rate 329

  varieties

    seeded types 324

    vegetatively produced 324

Biennial weeds 106

Big-eyed bugs 133

Billbugs 353

Binomial nomenclature 27

Binomial system 27

Biological control agents 131

Biological filtration 528

Blackberries 428

  erect 430

    pruning 430

  trailing 428

    pruning and training 428

Blackberries and raspberries 428 - *See also* **Bramble fruits**

  varieties 429

Blackberry psyllids 465

Black knot 290, 472

Black rot 412, 465, 470

Blister beetle 408

Blossom end rot 400

  pH and 387

Blueberries 431

  diseases 463

  fertilizing 432

  insects 463

  northern highbush varieties 431

  pH 427, 431

  pruning 432

  rabbiteye varieties 431

  row spacing 432

  soil preparation and planting 431

Blueberry bud mite 463

Blueberry gall midge 463

Bluegrass, Annual (*Poa annua*)

  identifying characteristics 322

Bluegrass, Kentucky (*Poa praetensis*)

  fertilizing 331

identifying characteristics 322

  seeding rate 328

Bog plants 526

Booklice 634

Bordeaux mixture 421

Botanical name 27

Botany, Basic (Chapter 2) 25–40

Botrytis 172, 272, 277, 281, 283, 463, 465, 466, 467, 470

Boxelder bugs 632

Boxwood leafminer 307

Boxwood psyllid 308

Bramble fruits 428 - *See also* Blackberries and raspberries

  diseases 464

    controlling 464

  insects 464

  pH for 428

  site selection 428

  trellis for 428

  varieties 429

Broadleaf weeds 106

Broccoli

  growing 373

  insect pest of 406

  planting dates 373

  problems 374

Brown patch 348

Brown recluse spider 627

Brown rot 471

Brussels sprouts 374

  insect pests of - *See* Cabbage, collards, broccoli and turnip pests

Bt - - *See Bacillus thuringiensis*

Budding 72, 73

Buds 29, 32

  adventitious 32

  lateral buds 29, 32

  scales 32

  terminal 29, 32

Bulb 32, 33

Bulbs

  bed preparation 184

  care and maintenance 184

  disease and insect control 185

  fertilizing 184

  for Georgia gardens 187

  pH for 184

planting 184

selecting 184

Bunch grapes 435

diseases 465

fertilization 439

plant spacing 436

problems

nutrient deficiencies 439

pruning 438

rootstocks 435

training young vines 437

trellis systems 437

varieties 436

weed control 439

C

Cabbage 374

diseases of 412

growing 374

problems 375

Cabbage (collards, broccoli and turnip) pests 406

Cabbage looper 406

Cabbage maggot 406

Cabbageworm 406

Cambium 26, 31, 32, 47, 72, 242, 243, 248, 254, 258, 656

Camellia

fertilizer 147

japonica 217

light requirements 49

propagating 70, 72

pruning 158, 160

renewal 156

sasanqua 208, 218

vernalis 218

Camellia, diseases of 289

algal leaf spot 290

canker and stem die back 289

leaf gall 289

oedema 290

petal blight 272, 290

viruses 290

Canada goose 579

Cane blight 466

Cankers 272

Cantaloupe - *See* Melons

Carbon-Nitrogen Ratio 562

Carpel 37

Carpenter ants 617

eliminating 618

Carpenter bees 614

Carpet beetles 633

Carpetgrass (*Axonopus affinis*) 325

fertilizing 331

identifying characteristics 322

pH for 325

Cat facing of tomato 400

Cation 2

Cation exchange capacity (CEC) 6

Cauliflower 375

blanching 375

growing 375

pests - *See* Cabbage, collards, broccoli and turnip pests

problems 375, 400

buttoning of 375

Cedar apple rust 296, 470

Centipedegrass, common diseases of

brown patch 348

centipedegrass decline 325

pH and 351

fading out 349

fairy ring 349

gray leaf spot 350

take all root rot 350

Centipedegrass (*Eremochloa ophiuroides*)

fertilization 331

and dormancy/green-up 110

herbicide tolerance 109

identifying characteristics 322

maintenance calendar 338

pH preferred 325, 338

seeding 329

weed control in 113

Centipedes 86, 357, 560, 630

Cercospora leafspot 412

Chill hours 55, 56, 451, 453

Chilopoda 83

Chinch Bugs 355

Chipmunks 580

Chlorophyll 42, 48, 654

Chloroplast 44

Choanephora 413

Cicada killer wasp 356, 623

Cigarette beetles 622

Classification, example of 83

Clone 29, 69

Clothes moths 632

Clover mites 631

C:N ratio 15, 19, 562, 567

Cockroaches
    control 621
    German 620
    smokybrown 621

Codling moth 472

Cold hardiness - *See* Hardiness

Cold protection 56

Cole crops - *See* Cabbage

Collar rot 451, 470

Colorado potato beetle 407

Commensalism 2, 14
    relationship example of 18

Common Bermudagrass (*Cynodon dactylon*) 323

Common names 27

Communications
    presentations 646
    written 642

Compost
    as source of nutrients 567
    increasing pH of 564

Composting
    anaerobic 556, 565
    bacteria 557

Composting (Chapter 26) 555–572

Cones 38

Contact poison 125

Cool season annuals 167

Cool season turfgrasses 321
    adaptation and characteristics 323
    pH 323
    planting 329

Copper 58, 59, 60, 61, 62, 63, 248, 275, 421

Corms 33

Corn
    growing 375
    insect pests 402, 403, 404, 407
    interplanting 371, 395
    interpollinating problems 395
    problems 376, 399, 400

Corn earworm 402

Corolla 35

Cottony maple scale 308

Cotyledon 38

Cover crops 363

Cowpea curculio 404

Crape myrtle
    light requirements 49
    organic pesticides for 421
    pests 311
        deer 601
        Japanese beetle 311
    propagating 70, 72
    pruning 155, 158, 161, 163
        renewal 156
    varieties 214, 235, 236
    water needs 493

Crape myrtle diseases 291
    powdery mildew 271, 291
        resistant cultivars 271

Creeping bentgrass (*Agrostis stolonifera*) 323

Crickets 630

Crop rotation 363

Crown gall 96, 267, 285, 293, 302, 464, 469

Cucumber beetles 405

Cucumber mosaic virus 273, 279, 412

Cucumbers
    diseases of 273, 412
    growing 367, 377
    insect pests of 403, 405, 406
    problems 377, 400
    row spacing for 367

Cultivar 29

Cutworm 408

D

Damsel bugs, predaceous 132

Day length 50

Day neutral plants 52

Deadheading
    annuals 170
    perennials 177

Deer 581

Deer-tolerant ornamental plants 599–606

Dermaptera 84

Diamondback moth caterpillar 406

Diatomaceous earth 420

Dicot 29
    floral organs of 35
    leaf venation 34

Dioecious plants 36
    holly as example of 36

Dipel 406, 420

Diplopoda 83
Diptera 85
Disease control
    chemical 275
    cultural 274
Disease cycle 92
Diseased plant 91
Diseases
    abiotic 270
    biotic 270
    chemical control 108
    of herbaceous ornamentals
        general 277
        specific 277
    of trees - *See* Diseases of woody ornamentals,
    specific
    of turf 347
    of woody ornamentals
        general 284
        specific 286
Disease triangle 92
Dogwood borer 308
Dogwood clubgall midge 309
Dollar spot 348
Dolomitic lime 149
Dormant oils 268, 312, 313, 314, 316, 473
Double-cropping 363
Double curtain trellis 437, 440, 441, 442
Downy mildew 91, 278, 282, 283, 302, 303, 412,
413, 465, 466
Drainage
    as disease-causing factor 270, 272
    improving 271, 274, 367, 427, 477, 481
Drip irrigation 496
Drip system
    components of a 496
Drupe 37

E

Early blight 95, 411
Earthworms 10, 393, 561
Earwigs 84
Eastern tent caterpillar 309
Ecosystem 2
Eggplant 378
    diseases of 411
    growing 378
    insect pests of 402, 403, 408

row spacing for 367
'El Toro' Zoysiagrass 326
'Emerald' zoysiagrass 326
Endophytes 94
Endosperm 39
English peas
    growing 378
    succession planting 363
Entomology 83
Entomology, Basic (Chapter 5) 77–88
Environmental stress 92, 139, 147
Essential elements 60, 246, 249 - *See also* Nutrients
Etiolation 50
Euonymus scale 309
European corn borer 404, 407
European hornet 624
Exotic pest plants 531

F

Fading out
    of turfgrasses 349
Fairy ring 349
Fall armyworm 407
Fall leaf color 55
Fall webworm 309
Female plant - *See* Dioecious
Fertilizer 11, 21
    applying to turfgrass 331
    banding 363
    IBDU 148, 500
    organic fertilizer 148, 164
    sidedressing 363
    slow-release 141, 146, 147, 148, 149, 150, 151,
    169, 331, 500
    specialty fertilizers 148
Fertilizer calculation 342
Fertilizer-herbicide mixtures 110
Fertilizer ratio 342
Fescue, red (*Festuca rubra*)
    identifying characteristics 322
Fescue, tall (*Festuca arundinacea*)
    identifying characteristics 322
    Kentucky 31 (K 31) 321
Field capacity of soil 2, 16
Figs 433
    diseases of 468
    growing in North Georgia 435
    growing in South Georgia 434

lack of fruiting 435
    pH for 433
    propagating 433
    soil preparation and planting 433
    spacing 433
    training and pruning 434
    variety selection 433, 434
Fire ants 618
    control 619
       two-step method 619
Firebrats 633
Fish 526
    feeding 527
    Japanese koi 526
    stocking 527
Flatheaded appletree borer 310
Flea beetles 403, 404
Fleas 82, 85, 120, 625, 634
Flies 85, 133
    parasitic 134
    predaceous 133
Floating plants 526
Floral organs
    of dicots 35
    of monocots 35
Flour beetles 622
Flower, botanical 34
    complete 36
    incomplete 36
    modifications 35
    pistillate 36
    sepal 35
    staminate 36
Flowers - *See* Annuals; *See* Perennials
Fog index 645
Food web 2
Fruit Gardening (Chapter 19) 425–460
Fruit, Insects and Diseases of (Chapter 20) 461–474
Fruits, botanical 36
    aggregate 37
    dehiscent 37
    indehiscent 37
    multiple 36
    simple 36
Fruit trees - *See also* specific fruits
    bearing tree care 448
    diseases of 469

fertilization 448, 449
    insect pests of 472
    key stages of development 470
    liming 450
    pH 427, 447, 450
    planting 447
    problems 468
    site preparation 446
    thinning fruit 450
    training 447
    tree spacing 451
Fungi 10, 15, 80, 93, 94, 271, 470
    and overhead irrigation 101
    and soil pH 11
    and soil temperature 14
    and tree decay 256
    as decomposers 17, 557, 559, 560
    as pesticide 124
    as plant pathogen 93, 95
    beneficial 94
    C:N ratio and 15
    disease development and 274
    diseases caused by 93, 93–102
    host specific 271
    in composting 558
    in soil 10, 15, 17, 95, 246, 272
    leafspots caused by 271
    mushroom 349
    mycorrhizal 94
    parasitic 94
    plant disease 17
    properties of 94
    reproduction of 17
    root rot 410
    rust 272
    seasonal activity 272
    slime mold 351
    soil-borne pathogens 95, 100, 410
    spores 17
    thermophilic 14, 558, 560
Fungicides 124
Fusarium 101, 277, 300, 386, 410, 411, 412, 413
Fusarium wilt 101, 411, 413

G

Geese - *See* Canada goose
Genera 83
Genus 28

Georgia Pest Management Handbook 124
Girdling
trunk 248
Girdling roots 256
Glomerella cingulata 469
Glossary 653–664
Glyphosate 109, 125
Gophers 582
bark graft 73
Grafting 72
cleft 72
four-flap 73
whip and tongue 72
Grain beetles 622
Grape root borers 467
Grapes - *See* Bunch grapes; *See* Muscadine grapes
bunch and European
pH 436
Grass clippings 500
Grasscycling 500
Grass weeds 105
Gravitational potential 2
Gray leaf spot 350
of turfgrass 350
Gray water, defined 501
Greenstriped mapleworm 310
Ground beetles 134, 630
Ground cover 200
for the landscape 204
Groundhog - *See* Woodchuck
Ground pearls 353
Group development
dealing with disruptive behavior 641
stages of 638
Growing medium
pH 538, 539
Gymnosperm 29
Gypsy moth 472

H

Half-runner beans 371
Hand watering 498
Hardiness 54
in plant selection 197
Hardiness zone map 55
Hardy annuals 167
Harlequin bug 407
Healthy plant 91

Heat hardiness zone map 55
Hemiptera 85
Herbaceous plants 32, 70, 167 - *See also* Annuals; *See also* Perennials
Herbicides 108
2,4-D 110
contact 109
for use in fruit gardens 115
for use in ornamentals 112
for use in turf 113
for use in vegetable gardens 114
landscape plant tolerance 109
nomenclature 109
nonselective 108
non-target plant tolerance 110
preemergence 108
fall application 111
spring application 111
selection of 109
selective 108
time of application 109
during hot and humid days 110
during turf green-up 110, 111, 336
Herbs 388
annual 390
grown in pots 389
harvesting 389
knot garden 390
perennial 390
pH for 389
HERL model 575
Holly (Ilex)
diseases 293
web blight 293
male and female 36
pests of
deer 600, 602
longtailed mealybug 312
native holly leafminer 310
nematodes 273
southern red mite 316
twolined spittlebug 317
and turfgrasses 355
wax scales 317
propagating 70, 71
pruning 155, 158, 161
seed dormancy 69
varieties 199, 209, 214, 219, 224, 235

Honey bees 624
Hornets 624
Hornworm 409
Horticultural oil 134, 306, 308, 309, 310, 311, 313, 314, 315, 316, 317, 318, 422
Host plant 270
House plants - *See* Indoor plants
Hybrid plants 28
Hymenoptera 85

I

Impatiens necrotic spot virus 280, 282, 283
Indianmeal moth 622
Indoor plants
    acclimatization 540
    factors affecting growth 535
    growing mixes for 538
    nutrition 538
    pests and diseases 541
    plant problems 542
    pruning, grooming, cleaning, and repotting 541
    relative humidity and 537
    selecting containers 540
    temperature requirements 536
    water and 537
Indoor Plants (Chapter 25) 533–554
Infection
    bacterial 96
    fungal 95
    viral 97
Inflorescence 35
    compact 38
Inflorescences
    types of 36
Inocula 561
Insect - *See also* Entomology
    classification 82
    metamorphosis 83
    orders 83, 84, 85
Insect damage on fruits 463
    blueberries 463
    fruit trees 472
Insect damage on ornamentals 79
    by chewing insects 79, 266, 304
        azalea caterpillar 306
        bagworms 307
        eastern tent caterpillar 309
        fall webworm 310

greenstriped mapleworm 310
Japanese beetle 311
    on turfgrass 351, 355
    orangestriped oakworm 313
    wood 614, 615, 616
by internal feeders 79
    azalea leafminer 307
    boxwood leafminer 307
    boxwood psyllid 308
    native holly leafminer 311
by laying eggs 80
by stem, twig, trunk or branch borers
    bark beetles 307
    dogwood borer 308
    dogwood clubgall midge 309
    flatheaded appletree borer 310
    Nantucket pine tip moth 312
    white pine weevil 318
by sucking insects 79, 353, 354, 355, 473, 542
    aphids 305, 542
    azalea bark scale 306
    azalea lace bug 306
    cottony maple scale 308
    euonymus scale 309
    juniper scale 311
    longtailed mealybug 312
    oak lecanium scale 313
    obscure scale 313
    pine needle scale 313
    pine spittlebug 314
    rhododendron lace bug 315
    southern red mite 316
    spruce spider mite 316
    thrips 316
    twolined spittlebug 317
    twospotted spider mite 317
    wax scales 317
    whiteflies 318
Insect damage on turf 353–358
Insect damage on vegetables
    by chewing/boring insects 402
        bean leaf beetle 404
        corn earworm 402
        European corn borer 404
        flea beetles 403
        lesser cornstalk borer 404
        lima bean borer 405
        Mexican bean beetle 404

spotted cucumber beetle 405

striped cucumber beetle 405

by internal feeders

leafminers 405

by sucking insects 403

southern green stink bug 403

spider mites 403

thrips 405

whiteflies 405

Insect form and structure 80

antennae 82

legs 81

mouthparts 82

wings 81

Insecticidal soap 78, 306, 420

Insect monitoring

flotation 352

irritation 352

sticky traps 317

using sweep net 352

Insects

as disease vectors 98, 403, 404

bacterial 264

biting or stinging 623

indoors 609

soil inhabiting 353

Integrated pest management (IPM) 119

components of 119

Integrated Pest Management, Principles of (Chapter 8) 117–136

International Code of Botanical Nomenclature 27

Internode 29

Invasive plant 176

IPM - *See* Integrated pest management

IPM strategies 263

Iron phosphate 420

Irrigating

herbaceous ornamentals 499

trees and shrubs 498

turfgrass 498

Irrigating the landscape

guidelines for 497

Irrigation 250 - *See also* Watering

J

Japanese beetle 79, 80, 185, 311, 354, 420, 464, 465, 467, 472

traps 420

Jump cut 155

Juniper scale 311

K

Kentucky bluegrass (Poa pratensis) 323

pH 323

Kingdom 82

Kudzu bugs 631

L

Lacewings 133

Lady beetles 134, 631

Land planaria 630

Landscape design

general principles of 479

helpful guidelines 481

implementation 482

maintenance considerations in 478

materials in 480

plant selection and use in 480

site analysis 477

sustainable 481

Landscape Design Principles (Chapter 21) 475–482

Landscape fabrics 107

Landscape maintenance - *See Ornamental Plants in the Landscape* Ch. 9

Landscape plant materials - *See Selecting Woody Plants* Ch. 11

Leadership 637

Leadership and Communication (Chapter 29) 635–652

Leaf

axils 32

blade 34

compound 34

form and structure 34

functions 34

parts of 34

petiole 34

simple 34

veins 34

Leafminers 306, 307, 310, 405, 409

Lepidoptera 85

Lesser cornstalk borer 404

Lesser peach tree borer 472

Lettuce

germination requirements 53, 54, 69

growing 379
    insect pests of 403
    problems 380
    saving seed 364
Lichens 268
Lifecycle 106
Light intensity
    measuring 48, 535
Lima beans 372
Lima bean vine borer 405
Lime
    when to apply 362
Lime-sulfur 421
Liming 149, 332, 362, 387, 400, 460
    for grape vines 439
    to increase boron uptake 61
    to maintain magnesium level 450
    turfgrass 332
Linnaeus, Carl 27
Lizards 583
Longtailed mealybug 312

M

Macronutrients 12, 658
Magnesium 6, 9, 12, 16, 20, 58, 59, 74, 148, 149, 246, 249, 264, 332, 362, 363, 381, 399, 436, 439, 443, 449, 450, 561, 658
Male plant - *See* Dioecious
Maple bladdergall mite 312
Maple spindlegall mite 312
Matric potential 2
Mealybugs 266, 312, 542
Mediterranean flour moth 622
Melons 380
    full-slip stage 381
    growing 380
    hill planting 367
    insect pests of 405
    problems 381, 400
Meristem 29
    apical 38
Metamorphosis 83
Mexican bean beetle 404
'Meyer' Zoysiagrass 326
Mice 583
Micronutrients 12, 16, 60, 363, 429, 430, 432, 445
Milky spore for Japanese beetle grubs - *See* Bacillus popillae

Millipedes 86, 357, 560, 629, 630
Mineralization 17
Minute pirate bugs 132
Mites 86
    predaceous 132
Mole crickets 353
Moles 584
Mollusca 83
Monocots 29
Monocotyledons - *See* Monocots
Monoecious 36
Mosquitoes 85
Mosquito larvaecide - *See* Bacillus thuringiensis israelensis
Moths 85
    mouthparts 82
    pollination 35
Mowing 107, 111, 114, 116, 158, 201, 248, 266, 320, 323, 325, 326, 330, 333, 334, 335, 347, 349, 350, 351, 352, 466, 471, 478, 484, 500, 557, 570, 625
    height for turfgrasses 332
    mower types 570
    mowing frequency 570
Mulch (-ing)
    applying 144, 570
    as disease control 100, 264
    for weed control 107
    materials 143, 568
        plastic 146
Mulch volcanoes 570
Mummyberry 463
Muscadine grapes
    diseases 466
    fertilizing 442
    insect pests of 467
    pH 440
    problems, nutrient deficiencies 443
    spacing 440
    training 441
    trellising 440
    varieties 441
Mutualism 14
Mycelium 10, 94, 95, 96, 262, 346, 411, 413, 466, 657
Mycorrhizae 17, 19, 31, 94, 246

N

Nantucket pine tip moth 312
Native holly leafminer 310

Native plant 177, 199
Natural controls 122
Nectarines 453 - *See also* Fruit trees
    diseases of 471
    rootstock selection 450
    training 448
    varieties 454
Neem 419
Nemaguard 427, 450, 471
Nematodes 10, 13, 19, 90, 93, 98, 100, 131, 264, 265, 269, 271, 273, 274, 275, 279, 280, 282, 283, 285, 289, 381, 400, 401, 409, 410, 414, 427, 435, 436, 443, 444, 446, 450, 467, 468, 471, 472, 559, 560, 561
    and fusarium wilt 411
    as pest of okra 381, 382, 413
    as pest of tomatoes 386
    as pests in vegetable garden 409
    as pests of bulbs 185
    as pests of figs 433, 435, 559
    as pests of fruit trees 427, 446, 471
    as pests of grapes 436
    as pests of ornamentals 270, 271, 273
    as pests of strawberries 443, 444
    as pests of trees 248, 269
    as predators in soil 15, 19
    assay 410, 446
    as soil organisms 10
    as vectors of viruses 98
    beneficial to control pests 124, 131, 132, 135
    foliar 273, 277, 278
    in compost 559
    in turf 347, 351
    marigolds for control of 410
    number in soil 11
    reducing populations 100, 363, 410
    reniform 409
    resistant tomatoes 411
    ring 446
    root knot 98, 100, 273, 409, 436, 446, 468, 471
        resistant roostocks 471
    selecting resistant rootstocks 450
    solarization to control 410
    sting 409
    symptoms of injury 98, 409
Neuroptera 86
Nitrogen
    fixation 17, 21, 247, 371, 561
Nitrogen cycle 527

bacteria in 527
Nitrogen 150, 305, 349, 385, 448, 463, 500, 563, 564, 566, 568, 569, 570
    slow-release 141, 146, 147, 148, 149, 150, 151, 169, 331, 500
Nodes 29
Non-pathogenic diseases 92
Nonselective 108
Nuisance Wildlife (Chapter 27) 573–606
Nutrient deficiencies 59, 60
    in annual and perennial flowers 265, 268
    in grapes 439, 443
    in trees 248, 249
    in turfgrass 351
    in vegetables 399
    pH and 149
Nutrients 3, 6, 7, 12, 15, 16, 17, 19, 20, 21, 92, 147, 148, 150, 342, 500, 567 - *See also* Essential elements; *See also* Fertilizer
    absorption during dormant season 148
    adsorption 6
    and fertilizer 147, 342, 362
    as pollutant 512
    competition for 19, 105, 141, 170, 389
    environmental stress and 92
    essential 16, 60–63
    for figs 434
    for pecan trees 459, 460
    high pH and 149
    in acclimatization 540
    in composting 562
    in container gardens 393
    indoor plants and 538
    in garden pond water 526, 529, 531
    in perlite 74
    in photosynthesis 44, 537
    in raised beds 393
    in sand 74
    in soilless mixes 392
    in vermiculite 94
    liquid fertilizers and 146, 148
    low pH and 149, 362
    macronutrients 16
    microbial activity 15
    micronutrient 16
    mycorrhizae and 31
    need for at transplant 144, 447
    organic fertilizers and 148
    organic matter and 362, 393, 427, 563

pH level and 7, 11, 59, 101, 264, 332, 399, 460
primary 149
recycling 333, 335, 500, 570
root function and 30, 57, 59, 272, 332
slow release fertilizers and 146, 148, 500
soil organisms and 12
soil test for 264, 399, 427
stem function and 31
symbiosis and 17
transport 46, 47, 56
trees and 151
water and 56, 57

O

Oak lecanium scale 312
Obscure scale 313
Okra
   diseases of 413
   growing 381
   harvesting 388
   insect pests of 402, 403
   nematodes 413
   problems 382
   row spacing for 367
One wire trellis 440, 442
Onion maggot 407
Onions 382
   growing 382
   insect pests of 407
    thrips 407
   problems 383
   row spacing 367
Oomycetes 95
Opossums 584
Orangestriped oakworm 313
Orchardgrass (Dactylis glomerata) 323
   identifying characteristics 322
Organic
   USDA National Organic Program 417
Organic bacteriacides 421
Organic fungicides 421
Organic Gardening, Principles of (Chapter 18) 415–424
Organic insecticide 419
Organic matter 3, 4, 6, 7, 8, 9, 11, 12, 18, 20, 141, 142, 146, 169, 177, 328, 360, 362, 363, 369, 410, 427, 431, 493, 557, 558, 560, 561, 567, 568, 570

Organic miticides 419
Oriental fruit moth 472
Ornamental grasses
   for the landscape 206
Ornamental Plant Problems, Diagnosing (Chapter 13)   261–318
Ornamental Plants in the Landscape (Chapter 9) 137–164
Orthoptera 86
Osmotic potential 2
Ovary 35

P

Paper wasps 623
Parasite
   obligate 94
Parasitic wasps 134
Parasitism 2
   soil organisms and 15
Parasitoids 132
Parthenocarpy 38
Pathogenic diseases 92
Pathogens 132
Peaches 453 - *See also* Fruit trees
   chill requirement 451
   diseases of 471
   rootstock selection 450
    nematode resistant 450
   training 448
   varieties 454
Peach tree borer 473
Peach tree short life 472
   pH and 472
Pea mosaic virus 413
   blackeye cowpea mosaic 413
   cucumber mosaic 413
   southern pea mosaic 413
Pear psylla 473
Pears 453 - *See also* Fruit trees
   diseases of 470
   pollinizing code 453, 457
   recommended varieties 457
   self-fruitful 453
   training 447
   zones for Georgia 451
Peas - *See* Beans; *See* English peas; *See* Southernpeas
Pecans 458
   care of bearing trees 460

fertilizing 460

    care of young trees 459

      fertilizing 459

    diseases 473

    insect pests of 473

    pH range 460

    planting 459

    site selection 458

    tree spacing 458

    varieties 459

    zinc nutrition 460

      foliar sampling for 460

Pecan weevils 474

Pedicel 35

Peduncle 35

Peppers

    diseases of 411

    growing 383

    insect pests of 402, 403, 408

    problems 383, 399, 400, 568

Percolation test 481, 513

Perennial ryegrass (*Lolium perenne*) 323

Perennials 176

    bed preparation 177

    deadheading 177

    diseases of - *See* Diseases, herbaceous ornamentals

    fertilizing 177

    for butterflies 173, 178, 182

    for Georgia gardens 182

    hardy 176

    planting 177

    tender 176

Perennial weeds 106

Permanent wilting point 16

Pest control 120

    goals of 120

    failures 123

Pest control products 609

    baits 609, 610

      ant 616

      fire ant 419, 619

      rats 587

      roaches 621

      slug 420

Pesticide

    application equipment 128, 129

      sprayers 128

      spreaders 129

    fire ant baits 619

    applied controls 122

    avoiding harmful effects 122

    disposal 130

    formulations 126

    labeling 127

Pesticide activity

    factors that affect 125

Pesticide exposure

    first aid for 130

Pesticide label 127

    active ingredients 127

    directions for use 128

    environmental hazards 128

    hazards to humans(and domestic animals) 128

    physical and chemical hazards 128

    signal words 127

    statement of practical treatment 128

Pesticides

    grouping 124

    protecting the body 130

    routes of exposure 129

    using safely 129

Pesticide spills 130

Pesticide toxicity 129

Pest identification 120

Pest monitoring 121

Pests

    types of 120

Petal 35

Petal blights 272

Petiole 34

pH 2, 5, 6, 7, 8, 10, 11, 15, 16, 19, 20, 46, 59

    adjusting 149

    and soil microbial activity 247

    and uncomposted amendments 142

    availability of elements 149

    calcium and 61

    defined 6

    environmental stress and 92

    for soil bacteria 11

    gypsum and 328

    of bark 74

    of compost 567

    of pond water 527

    perlite 74

    propagating medium 74

    raising 149

range for ornamental plants 149
range for vegetable gardens 362
sand 74
soil organism tolerance 11
sulfur to lower 149
using lime to raise 149
using sulfur to lower 149
Phloem 29, 31, 47, 72, 310
in bacterial infection 97
in phytoplasma infection 97
in viral infection 97
Phomopsis 287, 293, 295, 465, 466, 467
Phony peach 472
Photoperiodism 17, 50
Photosynthesis 34, 42, 43
Phototropism 50
Phyla 82
Physiological
disorders 400
Phythophthora 91, 95, 272, 277, 283, 284, 288, 432, 464, 470
Phytochrome 53, 54
Phytoplasmas 274
Pickleworm 405
Pillbugs 86, 357, 616, 629
Pine needle scale 313
Pine spittlebug 314
Pine voles 591
Pistil 35
Planning and site selection 521
Plant classification 27, 28
Plant diseases   - See also Plant Pathology
-See also Diseases
caused by bacteria 96 - See also Bacterial diseases
caused by fungi 93 - See also Fungi
caused by viruses 97 - See also Virus
types of
abiotic 91, 270, 273, 346, 608
Planting 250
direct seeding vegetables 367
herbaceous ornamentals
annuals 168
bulbs 184
perennials 177
herbs 389
ornamentals
amendments 142
best time of year 141

disturbing the root mass 143
hole size 142
procedures 142
vegetables in containers 392
vegetable transplants 366
Plant names - See plant nomenclature
Plant nomenclature 27
botanical name 27
common name 27
Plant parts 29
Plant Pathology, Basic (Chapter 6) 89–102
Plant Physiology (Chapter 3) 41–64
Plant propagation 66–76
bottom heat for 74
grafting 72
growing media for 74
leaf cuttings 71
sexual (seed) 67
shoot cuttings 71
taking cuttings 70
vegetative 32
Plant Propagation (Chapter 4) 65–76
Plant selection 140, 164, 167, 196, 197, 198, 199, 201, 233, 463, 476, 477, 479, 482, 484, 493
for specific uses 198
for the site 197
from the nursery 201
Platyhelminthes 83
Plum Curculio 473
Plum leaf scald 472
Plum pocket 472
Plum pox (Sharka) 471
Plums 458 - See also Fruit trees
diseases of 471
training 448
varieties 458
Pocket gopher - See Gopher
Polebeans 371
Pollination 19, 29, 35, 36, 38, 79, 364, 375, 376, 377, 378, 381, 385, 388, 400, 402, 405, 413, 431, 433, 435, 436, 440, 453, 457, 458, 459, 463, 655
Ponds and Water Gardening (Chapter 24) 519–532
Postemergence herbicides 108
Potassium Salts of Fatty Acids - See Insecticidal soap
Potatoes
growing 384
insect pests 403, 407, 408

lay by 384
   pH for 384
   problems 384, 400, 401
Potting soil - *See* Growing medium
Powderpost beetles 615
   Anobiid 616
   Lyctid 615
Powdery mildew 99, 225, 235, 265, 268, 271, 283, 284, 291, 293, 301, 413, 466, 469
Praying mantids 133
Predaceous mites 132
Predaceous plant bugs 133
Predation
   in soil organisms 15
Predators (Insects) 131, 132
Preemergence herbicides 108
Preventive practices 106
Primary dormancy 68
Propagation mix 74
Propagation systems 74
Protozoa 10, 11, 559
Pruning 247
   correct time for 157
   guidelines for specific plants 157
     conifers 159
     groundcovers 159
     trees 157, 158
     vines 159
   jump cut method 155
   renewal 156
   technique 154
     jump cut 155
     large limbs 155
     shearing 154
     thinning 154
Pruning tools 152, 153
Pruning compounds 155
Pumpkin - *See* Squash, winter
Pycnidia 95
Pyrethrins 124, 419
Pythium 95, 272, 277, 280, 284, 348, 349, 410, 412, 413
Pythium root rot 348

Q

Quiescent seeds 68

R

Rabbits 585
Raccoons 586
Rachis 34
Radicle 38
Rain Gardens 511
   benefits 512
   construction 516
   placement 513
   plants for 517
   ponding depth 514
   size calculation 513
Rainwater
   pH of 506
Rainwater harvesting 505
   estimating water demand 510
   mosquitoes 511
   system components 506
   system maintenance 510
   system sizing 509
   volume calculations 509
Rainwater Harvesting and Rain Gardens (Chapter 23) 503–518
Raspberries
   Dorman Red 428
   fall 430
   primocane 430
     pruning 431
Raspberry crown borer 465
Raster 311
Rats 586
Redhumped Caterpillar 314
Red-imported fire ant 618 - *See also* Fire ants
Red-necked cane borer 465
Redox potential 2
Respiration (plant) 42, 43, 45
   soil water and 16
Rhizoctonia 95, 100, 272, 277, 280, 285, 287, 293, 348, 410, 412, 467
Rhizomes 33
Rhizoplane 2
Rhizosphere 2
Rhododendron Borer 314
Rhododendron lace bug 315
Rice weevil 623
Root 30
   structure 30
Root and crown rots 272
Root cuttings 71

Root function 30
Root hairs 57
Rooting hormones 70
Rootstock 72, 73, 74, 426, 427, 436, 445, 446, 447, 448, 450, 451, 453, 469, 472
    nematode resistant 427, 450, 471
Rose diseases 285, 301
    black spot 271, 301
    common stem canker 302
    crown gall 285, 302
    downy mildew 302
    powdery mildew 271, 301
    rose mosaic virus 302
    rust 272, 302
Rose mosaic virus 302
Rose pests 311
    deer 600
    Japanese beetle 311
    redhumped caterpillar 314
    sawflies 315
    southern red mite 316
    whiteflies 318
Roses 212
    bare-root 141
    Cherokee rose (*Rosa laevigata*) 199
    diseases 100, 101
    fertilizer 147, 150, 151
    Lady Banks Rose 203
    light requirements 49
    organic pesticides for 421, 422
    phytotoxicity on 421
    propagation 73
    pruning 162
        climbing 158, 162
        floribunda 158
        grandiflora 158
Rough stalk bluegrass (Poa trivialis) 323
Rove beetles 134
Runners 33
Rust
    fungi 272
Ryegrass, Annual (*Lolium multiflorum*)
    identifying characteristics 322
    seeding rate 328
Ryegrass, Perennial (*Lolium perenne*)
    identifying characteristics 322
    seeding rate 328

Salamander - *See* Gopher
Samara 37
Sandy mounder - *See* Gopher
San Jose scale 473
Sawflies 315
Saw-toothed grain beetle 622
Scale insects 32, 33, 38, 79, 81, 82, 85, 134, 242, 266, 268, 281, 304, 306, 308, 311, 313, 317, 318, 353, 463, 470, 473, 526, 542, 620, 623, 654
    crawler stage of 134, 305
Scarification 68
Schizocarp 37
Sclerotia 95
Sclerotium 272
Sclerotium rolfsii 95
Scorpions 86, 630
Screening plants 197
Scuds 629
Seashore Paspalum (*Paspalum vaginatum*) 326
    cultivars 326
Secondary dormancy 68
Sedge weeds 105
Seed 38
    coat 38
    collecting 67–76
    germination 68
    recalcitrant 67
    storage 67
    viability 67–76
Seed coat 38, 54, 62, 66, 67, 68, 69, 75, 105
Seed dormancy 68
    types of 68
Seed propagation 67
Selective 108
Sepal 35
Septoria 271, 277, 284, 292, 464
Sessile 34
Sexual propagation 67
Shade
    effects on water loss 487
    incorporating into landscape design 487
Shearing 154
Shoot 29
    functions of 29
Shrubs
    for the landscape
        large shrubs (8 feet and up) 217
        medium shrubs (5-8 feet) 213

S

small shrubs (1-4 ft) 207
Signal words 127
Silverfish 633
Skunk 587
Slime mold 351
Slope, determining 514
Slug bait 420
Snakes 588
Sod webworms 355
Soil
    abiotic factors
      light 10
      nutrients 6
      oxygen 9
      pH 5
      temperature 10
      water 7
    cation 5
    cation exchange capacity 6
    describing 3
    describing soil 3
    mineral soil 3
    organic carbon 3
    organic soil 3
    oxygen 12
    pores 4
      organisms in 10
    redox 9
    series 3
    structure 5
    textural classes 3, 4
    water potential 8
Soil amendments 327
Soil analysis 492
Soil-borne diseases
    fungal 95
Soil-borne pathogen 95, 410
Soil bulk density 4
Soil Ecosystem, The (Chapter1) 1
Soilless mixture - *See* Growing medium
Soil organisms 10
    bacteria 10
    fungi 10
    abiotic factors for 11
    competition between 14
    nutrients for 12
    oxygen and 12
Soil testing 20, 22

Soil texture 2, 8, 9
Sooty blotch 471
Southern bacterial wilt 97
Southern blight 95, 410, 411, 412, 413
Southernpeas 372 - *See also* Beans and peas
    diseases of 413
Southern Pine Beetle 315
Southern Red Mite 316
Sowbugs 86, 357, 629
Species 28, 83
Spider mites 86, 266, 269, 317, 403, 465, 542
Spiders 86, 626
    brown recluse spiders 627
    cellar spiders 627
    jumping spiders 626
    sac spiders 627
    widow spiders 628
    wolf spiders 626
Spinosad 124, 419, 420
Spittlebugs
    in turfgrass 354
Spore 94, 95
Spreader - *See also* Pesticide application equipment
    for fertilizer 152, 331
    seeding with 329
Springtails 629
Spruce spider mite 316
Squash 385
    cross-pollination 80, 364, 400
    diseases of 364, 403, 413
    hill planting 367
    insect pests of 405, 406
    interplanting 395
    problems 385, 400
    summer 385
      harvesting 388
    winter 385
Squash bug 406
Squash mosaic virus 413
Squash vine borer 406
Squirrels 589
Stamen 35
State flower 199
St. Augustinegrass, common diseases of
    brown patch 348
    fairy ring 349
    pythium root rot 349
    St. Augustinegrass decline virus 327

take all root rot 350
St. Augustinegrass (*Stenotaphrum secundatum*)
  chinch bugs 355
  fertilizing 331
  herbicide tolerance 109
  identifying characteristics 322
  pH preferred 339
  varieties 327
Stem 31
  growth in 31
  modifications 32
  structure and function 31
Stigma 35
Stink bugs 403, 419, 473, 626, 631
  predaceous 132
Stipule 34
Stolons 33
Stomata 34
Stored product pests 621
Stratification 68
Strawberries 443
  annual hill system 443
  bed renovation 444
  bird control 445
  diseases 467
  matted row system 443
  varieties 443
Strawberry weevils 464
Structural and Household Pests (Chapter 28) 607–634
Style 35
Submerged plants 526
Subterranean termites 611
Suckers 33
Sulfur
  amount to lower pH 149
  as organic pesticide 420, 422
Surface plants 524
Sweetpotato
  growing 385
  insect pests of 404, 407, 408
  problems 386
Symbiosis 2
Systemic 109

T

Take all root rot
  of turfgrass 350

pH and 350
Tall fescue, common diseases of
  fading out 349
  gray leaf spot 350
  pythium root rot 348
Tall Fescue (*Festuca arundinacea*) 321
  fertilization 331
  maintenance calendar 341
  pH range 321, 341
  seeding rate 328
Tarnished plant bug 473
Temperature
  and plant growth 54
Terminal bud 29
Termite colony 612
Termites 611
  identification 612
  subterranean 611
Thatch 333
Threshold levels 121
Thrips 86, 316, 317, 405, 407, 419, 542
  monitoring for 317
Thuricide 406, 420
Thysanoptera 86
Ticks 86, 625
'TifBlair' Centipedegrass 325
'TifGrand' Bermudagrass 325
'Tifgreen' (Tifton 328) Bermudagrass 325
'TifSport' Bermudagrass 325
'Tifton 10' Bermudagrass 325
Tifton loamy sand 3
'Tifway' (Tifton 419 or Tif-419) Bermudagrass 324
Tiger beetles 134
Tobacco mosaic virus (TMV) 91, 98, 273, 412
Tomatoes 386
  determinate 386
  diseases of 386, 410, 411
  growing 386
  insect pests of 403, 408
    hornworm 409
  problems
    blossom end rot 388
    nutrient deficiencies 399, 400
    physiological 400
    cat facing 400
    cracking 400
  saving seed 365
  seed depth 367

transplanting 366, 387
VFNT 386
    VFNT resistant 410
Tomato fruitworm - *See* Corn earworm
Tomato leaf roll 400
Tomato spotted wilt virus 98, 386, 412
Topping 248
Transpiration 16, 34, 42, 44, 45, 54, 56
Transpiration-cohesion-tension 56
Tree care professional, selecting 257
Tree growth, pH and 247
Trees
    cabling and bracing 256
    care for mature 255
    fertilization 248
    for the landscape
        medium and large trees (40 feet and larger) 238
        small trees (10 - 40 feet) 223, 234
    growth 245
    hazardous trees 257
    hollow 255
    how they grow 242
    installation 250
    irrigation 250
    leaves and buds 242
    mulching 254
    pH range for 247
    planting 250
        balled and burlapped 251
        container grown 251
    pruning - *See* Pruning
        conifers 159
        deciduous 157
        evergreen 158
        flowering 157
        large limbs 155
    response to night lighting 244
    root control 255
    roots 244
        girdling 256
    selecting 233
    site consideration 233
    staking and guying 251
    water basins (saucers) 144, 250, 251, 252
    water sprouts 256
    wound paints 248
Trees (Chapter 12) 229–260
Tree wells 257

Trellising 362, 371, 377, 391, 440
Tuber 33
Turfgrass (Chapter 14) 319–344
Turfgrasses - *See also* specific species
    cultivation 333
        coring (core aeration) 333, 500
        vertical mowing 333
    establishment (planting) 327 - *See also* specific species
        plugging 330
        soil preparation for 327
    fertilization 330
        in absence of soil test 330
        when to apply 330
    Georgia Certified 327
    identifying characteristics 322
    insect pests of 351
    irrigation 332
    liming 332
    maintenance 330
    mowing 333
        during stress periods 333
    mowing frequency 332
    mowing height 332
    overseeding 336
    pest management/control 336, 352
    pH 324, 332
    renovation 334, 336
    seeding rates 328
    topdressing 333
    weed control 336
Turfgrasses, common diseases of 336, 347 - *See also* specific turf species
    brown patch 348
    centipedegrass decline 351
    dollar spot 348
    fading out or melting out 349
    fairy ring 349
    gray leaf spot 350
    pythium root rot 348
    slime mold 351
    take all root rot 350
Turfgrasses, Insects and Diseases of (Chapter 15) 345–358
Turf management calendar 335
    bermudagrass 337
    centipedegrass 338
    St. Augustinegrass 339

tall fescue 341
    zoysiagrass 340
Turnips 412 - *See also* Cabbage
Twolined spittlebug 317
Twospotted spider mite 317

U

Umbel 36

V

Vascular system 29
Vascular wilt 277
Vascular wilts 272
Vegetable diseases
    leaf, stem and fruit diseases 410
    soil-borne diseases 410
Vegetable gardening
    cool season crops 395
    cover crops 363
    crop rotation 363
    growing transplants 365
    insect pests and 402
    intensive gardening 395
    pH for 399
    problems 399
    raised bed 393
    warm season crops 395
    when to harvest 388
Vegetable Gardening (Chapter 16) 359–396
Vegetable Garden Problems, Diagnosing (Chapter 17) 397–414
Vegetative propagation 69
    cuttings 70
        herbaceous plants 70
        woody plants 70
    methods of 71
Venation 34, 81
Verticillium 272, 298, 410, 411
VFN 411
Vines 199
    for the landscape 202
Virus 97, 98, 273, 443
    as beneficial to control pests 135
    as plant pathogen 80, 273
    control 264, 273, 275
    insect vectors 413
    resistance 274
    seed transmission 413

symptoms 269, 273
    herbicide damage mimicking 412
Voles - *See* Pine voles

W

Warm season annuals 168
Warm-season turfgrasses 323
    planting 329
        sodding 330
        sprigging 329
        stolonizing 329
Wasps
    parasitic 134
Water
    absorption by roots 57
    as disseminating agent 272
    as environmental factor 56
Water garden
    installation 522
    pH in 527, 528, 529
    plants
        annual bog 526
        lotus 524
        perennial bog 525
        submerged plants 526
        surface 524
        water lilies 523
    tips 530
Water gardening 519
    helpful information 530
    materials and supplies 521
    mosquitoes 531
    water pH 527
    water quality 527
Water-holding capacity of soil - *See* field capacity
Watering - *See also* Irrigation
    during drought 501
    restricted or during ban 501
Watering fruit trees 331
Watering indoor plants 331
Watering ornamentals 331
Watering trees 331
Watering turf 331, 332, 335
    amount needed 332
    best time of day 332
Watering vegetables 331, 368
    in containers 392
    transplants 367

Water lilies 523
Watermelon - *See* Melons
Watermelon mosaic virus 413
Water pollutants 512
    bacteria 512
Water potential 2
Water quality 506
Water saucers 144 - *See also* Trees, water basins
Water Smart landscape
    planning and design 486
    practical turf areas 494
    use of mulches 499
    water-saving maintenance practices 500
Water Smart Landscape, Developing a
    (Chapter 22)   483–502
Wax scales 317
Weed control
    chemical 108
    cultivation 107
    in fruit gardens 116
    in perennial beds 177
    in turf 337
        bermudagrass 336
        centipedegrass 338
        St. Augustinegrass 339
        tall fescue 341
        zoysiagrass 340
    mechanical 107
    methods 106
    physical barriers 107
Weed killer products - *See* Postemergence herbicides
Weed-n-feed products 110
Weed preventer products - *See* Preemergence
herbicides
Weeds
    biennial 106
    broadleaf 106
    defined 105
    grassy weeds 322
    perennial 106
    reasons for control of 105
    reproduction 105
    sedge weeds 105
    summer annual 106
    weed types 105
    winter annual 106
Weed Science (Chapter 7) 103–116
Wheel bugs 626

Whiteflies 304, 318, 405, 409
White grubs 408
    in turfgrass 354
    in vegetable gardens 408
White peach scale 473
White pine weevil 318
Wilting point 2
Wirestem 412
Wireworm 408
Witches' broom 267, 274, 281, 283, 294, 300, 303
Wood boring beetles 615
Woodchuck 592, 593
Wood destroying insects 611
Woodpeckers 593
Woody ornamentals 197 - *See also* Ornamental Plants
in the Landscape (Chapter 9); *See also* Groundcovers;
See also Shrubs; *See also* Trees; *See also* Vines
    diseases of 284
    insects and related pests 304
Woody Plants for Georgia Landscapes, Selecting
    (Chapter 11) 195

X

Xeriscaping - *See* Water Smart landscape
Xylem 29, 31, 42, 46, 47, 57, 72, 97, 230, 472

Y

Yellow jackets 624
    traps 420

Z

'Zeon' Zoysiagrass 326
Zoysiagrasses, common diseases of
    brown patch 348
    dollar spot 348
    melting out 350
    pythium root rot 349
Zoysiagrasses (Zoysia Spp) 325
    fertilization 331
    identifying characteristics 322
    maintenance calendar 340
    pH preferred 340
    varieties 326